Handbook of Research on Knowledge-Intensive Organizations

Dariusz Jemielniak
Kozminski University, Poland

Jerzy Kociatkiewicz
University of Essex, UK

Information Science REFERENCE

INFORMATION SCIENCE REFERENCE

Hershey · New York

Director of Editorial Content: Kristin Klinger
Senior Managing Editor: Jamie Snavely
Managing Editor: Jeff Ash
Assistant Managing Editor: Carole Coulson
Typesetter: Larissa Vinci
Cover Design: Lisa Tosheff
Printed at: Yurchak Printing Inc.

Published in the United States of America by
Information Science Reference (an imprint of IGI Global)
701 E. Chocolate Avenue, Suite 200
Hershey PA 17033
Tel: 717-533-8845
Fax: 717-533-8661
E-mail: cust@igi-global.com
Web site: http://www.igi-global.com/reference

and in the United Kingdom by
Information Science Reference (an imprint of IGI Global)
3 Henrietta Street
Covent Garden
London WC2E 8LU
Tel: 44 20 7240 0856
Fax: 44 20 7379 0609
Web site: http://www.eurospanbookstore.com

Library of Congress Cataloging-in-Publication Data

Handbook of research on knowledge-intensive organizations / Dariusz Jemielniak and Jerzy Kociatkiewicz, editors.
p. cm.

Includes bibliographical references and index.

Summary: "This book encompasses a wide variety of research approaches and theoretical stances,that are united in their contributions to the study of the burgeoning field of knowledge intensive organizations"--Provided by publisher.

ISBN 978-1-60566-176-6 (hardcover) -- ISBN 978-1-60566-177-3 (ebook) 1. Knowledge management. 2. Organizational learning--Management. I. Jemielniak, Dariusz. II. Kociatkiewicz, Jerzy.

HD30.2.H36429 2009
658.4'038--dc22

2008047746

British Cataloguing in Publication Data
A Cataloguing in Publication record for this book is available from the British Library.

All work contributed to this book is new, previously-unpublished material. The views expressed in this book are those of the authors, but not necessarily of the publisher.

Editorial Advisory Board

List of Contributors

Andreeva, Tatiana / *Graduate School of Management, St. Petersburg State University, Russia*..... 459
Barinaga, Ester / *Copenhagen Business School, Denmark*.. 116
Böhm, Steffen / *University of Essex, UK*.. 479
Boje, David M. / *New Mexico State University, USA*.. 81
Bowman, Cliff / *Cranfield School of Management, UK*.. 330
Burke, Maria E. / *University of Salford, UK*.. 348
Claver-Cortés, Enrique / *University of Alicante, Spain*.. 311
D'Cruz, Premilla / *Indian Institute of Management, Ahmedabad, India*............................ 529
Ditillo, Angelo / *Università Bocconi and Sda Bocconi School of Management, Italy*.............. 243
Donate-Manzanares, Mario J. / *Universidad de Castilla-La Mancha, Spain*......................... 169
Gleadle, Pauline / *The Open University, UK*.. 330
Gold, Jeff / *Leeds Metropolitan University, UK*.. 30
Greenwood, Davydd J. / *Cornell University, USA*.. 1
Grisoni, Louise / *Bristol Business School, UK*.. 98
Guadamillas-Gómez, Fátima / *Universidad de Castilla-La Mancha, Spain*.......................... 169
Guthrie, James / *The University of Sydney, Australia*.. 375
Hepsø, Vidar / *Statoil Hydro Research and Norwegian School of Management, Norway*.......... 279
Hoecht, Andreas / *University of Portsmouth, UK*.. 47
Hong, Jianzhong / *Lappeenranta University of Technology, Finland*.................................. 259
Jemielniak, Dariusz / *Kozminski University, Poland*.. 552
Juntunen, Arla / *Helsinki School of Economics, Finland*.. 193
Kettunen, Juha / *Turku University of Applied Sciences, Finland*.. 19
Kianto, Aino / *Lappeenranta University of Technology, Finland*.. 259
Klincewicz, Krzysztof / *University of Warsaw, Poland*.. 152
Kociatkiewicz, Jerzy / *University of Essex, UK*... 552
Land, Chris / *University of Essex, UK*.. 479
Locker, Lawrence / *Georgia Southern University, USA*.. 414
MacGillivray, Alice / *www.4km.net, Canada*.. 440
Mehri, Darius / *University of California, Berkeley, USA*.. 363
Murray, John D. / *Georgia Southern University, USA*.. 414
Noronha, Ernesto / *Indian Institute of Management, Ahmedabad, India*............................. 529
Örtenblad, Anders / *Halmstad University, Sweden*.. 229

Owens, Jonathan D. / *University of Lincoln, UK* 208
Postuła, Agnieszka / *Uniwersytet Warszawski, Poland* 295
Prange, Christiane / *EM Lyon Business School, France* 394
Quer-Ramón, Diego / *University of Alicante, Spain* 311
Ricceri, Federica / *University of Padova, Italy* 375
Sevinc, Meryem / *Georgia Southern University, USA* 414
Sheard, Stephen / *Bradford University, UK* 133
Shih, Joanna / *Hofstra University, USA* 425
Steiner, Lars / *University of Gävle, Sweden* 67
Styhre, Alexander / *Chalmers University of Technology, Sweden* 495
Thorpe, Richard / *Leeds University, UK* 30
Tran, Ben / *Alliant International University, USA* 512
Trott, Paul / *University of Portsmouth, UK* 47
Tyler, Jo A. / *The Pennsylvania State University, USA* 81
Zaragoza-Sáez, Patrocinio / *University of Alicante, Spain* 311

Table of Contents

Foreword xxiv

Preface xxvi

Acknowledgment xxx

Section I
Learning and Innovation

Chapter I
Are Research Universities Knowledge-Intensive Learning Organizations? 1
Davydd J. Greenwood, Cornell University, USA

Chapter II
Construction of Knowledge-Intensive Organization in Higher Education 19
Juha Kettunen, Turku University of Applied Sciences, Finland

Chapter III
Collective CPD: Professional Learning in a Law Firm 30
Jeff Gold, Leeds Metropolitan University, UK
Richard Thorpe, Leeds University, UK

Chapter IV
Innovation Risks of Outsourcing within Knowledge Intensive Business Services (KIBS) 47
Paul Trott, University of Portsmouth, UK
Andreas Hoecht, University of Portsmouth, UK

Chapter V
Actor-Network Theory and Autopoiesis: A New Perspective on Knowledge Management 67
Lars Steiner, University of Gävle, Sweden

Section II
The Language of Knowledge

Chapter VI
Sorting the Relationship of Tacit Knowledge to Story and Narrative Knowing 81
Jo A. Tyler, The Pennsylvania State University, USA
David M. Boje, New Mexico State University, USA

Chapter VII
Exploring Organizational Learning and Knowledge Exchange through Poetry.................................. 98
Louise Grisoni, Bristol Business School, UK

Chapter VIII
Vagueness: The Role of Language in the Organizing Process of Knowledge Intensive Work 116
Ester Barinaga, Copenhagen Business School, Denmark

Chapter IX
Tyranny of the Eye? The Resurgence of the Proto-Alphabetic Sensibility in Contemporary Electronic Modes of Media (PC/Mobile Telephony); and its Significance for the Status of Knowledge.. 133
Stephen Sheard, Bradford University, UK

Section III
Managing Knowledge

Chapter X
Knowledge Management and IT Research and Analysis Firms: Agenda-Setters, Oracles and Judges.. 152
Krzysztof Klincewicz, University of Warsaw, Poland

Chapter XI
Knowledge Management Strategies Implementation in Innovation Intensive Firms......................... 169
Fátima Guadamillas-Gómez, Universidad de Castilla-La Mancha, Spain
Mario J. Donate-Manzanares, Universidad de Castilla-La Mancha, Spain

Chapter XII
Developing a Corporate Knowledge Management Platform in a Multibusiness Company............... 193
Arla Juntunen, Helsinki School of Economics, Finland

Chapter XIII
Modelling the New Product Development Process: The Value of a Product Development Process Model Approach as a Means for Business Survival in the 21st Century.............................. 208
Jonathan D. Owens, University of Lincoln, UK

Section IV
Management and Control

Chapter XIV
Achieving Organizational Independence of Employees' Knowledge using Knowledge Management, Organizational Learning, and the Learning Organization 229
Anders Örtenblad, Halmstad University, Sweden

Chapter XV
Balancing Stability and Innovation in Knowledge-Intensive Firms: The Role of Management Control Mechanisms 243
Angelo Ditillo, Università Bocconi and Sda Bocconi School of Management, Italy

Chapter XVI
The Knowledge-Based Approach to Organizational Measurement: Exploring the Future of Organizational Assessment 259
Aino Kianto, Lappeenranta University of Technology, Finland
Jianzhong Hong, Lappeenranta University of Technology, Finland

Chapter XVII
'Common' Information Spaces in Knowledge-Intensive Work: Representation and Negotiation of Meaning in Computer-Supported Collaboration Rooms 279
Vidar Hepsø, Statoil Hydro Research and Norwegian School of Management, Norway

Chapter XVIII
Creativity and Control in IT Professionals' Communities 295
Agnieszka Postuła, Uniwersytet Warszawski, Poland

Section V
The Culture of Knowledge

Chapter XIX
A Qualitative Study of Knowledge Management: The Multinational Firm Point of View 311
Patrocinio Zaragoza-Sáez, University of Alicante, Spain
Enrique Claver-Cortés, University of Alicante, Spain
Diego Quer-Ramón, University of Alicante, Spain

Chapter XX
Culture as a Dynamic Capability: The Case of 3M in the United Kingdom 330
Cliff Bowman, Cranfield School of Management, UK
Pauline Gleadle, The Open University, UK

Chapter XXI
Cultural Issues, Organizations and Information Fulfilment: An Exploration towards Improved Knowledge Management Relationships.......... 348
Maria E. Burke, University of Salford, UK

Chapter XXII
Engineering Design at a Toyota Company: Knowledge Management and the Innovative Process 363
Darius Mehri, University of California, Berkeley, USA

Chapter XXIII
Critical Analysis of International Guidelines for the Management of Knowledge Resources.......... 375
Federica Ricceri, University of Padova, Italy
James Guthrie, The University of Sydney, Australia

Section VI
The Knowledge Worker

Chapter XXIV
Strategic Alliance Capability: Bringing the Individual Back into Inter-Organizational Collaboration.......... 394
Christiane Prange, EM Lyon Business School, France

Chapter XXV
Automation vs. Human Intervention: Is There any Room Left for the Analyst in the Data Mining Process?.......... 414
Meryem Sevinc, Georgia Southern University, USA
Lawrence Locker, Georgia Southern University, USA
John D. Murray, Georgia Southern University, USA

Chapter XXVI
Temporality and Knowledge Work.......... 425
Joanna Shih, Hofstra University, USA

Chapter XXVII
Knowledge Intensive Work in a Network of Counter-Terrorism Communities.......... 440
Alice MacGillivray, www.4km.net, Canada

Chapter XXVIII
Tensions between Knowledge Creation and Knowledge Sharing: Individual Preferences of Employees in Knowledge-Intensive Organizations.......... 459
Tatiana Andreeva, Graduate School of Management, St. Petersburg State University, Russia

Section VII
Discussing Knowledge

Chapter XXIX
The 'Value' of Knowledge: Reappraising Labour in the Post-Industrial Economy 479
Steffen Böhm, University of Essex, UK
Chris Land, University of Essex, UK

Chapter XXX
New Media and Knowledge Work 495
Alexander Styhre, Chalmers University of Technology, Sweden

Chapter XXXI
Knowledge Management: The Construction of Knowledge in Organizations 512
Ben Tran, Alliant International University, USA

Chapter XXXII
Redefining Professional: The Case of India's Call Centre Agents... 529
Premilla D'Cruz, Indian Institute of Management, Ahmedabad, India
Ernesto Noronha, Indian Institute of Management, Ahmedabad, India

Chapter XXXIII
Knowledge Management: Fad or Enduring Organizational Concept? 552
Dariusz Jemielniak, Kozminski University, Poland
Jerzy Kociatkiewicz, University of Essex, UK

Compilation of References 562

About the Contributors 627

Index 636

Detailed Table of Contents

Foreword xxiv

Preface xxvi

Acknowledgment xxx

Section I
Learning and Innovation

Chapter I
Are Research Universities Knowledge-Intensive Learning Organizations? 1
Davydd J. Greenwood, Cornell University, USA

This chapter questions the clarity of the concepts of "knowledge society" and "knowledge-intensive organization". In particular, the author asserts that the notion that postindustrial society is more knowledge intensive than industrial society is a self-serving proposition made by academics and organizational consultants to emphasize the importance of their own industries. Since all organizations are knowledge-intensive in major ways, the specific meanings of a newly emergent kind of knowledge-intensive organization need to be clarified. The author undertakes this by means of an analysis of research universities.

Chapter II
Construction of Knowledge-Intensive Organization in Higher Education 19
Juha Kettunen, Turku University of Applied Sciences, Finland

The aims of knowledge management are to create knowledge and stimulate innovation. Knowledge management allows the knowledge of an organization to be located, shared, formalized, enhanced, and developed. The challenges of knowledge management lie in creating environments that support knowledge sharing, knowledge creation, and innovativeness. This chapter examines challenges faced by higher education institutions (HEI) in producing innovations and increasing their external impact on their regions. The most valuable assets of HEIs are the knowledge and skills embodied in human capital. The challenges of innovative HEIs can be derived from their customers' needs, which usually cannot be met within a single discipline. This chapter explores the multidisciplinary development projects at HEIs and presents implications for the organizational structure supporting innovation and engagement of the institution with its region.

Chapter III
Collective CPD: Professional Learning in a Law Firm 30
Jeff Gold, Leeds Metropolitan University, UK
Richard Thorpe, Leeds University, UK

Continuing professional development (CPD) is usually conceived as a planned and formulated process for individual members of professional associations. This chapter, by contrast, examines professional learning as a collective and distributed process, taking a whole firm, as the unit of analysis. Cultural historical activity theory is used to work with a law firm. The results show inherent tensions and contradiction in a process of knowledge sharing and practice improvement.

Chapter IV
Innovation Risks of Outsourcing within Knowledge Intensive Business Services (KIBS) 47
Paul Trott, University of Portsmouth, UK
Andreas Hoecht, University of Portsmouth, UK

The United States and European economies have witnessed an enormous increase in the amount of specialized business services, which now provide critical inputs to firms in all sectors. It is this area of the economy which has witnessed huge expansion and development. KIBS include traditional professional business services such as accountancy and law, but also a new generation of KIBS such as IT expertise and internet development. Coupled to this growth has been an increase in the level of outsourcing. Outsourcing was originally confined to peripheral business functions and mainly motivated by a cost saving logic, but has now developed into a routine strategic management move that affects not only peripheral functions but the heart of the competitive core of organisations. This chapter analyses previous research and adopts a conceptual perspective in investigating the innovation-related risks to the organisation that can arise from strategic outsourcing. It uses the example of KIBS outsourcing to highlight the increased risks that arise from a move from traditional to strategic outsourcing and discusses some measures that managers can take to attempt to control these risks.

Chapter V
Actor-Network Theory and Autopoiesis: A New Perspective on Knowledge Management 67
Lars Steiner, University of Gävle, Sweden

A new knowledge management perspective and tool, ANT/AUTOPOIESIS, for analysis of knowledge management in knowledge-intensive organizations is presented. An information technology (IT) research and innovation co-operation between university actors and companies interested in the area of smart home IT applications is used to illustrate analysis using this perspective. Actor-network theory (ANT) and the social theory of autopoiesis are used in analyzing knowledge management, starting from the foundation of a research co-operation. ANT provides the character of relations between actors and actants, how power is translated by actors and the transformation of relations over time. The social theory of autopoiesis provides the tools to analyze organizational closure and reproduction of organizational identity. The perspective used allows a process analysis, and at the same time analysis of structural characteristics of knowledge management. Knowledge management depends on powerful actors, whose power changes over time. Here this power is entrepreneurial and based on relations and actors' innovation knowledge.

Section II
The Language of Knowledge

Chapter VI
Sorting the Relationship of Tacit Knowledge to Story and Narrative Knowing 81
Jo A. Tyler, The Pennsylvania State University, USA
David M. Boje, New Mexico State University, USA

This chapter fits the theme, the interplay between creativity and control in organizations. Story is often claimed to be a way to elicit tacit knowledge from people, and their organization. The authors would like to suggest that this is impossibility. To story something is to shape it intuitively and willfully. Story shapes events into experience and into memory. Without story experience is just reenactment. To reenact is to relive the events, to feel the pain, fear, and terror.

Chapter VII
Exploring Organizational Learning and Knowledge Exchange through Poetry.................................. 98
Louise Grisoni, Bristol Business School, UK

The central discussion in this chapter is that poetry can be used to provide a bridge between tangible, rational, and explicit knowledge, and tacit or implicit knowledge, providing opportunities to access new organizational knowledge, understandings and learning. A study based on 60 middle and senior United Kingdom public service managers is presented. In this study managers worked together to explore how creative inquiry into their organizational experience might help address some of the problematic issues facing their organizations and learn how to develop new ideas about best practice. The challenge was to generate new knowledge about the organization. Poetry in the form of "haiku" was used as a creative research method to access tacit knowledge, which, when combined with explicit knowledge and understanding, led to new insights and organizational learning.

Chapter VIII
Vagueness: The Role of Language in the Organizing Process of Knowledge Intensive Work 116
Ester Barinaga, Copenhagen Business School, Denmark

"How do we define our project goal?" "How are we going to coordinate our independent national studies?" "Who is responsible for what?" "How are newcomers introduced to the project?" During the first year of co-operation among researchers from a variety of disciplines (labor law, sociology and organizational theory) and countries (Sweden, Spain, The Netherlands, UK, and United States) all efforts went to answer those, apparently simple, questions. Inspired by the late Wittgenstein's ideas on the performative character of language, the chapter follows the process by which an international and multidisciplinary group of researchers agree on a research goal, coordinate their work, distribute responsibilities, and socialize newcomers. That is, the process of organizing knowledge intensive work is approached from a performative view of language.

Chapter IX
Tyranny of the Eye? The Resurgence of the Proto-Alphabetic Sensibility in Contemporary Electronic Modes of Media (PC/Mobile Telephony); and its Significance for the Status of Knowledge.......... 133
Stephen Sheard, Bradford University, UK

In this chapter the author offers an argument towards the resurgence of a proto-alphabetic imagination in electronic and mobile communications. It is suggested that contemporary trends in mobile telephony which encapsulate the earlier advances in PC development are shifting electronic media – not towards a mythic culture of the aural (McLuhan) but towards an admixture of the aural and visual, aslant the controlling trope of the alphabetical. It is argued that this separation of technologies resembles the predecessors of writing technologies of a "proto"-alphabetic nature. This infuses the literature of management with a metaphysical animism, which is redolent of the faded animism, which marked the initial confluence of the pre-alphabetical sensibilities of Eye and Voice in the pre-alphabetic emergence of mankind. This is suggested as a fresh Symbolic form towards which mankind is advancing. The confluence of ideological tensions preceding these developments is traced; including debates as to conflicts of Word and Sacred (Ricoeur); or Postmodern aversion towards contemporary ocular dominance. This debate leads towards an evaluation of the role and significance of kinds of knowledge which underpin our knowledge society and the knowledge which we take to constitute "knowledge management".

Section III
Managing Knowledge

Chapter X
Knowledge Management and IT Research and Analysis Firms: Agenda-Setters, Oracles and Judges.......... 152
Krzysztof Klincewicz, University of Warsaw, Poland

The chapter discusses the role of IT Research & Analysis firms in the diffusion of knowledge management. The research is based on content analysis of reports and research notes concerning knowledge management, issued by the most influential analyst firm Gartner in years 1997-2003. It identifies three predominant roles of analysts: agenda-setters (focusing the public discourse on selected issues), oracles (offering ambiguous promises) and judges (selecting concepts, technologies and vendors). While critically evaluating the influence of IT Research & Analysis firms, the chapter documents important passages in the history of knowledge management.

Chapter XI
Knowledge Management Strategies Implementation in Innovation Intensive Firms........................ 169
Fátima Guadamillas-Gómez, Universidad de Castilla-La Mancha, Spain
Mario J. Donate-Manzanares, Universidad de Castilla-La Mancha, Spain

This chapter analyses the implementation of knowledge management strategies (KMS) in technology-intensive firms. Firstly, a review of KMS in the knowledge management (KM) literature is carried out in order to conceptually establish the focus of the chapter. Next, some key factors for successful KM implementation, such as corporate culture, technological systems, ethical leadership, human resources management practices and organizational flexibility are identified and explained. After that, the case study of two firms which have successfully implemented a KMS in innovation-intensive sectors, such as electronics and information technologies, is shown. Finally, and based on the results of the case study, some suggestions are extracted and recommendations are made from a managerial perspective in order to implement a KMS effectively.

Chapter XII
Developing a Corporate Knowledge Management Platform in a Multibusiness Company.............. 193
Arla Juntunen, Helsinki School of Economics, Finland

This chapter focuses on the development of the knowledge management (KM) platform, and, more generally, the knowledge- and resource-based view (RBV) of the firm. The knowledge is seen as a source of a competitive advantage. In high-velocity markets, like the ICT-sector, the knowledge is crucial in creating a long-term competitive advantage over the competitors. The study claims that corporate performance was improved when the case company simultaneously exploited a balanced set of related knowledge resources of the corporate KM Platfrom across its business areas.

Chapter XIII
Modelling the New Product Development Process: The Value of a Product Development
Process Model Approach as a Means for Business Survival in the 21st Century.............................. 208
Jonathan D. Owens, University of Lincoln, UK

Success in new product development (NPD) can be considered a general aim for any company wishing to survive in the 21st century. It has been found that positive effects can result from the existence of formal "blueprints" and "roadmaps" of the NPD process. This chapter discusses numerous NPD processes which can assist a company to capture what it does, and follow a structured development route, from which it is possible to gain a better understanding of how to improve the development process, and thus reap the potential and tangible benefits. This chapter's focus is at organisations that are considering implementing a new product development (NPD) process in order to improve repeatability and ultimately sustainability of their innovative capabilities, a necessary and vital component for survival. It aims to bring an understanding of the underlying characteristics that may contribute to a potential and successful outcome during the development process within organizations, through the adoption of a structured NPD process.

Section IV
Management and Control

Chapter XIV
Achieving Organizational Independence of Employees' Knowledge using Knowledge Management, Organizational Learning, and the Learning Organization 229
Anders Örtenblad, Halmstad University, Sweden

The ambition of this chapter is to pay some attention to more obvious, as well as more subtle, methods for organizations to become independent of the individual's subjective knowledge, from the employees' point of view. Terms such as "knowledge sharing", "knowledge transfer", and "learning for all" are almost always seen as being positive for both employers and employees. However, this chapter will critically examines those terms. Three popular management ideas relating to knowledge and/or learning have been analysed from a "knowledge control" perspective: knowledge management, organizational learning, and the learning organization. The main conclusion of this conceptual and elaborating chapter is that the more current and less academic ideas of the learning organization and knowledge management contain the same tools as the idea of "old" organizational learning as regards gaining control over knowledge, but that these two ideas additionally contain other knowledge control measures, which are more refined, in the sense that they are less obvious as knowledge control measures. The idea of "new" organizational learning, however, is less suited to knowledge control, since it implies that knowledge is not storable. In other words, the chapter's contribution is an analysis of some of the most popular management ideas that deal with knowledge and/or learning relating to the organizational/employer independence of subjective knowledge from the employees' point of view, something which is rarely seen.

Chapter XV
Balancing Stability and Innovation in Knowledge-Intensive Firms: The Role of Management Control Mechanisms 243
Angelo Ditillo, Università Bocconi and Sda Bocconi School of Management, Italy

Knowledge-intensive firms are composed of various communities, each characterized by specialized knowledge. These communities operate as critical agents in the organizational action because the relevant processes and the variety/variability of environment and technology are too complex for a single individual to understand in their entirety. They generate new models for interpreting reality and responding to customer needs thanks to the integration of knowledge taking place within and between them. The objective of this chapter is to provide some criteria for evaluating the comparative effectiveness and efficiency of combinations of control mechanisms in the regulation of these knowledge integration processes. On the basis of the characteristics of knowledge (level of complexity and diversity), a different set of control mechanisms is proposed, with a variation in their specific features to guarantee that the resulting modes of communication and cognition can guarantee the required level innovation, without however preventing a certain level of stability.

Chapter XVI
The Knowledge-Based Approach to Organizational Measurement: Exploring the Future of Organizational Assessment............ 259
Aino Kianto, Lappeenranta University of Technology, Finland
Jianzhong Hong, Lappeenranta University of Technology, Finland

Nowadays knowledge and competencies are the key productive factors, and the organizational capability for continuous learning, development and renewal has become the main driver of competitiveness. In this chapter the authors explore how organizational measurement should change in order to remain relevant in the face of the recent increase in the knowledge-intensiveness of work, organizing and value creation. First they argue that, while traditionally measurement has mostly been used for control purposes, recent changes in the nature of work have brought on new challenges which can no longer be met with old mindsets and measures. Then they focus on two novel approaches, intellectual capital and competence development, and examine the current state of the art. Finally, the authors construct foundations for a knowledge-based approach to organizational measurement and set some future directions in which measures should be developed in order to portray and enable knowledge work and knowledge-based value creation.

Chapter XVII
'Common' Information Spaces in Knowledge-Intensive Work: Representation and Negotiation of Meaning in Computer-Supported Collaboration Rooms............ 279
Vidar Hepsø, Statoil Hydro Research and Norwegian School of Management, Norway

In knowledge management literature, common information spaces (CIS) are believed to be instrumental in the development and sharing of knowledge. These information spaces provide the arena to facilitate knowledge creation, knowledge management, boost multidisciplinary collaboration and therefore increase the performance of the organization. In a global oil and gas industry an increasing part of the communication in day-to-day operations takes place in specially designed videoconferencing and collaboration rooms. This chapter addresses the role such information spaces play and some of the implications for practice when it comes to knowledge-intensive work: diversity, work relations and identity. What is regarded as "common" or "shared" among heterogeneous groups of professionals working within such information spaces is challenged.

Chapter XVIII
Creativity and Control in IT Professionals' Communities............ 295
Agnieszka Postuła, Uniwersytet Warszawski, Poland

This chapter presents and discusses two factors – creativity and control – which correspond to every organizational reality. IT specialists' professional communities are used as an example because of characteristic relationships between their members and their attitude to work. The chapter describes how combination of these two phenomena may build or destroy organizations. There is also an explanation of specific relations between IT professionals and beginning of further discussion based on these relationships, as well as analysis of consequences of inappropriate management practices. Creativity and control are presented as features of every common company with their special roles in organization. Also, main characteristics of well-organized practical communities are shown.

Section V
The Culture of Knowledge

Chapter XIX
A Qualitative Study of Knowledge Management: The Multinational Firm Point of View 311
Patrocinio Zaragoza-Sáez, University of Alicante, Spain
Enrique Claver-Cortés, University of Alicante, Spain
Diego Quer-Ramón, University of Alicante, Spain

Knowledge is one of the basic production factors owned by enterprises, and knowledge management is one of the main dynamic capabilities on which enterprises can base their competitive advantages. The creation, transfer, and later use of knowledge have become increasingly important, and multinational corporations (MNCs), being scattered in various places, constitute the appropriate environment to implement knowledge management processes meant to maximize their intellectual assets. This chapter has as its aim to answer three questions: (a) what actions do MNCs undertake in order to set knowledge management processes in motion; (b) what main variables impact on their knowledge creation capability; and (c) what main variables impact on their knowledge transfer capability? A qualitative research work based on a multiple case study has served to achieve that aim, allowing us to carry out an exploratory study of six MNCs which have shown their proactivity in the knowledge management area. The results of the analysis have led to eight propositions which highlight the most relevant variables facilitating the processes for the creation and transfer of knowledge within a MNC.

Chapter XX
Culture as a Dynamic Capability: The Case of 3M in the United Kingdom 330
Cliff Bowman, Cranfield School of Management, UK
Pauline Gleadle, The Open University, UK

The chapter addresses a central dilemma from the viewpoint of dynamic capabilities and the resource based view of the firm: how to manage creativity within New Product Development without sacrificing financial control. The empirical evidence examined concerns 3M's NPD activity in the United Kingdom from a holistically viewed management control perspective at the organizational level, and a study of the development and launch of a highly successful and radically new product, Genesis. It is concluded that NPD processes within 3M in the United Kingdom display a large measure of coherence juxtaposed with flexibility through the manner in which controls, holistically viewed, are embedded within organizational routines. Using case evidence clear distinctions can be made between dynamic capabilities, resources and product outcomes, and the elements of 3M's capability can be discerned. The authors conclude that a dynamic capability can consist of both replicable elements, and elements embedded in the culture and routines of the firm that are difficult to imitate.

Chapter XXI
Cultural Issues, Organizations and Information Fulfilment: An Exploration towards Improved Knowledge Management Relationships 348
Maria E. Burke, University of Salford, UK

The purpose of this chapter is to consider an original way of improving knowledge management relationships. This is done within the context of an aspect of Information behaviour, known as Information Fulfillment. The chapter presents the cultural results of a three-year study into the concept of information fulfillment, and considers the impact of culture on levels of information fulfillment. Ethnographic studies were undertaken within higher education institutions in four countries and the social and symbolic meanings that underpinned the culture of information in the chosen institutions are presented followed by a section of "raw data" from the ethnographic field. Culture impacted significantly in all the studies, and each study had its own unique character and provided rich insights into the culture and contexts of the fields. The relationships between the cultures and the levels of information fulfillment are reported with suggestions re helping build KM systems that deliver higher levels of information fulfillment.

Chapter XXII
Engineering Design at a Toyota Company: Knowledge Management and the Innovative Process 363
Darius Mehri, University of California, Berkeley, USA

The author worked in the research and design department at a large Toyota company in the late 1990s and experienced an innovative process where engineers worked in tightly knit groups where monitoring, the informal hierarchy and dependence resulted from an emphasis on collective work. In the approach to innovation during the design process, the Toyota engineers were found to engage in an inductive process that placed an emphasis on the concrete and an orientation toward the field as a result of an approach that relied on experience based knowledge. The use of tacit and explicit knowledge is discussed within the context of the design process and the author finds that explicit knowledge dominates the improvement of productivity and organizational learning. The latest research in the sociology of culture and cultural psychology is used to highlight the cognitive approach to problem solving during the innovative process.

Chapter XXIII
Critical Analysis of International Guidelines for the Management of Knowledge Resources........... 375
Federica Ricceri, University of Padova, Italy
James Guthrie, The University of Sydney, Australia

The shift towards a knowledge based economy is at the core of the debate of contemporary management and accounting literature and organisations are challenged by the need of managing their knowledge resources. Several national and international institutions have produced authoritative "guidelines" to facilitate the management and reporting of KR. Many of these guidelines are the result of co-operation between researchers, companies, industry organisations and consultants and have, therefore, been informed by practice. However, to date, there has been no serious critique of these guidelines. The main objective of this chapter is to provide an in-depth analysis of six contemporary guidelines. By reviewing these guidelines, this chapter explores how each of these addresses the MKR and therefore facilitates the management and reporting of KR. Therefore, this chapter will establish some of the key issues involved in understanding MKR. It will also provide an overview of how these issues are addressed or otherwise in the six guidelines. Two key messages of this chapter are the followings: first, MKR and its elements are embedded in various ways into the international guidelines examined; second, that a key policy issue is international harmonisation.

Section VI
The Knowledge Worker

Chapter XXIV
Strategic Alliance Capability: Bringing the Individual Back into Inter-Organizational Collaboration........ 394
Christiane Prange, EM Lyon Business School, France

Internationalisation has accelerated the speed of knowledge generation and innovation. Thus, companies increasingly need to pool and create new resources by engaging in alliances with various partners. However, high failure rates of strategic alliances imply that the degree of a company's collaboration success is related to the level of its alliance capability. While "alliance capability" has largely been conceptualized from within the resource based and the dynamic capability view, one of the major drawbacks is the lack of micro-foundations, i.e. an explanation of individual knowledge and actions, which drive the development of alliance capability. A modified approach to the capability life-cycle is introduced, which aims at filling this gap. Finally, some implications for managerial practice and for future research are addressed.

Chapter XXV
Automation vs. Human Intervention: Is There any Room Left for the Analyst in the Data Mining Process?........ 414
Meryem Sevinc, Georgia Southern University, USA
Lawrence Locker, Georgia Southern University, USA
John D. Murray, Georgia Southern University, USA

In the contemporary context of knowledge discovery, the amount of information and the process itself has increased in complexity. Relevant to the present chapter is the increased reliance on automaticity in knowledge discovery. Although, there are positive benefits of automation, there is reason to believe that a process that emphasizes greater human participation may produce more meaningful results. Through a description of the human information system and its attributes, this chapter discusses why an analyst-centered approach to a knowledge discovery system is a desirable goal. The authors argue that a perspective based on cognitive psychology can serve as a useful guide in achieving a desirable synergy between automated knowledge discovery tools and the human analyst.

Chapter XXVI
Temporality and Knowledge Work 425
Joanna Shih, Hofstra University, USA

The hi-tech firms that predominate in Silicon Valley contain a large proportion of knowledge workers—employees with high levels of education and expertise. The region is subsequently a useful prism by which to explore the shift in the pace of work and ideologies of labor control. Engineers in Silicon Valley are a prototypical example of "knowledge workers;" they are valued for their ability to contribute to firms' competitive advantage via their expertise and innovation. This chapter reports on fifty four semi-structured interviews of high-skilled, white and Asian men and women engineers who worked in the hi-tech industry of Silicon Valley, focusing on the issue of work temporality. Temporality has long been understood as central to the labor process, and as inextricably linked to the mode of production. Here, I highlight the problematic aspects of the shift from the routinized schedule of "clock time", characterized by rigid temporal boundaries between work and home, and "project time," characterized by an erratic and increasing pace of work that appears to be largely unfettered by boundaries between private and work time.

Chapter XXVII
Knowledge Intensive Work in a Network of Counter-Terrorism Communities................................ 440
Alice MacGillivray, www.4km.net, Canada

Knowledge management is often associated with the need for change and related shifts in ontologies, ways of knowing and ways of working. Combine the centuries-old debates about what defines knowledge with proposed paradigm shifts to become knowledge-oriented, focused on inter-relationships, and cognisant of the complex and voluntary nature of knowledge work, and there is bound to be controversy and ambiguity. However, knowledge management research and practice becomes more focused and less ambiguous when set in the context of an urgent need. This chapter describes a study of a Canadian public sector science initiative. The terrorist attacks of 9/11 catalyzed ripples of reflection and innovation over great distances. In Canada, the federal government initiated the chemical, biological, radiological and nuclear (CBRN) research and technology unitiative (CRTI) to enable learning and progress, using what is essentially a communities of practice model. CRTI established a knowledge management office, to help this network of communities generate, share and use tacit and explicit knowledge. Some aspects of the initiative were working better than others, and the author was asked to conduct research to explore how CRTI members understand their work in a complex, knowledge-rich environment.

Chapter XXVIII
Tensions between Knowledge Creation and Knowledge Sharing: Individual Preferences
of Employees in Knowledge-Intensive Organizations... 459
Tatiana Andreeva, Graduate School of Management, St. Petersburg State University, Russia

Contemporary literature usually views knowledge creation and knowledge sharing as either independent or positively related processes. However, based on the review of the literature on the organizational conditions aimed to support these processes, the author challenges this view at the individual level of analysis and suggests that an individual employee can hardly simultaneously combine features that support both knowledge creation and knowledge sharing and thus can hardly be efficient in both processes at the same time. The data from the survey of 120 employees from 5 knowledge-intensive companies supported this idea, and the author discusses its implications for further research and for management practice in knowledge-intensive organizations.

Section VII
Discussing Knowledge

Chapter XXIX
The 'Value' of Knowledge: Reappraising Labour in the Post-Industrial Economy 479
Steffen Böhm, University of Essex, UK
Chris Land, University of Essex, UK

Knowledge is implicitly assumed to form an increasingly important, or even the dominant source of values for today's knowledge based organizations. It is rare, however, to encounter writings questioning what is "value", enquiring into its provenance, or examining its distribution amongst organization's stakeholders. This chapter asks these very questions, focusing on Marx's (1976) formulation of value theory. Divided into four parts, it begins by giving a basic overview of the labour theory of value, as developed by Marx in mid 19th century, industrialised England. The second part examines Roy Jacques' (2000) critique of Marx, his rejection of the adequacy of "labour" as a concept for analysing contemporary value production, and his call for a "knowledge theory of value". The third section focuses on labour process theorist Paul Thompson (2005) and his challenge to the idea that labour and knowledge are fundamentally different. The fourth part extends this concern with "other" forms of contemporary labour to a more global level by examining De Angelis' (2006) and Retort's (2005) suggestion that the global economy today is driven by acts of enclosure and "primitive accumulation."

Chapter XXX
New Media and Knowledge Work.. 495
Alexander Styhre, Chalmers University of Technology, Sweden

This chapter discusses the use of media in knowledge-intensive organizations. Media is defined here as the integration of technologies, practices, and institutions serving to record, inscribe and circulate speech, writing, and images. The presence of media in organized activities remains relatively unexplored, even though various media "enframe" the life-world of the organization. New media do not only constitute assemblages of integrated technologies and tools (e.g. the telephone, the computer, pens and pencils) which are used en route in day-to-day work, they also gradually break down the line of demarcation between inside and outside, between embodied and technological matter.

Chapter XXXI
Knowledge Management: The Construction of Knowledge in Organizations.................................. 512
Ben Tran, Alliant International University, USA

This chapter examines knowledge and innovation as invaluable factors affecting the longevity of large organizations. It presents the history and evolution of the concepts of knowledge and learning within organizations to provide grounds for establishing crucial factors affecting the development and maintenance of competitive advantage for large contemporary organizations. Thus the purpose of this paper is to address the evolution of knowledge management, the meaning and purpose of knowledge management, and the organizational structure that supports such knowledge.

Chapter XXXII
Redefining Professional: The Case of India's Call Centre Agents.. 529
Premilla D'Cruz, Indian Institute of Management, Ahmedabad, India
Ernesto Noronha, Indian Institute of Management, Ahmedabad, India

Scholars researching the area of the sociology of professions had earlier predicted that as occupations seek to improve their public image, professionalism would embrace all their incumbents. It is therefore no revelation that call centre agents in India identify themselves as professionals. Using van Manen's hermeneutic phenomenological approach, the authors explored this dimension with 59 call centre agents located in Mumbai and Bangalore, India. The findings demonstrate that neither the trait nor the power approaches drawn from the traditional literature on the sociology of professions explain call centre agents' identification with professional work. Instead, agents' experiences validate the contemporary explanation that emphasizes the appeal of professionalism used by employer organisations as a means to convince, cajole, and persuade their employees to perform and behave in ways which the employer organization deems appropriate, effective and efficient. It is in this context that agents accept stringent work systems and job design elements, techno-bureaucratic controls and the primacy of the customer in return for the privileges bestowed upon them by way of being professionals. While professional identity thus serves as a means of socio-ideological control facilitating the realization of the organization agenda, it is not all-encompassing as agents simultaneously show signs of resistance.

Chapter XXXIII
Knowledge Management: Fad or Enduring Organizational Concept? 552
Dariusz Jemielniak, Kozminski University, Poland
Jerzy Kociatkiewicz, University of Essex, UK

Knowledge management and knowledge-intensive work are two of today's hot buzzwords, though both already have a history of managerial usage. While some authors claim that knowledge is the most important organizational asset in contemporary society, others retort that much of knowledge management literature and practical solutions are just perfunctory and propagandist and many, if not most, managerial polices rely on manipulation of emotions and identity creation. This chapter aims to capitalize on this fascinating and timely research area. The authors want to present the current business fad of knowledge-management in terms of excess and forgetful repetition of ideas. They look at knowledge management as an idea of highly suspect utility, and search for explanations for and possible counterbalances to its ubiquity.

Compilation of References 562

About the Contributors 627

Index 636

Foreword

Knowledge-intensive organizations (also, knowledge intensive firms, knowledge companies) spite being described by a rather vacuous and ill-defined term, have been the centre of much attention from management and organization scholars throughout the last two decades (e.g. Alvesson, 1995; Biljsma-Frankema et al., 2006; Schroeder and Pauleen, 2007). Definition-wise, Starbuck (1992) describes a Knowledge Intensive Firm as one in which knowledge has more importance than other inputs and outputs. As all judgments of importance are inevitably discretionary, this gives researchers a considerable leeway in circumscribing their field of study. Nevertheless, there exists a large body of literature (e.g. OECD, 1996; Neef, 1998; Schienstock, 2004) arguing that a radical transformation of global economy is underway, and knowledge-intensive organizations (by this or another name) are at the heart of the new resulting order.

The resulting knowledge economy is said to rely on knowledge as its most important resource (Rooney et al., 2005), and to form the basis of growth for developed economies in the foreseeable future. It can thus be expected to provide the basis for economic value creation (Lengrand & Chartrie, 1999). At the same time, knowledge work is rather unique in the fact that it is rarely precisely evaluated. In fact, quite often the employee's assessment is based more on symbolic sacrifices s/he makes and loyalty, rather than on actual work (Coser, 1974; Hochshild, 1997; Barley & Kunda, 2004). This is especially striking in high-tech corporations (Perlow, 1997, 1998; Cooper, 2000), where precise planning is not really possible (Brookes, 1995; Connel, 2000; Kesteloot, 2003), but increasingly present also in all other white-collar occupations (Barley, 1997). Knowledge-intensive workers spend more and more time at work (Schor, 1991; Jacobs & Gerson, 2001), and are being managed by the means of normative control, rather than the traditional hierarchical model. The old, bureaucratic understanding of management as standardization of work process, planning, structural design, control, and formalization, is no longer applicable (Kanter, 1977; Mintzberg, 1983). This change of organizational practices and of the meaning of management is happening in front of our eyes.

There are also many other paradoxes in knowledge work. For example, many innovation and knowledge management systems are designed to facilitate creativity (Gurteen, 1998), but at the same time by their sheer presence they deter many anti-bureaucrats from activity (Weick, 2006). Knowledge is described as organizational resource (Senge, 1990), and at the same time to reside primarily in individual knowledge workers (Leonard, 1998). These phenomena, while clearly observable, are new and still only perfunctorily researched or described.

Although there have been books related to the subject (Kunda, 1992; Hochshild, 1997; Perlow, 1997), in none this problem has been researched thoroughly from international comparative cross-cultural perspective. There was also no book presenting a juxtaposition of actual organizational practices (as observed in a solid field research) in knowledge-intensive organizations situated in different settings and based upon diverging organizing principles.

Last year, we have had the pleasure of publishing an edited volume entitled "Management Practices in High-Tech Environments" (Jemielniak & Kociatkiewicz, 2008). While that collection touched upon many of the themes also present here, we have come to believe that the subject of knowledge intensive organizations, spanning both high and low technology, for-profit and non-for-profit organizations, management-focused and critical perspectives, is both interesting and cohesive enough to warrant a research handbook of its own.

The present volume is the result of this idea, and the enthusiastic response we have met upon suggesting the topic appears to confirm our expectations. We can thus be proud to present a selection of texts that not only encompass a wide variety of research approaches and theoretical stances, but come together to chart the current boundaries of the study of knowledge intensive organizations. We are confident that this book can serve as an introduction to the field, as a guide to ongoing debates, and as inspiration for further research.

Dariusz Jemielniak, Kozminski University, Poland
Jerzy Kociatkiewicz, University of Essex, UK

Preface

This book is organized into seven sections. The first one is dedicated to **learning and innovation**, their rise within the management discourse, the possibilities of their analysis, as well as the varied ways in which they shape contemporary organizational realities. Davydd J. Greenwood shows how the idea of postindustrial society and knowledge-intensiveness is a tool used by scholars and consultants to promote their own means, despite the fact that research universities are neither knowledge-intensive nor eager to learn. Juha Kettunen continues the examination of higher education institutions and the problems they face in producing innovations, and the potential for knowledge management theory in enhancing them. His chapter focuses on human capital as the premier asset of these organizations, and the challenges appearing in the attempts to use it to foster innovation and inter-institutional cooperation.

Jeff Gold and Richard Thorpe delve into the subject of professional learning, using their action research-based study of a law firm to highlight and analyze its collective and distributive character. Paul Trott and Andreas Hoecht study the topic of innovation risks associated with strategic outsourcing, as well as the possible measures to keep them under control. Finally, Lars Steiner uses Actor-Network Theory, as well as the concept of autopoiesis to analyze knowledge management within a collaborative project uniting university and business actors. The study sheds light on both knowledge management and the possibilities of researching knowledge-intensive organizations and projects.

The second section explores the **language of knowledge**, both in terms of the discourse surrounding knowledge and language used to learn, innovate, and share experiences. Ester Barinaga studies performative aspects of international research team perceptions on project's development and construction, and by drawing on Wittgenstein's theory calls for studying knowledge-intensive work also from the linguistic angle. Jo A. Tyler and David M. Boje, conversely, argue that storytelling and narratives, as conscious creations, cannot be used to convey tacit knowledge, although they can help reflect on the already lived experience. Louise Grisoni continues the exploration of the relation between language and knowledge, positing that poetry as a possible link between explicit and implicit types of knowledge in organizations. Stephen Sheard, broadenig the focus of discussion, shows a resurgence of proto-alphabetic communication in contemporary technology, and argues for reexamination of the sources of symbolism animating contemporary discourse of knowledge management.

This discussion sets ground for the third section of the book which focuses on the issue of **managing knowledge** in organizations. Krzysztof Klincewicz analyzes the dissemination of particular forms of knowledge management discourse and ideologies by looking at the role IT Research companies and institutes play in promoting particular concepts, solutions, and perspectives. Fátima Guadamillas-Gómez and Mario J. Donate-Manzanares go into details of knowledge management strategies implementation in technology-intensive organizations, drawing from two success stories documented in research. Arla Juntunen continues a similar theme, reporting on a study of the modes for effective development of a knowledge management platform in high-velocity markets. Jonathan D. Owens concludes the section by arguing for the importance of modelling new process development in contemporary business environment, with particular emphasis on a structured approach involving the creation of roadmaps.

The fourth section of this volume picks up the theme of **management and control**, starting with Anders Örtenblad's critical study of knowledge sharing practices. Analyzing ideas within the dominant discourse of knowledge management, he highlights the dangers of taking these ideas at face value, without a thorough understanding of power relations embedded therein. Angelo Ditillo, also examining managerial control, uses his analysis to propose criteria for evaluating control measures used for knowledge sharing and development in organizations. Aino Kianto and Jianzhong Hong agree that the growth of knowledge-intensive companies and new organizational forms makes the traditional forms of control obsolete, and look at possible replacements, in this chapter they propose two new approaches, focusing on intellectual capital and competence development.

Vidar Hepsø takes a closer look at actual workings of organizational control mechanisms; in a chapter based on a field study in an oil and gas company, he analyzes collaboration and conflict in common information spaces, that is, places where knowledge is shared, negotiated, and disseminated throughout an organization. Agnieszka Postuła, in a chapter also based on a field study, contrasts tendencies for creativity and control in software development companies.

In the fifth section, we look at **the culture of knowledge**, working to situate knowledge-intensive organizations within a broader social context without abandoning focus on the managerial practices encountered in these organizations. In a chapter based on qualitative study of six multinational companies, Patrocinio Zaragoza-Sáez, Enrique Claver-Cortés, and Diego Quer-Ramón search out knowledge management practices conducive to the rise of a new knowledge society. Cliff Bowman and Pauline Gleadle also base their findings on a study of a large corporation, using the case of 3M in the United Kingdom to describe how corporate culture can help negotiate tensions between creativity and financial control. Maria E. Burke, reporting on a three-year international ethnographic study within higher education institutions, describes the interplay of culture and organizational structure, providing groundwork for building knowledge management systems allowing higher levels of information fulfillment.

Darius Mehri delivers a participant observation-based account of engineering work in Toyota Company, highlighting a culture of reliance on explicit knowledge, often undervalued in knowledge management literature, in an organization known for successful integration of innovation and product development processes. Federica Ricceri and James Guthrie also challenge dominant discourse on knowledge management, presenting a critical review of published guidelines for development of organizational policies regarding knowledge resource management in knowledge-intensive companies.

Having looks at management relations within knowledge-intensive organizations, in section six we turn towards the **knowledge workers** and issues concerning individuals taking part in knowledge economy. Christiane Prange discusses strategic alliances capability from knowledge-based view but, in contrast to traditional approaches, she does not take a macro perspective but rather concentrates on bringing the individual back into the equation. Meryem Sevinc, Lawrence Locker, and John D. Murray also look into a discourse commonly excluding the individual: they examine advantages and drawbacks of the ongoing automation of data mining processes. As a result of this analysis, they argue for the need of greater human participation in the form of an analyst-centered approach to knowledge discovery.

Johanna Shih moves the focus towards actual knowledge workers, presenting a study of the work lives of high-tech engineers in Silicon Valley. In particular, she highlights the details of temporal organization of work among these knowledge workers. Alice MacGillivray, maintaining a similar research sensibility, takes us to the public sector, reporting on a Canadian public sector science initiative. Drawing upon the community of practice perspective, she stresses the dynamic character of knowledge work. In another field study-based chapter, Tatiana Andreeva uses data from Russian companies to argue for distinguishing between knowledge creation and knowledge sharing in defining employee roles in knowledge-intensive settings.

The seventh and final section both sums up the major themes of the volume and opens up the field for further research and analysis. Called **discussing knowledge**, it groups together the broadest, theoretical contributions. Thus, Steffen Böhm and Chris Land take on the fundamental issue of value, its relation to knowledge and its status in contemporary economy, arguing for the continued relevance of the labour theory of value despite, or even because of, ongoing transformations of the global economy. Alexander Styhre examines the use of media in knowledge-intensive organizations, arguing for their role in not only integrating otherwise divergent technologies and tools, but also taking the lead in breaking down boundaries between inside and outside, between embodied and technological matter.

In the penultimate chapter, Ben Tran takes a step back to provide a thorough overview of knowledge management concept evolution, presenting the dominant ideas of the discourse as well as different organizational structures understood to enhance knowledge creation, management, and development.

Our own chapter concludes the volume with a critical overview of the knowledge management concept and its most common forms. Despite the prevalence of its usage in a simplistic rhetorical fashion in popular management, we argue that it also plays an important role in reinforcing managerial domination. As such, we believe this book constitutes not the final word on management in knowledge intensive organizations, but rather a recapitulation of the current state of research, as well as a demarcation of areas necessitating further study.

REFERENCES

Alvesson, M. (1995). *Management of Knowledge-Intensive Companies.* Walter de Gruyter, Berlin.

Barley, S. R. (1997). In L. A. Perlow (Foreowrd), *Finding Time. How Corporations, Individuals, and Families Can Benefit from New Work Practices*. Ithaca-London: ILR Press.

Barley, S. R., & Kunda, G. (2004). *Gurus, Hired Guns, and Warm Bodies. Itinerant Experts in a Knowledge Economy*. Princeton: Princeton University Press.

Bijlsma-Frankema, K., Rosendaal, B., & Taminiau, Y. (2006). Acting on Frictions: Learning Blocks and Flows in Knowledge Intensive Organizations. *Journal of European Industrial Training, 30*(4), 291-309.

Brookes, F. P. (1995). *The Mythical Man-Month.* Reading, Massachusetts: Addison- Wesley.

Cooper, M. (2000). Being the "Go-To Guy": Fatherhood, Masculinity, and the Organization of Work in Silicon Valley. *Qualitative Sociology,* 23/4: 379-405.

Coser, L. (1974). *Greedy Institutions.* New York: Free Press.

Connel, C. (2001). *Why Software Is (Almost) Always Late*. Presentation of CHC-3 Consulting at http://www.chc-3.com/talk/why_software_late.ppt. (accessed 01.10. 2008).

Gurteen, D. (1998). Knowledge, Creativity, and Innovation. *Journal of Knowledge Management, 2*(1), 5-13.

Hochshild, A. R. (1997). *The Time Bind: When Work Becomes Home and Home Becomes Work.* New York: Metropolitan.

Jacobs, J. A., & Gerson, K. (2001). Overworked Individuals or Overworked Families? *Work and Occupations, 28*(1), 40-63.

Jemielniak, D., & Kociatkiewicz, J. (Eds.) (2008). *Management Practices in High-Tech Environments*. Hershey: Information Science Reference.

Kanter, R. (1983). *The Changemasters*. New York: Simon and Schuster.

Kesteloot, L. (2003). *Why Software is Late?* http://www.teamten.com/lawrence/writings/late_software.html. (accessed 01.10.2008).

Kunda, G. (1992). *Engineering Culture: Control and Commitment in a High-Tech Corporation.* Philadelphia: Temple University Press

Lengrand, L., & Chartrie, I. (1999). *Business Networks and the Knowledge-Driven Economy*. Brussels: European Commission.

Leonard, D. A. (1998). *Wellsprings of Knowledge: Building and Sustaining the Sources of Innovation.* Boston: Harvard Business School Press.

Mintzberg, H. (1983). *Structure in fives: Designing effective organizations.* Englewood Cliffs, NJ: Prentice-Hall.

Neef, D. (1997). *The Knowledge Economy.* Oxford: Butterworth-Heinemann.

OECD. (1996). *The Knowledge-based Economy.* Paris: STI Outlook.

Perlow, L. A. (1997). *Finding Time. How Corporations, Individuals, and Families Can Benefit from New Work Practices*. Ithaca: ILR Press.

Perlow, L. A. (1998). Boundary Control: The Social Ordering of Work and Family Time in a High-tech Corporation. *Administrative Science Quarterly*, *43*, 328-357.

Rooney, D., Hearn, G., & Ninan, A. (2005). *Handbook on the Knowledge Economy*. Cheltenham: Edward Elgar.

Schienstock, G. (2004). *Embracing the Knowledge Economy*. Cheltenham: Edward Elgar.

Schor, J. (1991). *The Overworked American: The Unexpected Decline of Leisure*. New York: Basic Books.

Schroeder, A., & Pauleen, D. (2007). KM Governance: Investigating the Case of Knowledge Intensive Research Organization. *Journal of Enterprise Information, 20*(4), 414-431.

Senge, P. (1990). *The Fifth Discipline: The Art and Practice of the Learning Organization*. New York: Doubleday Currency.

Starbuck, W. H. (1992). Learning by Knowledge-Intensive Firms. *Journal of Management Studies, 29*(6), 713-740.

Weick, K. E. (2006). Organizing and Failures of Imagination. *Public Management Review, 8*(3), 425-439.

Acknowledgment

The authors would, first of all, like to thank all the members of the editorial board: Mats Alvesson (Lund University), Toru Ishida (Kyoto University), Monika Kostera (Warsaw University), John Van Maanen (MIT), Andrzej K. Koźmiński (Kozminski University), and Sarosh Kuruvilla (Cornell University) for their support and input in this book's formation. Jessica Thompson, Kirstin Roth, and Julia Mosemann of Information Science Reference also deserve our most heartfelt thanks.

Dariusz Jemielniak would also like to thank Center for European Studies (Harvard University), Institute for Research on Labor and Employment (University of California, Berkeley), Kosciuszko Foundation, as well as professor Neil Fligstein, without whose help and aid this project would not be possible. I am also grateful to Joanna, for her inspiration, love, and unconditional support.

Jerzy Kociatkiewicz extends his thanks to all the colleagues at Essex Business School, and particularly to Marjana Johansson, for her tolerance of his constantly missed deadlines, and to Martyna Śliwa of Northumbria University for inspiration and support. And the biggest debt of gratitude goes to Niq, as always.

Dariusz Jemielniak, Kozminski University, Poland
Jerzy Kociatkiewicz, University of Essex, UK

Section I
Learning and Innovation

Chapter I
Are Research Universities Knowledge-Intensive Learning Organizations?

Davydd J. Greenwood
Cornell University, USA

ABSTRACT

This chapter questions the clarity of the concepts of "knowledge society" and "knowledge-intensive organization". In particular, the author asserts that the notion that postindustrial society is more knowledge intensive than industrial society is a self-serving proposition made by academics and organizational consultants to emphasize the importance of their own industries. Since all organizations are knowledge-intensive in major ways, the specific meanings of a newly emergent kind of knowledge-intensive organization need to be clarified. The author undertakes this by means of an analysis of research universities.

INTRODUCTION

Research universities could seem to be among the best contemporary embodiments of knowledge-intensive organizations, given the vast quantities of people and knowledge resources at their disposal and their mission to expand and transmit knowledge. In addition, universities claim to be preparing students to work in the "knowledge society" of the future. Thus it would seem that universities are specially situated in a position of expertise about life in the knowledge society and in knowledge-intensive organizations. I do not believe this is the case.

Despite the many Ph.D.s awarded, students taught, research projects undertaken, and libraries/databases, universities generally do not embody the defining characteristics of knowledge-intensive organizations nor do they behave like learning organizations. Very little of the social science and humanistic knowledge universities have is deployed beyond the boundaries of the academic professional groups that generate it, few social scientists and humanists have the competence to act as thoughtful organizational participants in their own institutions or in the world beyond the university, and many of the students that universities train graduate lacking the competence to perform the jobs for which they are hired.

The situation of faculty and students in the sciences and engineering is somewhat better because they maintain multiple and continuing contacts with the world outside the university, often work in teams, and train students through participation in projects. However, in general, the effectiveness of research universities as contributors to the training of new participants in the knowledge society, beyond being successful businesses in their own right, is limited.

Against this backdrop, this paper provides a provisional analysis of what seems to be a key issue: If a high quantity of knowledge and a large staff of highly trained people automatically give rise to a knowledge-intensive organization, then research universities would be, by definition, knowledge-intensive organizations. However, since universities are not knowledge-intensive organizations by any reasonable definition, exploring why not reveals three things. First, it shows that knowledge-intensive organizations are a product of structures, relationships, and dynamics in the organization, not of the quanta of knowledge they contain, the level of education of their personnel, or their sectoral location. Second, a knowledge-intensive organization must have at least some of the key characteristics of learning organizations (Argyris and Schön, 1996). That is to say, unless organizations are capable of creatively modifying their structures, behavior, and alignment with the environment, then they simply cannot be knowledge- intensive organizations at all. Third, these characteristics of learning organizations are generally lacking in research universities which are Tayloristically- organized and yet loosely-coupled systems.

To make these points, I focus on research universities and compare some current models of knowledge-intensive organizations and learning organizations with the way knowledge and learning are organized in universities. To anticipate, my argument is that, though research universities are dedicated to the development and dissemination of knowledge, there are many ways that they do not function as knowledge-intensive organizations and they lack most of the characteristics of learning organizations.[a] Once this argument is made, I turn to asking if universities wished to become more predominantly knowledge-intensive organizations[b], how they would have to change and I close asking if these changes could be made while avoiding the further dilution of some of the key disciplinary knowledge development and management functions research universities perform.

Conceptual Background

The literature on the knowledge society and knowledge-intensive organizations is chaotic intellectual terrain. Beyond the inherent complexity of the issues, with so many disciplines and non-academic players engaged in the many dimensions of these topics, the subject itself is a labyrinth. To negotiate this terrain, I had to clarify for myself what I understand to be some of the key concepts and terms and will share the results of this effort as my point of departure.

It is necessary to begin with knowledge itself. Much of the literature takes particular views on knowledge for granted. Many academics have narrowed the notion of knowledge in ways that permit them to claim ownership over key forms of knowledge and to the right to arbitrate what is good and not so good knowledge in particular disciplines. I am especially sensitive to this because I am an action researcher. Action research is based on a considerably broader multi-disciplinary view and on profound respect for the knowledge of non-academic people (Greenwood and Levin, 2006).

I find it useful to treat knowledge as a broad and differentiated set of categories: knowledge about the world, knowledge about how the world works, knowledge that explains why particular things happen and others do not, and knowledge for particular purposes and practices. This is not the place for an essay on this topic. Good synthetic arguments about these distinctions are those found in Eikeland (2006), Flyvbjerg (2001), Ryle (1949), and Toulmin and Gustavsen (1996)[c]. While there are significant disagreements among these writers, the multiple dimensions of knowledge and the complexity of the knowledge/practice links are clear.

In addition, it is useful to distinguish between expert knowledge generated by professional groups with particular kinds of training and local knowledge developed over the course of life experience in particular situations. Everyone has local knowledge while expert knowledge is more narrowly distributed. It is also important to distinguish between tacit knowledge and explicit knowledge (Polanyi, 1964, 1966, Schön, 1983, 1987, 1991) and to problematize the links between these forms of knowledge[d]. It is also vital to follow Gilbert Ryle's distinctions between "knowing how" and "knowing that" to see that knowledge-intensive organizations actually must synthesize both forms of knowledge in order to operate successfully (Ryle, 1949).

One of the most intractable problems in this arena is many academics' powerful drive to segregate knowledge from practice, to separate thought from action. This has been widely noted by the pragmatists and neo-pragmatists and was nicely described by Toulmin as the "Cartesian wrong turn" (Toulmin, 1990). However, the efforts of generations of pragmatist thinkers have made little dent in the social science/humanities practice of rarifying knowledge into the realm of dematerialized theorizing that takes place and is validated in abstract disciplinary spaces. Such a view of knowledge is not only epistemologically flawed but it offers little that is of value for a discussion of the knowledge society, knowledge-intensive organizations, or learning organizations. Non-material or de-materialized knowledge, separate from thinking beings in the process of living their lives, is the root of the social and moral irrelevance of so work done in the social sciences and the humanities. Its only advantage is that it nicely allows academics to sit in their offices and libraries while imagining that somehow their work is meaningful to the world that provides them with a salary. In effect, this produces knowledge that without knowledge how, knowledge not tested in practice and not contextualized so that it can be more deeply understood. Such a narrow and uninteresting view of knowledge production dominates much of the social sciences and humanities. It also is widely distributed in the administrative ideologies by which institutions of higher education are managed.

Finally and again to suit the convenience of experts whose lives are lived in libraries, laboratories, and faculty offices, there is an overwhelming tendency to equate knowledge in all these discussions of the knowledge society with "explicit" knowledge. This restriction of the scope of the concept of knowledge reduces knowledge to a kind of explicitly produced and packaged commodity that is transacted by academics, consultants, and other kinds of experts as if useful knowledge in organizations is all explicit knowledge, as if implicit and tacit knowledge does not matter, as if non-formalized knowledge systems don't play a dominant organizational role[e]. Generations of field anthropologists, sociolinguists, and linguistic philosophers already rejected such simplistic claims.

Knowledge Society/Information Society/Technological Society/ Knowledge Workers/Knowledge-Intensive Organizations

It does not take long for a reader to discover that there is little conceptual agreement regarding the meaning of these terms. They need to be sorted out and others (e.g. Alvesson, 2004; Castells, 1999) are working on this. Here I only provide enough sense of my understanding of the various terms to anchor my analysis of universities.

One distinction analysts have invested in heavily is that between the information society and the knowledge society. Apparently Daniel Bell introduced the term Information society in 1973, in his book The Coming of Post-Industrial Society (Bell, 1973). He believed that theoretical knowledge would become more central to society's functioning and that knowledge-based production systems would supplant manufacturing in the new economy. With the coming of the IT age, this idea gained momentum and began circulating in international policy circles. Susan Burch argues that this concept became an ideological structure in support of the neo-liberal globalization of supposedly self-regulated markets (Burch, 2005). It appears that the concept of a knowledge society emerged partly to counter this ideological and political/economic tendency.

Knowledge society gestures in the direction of including more than the economic globalization of information systems in the notion of knowledge. It tries to capture a broader set of social and cultural dimensions that are relevant to the social transitions we are experiencing. People who use the term knowledge society often share an interest in empowerment and redistributive policies, take a critical attitude toward the processes at work, and contest the necessity of a link between the expansion of IT and of free market global capitalism (*e.g.* Zuboff, 1984).

The scope of Manuel Castells' work on these topics and the complexity of his arguments are daunting and he has become one of the most influential thinkers on this subject. According to him, information is actually a product of organizations in which information becomes the core source of productivity. Therefore, in Castells' view, IT is a set of processes to be developed in organizations and not simply some kind of technical tool (Castells, 1999: 5-6). Whatever else his view contains, it is important because it is a people-centered, society-centered view of the current processes amplifying the basis of the knowledge society view of the deployment of IT.

The competing techno/economic and social/ethical views of the information and knowledge societies have a direct impact on the contradictory literature on knowledge-intensive organizations. For some authors on knowledge-intensive organizations, a techno/economic view dominates; for others, a social/ethical view predominates. Of course, both dimensions are relevant and no account that ignores either side is likely to be useful.

However, returning to the point made by my colleague, Morten Levin, this whole discussion is heavily premised on the indefensible view that most knowledge that is relevant to this subject is explicit knowledge. That is certainly wrong. Explicit and tacit knowledge are mutually interdependent and necessary to the good functioning of organizations. Discussions of the knowledge society and knowledge intensive organizations that do not take account of the co-presence and importance of both tacit and explicit knowledge produce only a simulacrum of organizational life.

Knowledge-Intensive Organizations vs. What?

Having gotten to this point with the literature on the subject, I returned to the questions I started with: How can we distinguish a knowledge-intensive organization from any other? What is the relationship between the concepts of a knowledge-intensive organization and a learning organization? Do knowledge-intensive organizations learn better than others?

I already knew both from my own research experience and from the literature that non-knowledge-intensive organizations can be learning organizations. This has been made abundantly clear in the work of Argyris and Schön (1996), Senge (1990), and Jaworski and Scharmer (2000) and the other advocates of the concept of organizational learning. What has not been explored fully is whether knowledge-intensive organizations necessarily learn better than others and, in particular, whether the knowledge intensity of research universities is relevant to the notions of a knowledge society or to the training of "knowledge workers"[f].

One way to approach this is to examine the idealizations of conditions under which knowledge workers operate, conditions that supposedly create successful knowledge-intensive organizations. Like the conditions for the existence of a learning organization, these conditions are never fully met. Rather, they point to particular kinds of institutional arrangements that are logically necessary for knowledge-intensive organizations to function.

Knowledge workers and knowledge-intensive organizational environments necessarily operate within considerably less hierarchical structures than those found in bureaucratic chain-of-command organizations. This is not an ethical or political judgment; it is a structural consequence. If creativity and change are to be initiated and rewarded throughout an organization, then there has to be some autonomy of individuals and groups within the organizational structures both to determine their own courses of action and to assess and adjust to the conditions in the environment outside their organizations directly. Key prerogatives of upper management in bureaucratic organizations -- imposing decisions and direction from above and exclusive right to manage all external relations -- are, in knowledge-intensive organizations, diffused broadly throughout the organization. Self-control, self-evaluation and new and flatter systems of management and decision-making are vital. Even figuring out "what business we are in" is up for grabs in such situations. These dilemmas create many new organizational challenges and shift patterns of behavior and leadership in complex ways that are just now becoming more clear (Hirschhorn, 1997).

Another way to state these issues is to use the language that Morten Levin suggests for this. He calls the coordination that permits an organization to perform a particular service or to manufacture a specific product means that all the kinds and contexts of knowledge at the various positions in the organizational structure its "value chain". The virtue of this way of conceptualizing the matter is that it shows that knowledge-intensive organizations have to integrate and diffuse knowledge throughout the value chain. This kind of broadly diffused and integrated value chain becomes a defining characteristic of knowledge-intensive organizations.

Perspectives on Organization

Another key difficulty in the knowledge-intensive organization literature is a lack of agreement about how to conceptualize organizations in general. For those trained in the conventional social sciences (e.g. functionalist, structural-functionalist, social psychological, or political economic frameworks), the way organizations are understood is quite different from the way we understand them in the action research/socio-technical systems world where I work. For the conventional organizational thinkers, organizations mainly are combinations of rules, roles, social processes, psychological relationships and structured hierarchies that are amenable to positivist, structuralist, constructivist, and political economic analysis because they lie on the rule-driven and structured side of human behavior. Rules, functions, structures, infrastructures, superstructures, and ideologies are all conceptualized as products of human behavior and volition.

While action research does not deny the existence of these dimensions, action research perspectives growing out of the work of Eric Trist, Fred Emery, and Einar Thorsrud at the Tavistock Institute and in the Norwegian "industrial democracy" movement (see Greenwood and Levin, 2006), take quite a different view, one only found in some of the science and technology studies literature (e.g. David Noble, 1977, 1984). In this view, the technologies and materialities of organizations are intimately linked and interpenetrated with their social dimensions and integrated by the complex daily actions of the participants. Broadly called "socio-technical systems analysis," the emphasis is on the alternative ways of managing the integration and complex inter-relationships between social and technical systems.

The relationship between social and technical systems, even in highly complex technological environments, is always a contingent one, capable of being changed by conscious design to shift the linkages between social systems and technologies and create different kinds of working environments and human situations. Further, socio-technical analysis, as this is where it links to Science and Technology Studies, shows that the social relations of production are often designed, sometimes unintentionally or at least unconsciously, into the technologies used. In action research, this leads beyond the mere readjustment of social systems to existing technologies and into the redesign of technologies with human work systems themselves in mind.

From this work and the work done in the social studies of sciences, we know that the technologies, no matter how apparently deterministic and closed to human choice, often can be deployed in more and more diverse and complex ways than the designers of these systems ever imagined (Eijnatten, 1993). There is an immense literature on this subject, though its influence in Europe and Australia is much greater (England, Australia, Norway, Sweden, Finland, and Holland) than in North America where the technological determinist view still dominates and is supported by most of the conventional social science work on organizations (Eijnatten, 1993).

These perspectives are important because they complicate the relationships between organization and technology and because they have also been used to broaden and complicate the concept of technology itself. Technology is not limited to material artifacts (machines, tools, assembly lines) but includes a whole variety of technical routines and practices that involve material objects (information technology, paper, printers, networks, routinized practices that integrate thought and action, technology and knowledge in a seamless way. For people steeped in this approach to socio-technical systems, a hard and fast distinction between manufacturing organizations, service organizations, and knowledge-intensive organizations cannot be made. Human knowing, reflective practice, and human/technology interactions are central to all forms of organization and to all projects for organizational change and development.

As a result, for me this means that the implied distinction between knowledge-intensive organizations and other kinds of organizations needs to be worked at harder if it is to have useful meaning. We know that manufacturing organizations can be knowledge-intensive organizations and later I will argue that knowledge rich organizations like universities cannot currently be understood usefully as knowledge-intensive organizations.

Just to complicate matters more, it is important to introduce the concept of "loosely-coupled organizations". The concept of loose coupling, actually drawn from a particular IT context, was applied to universities in 1976 by Karl Weick. According to Weick's formulation, in loosely-coupled organizations, a variety of different means and units can produce a particular result, overall coordination of effort is lacking, regulations do not guide much of the conduct that goes on, and there is a profusion of networks but the feedback across them is slow and spotty. Weick also points out that these features, which a Tayloristic manager would view as negative can also have positive consequences because they permit survival through turbulent external situations, they do not suppress local creativity and responses, and they do mean that some parts of the organization can fail without compromising the whole organization.

It is abundantly clear to me that Weick is right that universities are loosely-coupled organizations. However, whatever their virtues, it means that the kind of value chains that are necessary for knowledge-intensive organizations and for learning organizations to flourish do not exist in this loosely-coupled world.

As a final preparatory step, I need to review some of the defining features of knowledge-intensive firms and of learning organizations to set some criteria for my discussion of universities. Among the central characteristics of knowledge-intensive firms are their focus on the value of the intelligence and engagement of their employees and the kinds of solidarities created among them. Technology is part of these relationships but the focus is explicitly on the creation on ongoing learning opportunities and communities of practice. Mentoring, sharing information, brainstorming, etc. are a central feature. They practice and encourage continuous learning, recognize knowledge sharing, mentoring and apprenticeship.[g]

Underlying this is the notion that the creation of value requires ongoing adaption to changing conditions through collaborative learning processes. This, in turn, places an emphasis on the people who work for the organization and the kinds of relationships and communication patterns they develop. People are also seen as the ultimate repositories of knowledge (both explicit and tacit) and the key source of value creation (Levin, ed., 2002). Finally, in such organizations, linkages to the clients and the external environments are multiple and occur at many levels of the organization. They are not limited only to those at the apex of the organizational system because adaptation to the external environment is a shared responsibility.

Learning Organizations

Another concept bearing a relationship to knowledge-intensive organizations is learning organizations and organizational learning (terms coined by and brought into major use by Chris Argyris and Donald Schön, *op. cit.* and then strongly promoted by Peter Senge, *op. cit.* and the Society for Organizational Learning). Learning organizations are not identical to knowledge-intensive organizations. Among the characteristics of learning organizations is the ability of the members to examine the situations they operate in openly and non-defensively. In conventional organizations, the hierarchical distribution of authority, defensiveness, and the "blame game" are key dynamics and they lead to erroneous analyses of problems and the repetition or even intensification of behavior that is counterproductive for the organization.

In a learning organization, non-defensive behavior based on open inquiry into the behavior and motives of others and transparency about one's own motives and actions is supported by managers and management systems that promote and reward interaction between people at different organizational levels. Learning experiences are widely shared, resulting in a good deal of feedback, commentary, and brainstorming about new organizational routines.

Learning organizations are able to engage in what Argyris and Schön call "double-loop learning" (following Gregory Bateson and cybernetics' emphasis on learning how to learn) to a greater extent than can non-learning organizations. No organization achieves perfection in double-loop learning and single-loop learning (responding to challenges by intensifying the actions that created the challenge without inquiring into their appropriateness) is always present.

I want to emphasize that double-loop learning involves reacting openly to challenges from within and without, examining the ways organization members' own behaviors are contributing to the problems faced, and then restructuring or resetting parameters of units or of the organization itself to achieve a more successful set of outcomes. It involves a good deal of online inquiry as a core organizational process and the expansion of discipline of reacting to challenges non-defensively while receiving encouragement to act in this non-defensive way from colleagues and superiors.

When these practices are successfully emphasized in an organization, the members develop a more widely shared vision of the organization's mission and they also develop a kind of solidarity and trust based on experience that enhances organizational flexibility and adaptiveness. In the end, operating this way requires the members of an organization to see the organization as an open system aligned with a complex and dynamic external environment. This is a clear example of a knowledge-intensive organization with an integrated value chain.

There are a fair number of cases of conventional manufacturing and materials processing companies that have managed to transition into becoming learning organizations without shifting into knowledge work *per se* (see Senge, *op. cit.*). By the same token, there is no inherent connection between having vast stores of non-material knowledge and being a knowledge-intensive organization or a learning organization. Thus the mere quantum of knowledge at a university in no way makes a university a knowledge-intensive organization and the loosely-coupled organizational structure of most universities makes it highly unlikely for universities to become learning organizations.

Knowledge at Research Universities

With these definitional matters now articulated, I can move to an explanation why I do not believe that research universities are knowledge-intensive organizations or learning organizations.

There can be no question that knowledge creation and transmission are central activities at such universities. A core activity is the preservation/archiving of knowledge in curricula and in libraries and databases. Considerable resources are devoted to the teaching and learning of knowledge in classrooms, laboratories, libraries, and studios. At most universities, a significant amount of time, infrastructure, and other resources are devoted to research processes that involve the organization of existing knowledge and the systematic effort to generate new knowledge. Some portion of most research universities' activities are devoted to fashioning existing knowledge into new and useful applications available to the private sector and/or to the public. What I have just written basically reproduces the commonsense version of what most people, including the faculty, staff, students, parents, and policymakers think of when they describe research universities. They are sites of knowledge creation, conservation, and knowledge transmission.

None of this means that university faculty are more intelligent or creative than other kinds of people, that university administrators apply rational and reflexively tested models to their decision-making, or that students are necessarily committed to the search for knowledge. All universities have faculty members, administrators, and students who are neither creative nor committed to the search for and transmission of knowledge. As in any organization, only a few of the members really press the boundaries in positive ways. Earning a Ph.D., Masters, or baccalaureate degree does not show that a person is intelligent or creative. It shows that they have certain work habits and have applied themselves sufficiently to earn the degrees. We have all met bus drivers, plumbers, and bricklayers who are at least as intelligent as any of our academic colleagues.

The role of technology and technical knowledge at universities heterogeneous and probably not very clear to most of the relevant stakeholders. For the administrative staff, having the requisite books, databases, information technology capacities, classrooms, laboratories, functioning utilities, and suitable built environment is an ongoing technical challenge of universities. For another part of the administrative staff and for many research faculty, having access to leading edge technologies and research infrastructure is a *sine qua non* for a university to be a major research institution. This group lives with something like an "arms race" among the top research universities to have and maintain the best research infrastructures to be competitive in the world of grant-getting, to recruit the most productive research faculty, to rank high among competing institutions, and to be credible with powerful actors in the public and private sectors. And even this is a minority activity with the bulk of the faculty doing very routine and repetitive work.

The teaching faculty and others concerned with teaching also have an interest in technologies. So-called "smart classrooms," online grading and examination systems, online student response systems, web-based instruction and course archives, on-line library access, and agile internet links widely distributed across campuses are key elements in the daily life of research universities as knowledge transmission institutions.

Administrative staff members rely heavily on information technology for data management, budgeting, planning, institutional research, and human resource actions. Most universities have transitioned into the use of some kind of complex management software systems such as those provided by SAP or PeopleSoft with lots of consequent reorganizations, confusions, difficulties, and incomplete deployment. Over time, IT professionals have come to play a more central role in university administrations than they once had but, as is the case in most private companies, the integration between management systems and IT structures is anything but perfect.

All dimensions of technology at universities can be analyzed usefully from a socio-technical perspective, though this is not a central point of the current essay. The match and mismatch between the organizational needs of knowledge generation, knowledge management, knowledge transmission, and institutional administration are constant features of contemporary university life. Many of the technical systems have inbuilt Tayloristic structures and yet there are ongoing pressures to operate in a much more decentralized and autonomous way. Many senior administrators lament that research universities are so egalitarian that they cannot "manage" the faculty successfully and yet the decision structure of most institutions, on paper, is intensely hierarchical. The lack of clarity about the contradictory uses of a command and control structure of administration and appeals to the autonomy and decisional power of the faculty is a feature of everyday life in academia.[h]

Disciplinary knowledge structures: One of the hallmarks of the modern and the contemporary research university (as well as of many teaching universities and liberal arts colleges) is the elaborate division of knowledge into disciplinary structures. The ideal model underlying this widespread organizational feature would have warmed the heart of the late Dame Mary Douglas because it is as good an example as one can find of the classificatory logic she described in her famous book, Purity and Danger (Douglas, 1966). Her basic premise is that most human societies operate as if the world were an orderly system of natural categories that do not overlap. Some version of the "great chain of being" conception of a world created by and held together by an omniscient and beneficent creator is necessary as an explanation for these features of the world (Lovejoy, 1936; Greenwood, 1985). Every academic discipline is asserted to correspond to a category of things in nature about which it has the obligation to know as much as possible. No one but a disciplinary specialist can possibly know as much and render competent judgments about their subject. Laid side by side, these disciplines cover the universe, giving a clear meaning to the idea of a "university".

Douglas' analysis, even though decidedly static in its view of nature and only dynamic in terms of the constant human efforts at sensemaking, showed clearly that such classificatory systems are inherently doomed to fail. When they fail, they give rise to what she called "dirt" (matter out of place, in her terminology). In Douglas' view, we humans spend most of our lives sweeping up this dirt, trying to tidy up the classifications. We work to adjust reality to the requirements of the classificatory system rather than observable state of the world.

When colleagues in anthropology assert that people in departments of literature have "stolen" the ideas of anthropology to invent a version of anthropology "lite" (e.g. cultural studies), they are speaking as if a particular set of subject matters and approaches inherently (in the nature of things) belonged to anthropology as a discipline. Such a view is a combination of arrant nonsense, cynical politics, and also an expression of the great chain of being view of the world. When students ask me, what exactly is the difference between sociology and anthropology, they make it clear that they have understood that the two are supposed to be inherently different and, because they cannot see the difference clearly, it must be their fault for not understanding the "disciplines". Thus this kind of disciplining encourages faculty and students to ignore the complexity and ambiguity of the observed world in favor of the classificatory scheme that justifies their actions.

These divisions are not just language games. They also have a political economy dimension. While within the disciplines, the experts assert their right to determine matters of content, interpretation, and quality and are backed up by national and international disciplinary professional societies and their journals, between the disciplines, there is a reasonably intense struggle to capture the resources of the institution at the expense of other disciplines. Since the disciplines are asserted to be completely distinct in this model, comparative judgments about their value or worthiness cannot be made (e.g. physics cannot be better than chemistry in principle) and so national and international "league tables" are used to argue that this physics department deserves more resources than the chemistry department because it is higher ranked nationally or internationally. Or the counter-argument is made that, since chemistry is not as well ranked, the administration should devote more resources to it and bring it up in the rankings. These disciplinary turf battles are adjudicated by the deans, provosts, presidents, rectors, and/or vice-rectors, giving the system its Tayloristic command and control structure.

This kind of university topography appears to be an ideal embodiment of Taylorism. It postulates a rigid division of labor based on separable categories of disciplinary expertise and delivers to the "experts" all decisions about content and quality within their categories. It also implies that disciplinary departments together do not form a university. For there to be a university, there must be a dean who oversees the division of labor and resources among departments and above the dean, a provost, president, vice-rector, or rector who oversees the division of labor among the colleges and faculties. Thus the disciplinary system involves a heavily hierarchical system of control and allocation of resources. It also means that key resource decisions are made at a very considerable distance from the point of academic value creation.

Yet universities are not really Tayloristic. In a Tayloristic system, a clearly defined product passes through the manufacturing or service development process from one unit to another until it emerges as a finished product. This has little or nothing to do with university life. There is no single product, no single market, and there is little that really integrates the units. While students may pass from unit to unit, they are hardly products of a tight Tayloristic system either. There are few real links between most of the "production" units and therefore no obvious "value chain" linking the parts in a coherent way. A loosely-coupled system of this sort simply does not have such value chains across its whole structure. Small and selective value chains leading from product inception to delivery may exist but none seem to operate at the level of the institution as a whole.

Forms of knowledge work: Research universities include a highly heterogeneous set of forms of knowledge work. These range from artistic creation in painting, sculpture, music, and creative writing taught through coaching, mentoring, and reflective practice to scientific discovery activities built around laboratories and engaged in by heterogeneous teams of professors, research associates, graduate students, and undergraduate students. They include a variety of fields engaged in social analysis, synthesis, critique, and reform that are largely organized by discipline and mainly enacted by solo practitioners. Universities also often include contract work for the public and private sectors in a wide variety of fields (e.g. applied sciences and engineering and the applied social sciences).

Purchase and sale of knowledge: As production systems, universities clearly engage in the purchase and sale of knowledge. As tuition charging institutions, universities are, in effect, "selling" knowledge transmission to students and their families on the promise that the development of particular competencies will assist the students in achieving a better future adult life. Universities also can be said to purchase knowledge when they pay faculty salaries and assert some financial stake in the intellectual property faculty produce (e.g. shared patent rights) or when they compete with other universities to recruit a prestigious faculty member in support of one of the university's research priorities.

Universities regularly sell their knowledge to the public sector as when universities do research financed by governmental research agencies (e.g. the National Science Foundation, the National Aerospace Administration, the National Institutes of Health, etc.). To be fair, universities also often donate knowledge to the public sector in areas where university expertise is needed. Still, as financial pressures increase, many research universities seek to make a significant income by selling their research capacities to the private sector (see Kirp, 2003; Washburn, 2005)

Steering mechanisms: Another feature of universities the overall way they guide themselves in relation to their external and internal environments, their steering mechanisms, to use Burton Clark's term[i]. While not entirely market-driven, universities do face markets of various sorts. There is a competitive market among the best institutions to enroll the best students. While prestigious institutions admit only a small percentage of the students who apply, they end up competing with other universities over that small number of the very best students in the applicant pool in any given year. In that competitive contest, curricula, faculty/student ratios, living arrangements, libraries, dining, and other services end up being important elements in a successful competitive strategy.

Universities also obviously compete for a limited number of highly visible faculty members. The competition takes the form of using salary and working condition considerations as elements in a package to recruit these elite faculty away from the institutions they currently work for. Young faculty who distinguish themselves and become highly visible receive offers from other institutions and their home institutions have to make decisions about the relative merits of meeting outside offers with reasonable counter-offers.

There is also another kind of disciplinary market in these institutions. In fields that bring in lots of external research money, faculty salaries and working conditions are sometimes viewed as university investments. In a "hot" scientific field like genomics, a university may be willing to offer a promising junior person they are trying to recruit not only a nice salary but a significant amount of money to set up a laboratory and start research projects. The administrators are betting that the success of these faculty in attracting outside money will both benefit the university financially and enhance its prestige.

Finally, and perhaps more obviously, there is an active competitive market in foundation grants, private sector research contracts, and public sector grants and contracts. Success rates in these grant-getting efforts are a major source of the prestige rankings among institutions, even though it is often the case that such grants cost universities more resources than they bring in.

However, all of these individual approaches to competitive situations do not add up to an integrated overall "business strategy". For the most part, these different competitive situations are addressed quasi-independently by individual units, often far down in the university hierarchy of management where individual faculty entrepreneurs, individual laboratories or research units, and programs set their own strategies and compete with extra-university peers for funding and prestige.

University management systems: While private sector companies rely on accounting systems and market analyses for decision support, university management is a more abstract exercise. To begin with, the products of a university are highly differentiated: undergraduate and graduate students, research outcomes, and public service in an immense and heterogeneous set of areas. A one-size-fits-all approach to decision-making simply cannot work.

Upper management is remote from the multiplicity of locations of value production and has little idea about the conditions of work, competitiveness, and difficulties being faced by most of the value producers in the system. In my own experience, I am regularly astonished by the poor and abstract information used by academic upper management to make major decisions about the allocation of university resources. By the time an issue manages to work its way up from a group of students or a faculty group to the central administration, it is often so completely deprived of context and meaning and thus the decisions made bear little relation to the problem to be addressed[j]. This situation is not surprising since no single accounting technology can provide accurate information about the operation of a great many of the key units of a university. In the absence of information that can be easily captured on spreadsheets and projections, it is not surprising that upper administrators often end up imitating the behavior of peer institutions or relying on the latest management nostrums like TQM or SAP applications, even if their deployment cannot be based on data analysis and is thus derisory or actually counterproductive[k].

I am not asserting that upper academic managers are fools. Rather I emphasize this point particularly because university administrators' ongoing reliance on structures of hierarchical and information poor decision-making is directly counter to the processes that organize a knowledge-intensive learning organization. It means that decisions are not well connected to most of the environments in which university generated knowledge is created or applied. Further, it means that relations with powerful public sector and community constituencies are not well managed and are often in the hands of people least able to know what substantively faculty and other personnel have to offer to these constituencies that would be of value to them.

Having a hierarchical organizational structure that reserves most adjustments to the external environment to central managers and that discourages direct connections between the broad array of staff and faculty who may be in a better position to know or find out the needs of key actors in the extra-university environment means that, while research universities contain lots of knowledge, they are not knowledge-intensive organizations.

Rather than adjusting to environmental challenges by inquiring into the causes of their problems and reflecting on their own behavior and organizational practices as contributors to the problem, university actors regularly try to deal with challenges by intensifying the very behavior that created the problem to begin with. For example, research universities that have embarked on a highly entrepreneurial approach to grant getting and patenting, when faced with declining revenues, rather than reconsidering their strategy and their mix of research/teaching products to find a more favorable income/expense balance, simply throw more institutional resources and effort into the competition for the ever more scarce resources, promoting a national race to the bottom in the process. This is classic single loop behavior.

Another way of framing these same issues is to examine these observations in the perspective provided by Nowotny, Gibbons, and Scott in Rethinking Science (2001)[i]. The core argument made in this work (and in an earlier work by Gibbons, Nowotny, and Limoges, 1994) and widely taken up by university administrators and policymakers in Europe is that there are two basic modes of knowledge production: Mode 1 and Mode 2. Mode 1 knowledge production is the kind of knowledge created in the Tayloristic university disciplinary structure in which the context of discovery and application is within the academy and judge by disciplinary peers. The connection between this knowledge and any extra-university application is tenuous and of relatively little interest to professors.

Mode 2 knowledge production is a process of producing knowledge "in the context of application". This means producing knowledge in the extra-university environment in the company of the relevant extra-university stakeholders. According to Nowotny, *et al*, this kind of knowledge is "socially robust" by which they mean that the knowledge works in ways that satisfy extra-university stakeholders.

It seems clear to me that the kind of knowledge production that Nowotny *et al.* characterize as Mode 2 is precisely the kind of knowledge that a knowledge-intensive learning organization with its relatively flat structures, freedom of action with external actors, and the general permeability of it boundaries at many levels would produce. Universities produce some Mode 2 knowledge, particularly in the applied sciences and engineering but rarely do so in the so-called "pure" sciences, even more rarely in the conventional social sciences, and almost never in the humanities. Thus if the production of Mode 2 knowledge is a defining characteristics of knowledge-intensive organizations, then universities mainly are not knowledge-intensive organizations.

What if Universities became Knowledge-Intensive Organizations?

There is little doubt that research universities are being pressed hard to develop more Mode 2 characteristics, though the story of the pressures to achieve this is contradictory. My recent research on policymakers' attempts to force public accountability on universities shows that these efforts have resulted in a combination of over-regulation and a deepening of disciplinary divisions. This is because the administration of this accountability is overwhelmingly based on a Tayloristic view of the university. Assessing universities by discipline and from the top down clearly reinforces their most conservative Mode 1 characteristics and the positions of the most conservative faculty members.

Despite this, change is afoot. The applied sciences and engineering have multiplex and fluid relationships with the world beyond the university. The combinations and recombinations of kinds of expertise are typical of what happens as these faculty members combine and recombine themselves across the boundaries of physics, chemistry, biology, medicine, information technology creating new research institutes and fields of study in their wake. This has been productive and patent offices and intellectual property officers, university science parks, and faculty as research entrepreneurs operating with the university's blessing are now increasingly commonplace.

The picture is less clear in the social sciences where the disciplinary divisions look very much as they did in 1910. Since then, the applied social sciences have been added, including education, commerce, and management programs, but they have all grown by exhibiting the abstracted and hermetic disciplinary characteristics of the original social sciences. The humanities present a mixed picture with many disciplines recognizably the same as they were nearly a century ago but with a strong emergence of comparative literature and cultural studies that has created complex combinations of history, social science, and humanistic analysis.

There are many laments about the "corporatization" or even "selling out" of the university under these new conditions. I have even written some of them. I think these perspectives have merit since it is clear that a headlong drive toward the commercialization of research universities is not much of an improvement over a having them operate as hidebound, isolated ivory towers. What is clear is that the *status quo* won't hold.

My analysis of universities and why they are not presently characterizable as knowledge-intensive organizations does not mean that I think they could quickly become knowledge-intensive organizations or that all of their operations should be subjected to this organizational model. Organizationally, a transition of universities to knowledge-intensive organizations would have quite significant organizational impacts. Meeting the criteria for knowledge-intensive organization would require universities to dismantle their departmental and collegiate structures to create opportunistically convened multi-disciplinary teams of experts that would collaborate with outside constituencies in the creation of Mode 2 knowledge. Students would be educated as apprentices to these multi-disciplinary teams. When the project was finished, the team would dissolve and, in response to new Mode 2 challenges, new teams would be configured.

Thinking this through organizationally shows that the full conversion of universities from Tayloristic organizations with hermetic disciplines into flat, agile, opportunistic organizations would be enormously challenging. But, in addition to the challenges, the knowledge-intensive learning organization model is not easily compatible with the creation and maintenance of deep disciplinary expertise that does not have immediate and obvious applications. The very important deep disciplinary expertise that would be called into action in the creation of Mode 2 teams would cease to exist after a generation of this kind of work unless some faculty members were occupied in the ongoing process of expertise creation. In a Mode 2 only university, only applied knowledge would be valued. It is a short step from this to the university as a research job shop and vocational training institute.

At the same time, we know that the Tayloristic structure itself cannot be allowed to rule universities as it has for so long. Bloated senior staffs, impossible turf battles, skyrocketing costs, isolated and out-of-touch faculty, and a loss of public and political confidence mandate change. The issue is how to steer a course between an investment in deep and not immediately relevant disciplinary expertise and the well-known knowledge development dynamics of that system and the need for agility, new combinations of expertise, strong external connections, and an enhanced capacity for autonomous decision-making throughout the university structure. For universities to have significant characteristics of knowledge-intensive institutions in parts of their operations, they have to continue investing in the deep disciplinary specialization and knowledge generation processes that made them Mode 1 institutions.

What this means to research universities is a difficult set of choices, no one of which can be optimized. To be a university and to be a deep knowledge generator/transmitter, a university must continue to invest in deep disciplinary specialization and structured peer review based evaluation systems that value specialization even when this specialization and expertise pays no immediate return. In so doing, university leaders must be smart enough to see through the elements of the peer review and ranking systems that simply reproduce the past and reward passivity and turf protection.

This is nothing new. The research university and institutions of higher education in general have lived partly on the creation of public goods the value of which is affirmed in the abstract, not proved by pecuniary calculation. Some of this deep knowledge will turn out to be crucial for the next generation of Mode 2 knowledge and some of it will not. But, if universities do not invest in deep, specialized knowledge creation, then they soon will have nothing at all to offer to the world beyond their walls and they will simply be private and public sector research shops and vocational schools.

On the other hand, if research universities do not engage actively and fully in Mode 2 knowledge creation and deployment "in the context of application", then their tax subsidies, public support, and institutional autonomy will be even more limited than it has become recently. Thus universities must also partly become knowledge-intensive organizations. Balancing these elements is harder than ever before. To become sustainable knowledge-intensive organizations, universities, in part, must resist becoming knowledge-intensive organizations while simultaneously creating significant institutional spaces for Mode 2 knowledge creation.

Unfortunately, there is little evidence that university leaders, creative and ambitious faculty members, or policymakers understand these challenges or are capable of rising to meet them. Instead, administrators and policymakers have given us lots of private sector management talk, the "new public management" language of neoliberalism, and nightmares like the Research Assessment Exercise and the most intrusive elements of the Bologna Process and the faculty winners in the current peer review system are hiding their heads in the sand while the rest of the world moves on. Unless there are some fundamental changes soon, it is hard to imagine that universities will remain key sites of knowledge creation and dissemination 50 years from now.

REFERENCES

Alvesson, M. (2004). *Knowledge Work and Knowledge-Intensive Firms.* Oxford, Oxford University Press.

Argyris, C., & Schön, D. (1996). *Organizational Learning II.* Reading, MA: Addison-Wesley.

Bell, D. (1973). *The Coming of Post-Industrial Society: A Venture in Social Forecasting.* New York: Basic Books.

Burch, S. (2005). The Information Society/ the Knowledge Society. In A. Ambrosi, V. Peugeot, & D. Pimienta (Eds.), *Word Matters: Multicultural perspectives on information societies.* Paris: C & F Éditions.

Castells, M. (1999). *The Information Age: Economy, Society and Culture.* Oxford: Blackwell Publishers.

Clark, B. (1983). *The Higher Education System: Academic Organization in Cross-National Perspective.* Berkeley: University of California Press.

Douglas, M. (1966). *Purity and Danger: An Analysis of the Concepts of Pollution and Taboo.* London: Routledge & Kegan Paul.

Drucker, P. (1959). *Landmarks of Tomorrow: A Report on the New "Post-Modern" World.* New York: Harper Colophon Books.

Eijnatten, F. M. van (1993). *The Paradigm That Changed the Work Place.* Assen, Van Gorcum.

Eikeland, O. (2006). Phrónêsis, Artistotle, and Action Research. *International Journal of Action Research, 2,* 15-53.

Flyvbjerg, B. (2001). Making Social Science Matter: Why Social Inquiry Fails and How It Can Succeed Again (Translated by Steven Sampson) Cambridge: Cambridge University Press.

Gibbons, M., Nowotny, H., & Limoges, C. (1994). *The New Production of Knowledge the New Production of Knowledge: The Dynamics of Science and Research in Contemporary Societies.* London: Sage.

Greenwood, D. (1985). *The Taming of Evolution: The Persistence of Nonevolutionary Views in the Study of Humans.* Ithaca, Cornell University Press.

Greenwood, D. (n.d.). *Why Universities are Not Learning Organizations and What Can Be Done About It: An International Action Research Approach to Higher Education Reform.* unpublished manuscript.

Greenwood, D., & Levin, M. (2006). *Introduction to Action Research: Social Research for Social Change,* 2nd edition. Thousand Oaks, CA: Sage Publications.

Hepsø, V., & Botnevik, R. (n.d.). *Improved Crane Operations and Competence Development in a Community of Practice through CSCW and CSCL.* unpublished manuscript.

Hirschhorn, L. (1997). *Reworking Authority: Leading and Following in the Post-Modern Organization.* Cambridge: MIT Press.

Jaworski, J., & Scharmer, C. O. (2000). *Leadership in the Digital Economy: Sensing and Seizing Emerging Futures.* http://www.ottoscharmer.com/LeadingDigitalEconomy.pdf.

Kirp, D. (2003). *Shakespeare, Einstein, and the Bottom Line: The Marketing of Higher Education.* Cambridge: Harvard University Press.

Levin, M. (2002) *Researching Enterprise Development - Action Research on the Cooperation Between Management and Labor in Norway.* Amsterdam: John Benjamins.

Lohmann, S. (n.d.). How Information Flows From Those Who Have It to Those Who Need It: The Information Ecology of the Large Public State University. *Conference on Herding Cats, Moving Cemeteries, and Hauling Academic Trunks: Managing Change in Higher Education,* UCLA.

Lovejoy, A. (1936). *The Great Chain of Being: A Study of the History of an Idea.* Cambridge: Harvard University Press.

Newfield, C. (2004). *Ivy and Industry: Business and the Making of the American University, 1880-1980.* Durham: Duke University Press.

Noble, D. (1977). *America By Design: Science, Technology, and the Rise of Corporate Capitalism.* New York: Alfred Knopf.

Noble, D. (1984). *Forces of Production: A Social History of Industrial Automation.* New York: Alfred Knopf.

Nowotny, H., Scott, P., & Gibbons, M. (2001). *Rethinking Science: Knowledge and the Public in an Age of Uncertainty.* London: Polity Press.

Polanyi, M. (1964). *Personal Knowledge.* New York: Harper and Row.

Polanyi, M. (1966). *The Tacit Dimension.* Gloucester, MA: P. Smith.

Ryle, G. (1949). *The Concept of Mind.* London: Hutchinson.

Schön, D. (1983). *The Reflective Practitioner: How Professionals Think in Action.* New York: Basic Books.

Schön, D. (1987). *Educating the Reflective Practitioner.* San Francisco: Jossey-Bass.

Schön, D. (Ed.) (1991). *The Reflective Turn.* New York: Teachers College Press.

Senge, P. (1990). *The Fifth Discipline: The Art and Practice of the Learning Organization.* New York: Doubleday.

Toulmin, S. (1990). *Cosmopolis: The Hidden Agenda of Modernity.* Chicago: University of Chicago Press.

Toulmin, S., & Gustavsen, B. (1996). *Beyond Theory: Changing Organizations Through Participation, Dialogues on Work and Innovation 2.* Amsterdam: John Benjamins.

Washburn, J. (2005). *University, Inc.: The Corporate Corruption of American Higher Education.* New York: Basic Books.

Weick, K. (1976). Educational organizations as loosely coupled systems. *Administrative Science Quarterly, 21,* 1-9.

Zuboff, S. (1984). *In the Age of the Smart Machine: The Future of Work and Power.* New York: Basic Books.

KEY TERMS

Defensive, defensively, defensiveness; also non-defensive, defensively- responding to organizational challenges by blaming external forces for problem rather than examining how individual and organizational behavior plays a role in creating the challenges

Discipline, Disciplines, Disciplinary: Knowledge and organizational structures that divide knowledge into putatively self-managing compartments; based on the erroneous assumption that a many individual non-interacting disciplines together add up to comprehensive understanding of complex systems

Knowing How: Gilbert Ryle's notion of knowledge embodied in the ability to accomplish a desired goal or outcome; contrasts with knowing that

Knowing That: Gilbert Ryle's notion of knowledge of discrete facts and the idea that knowledge is possible without actions other than thought; contrasts with knowing how

Learning Organizations: Organizations capable of responding to challenges by reorganizing internally and/or changing their parameters to bring their operations into a more adaptive and sustainable relationship with their environment

Loosely-Coupled Organizations, Systems: Karl Weick's term for organizations that are systems but systems in which the parts do not operate in tight functional coordination; universities are an example

Socio-Technical Perspective, Systems: An analytical and intervention approach pioneered in Europe linking technical systems and equipment with the social organizational characteristics and promoting a mutuality of design that alters the technology and the social organization to achieve a desired and more humane fit.

Taylorism, Tayloristic: From Frederick Winslow Taylor, the perspective on organizational design that treats organizations as an array of independent tasks, each to be designed for maximum efficiency according to a trained expert and then integrated into a production system by the system designer and the leader of the organization.

ENDNOTES

[a] This is actually another version of the argument of Christopher Newfield in Ivy and Industry where he argues that modern research universities were modeled on fordist factory structures and have yet to reorganize to approximate current global business models (Newfield, 2004).

[b] I seek to avoid the error of confusing models with existing organizations. No organization fully embodies the structures and dynamics of knowledge-intensive organizations or of learning organizations. It is more sensible to look for key characteristics of such organizational structures and dynamics rather than full-scale pure expressions of these characteristics.

[c] In addition to those cited, these distinctions rely heavily on the work of thinkers like John Dewey, Charles Pierce, William James, Michael Polanyi, Stephen Toulmin, Bent Flybjerg, Olav Eikeland, and Clifford Geertz.

[d] Expert knowledge is by no means superior. Many forms of knowledge created by academic disciplinary professionals do not pass serious tests of rigor or applicability and the publication of many manuscripts tell more about the social networks of the researcher than about the quality of the research.

[e] I directly indebted to Morten Levin for this argument.

[f] Peter Drucker (1959) invented the term to apply to workers to work mainly with information and who create and employ knowledge as their main job.

[g] Examples, Greenwood *et al.*, 1992; Hepsoe and Botnevik, n.d.)

[h] A socio-technical systems analysis of contemporary universities is a book-length project that I have begun.

[i] A term coined by Burton Clark (1983).

[j] Lohmann, How Information Flows From Those Who Have It to Those Who Need It: The Information Ecology of the Large Public State University, n.d.

[k] Of course, faculty and students are equally remote from the concerns and life issues of senior academic administrators.

[l] In another paper, as yet unpublished, I develop a detailed analysis of universities using the Nowotny et al framework (Greenwood, n.d.).

Chapter II
Construction of Knowledge-Intensive Organization in Higher Education

Juha Kettunen
Turku University of Applied Sciences, Finland

ABSTRACT

The aims of knowledge management are to create knowledge and stimulate innovation. Knowledge management allows the knowledge of an organization to be located, shared, formalized, enhanced and developed. The challenges of knowledge management lie in creating environments that support knowledge sharing, knowledge creation, and innovativeness. This chapter examines challenges faced by Higher education institutions (HEI) in producing innovations and increasing their external impact on their regions. The most valuable assets of HEIs are the knowledge and skills embodied in human capital. The challenges of innovative HEIs can be derived from their customers' needs, which usually cannot be met within a single discipline. This chapter explores the multidisciplinary development projects at HEIs and presents implications for the organizational structure supporting innovation and engagement of the institution with its region.

INTRODUCTION

Higher education institutions (HEIs) are facing challenges to produce innovations and increase their external impact on their regions. The most valuable assets of HEIs are the knowledge and skills embodied in human capital. The challenges of innovative HEIs can be derived from their customers' needs, which usually cannot be met within a single discipline. The aims of knowledge management are to create knowledge and stimulate innovation. Knowledge management allows the knowledge of an organization to be located, shared, formalized, enhanced and developed. The challenges of knowledge management lie in creating environments that support knowledge sharing, knowledge creation, and innovativeness.

HEIs must continually produce new knowledge and engage with their regions to remain competitive. An important by-product of knowledge creation is an innovation used in companies and by organizations outside of the institution. Companies and other organizations must continually innovate to remain competitive. A by-product of innovation is new knowledge (Matsumoto, Stapleton, Glass and Thorpe, 2005). HEIs assume entrepreneurial roles while companies develop an academic dimension to cooperate with HEIs (OECD, 2007).

This chapter will explore the multidisciplinary development projects at HEIs and present the implications for the organizational structure which supports innovation and the engagement of the institution with its region. This chapter is based on the foundations of knowledge management which support the cooperation of people from different backgrounds. The results of this study are useful to education administrators who aim to crate an innovative institution which will contribute to the positive development of its region.

The chapter is organized as follows. The next section introduces the main characteristics of knowledge creation. Then the nature of multidisciplinary applied research and development is described. Based on the background and the characteristics of project work, the chapter presents the multidisciplinary organization that supports innovations and increases the external impact of HEIs. Empirical evidence is presented from the Turku University of Applied Sciences (TUAS). Finally, the future trends and results of the study are summarized in the concluding section.

BACKGROUND: KNOWLEDGE MANAGEMENT IN DEVELOPMENT PROJECTS

The extreme complexity of many development projects causes problems if the internal processes do not support the development work. Although several studies have acknowledged the importance of multidisciplinary development projects and team learning (Drucker, 1998; Dyer and Hath, 2006; Koskinen, Pihlanto and Vanharanta, 2003; Ruuska and Vartiainen, 2005), sufficient attention has not been paid to the need to restructure HEIs to support knowledge creation and promote innovation.

The promotion of innovation can be planned and managed in a structured way. It is important that the internal processes and structures of the knowledge-intensive organizations support the rapid creation of innovations and ensure that the strategic objectives of an organization are achieved. Despite the need to manage the operations in a structured way, the organization must have flexibility and the ability to respond to customer needs, technological development and other environmental changes. The flexibility and ability to operate in a synergic and innovative way are competitive advantages of knowledge-intensive organizations.

Takeuchi and Nonaka (2004) argue that a key factor behind the success of Japan's innovation and of its research and development companies is the widespread process of socializing knowledge. That means sharing and articulating tacit knowledge within temporarily assembled project teams through effective dialogue. Tacit knowledge consists of individual ability, memory, know-how and experience, which have not been articulated in explicit form such as presentations, reports, journal, databanks, manuals and training materials. Even though knowledge management can be described using some formal procedures it is a very flexible framework in which the steps and tasks of the development project are continuously redefined.

It is important that the internal processes and structures and management methods support the effective creation of innovations and ensure that the strategic objectives can be achieved (Kettunen, 2005, 2006a, b, 2007a, b). Flexibility and the ability to operate rapidly are competitive advantages of research and development in universities of applied sciences. It is also important to support knowledge sharing and innovation creation. The spiral of knowledge conversion known in knowledge management can be used to describe the phases of development projects in order to build a structured view of the project management. This approach to knowledge conversion was developed by Nonaka and Takeuchi (1995) and it is applied in this study in the development projects of HEIs.

Figure 1 is adopted from Takeuchi and Nonaka (2004) and describes the spiral of knowledge conversion in development projects. The personal tacit knowledge is disseminated to the tacit knowledge of other people in the socialization phase. The tacit knowledge is transformed into explicit knowledge in the externalization phase. The explicit knowledge is disseminated to the explicit knowledge of other people in the combination phase. Finally, the explicit knowledge is transferred to tacit knowledge in the internalization phase. The spiral of knowledge conversion is a never-ending process which resumes when the previous cycle is finished and accumulates the knowledge of the organization.

Socialization is a process of sharing experiences, thereby creating tacit knowledge. Individual tacit knowledge becomes collective by observation, direct experience sharing, imitation and the other types of the individual exchanges of information. Tacit knowledge is disseminated in the form of shared mental models and technical skills. The original model of knowledge creation does not include any frictions or obstacles to team effectiveness (Fong, 2003; Tuomi, 1999). The experiences of knowledge management emphasize the importance of confidence and cooperation skills, which promote the dissemination of tacit knowledge. The informal meetings provide good opportunities to share experiences and exchange ideas.

Trust among the members of the project team supports the exchange of tacit knowledge. Therefore new development projects are often started using the existing networks. Project teams typically promote information and knowledge sharing through regular meetings, setting up

Figure 1. Spiral of knowledge conversion in development projects

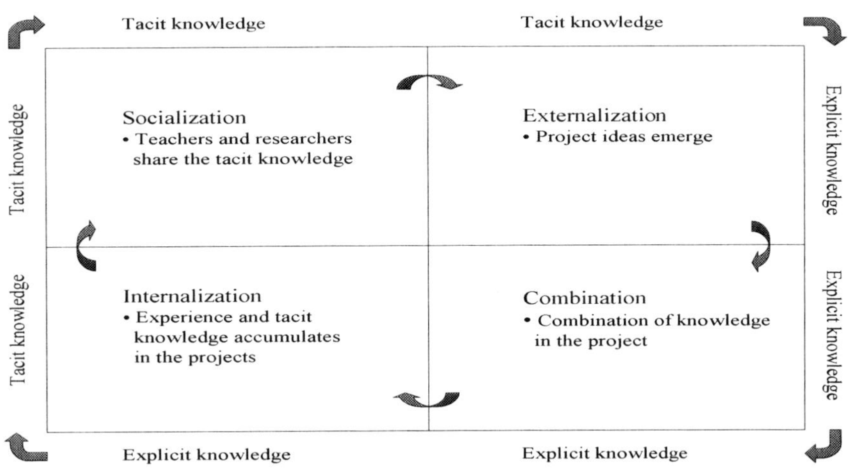

informal discussions and think-thanks. Open discussion and efficient knowledge sharing may impede the development of networks which can be used in the development projects. The projects can develop the assets of complementary tacit knowledge in this phase. Socialization is a phase in which new project ideas develop in networked circumstances.

Externalization is a phase which transforms tacit knowledge into explicit knowledge so that it can be communicated. Collective tacit knowledge then becomes explicit as it is formalized using adequate plans or other documentation. Identifying and locating tacit knowledge and making it explicit are necessary in creating inventions and innovations. Especially in short-term networked project teams it is important to document the projects, because knowledge may be lost when people start other projects or move to other organizations (Kasvi, Vartiainen and Halikari, 2003). The description of the conceivable invention or innovation is critical in the externalization phase. The management of the externalization phase can contribute to the knowledge description and sharing. When the knowledge is described, it is fairly easy to replicate, restore and disseminate throughout the organization or network.

Typically, HEIs apply for the funding for research and development projects. Usually, it must be an innovative and clear project idea if it is to motivate the funding body. A formally signed and submitted project plan is the basis for the funding decision. It is also the physical proof of the originality and invention. These matters may be important in the event of a possible infringement or dispute regarding the patent, because a new idea or invention cannot be protected by legal forms of protection as it may be still far from fully specific. The partners of the development project may write the letters of intent to participate in the project. They carefully plan and finalize the project plan before submitting the application.

Combination is a phase of knowledge creation where the knowledge of various partners is combined to create the new product, service or process. Many development projects are demand-oriented, producing improvements in the existing products or processes. As a result of this phase, an innovation can be expressed in systematic language in the forms of drawings and descriptions. In this phase, the business innovation is vulnerable, because it can be imitated by competitors (Arundel, 2001; Blind & Thumm, 2004, Striukova, 2007). Secrecy is not important in many organization-specific projects.

The obstacles of the combination phase relate in practice more to the multidisciplinary composition of the project team and less to the technological matters of the project. The obstacles are usually difficulties in setting up communication networks and information available to all the members of the project team. The development projects are described in a form that is easy to communicate and conductive to knowledge accumulation.

Internalization is a phase in which the experiences of the production process are internalized. The descriptions created in the combination phase are useful in the internalization phase, where the explicit knowledge is used in the production process. Learning by doing characterizes the internalization phase where explicit knowledge is used and new tacit knowledge emerges. The know-how of individuals accumulates and becomes a valuable asset of the organization.

Once a problem occurs, an experienced project team reflects on its past experiences and explores comparable problems and solutions. Project organizations know that they can no longer afford to reinvent the wheel. They must capture the knowledge accrued on projects to improve the quality and effectiveness of future projects. The tacit knowledge of the development project needs to be socialized again with the other members of the network or organization to start the new spiral of knowledge creation. This is done in dissemination seminars and in informal or formal meetings. Traditionally, knowledge has been transferred from one project to the next over time.

MULTIDISCIPLINARY ACTIVITIES AND STRUCTURE IN HIGHER EDUCATION

Multidisciplinary Activities

Knowledge is a context-dependent collective phenomenon arising from social interactions and effective dialogue among members of multidisciplinary project teams (Freyens and Martin, 2007). The task of the project manager is to unlock the potential of each discipline in a climate of cooperation rather than of the juxtaposition of different contributions to the project (Edmondson, 2003). Unfolding the potential is the core competence of the project manager of the project team. The recycling of knowledge includes the interactions of the dynamic social process which provides clear strategic opportunities for organizational success (Gray and Densten, 2005).

The active involvement of national governments and the European Union have set regional policy frameworks for regional development. These and many other funding bodies have created financial incentives for the regional engagement of HEIs. Many cities have an important role in financing the HEIs, which have established new branches. In Finland there are five university centers, which are strategic alliances among several university branches in cities which did not originally have a university. These centers are results of the active lobbying of towns and cities. A critical mass is required, because smaller university centers without a substantial research capacity will not be able to develop a strong regional economic base.

There are many reasons why the strictly defined industries or disciplines do not necessarily meet the needs of the regions and support innovations. Every HEI operates in an environment which has its own needs and characteristics. It is argued that better results can be achieved through institutional autonomy and strong management which takes into account the regional needs and enhanced cooperation between the institution and working life.

The concept of clusters introduced by Porter (1990, 1998) has been used as the basis of regional development. The concept has been developed to avoid the strictly limited concepts of industries, which do not describe well the real networked cooperation of organizations. Clusters are geographic concentrations of interconnected companies, specialized suppliers, service providers in related industries and associated institutions. They include, among others, publicly funded development companies, trade associations, HEIs and other education institutions that compete also in some fields but cooperate in others. A cluster increases the competitive advantage of the partners and provides the basis for an internationally competitive industry. Clearly the concept of the cluster emphasizes the multidisciplinary approach.

Projects in applied research and development involve several actors. Projects seek to add value to the normal operations of the partners. The objective of the cooperation is to find new ways of working in the network of HEIs, companies and other organizations. Innovation requires more than skills acquired in the course of education. It also requires tacit knowledge which can be gained or transmitted through interactions in networked cooperation. The density of interaction and the likelihood of change create favorable conditions for innovation (Burt, 2002). Better results can be achieved through enhanced cooperation between HEIs and other partners in the region.

The projects of applied research and development are often mixed with education, because the projects are not fully funded. Typically the costs are underestimated and the revenues generated disappointing. Therefore HEIs should enhance transversal mechanisms that combine education, research and development and may cut across disciplinary boundaries. A thesis written on working life as a part of a larger externally funded development project is one attempt by the universities of applied sciences to combine education and research. There are plenty of other projects in which students participate. Education and tacit knowledge gained through work-based learning in close interaction with working life represent "knowledge transfer on legs."

The physical proximity of research, businesses and intermediary support services is an important feature of partnership. The knowledge interchange with business becomes embedded in the internal processes and structures of HEIs embracing research, development, support services and education. Science, technology and business parks and innovation platforms combined with HEIs' aim to reach critical mass, create innovations and build partnerships with local businesses.

Institutional Structure

Finnish HEIs include the traditional universities and the universities of applied sciences which were formerly called "polytechnics." At the beginning of 2006 Finnish polytechnics adopted the name "university of applied sciences" a term commonly used in many other European countries. The traditional universities are science-oriented institutions, whereas the recently created universities of applied sciences have a professional orientation. They were created to support the development of their regions. There are currently 20 universities and 26 universities of applied sciences in Finland.

Research-oriented universities have tended to be self-contained entities focused on the creation and development of basic knowledge for the national and global economy and with limited emphasis on local and regional needs (OECD, 2007). The ideal of scientific enquiry embodied in the modern university is to strive for universalism. Scientific claims to truth were assumed to transcend time and place (Bender, 1998). When research was carried out in isolation from the context of application, the division of labour to single-field faculties was perceived as a problem when science policy was morphing into innovation policy. The traditional principle of "at a distance" is changing. Recently the decrease or slow increase in public funding for research and development has encouraged universities to look to external sources to maintain and expand their activities. They are increasingly engaged with the cities, companies and regions in which they are located.

The universities of applied sciences engage actively with their regions and contribute to the regional economic development and knowledge-intensive organizations and jobs. On the one hand, the focusing of education to meet the needs of the region helps the local companies and other organizations to find skilled labour force. On the other hand, the focusing helps graduates to find local employment and remain in their communities. Institutions must do more than simply educate if they want to contribute to regional economic development. They are expected to be involved in the application of knowledge with their local and regional communities. Institutions are expected to take a multidisciplinary approach in customer-oriented regional activities.

The TUAS is located in Southwest Finland, the country's second-largest economic area after Helsinki. The TUAS is a multidisciplinary institution and at the moment the largest university of applied sciences in Finland. It has about 9000 students in 35 degree programs leading to the bachelor's degree, and nine programs leading to the master's degree. The interaction of the institution with its operational environment is close. The purpose of the institution is to target its activities to the needs of the region and to respond flexibly to the changes in its environment.

HEIs must engage with large networks in their regions, provide opportunities for lifelong learning and contribute to the development of knowledge-intensive jobs which will enable graduates to find local employment and remain in their communities. For example, the TUAS targets its strategy and activities to the region.

About 75% of the graduates find employment in the region of Southwest Finland. The requirement of regional engagement has many implications for the activities and internal structures of these organizations.

The institution operates in seven fields of education: arts and media; business and administration; health care and social services; natural resources and the environment; natural sciences; technology, communication and transport; and tourism, catering and hospitality management. The fields of education have been defined by the Ministry of Education for statistical purposes. The institution was organized to support the innovations and the external impact on the region. The institution has four multidisciplinary faculties: Life Sciences and Business; Technology, Environment and Business; Telecommunication and e-Business and Well-Being Services. Arts Academy and Health Care are in a single field.

Many degree programs of the TUAS have planned their education provision around Problem Based Learning which supports cooperation with working life. The approach is one way to integrate education into multidisciplinary development projects. The Faculty of Health Care has developed its education and cooperation to meet the needs of hospitals and many organizations in the public and private sector following the examples in many other countries (Baker et al., 2007; Matthew-Maich et al., 2007). The institution is also creating more multidisciplinary entrepreneurship programs.

Applied research and development in the local labor market are left to institutions which often lack well-established strategic plans and organizational structures to support the regional development. Even when the engagement with working life has been recognized and laid upon HEIs as a duty by the national government, it has remained a "third task," which is not explicitly linked to the internal processes and organizational structures of every institution. The education, research and development of the TUAS are explicitly focused on the regional needs in the strategic plan.

Deregulation of traditional disciplines and the formation of multidisciplinary faculties (departments) to promote innovative applied research and development within an institution is a necessary step for the institution to gain a greater margin of manoeuvre to engage with the region and increase the external impact of the institution. Many countries have increased the autonomy and flexibility of their institutions to respond to the demands of the changing environment. The aim is to reach critical mass and combine it with commercial partners at the regional, national and international level and strengthen the economic base through spinoffs, transforming existing businesses and attracting inward investment. The new situation has opened the way to regional cooperation with companies and other organizations and made it possible for institutions to align their research portfolio to regional demand.

The increasing autonomy emphasizes the need for more accountability and stronger management of institutions. Increased regional responsibility means also reforming discipline-based structure that prevents multidisciplinary activities and the engagement with the region. Institutions wishing to see the regional engagement and innovations need to consider the strong leadership of HEIs to achieve these objectives. The discipline-oriented structures of traditional science-universities do not necessarily support the regional engagement.

The Board of the TUAS decided in 2004 to reconstruct the organization so that the multidisciplinary faculties assumed the leading role. Four of six faculties became multidisciplinary. The purpose was to increase the volume of research and development. That can be expected if the faculties were multidisciplinary and designed to meet the needs of the region. In addition, the new position of research and development manager was established and a full-time dean was recruited for each faculty.

Table 1 describes the share of multidisciplinary projects at the TUAS in 2007. The fields of education are defined by the Ministry of Education for statistical purposes. The single-discipline faculties only have only projects within a single field of education, but the multidisciplinary faculties have projects within many fields. Even though the data are limited, these results support the argument that the multidisciplinary faculties offer better service to their customers and regions. These results provide only rather coarse insight into the multidisciplinary innovative institutions, but the experience indicates that the degree programs of the multidisciplinary faculties are more inclined to cooperate with each other and with external partners.

Soon after the organizational change at the TUAS it became evident that there was potential to raise the volume of research and development. The expenditures, external revenue and the number of publications started to increase. The external revenue rose nearly 60% and expenditures over 40% annually in 2004-2006. The number of publications was only 98 in 2003, but 195 in 2006. Generally, the multidisciplinary faculties have been more successful in increasing the volume of research and development than single-field faculties have been. Networked projects are prevalent in the project database of the institution.

Figure 2 depicts the time series of the expenditures and external revenue from research and development at the TUAS in 1999-2006. The external revenue started to increase soon after the organizational change. The majority of the projects are funded by the European Union and domestic funding bodies. The innovativeness and added value of each project are evaluated before the funding decision is made. This finding supports the argument that the organizational structure promotes the creation of innovations. It seems evident that the transition to multidisciplinary faculties has been successful.

FUTURE TRENDS AND CONCLUSIONS

Strategic management should be aligned with knowledge management in knowledge-intensive organizations. Strategic plans should be designed to take knowledge sharing and creation into account. When strategic objectives have been defined, the structure of the organization should be analyzed and developed to achieve the strategic objectives. Often it is necessary to include the development of the organization in the strategic plans to promote the effective implementation of the strategic plan.

Efficient knowledge acquisition and sharing are crucial for the success of HEIs. Knowledge sharing prevents the development of closed knowledge pools and supports the creation of innovations. Knowledge is often too fragmented and there are no overlaps in small degree programs or other single-field units of HEIs. Therefore efficient knowledge sharing improves the competitive advantage of institutions to meet the needs of their environments.

Even though the knowledge creation cycle of knowledge management is widely understood, it provides a useful approach to develop the inter-

Table 1. Share of multidisciplinary projects at the TUAS in 2007

	Projects within many fields of education	Projects within a single field of education	Total
Multidisciplinary faculties	14	86	100
Single-discipline faculties	0	100	100
Total	11	89	100

Figure 2. Expenditure and external revenue from research and development at the TUAS

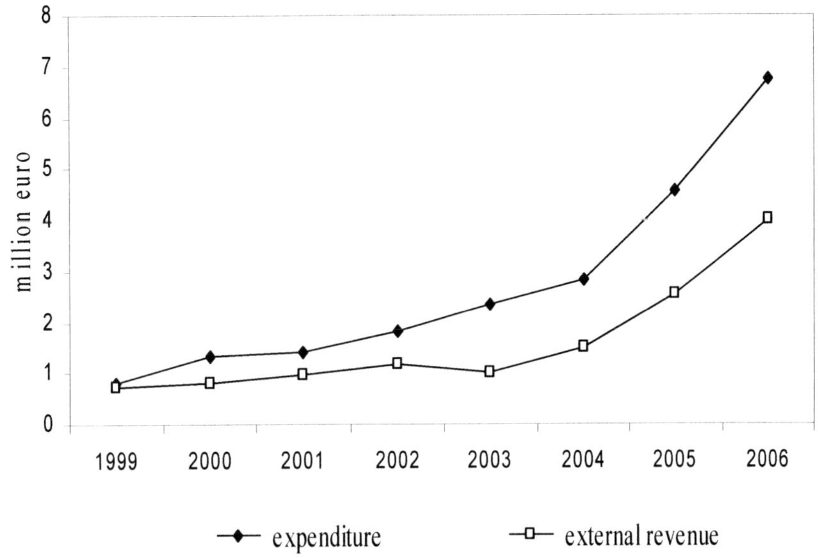

nal structures of HEIs to support the creation of multidisciplinary innovations and increase the external impact of the HEIs. Especially it provides a framework to identify the critical phases in innovation creation to develop the organizational structures that support applied research and development to create innovations.

The contribution of HEIs to innovations is achieved using new institutional links and a new type of cooperation. These new types of initiatives utilize a variety of modes of interchange between HEIs and working life. The interchange with working life reflects in the internal processes of HEIs. The institutions which aim to interchange effectively with working life have designed their structures to support innovations, synergies and cooperation with companies and other organizations. These kind of internal processes and structures are typically multidisciplinary.

On the other hand, the Finnish traditional science-universities have a national and international role. On the other hand, the Finnish universities of applied sciences direct their education, research and development to meeting the needs of their regions. The organizational structure of all these institutions does not support the regional development. In successful cases, the HEIs collaborate with regional development authorities to focus part of their activities on building stronger bridges between HEIs and business innovation.

The empirical evidence from the TUAS supports the argument that multidisciplinary faculties support the multidisciplinary projects of applied research and development and increase the external funding of the institution. The volume of research and development increased remarkably when the institution adopted the multidisciplinary structure of the organization. The results of this study challenge the management of HEIs to construct knowledge-intensive organizations to support innovations.

REFERENCES

Arundel, A. (2001). The relative effectiveness of patents and secrecy for appropriation. *Research Policy, 30*(4), 611-624.

Baker, C. M., Pesut, D. J., McDaniel, A. M. & Fisher, M. L. (2007). Evaluating the impact of problem-based learning on learning styles of master's students in nursing Administration. *Journal of Professional Nursing, 23*(4), 214-219.

Bender, T. (1988). Introduction. In T. Bender (Ed.), *The university and the city, from medical origins to the present* (pp. 3-10). New York: Oxford University Press.

Blind, K., & Thumm, N. (2004). Interrelation between patenting and standardisation strategies: Empirical evidence and policy implications. *Research Policy, 33*(10), 1583-1598.

Burt, R. (2002). *The social capital of structural holes, new directions in economic sociology*. New York: Russel Sage.

Drucker, P. F. (1998). The coming of the new organization. *Harvard Business Review, 66*(1), 1-19.

Dyer, J. H., & Hatch, N. W. (2006). Relation-specific capabilities and barriers to knowledge transfers: Creating advantage through network relationships. *Strategic Management Journal, 27*(8), 701-19.

Edmondson, A. C. (2003). Speaking up in the operating room: How team leaders promote learning in interdisciplinary action teams. *Journal of Management Studies, 40*(6), 1419-52.

Fong, P. S. W. (2003). Knowledge- creation in multidisciplinary project teams: An empirical study of the processes and their dynamic interrelationships. *International Journal of Project Management, 21*(7), 479-86.

Freyens, B., & Martin, M. (2007). Multidisciplinary knowledge transfer in training multimedia projects. *Journal of European Industrial Training, 31*(9), 680-705.

Gray, J. H., & Densten, I. L. (2006). Towards an integrative model of organizational culture and knowledge management. *International Journal of Organizational Behavior, 9*(2), 594-603.

Kasvi, J. J. J., Vartiainen, M., & Halikari, M. (2003). Managing knowledge and knowledge competences in projects and project organisations. *International Journal of Project Management, 21*(3), 571-82.

Kettunen, J. (2005). Implementation of strategies in continuing education. *The International Journal of Educational Management, 19*(3), 207-217.

Kettunen, J. (2006a). Strategies for the cooperation of educational institutions and companies in mechanical engineering. *The International Journal of Educational Management, 20*(1), 19-28.

Kettunen, J. (2006b). Strategic Planning of Regional Development in Higher Education. *Baltic Journal of Management, 1*(3), 259-269.

Kettunen, J. (2007a). Strategies of Regional Development. In A. Ghosh & G. Banerjee (Eds.), *Strategic Management for Firms in Developing Countries* (pp. 520-530). New Delhi: Allied Publishers.

Kettunen, J. (2007b). The Strategic Evaluation of Academic Libraries. *Library Hi Tech, 25*(3), 409-421.

Koskinen, K. U., Pihlanto, P., & Vanharanta, H. (2003). Tacit knowledge acquisitions and sharing in a project work context. *International Journal of Project Management, 21*(4), 281-90.

Matsumoto, I. T., Stapleton, J., Glass, J., & Thorpe, T. (2005). A knowledge-capture report for multidisciplinary design environments. *Journal of Knowledge Management, 8*(3), 83-92.

Matthew-Maich, N., Mines, C., Brown, B., Lunyk-Child, O., Carpio, B. Drummond-Young, M., Noesgaard, C., & Linton, J. (2007). Evolving as nurse educators in problem-based learning through a community of faculty development. *Journal of Professional Nursing, 23*(2), 75-82.

Nonaka, I., & Takeuchi, H. (1995). *The knowledge-creating company: How Japanese companies create the dynamics of innovation.* New York: Oxford University Press.

OECD (2007). *Higher education and regions, globally competitive, locally engaged.* Organisation for Economic Co-operation and Development, Paris.

Porter, M. (1990). *The competitive advantage of nations.* London: MacMillan.

Porter, M. (1998). *On competition.* Boston: Harvard Business School Press.

Ruuska, I. E., & Vartiainen, M. (2005). Characteristics of knowledge-sharing communities in project organizations. *International Journal of Project Management, 23*(5), 374-9.

Striukova, L. (2007). Patents and corporate value creation: theoretical approach. *Journal of Intellectual Capital, 8*(3), 431-443.

Takeuchi, H., & Nonaka, I. (2004). *Hitotsubashi on Knowledge Management.* Singapore: John Wiley & Sons.

Tuomi, I. (1999). *Corporate Knowledge: Theory and Practice of Intelligent Organizations.* Helsinki: Metaxis.

KEY TERMS

Combination Phase: New knowledge is combined with explicit knowledge of the organization in the combination phase of knowledge creation.

Explicit Knowledge: Explicit knowledge is easy to communicate. It can be expressed, for example, in written documents, tapes and databases.

Externalization Phase: The externalization phase transforms tacit knowledge into explicit knowledge so that it can be communicated.

Higher Education Institution: Higher education institutions include traditional universities and vocational institutions; in Finland these are referred to as "universities of applied sciences" or "polytechnics."

Internalization Phase: The explicit knowledge created in an organization is internalized in this phase. Learning by doing characterizes the emergence of tacit knowledge in this phase.

Knowledge Management: Knowledge management is a term applied to techniques used for the systematic collection, transfer, security and management of information within organizations, along with systems designed to assist the optimal use of that knowledge.

Socialization Phase: Socialization is a process of sharing experiences and creating tacit knowledge as shared mental models and technical skills.

Tacit Knowledge: Tacit knowledge consists of the culture of an organization and in the skills, habits and informal decisions of its individual members.

Chapter III
Collective CPD:
Professional Learning in a Law Firm

Jeff Gold
Leeds Metropolitan University, UK

Richard Thorpe
Leeds University, UK

ABSTRACT

Continuing Professional Development (CPD) is usually conceived as a planned and formulated process for individual members of professional associations. This chapter, by contrast, examines professional learning as a collective and distributed process, taking a whole firm, as the unit of analysis. Cultural Historical Activity Theory is used to work with a law firm. The results show inherent tensions and contradiction in a process of knowledge sharing and practice improvement.

INTRODUCTION

Continuing Professional Development (CPD)[a*] is usually conceived as a planned and formulated process for individual members of professional associations. Previous researchers in the field have focused on the methods used and issues of implementation (Sadler-Smith *et al*, 2000; Sadler-Smith and Badger, 1998). One consequence of this perspective is that scant attention is paid to more informal processes, including intuitive and implicit learning (Eraut 2000) and the way this learning is shared with others in local contexts and in turn, the way these local cultural and historical conditions enable or constrain such learning. Recent research by Gold *et al* (2007) highlighted a significant number of important ways in which professionals in a law firm frequently learned from key moments of their practice, 'on-the-run' so to speak, and the contextual nature of that learning. In particular, through the twin process of articulation and accumulation, learning was shared and became collective knowledge and understanding within the unit, a group of four employment lawyers within a department. This paper develops our understanding by examining professional learning as a collective and distributed process, one which affects subjects differently working within diverse but overlapping contexts. In this paper we take the whole firm as our unit of analysis and view the firm as an activity system (Engeström 2001). This paper, develops our understanding by examining professional learning as a collective and distributed process, one which affects subjects differently working within diverse but overlapping contexts. In this paper we take a whole firm, LawFirm, as our unit of analysis and view the firm as an activity system (Engeström, 2001). The findings are reported from a year-long study with a law firm in the north of England (LawFirm). Access was gained initially with the primary aim to improve the firm's competitive position. However, once close, we were able explore how learning emanates from practice through key moments with clients and how this learning becomes shared with others within the firm through meetings and other mediation means that cross functional boundaries. It also shows how tensions and difficulties that surfaced could also become a source of new knowledge that lead to changed actions and approach to business. We begin by considering the relationship between CPD and the law firm, and highlight the recent changes that affect the way in which law firms are organised. These changes have provided tensions and contradictions that require resolution and offer the potential for new learning. We then consider the findings from our involvement with LawFirm, and show how through the mediation of new tools which enable dialogue and debate to take place, a more collective approach to CPD is stimulated and developed.

CPD AND THE LEGAL PROFESSION

England and Wales has 116000 solicitors[b*], all of whom are regulated. They are represented by their professional association, the Law Society. As one of the original three professions, practising solicitors find themselves highly regulated by their professional body in all aspects of their work. Under the Solicitors Act 1974 any solicitor who is employed in the provision of legal services is required to hold a practising certificate and the Society has statutory powers to monitor compliance. There are a range of rules that relate to practice and professional conduct. CPD, since 1985, has been compulsory with solicitors being encouraged to take responsibility for their own professional development. The requirement is for a minimum of 16 hours of CPD per year; of which at least 25 per cent must consist of participation in accredited training courses. CPD operates on an annual cycle with each solicitor returning a completed training record, an example of which is shown at Figure 1.

The Law Society therefore, as with most professional bodies of a similar standing, attempt to 'manage' their members' CPD through a compulsory requirement in a planned and systematic process (Grant et al 1999). The logic and assumptions on which the training takes place and will eventually operate are based on mechanistic assumptions that serve bureaucratic control (Taylor, 1996). Not unsurprisingly, the focus of much CPD is focused on particular inputs of codified knowledge and skills; we notice in particular the way the CPD artefact is called a 'Training Record'. This inputs focus is also concomitant with the well-known difficulty of application in practice (Cantillon and Jones 1999). Partly in response to such difficulties, some professional associations, including the Law Society, have widened the scope of their schemes to incorporate evidence-based learning through the gathering of portfolios of evidence. However the individualised attribution

Figure 1. Sample training record for solicitors

Date	Training activity (for course attendance, indicate course title, provider name and reference otherwise state how activity was undertaken)	Comments	Number of hours credit
10.11.03	Attendance at update on Revenue Law (in-house) 123/ABCD video and discussion	Provided a review of the provisions in the budget which need to be taken into account when advising on personal investments and will planning	2 hours and 10 minutes
12.12.03	Time spent on building portfolio of evidence for NVQ in management	Prepared and gathered evidence in respect of units on budgeting and recruitment interviews	3 hours

Source: The Law Society

which distorts the social nature of professional practice still remains a problem. It is in order to counter these distortions that we have sought to explore collective learning, even though this is rarely recognised as CPD. To undertake this, we have by necessity moved to a level of collectivity that accounts for the practice of many solicitors, the Firm. Our research question is posed as follows: Could and should CPD be better conceived as a collective and distributed process affecting different subjects working within diverse but overlapping contexts?

Law Firms

The organisation of professional work at the level of the firm can be best understood as an effect of the successful employment of a message that persuades clients of their legitimacy in dealing with complex issues of law (Dietrich and Roberts 1997). As a credence good professional services are often taken on trust and the trust is placed by the client in the people who offer the service. Middlehurst and Kennie (1997) suggest the rhetoric which give the firm their credibility includes a. Technical and theoretical component and the authority and status flowing from the expertise and highly valued knowledge, understanding and skill of the partners; b. The establishment and the exercise of trust which forms the basis for professional relationships (with clients and professionals); c. The adherence to particular standards and professional ethics, often, but not always represented by a licence to practise; d. Independence, autonomy and discretion; e. Specific attitudes towards work, clients and peers involving dedication, reliability, flexibility and creativity in relation to the 'unknown'.

Client ignorance is also a feature of service operations and provides the condition for professional work, underpinning the emphasis that is placed on knowledge acquisition as the basis for practice and the accumulation of the social recognition of expertise allows a process of institutionalisation into firms and associations to unfold.

Our focus on LawFirm as the unit of activity requires attention to be given to the influence of culture and history, on the work that is completed, and the knowledge and learning necessary. Engeström (2004) and Warmington *et al* (2004) both have used the framework provided by Victor and Boynton (1998) that charts the historical trajectory of the organisation of industrial production. The value of this framework serves to emphasise the different types of knowledge and learning that need to be generated by different types of work, and the movement to more valuable types of work through the leveraging of knowledge (Warmington *et al,* 2004). However, notwithstanding the implication that these movements are usually towards higher levels of value, there always remains the link to the past and indeed, the need at each point of progression to provide a renewal process for each of the types that have gone before. Figure 2 shows the path of these movements and renewals.

Craft work, for example, requires knowledge of products and processes based on personal intuition and experience built up through practice. Such knowledge is often articulated verbally between co-workers but remains tacit to a greater or lesser extent. The legal profession, however, as a 'status profession' together with medicine and the church (Elliott 1972), take their origins as university disciplines, to be studied by the sons of the aristocracy. It was in its practice that the craft of the lawyer could be demonstrated. This is a reminder of the particular importance given to tacit knowledge within professional practice, which according to Eraut (2000a, p.128) 'cannot be accomplished by procedural knowledge alone or by following a manual'. This kind of knowledge is developed in situations within a field of practice, almost entirely informally (Cheetham and Chivers, 2000). The move towards mass production becomes possible through the leverage of tacit knowledge through articulation. Here, there is a dynamic process of exploration through practice which is exploited through the formulation of better ways of working, expressed as codified knowledge. However, because tacit knowledge is inherently ambiguous (with the potential for a variety of meanings and possible formulations), it is coded knowledge and especially abstract knowledge which came to provide the distinctive differentiator of professional occupations. As the economy grew during the eighteenth and nineteenth centuries and the market for expert and professional services developed, different professionals established their position in society by claiming a unique authority over particular 'disciplinary knowledge' (Fournier 2000, p.71).

Abstraction and codification of knowledge became the hallmark of professional status and the first ingredient of an ideal-type of profes-

Figure 2. Historical forms of work

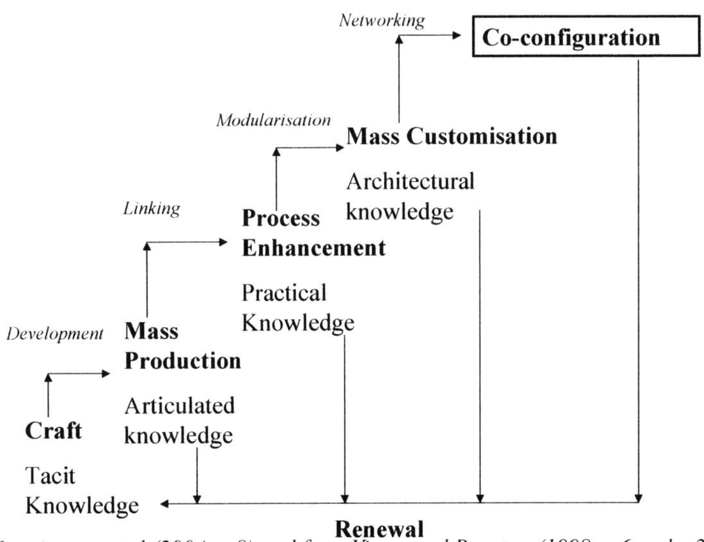

Source: Adapted from Warmington et al (2004, p.8) and from Victor and Boynton (1998, p.6 and p.223)

sionalism, that is, one in which 'specialized work that is grounded in a body of theoretically based, discretionary knowledge and skill and that is accordingly given special status in society' (Freidson 2001, p.129). However, far from making professions open to anyone, the process of mass production of codified knowledge provoked a defensive response from those in practice to make such practice exclusive to those they deemed fit and worthy enough to dispense it so as to avoid the disturbance of open market competition. As Abbott (1988) suggested, abstraction was important to define the boundaries of a profession. In other words, who was on the inside and who was not:

'.... *only a knowledge system governed by abstractions can redefine its problems and tasks, defend them from interlopers, and seize new problems...* '(p.8).

From the early nineteenth century, those who practised law became more concerned with protecting their status and interests than in making knowledge accessible. There were we understand many "pettifoggers and vipers' who brought disgrace to the profession[c*]. So ironically, while the dynamic between practice and articulation produced a growing stock of codified knowledge, the self-interest and concern to protect the work of solicitors from outside competition made professional law practice exclusive, resulting in growing regulation. In 1823 'The London Law Institution' was formed, becoming a national body in 1825. In 1831 a royal charter was awarded. From this time on, until the present, the legal profession has followed a path of development towards the 'ideal-type' of professionalism, as formulated by Friedson (2001). This includes, a formal education programme for members providing qualification credential; regulation at the point of entry to preserve exclusivity; an ideology to do good; and provide a framework of professional conduct. The Law Society's regulations provide professionals with a privileged position bordering on monopoly coupled with an apparent 'dislike of competition, advertising and profit' (Elliott 1972, p. 52).

At the level of the law firm, the mass production of codified knowledge resulted in functional specialisation but without the negative effects of tight rules to interfere with the practice of the professional. This was the start of the development of what Mintzberg (1983) called 'professional bureaucracy' and what Greenwood *et al* (1990) called 'professional partnership' or P^2. The key features of this form of organisation are that professional standards are expected but there is little central control and professionals are left to develop their own roles within decentralised units according to their preferences and specialisations. The traditional law firm that existed until the late 1970s and 1980's allowed the direction of the firm to be left to the partners however, so long as suffient fees are attracted and all the professionals can see a path of progression that will enhance their own status, there is little attempt to strategically control work or set stretching targets. During this period the protected and privileged position of professionals began to change, in response to a number of outside pressures which forced a move towards greater commercialisation, new definitions of professionalism came into being and challenges emerged to existing business (Hanlon 1998). For example, deregulation meant that solicitors lost the exclusive right to provide conveyancing which had been a staple earner for many 'high street' solicitors.

Perhaps the greatest challenge to the profession, and one that progressively blurred the boundary between professional firms and emerging knowledge intensive firms, has been the convergence of micro-technologies, computing, telecommunications and broadcasting and opto-electronics which form a part of the 'Information Technology Revolution' (Castells 1996). These developments dramatically add impetus to the articulation of codified knowledge and professional services in that they can now be mass-produced on a global scale via the access to such knowledge. For example, the public can access legal advice via such services as http://www.clsdirect.org.uk/, http://www.lawrights.co.uk/ and http://www.venables.co.uk/ in the way the public can access medical diagnoses online. There has always been a flow of new knowledge to practicing solicitors through the print media, but as Gold *et al* (2006) found, online and electronic mailing services now provide an even more rapid service to solicitors directly after decisions are made. The significance of this and other changes in the context of professional practice has meant that there has been a need for law firms to become much more commercial, more competitive and more market oriented. According to Cooper *et al* (1996), the consequence has been the emergence of new organizational forms, sometimes, referred to as the Managed Professional Business (MPB). These give far more emphasis to aspects of professional practice such as managing, planning and strategy. Targets, usually fee-related, are set for all staff and allow performance measurement. There is also more specialization in response to market changes. Staff, while still working within the framework of their professional standards, may also be accountable to a line manager or 'partner-in-charge' (Hinings *et al.* 1999).

While it has been argued that change in the professional organisation may be somewhat overstated, with evidence of partnership and consensus-seeking still remaining (Pinnington and Morris 2003), many professional firms have invested heavily in marketing and commercial awareness programmes and now seek to compete with other firms in the same profession but also stretching the boundaries of their own practice. Indeed, one source of efficiency is practice improvement and this is seen as the means of achieving an edge over others and requires a focus on process enhancement, involving professionals and support staff working together. In England and Wales, the Law Society provides a range of guidelines and events all aimed specifically at improving practice management. In addition, (and following the general trends in the 1990's for quality standards and process improvement) the Law Society has developed Lexcel, a quality standard for the legal profession. This requires an independent assessment of a law firm's practice.

The need for law firms generally to embrace 'commercialised professionalism' (Hanlon 1998, p.51) has been augmented by government policy that seeks to balance the need for the regulation of legal services on the one hand, with the promotion of competition that serves consumers on the other. In 2004, the Clementi Review of the regulatory framework of legal services recommended a more centralised and independent process for consumer redress whilst at the same time allowing non-lawyers to become partners in law firms. Indeed, it was envisaged that law firms could consist of a range of legal professionals which might include solicitors, barristers, licensed conveyancers as well as others. These were referred to as legal disciplinary practices or LDPs. In the future, it was thought it might be possible to allow different professions to establish a firm – these were referred to as multi-disciplinary practices or MDPs. The review was followed in 2006 with the publication of the Legal Services Bill, which set out the proposals recommended by Clementi. However a parliamentary Joint Committee which examined the bill advocated a more incremental approach to change, beginning with a model of a law firm that would be composed of different types of lawyers but without outside ownership or management, suggesting that the 'more complex forms' proposed by Clementi might result in problems of conflicts of interest. Nevertheless, it is clear that the framework for the provision of legal services is slowly moving in the direction of increased competition and in the removal of restrictive barriers so that clients can benefit. These changes which many law firms have already embraced (for example, the introduction of marketing expertise and greater attention to the outcomes achieved with clients) have meant there has had to be a change in the established relationships with clients (Hart and Hogg 1998) as well as client perceptions (Ellis and Waterson, 2001). In these ways, law firms have been building architectural knowledge to allow mass customisation.

In suggesting an organisational form that embraces different disciplines working together, Clementi may have been speculating on the future of legal services. However, it is an image of working that might be modelled as law firms attempt to leverage knowledge to ensure delivery of higher value-added services based on the integration of different forms of expertise. Such a model requires an ongoing learning process between professionals and their clients. This is a type of work that Victor and Boynton (1998) refer to as co-configuration. In a law firm, the traditional divisions of specialised provision, which respond to the requirements of clients for customisation, need also to consider how their interactions with clients provide opportunities for knowledge generation. However, for this knowledge to become known more widely within the organisation so that services to the client might be reshaped, it requires a process that takes professionals outside of their traditional disciplinary boundaries, and enables them to cross into the space between disciplines (Engeström, 1995). It is within these spaces, where knowledge can be shared, assumptions can be surfaced and new ideas can be challenged. The tensions and ambiguities that emerge can then be explored and new possibilities agreed. Using the image of tying different strands of expertise together to produce a new configuration, solicitors in a law firm become partners in a process of 'knotworking' (Engeström, 2004). The following section considers how one law firm in the North of England made inroads into reconfiguring its service so as to obtain greater flexibility and higher value-added for clients through 'knotworking'.

Methodology

Our work with LawFirm has been consistent with a methodology rooted in Cultural Historical Activity Theory (CHAT) (Engeström, 1995). Here researchers study the activity system of the firm, in a relevant and practical way so that interventions made contribute to the construction of new meanings which in turn lead towards greater understanding of the system. The approach is inherently multi-layered and multi-voiced, and considers the efforts of the different actors in the system as they pursue their work with clients and each other. The focus is always on how such work relates to the overall purpose for the firm or its object. This is a crucial feature of a CHAT approach and regarded as the key to understanding the change and learning (Leontyev, 1978) which we see as central to collective CPD. Specifically, the social organisation we define as LawFirm, achieves its unity and coherence in the production of professional services that provide definable outcomes when considered as object-oriented. Individuals within LawFirm, as they complete their work or pursue certain goals (even goals which fulfil the Law Society's compulsory CPD requirements) must connect to the object of the collective activity and its outcomes. In this way, the object becomes particular and very real for every work process that occurs in the firm (Engeström, 2004). Our study began with a study of the cultural and historical trajectory of LawFirm through an analysis of key documents and discussions with directors and staff. We also utilised previous data accumulation to consider how the firm moved from a reliance on a dwindling conveyancing market towards a fully-fledged commercial law firm to the market of regional owner-managed businesses and smaller PLCs to whom a quality service could be provided. Our study is also one of intervention. It is about working with participants as they seek to improve the firm. We achieve this through the introduction of new tools (to help managers to think and act), each with the potential to disturb existing patterns of working. Such disturbances also serve to produce confusions and contradictions, and these again allow the emergence of gaps in understanding to be resolved through new ways of proceeding, a process Engeström (1995) calls expansive learning.

Findings

LawFirm is a commercial legal services practice located in a city in the North of England. As with many firms in the city, LawFirm began in the late nineteenth century with two partners, and while the link with the originators has long disappeared, the firm still bears the name of the two partners. Until the 1950's, LawFirm focused mainly on conveyancing and probate work, but through a series of fortunate connections, it began to act for two major corporations. Until 1978 the amount of commercial work remained limited and conveyancing provided 60% of its work. However, through merger, acquisition and partner development, LawFirm sought to expand its activity, and although growth was not as fast as other similar firms in the city there remained a reliance on the dwindling conveyancing market. From 1987 onwards, LawFirm began to consciously focus its attention to becoming a commercial law firm to the market of regional owner-managed businesses and smaller PLCs to whom a quality service could be provided. At this time it might be said LawFirm took on the characteristics of a Managed Professional Business with a management team setting the strategic direction, and with department heads being responsible for the achievement of fee-earning targets. Features of a move to process enhancement were also in evidence during the 1990s. LawFirm gave increasingly more attention to marketing, with one of the senior partners taking responsibility for the marketing function. Its most recent push to improve its competitiveness has seen a prominent marketing campaign in the city region which, to quote the marketing partner (now director), 'upset the competition'. LawFirm has now seen itself winning more clients from their competitors through an emphasis on quality and its attention to its relationships. It prides itself in providing value for money and uses the intelligence gained from clients to provide an increased degree of customisation. Most recently, there has been an upgrade of premises, some new directors have been appointed, together with recruitment in appropriate areas and there has been a 'drive to improve and develop processes'. In addition, LawFirm has met the standard in Lexcel and Investors in People assessments. LawFirm continues to grow but not without the attendant tensions and contradictions, although as we consider below, these can provide the energy for learning and change (Blackler et al 1999).

By 2006, LawFirm had become a Limited Liability Partnership (LLP), a new legal entity in the UK allowing partnerships such as law firms to enjoy limited liability as a legal entity separated from its members, while enjoying the tax status of a partnership.

There are now 28 directors (previously partners) among 200 staff. The most recent strategic plan points to further growth, principally focused on improving the client base but also through offering new services, including quasi-legal and non-legal services.

In LawFirm, our cultural and historical consideration suggested the object to be 'to provide value for money and a professional service'. This was constantly articulated and reproduced in a variety of actions, ranging from the greetings of reception staff to clients entering the building to the provision of refreshing glasses of water on a hot day, to the many service actions undertaken with and for clients. We also considered how the firm's trajectory could be explicated by Victor and Boynton's (1998) types of work. At first glance, there was clearly still a great deal of reliance placed on tacit knowledge as the touchstone to practice, but as a firm, there had been considerable movement to embrace a number of new, non-standard legal solutions. Through its attention to process enhancement and its accumulation of architectural knowledge about clients, we could see that LawFirm was now operating on the 'cusp', between mass customisation and co-configuration (Warmington *et al*, 2004, p.8). Our intervention, therefore sought to work with LawFirm to bring about a further improvement and a move to co-configuration.

Co-configuration as explained is a form of work that matches LawFirm's aspirations to add value, particularly with relationships with clients and the leveraging the many cross-selling opportunities. As Victor and Boynten (1998, p.195) suggest,

'Mass customisation……requires the company to sense and respond to the individual customer's needs. But co-configuration work takes this relationship up one level-it brings the value of an intelligent and 'adapting' product'.

While staff in LawFirm were still mainly working under the old departmental headings and systems of control, a key feature of co-configuration is the bringing together of difference and apparently separate streams of knowledge so as to better respond to the needs of clients. This became apparent in an early exploration of the relationship with one client which LawFirm was particularly keen to improve relations with. The client (referred to as A) was an overseas bank with a UK presence including a local branch. It soon become clear that the relationship worked at different levels with different degrees of connection. The following diagram charts the relationships between nine professional staff at LawFirm and Firm A.

EG had a number of links with Firm A, ranging from Europe to London but also more locally in Regional. These links were with key gate-keepers and provide the necessary capital (human and social) for the referral of work to LawFirm. Although some members of the firm had links with the Europe HQ only – although these tended to be rather weak, others had particular links with Firm A staff in City North only. There had been a number of attempts to introduce LawFirm staff to Firm A headquarters staff in Europe. Staff had had to be ready to respond at short notice in order to demonstrate their expertise and explain what they could offer. This was necessary but not always successful, e.g. JO met a contact in

Figure 3. LawFirm and Firm A's relationship

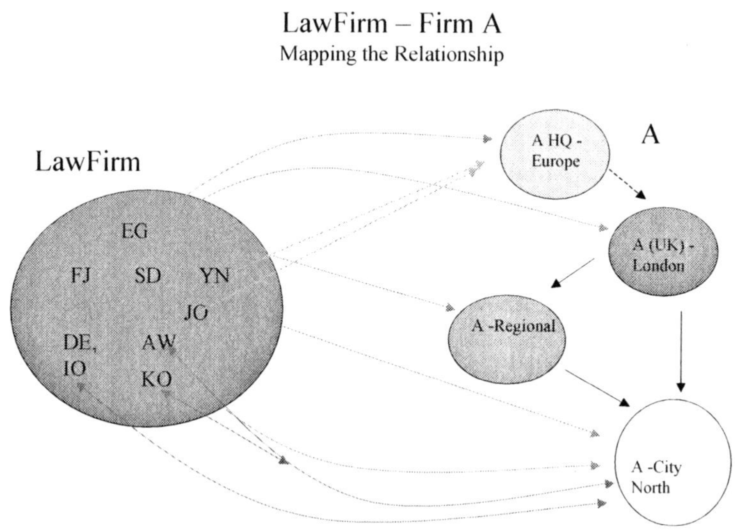

Europe HQ – 'great ideas' were discussed but there was no follow-up. A key comment at this level was that,' the people we meet can't necessarily deliver what they promise' although it was though necessary to keep trying to see if an opportunity arose, but the view was that there is little overall opportunity for LawFirm in Firm A's in European HQ. The relationships with Firm A's European HQ and especially the London office can be seen as part of the build-up of start-up capital and this was particularly important in providing permission for Firm A's staff in City North to include LawFirm in the local panel of approved solicitors. Similarly, LawFirm seemed to have met the criteria for panel membership in City North by placing a significant sum of money on deposit with Firm A. The relationship with Firm A at Regional level was seen as central in providing access to more work in City North and elsewhere. Other linkages were social and historical (DE- Rugby). These all served to 'put LawFirm in the frame' and 'keep the name there'. There have been a small but significant number of fee-earning projects completed in City North in three different departments. The importance of these projects was that they proved the expertise of LawFirm to Firm A staff in CityNorth and allowed the process of building social capital to begin. It became evident that working with clients such as Firm A and others in financial services was described as a 'constantly being in your face'. It was seen to be necessary to keep investing in start-up capital by being physically present in particular locations in City North on a Friday night after work. 'Being there' is another part of the process of keeping LawFirm's name alive.

There were some striking features of the linkages which demonstrated both vertical, horizontal and lateral dimensions of work with A and also the failure to 'tie things together' – a feature of co-configuration and knotworking ((Engeström, 2004). One identified weakness was that there seemed to be a lack of knowledge within LawFirm about 'who knows who' in A. The assumptions being used and a lack of common and agreed strategy of the 'bigger picture' to exert influence and share knowledge. LawFirm to this point lacked the necessary tools to bring together the variety of links that existed at different levels (Daniels 2004).

In another case different professionals from different departments in LawFirm were working at different levels with a client without any sharing of knowledge or attempts to co-ordinate actions. It was only after a series of important failures that reflection enabled them to see contradictions and tensions that cross-selling produced. It became apparent that early successful work with the client had established a particular storyline. In this storyline both the identity of the client and the professionals were established and the expectations understood. This was vital knowledge and formed the trajectory of future work. That is, the story evolved according to the core direction driven by the values of the participants in the story. Without knowledge of the past, new characters in the story ran the risk of disturbing the expectations, which is exactly what was happening. There was a failure to understand the storyline and knowledge of the expectations contained within it and this was the fundamental cause of negative outcomes and a loss of business with this client. Throughout, it was assumed that each professional who worked with the client, and there were up to six involved, had the required personal knowledge and experience to provide a service appropriate to the client's interests and in line with the storyline.

There was also a need to consider the voices of clients as potential partners in the reforming of services through the provision of feedback on how they perceived and valued the firm. To this end, we approached three clients regarded by LawFirm as 'friendly' and interested in playing a part in the development of future services. The particular focus was to consider each client's perception of professional services offered and how LawFirm compared against these expectations. We found that in all three cases, it was evident that a good relationship had been established with the client, although the extent and depth of the relationship varied. In all cases, there was a core relationship between senior directors and the client which has been established over a number of years. This continuity had engendered a sense of trust, honesty and integrity. All clients expressed confidence in LawFirm's ability to complete work and one client had been impressed by the work completed which was compared to another firm as being of 'more value' and 'pragmatic'. LawFirm provided good value for money; not the cheapest but not 'part of the magic circle'. There appeared however to be a number of doubts about LawFirm's provision:

Lack of specialism and a critical mass based on the presence of 'Big Names'

Questionable ability to cover more complex deals based on a reputation and track record of doing the 'donkey work'

A regional presence rather than simply a national one with no office in London and an ability to respond on a face to face basis outside the region location

One of the key features that we identified was the lack of depth the LawFirm had in terms of its ability to draw on 'social capital'. One client suggested that they had had little chance 'to scrum down' with members of the LawFirm such that relationships could be developed and confidence could be gained.

The above suggest that the LawFirm faced significant challenges if it wished to develop. As we indicated earlier in the chapter, contradictions and tension can be both a threat or an opportunity to address issues and develop the business. The research identified many instances where tension and ambiguity were present in relation to the object. These caused disturbances throughout the whole activity system. To facilitate the LawFirm to better exploit these opportunities, we suggested that we pilot a learning process for staff as part of their client engagement.

TOWARDS 'KNOTWORKING'

Co-configuration as a way of working with people's practice and learning and is synonymous with knowledge creation and knowledge sharing. It is oriented to both individuals and groups and has the potential to link learning at the individual level to that of the organisation. The processes by which this can be achieved are far from straightforward. For example, at the personal level, so much of what is practiced by individual professionals is considered to be a manifestation of their tacit knowing and there are, of course, different views on whether such knowing can ever be fully articulated. Beckett and Hager (2002), for example, argue that while tacit knowing is 'ambiguous' (p. 120), it can be made explicit and shared with others. Gold *et al* (2007), provide evidence of a process of knowledge creation and sharing among professionals from the same department which is used to illustrate this case. However, even the processes involved in sharing can be problematic when barriers exist between departments, as is the case in LawFirm. Daniels (2004) suggests that there are two features of learning required if co-configuration is to be successful. The first is, learning for co-configuration. This is where professionals from different departments find mechanisms (often dialogue) through which they can debate and negotiate their practices. The second is where professionals learn through interaction with clients (and others) and, more crucially, can be articulated so that sharing can take place. Both of the above need, it is argued, to become interdependent in a mutually reinforcing process of dialogue and debate about clients and practice with clients. Collective CPD in LawFirm we considered could occur if personal learning were to create knowledge which could then be shared horizontally across the divisional boundaries. This would allow the various strands of knowledge to be 'tied together'. New tools, rules or roles, could also be used to create the potential to broaden the perspective individuals have of the object across the whole firm.

To begin a process of learning for co-configuration, as part of a process of collaborative engagement to improve LawFirm's performance, we introduced a process we called 'Strategic Client Learning'. This process was specifically targeted at the firm's key clients. We agreed to pilot this process with two departments, both of which would identify up to four clients each for consideration. The key features of the process are shown in Figure 4:

The identification of a key client highlighted the need for a client team. In LawFirm, teams were not an unusual working structure, but the notion of team was now extended to include anybody in the firm who interacted with the particular client identified. For each client identified, the team that was formed debated the principal issues that related to the client before conducting an evaluation on a relationship index. This process surfaced the interdependence that existed within the team.

The next stage was to map the key actions that need to be taken over the next fee income period and the generation of action plans and targets that would close the gaps identified between the LawFirm's aspirations and the current reality (Thorpe and Cornelissen, 2003). As actions are gradually decided and taken, the team are able to capture important moments as critical incidents, provide stories (preferably in writing) to communicate the source of success and to learn from the issues as they occurred. We were again careful when we recognised that the different disciplinary backgrounds of LawFirm's staff lead to high levels of ambiguity and uncertainty. A further tool, and what proved to be a crucial one for client participation, was a review that was conducted on the relationship between completion of plans and learning from client feedback.

Although we did not specify that cross-department action should be a criteria for the selection of key clients (cross-selling was specified). Of the eight pilots, three involved cross-division team members from at least two departments and we found that these provided the greatest opportunity for learning to develop configuration; in these areas, knots were beginning to be tied.

Figure 4. A strategic client learning process

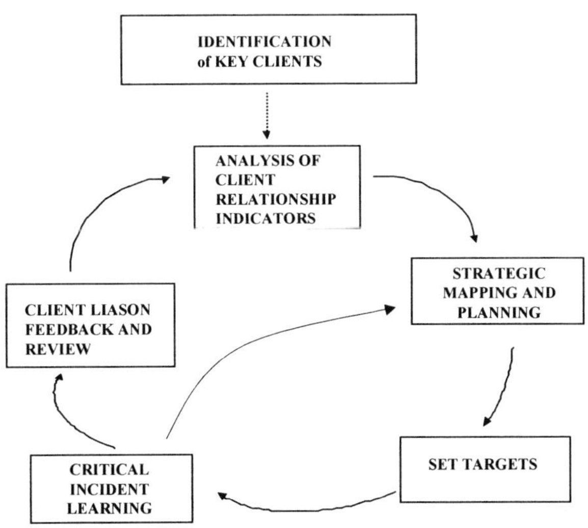

Of the identified clients, one was a fast-growing retail company we refer to as Client X. This organisation which LawFirm project-managed the contract work for a new property acquisition. In this case, the client team composed solicitors from three departments. Following their use of the new tools and their involvement in the debate and the completion of the relationship indicators, they agreed to develop new relationships with the client's board members, increase the number of people involved in client management and services provision. There was however, no recognition of the value-added by the client, particularly the Chief Executive. Actions planned were summarised in a map, as shown in Figure 5:

A crucial feature of the work in this case was the very demanding schedule set by the client. The debate that took place also brought to the fore the fact that the Chief Executive of the client had little appreciation of the way LawFirm added-value. The theme of adding value went wider than simply Client X and this indicates the ambiguities inherent in the object of this notion of adding value and giving value-for-money. An issue of intellectual property also existed and Client X was not yet aware of the value of this asset; this provided for them an opportunity for re-shaping a new service.

During a review conducted six weeks later, discussion of a number of the critical incidents identified when working with the client allowed LawFirm staff to articulate a need to 'streamline' the project management process and to move forward the development of an IT infrastructure to organise delivery. LawFirm agreed that a case for a project would be prepared and an emerging Unique Selling Proposition developed. We judged that as a consequence of the activity that had taken place the potential of this learning was transformative for the whole of LawFirm. The current level of thinking and ideas had stretched and broadened the object and provided a range of new artefacts, both physical and psychologically. At a subsequent review, it became clear that the client was seeing value in working with LawFirm and was beginning to compare the service provided, favourably, with others with whom they had worked.

After a six month period, LawFirm was reviewed again. On this occasion we reviewed the

Figure 5. Actions planned for Client X

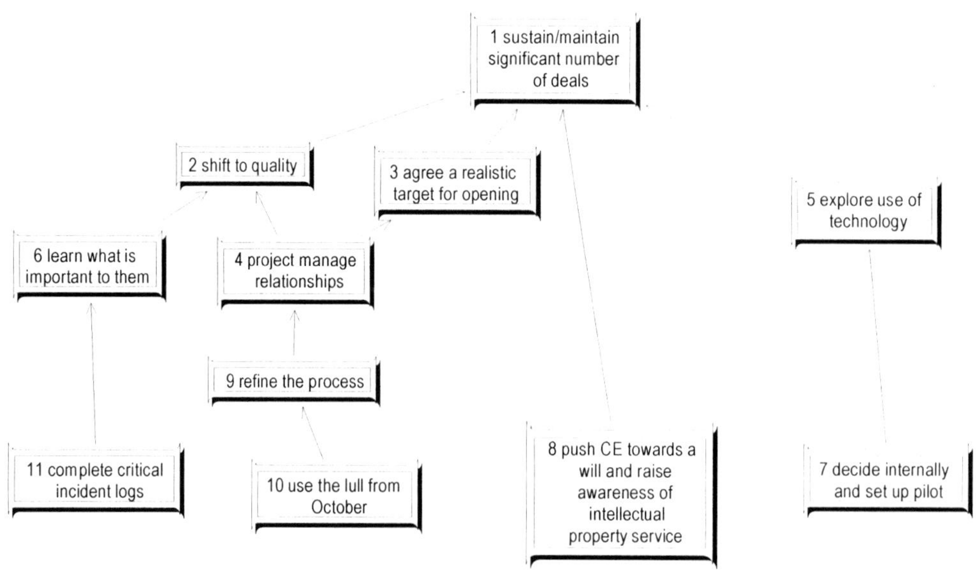

working of the process we have outlined with senior directors of LawFirm. Again it was evident, that by allowing departments to identify key clients, with whom they had potential to extend their services, moving towards a state of co-configuration could produce results. What was very encouraging to see was that individuals with very busy schedules and with very different views were able to meet the challenge to change, exchange knowledge and work to achieve new ways of working. Further the sharing of knowledge became more conscious and systematic even though it was face-to-face and the facilitation ensured that different views were heard and explained.

In two of the cases, unexpected events occurred. For example, the impending closure of a local branch of a multi-national finance firm required a swift and co-ordinated response to ensure that as much of the £100k+ fee income could be secured. For another client, one of the major banks, it was important to share with them vital information so that LawFirm's value could be appreciated. Difficulties such as these will always occur in any dynamic context, reinforcing the need to use a shared knowledge approach.

In a number of cases, new tools of mediation were introduced to energise and facilitate the learning process. Although these tools were not always fully developed, they were monitored and adjusted as events unfolded. One of the key ambiguities was the notion of value for money. For professional knowledge-based firms, the object of activity is invariably subjected to 'buffeting' in response to the changing expectations of clients. It is therefore incumbent on firms to move beyond basic services (i.e. those that are indistinguishable from competitor organisations) in order to add value. Adding value to clients requires an understanding of what value means for different individuals within the firm and between clients, as well as an awareness that value is being added in the delivery of the service. For example, involvement in solving key problems for a client and adding to a client's ability to make key decisions (Dawson 2000). Both require developing relationships with clients to more fully understand needs so that these can be targeted more carefully. As Victor and Boynton suggest:

'...co-configuration work never results in a 'finished' product. Instead, a growing network develops between customer, product and company' (p.195)

For LawFirm, extending the dialogue to clients through regular reviews and liaison meetings remained a challenge still to be realised and one that required the development of new tools. However, such is the success of the project so far, that LawFirm's management team have sought to extend the process throughout the firm. Each department now have a Strategic Client Learning facilitator, a qualified solicitor but now tasked to help departments identify key clients, form Client Learning Teams and follow the process identified in Figure 4. In this way, the project has moved learning beyond individuals towards a distributed and collective process.

CONCLUSION

This paper explores the changing nature of professional practice. It began by conceptualising the development of knowledge within the law profession. Using a historical analysis it traces the emergence of tacit knowledge (existing in professionals) into codified forms that helped firms exploit a growing market for professional advice. The control of the professional by the Law Society and the rules that allow lawyers to practice is explained. It is within the regulations of practice from which the requirements to undertake CPD emerge and in this context the view of knowledge as a configured resource rather than tacit, situated and emergent is developed. It is at this point in the paper that the threads of our argument are brought together. Namely how can increasingly deregulated law firms facing increasing competition structure themselves so as to leverage the key resource of knowledge to their commercial advantage.

The paper gives the case of one law firm with whom the authors have worked over a two year period. Using an activity theoretical perspective the paper examines a law firm located in the North of England. The methodological approach enables the researchers to use tools within an action research tradition to surface issues and ambiguities for discussion and debate. The case chosen and the illustrations provided not only demonstrate the value of this method of intervention, but specifically how CPD occurs at the level of the firm (an explicitly stated next stage of their development).

The case study evidence presented shows the way in which social capital with LawFirm is both generated and destroyed. Each phase of a four stage process of key client identification, stakeholder involvement client support and evaluation is described, the aim of which was to facilitate improved performance through producing a state of co-configuration. The evidence from the case presented indicated that this had indeed been achieved with LawFirm identifying a number of improvements in processes and performance. Two additional outcomes were identified. One, the trialling and development of new tools to aid reflection, the other the importance learnt about the need to understand the different ways individuals perceive value in the provision of a professional service. Both carry the potential for HRD practitioners within professional organisations to play a crucial and valued role in facilitating dialogic skills both for individuals and for groups composed of different specialists.

REFERENCES

Abbott, A. (1988). *The System of Professions.* Chicago: University of Chicago Press.

Beckett, D., & Hager, P. (2002). *Life, Work and Learning.* London: Routledge

Blacker, F., Crump, N., & McDonald, S. (1999). Managing experts and competing through innovation: an activity theoretical analysis. *Organization, 6*(1), 5-31.

Cantillon, P., & Jones, R. (1999). Does continuing medical education in general practice make a difference? *British Medical Journal, 318*, 1276-1277.

Castells, M. (1996). *The Rise of the Network Society.* Blackwell, Oxford

Cheetham, G., & Chivers, G. (2001). How professionals learn in practice. *Journal of European Industrial Training, 24*(7), 247-292.

Cooper, D., Greenwood, R., Hinings, C. R., & Brown, J. (1996). Sedimentation and transformation in organizational change: the case of Canadian law firms. *OrganizationStudies, 17*(4), 623-647

Dietrich, M., & Roberts, J. (1997). Beyond the Economics of Professionalism. In J. Broadbent, M. Dietrich, & J. Roberts, (Eds.), *The End of the Professions?* London: Routledge.

Daniels, H. (2004). Cultural historical activity theory and professional learning. *International Journal of Disability, Development and Education, 51*(2), 185-200.

Dawson, R. (2000). *Developing Knowledge-Based Client Relationships.* Butterworth-Heinemann, Woburn.

Elliott, P. (1972). *The Sociology Of The Professions.* Basingstoke: Macmillan.

Ellis, N., & Watterson, C. (2001). Client perceptions of regional law firms and their implications for marketing management. *Service Industries Journal, 21*(4), 100-118

Engeström, Y. (1995). Objects, contradictions and

collaboration in medical cognition: an activity-theoretical perspective. *Artificial Intelligence in Medicine, 7,* 395-412.

Engeström, Y. (2001). Expansive learning at work: toward an activity theoretical reconceptualisation. *Journal of Education and Work, 14*(1), 133-156.

Engeström, Y. (2004). New forms of learning in co-configuration work. Paper presented to the Department of Information Systems. *ICTs in the contemporary world.* seminar, LSE, January 2004

Eraut, M. (2000). Non-formal learning, implicit learning and tacit knowledge in professional work. In F. Coffield (Ed.), *The Necessity of Informal Learning.* Bristol: Policy Press.

Eraut, M. (2000a). Non-formal learning and tacit knowledge in professional work. *British Journal of Educational Psychology, 70,* 113-136.

Freidson, E. (2001). *Professionalism.* Cambridge: Polity Press

Gold, J., Thorpe, R., Woodall, J. & Sadler-Smith, E. (2007). Continuing professional development in the legal profession: a practice-based-learning perspective. *Management Learning, 38*(2), 235-250.

Grant, J., Chambers, E., & Jackson, G. (Eds) (1999). *The Good CPD Guide: A Practical Guide to Managed CPD.* Surrey: Reed Business Information.

Greenwood, R., Hinings, C. R., & Brown, J. (1990). P2 Form' strategic management: Corporate practices in professional partnerships. *Academy of Management Journal, 33*(4), 725-755.

Hanlon, G. (1998). Professionalism as enterprise: service class politics and the redefinition of professionalism. *Sociology, 32*(1), 43-63.

Hart, S., & Hogg, G. (1998). Relationship marketing in corporate legal services. *The Service Industries Journal, 18*(1), 55-69.

Hinings, C. R., Greenwood, R., & Cooper, D. (1999). The Dynamics of Change in Large Accounting Firms. In D. M. Brock, M. J. Powell & C. R. Hinings (Eds.), *Restructuring the Professional Organization.* London: Routledge.

Leontyev, A. N. (1978). *Activity, Consciousness and Personality.* Englewood Cliffs: Prentice-Hall.

Mintzberg, H. (1983). *Structure in Fives: Designing Effective Organisations.* Englewood Cliff, NJ: Prentice-Hall.

Pinnington, A., & Morris, T. (2003). Archetype change in professional organizations. *British Journal of Management, 14*(1), 85-99.

Sadler-Smith, E., & Badger, B. (1998). HR practitioners' attitudes to continuing professional development. *Human Resource Management Journal, 8,* 66-75.

Sadler-Smith, E., Allinson, C. W., & Hayes J. (2000). Cognitive style and learning preferences: some implications for CPD. *Management Learning, 31,* 239-256.

Taylor, N. (1996). Professionalism and Monitoring CPD: Kafka Revisited. *Planning Practice and Research, 11*(4), 379-389.

Thorpe, R., & Cornelissen, J. (2003). Visual media and the construction of meaning. In D. Holman & R. Thorpe (Eds.), *Management and Language.* London: Sage.

Warmington, P., Daniels, H., Edwards, Leadbetter, A., Martin, J., Brown, D., & Middleton, D. (2004). Learning in and for interagency working: conceptual tensions in 'joined up' practice. Paper presented to the *TLRP Annual Conference.* Cardiff, November

Victor, B., & Boynton, A. (1998). *Invented Here: Maximizing Your Organization's Internal Growth and Profitability.* Boston: Harvard Business School Press.

KEY TERMS

Co-Configuration: An ongoing learning process between organisation and their customers where interactions provide opportunities for knowledge generation.

Collective CPD: The creation of knowledge through personal learning which is shared and distributed across divisional boundaries.

Continuing Professional Development: A learning process for professionally qualified workers.

Cultural Historical Activity Theory (CHAT): The study of collective activity system of the firm, in a relevant and practical way so that interventions made contribute to the construction of new meanings which in turn lead towards greater understanding of the system.

Law Firms: The organisation of the delivery of legal services.

Legal Profession: Those qualified by a professional association to practice the delivery of legal services.

Strategic Client Learning: A team approach to identifying key clients, mapping and evaluating the current relationship before setting goals for action. Key incidents with the client are logged for learning and knowledge sharing.

ENDNOTES

[a] Elsewhere, outside the UK, CPD might be termed CPE or Continuing Professional Education

[b] Figures obtained from the Law Society website, http://www.lawsociety.org.uk/aboutlawsociety.law on 15 July 2006.

[c] A useful summary of the history of the Law Society can be found at http://www.lawsociety.org.uk/aboutlawsociety/whoweare/abouthistory.law

Chapter IV
Innovation Risks of Outsourcing within Knowledge Intensive Business Services (KIBS)

Paul Trott
University of Portsmouth, UK

Andreas Hoecht
University of Portsmouth, UK

ABSTRACT

The United States and European economies have witnessed an enormous increase in the amount of specialized business services, which now provide critical inputs to firms in all sectors. It is this area of the economy which has witnessed huge expansion and development. KIBS include traditional professional business services such as accountancy and law, but also a new generation of KIBS such as IT expertise and internet development. Coupled to this growth has been an increase in the level of outsourcing. Outsourcing was originally confined to peripheral business functions and mainly motivated by a cost saving logic, but has now developed into a routine strategic management move that affects not only peripheral functions but the heart of the competitive core of organisations. This chapter analyses previous research and adopts a conceptual perspective in investigating the innovation-related risks to the organisation that can arise from strategic outsourcing. It uses the example of KIBS outsourcing to highlight the increased risks that arise from a move from traditional to strategic outsourcing and discusses some measures that managers can take to attempt to control these risks.

INTRODUCTION

Occasionally one would be forgiven for thinking that in these advanced developed economies services had replaced all manufacturing activities, and there had simply been a huge growth in coffee bars, smoothie bars and hair salons. In the most advanced service economies in the world such as the USA and UK, services now account for up to three-quarters of the wealth and 85% of employment (Tidd and Hull, 2003). Within the EU services now account for 60% of GDP (Eurostat, 2006). The term knowledge based economy has been coined to characterize some of the main changes in the development of economies over the past twenty years. Similarly, the influence of technology in general and information communication technologies in particular cannot be overstated. In virtually all industries there has been a huge growth in specialist knowledge and skills being made available to firms. For example in civil engineering and architecture, where previously much of the input came from the architect now the architect employs a range of specialists from: fire engineering; acoustic engineers; lighting designers, etc. A new range of disciplines have emerged offering specialist knowledge and skills. This has been replicated in virtually all industries (Gann and Salter, 2003).

The development of these economies has led to a massive increase in the amount of specialized business services which now provide critical inputs to firms in all sectors. It is this area of the economy (US and Europe) which has witnessed huge expansion and development. It is not simply that people are spending more time and money in hair salons (though that may also be true). It is these knowledge intensive business services (KIBS) which are the key behind the development of the service side of the economies. KIBS include traditional professional business services such as accountancy and law, as well as services that have a scientific and technical knowledge base such as IT/IS (Miles, 2003; Alvesson, 2004). Other examples include a new generation of KIBS. For example the provision of specialist services to the Oil industry has led to huge growth for Halliburton and Schlumberger, the world market leader for oil services. Indeed, while the share prices of Exon and Shell have doubled over the past four years the share price of Halliburton and Schlumberger has tripled (Financial Times, 2007).

The growth in information communication technologies during the 1980s and the development of the internet in the 1990s and into the 21st century has led to enormous sums of money being spent by firms in order to ensure that they are equipped to compete. In addition, the introduction of some of these business systems such as Enterprise Resource Planning systems (ERP) have led to significant reductions in costs and improvements in efficiency. If one then adds to the KIBS the huge growth in entertainment industries including the gaming industry (Xbox, Nintendo, Playstation, PC games, etc), the new online gambling industry (Party-Gaming, Gaming Corporation) and the more recent social networking industry (which includes Myspace, Bebo and Mypages) one begins to recognize just how much change and growth there has been to economies over the past ten years.

The service sector is vast and it varies considerably from public services, in the form of state funded education for 97% of children in the UK, to specialist business services in the form of Internet web site design and maintenance. Each sector of the service economy (such as leisure, charities, public services, financial services) has its own set of specific challenges. Yet at the same time the distinctions between some of these sectors is blurring. Some charities and not-for profit organisations are offering their services to compete with the private sector. Health care provision is a prime example. Similarly some public funded organizations such as the BBC offer its services in the commercial world and generate large revenue streams. Table 1 offers a classification of services and includes professional business services, such

Table 1. Typology of services

	Business to business services (traditional)	Business to business services (KIBS)	Consumer services	Internal firm services	Public services	Not for profit services
Description	Services provided for businesses	Specialist services provided to businesses	Services provided to individuals	Services provided by internal functions	Services provided by local and national government	Services provided by charities
Examples	Accountancy Legal advice Training	Management consultancy IT consultancy	Shops Hotels Banking Health & beauty	Finance Personnel IT	Health Education Leisure Prisons	Hospices Counselling Aid agencies
Customers	Frequently purchased by professionals, who may not be end users	Frequently purchased by professionals, who may not be end users	Purchased by consumer of the service	Consumers of the service have no choice of provider	Funded through taxation and little choice for consumer	Funded through charities maybe government grants consumers chosen or choose.
Challenges	Providing high quality tailored and personal service	Providing high quality services to businesses who have high purchasing power	Providing a consistent service to a wide variety of customers	Delivering customised, personal service. And demonstrating value for money.	Delivering acceptable public services against a backcloth of political pressures.	Balancing needs of volunteers, donors and overwhelming needs of customers.

Adapted from Johnston & Clark (2005)

as accountancy and public services such as libraries. This overview helps demystify the service notion. It clarifies the different sectors within services and illustrates the different challenges facing each sector.

OUTSOURCING AND SERVICE GROWTH

Outsourcing has become very widespread in the last decade and has moved on from limited applications where peripheral business functions are "outsourced" to much more vital business functions being outsourced today, such as I.T. support (Jennings, 1997, Quelin and Duhamel, 2003). Despite the rather mixed record of large-scale long-term total outsourcing deals with single suppliers in particular in the IT/IS industry (Lacity & Willcocks, 1998), such contracts are still entered into in significant numbers. The academic literature has identified a number of expected gains that companies can derive from outsourcing. These include:

- the reduction of operational costs (Lacity & Hirschheim, 1993);
- the ability to transform fixed costs into variable costs (Alexander & Young, 1996);
- the ability to focus on core competencies (Quinn & Hilmer, 1994);
- access to the industry-leading external competencies and expertise (Kakabadse & Kakabadse, 2002).

There seems little doubt that the growth in services is linked to this enormous growth in outsourcing. With many firms now buying in "services" that were previously undertaken in-house. So whether its catering facilities within schools now being bought from local providers by the County Education Authority or whether it's a firm buying in information technology (IT) support rather than providing the service themselves, the evidence is overwhelming that this growth in outsourcing has contributed to the growth in services Davies, 2003). Coupled to this debate, however is the suggestion that manufacturers are now moving into highly profitable knowledge intensive services. This is certainly the case at IBM which has moved successfully from manufacturer to service solution provider with its profits now being dominated by IT services (FT.com, 2007). For some firms lower production costs in India and China are forcing them downstream into the provision of services. For other firms, like IBM and Ericsson, it is recognition that they can offer added value market offerings to their customers by providing additional services. Within sectors of complex products and systems (CoPS) buyers are outsourcing non-core activities and focusing on the provision of services to the final customer. In the pharmaceutical industry for example, clinical trials that were previously undertaken by the firm are now outsourced to clinical trial specialist firms.

There is, however, also an emerging literature that highlights the weaknesses and risks associated with large-scale outsourcing arrangements, in particular where non-peripheral business functions are concerned. This highlights the risk of becoming dependent on a supplier (Alexander and Young, 1996); Barthelemy (2001) draws our attention to the hidden costs of outsourcing and authors such as Doig et al (2001) and Quinn and Hilmer (1994) identify the possibility of a loss of vital know-how in particular with respect to core competencies as a major risk factor in outsourcing. There is also the problem of selecting the most suited supplier/service provider and their longer-term ability to offer the capabilities that are needed in particular in business environments with rapid technology change (Earl, 1996). Another risk that is often overlooked is linked to the broader area of information leakage that arises when business organisations collaborate in order to gain access to knowledge and expertise that they cannot develop on their own. Research by Hoecht & Trott (2006) has demonstrated that there is trade-off between access to cutting-edge knowledge via collaborative research and technology development in knowledge-intensive industries and the risk of losing commercially sensitive knowledge to competitors. This risk, they argue, cannot be

Table 2. Main outsourcing risks identified in the literature

	Main negative outcomes of outsourcing	**Research evidence**
1	Dependence on the supplier	Alexander and Young (1996); Aubert et al. (1998)
2	Hidden costs	Earl (1996); Alexander and Young (1996); Aubert et al. (1998); Lacity and Hirschheim (1993); Barthelemy (2001)
3	Loss of competencies	Bettis et al. (1992); Martisons (1993); Quinn and Hilmer (1994); Khosrowpour et al (1995); Alexander and Young (1996); Aubert et al. (1998); Doig et al. (2001)
4	Service provider's lack of necessary capabilities	Earl (1996); Aubert et al. (1998); Kaplan (2002)
5	Social risk	Lacity and Hirschheim (1993); Barthelemy and Geyer (2000)
6	Inefficient management	Wang and Regan (2003); Lynch (2002)

Adapted from Quélin and Duhamel (2003)

controlled by traditional management approaches and legal contracting alone, but requires the operation of social control and in particular the development of trust to be contained. Table 2 offers an overview of the main risks identified in the literature.

OUTSOURCING CORE CAPABILITIES

There is an additional specific risk associated with outsourcing that has yet to be fully explored. This may be classified under the general term of loss of competencies (Table 2 above), but precisely is innovative capability.

From a strategic management perspective, when considering a firm's innovation and long-term competitiveness, the traditional cost concerns are far less important than the question of how to identify and to retain a company's competitive core and not to lose its future ability to compete in fast-moving and unpredictable markets. The strategic management literature is divided on this issue. There are tools like Hamel and Prahalad's (1994) three tests for critical business processes, namely "customer value", "competitor differentiation" and "extendibility" that are claimed to be useful and reliable for identifying core competencies and authors like Quinnn (1999) are optimistic that these competencies can be identified but warn companies never to outsource their core (defined as "best in world") competencies. A number of researchers also believe that not only the core competences but also most special skills related to competitive advantage need to be kept in-house (Reve, 1990; Quinn, 1999). Nevertheless, there appears to be a general consensus in the strategic management literature that at least the complementary skills or organisational competences can be handled and developed by alliances and opened up to collaboration and that goods and services of little strategic value can be purchased on the open market (Brandes et al, 1997). The key strategic management controversy however, remains about the issue whether these core competencies and specialised skills can be reliable identified. McIvor (2000: 48), for example, is much less confident that other writers that these competencies can be accurately predicted:

"A current competency may cease to be a source of competitive advantage if there is a change in customer requirements or competitors develop innovative technologies".

There is also the important question of the potential for losing one's core skills and competitive advantage to competitors in the process of collaboration. Hamel (1991) maintains that core skills can be learnt form the other party and absorbed into one's own company just as much as one's own skills can be absorbed by a partner and one's unique competitive advantage lost in the process. Bower et al (1997) observed the behaviour of technology leaders in the close-knit North Sea upstream offshore oil and gas industry and found that participating in networks sharing leading edge technology was exposing firms to the risk of their competitive edge being lost to competitors. Interestingly, this risk was found to be much smaller for resourceful and influential companies benefiting form a network centrality position than for smaller and less well positioned companies.

The next section develops the above discussion further by exploring why outsourcing a firm's core capabilities may hinder its innovative capability.

THE MANAGEMENT OF INNOVATION WITHIN FIRMS: WHY OUTSOURCING MAY HINDER INNOVATION

The management of innovation is a large and diverse body of literature. It recognises that while

Table 3. Key studies studies of innovation management

	Study	Date	Focus
1	Carter & Williams	1957	Industry & technical progress
2	Project Hindsight- TRACES, (Isensen)	1968	Historical reviews of US government funded defence industry
3	Wealth from knowledge (Langrish et al.)	1972	Queen's Awards for technical innovation
4	Project Sappho (Rothwell, 1974)	1974	Success & failure factors in chemical industry
5	Stanford study (Madidique & Zirger)	1984	Success factors in US electronics industry
6	Minnesota Studies (Van de Ven)	1989	14 case studies of innovations
7	Rothwell	1992	25 yr review of studies
8	Sources of innovation (Wheelwright & Clark)	1992	Different levels of user involvement
9	MIT studies (Utterback)	1994	5 major industry-level cases
10	Project NEWPROD (Cooper)	1999	Longitudinal survey of success & failure in new products
11	Radical innovation (Leifer)	2000	Review of mature businesses
12	T.U.Delft study (Van der Panne et al.)	2003	A major literature review of success and failure factors.
13	Chesbrough	2003	Open innovation systems along the supply chain

Sources: van der panne et al., (2003) & Trott (2005)

there is much complexity and uncertainty in managing innovation and new product development much is known. There is considerable agreement on many of the factors that contribute to success and the activities and processes that need to be undertaken if innovation is to occur. Over the past fifty years there have been numerous studies of innovation attempting to understand not only the factors necessary for it to occur, but how they influence the process and when and where they are required and in what order. Table 3 captures some of the key studies that have influenced our understanding.

At the corporate level, a number of research paradigms have attempted to explain the international difference in technological development and innovation. Neo-classical economic theorists believe market structure, competition pressure, local supply of skills together with openness of communication are the most important factors (Stoneman, 1983; Geroski, 1993; Ansoff, 1965; Porter, 1980; 1985; 1990). However, this approach has not been able to fully explain the dynamics of innovation processes and the role played by firms and other institutions (Patel and Pavitt, 1984; Lundvall, 1988). In terms of firm specific characteristics that are required for firms to become more innovative much has been written about this (Quinn, 1991; Kanter, 1998; Wolfe, 1994). There is also significant amount of literature on the strategic dimension of competition (Porter, 1980; Pavitt, 1984; de Woot, 1990). Many writers on innovation consider it mainly as a process that needs careful management (Souder, 1987; Trott, 2004; Twiss, 1992), while others view innovation more as a cognitive and behavioural phenomenon (Van de Ven, 1988; Madique, 1988). Despite their differences, most of these writers seem to accept that innovation is a phenomenon that can be subjected to human control and is considerably affected by human interaction. We also know that individuals create knowledge through collaborating with others in groups/teams in an organisational context; helping individuals to achieve their full potential and contribute new knowledge is a critical management issue which has also received considerable attention in the literature (Tidd, 2000; Nonaka, 1991; Nonaka, & Takeuchi, 1995; Polyani, 1966).

The studies in Table 1 have contributed to the accepted view that a firm's ability to successfully develop innovative new products is not only the result of public and private investments in tangibles and intangibles by individual elements in the economy, but that it is also strongly influenced by the character and intensity of the interactions between the elements of the system. This position is strongly advocated in the literature on "National Innovation Systems" (Freeman, 1982; Lundvall, 1992; Nelson, 1993). In this view, innovation and technological development in particular depend increasingly on the ability to utilise new knowledge produced elsewhere and to combine this with knowledge already available in the economy and its actors. The capacity to absorb new knowledge, to transfer and diffuse knowledge and the ability to learn through interaction are crucial success factors in innovation (e.g. Cohen & Levinthal, 1989; Chesborough, 2003). New and commercially useful knowledge is not only the result of the conscious action of creative individuals. It is also the outcome of the interaction and learning processes among various actors in innovation systems, i.e. producers, users, suppliers, public authorities, and scientific institutions, which David & Foray (1995) have coined the "knowledge distribution power" of the innovation system. Indeed, Rothwell (1992) put forward the idea of a fifth-generation model of innovation management, based on inter-company networking facilitated by IT systems. More recently, the term network has become widely used. The need for connectivity and the complexity of the interactions it entails therefore emerges as a major factor influencing the management of innovation. While knowledge sharing across organisational boundaries is not an entirely new phenomenon the increasing emphasis on network forms of innovation in the innovation literature reflects the growth of KIBS for technology intensive sectors in the advanced economies.

Given the significance of the beneficial effect of effect of inter-firm collaboration and the role of networks for innovation and organisational learning (Hamel, 1991), it is necessary to explore this concept in more detail. March (1991) distinguishes between exploration and exploitation in organisational learning. He argues that there are major differences between experimentation with new alternatives (exploration) and the refinement of existing technologies and organisational competencies (exploitation). The latter can be conceived as a close relative of the keep in house-or outsource decision, where collaboration arises from an unwillingness to go-alone and a strong preference for risk-limitation will always be prevalent. On the other hand, explorative knowledge creation relies on much more "openness" and a dedicated participation in research communities, firms, universities, research laboratories, suppliers and customers (Powell, 1990). What is required here is a much more intimate form of collaboration where both parties are contributing, rather than the handing over of responsibility of an activity, which is often associated with the outsourcing decision. Furthermore, Powell at al (1996) argue that the locus of explorative innovations is to be found in networks of inter-organisational relationships and that a firm's success crucially depends on its "centrality-position" in such networks and the experience gained in managing its networks. They argue that internal capability and external collaboration rather than being substitutes are complementary:

" Internal capability is indispensable in evaluating research done outside, while external collaboration provides access to news and resources that cannot be generated internally... A network serves as a locus of innovation because it provides timely access to knowledge and resources that are otherwise unavailable, while also testing internal expertise and learning capabilities."

In their empirical study of the network behaviour of biotechnology firms operating in the human therapeutics and diagnostics field (1960-94) they found strong support for their hypothesis that a firm's centrality in network relationships and its incrementally acquired experience in managing network ties is a strong predictor for its growth and economic success. Network experience, it appears, should be considered as an incremental learning process both in terms of the management of collaborative ties and in terms of the actual technical learning of biotechnology innovations (Powell at al., 1996). The decision to outsource an activity includes the inherent risk of forgoing a firm's centrality of participation in valuable networks.

The development of network models of innovation have helped to illustrate further the prominence now given to internal and external interactions (networks) within the innovation process. All these knowledge flows contribute to the wealth of knowledge held by the organisation (Woolgar et al., 1998; Rothwell, 1992; Major and Cordey-Hayes, 2002). Recognising this, capturing and utilising it to develop successful new products is the difficult management process of innovation. Here then lies the potential problem for firms if key activities are outsourced: whether at the very least the firm risks disrupting the knowledge flows to the organisation and more worryingly for senior managers is whether it will isolate a firm from valuable networks.

Furthermore, the inability to retain a company's competitive core will not only endanger its future competitiveness, but can also create a serious risk of dependency on outside providers. A crucial question is whether the desired access to "best in industry" capabilities are sufficient to sustain its competitive advantage in particular where the provider serves "many masters" and the particular expertise ceases to be unique and becomes best- practice industry standard. While there is no shortage of advice in the literature on how to manage the risk of dependency from outside providers and suppliers in general (see for instance Currie & Willcocks, 1998 who suggest multi vendor approaches and shorter term contracts for handling large-scale long-term total outsourcing contracts with IT/IS providers), the specific problem that access to world-leading expertise via outsourcing may well be compromised by the "levelling-out" of unique advantages when leading service providers spread their world-leading expertise to several clients has not received much attention.

As a consequence of the problem of "levelling out" of leading edge expertise, the innovation impact of outsourcing is not limited to the issue of core competencies and the need of companies to retain at least the absorptive capacity to exploit innovations that have been developed by outside service providers. There is also the problematic assumption that service providers are always able to infuse best practice into the company. In a traditional outsourcing relationship, a long-term commitment is entered into that "locks" a company to a service provider for the length of the service contract. The ability to infuse best industry practice may not only depend on the relative competence of the provider, but the service providers may also be restricted in their ability to pass on best practices by confidentiality agreement with previous and other current clients. A significant dilemma emerges: Individual firms have a reasoned case against competitors gaining the fruits of their investment and innovation efforts, while at the same time the majority of companies choose outsourcing not least in the hope of gaining such advantages from other firms. This dilemma is mainly left to the service providers and the individual consultants they employ to resolve. It is, however, a very important issue from an organisational innovation perspective. We will see below that this issue becomes even more pressing when companies and industries move away from traditional long-term outsourcing relationships with single service providers to strategic outsourcing, i.e. to much more open, short-term relationships with multiple suppliers involving all business processes.

THE IMPORTANT ROLE OF TRUST IN THE MANAGEMENT OF OUTSOURCING RELATIONSHIPS: THE EXAMPLE OF INFORMATION SYSTEMS OUTSOURCING

Outsourcing has a long tradition in relation to the IT industry. Because of the high costs of IT infrastructure and the rapid change in technology, many organisations have been looking at external providers for the IT function since the early 1980s.

The reasons for this move are rational. If information services play a supporting role for the key business functions and this service can be bought in at higher quality of service delivery without having to commit substantial assets and resources, it makes good sense to look at the external market for providers.

In most cases, the outsourcing relationship goes further than just substituting for an internal IT service and a contractual relationship is sought where the service provider assumes responsibility for one or more of the organisation's IT or even business functions (Willcocks & Lacity, 1999). In this case, the relationship includes the transfer of resources of the outsourcing organisation to the external service provider and involves a long-term commitment with a detailed legally binding contract. Significant organisational changes are needed as the role of the internal IT department changes form being a supplier of its own services to assuming the function of a controller and broker of IT and/or business services. Because of the level of mutual commitment, lengthy contract negotiations (9-12 months) and detailed rules are the norm which later can become problematic as technology base and business requirement tend to change, at times even before the contract is finally signed (Gartner, Research Report, December 2001). As the original focus is traditionally on cost saving on the basis of existing solutions, both parties can be locked in inflexible arrangements that lead to a lack of satisfaction with the services received by the outsourcer and frustration with the constraints imposed by the service provider (Gartner, Research note, June 2001). Due to the long-term timeframe, the level of resources committed and the emphasis on cost efficiency, a bureaucracy-based approach to relationship management and management control is often pursued which as it is not well suited for coping with changing requirements and therefore leads to disappointment on both sides and further enforces the desire to impose a high level of management control. Ironically, despite a high level of dissatisfaction with current service providers, a high number of organisations stick with their existing provider when it comes to contract renewal because of the high level of sunk costs (Barthelemy and Geyer, 2000).

Outsourcing relationships need to be managed during the lifespan of the projects concerned. The costs involved and the complex nature of the projects that frequently involve the transfer of assets from the outsourcer to the provider call for detailed contractual arrangements. Theses are also in the interest of the service provider who does not wish to face spiralling costs due to ambiguities. In principle, detailed contractual arrangements are often considered good professional practice – the one who has good intentions can sign a detailed contract – and need not be considered as a substitute for or undermining trust in relationships. Detailed contracts and legal means are of course more of a background safeguard, providing contract parties with the confidence that although the law is slow and costly and seeking legal redress is not the best avenue to solve conflicts, they do have a safeguard against gross malfeasance (Sitkin & Roth,1993, Deakin & Wilkinson,1996). Beyond contract, however, a fair amount of trust [a] is required to make outsourcing relationships work. The outsourcing organisation must at least have trust in the service provider's competence and willingness to keep to contractual obligations. This will normally be based on the service provider's record of achievement and reputation. Most of the larger outsourcing contracts are awarded to the reputed and established players in the industry who can point towards a record of previous achievements or who have been directly recommended although the contract tendering process will be principally open to all contender who can meet the project requirements. As outsourcing involves close cooperation between internal and external staff, interpersonal trust relationships become very important for the success of the project. The long-term time frame of the contracts allow for interpersonal trust relationships to be built, but this trust-building can be undermined if the contractual terms do not sufficiently allow for a dynamic adjustment of the services to be delivered to changing circumstances of the outsourcing organisations (such as growth through acquisitions or moving into new markets) or to changes to the technology and products/services available at the cutting edge of the market. In such cases, rather than having governance procedures in place that allow for quick response and dynamic adjustment of terms, outsourcing contracts often are inflexible, require substantial renegotiation and lead to dissatisfaction on both sides. Once however, disagreements and tensions have set in, it becomes more difficult to renegotiate and find mutually beneficial solutions on the basis of trust (Sitkin & Stickel, 1996). Even worse, signals that relationships with service providers have become difficult seem to reinforce preferences for a bureaucracy-based approach to management control (van der Meer Koistra, 2000)[b] with closer supervision and monitoring and more direct intervention of the outsourcing company. Given that at least one of the causes of this adverse dynamic, the rate of technology change is bound to increase, the nature of IT outsourcing contracts is in need of flexibilisation. Rather than chasing "moving targets" with closer nets, a more developmental, trust-enabling approach to contact and relationship management is needed. A move towards a trust-enabling governance structure and management control approach would need to incorporate changes such as shared flexible decision-making and goal setting by a joint alliance board with backing from senior management level, open book accounting, outcome-based rewards with a clear recognition of a priority to meet dynamic goals rather than static contractual obligations (Dekker, 2001). Such an approach to management control, however, must be implemented before trust has been lost. It also requires a move away from a mainly tactical orientation towards cost efficiency to a more strategic consideration of overall business objectives and the role IT and IS can play to that end.

INFORMATION LEAKAGE, TRUST, REPUTATION AND THE INNOVATION DILEMMA

We have argued above that from an innovation perspective, the reliance on outside providers can be problematic, not only because key areas of expertise may be gradually lost to the outsourcing organisation but also because outside providers may not have the desired leading edge expertise over the long-term (Earl, 1996) or may spread their expertise among many clients so that it degrades from "best in world" to mere industry standard. The problem of information leakage lies at the heart of this dilemma. Companies want exclusivity in their relationship with their service providers, but consultants who work with many clients are unlikely to be able not be influenced and not to spread the best practice that they acquire when working with many client firms. Detailed legal contracts may offer short-term solutions as they can protect tangible outcomes from specific projects undertaken, but not every innovation related project outcome is tangible and can be clearly defined in legal contracts. And consultants are clearly expected to work at the cutting edge of their professional expertise for all of their clients.

The problem of information leakage in collaborative research and technology development has been investigated by Hoecht & Trott (1999). They contend that companies need to be outward-looking to gain access to new knowledge and that this openness comes at the risk of commercially sensitive information being leaked to competitors. Furthermore, the more dependent technology intensive industries are on "openness" in innovation related activities the higher the rate of information leakage is likely to be in these industries. The increasing role of KIBS for R&D in sectors such as the IT industry can be expected to increase this risk. The more outward-looking the R&D strategy of these companies, the less suitable are traditional approaches such as legal instruments for controlling this risk and the more these companies have to rely on mechanisms of social control, in particular trust and reputation concerns. When companies pursue an extrovert, the most outward-looking technology development strategy, they rely on the expertise of distinguished individual researchers, either as temporarily hired subject field experts or as prominent members of research community networks working within an organisation and acting as boundary spanners between the organisation and the scientific community. Because of their superior subject knowledge and their privileged position in the research community, which is after all the prime reasons for employing them, they have, at least in theory, ample opportunities to leak information to competitors and to betray the organisations hiring their services if they wish to do so. Direct, bureaucratic control is largely ineffective and non-implementable in situations where the controllers lack detailed understanding of the nature of the controlled person's work[c], legal contracts such as detailed secrecy clauses and intellectual property agreements are accepted as a matter of professional good practice, but detection of contravention would be very difficult and the contravention difficult to prove and any legal redress would not compensate for the commercial damage incurred. In such cases when legal instruments and direct, bureaucratic control are of limited effectiveness, companies need to rely on trust and social control in order to be able to work with the individuals in question. And although trust is always "ultimately a leap into the dark" (Luhmann, 1979), research organisations have good reasons to trust these individuals as their personal and professional integrity is based on their need to protect their professional reputation as the "social capital" (Coleman, 1990) which makes them so desirable to their employers. As a consequence of their self-awareness of the need to protect their reputation as their social capital, external hired experts and organisational boundary spanners more than any other group of scientists "internalise" proper professional conduct in themselves.

The problem of information leakage and how to control it also applies in the case of outsourcing of knowledge-sensitive business processes with high innovation potential.

We have encountered this issue as a pressing ethical and professional problem for a number of IS consultants that we interviewed for another innovation-related research project (Trott & Hoecht, 2004). With the move from traditional long-term single provider to strategic outsourcing, it will become much more of an issue as will be discussed in the next section.

STRATEGIC OUTSOURCING AND THE INNOVATION DILEMMA

Strategic outsourcing goes beyond traditional outsourcing in the sense that competitive advantages are being sought through opening up all business functions, including the core competencies which should provide competitive advantage to whoever can provide the perceived best solution, internal or external (Quelin and Duhamel, 2003). In contrast to traditional outsourcing, there are no protective boundaries around core activities in the hope that the organisations can maximise their innovative capacity by being an active part of a networked economy. This means that rather than having exclusive arrangements with one or very few service providers of long periods of time which will be expected to offer tailor-made solutions, strategic sourcing arrangements will be with multiple partners over short periods of time and with very little protection of internal core competency functions against outsiders (Gartner, Strategic Analysis Report, May 2001)[d].

There is a certain paradox inherent in this approach: a very high level of trust is required for such relationships as the risks involved are substantial while at the same time the conditions for building trust are undermined by a shorter-term orientation with less commitment compared to traditional outsourcing relationships.

If we are experiencing a move towards a global networked economy (Castells, 1996) with rapid technology change and an increasing need for sharing information and cooperative R&D, then long-term exclusive relationships between buyers and service providers may have too unsustainably high opportunity costs because of the inherent lock-in that can seriously hinder innovation. From a risk-control perspective exclusive relationships with clearly defined organisational boundaries may be preferable, but the cost of restricting information exchange among service providers in networks and limiting oneself to the expertise of just one firm can be significant. Furthermore, as discussed above, such exclusive relationships, when managed with a bureaucracy rather than trust-based approach to management control can be unproductive. The challenge then is to find ways in which more core business functions (but not all!) can be opened to the shared knowledge of the external service providers as a networked industry without losing core competitive capabilities, be it as a consequence of extensive reliance on outsiders, or through imitation by competitors as a consequence of information leakage.

The problem of information leakage is inherent in all outsourcing relationships, but the magnitude of this problem is greatly increased when dyadic relationships are replaced by multiple partner and network arrangements. There is some tentative evidence that "powerful" firms may be more able to protect their sensitive information than weaker ones, but this is far from certain and may well be influenced by managerial competence of the participating firms. It is also not always easy to determine the exact boundaries between the required up-to-date professional knowledge of individual consultants derived from current industry experience and cutting edge innovative practices exclusively developed for a particular client that have to be kept confidential. This boundary will become even more blurred the faster technology development progresses.

DISCUSSION AND MANAGERIAL IMPLICATIONS: INNOVATION, NETWORKS AND TRUST

Innovative capability of the firm is largely dependent on cumulative knowledge built up over many years of experience. Contrary to the model used by economists, innovative ability cannot be simply bought and sold. Hence, the need to remind senior managers of the unwitting harm that may be inflicted on the ability of the organisation to survive in the long term if its core competencies are slowly eroded through outsourcing. This chapter has put forward a different conceptual approach for how companies can view the role of outsourcing and its impact on innovative capability. We need to look again at what delivers long-term success as opposed to short-term gains.

This chapter has highlighted two particular strategic risks associated with outsourcing. Firstly, that not only does outsourcing involve the inherent risk of forgoing the development of the knowledge base of the firm but also that the firm's existing skills and core competencies may be unwittingly being leaked via the third party provider. The concept of trust is introduced as a possible mechanism for managers not only to understand the dynamics of knowledge leakage, but also as a means of managing the dilemma. From the point of view of the individual firm, the question is how it can maintain a commitment to secrecy and confidentiality from multiple partners. One solution would be their interest in repeat dealings. If the buyer firm is a significant player in its industry, the service providers may fear to loose it as a future customer and may therefore control their own behaviour. This would require a certain likelihood that potential betrayals would be noticed, which in terms depends on the nature of the relations between service providers. If there is sufficient competitive rivalry (despite the network cooperation) between service providers, some of their members may be prepared to "shop" the betraying service provider to the buyer in the hope of securing a future contract.

Another way of securing commitment would be for the buyer to acquire a stake in one or more of the service providers. Partial ownership may make the service provider as a consultant/provider less attractive to other buyers, but it would offer a degree of control in the sense that the buyer firm could exercise direct influence in managerial decisions and the employees of the service provider would be less likely to harm "part of their own" organisation. This is, however, a very costly way to buy loyalty and the associated costs could well be far higher than the benefits derived from strategic sourcing itself.

Tightening legal contracts would also be an option, at least in theory. In practice, the knowledge base of core competencies is often of a tacit nature and difficult to codify, and it is next to impossible to prove that betrayal has occurred. Furthermore, the essence of strategic sourcing is to move to shorter relationships including more flexible, less closely defined contracts.

To some extent, developments in IT may provide a solution. Those services which are mainly focused on IT (cost) efficiency (such as product support, network maintenance and help desk services) may well cease to require buyer-owned assets and to be firm specific altogether. Instead of longer-term service contracts, buyers may opt for a just in time/pay as you go "access" model where they tap into standardised solutions (Gartner, Strategic Analysis Report, May 2001). As this will normally not affect their core skills and competitive edge, the risks will be acceptable.

If networking and shared technology development is the future for the IT industry, another option would be for large buyers to retain the capacity to participate themselves directly in these networks. This could be achieved by either retaining or recruiting individuals into the buyer firms who have the ability to judge industry developments and to actively participate in industry networks. The task of these individuals, who have to be highly regarded experts in their field, would be to act as boundary spanners between scientific research, the service providing consultancy firms and their respective buyer firm. Their job would entail the definition and demarcation of high- risk areas within their home organisations and the selection and supervision of those "externals" who would be granted access to the business functions and processes identified as high risk. As external service providers can easily be made to specify the individuals assigned to specific tasks as part of the tendering process specification and as part of the final contract, the boundary spanner's judgement on the competence as well as trustworthiness of the specified individuals could be used as a device to control the risk of secrecy betrayal. As a consequence, it would be very much in the career interest of the staff of external service providers to keep and earn the trust of the boundary spanners of their main client firms as this would become a key selection criterion for the award of future contracts to their firms. As a consequence, the problem of trust would be transferred onto a higher level, from trust in service providers to trust in the controllers/boundary spanners. Although this resounds of Shapiro's (1987) observation that "one of the ironies of trust is that we frequently protect it and respond to its failure by bestowing even more trust"- onto regulators and guardians in this case, the experience of other industries such as biotechnology with boundary spanners as guardians of company secrets is positive (Liebeskind and Oliver, 1996; Hoecht& Trott, 1999). Boundary spanners have an overwhelming interest in guarding their reputation as being both trustworthy and competent as this reputation amounts to their "social capital" (Coleman, 1990). Naturally, the monitoring and supervision which can be exercised by boundary spanners themselves is limited to "working hours" and the "trusted externals" could still pass on information after hours and during future assignments with competing firms, in particular as there are no sufficiently effective legal sanctions to prevent this from happening. Therefore, in order to control this risk, some minimum level of exchange of information among boundary spanners of large buyers would be required. It is, after all, in the collective interest of buyers to limit the risk of betrayal and therefore to expel unreliable individuals from the circle of consultants with access to high risk areas in their clients' organisations. Whether this collective interest would prevail or the short-term benefits derivable from acts of betrayal would prove to be too tempting is very much a question of the character of the network of boundary spanners in question. Given that the collective sanctioning interest of networks cannot necessarily be relied upon particularly if detection is unlikely, other safeguards would be needed. Such as safeguard could be the external consultants own interest in protecting their reputation as their social capital. It may not be likely that a boundary spanner can be proven to have failed to inform his network colleagues of a betrayal, but the self-interest of the external consultants themselves is likely to stop them from committing acts of betrayal in the first place.

REFERENCES

Alexander, M., & Young, D. (1996). Outsourcing: Where's the Value? *Long Range Planning, 29*(5), 728-730.

Allen, T. J. (1977). *Managing the flow of technology.* Cambridge, MA, USA: MIT Press.

Alvesson, M. (2004). Knowledge Work and Knowledge-Intensive Firms. Oxford: Oxford University Press.

Ansoff, H. I. (1965). The firm of the future. *Harvard Business Review, 43*(5), (Sept-Oct), 162-178.

Barras, R. (1986). Towards a theory of innovation in services. *Research Policy, 15*(4), 161-173.

Barras, R. (1990). Interactive innovation in financial and business services: The vanguard of the service revolution. *Research Policy, 19*(3), 215-237.

Barthelemy, J., & Geyer, D. (2000). It outsourcing: findings from an empirical survey in France and Germany. *European Management Journal, 19*(2), 195-202.

Barthelemy, J. (2001). The hidden costs of IT outsourcing. *Sloan Management Review, 42*(3), 60-69.

Beveridge, W. I. B. (1957). *The art of scientific investigation* (3rd ed.). New York: Vintage.

Bower, D. J., & Keogh, W. (1997). Conflict and cooperation in technology-based alliances. *International Journal of Innovation Management, 11*(4), 387-409.

Brandes, H., Lilliecreutz, J., & Brege, S. (1997). Outsourcing- success or failure? Findings from five case studies. *European Journal of Purchasing & Supply Management, 3*(2),63-75.

Burns, T., & Stalker, G. M. (1961). *Managing innovation.* London: Tavistock.

Carter, C. F., & Williams, B. R. (1959). The characteristics of technically progressive firms. *Journal of Industrial Economics*, March, (pp. 87–104).

Castells, M. (1996). *The Information Age. Economy, Society and Culture, 1: The rise of the network society.* Oxford: Blackwell Publishers

Chesborough, H. (2003). *Open Innovation: The new imperative for creating and profiting from technology.* Boston, MA: Harvard Business School Press.

Cohen, W., & Levinthal, D. (1989). Innovation and Learning: the two faces of R&D. *The Economic Journal, 99,* 569-596.

Coleman, J. (1990). *Foundations of Social Theory.* Cambridge: MA: Harvard University Press.

Cooper, R. (1999). The invisible success factors in product innovation. *Journal of Product Innovation Management, 16*(2).

Currie, W. L., & Willcocks, L. P. (1998). Analysing four types of IT sourcing decisions in the context of scale, client/supplier interdependency and risk mitigation. *Information Systems Journal*, *8*(2), 119-1434.

Das, T. K., & Teng, B.-S. (1998). Between trust and control: developing confidence in partner cooperation in alliances. In *Academy of management review, 23*(3), 491-512 (Special topic forum on trust in and between organisations).

Das, T. K., & Teng, B.-S. (2001). Trust control and risk in strategic alliances: an integrated framework. *Organizational Studies, 22*(2), 251-283.

David, P. A., & Foray, D. (1995). Accessing and expanding the science and technology knowledge base. *STI-Review, 16,* 13-68.

de Woot, P. (1990). *High Technology Europe: Strategic issues for global competition.* Oxford: Basil Blackwell.

Deakin, S., Lane, C., & Wilkinson, F. (1994). 'Trust' or Law? Towards an integrated theory of contractual relations between firms. *Journal of Law and Society, 21*(1), 329-349.

Dekker, H. C. (2001). *Control of inter-organizational relationships.* Theoretical frameworks and an empirical investigation. ARCA Research Memoranda, Vrije Universiteit Amsterdam, ARCA-RM 01-12.

Doig, S. J., Ritter, R. C., Speckhals, K., & Woolson, D. (2001). Has outsourcing gone to far? *McKinsey Quarterly, 4,* 24-37.

Earl, M. (1996). The risks of outsourcing IT. *Sloan Management Review*, Spring 1996, (pp. 26-32).

Financial Times (2004, November). *Lex Column: Equity Research.*

Freeman, C. (1982). *The Economics of Industrial Innovation.* 2nd edn, Frances Pinter, London.

Gartner Research note. (2001, June).

Gartner Research report. (2001, December).

Gartner Strategic Analysis report. (2001, May).

Geroski, P. (1993). Technology and Markets. In P. Stoneman (Ed.), *Handbook of the Economics of Innovation and technical change.* London, Basil Blackwell.

Granovetter, M. (1985). Economic action and social structure: a theory of embeddedness. *American Journal of Sociology, 91,* 481-510.

Hamel, G. (1991). Competition for competence and interpartner learning within international strategic alliances. *Strategic Management Journal, 12.*

Hoecht, A. (2004). Control in collaborative research and technology development. A case study in the chemical industry. *Journal of Managerial Psychology, 19*(3), 218-234.

Hoecht, A., & Trott, P. (1999). Trust, risk and control in the management of collaborative technology development. *International Journal of Innovation Management, 3*(1), 257-270.

Humphrey, J., & Schmitz, H. (1996). *Trust in economic development.* Brighton, University of Sussex: IDS paper 355.

Isenson, R. (1968). *Technology in retrospect and critical events in science (Project Traces).* Chicago: Illinois Institute of Technology/National Science Foundation.

Jennings, D. (1997). Strategic guidelines for outsourcing decisions. *Journal of Strategic Change, 6*, 85-96.

Johannessen, J., Olaisen, J., & Olsen, B. (2001). Management of tacit knowledge: the importance of tacit knowledge, the danger of information technology, and what to do about it. *International Journal of Information Management, 21*(1), 3-20.

Kakabadse, A., & Kakabadse, N. (2002). Trends in outsourcing. *European Management journal, 20*(2), 189-198.

Kanter, R. M. (1984). *The change masters: Corporate Entrepreneurs at Work.* London, Routledge.

Kanter, R. M. (1998). When a thousand flowers bloom: structural, collective, and social conditions for innovation in organisation. *Research in Organisational Behaviour, 10*, 169-211.

Katz, R. (1997). *The human side of managing technological innovation.* New York: Oxford University Press.

Kelly, P., & Kranzberg, M. (Eds.) (1978). *Technological Innovation: A Critical Review of Current Knowledge.* San Francisco: San Francisco Press.

Kirton, M. (1980). Adaptors and innovators in organisations. *Human Relations, 3*(4), 213-224.

Lacity, M., & Hirschheim, R. (1993). Information Systems Outsourcing: Myths, Metaphors and Realities. Chichester: John Wiley Publishers.

Lacity, M., & Willcocks, L. (1998). An empirical investigation of information technology sourcing practices: lessons from experience. *MIS Quarterly, 22*(3), 363-408.

Langfield-Smith, K., & Smith, D. (2003). Management Control Systems and Trust in Outsourcing Relationships. *Management Accounting Research, 14*(3), *281-307.*

Lane, C., & Bachmann, R. (Eds) (1998). Trust within and between Organizations. *Conceptual Issues and empirical applications.* Oxford: Oxford University Press.

Langrish, J., Gibbons, M., Evans, W. G., & Jevons, F. R. (1972). *Wealth from Knowledge.* London: Macmillan.

Leifer, R., Colarelli O'Connor, G. Peters, L. S., Rice, M., Veryzer, R. W., McDermott, C. M., (2000). *Radical Innovation.* Boston, Mass.: Harvard Business School Press.

Liebeskind, J., & Oliver, A. (1998). From handshake to contract: intellectual property, trust and the social structure of academic research. In C. Lane & R. Bachman (Eds.), *Trust within and between organizations. Conceptual issues and empirical applications* (pp. 118-145). Oxford, Oxford University Press.

Luhmann, N. (1979). *Trust and Power.* Chichester: John Wiley.

Lundvall, B. A. (1988). Innovation as an interactive process: From user producer interaction to the national system of innovation. In Dosi et al., (Eds.), *Technical Change and economic Theory.* London and New York: Pinter Publishers.

Lundvall, B. A. (1992). Introduction to national systems of innovation. In B. A. Lundvall (Ed.), *National systems of innovation* (pp. 1-22). London: Pinter.

Madique, M. A. (1988). Entrepreneurs, champions and Technological development. In M. L. Tushman & W. L. Moore (Eds.), *Readings in the management of innovation* (2nd ed) (pp. 565-584). New York: Harper Business.

Major, E., & Cordey-Hayes, M. (2003). Encouraging innovation in small firms through externally generated knowledge. In L. Shavinina (Ed.), *International Handbook on Innovation*. Oxford: Elsevier.

March, J. G. (1991). Exploration and exploitation in organizational learning. *Organization Science, 2*, 71-87.

McIvor, R. (2000). Strategic Outsourcing: Lessons from a systems integrator. *Business Strategy Review, 11*(3), 41-50.

Miles, I. (2003). Services and the knowledge based economy. In J. Tidd & F. Hull (Eds.), *Service Innovation: Organizational Responses to Technological Opportunities and Market Imperatives* (pp. 1-34). London: Imperial College Press.

Moellering, G. (2006). Trust: Reason, Routine, Reflexivity. Oxford: Elsevier.

Nelson, R. R., & Winter, S. G. (1982). *An evolutionary theory of economic change*. Cambridge, MA: The Belknap Press of Harvard University.

Nelson, R. R. (Ed.) (1993). *National Systems of Innovation: A Comparative Study.* Oxford: Oxford University Press.

Nonaka, I., & Takeuchi, H. (1995). *The Knowledge-Creating Company.* Oxford: Oxford University Press.

Nonaka, I. (1991). *The knowledge creating company.* Harvard Business Review, *69*, Nov-Dec, 96-104.

Nonaka, I. (1994). A dynamic theory of organizational knowledge creation. *Organization Science, 5*, 67-77.

Nonaka, I., Sasaki, K., & Ahmed, M. (2003). Continuous innovation: The power of tacit knowledge. In L. Shavinina (Ed.), *International Handbook on Innovation.* Oxford: Elsevier Science.

Oliver, N., & Blakeborough, M. (1998). Innovation Networks: The view from inside. In J. Greive Smith & J. Michie (Eds.), *Innovation, co-operation and growth.* Oxford: Oxford University Press.

Patel, P., & Pavitt, K. (1994). The continuing widespread (and neglected) importance of improvements in mechanical technologies. *Research Policy, 23*, 533-545.

Pavitt, K. (1984). Patterns of technological change: towards a taxonomy and a theory. *Research Policy, 13*(6), 343-373.

Polyani, M. (1966). *The Tacit Dimension.* London: Routledge & Kegan.

Porter, M. (1980). *Competitive strategy: techniques for analysing industries and competitors.* New York: The Free Press.

Porter, M. (1985). *Competitive advantage.* New York: The Free Press.

Porter, M. (1990). *Competitive Advantage of Nations.* New York: Macmillan.

Powell W. W. (1990). Neither market nor hierarchy: network forms of organisations. In *Research in organisational behaviour, 12*, 95-336.

Powell, W., Koput, K., & Smith-Doerr, L. (1996). Interorganizational collaboration and the locus of innovation: networks of learning in biotechnology. In *Administrative Science Quarterly, 41*(1), 116-146.

Quelin, B., & Duhamel, F. (2003). Bringing together strategic outsourcing and corporate strategy: outsourcing motives and risks. *European Management Journal, 21*(5), 647-661.

Quinn, J., & Hilmer, F. (1994). Strategic outsourcing. *Sloan Management Review*, summer 1994, 43-55.

Quinn, J. B. (1991). Managing innovation: controlled chaos. In H. Mintzberg & J. B. Quinn (Eds.), *The strategy process: concepts, contexts & cases* (2nd ed) (pp. 746-758). Englewood Cliffs, NJ: Prentice Hall.

Quinn, J. B. (1999). Strategic outsourcing: leveraging knowledge capabilities. *Sloan Management Review*, summer 1999, (pp. 9-21).

Reve, T. (1990). The firm as a nexus of internal and external contracts. In M. Aoki (Ed.), *The firm as a nexus of treaties*. London: Sage.

Rothwell, R. (1992). Successful industrial innovation: critical success factors for the 1990s. *R&D Management*, *22*(2), 221-239.

Rothwell, R., Freeman, C., Horlsey, A., Jervis, V. T. P., Robertson, A. B., & Townsend, J. (1974). SAPPHO updated: Project SAPPHO phase II. *Research Policy*, *3*, 258–91.

Sako, M. (1992). Prices, Quality and Trust: interfirm relations in Britain and Japan.

Shapiro, S. (1987). The social control of impersonal trust. *American Journal of Sociology*, *93*(3), 623-58.

Sheth, J. (1996). Organizational buying behaviour: past performance and future expectations. *Journal of Business and Industrial Marketing*, *11*(1), 7-24.

Sitkin, S., & Roth, N. (1993). Explaining the limited effectiveness of legalistic "remedies" for trust/distrust. *Organization Science*, *4*, 367-392.

Sitkin, S., & Stickel, D. (1996). The road to hell: the dynamics of distrust in an era of quality. In R. Kramer & T. Tyler (Eds.), *Trust in Organizations. Frontiers of theory and Research*. Thousand Oaks: CA: Sage.

Souder, W. E. (1987). *Managing new product innovations*. Lexington, MA: Lexington Books.

Sternberg, R. J., Forsythe, G. B., Hedlund, J., Horvath, J. A., Wagner, R. K., Williams, W. M., Snook, S., & Grigorenko, E. L. (2000). *Practical Intelligence in everyday life*. Cambridge: Cambridge University Press.

Stoneman, P. (1983). *The Economic Analysis of Technological Change*. Cambridge: Cambridge University Press.

Tidd, J. (2000). *From knowledge management to strategic competence: Measuring technological, market and organisational innovation*. London: Imperial College Press.

Totterdell, P., Leach, D., Birdi, K., Clegg, C., & Wall, T. (2002). An investigation of the contents and consequences of major organizational innovations. *International Journal of Innovation Management*, *6*(4), 1-26.

Trott, P., & Hoecht, A. (2004). *A Preliminary study of Enterprise Resource Planning (ERP) and its impact on the innovative capability of firms*. Paper presented at Irish Academy of Management Conference, Trinity College, Dublin, Sept 2-4.

Trott, P. (2008). *Managing Innovation and New Product Development* 4th ed. London: Prentice Hall.

Tushman, M., & Nadler, D. (1986). Organizing for innovation. *California Management Review*, *28*(3) 74-88.

Twiss, B. (1992). *Managing Technological Innovation* 4th edn. London: Pitman.

Utterback, J. (1994). *Mastering the dynamics of innovation*. Boston, Mass: Harvard Business School Press.

Van de Ven, A. H. (1989). Central Problems in the management of Innovation. In M. L. Tushman & W. L. Moore (Eds.), *Readings in the management of innovation* (2nd ed) (pp. 103-122). New York: Harper Business.

Van de Ven, A., Polley, D., Garud, R., & Venkataraman, S. (1999). *Innovation Journey*. New York: Oxford University Press.

van der Meer-Kooistra, J., & Vosselman, E. G. (2000). Management control of interfirm transactional relationships: the case of industrial renovation and maintenance. *Accounting, Organizations and Society, 25,* 51-77.

Van der Panne, G., Van Beers, C., & Kleinknecht, A. (2003). Success and failure of innovation: A literature review. *International Journal of Innovation Management, 7*(3), 309-338.

Wheelwright, S., & Clark, K. (1992). *Revolutionising Product Development.* New York: Free Press.

Willcocks, L., & Lacity M. (1999). IT outsourcing in insurance services: risk, creative contracting and business advantage. *Information Systems Journal, 9*, 163-180.

Williamson, O. E. (1979). The economics of organization: the transaction cost approach. *American Journal of Sociology, 87,* 548-577

Williamson, O. E. (1993). Opportunism and its critics. *Managerial and Decision Economics, 14*, 97-107.

Wolfe, R. A. (1994). Organisational innovation: review and critique and suggested research directions. *Journal of Management Studies, 31*(3) 405–31.

Woolgar, S., Vaux J., Gomes, P., Ezingeard, J.-N., & Grieve, R. (1998). Knowledge and the speed of transfer and imitation of organisational capabilities: An empirical test. *Organisation Science, 6*(1), 76-92.

Zucker, L., Darby, M., & Yusheng, P. (1996). Collaboration structures and information dilemmas in biotechnology: organizational boundaries of trust production. In R. Kramer & T. Tyler (Eds.), *Trust in Organizations: Frontiers of theory and Research* (pp. 90-113). London: Sage.

Zucker, L. (1986). *Production of trust; institutional sources of economic structure, 1840-1920. Research in Organizational Behaviour, 8*, 53-111.

KEY TERMS

Core Capabilities: The knowledge and skill that resides in an organisation. Core capabilities include technical know-how, technical skills, business process know-how and business skills. Distinct capabilities are those things that the organisation is better at doing than its competitors.

Information Leakage: Information leakage refers to the unintended loss of information from an organization. This usually occurs as a result of employees passing information to others sometimes unwittingly sometimes wittingly.

Innovation: The process of developing and commercialising something new, usually a product, service or manufacturing process. The process is related to >invention but they are not identical twins. The management of innovation is a growing and significant subject in its own right. While there is continued debate in the literature about the range of activities covered by the term, there is broad agreement that successful innovation management involves research, technology development, marketing and manufacturing.

Knowledge Intensive Business Services: Knowledge intensive business services (KIBS) include traditional professional business services such as accountancy and law, as well as services that have a scientific and technical knowledge base such as IT/IS. Other examples include a new generation of KIBS. The growth in information communication technologies during the 1980s and the development of the internet in the 1990s and into the 21st century has led to enormous sums of money being spent by firms in order to ensure that they are equipped to compete.

Outsourcing: A term used to describe the process of using external organisations to provide the firm with the necessary services it requires, and that it previously supplied from within. Such as maintenance, cleaning, catering, computer support, telecommunications services. The benefits of outsourcing include reduced costs and increased services.

ENDNOTES

[a] There are literally hundreds of definitions of trust. A useful pragmatic definition of trust is that "an agent exhibits trust when he/she exposes herself/himself to the risk of opportunistic behaviour by others and when he/she has no reason to believe that the trusted other will exploit this opportunity" (Humphrey & Schmitz, 1996:4). A key point is that trust makes the trustor vulnerable to the behaviour of the trustee, but the trustor ignores this possibility. Moellering (2006: 111) defines trust as "an ongoing process of building on reason, routine, and reflexivity, suspending irreducible social vulnerability and uncertainty as if they were favourably resolved, and maintaining thereby a state of favourable expectation toward the actions and intentions of more or less specific others." Sako (1992) distinguishes between competence trust (confidence in the other parties ability to perform properly), contractual trust (honouring the accepting rules of exchange) and goodwill trust (mutual expectations of open commitment to each other beyond contractual obligations).

[b] Langfield-Smith and Smith (2003), following on from van der Meer-Kooistra and Vosselman (2000) distinguish between market-based, bureaucracy-based and trust-based control patterns of inter-firm transactional relationships. Trust plays no role in the first and only a limited role in the second control pattern (emphasis on outcome and behavioural control), but becomes central in the trust-based control pattern (emphasis on outcome and social control as well as trust). The relationship between trust and control is a complex one that can be either supplementary and or complementary depending on circumstances. The relationship between trust, risk and control in inter-firm relationships has been explored systematically and in considerable depth by Das and Teng (1998, 2001).

[c] Quinn (1999) acknowledges this as a major problem in controlling the risks involved in "intellectual outsourcing".

[d] While there is no accepted consensus in the literature regarding the exact nature of strategic outsourcing; Quélin and Duhamel (2003), for example, maintain that it involves a long-term commitment between the client and the service provider. Empirical research undertaken by Gartner suggests that strategic outsourcing can also involve short-term contracts with multiple partners in order to get access to the highest level of expertise from different specialist companies in their fields where such expertise is not available in any one particular company.

Chapter V
Actor-Network Theory and Autopoiesis:
A New Perspective on Knowledge Management

Lars Steiner
University of Gävle, Sweden

ABSTRACT

A new knowledge management perspective and tool, ANT/AUTOPOIESIS, for analysis of knowledge management in knowledge-intensive organizations is presented. An information technology (IT) research and innovation co-operation between university actors and companies interested in the area of smart home IT applications is used to illustrate analysis using this perspective. Actor-network theory (ANT) and the social theory of autopoiesis are used in analyzing knowledge management, starting from the foundation of a research co-operation. ANT provides the character of relations between actors and actants, how power is translated by actors and the transformation of relations over time. The social theory of autopoiesis provides the tools to analyze organizational closure and reproduction of organizational identity. The perspective used allows a process analysis, and at the same time analysis of structural characteristics of knowledge management. Knowledge management depends on powerful actors, whose power changes over time. Here this power is entrepreneurial and based on relations and actors' innovation knowledge.

INTRODUCTION: A DEFINITION OF KNOWLEDGE MANAGEMENT

The aim with this paper is to present a new perspective on knowledge management, a perspective that uses both actor network theory (ANT) and the social theory of autopoiesis (ANT/AUTOPOIESIS). Knowledge management is empirically presented as how a number of actors and actor companies collaboratively organized to increase specific knowledge and innovation capability. The co-operation, named KIT, aimed at research and innovations in home and buildings information technology (IT) products and services.

To know something is to interpret meaning and make sense of something from one's own experiences, information and data (Callon, 1986b). This is the ANT perspective of knowledge management which in this sense resembles a cognitive perspective where knowledge exists within a human brain. Managing knowledge is from a cognitive perspective impossible. Knowledge from a cognitive perspective is independent of others and socially closed. To be interesting from an organizational point of view, knowledge should be analysed in the light of goals and meaning not only for an individual, but also for an organization or as in this paper a collaboration of organizations. Knowledge is shown in the speech and activities of human actors. Argyris and Schön (1978/1995) called this visibility of knowledge; knowledge-in-action. Decision making is the most important act by which knowledge becomes apparent in organizations, according to Luhmann (2002). Acts, though, are also dependent on expectations of the future, power and human will. Non human actors do not have knowledge, since they cannot by themselves create meaning. To make machines "act" according to a human actor's wishes, knowledge might be inscribed into a machine, or a description of how to use a machine is prescribed for the user to read and follow. Also artifacts in buildings like doors, stairs, corridors, windows, etc, are shaped to fulfil certain functions decided by the designers. Prescriptions "give" non-humans ability to "act" on behalf of the humans that have written these. Machines and artifacts become agents for the will of human actors. Sveiby (2008) says that knowledge management is a poor term and that knowledge cannot be managed. Since knowledge is something inside a human brain, to claim that knowledge could be managed would mean to manipulate humans' brains. In spite of this the concept knowledge management is widely used. Wilson (2002) after a thorough review of the concept concludes that knowledge management is used about activities concerning management of information and work practices.

Social autopoiesis theory, being a general systems theory uses living systems as metaphor for describing social phenomena. Living cells communicates with its environment to survive (Maturana and Varela, 1987). The human brain is in social knowledge autopoiesis used as a metaphor for what happens in and between organizations (Morgan, 1986). Metaphors are often used in organizational theory and are for example used in the concept of the learning organization (Senge, 1990). Generative learning (Senge, 1990) imply that the organization as a whole is able to learn from experiences that actually are inherited from individuals and groups of human actors in the organization.

Burgoyne et al (1994) and Alvesson and Willmott (1996) claimed that knowledge is socially constructed in an organizational setting. With this view of knowledge management, power differences, conflict, domination, subordination and manipulation are considered as well as aspects that have to do with handling complex organizing processes efficiently, innovation capability and competitiveness. Knowledge actually expresses itself in multiple forms: propositional, theoretical, practical, experiential, and presentational (Marshall and Reason, 1993).

ANT draws on the relational aspects of human communication. Actor-networks inscribe the complex social processes underlying the construction, development and stabilization of forms of the social, the technological, the natural world and their combinations (Callon, 1986b). Humans make sense of language, texts (inscriptions) and actions. Relations between humans make the world meaningful by sensing and communication. In ANT actions are contingent phenomena, mediated by human actors and non-human actants. Power translation originally was the ontological interest in ANT (Callon, 1986a; 1986b). Power translation is explained in the following way:

'Spread in time and space of anything – claims, orders, artifacts and goods – is in the hands of people. Each of these people may act in many different ways, letting the token drop, or modifying it, or deflecting it, or betraying it, or adding to it, or appropriating it'. Latour (1986: 267)

Autopoiesis theory, originally biological, describes reproduction of a core structure, DNA/RNA (Maturana, 1981; Maturana & Varela, 1987/1992). The theory of autopoiesis has been used to describe social systems (Luhmann, 1995, 2002, Mingers, 1995). Communication/decision events construct organization according to Luhmann (1995: 287). The network of decisions produces decisions and communication channels to lock up further decision making and organizing. Maula (1999; 2000) use the social theory of autopoiesis by metaphorically describing companies' knowledge systems as autopoiesis systems that consist of two major knowledge flows, named the sensory function and the memory function. The sensory function gives an organization interactive openness, and the memory function is the company's access to its own knowledge, retrieved from experiences, expertise and knowledge bases. In autopoiesis theory this allows self-referentiality. Self-referentiality describes how

"the accumulated knowledge affects the firm's way to operate, and the way to operate affects the creation and acquisition of new knowledge." (Maula 2000: 159)

In the ANT/AUTOPOIESIS knowledge management perspective here presented I show how in an innovation co-operation the transformation functioned the way Maula's theory of self-referentiality prescribes. Knowledge management steered by human and artifactual power relations described by ANT determined the agenda until that some founders found themselves organized out of the innovation co-operation. Several actors were surprised, though, to find that in the end the accumulated knowledge or core competence survived and gave the studied co-operation a new identity, different from the one intended by the original founders.

ANT and the social theory of autopoiesis are both theoretical paradigms about human relations and organizing. Being ontologically different interpretations of organizing, these theories might be regarded as conflicting paradigms. There are some fundamental differences, but also similarities between these theories, which make them theoretically fruitful to use complementarily when we are to understand the concept of knowledge management in innovation co-operation. This paper could have stopped with an empirical description using ANT, which draws attention to differences in power between actors and a non-human "actant" (Greimas and Courtés, 1982), in this case an influential artifact; the e-box, a computer server. In order to fully understand the knowledge management in information intensive organizations I will with autopoiesis theory show how core competence was reproduced.

The structure of the paper is the following: First, there is an analysis of an innovation co-operation case using ANT/AUTOPOIESIS theory. Actors, managing events, artifacts and outcome of management are described as a time dependent narrative (Ricoeur, 1984/2003). Then there is a reflective part where ANT/AUTOPOIESIS theory is used as a complementary frame of reference for analyzing knowledge management. Finally, conclusions are drawn regarding the interpretation of data and knowledge management considerations.

METHODOLOGY

Research Approach

The research approach is to use an inductive qualitative method in a case study to develop a theoretical perspective based on the two paradigms, ANT and autopoiesis theory. The paradigms must be complementary since they are used in a theoretical framework to describe knowledge management. The case describes how the different paradigms are used when analyzing knowledge management complimentarily. Inductive reasoning has been used where interpretation of interview statements has given meaning to the theoretical concepts given by the theories. The interpretation process was done in two phases. First ANT was used to interpret the transformation of the studied case and the translation by actors of what happened in the process. Then, when ANT was not able to make sense of the process, autopoiesis theory was tried and offered an interpretation that gave meaning to the process.

Data Collection

Qualitative narrative data was collected from the foundation of KIT and the first four years of the collaboration association. The theoretical reflections using ANT and autopoiesis theory are based on twenty interviews, participative observation in a board meeting, document studies, and improvised talks with the founders, owners, managers, entrepreneurs and other employees on several occasions during the research period.

The case study method is closely related to narrative research (Yin, 1984/2003; Czarniawska, 1999; 2000). Like any other qualitative research methods the narrative does not seek generalization in a statistical sense, but inductively seeks knowledge about pieces and patterns of reality, which in this research has been knowledge management in innovation collaboration. Unlike logo-scientific knowledge (Lyotard, 1979/1984) narrative knowledge acknowledges that there are different experiences and expectations of reality and the future depending on who you are. This is also in line with the translation theory used by ANT. Narrative knowledge, according to Ricoeur (1984/2003), is connected to individual or organizational experiences from the past and expectations for the future. Ricoeur reflects on the inability of man to accommodate understanding of the present, because the present immediately becomes the past, and the future is unknown. Narrative approaches have so far mostly been used in organizational theory studies and in three ways: Research written in a story-like manner, research conceptualizing organizational life as story making and organization theory as story reading (Czarniawska, 1997: 26). The narrative is used here as a story to shed light on a new way of perceiving innovation knowledge in transforming organizational settings.

Case Study: KIT

KIT was planned to be a research and innovation co-operation situated close to a small Scandinavian University. Actors from ten different organizations were interviewed. They took part in KIT during shorter or longer time periods. The founding of KIT was preceded by fifteen years of research by the founder of KIT, a University professor interested in products and services to facilitate life at home by the help of IT.

As the development of the Internet opened up opportunities to distribute data about building status independent of space, KIT was started as an arena for further research by the University professor together with an IT corporation and the local municipal energy utility. Small and medium-sized entrepreneurial companies who developed IT products and services also became partners. KIT was planned to be active in three areas: as a meeting place, as a locus for development work, and as a forum for research and post-graduate studies. First, there was a research goal: to be an organization to explore possibilities to use Internet technology in buildings. Second, there was a well-being goal: to provide an environment for development of IT services to the home for the benefit of residents. Third, there was a welfare goal: to foster entrepreneurship and company start-ups, developing and selling IT services to the home.

As the Internet gave opportunity to distribute data about the status of buildings independent of space, KIT by the University professor was made the arena for further research, together with an information technology (IT) corporation and the local community energy organization. KIT was planned to be active in three areas: Meeting place, development work, research and post-graduate studies. Small and medium seized entrepreneurial companies who developed IT products and services also became parts of KIT. First, there was a research goal, an organization to explore possibilities to use Internet technology in buildings. Second, there was a well-being goal. To provide an environment for development of IT-services to the home for the benefit of residents. Third, there was a well-fare goal. To foster entrepreneurship and company start-ups, developing and selling IT services to the home.

ANALYSIS OF KIT KNOWLEDGE MANAGEMENT USING ANT

Actors came from different organizational cultures. They were academics, entrepreneurs, local government officials, and research financiers who normally do not work together. Around KIT, there were several small competing IT companies, innovative product and service companies pushing the technology forward and there were consulting companies acting as service providers. Communities housing companies, ISPs, and real estate consulting companies were interested in being part of KIT, testing new services and technologies in the new business. The service providers' mission was to fill the real estate owner's infrastructure with deep competitive service. Companies, specializing in a specific content, also chose to co-operate inside the co-operation organization.

KIT consisted of several types of system elements, such as companies, actors, artifacts, decisions and communication. The influence of the big IT corporations was profound by their technical developments and financial strength when KIT was founded. They functioned as magnets for IT entrepreneurs interested in the IT home area. The presence of dedicated persons in this area was important when founding the co-operation.

The E-Box, an Obligatory Passage Point

KIT was planned to be a place where researchers and doctoral students could meet with IT companies for mutual benefit. The knowledge management in this case became complex. The main reason for this was not a human, but an artifact. A non-human actant, the e-box, came to play a crucial role in the transformation of the co-operation. The fact that a computer server, a technical device that was installed for operating data on building status, came to be important was a surprise for non-business actors. This computer server was developed by the IT Corporation who was one of the founders. The e-box was more specifically inscribed to function as a switchbox between users in homes and suppliers of any kind of services that could be distributed via broadband or surveyed via Internet-based systems.

The co-operation organization KIT was the environment in which a scenario of operating the e-box was created. The e-box was a physical artifact, a hybrid (made by humans), that actors initially tried to bring forth, enframe and sustain (Heidegger, 1977: 19; Callon, 1987). Thanks to the central position that the e-box came to get, the e-box was a powerful actant, though it could not communicate by itself, only with the help of humans' inscriptions. Human actors (representatives of two of the participating companies) created inscriptions--instructions as to how to use the e-box. By doing this they put restrictions on the way the co-operation was to be organized and what role different actors were to play. The dominating actors strongly communicated how many complex IT problems the e-box could solve if it was to be installed as an operating computer server.

The big IT Corporation and the local municipality's energy company prescribed the e-box to be an obligatory passage point to the co-operation. The energy company invested in 20 e-boxes to operate for their customers. One of the founding entrepreneurs found this unacceptable:

"An industry standard is needed in this area. Companies that build operative systems have to themselves make box-independence with their technical products. Like with GSM-telephones, when you shall phone, you must be able to phone with a Nokia, Ericsson, Siemens, Bosch, Sony or a Motorola."

This entrepreneur left the co-operation, since the obligatory passage point discriminated against entrepreneurs interested in product development. The inscribed role of the e-box came to design the organizing of knowledge management, an interpretation the University professor explained as:

'The information technology corporation arrived with personnel and trucks loaded with computers and terminals, to be installed in the localities of KIT, but they never made this equipment function.'

The e-box did not even function the way the IT Corporation and the municipal energy utility company inscribed it to do, and the e-box became an artifact with the power to decide who was to be inside and who was to be outside the organization. All other academic founders left the board and another entrepreneur explained why he was not satisfied with the way KIT had transformed:

"Our company develops services and the platform for operators. We work in projects together with other companies. We should instead create an attractive work environment in KIT."

According to Callon (1987), there is a network if elements and relations hold and do not change. Though, White (1992: 102-115) with a network terminology argues;

"A phase transition in a network can be produced by two interacting kinds of uncertainty."

On the one side, there was ambiguity, designating uncertainty in purely cultural contexts. On the other side, there also was 'ambage,' designating uncertainty in purely social-structural contexts. Ambiguity is about fuzzy meanings and interpretations while ambage;

"concerns the concrete world of social ties, in networks of ties and among corporate nodes." (White, 1992: 107)

The founder professor expressed this ambiguity and ambage, explaining how he perceived the situation:

"With what people shall we co-operate? What's the purpose of our co-operation and communication? These questions popped up too often and made shared values diminish and changes take place everywhere."

When actors experienced ambiguity and ambage in their relations, the quality of these relations lost their value. Following Callon (1987), there was no network, since the relations did not hold. Following White (1992), we had a situation where a network might fall apart.

An actor-network is reducible neither to actor alone, nor to companies nor to a network. Like networks, it is composed of a series of heterogeneous elements linked to one another (Callon, 1987: 93). The first phases in managing this innovation co-operation were fragile and the intentions among actors did not hold. The circumstances became more like those of changing system elements and relations between actors. Baumann (2000) would describe what happened in terms of fluidity. Social structures today cannot easily hold their shape. Analogously, fluids neither fix space, nor bind time. Solid structures cancel time, while liquids constantly change.

Knowledge Sharing

The content of information and knowledge that was shared four years after the foundation of the research and innovation co-operation concerned ideas like fostering entrepreneurship and company start-ups, and developing and selling IT-services to the home (well-fare goal). Other ideas, considered by certain founders to be the most important, were completely neglected, like to provide an environment for development of IT services to the home for the benefit of residents (well-being goal), or to be a place for research and post-graduate studies (research goal).

The e-box never came to use. Unfortunately, over the course of fifteen months, these transitions gave the result that the former owners have now turned into non-active partners. Instead, two smaller companies, one service provider and one product manufacturer entered as active partners. Also, a number of small service providers still co-operated in KIT. The innovation co-operation survived, but with new actors, activities and goals.

Reflections Regarding the Transitory Stages

Any translation involves four stages through which an actor-network is configured by the negotiated alignment of allies (both human and non-human), according to Callon (1986b). In the Problematization stage, key actors are identified and persuaded that aligning themselves in the new network may provide solutions to their problems. This would involve that certain actors should become indispensable to others, and that access to obligatory passage points of the network should be negotiated. During this stage, actors from two Universities, a local municipal energy utility company, and two big IT corporations negotiated a co-operation association to benefit themselves and the local community. This stage was the foundation of KIT.

In the second stage, called stage of Interessement, actors are locked by other actors into prescribed roles so that old networks might dissolve and a new network might emerge. In this stage, the e-box played an important role as an obligatory passage point. During this stage of ambage and ambiguity the e-box never came to use, and the negotiated roles were changed. Certainly, quite a new network came to be.

According to Callon (1986b) next stage is the Proper enrollment in which the identity of the new network is achieved through consent, seduction or even coercion. The powerful act of inscribing the e-box to discriminate who would and who would not be participating in KIT activities by the IT corporation actor excluded all founders but IT entrepreneurs and the local municipality company. The situation had changed considerably. The former founders were no longer active. Instead, new entrepreneurs appeared on the scene generating ideas for new services. A consulting company, originally part of one of the big IT corporations, took a leading role together with representatives from the local municipality company. The owner of one small company in the new transformed KIT was a former development manager in the large IT Corporation. So this stage appeared with quite new actors.

Following Callon (1986b) there finally is the Mobilization. The established representation delegations are assured and the fear of betrayal is removed (Callon, 1986b); shared values and ideals exist that guide decisions and communication.

KIT eventually stabilized concerning ideas for co-operation, though changes in co-operating actors still occurred in the event of new projects and services. The roles that actor companies tried to reach as service providers, product, solutions, access, content, media, operations, billing, logistics or housing providers no longer existed. Instead, other actor roles developed. Borders were being crossed and contracts broken while old functions and roles were redefined. Relations and system elements changed. Newcomers established new relations.

ANALYSIS OF KIT AS A "LIVING SYSTEM" USING AUTOPOIESIS THEORY

KIT did not transform as the ordered network it initially was intended to be. Actors were never locked into prescribed roles. Actually, circumstances developed in such a way that the originally planned ideas for knowledge co-operation never were achieved. Instead, the original actors became inactive and entrepreneurial service provider actors replaced them. Important decision events were the regular board meetings where new business ideas were presented and discussed, and where new business relations were introduced. KIT transformed into a loose network where competence in IT smart home technology applications was the idea that organized knowledge. The managing director explains:

"A relation to a former partner that once was an operating relation still remains a possible speaking partnership after leaving the KIT board. The positions and the relations and competence this person has are still strengths for the operation."

The managing director thought of KIT in terms of a network of actors performing some kind of agency based on their competence and relations. The core competence was IT for the home, and this competence, independent of where actors had their organizational base, might be called upon for the benefit of KIT as a co-operating unit.

The story makes us interpret the ongoing process as rather like a continued stage of fluidity, with changes in system elements, actors, ideals and values taking place. New business co-operation was established, still in the IT home business area. The new actors were interested in a place where knowledge of interest for them was communicated. These new actors were entrepreneurs in small companies. By locating activities around KIT, companies were able to take part in the knowledge generation that was going on in the area of smart home IT products and services. By participating, cooperating and imitating each other, sharing knowledge and people, further knowledge generation were facilitated (Maula, 1999).

Making the analogy of a living system, the core competence was reproduced when KIT survived as an organization in spite of several founding actors leaving the co-operation. The core competence might be traced back to the foundation of KIT, where actors gathered around the organizing principles of being a meeting place for development work, research and post-graduate studies, even though there is only one of those principles that survived. Much research has been done on the survival of corporate identity, culture and core competence after structural changes (Penrose, 1959; Prahalad and Hamel, 1990). Core competence seems to be the remaining organizational value for further organizing. The corporate identity or the 'company blueprint' is reproduced (Stinchcombe, 1965; Steiner, 2003).

ANT/AUTOPOIESIS THEORY USED COMPLEMENTARILY WHEN ANALYZING KNOWLEDGE MANAGEMENT

When interpreting knowledge management in KIT, two ontologically different theories are used: ANT and the theory of autopoiesis. According to Kuhn (1962/1996), paradigms or theories might be incommensurable, meaning that they cannot be used for evaluation of each other's research. This though, does not mean that they are incompatible. Here a possibility is left open for coexistence of incommensurable paradigms for interpretation of empirical data (Elmholdt, 2003: 127; Bruun and Hukkinen, 2003). Metaphorical concepts are a natural part of a narrative approach. Both ANT and social autopoiesis theory use metaphorical concepts to describe complex phenomena. In ANT the "actor and actant" metaphor is used in order to reach consistency describing events with the human, nature, technical and social relations imbedded. The theory of autopoiesis uses the "living organization" metaphor. The epistemological differences between ANT and autopoiesis theory can be handled by considering agency as life, which is done in autopoiesis theory. Autopoiesis systems not only produce themselves, they also produce standards for how to handle input from the environment. Social autopoiesis theory uses the living system's metaphor, while ANT, besides relations between humans, also considers the effect that artifacts have on humans. According to Bruun and Langlais (2003: 37-38) the living beings demonstrate agency in the sense of singularity. This helps to identify the living from the environment. The term singularity is used since 'perspective' and 'subjective' are words used when consciousness is perceived. To produce standards for how to handle the environment is the basis for all other forms of agency, for instance that of being an agent who can act, which is the point of departure for ANT. Organizations consist of human beings, artifacts and machines. When ANT explain the living (humans, fauna and flora) and dead things (machines and building components), the theory uses the same concepts. In ANT a machine is considered to be able to "act" and "communicate" with humans. The way that is done is with the help of human inscriptions on how to use the machine. With a machine there is a document that explains how to use it and what it can do. Through human agency, machines are made "actants" in the world of humans. This 'ontological slipperiness' (Lee and Hassard, 1999) might be valuable in studying knowledge management, since we then are able to acknowledge that machines, buildings, computers like the e-box and other artifacts are parts of human life, affect human acts and decision-making and therefore also are important when trying to understand how to organize knowledge co-operation.

Lee and Hassard (1999: 402), and also Kickert (1993) claim that the more organizations can appear lively the less open to critique they are in a society demanding flexibility. ANT descriptions concern ambitions, enrolling new actors and actants by order, inscriptions, persuasion and use of artifacts. In autopoiesis, order in the living system originates from simple rules of connection. Synchronized behavior emerges without orchestrated planning, without a leader (Morgan, 1986; 1997). Meaningfulness recursively lies in the organizing ability of the system. The communication networks are held together by information that is interpreted and transformed inside the living system (Maturana, 1981).

Social autopoiesis theory recognizes certain organizational species, among which organizational identity is reproduced (Luhmann, 1995). The organizational continuity lays in the reproduction of a certain species' identity (Maturana, 1981; Maturana & Varela, 1992). Communication is the way an organization reproduces its identity. Communication is considered to be event-based. According to Luhmann (1995), the most important events in organizations are decisions. Meaning in the system is produced in relation to other system elements and relations, thereby the autopoiesis. That is, the unity of the organization is the unity of its reproduction.

ANT prescribes no law of unity, no structure to be reproduced. There are actors and actants influencing management in certain directions establishing organizing to implement ideas. Descriptions in ANT therefore become an inner landscape where nothing is clear beforehand. Everything is negotiable and could be affected. The local municipality energy company and an IT-company dominated the scene with the help of a non-human actant, the e-box. With the help of social autopoiesis theory structural patterns of the surviving system has been discerned, which was not to be done with ANT. Only one of the three founding ideas in KIT survived the management transformation, that of fostering entrepreneurship and company start-ups, developing and selling IT services to the home.

The narrative is therefore not only the one of powerful big companies setting their agenda. The events and decisions that guided KIT into the future were also the narrative of founding ideas of co-operative knowledge management that survived powerful actors' and actants' intentions, even though none of the founders survived into the new KIT co-operation.

CONCLUSION

ANT and social autopoiesis theory are presented to give a new perspective on knowledge management. A case is presented where these different paradigms are used complementarily to analyze knowledge management, and validate the theory. What is new in this perspective is that by using ANT, the power of an artifact to influence relations and events in innovation co-operation is shown. By using autopoiesis theory complementarily the survival power of the system itself is shown--the survival power of the core competence in the studied organization.

The power of an artifact, a computer server called the e-box, inscribed by two powerful actors, was found to be influential in the negotiations prior to the founding of the studied organization. When KIT was founded actors involved in the foundation came to an agreement on the goals of KIT and how to co-operate. Ambiguity in the identification process arose about the meaning and interpretation of actions. Ambage also occurred when the social-structural contexts became uncertain. Which companies and persons will share information and knowledge? How will relations develop further? These questions did pop up often.

When interpreting data from the case study using ANT, inscribed roles of humans and physical technical artifacts, as is shown in the empirical part above, have an impact on organizing and knowledge management. Closure and stabilization (Pinch & Bijker, 1987: 44) never was achieved in KIT. The e-box, which came to be the inscribed object to be tested and developed, never came to function the way it was intended, due to technical and relational problems. Since the e-box was not used commercially, KIT was translated by actors to be an organization to discuss, nourish and generate members' entrepreneurial ideas, and to develop IT services. These system elements formed the inscribed closure of the institutionalized KIT organization. When the artifact, the e-box, no longer played a role as problem solver in KIT, KIT lost the research ideals that earlier were communicated, and identified various IT innovations for the home in the interest of small entrepreneurial companies interested in co-operation. New relations were established over time as a result of altered positioning by participating members.

The survival capacity for collaboration in KIT was strong, even though the unique actor companies often did not survive in the collaboration. The survival capacity might be interpreted as an autopoietic social system, self-referential and recursive, being a product of its own operations (Maturana, 1981; Maturana & Varela, 1992; Luhmann, 2002: 103; Backen & Hernes, 2003). KIT as a system with an identity survives, though the elements of the system have changed and the activities the system performs are different. Foerster (1991) would say that KIT, viewed as a system, was an unpredictable historical machine that reproduced its own structure, to maintain its own survival.

A final reflection based on this research is that organizing small IT companies' knowledge co-operation here starts with a human idea and proceeds with the engagement of several actors and artifacts. Eventually the original idea transforms, allowing survival of the organization's core identity. Managing knowledge co-operation is as much managing actors and actor elements as it is to cultivate the organization's founding ideas. Using the ANT/AUTOPOIESIS perspective gives the means to analyze the complexity of management in a milieu of uncertainty and change.

REFERENCES

Alvesson, M., & Willmott, H. (1996). *Making Sense of Management.* London: Sage.

Argyris, C., & Schön, D. A. (1978/1996). *Organizational Learning II.* Reading, Mass: Addison-Wesley Pub.

Backen, T., & Hernes, T. (2003). *Autopoietic Organization Theory.* Copenhagen: Abstract, Liber, Copenhagen Business School.

Baumann, Z. (2000). *Liquid Modernity.* Cambridge: Policy Press.

Bruun, H., & Hukkinen, J. (2003). Crossing boundaries: An integrative framework for studying technological change. *Social Studies of Science, 33*(1), 95-116.

Bruun, H., & Langlais, R.(2003). On the Embodied Nature of Action. *Acta Sociologica, 46*(1), 31-49.

Burgoyne, J., Pedlar, M., & Boydell, T. (1994). *Towards the Learning Company.* McGraw Hill.

Callon, M. (1986a). The sociology of an Actor-network: The case of the electric vehicle. In M. Callon, J. Law, & A. Rip (Eds.), *Mapping the Dynamics of Science and Technology: Sociology of Science in the Real World* (pp. 19-34). London: Macmillan.

Callon, M. (1986b). Some Elements of a Sociology of Translation: Domestication of the Scallops and the Fisherman of St Brieuc Bay. In J. Law (Ed.), *Power, Action and Belief: A New Sociology of Knowledge* (pp. 196-233). London: Routledge & Kegan Paul.

Callon, M. (1987). Society in the Making. In W. E. Bijker, T. P. Hughes, & T. J. Pinch (Eds.), *The Social Construction of Technological Systems* (pp. 83-103). Cambridge: MIT Press.

Cyert, R. M., & March, J. G. (1963). *A Behavioral Theory of the Firm.* Englewood, NJ: Prentice-Hall.

Czarniawska, B. (1997). *Narrating the Organization: Dramas of Institutional Identity.*

Chicago: Univ. of Chicago Press.

Czarniawska, B. (1999). *Writing Management.* Oxford: Oxford University Press.

Czarniawska, B. (2000). *The uses of Narrative in Organization Research.* Gothenburg: GRI.

Elmholdt, C. (2003). Metaphors for Learning: cognitive acquisition versus social participation. *Scandinavian Journal of Educational Research, 47*(2), 115-131.

Foerster, H. von (1991). Through the Eyes of the Other. In F. Steier (Ed.), *Research and Reflexivity* (pp. 21-28). London: Sage.

Greimas, A. J., & Courtés, J. (1982). *Semiotics and Language. An Analytical Dictionary.* Bloomington, IN: Indiana University Press.

Heidegger, M. (1977). *The Question Concerning Technology and Other Essays.* W. Lovitt (transl.). New York: Harper & Low.

Kickert, W. J. M. (1993). Autopoiesis and the Science of (Public) Administration; Essence, Sense and Nonsense. In *Organisation Studies,* 14(2), 261-278.

Kuhn, T. S. (1962/1996). *The Structure of Scientific Revolutions.* Chicago, ILL.: University of Chicago Press.

Latour, B. (1986). The Powers of Association. In J. Law (Ed.), *Power, Action and Belief.* London: Routledge.

Latour, B. (1995). Mixing Humans and Nonhumans Together: The sociology of a Door-Closer. In S. L. Star (Ed.), *Ecologies of Knowledge, Work and Politics in Science and Technology.* New York: State University of New York Press.

Lee, N., & Hassard, J. (1999). *Organization Unbound: Actor-Network Theory, Research Strategy and Institutional Flexibility, 6*(3), 391-404.

Luhmann, N. (1995). *Social Systems.* Stanford, CA: Stanford University Press.

Luhmann, N. (ed.) (2002). *Theories of Distinction. Re-describing the Descriptions of Modernity.* Stanford, CA: Stanford University Press.

Lyotard, J-F. (1979/1987). *The Post-modern Condition: A Report on Knowledge.* Manchester: Manchester University Press.

Marshall, J., & Reason, P. (1993). Adult Learning in Collaborative Action Research:

Reflections on the supervision process. *Studies in Continuing Education, 15*(2), 117–132.

Maula, M. (1999). *Multinational Companies as Learning and Evolving Systems.* Helsinki: Helsinki School of Economics and Business Administration.

Maula, M. (2000). The senses and memory of a firm - implications of autopoiesis theory for knowledge management. *Journal of Knowledge Management, 4*(2), 157-161.

Maturana, H. R. (1981). Autopoiesis. In M. Zeleny (Ed.), *Autopoiesis: A theory of Living Organisation.* New York, North Holland.

Maturana, H. R. & Varela, F. J. (1987/1992). *The Tree of Knowledge: The Biological Roots of Human Understanding,* Transl. Paolucci, R. Boston. Shambhala, Boston & London: New Science Library.

Morgan, G. (1986). *Images of Organization.* Beverly Hills, CA: Sage.

Morgan, G. (1997). *Images of Organization. New Mindsets for Seeing, Organizing and Managing.* San Fransisco, Thousand Oaks, CA: Berrett-Koehler and Sage Publishers.

Mingers, J. (1995). *Self-Producing Systems. Implications and Applications of Autopoiesis.* New York and London: Plenum Press.

Penrose, E. T. (1959). *The Theory of the Growth of the Firm.* Oxford: Basil Blackwell.

Pinch, T. J., & Bijker, W. E. (1987). The Social Construction of Facts and Artifacts: Or How the Sociology of Science and the Sociology of Technology Might Benefit Each Other. In W. E. Bijker, T. P. Hughes, & T. J. Pinch (Eds.), *The Social Construction of Technological Systems* (pp 17-50). Cambridge: MIT Press.

Prahalad, C., & Hamel, G. (1990). The Core Competence of the Corporation. *Harvard Business Review, 68*(3), 79-93.

Ricoeur, P. (1984/2003). *Time and Narrative, 3.* Chicago: Univ. of Chicago Press.

Senge, P. (1990). *The Fifth Discipline-The Art and Practice of the Learning Organization.* New York: Doubleday/Currency, cop.

Steiner, L. (2003). Roots of Identity in Real Estate Industry. *Corporate Reputation Review, 6*(2) (March), 178-196.

Stinchcombe, A. L. (1965). Social Structure and Organizations. In J. G. March (Ed.), *Handbook of Organizations* (pp. 142-193). Chicago: Rand McNally.

Sveiby, K-E. (2008). www.sveiby.com, © March 1996. Updated 1 March 1998, 3 June 1998 20, March 1999, April 2000, and April 2001.

White, H. C. (1992). *Identity and Control: A Structural Theory of Social Action.* Princeton, NJ: Princeton University.

Wilson, T. D. (2002). The nonsense of 'knowledge management. *Information Research, 8*(1), 144. Available at http://InformationR.net/ir/8-1/paper144.html

Yin, R. K. (1984/2003). *Case Study Research: Design and Methods*. Thousand Oaks: Sage Publications.

Section II
The Language of Knowledge

Chapter VI
Sorting the Relationship of Tacit Knowledge to Story and Narrative Knowing

Jo A. Tyler
The Pennsylvania State University, USA

David M. Boje
New Mexico State University, USA

ABSTRACT

This chapter fits the theme, the interplay between creativity and control in organizations. Story is often claimed to be a way to elicit tacit knowledge from people and their organization. The authors would like to suggest that this is impossibility. To story something is to shape it intuitively and willfully. Story shapes events into experience and into memory. Without story experience is just reenactment. To reenact is to relive the events, to feel the pain, fear, and terror.

INTRODUCTION

The concepts of knowledge management, and knowledge-intensive work have been developing for quite some time. In both theory and the vernacular of practice, knowledge and the knowledge worker are claimed to be the most important asset of contemporary organizations (Stewart, 1997). Knowledge workers as said to possess tacit knowledge, which various knowledge methodologies and specialized knowledge workers such as the "integrators, librarians, synthesizers, reporters, and editors" (Prusak, 1998, p. 110) convert to explicit knowledge when they "extract knowledge from those who have it, put it in a structured form, and maintain it or refine it over time" (Prusak, 1998, p. 110). Critics suggest that such knowledge solutions are perfunctory and propagandist (Styhre & Sungren, 2005). Managerialist policies rely upon the manipulation of emotions and identity creation (Kärreman and Alvesson, 2004). Managerialism is the view from the top, from the perspective of the managers (owners & executives – or others with power to wield). It is a top-down logic, a one logic that becomes the logic of change. There is a major difference between official organizational rhetoric and common everyday practice (Höpfl 1995; Argyris and Schön, 1996; Knights and Willmott, 1999).

Knowledge-intensive companies, such as in high-tech environments, purport knowledge-workers to be highly valued members of an organization. At the same time, critics suggest that these same workers are being manipulated and even "engineered" to engage in such performativity that they burn-out, and are deprived of family life (Perlow, 2004). Managers interested in leveraging worker knowledge by transferring it are faced with "the challenge of detaching knowledge from some people and attaching it to others" (Seely-Brown, 2000, 123). The spirit of this sort of language establishes a fundamental tension where the worker must give up a part of herself, ostensibly for the greater good, and the manager necessarily "mines" the worker until the mine is exhausted, no longer useful. The worker in this way becomes a depreciating asset, unless she can simultaneously conjure a new vein of knowledge. Manager and worker conflict is often more obvious than in less knowledge-intensive settings (Roscigno & Hodson, 2004). So too may be conflicts between workers who are likely to be better rewarded for possessing knowledge that constitutes competitive advantage than they are for sharing it.

We propose to study a different paradox that marks knowledge work in knowledge-intensive companies. The purpose of the present work is to look at the quest for tacit knowledge in knowledge management. Storytelling is often said to be a way to elicit tacit knowledge from knowledge workers (Prusak, 1998; Gherardi & Nicolini, 2003; Bukowitz & Williams, 1999; von Krogh, Ichijo, and Nonaka, 2000) and to foster the internalizing of explicit knowledge, converting it to tacit knowledge (Nonaka and Takeuchi, 1995).

In this study we will first provide a brief overview of Polanyi's ideas about tacit knowledge and their implications. We will then establish the distinction between narrative and story, so that we can bring these ideas together to examine their interplay in the context of a small selection of popular, contemporary knowledge management and knowledge sharing theories and practices: Cooperrider's Appreciative Inquiry, Denning's Springboard stories and Wenger's Communities of Practice.

Polanyi's Theory of Tacit Knowing

Michael Polanyi's concepts of *tacit knowing* and *emergence* are foundational to knowledge management theory, research, and practice. Michael Polanyi (1891-1976) was born (Polányi Mihály) in Budapest. Polanyi's (1946) early work *Science, Faith and Society*, was followed in 1958 by *Personal Knowledge: Towards a Post-Critical Philosophy*, a short book *The Study of Man* (1959), and in 1966 to a book that is the central topic of this essay, *The Tacit Dimension* (based on the 1962 Terry Lectures at Yale University).[a]

In this 1966 work, the seminal book for Polanyi's work regarding tacit knowing and emergence, Polanyi argues against Existentialism, preferring to anchor his ideas in pragmatism. Polanyi (1966/1983) develops at least seven definitions and approaches to tacit knowing. Elsewhere Boje (2008a) has reviewed these in detail. We will summarize them briefly.

1. **Neural Processes of Tacit Knowing** - "Tacit knowing is the way in which we are aware of neural process in terms of perceived objects" (1966/1983: x). In the neural approach, tacit knowing is embodied in that "all thought dwells in its subsidiaries, as if they were

parts of our body" (p. x). From this basic definition, Polanyi begins to multiply the number of tacit approaches.

2. **Know More Than We Can Tell** -Polanyi states, "*we can know more than we can tell*" (1966/1983: 4). This tacit knowing is rooted in Gestalt psychology, and the study of subception (i.e. something perceived below the threshold of consciousness). Polanyi's model for this is the proximal/distal distinction. For example, in an electric shock experiment, at the *proximal level of awareness*, we know the electric shock, but at the *distal (subception) level* we cannot communicate what are the particulars of behavior that result in someone or something giving us the shock. Polanyi suggests that one disattends from the particulars to pay attention to the shock. The neural type of tacit knowing is related to the Gestalt type. We disattend to certain (Gestalt) things in order to attend or focus upon other things (p. 10). Or, we disattend to the "subliminal process inside our body" to attend to what is happening around us.
3. **Projection and Tacit Knowing:** Our projection of tacitness is a sentient extension of our body attending to a feeling (i.e. a relation between proximal awareness of the feeling and the distal particulars we can not tell about). However, *apriori* to, or *transcendent* to, the sensemaking (5 senses of perception), there can be various kinds of projections that follow, such as indwelling.
4. **Indwelling and Tacit Knowledge:** Indwelling then is a kind of reflexivity that has moral import. Indwelling is an attempt to understand the proximal terms of tacit knowing re relation to inquiry into the distal particulars. Indwelling goes beyond a neural, narrative, or projection type of tacit knowing, and Polanyi distinguishes it from empathy. Indwelling is "tacit framework for our moral acts and judgments" (1966, p. 17). It establishes moral knowledge (a framework for moral acts) in relation to practice. Here we begin to read in Polanyi, that tacit knowing is about a structure or more precisely, a theoretical-framework that is internalized for understanding the moral act. Polanyi is definite that this is bending his earlier conception of tacit knowing into a new type: "The identification with indwelling involves a shift of emphasis in our conception of tacit knowing" (p. 17). Polanyi assumes that it is not possible to recovery some original meaning (p. 19). At the same time, "the meticulous dismembering of a text, which can kill its appreciation can also supply material for a much deeper understanding of it" (p. 19). This brings us to the possibility of something in-between the unrecoverable origin, and a deeper understanding.
5. **Tacit Reintegration:** Tacit reintegration is an appreciation of how a coherent narrative (with its linear emplotment), sacrifices so many particulars that the indwellment of meaning in some new story, i.e. in a (tacit) reintegration of omitted particularities, is impossible. For Polanyi, tacit reintegration is a sort of reflexive practice, such as when the engineers understand more particularities than the non-engineer, and can afford therefore a deeper understanding. However, just as there is no recovery of an origin (due to complexity of movement), there is no "explicit integration that can replace the tacit counterparts of knowing (p. 20). It is here that Polanyi provides an insight into the contemporary knowledge management fallacy of trying to turn tacit knowing into explicit knowing (p. 20). To summarize, Polanyi claims modern science that tries to detach an objective knowledge by eliminating the tacit is misguided. Tacit is indispensable to all knowledge, so eliminating it would be a destruction of all knowledge (p. 20). It is one of the "devastating fallacies" (p. 20) of contemporary knowledge management theory and practice.

6. **Type Six – Past Lives:** Another kind of tacit projection is an act of reflexivity upon all that is hidden by the inanition of narrative "coherence" (p. 21). Narrative coherence can devitalize living (embodied-indwelling) story. The initiation of some originary narrative to supplant tacit reintegration ends the inquiry into discovery of what is hidden in all the discarded particularities. It is at this point that Polanyi pulls out yet another definition of tacit knowing: "... all discovery is a remembering of past lives" (1966/1983: 22). This is a very transcendental turn to defining tacit knowing in ways far beyond the previous five sorts of approaches. Sorting through the particulars discarded in narrative coherence (& control) will not give us an inkling of tacit reintegration that is rooted in past lives. Polanyi lists as one of his references for the 'past life' approach, Plato's *Meno* (p. 22). Plato's dialogue, known for the character *Meno*, is a theory of *anamnesis* (i.e. the recollection of past events). The soul knows that it has been incarnated before and conveys some of its recollections forward to the next incarnation. *Meno* is used by Polanyi to tease out the foreknowledge of tacit knowing: "we can have a tacit foreknowledge of yet undiscovered things" (p. 23). The insights of tacit knowing from past lives are "an indefinite range of unexpected manifestations" (p. 24). For Polanyi it is "foreknowledge which guides scientists to discovery" (p. 33). Whereas indwelling is paying attention to unspecifiable particulars, Meno is a conviction there is something more to be discover, as in a hidden truth which no positivist methodology or procedure will uncover. This transcendental turn to a recollection that recovers past memory of the eternal soul in its reincarnations is for Polanyi an alternative to positivism.
7. **Type Seven – Tacit Knowing Relation to Emergence:** Tacit knowing is related to emergence in a way that has not been noted or addressed in contemporary reviews of Polanyi. And it is a relationship that speaks directly to the transition from systems thinking to complexity thinking. For Polanyi has a foot in both ways of thinking. On one hand, Polanyi is caught up in systems thinking, where the "universe [is] filled with strata of realties" that are ordered, in "higher and lower strata" (p. 35, bracketed addition, mine). On the other hand, he theorizes the ills of [narrative] coherence that blind science to the more tacit acts of comprehending that are ontological (as well as transcendental aspects of complexity, of type six). For Polanyi, the systems thinking is revealed in the assumption that "principles of each level operate under the control of the next higher level" (p. 36). For Polanyi, the hierarchic orders of system-levels are a "process of morphogenesis" (p. 36) in which, for example, the sciences are ordered, where physics and chemistry cannot explain the complexities of biology and biophysics, or the perceptions and consciousness of ethnology and psychology. "The laws of physics and chemistry include no conception of sentience" (p. 37), nor do the principles of machine operation tell operators how to work the machine or the purposes the machine is to serve. In Polanyi's hierarchy-view, above the basic sciences is linguistics, where constituting speech making in words, sentences, style, and composition) makes literary criticism a higher order of systems than lexicography (vocabulary) or language-grammar. This hierarchic ordering of one systems relation to another of a different sort, is brought together in the "*principle of marginal control*" (p. 40), where "successive working principles control the boundary left indeterminate on the next lower level" (p. 41) and "each lower level imposes restrictions on the one above it" (p. 41). His example of speech acts

that control the order of utterance is that otherwise "words are drowned in a flow of random sounds, sentences in a series of random words, and so on" (p. 41).

In sum, Polanyi posits a special relationship between some types of tacit knowing and his concept of emergence. Tacit knowing (indwelling, projection, tacit reintegration & recollection of past lives) and emergence assume a hierarchic structure of stratas, as well as of alternative realities. Emergence, itself, is a function of the assumption of hierarchic relations among levels: "But the hierarchic structure of the higher forms of life necessitates the assumption of further processes of emergence" (pp. 44-45). More specifically, Polanyi's theory of emergence is complicity bound to hierarchic order assumptions:

Thus the logical structure of the hierarchy implies that a higher level can come into existence only through a process not manifest in the lower level, a process which thus qualifies as an emergence (p. 45).

And it is this structure of hierarchy in emergence that for Polanyi has its counterpart in the field of "tacit comprehension" (p. 45). Polanyi admits, that emergence represents yet another conception of tacit knowing: "I have included all stages of emergence in an enlarged conception of inventiveness achieved by tacit knowing" (p. 44). That is, the mental powers of tacit knowing are linked to an evolutionary emergence in an overall "theory of stratified universe" (p. 50).

Implications for Story, Narrative, and Knowledge Management

One way to extend Polanyi is to look more critically at his we "know more than we can tell" thesis. Another way to extend Polanyi is to look at his concept of integration in a more narrative conception of tacit knowing. We can look at the relationship of narrative-control (acts of explicitness) and story-diffusion (acts of reflexivity upon tacit reintegration). If narrative-order and story-tacitness are in a relationship it could be a handle on the very nature of self-organizing of knowledge. If narrative-explicit-coherence is a counterpart to story-tacit-reflexivity then it is important to not disembody the process of knowing. Eliminating story knowledge to make narrative-abstract-theoretic-explicitness is impersonal, misleading, and logically unsound because it collapses the counterforce of self-organization.

Third, is indwelling. It is a shift to an inquiry into the distance between unbridled lucidity of coherence (such as a simple narrative) and the complexity patterns (that simplifying narratives would destroy). While we can inquire into distal particulars of complex patterns,

Rather than a system thinking "hierarchy of controls" that Polanyi (p. 42) posits, it could be that systems are not so finalized, not so ordered, and could be more holographic such as Edgar Morin's (1973, 1996) approach to complexity. Positing a hierarchy of systems (Boulding or Polanyi, as examples) seems to remove the possibility of systems freely associating, or not being determined by principles of one level to another. It could be that there are more equipotential relationships between various modes and sorts of systems, and that the whole construct of levels (or strata) needs to be challenged and conceptualized non-hierarchically. Putting systems into level-by-level array is a definite form of linearization that does not allow for the possibility of self-organization in non-linear relationships. This is not saying there are no strata, and no important relational principles. Rather, the criticism is that there could be a relation between linear and nonlinear aspects of complexity, as force and counterforce of self-organizing processes.

TOWARDS A NARRATIVE AND STORY THEORY OF KNOWLEDGE

We will now turn our attention to the concepts of narrative and story, their connection to tacit knowing, and their relevance to the practice of knowledge management in organizations.

The Difference between Narrative and Story

Many authors (and practitioners) make no distinction whatsoever between narrative and story, using the words interchangeably (Tyler, 2007a). They accept Aristotle, or reinvent him, and see no difference. We prefer to follow Bakhtin, Derrida, Calvino and our own storytelling roots, and theorize a very important difference between narrative and story. In that difference is a very important lesson about change. Linear change is a 'systems thinking' that needs to wake up! There are non-linear change approaches that are dialectic and dialogical. The dialectic I have in mind is between narrative order (control) and living story differences (disorder). The dialogic I have in mind is a multiplicity of types of narratives and types of stories that consummate the essence of self-organization, emergence, and complexity. To see the dialectic and dialogic, you need to move out systems thinking into complexity thinking, and notice the dance of narrative and story.

For Mikhail Bakhtin (1973: 12), "narrative genres are always enclosed in a solid and unshakable monological framework." Narrative dances with a more dialogic manner of story. Story, for Bakhtin, is decidedly more dialogical than narrative, for example in the "polyphonic manner of the story" (Bakhtin, 1973: 60). And the two (narrative & story) are dialogical with each other.

Jacque Derrida also treats story and narrative as quite different.

Each "story" (and each occurrence of the word "story," (of itself), each story in the story) is part of the other, makes the other part (of itself), is at once larger and smaller than itself, includes itself without including (or comprehending) itself, identifies itself with itself even as it remains utterly different from its homonym. (Derrida, 1979: 99-100).

Derrida is more radical than Bakhtin, viewing narrative as an instrument of torture, and the way it is used in story consulting (particularly in Knowledge Management work), it is the torture of the Inquisition:

... The question-of-narrative covers with a certain modesty a demand for narrative, a violent putting-to-the-question an instrument of torture working to wring the narrative out of one as if it were a terrible secret in ways that can go from the most archaic police methods to refinements for making (and even letting) one talk that are unsurpassed in neutrality and politeness, that are most respectfully medical, psychiatric, and even psychoanalytic. (Derrida, 1979: 94).

Story Consulting that passes for Knowledge Management is a wringing of Living Story out of the Knowledge Workers, so it can be passed about as a tortured until death, Narrative Text.

Finally, Italo Calvino (1979: 109) imagines stories in relation to a space full of stories:

I'm producing too many stories at once because what I want is for you to feel, around the story, a saturation of other stories that I could tell... A space full of stories that perhaps is simply my lifetime where you can move in all directions, as in space, always finding stories that cannot be told until other stories are told first.

For Calvino, story necessarily opposes itself in a web of stories.

Implications for Knowledge Management, Narrative, and Story Consulting

Our main thesis is that none of these approaches to narrative and story differences appear in the knowledge management theory and consulting practice. We think that it is because of the way the managerialist writers shun any kind of dialectic relationship of narrative and story as agencies of change.

The upstart profession of story consulting began to specialize in something I call BME (Beginning, Middle, and End) narrative coherence. This idea comes to us from Aristotle (350 BCE), in his renditions of the Poetics of BME where he posits how proper story must have a narrative sequence of beginning, middle, and end, and thereby be a whole narrative with a plot sequence of events, characters, themes, dialogue, rhythm, and spectacle.

The field of narrative studies emerged from Aristotle's (350 BCE: section 1450b: lines 1-20: pp. 232-233) conception that narratives must be coherently plotted: "We have laid it down that a tragedy is an imitation of an action that is complete in itself, as a whole of some magnitude... Now a whole is that which has beginning, middle, and end" (1450b: 25-30: p. 233).

As Aristotle's mimetic of BME of linear, whole, representation becomes adopted by Russian Formalism, and other traditional narratologies, a double-move occurs. Story becomes relegated in the first move to a mere chronology of event. In the second move, narrative self-deconstructs its initial duality (the hierarchy of narrative over story), in order to double back to efface supposed underlying order of event (Culler, 1981: 171).

STORY AND NARRATIVE IN KNOWLEDGE MANAGEMENT

Schreyögg, Georg and Koch (2005) invited chapter writers for their edited book to answer two implicit questions: "*what is the relation between story and narrative?*" and "*how can Knowledge Management (KM) or Knowledge Engineers (KRs) explicit science protocol extract, codify, and disseminate tacitness using story/narrative?*"

Boje's (2006,a b) critique was that with two exceptions, the KM and KE writers craft a hegemonic commodification and colonization project that is decidedly managerialist. Secondly, chapter authors and editors leave the reader to sort out and interrelate *story and narrative* to what is *explicit and tacit knowledge*. Explicit knowledge is reasonably clear. Davenport and Prusak (1998) characterize it as knowledge which "can be embedded in procedures or represented in documents and databases and transferred with reasonable accuracy" (p. 95), and this will suffice for our purposes here. Tacit knowledge on the other hand is more complicated and we have already seen from the summary of Polanyi's work. Boje (2008, forthcoming book), linking to Polanyi's notions of tacit knowing, asserts there are at least five types of tacit sensemaking. They are: tacit mindfulness, an awareness of here-and-now (in the moment); retrospective sensemaking and codifying stories into coherence narratives; making sense of fragmentation, such as in terse narratives, and codifying fragments into proper narrative wholes; enactment sensemaking in ways of framing, such as unconscious logics, metaphors, or archetypes that precede retrospection; multiple discursive dialogisms, such as ways that Lyotard challenges the duality of explicit science versus tacit narrative (i.e. pointing out that science legitimates through narrating or being incredulous of grand narratives).

Boje's critique of the Schreyögg, Georg and Koch (2005) edited volume feels answerable to an examination of some of the popular approaches to knowledge management consulting that incorporate story, storytelling, and story consulting as central to their processes. We have chosen three reasonably well-known approaches to consider here: Denning's Springboard Story (2001), Cooperrider's Appreciative Inquiry (2000, 2003), and Wenger's Communities of Practice (Wenger, 1998; Wenger, McDermott & Snyder, 2002). We chose these based on three shared characteristics. First, they each enjoy a fair degree of popularity in practice. Second, each integrates story and narrative into their central thesis. Third, one of us (Tyler) has first-hand experience with them as an attendee in a workshop delivered by the central thought leader for each, and as a practitioner making choices about ways (and whether or not) to incorporate these approaches into practice in the Fortune 500. We will first discuss each approach briefly, with attention to their investment in story/narrative, tacit/explicit, and reflexive/coherent dualities, and then in our conclusion draw out some implications of our observations for knowledge intensive organizations.

Denning's Springboard Stories

Denning burst on to both the knowledge management and organizational storytelling landscapes in 2001 with his book, *The Springboard Story: How Storytelling Ignites Action in Knowledge-Era Organizations*, based on his work in implementing knowledge management at World Bank in the late 1990's. In the course of this organizational change effort, Denning stumbles on storytelling (p. 3) as an effective means to build understanding and ignite the action invoked by the title of the book. In the book, Denning essentializes storytelling as the key element to effective knowledge management strategy, though Denning makes no distinction between stories and narratives. He uses the terms interchangeably, as we see in this excerpt from the introduction: "The attractions of narrative are obvious. Storytelling is natural and easy and entertaining and energizing" (2001, p. xv).

A closer look at the constitution and role of the Springboard Story reveals that they are more narrative than story. Though he positions storytelling in organizations as the antidote to "reductionist simplicity" (p. xv) and a complement to analytical thinking in the introduction of his book, he goes on to provide a set of rules for developing and identifying Springboard Stories that move them toward the controlling nature of narrative. These stories are, for example, brief and explicit, contain sufficient specifics (particulars in the vernacular of Polanyi) so that the listener is "hooked by the conflict or problem" (p. 197), but not too much, so that the listener "doesn't get lost in the story, but can follow its meaning" (p. 197). They should contain actions that are challenging for the protagonist, contain a predicament that his addressed in an unusual manner, tension between characters in the story, events that happen in an unpredictable sequence, which Denning summarizes as "an element of strangeness" (p. 198). There are nine additional elements, including the notion that the stories should have happy endings, persuade listeners by encouraging them to identify with the protagonist, be specific and "prototypical of the organization's main business" (p. 199). In *The Springboard (2001)* Denning encourages the crafters of these stories to tell true stories rather than invented ones, and to "test, test, test" a story with individuals or small groups to ascertain whether it "is going to work with that audience or not" (p. 199).

Though Denning uses the terminology loosely, drawing on the prior discussion of the distinction between storytelling and narrative, he is primarily concerned with narrative. He is focused on instrumental, performed stories (Chapter IX is devoted to "Performing the Springboard Story" (p. 135)). that are practiced, rehearsed with the unabashed intention of persuading listeners in the spirit of change management. In one incident he relays, he accepts the point of a critic that "there are some analogies between persuading an organization to change and the subtleties of seduction" (p. 176). In another he suggests that "the less the listeners realize that they are listening to 'a story' the better" (180). While he concedes that there are two types of stories (p. 181), the distinction he makes are between what he calls "maximalist stories, or stories with a capital 's'" (p. 181) and "stories with a small 's'...mini-stories of less than fifty-five words" (p. 182) that he likens to "the spare stories of Raymond Carver, or the parables of Jesus Christ" (p. 182). While this may sound at first blush like Boje's "tersely told" stories (2006c, p. 29), it is quite different on the basis that the stories Denning is driving toward are carefully crafted, not implied (though he says the main message should be implicit and available for discovery by the listener) in a "you know the story" (2006, p. 29) understanding between the teller and the listener. Moreover, they are practiced, so as to be told in a manner consistent from one telling to the next, and consciously placed in the context of the persuasive presentation, not emergent in connection with the audiences' reaction and the flow of conversation.

Neither is Denning particularly concerned with expressing tacit knowledge in *The Springboard Story*. In two of his subsequent books (2005, 2007) targeting an audience interested in learning about leadership, Denning increases his use of the term narrative, perhaps because it is often perceived by management to be more serious and business-like (Tyler, 2007a). In the 2005 book, both storytelling and narrative appear in the title of the book, while in the 2007 book, only narrative makes the marquee. Even so, a reading of these two books indicates that the terms still feel synonymous to Denning. In the 2005 book, in his discussion of the relationship of storytelling to tacit and explicit knowledge, he indicates that we "have a certain amount of *tacit understanding*, which is acquired through experience and which we may [sic] be able to articulate explicitly....But a substantial part of our expertise also lies in *narratives* that describe how unusual situations have been handled in the past" (p. 178 *italics in original*). In this later work focused on leadership, we also see that while Denning is still advocating highly coherent narratives, crafted and rehearsed, he has moved ever so *slightly* in the direction of emergence and reflexivity, or at least toward a form of adaptive storytelling, at the same time continuing to provide allowances for fiction as a conscious tool in instrumental story performance. In talking about the "knowledge sharing story...the workhorse of narrative" (p. 181) for example, he instructs his readers that, "When you prepare a story version of an experience, you include some details from the actual experience, sometimes embellish it with potentially fictional details, and leave out much of the experience altogether. This process is called *leveling and sharpening*. You do this...so that you can give a coherent account of the experience to your listeners. Each time you find a reason to tell the story, you level and sharpen it in different ways to meet the current context" (p. 181).

In summary, Denning sees storytelling and narrative as interchangeable terms for oral conveyance of experiences, perhaps adapted with fiction to strengthen their ability to persuade listeners to be followers moving toward an organizational goal. These stories are explicit and formulaic – in Denning's 2001 "Storytelling Masterclass" (Nov. 15 in Washington DC) attended by Tyler, attendees were provided with a 12 step template for building a three-minute story – in an effort to drive coherency, lessen resistance, increase understanding of why the message of the story is worth following and inspire aligned action.

Cooperrider's Appreciative Inquiry

David Cooperrider is best known for his development of a method popular in the arena of organization development known as Appreciative Inquiry (Cooperrider, Sorensen Jr., Whitney, and Yaeger,

2000). Though Appreciative Inquiry (hereafter AI) is a method grounded in social construction that reverses the deficit problem solving model to focus on the "best in people, their organizations, and the relevant world around them" (2000, p. 5). It is variously considered not only a method for organizational change or transformation, but a "philosophy of knowing, a normative stance...and as an approach to leadership and human development" (p 5) that has attracted the attention of those interested in the design of Knowledge Management systems (Avital and Carlo, 2004). For our purposes here, we will consider it as a method for organization development. Like Denning, Cooperrider is also interested in mobilizing people in the interest of organization change, and like Denning, stories lie at the heart of his "four-D" (Discover, Dream, Design, Destiny) process (Cooperrider, Whitney and Stavros, 2003).

The process pivots on upfront interviews that may be conducted to choose a topic for intervention, or to explore a topic pre-determined by management. Cooperrider acknowledges that "topic choice is a fateful act" (2003, p. 38), but does not appear to be critical of the differences between topics that emerge from the interviews with employees and those pre-selected based on management decisions about what is in the interest of the organization. Instead he stresses only that "organizations move in direction of inquiry" (2003, p. 38). That inquiry involves the collection of stories from employees (and sometimes customers and suppliers since AI is a whole-system approach to change) in the initial interviews since, AI "assumes that every living system has many untapped and rich and inspiring accounts of the positive. Link the energy of this core directly to *any change agenda* and changes never thought possible are suddenly and *democratically* mobilized" (Cooperrider, Sorensen Jr., Whitney, and Yaeger, 2000, p. 6, *italics ours*). The irony of agendas set by management followed by a purportedly democratic process goes unnoticed in this text. The interview is structured to elicit this "positive change core" (2000, p. 9) through questions designed to elicit stories of positive experiences on which the organization could capitalize in the later stages of the process. Negative or shadow stories are not collected (Tyler, in press). Employees are asked to temporarily put these aside, and instead "share stories of exceptional accomplishments, discuss the core life-giving factors of their organizations, and deliberate upon the aspects of their organization's history that they most value" (Cooperrider, Whitney and Stavros, 2003, p. 39).

In describing the second stage, the Dream Phase, we see Cooperrider incorporate the use of the term narrative in a way that echoes a little the distinctions we made earlier in this essay: "As the various stories of the organization's history are shared and illuminated, a new historical narrative emerges. This narrative engages those involved in much the way a good mystery novel engages a reader" (2003, p. 39). We move from something that (though clearly manipulated by the nature of the questions chosen by those in power) was a personal story of experience with possibilities of tacit and reflexive properties, to a composite and compiled narrative, coalesced to suit a goal that is for the greater good of "the organization," and therefore subject to its hegemonic intentions. It is clearly intended to belong to and represent everyone, but in the process of amalgamating all stories into a narrative arc that will drive the remainder of the process, organizations end up with a story that belongs to and represents no one. While Cooperrider and his colleagues make no mention tacit or explicit elements of the process or the stories collected, this movement toward narrative coherence drives reflexivity out of the process and keeps the sensemaking explicit. In the 2004 workshop Tyler attended at the Taos institute, the process was taught as a series of mechanical steps akin to common approaches to narrative analysis. "Data can be reduced and displayed in diagrams, charts, tables, pictures, storybooks, newsletters, and other visual aids...look for common threads and anomalies in the data. Specifically, what are the best stories, practices and wishes that came out of the interviews?...A primary goal is to reduce and interpret the meanings and, through dialogue, make sure these are the interviewees' meanings" (Cooperrider, Whitney and Stavros, 2003, p. 98). This combination of reduction and interpretation may be done with the best of intentions, but it has at least two flaws.

First, it is grounded in a "Wholeness Principle" (Whitney and Trosten-Bloom, 2003, p. 69) drawn on what we consider to be a selective understanding of Bohm's assertion that the "wholeness or integrity [that] is an absolute necessity to make life worth living" (from Bohm, 1980, quoted in Whitney and Trosten-Bloom, 2003, p. 69). Bohm's paradigm is inherently in opposition to the reductionism that is evident in the Design phase of AI, and in any case, we believe that in the pursuit of only the positive stories about experience, the "whole story" is not made ever made available in the context of AI. Instead we end up with directed narratives that are, at best, a partial representation of the experience of an individual or of the organization at large. Cooperrider asserts the importance of the question and direction of the inquiry, but in the unrelenting focus on the positive, his process fails to gather the story in all its entirety. It splits the yin-yang diagram, ignoring the notion that the seeds of the opposite are contained within the other. For all of its nature-based metaphors, such as the principle of heliotropism, in which we turn toward the light, it ignores the practical reality that it is the very casting of the light which creates shadows (Tyler, in press). This tearing apart is a discursive manipulation by the process, and because of it, the sort of ontological holism that Bohm is interested in can never be achieved.

The second flaw in the reduction of the data into what is essentially a control narrative is that it ignores the implausibility of this in practice on the basis of social heteroglossia and the power structures (both overt and covert) inherent in the organization at large and especially in organizational change initiatives (Marshak, 2006). Reflexive storytelling can hardly stand its own ground in the face of such pressures and collapses into narrative-explicit-coherence.

Wenger's Communities of Practice

Etienne Wenger's work (Wenger,1998; Wenger, McDermott & Snyder, 2002) privileges Communities of Practice (hereafter CoP) over individuals and the organization at large as the prevailing social structure in which learning occurs, meaning is made and identity is formed. Wenger, in 1998, is compelled by the phenomenon of Communities of Practice and their inherent dynamics, which include knowledge exchange, stories (as a form of reification) (p. 59) and storytelling (as a form of participation) (p. 204). Wenger (1998) considers knowledge, both explicit and tacit, in the context of a duality between participation and reification, which he sees as distinct and complementary. Reification for Wenger is both "a process and its product" (p. 60), and requires the participation of humans to render them meaningful. He explains that "A certain understanding is given form. This form then becomes a focus for the negotiation of meaning, as people use [it]" to accomplish a task, e.g. "use the law to argue a point, use the procedure to know what to do, or use the tool to perform an action....Indeed, no abstraction, tool, or symbol actually captures in its form the practices in the context of which it contributes to an experience of meaning." (p. 58-59). Like the undulating interplay of participation and reification, wherein each "makes up for the inherent limitations" (p. 64) of the other, Wenger also considers knowledge to be not a continuum of explicit to tacit (or vice versa) wherein "moving to one side implies leaving the other" (p. 67), but also as an interacting duality. Here he supports Polanyi's notion that "the process of formalizing all knowledge to the exclusion of any tacit knowing is self-defeating" (1966, 1983, p. 20), contending that "classifying knowledge as explicit or tacit runs into difficulties...because both aspects are always present to some degree" (p. 69). In this context, he contends that "it is not possible to make everything explicit and thus get rid of the tacit....It is only possible to change their relation" (1998, p. 67). Wenger, in 1998, is not concerned so much with the management of knowledge (that interest comes later), but with the way it is put to work and the way it behaves in the social context of Communities of Practice. He is very precise in his use of language, giving cogent examples in the hopes of making his meaning clear. Indeed, Wenger echoes Polanyi's notion of the knowledge of the aforementioned machine operator versus the knowledge of the engineer (1966, 1983, p. 19) (as well as Polanyi's contention that "our body is the ultimate instrument of all our external knowledge, whether intellectual or practical" (p. 15)), raising the example of the embodied knowledge of walking and how "requiring only this [walking] yields a good enough relation between the explicit and the tacit for certain purpose, though probably not good enough for an orthopedist who needs to know which muscles I use to keep my balance and move my legs" (p. 69).

There is in Wenger also a metaphorical connection to Polanyi's proximal and distal noticing, when he asserts that learning depends on "locality, proximity, distance...the point is that learning is impaired when experience and competence are too close *and* when they are too distant. In either case they do not pull each other" (p. 140). When Wenger stresses that learning (and by extension transfer of knowledge) occurs "when participants are able to recognize and experience of meaning in each other" (p. 140), and that this occurs in "boundary encounters" (p. 140) between proximal CoPs, we begin to get a sense of the role that stories and storytelling can play in his theory.

For Wenger, stories are social events connected to imagination (and play) that can be "appropriated easily because they allow us to enter the events, the characters, and their plights by calling upon our imaginations. Stories can transport our experience into the situations they relate and involve us in producing the meanings of those events as though we were participants" (1998, p. 203). Taken together with his concept of stories as a process and product of reification we see that Wenger goes beyond the popular notion, challenged here, that stories can express tacit knowledge, that they are a vehicle for eliciting tacit knowledge from knowledge workers. Rather he sees stories and other products of reification as "tokens of vast expanses of human meaning" (p. 61), which inherently vesselize the tacit in its dualistic relationship to the explicit, along with "all the implicit relations....Most of these may never be articulated" (p. 47). In this way stories are negotiated, alive, and emergent (Tyler, 2007b) in a way that we have not seen in Denning or Cooperrider. Though Wenger uses narrative as a term interchangeable with stories (after Linde, 1993, who correctly, in our view, considers life histories a narrative attempt to create coherency), we find in his theory that stories and storytelling are simultaneously produced by members of CoPs and are the fabric that knits the CoP together relationally: "Old timers deliver the pas and offer the future, in the form of narratives and participation both. Each has a story to tell. In addition, the practice itself gives life to these stories, and the possibility of mutual engagement offers a way to enter these stories through one's own experience" (1998, p. 156). Here, along with the connection he makes with imagination, we see intimations in Wenger of reflexivity. Nowhere in the 1998 text does Wenger consider storytelling a tool for the purposes of persuasion (Denning), inspiring change (Cooperrider), or purposefully prompting action, as both Denning and Cooperrider intend. Stories are not instrumentalized through Wenger's 1998 lens, only considered as a social phenomenon supporting and creating the social fabric of the organizations.

So far, we have been considering Wenger's theoretical framework for CoPs from his seminal text, which explores the many facets of his theory deeply, with great care and careful articulation. In his follow-on book (2002), co-authored with two colleagues (McDermott and Snyder), the audience is practitioners rather than academics (2002, p. x) and the tone is decidedly different. Here, we see not just stories and storytelling instrumentalized, but the entire of concept of Communities of Practice is itself instrumentalized in the interest of knowledge management. Rather than a social phenomenon that is emergent, naturally occurring in organizations, that can be recognized and perhaps fostered, CoPs in *Cultivating Communities of Practice: A Guide to Managing Knowledge* (2002) are something to be planned and launched (p. 65). There are even "seven principles for cultivating Communities of Practice" (p. 49). Stories become one of several "communal resources....[that] include both the tacit and the explicit aspects of the community's knowledge" (p. 38). Now they are seen as a "mode of communicating and capturing knowledge" (p. 39). While they consider stories as a means of measurement, of "assessing the value of a community of practice" (p. 168), they maintain some of Wenger's original spirit; that stories can describe "complex causal relations while incorporating implicit contextual factors" (p. 168), but this aspect is teamed up with "a number of additional benefits....Stories provide recognition of the protagonists; they reinforce the importance of making one's practice visible in the organization; and they help build a culture that values innovation and knowledge sharing" (p. 169). We would agree with the authors contention that "stories are a powerful component of any culture" (p. 169), but Wenger et al are quickly distancing themselves from the reflexive nature of stories when they stress the importance of "legitimizing the storytelling process" (p. 169), a move which will almost certainly yield coherent narratives that align with the dominant texts of the organization. In this text we no longer get the sense conveyed by Wenger's seminal work (1998) that the tacit-explicit duality matters, or is even present. Instead there is movement toward a coherent (and repeated) narrative that will make a case, or prove a point. The authors ultimately confirming this trajectory when they cite Denning and provide their own version of a World Bank story (pp. 187-190) to illustrate stories as "instruments of change" (p. 188). Capitalizing on the knowledge management trend and the burgeoning interest in Communities of Practice appear (2002, p. x-xi) to have resulted in the development of templates, formulas, and recipes that leave little room for reflexivity, and little interest in emergent story.

Implications of Popular Knowledge Management Approaches for Story and Narrative

In the three popular approaches to knowledge management explored here with an eye toward their stance on stories and narrative, tacit and explicit knowledge, and reflexivity and coherency, there seems to be a force driving toward the a notion that the term *story* can be used interchangeably and therefore replaced with the term *narrative*. Attending this casual substitution of terms is a wish that narrative can somehow unearth the unarticulated secrets of the organization's members, that which Polanyi says we know, but cannot tell (1966, 1983, p. 4). But as we have shown, it cannot. Reflexivity in storytelling is expanded in the social aspects of living story, which is deadened by the attempts of the knowledge management process to develop explicit and coherent narratives that capture story.

The commoditizing of storytelling into coherent narrative approaches that can be delivered in templates and recipes with discreet steps are antithetical to reflexive storytelling. These approaches are about making storytelling efficient and speedy by molding it into palatable narrative shapes, but reflexive storytelling is about slowing down, and about noticing.

The temptation on the part of knowledge management professionals to seek out tidy answers to puzzles of knowledge management is great. The quest for solutions that can be packaged into training modules and rolled out to employees is ongoing in earnest. Polanyi, in considering the process of "tacit integration" (Polanyi and Prosch, 1975, p. 40), suggests that it "is intentional throughout, and as such can be carried out *only by a conscious act of the mind*....Such integration cannot be replaced by any explicit mechanical procedure....It can only be lived, can only be dwelt in" (p. 40-41). In the context of the knowledge management turn toward narrative coherency seen in the approaches of Denning, Cooperrider, and ultimately Wenger (as he departs from his study of the CoP phenomenon to a packaging of it for institutional implementation), knowledge managers may do well to consider the ways in which the move from reflexive storytelling to coherent narrative will leave behind much of the richness they seek.

CONCLUSION

Tacitness, is generally, considered, a pre-scientific knowledge, or a knowledge that is not explicit, because it is to taken-for-granted, it becomes inexplicable. However, in the case of story, the experience is already rendered explicit. Narrative is hegemonic to story, ever-controlling and disciplining story, to render events and characters into an emplotment that shapes memory into experiential representationalism. Without the shaping, it would be accurate to call the knowledge (more accurately pre-knowledge), tacit knowledge.

We would like to suggest a way out of this dilemma. We propose that tacitness is not the same thing as reflexivity. In tacitness, events are reenacted, but unshaped. In story, the events become shaped into experience. Reflexivity is the way meaning of events is being made meaningful, the way the language is making meaning in a particular way.

REFERENCES

Argyris, C., & Schön, D. A. (1996). *Organizational Learning II: Theory, Method and Practice.* Reading, MA: Addison-Wesley Publishing Company.

Boje, D. M. (2006a). Pitfalls in Storytelling Advice and Praxis. *Academy of Management Review, 31*(1), 218-224.

Boje, D. M. (2006b). The Dark Side of Knowledge Reengineering Meets Narrative/Story. *Organization: The Critical Journal of Organization, Theory and Society* (forthcoming, accepted 2006). http://business.nmsu.edu/~dboje/690/papers/Knowledge_Reengineering_Review_Boje.pdf

Boje, D. M. (2006c). Breaking out of narrative's prison: Improper story in Storytelling Organization. *Storytelling, Self, Society: An Interdisciplinary Journal of Storytelling Studies, 2*(2), 28-49.

Davenport, T. H., & Prusak, L. (1998). *Working Knowledge: How Organizations Manage What They Know.* Boston: Harvard Business School Press.

Denning, S. (2001). *The Springboard: How Storytelling Ignites Action in Knowledge-Era Organizations.* Boston: Butterworth-Heinemann.

Denning, S. (2005). *The Leaders's Guide to Storytelling: Mastering the Art and Discipline of Business Narrative.* San Francisco: Jossey-Bass.

Denning, S. (2007). *The Secret Language of Leadership: How Leaders Inspire Action through Narrative.* San Francisco: Jossey-Bass.

Cooperrider, D. L, Sorenson, P. F. Jr., Whitney, D., & Yaeger, T. F. (Eds.) (2000). *Appreciative Inquiry: Rethinking Human Organization Toward a Positive Theory of Change.* Champaign, IL: Stipes Publishing L.L.C.

Cooperrider, D. L., Whitney, D., & Stavros, J. M. (2003). *Appreciative Inquiry Handbook: The First in a Series of AI Workbooks for Leaders of Change.* Ohio: Lakeshore Publishers Inc.

Cooperrider, D. L., & Avital, M. (Eds.) (2004). *Advances in Appreciative Inquiry Volume 1: Constructive Discourse and Human Organization.* Oxford: Elsevier Ltd.

Gherardi, S., & Nocolini, D. (2001). The Sociological Foundations of Organizational Learning. In M. Dierkes, A. Berthoin Antal, J. Child, & I. Nonaka (Eds.), *Handbook of Organizational Learning and Knowledge.* Oxford: Oxford University Press.

Höpfl, H. (1995). Organizational rhetoric and the threat of ambivalence. *Studies in Cultures, Organizations and Societies, 1*(2), 175-187.

Jackall, R. (1988). *Moral Mazes: The World of Corporate Managers.* New York: Oxford University Press

Karreman, D., & Alvesson, M. (2004). *Cages in Tandem: Management Control, Social Identity, and Identification in a Knowledge-Intensive Firm Organization. 11*(1), 149 - 175.

Knights, D., & Willmott, H. (1999). *Management Lives: Power and Identity in Work Organisations.* London, Sage

Linde, C. (1993). *Life Stories: The Creation of Coherence.* New York: Oxford University Press.

Lyotard, J. F. (1979/1984). *The Postmodern Condition.* Translated by Geoff Bennington and Brian Massumi. Minneapolis, Minnesota: University of Minnesota Press. 1979 in French edition and 1984 English edition.

Perlow, L. A. (2004). *When You Say Yes But Mean No.* New York: Crowns Business

Roscigno, V. J., & Hodson, R. (2004). The Organizational and Social Foundations of Worker Resistance. *American Sociological Review, 69*(1), 14-39

Schreyögg, G., & Koch, J. (2005). *Knowledge Management and Narratives: Organizational Effectiveness Through Storytelling.* Edited by (Berlin: Erich Schmidt Verlag GmbH & Co).

Kurtz, C. F., & Snowden, D. J. (2003). The new dynamics of strategy: Sense-making in a complex and complicated world. *IBM Systems Journal,* 42(3).

Lazaroff, M., & Snowden, D. (2006). Anticipatory modes for Counter Terrorism. In R. Popp, & J. Yen (Eds.), *Emergent Information Technologies and Enabling Policies for Counter-Terrorism.* Wiley-IEEE Press http://www.research.ibm.com/journal/sj/423/kurtz.html

Mark, A., & Snowden, D. (2004). *Researching practice or practising research - innovating methods in healthcare the contribution of Cynefin.* Presented paper at the Organisational Behaviour in Health Care Conference on the theme of Innovation held by the Centre for Health and Policy Studies (CHAPS) University of Calgary at the Banff Centre Alberta Canada

Marshak, R. J. (2006). *Covert Processes at Work: Managing the Five Hidden Dimensions of Organizational Change.* San Francisco: Berret-Kohler.

Nonaka, I., & Takeuchi, H. (1995). *The Knowledge Creating Company: How Japanese Companies Create the Dynamics of Innovation.* Oxford: Oxford University Press.

Polanyi, M. (1966, 1983). *The Tacit Dimension.* Gloucester, MA: Doubleday and Company.

Polanyi, M., & Prosch, H. (1975). *Meaning.* Chicago: University of Chicago Press.

Seely-Brown, J., & Duguid, P. (2000). *The Social Life of Information.* Boston: Harvard Business School Press.

Snowden, D. (2000). Cynefin: a sense of time and space, the social ecology of knowledge management In C. Despres & D. Chauvel (Eds.), *Knowledge Horizons: The Present and the Promise of Knowledge Management.* Butterworth-Heinemann: Oxford.

Snowden, D., & Boone, M. (2007). A Leader's Framework for Decision Making. *Harvard Business Review.* November 2007.

Stewart, T. A. (1997/98). *Intellectual Capital: The New Wealth of Organizations.* London-Naperville: Nicholas Brealey Publishing

Styhre, A., & Sundgren, M. (2005). *Managing Creativity in Organizations. Critique and Practices.* New York: Palgrave Macmillan

Tyler, J. A. (2006). Only the shadow knows: Increasing organizational polyphony with liminal storytelling. *Tamara Journal, 5*(3)

Tyler, J. A. (2007a). Incorporating Storytelling into Practice: How HRD Practitioners Foster Strategic Storytelling. *Human Resource Development Journal, 18*(4).

Tyler, J. A. (2007b). Storyaliveness and powerful listening. *Electronic Journal of Radical Organizational Theory: Fifth International Conference on Critical Management Studies Proceedings.* Available online at http://www.mngt.waikato.ac.nz/ejrot/cmsconference/2007/proceedings.asp

Von Krogh, G., Ichijo, K., & Nonaka, I. (2000). *Enabling Knowledge Creation: How to Unlock the Mystery of Tacit Knowledge and Release the Power of Innovation.* Oxford: Oxford University Press.

Wenger, E. (1998). *Communities of Practice: Learning, Meaning, and Identity.* Cambridge: Cambridge University Press.

Wenger, E., McDermott, R., & Snyder, W. M. (2002). *Cultivating Communities of Practice: A Guide to Managing Knowledge.* Boston: Harvard University Press.

Whitney, D., & Trosten-Bloom, A. (2003). *The Power of Appreciative Inquiry: A Practical Guide to Positive Change.* San Francisco: Berret-Kohler.

KEY TERMS

Antenarrative: Defined as "nonlinear, incoherent, collective, unplotted, and prenarrative speculation, a bet, a proper narrative can be constituted" (Boje, 2001: 1). Antenarratives morph as they travel, picking up and depositing context as they move.

BME: Defined as Beginning, Middle and End progressive sequencing of retrospective narrative, the five-senses wholeness with imposed coherency that is in vogue since Aristotle.

Emergence: Defined as absolute novelty, spontaneity, and improvisation, without past/future.

Living Story Theory: Defined here as the emergence, trajectory, and morphing of living story from antenarrative-conception to the death of decomposition and forgetting to tell anymore (Boje, 2005e).

Narrative: Defined by Aristotle requiring "imitation of an action that is complete in itself, as a whole of some magnitude... Now a whole is that which has beginning, middle, and end" the definition of coherent narrative (Aristotle, 350 BCE: 1450b: 25, p. 233).

Story: Defined as "an oral or written performance involving two or more people interpreting past or anticipated experience" (Boje, 1991a: 111).

ENDNOTE

1 The following typology is adapted from foth-coming article Boje for E:CO (Emergence, Complexity & Organization Journal, due to publish in 2008)

Chapter VII
Exploring Organizational Learning and Knowledge Exchange through Poetry

Louise Grisoni
Bristol Business School, UK

ABSTRACT

The central discussion in this chapter is that poetry can be used to provide a bridge between tangible, rational and explicit knowledge and tacit or implicit knowledge, providing opportunities to access new organizational knowledge, understandings and learning. A study based on 60 middle and senior United Kingdom public services managers is presented. In this study managers worked together to explore how creative inquiry into their organizational experience might help address some of the problematic issues facing their organizations and learn how to develop new ideas about best practice. The challenge was to generate new knowledge about the organization. Poetry in the form of 'haiku' was used as a creative research method to access tacit knowledge, which, when combined with explicit knowledge and understanding, led to new insights and organizational learning.

INTRODUCTION

In a 'knowledge society' how organizations process knowledge and how they create new knowledge to meet the many competing challenges of organizational life are held as key issues (Drucker 1968, Bell 1973, Toffler 1990). The business case for innovation and creativity in modern organizations in a constantly changing environment has been well made (Stacey 2005, 2006, Shaw 2002, Weick and Quinn 1999). The general consensus from these authors is that organizations need to be flexible, flatter and ready to adapt when needed. Models of continuous change and adaptation provide opportunities to work with complex adaptive systems within organizations in order to stay competitive and knowledge creation is viewed as a source of competitive advantage (Von Krogh, Ichijo, Nonaka, Ichijo 2000). Organizational learning and knowledge exchange form part of the dynamic change process where organizational members work creatively together to find solutions to problems and create new organizational knowledge.

There is a tension both in management practice with its current focus in the public sector on performance indicators and evidence based practice, and in the literature - between explicit rational and measurable approaches to knowledge exchange and intangible, tacit and implicit including narrative approaches. Epistemological and ontological differences between approaches to knowledge creation are at the heart of the tension. Chia (2003) argues that new organizational knowledge can be accessed through exploration of intangible and tacit knowledge and an integration of organizational knowledge and organizational learning can be achieved using a 'social process perspective' (Chiva and Alegre 2006) where individual and organizational learning and knowledge exchange are viewed as mutually constitutive and constantly changing. Knowledge creation as an inter-subjective, aesthetic process is developed through narrative and story telling (Gabriel 2000, Banks and Banks 1997, Czarniawska 1998, Hatch, Kostera, Kozminski 2005) and I argue that working with poetry provides additional emotional richness and textured nuance to organizational knowledge and learning by distilling and refining story telling into a revised form - poetry, which then offers the potential for further levels of understanding, analysis and insight.

USING NARRATIVE AND POETRY TO CONTRIBUTE TO KNOWLEDGE CREATION AND ORGANIZATIONAL LEARNING

The contribution of narratives and story telling as ways of understanding organizations is well developed (Gabriel 2000, Banks and Banks 1997, Czarniawska 1998, Hatch, Kostera, Kozminski 2005) and has been used as the starting point for sense making (Weick, 1991) in organizations.

'Documenting and analyzing organizational stories can enhance our understanding of human behavior. It can also enrich our appreciation of what it means to be a participant in an organization. We gain insights into ways that people interact, communicate, project anxieties, cope with problems and solve dilemmas in human relations. We also discover how people view organizations and what they expect socially aesthetically and symbolically. Hence the information and hypothesis have a practical application'. (Jones, Moore, and Snyder, 1988:14).

Working with stories that are constructed between participants as part of an inquiry process draws on narrative analysis (Czarniawska 1998, 1999) where the stories contribute to the continual creation and re-creation of our understanding of organization and our place within them. Important stories are not so much the ones that have become part of an organization's mythology that persist within an organizational culture (Gabriel 1999), rather they are participants' stories that have been created with others with a particular focus and narrative. These stories tend to be immediate and relevant to current experience – they may be told relatively infrequently but have a relevance to the time place when they were created. As a result they are closely linked to experience and tend to contain an emotional element that would not otherwise find expression.

Story telling can be described as a 'poetic' form. According to Dilthey (1887), 'Poetic' is the term we use for the nature that enables us to enjoy vitality. 'Poetic' is above all the nourishing, strengthening and awakening within ourselves of this vitality, this energy of the life-sentiment; a sentiment that resonates in all images, music, words and is found in poetry. It is described as an experience, which can only be appropriated through reflexivity, by being set in relation to other lived experiences. It enables lived experience to be understood in its essence and as a result, in its meaning (in Strati, 1999:60).

The place of poetry in organizational life has been acknowledged in a special edition of *Management Decision* (James and Weir, 2006), which focused explicitly on the relations between poetry, organization, emotions, management and enterprise. The combined work in this issue demonstrates the richness that poetry brings to organizational life, as a way of exploring a range of management and organizational issues including culture, leadership and communications. Poetry is a particular and specialized form of narrative – and as such is an extension of story telling. Creating a poem involves crafting stories and transforming them. By immersing in the experience of organizational life through poetry, customary ways of making sense are suspended, and new insights into encountered reality become possible. Poetic expression therefore grasps at newly discovered reality. For example the story of a management 'Away Day' is turned into a 'playful' performance poem with an ironic twist (Grisoni, in Grisoni and Kirk 2006:519), which on analysis contains heightened double-edged meaning and foregrounds gender, competition, leadership, voice, separation and leaving, belonging and joining, that would have been lost through extended narrative and explanation. A fragment is provided for illustration below:

Away Day
.....
Heads: I win.
What?
Puppy dog – tails: you lose.
What?
Puppy dog tails – snip!

Sugar and spice.
Sacrifice
Three little mice
Roast them twice – nice.
......

In introducing poetry as a creative research method (Grisoni 2008), the argument is made that power of poetry lies in its ability to focus not only on events but also on behavioral and affective elements embedded in the experience. Poetry has been used to reveal hidden aspects of organizational life where the essence of an event or episode opens up an opportunity for greater understanding as well as the potential for change in individuals and organizations (Grisoni 2006, Grisoni and Kirk 2006). Whyte (1994) argues that we live in a time when idealism is out of fashion, where there is an absence of compassion and a failing of imagination. He argues that business and organizations need the poet's insight and powers of attention to 'weave the inner world of soul and creativity with the outer world of form and matter (1994:9).

A good poem seems to occupy a space beyond mere words especially when it is used to explore the full range of life's experience. According to Grisham:

"Poetry is by its nature a compressed communication of emotions and concepts that the listener must decompress and interpret. By participating in the process the listener must complete portions of the message, and thereby internalize, absorb, and reconstruct the message." (Grisham 2006:492).

The emphasis is on understanding as it appears from within an individual's own experience which on sharing becomes an example of organizational learning. Poems are also therefore an act of discovery, and require a degree of effort to write and to be understood. Poetry can cut through superficiality and help us to see the world differently. Grisham (2006), illustrates this well by drawing on Marchant (2005) who refers to the last few lines of a poem by Komumunyakaa (2001) about seeing the Vietnam Veteran's Memorial in Washington DC:

In the black mirror

A woman's trying to erase names:
No, She's brushing a boy's hair

Poetic methods of extended metaphor, broken cadence, juxtaposition and overlay are used to evoke emotions and contain several layers of potential meaning.

Kostera's (1997) work develops the contribution of poetry to research the relationship between feelings and organizing. She argues that poetry, as an approach is well suited for expressing the ambivalence and volatility of the managerial experience. Its strength is that it does not *'flatten out'* the domains of organizing or *'translate them into rationality'* (1997:343). As a result she proposes that poetry can be used to understand more about organizational realities. Her aim in using poetry was to learn about the subversive and subjective experience of talking about management topics. She argues that poetry is particularly powerful in that it does not avoid passion and it is disruptive because it is inconclusive. As such poetry does not provide rational answers – it creates and evokes feelings and its form and shape acts as a container to encourage exploration of a range of possibilities, lines of inquiry, analysis, interpretation, understanding and meaning. To illustrate this point I have chosen Kostera's (1997:351-352) summary of her reading of the contributions from others in her article:

Management is
about dreams, nets, growing seeds
out of chaos comes liberation
and the god's listen
to deserters' prayers
(sometimes)

Ambiguity is painful
but also sensual; a necessity
a falling angel, falling veil
curtain falling down onto the stage
(falling in love)

Soon its time
The rest is science.

Analysis of organizational life is complex and multilayered as it involves acknowledgement of emotions and relationships. Choosing to work with poetry in the research process to explore these issues is powerful as poetry captures both the richness of language and harnesses reflective processes that encourage expression of the complexity of organizational experience. As a consequence there is potential for poetry to access tacit organizational knowledge both in the words used the form and in the emotions evoked that lie behind and between them.

INTRODUCING HAIKU

The particular form of poetry selected for the research-based case study was haiku. This form was purposely chosen for its structure and brevity, which results in a focused and concentrated capturing of the essence of a situation. Haiku originated in Japan, around the 15th century. It is a specific form of poetry containing seventeen syllables, in three phrases of five-seven-five syllables. It usually presents a moment of heightened awareness in simple imagery, originally using an image from nature. Traditional haiku requires a long period of learning, practise and maturity. The mastery of this form exemplifies Chia's (2003) discussion relating to eastern forms of knowledge creation concerned with flux and transformation, and where indirect, suggestive and symbolic meaning is privileged over literal meaning. The concept of 'being-in-the-world' is important here and relates closely to approaches taken by many Western artists and poets.

Fermine (2001) in a short novel entitled 'Snow' captures the essence of haiku beautifully drawing on the work of one of the earliest Haiku writers, Matsuo Basho (1644-1694).

Frozen in the night
The water-jar cracks
Wakes me

One morning a water jar cracks and a drop of poetry forms:

'Its beauty touches the soul. It is the moment of saying what cannot be said, of making a journey without taking a step. It is the moment of becoming a poet. Do not break the silence. Just watch and write'. (Fermine, 2001:14)

The haiku form has been developed and experimented with over many hundreds of years and different fashions, variations, styles and techniques have come and gone. Contemporary haiku is often regarded as an "instant" form of brief verse that can be written by anyone from schoolchildren to professionals. Many present-day writers have dropped traditional standards, emphasizing personal freedom and pursuing ongoing exploration in both form and subject matter. Due to the various views and practices today, it is impossible to single out any current style or format or subject matter as definitive haiku. The term has broadened greatly in modern usage to cover nearly any short verse. According to Pio:

"It is a way of calling the spirit of the thing named, with the eternal and momentary juxtaposed. It is considered the poetry of ahness, because it makes you say, 'Aha, now I see it!'." (Pio 2004:16).

Another example, this time of an organizational haiku:

Three things are certain:
Death, taxes, and lost data.
Guess which has occurred.
(David Dixon)

There is a clear qualitative difference between the beautiful Japanese haiku, about elements that address human existence and the states of nature and the 'office haiku' about topics such as money, power, process and partnerships which may seem - as one anonymous reviewer put it – *'miserable'* by comparison. Nevertheless, the haiku form captures in a minimal way, a sense of depth and communion that reaches beyond formal parsimony. Rather than making anything explicit in the sense of formalized transferable knowledge it encourages personal awareness, depth, beauty and instant knowledge and this in turn impacts on organizational knowledge creation. To this end, working with haiku poetry as direct experimental action, is introduced as a creative form of expression within the enabling context of a workshop intervention, and provides the conditions for new ways of working which surface emotions and learning through insights provoked by organizational experiences thereby contributing to fostering emerging relationships and new knowledge creation.

Creating haiku provides the focus for attention through instructive forms of talk and relationships (Tsoukas 2003). Through this method the distinctions, which we had previously not noticed, and features, which had previously escaped our attention, are brought into focus. Whilst tacit knowledge cannot be made operational (Chia 2003), new ways of talking, fresh forms of interacting and novel ways of distinguishing and connecting can be achieved. Reason (2001) also supports the use of creative methods arguing that they enable researchers and participants access a richer, deeper, more true to life and more useful knowing when constituted in a complex relationship between different forms of knowing.

CREATING A POETIC PROCESS

The Chief Executive of a public service organization requested a workshop for all middle and senior managers and staff in a UK county council and partner organizations. It is important to mention at this point that the organization concerned had been recently 'inspected' by the Government and was officially rated as a 'successful, performing authority' and that the request was made following several years of close association with colleagues in the Business School. The overall aim of the workshop was to provide an opportunity for researchers and practitioners to engage in dialogue in an exploratory way to see how current research and thinking might help address the problematic change issues which are typical of many UK public service organizations, including; performance cultures based on targets, managing increasing client expectations and demands, reducing costs whilst maintaining service levels, working in partnership on new initiatives, and the need to demonstrate added value.

A collaborative inquiry (Reason 2001) based on action research (Coghlan and Brannick 2005) was adopted and is particularly suited to action research where the aim is to be critical of the familiar and taken for granted. A collaborative process of inquiry through action research facilitates an engagement of all participants in a process that aims to take action and create knowledge or theory about that action. Working with participants as co-researchers the action research cycle (plan action, act thoughtfully, research action, and evaluate action) is combined with reflective and interpretive practice in a collaborative process. In this way the stories, recreated in poetic form, fit well with a social-process perspective to organizational knowledge and learning. The workshop approach developed for this research project provides an opportunity to explore organizational issues in a way that echoes Elkjaer's (2004) call for the development of knowledge and experience by inquiry, 'to work with situations and events as units of analysis in order to understand individuals and organizations as being mutually formed and forming' (2004:419).

Facilitating a workshop designed to share experiences and create new energy for working with the challenges of the public services agenda was a priority as well as attempting to develop a contribution to new organizational knowledge and learning. The workshop could be described as an example of 'researched action' (Tripp 1996) a particular form of action inquiry, planned as research as well as an improvement to practice where:

'the main aim is to increase our knowledge about a problem or issue, so the action may be primarily an intervention designed to illuminate a research question' (Tripp, 1996:17).

In 'researched action' two cycles of inquiry are simultaneously in operation, one in the field of practice and the other in the field of research. It was important to design a workshop that was both consistent with the principles of action research and was innovative in that it would experiment with interpretive processes creating the potential for developing new ways of thinking about and working with change issues. A realization occurred during a planning group meeting that, in order to explore ways of sustaining levels of energy and continuing successful achievement of organizational goals it would be important to access new organizational knowledge. An approach that would cut through accustomed and patterned ways of thinking would be required and at this point my colleague, knowing my interest in working with poetry, recommended that I facilitate 'poetic' workshops as part of the day.

The poetic process workshop was repeated three times during the day to allow groups of around 20 managers per workshop (60 managers in total) explore their experiences of the organization. At the same time that this poetic workshop was running other activities were on offer to the group of managers focusing on different aspects of the service, which were viewed as priorities. These included sessions on: increasing client needs and expectations, collaborative leadership in partnerships, and action planning to meet government targets. Each of the sessions were planned and run jointly with a member of the organization, and I was paired with a manager from the library service who was also particularly interested in the poetic process.

In the early stages of planning the workshop there was a pull to design something that fitted existing ways of thinking about new policy implementation with an overriding concern that the workshop would offer value in terms of tangible outputs and plans. This pull towards what was already known by the organization seemed to contradict the requirement to generate new knowledge and understanding. We were concerned to meet the Chief Executive's needs (our sponsoring client) in a way that would be deemed acceptable to the organization and at the same time meet her aspiration to introduce new ways of thinking and working that might break through some of the established patterns and behaviours in order to access new possibilities for working with change and meeting the challenges facing the public sector. This would help re-energise and re-vitalise participants who were described as *'exhausted by policy and initiative overload'*. The design that emerged was to develop a collaborative inquiry with what Reason (2001) has identified as working at a deeper level encouraging participants through the processes of constructing and using their own knowledge to "see through" the ways in which the establishment monopolizes the production and use of knowledge for the benefit of only some of its members.

As workshop facilitators we recognized that some risk taking and a 'leap of faith' (Schon 1985) was required in order to discover whether new ways of working that would cut across the well established patterns in thinking, relating, behaving and understanding would be achieved. The planning group comprising the Chief Executive, representatives of the organizations involved and fellow academics judged that the risks of trying a different approach was important and supported the poetic workshops in the spirit of creative experimentation, innovation and discovery.

An action research process for the poetry workshops, capturing each of these activities was developed. Each cycle of the workshop lasted one and a half hours. In small groups of three, participants in the workshop were invited to tell each other stories of significant events from their recent organizational experiences. Listeners noted key words from these stories and together the small group developed short poems using the haiku poetic form. Participants were encouraged to play with words rather than worry about whether the poems they created were good examples of poetry (mastery only comes through repeated practice!) The process of creating poems was new to most participants and this created some anxiety in the groups as tried and tested methods of exploring work related issues had been removed. In this way all were new to the process and needed reassuring – the element of being surprised by what was created was important as the new way of working resulted in new conversations, understandings and insights. The structure for a haiku was useful in that it channeled anxiety into the need to count syllables and ensure that the haiku created met the numeric criteria set. The poems were then read back to the whole group and participants invited to capture the thoughts, feelings that emerged in the hearing and understanding of the new knowledge presented to them. Through this process of 'double reflection'- reflection following the story and then reflection on reflection of the haiku, a revised sense of the issues and priorities held in the organization was discovered. Feedback on working with the poetic process of knowledge sharing and creation was also gathered.

Presentation of Haiku

The haiku developed by the managers can be grouped in many different ways; collectively they may be read as a *renga*[a]. The haiku were written up and presented back to all the workshop participants as a small booklet, as a record of the day. Examples from the 25 haiku that were jointly created are shown below and allocated to groupings identifying intangible assets. Categories for intangible assets can be divided into three types: employee competence, internal structures and external structures (Sveiby 1997). Employee competence involves the capacity to act in a wide variety of situations to create value. Internal structures include such things as processes; ways of working, new designs or models. External structures include relationships with customers and other stakeholders, reputation and image. All of these assets are based on the relationship between tacit and explicit knowledge.

- Employee Competence

The group acknowledged the extent of personal learning. Personal learning was identified as relating to periods of study on professional courses, achieving clarity around roles and different working patterns arising from an absence from work (e.g. maternity leave) or as a result of organizational restructuring. There were positive endings and a sense of achievement for many although there were other examples that were more ambiguous where particular challenges had been posed. Many participants referred to their own and other's enhanced competence, arising from acquisition of information, skills and experience and exploration of shared values. The importance of this enhanced competence described by Sveiby (2001) is the capacity to act in a variety of situations in order to add value to the organization.

Son's nursery trial
Dumped apprehensive parents
No-cry, relief.

Out of date, away
briefing shouting discussion,
back now – enjoy!

Member of team
Develop role, career
Encouraged, valued.

This last example of a 'one-line' haiku illustrates a less positive outcome:

Meeting Outside, Plan Next Week, Time, Unsure, Beyond Skills, Used, Upset.

It is interesting to note in the examples above how the boundary between being in the organization and what goes on outside is referred to more than once. Participants were surprised that they felt able to talk about the emotions involved, for example, in dropping their son at nursery – it's hard to tell whether its relief that the parents didn't cry or the child. In the second one the contrast between being out of the organization for a period and out of date sits next to enjoyment of being back - the noise of discussion and shouting acts as a bridge to the two experiences. The third haiku catches the sense of being valued as a member of the team this was after a period of absence. In all three cases the issue of being away from the organization and returning is a common theme with different details and a range of emotional expression. A focus on competence, being up to date, coping well and performing pervades all four examples with the last one expressing more negative emotions. Creating the haiku facilitated a focus on the emotional aspects of participants' experiences and confronted previously unchallenged norms in the organization such as whether it was legitimate to talk about life outside the organization and use those experiences to make sense of their current engagement with the organization.

- Internal structures: Team Level and Organizational Issues

The second grouping seemed to cohere around team level change issues where there were difficulties but achievement of a shared task and sense of working together seemed to be a focus. Pride in organizational achievement was identified as an important outcome of collaborative efforts and many noticed the positive ends in the last line of the haiku and use of positive words throughout the collected haiku. There was a strong desire to associate the organization with success. Losses and gains were evident in many of the examples perhaps pointing to ambivalence in relation to the pressures participants were experiencing in their efforts to make the organization successful which sits in contrast to the positive achievements and external validation that the organization had recently realized. Internal structures referred to the complexity of change, restructuring and technological developments and finance is specifically mentioned as a disabling factor. Emotions and relationships figure significantly, both positively and negatively – feeling proud for others as a result of a positive outcome begs the question of how those expressing the pride might be feeling. As one participant commented, *'Sometimes what's not said but implied opens up new avenues for discussion'.* The juxtaposition of brief words and phrases seemed to bring this hidden dimension to the fore and created the space for difficult conversations where different views of similar episodes, such as experiences of organizational restructuring - 'Change risk frightened us' could be explored.

Project completed
Feeling proud for others
Outcome positive

Understanding loss
Care to build relationships
Finance frustrates

Change risk frightened us
Thought safe, but hidden fear revealed.
Moved into sparkling sunshine

December, budgets bring
High expectations. Service provision
No money, disappointments.

Power-mongers gathered
Eloquent, compliments, coup
Proud: top partnership

- External Client Focus

Examples of external structures, which were identified in the poems, include development of relationships and networks and reputation.

Fog pulling together
Positive partnership passion
Long way to go

Ongoing concern – always
People in need, a start
Towards positive change!

Gentleman, complaint, made safe
Confused, concerned, angry, resolved
Not what it seemed.

Strangers making time
Trust the process, insights
Carers listening

The sense of long term commitment to the client group is expressed in several of these haiku – 'long way to go', 'a start', 'ongoing concern', 'carers listening' which also indicate that whilst working in partnership and commitment to the clients is present there is still more to be done. This was problematic for participants as when combined with the frustrations of lack of finance and emotional exhaustion from change initiatives what participants wanted was some sense of scale and scope and ultimately sets of priorities on which to focus their depleted energy. This became an important action point from the workshop. At the same time there was an appreciation of what had been achieved and sense of mutual congratulation that spread through the group in a way that the news of the recent successful government inspection had failed to achieve. Participants resolved to maintain levels of appreciation of effort and acknowledgement of hard work and the emotional labour involved in working through multiple sets of change initiatives.

WORKING AT THE BOUNDARY OF EXPLICIT AND TACIT ORGANIZATIONAL KNOWLEDGE FOR NEW KNOWLEDGE CREATION IN PUBLIC SERVICES

The context facing public services in the UK is one of continual change in the delivery of services driven centrally by the Labour Government's modernization agenda. Central to this strategy is the rhetoric of renewal through partnership and inclusion. A significant challenge for senior managers in public services is to work in partnership on new initiatives in the management and delivery of public services that need to demonstrate added value. Fenwick and McMillan (2005) suggest that the assumptions of current government thinking on partnership and the way they can enable learning through knowledge exchange are predicated in the notion that good practice can only be provided by external opinion, in other words through evidence-based thinking. The search for ways to account for the value of services provided has therefore resulted in the rise of evidence-based management techniques. This has established a 'performativity' culture, which relies on explicit knowledge to identify tangible outputs that measure the added value of the work of these organizations. (Allee 2000, 2003). This 'performativity' culture is underpinned by a view of knowledge as cognitive acquisition - a commodity, and as a result much organizational knowledge exchange and learning is based on adaptive behaviour (Common 2004). There is an alternative, counter-cultural view, which argues that knowledge is socially constructed (Spender 1996) and Von Krogh et al. (2000) by highlighting the limits of an evidence-based approach, shift attention away from tangible outputs and explicit knowledge and turn the focus towards the value of accessing tacit organizational knowledge and intangible outputs (Sveiby 1997) as an alternative way of influencing organizational effectiveness.

The haiku developed by the managers and presented above point to the significance of emotions and work life balance as they affect employee competence. The impact that structural change and reorganization has on internal structures in teams and departments emerges as a significant issue, and where a sense of achievement and success seems to be fundamental to the ability to cope with the down sides of the change agenda. Finally the external focus particularly on clients is present and provides the reminder of the main purpose and function of the organization – to provide a range of services. Key areas of knowing for the managers on the workshop include knowledge of local community needs, of policy, of local infrastructure and context. The value of the diversity within the organizational partnership is that it provides a range of people with different information, skills and experience to help the transition of information to knowledge. Clearly, a better balance needs to be found between the demands for tangible measurable outputs and finding voice and recognition for the emotion work involved in leading change (Hochschild 1983, Fisher and Ashkanasy, 2000).

It is too simple to say that poetry in the form of haiku provides a mechanism for translating tacit knowledge into explicit knowledge. The relation of explicit to tacit knowledge and explanations of conversion of one form to the other is complex, problematic and has been criticized

(Tsoukas 2003). One key issue is the methodological standpoint adopted for understanding the nature of knowledge is critical as it provides clarity regarding how knowledge is discussed and claims for the generation of new knowledge made. Chia (2003) explores this as a dichotomy where he describes differences between 'western' and 'eastern' epistemological and ontological underpinnings that characterize the creation of knowledge. In Western approaches knowledge is produced through the process of observation, reflection and reasoning. It is systematically articulated in written form through the medium of language. As a result, reasoning and knowing the cause of a thing is privileged over action. Documented knowledge precedes and therefore predetermines action and performance hence the focus on explicit knowledge. Eastern approaches contain an ontological commitment to flux and transformation, (this is an epistemological reversal to the western approach), where indirect, suggestive and symbolic meaning is privileged over literal meaning. Immediate engagement with tasks and lengthy apprenticeship through sustained experimental practice develops proficiency into mastery. The concept of 'Being-in-the-world' is important where:

"Such a view would privilege a directness of experiencing and it is this unmeditated directness that encapsulates what we mean here by the broad term 'eastern'." (Chia, 2003:956)

The focus from this perspective concerns tacit forms of knowledge and the contribution tacit knowledge makes to organizational learning. Tsoukas (2003) develops further clarity into the nature of tacit knowledge arguing that it has been greatly misunderstood in that the essential 'ineffability' of tacit knowledge has been ignored. When viewed from this perspective tacit knowledge cannot be captured, translated, or converted in the way Nonaka (1994) originally proposed, but only displayed and manifested in what we do. Tsoukas argues that we need to focus on how we draw each other's attention to things - instructive forms of talk help us to re-orientate ourselves to how we relate to others and the world around us, thus enabling us to talk and act differently. Distinctions, which we had previously not noticed, and features, which had previously escaped our attention, may be brought forward. We cannot make tacit knowledge operational, but we can find new ways of talking, fresh forms of interacting and novel ways of distinguishing and connecting.

Sveiby (1997) makes an additional contribution here and describes four characteristics of knowledge, which include: tacit, action-oriented, supported by rules and constantly changing. All knowledge is either tacit or located in tacit knowledge which means it is rooted in practice and once assimilated, is usually taken for granted. Tacit knowledge is likened to a tool with a focus on a particular object or phenomenon without consciously thinking about the background knowledge brought from experience, enacted, for example, in something like 'bicycling on the moon' (Collins 2007). Knowledge from this perspective is action-oriented, meaning that there is a continuous processing and categorising of perceptions into existing theories, methods, feelings, values and skills, for future use. The rules that support knowledge enable people to act skillfully without thinking and automatically filter all new knowledge through the rules already acquired. These rules are generally unknown to the person observing them since:

"skills retain an element of opacity and unspecificity; they cannot be fully accounted for in terms of their particulars, since their practitioners do not ordinarily know what those particulars are" (Tsoukas, 2005:145).

Developing the discussion further, Collins (2007) distinguishes two forms of tacit knowledge each with different causes and consequences. The first kind he calls 'somatic-limit tacit knowledge' has to do with the cognitive limitations of the human brain and body, the second 'collective tacit knowledge' he argues is ontological – being concerned with its location in the social collectivity. He argues that both forms are rarely distinguished because they are experienced and acquired in the same way; nevertheless, they have different causes and different consequences. The concept of 'collective tacit knowledge' is of most relevance to this paper in that it relates to the cultural, relational and situated nature of learning:

"This knowledge has to be known tacitly, because it is located in human collectivities and, therefore can never be the property of any one individual. The simplest way to see this is to note the changes in content of the knowledge belonging to communities is beyond the control of the individuals within the communities." (Collins, 2007:260)

This proposition supports the view that knowledge is constantly changing. As soon as it is made explicit it becomes static and what is articulated is always less than what is tacitly known. Accessing tacit knowledge held by individuals' lies at the heart of the knowledge creation process and finding ways to verbalise and share tacit knowledge is an important first step on the way to new organizational knowledge. In addition, Chia argues that the current preoccupation with explicit knowledge-creation and management may need to be balanced with an equally important emphasis on direct experimental action as a valuable source of meaning innovation and enhanced performance (2003:959). Effective knowledge creation therefore depends on establishing an enabling context for communication and dialogue where emerging relationships can be fostered.

The workshop provided the enabling context (Chia 2003) and was characterized by sharing stories that created an energized atmosphere where participants engaged in dialogue to access collective tacit knowledge (Collins 2007) to explore organizational experiences. This shared process of sense-making is an important part of knowledge generation and exchange between all participants and from a social process perspective (Chiva and Allegre 2006) provides the possibility for greater integration of organizational knowledge and learning. An important role played by introducing haiku poetry was to emphasize the 'eastern' approaches to knowledge described by Chia (2003) emphasizing that knowledge is embedded in experience.

In order to maximize the value of knowledge as an intangible asset, the main strategy must be one of enabling rather than controlling (Sveiby 2001). Such a strategy is aimed towards improving what Sveiby refers to, as people's capacity-to-act, either inside or outside the organization. Allee (2003) emphasizes that attempts to assign monetary value or other hard measures to intangible assets miss the point. If such a value could be attached to them, they would no longer be intangible. The point is not their current value or their ability to reflect past performance, but their potential for future value creation or in the context of public service, future contribution to the public good principally through the actions taken as a result of new insights. The insights gained through the development of haiku during the workshops whilst interesting and revelationary at the time for participants would hold no real value unless translated into future actions. There was clearly a commitment to take the new knowledge about the significance of emotional labour and other key insights back into the organization, however there would need to be detailed follow up to discover whether this has had any real impact. Anecdotally, the Chief Executive resigned recently to follow an alternative career and achieve a childhood ambition to run a teashop. Rumour has it that she was burnt out by the constant pressures of her role.

At this point it seems possible to move to the dimension of organizational learning and understand it in terms that Clegg et al (2005) articulate:

"Here learning is not something that is done to organizations, nor is it something that an organization does; rather learning and organizing are seen as mutually constitutive and unstable, yet pragmatic constructs that might enable a dynamic appreciation of organizational life." (2005:150)

Discussions in groups following the reading of all the haiku instigated a range of thoughts and ideas about the organization. As a result of the workshop there was a realisation that everyone had a story to tell of their experiences and that the organization is made up of individuals who all have a voice and a view. There were some common threads, but many variations and whilst all could be voiced, there was a realisation that some held more 'organizational currency' in that they were politically or culturally more acceptable (struggles for resources on behalf of the organization) than others (personal issues), *'I didn't realise how emotional I felt about coming back to work'* that were viewed as marginal and therefore less important. This felt like a new realisation for many, brought into focus by using a form that requires brevity, which one participant described as *'cutting to the chase'*. The participants were aware of their well-honed skills of storytelling that had been developed to provide lengthy and detailed articulations of how to account for what they do.

The significance of working on an unfamiliar task (creating haiku) helped to disturb established patterns of thinking, explaining and understanding, this allowed a different perspective to enter the interactions leading to 'truly effective and insightful action' (Chia 2003:956). Standing back to review the poems providing a 'double reflection' also gave a different perspective on the organization to many enabling the celebration of success and as one participant commented, *'Playfulness is possible in a contained way'*. These seems to confirm that the conditions necessary for enabling new knowledge creation (Von Krogh et al 2000) had been met. Through a process of poetry creation conversations sharing local knowledge, understandings and experiences were facilitated and new relationships established. Stacey's (2003) complexity view of organizational learning provides a useful explanation from which the reflective comments made by participants can be understood:

"[L]earning is the emerging transformation of inseparable individual and collective identities. Learning occurs in shifts in meaning and it is simultaneously individual and social. Learning is the activity of interdependent people and can only be understood in terms of self organising communicative interaction and power relating in which identities are potentially transformed." (2003:8)

It was noticed by the group that the use of poetry enabled a surfacing and discussion of emotions and emotional engagement with the organization in a new and different - more accessible way. Clegg et al (2005) draws on work by Antonacopoulou and Gabriel (2001:48) to illustrate that organizational learning is full of a range of emotions involving an "inner world of passion, ambivalence and contradiction which may be experienced as repressed, expressed or controlled, diffused or diluted, but never actually obliterated" (2005:152). Elkjaer (2004) speaks of the development of experience and knowledge by inquiry and reflection, emphasising the place of intuition and emotion in the process. Anxiety arising from organizational change and the uncertainty challenging a previously held sense of security was identified by the managers during the workshop and discussed as an issue. Alongside this was a sense of hope for the organization and pride in the achievements gained so far. A deeper sense of new emotional knowledge and care emerged from the poems highlighting a need to tend to how people treated each other. The process created was one of encouraging creativity and playfulness and would appear, in the moment, to have contributed to both knowledge creation and organizational learning.

CONCLUSION

Organizational learning and knowledge exchange form part of the dynamic change process where organizational members work creatively together to find solutions to problems and create new organizational knowledge. I have argued that learning and organizing are mutually constitutive and unstable and that working with poetry can provide emotional richness and textured nuance to organizational knowledge and learning. In particular, this chapter has provided an opportunity to further examine the claim that poetry when used as a creative research method, combined with processes of collaborative inquiry, facilitates new organizational knowledge, understanding and learning.

An early proposition was that poetry would provide a way of making tacit knowledge about current organizational challenges and experiences explicit and facilitate new organizational knowledge. Through the poetic process established for the workshops new understandings about the organization and its priorities were raised. The general level of appreciation of individual and organizational effort that was being made to demonstrate added value in order to meet performativity targets was high. As a consequence it was possible to identify a range of intangible values and assets, which supplement the explicit or tangible knowledge used to measure organizational performance and gain an understanding of an approach to organizational learning that emphasizes interdependence. The collaborative inquiry using action research facilitated new approaches to knowledge creation through poetry, enabling different stories and voices to emerge. The process facilitated new understandings and relationships by cutting across established patterns or relating and communicating. In terms of action research however, the extent to which these new insights were taken back into the organization to instigate further change requires further investigation.

Working with poetry clearly holds the potential to capture emotion and express the unsayable with passion, truth and intensity. The choice about when to use poetry relates to whether the topic or issue to be researched requires a reflective space that taps into emotions and uncovers layers of thought and feelings. The haiku demonstrate an ability to explore the dark side of experience as well as the light and juxtapose the rational realm with the emotional. Creative forms of research invite active engagement, where those who participate in the process become co-creators of meaning. Configuring and reconfiguring words in different ways, in poetic forms, enabled the managers to understand and feel the world differently. Haiku with their particular structure provide a supportive container to discussions relating to emotions, which forms an important part of the organizational learning literature, surfacing and facilitating dialogue about these issues in a way that other processes may not access so directly.

Poetry, haiku or otherwise, taps into emotions and cognitions that have not yet been articulated explicitly. However, I would not recommend using poetry for all organizational interventions or even recommend that anyone can adopt these methods. The first danger is that using poetry all the time could be viewed as just another 'gimmicky' method and as a consequence the approach could be undermined and cast into that dread place - the 'toolkit' of management consultants. In this study there was clear 'buy in' to trying a different approach that appeared to meet the organizational need to think and work differently. Most managers in the study were unfamiliar and relatively uncomfortable with poetry but prepared to take the risk to engage with it and this was an important dimension to accessing new knowledge. Not all felt overwhelmed by what they produced, but most were able to be surprised and all felt the haiku had initiated new levels of communication and new ideas about the organization and what was important in it. Finally poetry is my passion and bringing poetry and management closer together is one of my principal research interests. However, I remain selective about how and when to introduce poetry to groups that I work with. Further inquiry is recommended in order to continue the development of the contribution poetry can bring to understandings and interpretations of organizational experiences, learning and knowledge and close with a final reflection.

Poetic breezes
Release management insights
More change expected.

REFERENCES

Allee, V. (2000). The value evolution: addressing the larger implications of an intellectual capital and intangibles perspective. *Journal of Intellectual Capital 1*(1), 17-32.

Allee, V. (2003). *The future of knowledge: increasing prosperity through value networks.* Burlington: Butterworth-Heinemann.

Antonacopoulou, E. P., & Gabriel, Y. (2001). Emotion, Learning and Organizational Change: Towards an integration of Psychoanalytic and Other Perspectives. *Journal of Organizational Change Management, 14*(5). 435-451.

Bell, D. (1973). *Coming of Post-industrial Society: A venture in social forecasting.* New York, NY.

Banks, A., & Banks, S. P. (1998). *Fiction and research By Ice or Fire.* Walnut Creek: Sage publications.

Chia, R. (2003). From knowledge creation to the perfection of action: Tao, Basho and pure experience as the ultimate ground of knowing. *Human Relations, 56*(8): 953-981

Chiva, R., & Alegre, J. (2006). Organizational Learning and Organizational Knowledge. Towards the Integration of Two Approaches. *Management Learning 36*(1), 49-68.

Clegg, S. R. (2005). Learning/Becoming/Organizing. *Organization, 12*(2), 147-167.

Coghlan, D., & Brannick, T. (2005). *Doing Action Research in your own Organization.* London: Sage publishers

Collins, H. (2007). Bicycling on the Moon: Collective Tacit Knowledge and Somatic-limit Tacit Knowledge. *Organization Studies, 28*(2), 257-262.

Common, R. (2004). Organizational Learning in a Political environment. *Policy Studies, 25*(1), 35-49

Czarniawska, B. (1998). *A Narrative Approach to Organization Studies.* Thousand Oaks, CA: Sage Publications.

Drucker, P. F. (1968). *The Age of Discontinuity.* New York: Harper and Row

Elkjaer, B. (2004). Organizational Learning. The 'Third Way'. *Management Learning, 35*(4), 419-434.

Fisher, C. D., & Ashkanasy, N. M. (2000). The emerging role of emotions in working life: An introduction. *Journal of Organizational Behavior, 21,* 123-129.

Fenwick, J., & McMillan, J. (2005). Organizational Learning and Public Sector Management: An alternative view. *Public Policy Administration, 20*(3), 42-55.

Fermine, M. (2001). *Snow.* Surrey, UK: Acorn Book Company.

Gabriel, Y. (2000). *Storytelling in Organizations: Facts, Fictions, and Fantasies.* Oxford University Press.

Grisham, G. (2006). Metaphor, poetry, story telling and cross-cultural leadership. *Management Decision, 44*(4), 486-503.

Grisoni, L. (2008). Poetry. In M. Broussine (Ed.), *Creative methods in Organizational Research* (pp. 108-127). London: Sage publications.

Grisoni, L. (2006). *Poetic bridges between Knowledge and Practice.* Art of Management Conference Krakow, Poland 5-8 September 2006.

Grisoni, L., & Kirk P. (2006). Voice, Verse and Va va voom: Iluminating Management processes through Poetry. *Management Decision, 44*(4), 512 -525.

Hatch, M. J., Kostera, M., & Kozminski, A. (2005). *The Three Faces of Leadership: Manager, Artist, Priest.* Oxford: Blackwell Publishing

Hochschild, A. (1983). *The Managed Heart Commercialization of Human Feeling.* Berkeley: The University of California Press.

Jones, M. O., Moore, M. D., & Snyder, R. C. (1988). *Inside Organizations Understanding the Human dimension.* New York: Sage publications.

James, J., & Weir, D. (2006). Special issue on poetry, organization, emotions, management and enterprise – POEME. *Management Decision, 44*(4).

Komumunyakaa, Y. (2001). *Pleasure Dome: New and Collected Poems.* In G. Grisham (2006) *Metaphor, poetry, story telling and cross-cultural leadership', Management Decision, 44*(4), 486-503. Wesleyan University Press, Middletown CT cited.

Kostera, M. (1997). Personal Performatives: Collecting Poetical Definitions of Management. *Organization, 4*(3), 345-353.

Marchant, F. (2005). Night Visions. *New England Journal of Public Policy, 19*(2), 285-295. In G. Grisham (2006). *Metaphor, poetry, story telling and cross-cultural leadership. Management Decision, 44*(4), 486-503.

Nonaka, I. (1994). A dynamic Theory of Organizational Knowledge Creation. *Organization Science, 5*(1), 14-37.

Pio, E. (2005). What's Stopping you? Find out through Haiku. *Workplace Spirituality.* www.workplacespirituality.info/haiku.html. (Accessed 02.02.05)

Reason, P. (2001). Learning and Change through action research. In J. Henry (Ed.), *Creative Management.* London: Sage Publications.

Schon, D. (1985). *The Design Studio.* London: RIBA Publications.

Shaw, P. (2002). *Changing Conversations in Organizations: A complexity Approach to Change.* London: Routledge.

Spender, J. C. (1996). Competitive Advantage form Tacit Knowledge? Unpacking the Concept and Its Strategic Implications. In B. Moingeon & A, Edmondson (Eds.), *Organizational Learning Competitive Advantage*, (pp. 56-73). London: Sage Publications.

Stacey, R. D. (2006). The Science of Complexity: An Alternative Perspective for Strategic Change Processes. In R. MacIntosh *et al* (Eds.), *Complexity and Organizations: Readings and Conversations.* Abingdon: Routledge.

Stacey, R. D. (2005). *Experiencing Emergence in Organizations: Local Interactions and the Emergence of Global Pattern.* Abingdon: Routledge.

Stacey, R. D. (2003). Learning as an Activity of Interdependent People. *The Learning Organization, 10*(6), 325-331.

Strati, A. (1999). *Organization and Aesthetics.* London, Sage publishing.

Sveiby, K. E. (1997). *The new organizational wealth: managing and measuring knowledge-based assets.* San Fransisco: Berrett-Koehler.

Sveiby, K. E. (2001). *A knowledge-based theory of the firm to guide strategy formulation.* Journal of Intellectual Capital, *2*(4), 344-358.

Toffler, A. (1990). *Powershift: knowledge wealth and violence at the edge of the 21st century.* New York: Bantam Books.

Tripp, R. (1996). *Action Inquiry* www.parnetorg/PARchive/docs/tripp_96/ (Accessed 05.05.2007).

Tsoukas, H. (2003). *Handbook of Organizational Knowledge.* London: Blackwell.

Tsoukas, H. (2005). *Complex knowledge: studies of organizational epistemology.* Oxford, UK: Oxford University Press.

Von Krogh, G., Ichijo, J., Nonaka, I., & Ichijo, K. (2000). Enabling Knowledge Creation: How to Unlock the Mystery of Tacit Knowledge and Release the Power of Innovation. Oxford, UK: Oxford University Press.

Weick, K. E. (1991). The Nontraditional Quality of Organizational Learning. *Organization Scienc, 2*(1), 116-123.

Weick, K. E., & Quinn, R. E. (1999). Organizational Change and Development' *Annual Review of Psychology, 50*(1), 361-386.

Whyte, D. (1994). *The Heart Aroused: Poetry and the Preservation of the Soul in Corporate America.* New York: Doubleday.

KEY TERMS

Haiku: Haiku originated in Japan, around the 15th century. It is a specific form of poetry, originally of jesting character, containing seventeen syllables, in three phrases of five-seven-five syllables. It usually presents a moment of heightened awareness in simple imagery, originally using an image from nature. Writing traditional haiku requires a long period of learning, practise and maturity. Modern Haiku are less exacting in their development and use.

Knowledge Creation, Exchange, and Organizational Learning: There are epistemological and ontological differences between approaches to knowledge creation. The definition which this chapter works with follows Chia's (2003) argument that new organizational knowledge can be accessed through exploration of intangible and tacit knowledge and an integration of organizational knowledge. Organizational learning and knowledge exchange are viewed as social constructions which are mutually constitutive and constantly changing. Knowledge creation is an inter-subjective, aesthetic process which is developed through narrative and story telling and in this chapter: poetry.

Poem: http://dictionary.oed.com. A piece of writing or an oral composition, often characterized by a metrical structure, in which the expression of feelings, ideas, etc., is typically given intensity or flavour by distinctive diction, rhythm, imagery, etc.; a composition in poetry or verse. A good poem seems to occupy a space beyond mere words especially when it is used to explore the full range of life's experience. According to Grisham:

"Poetry is by its nature a compressed communication of emotions and concepts that the listener must decompress and interpret. By participating in the process the listener must complete portions of the message, and thereby internalize, absorb, and reconstruct the message." (Grisham 2006:492).

Poetic: http://dictionary.oed.com.

A. (adjective) Composed as poetry; consisting of or written in verse and having the style or character proper to poetry. Making, creative, formative; relating to artistic creation or composition.

B.(noun) The aspect of literary criticism that deals with poetry; the branch of knowledge that deals with the techniques of poetry. The creative principles informing any literary, social or cultural construction, or the theoretical study of these; a theory of form.

In the context of this chapter a **poetic process** is defined as the creation of poems (haiku) from organizational stories: inquiring into their meaning through dialogue for new knowledge creation.

Poetry: http://contemporarylit.about.com/cs/literaryterms/g/poetry.htm. Poetry is an imaginative awareness of experience expressed through meaning, sound, and rhythmic language choices so as to evoke an emotional response. Poetry has been known to employ meter and rhyme, but this is by no means necessary. Poetry is an ancient form that has gone through numerous and drastic reinvention over time. The very nature of poetry as an authentic and individual mode of expression makes it nearly impossible to define.

ENDNOTE

[a] *Renga* is a poem several poets create co-operatively and comprise often up to 100 haiku.

Chapter VIII
Vagueness:
The Role of Language in the Organizing Process of Knowledge Intensive Work

Ester Barinaga
Copenhagen Business School, Denmark

ABSTRACT

"How do we define our project goal?" "How are we going to coordinate our independent national studies?" "Who is responsible for what?" "How are newcomers introduced to the project?" During the first year of co-operation among researchers from a variety of disciplines (labor law, sociology and organizational theory) and countries (Sweden, Spain, The Netherlands, United Kingdom and United States) all efforts went to answer those, apparently simple, questions. Inspired by the late Wittgenstein's ideas on the performative character of language, the chapter follows the process by which an international and multidisciplinary group of researchers agree on a research goal, coordinate their work, distribute responsibilities, and socialize newcomers. That is, the process of organizing knowledge intensive work is approached from a performative view of language.

INTRODUCTION

The last 20 years have seen a growth in interest in the role played by language in the social sciences (Deetz, 1992; Potter & Wetherell, 1987; Silverman, 1993). The linguistic fervour has taken upon organizational studies in the form of critical discourse analysis (Fairclough, 1995; Chia, 2000), conversation analysis (Tulin ,1997; Woodilla, 1998), narrative analysis (Boje, 1991; Czarniawska, 1997), and more recently, textual agency analysis (Cooren, 2000; Cooren, 2004).

Students of organization taking a linguistic approach to the field focus, most often than not, on the referential aspects of language. That is, studies aim at denoting, depicting or revealing a referent outside the actual speech situation – institutionalized discourses (Silverman, 1993, Tienari et al. 2005), prevailing ideologies (for an example see, Barley and Kunda, 1992), accounts from the field (Czarniawska, 1998), a set of representations (for an example, see Van Dijk, 1993), or the rhetorics of power. As Mats Alvesson and Dan Kärreman (2000) argue, these studies represent an incomplete linguistic approach since they focus not so much on language per se as on other phenomena (such as ideas, representations, meanings, etc.).

During the last thirty years, however, philosophers of language have stressed the importance of uncovering the performative aspects of language; that is, how the use of language in a particular situation in a given moment constructs the very situation and the actors engaged in it. Initiated by Austin (1975) and formalized by Searle (1969, 1995), speech act theory shows that talking is not merely about semantics, but about acting and sense-making. In this perspective, language use (in the form of oral or written texts) participates in the construction of social and organizational reality. As Potter argues, analysis of language becomes analysis of what people do with it in particular social settings (Potter, 1997).

The first and most immediate consequence of concentrating on the performative aspects of language is that, since focus is set on performativity, the researcher is suddenly attending to organizing processes. Focus moves away from organizations, the ready-made products of such processes. Instead of static institutions, discourses or ideologies, focus is addressed towards (active) speech acts or language games.

An attempt to move in such direction is made by François Cooren (2000). Trained within the field of communication, Cooren combines speech act theory with Greimas' semio-narrative model to show how narrative structure can help understand organizing. Texts, he contends, participate in the production of organizations.

This chapter is an attempt to bring into focus the performative aspects of language in the organization of knowledge intensive work. Whereas Cooren focuses his analysis on ready-made texts (in the form of memory traces, written documents, or graphical devices) and how these can function as agents that drive the organizing process, I concentrate on the very acts of language use and how these participate in constituting organization. In this way, the chapter aims at contributing to a discussion on how a performative view of language can allow the researcher to follow and interpret such elusive a phenomenon as the process of organising knowledge intensive work. By looking at what actors do with words, what linguistic resources they use in their everyday life, and how these are used through a more or less prolonged period of time, it is possible to give an alternative account of knowledge intensive work.

After presenting the theoretical background of the study, Wittgenstein's performative approach to language, I will show how such an approach can be used to follow and describe the organizing process of knowledge work. The case presented is an international group organizing a broad research collaboration on contingent employment. Empirical material comes from 17 months of participant observation.

THEORETICAL BACKGROUND: FOLLOWING AN ORGANIZING PROCESS

According to the traditional view of language the meaning of a word is the object, physical or mental, pointed out by the word. This is a referential view of language, in which meaning is a one to one relationship where words lie on the side of humans and language, and what they stand for lies on the side of artefacts and non-humans.

Wittgenstein revolted against the previous Augustinus view of language, where words were the mere labels of things (Wittgenstein, 1953, §1).

Whoever defends a referential view of language, Wittgenstein observed, "... has in mind the way in which a child learns such words as 'man', 'sugar', 'table', etc. He does not primarily think of such words as 'today', 'not', 'but', 'perhaps.'" Such a description of language would be incomplete (Wittgenstein, 1958, p.77).

Wittgenstein's criticism of the traditional view of language goes further. Do words just name and designate? Think of statements such as "Fire!," "Out," "Very good" or "I love you." "Are you inclined still to call these words 'names of objects'?" (Wittgenstein, 1953, §27). In fact, as Austin would reply, these words are *doing* very heterogeneous things: warning, ordering, praising or declaring a beautiful feeling. *How To Do Things With Words*, the title of Austin's book, very well illuminates the performative function of language. The meaning of a word is not, as Augustinus thought, an outside reality.

If meaning is not the referent of the outside world, what is the meaning of a word? A common temptation is to answer the question by pointing to the mind, as if meaning, and the understanding of it, were some sort of mental processes, or hidden mechanisms. However, Wittgenstein opposes the idea of a private meaning; a meaning only known by the person who utters the word or sentence. That would be, he compares, as if the person he is playing chess with gives the white king a paper crown, leaving the use of the piece unaltered, but telling Wittgenstein that the crown has a meaning to him which he cannot explain by rules. Wittgenstein replies, "as long as it doesn't alter the use of the piece, it hasn't what I call a meaning" (Wittgenstein, 1958, p. 65). We see that meaning has to do with use. The meaning of a word is not inside our heads, no matter how strongly we may feel it; nor is understanding a mental process.

So far we have seen that the belief in meaning as an object existing in an outside reality, and the belief in meaning as some sort of image existing in our heads are both misleading beliefs. Both beliefs steam from the same mistake: We are looking for the use of a sign, but we look for it as though it were an object *co-existing* with the sign. One of the reasons for this mistake is again that we are looking for a thing corresponding to a substantive.

Still, the question remains unanswered. In fact, in the hands of Wittgenstein, the question "What is the meaning of a word?" transforms into the question "What is an explanation of meaning?" (Wittgenstein, 1958, p.1).

Having transformed the question, the answer indeed sounds trivial. "The meaning of a word is what is explained by the explanation of the meaning" (Wittgenstein, 1953, §560). Yet, what is explained when we explain the meaning of a word? Its use (§ 432), the rules governing the use of the explained word (§81-82). More often than not, we explain the meaning of a word or of an expression by giving examples of various cases where the word is used (§71-75). For instance, to explain the meaning of the term "game," we talk of board games, card games, ball games, Olympic Games and so on; we present a wide variety of instances were the word "game" is used correctly. We would however be unable to put into words what is common to all those uses, because, Wittgenstein notes, there is no single characteristic that is shared by all of them.

Wittgenstein's advice if we want to understand the meaning of a word or expression is to *look and see* how it is used. To study how the meaning of a particular word is understood, Wittgenstein observes how the staging of the word is performed, chases the praxis of its use, analyses the circumstances under which the word is applied and describes the immediate experience surrounding it; that is, he follows the language game in which the word/expression is inserted. He takes us back to ordinary linguistic practices – such as explanations –, which renders meaning public (shared by all speakers of a language) and immanent (accessible to us and surveyable by us). This gives way to consensual action because where an explanation ends, there is agreement about the use of the word in the language of the speakers (ibid, §241).

Bruno Latour has applied Wittgenstein's ideas to his studies of natural scientists. He, however, follows circulating references instead of words and language games. "Circulating reference" is the series of translations of the referent; that is, of the specific natural phenomenon studied by Latour's scientists. To study how natural scientists construct knowledge Latour traces the transformation of a crumb of earth in the Amazons to a scientific journal in France (Latour, 1999, Ch. 2.), or tracks the transformations of rats and chemicals into a scientific article (Latour &Woolgar, 1979). He turns his eyes towards the place indicated by the finger tip; he follows the tiny gesture pointing at the referred thing; he sees the differences, acknowledging the nuances of their use, the circumstances of term-giving and the varying shapes it takes along the process of mutations. "Acts of reference [...] rely not so much on resemblance as on a regulated series of transformations, transmutations and translations" (Latour, 1999, p. 58). Wittgenstein taught us differences; Latour points them to us. Following and deploying the circulating reference is analogous to tracing and describing the language game through which meaning is performed, knowledge is negotiated and the world is organized.

Armed with Wittgenstein's advice, Latour is able to catch the dynamism of the process of knowledge construction. Similarly, I followed the process by which a group of social scientists, diverse in many aspects, developed an understanding of what they were to study and organized a their work. Inspired by Wittgentein's later philosophy and Latour's empirical implementation of it, I follow a circulating reference. My reference, however, is of a different nature than that of Latour's natural scientists. Mine is not tangible in the same sense a crumb of earth, or rats, can be, but as intangible as words and concepts are. My referent is the expression "contingent employment," a phenomenon that the group of researchers studied tried to understand. This helped me select and prioritize among the immense amount of empirical material. More importantly, "contingent employment" became the link across micro-episodes. By following it, and looking at the circumstances of its use, I have been able to see the process through which understanding is developed, knowledge constructed and an international research collaboration organized.

SETTING AND METHOD

General, all-encompassing definitions are often the first step to design international research collaborations. They are the ground block upon which to build the research project and co-ordinate the various national studies. In the case here studied, the countries the definition had to consider were Spain, Sweden, The Netherlands, UK and US. The term to define "contingent employment." Contingent employment however looked slightly different in those countries. For instance, contingent employment could not be used in the Spanish hospitals, while it was a common use in the Swedish ones. Contingent employees had a fix contract at the Swedish intermediaries, while in the US "contingent employment" was not used together with "fix contract." The here and now where the expression "contingent employment" was used varied across geographical realities and thus, to accommodate the abundance of reality our language is doomed to be vague.

To the abundance of reality you can add the variety of perspectives. The circumstances at home of the members of a research collaboration are very seldom the same. In some countries the amount of teaching hours might be burdening whereas in others researchers can dedicate all their time to research. Some might already have matching projects running at home, whereas for others it might be the first research project in the subject. Moreover, not always do all participants come from the same research perspective. In the case of this paper, some were sociologists, some organizational theorists, and still some jurists. Nevertheless, for the sake of comparison across countries, a common perspective is often encouraged in international research collaborations.

Despite the abundance of cases, the vagueness of language, and the variety of research perspectives, how is agreement about what is to be studied and how it is to be studied negotiated? To reach that agreement the group studied could not refer to a common reality. The diversity of the group brought to their discussions a variety of situations and perspectives. Contingent employment looked slightly different in their home countries, and the way to approach the phenomenon varied according to their research disciplines. The realities of group members differed and so did the tools to negotiate their differences (Bruner 1990). In such circumstances, how is a project organized? What does the process leading to some sort of agreement about what counts as knowledge look?

Generation of Empirical Material

Participation in the activities of the actors is as much a way of generating research material as it is getting access to the meaning that situations have for the actors studied (Baszanger & Dodier, 1997). The ethnographical approach elevates the micro-situation, facilitating the researcher in tracing the chain of events. It makes it possible to observe the organizing process prospectively; in the making. Focus is set on the performative aspect.

The concrete characteristics of my field influenced the choice of methods used to generate data. The organizing process I was to follow was fragmented in time, condensed in space and the interacting partners were geographically dispersed. The group came together for the workshops, dissolved after each workshop and regrouped again at the next workshop.

Between workshops group members worked at home and all contact among them was via e-mail or telephone. This meant that if I wanted to follow the group as such, when all members (or most of them) met, I had to participate in every workshop. That turned out to be an advantage: I could register a 17-month long interacting process without long months of participation in the field. I followed the group of researchers wherever they met and took part in all workshop activities. I participated in every work meeting and social event, registered all the meetings and filmed some of them, talked to each group member, took notes frantically, and collected every single document that was written by, or distributed in, the group.

In between workshops group members were geographically dispersed, and thus the contexts in which they mainly worked were inaccessible to me. To compensate for this lack of access, following each workshop I sent an e-mail to every participant asking them to describe their impressions of and reflections on the workshop. "If you took the workshop as a trip, how would you describe your trip?" In this way I got the participants to make sense of the recent workshop from the contexts of their home offices. The diversity of national contexts shone through the personal experiences, giving space to the plurality of voices and accounts coming from the field (Salzer-Mörling, 1998).

Time fragmentation and geographical dispersion had another consequence. How could I observe the interaction process while group members were at home? In addition to the returned e-mails with thoughts and accounts of the last workshop, I got access to the e-mails exchanged among them between the workshops. That gave me the possibility of following the doings of the group while its members were scattered.[a]

Time and Places of the Study

The study began in a hotel room in Uppsala, January 1999. SALTSA, a collaboration between the

Swedish National Institute for Working Life and Sweden's central trade unions, had joined them there to talk about the state of the art concerning working life in Europe. For some of the persons in the hotel room (including myself) it was the first time they met. For others, the second. Following that workshop in Uppsala, others were to come: Marstrand, April 1999; Bath, September that same year; Seville, April 2000. The formal study ended in Bath.

At the workshop in Uppsala the nature of their future co-operation was still unclear. SALTSA only financed their travel and hotel expenses for more or less a year. If they wanted to carry out a long-term international research collaborations, employ research assistants and Ph.D. students, organize conferences, go to other research forums, and get their salary for the coming years, they needed extra funding. It is in Uppsala where this need was evidenced, and where they decided to apply for EU research grants. This is the time span of the study here presented: from the moment they decided to collaborate in a long-term joint research project and apply for EU funds till the day they were awarded those funds. Although I have had contact with the group posterior to the EU acceptance of their research proposal, the study ends with that acceptance. They had agreed on the aim as well as on the organization of their collaboration.

A DIFFICULTY OF AGREEING ON A COMMON GOAL IN KNOWLEDGE INTENSIVE WORK

January 29, 1999, Uppsala, Sweden. Tables have been arranged in the form of a big "U." In the open side of the "U" there is a blackboard and an overhead PROJECTOR. Per stands by the projector. The rest of the group sits around the arranged table. They are all deeply absorbed in an animated discussion.

PER: Until now, we have only talked about the increasing use of contingent employment. But we should try to define what the phenomenon includes and doesn't include.

JOANNE: In the States, contingent employment is a contract of leasing. You lease some employees for a period of time....

PER: But first we have to see what are the phenomena that we're gonna study. And only then we can compare between countries.

ERIK: Maybe we should include seasonal employment

PER: Yes. That could be something to include. Also, another phenomenon to study is the marketization of employment, that is, that the employer buys the employee's services.

ROBERT: Why should we consider that?

PER: In my mind, we are talking about structural change, the way the labour market handles the employment contract.

ROBERT: What about students? We could also include them.

ERIK: Yes. That would be a type of contract with no regularity.

PAAL: Is that your definition of contingent employment? As employment with no regularity, employment you cannot predict? But, if it were so, then you would rule out all seasonal work! Seasonal work means that they go back to the same boss, and thus there is regularity there.

PER: In my mind, it is not contingent employment if it is for instance a boom in the business. On the contrary, there has to be some regularity, 'cause otherwise we don't have any phenomena to study.

CATHERINE: What about outsourcing? Are we including it in the phenomenon?

ROBERT: There's no reason why outsourcing would mean lack of regularity. So you're right not to include it. On the other hand, there is more outsourcing because it is cheaper that way, and it is cheaper because they use contingent employment.

PER: Outsourcing may be a previous form, or maybe a start in the process...

"What is contingent employment?" The first workshop was intended to answer that, apparently simple, question. Still without any vision of what they were to study, the discussion about contingent employment was meant to define an objective for the group; to somehow establish where the group was going and what they were there for.

However, as Wittgenstein very well notes, questions like "What is contingent employment?," "What is X?," "What is the object of thought?" are a chimera. They adopt the form of scientific questions; their answers point to unique, precise, general definitions, definitions that will embrace all possible cases for contingent employment, X or the object of thought. A deeply rooted confusion lies there. Such questions are mere expressions of puzzlement: That which is brought forward by an unclear use of the questioned terms. To clear up the puzzlement, the answers are not to be found in any single rule or criterion of definition. Instead, the answers are to be found by looking at the grammar of those terms. "Contingent employment," "X" and "object of thought" remain vague until their actual uses are observed.

An added difficulty is inherent to the group of researchers studied. The terms used in the researchers' native tongues to refer to "contingent employment" are not always synonymous. Literally, the Swedish *tillfälligt arbete* translates to "temporary work," and so do the Spanish expression *trabajo temporal* and the Dutch term *tijdelijke arbeid*. *Flexibele arbeid*, another common Dutch term, translates to "flexible labor."

Yet "contingent," "temporary" and "flexible" carry different nuances. A quick look in The Merriam-Webster's Collegiate Dictionary[b] gives us the following acceptations for the term "contingent:"

1. likely but not certain to happen. See "possible."
2. not logically necessary; especially. See "empirical."
3. happening by chance or unforeseen causes. Subject to chance or unseen effects. See "unpredictable." Intended for use in circumstances not completely foreseen
4. dependent on or conditioned by something else.
5. not necessitated; determined by free choice. Synonym. See "accidental."

Unpredictable, accidental, possible, conditional – all these significations may lead to temporality, but do not necessarily do so. In any case, the temporary aspect is not stressed. The word "temporary," however, stresses very clearly such an aspect, its definition in the dictionary leaving no room for doubts: "lasting for a limited time." And neither temporality, nor unpredictability or conditionally are nuances associated with the term "flexible" which in turn puts the accent on the "capability to adapt to new, different, or changing requirements."

A single, general definition of "contingent employment" proved, as we will see, troublesome. Not only did their home country situations and their national institutions differ. Equivalent terms in their native languages stressed various aspects of what they took to be the same phenomenon.

Later on in that first workshop, Per suggested the following image as a way of thinking about their phenomenon of interest and go around the problem of definition:

Pointing to the image projected by the overhead, Per announced "this is a proposal for a model of how the relationships between those involved in contingent employment go." The discussion then switched character, becoming more concerned with what should be the focus of study: the organizational level? The employee relationships? Why not the relationship between the trade union and the employer? The final focus of their study is, however, not of interest here.

Figure 1.

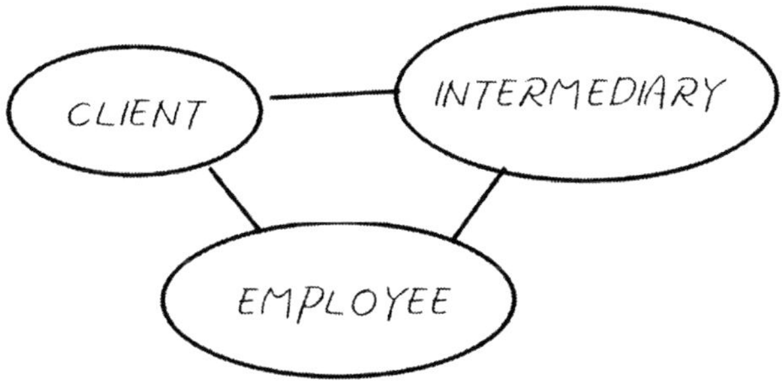

Let us look instead at how that image came to life, and entered the process of organizing the project and coordinating the group.

DEFINING THE GOAL: NEGOTIATING KNOWLEDGE

The vague and evasive nature of the term "contingent employment" was evident to the group from the very beginning. How were they going to consider the phenomenon – statically or dynamically; as a labor market, social or organizational solution to certain circumstances; a conjunctural or structural situation? How did trade unions come in? Besides its puzzling nature, "contingent employment" was an arduous concept to define. Initially, they tried to come up with some sort of criterion telling them when to include, and when not to include a labor relationship under the term "contingent employment." Could such a criterion be the duration of the employment relationship, its regularity, or, maybe, the existence of an intermediary? Rather, shouldn't it be more accurate to pay attention to the reason for the relationship, such as covering sickness, maternity leave or a business pick? There was not any clear-cut defining criterion. "Contingent employment" proved to be a slippery phenomenon that did not let itself be neither caught nor closed into a sharp and narrow definition.

Vacillations being too many, the group started dividing the phenomenon into parts (first named as "employee," "client" and "intermediary") and the relationships among these. In this way, "contingent employment" suddenly took the analytical shape of independent, although related, entities. Analysis, the division of the whole into parts, became the group's way of managing the confusion and vagueness that seemed inherent to their research area. Instead of having a single contourless phenomenon, they had several bordered entities – although bordered only in appearance, as the researchers soon discovered.

Back in the conference room:

JOSÉ: We use two terms: temporary employer and user employer, because the functions of the real, the true employer are shared between the temporary employer and the user employer.

ROBERT: I do not understand that.

JOANNE: Temporary employer is the agency?

JOSÉ: Yes, the agency. Temporary employer and real employer. The intermediary. But the term intermediary has negative connotations in Spain because before 1994 it was forbidden.

PER: An interesting distinction the term 'intermediary' permits including is that between intermediaries, public agencies… – what do you call them? Arbetsförmedling … – and I would also suggest to include recruitment consultants. It could be other kind of institutes and organizations that matches employer-employee together. It does not have to be a temporary agency.

ROBERT: I am just worried that we might get lost with definitions. I thought that what we were saying about labor agency or intermediary was that they would both employ and supply a number of people required by the user. Ok. Now, that is different from the public sector or the recruitment agency, which simply says "We have a number of people in our books and we interview them and you can employ them." That's a normal... there is nothing new about that. What is new, what is structurally different, is then that the agency says, "We will supply you and your company with the people you need and supply it everyday." And that's what is different, the labor supply.

PER: The important is the term 'intermediary' because it is the agent that mediates between employee and user. Then, there are different functions of intermediary. It might be a recruiter consultant which makes the selection, helps the selection process or job search process or something like that. It might be a public work agency which helps the individual to find a job. For example Manpower, which is what we'll call work firm, or temporary work firm, or temporary help industry firm or help service industry... whatever. It needs to be defined. That means if we have the term 'intermediary', it could have different functions and each individual [employee] could have different relationships to their intermediary so there is an industry of intermediaries, which have certain strategies.

PAAL: But I still don't see how the pure recruiters are agencies since they just provide labor, connect people. Nothing to do with contingent labor!

ROBERT: But, but... I think we have to then include these recruitment agencies even if they just do the recruitment. Even if they simply link up people who want jobs with employers who want workers. Is that relevant to the study? My answer would be: it is only relevant to the study if it's then associated with the greater use of contingent labor by the employer, because the employer says, "Ok, I'll give you a job of six months... and I'll do that because I have a constant supply of people coming in. If I didn't have a constant supply then I might want to keep you for a long time." And what I am also saying is that, of course, people like Manpower, Decco, all the big players, play all of these functions.

ERIK: From the beginning we've been discussing how to describe the intermediary. We gave all these different forms, and there are very many different terms to describe intermediaries. That's why we could try to describe them in terms of function. What kind of function does the intermediary have in the labor market in relationship to contingent work?

Having agreed on the entities into which they had divided the wider research phenomenon, the group of researchers faced similar difficulties as before. The "whos" inside the circles were unclear. Who were to be included within the "intermediary"? Selection agencies? Head hunters? Public services? Consultancies? After all, the discussion continued, consultancies worked similarly to intermediaries: they rented out their own employees to work at another company. Who were to be considered under the "employee" label? Students in their summer jobs? Stationary workers? Consultants? If the defining criterion for "contingent employment" was the existence of an intermediary that rented out its employees to another company for a limited period of time, then consultants had to be considered temporary workers. This, however, went against normal use. Consultants were never seen as contingent employees! A similar difficulty lied in who used such type of employees. Along with the vagueness of each "who" came the dubiousness of the relationships among those "whos:" what types of contracts were to be included? Commercial? Labor? Subcontracting of services? Other areas that also remained vague lied outside the analytical-shaped image, such as the role played by trade unions. What seemed to be a sharp image proved to have blurred and diffused contours. Vagueness had moved from the whole to each of its parts. That vagueness manifested itself into a discomfort towards the labels used, a discomfort grounded in the indeterminacy of the terms, which led the group to discuss them over and over. "Employee" transformed into "worker," then "individual," and again into "employee"; "client" changed to "user" having been "employer" in between; "intermediary" remained throughout the research collaboration although not without agitated arguments and much discontent. "Contingent employment" had now a more or less precise form, three-circles joined by three lines, but its meaning (read use) remained vague and open, and so did the meaning of the diagram.

Another salient trait of their particular way of looking at "contingent employment" is its image appearance. The three-circles-three-lines image visualizes a term which, given its slippery nature, had proven to be very hard to put into words. As the popular saying goes... The image allowed them to handle vagueness. It allowed them to get a firm grip on a phenomenon that obstinately remained indefinite. A textual explanation did not provide them with a unified answer to the question of what "contingent employment" was. They could not agree on a wordily explanation. Furnished with an image, however, the group could then deal with vagueness and answer the query.

Meanwhile:

Paal: In practice, it might not be possible to find a coherent definition, but I think we have to understand the types of a new phenomenon. We have a new pattern. Maybe, for definition, we could work with the dichotomy core/periphery: what has moved out to the periphery and what never will.

Per: It's in our interest to broaden up the definition of contingent employment 'cause it enhances the relevance of our work.

Erik: Even more important. With a broad definition, the research can take several perspectives.

Per: Important because if a narrow definition then... It is a methodology for all countries. We'll have to study the same for all countries, which might be absurd. Maybe a country wants to study other specific phenomena... So it's good with as broad a definition as possible.

All in all, maybe it was not a precise definition the researchers were looking for. As long as its form was sharp enough to allow the project to move on, the group was ready to accept, at least for the time being, a representation which remained vague. "Need the ostensive definition itself be understood?" Wittgenstein asks in *The Blue Book* (Wittgenstein, 1958, p.1), to which he answers in a marginal note in *Philosophical Investigations*. "Remember that we sometimes demand definitions for the sake not of their content, but of their form. Our requirement is an architectural one; the definition a kind of ornamental coping that supports nothing" (Wittgenstein, 1953, § 217). The group of researchers simply needed to have some common idea, however vague and imprecise it may have been, as the cornerstone of the research proposal. That is how I understand Wittgenstein's comment. The members would use the image as a building block for the future research collaboration. In other words, without some sort of definition, without a common way of looking at contingent employment, there was nowhere to start the research collaboration. Moreover, a research project with no clear description of its research object would, in the eyes of the EU, not be credible. The three-circle image is thus a practical solution to the managerial dilemma articulated by Stone and Brush (Stone & Brush, 1996): The conflict between the need to use informality and vagueness to gain commitment from diverse interests (in this case, those of all group members), and the need to demonstrate formalization to acquire legitimacy from critical resource suppliers (in this case, the EU funding organ).

During the first workshops the researchers discussed and tried to agree on what "contingent employment" was, and what it was not. They engaged in an intellectual argument, which was meant to settle a working definition that they could use to ground the international collaboration. They needed to agree on a single definition, one they would all build upon in their subsequent national research projects. However, the definition had to be broad enough to permit several perspectives and to allow for the peculiarities of each participating country.

Inherent vagueness, analytic form and image appearance were the three central aspects of the knowledge negotiated by the international group of researchers, a knowledge that would serve as the building block of their collaboration. Although all three characteristics play an important role in how the project came to be organized (Barinaga, 2002), it suffices to keep the three aspects in mind. In what remains, I will concentrate on the process of organizing and coordinating knowledge intensive work.

ORGANIZING KNOWLEDGE WORK AND DISTRIBUTING RESPONSIBILITIES – OR, TWO USES OF THE IMAGE

On June 2nd, three months after the meeting in Marstrand and five months after Uppsala, the final research proposal was submitted to apply for EU funds. Under the introductory section "Understanding Contingent Employment: Contingent Employment and the Labour Market," the text presented the research phenomenonäs background and some literature related to it. It described recent changes in the labour market and suggested possible causes of the increased use of contingent employment. Nowhere, however, did the proposal ever make explicit what they understood with "contingent employment," nor who the term "intermediary" referred to. Next, the text exposes the model on which they would base the project:

That section ended with comments on the consequences of looking at contingent employment through the three-circles image. Mainly, that the relationships between the three actors were considered to be market relationships.

There is nothing remarkable up until this point. In fact, it is quite natural to start a research proposal presenting some background on the phenomenon to study and then proposing a model conceptualising such a phenomenon. What I find interesting comes next, under the section "Project Plan." There knowledge work is structured into work packages,[c] the deadlines of the work packages are settled, and responsibility for the coordination of packages is distributed among the participating countries.

The titles of work packages I, II and VII state very clearly the matter these packages were going to consider. That is nevertheless confirmed later in the separate descriptions of each work package.

Figure 2.

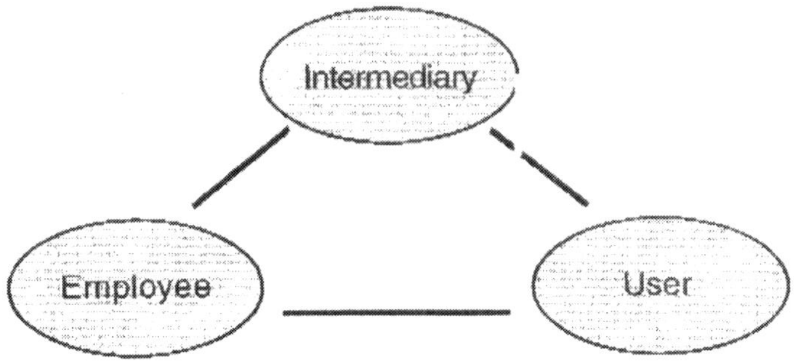

Figure 3. Work package list

No	Work package title	Lead partner No	Person months	Start month	End month	Deliverables
I	Legal, Social and Economic Context of Contingent Employment	1	3	000101	000630	I:1-2
II	The Role of Intermediaries in the Employment Relationship	3	10	000101	020630	II:1-3
III	Contingent Employment in the Health Care Service Sector	1	6	000101	011231	III:1-3
IV	Contingent Employment in the Food Manufacturing Industry	4	6	000701	020630	IV:1-3
V	Contingent Employment in the Financial Industry	2	6	000701	020630	V:1-3
VI	Contingent Employment in the ICT-Industry	5	6	000701	020630	VI:1-3
VII	Implications for European Labour Markets	1	11	010701	021231	VII:1-6
	TOTAL		48		36	23

Work package I concerned the institutional context of each country. Work package II described the intermediary sector and carried out four or five case studies, two of multinational generalist intermediaries and three of more sector specific intermediaries. Work package VII compares and synthesises the findings of the previous work packages. Doubts arise however for work packages III, IV, V and VI, as all that is said in their title is that they are going to study contingent employment in a given sector or industry. However, what aspect of contingent employment are they going to deal with? Are they going to study the three components of their representation in each industry – or only one of them, as in work package II?

Looking closer at the description of these work packages the research proposal maintained that the group would "compare the *use* of contingent employment in the x industry between different countries and its effects on employee relations" (emphasis is mine). Getting down to the activities of the work packages, each included:

Activity 1: Sectoral Overview
Activity 2: *User* Case Study (emphasis is mine)

These work packages referred exclusively to the "user." The distinction among packages III through VI is the "X," the industry where the case study was to be carried out, but in each of them the focus lied on the same actor/component of group's model for conceptualizing contingent employment.

Getting to the point. The three-circles image was used to structure knowledge work into work packages as well as to decide a time limit for those work packages. Work package II was devoted to the "intermediary" component, whereas work packages III, IV, V and VI were consecrated to the "user." The very same analytical division that once helped the group of researchers to represent a concept they could not define was helping them to structure knowledge work. It could almost be said that the three-circles transformed into their *project agenda*, designing stages and setting deadlines.

In addition, the table above also distributed responsibility among group partners for the coordination of the packages. Coordination involved, in their case, being the member that the rest of the group could turn to in case of complications or doubts in any part of the project related to that work package, collecting from all countries the deliverables[d] of that package, and seeing to it that the package deadlines were met. Since the image structured the project into work packages (or areas of knowledge work), and since responsibility for those work packages was distributed among countries, indirectly, the image was used to distribute responsibility for the various areas of knowledge work. Once more, the image was used. This time as an *organisational chart*, telling them who was responsible for what.

SOCIALIZING NEWCOMERS: OR, A THIRD USE OF THE IMAGE

October 1, 1999, 18:30, Bath, UK. Ten months after the first meeting in Uppsala, the research proposal had formally been approved for EU funding, administrative responsibilities for the many work packages had been distributed, Ph.D research had started, addi-tional research assistants had already been recruited, and some countries had even begun interviewing. Some new faces were seen around the table: Laura, Aalbert and Susanne. It is still rainy and grey outside.

PER: One of the important things of this meeting in Bath is building up the groups; putting the people together. That everybody meets and knows each other. I think that is the most important thing of this workshop, to know whom we are going to work with and to talk to. So, it is already decided that the responsible for work package I is me, for work package II is Paal, for work package III is Erik… is that a deal?

ROBERT & OTHERS: Yes

PER: Then tomorrow, we are splitting in smaller groups to discuss the different work packages. In the morning, Robert, Joanne, Laura, Susanne, Aalbert, and me will go to the group discussing work package I…

(Meanwhile, Fredrick notes on the board who will go to what group.)

PER: … and Paal, Catherine, Erik, José and Anne will discuss work package II.

Newcomers were from their very first day placed in a smaller group to discuss one of the work packages. In the previous scene, Laura, Aalbert and Susanne, all new-comers, were included into the group working on work package I; that is, on the legal, social and economic context of contingent employment. From that their first meeting they heard of the intermediary, the user and the employee. That same morning, the other group worked on the intermediary (work package II), whereas in the afternoon both groups worked on the user, one group on the health care sector and the other on the food industry. Newcomers immediately learnt that contingent employment was conceptualised as a phenomenon with three actors. All they heard about and discussed were the terms "user," "intermediary" and "employee;" three specific actors, no less, no more. Trade unions were, for instance, left out of the discussions. At once, they were introduced into looking at contingent employment through the three-circles image.

As we have seen, the image was a representation of what they were to study; a sort of enactment of the field. However, it was also used as a project agenda and an organisational chart. This double character made it ideal to transmit to newcomers the knowledge developed in the course of the various workshops. Laura, Aalbert and Susanne in Bath, and Axel, Felix and Eve in Seville were new to the discussion. Despite their newness, they did not encounter the paralysing vagueness the group of researchers faced at the beginning. They already had a representation, something telling them how to look at contingent employment, even if that something was wordless. They also knew what the structure of the project was and the steps the group was going to take. Even more. They knew who they could turn to if questions arose about a given work package. They knew what to expect and what was expected from them.

Nonaka talks about knowledge creation as a dynamic and ongoing transformation in the form of knowledge (Nonaka, 1994; Nonaka & Takeuchi, 1995), from implicit to explicit and back to implicit. Initially, the researcher group seemed to know what contingent employment was. Even if such knowledge was difficult to verbalise they still could tell what was a case of contingent employment from what was not. After much effort, that tacit knowledge was formalised into an image. What first had the character of a representation, later transformed into a project agenda and an organising device. Knowledge had thus been transformed once again, from explicit into tacit. Finally, by merely fitting into the discussion groups, following the stages of the project and accepting the responsibilities distributed, newcomers slowly absorbed the tacit knowledge embedded in the image, the project design and the organisation of the group. The image worked as a socialising device. It told newcomers how to think about what they were to study, how to study it, how to organize work and who was responsible for what in the coordination of the study.

CONCLUSION

The perspective I propose, a performative view of language that places meaning neither in the mind nor in the world but in the linguistic practices and actions around the use of words, led me headlong into vagueness. The focus on the pragmatics of words, acknowledging the tight twine between words and deeds, talk and action, the meaning of an expression and group interaction, translates into a method that attempts to follow human interaction by following the use of words, closely studying contexts, situations and actions where they are inserted. For the study presented in this chapter I followed the use, by an international group of researchers, of the expression "contingent employment." The contexts, situations and actions into which the expression was inserted varied across countries and disciplines. Contingent employment, the phenomena they were to study, could be defined only vaguely. The aim of the project and the degree of future cooperation had, initially, a vague confine. Individual commitment to the project and the extent of research skills and knowledge in the relevant field were vaguely known.

How was knowledge work organised in that sea of vagueness? Group members proceeded by trying to make sense of the vagueness that paralysed them. In their attempt, they indistinctly used different rationalities or modes of knowledge (Bruner, 1986): analysis and metaphor (images are but a form of metaphor, McCloskey, 1986). Analysis and metaphor were steadily used to cope with vagueness.

Analysis balanced the vagueness of concepts by dividing and categorising them into smaller boxes that were easier to manage. It also balanced the vagueness of the collaboration by structuring it, setting deadlines and distributing responsibilities. Analysis did not reduce vagueness. It made vagueness manageable. Metaphor balanced the vagueness of the core issue by visualising it and by materialising a consensus – a consensus that was not grounded on a unique meaning of "contingent employment" for all group members in all work contexts but on heterogeneity, the acceptance of everyone's peculiarities. The analytical shape of the image permitted structuring the project and organising the group's knowledge work during the meetings. In this sense, the image became the organising rule when group members were together. In short, organising knowledge work proceeded by dividing and visualising.

How did the organising process of knowledge work look in the international research collaboration? It was neither linear, nor circular (which is but a bent sort of linearity). Analysis and metaphor were not strictly used one after another. No ordered sequence was in place. Rather, the two forms of sense-making were tightly braided together

– even interdependent. Without the division of analysis the metaphor could not have been drawn, and vice-versa. Without the visualisation of the metaphor the aim of the project would not have been grasped, and analysis would have had no project to structure. Analysis and metaphor, two forms of structuring knowledge, iterated.

Further, the two organising processes described directed the group to discuss things in smaller groups, it directed them not to ask certain uncomfortable question and to draw instead of theorise. Each group member knew whom to ask what, how to excuse confusion, how to argue the worth of the project, how much was enough and when to take a break. Analysis and metaphor shaped the group's routines and habits. They gave group members a guide for acting, reacting, behaving and speaking; and for not speaking, not asking, not reacting and not acting. They got a regularity for what words to use and how; a regularity reflecting "the way to do things around here," the accepted, the ungrounded, the taken for granted that cannot be justified. It is a form of life, as Wittgenstein might have put it, since it is that regularity that made each researcher a member of a community – the research collaboration.

Analysis and metaphor balanced vagueness by shaping the rules of the game group members were to play together. Analysis and metaphor contributed to the organizing process of the research collaboration and the group's knowledge work. The group of researchers developed language, and inherent to it, a form of life (Wittgenstein, 1953, §9, §23, §241).

Returning to the original debate of this paper. As Cooren has argued, a representational view of language maintains traditional oppositions - those between action and structure, micro and macro, local and global (Cooren, 2001). Assuming a performative view of language and focusing on the active contribution of texts to organizational processes, Cooren manages to bridge the gap between agency and structure (Cooren, 2004). Likewise, the approach in this paper bridges the micro and macro levels by following the chain of micro-episodes that constitute structure.

REFERENCES

Alvesson, M., & Kärreman, D. (2000). Varieties of discourse: On the study of organizations through discourse analysis. *Human Relations*, *53*(9), 1125-1149.

Austin, J. L. (1975). How to do things with words. In J. O. Urmson & M. Sbisà, (Eds.), *The William James Lectures delivered at Harvard University in 1955.* Oxford University Press,.

Barinaga, E. (2002). *Levelling Vagueness – A study of cultural diversity in an international project group.* Stockholm: EFI.

Barley, S., & Kunda, G. (1992). Design and Devotion: Surges of Rational and Normative Ideologies of Control in Managerial Discourse. *Administrative Science Quarterly*, *37*, 363-399.

Baszanger, I., & Dodier, N. (1997). Ethnography. Relating the Part to the Whole. In D. Silverman (Ed.), *Qualitative Research. Theory, Method and Practice* (pp. 8-23). London: SAGE.

Boje, D. M. (1991). The storytelling organization: A study of story performance in an office-supply firm. *Administrative Science Quarterly*, *36*, 106-126.

Bruner, J. (1990). *Acts of Meaning.* Cambridge, Mass: Harvard University Press.

Bruner, J. (1986). *Actual Minds, Possible Worlds Cambridge*. Massachusetts: Harvard University Press.

Chia, R. (2000). Discourse analysis as organizational analysis. *Organization*, *7*(3), 513-518.

Cooren, F. (2000). The organizing property of language. Philadelphia: John Benjamins.

Cooren, F. (2001). Acting and Organizing: How speech acts structure organizational interactions. *Concepts and Transformations*, *6*(3), 275-293.

Cooren, F. (2004). Textual agency: How texts do things in organizational settings. *Organization*, *11*(3), 373-393.

Czarniawska, B. (1998). A Narrative Approach to Organization Studies. Thousand Oaks, CA: Sage.

Czarniawska, B. (1997). Narrating the organization: Dramas of institutional identity. Chicago: University of Chicago Press.

Deetz, S. (2003). Reclaiming the legacy of the linguistic turn. *Organization*, *10*(3), 421-429.

Fairclough, N. (1995). *Critical discourse analysis: The Critical Study of Language*. London: Longman.

Latour, B. (1999). *Pandora's Hope. Essays on the Reality of Science Studies.* Harvard University Press.

Latour, B., & Woolgar, S. (1979). *Laboratory life: the social construction of scientific facts.* Beverly Hills: Sage.

McCloskey, d. N. (1986). *The Rhetoric of Economics.* Brighton: Wreatsheaf Books Ltd.

Nonaka, I., & Takeuchi, H. (1995). *The Knowledge-Creating Company.* New York: Oxford University Press.

Nonaka, I. (1994). A Dynamic Theory of Organizational Knowledge Creation. *Organization Science*, *5*, 14-37.

Potter, J. (1997). Discourse analysis as a way of analysing naturally occurring talk. In D. Silverman (Ed.), *Qualitative research* (pp. 144-160). London: Sage.

Potter, J., & Wetherell, M. (1987). *Discourse and social psychology. Beyond attitudes and behaviour.* London: Sage.

Salzer-Mörling, M. (1998). Murderous Ink: A Case of Rhetorical Killing. *Studies in Cultures, Organizations and Societies*, *4*, 125-145.

Searle, J. R. (1995). *The construction of social reality.* New York: Free Press.

Searle, J. R. (1969). *Speech Acts: An Essay in the Philosophy of Language*. London: Cambridge University Press.

Silverman, D. (1993). *Interpreting qualitative data: Methods for analysing talk, text and interaction*. London: Sage.

Tienari, J., Holgersson, C., Meriläinen, S., & Höök P. (n.d.). *Gender relations and market discourse: the case of gender quotas in the Swedish and Finnish media.*

Tulin, M. F. (1997). Talking organization: Possibilities for conversation analysis in organizational behavior research. *Journal of Management Inquiry*, *6*, 101-119.

Van Dijk, T. (1993). Principles of critical discourse analysis. *Discourse & Society*, *4*, 249-283.

Wittgenstein, L. (1958). *The Blue and Brown Books*. HarperCollins Publishers.

Wittgenstein, L. (1953). *Philosophical Investigations*. G. E. M. Anscombe (transl.). Oxford: Blackwell.

Woodilla, J. (1998). Workplace conversations: The text of organizing. In D. Grant, D., Keenoy, T., & Oswick, C. (Eds.), *Discourse and Organization* (pp. 31-50). London: Sage.

KEY TERMS

Analysis: The term "analysis" comes from the Greek *ana-lyein*: to unloosen, to break up, to divide the whole into its components, breaking up a complex concetp into smaller parts to gain a better understanding.

Circulating Reference: Series of translations and mutations of the referent. Focus is set on the net of transformations.

Language Game: Key term in Ludwig Wittgenstein's later philosophy, which challenges established notions about language. It refers to the linguistic practices around the use of words, pragmatics that determine the meaning of the particular word in the particular situation.

Meaning of a word (in the Performative Perspective): The meaning of a word is understood by how the word is used within their social context; that is, the meaning of a word is given by the function the word plays in the language game of the speakers; it is related to the rules of use of the word.

Metaphor: From the Greek *metaphora*: to transfer. Metaphors talk about how things are, not what they are. More generically, a metaphor is a rhetorical trope that describes a first object/subject as being equal to a second object/subject in some way. Metaphors connect disparate symbols, are shortcut explanations, and cannot be empirically tested.

Performative Perspective of Language: Perspective that focus on how the use of language in a particular situation and in a given moment constructs the very situation and the actors engaged in it.

Referential Perspective on Language: Perspective in which language is a mirror of reality and meaning a one to one relationship between words and the outside world.

ENDNOTES

[a] In her doctoral thesis, Galit Ailon-Souday observes how technologically-mediated communication, such as e-mail and conference calls, are used to manage identity boundaries. With the help of the mute button in conference calls and the addressee selection option in e-mail exchange, participants can be included or excluded in a conversation, narrowing down communication channels and enabling the manipulation of boundaries of identity to a member's own advantage (Ailon-Souday, 2001). In this sense, I might be unaware of whether or not the international researcher group studied took advantage of the e-mail addressee selection option to exclude me from their conversations, drawing a boundary between "us" and "her."

[b] http://www.m-w.com

[c] "Work package" is the terminology imposed by EU requirements when writing a research proposal. It corresponds to a set of activities to carry out within the project. In this way, a project is structured into several work packages, and a work package into several activities.

[d] "Deliverable" is another EU term. It refers to any kind of paper, report or document synthetising the work and the findings of a given part of the research project.

Chapter IX
Tyranny of the Eye?
The Resurgence of the Proto-Alphabetic Sensibility in Contemporary Electronic Modes of Media (PC/Mobile Telephony); and its Significance for the Status of Knowledge

Stephen Sheard
Bradford University, UK

ABSTRACT

In this chapter the author offers an argument towards the resurgence of a proto-alphabetic imagination in electronic and mobile communications. It is suggested that contemporary trends in mobile telephony which encapsulate the earlier advances in PC development are shifting electronic media – not towards a mythic culture of the aural (McLuhan) but towards an admixture of the aural and visual, aslant the controlling trope of the alphabetical. It is argued that this separation of technologies resembles the predecessors of writing technologies of a "proto"-alphabetic nature. This infuses the literature of management with a metaphysical animism, which is redolent of the faded animism, which marked the initial confluence of the pre-alphabetical sensibilities of Eye and Voice in the pre-alphabetic emergence of mankind. This is suggested as a fresh Symbolic form towards which mankind is advancing. The confluence of ideological tensions preceding these developments is traced; including debates as to conflicts of Word and Sacred (Ricoeur); or Postmodern aversion towards contemporary ocular dominance. This debate leads towards an evaluation of the role and significance of kinds of knowledge which underpin our knowledge society and the knowledge which we take to constitute "knowledge management".

INTRODUCTION

In this chapter I examine a range of theories related to the adjustment of technologies and their effects on sensibilities – both ancient and new. The chapter therefore has a historiographic aspect. I especially look at the confluence of mobile telephony and the Internet. I consider the emergence of an alphabetical culture and the deviation from that suggested by both cyberspace and the new technological forms – specifically mobile telephony and the PC. I examine the role of confluences that are pre-alphabetic in nature and how they lead towards a proto-alphabetical sensibility (as I define it), which (I argue) is able to recrudesce in contemporary forms of media (especially cyberspace and internet related prosthetic devices related to mobile telephony)

My aim is to examine the inter-relationship of sensibilities which show a bias towards aural or visual emphasis, and aspects of technology especially that are established by the use of the internet. This leads to a further evaluation of contemporary arguments related to the role of knowledge (alphabetic) primarily and the elements of visual and oral which are composed thereby. I address features of argument which dispose themselves towards particular views towards the pre-alphabetic and its revival (McLuhan and Shlain); theorists who argue for an element of vitality in what I define as proto-alphabetical animism (Davis and Jaynes); I also obtain an evaluation of the postmodern "fix" on the Eye or scopic; evaluating this critically relative to a historiographic sense of development of the conflicting traditions of Eye and Voice.

It has been suggested that a bias exists towards the visual as opposed to the aural, in modern sensibility and that the visual bias can be identified with features such as positivism, objectivism, and modern technologies associated with rationalism; that the post-enlightenment legacy was "to de-carnalize the eye and foreground the perspectival scopic regime" (Burrell, 1998; following Jay, 1994). I aim to refine this thesis and show a more sophisticated narration of the inter-relationship of visual and aural modes of sensibility. Thereby, relative to organizational theories, this chapter moves to challenge the notion that a complete tyranny of the eye obtains in modern management research and that this underpins positivistic and empirical approaches towards management science. Knowledge management might be seen as an exemplar of management science in that respect, in that it adopts an approach which emphasizes the significance of control over the management of knowledge and the adoption of forms of knowledge which are amenable to storage and manipulation. By inference, my view is that knowledge management itself follows the shifts in sensibility which I describe in this chapter, and that those perceptual shifts underpin our treatment and conception of information which causally must be defined as originating in the mind, and hence a feature of the human psyche.

European Electronic commerce and, specifically commerce related towards the use of mobile telephony (in commercial terms: E and M Commerce) is marked by the confluence of visual and auditory technologies; this has resulted in massive investment into areas of telecommunications as phone company's shift towards the inclusion of the Internet within the context of their services. Mobile telephony itself seems to present a variety of technological features: email; games; enhanced visual downloads such as colour photographs. These features have become realized to a significant extent with 3rd generation mobile telephony. By 2003, 2 or 2.5 Generation technologies were main sellers (Budden, FT, January 6, 2003). At that point multimedia made a significant inroad into the personal user market of mobile phones (Hunt, FT, May 15, 2003). A striking feature therefore as between the earliest mobile phones and the newer varieties is the increased sophistication of the service; incorporation of features such as the camera; and integration of Internet activity.

Most of these services have been readily available for some time in computer technology linked to PC based application. The M-commerce miniaturization of these technologies initially fell considerably short of the online experience of a PC but recent mobile technology has gone someway to reduce this gap through clever adaptation of menu and limited screen space. Despite this certain predominant modes of domestic exchange such as the text are less rich as modes of communication than for instance email, but find counterparts in aspects of PC communication such as instant messaging. Nevertheless, increased sophistication of potential use of the mobile phone within the domestic market has proved a feature of the incorporation of multimedia with visual appeal, formerly the province of the PC. A striking feature therefore as between the earliest mobile phones such as WAP,(wireless aided protocol) and the newer varieties is the increased sophistication of the service; incorporation of features such as the camera; and integration of Internet activity.

What can we then make of these advances relative to the contemporary sensibility? The mobile phone is a ubiquitous piece of technology and therefore can lay claim to being a technological innovation which is almost a prosthetic addition to the psyche of many individuals. McLuhan noted that "alphabets transformed acoustic sound into visual terms and by so doing gave "the barbarian or tribal man an eye for an ear" (McLuhan, 1967: 26). As Chia notes, "the interiorization of the technology of phonetic alphabet 'delivered' man (sic) from the magical acoustic world to a world dominated by vision and abstract visual space (Chia, 2001, p13). Does M-Commerce now promise a greater integration of computer mediated and Internet related technology in our daily lives? Prior mobile telephony has emphasized the combination of oral (auditory) and textual (alphabetic) rather than more purely visual stimulus. More advanced mobile technology accompanies the widespread use of computer technology, to emphasise the visual as well as the oral and textual.

Shlain argues that the predominantly visual and therefore feminine sensibility is advanced by predominantly visual computer modes (Shlain, 1998). This in contradistinction to a masculine sensibility ensconced in alphabetical writing with the Phoenician/Canaanite/Grecian confluence of the thought in early-recorded history. It could be suggested that the confluence of visual technology in the form of multimedia, and auditory/alphabetic technology in mobile telephony, is a synthesis of varying modes of technology which shifts the balance away from the alphabetic/visual of the PC towards a greater incorporation of aural information with that type of media, in miniaturized computer representation. How can one read this in terms of a shift in sensibility?

First, the presence of the visual in hand-held multimedia can be said to echo Shlain's suggestion of a pro-visual, pre-Masculinized sensibility (contra Burrell's argument for visual modes as being a feature of post-enlightenment man). However, this visual aspect is incipient in media that is very much also textual and aural (hand-held mobile). There is a sense in which the visual bias of the PC has been redressed by an aural confluence with the mobile telephony.

Second, miniaturization of the computer especially promises the prosthetic extension of computer technology within the self (McLuhan, 1962/1964). Shlain suggests that computers return us towards a pre-alphabetic sensibility which is marked by a fusion of eye and voice in that it represents an admixture of pre-alphabetic technological sensibilities. Contemporary sensibility is clearly post-alphabetic and any "return" to a pre-alphabetical culture can only be a partial feature. So, in the case of the Internet, much navigation is alphabetically mediated despite the visual content which accompanies that navigation. Linkage is via the indexical hypertext links of alphabetical constitution of a hypertext shell (Shields, p177). Hypertext is at the root of the modes of navigation of the Internet and cyberspace. The non-lineal aspect of hypertext – the sense of Internet space as being ordered by a series of leaps or jumps, creates a series of jumps or leaps which "involve a sense of space" and also create a magical effect by conjuring websites through naming (Shields, p176).

Third: the role of the internet relative to these aspects might be clarified, and set against the historical scale which narrates the evolution of sensibilities from pre- to post- alphabetic man/woman. The alphabet represented a considerable simplification of early languages such as hieroglyphics and cuneiform. This simplification led to eventual widespread dissemination (Gutenberg). The Internet is the latest form of that dissemination; it embodies pictorial forms of representation and non-lineal modes of organization as a communication device. It follows the admixture of non-lineal and lineal forms of language expressed in cuneiform; and also, the visual or pictorial features are redolent of the hieroglyphic functions. Hypertext representation especially (being non-lineal) suggests a variation of the predominantly lineal modes of ordering our world (McKnight, 1991).

Mobile telephony integrates the Internet organization to a certain extent but perhaps more seamlessly in our lives than the PC (the aspect of a prosthetic extension of our sensibility). Apart from this quasi-visual/alphabetic extension of the Internet and online experience of navigation, mobile telephony seems to add an array of visual gimmicks to its prior dominance of aural (voice) or alphabetic (text-message) based emphasis of prior applications. It is worth dwelling on the feature of the difference that technology makes if it becomes part of a daily pattern of life. McLuhan argued that technological forms are self-extensions; and that this feature of self-extension becomes a feature of self-intrigue. That men "become fascinated by any extension of themselves in any material other than themselves…" a la Narcissus (McLuhan, 1964, p5). This is a feature of objectification which seems to hold a magical allure.

MOBILE TELEPHONY AND ITS ROLE IN PAST/PRESENT SENSIBILITY

To resume: so far in this chapter we have introduced a discussion of the role of mobile telephony relative towards conjecture relative to the topic of shifts in sensibility. That conjecture has linked with certain authors: Burrell, Shlain, McLuhan. It is suggested that purchase can be gained on the issue of the significance of the introduction of mobile telephony as being an admixture of technological sensibilities. More needs to be said at this stage, about the historical aspect of the emergence of the distinct types of sensibility which have contributed towards the contemporary psyche.

Scanning of writing produces phonetic elucidation which occurs as a form of interiorized patterning. This is a reflexivity that proceeds from "pictures of visual events to symbols of phonetic events" (Jaynes, 1977/1990). This is the reflexivity that we take for granted as *reading*. It is possible to view the alphabetical means of communication as a form of animism:

…just as a Zuni elder might focus her eyes upon a cactus and hear the succulent begin to speak, so do we hear voices pouring out of our printed alphabets. "This is a form of animism that we take for granted, but it is animism nonetheless – as mysterious as a talking stone." Abram, p131, (citing Davis, 1998, p23).

Initially early modes of writing such as cuneiform and hieroglyphics were distinct from the phenomena of auditory expression expressing phonetic sounds. This meant that a disjunction of the visual and auditory worlds was a feature of the pre-alphabetical sensibility. Early writing (cuneiform/hieroglyphics) included signs which symbolized objects but which did not represent a pronunciation of the objects in question (pictographic systems). On this basis, alphabetical writing was the bud of distinct kind of unification of the auditory and visual sensibilities. This conjunction emerged from the early pictograms of Sumeria, and hieroglyphs of Egypt, to reach full expression in the formation of the alphabetic code. The culmination of the alphabetic enterprise may be said to have occurred with the Grecian replacement of vowels for Phoenician guttural stops (Thomas, 1992/1995).

The association has been made between the alphabetical system and the advent of western rationality. This forms a principle plank of the postmodern thesis of authors like Burrell and Chia. However, the alphabet was often used for non-rational purposes from its inception. Thomas notes that alphabetical writings were frequently used in a semi-magical manner and in symbolical and magical modes (an example being the "curse" tablet). Hence it would be a mistake to assume that rationality and the alphabet were identical and consistently rational in their applications in early Grecian culture. Shlain argues that the bias of the alphabet was towards the left-brain and towards patriarchal modes of thinking (contra the earlier emphasis on the visual in societies orientated towards fertility and maternal features of worship).

A precursor of the alphabetic form was the evolution of cuneiform; this may be interpreted as admixtures of mental processes of the brain – right sided in terms of symbolic representation but left-sided in terms of the non-linear arrangement of the marks or ideograms (chiefly used for records of transactions). Innovatory deployment of the cuneiform method occurred in Akkadia, with the invention of phonograms (symbols representing syllables); as Shlain notes: "Cuneiform characters now served two purposes: a single character often represented both the image of the noun and the sound of the word…" (Slain, 1998, p46). Subsequently these types of character were represented in a linear manner; however, as cuneiform is an extensive language (like Chinese), the innovation was confined towards an elite. It is tempting to see in languages like cuneiform the origins of alphabetical literacy but the topic of the origins of the alphabet is fraught with scholarly controversy.[a]

If the alphabet shattered any charmed circle of a magical "tribal" world it was not the world that McLuhan conceived as an orally dominated world of magic ("the Africa Within") but rather an oracular animism that lay as an inherent feature in the confluence of cuneiform and hieroglyphics which influence the formation of the alphabet (above). McLuhan perhaps saw the contest between the cultural aspects of western and non-western civilizations in terms which overlaid the real and earlier transition towards a post-alphabetic man/woman.

This perhaps suggests a refinement of McLuhan's own view.

In summary: literacy has the quality of animism: its origins are occluded in the past – but represent an emergence from pro-visual or symbolic literature with distinct aural and visual content, towards a more abstract media (the alphabet). However, it has been suggested that the computer (PC) by virtue of its creation of a further space (cyberspace) has advanced a pro-visual pre-alphabetic world-view (Shlain). [b] Similarly Burke and Ornstein argue for the computer as a kind of "ultimate Ax", which may "take us back to what we were, mentally, before the axemaker's first gift changed the way our minds got developed and selected…"(Davis, citing Burke and Ornstein, 1995). On this account "icons, associative links (hypertext), virtual spaces, and parallel processing of multimedia computing may resurrect the "arational thinking" of earlier days, a mode of consciousness based on intuition, imaginative leaps, and fuzzy rules of hand." (Davis, 1998, p194).

The implications of these speculations are significant, in the sense that the PC itself is the means by which the data and information flows of an ordered commercial world (E-Commerce) are stratified. Knowledge Management is the theoretical edifice which strides above these forms of sensibility. Viewed as the embodiment of rationalism and a kind of controlling presence; the ordering of knowledge assumes the media which has perceptual implications. If this is the "Cartesian scopic regime in which the individual human being inhabits a uniform, infinite, isotropic space... (in which)... the key sensory device is the eye" (Burrell, 1998, 138); one must ask: what is the status of the visual media (the eye) in advancing a pre or pro-rationalistic sensibility. Shlain and Burke and Ornstein speak of visual media promoting right-brain features, Burrell of the eye in association with the perspectival displacement of the aural and linked to rationalism – which is correct?

In this next section I move towards a further description of the theories of Marshal McLuhan in relation to the other theorists described, before returning to discuss this question – as to the status of a pro-visual media (bearing in mind our caveat that mobile telephony incorporates other media, alphabetic and aural also).

McLUHAN AS A STARTING POINT FOR DISCUSSION

McLuhan saw a reversion from the process of visualization which the alphabetic system has inaugurated in the popular consciousness of mankind (with the printing press). This is of immediate interest to our theme, because it points towards the alphabet as a visual medium. The gradual achievement of the ascendancy of an admixture of the visual and the auditory is marked by the rise of the alphabet (Ong, 1956) and the renaissance attainment of 3-D perspectival forms of thinking is a kind of triumph of western reasoning which began with modes of spatial manipulation exemplified by Euclidean geometry, (Edgerton, 1975; and Burrell, 1998). McLuhan argues that three-dimensional perspective is a "conventionally acquired mode of seeing" (McLuhan, 1962, p17).[c] The dominance of (renaissance) perspective may be seen as a marked break with the pre-alphabetical form of sensibility which separated visual and auditory space; rather, an alphabetical sensibility may be seen to unify them with a left-brain (or rationalistic) emphasis (Shlain, 1988).

McLuhan's conceptualization of the process of pictorialization (acquisition of three-dimensional perspective) may be conceived as the culmination of a process of "detribalisation", or shift from the aural which began with alphabetic literacy. With the advent of the printing press this tendency was instantiated in a more widespread fashion across society, as literacy was increasingly disseminated. McLuhan envisaged that the oncoming forms of "electronic interdependence", would challenge a predominantly visual mental space (in that McLuhan envisaged the interiorization of wireless related "electro-magnetic" media (the radio), as likely to disturb the social psyche). Clearly, McLuhan did not conceive of a PC led visual sensibility or the profound significance of the television either; his vision was in that sense incorrect and did not foresee the future. What was interesting was his method of linking a particular technological development with specific (seemingly unconscious) developing sensibilities. It is not purely that the PC is a visual medium but also that cyberspace as organized on the PC as a pro-visual, non-lineal mode of ordering of cyberspace (hypertext), which attenuates the left-brain bias, towards a closer equation with the more holistic feminine sensibility which is pre-alphabetic (a la Shlain). This feature, which fed into the Canaanite origins of the alphabetical, contains a visual and symbolical element which was distinct from the alignment of sound and meaning.

To recapitulate: we have envisaged a pre-alphabetical culture in which the auditory and the visual were separated. The advent of the alphabet united those two media and that tendency I define as "proto-alphabetic". In this argument, Shlain's position emphasizing the visual as a feature of fresh dominance with the PC is as over-simplistic as McLuhan's emphasis of the aural with the radio; whether PC or radio, both are interdependent for conceptual understanding with the alphabet. We cannot return to pre-alphabetical forms of understanding or sensibility but we may return to those tendencies inimical in those confluences – these *tendencies* I term "proto-alphabetical". We do not see a return to a pre-alphabetical visual culture which separated the auditory from the visual because the alphabet is thoroughly with us. The Internet and its forms are quasi-visual and contain an admixture of the alphabetical.

Developing this argument further: I would argue that we do see an increased parallel between a culture that was emergent as auditory animism ("proto" - alphabetical) and the contemporary influence of cyberspace on the modern mentality (I will expand discussion of that point throughout this chapter). In that respect, the mental space which is cyberspace I conceive as a kind of step back from the total unity of the word and image represented by the alphabetical.

To return to the theme of mobile telephony: the mobile is an even closer synthesis at a prosthetic level of the aural and visual features which are present in the PC (and thereby available as cyberspace).Therefore mobile telephony puts ready to hand and perhaps closer to habit and a perceptual ensemble the forms which are already present in the world of cyberspace; adding the distinct forms of pure alphabetic transfer (texts) and pure visual transfer (pictures) which of course have their counterparts in Internet activity also.

But what is the significance of this element of animism which I have argued is a feature which was inherent within the amalgam of the features of cuneiform and hieroglyphics (above) which preceded the cognitive unity which is the alphabet? This feature fulfills a vital role in this theorization because the animism is the content which exceeds the bounds of language when language forms solidified in the phonetic alphabet. Auditory animism may be said to find an objective correlation with the alphabet.[d] The *book* is therefore both source of the animistic voice and a precise invocation of the words that are read. The alphabet precisely displaces that animism to a confined or defined meaning (an explication of prose in *the book).*In this sense, the alphabetical incorporates the essence of a pre-alphabetical animism which conjecturally attended a "mythic" state of immersion between self and world. Such a state was not lost thereby or erased but sublimated. Recognition of this is vital for an understanding of subsequent conflicts around the nature and value of language. On this theme, Cassirer notes that:

The crucial achievement of every symbolic form lies precisely in the fact that it does not have the limit between I and reality as pre-existent and established for all time but must itself create this limit – and that each fundamental form creates it in a different way...(Cassirer, 1954; cited in Baeten, 1996, 59)[e]

On Cassirer's account, a mythic symbolic form underpins subsequent refinements in consciousness, and is prone to re-occur in some form or another. It is possible to suggest that the forms of cyberspace can be suggested as a mode of subjectivisation of the pro-lineal left brain emphasis on processes of alphabetical influence. One can read "subjectivisation" in this context as a return to the visual or "feminine" if one follows the association between these features at an experiential level (Shlain, 1998). However, it is important to demarcate Cassirer's conception from that of Shlain. We can perhaps speculate that animism is a kind of semantic equivalent to a kind of mythic symbolic form, inchoate within subsequent cognitive development, represented by literacy. My view is that debates as to the status of language may correlate with a perceptual ensemble of changes as the balance shifts between Eye and Voice; a shift to voice is a shift towards a more personal or inner world; a mode of introspection in a sense (as akin to that which Ong described as related to the medieval world).

If alphabetical animism can be suggested as a mode of objectification of auditory animism which had initially no external locus or form of displacement; then the alphabetical pins or fixes an earlier sensibility of animistic disposition. But why should we associate this sensibility with the "mythic"? The association takes strength because of the characteristics of rational equation between meaning and word which is part of the modernist heritage of interpretation of the alphabet. The "mythic" can be conceived as a lack of consciousness of such symbolic form (following Cassirer). Such close equations (symmetry of word with an exact "essence" of meaning), have only recently been challenged, partly through the relativisation of Saussurian linguistics and more extreme forms of emphasis on metonymy in semiotics (post-structuralism). More generally, and in populist terms, we take the precise equation of word and meaning (signified and signifier) to represent a correlation of meaning and representation. The alphabetical underpins a theory of meaning which in western metaphysics gives us the basis of a conception of objective formal interpretation of things and their (locatable) place in our own more rational world order.

Relative to these arguments, the alphabet has become a feature of western rationality (I speak here of the western or phonetic alphabet rather than pictorial languages such as Chinese). It is possible to argue that the aspect of animism was imprisoned within the word, but that the power of the word was a feature of the color and magic of the animistic being spilled as meaning was conveyed from sensibility to sensibility. In this sense, words convey more than they say in precise cognitive terms. As said, the alphabet may be said to resolve the separateness of visual and aural forms of expression unlike proto-alphabetical forms such as hieroglyphics or cuneiform. Letters are at first, of course, visually conceived – though with reading that process becomes a tacit feature of the action of comprehension.

In its increased emphasis on distinct aural and visual modes of communication (in contrast to), mobile telephony in the wake of the PC emphasis non-unified aural/visual forms, alongside their unified partner (the alphabetical qua *the book*). An admixture of the hypertext and the Internet - alongside the deployment of the alphabet (as a mode of ordering in cyberspace) adds to this effect to create an ensemble of technologies. This loosens the alphabetical grip of technological sensibility. This suggests in line with the kind of methodology of reasoning which McLuhan inaugurated that the confluence of PC and mobile telephony is modifying the ratio of technology and our senses; this might be said to represent the emergence of a fresh symbolic form in humanity. Conjecturally, I suggest that this amounts to an element of atavism to a proto-alphabetical culture.

It is I think wrong to call the Internet a shift to a pure visual or "mythic" sensibility of a feminine disposition as opposed to a masculine alphabetical culture (Shlain). This oversimplifies the influence of the pre-alphabetic. These pre-alphabetic forms are no longer held in separateness in our sensibilities though they may be emphasized as so in our conceptions of sensibility, and strict gender equivalence is to my mind a confusion of the governing aspects of the cultures that identified with Eye as opposed to Voice (some of these cultures may have been more akin to goddess worship). Ordered by alphabetical means and navigated from site to site by alphabetic signs; the Internet is nevertheless a pool of rich visual stimulus. Mobile telephony takes of that ordering incompletely in that textual navigation is perhaps less refined (simple hypertext trees as in the case of a PC in many applications), but contemporary advances are mitigating the distance between PC and mobile.

One might ask what the significance of these distinctions is. McLuhan is clearly "dated"; though a novel approach at its time. What does it matter that Shlain's case or Burrell's for that matter, are refined or challenged? What does it mean to say we are in some sense, shifting to a proto-alphabetical sensibility? I think it is important to retain a sense that by moving towards a proto-alphabetical confluence of forms, we are moving as far as we can towards an admixture of sensibilities which is pre-rational – in so far as the creation of phonetic literacy was the inauguration of a rational influence. I argue that it is not possible to move beyond that towards a sensibility which separates eye and voice or which places them in complete antithesis.

IMPLICATIONS OF A PROTO-ALPHABETICAL CULTURE BY CYBERSPACE

At the heart of Shlain's conception it is envisaged the advent of literacy as antagonistic to those cultures of a matriarchal nature in which worship of Goddesses was primary. In other words the "Word" became antithetical to the image. Similar accounts can be found in terms of the opposition of Logos and Bios (Labouvie-Vief, 1994); and in terms of the conflict of the "Word" and the "Sacred" (Ricoeur, 1995). The essence of these accounts is to argue that the alphabetic literacy emerged in conflict with a "mythic" or pro-sacral culture based on the visual or pro-feminine (bios versus logos). One can see later recrudescence of these tensions, for instance at the time of the reformation and the destruction of icons. The rise of monotheism may also be traced to the rise of the alphabetical; as the idea of an abstract monotheistic god became thinkable in the mental space increasingly dominated by abstract and lineal modes of thinking of western reason (Burke & Ornstein, 1995; and Davis, 1998, p29, citing Porush). What I define as "tensions" here are perceptual revenants of earlier societal conflict related to the emphasis placed on pro-visual as opposed to pro-aural sensibilities; the breaking of the golden calf by the Hebrew is such a tension (bible); its modern equivalent is the castigation of the Ocular (postmodern theorization). It is interesting as to "why" word and image or Eye and Voice became principle themes of tension; it infers a kind of synaesthetic or bodily-led determinism of ideological conflicts within mankind, but this has to be a mode of speculative reasoning as to the causal features of this "conflict."

Whereas mythic cultures have observed a tradition of oral narrative, (for instance the Homeric); an emphasis on a visual representation of the auditory shifts that display into an exterior form (the alphabetical). Writing becomes a spatial analogue for a process that previously occurred as a process of interiorization. I have described this spatial analogue in terms of an objective correlate of the element of aural animism. Systems such as cuneiform represent a shift towards a linear mode of representation but still embed non-lineal elements of representation (Shlain, 1998, p46). I would suggest that hypertext becomes a kind of infrastructure for shifting the alphabetical towards an amalgam via cyberspace with technology which is more iconic or symbolic and also mixed with pure visual/aural communications. The skeletal forms of hypertext may be largely embedded or become discrete within contemporary PC programs. Therefore, the hypertext arrangement is only partially registered as a perceptual ensemble relative to the Internet browser and in this respect has a tacit dimension which aids the prosthetic feature in mobile telephony. [f]

It is possible to suggest that the pro-visual element in contemporary Internet and Mobile telephony introduce partly via the visual features associated with cyberspace – a fragmenting of the auditory animism. The objective correlate is no longer the alphabetic pure but an amalgam of visual and iconic modes alongside the alphabetic structures. As far as this proto-alphabetical sensibility is concerned - what I think we can say is that the visual and the auditory are distinct forms. One of the features we have noted is the tendency of authors to view the visual and aural as in tension (McLuhan and Shlain), or view the traditions of word and sacred as in conflict (Ricoeur, 1995). The postmodern OS case (for instance Burrell, 1998 but also Chia) tend to follow that kind of dichotomy, but adapts it towards a case synonymous with post-structural challenges towards the equivalence of "truth" essences and language formation:

...from this commitment to a becoming ontology (his process metaphysics derived from White-head/Bergson)... it follows that language, and in particular the activities of naming and symbolic representation, provide the first ordering impulse for the systematic fixing and structuring of our human lifeworld. Language, and in particular the alphabetic system, are technologies of organization that help us portion off, fix, locate and represent different aspects of our phenomenal experiences from ourselves. They do not, in any way, mirror the going-on's in the world. Post-modernists therefore reject the kind of representationalist epistemology championed by modern science. Chia, 2003, 128-129

It is not my purpose to examine the role of process metaphysics in too great a detail in this chapter,[g] however, it is important to note that the adherence towards Bergson's dualist phenomenology represents a belief in an inaccessible inner world (that of duree) which cleaves the extrinsic visual world from that of the inner phenomenology of the individual. Similarly language is seen as having a visual form which is distinct from the sounds heard; in this respect it is argued that "the sound heard and word which is seen are distinctly different experiences". The semantic unity of meaning is not focused on, rather that "the phonetic alphabet, as a system of communication, works by breaking up the seamless flow of speech into arbitrary consonants and individual word syllables..." (Chia, 2003, 113). The emphasis therefore is akin to that described by Burrell as rendering in two dimensions (visually) a three dimensional world. Language as typified in the alphabet is viewed as a mode of declension from a pristine state (spelt out in terms of phenomenology rather than the symbolic form of "myth" a la Cassirer it may be noted).

What is then interesting, following this – is how one would typify the modes of ordering of information accomplished in modern society. The kind of information which is captured in the processes of tabulation occasioned by Intellectual Capital processes as a function of contemporary knowledge management/manipulation is refined and rationally orientated in nature. This is the word drained of its animistic power, or so it seems. The knowledge is depersonalized. To the postmodern analysis (as represented by Chia and Burrell) the emphasis is on the forms of language as a mode of ratiocination which is an impoverishment of the full human experience (or its potentiality). The emphasis is on the organization as a function of an illusory stability; as Clegg notes: "paradoxically, the seemingly solid elements and structures are characterized by their immanent instability..." (Clegg, 2005, 60). The view is one in which the emphasis on the ocular is a form of "division" of over-determination of elements into entitative and controllable form (Cooper, 1989). Of course, as noted, this is not the place to exhaustively dwell on these theses, but it is notable that they emphasize an inner private world; one which is excoriated from the processes of knowledge formation and reformation as amenable to the processes of contemporary capitalism. It is therefore possible to operate a perception of the broadly "postmodern" ideas summarized here as compatible with a view of language as essentially an imposition, and unlike the natural order.

ORIGINS OF DUALISM AND THE NOTION OF LANGUAGE AS ALIEN OR ENTITATIVE

It is possible to argue that the left-brain-orientated processes (the word/alphabetic literacy) create a sense of detachment from reality. The correlation which Chia (and others) establishes between language and its alien or entitative aspect, inclined to encapsulate and somehow diminish the experience of reality in a further sense, is expressed elsewhere. Davis notes that:

"The singular self-knowledge sought by the Gnostic, which reveals the self to belong to a transcendent order estranged from the mundane world, can be seen partly as a Platonic by-product of the phenomenology of alphabetic reading, whose artificial shapes are essentially alien to the natural order... (Davis, 1998, p98).

Davis essentially suggests that the Gnostic movement encouraged towards a dualistic sensibility by the advent of alphabetic reading. Hence the alphabetical animism may locate or "fix" the auditory animism which is a feature of a sensibility which cleaves aural and visual aspects of experience. This feature of cleavage was emergent but not salient in the early writing technologies (hieroglyphics or cuneiform). The objective sense (locus) which creates the written word comes at a price. Another theorist, Jaynes, notes that the progression of literacy towards cuneiform and more advanced forms of literacy especially was partially responsible for a breakdown in the sensibility he terms "bicameral", but which we might alternately correlate with the "mythic" sensibility.

...the input to the divine hallucinatory aspect of the bicameral mind was auditory. It used cortical areas more closely connected to the auditory parts of the brain. At once the word of god was silent, written on dumb clay tablets or incised into speechless stone, the god's commands or king's directives could be turned to or avoided by one's own efforts in a way that auditory hallucinations could never be. (Jaynes, 1977/1990, p208).

The book (alphabetic literacy) is a mode of excising the auditory compulsions, which Jaynes argues – governed pre-literate man. *The book* objectively displaces these compulsions. Literacy creates the presence of an extrinsic locus that transmutes the animistic influence which is the legacy of the bicameral sensibility. Hence, one now hears the voice of God from the book (Hebraic tradition) rather than the stones or trees; the gods have retreated with the advent of monotheism – away from a mythic integration with nature (pantheism) towards *the book*. It is possible to describe Cyberspace as a form of atavism – and is the confluence of new technologies inclined towards a proto-alphabetic form but not purely by virtue of a pro-visual component (as Shlain suggests), nor by virtue of a revival of "mythic-aurality" (McLuhan). I have elsewhere described perspectives which interpret the forms and symbolism of cyberspace in terms of mythic avatars.[h] McLuhan (following Carothers) notes that "phonetic writing split apart thought and action" and that from the advent of literacy the "tribal" man became schizophrenic. In contrast to Jaynes; who perceives schizophrenia as the maladjustment of a mythic or bicameral sensibility in post-bicameral society; McLuhan conceives of the departure from a pre-literate aural state as being a function of technological advance. Jaynes might be said to conceive of the departure from bicamerality as a physiological shift which resulted in a change of relationship leading to alphabetic literacy (ideological stance).

Conjecturally, one can note that these theories focus in their different ways on the evolution of consciousness – alphabetic literacy becomes the archetypal knowledge management – the progenitor of subsequent modes of management which are functions of organization throughout civilized history. It can be seen that different values or ideologies view the touchstone of that development as either a progression (for instance Cassirer or Jaynes) or a kind of mute but unacknowledged declension (we have cited the cases of postmodern theorists of contemporary organizational theory); regardless of their emphasis, they tend to recreate the context of language transformation and its subsequent dominance in terms of their respective ideologies.

To summarize: it could be argued that the unconscious animism which Davis mentions as occurring in the act of reading, or the sense of separateness which Havelok describes as occurring with the advent of the book – are all forms of transmutation of an ancient state. That "ancient state" might also be viewed as in intrinsic state which is thereby in an important sense thereby no longer ancient as contemporary and continuing (Bergsonian dualism as informing phenomenology). In terms of the parlance of Jaynes: *The book* becomes a surrogate form of the prior experiential state of auditory hallucination (which Jaynes links to bicamerality). In other words, an ancient animism becomes refined and to some extent suppressed with the alphabetic mode of depiction. On this account, the left-brain modes of dominance are therefore a further working on their objectified mode of thinking (the *book),* whose nature is to indirectly express an ancient animism – from which "we hear voices pouring out of our printed alphabets" (Abram, in Davis, 1998). Such a working is the conscious evolution of technological advance, which meld visualist and aural media (in separateness) with their (relatively) unified form (the alphabetical).

Whereas the evolution of literacy may be viewed as a form of suppression of a tendency towards an auditory compulsion (Davis) or possession (Jaynes); that same suppression of animism may be viewed as an aspect of the impossibility of language as achieving coeval expression with essence (post-structural approaches) and that in turn interestingly relates at the level of identity towards the dualism incipient in the views of certain forms of phenomenology which have informed contemporary organization studies via the ideologies of "postmodernism". The fire or flare of the nature of language I have suggested, takes of the ancient roots of language (defined for instance by Davis in terms of animism). Language obviously takes a visual form but each word chimes with a resonance which semantic form can barely encapsulate. As form and content press against each other, so these opposing tendencies can be read in terms of cruder ideologies as either the power of the voice or auditory possession or the worship of the image (Jaynes); hence the tension of monotheistic and polytheistic forms of worship in western society (see above).

The significance of the proto-alphabetical and cyberspace is the extension of these tendencies, and more overt conceptual discussion following those tensions of sensibility – for example in theoretic or philosophical terms. Language in that sense is a forum for continuing debate relative to what it reveals and conceals. Mobile telephony mirrors these tendencies in part; it is kind of epiphenomena of perceptual changes extrinsically located in technology which is so prosthetic as to lack that element of detachment which is inferred by an artifact. Such advances incorporate older tendencies towards the aural mode of communication more purely than the PC but the chief significance lies in their seamless proximity with daily life. All these advances are held or checked within the power of language (the alphabet). That is a visual and oral power to the extent that these cannot be other than conceptually regarded in separateness; they are not experientially so.

It is on that significance and the interpretation of that, which this account has led. I argue that even when relatively "anemic" or literal, language retains the power of the element of animism incorporated therein. That cyberspace is in one sense a feature of control of communication of tamed information (in the mode of knowledge which is "managed") and in that sense a feature of technocratic advance; but that this is the use to which technology is put and the visual per se is not a feature which ought to be viewed in a negative manner as a mode of fetishization which has accompanied the mode of rationalization (as in the postmodern thesis, Burrell, 1998, etc). Rather, the visual is an inimical mode of conveying the dynamism of the voice.

VISUALISM AND CYBERSPACE

It might be tentatively suggested that the sense of the cyber-self as a separate entity is an ontological embodiment of the development of the sense of space which is evolved with the Internet. In this context we might consider the suggestion of Cyberspace as kind of alternate realm. In this case we are conceiving very much of Cyberspace as an aspect of being, very much like the reflection of the self in the pool which Narcissus found – rather than a theatre of action. It has been stressed that Cyberspace – deploys itself as activities on the Internet which show varying biases towards visual and oral engagement in some admixture.

It is possible to conceive of Cyberspace in terms of a metaphysical entity (pro-holistic) or as a theatre for action - but not easily both. But, the realm of metaphors, Shields argues – tends to misrepresent the actuality of the experience of "going online" and that cyberspace itself is something of a popular trope, aligning itself to a quasi-Platonic conception of cyberspace as a separate space or world. In this sense: "cyberspace returns us to a dualistic theater of reality..."(Wertheim, 1998, p227); this is a feature of quasi-rhetorical status. "Space" in this context is a pro-visualist metaphor, and one in which we have taught ourselves to think. Ong notes, we have an "immeasurably greater exploitation today of visualist metaphors and of imagery which in one way or another admits of diagrammatic analysis (Ong, 1956, p231). His theme - the quantification of mental logic in visual terms - argues a shift in social psychology towards a culture, which displaced mental forms towards visualist media.

An associated feature was the tendency to systematize that transition - which amounts to a mode of apperception. Such systematization might be said to take the form of "a free-floating "virtual-eye" roving in space" (Wertheim, 1998, p115) - and precursor of Galilean and Cartesian approaches to science. The rise of rationality may have attuned itself to such developments, but also refined its applications - so that an inner mental enquiry (res cogitans) was facilitated in something very much like the blankness or two dimensionality of a more aurally disposed world; whereas the carving of scientific space - of matter - proceeded in systematic form (res extensa). On this account the mind comes to "contain knowledge" as the "whole intellectual world goes hollow" (Ong, 1956). Letterpress printing is argued to give permanence to sound – "transmuting it more perfectly into silence, a technique for fixing the words in space more adroitly than ever before" (Ong, 1956, p228). The sense of the book as both animistic voice and displaced aural hallucination (Jaynes/Davis) is rendered a popular rather than select medium. The pro-visualist emergence which Ong suggests is towards the mind as container but also within the context of the popularization and technologization of alphabetical forms which despite the advent of the alphabetical media in BC had never really seized popular consciousness. The visualist evolution and grip of space in the renaissance was fast affecting the whole of culture and not just a minority. Ong's pro-visualist sensibility presents a new orientation in which one no longer holds converse with oneself – a dialogic state but one in which one thinks of what is in "one's mind". A step towards the dilution of the post-renaissance visualist state is permitted by virtue of a dislocated space (Cyberspace) which allows a dialogic second-self (the cyber-self). Its rhetoric dominated by the tropes of space; they pervade the conception of Internet related tropes, which can be said to influence commercial literature also.

CONCLUSION

It is suggested that the shift towards the increased emphasis of the visual in the admixture of visual/pictorial/alphabetic in the Internet takes us one step back from the alphabetic towards the pro-visual cultures which were pre-alphabetical; towards the state in which auditory compulsion was a feature of the separateness of visual and auditory senses. This I have defined in terms of its proto-alphabetical nature, in contradistinction to other theorists (Shlain/McLuhan) who have followed this mode of analysis.

Jaynes argued that the ancient sensibility was bedeviled by auditory hallucinations which forms of writing exerted a force towards breaking the left-brain from the thrall of the right (bicamerality thesis). The right brain is not purely pro-visual but also the domain of intuition; its commands to act may be said to be executed by the left brain as a feature of logic and deduction. The sense that one can suspend action or choose not to obey such precepts is an important feature of modern consciousness. The book was a form of exorcism of auditory compulsion, whereas the Internet renders plastic and malleable the book – rather like the melting clocks of a Dali landscape. In this new forum the demon of auditory compulsion writhes a little less fixedly. This is the role I have given to the phenomena of cyberspace; which adds a feature to the prosthetic advance of the mobile; via the conduit of a hand-held PC (in effect).

In this sense Cyberspace maybe viewed as further acquisitive of the self in a manner which the modes of alphabetical union of the visual and auditory represented in the alphabet, are not. As *the book* is a surrogate form of the auditory hallucination which Jaynes suggested beset the pre-alphabetical consciousness, so the fluid *book* (the Internet) which is not purely at our desks (computer) but by our ears and hands (mobiles which encapsulate cyberspace) may be suggested as further devouring of our consciousness. It might be noted that the Internet and Cyberspace is a product of a consciousness which is emerging from an age of unconscious (if the ancient pre-literate state maybe said to be that). The products of left-brain consciousness dispossess themselves of the awareness of man and distance that awareness in objectified media. *The book* is perhaps the start of that process. We are then met with a dilemma; the dissemination of the products of consciousness – the book, the Internet – lead towards a diminution of self-awareness in that they are prosthetic removals of consciousness from self towards other "containers."

The conflict characterized by Ricoeur as a tension between the Word and the Sacred symbolize the polar forces which will always move to pull language apart from its alphabetical moorings. It might be speculated that the status of knowledge takes from the status of language on this equation; and that knowledge management is a vehicle for the shift towards the retention of the cognitive anchor which holds consciousness within the sway of the left-brain (cognitive dimension). "Knowledge Management" can be interpreted as being the emergence of communication as language; and the latest contemporary variant of that – knowledge management as an ideological organizational feature of capitalist economy, is perhaps purely a bud on a greater tree. Cyberspace might then be said to express a dual function; at once shifting sensibility (including in prosthetic mobile forms) away from post-alphabetic consciousness, but also the medium for the exploitation of the modes of dominance suggested by that consciousness – of which knowledge management is an expression within contemporary capitalist society.

So, the cyberspace prosthetics suggest a modified hermeneutic between the self and the book; it is a relationship which shifts more closely towards the proto-alphabetical visual phenomenology of being in which voice and eye were melded towards unity in alphabetic communication. The cyberspace experience may therefore be said to be a moderate form of disruption of pro-conscious modes of activity; visual and aural experience becomes layered akin to its confluences which led towards the unity of alphabetic seizure. This does not bring about the tyranny of the eye or that ancient tyranny of the voice, features which arguably accompanied pre-alphabetical man (Jaynes/Davis), but it does represent the partial elision of the alphabetical modes of seizure of consciousness. The Internet is then like the pool of Narcissus – it holds the self at one remove by the eye; and thence devours of the consciousness. One might say that in the eye of the pool the voice becomes freer, more elastic. But, the frame of the pool is language.

REFERENCES

Abram, D. (1996). *The Spell of the Sensuous.* New York: Pantheon Press.

Baeten, E. M. (1996). The Magic Mirror: Myth's Abiding Power. *Suny series in the Philosophy of the Social Sciences.* New York Press.

Bergson, H. (2001). *Time and Free Will: An essay on the immediate Data of Consciousness.* Dover Publications (ISBN: 0480417670).

Budden, R. (January 6, 2003). Life for 3 G without Killer Application. *Financial Times.*

Burke, J., & Ornstein, R. (1995/1997). *The Axemaker's Gift: Technology's Capture and Control of Our Minds and Culture.* New York: Penguin Putnam.

Burrell, G. (1998). Linearity, control and Death. In D. Grant, T. Keenoy, & C. Oswick (Eds), *Discourse and Organization.* In London: Sage.

Chia, R. (1992). Foundations of Management Knowledge: Assumptions and Limitations. Paper number 01/ 04, University of Exeter paper series.

Chia, R. (2003). Organization Theory as a Post-modern Science. In H. Tsoukas & C. Knudsen, (Eds.), *The Oxford Handbook of Organization Theory: Meta-theoretical Pespectives* (pp. 113-143). Oxford: Oxford University Press (2005 paperback edition).

Clegg, R. S., Kornberger, M., & Rhodes, C. (2005). (referred to as Clegg, 2005). Learning/Becoming/ Organizing. Organization, *12*(2), 147-167.

Cooper, R. (1989). The visibility of the Social Sciences. In M. C. Jackson, P. Keys, & S. A. Cropper (Eds.), *Operational Research and the Social Sciences* (pp. 51-57). New York and London: Plenum Press.

Cooper, R. (1992). Formal Organization as Representation: Remote Control, Displacement and Abbreviation. In J. Hassard & D. Pym (1990, reprinted 1992), (Eds.), *Theory and Philosophy of Organizations.* London: Routledge.

Davis, E. (1998). *TechGnosis: Myth, Magic and Mysticism in the age of Information.* New York: Harmony Books, Crown Publishers.

Drucker, J. (1999). *The Alphabetic Labyrinth: the letters in History and Imagination.* London: Thames and Hudson.

Edgerton Jr., S. Y. (1975). *The Renaissance Rediscovery of Linear Perspective.* New York: Icon Editions, Harper and Row.

Gombrich, E. H. (1960). *Art and Illusion.* New York: Pantheon Books, Bollinger Series xxxc. 5.

Havelok, E. A. (n.d.). *The Muse Learns to Write; Reflections on Orality and Literacy from Antiquity to the Present.* New Haven, USA: Yale University Press.

Hunt, B. (May 15, 2002). Multimedia Messaging: Operators hope for Many Happy Returns. *Financial Times.*

Jaynes, J. (1976, reprinted 1991). *The Origin of Consciousness in the breakdown of the Bicameral Mind.* London: Penguin.

Labouvie-Vief, G. (1994). *Psyche and Eros: Mind and Gender in the Life Course*. New York: Cambridge University Press.

McKnight, C., Dillon, A., & Richardson, J. (1991). *Hypertext in Context.* Cambridge: Cambridge University Press.

McLuhan, M. (1962 reprinted 1967). *The Gutenberg Galaxy: The making of Typographic Man.* London: Routledge and Kegan Paul.

McLuhan, M. (1964). *Understanding Media: The extensions of Man.* McGraw-Hill, Toronto.

McLuhan, M. (1969). *Counter Blast.* Toronto: McClelland and Stewart.

Ong, W. (1956). System, Space, and Intellect in Renaissance Symbolism. Bibliotheque d' Humanisme et Renaissance, no. 18, (pp. 222-239).

Pirenne, M. H. (1964). The Scientific Basis for Leonardo Da Vinci's Theory of Perspective. *The British Journal for the Philosophy of Science, 3* (1952-1953), 169-185.

Ricoeur, P. (1995). Manifestation and Proclamation. In D. M. Pellauer (trans.) & I Wallace (Ed.), *Figuring the Sacred.* U.S.A.: Fortress Press.

Shields, R. (n.d.). The Ethic of the Index and its space-time effects. (details of paper not known at this point).

Shlain, L, (1998). *The Alphabet versus the Goddess: Male Words and Female Images.* London: Allen Lane, The Penguin Press.

Thomas, R. (1992/1995). *Literacy and Orality in Ancient Greece.* Cambridge, England: Cambridge University Press.

Wertheim, M. (1999). *The Pearly Gates of Cyberspace: A history of space from Dante to the Internet.* England: Little Brown and Company, Virago Press.

KEY TERMS

The Book: Literacy and the written word; the book ensconces the new alphabetical media in a fixed creation. The book embodies the transmogrified animism which was previously separate to the written media and in the sense that the alphabet unifies or reconciles pre-alphabetic modes of literacy with conflicting visual or oral emphasis, the book represents the culmination of the proto-alphabetical in those "technologies" – representing a shift in sensibility.

Alphabetic sensibilities of Eye and Voice: Expressing the twin poles of human sensibility which modes of pre-alphabetic expression were torn between; now reconciled in language of a Hebraic nature (in terms of origin). The "Eye" expresses pro-visual tendencies, whereas the "Voice" pro-aural tendencies. Within the context of their enclosure within the alphabetical media, these sensibilities are to some extent reconciled and unified but nevertheless pull in opposite directions, in consistency with their ancient roots.

Animism: The alphabet maybe viewed as a form of animism; words on a page speak as one reads. This is viewed as originating in a pre-auditory animism which became expressed in media with distinct aural and visual content (cuneiform and hieroglyphics), and thence fed into the evolution of literacy as represented in the alphabet. Animism is viewed as a vital force contained within language; partly sublimated by the forms of rational description but nevertheless containing the embers of an earlier pre-alphabetical mental seizure of the mind by voices perceived in separateness in nature; now harnessed to the "book".

Bicamerality: Julian Jaynes coined this phrase to express the view that Ancient man was originally possessed of a dual-mind; expressed in modern parlance by the heritage of both compulsive belief (faith) and, schizophrenia. Schizophrenia in that sense is the certainty of faith without the external and verifiable personal locus of societal reinforcement in one's convictions. Bicameral society broke down when the brain evolved so as to link the separate halves; thereby freeing humanity from the thrall of "external voices" which had the force of auditory compulsion. This compulsion can be associated also with external location of voices within nature or human edifices such as the statues of gods.

E and M Commerce: "Electronic" as distinct from "Mobile" Commerce. Electronic Commerce is a generic term for modes of electronic communication; I use in the specific sense of the Internet. M-Commerce is used to describe recent advances in mobile telephony which may also include internet access but in a miniaturized and hand-held form. Both terms may also be detached from the term "commerce" in the sense that they can become features of everyday life (prosthetic extensions of sensibility) but also linking humanity to the capitalist and consumer societies.

Knowledge Management: Knowledge underpinning a knowledge society: expressing itself within management science as a methodology of a positivistic nature with empirical forms of evidence highlighted. Related as a practice to the storage, codification and regulation of knowledge and, closely linked to modes of societal regulation, control and governing meta-ideologies, especially rationality. Alphabetic literacy is viewed as a mode of knowledge management at a more fundamental level, than that ensconced in recent management literature; in that respect "knowledge management" is also viewed as a mode of development in human sensibility as well as an ideology.

Pre/Proto-Alphabetic Technologies: A pre-alphabetic technology expresses the types of writing technologies which existed prior to the amalgam of visual and oral tendencies within early forms of writing, within the early alphabet. This expressed as the Hebraic alphabet which incorporated the deployment of Phoenician/Canaanite/Grecian confluence of the thought in early-recorded history. The replacement of vowels for Phoenician guttural stops (Thomas, 1992/1995); marks a key-point in this development.

Process Metaphysics: A kind of approach to matter and ontology which emphasizes "flow" rather than permanence and can be traced ultimately back to the contrast between the writings of Heraclitus as opposed to those of Democritus, in early Greek Philosophy. The writings of both Bergson and Whitehead are therefore said to express this emphasis on flow and on the transient status of reality, in the case of Bergson linked to the belief that a further state known as "duree" is overlaid by our rational conceptions and that this represents a truer conception of reality, and hence becomes the basis for his ontology. Certain postmodern theorists follow these beliefs (example: Robert Chia).

Symbolic Form: Ernst Cassirer used this term to express distinct stages of human evolution represented by different modes of belief. They "mythic" stage was accompanied by a lack of human self-consciousness, as we conceive modern man possesses this. I equate the animistic impulse with this mythic state. I conceive that as man advances from the sensibility of the "book" towards the sensibility of the Internet, the current hegemony of post-mythic symbolic form is affected; infused with a re-awakened animism as the forces inchoate in the alphabetical imprisonment of the "book" sleep less deeply.

Word and Sacred: Envisaged as a conflict between conflicting media; the "Word" associated with monotheism and the "book" (alphabetic literacy); the "Sacred" envisaged as pro-visual traditions of worship including that of early mother worship and forms of pagan belief (pro-feminine in nature). Finds expression in the theories of the French theorist – Ricoeur.

ENDNOTES

[a] It is probable that a link exists between Cuneiform and Canaanite linear-alphabet at 1400-1100 BC but this is not the only influence perceived; a second influence being the Proto-Sinaitic language (1700-1500 BC) and a third being hieroglyphics (Drucker, 1995/1999). This is expressed as being derived from Byblos-Pseudo Hieroglyphics (1800-1500 BC).

[b] "The World of cyberspace is a computer-generated extension of the human mind into another dimension. The computer has carried human communication across a threshold as significant of writing, and cyberspace's reliance on electromagnetism and photographic reduction will only lead to further adjustments that favor a feminine worldview…" (Shlain, 1998, p418).

[c] McLuhan follows Gombrich (1960) in this view. Variants exist: Damish stating the acquisition of perspective as a kind of cultural choice (cited in Wertheim, 1999, p84). Edgerton (1975) cites the antagonistic positions of Panofsky - arguing (in the wake of Cassirer) that renaissance perspective was a "symbolic form", and Pirenne argues that perspective is the "fascination of truth" (Pirenne, 1964).

[d] The Oxford English Dictionary simply defines animism as the attribution of a living soul to plants or inanimate objects in accordance with the doctrine of the anima mundi (a regulatory power of the material world).

[e] Cassirer, The Myth of the State, 43.

[f] Hypertext as non-lineal browsing is only one feature of this shift in sensibility. Non-linear as a mode of organization; hypertext represents a mode of traversing text of a linear variety but text increasingly entwined with images. McKnight notes that "linear argumentation is more a consequence of alphabetic writing than of printed books and it remains to be seen if hypertext presentation will significantly erode this predominant convention of mentally ordering our world..." (McKnight, 1991, p41

[g] See Sheard, S, Continental Philosophy and Organizational Studies: A critique of selected aspects of Postmodern thought in Organization Studies, Process Metaphysics, Journal of Philosophy of Management, Volume 7/2 (2009); accepted pending publication.

[h] Managers and the Heavenly City: How E-Commerce Metaphors shape management thought`, *The Journal of Philosophy of Management,* Volume 5, No.3, 2005, pp91-103.

Section III
Managing Knowledge

Chapter X
Knowledge Management and IT Research and Analysis Firms: Agenda-Setters, Oracles and Judges

Krzysztof Klincewicz
University of Warsaw, Poland

ABSTRACT

The chapter discusses the role of IT Research & Analysis firms in the diffusion of knowledge management. The research is based on content analysis of reports and research notes concerning knowledge management, issued by the most influential analyst firm Gartner in years 1997-2003. It identifies three predominant roles of analysts: agenda-setters (focusing the public discourse on selected issues), oracles (offering ambiguous promises) and judges (selecting concepts, technologies and vendors). While critically evaluating the influence of IT Research & Analysis firms, the chapter documents important passages in the history of knowledge management.

INTRODUCTION

The chapter presents a critical perspective on knowledge management, analyzing the involvement of IT Research & Analysis companies in promotion and subsequent rejection of the approach to organizational IT-enabled changes. Literature emphasizes the rhetorical aspects of recommendations and points to fundamental errors in knowledge management initiatives (Fahey, Prusak 1998; Nonaka, Reinmöller 2001). Dramatic changes in the adoption of this approach can also be interpreted using the model of management fashions (Abrahamson 1991; Kieser 1996; Czarniawska, Joerges 1996; Swanson, Ramiller 1997). Faced with the stunning popularity of knowledge management, consulting firms and software vendors started re-branding solutions and services, previously offered under other „labels". They were joining the bandwagon since 1996, but later modified their marketing literature once again as soon as the concept lost its commercial appeal around 2001 (Klincewicz 2006). The inherent „interpretative flexibility" of knowledge management opened opportunities for its incommensurable interpretations by various professional communities (Swan, Robertson 2001). Management ideas diffuse through translations into objects and institutions (Czarniawska, Joerges 1996), and the original concepts may acquire new meanings in this process.

Management fashion arena brings together multiple parties, deriving commercial or other interests from promoting the fashion (Kieser 1996), among them: book authors, consultants, academics, software vendors, website owners, conference organizers, publishers and headhunters. The chapter focuses on a selected group of players in the arena: IT Research & Analysis (IT R&A) firms such as Gartner, IDC or Forrester Research. They monitor and interpret industry events and trends. Even though often perceived as „*the voices of independent reason, interpretation and analysis*" (Franson 1997), their interpretative activities can also make sense of technologies, establish markets and create new value (Swanson 2000). As the research will demonstrate, they played an underestimated role in defining the concept of knowledge management, promoting related technology solutions and re-defining the market several years later to trigger the abandonment of the knowledge management theme by IT vendors and customers.

The chapter discusses revenues streams and scope of activities of IT R&A firms, as well as differences from traditional market research and consulting firms. It outlines their difficulties in balancing between two sometimes contradictory tasks. IT R&A firms serve the general public by publishing impartial technology and market reports, including quantitative forecasts and vendor evaluations. The reports are used by technology customers as „shopping lists", and by the financial community as indicators of potential future investments (Franson 1997). At the same time, IT R&A firms work closely on consulting or copywriting assignments with individual customers - technology companies, which are at the same time evaluated in published reports (Konicki 2001). The arising ethical dilemma is parallel to experiences of the investment banking industry, especially as IT R&A firms cannot actually be held accountable for their predictions and recommendations.

The case of knowledge management popularity seems particularly well-suited for the analysis. The concept has multiple interpretations, is very popular but promoted in incommensurable ways by diverse professional communities. The analysis helps identify direct influences of IT Research & Analysis firms, contributing to the conceptual „buzz".

The chapter presents translations of ideas into objects and institutions. It does not intend to criticize IT Research & Analysis companies, nor „denounce their wrongdoings". Proposed interpretations would rather focus on the intertextual character of these translations and unintended influence mechanisms. From this analytical perspective, „being objective" is not a feasible intent for market participants due to the nature of perception and decision making processes, and the interpretative role of opinion leaders can become an important source of power.

IT RESEARCH AND ANALYSIS FIRMS

Analyst firms, which specialize in high-technology markets, are often referred to as IT Research and Analysis Services or IT R&A (comp. Firth, Swanson 2005). They inform potential technology customers and vendors about changes in the marketplace, including opportunities and challenges related to innovations, thus influencing customers' purchasing decisions and vendors' product strategies. IT R&A reports include: market sizing, trend forecasting, and comparisons of competing vendors in the market used to facilitate product selection decisions by explaining complex innovations and their possible benefits. A survey of the largest US companies, conducted in 1997 by IT magazine Computerworld, revealed that the majority of respondents believed that Gartner, the leading IT R&A firm, was influential in shaping their information systems strategy (Anthes 1997: 88). Other well-known firms are IDC, Forrester Research, META Group and Ovum.

IT Research and Analysis firms differ from traditional market research companies, which are focused on clients, product selection and usage patterns. IT R&A firms focus on the supply side of markets – technologies, vendors and products. Their findings are frequently used both by technology clients and suppliers. The research is prepared regularly and sold as a ready-to-use intellectual product – thus making the operations of IT R&A firms closer to literary or art criticism than disciplined market research. The analogy refers also to the potential influence – both literary critics and technology analysts can influence the fates of products and their authors by publishing their own opinions.

Analyst companies derive their revenues from interdependent services:

- **Research:** Produced on a regular basis to keep up with market changes, and sold as standard products to subscribers or one-time customers (with research notes, market forecasts, user studies, vendor evaluations as well as comments on current events in the market),
- **Advisory services:** Custom offering for clients, planning purchases or setting directions for future IT development, as well as for vendors deciding about product strategies,
- **Events:** Paid seminars and conferences, where research findings are previewed, and attendees can directly communicate with leading analysts.

In the case of Gartner, its revenues in 2002 were composed of research (54.7%), advisory services (30%), events (1.6%) as well as other sources (Gartner 2002 Annual Report). Interestingly, Gartner has been reported to receive approximately 25% of its annual revenues from technology vendors (Konicki 2001). This relatively high percentage accounts for product evaluations, reprints of reports used by vendors for marketing purposes, as well as special vendor-focused publications (e.g. Gartner Connect, a vendor's marketing brochure supplemented by Gartner's market report).

A very important and often unnoticed aspect of analysts' work are individual contacts with key customers. Apart from purchasing standard reports, large customers are also entitled to telephone enquiries related to these materials. An important reason to subscribe to a report category is therefore the opportunity for individual contacts. Gartner's VP and research area director was reported to be spending 80% of his day on answering such client phone calls (Anthes 1997: 89).

Analyses of the usage patterns of IT R&A products and services are fairly limited. Research on environmental scanning for IT revealed that analyst reports had slightly less impact on IT-related decisions than articles published in industry magazines (Maier, Rajner 1997: 194). The only detailed research piece is a survey, administered in 2001 to IT directors of California-based companies (Firth, Swanson 2002; Firth, Swanson 2005). The sample was not representative, so the validity of findings could be questioned – nevertheless, it revealed that Gartner was by far the most frequently used provider (Firth, Swanson 2002: 6). The most frequently cited use of IT R&A reports was "*innovation comprehension: monitoring trends, learning about new IT innovations, and identifying emergent IT standards*" (Firth, Swanson 2002: 8). Research reports are also used by financial community, supporting their decisions about investments in high-tech companies. Likewise, technology companies resort to these reports when looking for additional funds: "*start-up companies visit venture capitalists and other investors armed with numbers that ‹prove› how big their chosen markets are*" (Franson 1997: 78). The findings are also frequently summarized by management and IT magazines, where quotations from analysts tend to be regarded as "*the voices of independent reason, interpretation and analysis*" (Franson 1997: 78).

CRITICISM OF IT R&A INFLUENCE

Power is usually accompanied by augmented liability, which explains the frequent criticism of IT R&A firms, voiced by media, customers and technology vendors, watching out for mistakes or incoherence in influential opinions. According to a popular interpretation, "*modern high-tech market researchers have become the high priests of high technology. They can influence the buying public's perceptions of companies and technology, affect executive careers and change the stock market*" (Franson 1997: 78).

IT R&A firms are fallible – there have been numerous examples of erroneous predictions, generating substantial sunk costs for clients and vendors. Historical examples include: Gartner's mistake in the late 1980s, when its analysts predicted that OS/2, an operating system of IBM, would dominate the desktop computer market within five years (Anthes 1997: 89), Dataquest's overoptimistic forecast of the future size of the gigabit Ethernet market (Franson 1997), or Gartner overestimating the cost of maintaining a personal computer (Anthes 1997: 89). According to a survey of IT R&A users, conducted by InformationWeek, analysts are considered to frequently fail in providing insights about technology markets or anticipating strategic business changes (Konicki 2001).

Secondly, the analysts are criticized because of their relatively limited experience and lack of reliable, transparent, and scientifically grounded research methods. "*‹We used to joke that every market would be $1 billion by the year 2000, › says Scott McCready, who logged nearly 12 years as an analyst of Yankee Group, IDC and Giga before becoming CEO of CIOview, a Boxborough, Mass., software vendor. ‹Once you come up with some kind of growth rate, all you have to do is compound that over several years and you're going to come up with a pretty big number. But [analysts] don't do a good job getting the constraints of the market right. I honestly think [most forecasters] sit around a campfire›*" (Paul 2001). Market sizing exercises are often distant from reality and thus criticized by multiple parties (Franson 1997: 80). Unlike investment banks, advising clients how to invest money, IT R&A firms cannot be held accountable for the accuracy of their predictions. Moreover, 5 years forecasts of dynamically changing markets cannot actually be considered reliable.

The third reason for criticism is the analysts' relations with technology vendors, often leading to a biased advice. A relevant analogy is the capital market, where overlapping roles of underwriters, investors and analysts were found to generate incentives for biased research (Bradshaw 2004; Irvine 2004). As an example, Gartner is reported to derive 25% of its annual revenue from vendors (Konicki 2001), while for other companies this percentage may even be higher though it never is officially reported. Anecdotic evidence suggested that some market forecasts had been modified in reply to requests by large and influential IT firms (Franson 1997: 114; Paul 2001) that wanted their customers or investors to believe in a more promising future for certain product lines. Another scenario concerned the conflict between Gartner and a large software company Computer Associates, which complained about negligent analyses of its products, and an obvious conflict of interests, as persons laid off by Computer Associates were later analyzing the company's products on behalf of Gartner (Anthes 1997: 89).

If a technology company wants to attract favorable press attention, it should start by approaching the analysts. Nowadays, a costly subscription to analyst services for internal use may be a door-opener for smaller vendors, helping them establish contacts and have their products reviewed in the future (Franson 1997: 80, 106). Even though analysts put a lot of effort to ensure clients that they are not manipulated by vendors, quoting one of clients: "*some research he sees reminds him more of advertising than independent analysis, with a few product weaknesses or problems thrown in ‹to balance things out a little so you believe the rest of it›*" (Konicki 2001).

RESEARCH PROBLEM AND METHODS

Using the case of knowledge management, the chapter discusses how perceptions and interpretations of market players can be influenced by analysts. The research problem concerns the contributions of IT Research & Analysis firms to the hype and to the subsequent decline of knowledge management popularity. The research will demonstrate mechanisms, which were used by a selected IT R&A firm to influence the perceptions and decisions of technology clients and vendors.

The empirical research is based on qualitative content analysis of relevant reports and research notes from the leading IT R&A company Gartner concerning knowledge management, published in years 1997-2003. The primary reason for using the technique was its unobtrusiveness. The discussed research problem is controversial and individual interpretations of past events, collected through interviews, might be biased unless supported by documentary evidence.

The document sample included all available Gartner documents from years 1997-2003, referring to knowledge management and several related terms (such as information, document and content management), identified by full-text searches in Gartner online archive. Altogether 38 documents were collected. Various forms of written communication such as reports, research notes and articles were treated equally. This systematic data collection process was enriched by several comparable reports from other IT R&A firms.

The subsequent analysis was based on typological strategy (Lindlof 1995: 230), attempts to interpret data by means of a developed and constantly refined typology. Documents were coded and the coding process resembled methods of grounded theory by constantly comparing instances, which may apply to specific types, searching for contradictions and iteratively constructing new types. Codebook consisted of 18 instances, with codes denoting: explicit and implicit definitions of knowledge management, reference to processes or products, occurrence of surfing (diluting previous definitions or normative statements to avoid their definite rejection, comp. Abrahamson, Fairchild 1999: 729-730), market forecasts and various types of technologies and business domains.

The further analysis of documents involved tracking historical developments (based on timelines and sequence of events) using dramatistic strategy of content analysis (Lindlof 1995: 233) and historiographical methods (Goodman, Kruger 1988). Publication dates of documents were used to structure this part of analysis. An important aspect of the document sample was its intertextuality – production, distribution and consumption of texts by multiple parties (Boje 2001: 76), establishing new meanings and changing previous recommendations. In mass communications such as published research reports, „each release is a link in a never-ending chain of releases that will become part of news columns" (Boje 2001: 86), purchasing decisions or strategies of IT vendors. The market changes, documented in another study of knowledge management history (Klincewicz

2006), were contrasted with contents of Gartner's documents. Finally, by refining the initial codebook and aggregating the collected data into categories, three roles of IT R&A firms were identified, and they will be characterized below as: agenda setters, oracles and judges.

The adopted research methods suffer from limitations typical for all content analysis studies: the limited representativeness of document samples and lack of proof for the correctness of inferences (Berger 1998: 117). The study also has limited generalization potential, as it concerns only one topic (knowledge management), one IT R&A firm (Gartner), written publications (while IT R&A firms influence clients and vendors also by means of verbal communications and staged events). In addition, the analyzed events coincided with the Internet bubble and changes in popularity of knowledge management, which made all industry participants re-evaluate their strategies. The study identified nevertheless distinctive mechanisms, used by Gartner to form opinions about knowledge management, and offers a point of departure for future replications, verifying the existence of similar mechanisms related to other management fashions or technologies.

IT R&A FIRMS AS AGENDA SETTERS

IT R&A firms can focus the attention of customers and vendors on specific issues, highlighted in the research. The mechanism has a useful analogy in the domain of mass media. Patterns of media influence on society are rooted in the psychological concept of *framing* – selecting some aspects of perceived reality and making them more salient in the communicated message, so that particular interpretations or evaluations are inclined (Entman 1993: 52). This approach was complemented by early 1970s studies of how mass media determine the importance of certain issues in pre-elections debates and thus define the focus of political campaigns, and the phenomenon was referred to as their *agenda-setting role* (McCombs, Shaw 1972: 176-177; McCombs 1997: 433).

From mass media, "*readers learn not only about a given issue, but also how much importance to attach to that issue from the amount of information in a news story and its position*" (McCombs, Shaw 1972: 176) so that the press "*may not be successful much of the time in telling people what to think, but it is stunningly successful in telling its readers what to think about*" (Rogers, Dearing 1993: 72). Media select objects and decide, which frames should be used to think about these objects (McCombs, Shaw 1993: 62). If the audience is deprived of alternatives to the given interpretation, the influence of agenda-setters is particularly effective (Entman 1993: 54).

In the 1980s, findings of the agenda-setting research were applied to aspects other than political campaigns, such as advertising (McCombs, Shaw 1993: 58). The mass media model is highly relevant for IT R&A firms, operating in ways similar to news organizations, i.e. deciding arbitrarily about the importance of events, technologies or tendencies. Apart from researching and analyzing the markets, IT R&A firms play an important role in shaping the market structures, investments and technology development directions. Analysts influence the diffusion of innovations by using frames that influence "shopping lists" and development plans in technology markets.

As the knowledge management popularity was dramatically growing in 1997-98, leading IT R&A firms issued their forecasts of knowledge management market size, which in turn influenced specialist press, vendors and of course customers. In June 1997, Gartner's research director Jim Bair was quoted as saying that the market for knowledge management software and services was expected to reach $5 billion by 2000 (Nerney 1997; Nerney 1998: 26). Gartner Dataquest issued a similar forecast in October 1997, predicting that "*businesses will spend $4.5 billion on knowledge management products and services by 1999*" (Hibbard 1997:

68). Other firms issued similar forecasts. Ovum anticipated in 1998 that knowledge management applications market would exceed $1 billion worldwide by 2002, while accompanying services would grow to more than $5 billion (Romberg 1998). Delphi Consulting Group evaluated only the relative value of the market, stating that the penetration of knowledge management solutions among business organizations would increase from 28% in 1997 to 77% by 1999 (Knowledge Management 1997).

The figures were subsequently used by IT magazines to interpret changes in the software market and comment on strategies of individual technology vendors (Nerney 1997; Hibbard 1997; Nerney 1998). It is difficult to demonstrate direct linkages between IT R&A forecasts and vendors' decisions. One cannot establish, to what extent the forecasts interpreted changes in the marketplace, and to what extent influenced these changes, acting as self-fulfilling prophecies[a]. The optimistic findings of IT R&A firms coincided with launches and re-positionings of software products intended to "manage knowledge" in 1997-98.

Figure 1. "Waterfall" model of IT Research & Analysis firms' influence in the IT market

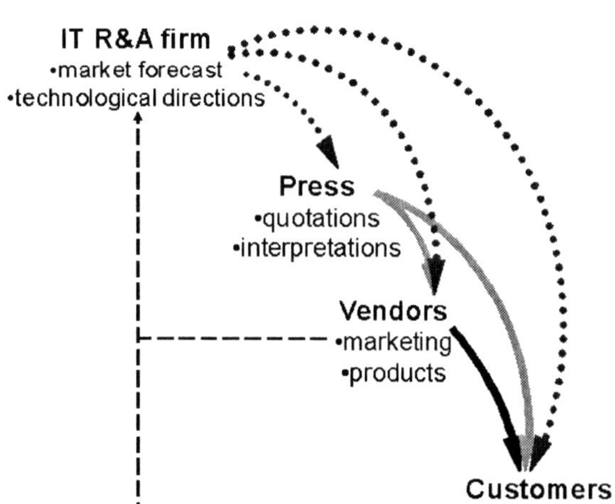

The hypothesized influence of IT R&A firms on press, vendors and customers is presented in the "waterfall" model (Figure 1), where positive predictions of analysts are further transmitted by other market participants so that a management fashion is amplified. IT R&A firms clearly succeeded in focusing the attention of market participants on knowledge management-related topics – while not offering guidelines or precise recommendations for strategic action. The "waterfall" model relies on mere amplification of concepts, but mechanisms described in the following sections will also involve modifications of these concepts.

IT R&A FIRMS AS ORACLES

The second role of IT R&A firms with reference to knowledge management can be characterized as an oracle, using the power of interpretation to impose new definitions and concepts upon market participants. The research will demonstrate how Gartner was re-defining established and introducing new concepts, thus setting directions for product development activities of software vendors.

This resembles Weick's notion of *enactment* (Weick 1979: 122-123), which is based on *bracketing*, emphasizing selected aspects of reality, and *sense-making*, making these aspects meaningful for other people and inducing their actions. According to Weick, "*when you pull out some portion of the text of the speech from its surrounding context, then the environment that you have bracketed for inspection is a different environment that the original one*" (Weick 1979: 154). Intentional selection of certain approaches and proposing their new interpretations present examples of enactment activities, in which IT R&A firms engage. Effectiveness of enactment depends on access to power (Weick 1979: 168), and the largest firms such as Gartner can benefit from their privileged positions.

The coding procedures adopted in the study were comparing knowledge management interpretations, offered by Gartner at specific points of time, as well as looking for inconsistencies or modifications, as well as instances of *surfing*, smooth moves from the concept to promote alternatives, deemphasizing their differences (Abrahamson, Fairchild 1999: 729-730). Similarly to mythical oracles, analyst firms use intentional ambiguity as a source of power: unclear problems are perceived as complex by potential clients, who turn to IT R&A firms for costly advice. The confusion restricts individual responsibility for actual technology-related decisions, made by clients based on analyst reports. The study revealed a surprising lack of reinterpretation of past statements and opinions of analysts, which in the course of time turned out to be inaccurate. Oracles do not like to be reminded of mistakes, and prefer discussing the future. While "historicizing", retrospective thinking plays an important role in Weick's enactment and selection processes (Weick 1979: 195), Gartner's analysts seem to intentionally avoid it. This leads at times to inconsistencies and radical conceptual changes, which were identified in the analyzed documents.

The over-optimistic predictions and knowledge management market forecasts did not precisely stated which technologies, products and services were actually concerned. As META Group admitted in 2003 (5 years after the knowledge management hype), "*journalists often ask us for research quantifying the size of the knowledge management (KM) ‹market›. However, our research shows this to be a meaningless question because it is impossible to define a discrete market that corresponds to KM. Defined narrowly (semantic analysis and reasoning engines, for example), this phantom market could be as small as several million dollars worldwide. Defined broadly (to include collaboration, document management, services, data warehouses, business intelligence, etc.), it could legitimately be pegged at several hundred billion dollars. Ultimately, it is not the size of the KM market that is important, but what you do with KM.*" (Mann 2003)

IT R&A firms were re-defining established concepts and introducing new ones, thus setting directions for product development activities, legitimizing or undermining strategies of software vendors. This phenomenon can easily be observed with reference to Gartner, as the firm was changing its interpretations of knowledge management and relations between the concept and new technologies over time.

In the initial phase of the concept's diffusion, Gartner analysts were confident about the rosy future of the knowledge management market, as the previously quoted market forecasts from 1997 demonstrated. One of Gartner Dataquest's documents from 1999 defined what was meant by the term in question: "*Knowledge management software allows organizations and end users to organize, access, and use information regardless of location and format*" (Gartner 1999). Based on this definition, knowledge management applications included solutions handling "*data and content from both internal and external sources, including the Internet, workgroup files, documents, and so on*" (Gartner 1999), while no specific reference was made to the concept of knowledge management, its particular business benefits or links to other organizational practices. The definition was difficult to tell apart from that of "information management", underestimating the differences between knowledge and information. The imprecise market definition turned knowledge management into a buzzword, to which almost every IT company could easily refer. In 2000, Gartner issued a review of document management market, where it presented knowledge management as value-added application for traditional document management systems (Weintraub, Shegda, Landers 2000). Interestingly, knowledge management remained an undefined set of functionalities and benefits, as Gartner did not elaborate on any specific examples of such applications.

When the popularity of knowledge management started fading, Gartner introduced strict terminological distinctions. The change might be linked to the failure of previous market forecasts – in 2000, the knowledge management market was supposed to reach the $5 billion size based on earlier Gartner estimates, and the promises did not materialize. In November 2000, Gartner finally issued a document explaining the differences between "knowledge management" and "information management" (Harris, Jacobs 2000) – the former was related to business operations, including procedures, cultural elements and tacit knowledge, while the latter was surprisingly similar to what only a year earlier was touted by Gartner Dataquest as "knowledge management". According to the new interpretation, both types of technologies were co-dependent, as "*information access is the element that links IM and KM*" (Harris, Jacobs 2000). Two months later, the approach was refined by stating that "*Gartner considers KM a sophisticated business process rather than a type of product or technology*" (Carreau, Logan 2001). This interpretation was repeatedly confirmed in following documents (comp. Logan, Caldwell, Young 2001; Caldwell, Andrews 2002; Logan, Caldwell 2002; Caldwell 2002; Harris, Kolsky, Lundy 2003). With the new understanding, it was no longer possible to size the knowledge management market, even though the same IT R&A firm used to issue such market sizing statements in the past. Gartner started even opposing its own previous judgments: when analyzing the strategy of Lotus IBM in January 2001, the analyst argued that knowledge management cannot be considered a product – according to the review, Lotus made a strategic mistake as it "*has tried to use collaboration and knowledge management (KM) to differentiate itself beyond simply selling e-mail seats, but both areas (particularly KM) call for a focus more on services than products*" (Hayward, Austin 2001). The very same strategy would have been rewarded by Gartner as progressive before 2000.

Parallel to the re-interpretation of knowledge management, Gartner introduced the notion of "*functions needed to support KM*" (Carreau, Logan 2001) or "*KM technologies*" (Caldwell et al. 2002; Caldwell, Shegda 2002; Caldwell, Andrews 2002), naming specific relevant product categories. In November 2002, Gartner confessed that "*much of the technology used to support knowledge management may not be unique to knowledge management or always have knowledge management as the motivation for its implementation*" (Logan, Caldwell 2002). Other documents proposed five "lenses" (Caldwell 2002) or practices of knowledge management (Caldwell, Harris 2002), defining the technological offerings: e-commerce, process knowledge, intellectual capital management, information management and access, and knowledge workplace. Gartner noticed shifts in software solutions from managing explicit knowledge ("*Early KM efforts often focus on information access and move quickly to building a ‹knowledge base›*" (Caldwell 2002: 16)), towards applications supporting tacit knowledge (Caldwell 2002: 9). Knowledge management applications differed clearly from software managing structured data (Caldwell, Logan 2002) and line-of-business applications, "*conventionally focused on transactional data and operations*" (Logan, Caldwell 2002)[b], while Gartner witnessed certain convergence between solutions managing structured data and unstructured information, thus supplementing organizational processes by the knowledge-related dimensions (Logan, Caldwell 2002; Lundy, Herschel 2003).

With the implicitly defined knowledge management market, Gartner was able to claim in 2003 that knowledge management was experiencing a "*technology renaissance*" (Caldwell et al. 2003), with the KM practices supported by technology better than before. It stated that "*knowledge management is continuing to evolve into richer, more-complex, and higher-value applications*" (Harris 2003), and for the first time revealed that "*KM is critically dependent on technology. In the absence of technology, many KM processes would exist only in narrow domains and with limited capabilities*" (Harris, Kolsky, Lundy 2003). The shift in interpretations resulted in supplementing a business process by a set of indispensable technologies, which had to be implemented to support enterprise-wide knowledge management efforts. The technologies were presented as important add-ons to existing solutions, offered by "*powerhouse vendors*" (Caldwell, French 2002), companies selling enterprise-wide solutions such as databases, ERP and CRM systems, with predictions that future solutions would integrate various aspects and categories of information and knowledge to offer a more comprehensive picture of the organization and its environment (particularly of customers (Lundy, Herschel 2003)), so that knowledge management technologies in 2003 seemed to be developing into all-encompassing solutions.

The examples demonstrate that apart from acting as agenda-setters, IT R&A firms enriched the knowledge management arena by interpreting the business concept and its links to technologies. They creatively enriched the original notions and adjusted them to suit the needs of particular audiences, i.e. translated into localized ideas (Czarniawska, Joerges 1996: 36). Gartner set functional requirements for software products, used for knowledge management purposes, classifying products from specific vendors as matching or not these requirements – thus practically deciding about the fates of individual products and their future development. These interpretations and terminology, introduced by IT R&A firms, were subsequently used by specialist press, technology vendors and customers. The role of oracle is also based on intentional ambiguity and the vagueness of definitions, changing over time. Once enthusiastically praised, technology strategies and solutions were later criticized as soon as the conceptual frames imposed by analysts on knowledge management arena were changed. The oracle seems to be beyond right and wrong – she does not assume responsibility for past opinions or recommendations, and answers to potential complaints with mysterious indifference.

IT R&A FIRMS AS JUDGES

IT R&A firms act also as judges, deciding about leading positions of some products and discouraging customers from buying other solutions. The structure of these comparisons, limited sets of compared vendors, definition of alternatives and of comparison criteria could be regarded as important sources of power (Rogers, Dearing 1993; Entman 1993). The role corresponds to Weick's notion of *selection* as the next step in organizing process, following the previously described enactment: decisions to select and support specific interpretations "*prove helpful in reducing the equivocality of displays*" (Weick 1979: 123). They can offer guidance, straightforward answers and support for certain courses of action, positioned as preferable to others.

Analysts facilitate technology selection decisions of clients by providing direct recommendations – they "judge" products and suppliers, and these "judgments" tend to be unquestionably followed by technology buyers. Analysts can thus reduce uncertainty by incorporating new solutions in existing mental structures, used by clients to solve practical business problems. Gartner publishes "*Magic Quadrant*" reports, comparing vendors in certain product categories and indicating category leaders. These reports contain arbitrarily selected vendors - mostly the largest, US-focused companies. In certain cases the sole definition of product category may seem original and questionable.

In 2002-2003, Gartner introduced alternative terminology to replace the term "knowledge management", which as a buzzword lost its appeal to client organizations, and seemed confusing after numerous attempts at defining it. In January 2002, Gartner predicted a birth of "*packaged ‹smart enterprise› portfolios of portal, content, document management, KM and collaboration products*" (Caldwell et al. 2002) – this conclusion was based on the witnessed convergence of technologies, blurring the boundaries between portals, document management and other traditional applications. In May 2002, Gartner defined this new software system category as Smart Enterprise Suite (SES) – "*it covers enterprise needs for content management, knowledge management and collaboration, and supports the extended virtual workplace – inside and between enterprises*" (Gilbert, Caldwell, Hayward 2002). SES would have a similar impact on enterprises as another class of software – ERP – had years before in the area of managing structured data (Caldwell, Gilbert, Hayward 2002). The new category covered a set of functions, which were delivered by products, previously described by Gartner as knowledge management technologies (comp. Caldwell, Harris 2002; Caldwell 2002). The notion of Smart Enterprise Suite was gradually replacing references to knowledge management technologies in Gartner's documents, especially when a comprehensive generic system, not just specific support for a selected knowledge management process was concerned. According to some reports, "*SES has the potential to substantially reduce implementation and integration costs for enterprise KM*" (Caldwell 2002: 14), such systems are "*sophisticated suites of applications that, if used together, might be said to comprise a knowledge management technology stack*" (Logan, Caldwell 2002), and are developed by vendors "*to support enterprise KM and collaboration needs*" (Caldwell, Logan 2002). While reviewing product development from major vendors, Gartner compared their roadmap status against the benchmark of an ideal Smart Enterprise Suite (comp. Hayward, Graff, Grey 2002; Hayward, Shegda, Logan 2002; Gilbert et al. 2002). Open Text – a historical pioneer in delivering knowledge management solutions – was presented by Gartner as the first vendor offering SES already in 1999 (Landers 2002: 7). This shows the power of framing, applied by the IT Research & Analysis firm to reinterpret the already established software categories.

In order to support its story about the emerging SES market, Gartner listed in October 2002 eight vendors, whom it considered to strive for SES status with their solutions (Caldwell 2002: 14), and in March 2003, it published "*The Smart Enterprise Suite Magic Quadrant*", its first report reviewing offerings of 20 competing vendors in the new market (Hayward et al. 2003). SES was presented as a technological solution in a report from 2003, concerning the development of knowledge management market ("*hype cycle*") (Caldwell et al. 2003). According to a prediction from March 2003, "*by 2004, the smart enterprise suite will emerge as a superset of content management, collaboration and portal frameworks*" (Caldwell 2003: 8), while still being "*an ideal state, a "nirvana" for information sharing across, and possibly between, the enterprise and its partners*" (Caldwell 2003: 8) in 2003.

Some I.C.T. vendors applied SES category name to their products early on – for example SAP used the term already in September 2002 when referring to mySAP Portal at Lisbon SAPPHIRE conference for SAP customers (comp. Haendly 2002). By October 2003, out of 20 vendors classified by Gartner as striving for SES development, 6 referred to the term in own press releases or other materials available from their websites, and 4 were using the Smart Enterprise Suite concept in their literature to strengthen the definition of product offering. Two vendors decided to change their products' names to match the SES concept: it was the case of Hummingbird Smart Enterprise Suite and Open Text Livelink Enterprise Suite.

The discussion of the roles of IT R&A firms resembles Weick's presentation of the process of organizing, consisting of ecological change, enactment, selection and retention (Weick 1979: 122-123). In reply to new concepts, products and technologies (ecological change), firms such as Gartner act as agenda setters: highlight certain tendencies and put them under scrutiny. This initial interest stimulates further ecological change (Weick 1979: 122), as market participants learn about apparently important and profitable technologies, trying to re-evaluate own product strategies. Agenda setting is followed by the role of the oracle, actively enacting the market reality by means of bracketing and interpretations. Weick points to the possible "deviation-amplifying circuit" (Weick 1979: 132), when enacted elements of reality affect the actions of other parties and induce new waves of enactment. Subsequently, analysts assume the role of the judge. They engage in selection, i.e. propose specific solutions and courses of actions, thus influencing strategies of technology buyers and vendors, as well as opinions of other analysts or journalists.

The selection stage can be illustrated by a metaphor of lens (Figure 2), which has the potential to magnify perceived objects. As the lens can be used to observe the environment, IT R&A firms collect information from different sources, transform and magnify it, making the messages more powerful. Another characteristic of the lens is however its potential for distortion of the observed picture. Weick quotes Tom Lodahl, suggesting that "*organizations paint their own scenery, observe it through binoculars, and try to find a path through the landscape*" (Weick 1979: 136) and explains that for organizations "maps are the territory" (Weick 1979: 249-250), as organizational participants act based on distorted and incomplete representations of their environment. In analogous ways, IT buyers and vendors rely on arbitrary and fragmented representations of the market, provided by IT R&A firms.

The proposed metaphor is also related to the social construction of technology model, proposing that technological artifacts are developed as „an alteration of variation and selection" (Pinch, Bijker 1987: 28). The use of the lens, involving focus and distortion, brings about demise of some solutions, and strengthens demand for others. As previously described with reference to the role of the oracle and Weick's concept of enactment, the artifacts start addressing problems of specific social groups, i.e. acquire meaning in social context (Pinch, Bijker 1987: 32-34), and are subject to "interpretative flexibility" (Pinch, Bijker 1987: 40), exploited by the analysts. IT R&A firms acting as judges can directly influence investment decisions by technology buyers and vendors, presenting not only own interpretations but also specific recommendations for action. They interpreted the concept of knowledge management, changed its original meaning, introduced new terminology and put the established body of knowledge in new contexts. The discussed Gartner's reports offered a new vision of technologies supporting knowledge management. They replaced traditional categories by an all-encompassing notion of Smart Enterprise Suite, recommending vendors that complied with

Figure 2. IT research and analysis firm as a lens in the management fashion arena

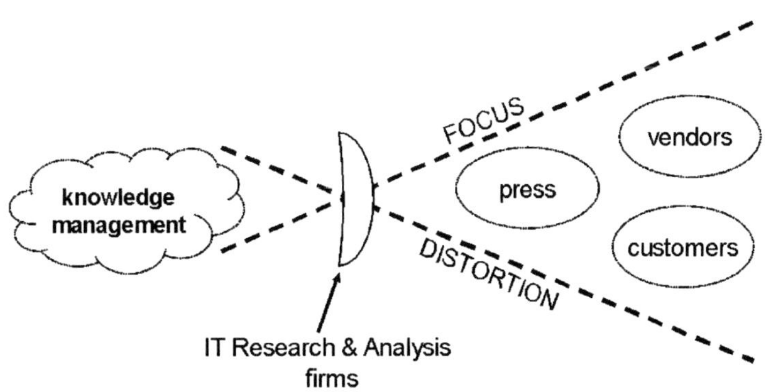

the vision. At the same time, judges act as gatekeepers: they restrict access to clients' minds and "shopping lists", keeping away products that they consider incommensurable or incompliant with specific visions or technology strategies.

CONCLUSION

The chapter demonstrated how one of IT R&A firms participated in the evolution of the concept of knowledge management. Using the example of Gartner's opinions and influences on strategies of technology vendors, three roles of agenda setters, oracles and judges were described. Agenda setters amplified and legitimized the new concept, oracles offered interpretations of knowledge management, thus adding to the conceptual ambiguity, and judges were influencing commercial decisions of technology clients and vendors. The process resembles Weick's understanding of the process of organizing, defined as "*consensually validated grammar for reducing equivocality by means of sensible interlocked behaviors*" (Weick 1979: 3). The "*consensually validated grammar*" corresponds to market definitions, forecasts, predictions and technological categories proposed by Gartner and commonly accepted by the IT industry. The communications initiated by IT R&A firms are intended to offer uniform, all-encompassing interpretations of new concepts and technologies ("*reducing equivocality*") and are particularly effective thanks to the use of "*sensible interlocked behaviors*" (i.e. influencing both IT buyers and vendors by visionary interpretations). As the research revealed, Gartner's statements were often flawed, and the firm frequently modified its official technology definitions and business recommendations. Nevertheless, these shortcomings did not undermine the firm's expert status in technology evaluation and forecasting. This phenomenon could be explained by the implicit acceptance of the three above-described roles by other technology market participants.

Knowledge management is a specific example of management fashion, linked to Information Technology and therefore particularly prone to influences of technical authorities. IT R&A firms are previously overlooked yet important players in the management fashion arena. The chapter modeled their involvement using the metaphors of waterfall (denoting staged diffusion of opinions and interpretations) and lens (offering at the same time both focus and distortion). The diffusion of complex concepts such as knowledge management differs from the traditional, one-dimensional model of management fashion (Abrahamson 1991), multiplied and adopted by organizations. Various agents in the fashion arena offer their own interpretations, linked to their individual interests and competences (Kieser 1996). Specific professional communities focus on specific, divergent understandings of knowledge management (Swan, Robertson 2001). The initial concept underwent multiple translations over time (Czarniawska, Joerges 1996), acquiring new meanings and applications. IT Research & Analysis firms such as Gartner contributed to this process of social construction of knowledge management concepts and practices. The presented study analyzed one management fashion, interpreted by one selected IT R&A firm. This limited scope restricts the generalization potential, but the method could be used to replicate the research for other concepts, technologies and analyst firms.

Finally, the chapter outlined selected aspects of the knowledge management history. It traced the roots of the concept from the perspective of the analyst firms. Knowledge management hype started in the 1990s and lasted until 2001. In this initial period, Gartner glorified the benefits of the concept, ambiguously linking it to existing technologies and business approaches. The firm was evangelizing client organizations and stimulating technology investments by means of promising market forecasts. The disillusionment of clients and vendors with this vague, all-encompassing notion of knowledge management motivated Gartner to elaborate the concept and introduce important terminological distinctions. In the 21st century, knowledge management regained its popularity in IT markets, even though analysts and vendors intentionally replaced its label with other names such as "Smart Enterprise Suite". These painful transitions in knowledge management lifecycle have made the concept more responsive to the needs of organizations, eliminated its faddish elements and emphasized the actual business benefits.

REFERENCES

Abrahamson, E. (1991). Managerial fads and fashions: the diffusion and rejection of innovations. *Academy of Management Review, 16*(3), 586-612

Abrahamson, E., & Fairchild, G. (1999). Management Fashions: Lifecycles, Triggers, and Collective Learning Processes. *Administrative Sciences Quarterly, 44*, 708-740

Anthes, G. H. (1997). The Gartner Gods. *Computerworld*, March 3, 87-89

Berger, A. A. (1998). *Media Analysis Techniques*. Thousand Oaks-London-New Delhi: Sage Publications.

Boje, D. M. (2001). *Narrative Methods for Organizational & Communication Research*. London-Thousand Oaks-New Delhi: Sage Publications.

Bradshaw, M. T. (2004). How Do Analysts Use Their Earnings Forecasts in Generating Stock Recommendations. *The Accounting Review, 79*(1), 25-50.

Caldwell, F. (2002). *Knowledge Management Scenario: What's Next*? Gartner Symposium ITxpo (Orlando, Florida), 26F-SYM12, October 6-11, 2002.

Caldwell, F. (2003). *From Enterprise Content Management to the SES and Beyond*. Gartner Symposium ITxpo (Florence, Italy), 26F-SPR4, March 10-12, 2003.

Caldwell, F., & Andrews, W. (2002). Update on Search Technology. *Gartner Letter From the Editor, LE-16-9553*, June 7, 2002.

Caldwell, F., Gilbert, M., & Hayward, S. (2002). CM, Portals and Collaboration Fading: Enter 'Smart' Suite. *Gartner Letter From the Editor, LE-16-6229*, May 10, 2002.

Caldwell, F., Gilbert, M., Hayward, S., Logan, D., & Lundy, J. (2002). *New Focus on Knowledge and Collaboration Begins in 2002*. January 7, 2002.

Caldwell, F., & Harris, K. (2002). Hype Cycle for Knowledge Management 2002. *Gartner Research Note, SPA-15-0651*, January 3, 2002.

Caldwell, F., Linden, A., Miklovic, D., Morello, D., Knox, R., Logan, D., Grey, M., Gilbert, M., Harris, K., Andrews, W., Lundy, J., Hayward, S., Bell, M., Latham, L., & Shegda, K. (2003). Hype Cycle for Knowledge Management 2003. *Gartner Strategic Analysis Report, R-20-0010*, June 6, 2003.

Caldwell, F., & Logan, D. (2002). Powerhouse Vendors Move to Knowledge Management. *Gartner Letter From the Editor, LE-18-6080*, November 12, 2002.

Caldwell, F., & Shegda, K. (2002). BEA Participates in High-Growth Area of Knowledge Management. *Gartner FirstTake, FT-15-3652*, January 25, 2002.

Carreau, D., & Logan, D. (2001). With SharePoint, Microsoft Blurs Portals and Knowledge Management. *Gartner FirstTake, FT-12-9070*, January 25, 2001.

Czarniawska, B., & Joerges, B. (1996). Travels of Ideas. In B.Czarniawska & G. Sevón, (Eds.), *Translating Organizational Change* (pp. 13-48). Berlin-New York: de Guyter.

Entman, R. M. (1993). Framing: Toward Clarification of a Fractured Paradigm. *Journal of Communication, 43*(4), 51-58

Fahey, L., & Prusak, L. (1998). The Eleven Deadliest Sins of Knowledge Management. *California Management Review, 40*(3), 265-276.

Firth, D. R., & Swanson, E. B. (2002). *IT Research and Analysis Services: Surveying their Use and Usefulness*. Working Paper, May 2002, Los Angeles: The Anderson School at UCLA

Firth, D. R., & Swanson, E. B. (2005). How useful are IT research and analysis services? *Business Horizons, 48*, 151-159

Franson, P. (1997). The Market Research Shell Game. Upside, March 1997, (pp. 78-82 & 106-116).

Gartner (1999). 1999 Worldwide Collaborative Workplace Software Program Market Definitions. *Gartner Dataquest Guide,* January 11, 1999.

Gilbert, M., Caldwell, F., & Hayward, S. (2002). The Smart Enterprise Suite Is Coming: Do We Need It? *Gartner Article Top View, AV-16-2189*, May 10, 2002.

Gilbert, M., Phifer, G., Hayward, S., Latham, L., & Lheureux, B. (2002). Vignette to Buy Epicentric, Move Toward Smart Enterprise Suite. *Gartner FirstTake, FT-18-7281*, November 4, 2002.

Goodman, R. S., & Kruger, E. J. (1988). Data Dredging or Legitimate Research Method? Historiography and Its Potential for Management Research. *The Academy of Management Review, 13*(2), 315-325.

Haendly, M. (2002). *SAP Exchange Infrastructure. Enabling Process-Centric Collaboration.* Presentation at SAPPHIRE, Lisbon, September 4-6, 2002, http://www.sap.com/community/events/2002_lisbon/pdf/d2_t12_17.pdf, access date 3.10.2003.

Harris, K. (2003). Success or Failure in KM, CM, Collaboration and E-Learning. *Gartner Article Top View, AV-19-2417*, February 11, 2003.

Harris, K., & Jacobs, J. (2000). Knowledge Management vs. Information Management. *Gartner Commentary, COM-11-9460*, November 3, 2000.

Harris, K., Kolsky, E., & Lundy, J. (2003). The Case for Knowledge Management in CRM. *Gartner Article Top View, AV-19-5592*, April 21, 2003

Hayward, S., & Austin, T. (2001). IBM to Integrate Lotus More Closely. *Gartner FirstTake, FT-12-8860*, January 12, 2001

Hayward, S., Gilbert, M., Phifer, G., & Caldwell, F. (2003). The Smart Enterprise Suite Magic Quadrant for 2003. *Gartner Research Note M-19-3949*, March 4, 2003

Hayward, S., Graff, J., & Grey, M. (2002). Oracle Has a Chance to Challenge in the Collaboration Market. *Gartner FirstTake, FT-17-4164*, July 12, 2002

Hayward, S., Shegda, K., Logan, D., & Gilbert, M. (2002). Documentum Aims for Smart Enterprise Suite with eRoom Deal. *Gartner FirstTake, FT-18-4537*, October 8, 2002

Hibbard, J. (1997). Search for Differentiation. *InformationWeek*, October 6, 68 and 72.

Irvine, P. J. (2004). Analysts' Forecasts and Brokerage-Firm Trading. *The Accounting Review, 79*(1), 125-149.

Kieser, A. (1996). Moden & Mythen des Organisierens. *Die Betriebswirtschaft, 56*(1), 21-39.

Klincewicz, K. (2006). *Management Fashions. Turning Bestselling Ideas into Objects and Institutions.* New Brunswick: Transaction Publishers.

Knowledge Management (1997). 1997 Knowledge Management Insight Report – Summary,

PC Week, August 18, http://ntsrv2000.educ.ualberta.ca/nethowto/urlsubmit/knowledge/hype/delphi%20survey.htm, access date 20.08.2003

Konicki, S. (2003). The Reality of Research. *InformationWeek*, September 10, 2001, www.informationweek.com, access date: 14:08.2003

Landers, G. (2002). *Extracting Value: Document Management and Imaging*. Gartner Symposium ITxpo (Orlando, Florida), 02E-SYM12, October 6-11, 2002

Lindlof, T. R. (1995). Qualitative Communication Research Methods. Thousand Oaks-London-New Delhi: Sage Publications.

Logan, D., Caldwell, F., & Young, C. (2001). New Rules for Measuring and Managing Intellectual Capital. *Gartner Research Note, SPA-12-7644*, March 13, 2001,

Logan, D., & Caldwell, F. (2002). Knowledge Management Attracts Powerhouse Vendors. *Gartner Article Top View, AV-17-7196*, November 12, 2002,

Lundy, J., & Herschel, G. (2003). Making Knowledge Part of CRM. *Gartner Letter From the Editor, LE-19-8729*, April 21, 2003

Maier, J. L., Rajner Jr., R. K., & Snyder, C. A. (1997). Environmental scanning for information technology: An empirical investigation. *Journal of Management Information Systems, 14*(2), 177-200.

Mann, J. (2003). Knowledge Management Is Not a „Market". *META Group Analyst Insights* (METAbits), 21 February, www.metagroup.com, access date: 8.08.2003

McCombs, M. E., & Shaw, D. L. (1972). The Agenda-setting Function of Mass Media. *Public Opinion Quarterly, 36*(2), 176-187.

McCombs, M. E. (1997). Building Consensus: The News Media's Agenda-Setting Roles. *Political Communication, 14,* 433-443

McDonough, B. (2002). Knowledge Management. *eINFORM, 3*(8). http://www.kmcenter.info/Documents/IDC_april_2002.pdf, access date: 12.05.2003

Nerney, C. (1997). Search Engines. Searching for true knowledge. *Network World, 42.*

Nerney, C. (1998). They're not start-ups anymore. BackWeb pulls back on push. *Network World, 26.*

Nonaka, I., Reinmöller, P., & Toyama, R. (2001). Integrated Information Technology Systems for Knowledge Creation. In M. Dierkes, B. A. Antal, J. Child, & I. Nonaka (Eds.), *Handbook of organizational learning & knowledge*. New York: Oxford University Press, (pp. 827-848).

Paul, L. G. (2001). *How IT Managers Can Get The Most Out of Analyst Services Firms*. CIO, July 15, http://www.cio.com/article/30383/How_IT_Managers_Can_Get_The_Most_Out_of_Analyst_Services_Firms, access date: 21.11.2007

Pinch, T. J., & Bijker, W. E. (1987). The Social Construction of Facts and Artifacts: Or How the Sociology of Science and the Sociology of Technology Might Benefit Each Other. In E. B. W. Hughes, P. Thomas, & T. Pinch (Eds.), *The Social Construction of Technological Systems* (pp. 17-50). New Directions in the Sociology and History of Technology, Cambridge, Massachusetts – London: The MIT Press.

Rogers, E. M., Dearing, J. W., & Bregman, D. (1993). The Anatomy of Agenda-Setting Research. *Journal of Communication, 43*(2), 68-84.

Romberg, D. (1998). *Knowledge management market to hit $5 billion*. Computing Canada, September 11, http://ntsrv2000.educ.ualberta.ca/nethowto/urlsubmit/knowledge/hype/5%20billion.htm, access date: 5.05.2003

Swan, J., Robertson, M., & Bresnen, M. (2001). Knowledge Management and the colonization of knowledge. *CMS Conference: The Dissemination of Management Knowledge Stream*, July 2001

Swanson, E. B., & Ramiller, N. C. (1997). The Organizing Vision in Information Systems Innovation. *Organization Science, 8*(5), 458-474.

Swanson, E. B. (2000). *Information Systems as Buzz.* Information Systems Working Paper 1-00. Los Angeles: The Anderson School at UCLA.

Weick, K. E. (1979). *The Social Psychology of Organizing.* Reading Massachusetts; Menlo Park CA: Addison-Wesley Publishing.

Weintraub, A., Shegda, K., & Landers, G. (2000). Universal IDM Vendors Define Their Survival Strategies. *Gartner Research Note, M-10-4123,* November 1, 2000.

KEY TERMS

Agenda-Setting: Attaching relatively more attention to selected topics in public discourse. For example, journalists may not effectively convince the public opinion what to think, but as agenda-setters they can suggest what to think *about.*

Enactment: Emphasizing selected aspects of reality, making these aspects meaningful for other people and thus inducing their actions. The enacted reality is changed through these sense-making processes.

Framing: Selecting some aspects of perceived reality and making them more salient in the communicated message, so that particular interpretations or evaluations are inclined.

IT Research & Analysis Firms: Analyst firms specializing in high-technology markets. They analyze technological developments, forecast market sizes, evaluate products and help clients understand product innovations.

Management Fashion: A concept describing swings in popularity of specific management techniques and of related management bestsellers, approaches to organizational change, consulting services and software solutions. Management fashions differ from management theories as they are centered around pseudo-scientific concepts, usually promoted by consultants and summarized with buzzwords.

ENDNOTES

[a] The question about the basis and effects of market forecasts, issued by IT R&A firms, had already been raised with respect to other markets – comp. Franson (1997) elaborating on PDA market in 1997 and not being able to give a definite answer to the question: "*Did companies start up to make PDAs because Dataquest published great numbers, or did it start covering the market segment because there were companies to sell reports to?*" (Franson 1997: 80). The situation is different for two remaining roles (oracle and judge), as interpretations and recommendations can be directly linked to decisions by technology vendors and buyers.

[b] Gartner's definition and interpretations of knowledge management technologies differ from those by other IT R&A firms – for example, IDC in 2002 included in its list of technologies supporting KM also solutions dealing with structured data – data warehousing, analytic applications, reporting and OLAP (McDonough 2002: 10).

Chapter XI
Knowledge Management Strategies Implementation in Innovation Intensive Firms

Fátima Guadamillas-Gómez
Universidad de Castilla-La Mancha, Spain

Mario J. Donate-Manzanares
Universidad de Castilla-La Mancha, Spain

ABSTRACT

This chapter analyses the implementation of knowledge management strategies (KMS) in technology-intensive firms. Firstly, a review of KMS in the knowledge management (KM) literature is carried out in order to conceptually establish the focus of the chapter. Next, some key factors for successful KM implementation, such as corporate culture, technological systems, ethical leadership, human resources management practices and organizational flexibility are identified and explained. After that, the case study of two firms which have successfully implemented a KMS in innovation-intensive industries, such as electronics and information technologies, is shown. Finally, and based on the results of the case study, some suggestions are extracted and recommendations are made from a managerial perspective in order to implement a KMS effectively.

INTRODUCTION

The knowledge-based view of the firm, in line with the resource-based view, considers knowledge as the most important strategic resource for ensuring an organization's long-term success and survival, because it is unique and difficult to imitate (Winter, 1987; Kogut and Zander, 1992; Grant, 1996; Conner and Prahalad, 1996; DeCarolis and Deeds, 1999). Hence, processes to manage this asset–e.g., transfer, storage and application– are recognised to be basic for the firm, and their strategic consideration imply they are fundamental to attain a firm's objectives (Zack, 1999a; Earl, 2001). In relation to this, some researchers understand knowledge management strategy (KMS) as the design of the processes related to the management of organizational knowledge and their implementation for the fulfilment of a firm's goals, among which innovation is included (e.g., Bierly and Chakrabarti, 1996; Hansen, Nohria and Tierney, 1999; Earl, 2001; Schulz and Jobe, 2001; Clarke and Turner, 2002; Maier and Remus, 2002; Choi and Lee, 2003; Garavelli, Gorgoglione and Scozzi, 2004; Donate and Guadamillas, 2007).

Research interest and empirical efforts in the study of the relationship between knowledge management (KM), innovation and competitive advantage have grown recently, and significant contributions have been made (see e.g., Gopalakrishnan and Bierly, 2001; Thomke and Kuemmerle, 2002; Nerkar and Roberts, 2004; Kor and Mahoney, 2005; Smith, Collins and Clarke, 2005; Subramanian and Youndt, 2005). Essentially, these works show that the knowledge base of the firm determines innovation efforts and may have a strong influence on their cost and performance. Thus, one firm can also achieve superior performance on the basis of its ability to generate new knowledge and utilize the existing base more effectively and efficiently than competitors (Grant, 1996; DeCarolis and Deeds, 1999). In this sense, the development of an effective KMS can be regarded as an important factor in contributing to a firm's pursuit of competitive advantage based on innovation (Zack, 1999a; Donate and Guadamillas, 2007).

For a KMS to be effective an adequate implementation approach is required (Donate and Guadamillas, 2007). For example culture, leadership or the kind of organizational structure are aspects, among others, which the companies have to take into account in order to put its selected KMS into practice. But although certain researchers in KM have broadly highlighted the role of the KMS formulation (see e.g., Bierly and Chakrabarti, 1996; Hansen et al., 1999; Choi and Lee, 2003) to date less has been published on the issue of the implementation. In this sense, more research on KMS implementation frameworks and the key elements that should be including in them is still necessary to ensure firms the success of their KM endeavours (Wong and Aspinwall, 2004: 94). Moreover, the analysis of such elements can help to better understand the main difficulties associated with this process –i.e., implementation– and identify how the firm can encourage its staff to use certain formal instruments in order to make the KMS implementation easier. Thus, the aim of this work is to explore what factors were present in two innovative firms that made significant progress in achieving their strategic objectives through appropriate implementation of KM strategies.

Therefore, in this chapter the implementation of the KMS in the firm will be analysed. Firstly, a brief review on KMS will be given. From the establishment of KMS, which is integrated by four main dimensions –objectives, conception of KM for firm managers, KM tools, and implementation support systems (Donate and Guadamillas, 2007)– we will focus in the last of these, the implementation support systems of KMS. Consequently, we include some important aspects which are needed to enable the firm to make its strategy possible to accomplish, such as cultural elements, ethical leadership, flexible structure, technological support or the promotion of some human resources (HR) practices. All these elements should help to make the development of KM processes easier, and in doing so, to spread innovation and to make KM more efficient for the firm. Finally, the implementation of a KMS oriented towards innovation is analyzed in two Spanish firms, which belong to technology-intensive industries. Thus, how these implementation aspects have been managed and the way they have contributed to the attainment of the strategic objectives of these organizations will be explained.

The first company –Indra– operates in some industries such as consultancy services, military defence systems and information technology (IT) developments. This company stands out for considering knowledge as its main productive asset and as being an innovation-intensive firm. Thus, knowledge creation, in which the continuous development of innovations is based, is an essential requirement to attain a competitive advantage (Grant, 2002). Due to this, KM in Indra is encouraged by strong cultural principles and HR practices based on the impulse of creativity with the aim of linking knowledge with innovation, all of which is supported by the firm's technological infrastructure.

The second firm is Tecnobit, which has developed a successful growth strategy by related diversification in electronics and information technologies, based on its organizational KM. For this firm, implementation processes to make this strategy possible have been essential, especially certain factors such as its flexible structure, the cultural values and the technological systems to integrate knowledge from different sources.

Overall, the study of the two cases will show some tools through which the KMS is implemented in the firm and the way they are employed according to the firm's objectives, conception (and importance) of KM for managers and some contingent aspects such as the conditions of the competitive environment, among others. Finally, some practical implications are given about the key factors in which the development of innovations is based. Furthermore, the most relevant aspects of the study will be discussed.

KNOWLEDGE MANAGEMENT STRATEGIES: A BRIEF REVIEW

The Knowledge Management Strategy (KMS) of a firm is based on the best possible strategic design in order to create, maintain, transfer and apply organizational knowledge to achieve competitive goals (Earl, 2001; Maier and Remus, 2002; Choi and Lee, 2003; Garavelli et al., 2004; Donate and Guadamillas, 2007). The development of a KMS includes all the operations related to the creation, acquisition, integration, storage, transmission, protection and application of knowledge (Day and Wendler, 1998). The management of this array of organizational knowledge processes is increasingly regarded as an important factor for contributing to a firm's pursuit of competitive advantage through innovation (Maier and Remus, 2002). A firm can achieve superior performance on the basis of its ability to generate new knowledge, and to utilize the current base more effectively and efficiently than its competitors (Quinn, Anderson and Finkelstein, 1996; DeCarolis and Deeds, 1999; Grant, 2002; Almeida, Phene and Grant, 2003).

Overall, a number of researches on KMS consider it integrates certain dimensions, recognising it as a complex concept (Bierly and Chakrabarti, 1996; Zack, 1999a; Earl, 2001; Maier and Remus, 2002; Garavelli et al., 2004). Some of these works incorporate a wide number of these dimensions, trying to include various KM processes developed by the firm (see e.g., Bierly and Chakrabarti, 1996; Zack, 1999a; Maier and Remus, 2002; Garavelli et al., 2004), while others are focused on one or a small number of these processes (see, e.g., Hansen *et al.*, 1999; Schulz and Jobe, 2001; Clarke and Turner, 2004; Un and Cuervo-Cazurra, 2004). Generally, the majority of these works elaborates different typologies of KMS, as a function of the selected dimensions, as table 1 shows.

Furthermore, most of these works shows that companies can obtain different performance levels by carrying out alternative strategic decisions in relation to KM, with the aim of attaining certain objectives are also guided by aspects such as the availability of learning sources and the extent of the knowledge base (Bierly and Chakrabarti, 1996), the preference of the firm towards the codification or personalisation of the organizational knowledge (Hansen et al., 1999; Schulz

Table 1. Some KMS typologies

Author/s	Dimensions	KMS typology
Bierly and Chakrabarti (1996)	• External *versus* internal learning • Radical *versus* incremental learning • Learning speed • Knowledge base extent	• Explorers • Exploiters • Loners • Innovators
Hansen, Nohria and Tierney (1999)	• Knowledge storage • Transfer and sharing	• Codification • Personalisation
Zack (1999a)	• External *versus* internal knowledge • Exploration *versus* exploitation • Conservative *versus* aggressive posture	• Explorers • Exploiters • Innovators • External acquisition • Internal development • Unlimited
Earl (2001)	• Focus • Interest • Unit • Successful critical factors • IT main contribution • "Philosophy"	• *Technocratic* -Systems -Cartographic -Engineering • *Economic* -Commercial • *Behaviourist* -Organizational -Spatial -Strategic
Schulz and Jobe (2001)	• Knowledge storage • Transfer and sharing	• Codification • Tacitness • Focused • Unfocused
Von Krogh, Ichijo and Nonaka (2001)	• Knowledge creation • Knowledge transfer	• Survival • Advanced
Maier and Remus (2002)	• Knowledge type (content) • Target group • Tools and technologies • Culture • Processes and organization of KM	• Several KMS in relation to each dimension
Choi and Lee (2003)	• Knowledge type (explicit vs. tacit)	• Passive • Persons centred • Systems centred • Dynamic
Clarke and Turner (2004)	• Knowledge source	• External acquisition • Internal development
Garavelli, Gorgoglioni and Scozzi (2004)	• Variety and relevance of the abilities (specific knowledge) • Abilities applicability • Compromise • Behaviour • Atmosphere • Management style • Type of knowledge • Source of knowledge	• Knowledge community • Knowledge market
Un and Cuervo-Cazurra (2004)	• Knowledge creation capacity	• Project teams • Knowledge organization

continued on following page

Table 1. continued

Leidner, Alavi and Kayworth (2006)	• Storage • Transfer	• Codification • Personalisation • Mixed
Donate and Guadamillas (2007)	• KM conception • KM objectives • KM tools • KM implementation support systems	• Proactive • Passive • Moderated • Inconsistent

and Jobe, 2001; Choi and Lee, 2003; Leidner et al., 2006), or the orientation in the development of the knowledge creation capacity (Un and Cuervo-Cazurra, 2004).

However, the development of strategies based on organizational knowledge and its effect on financial performance is a new line of research, which has not yet generated notable empirical findings (McEvily and Chakravarthy, 2002). For example, Teece (1998) points out, from a Resource-based View, that (1) few studies have found a clear relationship between knowledge management and performance, and (2) few studies have investigated how a knowledge-based advantage can be sustained. Specifically, the empirical work carried out on KMS focuses on some critical aspects, such as learning (Bierly and Chakrabarti, 1996), knowledge storage and distribution (Hansen, Nohria and Tierney, 1999; Schulz and Jobe, 2001) or the way in which knowledge is acquired or developed (Clarke and Turner, 2004). Also, its effects on competitive advantage and performance have been studied (Bierly and Chakrabarty, 1996; Choi and Lee, 2003; Donate and Guadamillas, 2007). From our viewpoint, two problems arise from these works: (1) they focus on specific aspects of organizational knowledge management and, in doing so, give a partial vision of the concept; and (2) these works do not consider other related aspects that are of great importance in the fulfilment of the strategic objectives of the organization (e.g., implementation issues).

Therefore, and from a more comprehensive perspective, the KMS design is based on the planning and starting up of all activities included in the knowledge management cycle–creation, storage, distribution and application–, in a manner that can contribute to the attainment of organizational goals (Earl, 2001; Donate and Guadamillas, 2007). In accordance with the prior literature, and from a classical content-strategy design (e.g., Ansoff, 1967; Andrews, 1971), we consider that several dimensions make up the KMS of the firm.

KM conception refers to the company's strategic orientation with respect to knowledge, which is reflected in the way the board of managers understand the potential contribution of KM for the firm. For example, they could understand that KM is just related to the use of information technologies or, conversely, be aware that it is a wider concept that includes both human and technical aspects (Huplic, Pouloudi and Rzevski, 2002). Therefore, it would express the main role that KM plays in the organizational system (Choi and Lee, 2003).

KMS objectives could be understood as the company's orientation towards the solution of the "gap" of knowledge in different operative and strategic areas within the organization: quality problems, efficiency searching, new product development, solutions to customer service failures, etc. (Zack, 1999a; Earl, 2001: 229). Generally, organizations attach a greater importance to the accomplishment of certain objectives over others. Moreover, managers will consider that KS can contribute to this fulfilment to a greater or a lesser degree. This fact can influence the way KM tools are designed and used in order to accomplish these objectives (Davenport, DeLong and Beers, 1998). Therefore, it would express

Table 2. Knowledge management strategy dimensions

- *Knowledge Management Conception*
-*Knowledge Management Strategy Objectives*
-*Knowledge Management Policies*: • Creation • Storage and retrieval • Transfer/sharing • Application • Protection
-*Implementation Support Systems*: • Leadership • Culture • HR practices • Flexible structure • Technological systems

the perceived –relative– importance of KM for the organization because it would establish how KS could contribute to the fulfilment of strategic objectives.

Knowledge management policies are the specific methods or initiatives used by the organization to support the creation, transfer, storage, retrieval and application of knowledge, and they can include technical as well as human components (Alavi and Leidner, 2001; Alavi and Tiwana, 2003). As Davenport et al. (1998: 44-45) indicate, these KM initiatives specifically seek to create knowledge repositories, to improve knowledge access and transfer or to manage knowledge as an asset –including its protection. Besides, the organization could focus on several procedures in a comprehensive manner, or on using some of its tools in a specific way.

Finally, in relation to *implementation support systems*, we consider organizational aspects that should make the development of KM processes easier, such as culture, leadership human resources practices, flexible structures, and technical systems. Culture should promote knowledge exchange and sharing in order to allow continuous innovation and change (Nonaka, 1994). Leadership is necessary to build the right context so different knowledge processes can be successfully developed. Therefore, knowledge "managers" must be aware of their "facilitator" role, promoting work independence, as well as the experimentation that is necessary to stimulate creativity (Davenport et al., 1998). Moreover, Quinn, Anderson and Finkelstein (1996) point out a number of essential changes that KM initiatives imply in human resources practices to make implementation possible. Thus, those related to the promotion of access/availability to the knowledge of experts, the development of work teams and communities of practices, or incentive methods, monitoring and control process systems, among others, stand out as important elements to accomplish the strategic –knowledge– objectives of the organization. Also, the implementation of a KMS should be supported by an adequate structure, which encourages the attainment of objectives and the development of the different knowledge processes in the firm. Thus, high-flexible structures will promote innovation because they push people to interact and encourage creativity, while others, that are more rigid, will be oriented towards searching for the greatest efficiency. Finally, technical systems are those tools based on information technologies (IT) used for developing (and making easier) certain knowledge processes, such as data bases, e-learning tools, intranets or other communication instruments.

This last dimension is analysed in depth next. The importance of all these elements in KMS implementation has briefly been shown and because of this, in the next point each element will be explained in more detail.

ELEMENTS OF KMS IMPLEMENTATION

As elements of the implementation of KMS support systems that stand out are those which have to make the development of KM processes easier with the aim of generating synergies and taking advantage of the creative and innovative capacity of employees and managers (Malhotra, 1998; Alavi and Leidner, 2001). Thus, support based on human resources practices, culture, flexible structures, leadership and technological systems stand out as being the most important for the firm.

Culture

For Guadamillas and Donate (2006: 57) the culture of firms that centre their strategy on KM display certain distinctive features: it is focused on satisfying customer needs; important endeavours are made towards developing technological aspects; and creativity is strongly promoted and encouraged. Therefore, culture must promote the sharing of knowledge and tolerance of mistakes –up to a certain point– and it must make easier changes that arise because of continuous innovation promoted by the creation and application of knowledge in the firm (Alavi and Leidner, 2001; Gopalakrishnan and Bierly, 2001).

The existence of a common language with the aim that the receiver knows the code and the context in which the knowledge that is transmitted arises (how this knowledge can be used) is essential as well (Kogut and Zander, 1992; Teece, 1998: 63). This common language is one part of a necessary level of common knowledge which allows the different specialists of the firm to collaborate and interact, looking for the integration and application of knowledge to be carried out efficiently (Grant, 1996; 2002: 184). Some of the principles of culture promoting knowledge processes are:

- The knowledge exchange among areas is supported by a common language
- The employees experiment and implement their ideas in the work journal.
- Mistakes are part of learning and they are tolerated up to a certain level.
- Culture is characterised by openness and trust among employees.
- Employees have a responsible behaviour and a high capacity for learning.
- The exchange of knowledge is encouraged by the firm, at informal level.
- The members of the organization perceive the same company intention, with which they feel compromised.

(Ethical) Leadership

Another way of supporting KMS implementation should be based on an effective orientation towards knowledge objectives through exercising leadership. This leadership should be furthermore based on ethical principles (Margolis and Walsh, 2003). The managers in charge of KMS implementation must assume their role as facilitators of the knowledge processes in the firm (Guadamillas and Donate, 2006; Leidner *et al.*, 2006). Thus, their efforts are centred on building an adequate setting for the diffusion, creation and application of knowledge. In this sense, Spender (1996: 47) asserts that managers should promote a certain level of independence at work, the assumption of responsibility and experimentation as well.

For example, Haas and Hansen (2005: 20) suggest that leaders should create high expectations in relation to the quality of work they expect of their teams, which promotes a continuous questioning

Figure 1. Knowledge processes and implementation support systems

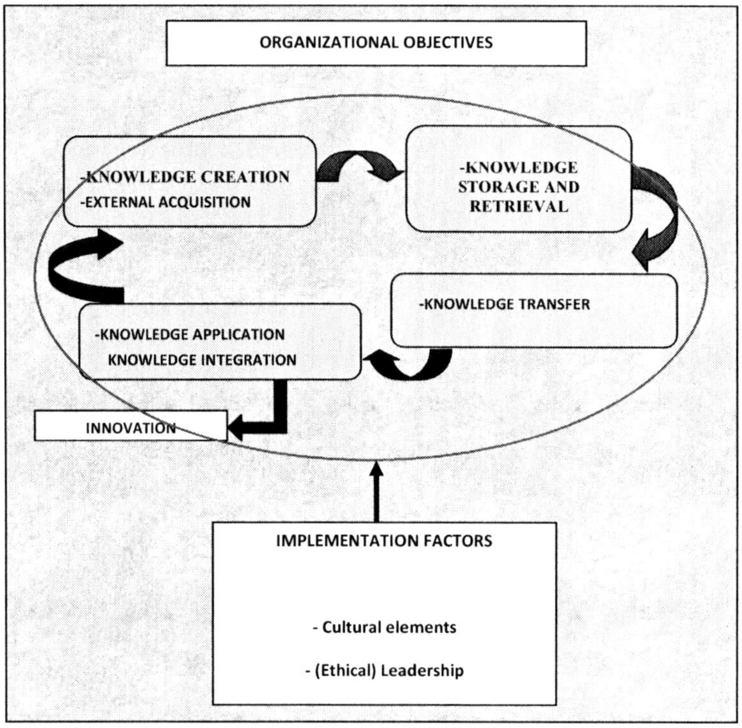

of the previously gathered knowledge, and thus the creativity is encouraged. Therefore, leaders are very important in this process, since they push for the necessity of introducing changes in the firm and in facing uncertain situations, all of which involves the development of new knowledge and innovation (Rosenbloom, 2000).

Moreover, in the promotion of these knowledge processes through leadership, certain ethical and social responsibility principles should also be considered. This is because the way the company applies these principles, values and ethical practices affects the relationships with its stakeholders: shareholders and other investors, customers, suppliers, employees, communities and the Government. This application can lead to social benefits and legitimacy for the firm, since it can consider itself as a coalition in which the different stakeholders participate to gain their own benefit (Douma and Schreuder, 2004). For instance, when a firm satisfies customer needs, it generates an intangible asset, that is, the customer's trust, and when it satisfies the employee's needs it builds commitment, identification and trust in relation to the firm.

Therefore, the application of ethical principles and corporate social responsibility (CSR) activities to the development of innovations and new knowledge can contribute to value creation. Some contributors to the knowledge-based theory of the firm (e.g., Kogut and Zander, 1992, 1996; Grant, 1996; Conner and Prahalad, 1996; Spender, 1996) highlight the necessity of giving a social vision to KM, because firms handle knowledge from individuals who are responsible for its productive application within the firm. It also helps to explain the nature and boundaries of the firm (Kogut and Zander, 1992; Conner and Prahalad, 1996; Ghoshal and Moran, 1996). On this point, it is important not to forget the motivational effects of the application of CSR activities that concern employees, because profits that the firm will be able to generate and keep for itself depends on the application of their knowledge, over which the firm does not have entirely effective control (Grant, 2002).

Support Based on Human Resources Practices

O'Dell and Grayson (1998) point out that learning and sharing –all that which it has been learned– is a social act, and that knowledge transmission implies willingness and positive attitudes both in the receiver and in the person (or group) who transfers the knowledge. In the same vein, Gupta and Govindarajan (2000) also indicate this motivational willingness in both directions as one of the key questions in the knowledge transfer and sharing processes. The accessibility to the knowledge of organizational members is one of the key objectives of KM, because capabilities, experience, abilities and the "know-how" of individuals are the essence of a firm's competitive advantage (Guadamillas and Donate, 2006: 59). On the other hand, the generation and integration of knowledge among individuals requires practices that encourage the socialization and externalization of tacit knowledge (Nonaka and Takeuchi, 1995; Nonaka and Konno, 1998). Quinn et al. (1996) expose an array of important changes that a KMS implies for HR management, all of which stand out in this context: the improvement of the access to/availability of expert knowledge; the promotion of team work –as a means of sharing experiences and making interaction and dialogue easier–; incentives systems based on the promotion of knowledge sharing and application and rewards for the team work; training to develop abilities and for the handling of IT tools; and the assessment of processes as a way of controlling them jointly through the promotion of empowerment and self-control.

Flexible Structure

Organizational flexibility, needed in companies whose competitive advantage is based on innovation and constant knowledge creation, can be promoted in different forms, and its basic principles are those associated with what is typically referred to as the "organic" structure (Burns and Stalker, 1961). Therefore, a high decentralization, fluid horizontal communications, flexible and narrowly defined tasks, a small number of hierarchical levels, organization in projects or team work, and a number of strategic alliances stand out as elements that offer a considerable flexibility to organizations developing their activities in unstable environments with a significant level of technological uncertainty and ambiguity (Butler, 1991: 76; Grant, 2002: 201).

Certain initiatives developed to encourage knowledge transfer and sharing, which group the individuals in teams or projects with different kinds of objectives, deserve a special mention. For instance, the *communities of practice* are defined by Brown and Duguid (1991) as organizational groups in which the interest for the improvement of work practices, learning and innovation are the main objective. In these communities, the knowledge is shared by its members and has to be used for executing a concrete job with pre-specified tasks and a pre-defined performance[a]. On the other hand, Foss and Manhke (2003) point out the *epistemological communities* as another kind of team which –unlike communities of practice– does not have specified *ex-ante* means or goals. Their main advantage is based on the lack of specifications, which can promote creativity to generate knowledge that gives solution to non-routine problems (Foss and Manhke, 2003: 94). The problem, in this case, could arise from the lack of clear objectives and an established hierarchy in the teams, which could force it to look for in-between solutions that tend to establish limited structures (responsibility, hierarchy) with some freedom for experimentation; i.e., structures not so rigid as to strictly control the processes nor so chaotic that everything is left to improvisation (Brown and Eisenhardt, 1997: 2-3). Whatever the teams orientation, knowledge creation and sharing in these are two tasks that tend to be undivided due to the principles, language and shared beliefs about the work and the vision of the world held by the team (Oliveira, 1999: 27).

The strategic alliances are another aspect that stands out in flexible organizations (Grant and Baden-Fuller, 2004). However, while is undisputable that these give great flexibility to the organizations, one feature which is of special importance for the KMS is the manner in which knowledge is transferred and shared between the agreement members (Hitt, Ireland and Santoro, 2004). The key question is how to share the agreed knowledge without transferring the core knowledge of the implicated firms, although the characteristics of the agreement (e.g., exploration *versus* exploitation) have an important influence as well. The government structure of the alliance and other aspects such as partner confidence, the investments in specific assets, or the previous agreements carried out by the firm will be essential in order to obtain relational rents[b] in the strategic alliance (Dyer and Singh, 1998).

Technological Systems

Technological systems are those tools based on information technologies (IT) which are used to develop (and to make easier) knowledge processes. They support and, in some cases, systematize some processes of creation, storage, transfer and application of knowledge (Davenport and Prusak, 1998). Although tools based on IT are not applicable to all aspects of KM, they can support it in diverse ways. For instance, tools based on IT can help to develop a support infrastructure in relation to the improvement of speed, scope, dynamics and efficiency of KM processes (Davenport and Prusak, 1998; Zack, 1999b; Alavi and Leidner, 2001; Alavi and Tiwana, 2003).

Alavi and Leidner (2001) refer to knowledge management systems as all those applications based on IT which are used by the firm in its KM tasks. Following Alavi and Leidner (2001) and

Table 3. Tools based on IT (supporting KMS)

KM process	*Creation*	*Storage and retrieval*	*Transfer/sharing*	*Application*
KM tools (IT)	-E-learning -Collaboration support systems	-Data warehousing -Data mining -Repositories	-Communication support systems -Information company site -Knowledge directories	-Expert systems -Support systems to the decision making -Work-flow systems
IT make easier...	-Combination of new knowledge sources -"Just in time" learning	-Support to the organizational memory -Knowledge access among groups	-More wide internal network -More availability of communication channels -Rapid access to knowledge sources	-Knowledge can be applied in a number of localizations -Rapid application of new knowledge through the work-flow automation

Source: adapted from Alavi and Leidner (2001:125) and Alavi and Tiwana (2003: 115)

Alavi and Tiwana (2003), the tools of the knowledge management system can be grouped around four basic KM processes: creation, storage and retrieval, transfer/sharing and application. Table 3 shows some examples of these tools related to each KM process.

CASE STUDIES: IMPLEMENTATION OF KMS

Methodology

The implementation of a KMS oriented towards innovation is next analyzed in two Spanish companies, which belong to technology-intensive industries. The case studies will show some tools through which the KMS is implemented in the firm and the way they are employed according to aspects such as the company objectives and the conception (and importance) of KM for managers, among others. Finally, some practical implications will be given regarding the key factors in which the technology development is based.

In general, a case study aims to examine a "contemporary phenomenon within its real life context" (Yin, 1994: 13). As a research method, it is viewed as improving our knowledge of individual and organizational phenomena (Van Maanen, 1979; Yin, 1994). Case studies primarily involve researchers undertaking an in-depth study of particular organizations with a wide variety of evidence being collected as a result. In our case, we collected multiple data and information from interviews with one of the main directors of each firm and other companies' documents. In interviews, questions were of an unrestricted nature in order to encourage the manager to converse freely (Maykut and Morehouse, 1994). These interviews were carried out on September 2006 (Indra) and June 2006 and October 2007 (Tecnobit). In relation to documents, extracts from internal reports, the companies web sites and other relevant information from secondary sources (e.g., financial press), were also used to elaborate both case studies.

The INDRA Case

Indra is a leading corporation in IT development and military defence systems in Spain[c], and also operates in other industries such as consultancy services. In 1991, it managed to overcome a crisis situation with several problems among the companies of the group, as it counted on great potential in terms of resources and capabilities, having taken a set of decisions that year with the aim of reorganizing its activities, such as mergers, sale of divisions and spins-off. In addition to this, it restructured its internal organization reducing the size of some divisions along with its productive capacity and staff, it limited its debts and it consolidated its market position. Recently, Indra has reinforced its leadership position in the IT sector in Spain, through the acquisition of SOLUZIONA's consultancy and IT businesses[d] and the purchase of the Spanish firm AZERTIA, which was formalized in September of 2006. Nowadays, it holds a strong competitive position in some national and international markets[e].

The IT industry, which Indra forms part of, has made advances in important organizational themes in comparison to other industries, such as the prominence of horizontal structures and self-managed work teams. At the same time, knowledge creation, in which the process of continuous innovation in the company is based, is a fundamental requirement to attain competitive advantages in the market. For Indra, these aspects are all considered as strategic objectives and so form part of its business model.

The success factors in the implementation of the knowledge management model in Indra are mainly its corporate culture, the support of ethical leadership, the development of its innovation capacity, the involvement of employees and the

Figure 2. Indra's business model

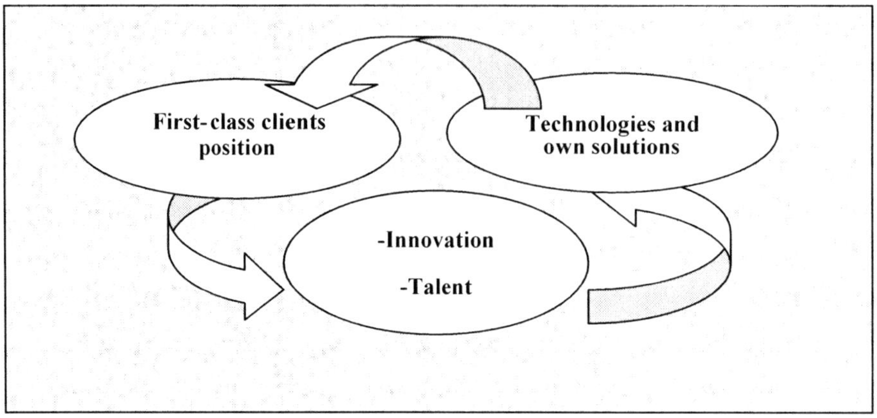

Source: Indra, 2005, 2006

coherency between strategic and organizational issues.

Corporate Culture

One of the main aspects that explain the current strong competitive position of the firm is its corporate culture. This is based on different elements that try to benefit the stakeholders, its orientation to product and customer, the global conception of problems, and innovation[f]. This company stands out for considering knowledge as its main productive asset and being an innovation-intensive firm. Thus, knowledge creation, on which the continuous development of innovations is based, is an essential requirement for attaining competitive advantages in markets in which it competes. Due to this, KM in Indra is supported by cultural principles and human resources practices based on the impulse for creativity with the aim of linking knowledge with innovation, all of which is supported by the firm's technological infrastructure.

Also, another main principle of Indra's corporate culture is the application of ethical values and CSR (Corporate Social Responsibility) in relation to the development of new knowledge and innovation. The corporate culture stimulates the consideration of CSR as a basic aspect of its KMS. Other essential cultural aspects are the shared vision, the commitment to common projects, team-work, independence in decision making, tolerance of mistakes which is implicit in innovation, shared learning and ethical values. To disseminate these principles and values some initiatives stand out, such as institutional declarations about the mission and the firm's values, the elaboration of ethical codes and training actions on social responsibility themes.

Indra considers the creation of knowledge to be a key element of its strategy and a key responsibility in order to generate technologies and solutions which provide value to the stakeholders, especially customers, suppliers and communities in which it operates. Established relationships with these stakeholders also offer Indra relevant knowledge about their needs and the market's evolution. Due to this, the strengthening of the firm's participation in agreements and alliances with stakeholders and its ethical performance in these is very important. This allows Indra to learn "best practices" identify their needs and reinforce relationships with them and to drive its innovative efforts in the correct direction.

(Ethical) Leadership

The responsibility of the company's decisions correspond to all the individuals who participate in the decision making process. Thus, managers are morally responsible and because of this, their behaviour should be an example for other employees in an attempt to achieve the vision or strategic intent of the firm (Hamel and Prahalad, 1989). Also, responsibility of the managers is derived from the promotion of a culture which highlights knowledge and innovation.

The Improvement of the Innovation Capacity through Flexible Structure

The innovation capacity is understood in Indra in a wide sense, including the improvement of products and processes and those innovations which are refer to the strategic management area. Thus, KMS implementation through flexible structural elements such as team-work, communities of practice and strategic alliances, among others, are seen as an essential issue in the strategy which leads to the development of knowledge and innovations.

A prominent initiative is the organization of work in *multidisciplinary teams*, which facilitate knowledge exchange, even that of a tacit nature. When teams are self-managed or when they have a high level of independence to take decisions regarding objectives and processes to achieve them, they themselves become an important factor for motivation, because they reinforce participation, independence and consensus about objectives and methods. This allows employees to actively involve themselves in the creation, acquisition and transfer of knowledge in which innovation is based. Teams also contribute to the dissemination of cultural values of innovation, and in doing so, meet with Indra's essential objectives. All this implies an improvement in the working environment and the reduction of conflicts –jointly with the cost that they imply.

Employees Commitment through Human Resource Practices

Employees are an essential group for Indra because they are directly affected by most of the firm's decisions that refer to KMS implementation. This produces a positive influence on employees –e.g., practices based on a proper communication, the improvement of the work climate– or trying to avoid negative tendencies –e.g., problems related to sharing knowledge or lack of willingness to do so. Moreover, employees actively participate in the KMS implementation and assume cultural values as an essential part of their work only when they have a high level of motivation. Also, their active participation in the innovation process is indispensable, because they hold skills, abilities, creativity and tacit knowledge of high strategic value, all which they have to be willing to share and apply to their work. Likewise, employees must individually assume part of the responsibility for their learning and performance, although the organization should make their training and professional development easier (Quinn et al., 1996).

The most important practices which Indra develops in relation to employees participation in KMS implementation, motivating their work are:

- Systems to promote learning and professional development.
- Fixed and variable incentives in relation to achieving results.
- Active participation in some of the company's decisions, relating to specialization and the way that decisions affect to their objectives.
- Systems which promote fluid communication among employees and other stakeholders regarding the strategic objectives, activities

and company results. The initiatives range from formal documents (e.g., the strategic plans or the conduct codes) to meetings which promote informal communication.

- Programs of equality for opportunities, non-discrimination and labour conciliation, based on mutual respect for the rights of the individuals and which allow the better qualified and more motivated employees to occupy the most adequate position in the firm.

The TECNOBIT Case

Tecnobit is a Spanish company which has developed a growth strategy by related diversification based on the management of its organizational knowledge. Specifically, Tecnobit has based its strategy on the utilization and application of the accumulated knowledge within its own organization, jointly with the acquisition of external knowledge through cooperation agreements and certain purchases of companies. These aspects have contributed towards improve its strategic position in the markets in which it competes.

Tecnobit has five lines of activity with the following sales income distribution (2006): Avionics (49%); command and control systems (21%); simulation systems (14%); optronics (8%), and IT systems (8%) (Figure 3). The diversification strategy of the Company, starting from its main activity of aviation electronics, has evolved towards new simulation and training projects in the same industry[g], as well as towards the IT field, through the creation of command and control systems, the development of software, and knowledge management projects. With the purchase of certain enterprises, the company has extended its activities beyond the electronics industry, to provide maintenance and technical support to other companies. Specifically, Tecnobit incorporated a computer services enterprise into the company, and currently continues to consolidate its growth in related industries. In 2007, the Company had more than 300 employees[h], and its growth continues.

Competitive conditions are changing within the industries that Tecnobit operates. Firms are intensive in knowledge and innovation is a very dynamic process. To face these competitive conditions and the innovation challenge, Tecnobit has designed a dynamic and aggressive growth strategy. The objective is to generate synergies in knowledge and to improve the value of the company through internal development and related diversification. Currently, its financial position is healthy, and it has improved its efficiency due to the reduction of commercial and general expenses, through a functional and organizational restructuring. Nowadays, Tecnobit faces new growth challenges from the success of its R&D projects that imply to have a financial and industrial size wide enough for access to new projects; to develop new technological products and to promote its

Figure 3. Tecnobit's activity lines

Avionics	Optronics	Command and control systems	Simulation	Information systems
-EF-2000 -Avionics equipment -Manufacturing	-Thermal Chambers -IR Systems	-Command and control -Tactical communication -Maintenance tools	-Operational simulators -Tactical simulators -Civil simulation	-Systems/ Applications -Tools -Services

Source: Tecnobit Report (2007)

commercial activity; to offer new solutions and products to its main customers; and to promote its presence in international markets[i].

A deeper analysis of the success factors involved in the process of creating and developing IT knowledge and skills and turning them into new products and services allows a deeper understanding of the process of organizational growth. In this process, strategic and organizational elements interact in the development of new knowledge and innovations. For this company, certain factors of KM implementation have been essential in order to make this strategy possible: the development and integration of IT and technological resources for KMS, the human resources policies, organizational flexibility, knowledge management tools and activities, cultural values and the integration of knowledge from different sources. Also, a key factor analyzed is the successful governing of cooperation agreements with other firms and institutions for the acquisition of external knowledge regarding IT opportunities, which gives Tecnobit great flexibility in its structure.

Information Technologies for Knowledge Management

Tecnobit has based its growth on the application of available resources and the expertise and knowledge about IT, internally developed or acquired, for the development of new products and services. Owing to this, it manages to take advantage of the great potential which, from a strategic and organizational viewpoint, IT can offer to some critical activities for knowledge management –to ease the access to, the transfer of and the storage of knowledge and information within the firm. The diversification strategy of the group is based on the application of IT to the following branches of activity:

- Development of Information and Control Systems.
- Simulation and Training Systems.
- IT for Document Management.
- Tools for Technical Documentation.
- IT for software development in knowledge management activities: storage and knowledge linkages, distribution, and systems to facilitate the application of newly created knowledge.

The continuous innovation in Tecnobit is based on the appropriate use of the capabilities and knowledge about IT that it develops and applies to projects and products. All of these have a high technological content, especially in its principal activity of defense electronics, as well as the new technological developments in aviation, in electro-optical sensors, in simulation and training tools, in command and control systems, in software development and in other products related to IT (Figure 3). All of this requires continuous investment in R&D in order to technically update products and develop new technologies[j]. Also, the implementation of different quality regulations, which have to be continuously updated, is very important.

IT development for KM in Tecnobit has been built up since the incorporation of the SIDOCOR company, which was founded in 1988 and was dedicated to IT and knowledge management tools and systems development. Currently, its activities (as a Tecnobit's division) are based on the use of web technologies in open and multi-platform systems. Moreover, the development of applications and content with international standards are carried out through the use of document management and content tools, designed to serve as a help in the creation, storage, retrieval, transfer and application processes of knowledge management. In general, it has developed different tools based on IT for all knowledge management activities, especially for storage and transfer. They are shown in Table 4, and their utility and application for KMS implementation are explained next.

Information and control systems are based on IT and communication technologies, adapted

Table 4. IT for knowledge management

- Information and Control Systems - Document Management Tools - Storage Systems - Other Archive Systems

to the commercial, security and defense sectors. Among these, the Incidence Management Systems (IMS) stands out, which are applied to the financial sector to unify and relate, with the help of the client, operative and technical control information and data. Along the same lines, control systems have been developed to integrate different airport systems and the Aerial Operations Control Systems, capable of quickly integrating very diverse information and explicit knowledge about air traffic and incidents. Moreover, it has developed Decision Support Systems, which facilitate the creation and application of new knowledge. These are based on the use of databases and simulation procedures to construct scenarios to make decision-taking easier.

Document management systems are used for knowledge storage activities, such as digitalization, structuring, filing according to selected standards, control of the authorship of documents, and the management and electronic editing of databases. Since 2000, these systems have been used by public organizations of different countries, and are now also applied within the own company.

The development of technical documentation consists of the creation of knowledge archive systems – specifically technical manuals – for the documentation of "software" products, or for equipment and systems for the aeronautical sector. These are specific projects for client companies, and they are applied in Tecnobit as well.

Finally, it has created *systems to store and to relate all the information and accumulated knowledge*. The main goal is to make their transfer and user access easier, for their subsequent use. To make this possible, the contents are structured as a web site, where authorized users can access all knowledge and updated information which the company possesses on one subject, and improve it through their contribution of new data or information. Another use of these systems is to make electronic training for employees easier. Thus, it has developed systems adapted to the user's needs, through the application of Intra/Extranet solutions and SGML/XML document databases.

Also, the firm exclusively commercializes and implements the *HYPERWAVE tool*, which offers knowledge management solutions, electronic learning, and corporate sites. Through this product, Tecnobit continues its related diversification strategy, securing its strategic positioning in the aeronautical field and introducing itself into the civil commercial field. It is a help tool for operations related to document management (indexation, authorship control, versions control, etc.), web content management (linking, presentation, upgrading, security, etc.), the creation and management of a corporate site, information search in a structured manner, work-flow management, assistance for team work and assistance for learning at a distance (courses, forums, libraries, searches, course support, etc.), among others.

The development of these tools based on IT and the accumulated knowledge about them is a basic factor for the development of its growth strategy by related diversification, since they have been successfully applied in new business and markets.

HR Practices for Organizational Knowledge Management

The employees' knowledge is one of the main resources for the firm, because experience, expertise, abilities, skills, and the "know-how" of individuals are the essence of a firm's competitive advantage when it is coordinated, combined, and applied for creating value (Grant, 1996; Kogut and Zander, 1992). Also, as a result of this combination and coordination, new valuable knowledge is created, both in an individual and in a collective sense as well (Grant, 1996; Spender, 1996). However, the generation and integration of knowledge among individuals need practices that encourage the socialization and externalization of tacit knowledge, access and availability to the knowledge of experts, or the training of the firm's employees (Nonaka and Takeuchi, 1995; Quinn *et al*., 1996). In this case, the main HR practices that support the knowledge management processes and the development of technological capabilities of Tecnobit are: the contracting of highly qualified employees, the implementation of appropriate and extensive training practices, the use of teamwork, and the design and implementation of various incentive systems to promote specific aspects in the organization, such as knowledge sharing or the extensive use of IT. It is important to note that these practices allow for some degree of individual and group autonomy while ensuring the achievement of organizational goals.

Due to the high technological level of the industries in which the company operates and the continuous innovation activities carried out, it is essential to have highly qualified employees. Moreover, the organization of work is based on *multidisciplinary teams*. These are work groups that have been designed to make knowledge creation and its transfer in the firm easier. They constitute one of the continuous and intensive collaboration tools among different professionals, who possess very distinct knowledge. This fact characterizes the process of innovation and the creation, accumulation and transfer of knowledge in the firm. Also, in Tecnobit, work in teams is very set in the culture of the firm. The employees have great motivation and are acquainted in depth with the productive processes of the firm.

Another system used is the *contribution of suggestions* by employees. In addition, to encourage the effective storage and transfer of knowledge some databases have been designed. Principally two exist: the *good practices* database and the *failures* database. The latter is used more when the objective is to learn from former mistakes and to minimize future failures. In these databases, tacit knowledge is transformed into explicit knowledge and is applied in practice to activities by combining it with the existing knowledge (the accumulated knowledge base of the firm). The key aspect to make the system useful – and successful – is that employees use it frequently, because this enriches its content and utility.

Moreover, the firm carries out *continuous training programs*. Staff in charge for HR organize these programs, but in a flexible form, because it is the departments which request training on specific themes, either of a technical or managerial nature (quality, work risks, logistics, office applications, process management, or business administration, among others). Any of the employees can participate in them, and this fact makes the increase and updating of their knowledge and the development of their abilities easier. In many cases, in order to promote participation, distance-learning courses are given through computer systems. Training plans enable employees to develop an individualized career plan, and are critical in achieving the consolidation of knowledge, technical know-how and the improvement of work in all organizational areas. Also, the company gives training in topics concerning quality to all employees, especially in relation to quality policies, procedures or control methods.

Furthermore, Tecnobit has established motivation and incentive systems to promote work improvement and knowledge transfer, especially tacit knowledge. Monetary incentives exist which involve 2-3% of the profits, which go to the different departments. The department head decides the amount that goes to each person, without considering the hierarchical level, but based on production and contribution to the improvement of work in the firm, and participation in knowledge management. The latter aspect is very important in Tecnobit, so a monetary incentive for the best suggestion of the month has been set, which can refer to any technical or administrative subject.

Incentive systems motivate employees to share their knowledge, even though it entails an additional cost in the management process.

All the analyzed aspects are supported by a strong *corporate culture,* which promote active participation in knowledge sharing and innovation. This is one of the most important organizational elements, due to its influence on the functioning of the company structure and human resources management.

Flexible Structure

The growth of Tecnobit since 2000 has involved new management problems, due to a significant increase in its size and changes in its strategy, all of which was essentially caused by the necessity to coordinate companies with different cultures and backgrounds, which were purchased by the company in order to grow and go into new business areas.

To solve these problems, Tecnobit has implemented a kind of flexible organization based on the decentralization of those functions which can be carried out more efficiently in the divisions, even if in some cases some functions are jointly developed by the divisions and the central office. Thus, albeit certain decisions about financial topics and human resources remain centralized, in some cases divisions negotiate their long term debts, develop or seek training activities, or start the selection process for a particular employee. This allows the firm to obtain flexibility in its organizational structure and a high efficiency level, which is essential for making the creation, application and integration of new knowledge easier.

Also, a key aspect in making Tecnobit's structure more flexible is the successful governing of cooperation agreements with other firms and institutions for the acquisition of external knowledge regarding IT opportunities.

IMPLICATIONS AND CONCLUSION

The elements of KMS implementation are recognized by the firms of the study as playing an important role in innovation development and the attainment of other objectives. The two case studies show that the implementation of a KMS must be carried out in a coherent manner in relation to corporate culture, leadership, human resources practices, flexible structure and technological systems, all which will positively influence a firm's performance.

The Tecnobit case shows the way organizational and strategic elements interact for the development of new knowledge and innovation. These are: the development and integration of IT and technological resources (Alavi and Leidner, 2001); human resources policies (Andreu and Ciborra, 2001; Tannenbaum, 1997); organizational flexibility; and knowledge management activities and tools. Also, the successful management of cooperation agreements in order to acquire external knowledge about IT related opportunities or to generate knowledge jointly stands out (Kessler, Bierly and Gopalakrishnan, 2000). These agreements are of growing importance, because the synergies and risk reduction that they involve allow a number of companies to decide on growth through technological cooperation.

One of the most interesting conclusions of the Indra case is the involvement of CSR in KMS. Firms face CSR problems in all of the activities they develop, especially in their relationships with stakeholders, KM and innovation. Integration of CSR in corporate and business strategy implies the belief that, in some manner, responsible behaviour helps to achieve the organizational objectives and to solve problems, with higher economic efficiency and less social costs (Lyon, 2004; Anderson and Bieniaszewska, 2005). Additionally, the ethical values of managers determine their vision on what the organizational objectives should be and the appropriate way to attain them. Due to this, the achievements of firms can not be explained without CSR considerations (Margolis and Walsh, 2003). Thus, the analyzed company has acquired an essential knowledge on stakeholders' needs and problems from its relationships with them, which allow it to identify new business opportunities. This knowledge is integrated in the organizational base (of knowledge) and, as a result of this, the objectives of the firm are established through the consideration of the stakeholders' goals. Later, this knowledge is applied to the development of innovations. Overall, social responsibility, KM and innovation are integrated in the strategic management of the firm and they jointly contribute to promote confidence and a reputation as a responsible company.

Because of this, it should be pointed out that the most innovative firms which are managed by ethical leaders have an opportunity of ensuring that social responsibility and ethical principles are implemented in a coherent manner and, in doing so, contribute to the attainment of economic efficiency, confidence and culture identification. As a direct result of this, these aspects turn into knowledge and innovation propellants and thus, form part of the basis of a firm's competitive advantage.

Based on the two companies studied, the main implications and key factors to promote and support KM initiatives will be highlighted next:

Shared and strong corporate culture. The values system to support KMS implementation include aspects such as continuous and intense communication between employees at different levels, incentives for sharing knowledge, considerable efforts to develop and improve technological tools for KM and openness to innovation through the promotion of creativity.

(Ethical) leadership. Leaders must facilitate the development of KM, promoting collaboration and participation between employees, the sharing, transfer and application of knowledge, and closer collaboration with stakeholders, all which implies making ethics and KMS coherent and compatible.

Human resources practices. Some human resources practices like training and education are needed to implement the KMS. Employees must improve their skills and abilities in order to make valuable contributions to the innovation process. They should be trained and motivated to increase their participation and provide more flexibility. Also, training and reinforcement in cultural and ethical values is essential in order to achieve an adequate KMS implementation.

Flexible structure. KMS should be implemented at all levels of the organization, from the team work to the top strategic levels. This is difficult to do for organizations that compete in global markets (such as Tecnobit and Indra) and also for large size firms such as Indra. Self-managed teams, high level of decentralization in the decision-making, fluid communication, flexible tasks, a small number of hierarchical levels, and strategic and corporate agreement with stakeholders are the main elements that are used to provide flexibility to the organization in order to implement KMS.

Technological systems. When applied in coherence with all the previous elements, technological systems contribute to KMS implementation because they make easier the combination of knowledge from different sources, learning and the access to the employees' knowledge, their storage and application, and a more fluid communication.

Overall, the experience of Tecnobit and Indra shows how KMS must be implemented in a coherent, strategic, holistic and progressive manner. The agreement and involvement of all the organizational members is essential, jointly with the assumption of the firm's cultural values, all which it has to be supported by an ethical leadership.

ACKNOWLEDGMENT

Authors wish to thank Antonio Cuquerella (Tecnobit's plant director at Valdepeñas, Spain), Emma Fernández (Indra's Corporate Strategy and Marketing Director at Madrid, Spain) and Beatriz Sánchez Guitián (Indra's Corporate Development and Marketing Manager at Madrid, Spain) for their support in the development of this research. We also thank two anonymous reviewers for their helpful comments and suggestions, and Rachel Davy for her assistance in preparing this book chapter for publication.

REFERENCES

Alavi, M., & Leidner, D. (2001). Knowledge Management and Knowledge Management Systems: Conceptual Foundations and Research Issues. *MIS Quarterly, 25*(1), 107-136.

Alavi, M., & Tiwana, A. (2003). Knowledge Management: The Information Technology Dimension. In M. Easterby-Smith & M. A. Lyles (Eds.), *Organizational Learning and Knowledge Management* (pp. 104-121). London: Blackwell Publishing.

Almeida, P., Phene, A., & Grant, R. (2003). Innovation and Knowledge Management: Scanning, Sourcing and Integration. In M. Easterby-Smith & M. A. Lyles (Eds.), *Organizational Learning and Knowledge Management*, (pp. 356-371). London: Blackwell Publishing.

Anderson, C., & Bieniaszewska, R. (2005). The Role of Corporate Social Responsibility in an Oil Company's Expansion into New Territories. *Corporate Social Responsibility and Environmental Management, 12*, 1-9.

Andreu, R., & Ciborra, C. (1996). Organizational Learning and Core Capabilities Development: The Role of Information Technology. *Journal of Strategic Information Systems*, June, (pp. 117-127).

Andrews, K. (1971). *The Concept of the Corporate Strategy.* Homewood: IL, Irwin.

Ansoff, H. I. (1965). *Corporate Strategy.* New York: McGraw-Hill.

Bierly, P., & Chakrabarti, A. (1996). Generic Knowledge Strategies in the US Pharmaceutical Industry. *Strategic Management Journal, 17*(1), 123-135.

Brown, J., & Duguid, P. (1991). Organizational Learning and Communities of Practice: Toward a Unified View of Working, Learning and Innovation. *Organization Science, 2*(1), 40-57.

Brown, S. L., & Eisenhardt, K. M. (1997). The Art of Continuous Change: Linking Complexity Theory and Time-paced Evolution in Relentlessly Shifting Organizations. *Administrative Science Quarterly, 42*, 1-34.

Burns, T., & Stalker, G. M. (1961). *The Management of Innovation.* London: Tavistock Institute.

Butler, R. (1991). *Designing Organizations: A Decision Making Perspective.* London: Routledge.

Choi, B., & Lee, H. (2003). An Empirical Investigation of Knowledge Management Styles and Their Effect on Corporate Performance. *Information & Management, 40*, 403-417.

Clarke, J., & Turner, P. (2004). Global Competition and the Australian Biotechnology Industry: Developing a Model of SMEs Knowledge Management Strategies. *Knowledge and Management Process, 11*(1), 38-46.

Conner, K. R., & Prahalad, C. (1996). A Resource-Based Theory of the Firm: Knowledge *versus* Opportunism. *Organization Science, 7*, 477-501.

Davenport, T., & Prusak, L. (1998). *Working Knowledge.* Cambridge, MA: Harvard Business School Press.

Davenport, T., DeLong, D., & Beers, M. (1998). Successful Knowledge Management Projects. *Sloan Management Review, 39*(2), 43-57.

Day, J. D., & Wendler, J. C. (1998). Best practices and Beyond: Knowledge Strategies. *The McKinsey Quarterly, 1*, 19-25.

DeCarolis, D. M., & Deeds, D. (1999). The Impact of Stocks and Flows of Organizational Knowledge on Firm Performance: An Empirical Investigation of the Biotechnology Industry. *Strategic Management Journal, 20*, 953-968.

Donate, M., & Guadamillas, F. (2007). The Relationship between Innovation and Knowledge Strategies: its Impacts on Business Performance. *International Journal of Knowledge Management Studies, 1*(3/4), 388-422.

Douma, S., & Schreuder, H. (2004). *Economic Approaches to Organizations*. Third Edition, New York: Prentice Hall.

Dyer, J. H., & Singh, H. (1998). The relational View: Cooperative Strategy and Sources of Competitive Advantage. *Academy of Management Review, 23*, 660-679.

Earl, M. (2001). Knowledge Management Strategies: Toward a Taxonomy. *Journal of Management Information Systems, 18*(1), 215-233.

Foss, N. J., & Mahnke, V. (2003). Knowledge Management: What Can Organizational Economics Contribute? In M. Easterby-Smith & M. A. Lyles (Eds.), *Organizational Learning and Knowledge Management*. (pp. 78-103). London: Blackwell Publishing.

Garavelli, C., Gorgoglione, M., & Scozzi, B. (2004). Knowledge Management Strategy and Organization: a Perspective of Analysis. *Knowledge and Process Management*, *11*(4), 273-282.

Ghoshal, S., & Moran, P. (1996). Bad for Practice: A Critique of the Transaction Cost Theory. *Academy of Management Review, 21*(1), 13-47.

Gopalakrishnan, S., & Bierly, P. (2001). Analysing Innovation Adoption Using a Knowledge-based Approach. *Journal of Engineering and Technology Management, 18*, 107-130.

Grant, R. M. (1996). Toward a Knowledge Based Theory of the Firm. *Strategic Management Journal, 17*, 109-122.

Grant, R. M. (2002). *Contemporary Strategy Analysis. Concepts, Techniques and Applications (Fourth Edition).* Boston: MA, Blackwell Publishers.

Grant, R. M., & Baden-Fuller, C. (2004). A Knowledge Accessing Theory of Strategic Alliances. *Journal of Management Studies, 41*(1), 61-79.

Guadamillas, F., & Donate, M. (2006). Conocimiento organizativo, innovación y crecimiento empresarial: el caso del Grupo Tecnobit. *Universia Business Review, 12*, 50-65.

Gupta, A., & Govindarajan, V. (2000). Knowledge Flows within Multinational Corporations. *Strategic Management Journal, 21*, 473-496.

Haas, M. R., & Hansen, M. T. (2005). When Using Knowledge Can Hurt Performance: The Value of Organizational Capabilities in a Management Consulting Company. *Strategic Management Journal, 26*, 1-24.

Hamel, G., & Prahalad, C. K. (1989). Strategic Intent. *Harvard Business Review, 67*, May-June, 63-78.

Hansen, M. T., Nohria, N., & Tierney, T. (1999). What's Your Strategy for Managing Knowledge. *Harvard Business Review*, March-April, (pp. 106-116).

Hitt, M. A., Ireland, R. D., & Santoro, M. D. (2004). Developing and Managing Strategic Alliances, Building Social Capital and Creating Value. In A. Ghobadian *et al.* (Eds.), *Strategy and Performance: Achieving Competitive Advantage in the Global Marketplace*. New York: Palgrave, (pp. 1-14).

Huplic, V., Pouloudi, A., & Rzevski, G. (2002). Towards an Integrated Approach to Knowledge Management: 'Hard', 'Soft' and 'Abstract' Issues. *Knowledge and Process Management, 9*(2), 90-102.

Kessler, E. H., Bierly, P. E., & Gopalakrishnan S. (2000). Internal vs. External Learning in New Product Development: Effects on Speed, Cost and Competitive Advantage. *R& D Management, 30*(3), 213-223.

Kogut, B., Zander, U. (1992). Knowledge of the Firm, Combinative Capabilities and Replication of Technology. *Organization Science, 3*(3), 383-397.

Kogut, B., & Zander, U. (1996). What Firms Do? Coordination, Identity, and Learning. *Organization Science, 7*(5), 502-518.

Kor, Y. Y., & Mahoney, J. T. (2005). How Dynamics, Management, and Governance of Resource Deployments Influence Firm-Level Performance. *Strategic Management Journal, 26*, 489-496.

Leidner, D., Alavi, M., & Kayworth, T. (2006). The Role of Culture in Knowledge Management: A Case Study of Two Global Firms. *International Journal of e-Collaboration, 2*(nº 1) 17-40.

Lyon, D. (2004). How Can You Help Organisations Change to Meet the Corporate Responsibility Agenda? *Corporate Social Responsibility and Environmental Management, 11*, 133-139.

Maier, R., & Remus, U. (2002). Defining Process-Oriented Knowledge Management Strategies". *Knowledge and Process Management, 9*(2), 103-118.

Malhotra, Y. (1998). Knowledge Management for the New World of Business. *Asian Leadership Institute Review (Business Studies Special Issue), 20*, 489-514.

Margolis, J., & Walsh, J. P. (2003). Misery Loves Companies: Rethinking Social Initiatives by Business. *Administrative Science Quarterly, 48*, 268-305.

Maykut, R., & Morehouse, R. (1994). *Beginning Qualitative Research: A Philosophical and Practical Guide*. London: The Falmer Press.

McEvily, S. K., & Chakravarthy, B. (2002). The Persistence of Knowledge-based Advantage: An Empirical Test for Product performance and Technological Knowledge. *Strategic Management Journal*, *23*(4), 285-305.

Nerkar, A., & Roberts, P. W. (2004). Technological and Product-Market Experience and the Success of New Product Introductions in the Pharmaceutical Industry. *Strategic Management Journal, 25*, 779-799.

Nonaka, I. (1994). A Dynamic Theory of Organizational Knowledge Creation. *Organization Science, 5*(1), 14-37.

Nonaka, I., & Konno, N. (1998). The Concept of "Ba": Building a Foundation for Knowledge Creation. *California Management Review, 40*(3), 1-15.

Nonaka, I., & Takeuchi, H. (1995). *The Knowledge Creating Company: How Japanese Companies Create the Dynamics of Innovation*. New York: Oxford University Press.

Oliveira, M. (1999). Core Competencies and the Knowledge of the Firm. in Hitt, M.A. *et al.* (Eds.): *Dynamic Strategic Resources: Development, Diffusion and Integration*. (pp. 17-41). New York: John Wiley & Sons.

O'Dell, C., & Grayson, C. J. (1998). If Only We Knew What We Know: Identification and Transfer of Internal Best Practices. *California Management Review, 40*(3), 154-174.

Pearce, C. L. (2004). The Future of Leadership: Combining Vertical and Shared Leadership to Transform Knowledge Work. *Academy of Management Executive, 18*(1), 47-57.

Quinn, J. B., Anderson, P., & Finkelstein, S. (1996). Leveraging Intellect. *Academy of Management Executive, 10*(3), 7-27.

Rosenbloom, R. S. (2000). Leadership, Capabilities, and Technological Change: The Transformation of NCR in the Electronic Era. *Strategic Management Journal, 21*, 1083-1103.

Schulz, M., & Jobe, L. A. (2001). Codification and Tacitness as Knowledge Management Strategies: An Empirical Exploration. *Journal of High Technology Management Research, 12*, 139-165.

Smith, K. G., Collins, C. J., & Clark, K. D. (2005). Existing Knowledge, Knowledge Creation Capability, and the Rate of New Product Introduction in High-Technology Firms. *Academy of Management Journal, 48*(2), 346-357.

Spender, J-C. (1996). Making Knowledge the Basis of a Dynamic Theory of the Firm. *Strategic Management Journal, 17*, 45-62.

Subramanian, M., & Youndt, M. A. (2005). The Influence of Intellectual Capital on the Types of Innovative Capabilities. *Academy of Management Journal, 48*(3), 450-463.

Tannenbaum S. I. (1997). Enhancing Continuous Learning: Diagnosis Finding from Multiple Companies. *Human Resource Management, 36*(4), 437-452.

Teece, D. J. (1998). Research Directions for Knowledge Management. *California Management Review, 40*(3), 289-292.

Tecnobit (2007). *Tecnobit Report.*

Thomke, S., & Kuemmerle, W. (2002). Asset Accumulation, Interdependence and Technological Change: Evidence from Pharmaceutical Drug Discovery. *Strategic Management Journal, 23*, 619-635.

Un, C. A., & Cuervo-Cazurra, A. (2004). Strategies for Knowledge Creation in Firms. *British Journal of Management, 15*, 27-41.

Van Maanen, J. (1979). Reclaiming qualitative methods for organizational research: a preface. *Administrative Science Quarterly, 24*, 520-526.

Von Krogh, G., Ichijo, K., & Nonaka, I. (2001). *Facilitar la Creación de Conocimiento.* México: Oxford University Press.

Winter, S. G. (1987). Knowledge and Competence as Strategic Assets. In D. J. Teece (Ed.), *The Competitive Challenge: Strategies for Industrial Innovation and Renewal.* (pp. 159-184). Cambridge, MA: Ballinger Publishing Company.

Wong, K. Y., & Aspinwall, E. (2004). Knowledge Management Implementation Frameworks: A Review. *Knowledge and Process Management, 11*(2), 93-104.

Yin, R. K. (1994). *Case Study Research: Design and Methods.* Sage: London.

Zack, M. (1999a). Developing a Knowledge Strategy. *California Management Review, 41*, 125-145.

Zack, M. (1999b). Managing Codified Knowledge. *Sloan Management Review*, summer, (pp. 45-58).

KEY TERMS

Case Study: Methodology of research which involves researchers undertaking an in-depth study of particular organizations with a wide variety of evidence being collected as a result.

Innovation-Intensive Firm: A company developing businesses in technology-intensive industries with knowledge considered as the main productive asset.

KMS Implementation Support Systems: Organizational aspects that should make the development of knowledge management processes easier, such as culture, leadership human resources practices, flexible structures, and technical systems.

KMS Objectives: A company's orientation towards the solution of the "gap" of knowledge in different operative and strategic areas within the organization.

Knowledge Management Practices: Specific methods or initiatives used by the organization to support the creation, transfer, storage, retrieval and application of knowledge, and they can include technical as well as human components.

Knowledge Management Strategy (KMS): Design of processes related to the management of organizational knowledge and their implementation for the fulfilment of a firm's strategic goals.

Knowledge Management Systems: All those applications based on information technologies which are used by the firm in its knowledge management tasks

ENDNOTES

[a] These teams, through the interactions that take place among its members, are knowledge generators in the sense pointed out by Nonaka and Takeuchi (1995), because they generate a common space in which socialization processes are developed.

[b] Relational rents can be understood as "supernormal profit jointly generated in an exchange relationship that cannot be produced by either firm in isolation and can only be created through the joint idiosyncratic contributions of the specific alliance partners" (Dyer and Singh, 1998: 662). Management of strategic alliances involves four aspects that directly affect the possibility of achieving *relational rents* (Dyer and Singh, 1998): (1) Investments in relation-specific assets; (2) Management of knowledge exchange, including that which results in joint learning and routines; (3) Adequate combining of complementary resources and capabilities that result in the joint creation of new products, services or technologies; (4) Effective governing mechanisms of inter-firm alliance that results in a lower transaction cost than cooperative arrangements of competitors.

[c] Its growth path responds to a related diversification through knowledge on IT and developments in this area.

[d] Soluziona is a technological-intensive company which formed part of the Union Fenosa Group, in Spain.

[e] In 2007, Indra achieved around about € 2.150 million in sales, had close to 23,000 employees, and developed projects in more than 80 countries over four continents.

[f] Activities Report of Indra (2005, 2006).

[g] Some examples are: electro-optical sensors, Command Systems, and Naval Control or Aerial Operations Control Systems.

[h] 80% of the employees have a university degree in engineering and IT fields.

[i] Memory Report from Tecnobit (2007).

[j] During the course of the last years Tecnobit has devoted, on average, 8.5 % of sales income to R&D .

Chapter XII
Developing a Corporate Knowledge Management Platform in a Multibusiness Company

Arla Juntunen
Helsinki School of Economics, Finland

ABSTRACT

This chapter focuses on the development of the Knowledge Management (KM) platform, and, more generally, the knowledge- and resource based view (RBV) of the firm. The knowledge is seen as a source of a competitive advantage. In high-velocity markets, like the ICT-sector, the knowledge is crucial in creating a long-term competitive advantage over the competitors. The study claims that corporate performance was improved when the case company simultaneously exploited a balanced set of related knowledge resources of the corporate KM Platfrom across its business areas.

INTRODUCTION

Managing the data, information and knowledge in a business as well as using it to gain a sustainable competitive advantage, is a challenging assignment in any organization. Knowledge management essentially consists of tools, practices and processes to efficiently capture, store and share data and knowledge between individuals within an organization. The last decade has witnessed a growth of information generated within organizations due to the increased use of technology and the internet. In the 1990s, companies discovered knowledge as a new source of competitive advantage (See e.g. Davenport, 2001; Möller & Svahn, 2006; Nonaka et al., 2001) The concept of knowledge management was widely discussed in the information technology and management literature. Sharing, transferring and storing knowledge has highlighted the need to further develop data warehousing to support learning and knowledge management within the organization. Exploiting information and knowledge within data warehouses is one method to attain industry-leading performance (Juntunen, 2008; Matusik & Hill, 1998; Törmänen, 2003) and a competitive advantage in markets. Organizations that develop and leverage knowledge resources are more likely to achieve success than organizations with a greater dependence on tangible resources (Autio et al., 2000; Yli-Renko et al., 2002).

Also, the spirit of the knowledge-based view must be fully understood in order to truly conceptualize the value of knowledge to organizations that operate in dynamically changing environment, as exemplified by the ICT sector. The increasing importance of innovation and rapid product development in the ICT-sector has made an awareness of knowledge creation and innovative organizational transformations a critical issue in an organization. Therefore, knowledge management (KM) is not a narrow information technology (IT) related function within an organization, but rather an integration of strategic management, learning, R&D, use of different technologies, human capital and business management. From this perspective, knowledge creation and management in an organization is not purely a problem of product development, but also a question of mastering the renewal and transfer of information both within all hierarchic levels of an organization and between different communities of practice, forming a continuous organizational development process and a way to rapidly capitalize on innovations. An organization with valuable, rare, inimitable and non-substitutable resources can generate a sustainable competitive advantage over its rivals, thus resulting in better financial performance (See e.g. Barney, 1991; Conner, 1991; Hatch & Dyer, 2004; Wernerfelt, 1984).

Moreover, the introduction of Internet and web-based tools haves given rise to many forms of online interactions, including e-mail, instant messaging, blogging, and community based online services. In addition to descriptive personal profiles, members of such online communities publicly articulate mutual "friendship" links with other members, creating a browseable network of social relations (Heer & Boyd, 2005). The KM Platform concept in the case corporation included tools for different communities: for work projects, for teams and for leisure time-related online societies and individuals.

The following sections will begin with an overview of the development of Knowledge Management platform (KM Platform) concept and then proceed to explain the development, benefits and consequences of its implementation.

BACKGROUND

The case organization is Elisa. Elisa, formerly known as Helsinki Telephone Corporation, has been on the forefront of telephone and service development in Finland since 1882 (Juntunen, 2005). Elisa is a leading Finnish communications service company whose shares are quoted on the Helsinki Exchanges. Its core business areas are Consumer and Small Enterprise Customers, Business Customers and Production. The Group's revenue in 2007 amounted to EUR 1.57 billion. In the end of 2007 the Elisa Group employed approximately 3,000 people. In 2007, Elisa's operational model was based on two business units, production and support functions. The aim of the new operational model is to further increase customer orientation and cost efficiency. (Elisa, 2006, 2007) Elisa is the Finnish market leader in broadband subscriptions. Its vision is to be the most attractive and effective operator. Elisa operates in Finland and in carefully selected international market areas, and provides international services in association with its partners Vodafone and Telenor (Elisa, 2006). During the years 2003-2007 Elisa unified its organizational structure, strengthened its market position in chosen core markets, added new services in its service portfolio and launched itself into new markets (Elisa, 2007).

The case corporation's approach to organizational learning and to knowledge management was based on the KM Platform concept (see Figure 1). The KM Platform concept outlined different areas of information, and knowledge sharing for communities, individuals and for work and leisure time. The Community element of the KM Platform concept consisted of tools for business management and learning, such as benchmarking information, best practices, and listings of different competence laboratories and projects. It also included internal surveys, news of competitors and products, and access to e-libraries. The individual part of the platform concept consisted of tools for self-learning, education, recruitment and job rotation. During the initial phase of the KM Platform concept between 1999 and 2001, an attempt was made to understand the key factors and events affecting development. The resultant KM Platform concept developed during this time still supports the current strategy of the case corporation, its knowledge management initiatives and needs.

The preliminary analysis of the development of KM platform concept was part of a longitudinal qualitative study of the years 1990-2003 (Juntunen, 2005). Research documentation consisted of both information about the telecommunication industry and the case corporation's development. Interviews were undertaken during 1999 to 2005 with personnel sourced from various levels of the organization as well as from the network partners and from Elisa's main competitor. Data gathered consisted of articles, project documents, memorandums relating to strategies, businesses and competence laboratories in different communities of practice. It must also be noted that this study focuses on the experiences of a large company with a multi-business organization. Additional information was acquired of the years 2005-2007 for this chapter.

It can be claimed that the findings of this study have a general relevance, particularly for organizations operating in dynamic, rapidly changing fields characterized by several interlinked technologies. The relevance of this study can reach beyond the limited time period. The research design is based on a logical sequence to connect empirical data to the initial research questions (Miles & Huberman, 1994; Yin, 1994). The qualitative methods make it possible to develop a thorough understanding of a complex and a multi-dimensional phenomenon in a specific context. The case design here is a single case study based on one corporation. The reason for choosing a case study approach lies in the in-depth knowledge required regarding the evolution of different collaborative forms and their managerial processes. Information about these phenomena requires intensive access to an organization in order to be able to identify them (Heide & John, 1995; Yin, 1994). A case study is claimed to assist understanding of the complexity of process and change (Cassel & Symon, 1994; Pettigrew, 1990; Van de Ven & Poole, 1990), as confirmed by Hartley (1994) who emphasized the tailor-made nature of a case study as allowing observation within a real-life context. Follwing these contextual approaches by Pettigrew (1985, 1987) this study argues that the multibusiness knowledge management and organizational capability development cannot be understood unless one examines it over longer period of time. Moreover, the network theory suggests that the ties within multi-business firms such as business groups create both opportunities and constraints for innovation: opportunities that arise from resource access and availability (Coleman, 1990; Håkansson & Lundgren, 1995).

In this study, the two diverse fields of research, namely the knowledge management (KM) and resource-based view of the firm (RBV), were synthesized. Literature review on knowledge management depicts the different views of the concept of knowledge management and its objectives. Many authors discuss just on coding and measuring knowledge as intangible asset that an organization can exploit focusing on individual as the unit of analysis and conceptualizing knowledge as an objective and easily measurable (Davenport,1998; Malhotra, 2000). Other researchers argue that knowledge management is closely related to learning organization and that it should also consider the social aspect of knowledge management (Nonaka & Takeuchi 1995). Some consider knowledge management as a way to capture knowledge embedded in collective practices and they also consider the community of practice as the unit of analysis (Virkkunen & Ahonen, 2000). This study discusses both the codified knowledge and knowledge embedded in collective practices.

The resource-based view (RBV) is view used to determine the strategic resources available to a firm. The fundamental principle of the RBV is that the available capabilities are the basis for a competitive advantage of a firm (Wernerfelt, 1984, p.172; Rumelt, 1984, p.557-558)

The interaction between the KM technology and inter- and intra-organizational relationships were examined as part of understanding multibusiness synergies. In a dynamically changing environment it is challenging for any organization to pursue major innovations or systemic product offerings because of the dispersion of knowledge and technological resources. Companies try to overcome this by seeking knowledge transfer and, more ambitiously, joint ventures or alliances to create knowledge and innovations through collaboration (Kogut & Zander, 1997; Teece, 2000).

In general, this study discusses of the cross-business knowledge synergies (See Goold and Luchs, 1993). Theoretically, this study tries to synthesize the resource-based views (RBV) of diversification and knowledge management theory to conceptualize cross-business knowledge synergies of a multibusiness company, like the case company Elisa, in terms of the complementarity of knowledge resources, like customer and technology knowledge, of different business areas when developing a corporate KM Platform.

DEVELOPMENT AND IMPLEMENTATION OF THE KM PLATFORM

The KM platform concept was developed to support a multibusiness organization in acquiring and collecting diverse information and knowledge from within the corporation and from the surrounding competitive environment.

The KM platform represented different views of knowledge sharing and exchange across the multibusiness organization. It also denoted the different knowledge management perspectives and roles of the various actors involved in order to develop a shared view of KM within the organization. The existing legacy systems held a lot of information from different business processes. However, not all the information was used or was analyzed to guide the business or to predict the business trends. The developers of the KM platform wanted to ensure that the existing legacy systems would be able to capture and encode knowledge for further business applications.

The Information Technology Architecture in the KM platform concept assisted in codifying, storing and delivering the knowledge to different organizational parts. KM tools also assisted in locating knowledge and information within the company and accelerating the creation and acquisition of knowledge within the case organization.

The platform concept was created to leverage organizational knowledge across business areas. Knowledge could be transferred directly, through education and training, or indirectly. The KM platform was divided into four parts (see Figure 1): Community (*C*), Individual (*I*),

Work & Management (*WM*) and Learning & Developing (*LD*).

The KM platform consisted of the following parts (see Figure 1):

1. (I) consisted of personal-level information such as recruitment and training opportunities in addition to organizational information.
2. (LD) was the corporate e-learning platform. There was an internet based academy which was created in conjunction with universities and other research foundations and institutes. Since 1990, continuous cooperation with Finnish and international research organizations formed an integral part in adopting and implementing new technologies at Elisa and these technologies were also used to assist organizational learning and capability and skill development. (Juntunen, 2005; Elisa, 2005).
3. (WM) consisted of a managers' toolkit consisting of essential documents and information, related to the methods for improving administrative or operational managerial work.
4. (C) consisted of access to e-libraries, news, business intelligence (BI) information, industry-level surveys and other useful material from both domestic and international partners and research networks. Domestic R&D partners included universities, higher education institutions, the VTT - Technical Research Centre of Finland and innovative

Figure 1. KM-platform in Elisa (© Liisa Varjokallio, Elisa: the pictures of Elisa are published with the courtesy of Elisa, with permission of Elisa) (published in Juntunen, 2005, p.141)

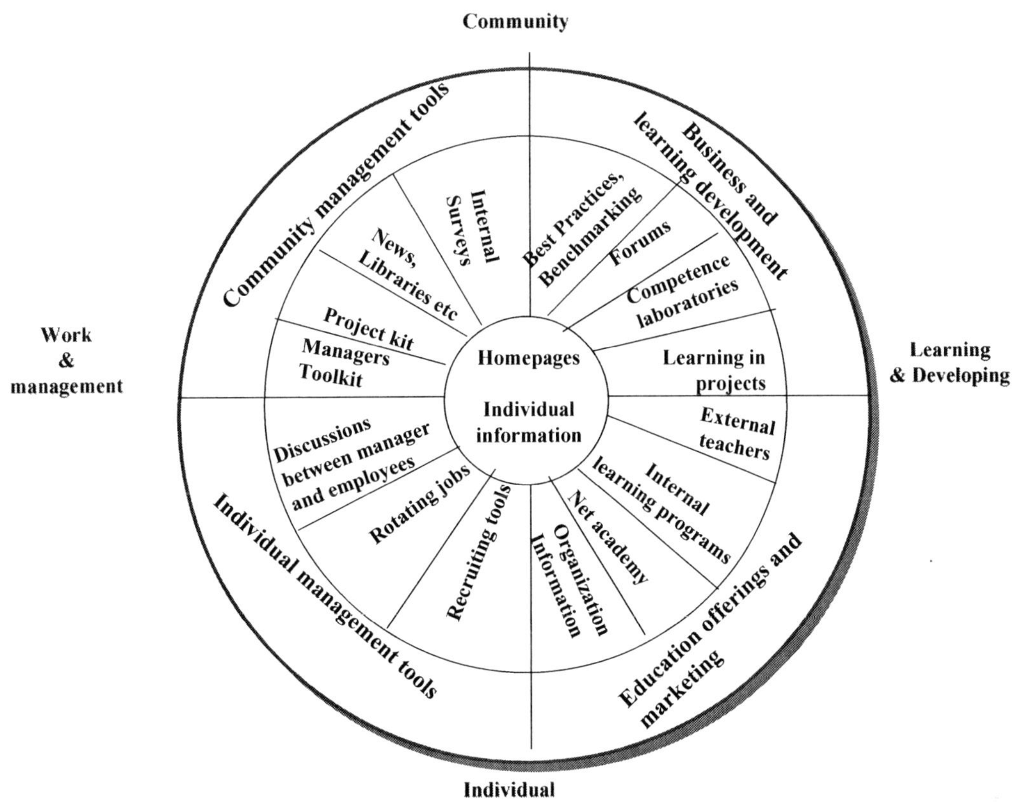

private sector companies, like Nokia and Cisco. (www.elisa.com, 2008) International collaboration partners were: IETF (Internet Engineering Task Force), ITU (International Telecommunication Union), OMA (The Open Mobile Alliance Ltd, W3C (The World Wide Web Consortium) and WWI (Wireless World Initiative). (www.elisa.com, 2008)

A new version of a change laboratory model for team-level (see Virkkunen & Ahonen, 2004) called the competence laboratory was also tested in the case organization. The competence laboratories model was part of the KM Platform and its community tools. Current methods of grassroots level organizational learning connect learning to the incremental, linear expertise development and processes management. (Virkkunen & Ahonen, 2004) The competence laboratories model was developed at the University of Helsinki. It was a bottom-up approach to facilitate the learning process within and between the communities of practices within an organization (cf. Ahonen et al., 2000). In the competence laboratories-model, roots of recurrent problems occurring in work processes were traced and conceptualized. The model was also used to evaluate potential for change and to develop a long term activity plan. (Virkkunen & Ahonen, 2000) The competence laboratories were tested in several functional areas in the case company between 1990 and 2000, including customer service, installation and product maintenance. Specifically, this model was employed in customer service and help desk areas to fine tune interaction between the various elements of help desk functionality and associated processes, from sales to delivering the service to customers. The competence laboratory model was useful in change management and transferring existing knowledge across the organizational boundaries in a change situation or in a business transformation.

The organization of the KM process and KM technology support within the case company were assigned to trained KM network personnel. Training sessions and competence laboratories were held within the organization. The organizational management was interested in KM development and supported it. The Human Resources Director Liisa Varjokallio championed KM within the organization and fostered the KM development.

In the case company, a new business creation and development was seen as a collective process that required interaction and cooperation with internal and external partners, particularly because of the managerial challenges of a fast changing technological environment. Therefore, it was necessary to disseminate managerial experience and practices throughout the organization. The case organization believed that managers should not be bound by past experience but should examine the implications of future business scenarios and encourage innovativeness. In addition, the managers performed an important role within the organization in fostering the organizational knowledge of employees and supporting the vision and strategies selected by management. However, mentoring between managers was equally important in order to support common goals and to share knowledge of best practices. The case organization used the so called manager's toolkit to assist young/new managers in the enhancement of their managerial and networking skills. Nevertheless, access to knowledge and information still required the users of the KM Platform to have both the capacity and competence for understanding, assimilating, compiling and using the retrieved knowledge, and the skill to be able to adapt the information and to their specific issues. For example, it seemed to be very difficult to provide any kind of fixed managerial toolkits for handling business network management issues. All strategic business decisions and subsequent business situations are unique and could only be understood in the context of the business network situation and the business history that has produced the current partners and services. The management toolkit therefore consisted of best practices and administrative documentations, like rules and procedures.

USAGE AND BENEFITS OF THE KM PLATFORM

With the help of corporate KM Platform, the case organization managed to create new forms of joint learning and collaborative networks. Knowledge creation, exchange and transfer played a crucial role in the various collaborative forms. In the case corporation different types of knowledge bases had been created over time: some were based on mobile-technologies, some on the Internet and some from the integration of several technologies. These were incorporated with the KM Platform.

Knowledge exchange was limited in some of the collaborative networks because the participants were unwilling to share crucial information, especially in situations where competitors were acting as coopetitors. Knowledge and information sharing happened with known and trusted partners. These formed the basis for the future competitive advantage. Historical development and past experiences influenced the actors' use of new technologies and solutions and also the partners chosen. If past experiences with actors in projects had been good, those actors were likely to be used again. If the experiences had been less positive, those actors were stringently assessed before being selected to participate in projects. However, the limited number of individuals or organizations with the requisite knowledge of home networking and related technologies meant they were not completely out of consideration. It was essential to keep solid working relationships with everyone. The different experiences of partnerships and collaborations were also documented in the KM platform as best practices or lessons learned.

The KM Platform seemed to support the creation of a new business and business networking strategy within the case corporation. The most successful new service and technology platform ideas were created while the KM platform was being developed. Personnel in R&D and in new business development understood that cooperation and corporate synergy was, in most cases, advantageous for any new business. The R&D personnel that took part of the KM development were successful both in product development and innovation. These ideas, processes and platforms were the most profitable ones in Elisa between 2000 and 2007. These included: Elisa's DSL-solutions and Kotiportti™ which consists of various subscriber connections and community services, household monitoring and security systems; Efodi – the learning space; and the technical solutions used in mobile and DSL-services offered to consumers and business customers today.

Management noticed that there were different reasons to use the KM Platform in new business development and in collaborative business networking. There appeared to be different types of knowledge and information requirements relating to capability creation and utilization in business development and R&D. The key objectives common to the R&D alliances during 1999 to 2000 included the utilization and development of core capabilities in both network and communication technologies (Hölttä, 2000). The case company had realized that the competitive advantage of companies relied on its managerial and organizational processes, supported by dynamic capabilities. They had also collaborated with universities to access the most recent studies of dynamic capabilities (See Juntunen, 2005). These dynamic capabilities reflected the organization's ability to integrate, build, reconfigure and renew internal and external competences to address changes in its competitive environment (cf. Teece et al. 1997, Teece, 2003). Elisa's particular goal in the R&D alliances was to fine-tune product concepts generated from earlier R&D projects between 1990 and 1999. These ideas related to educational platforms in the Internet, self-learning in the

Internet, home automation, data security issues, and VOIP-technology[a]. The case organization also tried to establish a best practice method, with which they could manage either several concurrent R&D processes in different business units, or R&D projects concerning multiple products and services within the case company (Hölttä, 2000). Since 2005, Elisa's greatest investment target in long-term research was MobiLife, the EU's large-scale sixth generation framework project. MobiLife investigates everyday customer-centric applications and services enabled by technological development. The key areas of study included personalization and adaptable interfaces, as well as privacy, security and trust. Moreover, Elisa was one of the initiators of Forum Virium Helsinki, a cluster project concerned with digital content and services. The aim of the first Forum Virium project in 2005, called Finnish MobileTV Forum, was to establish a cluster of enterprises to develop mobile TV services and to introduce and to commercialize them. Moreover, Dimes Association cooperation project promoted the development of technology and service innovations related to the ICT field in Finland. (www.elisa.com, 2008)

The R&D projects formed so-called collaborative innovation networks (COINs) (cf. Gloor et al. 2003) based on knowledge, technologies and capabilities required. They consisted of self-motivated individuals drawn from different business areas of the case company and also sometimes from multiple organizations, driven by an idea or a vision. By locating and analyzing the work methods and processes of COINs in the organization with the help of the KM Platform concept, the case company was able to streamline R&D processes of different strategic business areas between 1999 and 2001, also managing to create competitive advantage in markets. In addition, according to Timo Simula (2003), who was a manager in several new business networks and involved in R&D, those people who were involved in projects and business networks learned and were capable of finding, using and adapting the new knowledge, but it also seemed as if the company itself did not learn or that the learning cycle was unbelievably slow.

Moreover, the transformation points of a business where happens organizational and processual changes can cause causal ambiguity in capabilities and knowledge sharing and trasferring in the company. In the case company, these transformational points were the changes of the CEO and corporate strategy in 1990, 1994, 1997 and 2003 and major organizational structural changes in 2000, 2003 and 2005.

CONCLUSION

As a summary, it seems that companies that are good in managing knowledge within the organization tend to be good at other things, too, like for example, they, can speed products into the markets, and respond quickly in competitors' challenges and exploit emerging markets faster than the competitors. It also seems that the knowledge transfer within a multi-business company can create opportunities for new product development and innovation: opportunities that arise from resource access and availability (cf. Håkansson & Lundgren, 1995). This is an expression of a new characteristic of a corporate strategy; namely the knowledge- and capability-based competition.

Knowledge management is increasingly involved in the creation of new collective capabilities. This calls for a new form of collaborative learning activity and dialogue between management and other employees. This supports the studies of competence and change laboratories by Virkkunen and Ahonen (2004). In a rapidly changing technological environment, the challenges of learning that employees encounter changes as businesses develop. Different forms of learning are required in different phases of the business life-cycle, organizational and/or environmental transformation. This study supports the studies of Virkkunen and Ahonen (2004) because learning in an incremental process improvement is also a part of a business change cycle, and a renewal of a business concept (cf. studies of Hong & Ståhle, 2005).

Additionally, since organizations in high-velocity markets exist to achieve predictable and superior results than the competitors, the employees are encouraged to share their knowledge. This takes place through improved information management about where knowledge resides, how it can be used and reused, and where or when it can create greater business value through new ideas and innovations. That was the basic reason for the case company to develop the KM platform The greatest challenge for the case company is still the renewal of the knowledge base in the KM platform because it needs to be updated and knowledge and information need to be there in-time otherwise it is not useful for anybody.

This study also claimed that corporate performance was improved when the case company simultaneously exploited a balanced set of related knowledge resources of the corporate KM Platfrom across its business areas with diverse business portfolios. This supports the previous research by Goold and Luchs, 1993. The development of the KM Platform resulted from the need for knowledge transfer both within and between different organizational units. Elisa's management clearly understood that knowledge transfer could create or reveal existing synergies between different businesses and business networks, thus, creating a competitive advantage at market. Therefore, either creating or locating the cross-business synergies was central to the performance of multi-unit and multi-business organization, characterized by diverse business models, technology platforms and service portfolios (Goold & Luchs, 1993). It seemed that when the case company aimed at leveraging its capabilities and finding synergies in a multibusiness environment, management focused on process efficiency especially in R&D. This supports also studies by Mintzberg, Ahlstrand and Lampel (1998, 175-231), claiming that the collective learning and knowledge management are essential in professional organizations that operate in high-velocity business environment.

As this chapter discussed the issue of developing and implementing a KM platform, it managed to touch on several important factors, including the benefits of a corporate level KM Platform and strategy planning, the management roles in this process and synergies with R&D and knowledge transfer within the organization. Future studies can assess whether the exploitation of a common corporate KM Platform and common practises and processes to manage knowledge and information across multiple businesses creates synergies or are there other factors, like specific business related capabilities that can explain the creation of competitive advantage over the competitors in markets. Broadly speaking, this study suggests that competitive environment, knowledge requirements and the existing capabilities are influential factors driving firms towards different forms of collaboration in order to gain more knowledge and lacking resources. Empowered by the digital media, business networks are expected to take the leading role in innovation development in knowledge-driven society (Castells,1996,; Parolini, 1999). This study therefore also suggests that high-tech organizations have capabilities and specific business-related knowledge that seem to arise from managing a complex web of relationships of teams and coordinating a large number of interdependent processes. Managers should consider the organization as a set of capabilities and knowledge assets in order to integrate these assets and capabilities in different situations in R&D, customer service, manufacturing or production needs.

REFERENCES

Ahonen, H., Engeström, Y., & Virkkunen, J. (2000). Knowledge management – The Second Generation: Creating Competencies Within and

Between Work Communities in the Competence Laboratory. In Y. Malhotra (Ed.), *Knowledge Management and Virtual Organizations*. London, UK: Idea Group Publishing (IGP).

Autio, E., Sapienza, H. J., & Almeida, J. G. (2000). Effects of Age at Entry, Knowledge Intensity, and Imitability on International Growth. *Academy of Management Journal, 43*(5), 909-924.

Barney, J. B. (1991). Firm resources and sustained competitive advantage. *Journal of Management, 17*(1), 99–120.

Castells, M. (1996). *The Rise of Network Society*. MA: Blackwell, Cambridge.

Cassel, C., & Gillian, S.(Eds.) (1994). *Qualitative Methods in Organisational Research: A Practical Guide*. London: Sage.

Coleman, J. S. (1990). *Foundations of Social Theory*. Cambridge, MA: Harvard University Press.

Conner, K. (1991). A historical comparison of resource-based theory and five schools of thought within industrial organization economics: do we have a new theory of the firm? *Journal of Management, 17*(1), 121–154.

Davenport, T. H. (2001). *From Data to Knowledge*. San Jose, CA: Oracle Inc.

Elisa (2006). *Annual Report*. [http://www.elisa.com/english/docimages/attachment/Elisa_vk2006_uk.pdf].

Elisa (2007). *Presentation*. [http://www.elisa.com/english/docimages/attachment/Q2%202007%20English.pdf]

Elisa (2008). [http://www.elisa.com/english/]

Goold M., & Luchs, K. (1993). Why diversify? Four decades of management thinking. *Academy of Management Executive, 7*(3), 7–25.

Gloor, P., Laubacher, R., Dynes, S., & Zhao, Y. (2003). Visualization of Communication Patterns in Collaborative Innovation Networks: Analysis of some W3C working groups. *Proc. ACM CIKM 2003*, New Orleans, November 5-6.

Håkansson, H., & Lundgren, A. (1995). Industrial Networks and Technological Innovation. In K. Möller & D. Wilson (Eds.), *Business Marketing: An Interaction and Network Perspective*. London: Kluwer Academic Publishers.

Hartley, J. F. (1994). Case studies in organisational research. In C. Cassel & G. Symon, (Eds.), *Qualitative Methods in Organisational Research: A Practical Guide*. London: Sage.

Hatch, N. W., & Dyer, J. H. (2004). Human Capital and Learning as a Source of Sustainable Competitive Advantage. *Strategic Management Journal, 25*, 1155–1178.

Heer, J., & Boyd, D. (2005). *Vizster: Visualizing Online Social Networks. In InfoVis 2005, IEEE Symposium on Information Visualization.*

Heide, J. B., & John, G. (1995). Measurement issues in research on interfirm relations. In K. Möller & D. Wilson (Eds.), *Business Marketing: An interaction and network perspective* (pp. 531-554). Boston: Kluwer Academic Publishing.

Hölttä, P. (2000). *Piimäki 2000: Laajakaistaisen alueverkon uudet palvelut. tuotekehityshakemuksen liite 2.* Tutkimus- ja kehitysprojektisuunnitelma TEKESin 'Tietoliikenteellä maailmalle' teknologiaohjelmaan. HPY Tutkimuskeskus. (Unpublished reference).

Hong, J., & Ståhle, P. (2005). The Coevolution of Knowledge and Competence Management. *Int. J. Management Concepts and Philosophy, 1*(2).

Juntunen, A. (2005). *The emergence of a new business through collaborative networks: a longitudinal study in the ICT sector.* Acta Universitatis Oeconomicae Helsingiensis. Printed in HSEPrint. A-series, no 256, ISSN 1237-556X. ISBN: 951-791-957-3/1.

Juntunen, A. (2008). Data Warehouse in the Finnish Police - A Case Study, In John Wang (Ed.) *Encyclopedia of Data Warehousing and Mining: 2nd Edition.* Idea Group Publishing. Forthcoming.

Kogut, B., & Zander, U. (1997). Knowledge of the Firm, Combinative Capabilities, and the Replication of Technology. In N. J. Foss (Ed.), *Resources, Fims and Strategies – A Reader in the Resource-Based Perspective*. Oxford: Oxford University Press.

Malhotra, Y. (2000). Knowledge Management and New Organization Forms: A Framework for Business Model Innovation. *Information Resources Management Journal, 13*(1), 5-14.

Miles, M. B., & Huberman, A. M. (1994). *Qualitative data analysis: an expanded sourcebook*. 2nd edition. CA: Sage Publications.

Mintzberg, H., Ahlstrand, B., & Lampe, J. (1998). *Strategy Safari. The complete guide through the wilds of strategic management*. London: Prentice Hall Financial Times.

Möller, K., & Svahn, S. (2006). Role of Knowledge in Value Creation in Business Nets. *Journal of Management Studies, 43*(5), 985-1007.

Nonaka, I., & Takeuchi, H. (1995). *The Knowledge Creating Company*. NY: Oxford University Press.

Nonaka, I., Toyama, R., & Konno, N. (2001). SECI, Ba and leadership: a unified model of dynamic knowledge creation. In: I. Nonaka & D. J. Teece (Eds.), *Managing industrial knowledge. Creation, transfer and utilization* (pp. 13-43). London: Sage.

Parolini, C. (1999). *The Value Net: A Tool for Competitive Strategy*. Chichester: Wiley.

Pettigrew, A. M. (1997). What is a processual Analysis? *Scandinavian Journal of Management, 13*, 337-348.

Rumelt, D. P. (1984). Towards a Strategic Theory of the Firm. Alternative theories of the firm, (2), 286-300, *Elgar Reference Collection. International Library of Critical Writings in Economics, 154*. Cheltenham, U.K. and Northampton, Mass.: Elgar; distributed by American International Distribution Corporation, Williston.

Teece, D. J. (2000). *Managing Intellectual Capital.* Great Britain: Biddles Ltd., Guildford & King's Lynn.

Teece, D. J. (2003). Explicating Dynamic Capabilities: Asset Selection, Coordination, and Entrepreneurship. *Strategic Management Theory* (August 2003).

Teece, D. J., Pisano, G., & Shuen, A. (1997). Dynamic Capabilities and Strategic Management. *Strategic Management Journal, 18*(7), 509-533.

Törmänen, A. (2003). *Tietovarastoinnin kehitys poliisiorganisaatiossa 1992-2002.* Sisäasiainministeriö, poliisiosaston julkaisusarja 11/2003. ISBN 951-734-513-5.

Van de Ven, A. H., & Poole, M. S. (1990). Methods for Studying Innovation Development in the Minnnesota Innovation Research Program. *Organization Science, 1*(3), 313-335.

Virkkunen, J., & Ahonen, H. (2000). *Knowledge Management as Creative Dialogue about the Future*. Paper presented in Knowledge Management conference in Sao Paulo, Brazil, 7/2000.

Virkkunen, J., & Ahonen, H. (2004). Transforming learning and knowledge creation on the shop floor. *International Journal of Human Resources Development and Management 2004, 4(1*), 57–72.

Wernerfelt, B. (1984). A resource-based view of the firm. *Strategic Management Journal, 5*(2), 171–180.

Yin, R. K. (1994). *Case Study Research: design and methods*. Thousand Oaks, CA: Sage.

Yli-Renko, H., Autio, E., & Tontti, V. (2002). Social Capital, Knowledge, and the International Growth of Technology-Based Firms. *International Business Review, 11*, 279-304.

INTERNET SITES

www.iec.org.online/tutorials/int_tele. Retrieved 05/2003.

KEY TERMS

Capabilities: Capabilities can be defined as intangible knowledge resources, and physical and non-physical resources as tangible and intangible assets. The difference between resources and capabilities in a firm is that capabilities deploy or coordinate different resources, and therefore, capabilities are involved in the activities of the whole value chain of the company.

ICT sector: ICT sector includes both the Information Technology (IT) and telecommunication sector. The latter includes both the service and the manufacturing industry. The previous includes all the software and hardware manufacturing and developing companies.

Knowledge Management: The Process responsible for gathering, analysing, storing and sharing knowledge and information within an Organisation. Knowledge management is seen as a way to enhance the performance in many organizations.

Knowledge Sharing: Knowledge sharing refers to not only codified information, like product specifications, but also beliefs and experiences. Seen from this perspective, knowledge creation, management and sharing are a question of mastering the renewal and change in all the activities within an organization and in a network of organizations.

Knowledge: Nonaka and Takeuchi (1995) explicated the concept of knowledge by contrasting knowledge and information. "First, knowledge unlike information, is about beliefs and commitment. Knowledge is a function of a particular stance, perspective, or intention. Second, knowledge unlike information, is about action. It is always knowledge 'to some end', and third, knowledge, unlike information, is about meaning. It is context specific and relational" (Nonaka –Takeuchi 1995, 58). Instead of the absolute, static view of knowledge, Nonaka and Takeuchi consider knowledge as "a dynamic human process of justifying personal belief toward the 'truth' ". Knowledge is created dynamically in social interaction among people

Organizational Learning: *Organizational Learning* can be defined as the organization's ability to gain understanding from experience through experimentation, observation, analysis, and a willingness to examine both successes and failures

ENDNOTE

[a] VOIP = *Voice over IP*, a VoIP-device and -service to send and to receive IP-voice. Internet telephone refers to communication services – voice, facsimile, and/or voice-messaging applications – that are transported via the Internet, rather than the *public switched telephone network* (PSTN). The basic steps involved in originating an Internet telephone call are conversion of the analog voice signal to digital format and compression/translation of the signal into *Internet protocol (IP) packets* for transmission over the Internet. The process is reversed at the receiving end. (www.iec.org.online/tutorials/int_tele)

APPENDIX: INTERVIEWS

Name (Interviewee)	Position	Organization	Interview	Time
Ahlstrand, Klaus	Business Development Manager	Datatie	in person e-mails	February 11th 2001, October 31st 2001, November 1st 2001 March 29th 2000, October 31st 2001, November 1st 2001, November 12th 2001, December 5th 2001, January 5th 2002
Arhi, Mika	BI, Analyst	Elisa Corporation	in person e-mails	May 2001 July 7th 2002, August 1st 2002
Buuri, Marko	Product Development	Elisa, HCB	in person, cooperation meeting	September 7th, 2001
Grönroos, Timo	Development Manager	Radiolinja	in person	May 5th, 1999
Hakanen, Seppo	Marketing Manager	Elisa, PCS	in person cooperation meeting	March 30th 2000 April 17th 2000
Hedberg, Nina	Voice Services, Manager	Elisa, Traffic and Subscriber connections	in person, cooperation meeting	June 2nd 1999, November 20th 1999
Hedberg, Nina	Manager	Elisa, PCS	in person, cooperation meeting	,March 30th 2000, April 17th 2000
Hietanen, Petri	Development Manager	Elisa, HCB	in person, cooperation meeting	September 2nd 2001, October 3rd 2001
Hölttä, Pertti	Research Center	Elisa, Research Center	in person, cooperation meeting	January 31st 2000, January 21st, 2001, January 25th 2001
Jokinen, Juha	Manager (IM)	Elisa, BS	in person, cooperation meeting email updates	September 5th 2001, September 27th 2001, June 18th 2004, January 12th 2005 October 20th 2001, May 15th 2002, January 12th 2003, March 10th 2004
Jäntere, Kirsi	Development Manager	Elisa, PCS	in person, cooperation meeting	March 3rd 2000, April 5th 2000
Kaasinen, Katariina	Student	Elisa, HCB	in person	November 30th 2001
Kaasinen, Katariina	R&D developer	Nokia, R&D	e-mail	August 4th 2003
Karjalainen, Ismo	Product Manager (Kotiportti™)	Elisa, PCS	in person, cooperation meeting	June 1st 2001
Kautto, Antti	Management Consultant	Comptel	in person	December 18th 2001

continued on following page

APPENDIX: CONTINUED

Lehmus, Pasi	Director	Elisa	in person, cooperation meeting	January 15th 2002 March 3rd 2003
Malmberg, Juha	Director	Elisa, Traffic and Subscriber connections	in person	May 1999
Malmberg, Juha	Director	Elisa, PCS	in person	March 30th 2000, April 17th 2000, November 20th 2001, December 17th 2001
Masala, Sami	Business Development Manager	Elisa, HCB	e-mails	March 30th 2000, April 17th 2000, November 26th 2002, December 12th 2002, January 23rd 2003, February 27th 2003, November 13th 2003, December 16th 2003
Masala, Sami	Business Development Manager	Elisa, HCB	in person	March 29th 2000, April 18th-19th 2000, November 24th 2002, December 12th 2002, January 20th 2003, February 25th 2003, November 10th 2003, December 15th 2003, January 12th 2004, May 21st 2004, August 18th 2004, May 13th 2005
Peltola, Hannu	Product Development	Elisa, Traffic and Subscriber connections	in person, cooperation meeting	May 20th 1999
Pohtola, Raili	Director	Elisa, PCM	in person	May 15th 2002
Rasia, Olli	Multimedia Access, Manager	Elisa, Traffic and Subscriber connections	in person, cooperation meeting	May 5th 1999
Rasia, Olli	Department Manager	Elisa, PCS	in person, cooperation meeting	March 30th 2000, April 17th 2000, April 9th 2001, August 28th 2001
Riipinen, Jarmo	Business Manager	Elisa, BS	phone	November 7th 2001

continued on following page

APPENDIX: CONTINUED

Simula, Timo	Head of Development, HCB's Manager	Elisa, HCB	in person, cooperation meeting e-mails e-mails, updates in meetings	March 30th 2000, April 17th 2000, November 7th 2001, December 2nd 2001, December 20th 2001 November 26th 2002, December 12th 2002, January 30th 2003, March 14th 2003, September 9th 2003, October 13th 2003, November 3rd 2003, December 18th 2003, January 12th 2004, February 13th 2004 June 18th 2005, September 30th 2005, May, 15th 2006, January 12th 2007
Tirkkonen, Piia	Student	Elisa, HCB	in person	November 22nd 2002
Tirkkonen, Piia	R&D	Nokia	e-mail	July 22nd 2003
Yli-Äyhö, Janne	Manager	Telia-Sonera	e-mail	June 24th 2002
Varjokallio, Liisa	Manager	Elisa, HR	in person	January 25th 2001
Vainionpää, Sami	Multimedia Access, Development Manager	Elisa, PCS	in person, cooperation meeting	January 15th 2001
Viitala, Erkki	Customer Service Manager	Comptel	in person	December 2001 July 7th 2003
Vuolteenaho, Petri	Product Development, Manager	Elisa, PCS	in person, cooperation meeting	March 30th 2000 April 17th 2000
Weckström, J-P.	Manager	Telia-Sonera, BI	e-mail	June 18th 2002

Chapter XIII
Modelling the New Product Development Process:
The Value of a Product Development Process Model Approach, as a Means for Business Survival in the 21st Century

Jonathan D. Owens
University of Lincoln, UK

ABSTRACT

Success in new product development (NPD) can be considered a general aim for any company wishing to survive in the 21st Century. It has been found that positive effects can result from the existence of formal "blueprints" and "roadmaps" of the NPD process. This chapter discusses numerous NPD processes which can assist a company to capture what it does, and follow a structured development route, from which it is possible to gain a better understanding of how to improve the development process, and thus reap the potential and tangible benefits. This chapter's focus is at organisations that are considering implementing a new product development (NPD) process in order to improve repeatability and ultimately sustainability of their innovative capabilities, a necessary and vital component for survival. It aims to bring an understanding of the underlying characteristics that may contribute to a potential and successful outcome during the development process within organizations, through the adoption of a structured NPD process.

INTRODUCTION

The design and development of products has been, and is continually the focus for many different authors. The pre-occupation with design and development exists because getting it right is so important. A revealing comment from Norman and Peterson (1999, p65) advises why companies are so desperate to understand what they do, and how they can make things better: *"...all good companies can innovate, but fewer are able to be innovative again and again."* No one has been able to capture the ultimate prescription for success, even some of the same authors publish different observations, depending upon the orientation and audience.

WHAT IS A NEW PRODUCT?

There are numerous definitions by various authors (Cooper, 1999, 2001; Cooper *et al*, 1997; Hart, 1996; Ozer, 1999, 2004; Tracey, 2004) however one common similarity characterises a new product as 'one not previously manufactured by a company'. One of the foremost aims of any development programme should be to get the right product or service, to the market or customer as quickly as possible. This can limit the chance of a competitor gaining an advantage by first entry, and therefore one enjoying an early market position. The cost of development, whether large or small, is a burden on the cash flow of an organisation and pressure will be applied for an early payback of cash spent (Hultink and Hart, 1998). For example, marketing functions can expend vast resources, determining which products should be offered to particular markets and at what price. Restrictions on new product scope that are imposed are usually derived from a combination of the mission statement, or strategy of a company and the attractiveness of the market (Cooper and Kleinschmidt, 2000).

THE NEW PRODUCT DEVELOPMENT PROCESS

The potential for innovation is considered to be a fusion of a perceived user needs and a technological opportunity for fulfilment of this need (Jenkins *et al*, 1997). Innovation is often used interchangeably with other words and phrases, or can be used with varying emphasis, depending upon the subjects that are under consideration (Hutlink and Hart, 1998). It has been discussed (Wright and Swain, 1995) that 'innovation' is a term invariably used by research and design people; 'new product development' is a phrase generally referred to more in marketing and management; and 'design' is a common word in engineering. However, to many who are embroiled in the act of NPD, they will note that the three have subtle, but important differences. There appears to be a hierarchy of activities that these phrases encompass. 'Innovation' can be considered as the unit of technological change and an invention, if one exists in the situation, it is part of the process of innovation (Harborne and Johne, 2003). New product development, for all intents and purposes, can be viewed as a slightly less radical phrase such that the development of a 'new' product does not have to involve innovation. New products are different from those, which already exist, in terms of major or minor changes (Noke and Radnor, 2004). The 'newness' may be new creations (such as original innovations; or products new to the world or new to the company); additions, improvements and revisions (with greater emphasis on particular values); repositioning of the product (e.g. novel ways to use it in a different market segment, or possibly the use of branding); or simply cost reductions (lower price, or improvement in through life costs) (Booz, Allen and Hamilton, 1991). Figure 1 illustrates a typology for product 'newness' categories. It is thc product design and development that is the interest of this research.

Figure 1. Classification of New Products (Booz, Allen and Hamilton, 1991)

New to the World Products.

These new products are the first of their kind and create an entirely new market. Examples of products in this category are the Sony Walkman and 3M's Post-It notes. This category represents up to ten percent of all new products.

New to the Company.

These are products new to a company, but not to the marketplace, enabling a company to enter an established market for the first time. For example, IBM was not the first to launch an office version laser printer, Hewlett Packard (HP) were, therefore it was not an innovation, but it did however represent a new product line for IBM. Approximately twenty percent of all new products correspond with this category.

Additions to existing Product Lines.

These are new items to a company that fit within an existing product line the company manufactures. They may also represent a fairly new product to the market place. For example, the introduction of HP smaller and considerably less expensive version of its laser printer, that was suitable for home computers. The printer was a new item to the LaserJet line. This product type represents approximately twenty-six percent of all new product launches.

Improvements in revisions to existing products.

These are essentially replacements of existing products. They offer improved performance or greater perceived value over the previous product. Similarly, this product type can represent up to twenty six percent of all new product launches.

Repositioning.

These are essentially new applications for existing products, and involve retargeting an old product to a new market segment for a different application. For example aspirin was considered a standard reliever for headache and fever symptoms, but due to safer, more effective and cheaper products it (aspirin) was superseded. However, new research demonstrated this product had other benefits, and resulted with the aspirin being marketed as prevention against blood clots, strokes and heart attacks. This product type can account for up to seven percent of all new product launches.

Cost Reductions.

These are new products designed to replace existing products in the line, and can yield similar benefits and performance. From a marketing perspective they are not new products but from a design and production perspective, they could represent significant change(s) to the company. This product type can account for up to eleven percent of all new product launches.

However, the driving force for this product innovation may be varied: anything from market and competitor action and reaction; information on customers' needs; technical fine tuning of the process; or entrepreneurial inspiration.

According to Kalyanaram and Krishnan (1997) "Good design" can be achieved when the product not only looks good, but it also does the job well. Indeed, "*design can often add something to a product or service which the customer never expected, thus improving the overall customer experience*" (Cooper, 1999, pg 26). Thus, here 'designing' is differentiated, because it is a tool which can be applied during NPD to help turn an invention into a successful product, or to extend the usefulness of an existing innovation (Osterlund, 1997). Subsequently, NPD is a most appropriate term for this research, because it relies upon "design" activities carried out to deliver a product, which may, or may not, be an "innovation".

In order to undertake NPD, it would be prudent to have a formal blueprint, roadmap, template or thought process for driving a new product project team from the idea stage, through to market launch and beyond (Cooper, 1994). However, as with many other things in the business world, a definitive process that provides continual success has not been forthcoming. This section reviews some of the different models that have been put forward to describe the process and further examines activities, methods and techniques, which have direct relevance to the area of developing quality products.

MODELLING THE NEW PRODUCT DEVELOPMENT PROCESS

Many researchers have found the need to try and capture the progression of the product during development either prescriptively, to inform students and industrialists how it should best be done; or descriptively, to define what actually happens in real life. Also, there are many researchers who discuss the NPD process models and take differing opinions upon what these 'models' actually look like. However, most are in agreement on one thing; that a definitive NPD model which is applicable for every situation cannot be produced.

There are a plethora of examples of different NPD models given by different researchers. Indeed, even in a single study by Cooper (1999) no two product processes were identified as being exactly the same and seven separate general types of processes were outlined from the fifty eight companies involved. Saren (1984) undertook a study of the available NPD process models and classified them into five categories:

1. Departmental-stage models.
2. Activity-stage models.
3. Decision-stage models.
4. Conversion process models
5. Response models.

Figure 2 provides a summary of these different models by type. Discussion points on the usefulness of each model for research work and their practical use in the management of NPD are also illustrated.

Saren (1984) suggests that dividing methods into groups provides a useful point for an examination of how each model might purposefully be used in research; for example, who is involved in the innovation; at what point and in what order are specified tasks undertaken; upon what basis decisions are made; how inputs to a process become outputs; or the reactions to specified stimuli. However, he concluded that although each individual model is valid, in that it indicates something of the characteristics of the process, more work needs to be done on the holistic process of innovation in companies; this is something that is reiterated in further research carried out by Cooper (2001).

More recent research by Noke and Radnor (2004) uses the nineteen sixties phased development model as a starting point for a comparison with some of the NPD process model ideas which have been progressing from the late nineteen eighties in to the early twenty first century. They also claim that modern stage gate methodologies, product and cycle-time excellence; and total design as the main examples of advancement in processes aimed at improving product success. Since there is a number of different ways to model the NPD process, and each way has associated with it its own specific strengths and weaknesses, this paper will cover those that are recurrent in the most recent literature. Therefore, the following will briefly outline the origins, uses and limitations of five generalised modelling techniques, which are common and progressive:

Figure 2. Summary of some NPD process models (after Saren, 1984)

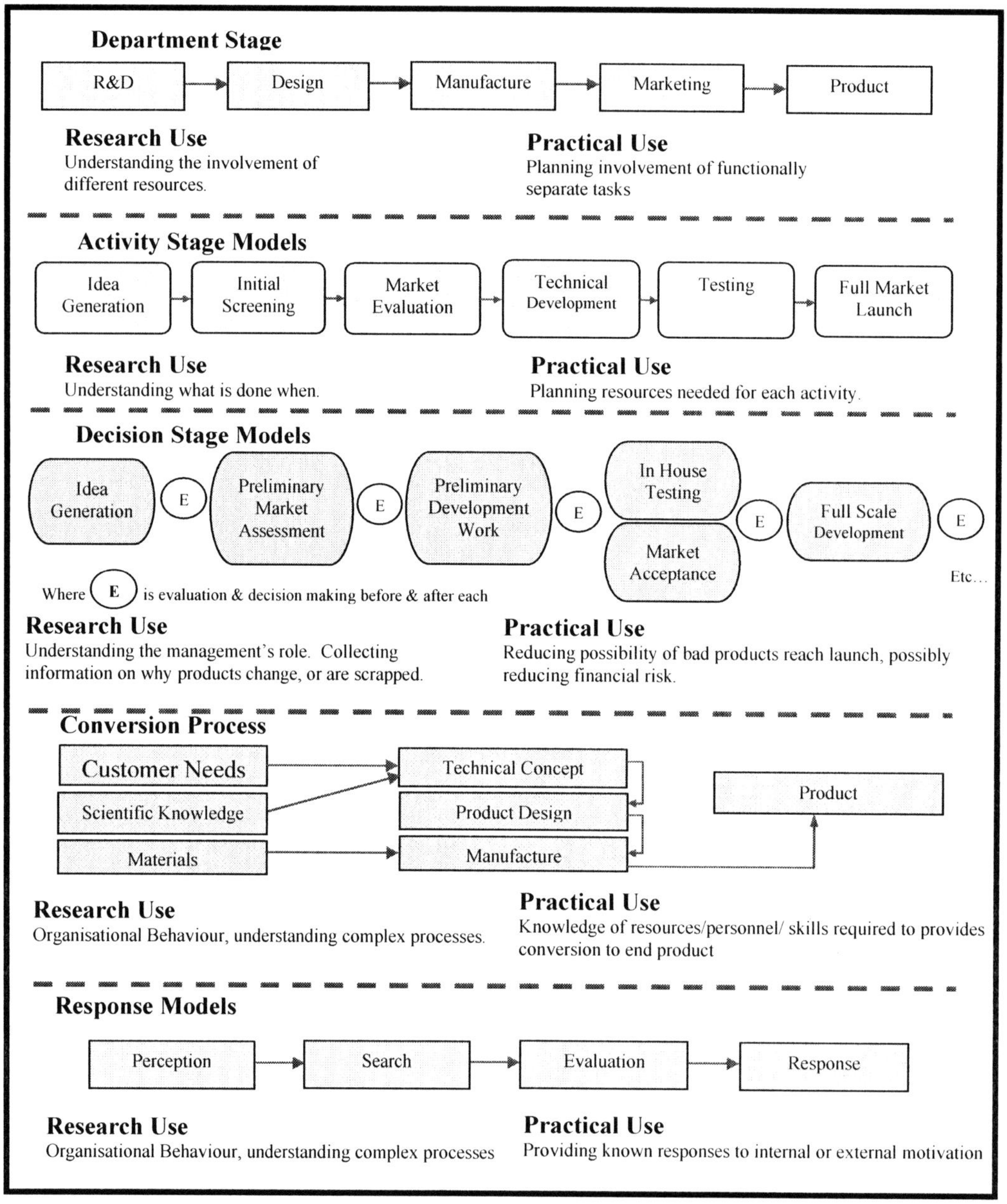

1. Stage gate models.
2. Multiple convergent process.
3. Product and cycle-time excellence.
4. Total design.
5. Third generation NPD process.

THE STAGE GATE MODEL

The stage gate model takes the process as an alternate series of activity stages followed by decision gates (see figure 3). The decision gate allows or prevents the following activity stage being initiated, depending upon whether it meets the evaluation criteria. At any stage the project may be terminated, suspended or rejected for rework or improvement until it can finally pass the gate. It may even have to go back further, to a previous stage. Therefore, the stage gate process facilitates iteration, with built-in feedback loops in each stage, and among stages (Zhao *et al*, 1999). In recent years some researchers (Baldwin and Clark, 2000; Cooper *et al*, 2002; Gerwin and Barrowman, 2002) have suggested that successful product development is aided by following a stage gate decision process because it encourages activities to be undertaken by a core team of representatives from all functional departments. The stage gate models may help the reader to understand the management of the process and may also help prevent losses made by revealing early on, and before market launch, the products which will fail in an industrial situation by reducing failure risk in the comprehensive review implemented at the gate of each stage (Zhao *et al*, 1999).

However, the model does not lead us to a means of ensuring that the product will meet the need of the user(s), or indeed the final customer. This kind of system does have the potential to include "*go/no go*" decisions, based on whether the product is being designed to a high enough quality and will satisfy the user(s) and ultimately the customer. On the other hand, without elucidation from someone providing a customer needs compliance emphasis, there is not necessarily any strong incentive to use this as a basis for what the product "*must meet*" or "*should meet*" when product management decision are being made at each of the gates.

Although some forms of this model can be seen widely in practical use today in some industrial organisations (Owens and Davies, 2000; Owens, 2004a) there are some general problems which occur when following a stage gate model which are indicated by Cooper (1999). Cooper adds later (2001) that even though the idea has been taken up in the last decade with positive effect, stage gate process models are still not really usable because they are too time consuming, often have too many ways of waiting time, are too bureaucratic and have no provision for focus. Also, one author (Himmelfarb, 1992, p.10) provides a fairly severe and emotive set of comments by claiming that it "*creates products that are hard to make, that cost too much, that require too many expensive design changes, and that may or may not meet*

Figure 3. Overview of a Stage-Gate NPD process (after Cooper, 2001)

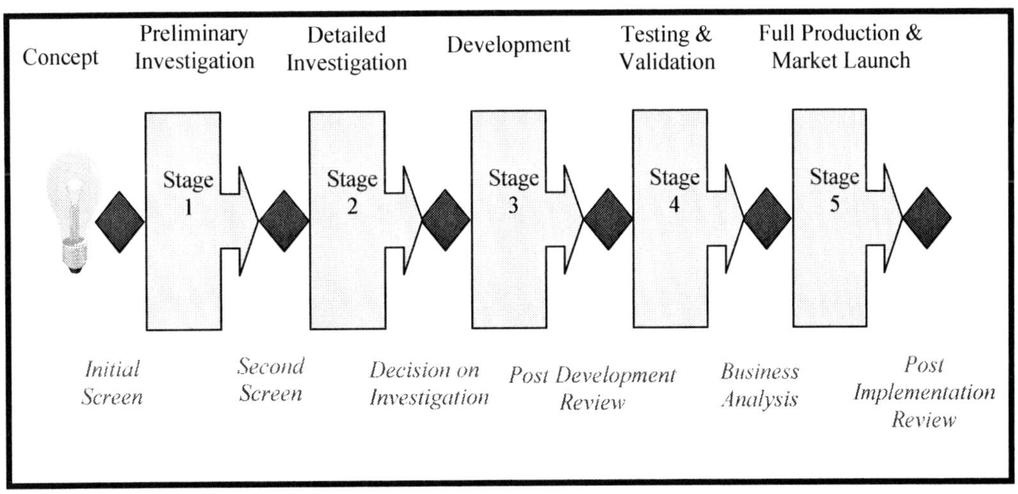

marketplace needs. It encourages isolation of functional areas and, worst of all, it is very slow." All of these observations do not bode well for the extra and important inclusion of both usability and customer needs compliance in this particular process model.

MULTIPLE CONVERGENT MODEL

Problems of the stage gate model and other linearly defined process models have been recognised by those who have been researching the interaction of the process and the people involved with them

Figure 4. The early stage of the multiple convergent model (after Hart and Baker, 1996)

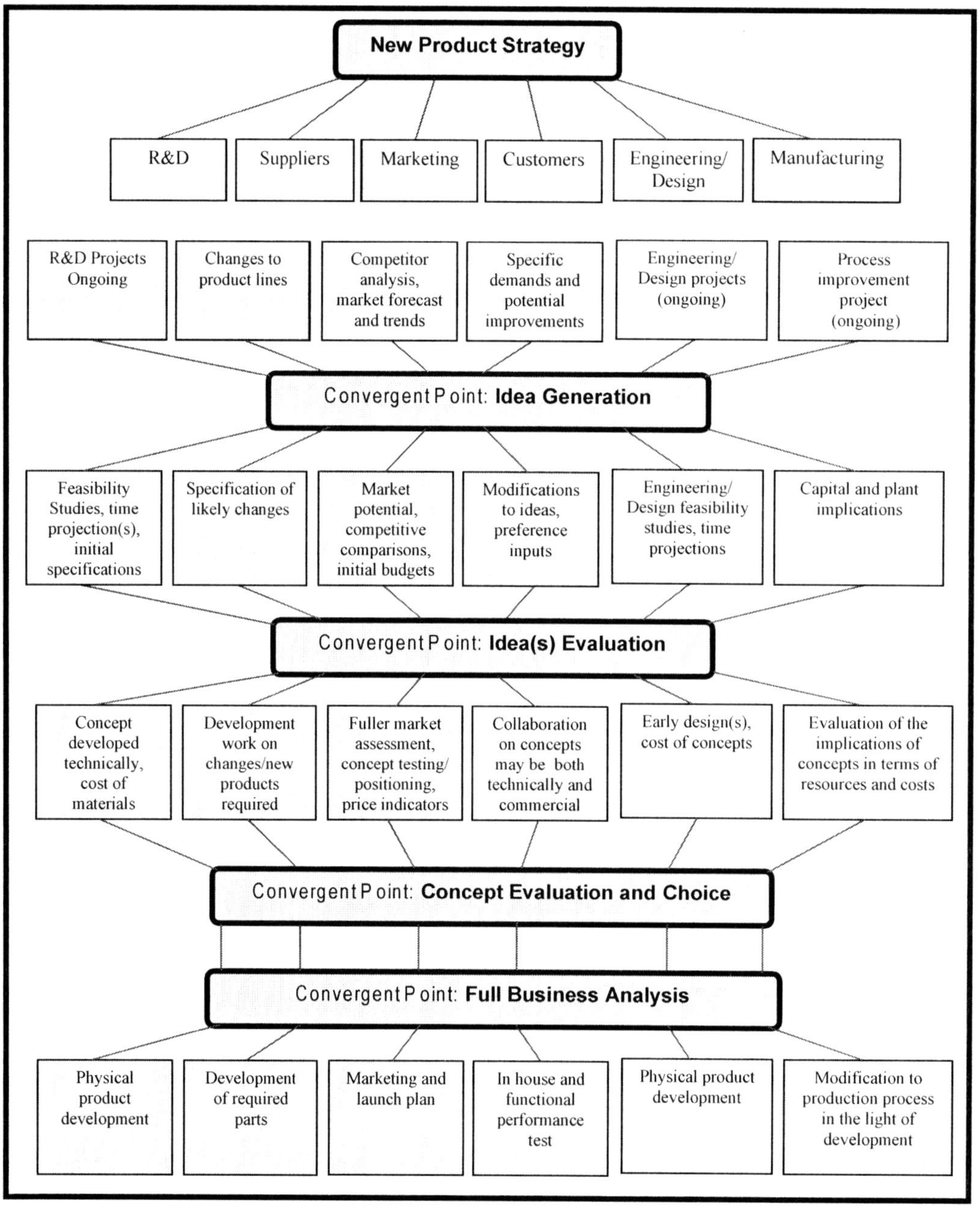

(Hart, 1996; Griffin, 1997; Shenhar, 2001; Hart *et al*, 2003). The multiple convergent model aims to directly and explicitly integrate people into the process and overcome the reported shortcomings in other NPD process models (Hart, 1995; Hart and Baker, 1996).

The model takes into account the lessons learned from reports in literature that suggest success comes from having quality inputs that are valid from multidisciplinary areas. There is much importance placed on the use of networks and the production of a model that breaks down multidisciplinary boundaries (Hart and Baker, 1996). The model views NPD as tasks with areas leading towards a common conclusion, but are required to come together at a number of different natural and integrative points for evaluation, as illustrated in figure 4. In this way the multiple convergent model is similar to the stage gate models. However, where it differs is that the convergent model has multiple points, which it recognises as important to an iterative process. According to Hart (1995) the advantages of taking the process as a series of converging points for evaluation, followed by diversion into functional activities are:

Figure 5. The phase review process within the product and cycle time excellence model (after Jenkins et al, 1997)

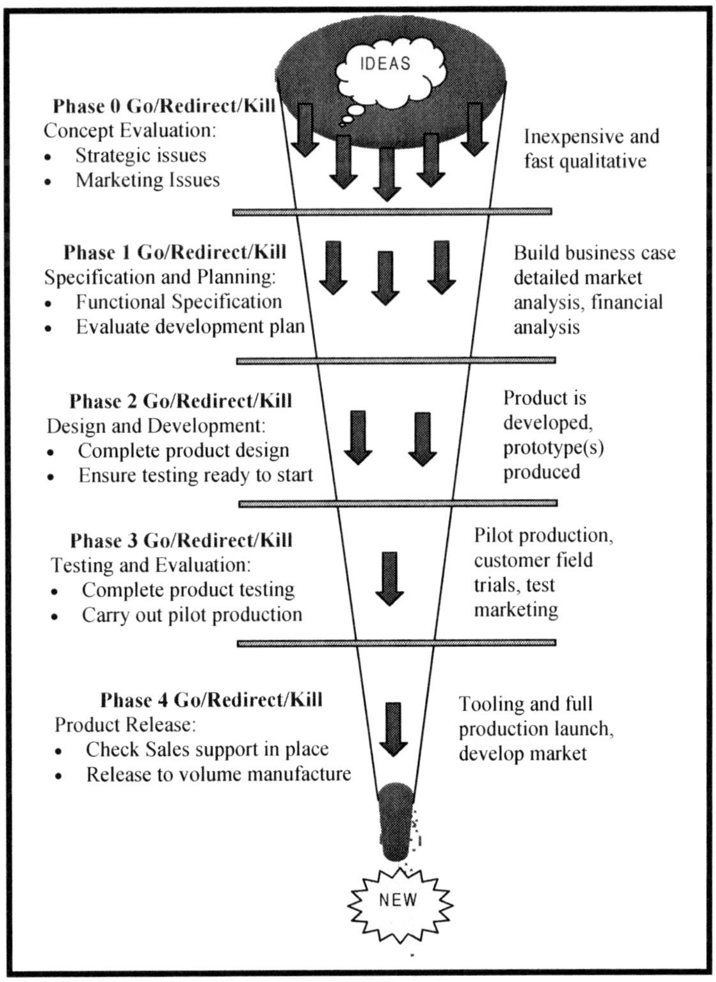

- It accommodates iteration.
- It allows for iterative communication and evaluation within the functional groups.
- The framework can accommodate third parties easily.
- Methods for real integration of work from functional groups can be provided in the convergent points.

Despite the model being driven by converging points, the main disadvantage in practical use appears to be, ironically, that it may be too divergent. It converges for cross-functional decisions, but then separates out into each of the different functions to carry out the tasks. Hart *et al* (2003) describe a key element as the amount of information sharing that is modelled, however, horizontal communications between functional areas, are only modelled as happening during the evaluation or collation points and not during other activities. With so many points of convergence during the process, this model does not appear to be conducive with efficiency and it seems to require a large amount of management effort to keep the process on track.

PRODUCT AND CYCLE-TIME EXCELLENCE MODEL

In contrast to the multiple convergent model, there are models that have been developed which are driven by the need to reduce time to market. These models concentrate on the control of economics of the design process. One such example is that of the product and cycle-time excellence model developed by Pittiglio Rabin and McGrath (McGrath *et al,* 1992). This particular model follows a stage gate analogy, with 'phase reviews' providing the decision points, at which the project should continue to go on, be redirected or terminated. However, during phase reviews the decisions are not made by the multidisciplinary core team carrying out the work, as with multiple convergent theory, but a group of four or five senior managers known as the 'Product Approval Committee' (Robinson and Chiang, 2002). Under product and cycle time excellence, the process is seen as a funnel taking in lots of ideas, following the completion of five phases, producing new products, as illustrated in figure 5. In an attempt to reduce the time it takes to develop a new product, the productivity model breaks down each of the five phases in the process into fifteen or twenty steps and then each of these steps into ten to thirty tasks. Database records can be kept on the timing for each of the tasks and thus the total development time can be judged for each new product (Suomala and Jokioinen, 2003).

The productivity and cycle time concepts also pay attention to the management of the process in more holistic ways. According to Jenkins *et al* (1997) of the seven major elements for this model, four are directly overseeing the whole of the product development process in the company:

1. The provision of core teams during development
2. The use of a product strategy
3. The review and correct implementation of technology management
4. The endorsement of cross project management

The authors of the product and cycle time excellence model also advocate the use of design techniques and automatic development tools that will help focus and streamline the development of the product (McGrath *et al,* 1992).

The product and cycle time excellence model is more than just a definition of the development process. It is aimed at efficiently managing the development of new products such that the product is produced on time and within budget, whilst using the optimum balance of skills and methods at the right point during the projects' progression (Lynn and Akgun, 1999). However, these types of models, which are driven by productivity and cycle time reduction, rely upon putting senior management in an overriding position of authority and also upon splitting down the design process to a level so low that it can be timed. As well as the obvious philosophical discussions about specifying exactly the creative nature of design that these issues incite, both of these ideas seem regressive and are reminiscent of the work-study principles, based on Taylorism, which had its 'glory days' at the beginning of the twentieth century.

TOTAL DESIGN

"Total design is seen as a broadly based business activity in which specialists collaborate in the investigation of a market, the selection of a project, the conception and manufacture of a product, and in the provision of various kind of user support." (Pugh and Moreley, 1988, p1)

The models discussed revolve around breaking down the process into manageable portions by seeing the development process as a series of problems to be solved (Wright, 1998). Various authors (Cooper and Edgett, 2003; Hart *et al*, 2003; Griffin, 1997) have criticised the way of focussing on parts of the problem and solving them one-by-one because they have found that they are often used without paying sufficient attention to the aspects of assimilating all of the problems together. A slightly different outlook to view design and development as a converging spiral, the spiral from the design process attempts to emulate real-life, in that the design process is evolving (Oakley, 1990). The spiral moves from a formulations stage, to an evolution stage, through to a stage where transfer takes place and is followed by a reaction stage that returns the development to the formulation stage, as illustrated in figure 6. This is different to other series or stage gate models as it relies upon interactive and overlapping stages that evolve.

The spiral form was a depiction used for Acar's (1966) triple-helix model of the product development process that can be cross-sectioned at any point to reveal the interaction between

Figure 6.

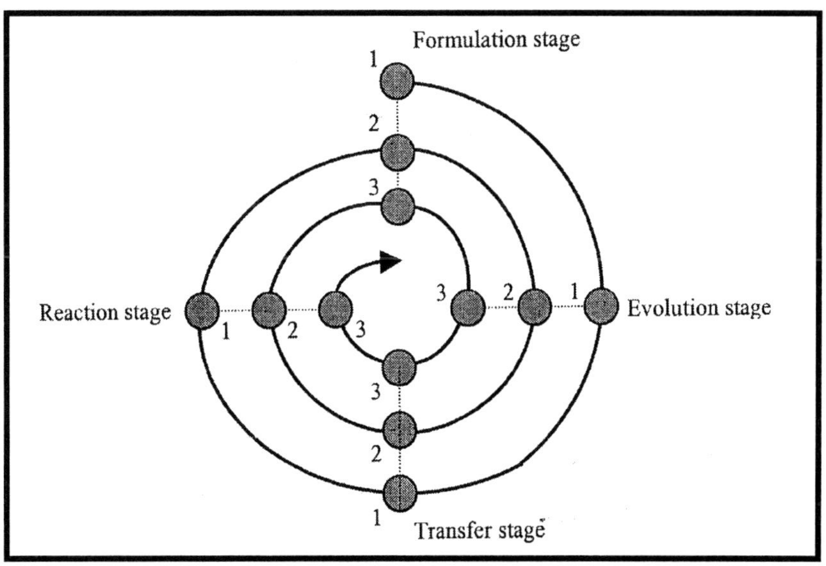

Figure 7. The total design activity model (Pugh, 1991, p11)

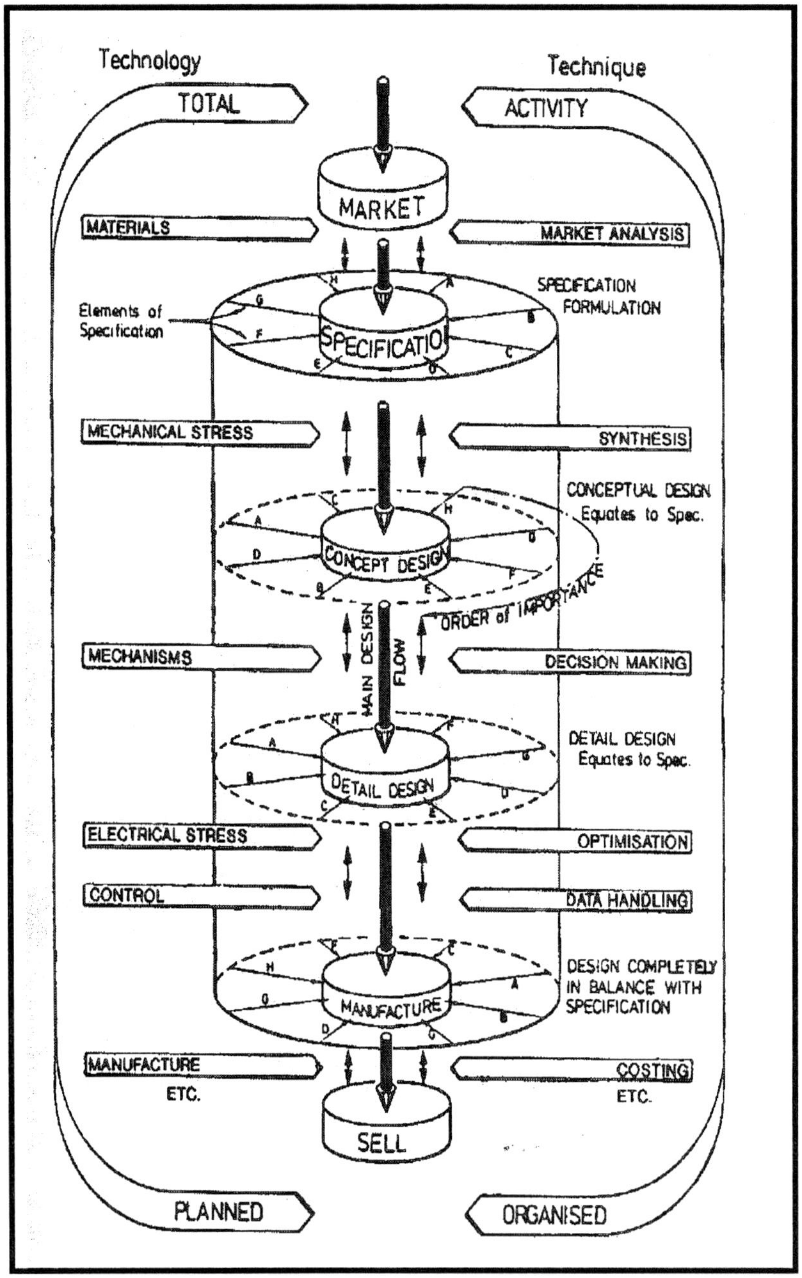

specification, conceptual design and embodiment design. In the total design model championed by Pugh and his colleagues, the spiral is taken into more depth (Pugh, 1991; Pugh and Moreley, 1988; Hollins and Pugh, 1990).

The development of the total design model and subsequent publishing of Pugh have stimulated much discussion within engineering design circles (Pugh and Moreley, 1988; Pugh, 1991; Hollins and Pugh, 1990; Jenkins *et al*, 1997). Also, the total

Figure 8. Theoretical requirements capture process model (Cooper et al, 1998, p 510)

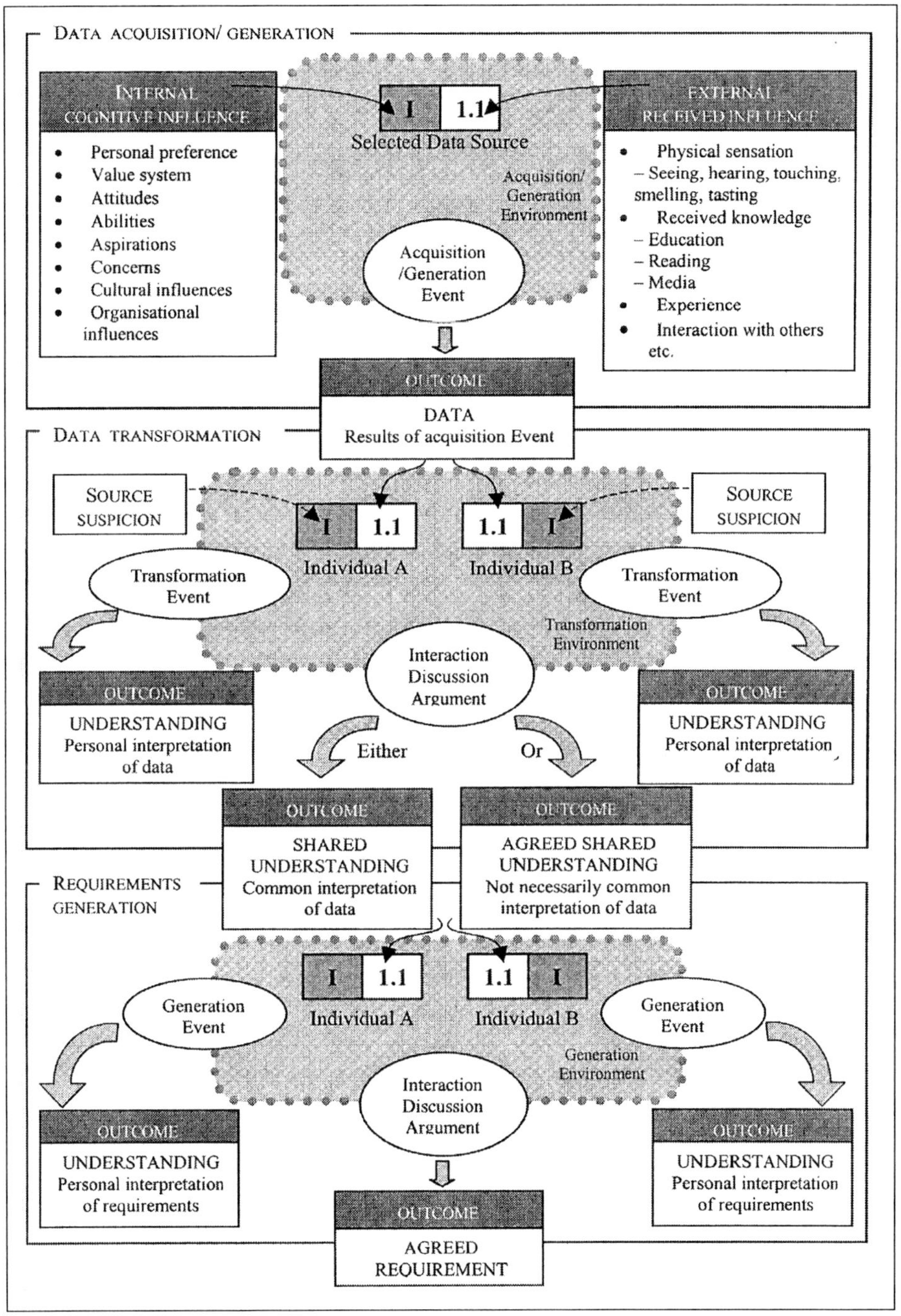

design philosophy is taught as a useful and useable model of best practices on a number of UK higher education institutes' engineering courses, especially because it emphasises the use of many different discipline independent tools and methods (Wright, 1998).

The total design model outlines six nominal spirals, which attempt to capture the main undertakings during the design process, all within an iterative environment. These "design cores" are presented by Pugh (1991) as:

- Investigation of market/user needs and demands
- The development of the product design specification
- Conceptual design
- Detailed (technical) design
- Manufacture
- Selling (marketing)

Figure 7 illustrates how Pugh visualises the whole package of design activities, within a "...framework of planning and organisation...and how they fit into a business structure" (Pugh, 1991, p8).

The total design and its embellishment with detailed information on how to approach each of the "design cores" goes a long way to assist engineering designers practically undertake product design systemically. Pugh and his colleagues have devoted much literature (Pugh and Moreley, 1988; Pugh, 1991; Hollins and Pugh, 1990) to explaining methods and tools that can be used in conjunction with the total design philosophy. The model does acknowledge and capture many of the complexities of NPD and attempts to attract a cross discipline audience. It also explicitly acknowledges the place of design within the company's structure and long-term strategy (Sethi, 2000). However, much of the work is essentially a model and text for engineers, and gears itself more towards explaining business requirements to a technical audience, rather than explaining technical issues to a business audience.

The market and user needs "design core" does not clarify well enough for an inexperienced company or researcher to fully comprehend the importance of meeting customer needs to the success of the product. However, having said that, there are numerous issues that have arisen from studying this approach, such as the strong emphasis on the Product Design Specification (PDS) and the recognition of informal paths of communication within the design team, which have directed some of this particular research and will be discussed in the following section of the thesis.

REQUIREMENTS CAPTURE PROCESS MODEL

Cooper *et al.* (1998) have produced a theoretical model of the requirements capture process and have included the aspects of individual and group understandings for customer requirements, this is illustrated in figure 8. They discuss both internal and external variables that can influence the personal interpretation of data. They look at the outcomes of three levels:

1. Acquisition of data
2. Transformation of data
3. Generation of requirements

They concentrate upon considering the situation where individuals come together to gain a shared understanding of customer needs, and then generate an agreed requirement. Cooper *et al's* (1998) is important, because it deals with the handling of customer information and the definition by the NPD team of requirements for the customer. Issues that are addressed in the model, that are particularly pertinent to this research are:

- Different views and understandings (perceptions) of the same data are included
- Activities and events change the understating (perception) of a customer requirement(s)
- Data acquisition and transformation events are required to gain an agreement on the definition of a product requirement(s)

Figure 9. "Over the wall" Concept (after Gehani, 1996)

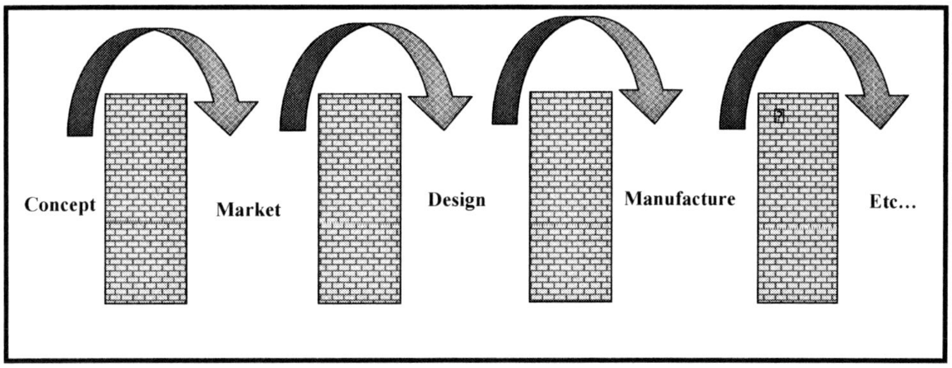

THIRD GENERATION NEW PRODUCT PROCESSES

The phase development models of the nineteen-sixties are referred to as the first generation of defined product processes (Dillon *et al*, 2005). The phase review process advocates sequential development stages, each carried out by different functional groups that complete their phase then pass on the results to the next phase and function (Ahmed, 1998). First generation development processes are often referred to as "*over the wall*" (illustrated in figure 9) processes because development is handed onto the next group, when the last has finished, with an obvious lack of interaction between each phase (Gehani, 1996). The second generation of product development processes are the processes of today – which are mainly based upon stage gate type models involving a cross discipline structure of one type or another. According to Cooper (2001) the third generation are the future way in which products should be produced. He suggests third generation processes are relatively inadequately defined because they are still in development and should be developed and grown around the specific company. They are driven by the need to efficiently create new products and get them to market as quickly as possible, but with a much greater tolerance for calculating risk taking, which is a conflicting view to that of the previously discussed models driven by cycle time.

Cooper *et al* (2002) suggests there is a distinct need to redress the balance from a restrictive linear process that only moves the product development forward when a decision is made on the outcome

Figure 10. Third generation process (Cooper, 2001)

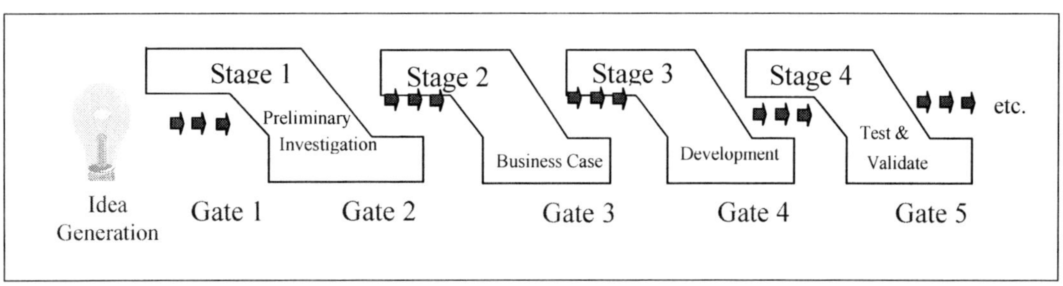

of a preceding activity, as illustrate in figure 10. The ideas put forward by these third generation models tie in with the management practices of concurrent and simultaneous engineering.

This model would, inevitably require integration through software, hardware and 'human ware' or team facilitation (Sethi, 2000; Reid and Brentani, 2004). It will allegedly work from a premise that attempts to maintain discipline, but allows a balance of action thoroughness and the need to move quickly (Cooper and Edgett, 2003). To answer problems that may arise from this basis of reasoning, four fundamental 'F's' have been defined (Cooper, 2001):

1. **Fluidity**. The model is fluid and adaptable, with overlapping and fluid stages for greater speed.
2. **Fuzzy Gates**. The model features conditional go decisions (rather than absolute ones), which are dependant on the situation.
3. **Focused**. The model builds in prioritisation methods that look at the entire portfolio of projects (rather than one at a time) and focuses resources on the "best bets".
4. **Flexible**. The model is not a rigid stage gate process, each project is unique and has its own routing through the process.

The implications from the use of such a model is that everything becomes so much more difficult to define in absolute terms, making devising and understanding the product development process a more daunting task (Zollo *et al*, 2002). As a project progresses, the decisions made will be more complex and sophisticated and may be hard to place in context if the stages overlap too readily (Gerwin and Ferris, 2004). Thus, falling into an ad-hoc, free-for-all system of product development seems a distinct possibility. Cooper (2001) has also made some of these observations and suggests that this model will only work within a framework based on the second-generation stage gate models. He does not advocate a withdrawal from stages and gates, instead he realises that to make these systems really work, product development must allow much more flexibility. A potential way of achieving this could be a move towards reducing the authoritative role of senior management and pushing the decision-making role of the NPD project team members and leaders.

DISCUSSION: THE USEFULNESS OF A PRODUCT DEVELOPMENT PROCESS MODEL APPROACH

The previous discussions provide a good example of the abundance and variation in the different ways of modelling the product development process. It is by no means exhaustive, but rather reflects upon the importance of the diversity that exists in this one area alone. The necessity to examine these different types of models and ways of describing the product development process is that of practicality. For example, if one can somehow capture what it is one's company does, and can follow the path the product development process takes, then one could have a better understanding of how to improve the process and can reap tangible benefits. It has been found that positive consequences result from the existence of formal NPD processes (Cooper *et al*, 2002; Harborne and Johne, 2003; Wong, 2002). Also, research (Cooper, 2001; Gehani, 1996; Reid and Brentani, 2004; Meyer *et al*, 2005; Sethi, 2000) has suggested that the lack of understanding and implementation of product development processes in industry can account for poor product development performance.

Since many product development authors and practitioners have reported these positive results, it is no wonder that they are driven to try and capture the essence of good product development practices and processes. Therefore, in an effort to make the task of modelling the process more manageable, different authors have tried to summarise their complexities by generalising

Figure 11. Model of the need assessment process (Holt et al, 1984)

Need Identification	A problem or a user need is perceived, often in a vague form. This is usually the initiation of the product innovation process.
Need Evaluation	Based on available information, the perceived need is analysed and evaluated; for example in connection with preparation of the proposal.
Need Clarification	This involves a systematic study of the user needs involved. It may be undertaken in connection with a feasibility study in the last part of the idea generation stage.
Need Specification	Based on assessed needs and their relative strength, relevant need requirements are specified.
Need Up-Dating	As the project moves ahead, the needs specified are up-dated at intervals in connection with development of the technology and planning of the marketing and manufacturing operations.

and minimising differences between companies and products (Noke and Radnor, 2004). However, because of this the models are often only a representation of the process and are regularly produced by individual researchers as tools to investigate specific phenomenas that occur during product development. Also, the reality of producing working models is the consideration of differences, which occur between what the literature describes and/or prescribes and what is actually done in reality because the nuances within each company are so difficult to encapsulate (Cooper *et al,* 1998).

Given the plethora of product development models available and reviewed here, it would be reasonable to assume that there would be one, which specifically follows a customer's need through product development. However, although many pay more than just 'lip-service' to customer needs. None have been found that depict the whole of the process for NPD, with explicit emphasis on customer needs compliance. The closest is a descriptive list suggested by Holt *et al* (1984). Their list of stages during which different user needs issues are addressed is illustrated in figure 11. This is a useful list, and does highlight different periods of need recognition, assessment and appraisal. Yet, it does not get to grips with the essence of product development interaction, process, iteration and communications required. These are issues that must first be identified by the company in order to be able to understand at least some of the facets of customer needs compliance during the product development process.

CONCLUSION

In summary, from the discussions it is apparent various investigators have provided a lot of different methods for depicting the NPD process. It has examined the areas of product definition, NPD process modelling and activities, together with a discussion of management issues and matters of information production and use during product design. In short, it has explained some of the principles involved and concepts that are generally referred to in the field of NPD and marketing. However, thus far, none of the methods have been specifically developed for following customers' needs through the NPD process from concept to launch.

The representation of the linkages within NPD practice these models demonstrate a useful starting point for further examination and research, as long as they are taken within their context and understanding of their limitations.

It is evident there is much anecdotal evidence, postulation and idea generation around the area of NPD processes and designing new products. Yet it also indicates the lack of research that has been specifically carried out, that looks at customer needs during NPD. The requirement for further study is evident in a number of particular areas:

- Customer needs literature is mainly restricted to marketing and marketing research literature. There is little research in engineering and design that acknowledges the importance of the customer as the end recipient of the product's quality.
- There is much NPD literature that concentrates upon the general NPD and, in particular, the success and failure of products, broad NPD processes and the overall management of new product ideas. However, specific attention to the customer during success or failure, NPD process, or management of design is minimal.
- There are no apparent NPD modelling methods that have been specifically designed to capture and show the development of new products to meet customer needs requirements. Those models that are available may be used as a basis, but definition of how and what should be modelled to capture information on these aspects is required.
- It has been discussed that the most successful companies undertake both marketing and technical activities well. It has been noted that good market research is a key to achievement, together with practical application of quality techniques. However, little empirical casework has been carried out to discover the effect these issues may have upon customer needs compliance and customer satisfaction.
- The strategy and structural linking mechanism adopted at company and project level has been discussed in the management literature, but still little empirical studies in design research acknowledge links between strategically valuable NPD processes and the customer needs.
- The production, transfer and use of information on customer needs has been included by a number of authors. However, Hart (1995) notes that much research is still warranted into how information is generated and what contingencies might affect information-gathering activities. Also, Davis (2002) identifies numerous areas worth researching with respect to information and knowledge presentation within the design process during NPD.
- A quality gap has been recognised and discussed by previous researchers. However, there is certainly a requirement for more empirical research to investigate the role of the perceptions that the designers have of the product's quality during NPD.

Subsequently, there are numerous gaps in the current NPD research, and therefore, potentially a large number of definitive areas for research in the field of customer needs compliance, product quality and NPD. However, much of the work undertaken by previous authors can be used as a basis to start a novel project.

REFERENCES

Acar, B. S. (1966). A new model for the design process. *Proceedings of the Institute of Mechanical Engineers, Series E*(210), 135-138.

Ahmed, P. X. (1998). Culture and climate for innovation. *European Journal of Innovation Management, 1*(1), 30-43.

Akgun, A. E., Lynn, G. S., & Byrne, J. C. (2004). Taking the guesswork out of new product development: how successful high-tech companies get that way. *The Journal of Business Strategy, 25*(4), 41-48.

Beard, C., & Easingwood, C. (1996). New Product Launch: Marketing Action and launch tactics for high technology products. *Journal of Industrial marketing Management, 25*, 87-103.

Booz, A., & Hamilton (1991). *New Product Management.* New York, USA: Booz, Allen and Hamilton Inc.

Cooper, R. G., & Kleinschmidt, E. J. (1996). Winning businesses in product development: The critical success factors. *Research Technology Management, Jul/Aug, 39*(4), 18-30.

Cooper, R. G., Edgett, S. J., & Kleinschmidt, E. J. (1997). Portfolio management in new product development: Lessons from the leaders – Part I. *Research Technology Management, Sep/Oct, 40*(5), 16- 30.

Cooper, R. G., & Kleinschmidt, E. J. (2000). New product performance: What distinguishes the star products? *Australian Journal of Management, 25*(1), 17-46.

Cooper, R. G., Edgett, S. J., & Kleinschmidt, E. J. (2002). Optimising the stage-gate process: What best practice companies do – II. *Research Technology Management,* Nov/Dec, *45*(6), 43-51.

Cooper, R. G., & Edgett, S. J. (2003). Overcoming the crunch in resources for new product development. *Research Technology Management, 46*(3), 48-59.

Cooper, R., Wooton, B., & Bruce, M. (1998). Requirements Capture: Theory and Practice. *Technovation, 18*(8/9), 497-511.

Cooper, R. G. (1994). Perspective: Third generation new product processes. *Journal of Product Innovation Management, 11*(1), 3-14.

Cooper, R. G. (1999). From Experience: the invisible success factors in product innovation. *Journal of Product innovation Management, 16*(4), 333-351.

Cooper, R. G. (2001). *Winning at New Products: Accelerating the process from idea to launch*, 3rd Edition. Perseus Books.

Dillon, T. A., Lee, R. K., & Matheson, D. (2005). Value Innovation: Passport to wealth creation. *Research Technology Management, 48*(2), 22-36.

Gehani, R. R. (1996). Concurrent product development for fast track corporations. In S. J. Hart (Ed.), *New product development* (pp. 184-197). Dryden Press.

Gerwin, D., & Barrowman, N. J. (2002). An evaluation of research on integrated product development. *Management Science, 47*(7), 938-953.

Gerwin, D., & Ferris, S. J. (2004). Organising New Product Development Projects in Strategic Alliances. *Organisation Science, 15*(1), 22-38.

Griffin, A. (1997). PDMA research on new product development practices. *Journal of Product Innovation Management, 14*(6), 429-458.

Harborne, P., & Johne, A. (2003). Creating a project climate for successful product innovation. *European Journal of Innovation Management, 6*(2), 118-133.

Hart, S. J., & Baker, M. J. (1996). The multiple convergent processing model of new product development. In S. J. Hart (Ed.), *New Product Development* (pp 151-166). London: TheDryden Press.

Hart, S. J., Hutlink, E., Tzokas, N., & Commandeur, H. (2003). Industrial Companies' Evaluation Criteria in new Product Development gates. *Journal of Product Innovation Management, 20*(1), 22-36.

Hart, S. J. (1995). Where we've been and where we're going in new product development research. In M. Bruce & W. G. Biemens (Eds.), *Product development – Meeting the challenge of the design-marketing interface* (pp. 13-43). Chichester, UK: John Wiley and Sons.

Hart, S. J. (1996). *New Product Development: A Reader.* The Dryden Press, Harcourt Brace and Company Limited.

Himmelfarb, P. A. (1992). *Survival of the fittest – New product development during the 90's.* Englewood Cliffs, NJ, USA: Prentice-Hall International.

Hollins, W., & Pugh, S. (1990). *Successful product design*. London, UK: Butterworth.

Holt, K., Geschka, H., & Peterlongo, G. (1984). *Need assessment – A key to user orientated product innovation.* John Wiley and Sons Ltd.

Hultink, E. J., & Hart, S. (1998). The world's path to the better mousetrap: myth or reality? An empirical investigation into the launch strategies of high and low advantage new products. *European Journal of Innovation Management, 1*(3), 106-121.

Jenkins, S., Forbes, S., Durrani, T. S., & Banerjee, S. K. (1997). Managing the product development process [Part I: An assessment]. *International Journal of Technology Management, 13*(4), 359-378.

Jobber, D. (1998). *Principles and Practice of Marketing,* Second Edition. McGraw-Hill Publishing Company, International Editions.

Kalyanaram, G., & Krishnan, V. (1997). Deliberate product definition: Customising the product definition process. *Journal of Marketing Research, 34*(2), 276-286.

Li, T. (1999). The impact of the marketing-R&D interface on new product export performance: A contingency analysis. *Journal of International Marketing, 7*(1), 10-34.

Lynn, G. S., & Akgun, A. E. (1999). Launch your new products/services better, faster. Research Technology Management, 46(3), 21-26.

McGrath, M. E., Anthony, M. T., & Shipiro, A. R. (1992). Product development: Success through cycle time excellence. PRTM Butterworth-Heinemann Publishing.

Meyer, M. H., Anzani, M., & Walsh, G. (2005). Innovation and Enterprise Growth: It took courage, focus and commitment at all levels for IBM to develop its next-generation product lines. *Research Technology Management, 48*(4), 34-44.

Noke, H., & Radnor, Z. J. (2004). Navigating innovation: a diagnostic tool supporting the process. *Journal of Manufacturing Technology Management, 15*(2), 172-185.

Norman, P. A., & Peterson, T. (1999). Quality improvement through innovation. In S. K. Ho (Ed.), *TQM and Innovation Proceedings of the fourth international conference on ISO 9000 and TQM* (pp 64-70). HKBU press.

Oakley, M. (1990). Design and design management. In M. Oakley (Ed.), *Design management: A handbook of issues and methods* (pp 3-15). Oxford, UK: Basil Blackwell Ltd.

Osterlund, J. (1997). Competence management by informatics in R&D: The corporate level. *IEEE transactions on Engineering Management, 44*(2), 135-145.

Owens, J. D. (2004a). An evaluation of Organisational groundwork and learning objectives for New Product Development. *Journal of Enterprising Culture, 12*, 303-325.

Owens, J. D. (2004b). World Class Supply: Is it just a question of effective partnership? *Management Services Journal, 48, 8-15.*

Owens, J. D., & Davies, J. (2000). The Importance of a New Product Development (NPD) Process: Getting Started. *First European Conference on Knowledge Management,* Bled School of Management, Bled, Slovenia, 26-27 October.

Ozer, M. (1999). A Survey of New Product Evaluation Models. *Journal of Product Innovation Management, 16*, 77-94.

Ozer, M. (2004). Managing the selection process for new product ideas. *Research Technology Management, 47*(4), 10-15.

Pugh, S., & Moreley, I. E. (1988). *Total Design: Towards a theory of total design and Total Design: Some questions and some answers.* Design division, University of Strathclyde, UK.

Pugh, S. (1991). *Total design – Integrated methods for successful product engineering.* UK: Addison-Wesley Publishing.

Reid, S. E., & Brentani, U. de (2004). The fuzzy front end of the new product development for discontinuous innovations: a theoretical model. *Journal of Product Innovation Management, 21*(3), 170-198.

Robinson, W. T., & Chiang, J. (2002). Product development strategies for established market pioneers, early followers, and late entrants. *Strategic Management Journal, 23*(9), 855-864.

Saren, M. A. (1984). A classification and review of models of the intra-firm innovation process. *R&D Magazine, 14*(1), 11-24.

Sethi, R. (2000). New product Quality and Product Development Teams. *Journal of Marketing, 64*(2), 1-14.

Shenhar, A. J. (2001). One size does not fit all projects: Exploring classical contingency domains. *Management Science, 47*(3), 394-414.

Suomala, P., & Jokionen, I. (2003). The pattern of success in product development: a case study. *European Journal of Innovation Management, 6*(4), 213-227.

Tracey, M. (2004). A holistic approach to New Product Development: New Insights. *Journal of Supply Chain Management, 40*(4), 37-56.

Wong, V. (2002). Antecedents of international new product rollout timeliness. *International Marketing Review, 19*(2/3), 12-132.

Wright, I. C., & Swain, E. (1995). New product engineering: The quality paradox. *Journal of Engineering Design, 6*(1), 49-56.

Wright, I. C. (1998). *Design Methods in engineering and product design.* UK: McGraw Hill.

Zhao, Z., Yap, C. M., & Ang, B. W. (1999). A framework for facilitating quality tools' applications in new product development. In S. K. Ho (Ed.), *TQM and Innovation proceedings of the fourth international conference on ISO 9000 and TQM* (pp. 455-461). HKBU press.

Zollo, M., Reuer, J. J., & Singh, H. (2002). Interorganisational routines and performance in strategic alliances. *Organisational Science, 13*(6), 701-713.

KEY TERMS

New Products: There are numerous definitions however one common similarity characterises a new product as 'one not previously manufactured by a company'.

Innovation: "Innovation' can be considered as the unit of technological change and an invention, if one exists in the situation, it is part of the process of innovation.

Newness: 'Newness' may be new creations, such as original innovations; or products new to the world or new to the company. Additions, improvements and revisions, with greater emphasis on particular values. Repositioning of the product, for example, novel ways to use it in a different market segment, or possibly the use of branding. Cost reductions, lower price, or improvement in through life costs.

New Product Development: New Product Development (NPD) is the term used to describe the complete process of bringing a new product or service to market. There are two parallel paths involved in the NPD process: one involves the idea generation, product design, and detail engineering; the other involves market research and marketing analysis.

Product Development: The development of new, improved, or replacement product or service

Section IV
Management and Control

Chapter XIV
Achieving Organizational Independence of Employees' Knowledge using Knowledge Management, Organizational Learning, and the Learning Organization

Anders Örtenblad
Halmstad University, Sweden

ABSTRACT

The ambition of this chapter is to pay some attention to more obvious, as well as more subtle, methods for organizations to become independent of the individual's subjective knowledge, from the employees' point of view. Terms such as 'knowledge sharing', 'knowledge transfer', and 'learning for all' are almost always seen as being positive for both employers and employees. However, this chapter will critically examines those terms. Three popular management ideas relating to knowledge and/or learning have been analysed from a 'knowledge control' perspective: knowledge management, organizational learning, and the learning organization. The main conclusion of this conceptual and elaborating chapter is that the more current and less academic ideas of the learning organization and knowledge management contain the same tools as the idea of 'old' organizational learning as regards gaining control over knowledge, but that these two ideas additionally contain other knowledge control measures, which are more refined, in the sense that they are less obvious as knowledge control measures. The idea of 'new' organizational learning, however, is less suited to knowledge control, since it implies that knowledge is not storable. In other words, the chapter's contribution is an analysis of some of the most popular management ideas that deal with knowledge and/or learning relating to the organizational/employer independence of subjective knowledge, from the employees' point of view, something which is rarely seen.

INTRODUCTION

We are said to live in a 'knowledge society'. If this is true, it would mean, among other things, that individuals and their subjective knowledge are becoming more important at the expense of machines and other so called 'resources'. Droege and Hoobler recently (2003: 50) described one of the problems of the 'knowledge economy' stating that employees' knowledge 'is rarely shared, swapped, traced, and fertilized to ensure that it remains, at least in part, with the firm when employees leave'.

There are, however, ways for organizations to become more or less independent of any one individual and her or his subjective knowledge. The aim of this chapter is to identify and draw attention to such means, which are sometimes obvious but often quite subtle, in the following management ideas concerning knowledge and/or learning in an organizational context: organizational learning, the learning organization, and knowledge management. I have analysed literature on these ideas in order to highlight and 'unveil' means enabling organizations to become independent of the individual's subjective knowledge.

Organizations interfere a lot in every single person's life; Deetz (1992) has even claimed that organizations 'colonize' us and our world – we grow up in organizations (child care centres, schools, etc.), we shop in them, we work there, etc. They can easily – like giants – in one way or another destroy the originality of the only thing that makes individuals unique on the labour market: subjective knowledge. There is always a risk that all knowledge will stay within, or be transferred to, organizations. The employees – and especially their subjective knowledge – run the risk of being exploited. Therefore, it is so important to unveil all the means enabling employers to become independent of the individual's subjective knowledge, for instance in popular management ideas, which this chapter is about.

Most of the management literature generally seems to view the struggle to become independent of subjective knowledge as risk reduction, if it is acknowledged at all. From such a functionalistic perspective, independence struggles are thus a necessity that organizations – and in particular employers – would not be able to cope without. For instance, Bonora and Revang (1993) discussed strategies for reducing firms' dependence on subjective knowledge, by building knowledge into the organization and by building exit barriers. Clegg argued that:

> *If management can reduce their dependency on individuals as the bearers of knowledge and skills by rendering these skills into computer-based artifacts, it is possible to manipulate and combine these with other factors of production in ways that are impossible if these skills remain a human possession.* (Clegg, 2000: 87-88)

Stovel and Bontis (2002: 310) argued that 'senior managers must implement knowledge management strategies to ensure that monies they have spent on the training and operation of departments are not wasted when voluntary turnover occurs within the firm'.

I will instead view the means enabling organizations to become independent of subjective knowledge from a more critical perspective, thus following in the footsteps of pioneers such as Braverman (1974), and view them as concrete tools for gaining control over knowledge. From such a critical perspective, current and more hidden means of controlling knowledge are hardly signs of a new trend, rather they are extensions of earlier ways of controlling knowledge, such as slavery, where the workforce was (and at some places in the world still is) owned, and Taylorism, where the employees are alienated from knowledge of the whole product/service and are only allowed to learn and master narrow, specialised work tasks, which could also be expressed in terms of control by deskilling the employees (Braverman,

1974). I see it as a continuous struggle between organizations on the one hand, mainly represented by the employers, trying to remain or become independent, and on the other, the individual's (which, of course, in some cases might at the same time represent an employer) struggle not to become redundant. Both the organization and the individuals have their passions for knowledge, or should I say *possessions* for knowledge. In this chapter, however, the conflict in focus is that between the organization and the individual. I will, however, assume that employers are more interested in organizational independence than employees are. Consequently, the conflict at stake is also that between employers and employees.

The standpoint that I take in this chapter is that of the individual (the employee). The main reason for this is that the employee perspective has thus far been rather neglected, and the employer perspective has instead been the most common one by far in management studies of knowledge sharing. The main perspective in the area of knowledge sharing and knowledge transfer is still that of management/employers. For instance, the knowledge-based theory of the firm, which is more of a normative management theory than a descriptive theory (see, for instance, Grant, 1996). There is definitely a need for a critical examination of this perspective, as well as how it affects employees. Burgoyne (1999) acknowledged the importance of the question of whether the organization is in control of knowledge within the organization or not. Moreover, Easterby-Smith, Crossan and Nicolini claimed that

The time is ripe to start addressing learning and knowing in the light of the inherent conflicts between shareholders' goals, economic pressure, institutionalised professional interests and political agendas. (Easterby-Smith et al., 2000: 793)

There is some literature, however, that deals with knowledge sharing in general, which is more critical (e.g. Lam, 2000). I have used more management-oriented as well as more critical literature on knowledge sharing when analysing knowledge management, organizational learning, and the learning organization. Actually, there is even some literature in which these ideas are critically examined with regard to knowledge sharing (e.g. Akella, 2003; Filion & Rudolph, 1999; Scultze & Stabell, 2004). However, this chapter takes a more general grasp of management ideas connected to knowledge and/or learning, compares them, and provides an overview of possible knowledge-controlling mechanisms, whereas previous studies have tended to study only one management idea each. In addition, this study focuses on the employers' struggles to make their organizations independent of subjective knowledge (although I will also discuss employee independence), in order to clarify and unmask them, since they are not always that obvious. Many previous critical studies have instead aspired to present employee resistance to employers' struggles to become independent of their employees. I believe that it is more important to understand and unveil the many subtle techniques used by employers to achieve such independence than it is to discuss resistance to them or coping strategies. The measures must first be acknowledged before any struggles to cope with them or fight them can be initiated.

Knowledge management, organizational learning, and the learning organization are all important management ideas, because at least some of them are often sold to many organizations as possible answers to *all* of their problems – they are nothing but 'management fashions'. I believe that most academics would regard the ideas of the learning organization and knowledge management as fashions. At the other end of a continuum, there is 'new organizational learning', which has hardly become very popular among consultants and so called practitioners. And in the middle, I would say that we would find 'old organizational learning', with some attraction, but it is definitely a more academic idea than the learning organization and knowledge management.

It is of great importance to investigate management ideas relating to knowledge and/or learning, since these might influence people's lives in general and their right to have their own knowledge in particular. These ideas can, in different ways, exert an influence on who is in control of knowledge: the organization/employer or the individuals/employees. The unveiling of means enabling organizations to stay or to become independent of the individual's subjective knowledge is extremely important, since these organizations, with the employers at the forefront, might fool us – especially using less obvious means – and make sure that they are in control of the knowledge, not the individual. This might, of course, be fatal for all the individuals/employees who may lose their only means (subjective knowledge), perhaps, of competing on the labour market, as well as competing with organizations. Without their subjective knowledge, individuals will be very small and insignificant on the labour market, and easy to outmanoeuvre.

In general, popular management ideas are often ambiguous and thus not easily defined. Extensive deliberations regarding what the three ideas actually mean would not, however, help in this case – these would instead guarantee missing the point on my part. Some general definitions are needed, however, in order to make it possible to follow the line of reasoning. Organizational learning will be divided, in accordance with Turner referred to in Gherardi (1999), into two sub-ideas: 'old organizational learning' and 'new organizational learning'. In this chapter, in using the term 'old organizational learning', I mean the embedding of what the organization's individuals have learnt, as agents of the organization, into different kinds of Standard Operating Procedures (SOPs) which in turn direct the individual's actions (and further learning) (see Argyris and Schön, 1978). The idea of the 'learning organization' will be defined as a flexible organization, with a relatively flat structure and empowered employees, which implies that the individuals have learnt from one another so that everyone can perform each other's work tasks, and that the employees continuously learn from their customers what (altered) needs the customers have as well as learn lessons enabling them to satisfy these needs, and also that the learning takes place during work – not during formal education (see Senge, 1990; Watkins and Marsick, 1993). 'Knowledge management' will be defined as the dissemination of the knowledge created in one place or within one group at the organization to as many individuals within the organization as possible, as well as the process of informing everyone within the organization about who knows what (see Ives, Torrey and Gordon, 1998). 'New organizational learning' will be defined as situated, collective learning (see Cook and Yanow, 1993; Gherardi, Nicolini and Odella, 1998).

The next part of the chapter highlights what is probably the most common way for organizations to become independent of and to control subjective knowledge, described in the studied literature, namely storing it outside the individual. Thereafter, I present other and probably less apparent means of becoming independent and taking control, shown by the analyses of the three ideas. In the third part of the chapter, I present (a perspective of) an idea that does not seem to involve any means of knowledge control whatsoever. The final part of the chapter is devoted to a discussion about and a comparison between the three studied management ideas, and how they differ in terms of the means of the organizational independence of subjective knowledge that they provide.

INDEPENDENCE AND CONTROL BY STORING KNOWLEDGE OUTSIDE THE INDIVIDUAL

One way for organizations to remain, or become, independent of the individual and her or his subjective knowledge, and thus in control of knowledge, is to store knowledge outside the individual in what is often called the 'organizational memory' (Argyris and Schön, 1978; Cyert and March, 1963; Hedberg, 1981). This consists of routines, SOPs, manuals, shared mental models, etc. An image that comes to mind here is the assembly line, where all the workers are competent enough to add their specific piece to what is going to become a car; but one by one, they are totally unable to build a whole car. The knowledge of how to build a car is stored in the assembly line in itself, together with the workers' routines and procedures. Argote and McGrath (1993: 366) argued that the effects of turnover on knowledge depreciation are smaller when knowledge is stored in the organization than if it is stored in individuals. Lam (2000: 492) claimed that '[t]he abstraction of individuals' experience and knowledge into encoded knowledge also facilitates centralisation and control in organizations' (see also Grant 1991: 128). Prichard, Hull, Chumer and Willmott argued that 'if a worker's tacit knowledge and know-how can be codified and tucked into databases for access by anyone at any time from any place, then what is the value of that worker to the organization?' (Prichard et al., 2000: xxii). Yakhlef and Salzer-Mörling (2000: 32) claimed that '[i]f knowledge is safely stored in the organizational databases and structures, an organization stands to lose less money if one of its experts leaves it with all the knowledge and information that he or she may have.' When it comes to the three management ideas I have studied, the storing of knowledge in the organizational memory in fact seems to be the cornerstone of the idea of organizational learning:

[I]n order for organizational learning to occur, learning agents' discoveries, inventions, and evaluations must be embedded in organizational memory. They must be encoded in the individual images and the shared maps of organizational theory-in-use from which individual members will subsequently act. If this encoding does not occur, individuals will have learned but the organization will not have done so. (Argyris and Schön, 1978: 19; see also Kim, 1993: 37)

According to Levitt and March (1988: 320), '[r]outines are independent of the individual actors who execute them and are capable of surviving considerable turnover in individual actors'.

Knowledge storing in the organizational memory is also important in the idea of the learning organization. For instance, Marquardt and Reynolds (1994: 25-26) argued that the meaning and memory subsystem of the learning organization stores what they called 'organizational knowledge'. This is also apparent in the literature on knowledge management, where Templeton and Snyder (1999: 706) argued that 'knowledge embedding is an important and desired outcome of knowledge management in organizations'.

One can, of course, argue that if every member of an organization were to leave that organization, then the knowledge would also disappear due to the fact that documents, routines, etc. would have to be interpreted by people who are familiar with the culture of the organization in order to understand that knowledge (cf. Kim, 1993; Scarbrough, 1998). This would mean that the organization is able to learn independently of specific individuals, but not independently of all of the individuals (Kim, 1993). However, it is a relatively rare phenomenon that all employees leave at the same time. Accordingly, one way for organizations to make sure that they are in control of subjective knowledge is to store it in the organizational memory, outside the individual.

However, some have argued that it is impossible to store knowledge outside the individual (e.g. Alvesson and Kärreman, 2001: 999), and that knowledge is always context-dependent (cf. the socio-cultural perspective of organizational learning, see below). More recent management ideas regarding knowledge and/or learning seem, however, to have taken this criticism into account, involving other ways for organizations to become and stay independent of individuals and their subjective knowledge that do not imply that knowledge is stored outside the individual. Instead, knowledge remains – as it would seem – in the possession of the individual and, as we shall see next, many of the means connected with these ideas differ from the means dominating the literature on organizational learning.

MORE REFINED MEANS FOR INDEPENDENCE AND CONTROL

Although also the ideas of the learning organization and knowledge management involve knowledge storing outside the individual, as shown above, these ideas largely seem to accept the fact that knowledge remains subjective and is thus tightly intertwined with the individual. Consequently, these ideas instead involve techniques of making organizations independent of subjective knowledge, techniques that deal with controlling these individuals and their knowledge. Such means, found in the literature on the learning organization and knowledge management – but also on organizational learning – can be categorised into various types: 'mind control', 'knowledge redundancy', 'complete transparency and accessibility', and 'contextual knowledge'. These types will be presented in more depth below.

I call these specific means of achieving independence and control 'more refined means', compared with storing knowledge outside the individual. The latter means is an older one, it is better known and probably more obvious. The former type of means is, as far as I am concerned, more refined in that it is not immediately understood as means of independence and controlling knowledge. It has to be revealed as means of independence and control, which is one of the contributions of this chapter.

Mind Control

Mind control, i.e. the controlling of individuals so that they learn the right things – i.e. what the organization which they are members of needs – is probably the second most common means of knowledge control in the studied literature. It can, for instance, be the case that individuals working for an advertising agency automatically focus on other agencies' advertisements, when watching TV, for instance, in their spare time, and thus obtain ideas regarding how an advertisement that their own agency is selling can be improved. This is quite common in the literature on organizational learning and is often closely connected with the storing of knowledge outside the individual. Before any knowledge can be stored in the organizational memory, the individuals will have to learn this particular knowledge, which will later be embedded in routines, rules, etc. Argyris and Schön (1978) expressed this in terms of the individuals learning as agents of the organization, claiming that 'organizational learning occurs when individuals within an organization experience a problematic situation and inquire into it on the organization's behalf' (Argyris and Schön, 1996: 16). It is presumed, here, that the individuals pay attention to and learn things that are of importance to the organization. This is accomplished by means of 'shared mental models' (Filion and Rudolph, 1999). Accordingly, 'mind control' is an important element of the idea of organizational learning. By controlling what the individuals learn, the knowledge that they learn will be well adapted to the organization's needs, and the risk that they learn things that they do not want to share, when it is time to embed it, will be minimized.

'Mind control' also seems to be occurring in the idea of the learning organization. Jones and Hendry (1994), for instance, have argued that the individuals are supposed to focus on things in their environment that are of interest to the organization. A 'shared vision', which has been described by, for instance, Senge (1990) as an important ingredient of the learning organization, can also be understood as 'mind control' in that it is assumed to achieve everyone working in a common direction towards a common goal (cf. Akella, 2007; Filion and Rudolph, 1999). The individuals' learning will probably be directed by such a shared vision.

Knowledge Redundancy

'Knowledge redundancy' means that more than one individual possesses the same knowledge, so that the organization is made less dependent on employees who possess unique knowledge. For instance, if the architect, in a team of architects, who has the highest level of expertise, when it comes to drawing and designing houseboats, is busy with another urgent project (or is simply away from work due to being on sick leave), another architect in the team has enough expertise to fill in for the most competent architect and the team will be able to meet the customer's requirements nevertheless. In some cases, the organization makes sure that at least some other individuals possess the same knowledge, while in other cases, it seems to be the objective that as many people within the organization as possible share specific knowledge. This is apparent in both the idea of the learning organization and in the idea of knowledge management.

The learning organization is often described in terms of self-organizing and relatively independent teams. The individuals in the teams are supposed to learn from each other in order to create flexibility, in that every team member has acquired the knowledge necessary to perform the tasks of the other team members, if there is a lot to do and the other members are busy (see, for instance, Garratt, 1990; McGill and Slocum, 1993; Senge, 1990; Swieringa and Wierdsma, 1992; Watkins and Marsick, 1993). Not only are the individual teams supposed to possess such redundant capacity (cf. Morgan, 1997), but also the whole organization – the teams are supposed to fill in for each other. This makes the organization less dependent upon any one individual and less vulnerable to turnover (cf. Bonora and Revang, 1993: 200). Another, similar way for the organization to become independent of individuals, one which is also present in the learning organization literature, is work rotation (see, for instance, Kiechel, 1990: 76; Watkins and Marsick, 1993: 25-26). The same can be accomplished via personnel rotation programmes, something which is also mentioned in the learning organization literature (e.g. Garvin, 1993: 87).

The focus on knowledge sharing in the idea of knowledge management (see, for instance, Civi, 2000: 173; Hermans, 1999: 161) is another way of ensuring that more than one individual possesses a particular item of knowledge. Sometimes this knowledge is described as being in need of facilitating measures, such as a harmonious climate:

> *...because knowledge needs to be shared to be created and exploited, it is important for leaders to ensure that there is an atmosphere in which an organization's members feel safe sharing their knowledge. It is also important for leaders to cultivate commitment among organization members to motivate the sharing and creation of knowledge based on the knowledge vision.* (Nonaka, Toyama and Konno, 2001: 37)

This facilitating culture – which might seem to be good and harmless – further increases the employers' control of knowledge, in that it facilitates the dissemination of knowledge to everyone and thus makes the individual less important to the organization, while people are supposed to feel 'safe' as Nonaka et al. express it (see the citation above).

Complete Transparency and Accessibility

Knowledge management is not only about sharing knowledge with others, i.e. everyone learning everything. It is also about informing others – or ideally everyone – within the organization that a specific employee possesses knowledge in a particular area so that it becomes widely available to others who might need it. Ives, Torrey, and Gordon (1998: 272), for instance, describe knowledge management as 'the effort to make the knowledge of an organization available to those within the organization who need it, where they need it, when they need it, and in the form in which they need it'. In this case, the knowledge still seems to be 'stuck within' a few individuals – and not disseminated to everyone, as was the case with the means of 'knowledge redundancy' outlined above – but there is supposed to be an awareness in everyone regarding the knowledge that exists within the organization, i.e. who knows what. In this manner, one can more easily make an inventory of all the knowledge within the organization, thus replacements – for instance in the form of substitutes – can be planned for in detail in the case of turnover. It could, for instance, be the case that everybody at an accountancy firm knows which of their colleagues specialize in groups and major companies, which specialize in medium-sized companies, which specialize in small companies, and which specialize in other associations, etc. In that way, any employee of the accountancy firm can direct the customer to the right accountant, who can then help to solve the problems of the customer. In fact, a group of commentators have described the aim of knowledge management as making 'the knowledge inside people's heads (i.e. cognitive knowledge) widely available to reduce the threat of valuable knowledge assets literally "walking out of the door"' (Swan, Newell, Scarbrough and Hislop, 1999: 265).

A similar way for organizations to obtain relative independence as regards subjective knowledge is apparent in the learning organization literature. Several authors have described the importance of a holistic way of thinking in the learning organization (e.g. Senge, 1990; Watkins and Marsick, 1993). In essence, everyone should be aware of what the other members of the organization are doing and whether they are in need of any help, so that they can be helped out when necessary. This makes the organization less dependent on the individual, in that everyone knows what is going on in other parts of the organization and is thus able to help to recreate the whole, although remaining unable to perform others' work tasks themselves.

Contextual Knowledge

A rather common theme in the learning organization literature is 'learning at work' or 'on-the-job learning' (e.g. Jones and Hendry, 1992; Jones and Hendry, 1994; Watkins and Marsick, 1993). The intention of this theme is that employees learn more valuable knowledge while learning from day-to-day work, instead of learning general (decontextualised) knowledge on formal courses. We have probably all heard of managers who go away on formal courses, away from the workplace, preferably to a nice little conference centre, to learn more and/or better leadership, and how difficult it is for them to integrate their newly-acquired knowledge into their leadership upon returning. They might be excited for a couple of weeks, and they may plan to change their leadership style – which usually also makes the employees excited for a while – but after a short time, everything is back to normal again – nothing is new under the sun. Thus, this theme is based upon the premise that there is such a thing as general knowledge, and consequently, that there is a division between context-specific and non-contextual (or general) knowledge.

By allowing employees to learn on-the-job, instead of on courses away from work, knowledge is made less general and more specific to the context in which the learning takes place. Therefore, it might be more difficult for the individual employee to transfer this knowledge to another organizational context. Thus, the organization remains, to some extent, in control of knowledge (and hence of the individual) since it cannot easily be used elsewhere (cf. Lam, 2000: 504; Scarbrough, 1995: 1012). This reasoning is based on the assumption that organizations are more vulnerable to staff turnover when knowledge is organization-specific, and that individuals gain by learning general knowledge that they can use elsewhere (cf. Lam, 2000).

AN IDEA WITHOUT ANY MEANS OF INDEPENDENCE OR CONTROL

There is, however, a perspective on organizational learning that does not seem to involve any tools aimed at making organizations independent from subjective knowledge – the so-called 'new' or 'socio-cultural' perspective of organizational learning. Instead of emphasising cognitive learning on the part of individuals or cognitive learning on the part of the organization as if it were an individual, as organizational learning researchers have traditionally done (Cook and Yanow, 1993), the new perspective sees organizational learning as collective learning. For instance, Cook and Yanow (1993) describe learning by the collective, and several other authors have described the learning in and by communities of practice (e.g. Brown and Duguid, 1991; Lave and Wenger, 1991; Richter, 1998; Wenger, 1991). According to Gherardi et al. (1998: 274), another main difference between old and new organizational learning has to do with contextual dependence. They claim that all knowledge is context-dependent in the socio-cultural perspective of organizational learning – learning is situated (Lave and Wenger, 1991). According to the socio-cultural perspective of organizational learning, there is no such thing as 'knowledge', in terms of being a noun. Instead, knowledge is as much a process as learning is, and should thus be called 'knowing' instead (see Blackler, 1995). According to Orlikowski (2002), 'knowing' cannot be transferred or moved. In Cook and Brown's (1999) terms, knowing is action, and cannot be possessed. Thus, knowledge as knowing is a process and a verb, not a noun, and not something that can be stored or transferred.

Consequently, as I have understood this perspective of organizational learning, the collective per se learns to perform its task in a unique way; for instance, a symphony orchestra that learns to play a specific symphony in its own particular and unique way. In addition, as the orchestra performs the symphony, which it has been learning or practicing for a long period of time, it performs what it has learnt, and this process is called *knowing*. Knowing builds on and is dependent on all previous learning, although no knowledge in the normal sense has been stored, since that is an impossibility in this perspective. Instead, knowing is the collective creation of the symphony at that moment, based on the learning that has taken place previously. The knowing *happens*, or perhaps better, is *created* by a group while performing its task, and it might never happen again in exactly the same way. Although a symphony orchestra has learnt to play a symphony in a specific way, no two performances will be exactly the same, and it would not be possible to reproduce a performance – not even with the same orchestra (i.e. the same collective).

Furthermore, as Cook and Yanow (1993) explain, no two symphony orchestras play the same symphony in the same way. Therefore, a musician who leaves one orchestra for another must learn to play the symphony in the same manner that the new orchestra uses, not to mention the orchestra having to learn to play the symphony anew with its new member. Knowledge (in the sense of *knowing*) that has been developed (or should I say has happened) in one context does not make sense in any other context, and cannot thus be disseminated to, or used in, these contexts (cf. Swan et al., 1999: 270). The process of collective organizational learning – and even that of knowing – might seem to be harmonious, but that does not have to be the case at all. Although the learning takes place collectively, relations within the group or collective might be experiencing conflict, which in turn may be constructive as regards the development of the learning processes (Contu and Willmott, 2003).

Accordingly, the employees cannot take 'knowing' with them, to other organizations, hence the organization will not have to fear turnover. However, since 'knowing' cannot be stored, and in this sense, does not even exist in the individual (Fisher and White, 2000, argue, however, that knowledge in this perspective exists in the relationships between individuals), this perspective of organizational learning provides no means for organizations to stay or become independent vis-à-vis the individuals. In order to remain in control of knowledge, the organization would have to find other ways of controlling the collectives and communities of practice wherein this 'knowing' happens. Accordingly, it is – by definition – impossible to be in control of knowledge in this perspective, since there is no such thing as knowledge; however, it might be possible, but difficult, to control the process of knowing. Knowing is something people do, not something they have or possess.

DISCUSSION AND CONCLUSIONS

There are many different ways of explaining the continuous stream of 'new' management ideas. One way of explaining the appearance of the ideas of the learning organization and knowledge management, is that these two ideas are better adapted to the knowledge society than the idea of organizational learning – especially the older, traditional perspective, in which knowledge is assumed to be routinized and stored outside the individual. As it would seem, knowledge is more often possessed by the individuals in the ideas of the learning organization and knowledge management, making them more suited to a society in which knowledge is needed on every level, promptly. In fact, the learning organization and knowledge management have been contaminated to varying degrees by means of becoming or remaining independent of individual employees and their subjective knowledge.

Another explanation, however, might be that the ideas of the learning organization and knowledge management appear to be more democratic, in that knowledge is understood to exist within the individual. Indeed, the idea of the learning organization in particular is often connected with democracy and empowerment, as, for instance, Snell and Chak (1998) and Coopey (1998) have argued, and according to Fenwick (1998), the literature on the learning organization promises a humanistic workplace. Also knowledge management is often depicted in beautiful words such as 'knowledge sharing'.

However, this seems to be a somewhat superficial image of these ideas, according to the analysis of the means of independence in the literature regarding these ideas. The means of independence are often subtle, but apparent. Moreover, it is precisely the idea of the learning organization – which is certainly the one idea of the three most associated with democracy – that contains the largest number of means whereby organizations can make themselves independent of individual employees and their subjective knowledge, and hence put them in control of this knowledge. These means, however, are often quite subtle, and they must probably be a part of an idea that signals democracy, yet provides many means of controlling knowledge. In this chapter, I have contributed towards unveiling the subtle, less obvious, and more refined means enabling organizations to stay or become independent of individuals' subjective knowledge, which they can find in the ideas of the learning organization and knowledge management. These subtle means are mind control, knowledge redundancy, complete transparency and accessibility, and contextual knowledge. By that, the chances for individuals on the labour market – against all the organizations that tend to seize all knowledge – have hopefully increased a bit. The unveiling that I have dedicated my time to in this chapter, and the advice that I have offered, are based, however, on the premise that the older, functionalistic perspective on knowledge, as something that exists somewhere, still rules.

But what about the socio-cultural perspective of organizational learning? It has not yet become, as far as I am aware, particularly popular among practitioners. This idea (or sub-idea of the idea of organizational learning) differs from the other ideas, in that it involves – as it would seem – no means of knowledge storing, and thus no tools aimed at controlling subjective knowledge. Thus, one scenario is that this idea will never become popular among employers (and, consequently, not in the management literature either). Another possible scenario is that – if new organizational learning becomes a more widely-disseminated perspective than it has hitherto been – then employers, instead of controlling the knowledge, will increase their control over the employees. This could be achieved by offering them partnerships, or the employers could be even more careful regarding whom they employ, in order to have staff with good prerequisites for creating 'knowing' together, in communities of practice. Thus, even if the socio-cultural perspective of organizational learning implies less means of controlling knowledge, it might result in less democratic organizations. A third scenario is that this perspective of organizational learning develops towards a state of harmony with management, i.e. involving means by which it is possible to store knowledge, or in other ways control it, thus increasing its chances of becoming a really popular management idea. In this way, the idea would be 'colonized' by functionalists. One sign of this is that the term 'communities-of-practice' is today being used as a management term, implying that knowledge can be stored (see, for instance, Saint-Onge and Wallace, 2003). Alternatively, but less likely, the increased popularity of this idea will result in more equality between organizations and individuals, especially as regards who is in control of knowledge.

I see this, the new perspective of organizational learning, as a new perspective on learning and knowledge in organizations, one which, in fact, is the result of a paradigmatic shift, and hardly just a matter of a complementary perspective. Therefore, if this new perspective outmanoeuvres the ideas of the learning organization, knowledge management and the old perspective of organizational learning, there will not be a problem, from the employees' point of view. When knowledge is seen as knowing, which cannot be created and thus not owned either, a lot fewer capitalists will take an interest in it. And the odds of people creating something jointly, without having greedy employers after them, hot on their heels all the time, will increase dramatically. Let us hope, for the future, that this new perspective receives more attention, so that the labour market will finally be the employees' market, or at least that the conditions for employers and employees will be more equal than they are now.

In conclusion, employees should be more suspicious about new management ideas that deal with knowledge and/or learning, which seem fine but can be fatal for them. They should look after their subjective knowledge more carefully.

REFERENCES

Akella, D. (2003). *Unlearning the Fifth discipline: Power, Politics and Control in Organizations*. New Delhi: Response Books.

Akella, D. (2007). Learning organizations: managerial control systems? *Global Business Review, 8*, 13-28.

Alvesson, M., & Kärreman, D. (2001). Odd couple: making sense of the curious concept of knowledge management. *Journal of Management Studies, 38,* 995-1018.

Argote, L., & McGrath, J. E. (1993). Group processes in organizations: continuity and change. *International Review of Industrial and Organizational Psychology, 8,* 333-389.

Argyris, C., & Schön, D. A. (1978). *Organizational Learning: A Theory of Action Perspective*. London: Addison-Wesley.

Argyris, C., & Schön, D. A. (1996). *Organizational Learning II: Theory, Method, and Practice*. Reading, MA: Addison-Wesley.

Blackler, F. (1995). Knowledge, knowledge work and organizations: an overview and interpretation. *Organization Studies, 16*, 1021-1046.

Bonora, E. A., & Revang, O. (1993). A framework for analysing the storage and protection of knowledge in organizations: strategic implications and structural arrangements. In P. Lorange, B. Chakravarthy, J. Roos, & A. Van de Ven (Eds.), *Implementing Strategic Processes: Change, Learning and Co-operation* (pp. 190-213). Oxford: Blackwell.

Braverman, H. (1974). *Labor and Monopoly Capital: The Degradation of Work in the Twentieth Century*. New York and London: Monthly Review Press.

Brown, J. S., & Duguid, P. (1991). Organizational learning and communities-of-practice: toward a unified view of working, learning, and innovation. *Organization Science, 2*, 40-57.

Burgoyne, J. (1999). Design of the times. *People Management, 5*(11), 38-44.

Civi, E. (2000). Knowledge management as a competitive asset: a review. *Market Intelligence & Planning, 18*, 166-174.

Clegg, S. (2000). Globalising the intelligent organisation. In J. Garrick & C. Rhodes (Eds.), *Research and Knowledge at Work: Perspectives, Case-studies and Innovative Strategies* (pp. 77-99). London and New York: Routledge.

Contu, A., & Willmott, H. (2003). Re-embedding situatedness: the importance of power relations in learning theory. *Organization Science, 14*, 283-296.

Cook, S. D. N., & Brown, J. S. (1999). Bridging epistemologies: the generative dance between organizational knowledge and organizational knowing. *Organization Science 10*, 381-400.

Cook, S. D. N., & Yanow, D. (1993). Culture and organizational learning. *Journal of Management Inquiry, 2*, 373-390.

Coopey, J. (1998). Learning to trust and trusting to learn: a role for radical theatre. *Management Learning, 29*, 365-382.

Cyert, R. M., & March, J. G. (1963). *A Behavioral Theory of the Firm*. Englewood Cliffs, NJ: Prentice-Hall.

Deetz, S. (1992). *Democracy in an Age of Corporate Colonization: Developments in Communication and the Politics of Everyday Life*. Albany, NY: State University of New York Press.

Droege, S. B., & Hoobler, J. M. (2003). Employee turnover and tacit knowledge diffusion: a network perspective. *Journal of Managerial Issues, 15*(1), 50-64.

Easterby-Smith, M., Crossan, M., & Nicolini, D. (2000). Organizational learning: debates past, present and future. *Journal of Management Studies, 37*, 783-796.

Fenwick, T. (1998). Questioning the concept of the learning organization. In S. M. Scott, B. Spencer, & A. M. Thomas (Eds.), *Learning for Life: Canadian Readings in Adult Education*, (pp. 140-152). Toronto: Thompson.

Filion, N., & Rudolph, H. (1999). *Power, Control and Organisational Learning*. Discussion paper no. FS I 99 - 104. Institut de sciences sociales Raymond-Ledrut.

Fisher, S. R., & White, M. A. (2000). Downsizing in a learning organization: are there hidden costs? *Academy of Management Review, 25*, 244-251.

Garratt, B. (1990). *Creating a Learning Organisation: A Guide to Leadership, Learning and Development.* Cambridge, UK: Director Books.

Garvin, D. A. (1993). Building a learning organization. *Harvard Business Review, 71*(4), 78-91.

Gherardi, S. (1999). Learning as problem-driven or learning in the face of mystery. *Organization Studies, 20*, 101-124.

Gherardi, S., Nicolini, D., & Odella, F. (1998). Toward a social understanding of how people learn in organizations: the notion of situated curriculum. *Management Learning, 29*, 273-297.

Grant, R. M. (1991). The resource-based theory of competitive advantage: implications for strategy formulation. *California Management Review, 33*(3), 114-135.

Grant, R. M. (1996). Toward a knowledge based theory of the firm. *Strategic Management Journal, 17*, 109-122

Hedberg, B. (1981). How organizations learn and unlearn. In P. C. Nystrom, & W. H. Starbuck (Eds.), *Handbook of Organizational Design* (pp. 3-27). Oxford: Oxford University Press.

Hermans, J. A. (1999). Catch the knowledge management wave. *Library Journal, 124*(14), 161-163.

Jones, A. M., & Hendry, C. (1992). *The Learning Organization: A Review of Literature and Practice*. Unpublished report. The HRD Partnership, London.

Jones, A. M., & Hendry, C. (1994). The learning organization: adult learning and organizational transformation. *British Journal of Management, 5*, 153-162.

Ives, W., Torrey, B., & Gordon, C. (1998). Knowledge management: an emerging discipline with a long history. *Journal of Knowledge Management, 1*, 269-274.

Kiechel III, W. (1990). The organization that learns. *Fortune, 121*(6), 75-77.

Kim, D. H. (1993). The link between individual and organizational learning. *Sloan Management Review, 35*, 37-50.

Lam, A. (2000). Tacit knowledge, organizational learning and societal institutions: an integrated framework. *Organization Studies, 21*, 487-513.

Lave, J., & Wenger, E. (1991). *Situated Learning: Legitimate Peripheral Participation*. Cambridge, UK: Cambridge University Press.

Levitt, B., & March J. G. (1988). Organizational learning. *Annual Review of Sociology, 14*, 319-340.

Marquardt, M., & Reynolds, A. (1994). *Global Learning Organization: Gaining Advantage through Continuous Learning.* New York: Irwin.

McGill, M. E., & Slocum Jr., J. W. (1993). Unlearning the organization. *Organizational Dynamics, 22*(2), 52-66.

Morgan, G. (1997). *Images of Organization.* London: Sage.

Nonaka, I., Toyama, R., & Konno, N. (2001). SECI, ba and leadership: a unified model of dynamic knowledge creation. In I. Nonaka, & D. Teece (Eds.), *Managing Industrial Knowledge: Creation, Transfer and Utilization* (pp. 13-43). London: Sage.

Orlikowski, W. J. (2002). Knowing in practice: enacting a collective capability in distributed organizing. *Organization Science, 13*, 249-273.

Prichard, C., Hull, R., Chumer, M., & Willmott, H. (Eds.) (2000). *Managing Knowledge: Critical Investigations of Work and Learning.* London: MacMillan.

Richter, I. (1998). Individual and organizational learning at the executive level: towards a research agenda. *Management Learning, 29*, 299-316.

Saint-Onge, H., & Wallace, D. (2003). *Leveraging Communities of Practice for Strategic Advantage*. Amsterdam: Butterworth-Heinemann.

Scarbrough, H. (1995). Blackboxes, hostages and prisoners. *Organization Studies, 16*, 991-1019.

Scarbrough, H. (1998). Path(ological) dependence? Core competencies from an organizational perspective. *British Journal of Management, 9*, 219-232.

Schultze, U., & Stabell, C. (2004). Knowing what you don't know? Discourses and contradictions in knowledge management research. *Journal of Management Studies, 41*, 549-573.

Senge, P. M. (1990). *The Fifth Discipline: The Art and Practice of the Learning Organization*. London: Century Business.

Snell, R., & Chak A. M. (1998). The learning organization: learning and empowerment for whom? *Management Learning, 29*, 337-364.

Stovel, M., & Bontis, N. (2002). Voluntary turnover: knowledge management – friend or foe? *Journal of Intellectual Capital, 3*, 303-322.

Swan, J., Newell, S., Scarbrough, H., & Hislop, D. (1999). Knowledge management and innovation: networks and networking. *Journal of Knowledge Management, 3*, 262-275.

Swieringa, J., & Wierdsma, A. (1992). *Becoming a Learning Organization: Beyond the Learning Curve*. Wokingham, UK: Addison-Wesley.

Templeton, G., & Snyder, C. (1999). A model of organizational learning based on control. *International Journal of Technology Management, 18*, 705-719.

Watkins, K. E., & Marsick, V. J. (1993). *Sculpting the Learning Organization: Lessons in the Art and Science of Systemic Change*. San Francisco: Jossey-Bass.

Wenger, E. (1991). Communities of practice: where learning happens. *Benchmark, Fall*, 6-8.

Yakhlef, A., & Salzer-Mörling, M. (2000). Intellectual capital: managing by numbers. In C. Prichard, R. Hull, M. Chumer, & H. Willmott (Eds.), *Managing Knowledge: Critical Investigations of Work and Learning* (pp. 20-36). London: MacMillan.

KEY TERMS

Knowledge Control: Accessibility and possession of knowledge.

Knowledge Management: The dissemination of knowledge throughout the organization.

Leaning Organization: A flexible organization with a relatively flat structure and empowered employees.

New Organizational Learning: Situated, collective learning.

Old Organizational Learning: The storing of knowledge in the organizational memory.

Organizational Independence: A state in which the organization is not vulnerable for personnel turnover.

Organizational Memory: Embedded, encoded and encultured knowledge.

Subjective Knowledge: Knowledge that is possessed by the individual and that no others have access to.

Chapter XV
Balancing Stability and Innovation in Knowledge-Intensive Firms:
The Role of Management Control Mechanisms

Angelo Ditillo
Università Bocconi and Sda Bocconi School of Management, Italy

ABSTRACT

Knowledge-intensive firms are composed of various communities, each characterized by specialized knowledge. These communities operate as critical agents in the organizational action because the relevant processes and the variety/variability of environment and technology are too complex for a single individual to understand in their entirety. They generate new models for interpreting reality and responding to customer needs thanks to the integration of knowledge taking place within and between them. The objective of this chapter is to provide some criteria for evaluating the comparative effectiveness and efficiency of combinations of control mechanisms in the regulation of these knowledge integration processes. On the basis of the characteristics of knowledge (level of complexity and diversity), a different set of control mechanisms is proposed, with a variation in their specific features to guarantee that the resulting modes of communication and cognition can guarantee the required level innovation, without however preventing a certain level of stability.

INTRODUCTION

Over the last twenty years, management scholars have focused their attention on how knowledge-intensive firms, as a distinct category of organizations characterized by specific features, are managed (Nurmi, 1998; Alvesson, 2000; 2004; Ditillo, 2004; 2005; Barber and Strack, 2005).

A substantial amount of the literature on these firms assumes that a knowledge base exists in their organization – either as individual specialized skills and competencies (e.g., Tsoukas, 1996) or as capabilities embedded in organizational practices and in systems and structures – and that the continuous combination and recombination of this knowledge is the basis of continuous renewal and innovation (Kusunoki *et al.*, 1998). The effective integration of this internal knowledge is seen as an essential base for providing innovative solutions for customers and for enhancing the survival chances and the prosperity of the organization (Grant, 1996a). This recognition has spawned substantial interest in the factors that influence the potential (or feasible) integration of knowledge of different kinds within the organization (Grant, 1996a; 1996b; Szulanski *et al.*, 2004).

However, very little is known about whether management control mechanisms play a role in fostering knowledge integration, their different degrees of relevance to various situations and the ways in which they can be combined in practice.

The objective of this chapter is, therefore, first to provide a useful framework for understanding the existence and organization of knowledge-intensive firms, and, second, to suggest some criteria for evaluating the comparative effectiveness and efficiency of combinations of management mechanisms in pursuing control and knowledge integration as ways to achieve stability and innovation at the same time.

EXISTENCE AND ORGANIZATION OF KNOWLEDGE-INTENSIVE FIRMS

A recent approach that helps to shed some light on the reasons for the *existence and organization of knowledge-intensive firms*, and to some extent for all firms in general, is represented by the knowledge-based theory of the firm (Zander and Kogut, 1995; Kogut and Zander, 1996; Conner and Prahalad, 1996; Grant, 1996a; 1996b; 1997). Even if this approach has been criticized (Foss, 1996a; 1996b), and refers to any kind of firm, it may help explain the emergence of knowledge-intensive firms and the way in which they are organized. Central to the knowledge-based theory of the firm is the argument that increasing turbulence in the external business environment has focused attention on resources and organizational capabilities as the principal sources of sustainable competitive advantage and the foundation for strategy formulation (Peteraf, 1993; Teece and Pisano, 1994; Kim and Mauborgne, 1999; Morris *et al.*, 2006). As the markets for resources have become subject to the same dynamically competitive conditions that have afflicted product markets, so knowledge has emerged as the most strategically significant resource of the firm (Vicari, 1992; Drucker, 1993).

This perspective suggests the idea that the primary role of firms, and the essence of organizational capability, is the *integration of knowledge* (Nonaka, 1994; Grant, 1996a; 1996b; Kogut and Zander, 1996; Nonaka *et al.*, 2000). Firms structure, coordinate and communicate individual and functional expertise by defining organizing principles that underlie what firms can do. Being flexible requires rules by which work is coordinated and by which information on the market is gathered and communicated. Just-in-time operations, designing for flexibility and decreasing time to the market are capabilities which presuppose a certain social knowledge regarding who is competent, how work is coordinated and what information is shared. In this respect, firms are social communities, which use their relational structure and share coding schemes to enhance the development and communication of new skills and competencies (Zander and Kogut, 1995: pp. 76–77). According to this view, the management of knowledge-intensive firms is directed to fostering the integration of knowledge.

To foster *knowledge integration*, knowledge-intensive firms need to adopt specific organizational structures. The literature on the topic has always suggested for knowledge-intensive firms the use of *adhocratic organizational forms*. These are claimed to be the effective organizational configuration for this kind of firm because they need to innovate continuously by breaking away from established patterns and therefore cannot rely on any form of standardization for coordination. They are characterized by a highly organic structure, with little formalization of behaviour; a high horizontal job specialization based on formal training; a tendency to group specialists into functional units for housekeeping purposes but to deploy them in small market-based project teams to do their work; a reliance on liaison devices to encourage mutual adjustment – the key coordinating mechanism – within and between these teams; and selective decentralization to and within these teams, which are located at various places in the organization and involve various mixtures of line managers, staff and operating experts (Mintzberg, 1983; 1989).

Similar arguments have been proposed by the authors of the knowledge-based theory of the firm, who propose a *team-based structure* for knowledge-intensive firms where team membership is fluid depending upon the knowledge requirements of the task to be performed. The essence of a team-based organization is the recognition that integration is best achieved through the direct involvement of individual specialists because official coordinators ('managers') cannot effectively coordinate if they cannot access the range of specialist knowledge that a task requires. At the same time, the individuals' ability to integrate is constrained by cognitive limits: it is not possible for each individual to try to learn the knowledge possessed by other specialists. Therefore, integration takes place within team-organized processes (Grant, 1996a: p. 377; Grant, 1997: p. 453).[a]

A complementary perspective that emphasizes the process dimension of teams is the community of practice theory (Brown and Duguid, 1991; Easterby-Smith *et al.*, 2000). According to this approach, teams are an organization's communities who, at all levels, are in contact with the environment and involved in interpretive sense making, congruence finding and adapting. It is from any site of such interactions that new insights can be co-produced. If an organizational core overlooks or curtails the enacting in its midst by ignoring or disrupting its *communities of practice*, it threatens its own survival in two ways. It will not only threaten to destroy the very working and learning practices by which it, knowingly or unknowingly, survives, but it will also cut itself off from a major source of potential innovation that inevitably arises in the course of that working and learning. Every organization is made up of various communities of practice that are committed to the same practice and where learning is not the result of conscious design or recognizable rationality and cognitive frames, but emerges from new meanings and emergent structures arising out of common enterprise, experience and sociability (learning by doing) (Ancori *et al.*, 2000). A community of practice – drawing on the subconscious interaction, participation and reified knowledge to act, interpret, innovate and communicate – acts as 'a locally negotiated regime of competence', as 'shared histories of learning'. This concept of community is mainly based on the socialization of knowledge emerging from routines and repeated interactions more than embedded in rules or in an organizational design. It includes agents who operate on a jointly recognised subset of knowledge problems, and who accept some shared procedural authority as key to the success of their collective building activities

(Wenger, 1998; Cowan *et al.*, 2000). Two points are worth mentioning here. First of all, the social construction of knowledge relies not only on how existing knowledge is shared, but also on the processes through which the knowledge is obtained. The analysis of the way in which knowledge is exchanged and managed is a way to include this dimension. Second, the community is more than simply a coordination mechanism, because it incorporates learning infrastructures. These are embedded in the routines and daily practices of members and characterize all the communities belonging to a specific organization.

Also, Boland and Tenkasi (1995) suggest that knowledge-intensive firms are characterized by communities. They develop a process of distributed cognition in which multiple groups of specialized knowledge workers (*communities of knowing*), each dealing with a part of an overall organizational problem, interact to create the patterns of sense making and behaviour displayed by the organization as a whole. This distributed cognition is necessary because the critically important processes and the diversity of environments and technologies to be dealt with are too varied and complex for an individual to understand in their entirety. This is particularly true in knowledge-intensive firms because they rely on multiple specialities and knowledge disciplines to achieve their objectives.

Examples of these communities can be found in all types of knowledge-intensive firms. They relate to the organization of experts around various projects activated by the firm to solve the specific problems of customers. Projects to develop an advertising campaign, to develop new software, to implement a new information system and to define a new product strategy are all instances of teams that normally combine multifunctional expertise to develop a new solution to the customers' needs and that originate communities.

The interaction between communities[b] takes place by means of the following processes.

Exchanging memories, to reduce the costs of 'developing' solutions to problems that had already been discovered and experimented with. This reduction is a result of saving time and efforts devoted to reinventing existing solutions. Collective memory signals the availability of previous work and solutions to a problem that might arise again either within the same community or in another (Steinmueller, 2000).

Dynamic interaction, which creates new meanings, new linguistic routines and new knowledge. In contrast, the maintenance and refinement of existing knowledge in a single community is left to the feedback processes of established routines and policies. The generation of new knowledge is guaranteed through the transformation of communities of knowing as they change and revise their procedures, processes and relationships between themselves (Boland and Tenkasi, 1995). In addition, knowledge creation can be achieved by dividing problems into parts, represented either by competing possible advances or by components that can be combined into an articulated whole. In both cases, the ability to share preliminary results and conjectures and to discover the rate at which individual groups are progressing has important consequences for the productivity of the collective effort (Steinmueller, 2000).

Collective sense-making provision, which homogenizes the way individual and collective knowledge is extracted and used (Ancori *et al.*, 2000).

INTEGRATING KNOWLEDGE THROUGH DIFFERENT FORMS OF COMMUNICATION AND COGNITION

In order to explain further how communities work and interact with each other, Boland and Tenkasi (1995) introduce the concepts of perspective making and perspective taking, which are the basis for transformations within and between epistemic communities.

On the one hand, *perspective making* is 'the process whereby a community of knowing develops and strengthens its own knowledge domain and practices'. As a perspective becomes more consolidated and complex, it contributes better to knowledge work. This complexification occurs through the use of paradigmatic analysis within a narrative framing of experience. It is the process of developing a new language and of defining the causal laws of events in order to find better explanations of reality and more coherent meaning structures.

On the other hand, *perspective taking* is the process by which individual knowledge is acquired, evaluated and integrated with that of other individuals and communities in the organization. It is the process of taking knowledge from a different context (a different community, in this case) and re-adapting it in the local context. In order to take place, perspective making and perspective taking require *communication* within and between the different communities inside the firm.

Boland and Tenkasi (1995) present two different models of communication and corresponding modes of cognition for the interaction within and between communities. The first model is the *conduit model of communication*. On the basis of this, communication is viewed as a message-sending and message-receiving process, which has a limited capacity of transmission. Communication is effective if the errors contaminating the message from the sender to the receiver are completely eliminated. It can be improved by increasing the channel capacity, refining the procedures for encoding and decoding messages, providing more reliable data storage and retrieval facilities and making the channel of communication more universally available. Yet, the major defect of this model of communication is that it treats messages unproblematically, that is to say without considering their symbolic or interpretive characteristics. Encoding and decoding activities are considered as discrete selections from a predefined set of messages, which are unambiguous and steady over time.

The conduit model of communication is consistent with an *information-processing mode of cognition*. This is characterized by the rational analysis of data and the deductive way of reasoning. It emphasizes logical, coherent, consistent and non-contradictory arguments. It assumes the existence of an a priori external reality which is truc at all times and in all places and which is the highest grade of knowledge. Such knowledge does not need to be justified by any sensory experience. Thus, words point at things, meanings are not problematic and deductive logic is the most effective way of analysing reality. Knowledge can be achieved by using mental constructs such as concepts, laws and theories and supposes a distinction between the knower and the known. In addition, knowledge formation can be described as a linear process of transformation: data are turned into information, information into knowledge and finally knowledge is confronted with 'wisdom' (or 'meta-knowledge' that encompasses beliefs and judgements). This perspective focuses on the role of information processing as a key step in the formation of knowledge. It assumes that a linear process is involved in increasing the complexity of the search for knowledge, and the first step is transforming 'data' into structured pieces of information that are then addressed to the search for knowledge. Each piece of information carries a 'quantum of novelty' that helps increase the stock of knowledge and the combinatorial complexity of this knowledge stock. As a consequence, information can be measured quantitatively and knowledge is the result of the codification and classification of information. Therefore, the quality and accuracy of knowledge formation depends strictly on the way information is treated (Ancori *et al.*, 2000). See Figure 1.

The second model considered by Boland and Tenkasi (1995) is the *language games model of communication*. This model assumes that language is strictly inter-linked and embedded in the situated action of the communities. Action is the locus of language generation and use.

Figure 1. Knowledge formation according to a conduit model of communication and an information-processing mode of cognition

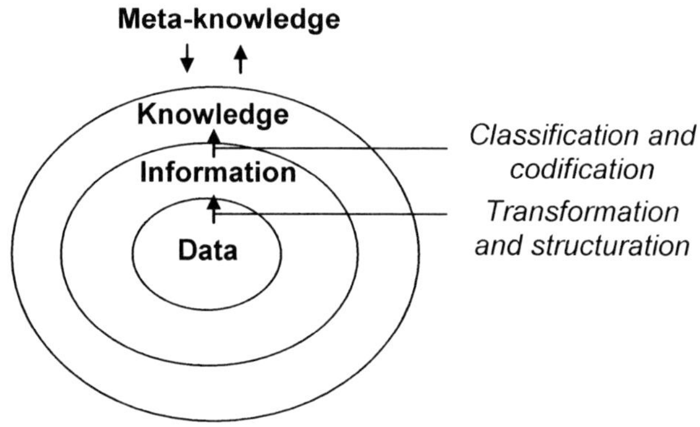

Source: adapted from Ancori et al. (2000)

Conversations and activities are language games that create meanings for words and speeches in an evolutionary process of talking and acting together. In this case, language is not understandable without reference to experience, and words are characterized by ambiguous meanings. Language and words evolve together with the activities of the communities. As a result, there are no fixed sets of messages or meanings to use for communication.

The language games model is consistent with a *narrative mode of cognition*. This is characterized by the recognition that individuals narrativize their experience continuously when they experiment with unusual and unexpected events and construct stories that make sense of them. It emphasizes interesting, plausible and believable arguments. It challenges the often implicit assumptions of information processing arguments, thus contributing to innovative knowledge work. It assumes that words gain sense only through actual use in a community, meanings are symbolic and inherently ambiguous and social processes, storytelling and conversation are the most effective means for facing reality. In this case, knowledge is not regarded as simply the accumulation of information in a stockpile, but requires continuous feedback loops between the various elements involved (data, knowledge, wisdom). Each element interacts with the others and 'transforms' the other both quantitatively and qualitatively. See Figure 2.

From this perspective, the various components of knowledge formation are considered differently. Firstly, 'data' can be distinguished in terms of a 'stimulus' in the case of an emission of data from nature, and a 'message' in the case of an emission of data from a human emitter. The main difference between the two kinds of 'data' is that while stimuli are not being organized a priori but are interpreted and classified *ex post* by the cognitive agent, messages are organized a priori by a cognitive building such as language, categorization or classification, even if they also need further interpretation by the cognitive agent. Secondly, 'knowledge and representation' result in forming a specific structuring of stimuli and messages depending on the cognitive model of the agent. Knowledge and representation are distinguished here to emphasize the separation between short-term and long-term memories. Both derive from the cognitive structuring of the agent, but while representation is contextual and temporary and has to do with the mental attitudes in a given context, knowledge corresponds to a more long-term 'sedimentation'. Thirdly, the cognitive framework of the agent corresponds to his/her wisdom that

Figure 2. Knowledge formation according to a language games model of communication and a narrative mode of cognition

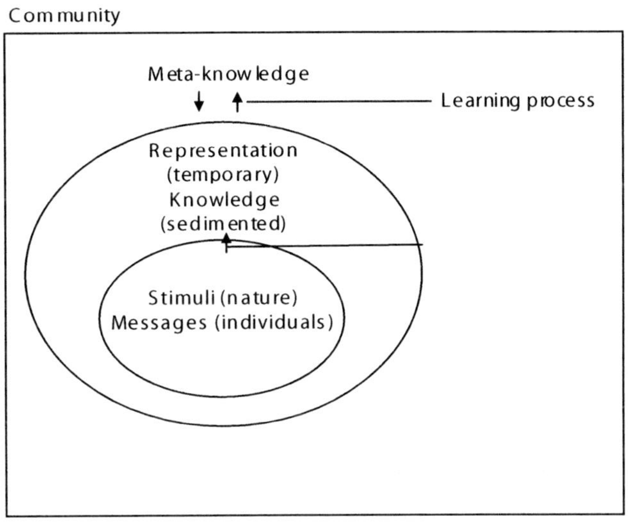

Source: adapted from Ancori et al. (2000)

includes beliefs, judgements and values. These are meta-categories which determine the nature of the rules and the direction of the learning processes to be followed by the agent. Finally, the relationship between the different elements of the system shows the processes intervening in the dynamics of the systems – classification/categorization, interpretation, application of rules and heuristics, learning processes and so on – that are instrumental in the interaction between experience and practice on the one side and beliefs and judgements on the other (Ancori *et al.*, 2000).

For the key assumptions of the characteristics of the two models of communication and cognition and the characteristics of knowledge, see Table 1.

Table 1. Key ideas behind the two different models of communication and cognition

The conduit model of communication and the information-processing mode of cognition	**The language games model of communication and the narrative mode of cognition**
◊ Knowledge is objective and the language is a medium for representing it.	◊ Knowledge is subjective and is the result of a consensus achieved within a specific community.
◊ Knowledge can be acquired and evolves by means of a rational process.	◊ Knowledge can be acquired through narrativizing the familiar or explaining the unfamiliar, and it evolves by means of new languages and narrative forms.
◊ Individuals can achieve universal understanding as communication between them takes place in an objective way.	◊ Individuals can achieve only partial understanding as language and narrative forms are characterized by some limitations.

Source: adapted from Boland and Tenkasi (1995)

To sum up, knowledge-intensive firms are composed of various communities and integrate knowledge by developing strong perspectives (*perspective making*) within the communities and by taking into consideration the perspectives of other communities (*perspective taking*). The exchange of perspectives between these communities requires adequate models of communication and cognition. At first glance, communication and cognition seem to regard only the selection from a predefined set of messages and refer mainly to the exchange of information. Yet, the same processes can be seen in terms of questioning and changing perspective. This is because language and practices are evolving continuously and communication and cognition cannot be separated from the shifting context in which they take place. There is no predefined set of messages but these emerge from the evolving form the community is assuming. Both models of communication and cognition contribute to understanding the interaction within and between the various communities within knowledge-intensive firms necessary to maintain stability, integrate knowledge and, through this integration, innovate.

COMBINING FORMS OF COMMUNICATION AND COGNITION THROUGH CONTROL MECHANISMS TO BALANCE STABILITY AND INNOVATION

The study of control mechanisms (Ouchi, 1979; Merchant, 1985) can be conducted by taking into consideration the contexts in which they contribute to coordinating action to maintain stability, while at the same time allowing knowledge integration to achieve innovation (Raelin, 1985; Ancori *et al.*, 2000; Ditillo, 2004; 2005). Different mechanisms can achieve these objectives:

Social mechanisms: in some situations, some pieces of knowledge remain tacit because they are part of a wider knowledge structure (as is the case of the knowledge held by an expert). The reason for keeping this knowledge tacit is that, even if it were possible to formalize and transmit part of it, thanks to the existence of codes of communication, in practice most of the knowledge about how to manage it would remain tacit. Only experience would suggest which knowledge has to be mobilized and which has to be left in the background in order to act or learn properly. This happens when knowledge is part of a complex structure and remains sticky (von Hippel, 1993; Grandori, 1997; Cowan *et al.*, 2000). In this case, knowledge is characterized by cognitional complexity: neither inputs nor outputs of knowledge processes can be observed (at a reasonable cost and in a reasonable time). The processes are either new to the agents involved or entail innovative problem solving and are characterized by many possible 'serendipities' and unexpected outcomes. This implies the discovery of cause–effect relations and relevant goals, and the transformation in explicit knowledge is expected to fail (Grandori, 1997; Burns and Stalker, 1961). Therefore, such a form of knowledge is communicated between the members of a community (if these members have the time, the occasions for socialization and the broader institutional incentives to perceive the game as basically integrative) (Ouchi, 1980; Grandori, 1997) by means of a common history, shared experiences and collective social and organizational frames. Its possession determines who does belong to the community and who does not, and is a function of the historical process of tacit knowledge creation. The socialization control mechanism applied in this case maintains stability and is consistent with intensifying interactions between individuals more than transforming the nature of knowledge itself, allowing in this way the process of knowledge integration and innovation (Ancori *et al.*, 2000).

Action and result control mechanisms: what matters here is the degree of diversity of tacit knowledge (Cohen and Levinthal, 1990; Iansiti and Clark, 1994). The more knowledge is differentiated among agents, the more it fosters interactions and triggers mechanisms for knowledge creation, due to the multiplicity of ways the problems are perceived and dealt with. Integration is *not* achieved by the *transmission of tacit knowledge* (and by its formalization) but by its coordination aimed at pursuing a common objective. In other words, in a context of diversified knowledge, the 'constraint' of tacit knowledge can be solved by means of coordination mechanisms more than codification processes. Control can be achieved in this case by either organizational routines (Grant, 1996a; 1996b) or administrative mechanisms. The first can be defined as '[...] relatively complex patterns of behavior [...] triggered by a small number of initiating signals or choices and functioning as a recognizable unit in a relatively automatic fashion' (Winter, 1987: p. 165). Knowledge-intensive firms learn by creating routines (Nelson and Winter, 1982). Routines represent the guidelines that have provided knowledge integrating solutions to past problem solving. They make up the historical memory of the firm: they 'remember' how conflicts were solved between the firm's parts and provide the same solutions again; they 'remember' the reactions to past problems and retain the solutions that worked; they make the firm's individual behaviour predictable, contributing to reducing the level of general uncertainty (Di Bernardo and Rullani, 1990: p. 50). The second include both *formal rules* and *standard procedures*, and *plans*, *budgets* and *reporting systems* to regulate interactions between managers and employees of different units of the same organization (Hopwood, 1976; Amigoni, 1979). The adoption of a combination of these mechanisms guarantees a certain level of stability, while at the same time proposing a structure for integrating knowledge and innovating.

Codification mechanisms: another way of achieving integration is through pure knowledge codification, which requires adapted codes and media (Boisot, 1998; Nonaka *et al.*, 2000; Ancori *et al.*, 2000; Cowan *et al.*, 2000; Cohendet and Steinmuller., 2000; Malerba and Orsenigo, 2000). Codification can be defined as the process that 'creates perceptual and conceptual categories that facilitate the classification of phenomena' and 'the act of assigning phenomena to categories once these have been created' (Boisot, 1998). Codification is a useful integrating mechanism when different pieces of *knowledge need to be complementarily integrated* (Cowan *et al.*, 2000), and when knowledge is characterized by computational complexity, arising from the high number of actors and activities and their interconnections (Simon, 1979; Grandori, 1997). This argument is supported by the classic organization theory, which has shown that an increase in computational complexity can be managed by extending the use of formal information processing tools (Simon, 1979; Galbraith, 1974). Two problems arise in this respect: on the one hand, the cost and control of the creation, diffusion and storage of codes, languages and models make this process difficult. On the other hand, the same codes, languages and models strongly influence the individual potentiality for knowledge creation, because they act as inertial forces in the generation of new knowledge if they do not leave enough freedom and ambiguity in interpretation (Ancori *et al.*, 2000). In a context of change, the accumulation of a successive generation of codes can prevent the development of radically new knowledge, which would require entirely new codes and languages. As proposed by Arrow (1974, p. 56), codification fosters increasing communication and transaction efficiency but leads to organizational rigidity and uniformity: 'the need for codes mutually understandable within an organization imposes a uniformity requirement on the behavior of participants. They are specialized in the information capable of being transmitted by the codes, so that they learn more in the direction of their activity and become less efficient in acquiring and transmitting information not easily fitted into the code'. Therefore, codification can have some undesired effects on creativity and innovation. It encapsulates the influences of essentially transient and possibly extraneous phenomena that were present in the circumstances where specific codes and languages were developed, becoming a source of *path-dependence* (Cowan *et al.*, 2000).

Examples of the different weights assigned to the different control mechanisms, depending on the context in which they are applied, can be found in a software firm. Depending on the characteristics of knowledge, the coordination of the project tends to be centred around social mechanisms based on common values/beliefs, action as well as output control, and codification. More specifically, while all the mechanisms tend to be present at the same time in all projects to maintain the necessary balance between stability and innovation, in the development of software that requires the contribution of many developers and is the revision of previously developed software (computational complexity), codification plays a key role in coordinating the efforts of many individuals and in integrating their knowledge. In the development of software that requires the combination of many different forms of expertise, the organization of activities tends to be focused on action and result control. For instance, the writing of software for managing financial transactions on a mobile phone, which requires technical mobile expertise, financial expertise and communication expertise, requires that work is organized around independent groups which combine their activities and outputs through action and result mechanisms. These operate as levers for coordinating efforts and maintaining stability as well as tools for favouring a certain way of integrating knowledge. Finally, the development of completely new software (cognitional complexity) needs a high level of exploration and flexibility which can be achieved by means of social mechanisms that intervene as stabilizing mechanisms through mutual adjustment and as knowledge integration mechanisms by means of the flexible interaction of individuals (Ditillo, 2004).

While action and result mechanisms and codification assume relevant roles in the integration of knowledge within and between different communities, social control is consistent with and fosters knowledge integration mainly within the same community. Only by composing the right mix of these mechanisms according to knowledge characteristics is the firm able to foster an effective flowing of knowledge within and between the various communities of knowing, and the lack of both awareness of their role, and consistency between them can prevent the natural processes of stability and innovation which guarantee the long-term survival of the firm.

In addition, the three different mechanisms can be designed and implemented with greater reference to either a conduit model of communication and an information processing mode of cognition or a language games model of communication and a narrative model of cognition. The choice seems to be related to the specific characteristics of knowledge. When knowledge is characterized by a low level of computational and cognitional complexity and a low degree of diversity (typical of a stable context), the first model of communication and cognition is able to grasp the consistency and linearity of phenomena and to integrate knowledge by means of a simple information exchange. By contrast, when a high level of computational and cognitional complexity and a high degree of diversity is characteristic of knowledge (typical of a relentless changing environment), then communication becomes a much more complicated process that emphasizes the symbolic nature and ambiguity of phenomena and that achieves knowledge integration by means of narrating experience.

This is not to say that the various control mechanisms incorporate either one or the other model of communication and cognition. Instead, they need to combine elements of both models of communication and cognition in accordance with the different characteristics of the pieces of knowledge they contribute to integrating. So, social control may simply result in an exchange of information between individuals and imply a language game process when dealing with unusual and unexpected events. Action and results control mechanisms incorporate a fixed number of messages expressed in a uniform language, or imply a combination of different languages that incorporate different perspectives on a specific problem. Consider, for example, the initiatives undertaken by firms with reference to performance measurement systems. These systems were mainly based on financial information in the past and are now evolving towards a balance between different views and a more articulated set of indicators. Total quality, productivity, customer satisfaction and innovation have integrated the traditional financial measures of performance used by organizations (Eccles, 1991; Maskell, 1991; Kaplan and Norton, 1992; 1993; Zenger and Hesterly, 1997). Finally, codification can be achieved by means of a predefined set of codes or by trying to develop new codes and languages deriving from new and unexpected events. It is the combination of these mechanisms and the incorporation of the various models of communication and cognition within these mechanisms that make knowledge integration effective and functional to the long-term stability and innovation of knowledge-intensive firms.

CONCLUSION

Knowledge-intensive firms are composed of various communities, each characterized by specialized knowledge. These communities operate as critical agents in the organizational action because the relevant processes and the variety/variability of environment and technology are too complex for a single individual to understand in their entirety. The communities are places where new models for interpreting reality are gradually tested, validated and compared. They represent the level where the conversion and diffusion of knowledge from the individual to the organization (and vice versa) take place, where the modes of knowledge conversion are activated and where the translation of local codes to the organization language (and reciprocally) is made.

Innovation requires integration within and between a firm's multiple communities. It is by means of this dynamic process that new configurations of knowledge emerge by creating new meanings, new linguistic routines and new knowledge. Yet, in order to avoid communication becoming a source of organizational *inertia* and rigid *path-dependence*, it is necessary that combined models of communication and modes of cognition are used. A conduit model of communication with the corresponding paradigmatic mode of cognition, on the one hand, and a language games model of communication with the corresponding narrative mode of cognition, on the other, only if taken together contribute to making a strong perspective within a community of knowing and to taking another perspective into account as a means by which more complex knowledge and improved possibilities for product/service or process innovation are achieved, while at the same time maintaining stability.

Depending on the characteristics of knowledge, perspective making and perspective taking are managed and valorized through socialization, action and result control mechanisms and codification processes. When knowledge is part of a *complex structure* and remains sticky (von Hippel, 1993; Grandori, 1997; Cowan *et al.*, 2000), it is communicated between the members of a community by means of a common history, shared experiences and collective social and organizational frames. On the other hand, if the *degree of diversity* of knowledge (Cohen and Levinthal, 1990) is high, integration is *not* achieved by the *knowledge transmission* but by either organizational routines or administrative controls. Finally, in *large systems* that must coordinate the *complementary knowledge* of *many agents*, the communication of knowledge is achieved through codification.

The above developments suggest that knowledge-intensive firms manage their knowledge integration processes as conducive to innovation, yet without neglecting the need for coordination to maintain a certain level of stability. It is our contention here, as Amin and Cohendet (2000), that firms manage knowledge integration to innovate, and control to maintain stability, at the same time. Firstly, they select their knowledge domains, which need different mechanisms for their integration. Secondly, after selecting the knowledge domains and the direction they want to undertake to create and sustain a competitive advantage, they control their transactions in order to adapt to the specific needs of the environment. This signifies that the organization of the firm requires a dual structure of governance: one dedicated to knowledge integration and one devoted to control transactions. In this respect, administrative mechanisms can play an important role because, on the one hand, they have always been recognized as means for controlling transactions; on the other, they may contribute to integrating complementary and diversified knowledge of agents operating in different communities. They codify a specific language and frame for interpreting reality. The advancements in their content and articulation have transformed them from simple message-sending and message-receiving channels to more complex communication languages that emphasize the symbolic or interpretive character of messages. One example of this transformation is represented by the introduction of a more balanced model of reporting (e.g. Mourtisen and Thorsgaard Larsen, 2005), promoting different perspectives in the evaluation of performance.

From a managerial point of view, the implications deriving from this analysis are that, depending on the characteristics of knowledge (level of complexity and diversity) to integrate and use to meet customers' needs, a different set of control mechanisms needs to be adopted, with a variation in their specific features to guarantee that the resulting modes of communication and cognition emphasize the required level of stability and innovation.

The enrichment of approaches introduced here to study knowledge-intensive firms should open some promising avenues of research aiming at both better understanding of complementary perspectives and mechanisms involved in the functioning of the firm and grasping the roots of new knowledge phenomena.

REFERENCES

Alvesson M.(1995). *Management of Knowledge-Intensive Companies*. Berlin: Walter de Gruyter.

Alvesson M. (2000). Social Identity and the Problem of Loyalty in Knowledge-Intensive Companies). (8), December. *Journal of Management Studies, 37.*

Alvesson M., 2004, 'Interfaces of control. Technocratic and socio-ideological control in a global management consultancy firm', *Accounting, Organizations and Society*, 29:3-4, April/May.

Amigoni F. (1979). *I sistemi di controllo direzionale.* Giuffré, Varese.

Amin A., & Cohendet P. (2000). How to Govern Simultaneously Transactions and Competencies: Should Organisational Learning Rely on Isolated Properties or Embedded Practices. *Journal of Management and Governance.*

Ancori, B., Bureth, A., & Cohendet, P. (2000). The Economics of Knowledge: The Debate about Codification and Tacit Knowledge. *Industrial and Corporate Change*, *9*(2).

Arrow, K. J. (1974). *The Limits of Organization.* New York: Norton.

Barber, F., & Strack, R. (2005).The surprising economics of a "People Business". *Harvard Business Review*, June.

Boisot M. H. (1998). *Knowledge assets – Securing Competitive Advantage in the Information Economy.* Oxford: Oxford University Press..

Boland Jr., R. J., & Tenkasi, R. V. (1995). Perspective Making and Perspective Taking in Communities of Knowing. *Organization Science*, *6*(4), July-August, 350-372.

Brown, J. S., & Duguid, P. (1991). Organizational Learning and Communities-of-Practice: Toward a Unified View of Working, Learning, and Innovation. *Organization Science*, *2*(1), 40-57.

Burns, T., & Stalker, G. M. (1961). *The Management of Innovation.* Tavistock, London.

Chandler, A. D. (1962). *Strategy and Structur.* Caembridge, MA: The MIT Press..

Cohen, W. M., & Levinthal, D. A. (1990). Absorptive capacity: A new perspective on learning and innovation. *Administrative Science Quarterly*, *35*, 128-152.

Cohendet, P., & Steinmuller, E. (2000). The Codification of Knowledge: A Conceptual and Empirical Exploration. *Industrial and Corporate Change, 9*(1), March.

Conner, K. R., & Prahalad, C. K. (1996). A Resource-based Theory of the Firm: Knowledge Versus Opportunism. *Organization Science*, *7*(5), September-October, 477-501.

Cowan, R., David, P. A., & Foray, D. (2000). The Explicit Economics of Knowledge Codification and Tacitness. *Industrial and Corporate Change*, 9(2).

Di Bernardo, B., & Rullani, E. (1990). *Il management e le macchine. Teoria evolutiva dell'impresa*, Il Mulino, Bologna.

Ditillo, A. (2004). Dealing with uncertainty in knowledge-intensive firms: the role of management control systems as knowledge integration mechanism. *Accounting, Organizations and Society*, *29*(3-4), April/May.

Ditillo A. (2005). Management control in knowledge-based organizations. In C. Clubb (Ed), *Accounting – The Blackwell Encyclopaedia of Management.* Second Edition, Blackwell Publishing.

Drucker, P. (1993). *Post-Capitalist Society.* London: Butterworth Heinemann..

Easterby-Smith, M., Crossan, M., Nicolini, D. (2000). Organizational learning: Debates past, present and future. *Journal of Management Studies*, *37*(6), 783-796.

Eccles, R. G. (1991). The Performance Measurement Manifesto. *Harvard Business Review*, *69*, January-February, 131-137.

Foss, N. J. (1996a). Knowledge-based Approaches to the Theory of the Firm: Some Critical Comments. *Organization Science*, *7*(5), September-October, 470-476.

Foss, N. J. (1996b). Critical Comments on Knowledge-based Theories of the Firm.*Organization Science*, 7(5), September-October, 519-523.

Galbraith, J. R. (1974). Organization design: An information processing view. *Interfaces*, *3*, 28-36.

Grandori, A. (1997). An Organizational Assessment of Inter-Firm Coordination Modes.*Organization Studies* (pp. 897-925).

Grant, R. M. (1996a). Prospering in Dynamically-competitive Environments: Organizational Capability as Knowledge Integration. *Organization Science*, 7(4), July-August, 375-387.

Grant, R. M. (1996b). Toward a Knowledge-Based Theory of the Firm. *Strategic Management Journal*, *17*, Winter Special Issue, 109-122.

Grant, R. M. (1997). The Knowledge-based View of the Firm: Implications for Management Practice. *Long Range Planning*, *30*(3), 450-454.

Hopwood, A. G. (1976). *Accounting and Human Behavior.* Englewood Cliffs: NJ: Prentice Hall.

Kaplan, R. S., & Norton, D. P. (1993). The Balanced Scorecard – Measures That Drive Performance. *Harvard Business Review.*

Kaplan, R. S., & Norton, D. P. (1993). Putting the Balanced Scorecard to Work'. *Harvard Business Review.*

Kusunoki, K., Nonaka, I., & Nagata, A. (1998). Organizational capabilities in product development of Japanese firms: a conceptual framework and empirical analysis. *Organization Science, 9*(6), 699-718.

Iansiti, M., & Clark, K. B. (1994). Integration and Dynamic Capability: Evidence from Product Development in Automobiles and Mainframe Computers. *Industrial and Corporate Change, 3*(3).

Kim, C. W., & Mauborgne, R. (1999). Strategy, Value Innovation, and the Knowledge Economy. *Sloan Management Review, 40*(3), 41-54.

Kogut, B., & Zander, U. (1996). What Firms Do? Coordination, Identity, and Learning. *Organization Science, 7*(5), September-October, 502-518.

Malerba, F., & Orsenigo, L. (2000). Knowledge, Innovative Activities and Industrial Evolution. *Industrial and Corporate Change, 9*(2).

Maskell, B. H. (1991). *Performance Measurement for World Class Manufacturing.* Cambbridge, MA: Productivity Press, Inc.

Merchant, K. A. (1985). Control in business organizations. Boston: Pitman.

Mintzberg, H. (1983). *Structure in Fives.* Englewood: Prentice-Hall, Inc.

Mintzberg, H. (1989). *Mintzberg on management.* New York: The Free Press.

Morris, M. H., Allen, J., Schindeutte, M., & Avila, R. (2006). Balanced Management Control Systems as a Mechanism for Achieving Corporae Entrepreneurship. *Journal of Managerial Issues, XVIII*(4), 468-493.

Mouritsen J., & Thorsgaard Larsen H., (2005). 'The 2nd wave of knowledge management: The management control of knowledge resources through intellectual capital information'. *Management Accounting Research, 16*, 371-394.

Nelson R. R., & Winter, S. G., (1982). *An Evolutionary Theory of Economic Change.* Belknap Press, Cambridge.

Nonaka I., (1994). 'A Dynamic Theory of Organizational Knowledge Creation', *Organization Science, 5*(1), 15-37.

Nonaka I., Toyama R., & Nagata A., (2000). 'A Firm as a Knowledge-creating Entity: A New Perspective on the Theory of the Firm, *Industrial and Corporate Change, 9*(1), March.

Nurmi R., (1998). ' Knowledge-Intensive Firms', *Business Horizons*, May-June.

Ouchi, W. G., (1979). 'A conceptual framework for the design of organizational control mechanisms', *Management Science, 25*(9), 833-848.

Peteraf M. A., (1993). 'The Cornerstones of Competitive Advantage: a Resource-based View', *Strategic Management Journal*, Vol. 14: pp. 179-191.

Raelin J. A., (1985). 'The Basis for the Professional's Resistance to Managerial Control', *Human Resource Management*, Summer, Vol. 24, Number 2: pp. 147-175.

Simon H. A. (1979), 'The architecture of complexity the sciences of artificial', Cambridge: MIT Press.

Steinmueller W. E, (2000). 'Will New Information and Communication Technologies Improve 'Codification' of Knowledge?', *Industrial and Corporate Change*, Vol. 9, No. 2, March.

Szulanski, G., Cappetta R., Jensen R. J., (2004). 'When and how trustworthiness matters: knowledge transfer and the moderating effect of causal ambiguity', *Organization Science*, *15*(5), pp. 600-613.

Teece D. J. & Pisano G., (1994). 'The Dynamic Capabilities of Firms: an Introduction', *Industrial and Corporate Change*, *3*(3).

Tsoukas, H., (1996). 'The firm as a distributed knowledge system: a constructionist approach', *Strategic Management Journal*, *17*(1), 11-25.

Vicari S., (1992). 'Risorse aziendali e valore', *Sinergie*, n. 29 Settembre-Dicembre: pp. 81-94.

von Hippel E., (1993). 'Trading in Trade Secrets', *Harvard Business Review*, February/March.

Wenger E., (1998). 'Communities of Practice; Learning as a Social System', *Systems Thinker*, June.

Winter S., (1987). Knowledge and Competence as Strategic Assets. In D. Teece (Ed.), *The competitive Challenge*. Ballinger, Cambridge.

Zander U. & Kogut B., (1995). 'Knowledge and the Speed of the Transfer and Imitation of Organizational Capabilities: An Empirical Test', *Organization Science*, *6*(1), 76-92.

Zenger T. R. & Hesterly W. S., (2007). 'The Disaggregation of Corporations: Selective Intervention, High-powered Incentives, and Molecular Units', *Organization Science*, *8*(3).

KEY TERMS

Codification: It is the process of defining perceptual and conceptual categories that facilitate the classification of phenomena and of linking these phenomena to categories, once they have been developed.

Communities of Practice: They are the teams that are linked to the environment and that aim at finding a match with it by means of interpretive sense-making and congruence finding.

Control Mechanisms: They refer to a set of integrated tools for steering an organization toward the achievement of its objectives, by influencing managers' behaviour.

Innovation: It is the process through which new ideas, goods, services, processes and activities are created, developed or redefined.

Knowledge-Based Theory of the Firm: It is the theory of the firm that focuses attention on the resources and organizational capabilities as the principal sources of sustainable competitive advantage and the foundation for strategy formulation.

Knowledge-Intensive Firms: They are the firms that employ mainly the knowledge of people to develop and trade immaterial solutions for customers.

Knowledge Complexity: It is the characteristic of knowledge that derives from the fact that either a high number of actors and activities are involved in a knowledge process or knowledge is differentiated among agents or, finally, neither inputs nor outputs of knowledge processes can be observed.

ENDNOTES

[a] However, even within team-based structures, hierarchy is still necessary in order to link different sub-systems (e.g. the various team projects) together. The principles of hierarchical design are fundamental to 'modular' design in organizational structures. Critical to the design of modular structures is the separation of the total system into a number of modular sub-systems and then the design and standardization of the *interfaces* between these sub-systems. A key

distinction here is between the *component knowledge* required by the sub-systems and the *architectural knowledge* required for the linking of the various sub-systems (Grant, 1997: p. 453). Therefore, we can imagine knowledge-intensive firms' structure as a mixture of hierarchical elements to define the general architecture of the firm and project teams as locations of operating activities.

[b] The community represents the elementary unit for understanding the process of the transformation and transmission of knowledge from the individual to the organization (and reciprocally). This is the level at which the processes of knowledge conversion are activated and the translation of local codes to organizational language (and reciprocally) is made (Ancori *et al.*, 2000).

Chapter XVI
The Knowledge-Based Approach to Organizational Measurement:
Exploring the Future of Organizational Assessment

Aino Kianto
Lappeenranta University of Technology, Finland

Jianzhong Hong
Lappeenranta University of Technology, Finland

ABSTRACT

Nowadays knowledge and competencies are the key productive factors, and the organizational capability for continuous learning, development and renewal has become the main driver of competitiveness. In this chapter the authors explore how organizational measurement should change in order to remain relevant in the face of the recent increase in the knowledge-intensiveness of work, organizing and value creation. First they argue that, while traditionally measurement has mostly been used for control purposes, recent changes in the nature of work have brought on new challenges which can no longer be met with old mindsets and measures. Then they focus on two novel approaches, intellectual capital and competence development, and examine the current state of the art. Finally, the authors construct foundations for a knowledge-based approach to organizational measurement and set some future directions in which measures should be developed in order to portray and enable knowledge work and knowledge-based value creation.

INTRODUCTION

It is widely agreed that nowadays knowledge and competencies are the key productive factors, and the organizational capability for continuous learning, development and renewal has become the main driver of competitiveness (Drucker, 1988; Prahalad & Hamel, 1990; Kogut & Zander, 1992; Grant, 1996b; Teece et al., 1997). Thus, organizations are increasingly interested in assessing, managing and developing what they know and can do. This chapter explores how organizational measurement should change in order to remain relevant in the face of the recent increase in the knowledge-intensiveness of work, organizing and value creation. Traditionally measurement has mostly been used for hierarchical control purposes with regard to material and financial stocks and flows, but we argue that recent changes in the nature of work have brought on new challenges which can no longer be met with old mindsets and measures.

"You can only manage what you can measure." Undoubtedly one of the oldest clichés of management science, it embodies an assumption that once something can be measured, it can also be managed. This type of an assumption is based on the idea that optimal performance can be totally standardized. It is also connected with the view that the expertise about the nature of optimal performance is located at the top of the organizational hierarchy. Thus, management is reduced to giving orders and enforcing control, and the role of employees is that of obedient implementers.

Even though this may have been a justified view in the Fordist era of mass production, current changes in the nature of work have created new challenges. Knowledge work implies different performance criteria and a different type of management than other types of work (e.g., Blackler, 1995; Davenport, 2001; Snowden, 2002). This entails changes for measurement on two levels. First, the actual measures themselves have to change. For example, knowledge worker productivity is more related to the quality than the quantity of output (Drucker, 1999), which makes most traditional performance measures inadequate. Second, the whole goal of measurement has to be seen differently: not as to control but to foster continuous learning and renewal of the whole organization.

In this chapter, we first examine the nature of knowledge work and knowledge-based organizing in the light of recent management science literature. We argue that as organizations have changed, so should the measures used in them. Performance measurement was developed for the needs of organizations in the pre-knowledge era and cannot adequately capture the essential characteristics of knowledge work and knowledge-based value creation.

We also shed light on the novel approaches brought about by scholars working in the fields of intellectual capital (e.g., Edvinsson & Malone, 1997; Sveiby, 1997; Roos et al., 1998; Stewart, 1997; Bontis, 1999) and competence development (e.g. Snow & Hrebiniak, 1980; Henderson & Cockburn, 1994; McGrath et al., 1995; Riiter et al., 2002), and examine the current state of the art. These two modern schools of thought are mindful of the special qualities of knowledge as opposed to other types of resources. Interestingly, in these postulations there is also a different kind of twist when compared to the traditional measures: traditionally measurement was mostly aimed at controlling, whereas these new approaches are, more or less explicitly, aiming to measure learning. So, rather than control the intangible resources and competencies, the novel metrics are meant to foster development and learning.

Even though these new branches of management have set to expand the scope of measurement to knowledge-related issues, there is however still room for improvement in the measurement frameworks as well as the specific indicators. Finally, based on the knowledge-based view of work and organizing, we propose criteria for more adequate measurement of knowledge and competence. We set some future directions in which measures should be developed in order to better reflect the change towards knowledge work and knowledge-based value creation in organizations.

THE RISE OF KNOWLEDGE WORK AND IMPLICATIONS FOR MEASUREMENT

There exists a widespread agreement that knowledge is the new fundamental basis of competition: it is the most important factor in the creation of economic value and competitive advantage (e.g., Drucker, 1993; Stewart, 1997). Nowadays organizations are routinely viewed as collections of knowledge assets, compentences and capabilities (e.g., Kogut & Zander, 1992; Prahalad & Hamel, 1990) which are populated by knowledge workers (e.g., Drucker, 1999) and located in the wider context of information society (e.g., Castells & Himanen, 2002). Knowledge has replaced land, labor and physical capital as the most important factor of production (Drucker, 1988), and the ability to manage and create intellectual capital (IC) is recognized as the foundation of the productive capacity of all types of organizations (e.g., Edvinsson & Malone, 1997; Marr, 2005).

Knowledge has always been at the heart of organizations, but it is during the past two decades that the significance of knowledge as the most important source of economic value has really been unleashed (Foray, 2004). Peter Drucker (1959) predicted the rise of knowledge workers already in the late 1950s. Recently, he stated that the main economic challenge of the 21st century will be increasing their productivity (Drucker, 1999). Knowledge workers are the fastest growing segment in the developed countries (Campion et al., 1996; Janz et al., 1997; Drucker, 1999; Foss, 2005; OECD, 2005), and they produce most of the value added in companies (Stewart, 1997).

Knowledge workers are highly educated employees who apply theoretical and analytical knowledge to developing new products, services, processes and procedures (e.g., Janz et al., 1996). The essence of knowledge work lies in the manipulation of symbols that convey data, information and ideas into new information and knowledge, in contrast to the manipulation of concrete materials (Reich, 1992). Consequently, knowledge workers must master, for example, information processing, knowledge integration, knowledge creation and abstract thinking (e.g., Tynjälä, 2003).

In addition to posing new demands for the individual employee, knowledge work also challenges the traditional conceptions of management. In fact, managing knowledge and knowledge work requires that most of the traditional assumptions about what effective management consists of must change. As Davenport (2001, 44) puts it, management in the knowledge economy is "a different game with different rules."

Modern management was developed for the needs of Fordist mass production organizations. Ideally, this kind of an organization functions as a perfect piece of machinery, which efficiently produces permanent quality and achieves pre-determined goals (see, e.g., Burns & Stalker, 1961; Grant, 1996a; Spender, 1996b; Ståhle & Grönroos, 2000; Davenport, 2001). All the essential knowledge is seen to be located at the higher levels of the organization, and there is a strict separation into thinkers and doers; hence the famous outburst of Henry Ford: "What I want is a good pair of hands; unfortunately I must take them with a person attached." The managerially created knowledge is passed downwards in the form of rules and regulations, and the task of employees is the obedient execution of the set criteria. Possibilities for new interpretations, elaborations and modifications by the employees are minimized, because these would merely disturb the efficiency of the pre-designed operating methods and hinder productivity. The hierarchical structure and centralized control ensure efficient steering of the organization.

In contrast, in knowledge-based organizations the locus of knowledge is no longer solely at the higher levels of the organization and in specialized functional units. Rather, knowledge is dispersed and distributed all around the organization (Brown & Duguid, 1991; Blackler, 1995; Tsoukas, 1996). Sometimes the relevant knowledge is in the customer interface or the marketing and sales department, sometimes on the shop floor. Each member of the organization is likely to have some important knowledge that no one else in the firm possesses. Front-line employees are often perceived to be in a crucial position, as they directly interact with customers and production processes, and therefore they can continuously develop organizational functioning if empowered to make decisions.

As knowledge workers by definition are the experts of their own jobs, much of the decision-making and job design has to be relocated where the expertise lies (see, e.g., Blomqvist & Pöyhönen, 2006). This signifies a shift toward a more organic view of management (Spender & Grant, 1996) in which employees are seen as active, intentional and intelligent agents that are capable of learning and making decisions based on their specialized and local knowledge. Then the role of management is to provide the "context in which employees at every level become independent agents, take responsibility, experiment and make mistakes and learn as they strive for continuous improvement in every aspect of the firm's total transformation process" (Spender, 1996b, 48).

In traditional management, the role of measurement is to provide the management with information about whether the set goals are being met and the standardized operating methods being followed, and thereby to enable timely and just monitoring of execution. The measurement objects are tangible, namely, financial or material resources and liabilities of the organization. In contrast, from the perspective of knowledge work, the role of organizational measurement is to enable knowledge workers to develop their own working methods and conditions, and to inform the management of how to support employees better in creating, sharing and integrating knowledge for productive ends. The focus of measurement should be on knowledge resources instead of material ones.

Measures have long been used to assess and manage organizations. Organizational measurement simply refers to assigning numbers to observations about organizations (e.g. Price, 1997). The most commonly used organizational measures relate to assessing organizational performance. Furthermore, the great majority of such measures are financial in nature and based on cost accounting (Kaplan, 1986; Eccles, 1991).

As organizational realities change, so should the measures used in assessing them (Neely, 1999). However, performance measures were developed for the needs of organizations in the pre-knowledge era, and it is doubtful how well they can portray those characteristics of organizations that are most important in knowledge-intensive contexts. The roots of the modern accounting system date back to the 15th century, and the most widely used performance measures have stayed similar since the beginning of the 20th century (Eccles, 1991; Ghalayini & Noble, 1996). The increasing irrelevance of traditional performance measures has been discussed since the 80s (e.g., Kaplan 1986), and the field of performance measurement is said to be in the midst of a revolution (Neely, 1999).

Indeed there are problems associated with the traditional performance measures (e.g., Kaplan, 1986; Eccles, 1991; Kaplan & Norton, 1992; Ghalayini & Noble, 1996; Neely, 1999; Kennerley & Neely, 2003) because they

- are historical,
- provide little indication of future performance,
- encourage short termism,

- neglect customers and competitors,
- lack strategic focus,
- inhibit innovation,
- do not indicate how performance is achieved,
- do not offer advice on how to improve, and
- are especially irrelevant in rapidly changing and highly competitive markets.

It is very important that the measurement systems reflect the context in which they are applied, namely, the objectives and priorities of the organization (Neely, 1999). As organizations become more focused on the productivity of knowledge rather than the manipulation of physical resources, their measurement systems should be modified to focus on knowledge outcomes and processes. Already in 1776, Adam Smith posited that learning improves the performance of workers and thereby increases productivity. How to measure intangible assets in addition to the tangible ones still, however, remains one of the most pressing concerns in the development of research on performance measurement (Neely, 2005). For the moment, organizational measures lag behind the reality they aim to capture.

NEW APPROACHES TO ORGANIZATIONAL MEASUREMENT: INTELLECTUAL CAPITAL AND COMPETENCE DEVELOPMENT

As knowledge has become the primary driver of competitive advantage in the contemporary economy, new approaches for measuring organizations are needed which recognize the knowledge-based aspects of value creation. Especially two relatively novel strands of research[a], intellectual capital and competence development, have set out to understand the productive capacity of knowledge-based organizations through developing measurement frameworks. Both schools of thought are mindful of the special qualities of knowledge and competence as opposed to other types of resources, and the measurement frameworks created within them aim, more or less explicitly, to foster development and learning. Both traditions are interested in knowledge in organizations, but there is a difference in their preferred analytical level: the intellectual capital literature addresses the whole organization as a single unit, and the competence development literature typically focuses on the individual employee.

Intellectual Capital

Research on intellectual capital (IC) is explicitly based on the assumption that the logic of doing business and creating value has changed fundamentally and knowledge has taken the place of land, labor and economic capital as the main source of corporate wealth creation. The success of modern organizations is seen to depend on their ability to gather and create knowledge, to share it and integrate it into the existing organizational knowledge base, and to apply it in a profitable manner. Even though financial capital and other resources can also be important, the primary resources are intangible.

The school attempts to overcome the limitations of conventional indicators that are used to explain, measure and manage organizational performance, and to provide classifications for intangibles that allow examining intellectual wealth from a comprehensive perspective. Research in this tradition focuses on constructing methods for identifying, describing, measuring, reporting and valuating intangibles in organizations, regions, networks and nations.

The field of IC is multidisciplinary, and the views of the nature and composition of intellectual capital tend to vary from one author to another. One definition of intellectual capital is that it is "the possession of the knowledge, applied experience, organizational technology, customer relationships and professional skills that provide a company with a competitive edge in the market" (Edvinsson & Malone, 1997). According to another definition, intellectual capital consists of "knowledge-based resources that contribute to the sustained competitive advantage of the firm," or simply "knowledge that can be converted into profits" (Sullivan, 1998).

Attempts to understand and conceptualize intellectual capital have yielded many theoretical frameworks (e.g., Edvinsson & Malone, 1997; Sveiby, 1997; Stewart, 1997; Roos et al., 1998; Sullivan, 1998; OECD, 2000) all of which divide IC into several components. The most commonly shared view is that IC is constructed of three parts: human capital (skills and know-how of the people in the organization), structural capital (organizational infrastructures and processes) and relational capital (relationships with clients, suppliers and other significant stakeholders, image, brand) (e.g., Edvinsson & Malone, 1997; Sveiby, 1997; Bontis, 1999).

Specifically, the criticism of the IC school on traditional performance measurement is mainly aimed at three intertwined issues. First, instead of relying on traditional accounting indicators, performance measurement should focus on the intangible properties of organizations. The difference between companies' book values and their market values has increased: for example, in the US the ratio of market value to book value had risen from 1:1 in 1980 to 5:1 in 2000. This indicates that traditional accounting is unable to address most of the essential dimensions of organizational value creation. Second, the perspective should be oriented towards the future rather than the past. From looking at the past achievements the view should be directed to assessing capabilities that foster competitiveness in the future. Third, financial information should be complemented and even replaced by non-financial information. As it is human knowledge that creates revenue, measurement should focus on the enabling conditions and proxies of human knowledge.

Many measurement frameworks have been created for assessing IC. For example, Andriessen (2004) reviews 25 IC measurement systems, whereas Lönnqvist (2004) divides IC measures into five classes:

- Multidimensional measurement systems that measure IC by assessing components that IC is built of: for example, human, structural and relational capital.
- Management processes that are wider operational models that encompass several phases related to the development of IC.
- Reporting models that guide how IC can be communicated to various reference groups.
- Indicators that portray IC through single measures.
- Other approaches that include general management methods with facets that can also be used in IC management (e.g., quality systems).

Competence Measurement and Development

The dominant line of competence management research and practice adopts a conventional psychological approach, seeing individual employees and managers as prime knowledge and competence carriers. The competence measurement within this framework is very much related to the so-called competence matrix or mapping in which individual knowledge, skills and competences are codified, assessed and recorded. With the introduction of the concept of core competence by Prahalad and Hamel (1990), a profoundly new type of competence understanding and measurement with a clearer focus on corporation wide strategic competence and collective practices was initiated.

Competence Matrix

The competence matrix is sometimes also called competence mapping or competence analysis. It is the most common tool used in work organizations for competence measurement and development, and it focuses entirely on the personal and cognitive traits of so-called competent managers or employees in relation to their job performance (e.g., Boyatzis, 1982; Klemp, 1980; McClelland, 1973; Morgan, 1988; Spencer & Spencer, 1993). Those skills and competences include technical or professional skills, human competence (e.g., interpersonal communication skills) and business know-how. In this connection, common competence management practices discussed in the literature include 1) making individual competence profiles visible by the company's intranet or data systems, so that people's talents and expertise can easily be traced when needed, and 2) identifying the gaps between current and required competences through development meetings and discussion between managers and subordinates, and setting up training and development programs for building up employee competences.

The competence matrix represents the mainstream of competence measurement and is still popular in today's organizations. In most cases, such a practice is initiated in a top-down manner and developed by the HR department of an organization. Nowadays organizations put more and more efforts in integrating HR functioning into business and strategic development in order to conduct a more profound and effective development program. However, the integration of the development of individual or employee competence with the organization's business and strategic development demands competence measurement on a different level, where organizations rather than individuals become the focus of the analysis.

Competence Measurement on an Organizational Level

Competence measurement on an organizational level is likely to tackle and focus on the firm's distinctive or core competence, which yields a more competitive performance. Key features of such a competence include potential access to a wide variety of markets, a significant contribution to the perceived customer benefits of the end product and inimitability from the competitors' perspective (Prahalad & Hamel, 1990).

Several attempts are remarkable in measuring the firm's distinctive competence on a more organizational or collective level (Henderson and Cockburn, 1994; McGrath et al., 1995; Ritter et al., 2002; Snow and Hrebiniak, 1980). Snow and Hrebiniak's research (1980) is perhaps one of those earliest attempts. They focused on the measurement of the distinctive competence of an organization, which refers to the things an organization does especially well in comparison to its competitors. The interesting and significant point of their work lies in their exploration into the relationship between the strategy, distinctive competence and organizational performance, conducted already in the 1980s. For some reason, this has been neglected for decades, and lately there seems to have been a renewed interest in the issue.

McGrath et al. (1995) identified two antecedents or processes which are central to the emergence of competence and its measurement in organizations: the emergence of comprehension (the comprehension of the management team working on developing competence) and deftness (deftness of their task execution). In the treatment of both comprehension and deftness, they consider and measure the relative impact of the content and process upon the emergence of competence, where the comprehension score is a measure of content understanding (what we know and how well we know it), and the deftness score is a measure for how well group processes are operating. Further, both the content and process are moderated by the inclusion of contextual variables.

Several contributions of the work by McGrath et al. are worth mentioning. Firstly, their research draws attention to the comprehensive and holistic nature of competence development. Secondly, it emphasizes the collective nature of competence formation while pointing out that "individuals are poor processors of complexity" (p. 55). Thirdly, it lays stress on the dynamic nature of competence and process, and a process-centered paradigm is accentuated; and finally, objectives and strategic process are emphasized in defining and measuring the competence content and process.

Henderson and Cockburn (1994) further elaborate the concept of core competence and divide it into two critical elements or forms of competence to be measured: component and architectural competence. Component competence is the local abilities and knowledge that are fundamental in day-to-day problem solving, and architectural competence is the ability to use these component competencies – to integrate them effectively and to develop fresh component competencies as they are required.

Ritter et al. (2002) have provided another research attempt to measure network competence. For them, the core competence is the ability of a firm to develop and manage relations with their key suppliers, customers and other organizations, and to deal effectively with the interactions in these relations. The measurement they developed focuses on two dimensions: network management task implementation or execution and the network management qualifications possessed by the people handling a company's relationships.

The shift of competence measurement, as reviewed above, is evident from the dominated line of focusing on individuals (e.g., employee competence followed the tradition of psychological & cognitive science studies) to the focus on collective competence practices (e.g., identification of core competence and stress on network competence measurement). This, as pointed out by Ahonen et al. (2000), indicates a major transition in knowledge management theories. The first generation in knowledge management theories took the knowledge-carrying individual as the unit of analysis and defined knowledge and competence in terms of discrete skills that could be codified and measured. The second generation theories focused more on networking, communication and collective practices rather than the things people apparently know and the information they possess. The key idea behind the second generation theories is that knowledge is embedded in collective practices and becomes constructed in them. This transition in knowledge and competence thinking has also been noted by a number of other authors (Snowden, 2002; Tuomi, 2002; von Krogh, 1999).

TOWARDS A KNOWLEDGE-BASED APPROACH TO ORGANIZATIONAL MEASUREMENT

Even though the research traditions in intellectual capital and competence development have set out to expand organizational measurement from command and control purposes towards enabling learning, there is still room for a lot of improvement if they are to deliver their full potential. We claim that using the knowledge-based view (KBV) of the firm as a background ideology it is possible to construct measures that are relevant and useful for knowledge-based organizations. In this chapter we examine the essential features of the KBV and then point out six consequences it has for organizational measurement.

Foundations of the Knowledge-Based View of the Firm

Along with the rise of knowledge work, a novel approach to organizations, the knowledge-based view of the firm, has emerged bringing significant changes to the way in which organizations are understood. The KBV addresses the issues of the existence, the boundaries and the internal organization of the multi-person firm (Foss, 1996). According to the KBV, organizations exist to create, transfer and transform knowledge into competitive advantage (Kogut & Zander, 1992), and performance differences between firms derive from their differing stocks of knowledge and capabilities in using and developing knowledge (Nonaka & Takeuchi, 1995; Grant, 1996b; Grant & Spender, 1996).

According to the latest management science understanding, the integral characteristic of knowledge is its human nature (e.g. Nonaka & Takeuchi, 1995; Spender, 1996a). Knowledge does not exist apart from the knowing subject – as universal abstractions floating somewhere out there – but is always tied to a particular viewpoint and practical application. In other words, knowledge is a fundamentally human issue: it is a product and vehicle of human activity, bounded by the limitations of human cognitive and other psychological capacities and by the social and cultural environment of the activity. Information technology systems and other related mediating tools can act as vehicles for transferring knowledge or as repositories for storing knowledge, but in knowledge-based management the role of these is secondary compared with knowledgeable human actors.

Also, humans are seen as active constructors of knowledge, who use knowledge for achieving certain goals, rather than naive recipients of externally created knowledge or "garbage cans" into whose minds information is inserted and where it exerts a stable and predictable influence. Learning is a situated process of knowledge construction based on action (Berger & Luckmann, 1966; Kolb, 1984; Schön, 1987). In fact, to learn is to be able to make use of the newly acquired knowledge in one's behavior.

Furthermore, humans are always located in a social context, or as Marx put it, human beings are social animals (Eskola, 1982). The particular socio-historical context sets the boundaries for individual understanding and behavior, while individuals regenerate and modify the context by enacting it (e.g., Giddens, 1984). Even when we are alone, our culture and communities influence us both from the outside and inside as internalized conceptions, mental models, attitudes and values. This is not to say that knowledge would not exist on the personal level, but that even individually held knowledge has a fundamentally inter-subjective quality to it. Individuals neither think nor take action in a vacuum; knowledge is embedded and constructed in shared practices by interacting individuals who combine their efforts while striving towards more or less common goals (e.g., Berger & Luckmann, 1966; Crossan et al., 1999). As Spender (1996a, 64) argues, "knowledge is less about truth and reason and more about the practice of intervening knowledgeably and purposefully in the world." Moreover, to intervene in the world one has to be able to communicate with others and understand the particular context of activity. In this sense, knowledge essentially exists between individuals and not within them.

To summarize, knowledge, from a management perspective, is not something objective, free-floating, abstract and universal as portrayed by the traditional western epistemology; but neither is it only subjective, residing solely in the minds of individuals as their personal experience. Rather, knowledge is something that is constructed in the social practices of actors embedded in a particular social context. Knowledge emerges from the social interactions between various parties within and across the organizational borders. It is continuously re-interpreted and modified, and continuously changing and developing (e.g.,

Blackler, 1995; Drucker, 1997; Tsoukas & Chia, 2002; Orlikowski, 2002). In other words, knowledge is fundamentally dynamic in nature: it is the subject of constant negotiations, modifications and alterations. It is also related to the issues of power and control (Blackler, 1995).

Tacit knowledge is demonstrated in skilled action and unconscious judgments, and it is very hard to separate it from the activity in which it is demonstrated (Polanyi, 1966). Cognition and action go hand in hand: knowledge is both acquired and demonstrated in action (Dougherty, 1992; Spender, 1996a; Crossan et al., 1999; Orlikowski, 2002). Even though knowledge is demonstrated in many forms (e.g., explicit and tacit) and located on many levels (e.g., individual and social), the most valuable kind of knowledge is what is demonstrated in the process of "knowing" and the formation of skillful behavior, rather than that which is stored in, for example, databases and patents. On the level of the whole organization, competitive advantage flows not from the resources themselves but from the firm capabilities to use these resources for productive purposes (e.g., Penrose, 1959; Kogut & Zander, 1992; Grant & Spender, 1996; Grant, 1996b).

Humans are bounded by cognitive limitations as to how much and what they can know, and therefore they have to specialize (Simon, 1955). Especially in complex issues which cannot be understood by any single individual, there is a need for the integration and coordination of knowledge (Grant, 1996b). Producing a good or service typically requires the application of many types of knowledge resources (Kogut & Zander, 1992; Grant, 1996b; Grant & Baden-Fuller, 2004). This means that the organization also has to be able to manage, integrate and coordinate the knowledge of its employees (Penrose, 1959; Kogut & Zander, 1992; Grant, 1996b). For a firm to be knowledgeable, it is not enough that its individual employees are skilled and educated. The scattered, uncoordinated insights of individual organizational members are not enough to produce competitive advantage; in order to produce sustainable value, they must be combined into a synergistic whole. This does not mean a mechanistic aggregation or synthesis of what the individual members of the organization know. The pattern and mechanisms of the integration of knowledge cannot be reduced to the level of individual actions, but have to be analyzed in their own right, on the level of shared practices. The crucial issue is how the employees work together, how their tasks interrelate and how their individual knowledge is integrated to produce value for the company (Grant, 1996a; 1996b). This entails that, from the knowledge-based view, organizations are above all social entities "specializing in the creation and transfer of knowledge" (Kogut & Zander, 1996, 503).

The Knowledge-Based Criteria for Measurement

Based on the key ideas of the knowledge-based view of organizations, we can outline six more specific implications for measurement.

Dynamic Perspective

For knowledge work, it is hard to craft a set of performance measures following the traditional logic of performance assessment. Defining the precise goals and criteria of good performance for knowledge work is problematic. In knowledge work, the tasks are likely to be non-repetitive and cannot be standardized. Furthermore, performance criteria mostly concern the quality rather than the quantity of output (Drucker, 1999). As is well known, quality is hard to define in general terms and even harder, if not impossible, to measure. The primary means to evaluate the output quality is probably customer satisfaction or peer review instead of some objective criteria. The dynamic nature of knowledge makes it even harder to pin down: since knowledge is altered, re-interpreted and modified as it is used, it is quite impossible to define stable content-based yardsticks for judging knowledge worker performance.

A more viable option would hence be to examine the processes of knowledge work rather than its outcomes. In fact, according to the knowledge-based view of strategy (e.g., Penrose, 1959; Kogut & Zander, 1992; Grant & Spender, 1996; Grant, 1996b), value creation depends not so much on the knowledge resources *per se* but on how they are used. Therefore, if the core rationale of organizational measurement is to improve the firm's value creation capabilities, they should be focused on the organizational practices in which resources are used rather than the resources or assets *per se*, no matter how intangible and knowledge-related these may be.

However, the existing measures in both IC and competence development traditions tend to examine knowledge and competencies as the static possessions of the organization, and not as activities conducted by the actors or brought about by the act of organizing itself (cf. Blackler, 1995; Tsoukas, 1996; Orlikowski, 2002; Kianto, 2007). For example, most of the literature on intellectual capital conceptualizes intellectual capital as a static asset or a "stock" (Bontis, 1999) and assumes that it is something that can be relatively easily identified, located, moved and traded, much like some sort of a package, be it an intangible one. Alternatively, knowledge could be understood to emerge from ongoing social interactions, and the focus could be not on the knowledge resources as static assets or outcomes *per se* but on the capabilities to leverage, develop and change them. There are some recently constructed measures which address this dynamic dimension of knowledge (Ståhle et al., 2003; Pöyhönen, 2004; Kianto, 2008).

Emic Approach

Knowledge is situated in specific local contexts and distributed across the organization among individual knowledge workers and communities of practice (e.g., Lave & Wenger, 1990; Brown & Duguid, 1991; Blackler, 1995; Tsoukas, 1996). The locus of expertise is viewed fundamentally differently in knowledge work versus traditional work: in the latter it is located on the top of the hierarchy, whereas in the former it is seen to be in the hands of knowledge workers themselves, namely, distributed across the organization. To improve reflexivity and learning, what gets measured and how it is measured should make sense to those that are meant to be the ones learning. In knowledge work, the core rationality is that it is the employees themselves who are the best experts and developers of their work; so they are the ones that should have a say in deciding the measures. This implies an emic rather than an etic approach towards measurement which should not aim to serve the scrutiny of an external evaluator or supervisor looking at the system from above and outside the system, but the contextualized self-understanding of the local actors themselves.

Particular Practices

Tacit knowledge is demonstrated in skilled action, and it is very hard to separate it from the activity in which it is demonstrated (Dougherty, 1992; Spender, 1996a; Crossan et al., 1999; Orlikowski, 2002). The most valuable kind of knowledge is that which is demonstrated in knowing and skillful performance. There is no pure or stand-alone performance; to understand how proficient a performance is, one needs to understand the context in which it takes place. This implies a focus on particular practices rather than universal abstractions and generalized criteria.

Based on the knowledge-based view of the firm, Spender and Marr (2006) argue that human capital is demonstrated in skilled performance and that it can only be addressed by looking into the particular work practice in detail. Performance "needs to be understood in the context of its being integrated into, and as a constituting part of, the production function. Hence, performance measurement and human capital must be based on the specific system of practices internal to the firm" (p. 265). Spender and Marr offer activity-based accounting as a possible solution, but note that this strand of research is in its infancy and does not yet offer developed tools. Thus, because the identification of tacit knowledge is difficult, if not impossible, its measurement promises to be even more so.

Strategy-Based Indicators

According to the resource-based view of strategy (of which the knowledge-based view is an outgrowth), performance differences among firms are due to the differences in intra-firm characteristics instead of market positioning. Consequently, the most important information for strategic decision-making is provided by understanding the firm's resources and capabilities rather than external market-based evaluations.

This implies that to allow learning and development, indicators should be chosen based on the organizational strategy, and not on external needs and demands. The organizational strategy should function as a frame of reference that determines what factors to measure. In the intellectual capital literature there is a strong conviction that the measures should be derived from the organizational strategy and be connected with the value creation logic of the firm (Sveiby, 1997; Stewart, 1997; Sullivan, 1998). Organizations are emphasized as strategic, goal-oriented entities rather than a free-floating collection of stocks and flows. The drawback of this is that intellectual capital measurement systems and reports tend to be so idiosyncratic that it is hard to make cross-comparisons between several organizations and to interpret whether a given measurement indicates a positive or a negative tendency.

Concerning competence development in their early article, Snow and Hrebiniak (1980) already emphasized the importance of identifying and assessing the distinctive competencies of the firm. This of course is the main thrust of the resource-based view (RBV) of the firm: the creation of supernormal returns is based on the heterogeneous and inimitable resources. However, looking at the competence development literature and assessment systems in the literature and in use, it seems that this lesson has been lost on the way. It should be clear that it makes little sense to map competencies in general; instead, what is measured should be related to the value creation logic of the firm. In sum, indicators should be drawn from the strategy and distinctive competencies of the firm, namely, be grounded on internal features.

Potential Skills

In the intellectual capital literature, authors often note that an important drawback of the traditional performance measures is that they are past-oriented – they show changes in performance only when it is too late to influence the situation (e.g., Sveiby, 1997; Edvinsson & Malone, 1997). In contrast, monitoring the intellectual qualities and properties of a firm should allow the rapid re-steering and a more realistic evaluation of the available alternatives. Furthermore, as knowledge-intensive businesses are increasingly characterized by rapid changes and nonlinearity, it is impossible to predict which specific competencies and resources are the ones that will emerge to rule in a given business area. Therefore, the success factors have to relate to organizations' dynamic capabilities for mastering change and adaptation and continuous renewal (Teece et al., 1997; Eisenhardt & Martin, 2000; Pöyhönen, 2004).

In addition to examining the actualized, existing skills, it would also be important to address potential knowledge and competencies. Knowledge is not only related to action and already made decisions and sought for possibilities, but also to the emergent future possibilities and potential, the not yet embodied or the self-transcendent (Scharmer, 2001). Spender and Marr (2006) underline that in measuring human capital, understanding what constitutes skilled performance in the context of current circumstances is only the first step. What would also be needed is understanding the potential for skilled performance under circumstances that have not yet come to be. That is, while it is important to understand what is known at present, it is also important to understand what is in the "zone of proximal development" (Engeström, 2001) or in the space of potential possibilities, what kinds of paths or real options (Kogut & Kulatilaka, 2001) there are open for the actor or the firm in the (near) future. Grasping the potential capabilities is more important to the extent that the environment is non-predictable and rapidly changing.

The Collective Dimension

Knowledge is fundamentally inter-subjective: it is embedded and crafted in continuous social interaction among the members of the organization. Rather than residing in the minds of individuals or in databases, the most important type of knowledge is that which is located between people (e.g., Spender, 1996b). This means that its measurement should emphasize inter-subjective factors and social interaction, instead of individual propensities. The problem with current competence development metrics is that they are exceedingly individualistic and fail to examine knowledge and capabilities on the collective level. The same applies to the human capital measures of the intellectual capital measurement frameworks which (in both IC and competence development frameworks) tend to focus on such factors as age and educational background.

The problem is two-fold. First, it is well reported that the social environment significantly influences the extent to which individuals actually invest their time and effort in reaching organizational goals. Measures depicting individual propensities only tell what the individual potential is – and even this defined in quite a narrow manner. They do not address whether or how widely the individual really directs these latent capacities to performing a given task. By assessing the features of the socio-psychological environment, a more valid analysis could be provided that would also help in determining how the situation could be improved so as to better allow and encourage the enactment of individual skills and competencies.

Second, collective knowledge or shared tacit knowledge is the strategically most important type of knowledge (e.g., Spender, 1996a; Bollinger & Smith, 2001) and should therefore be measured in itself. Collective knowledge consists of the knowledge that is embedded in the forms of social and organizational practice, residing in the tacit experiences and enactment of the collective, such as routines (Nelson & Winter, 1982). Individual actors may be unconscious of such knowledge, even though it is accessible and sustained through their interaction. (Spender, 1996a; 1996b.) Consequently, the manner in which it can be studied is by examining the relational patterns among the organizational actors and the coordination principles by which they collaborate (Kogut & Zander, 1992; Grant, 1996). Shared operating methods are inimitable across firms, and therefore they are the main source of sustained competitive advantage. For example, innovations can be copied by competitors, whereas innovativeness as an organizational characteristic embedded in the organizing principles and patterns of social interaction cannot. However, there are very few measures that have been created for collective knowledge, and indeed it seems like a very demanding issue to quantify.

CONCLUSION

The crucial importance of knowledge as a factor of production means that the basis of competition has shifted from striving to achieve maximal ef-

Table 1. A comparison of measurement approaches

	Traditional view of measurement	**Intellectual capital measures**	**Competence development measures**	**Knowledge-based approach to measurement**
Goal of measurement	Allowing control by management	Allowing learning and development	Allowing learning and competence development	Allowing learning and development
Knowledge understood as	Knowledge not discussed	Static asset, stock	Professional skills and production technologies	Emergent and socially constructed process
Essential form of knowledge	Knowledge not discussed	Explicit, know-that	Explicit, know-that	Tacit, potential, know-how
Epistemological assumption	Positivist (even though knowledge not explicitly discussed)	Positivist view of knowledge	Constructivist view of knowledge	Constructionist view of knowledge
Locus of expertise in the organization	Expertise located at the top of the organizational hierarchy	Knowledge is embedded in employees, structures and relationships	Knowledge is embedded in the heads of employees, working artefacts, strategic structures and network relationships	Knowledge is dispersed and contextual, embedded in individuals and shared practices
View of employees	Naive recipients and implementers of managerially crafted knowledge	Intelligent agents	Active, collaborative and intelligent agents	Active, intentional and intelligent agents
Main interest	Leveraging existing factors of production	Identifying and leveraging existing intellectual capital	Identifying existing knowledge and skills and developing core competences	Improving existing knowledge and competencies, creating new ones
Measurement focus on	Financial variables	Intangible property, investments in intangibles, human, structural and relational capital	Individual skills and organizational core competences	Particular activities, social processes and organizational characteristics
Quantification of objects of measurement	Easy	Moderate	Moderate	Difficult

ficiency in mass production towards generating an organization-wide capability for the effective exploitation of knowledge, continuous learning and self-directed development. To assist in this new strategic focus, the underpinning logic of organizational measurement also has to change. In this chapter we have explored what the knowledge-based approach to measurement should look like and constructed its foundations. Table 1 summarizes the key characteristics of this new paradigm and contrasts it with the traditional view of measurement and with the recent developments in the fields of intellectual capital and competence development.

If organizational measures are to reflect the change in the organizational reality they aim to capture, the measurement system has to be changed on two levels. First, the goal of measurement has to be seen differently: not as to control but to allow the continuous learning and renewal of the whole organization. At its best, measurement can facilitate the development of a meta-competence through providing "mirror materials" in an organizational change laboratory (Engeström et al., 1996) and the narrative for improved reflective learning (Ramsey, 2005). Meta-competence is the ability to assess the existence, exploitation and development potential of one's own competences (Morgan, 1988; Nordhaug, 1998; Weinert, 2001), and it constitutes a capability to facilitate organizational and strategic change (e.g., learning ability, mastering of uncertainty and the ability to tolerate change). Moreover, meta-competence is crucial, not exclusively to managers, but also for subordinate employees at all the levels in firms that have to accomplish organizational change (Nordhaug, 1998). In recent strategic management literature, meta-competence for change has been conceptualized as a dynamic capability which allows the firm to survive in turbulent environments (Teece et al., 1997; Zollo & Winter, 2002).

Second, in order to achieve the new goal, the actual measures themselves have to change. On the most obvious level, the focus has to be changed from assessing financial and material resources towards examining knowledge resources. In addition, based on the knowledge-based view of the firm, we have proposed that such measures should be dynamic, collective, localized, based on the organizational strategy and oriented towards the future. The two relatively novel approaches to organizational measurement, intellectual capital and competence development, meet these criteria much better than the traditional performance measures. However, when assessed with the knowledge-based criteria, it is evident that there is still much room for improvement. The knowledge-based measurement criteria are demanding to satisfy, and improving organizational measures so that they capture organizational knowledge processes and outcomes remains a taxing challenge for future research to tackle.

It should be noted that this chapter has intentionally painted quite a rosy picture of the knowledge-based approach in order to underline its potential differences with the more traditional approach to organizational measurement. However, clearly not all human undertaking will ever take place only in the intangible realm. Nor are the knowledge-based organizations necessarily any more equalitarian and democratic than the Fordist manufacturing companies. For the best results, the knowledge-based approach should be wisely complemented with the more traditional approaches as well as with a continuing concern for ethical integrity in worker–management relationships.

REFERENCES

Ahonen, H., Engeström, Y., & Virkkunen, J. (2000). Knowledge management - the second generation: creating competencies within and between work communities in competence laboratory. In Y. Malhotra (Ed.), *Knowledge Management and Virtual Organizations*, (pp. 282–305) Hershey and London: Idea Group Publishing.

Andriessen, D. (2004). IC Valuation and Measurement: Classifying the State of the Art. Journal of Intellectual capital, *5*(2), 230-242.

Berger, P., & Luckmann, T. (1966). *The Social Construction of Reality.* New York: Anchor Books.

Blackler, F. (1995). Knowledge, Knowledge Work and Organizations: An Overview and Interpretation. Organization Studies, *16*(6),1021-1046.

Blomqvist, K.-M., & Pöyhönen, A. (2006). *Knowledge-Based View of the Firm – Theoretical Notions and Implications for Management.* Working paper, Lappeenranta University of Technology.

Bollinger, A. S., & Smith, R. D. (2001). Managing Organizational Knowledge as a Strategic Asset. *Journal of Knowledge Management, 5*(1), 8-18.

Bontis, N. (1999). Managing Organizational Knowledge by Diagnosing Intellectual capital: Framing and Advancing the State of the Field. *International Journal of Technology Management, 18*(5-8), 433-462.

Boyatzis, R. E. (1982). *The Competent Manager.* New York: John Wiley & Sons.

Brown, J., & Duguid, P. (1991). Organizational Learning and Communities of Practice', Organization Science 2 (1): 40-57.

Burns, T. R., & Stalker, G. M. (1961). *The Management of Innovation.* London: Tavistock.

Campion, M. A., Papper, E. M., & Medsker, G. J. (1996). Relations Between Work Team Characteristics and Effectiveness: A Replication and Extension. Personnel Psychology, *49*(2), 429-440.

Castells, M., & Himanen, P. (2002). *The Information Society and the Welfare State: The Finnish Model.* Oxford: Oxford University Press.

Crossan, M., Lane, H., & White, R. (1999). *An Organizational Learning Framework: from Intuition to Institution.* Academy of Management Review, *24*(3), 522-537.

Davenport, T. (2001). Knowledge Workers and the Future of Management. In W. Bennis, G. Spreitzer, & T. Cummings (Eds.), *The Future of Leadership – Today's Top Leadership Thinkers Speak to Tomorrow's Leaders* (pp. 41-58).

Dougherty, D. (1992). A Practice-Centered Model of Organizational Renewal through Product Innovation. *Strategic Management Journal, 13,* 77-92.

Drucker, P. F. (1999). Knowledge-Worker Productivity: The Biggest Challenge. *California Management Review, 41*(2),: 79-95.

Drucker, P. F. (1993). The Rise of the Knowledge Society. *Wilson Quarterly, 17*(2), 52-70.

Drucker, P. F. (1988). The Coming of the New Organization. *Harvard Business Review, 66*(1), 45-54.

Drucker, P. F. (1959). *Landmarks of Tomorrow: A Report on the New "Post-Modern" World.* New York: Harper & Row.

Eccles, R. (1991). The Performance Measurement Manifesto. *Harvard Business Review,* Jan-Feb, 131-137.

Edvinsson, L., & Malone, M. (1997). *Intellectual capital: Realising Your Company's True Value by Finding its Hidden Brainpower.* New York: Harper Collins.

Eisenhardt, K., & Martin, J. (2000). Dynamic Capabilities: What Are They? *Strategic Management Journal, 21,* 1105-1121.

Engeström, Y. (2001). Expansive learning at work: toward an activity theoretical reconceptualization. *Journal of Education and Work, 14*(1), 133-156.

Engeström, Y., Virkkunen, J., Helle M., Pihlaja J., & Poikela, R. (1996). The change laboratory as a tool for transforming work. *Lifelong Learning in Europe, 2,* 10-16.

Eskola, A. (1982). *Vuorovaikutus, muutos, merkitys* [Interaction, Change, Significance]. Helsinki: Tammi.

Foray, D. (2004). *The Economics of Knowledge.* Cambridge: MIT Press.

Foss, N. (2005). *Strategy, Economic Organization and the Knowledge Economy.* The Coordination of Firms and Resources. Oxford: Oxford University Press.

Foss, N. (1996). Knowledge-Based Approaches to the Theory of the Firm: Some Critical Comments. *Organization Science, 7*(5), 470-476.

Ghalayini, A., & Noble, J. (1996). The Changing Basis of Performance Measurement. *International Journal of Operations & Production Management, 16*(8): 63-80.

Giddens, A. (1984). *The Constitution of Society. Outline of the Theory of Structuration.* Cambridge: Polity Press.

Grant, R. (1996a). Prospering in Dynamically-Competitive Environments: Organizational Capability as Knowledge Integration. *Organization Science, 7*(4), 375-387.

Grant, R. (1996b). Toward a Knowledge-Based Theory of the Firm. *Strategic Management Journal, 17,* 109-122.

Grant, R., & Baden-Fuller, C. (2004). A Knowledge Accessing Theory of Strategic Alliances. *Journal of Management Studies, 41*(1), 61-84.

Henderson, R. M., & Cockburn, I. (1994). Measuring competence? Exploring firm effects in pharmaceutical research. *Strategic Management Journal, 15*(Winter Special Issue), 63-84.

Janz, B. D., Colquitt, J. A., & Noe, R. A. (1997). Knowledge Worker Team Effectiveness: The Role of Autonomy, Interdependence, team Development, and Contextual Support Variables. *Personnel Psychology, 50*(4).

Kaplan, R., & Norton, D. (1992). The Balanced Scorecard: Measures that Drive Performance. *Harvard Business Review* Jan-Feb, (pp. 71-79).

Kaplan, R. (1986). Accounting Lag: The Obsolescence of Cost Accounting Systems. *California Management Review, 28*(2):174-199.

Kennerley, M., & Neely, A. (2003). Measuring Performance in a Changing Business Environment. *International Journal of Operations & Production Management, 23*(3): 213-229.

Kianto, A. (2007). What do we really mean by dynamic intellectual capital? *International Journal of Learning and Intellectual Capital, 4*(4), 342-356.

Kianto, A. (2008). Development and validation of a survey instrument for measuring organizational renewal capability. *International Journal of Technology Management, 42*(1/2): 69-88.

Klemp, G. O. Jr. (Ed.) (1980). *The Assessment of Occupational Competence.* Washington, DC: National Institute of Education.

Kogut, B., & Kulatilaka, N. (2001). Capabilities as Real Options. *Organization Science, 12*(6), 744-759.

Kogut, B., & Zander, U. (1996). What Firms Do? Coordination, Identity and Learning. *Organization Science, 7*(5), 502-518.

Kogut, B., & Zander, U. (1992). Knowledge of the Firm, Combinative Capabilities, and the Replication of Technology. *Organization Science, 3*(3), 383-397.

Kolb, D. (1984). *Experiential Learning.* Englewood Cliffs: Prentice Hall.

Lave, J., & Wenger, E. (1991). *Situated Learning: Legitimate Peripheral Participation.* Cambridge: Cambridge University Press.

Lönnqvist, A. (2004). *Measurement of Intangible Success Factors: Case Studies on the Design, Implementation and Use of Measures.* Tampere University of Technology, Publication 475. Tampere: Tampere University of Technology.

Marr, B. (2005) (Ed) *Perspectives on Intellectual capital.* Oxford: Elsevier.

McClelland, D. C. (1973). Testing for competence rather than for "intelligence'. *American Psychologist, 1*,1-14.

McGrath, R., MacMillan, G., & Venkataraman, S. (1995). Defining and developing competence: A strategic process paradigm. *Strategic Management Journal, 16*, 251-275.

Miles, R. E., Snow C. C., & Miles, G. (2000). The-Future.org. *Long range Planning, 33*, 300-321.

Morgan, G. (1988). *Riding the waves of change: Developing managerial competences for a turbulent world.* San Francisco: Jossey-Bass.

Neely, A. (2005). The Evolution of Performance Measurement Research. Developments in the Last Decade and a Research Agenda for the Next. *International Journal of Operations & Production Management, 25*(12), 1264-1277.

Neely, A. (1999). The Performance Measurement Revolution: Why Now and What Next? *Inter-*

national Journal of Operations & Production Management, 19(2), 205-228.

Nelson, R., & Winter, S. (1982). *An Evolutionary Theory of Economic Change*. Cambridge: Harvard University Press.

Nonaka, I., & Takeuchi, H. (1995). *The Knowledge-Creating Company*. New York: Oxford University Press.

Nordhaug, O. (1998). Competence specificities in organizations. *International Studies of Management and Organization, 28*(1), 8-29.

OECD (2005). OECD Science, Technology and Industry Scoreboard 2005. Executive Summary. Available at: http://www.oecd.org/dataoecd/59/52/35465901.pdf.

OECD (2000). *Chairman's conclusions. International symposium Measuring and Reporting Intellectual capital: Experiences, Issues, and Prospects.* 9-11 June, Amsterdam, Netherlands. Available at: http://www.oecd.org//dsti/sti/industry/indcomp/act/ams-conf/conclusions.htm.

Orlikowski, W. (2002). Knowing in Practice: Enacting a Collective Capability in Distributed Organizing. *Organization Science, 13*(3), 249-273.

Penrose, E. (1959). *The Theory of the Growth of the Firm*. Oxford: Oxford University Press.

Polanyi, M. (1966). *The tacit dimension*. New York: Double Day.

Prahalad, C., & Hamel, G. (1990). 'The Core Competence of the Corporation. *Harvard Business Review* May-June: (pp. 79-91).

Price, J. (1997). Handbook of Organizational Measurement. *International Journal of Manpower, 18*(4/5/6), 305-558.

Pöyhönen, A. (forthcoming). *Development and Validation of a Method for Measuring Organizational Renewal Capability.*

Pöyhönen, A. (2004). *Modeling and Measuring Organizational Renewal Capability.* Doctoral Dissertation. Acta Universitatis Lappeenrantaensis 200. Lappeenranta: Lappeenranta University of Technology.

Ramsey, C. (2005). Narrative: From Learning in Reflection to Learning in Performance. *Management Learning, 36*, 219 - 235.

Reich, R. (1992). *The Work of Nations*. New York: Random House.

Riiter, T. et al (2002). Measuring network competence: some international evidence. *Journal of Business & Industrial Marketing, 17*(2/3), 119-138.

Roos, J., Roos, G., Dragonetti, N. C., & Edvinsson, L. (1998). *Intellectual capital: Navigating in the New Business Landscape*. New York: New York University Press.

Scharmer, O. (2001). Self-Transcending Knowledge: Sensing and Organizing around Emerging Opportunities. *Journal of Knowledge Management, 5*(2), 137-151.

Schön, D. (1987). *Educating the Reflective Practitioner*. San Francisco: Jossey-Bass.

Simon, H. (1955. A Behavioral Model of Rational Choice. *Quarterly Journal of Economics, 69*, 99-118.

Snow, C. C., & Hrebiniak, L. G. (1980). Strategy, distinctive competence, and organizational performance. *Administrative Science Quarterly, 25*, 317-336.

Snowden, D. (2002). Complex Acts of Knowing: Paradox and Descriptive Self-Awareness. *Journal of Knowledge Management, 6*(2), 100-111.

Spencer, L. M., & Spencer, S. M. (1993). *Competence at Work: Models for Superior Performance*. New York: John Wiley & Sons.

Spender, J.-C. (1996a). Organizational Knowledge, Learning and Memory: Three Concepts in Search of a Theory. *Journal of Organizational Change, 9*(1), 63-78.

Spender, J.-C. (1996b). Making Knowledge the Basis of a Dynamic Theory of the Firm. *Strategic Management Journal, 17*, 45-62.

Spender, J.-C., & Grant, R. (1996). Knowledge and the Firm: An Overview. *Strategic Management Journal, 17*, 5-9.

Spender. J.-C., & Marr, B. (2006). How a Knowledge-Based Approach Might Illuminate the Notion of Human Capital and its Measurement. *Expert Systems with Applications, 30(*2), 265-271.

Stewart, T. A. (1997). *Intellectual capital: The New Wealth of Organizations*. New York: Doubleday

Ståhle, P., & Grönroos, M. (2000). *Dynamic Intellectual capital*. Knowledge Management in Theory and Practice. Porvoo: WSOY.

Ståhle, P., Ståhle, S., & Pöyhönen, A. (2003). *Analyzing Dynamic Intellectual capital: System-Based Theory and Application*. Acta Universitatis Lappeenrantaensis, 152. Lappeenranta: Lappeenranta University of Technology.

Sullivan, P. H. (1998). *Profiting from Intellectual capital - Extracting Value from Innovation*. New York: Wiley.

Sveiby, K. E. (1997). *The New Organizational Wealth: Managing and Measuring Knowledge-Based Assets*. San Francisco: Berret-Koehler.

Teece, D., Pisano, G., & Shuen, A. (1997). Dynamic Capabilities and Strategic Management. *Strategic Management Journal, 18*, 509-533.

Tsoukas, H. (1996. Firm as a Distributed Knowledge System: A Constructionist Approach. *Strategic Management Journal, 17*, 11-25.

Tsoukas, H., & Chia, R. (2002). On Organizational Becoming: Rethinking Organizational Change. *Organization Science, 13*(5), 567-582.

Tuomi, I. (2002). The future of knowledge management. *Lifelong Learning in Europe, 2*, 69-79.

Tynjälä, P. (2003). Developing Vocational Expertise in the Knowledge Society. In J. Kirjonen (Ed.), *Knowledge Work and Occupational Competence*, (pp. 85-108).

von Krogh, G. (1999). *Developing a knowledge-based theory of the firm*. Available at: http://www.dialogonleadership.org/vonKrogh-1999cp.html.

Weinert, F. E. (2001). Concept of competence: a conceptual clarification. In D.S. Rychen & L. H. Salganik (Eds.), Defining and Selecting Key Competence, (pp. 45-65). Seattle: Hogrefe & Huber Publishers.

Zollo, M., & Winter, S. (2002). Deliberate Learning and the Evolution of Dynamic Capabilities. *Organization Science, 13*(3), 339-351.

KEY TERMS

Competence Development: Competence is more like an asset, while competence development is a more practical or at least action-oriented approach which aims to develop these assets or competences. Competence development has set out to expand organizational measurement from command and control purposes towards enabling learning and self-renewal.

Competence Matrix: The competence matrix is sometimes also called competence mapping or competence analysis. It is the most common tool used in work organizations for competence measurement and development of individual skills, knowledge and competences including technical or professional skills, human competence (e.g., interpersonal communication skills) and business know-how.

Competence: Competence can be either individual one that focuses on the personal and cognitive traits of so-called competent managers or employees in relation to their job performance, or organizational one that focuses on corporation wide strategic competence and collective practices. It can also be a comprehensive one that integrates both individual and organizational strategic competences together.

Intellectual Capital: Intellectual capital is a set of knowledge-based resources and processes that contribute to the sustained competitive advantage of the firm. The most commonly shared view is that intellectual capital consists of three basic elements: human capital (skills and know-how of the people in the organization), structural capital (organizational infrastructures and processes) and relational capital (relationships with clients, suppliers and other significant stakeholders, image, brand).

Knowledge Workers: Knowledge workers are highly educated employees who apply theoretical and analytical knowledge to developing new products, services, processes and procedures. As knowledge workers by definition are the experts of their own jobs, much of the decision-making and job design has to be relocated where the expertise lies.

Knowledge-Based View: According to the knowledge-based view, organizations are communities of knowledge and innovation that constantly create, transfer and transform knowledge into sustainable competitive advantage, and performance differences between firms derive from their differing stocks of knowledge and capabilities in using and developing knowledge.

Measurement: In traditional management, the role of measurement is to provide the management with information about whether the set goals are being met and the standardized operating methods being followed, and thereby to enable timely and just monitoring of execution. The measurement objects are tangible, namely, financial or material resources and liabilities of the organization. In contrast, from the knowledge-based view, the role of organizational measurement is to enable knowledge workers to develop their own working methods and conditions, and to inform the management of how to support employees better in creating, sharing and integrating knowledge for productive ends. The focus of measurement shifts from material or tangible resources to knowledge.

ENDNOTE

[a] It should be noted that in some contexts these approaches are quite prevalent in practice and even fairly institutionalized.

Chapter XVII
'Common' Information Spaces in Knowledge-Intensive Work:
Representation and Negotiation of Meaning in Computer-Supported Collaboration Rooms

Vidar Hepsø
Statoil Hydro Research and Norwegian School of Management, Norway

ABSTRACT

In knowledge management literature, common information spaces (CIS) are believed to be instrumental in the development and sharing of knowledge. These information spaces provide the arena to facilitate knowledge creation, knowledge management, boost multidisciplinary collaboration and therefore increase the performance of the organization. In a global oil and gas industry an increasing part of the communication in day-to-day operations takes place in specially designed videoconferencing and collaboration rooms. This chapter addresses the role such information spaces play and some of the implications for practice when it comes to knowledge-intensive work: diversity, work relations and identity. What is regarded as "common" or "shared" among heterogeneous groups of professionals working within such information spaces is challenged.

INTRODUCTION TO 'COMMON' INFORMATION SPACES

The need to have a strong integration between collaborative knowledge work and common information spaces has been apparent in the business literature since the development of theories of information management and BPR (Hammer & Champy, 1993) in the 1980s and 1990s. From there it has spread to knowledge management

(Davenport, 2005; Ciborra, 2000). Boland and Tenkasi (1995) have argued that knowledge production requires communication within and between an organization's multiple communities of knowing. The most important challenge for knowledge-intensive organizations is to make each community strong while at the same time nurturing the ability to take the perspectives of other communities of knowing into consideration. Before considering common information spaces (CIS) it is worth considering Boland and Tenkasi's conception of perspective taking and perspective making since these two concepts are important in what follows. Communication that strengthens the unique knowledge and practice of a community of knowing is perspective making. As the community's perspective grows stronger it becomes more complex and more able to meet the knowledge work requirements. Unexpected events or findings can only be recognized as such from within a perspective. Boland and Tenkasi argue that without a strong perspective a community of knowing cannot create important knowledge. The relevance for a discussion on CIS is that the community must have a 'space' for conversation and action that is isolated from other communities to be able to nurture their vocabulary, methods, theories, values and logic. Perspective taking is communication that makes it possible for the community to take the knowledge of other communities into account. This means that the community must be able to overcome the incommensurability between communities without sacrificing the integrity and distinctiveness of their own perspective. The main challenge for perspective taking is that communication must first support perspective making processes: "Only after a perspective is differentiated and strengthened can it be reflected upon and represented so the actors in other communities of knowing have something to integrate through a perspective taking communication" (Boland & Tenkasi, 1995, p. 359).

Let us now turn to CIS. I assert that there are two major literature 'clusters' of importance that will enable us to grasp the essence of work practices associated with CIS. The first is the interdisciplinary study of computer-supported cooperative work (CSCW) and the other is science studies/the social construction of technology. Each of these has the potential to go beneath the simplified notion of CIS that is often found in the management literature. These two clusters of thinking will be elaborated upon.

The CIS approach in CSCW was initiated by Kjeld Schmidt and Liam Bannon (1992). They were the first to link the conceptualization of co-operative knowledge work and common information spaces (CIS) across people in heterogeneous communities. In their work they stressed the practices associated with CIS: ..."how people in a distributed setting can work cooperatively in a common information space - i.e. by maintaining a central archive of organisational information with some level of 'shared' agreement as to the meaning of this information (locally constructed), despite the marked differences concerning the origins and context of these information items. The space is constituted and maintained by different actors employing different conceptualizations and multiple decision making strategies, supported by technology."(Schmidt & Bannon, 1992, p.22). They argue that embedded in the CIS concept is a 'shared agreement as to the meaning of information'.

The major lesson that I have learned from the CSCW literature and Boland and Tenkasi concerning knowledge-intensive work is that simply providing a common technology platform or shared access to new information resources will not necessarily lead to fruitful collaboration and the sharing of information. Such a belief is too simple, since according to Schmidt and Bannon the development of a CIS requires:..."the active construction by the participants of this common information space where the meanings of the shared objects are debated and resolved, at least locally and temporarily" (Schmidt & Bannon, 1992, p. 27). This means in Boland and Tenkasi's

(1995) terms; active perspective making followed by active perspective taking.

The CIS concept originating from Schmidt and Bannon has been heavily debated in the CSCW community over the years. The literature has focused on various types of CIS in different contexts, issues of heterogeneity, the degree of work distribution, and the varying need for articulation work – to mention just a few aspects. Readers are advised to consult this literature for more details (Harrison & Dourish, 1996; Bannon & Bødker, 1997; Bannon, 2000; Bertelsen & Bødker, 2001; Bossen, 2002; Erickson, et al., 2003; Rolland, Hepsø & Monteiro, 2006). I have argued elsewhere (Rolland, Hepsø & Monteiro, 2006) that in spite of recent contributions to the CSCW literature the 'shared' aspect of CIS (or the 'C') remains slippery and is a source of debate. This is also the situation in most knowledge management literature. What constitutes the 'common' or 'shared' is therefore of great importance if we are going to understand the difference between official organizational rhetoric and common practice in knowledge-intensive work. It is also important to ask what needs to be shared and what is the minimum threshold of shared meaning associated with activities between communities of knowing? The insight from Boland and Tenkasi adds up to this. Since perspective making is a pre-requisite for perspective taking, the 'shared' in an information space will always have connections to particular communities of knowing. 'Shared' elements in an information space have no meaning in themselves.

If we want to get a grip on what is 'shared' in such information spaces and go beyond the rhetoric, there are at least two possible tracks. The first starts with Schmidt and Bannon (1992) and Bannon and Bødker (1997). Bannon and Bødker address the notion of 'immutable mobile' originating in actor-network theory (ANT) to address differences in perspectives and meaning when objects in information spaces cross communities, or how communities develop means for sharing items in a common information space. 'Immutable mobiles' (Latour, 1987) in ANT refers to objects that are shared across heterogeneous contexts, but have a relatively stable meaning across contexts. Based on the insight of Latour, Bannon and Bødker (1997) argue that CIS display their dialectical nature. On the one hand, they are open and malleable, and on the other hand they are packaged and are turned into things that are immutable to allow sharing across contexts and communities of practice. A key issue is to study the closure processes of CIS or how people and different groups that are involved create and maintain a CIS over time and space. It is necessarily to look at the alignment of human and technical forces and the way artefacts both shape and are shaped by the actor networks in which they participate (Bannon, 2000). There is a process of black-boxing or closure associated with common information spaces where both the objects and the practices of the associated information space develop a stable configuration. In their work Bannon and Bødker (1997) also give the well-known concept of 'boundary objects' an important role. Boundary objects are especially mouldable objects that can be interpreted differently in various communities. At the same time they appear stable enough to maintain their integrity as 'common' objects across different communities. They facilitate across the boundaries of different communities and due to their flexibility they can take up local interpretations. Boundary objects hardly convey unambiguous meaning but they inhabit a symbolic adequacy that enables conversation without enforcing commonly shared meanings (Star & Griesemer, 1989). Boland and Tenkasi (1995) argue that when there is an absence of boundary objects, perspective taking and consequently the opportunity for knowledge work will be severely limited.

The other track to clarify the concept of a common information space is more deeply embedded in science studies and social construction of technology. This tradition emphasizes the mutability, as opposed to the stability and immutability of objects. A CIS is always in the making. Key characteristics of CIS in heterogeneous knowledge-intensive settings are their malleability and momentary character. Thus, in contrast to what was argued previously by Bannon and Bødker (1997), a CIS only seldom and momentary arrives at a closure (Rolland, Hepsø & Monteiro, 2006). The notion of closure fails to accommodate all the real-life instances where black-boxed solutions and decisions are reconsidered and possibly redone. Bijker (1993) proposes the notion of stabilization as a time-dependent form of closure, where a CIS remains stable for some time but is reopened again later. This is a different CIS approach, where a 'closure' is achieved in relation to a particular configuration of the technologies or resources, but this only lasts for a short period. In a new situation the issues, the shared objects and practices are reopened for negotiation. An essential aspect of CIS is therefore that they tend to remain open and malleable. In addition, they only provide shared understanding between actors at the exact moment when information is used in a specific temporary arrangement. This perspective challenges the conceptions of boundary objects presented in the first track. Anne Marie Mol (2003, p. 35) challenges key assumptions underpinning boundary objects and argues that communities quite routinely are capable of working independently around a given object. The meaning ascribed to objects goes well beyond the notion of 'perspectives' associated with boundary objects. She shows how different work practices exclude one another; create incompatible differences that in the end mould multiple objects and 'make a patchwork' (Mol 2003, p. 72). Still, when required in given circumstances, compatibility is produced as a practical task. Elsewhere I have indicated the importance of this insight in relation to achieving compatibility as a practical task in CIS (Rolland, Hepsø & Monteiro, 2006). In the context of CIS, this insight implies bracketing foundational concerns regarding exactly how much needs to be common for information to be shared, and instead tracing the ongoing, fragile and contingent performances that make up instances of collaboration. This approach enables us to study the continuous perspective making and perspective taking process in detail.

Work in real-life situations has to handle resource slips, or the under-supply or misalignment of resources needed or expected to carry out a work task (Gasser, 1986). Perspective making and taking occur within one or across several communities of knowing. Thus production optimization can make such slips occur in several dimensions. In the organizational dimension there can be too little time to follow up all the wells, poor reservoir model updates, small budgets for long-term optimization work vs. daily optimization and 'fire-fighting'. Other challenges are inaccurate data due to poor reliability of sensors, and software-hardware incompatibilities. These resource slips (Gasser, 1986) lead to contingencies that must be handled in the perspective making and taking processes of the communities of knowing.

For people that work with knowledge management and knowledge-intensive work, what is the importance of the discussion of perspective making/taking and what constitutes a common information space? In most knowledge management literature and also in much of the rhetoric of knowledge-intensive work we find a strong belief in the development of common information spaces (CIS) that are believed to be instrumental in the development and sharing of knowledge in today's organizations (Davenport, 2005; OLF, 2005). These information spaces provide the arena or the infrastructure to facilitate knowledge creation, knowledge management, boost multidisciplinary collaboration and therefore increase the performance of the organization. Professionals involved in change management initiatives especially those that try to develop the new ways of collaboration enabled by new information and communication technology should be particularly attentive to the discussion of CIS as it is presented and discussed in this chapter.

The Norwegian Oil Industry Association (OLF) reports on the importance and consequences of these common information spaces (OLF, 2005). It is not my task to challenge the importance of CIS. CIS fill important functions for collaboration and information sharing in knowledge-intensive work. Instead this chapter challenges the simplified notions of what is regarded as 'common' or 'shared' among heterogeneous professionals that work in such information spaces. The approach discusses how heterogeneous groups in organizations construct knowledge and shows how knowledge becomes a property of organizations via the objects brought forward by these information spaces. Perspective making and perspective taking are key processes in this development. By investigating CIS of a particular kind, tagged collaboration rooms, the chapter provides empirical examples of some of the work practices associated with common information spaces. The first research question that is addressed considers the role such 'shared' information spaces play in the knowledge intensive oil and gas industry; implications for knowledge-intensive work: diversity, work relations and identity? The second research question follows the first; how is the notion of a 'shared' CIS enacted in practice? The structure of the rest of the chapter is as follows. I start by presenting the methodology employed in the case. Then I present the case around a common information space in the Norwegian oil and gas industry to reveal the practice. I analyse the case in the light of the two tracks of CIS presented in this introduction; in relation to perspective making/taking, what is shared, (meaning the characteristics of the objects shared in the CIS) and the consequences for identity among the communities of knowing. Finally I analyse the lessons learnt in relation to the construction of knowledge and knowledge as a property of organizations. Here the strong relationship between technology and knowledge is presented.

METHODOLOGY

This chapter is the consequence of my participation as facilitator and change agent/action researcher within projects soon to be described as 'integrated operations'. Through this work I have been given access to the arenas where these CIS are planned, implemented and negotiated. This participation has been both local/practice oriented, in the sense of participation in user driven action research projects and official/policy oriented in the sense of taking part in Statoil corporate initiatives, Norwegian Petroleum Authority (E-driftsforum) and Norwegian Oil Industry Association work groups (OLF) on these issues. The action research (Greenwood & Levin, 2006) aspect of this work is not covered this chapter. Here the aim has been to focus on the CIS and collaboration between heterogeneous groups of the kind described here. The case presented is from a 3-month pilot in 2005 (with 2 days of observations every week, totally 30-35 full work days) within the domain of production optimization that tested a new CIS. Here I had the role of observing collaboration in the CIS and helping the people involved to document the pilot in a company internal report. In addition to the action research input, there is also participant observation of collaboration rooms in Statoil assets for almost three years, 40 days in 2006 and 20 days in 2007. In addition, 35 interviews have been conducted with people working in such facilities over a period of 2 years. Digital archives of e-mail, internal reports and project communication from internal logs, intranets and databases (Lotus Notes and MS SharePoint) have been available to me during this period. Statoil is a partly state owned Norwegian oil and gas company with around 17 000 employees but operates globally. The main business areas of the company are exploration and development of new oil and gas fields, operations and maintenance of a number of oil and gas assets. The company also has refineries and operates a leading petrol station chain in Scandinavia and the Baltic states.

DEVELOPMENT OF A COMMON INFORMATION SPACE IN THE NORWEGIAN OIL AND GAS INDUSTRY

Most major oil companies and globally operating service companies address their future way of doing business as oil exploration and operation enabled by information and communication technology. In the espoused version this is the integration of people across geographical, organizational and disciplinary boundaries, integration of processes in terms of business alignment and vendor collaboration. This integration process also closely involves technology: data, sensors, protocols, fibre-optics, standards and others (OLF, 2005). Real-time data and information are made available from a remote location, typically the down-hole reservoir/well of an oil and gas asset or from a process facility through a high-capacity fibre-optic infrastructure. Various professionals with multidisciplinary backgrounds onshore-offshore, inside or outside the oil companies/vendors analyse the data in collaborative environments and take decisions to support and optimize the production of oil and gas, see Figure 1.

This hybrid network of sensors, equipment, hardware and people taking and acting on decisions is the field the oil and gas industry in Norway describes as 'integrated operations'. The backbone infrastructure associated with integrated operations is a number of collaboration rooms or common information spaces where heterogeneous professionals collaborate to optimize oil and gas production; see Figure 1. These types of collaborative spaces are addressed in this chapter. However, readers must be aware that these collaboration rooms are part of a larger network structure that I have had to omit for heuristic reasons in this chapter.

THE CASE: PRODUCTION OPTIMIZATION IN AND OIL AND GAS ASSET

Production optimization can be defined as the process for short- and long-term control and optimization of oil and gas flow in a value chain from the reservoir, via offshore facilities to export from installations. This is probably the most important value-adding process for all oil companies and there is a shared understanding in the business that this process has substantial potential for improvement (OLF, 2005). The Norwegian Oil Industry Association has argued (OLF 2005, pp.6-10) that there is a gap in the practices between reservoir engineers who set well production targets and the engineers that are responsible for topside process facilities. In this situation most operative decisions are made offshore, in isolation or with limited support from experts onshore. At the same time plans are relatively rigid and are only changed at fixed intervals.

THE PARTICIPANTS IN THE SETTING

This also means that plans are made by each discipline and problems are solved fragmentally. The organizational structure tends to be traditional, meaning that personnel onshore and offshore belong to several organizational units. OLF shows how meetings are held onshore as well as offshore just to inform each other and coordinate activities. At the same time OLF argues that the competence development programmes in the oil companies focus on developing domain specialists. They do not prioritize developing professionals with a good understanding of the value chain and the key decision and work processes. Finally, OLF argues that the IT systems for production optimization are specialized or silo-focused. The consequence is that it becomes time consuming and difficult

Figure 1. Integrated operations, from reservoir and process facility sensors to integrated collaboration among operators and vendors

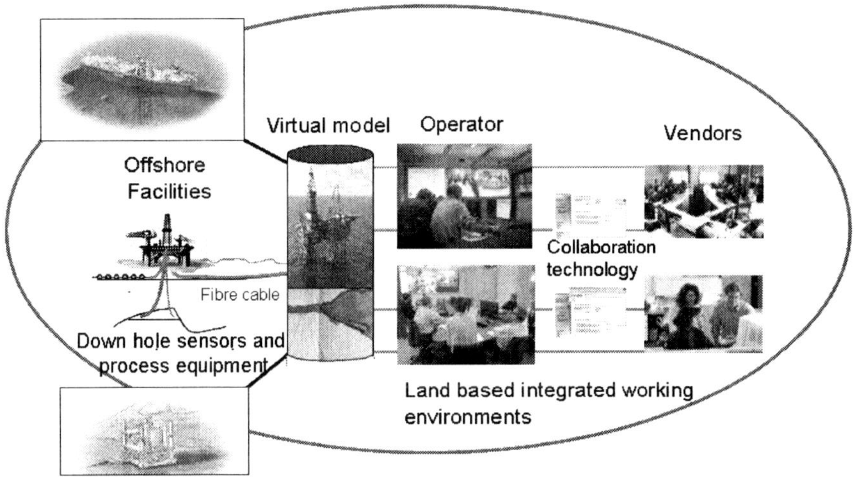

to gather data for production analysis and optimization purposes. Each technical discipline involved should address its work in a total value chain perspective.

There are at least three major communities of knowing involved in production optimization: reservoir engineers, production engineers and process engineers. These three communities inhabit different parts of the oil and gas value chain and are located onshore. The reservoir engineers are responsible for updates of the subsurface model when production output changes the properties of the reservoir. The production community is responsible from reservoir, meaning to maximize the production from the existing wells to the separators (separate oil-gas-water) on the platform. The process community is responsible for modelling the flow from the separation facilities on the platform onwards. While the reservoir models have a long time constant (usually changes in drainage strategy take months/years to show effect), changes in process and production are almost instantaneous. Reservoir management aims at optimizing the reservoir performance over the life of the field, while production management is optimizing the well production and injection, production network and process facilities on a day-to-day basis. Daily process control and optimization is handled by offshore control room operators. These offshore operators are monitoring technical systems and equipment, critical issues related to safety, emergency and process shut-down alarms and minute-to-minute production. In sum, these communities need tight integration and coordination since their activities are closely connected. Sufficient perspective taking is vital for their work. Much of the perspective taking here is based on sharing the material that is suitable for the purpose of computer and simulation models. At the same time the companies rely upon specialist skills of each community of knowing to address specific challenges in various parts of the reservoir to the market value chain. Strong perspective making is therefore of vital importance to develop long-term community robustness.

Most oil companies have initiatives that address these challenges (Hepsø, 2006). This is also the setting for the case in one of Statoil's assets. Before the 3-month pilot, the production engineers were located in cell offices and worked in a traditional functional organization. Their focus was on individual wells and production according to overall schedules and plans. The operating limits of the wells and networks of wells were not systematically challenged. Few arenas for collaboration existed and sharing of information within and across communities was complicated. The physical layout of their cell offices made collaboration difficult. Production engineers had poor contact with other communities of knowing due to lack of spaces for collaboration. They also had limited access to real-time data. During the pilot they moved to a collaboration room and had increased access to real-time production data. The collaboration room had workstations with PCs, whiteboards, Smartboards, large visual displays and telephone-videoconferencing facilities; see Figure 2. The room was supposed to be used by the asset during drilling operations but was 'borrowed' by the production engineers during the pilot period; see Figure 2.

During the pilot the space became the day-to-day work environment for the production engineers. It was soon domesticated as their space. The production engineers in the asset were a group of young people that took interest in sitting and working together. They argued it was a more social and fun way of working where they could learn from and get help from their colleagues. Here they could discuss their ideas, conduct analytic work among peers much easier than before. As a rookie production engineer argued: "My learning curve has increased substantially during these months, after we moved together. We get along very well". The work also boosted the confidence of production engineers. In many assets this is a rookie job with poor status. The room had separate PC workstations that were made available for process engineers and reservoir engineers. These two disciplines were not to sit in the collaboration room continuously but come to the room when their skills were needed. The intention was that they should also sit in the room permanently to have ongoing discussions with the production engineers. To a certain extent this happened but they also had obligations towards their own communities and much production engineering work is not relevant for reservoir engineers. Process engineers had the same obligations and also served several assets.

The following two examples describe the role of this new shared information space and some of the implications this information space had for knowledge-intensive work in these communities of knowing. I relate this to diversity and identity. Here I present how the 'shared CIS' is enacted

Figure 2. Layout of the collaboration room (CIS) during the pilot

in practice. To address this I look at perspective making/taking, what is shared, (meaning the characteristics of the objects shared in the CIS) and the consequences for identity among the communities of knowing. The first example is within the production engineers' community of knowing and represents the way the CIS was used for perspective making among peers. The second example shows the interaction of the production engineers with the two other heterogeneous communities of knowing and represents CIS usage in relation to perspective taking.

THE COLLABORATION ROOM AS CIS ENABLING PERSPECTIVE MAKING IN THE COMMUNITY OF PRODUCTION ENGINEERS

The production engineers located in the CIS have close to fifty wells to follow up, 30 of these wells are producers and the rest are injectors. The injectors are used to pump water back into the reservoir to keep up the reservoir pressure. Each well in this dispersed network is located at strategic points in the reservoir. Contrary to the belief that an oil reservoir is a homogeneous 'tank of oil' the reservoir is complex with faults splitting it into segments with diverging vertical and horizontal flow conditions. A production engineer explains: "We develop an increased understanding of how wells interact through the production history. The key is to see the wells together since the optimization of one well might lead to loss of overall production given the right circumstances. When doing this evaluation and analysis work we juggle between parameters; temperature, pressure, water production, production rates, gas and availability of equipment in the offshore process plant". They use real-time data that are analysed and aggregated via numerous production engineering software tools to develop this understanding. Important articulation activities to understand this work will involve activities such as the validation of information and data, comparing-contrasting and double checking the information. Different representations are used to develop a useful understanding of data and information before they are applied in their well settings. The main activities of the group are to monitor well performance and flowline performance, diagnose wells with deviating behaviour and monitor water breakthrough in the wells: "When we do this work we are also identifying constraining elements and the effect these elements can have on production vis-à-vis increased well potential, flow restrictions, reservoir drainage strategy and process limitations. We give various types of input to both reservoir engineers and people responsible for running the oil installations operations onshore and offshore". Several morning and ad-hoc coordination meetings are held with various groups onshore and offshore. During these meetings wells are on the agenda and some short and long-term action points are taken back to the community for more detailed analysis or immediate trouble-shooting.

Production optimization has a short time frame, where things can happen very fast. Production engineers need to have a shared situational awareness of what is going on in the whole network of wells so that they are able to take quick action when the performance from the current configuration of wells changes. The CIS eases each individual's ability to share and discuss alternatives with peers. During these discussions, the production engineers use information from very different sources in order to evaluate alternative solutions to a particular complex problem. Production engineers draw on the distributed knowledge of each other and couple encoded information in databases. Visual displays of production data are presented as plots by means of specialist software; see Figure 4. The making of such production and injection plots is more than just perspective making. They also create a shared identity since production engineers favour a particular genre of these shared artefacts made visible for self-reflection; representations favoured by the production engineers and are not used by other communities.

THE COLLABORATION ROOM AS CIS IN ENABLING PERSPECTIVE TAKING BETWEEN HETEROGENEOUS COMMUNITIES OF KNOWING

Other communities of knowing were not present in the collaboration room continuously. The room was quickly regarded as production engineer space and the others regarded themselves as guests. There were also pragmatic reasons for the other communities not being there continuously. Both reservoir engineers and process engineers can work with issues that are of little relevance to production engineers and would distract the situation awareness around the CIS. Let me present some examples that show how collaboration across communities of knowing developed. However, it is necessary to point out that there are stable features that can be denoted as boundary objects or immutable mobiles across the involved disciplines. These are of several types, ranging from naming conventions/standards as those described in Figure 3, espoused work descriptions, minutes of meetings, MS PowerPoint presentations, production and injection plans, Intranet visualization of key asset production data, shared document workspaces and others. These are key objects that ease coordination between the communities of knowing but will not be handled directly in these examples.

During a discussion among production and reservoir engineers in the collaboration space the production challenges from wells in a particular reservoir segment were addressed. A simplified map of a particular part of the reservoir (a segment) was drawn on the Smartboard, see the left-hand part of Figure 3. In this situation, to enable discussion between production and reservoir engineers, the reservoir is simplified into a few but important parameters, of which the most important is pressure. The following details might be complex to understand for the readers, but bear in mind the need to have a representation of the problem and a minimum of shared language or understanding between the domain experts.

The circle in Figure 3 (left) is the bottom-hole pressure (the pressure in the bottom of the well), Qo is the oil rate and WC is water cut in the well. A-54 is an important well in this segment. There were indications of previous unknown flow connections with a nearby water injector A-56. A-54 is part of the I-segment and produces in Åre and lower Tilje; see Figure 3. Åre and Tilje are suitable purpose names to describe layers in the reservoir that represent a particular reservoir depth and sedimentary history. In this situation there is a high water cut in Åre (70%) and the pressure is 20 bar higher than in lower Tilje formation. The oil production (Qo) in the three wells producing in the different formation levels produce from 450 to 900 Sm3/d. After a production logging where measurement equipment was put into the well there was a dramatic increase in water production. They agreed to reduce the reservoir pressure in injector A-56, by reducing the water injection in this well. At the same time they increased the production in A-26 that also produced in the Åre formation. This should reduce the pressure in the Åre formation, move the gas cap in the direction of Tilje and secure drawdown (the lowering of the water level in the reservoir zone).

The subsurface details are not important for our purpose, but production engineers with the help of a reservoir engineer that had the necessary reservoir understanding analysed the connections between the wells A50a, A49, A56, A23) in the I-segment. The communities of knowing shared vital parameters; naming conventions like Åre-Tilje, position of well in segment, flowing connections, pressure, water cut and others. The total relationship among producers and injectors in the segment was addressed, simplified and through perspective taking they were able to get the well back into the same production level again. Still, this perspective taking process was never a fusion of communities of knowing but a pragmatic agreement related to a specific situation that developed in time.

One production engineer said: "I do not know the reservoir model and the uncertainties associated with it. The reservoir engineer has given me some key data that I use in my spreadsheet". This was followed up by a reservoir engineer: "What we share is some overall understanding of the hydrocarbon value-chain. I know my goals and targets. We know where we fit in and what types of data and input we must give the other domains".

Let me now present an example that shows the interaction of the production engineers with the process engineers. After the start-up of well X, pressure support from water injector well Y was increased by the central control room. This led to a higher water cut in well Y. The tail producer well Z was already producing at a high water cut, and the well had no gas lift to maintain its pressure. At the next maintenance turn around on the installation a few weeks ahead, all wells would be shut down for several days. It was anticipated that well Z would not be able to get back on production after the production stop due to severe lift problems. Well X would not be able to drain all the remaining oil from its current position. Well Z was producing at a minimum wellhead pressure (14.6 bar) that was hardly enough to lift the oil into the installation. The process engineer together with the production engineers discussed the possibility of putting the well on low pressure via the test separator. Was it possible to increase the drawdown and thereby accelerate the oil production before the turn around? The idea being put forward by the topside process engineer in collaboration with the production engineer was therefore to route the production from the test separator directly to the 2nd stage separator that could handle wells with lower pressure. The process engineer had previously discussed this possibility with the offshore control room operators, and actions were taken immediately after the idea was raised. The inlet pressure on the 2nd stage separator was 7 bar and wellhead pressure could therefore be reduced by approximately 7 bar. These possibilities between different communities of knowing were available only in a

Figure 3. Two boundary objects that enabled perspective taking between the production engineers and reservoir engineers (left) and process engineers (right)

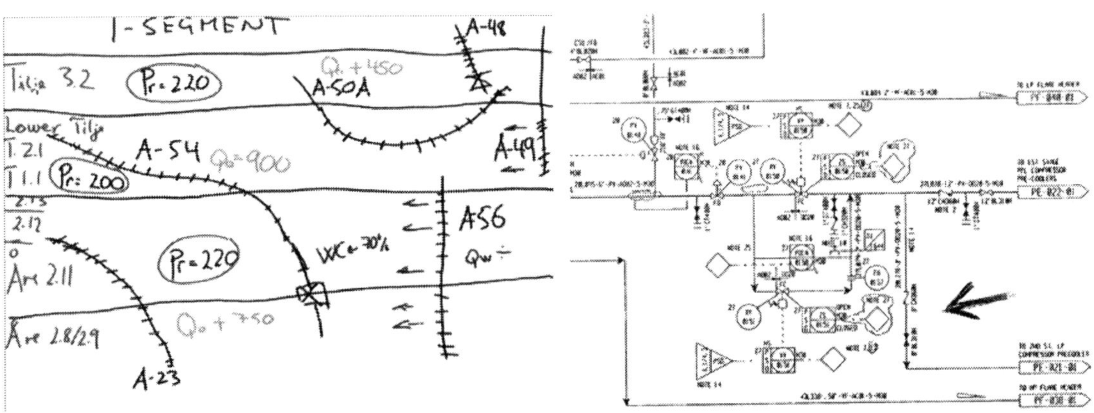

temporary time window and had to be exploited in that period. The production and process engineers discussed the possibility to re-route the well in the process plant. A P&ID-drawing with annotations played an important part in a discussion between the production engineer, the topside process engineer and the offshore control room. The drawing was a systemic flow chart representation of the process facility with the test separator, the first and second stage separation, the piping

Figure 4. Above-left: a drawing of a stratigraphic map of layers and a position of a well comparable to the object in Figure 3. Above-right: a messy seismic or geophysical map of the same structure with graphical annotations. Below: a production engineer plot used to analyse the performance of a well.

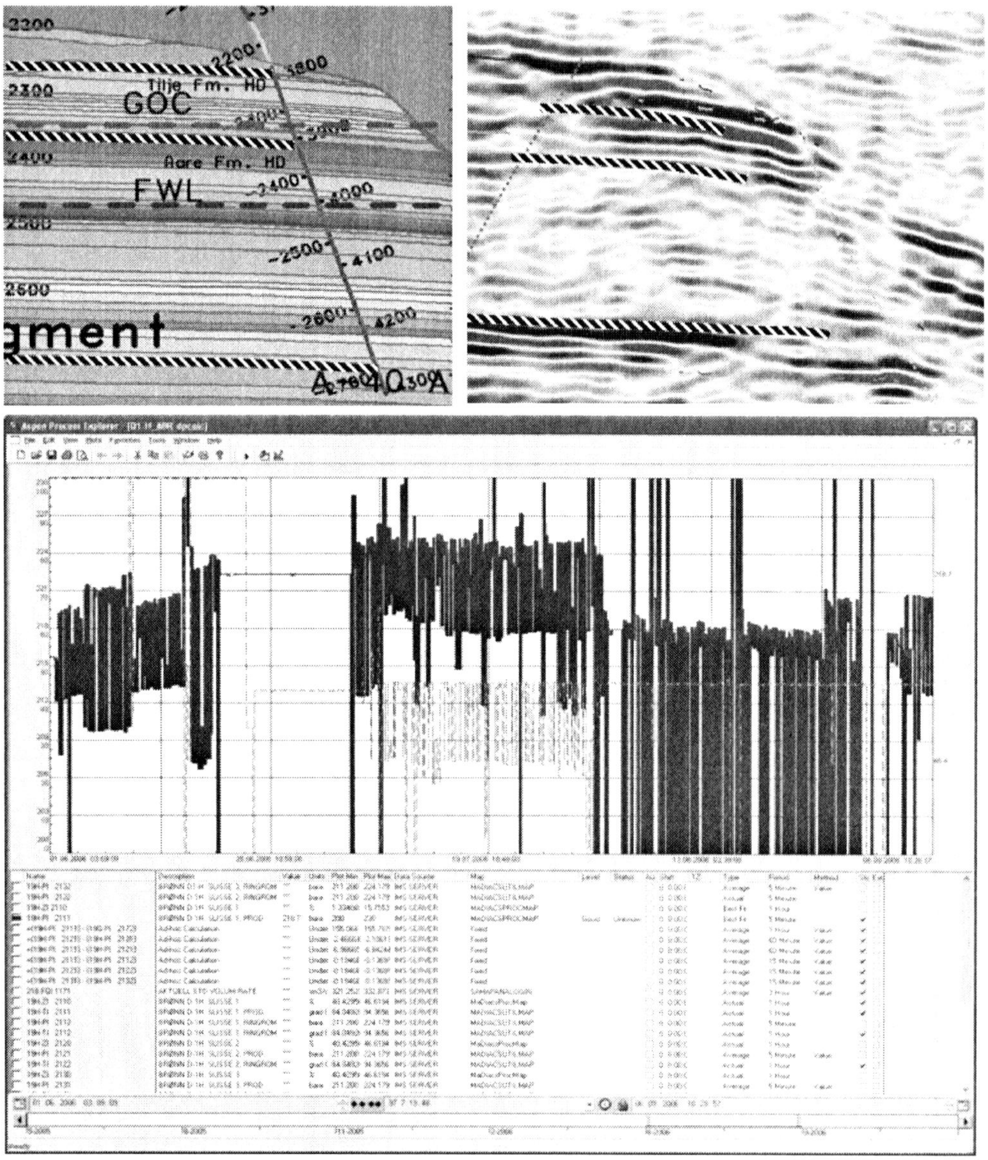

and valves. This P&ID, see Figure 3 (right), was used in a perspective making and taking process between the representatives from the different communities and led to increased production in the available time window. As with the I-segment example the production engineers shared some vital parameters like pressure in the separators, sufficient understanding of the construction of the platform for re-routing via test separator. As in the previous example this was not a fusion of communities but a pragmatic agreement developed because they had to respond to a window of opportunity that only existed for a short time. In both cases compatibility were practical tasks of accomplishment.

The ambition of the engineering community is to have mathematical models that integrate across contexts and communities of knowing. These are large-scale mathematical models that emulate processes from the reservoir to the market. This is not the situation today even though each community can use input data made by another community; "As a production engineer I can use reservoir model data in a spreadsheet during my production analysis. This is still a tiresome process that requires many workarounds between various types of software tools". In this pilot and also in work I have done subsequently, spreadsheets are the 'tool of tools' for all engineers (Hepsø, 2006) since this is the only tool that has the adaptability to match all these divergent needs and expectations. Workarounds with spreadsheets create compatibility.

DISCUSSION OF THE CASE

The subsurface communities of production and reservoir engineers are never able to see the reservoir they assess via their perspective making directly. It is only through calculations, plots and models they see it indirectly and can create an understanding of the reservoir and production performance. Their production and reservoir knowledge is shared via objects that are denoted by attributes that are mainly calculated from measured or modelled data. A goal oriented and pragmatic way of thinking (about what is good enough) guides what type of objects will suffice to discuss the reservoir in each particular situation. A manager gets a different version from the reservoir engineer.

I will end this chapter by considering the implications of this case for common information spaces in relation to information sharing and knowledge management in more general terms. The case shows that the collaboration room does not become a CIS by itself but must be made into a CIS through the active sense-making processes of the communities of knowing. The space in the pilot was originally owned by the drilling community and the production engineers had to domesticate it, fill it with meaning, behavioural appropriateness and cultural expectations – root it in the practice and understanding of their community (Harrison & Dourish, 1996) in order to make it become their own and a part of their identity. Perspective making and perspective taking have been used to understand the development of meaning in these processes and the strategies various communities employ when interacting in such spaces. Our first research question was to address what role such 'shared' information spaces play and some of the implications such information spaces have for knowledge-intensive work: diversity, work relations and identity. We see that the collaboration room filled different functions according to which community of knowing it involved. In this sense it was an aggregated boundary object. Among production engineers it enabled perspective making. It became an arena that enabled the improvement of identity, self-confidence in addition to improving the language, tools and practices of the production engineers. The CIS became 'shared' because it was the language, models, theories of a homogeneous community that were embedded in the interaction and the objects of the CIS. In this community it soon developed into a stabilized configuration.

Basically this type of collaboration room with its objects became a symbol of a new generation of production engineers, their domain with objects and practices. The CIS helped to develop a shared situational awareness of what was going on within production optimization in the asset and was eased by numerous shared objects or immutable objects that helped production engineers in this process: software tools with spreadsheets, plots, models and specialist tools for production management. These were immutable objects with a largely converged meaning since they were developed and used by the same homogeneous community of knowing.

The production engineers' collaboration room (as a CIS in relation to the heterogeneous groups of reservoir engineers or the process engineers) represents a sharedness of a different kind. It also shows how diversity between various communities of knowing was handled in collaboration where mutable mobiles enabled different temporary forms of collaboration and sharing. The I-segment sketch on the left in Figure 3 is only used in perspective taking on the spur of the moment, and the collaboration room (as a CIS vis-à-vis these two communities) has very few stable boundary objects. In this setting the shared CIS is a short-lived arrangement that constantly needs to be re-negotiated from situation to situation. It represents a short-lived common ground for decision making in the cross-disciplinary team of engineers. It is important to recognize that this work has to be undertaken each time. Ambiguities are seldom sorted out once and for all (Rolland, Hepsø & Monteiro, 2006). As the collaboration room was used by the production engineers for perspective making, the space in this context also fulfilled perspective taking. The different communities of knowing used the collaboration room to constitute a shared context in which a wide range of heterogeneous information could be interpreted and improvised. Even though computers were used in the same way during the meeting it was mainly general tools like spreadsheets, MS Word documents and MS PowerPoint presentations that were in use. They hardly used the specialist tools in discussions with other communities of knowing. As one production engineer said: "EXCEL is king". The CIS in these examples never achieved a closure in the sense that it established a common understanding once and for all between the heterogeneous communities. When production engineers discussed issues with reservoir or process engineers they all had to improvise to make their representations less complex. Some important information and uncertainties will almost inevitably be lost in the process and the participants will get ambiguous information and representations. However, the examples showed that the collaboration room provided a shared arena for discussion and provided an additional context to representations that made it easier to interpret the phenomenon they were discussing.

CONCLUSION

If the communication between the different communities of knowing is so temporary, full of ambiguity and re-negotiated from situation to situation, why is the heterogeneous organization as stable as it seems to be? The communities seem to be able to maintain their identity and community of knowing and at the same time meet the business objectives. The organization has boundary objects and organizational mechanisms and systems across the communities. This heterogeneous environment is torn on the one hand between the challenge of maintaining their own separate identity, skills and competence as production, process and reservoir engineers. On the other hand, they must develop a kind of 'common' understanding to be able to fulfil the tasks of their formal organization and live with the management demands of having a proper 'business' value-chain understanding. The primary goal is always to boost existing oil and gas resources. Such pragmatism is also fundamental to understand the processes of perspective taking. It not only for academic reasons they try to understand the perspective of the reservoir engineer. It is also an obligation vis-à-vis their company as employees of Statoil. Mol's (2003, p.72) practical accomplishment presented in the introduction is undertaken by perspective taking and making put under pressure by deliverables, measurements and organizational management systems. The communities share each others' output but they black-box the processes associated with creating the output since it is outside their functional domain. In most cases this is a practical accomplishment that works. The communities of reservoir, production and process engineers are expert and domain focused and highly knowledge intensive. At the same time they manage to take commercial interests into consideration across these functional domains when needed. I have presented a case from the oil industry but collaboration within other knowledge-intensive industries will most likely have the same challenges. They will have to handle the same perspective making/taking processes among domain experts. They must address what needs to be shared and is stable and contrast them with the temporal features of the collaboration processes.

REFERENCES

Bannon, L. (2000). Understanding Common Information Spaces in CSCW. Paper presented at the Workshop on Cooperative Organisation of Common Information Spaces. Technical University of Denmark. Available at http://dmm.cti.dtu.dk/position/bannon.pdf.

Bannon, L., & Bødker, S. (1997). Constructing common information spaces. In Proceedings of the 5th European Conference on CSCW (ECSCW'97) Dordrecht/Kluver, (pp. 81-96).

Bertelsen, O., & Bødker, S. (2001). Cooperation in Massively Distributed Information Spaces. In Proceedings of the European Conference on Computer Supported Cooperative Work (ECSCW'01), Dordrecht/Kluver, (pp. 1-17).

Bijker, W. E. (1993). Do not despair: there is life after constructivism. Science, Technology, & Human values, 18(1), 113-138.

Boland, R. J., & Tenkasi, R. V. (1995). Perspective Making and Perspective Taking in Communities of Knowing. Organization Science, 6(4), 350-372.

Bossen, C. (2002). The Parameters of Common Information Spaces: The Heterogeneity of Cooperative Work at a Hospital Ward. In Proceedings of Computer Supported Cooperative Work (CSCW'02), (pp. 176-185). New York: ACM Press.

Ciborra, C. U. (Ed) (2000). From Control to Drift: The Dynamics of Corporate Information Infrastructures. Oxford: Oxford University Press.

Davenport, T. H. (2005). Thinking for a living: how to get better performances and results from knowledge workers. Cambridge: Harvard Business School Press.

Erickson, T., &. Kellog, W. A. (2003). Social Translucence: Using Minimalist Visualisations of Social Activity to Support Collective Interaction. In K. Höök, D. Benyon, & A. J. Munro (Eds.), Designing Information Spaces: The Social Navigation Approach (pp. 17-42). Berlin: Springer.

Gasser, L. (1986). The Integration of Computing and Routine Work. ACM Transactions on Office Information Systems 4(3), 205-225.

Greenwood, D., & Levin, M. (2006). Introduction to Action Research. London: Sage.

Hammer, M., & Champy, T. (1993). Reengineering the Corporation: a manifesto for business revolutions. New York: Nicolas Brealey.

Harrison, S., & Dourish, P. (1996). Re-Placing Space: The Roles of Place and Space in Collaboration Systems. In Proceedings of the CSCW 96, New York: ACM Press.

Hepsø, V. (2006). When are we going to address organizational robustness and collaboration as something else than a residual factor? Society of Petroleum Engineers-paper SPE-100712.

Laet, M., & Mol, A. (2000). The Zimbabwe Bush Pump: Mechanics of a fluid technology. Social Studies of Science, 30(2), 225-263.

Latour, B. (1987). Science in Action. Cambridge: Harvard University Press.

Law, J. (2003). Ladbroke grove, or how to thing about failing systems. http://www.comp.lancs.ac.uk/sociology/papers/lawladbroke-grove-failing-systems.pdf Revised December 2003, (last accessed December 2004).

Law, J., & Singleton, W. (2005). Objects lessons. Organization, 12(3), 331-355.

Mol, A. M. (2003). The Body Multiple: Ontology in Medical Practice. New York: Duke University Press.

OLF (2005). Integrated Work Processes: Future work processes on the Norwegian continental shelf. On-line: http://www.olf.no/?28867.pdf.

Rolland, K., Hepsø, V., & Monteiro, E. (2006). (Re)conceptualizing Common Information Spaces Across Heterogeneous Contexts: im/mutable mobiles and imperfection. Proceedings of the CSCW 2006 New York: ACM Press.

Schmidt, K., & Bannon, L. (1992). Taking CSCW seriously - Supporting articulation work. Computer Supported Cooperative Work (CSCW), 1(1), 7-40.

Star, S. L., & Griesemer, J. R. (1989). Institutional Ecology, Translations, and Boundary Objects: Amateurs and Professionals in Berkeley's Museum of Vertebrate Zoology, 1907-1939. Social Studies of Science, 19(3), 387-420.

KEY TERMS

Boundary Object: Concept intended to describe information used in different ways by different communities. Such objects are plastic, interpreted differently across communities but has enough immutable content to maintain integrity.

Common Information Space (CIS): Virtual or actual space constituted for people that collaborate whether co-present or distributed in time and space. A CIS contains shared information resources for those that participate in the activities of the space and facilitate their work.

Communities of Knowing: A particular group or collection of people that shares a similar educational background, language, interest and a practice

Immutable Mobiles: An object or artefact that moves around but keeps its shape, like a map or a newspaper

Perspective Making and Taking: Concepts used to characterize the learning processes within and across various communities of knowing

Shared Situational Awareness: Shared perceptions of environmental elements among a group of people within a given context of time and space, the comprehension of the elements meaning, and the projection of their status in the near future.

Chapter XVIII
Creativity and Control in IT Professionals' Communities

Agnieszka Postuła
Uniwersytet Warszawski, Poland

ABSTRACT

This chapter presents and discusses two factors – creativity and control – which correspond to every organizational reality. IT specialists' professional communities are used as an example because of characteristic relationships between their members and their attitude to work. The chapter describes how combination of these two phenomena may build or destroy organizations. There is also an explanation of specific relations between IT professionals and beginning of further discussion based on these relationships, as well as analysis of consequences of inappropriate management practices. Creativity and control are presented as features of every common company with their special roles in organization. Also, main characteristics of well-organized practical communities are shown.

INTRODUCTION

The reason why IT specialists were chosen as the best example of the main topic of this article seems quite obvious. Every IT specialist – regardless of certain specialization – should present at least a bit of creativity in his work. IT specializations are based on scientific knowledge developed during processes of creating and innovating. Interviewees mentioned that their work may be compared to some kind of artistic activity with regard to a need of creating skills, open minded state and improvisation. However, IT professionals are ascribed in a certain reality – different organizations operating in various branches. They are embedded in complicated organizational networks which they developed themselves (Latour, 1987). The need of control is one of the network's features. Especially in bigger, more complex organizations this demand is truly justified. Combination of these two factors would be the topic of this paper.

This chapter consists of few connected parts. The first one considers methodological notes and theoretical background (IT professionals' communities, creativity and control). Then, selected field material is presented, where IT professionals are the main actors of the stories. After empirical part discussion follows.

METHODOLOGY

Data presented in this paper are the result of an ethnographic project conducted in Poland in 2002-2004. There were two levels of gathering field material. The first one was concentrated on exploration of a medium company producing business software "to the client's needs" and took about half a year. The second stage was based on interviews with IT specialists working in several organizations. The research on this level embraced workers from bigger and smaller software companies, international corporations and IT departments in organizations from various branches.

The first step lasted about half a year and considered deep ethnographic inquiry of organizational reality, the second one was a continuation of plots revealed in the first part. The research method was based on open-ended, non-structured interviews, mainly ethnographic (unstructured and unstandardized) which allowed interlocutors to express thoughts freely. Other methods were 10 hours of non-participant observations on the first level and shadowing (2 working weekdays) on the second. Triangulation of data and methods was used to increase the richness of data, as well as to add other perspectives to the study (Konecki, 2000). Data triangulation was based on using data from different organizations (on the second level). Methodological triangulation was based on using several methods (interviews, observations, shadowing) for investigating one single issue.

All conversations were conducted in a form as open as possible, and often informally (during observations or shadowing). Interlocutors took up topics themselves, without or with only few general directions from the researcher. Thus, the gathered material reflects the topics and notions particularly important for workers, and is not meant to fit into any prior theoretical framework. All field material was analyzed and interpreted through categorizations, close to grounded theory manner. As a result, the categories, among which control and creativeness at work, emerged.

In order to keep being open to the field, stay within the "anthropological frame of mind" and to follow the social structures as perceived by the informants, researcher used both of the two typical methods of interviewees selection : "contact person" method helped in finding new interlocutors and in general reconnaissance of the organization, while "snowball" method was used to extend circles of interlocutors and deepen the topics.

The studied interviewees come from 13 companies, from various departments and represent many IT specializations (mostly programmers, but also designers, administrators, IT consultants and others). All, however, identified themselves with software engineering profession. In total, 34 interviews were conducted (18 at the first stage and 14 at the second). The research material includes over 400 pages of transcriptions and over 50 pages of field notes.

The research problem of the study concerned the systemization of organizational roles played by IT professionals in their job and the analysis of the social IT professionals' reality. On the basis of the research results a model of the social construction of the IT profession was presented.

The author was particularly interested in the roles played by IT professionals in the organizations within their everyday activities as well as their job attitudes and relationships between professionals in IT branch. The purpose of the thesis was to find a tentative answer to the question of how the role of IT professional is constructed, what elements the role consists of, and what factors have the major impact on its creating process.

Besides addressing the research questions, this project resulted in revealing and understanding a typical IT specialists' work day, including their attitude to control issue in the organizations and its relation to creativeness.

IT PROFESSIONALS' COMMUNITIES

IT specialists are members of a specific professional community, which means that it has certain features distinguishing them from other groups or communities. Term "professional community" was developed by Van Maanen and Barley (1984) who defined their approach that way:

We define occupational community as a group of people who consider themselves to be engaged in the same sort of work; whose identity is drawn from the work; who share with one another a set of values, norms and perspectives that apply to but extend beyond work related matters; and whose relationships meld work and leisure. (ibidem: 287)

Professional community considers more specialized (relative to a job) work teams. Also, it is defined differently than an occupation. Precisely

[p]rofession [...] refers to a broad stratum of relatively prestigious but quite varied occupations whose members have all had some kind of a higher education and who are identified more by their educational status than by their specific occupational skills. (Freidson, 1994)

Therefore, professional communities provide environment for IT professionals to share the body of knowledge of their profession such as similar working cultures, problem perceptions, problem-solving techniques, professional values, and behavior. Professional community helps to support IT specialists' practices, and helps them in addressing the uncertainty that accompanies non-routine working. The community is characterized by numerous factors from which confidence and freedom are of the greatest significance. Confidence understood as a relationship of reliance which is based on honesty, truth, friendship and common rules. Freedom is considered rather as a lack of control (or minimum control). These two factors connected together give basic background for creative work for IT professionals.

However, in this paper author will not concentrate on differences between terms "occupation" and "profession", thus they will be used alternatively (Freidson, 1994).

CREATIVITY AND/VERSUS CONTROL

Creativity is a specific feature describing many IT specializations. IT problems that occur in the system or challenges of building a new one need permanent presence of creativity. Creativity is understood as "the human impulse to organize, but to improvise rather than to locate, divide and control" (Linstead & Mullarkey, 2003). It is extremely important to have a different perspective of seeing things in programmers work (as well as in many other IT specializations). Solving system problems requires using imagination (Morgan, 2001). Moreover, imagination and creativity should accompany every team work. Making an IT system is predominantly based on working together in a team of people representing different specializations, also professions. This is typical feature especially for project teams constructing IT systems. Each member of the team should be "prepared to be wrong" in a certain moment to develop both system and a group work. They have to be ready to deal with mistakes and be as open as possible to enter new areas, gain new ideas. In some kind of way IT professional should behave like an artist who designs pieces of work with wide open mind.

Project manager's challenge is to guide all team members in a proper direction. He or she should plan work precisely and definitely leave the space for play (Strannegård & Friberg, 2001) which is the factor stimulating creativity. Play is the condition which enables IT specialists to work innovatively and think openly. Both features are connected with creativity. Requirement of innovativeness and creativeness on the one hand as well as managing on the other are the reason why IT professionals need to be controlled but in a very unique way with a wide space for entertainment (which means flexible time schedule among others) at work. So, the bosses' role is very significant here.

The second element described here – control – has been discussed widely in numerous publications on organizational and management theories. It seems quite obvious that first who touched and developed issue of control in organizations was Henri Fayol (1987). He proposed 5 main functions of management among which controlling found its place. Another classic author was Max Weber (1922/2002) who stated that power (which lied in the area of his main interests) is principally exemplified within organizations by the process of control. Weber outlined the characteristics of bureaucracy (which he explored) among which he enumerates:

- a clearly defined hierarchy of offices: organization system of supervision based on clear levels of authority. Each official knows whom to report to with specified rights of control and complaint procedures;
- a strict, systematic discipline and control of the official's work.

Analyzing the concept of bureaucracy Weber had idealistic assumptions. He omitted some of the negative consequences of his system, like relation between control and creativity.

Later, modernists added a lot of ideas and research results to the issue of control. Arnold Tannenbaum (1968, cited by Hatch, 1997/2002) said that "organization means control" (p.323), it is something more that Fayol's organizational function. Social organization is a particular system of human interactions which needs to be managed. Processes of control help to minimize idiosyncratic behavior and keep it in order to rational plan of the organization. The cybernetic model assumes that current state should be compared to desired state and any discrepancy between them has to be adjusted. It reveals one problem: control seems to evoke negative reaction of people and it's a threat to innovativeness and creativity. Kathleen Eisenhardt (1985, cited by Hatch, 1997/2002) – representing agency theory – is the one who enumerated strategies of control. The problem of uncertainty with reference to control was analyzed for the first time. She showed that more complex and interesting works should be controlled in different way (information systems, additional management levels, observation of behavior) than routine, easy works (only observation may give a lot of data). The third modernist theory represented by Ouchi (1979, cited by Hatch, 1997/2002) approaches issue of control as "attaining cooperation between different units which has partially divergent goals" (p. 332). Again, the problem of consequences of controlling people at work is not analyzed enough. All these theories are concentrated on organizations as a whole. They don't perceive an individual worker as a subject of important discussion on control.

Finally, interpretivists – as Kunda and Van Maanen (1989) – started to notice the role of single worker in the organizations. They discussed the impact of culture in the process of control. Paradox of "cultural control" is being revealed, which means that culture is controlling people, not vice versa. Czarniawska-Joerges (1988) deepens the issue settling dilemma of autonomy and control. She is confronting two sides of organizational reality. As she states, autonomy leads to creativity and flexibility, but also unpredictability, on the one hand; control leads to predictability, but also kills creativity, on the other.

Personally, I also find interesting Drucker's (1993/1999) approach where he uses interpretation of Schumpeter. Drucker treats phenomena of organizing as a destabilizing factor, especially in postcapitalistic society. He argues that one of the organizational functions is using knowledge for working – tools, products, processes and actions – and it has to be prepared to continuous change. It has to be organized for innovation. And Schumpeter states that innovation is a "creative destruction". Thus, organization has to be prepared to reject things that are established – services, products, processes and relations etc. – everything what is well-known, comfortable and what we get used to. As Drucker says, knowledge cannot be separated from quick changes and these are the foundations of contemporary organization. And as the case shows, this is also the reality of IT professionals' communities.

Here, I will mention two more perspectives on control, both developing Weber's analysis in a different way. Hochschild's (1983) approach assumes that control exists in two forms: positional and personal. First one considers traditional working class and technical sector of middle class, second one – upper and middle class and new working class. The aim of social control in the first group is related to behavior of workers, in the second – to the feelings, thoughts and intentions. IT specialists' profession distinctly refers to the second one. That means that control in IT companies should be different from that one we know from a classic theories. That is why so many complex factors (mentioned in this chapter) play important role in IT professionals' work.

In some kind of way Senge (1990/2006) is using this approach to write about management nature. In his opinion management process may be rational or emotional. The force driving people to do something is power. Bosses are able to do everything just to be powerful. But "being on the top" of the organizational structure doesn't mean to have power and to be able to control people effectively. Senge calls it "illusion of being powerful". Bosses are giving orders, workers are following them but this is not the same as being powerful. I think, this phenomenon considers IT specialists very strictly. They have bosses as any worker in every other organization but still it doesn't mean they are controlling anything. So, the role of the boss in IT companies is very important from the managerial point of view.

After short historical view, we may try to get closer to understand IT professionals' communities. As it was mentioned, every team work requires control to a certain degree. But the question is how far control should reach in every company, in different branches or professional communities? IT specialists are definitely kind of professionals who should be driven by a wise manager in a proper direction. In this case – concerning IT specialists – proper means connected with play, with large space for freedom and being together with other community members. Working in groups allows to exchange thoughts freely and care for innovative ideas. Notes from the field would be drawn for showing the example of specific organization of certain company where work and play get similar status. Here, control is perceived as an intrinsic element of working time and it relies on preparing by a (project) manager comfortable place and space for IT specialist. This should be an implication of Foucault's (1969/2002) theory about controlling time and space at work.

Whereas outsiders may be confused with IT professionals' work and behavior, programmers are happy with the essence of their job. The asset of programmers' work reality is constructing new systems, new products done according to what the client wants. Creativity is the reason why IT specialists cherish this profession so high.

Creativeness. When there is creation, production in it, it's great. And such work gives pleasure. You have a chance to create something new. It's not schematic, something new emerges. [...] when someone works in one department, you have to move him to another [...] to avoid a situation when he gets crazy. [...] I'm working in a place where every moment brings new challenges, something is changing, something new appears, new ideas arise and we have one more new project. And this is great. Every day brings something new. You never know what are you gonna get. (LMI)

There is just one problem with creating new systems and implementing new ideas. After finishing the system it is extremely difficult for IT specialists to give the project away. Besides implementing the project some of them may be "shelved" or "thrown away" as interlocutors said. Sometimes systems are not used by the client because of many reasons, such as client's retreating or – which is rare – system is mismatched with a client's needs, outdated system is too old to implement etc. In such cases all creativity and work seems useless. Most of IT professionals describe this situation as the most predicaments. The citation below shows the IT specialists' approach.

I think that parts of IT systems created by us are like our children. I like it and I'm watching how it works, and I'm happy when it works properly, when not – I'm angry. I'm attached to it somehow. It's not like that I can throw it out and go away doing something completely different. Of course I can do it theoretically but I feel attached to each project and that's why I prefer the system to turn out all right. (NKI)

Bosses' Role

Part of programmers' working reality is the role of their bosses (mainly project managers) who have power to control. They are not only simple managers but also some kind of mentors for them. They are planning work, they secure the place and remain even the best friends for the programmers sometimes. Bosses have power to manage level of control and thus influence workers' creativity.

Project managers state that designing is a theoretical activity to a large degree. Programming begins with the long process of planning each activity and project structure. Every team member is a part of a project and takes decisions in a long process of discussion. Project managers claim that they are trying to avoid imposing rigid roles and forcing own ideas in place of common problem solving. Such approach helps to develop creativity and encourage workers to reveal their ideas openly. Moreover, it may positively influence the relationships between team members. Therefore, project managers' role at this initial stage is often reduced only to monitoring and planning actions.

Actually, now I'm mainly controlling everything to be right – unfortunately it is expanding now – and I have to care about everything, remember that this should be done, here I should take a look from aside because when someone is writing this front-end – that is everything you can see – not everyone has the sense, [...] so I have to take decision what would be easier, and also plan some shows [...] for the clients, listen to his comments, to his needs and his reflection so that should be like that and this should be different... (LHS)

Often, project managers take active part in project execution . Preparing a project consists mainly of programming and construing parts of the system. These activities are not a strict job of the mangers but many of them strive for programming (even if they are not working as a programmer). Career path is the reason of this situation. Most of the managers who started their careers with programming cannot fully abstain from doing it while climbing up the organizational structure. Interlocutors who already became managers state that programming in spite of its boredom and routine – as some of them believe – is the most interesting and creative activity in IT professionals' work. Only lack of time at work may interrupt following that path.

Sometimes I also deal with programming. Mainly the project manager – at least in my opinion – should be a designer of the system. He shouldn't only be a boss but he also has to think about the general view. Sometimes he should do the small things like technical pieces of the system. (RBL)

IMPLICATIONS AND CONCLUSION

IT specialists constitute specific professional community which is characterized by high level of flexibility in taking upon professional roles. Certainly, these roles should be related to actor's specialization. Such an approach conduces work team activity and stimulates entrepreneurial attitudes. During realization of the project there is a lot of space for taking actions freely and the main actor (see Latour, 1987) is not (should not be) gendarme/policeman who imposes certain roles but rather a supervisor who negotiates these roles with other actors. Like Streatfield (2001) states, conversation is a self-organizing phenomenon in which meaning emerges. This is the most efficient way of behavior which doesn't cause conflicts and misunderstandings. This approach leaves enough space for organizing time in a project by all actors which allows them for adaptation of social role to the individual predispositions (see Foucault, 1969/2002). Thanks to this, entrepreneurial and creative actions are possible (Hjorth, 2005). All these factors (simplicity in social role taking, entrepreneurship, creative activity) are connected together with one more element – often enumerated during interviews – IT organizations' atmosphere. Interlocutors put emphasis on shaping such organizational culture which favors activating work creativeness and efficiency. It refers to Streatfield (2001). Author is naming elements significant to the professional culture and calling them patterns. Patterns are about relationships and they emerge in conversations and actions. Therefore, they have to form and change continually through these activities. Moreover, there have to be several actors taking part in organizing in the process of making patterns. That is why IT professionals' communities are so proper example to explain such relationships. IT specialists need place and space for exchanging thoughts and this is community which allows this process to take place.

As it was described above, creativity is inherent feature of IT specialists and their organizations. Now, the question is how to stimulate creativity with simultaneous control which is also an important element in each social community. Control should be cautious and fitted to the organization type and style of its members (Hochschild, 1983). IT type organizations needs just little positional control (of course depending on how large the company is) and therefore flat structure. Personal control is much more important because it creates specific organizational climate. Members of such organizations are IT specialists who prefer to work in a certain culture. There are some more crucial factors which should be considered from the management point of view. One of them is stadium of organizational life. On each stage different elements dominate and cause crisis, if organization is not well- managed. Entrepreneurial stage, which seems to be suited the best for IT professionals, is on the very beginning of the organizational life cycle. It means that young IT organizations have a great chance to develop at that stage and care for all the members who desire innovation and creativeness at work. Especially small and medium IT companies which develop very dynamically have the greatest possibilities to attract attention of young programmers and other young IT university graduates. Young IT workers may find in these companies anticipated work conditions – physically and psychologically comfortable environment – and they may build professional relationships. Young IT specialists have a chance to develop practical skills, knowledge and relationships. Moreover, their entrepreneurial attitude may flourish thanks to favorable conditions: lots of new challenges, little limits from the management, boss concession (and understanding the need) for high creativity at work. These conditions allow for taking an advantage of young IT professionals' dynamic attitude in a process of acquiring new clients. This directly leads to strengthening the organization's position on the market. High range and variety of clients gives the organization opportunity to gather the experience and practicing skills. That's how IT specialists have possibility to build base of knowledge which is the most important factor in their profession (Abbott, 1988, MacDonald, 1995). Thus, at the entrepreneurial stage of organizational life cycle this is the mutual benefit for all organization's members.

On the next stages of organizational life cycle other elements influence company's development. Leadership crisis should form more systematized management group. Centralized authority may bear fruits of concentration on goals. Direction of organizational development is then more clear and comprehensible for the workers. It may cause better integrity of organizational work teams. That is why after leadership crisis collectivity stage follows, where IT professionals still may have a chance to develop entrepreneurial postures (on the higher level of cooperation). Even if organization is growing and more workers join the company everything stays under management's control. Control is needed for managing bigger organization on the one hand, but it causes misunderstandings and situation when workers do not keep up with execution of supervisors' decisions, on the other. Moreover, IT professionals generally do not like to take managerial roles. There may be even lack of workers on executive posts in some programming organizations. Work teams prefer to have bosses who are former programmers. Interlocutors claim that it is making the communication process easier and increases mutual understanding. Thus, the problem of management is to find team manager with a certain predispositions who may control the group of IT specialists. One of the greatest challenges of the boss may be persuading subordinates to necessary changes in organization. It is difficult task because IT specialists do not like to change anything in their work life. The biggest problem may be initiating any change slenderizing the organizational structure. More hierarchical levels disturb IT specialists' work order valuing individualism and creativeness. That is why it is difficult to develop IT company on this stage of organizational life cycle. Too high centralization and too strong ordered rules may lead organization to another crisis – autonomy. The main challenge for the management is to reduce control. This crisis may be solved by delegating decision processes and entering the next stage which is delegation. Decentralization process lasts until the need of control integration reveals. These are the processes which do not attract attention of IT professionals. Matters of power and control are not interesting for them. Main goal of IT specialists is work under the supremacy of manager (desirable IT specialist). Similarly to stage of collective action the stage of delegation takes rather little time in IT companies. Then the crisis of control follows manifesting itself with numerous schedules and regulations which allow the organization to enter the formalization stage. As it was mentioned earlier, IT specialists do not like to stick to the formal, written rules. They prefer to create the informal rules of comfort, while working by themselves. That is why not every IT professional may work in the company on that stage of organizational life cycle. It is very possible that strong crisis

Figure 1. Priorities in IT specialist profession in organization outside the IT branch

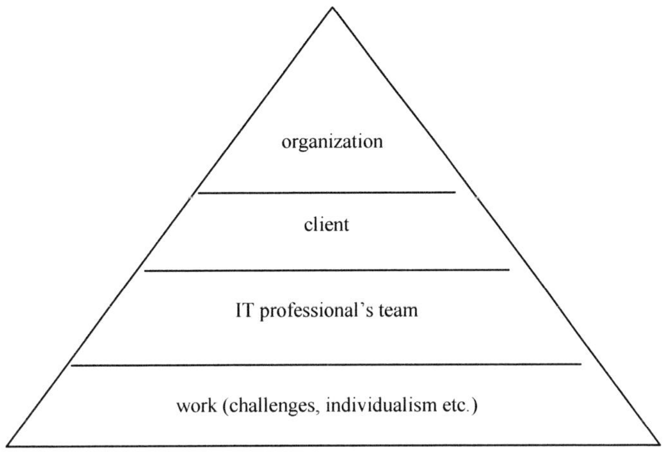

may happen in IT companies. IT professionals are more able to open resistance than obedience applied to incomprehensible or redundant rules. If organization is able to survive this crisis it may enter very useful stage of cooperation. Company starts organizing itself, work teams find their place and all factors tend to effectiveness. Trust and cooperation become the crucial characteristics. For IT professionals it is a very conducive stage because it allows them for natural (the most comfortable) working style and gives a chance for further development and efficiency improvement. Highly valued entrepreneurial (creative) postures are developing.

Thus, on every stage of organizational life cycle mangers of IT companies should analyze which factors are the most important and what hierarchy is the best for preparing the best conditions for workers. Combination of creativity and control should fit in organizational life and favor culture of efficiency and cooperation.

Managers in IT companies should carefully scrutinize priorities of their workers. They are completely different for IT professionals hired in organizations outside the IT branch and for those working in software companies where IT professionals constitute the majority of employees. Priorities of IT specialists in the first type of organizations are illustrated in the form of pyramid:

On the top of the pyramid – on the first place of importance priorities – is an organization (organizational role) and an IT professional's affiliation to the certain group (IT department or project team) and the position. A little bit lower in this hierarchy is a client who places orders for IT systems or another IT products or services. A client is an actor who allows IT specialists to play their social role in the environment. In the organizations outside the IT branch those can be orders from marketing, sales, financial and other departments. Those can be also fixed orders related to regular organizational activity. Organization and client are the two most important factors which influence the quality of IT professional's work and his global organizational status. Below, in the pyramid there is a team which helps IT professional to finalize all tasks and other workers needs. Only at the bottom of the pyramid there is work of IT professional, its quality, adaptation to ways of doing work, accounting individual needs of IT specialist. Research results show that it is an extreme ineffective division for the employees as well as for the organization which rely on productivity of its employees. It is variance with professional role of IT specialists, what is at the first place in hierarchy of relevance (see figure 1). Priorities in system of IT professionals' needs and values should be placed in reverse order. That composes opposite pyramid of IT professionals' needs. Such a system shows how much time and social space is dedicated to each element. It means that top of the pyramid is not only the most important but it takes majority of time and attention of an IT specialist.

This system is distinctive for software companies, where individual needs and predispositions such as free working hours, entertainment during the breaks (Strannegård & Friberg, 2001), physical environment etc. occupy first place in the hierarchy of priorities. This gives worker greater job satisfaction and allows organization for taking advantage of the workers' productivity. Pyramid shows that software companies allow IT specialists working in favorable conditions. That is why the work is placed on the top, which means caring about IT professionals' physical and psychological comfort. It embraces good arrangement of hardware at workplaces as well as preparing work environment in the best possible way. IT professionals are occupational group which prefers to act in a selected time of a day without harrying up too much. Composure and concentration are characteristic features of favorable environment for the IT professional's work. That is why they do not like any schedules (besides these absolutely necessary like the deadline of a project and implementation of a system). One step lower in the pyramid there is a project or department team, which support the completion of all tasks arising from different functions of a group. Collective work is right after IT specialists' individual needs. What may be surprising just on a third level a client with his/her demands is placed. Research material shows that caring about client's satisfaction is not a goal of IT professionals' work. Their aim is to prepare a system (or any other IT project) as good as possible. These interests coincide in the moment of getting client's satisfaction. But way of pursuing this goal is different for both sides. IT professionals concentrate on their work, which eventually ends up with a ready system. Client's organization concentrates on correct relations with IT specialists and pursuing their demands in specific way of treating. This divergence may cause conflicts because it is easy to reach the moment when a client feels that IT professional's company shows an insufficient interest. That is why project managers or other professionals responsible for contacts with a client play so important role. Their goal is to minimize contradiction between interests of both parties

Figure 2. Priorities in IT specialist profession in software companies

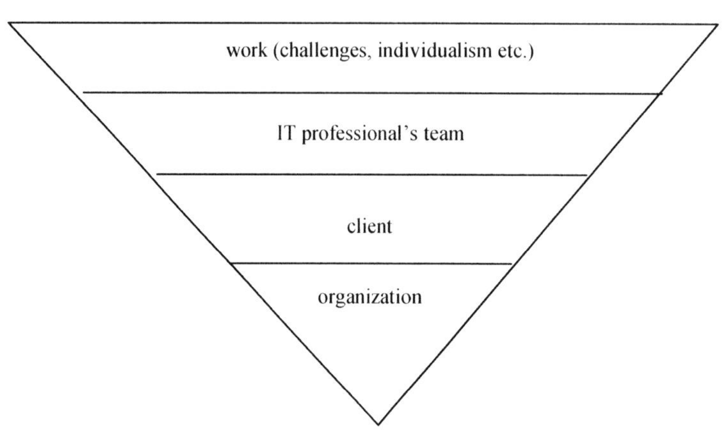

(client's organization and IT company). Finally, on the bottom of the pyramid there is an organization hiring IT specialists. Definitely the minority of their time IT professionals dedicate to goals and values of a particular organization. IT specialists working in software companies usually share professional values with their organization, so it is easier to prevent conflicts. Some of software companies create such favorable atmosphere for IT professionals' work but the norms and values of both parties coincide. In general, occupational community predominates over organization in IT specialist's hierarchy of priorities.

After this analysis, it is possible to enumerate factors indispensable in IT professionals' work accordingly to interlocutors' opinions. First of all, they have to work in favorable conditions, which means e.g. office in a building that is quiet, relatively small and preferably not in the center of the big city. IT professionals do not like to be striking in general and they prefer to work in seclusion. For the same reasons most of IT specialists do not like to meet clients and they deliberately avoid promotion because they do not want to become managers whose contacts with contractors are rather wide and often. Also, IT professionals prefer to meet people of the same interests, whose work, skills and knowledge they mutually value and respect. The reason of such kind a idiosyncrasy is being closed for new people, but being open for changing thoughts. Thus, IT professionals find a place to exchange ideas and therefore develop creativity. All these should be organized without often meetings which are not desirable for interviewees. Lack of control (in the old meaning) reveals again. IT professionals' communities are groups which do not like to be driven and controlled. Actions are taken individually and confronted with management very rarely. This issue is also referring to methods of solving problem. "If you have any, do it by yourself" – seems to be the general motto of IT workers. And if IT professional is not handling the problem, he asks a friend (co-worker) for help. IT specialists usually do not ask their supervisors for help . In average Polish software company there are only few supervisors. They are not necessary in the process of work control. That's why the organizational structure is flat and all the hierarchy very straight and clear. IT professionals require only temporary control because their work bases on trust and friendship (see table 1). Thanks to this structure and relations creativity may develop besides rational control.

Summarizing, key elements of control were described and analyzed in this chapter. It is choice of management (or any decision-making unit) what kind of control should they implement in the organization to be effective and not kill creativity of workers, the same time. Every time there is a choice between positional control system and personal control system (Hochschild, 1983). Management should be just aware of consequences of using certain way of controlling workers.

Concluding, how to perceive creativity and control and how to conduct any research of this very important part of organizational life? Some authors state that creativity and control should be connected with a word "versus" and that is how it is presented and analyzed here. It means that control kills creativity, ruins relationships and plays explicitly negative role in organizations. Another approach points out that control may be a pair for creativity if connected under proper conditions. In authors' opinion, IT professionals' communities are the best example for this combination. IT specialists belong to the profession which cannot exist without creativity on one hand. On the other, these are people who demand minimum of control. Thus, the control should be reasonable and concentrated on reaching a goal (i.e. making IT systems, servicing etc.), allowing for building extensive relationships inside professional community, leaving a space for creating specific professional culture (with all its artifacts, norms, values) and finally lead by a wise manager.

REFERENCES

Abbott, A. (1988). *The system of professions. An essay on the division of expert labor.* The University of Chicago Press.

Czarniawska-Joerges, B. (1992). *Exploring complex organizations: a cultural perspective.* Newbury Park, CA: Sage Publications.

Czarniawska-Joerges, B. (1988). *Ideological control in non-ideological organizations.* New York: Praeger.

Drucker, P. (1993/1999). *Społeczeństwo pokapitalistyczne.* Warszawa: PWN.

Fayol, H. (1987). *General and industrial management: Henri Fayol's classic revised by Irwin Gray.* Belmont, CA: David S. Lake Publishers.

Fontana, A., & Frey, J. (1994). „Interviewing. The art of science". In Denzin, N. & Lincoln, Y. (eds.) *Handbook of Qualitative Research* (pp. 361-376). Thousand Oaks, London, New Delhi: Sage.

Foucault, M. (1969/2002). *Archeologia wiedzy.* Warszawa: De Agostini.

Freidson, E. (1994). *Professionalism reborn. Theory, prophecy and policy.* The University of Chicago Press.

Glaser, B. G., & Strauss, A. L. (1967). *The discovery of grounded theory: strategies for qualitative research.* Hawthorne, NY: Aldine de Gruyter.

Hammersley, M., & Atkinson, P. (1995). Ethnography: principles in practice (2nd ed.). London, New York: Routledge.

Hatch, M. J. (1997/2002). *Teoria organizacji.* Warszawa: PWN.

Hjorth, D. (2005). Organizational entrepreneurship with de Certeau on creating heterotopias (or spaces for play). *Journal of Management Inquiry, 14*(4), 386-398.

Hochschild, A. R. (1983). *The managed heart. Commercialization of human feeling.* Berkley, Los Angeles, London: University of California Press.

Konecki, K. (2000). *Studia z metodologii badań jakościowych. Teoria ugruntowana.* Warszawa: PWN.

Latour, B. (1987). *Science in action. How to follow scientists and engineers through society.* Cambridge, Mass: Harvard University Press.

Linstead, S., & Mullarkey, J. (2003). Time, creativity and culture: introducing Bergson. *Culture and Organization, 9*(1), 3-13.

MacDonald, K. M. (1995). *The sociology of the professions.* London, Thousand Oaks, New Delhi: Sage Publications.

Morgan, G. (1997/2001). *Wyobraźnia organizacyjna. Nowe sposoby postrzegania, organizowania i zarządzania.* Warszawa: PWN.

Schein, E. H. (1985). *Organizational culture and leadership.* San Francisco: Jossey-Bass.

Senge, P. (1990/2006). *Piąta dyscyplina. Teoria i praktyka organizacji uczących się.* Kraków: Wolters Kluwer.

Strannegård, L., & Friberg, M. (2001). *Already elsewhere. Play, identity and speed in the business world.* Sweden: Raster Forlag.

Streatfield, P. J. (2001). *The Paradox of Control in Organizations.* London: Routledge.

Van Maanen, J. & Barley, S. R. (1984). Occupational communities: Culture and control in organizations. In L. L. Cummings & B. M. I. Staw (Eds.), *Research in organizational behavior, 6*, 287-365. Greenwich, CT: JAI Press.

Van Maanen, J., & Kunda, G. (1989). Real feelings: Emotional expression and organizational culture. In L.L. Cummings & B.M. I. Staw (Eds.), *Research in organizational behavior, 11*, 43-103. Greenwich, CT: JAI Press.

Weber, M. (1922/2002). *Gospodarka i społeczeństwo.* Warszawa: PWN.

Whyte, W. F., & Whyte, K. K. (1984). *Learning from the field: a guide from experience.* Beverly Hills: Sage Publications.

KEY TERMS

Control: One of the fundamental functions of management. It can be defined as an mechanism of strategy implementation (modernists' theory) or legitimizing tool which hides influences of power and political behavior of managers (post-modernists' theory).

Creativity: The human impulse to organize, but to improvise rather than to locate, divide and control. Seeing things from a different perspective.

Entrepreneur/Entrepreneurship: Following Schumpeter, an entrepreneur is a person who is willing and able to convert a new idea or invention into a successful innovation. Entrepreneurship forces "creative destruction" across markets and industries, simultaneously creating new products and business models. For Peter Drucker entrepreneurship is also about taking risk.

Ethnographic Research: Is a methodological tradition of qualitative study. It can be used for discovering every social reality and organizations as well. Ethnographic researcher uses all methods characteristic of social inquiry.

Occupational Community: Occupational communities represent bounded work cultures populated by people who share similar identities and values that transcendent specific organizational settings.

Organizational Life Cycle: Larry Greiner defined 5 stages of organizational life. In order to grow, the organization is supposed to pass through a series of identifiable phases or stages of development (creativity, direction, delegation, collaboration, coordination) and crisis (leadership, autonomy, control, staff, unknown).

Organizations/Organizing: Here, organizations are seen as cultures. Therefore, organizing, in short, means constructing specific reality with its artifacts, norms and values. It is a complex process which can be discovered deeply with ethnographic methods.

Professional Community: Refers to specialized working teams whose members have all had some kind of a higher education and who are identified more by their educational status than by their specific occupational skills.

Section V
The Culture of Knowledge

Chapter XIX
A Qualitative Study of Knowledge Management:
The Multinational Firm Point of View

Patrocinio Zaragoza-Sáez
University of Alicante, Spain

Enrique Claver-Cortés
University of Alicante, Spain

Diego Quer-Ramón
University of Alicante, Spain

ABSTRACT

Knowledge is one of the basic production factors owned by enterprises, and knowledge management is one of the main dynamic capabilities on which enterprises can base their competitive advantages. The creation, transfer, and later use of knowledge have become increasingly important, and multinational corporations (MNCs), being scattered in various places, constitute the appropriate environment to implement knowledge management processes meant to maximize their intellectual assets. This chapter has as its aim to answer three questions: (a) what actions do MNCs undertake in order to set knowledge management processes in motion; (b) what main variables impact on their knowledge creation capability; and (c) what main variables impact on their knowledge transfer capability? A qualitative research work based on a multiple case study has served to achieve that aim, allowing us to carry out an exploratory study of six MNCs which have shown their proactivity in the knowledge management area. The results of the analysis have led to eight propositions which highlight the most relevant variables facilitating the processes for the creation and transfer of knowledge within a MNC.

INTRODUCTION

In recent years, the environment surrounding enterprises has characterized by high levels of dynamism and complexity. The accelerated globalization, the widespread business restructuring and the strong competition in practically every economic sector have forced enterprises to become highly flexible and able to react before the new dynamics that may arise. These ingredients have led to the appearance of *the knowledge society*, which imposes new requirements on organizations. In order to compete effectively, the organizations need to learn new skills to be able to find, manage, share and use both information and knowledge (Abell & Oxbrow, 1999). As a result, competitive advantages increasingly derive from strategic assets, such as knowledge, and from a set of dynamic capabilities which mainly materialize in innovation and learning. Due to all this, knowledge management is now of paramount importance within organizations.

Firms have to face another unquestionable fact, namely, the ever-increasing level of globalization which is causing practically all economic sectors to shift from a local market toward a global one. The MNC, which has as one of its main characteristics the possession of scattered resources in various countries, appears as a diversified-knowledge corporation and provides the ideal environment to implement knowledge management processes, as it will be necessary to coordinate the creation and transfer of this resource between its various locations for the purpose of leveraging and achieving the maximum global performance.

In accordance with these ideas and taking as a reference the knowledge theory as well as the MNC theory, this study seeks to answer the following three questions: (a) what actions do MNCs undertake to set knowledge management processes in motion? (b) what main variables impact on their knowledge creation capability? and (c) what main variables impact on their knowledge transfer capability? In our opinion, the answers to these questions can make a contribution to the literature in two ways: from the empirical point of view, they will provide further empirical evidence of the knowledge-MNC link through a focus on the actions undertaken for the purpose of managing knowledge and on the mechanisms which make possible the generation and transfer of this resource; and from a practical perspective, they will be the basis of an exploratory study which shows that management is facing new patterns. One of the main challenges lies in understanding the role of knowledge as a strategic intangible resource and, once managers have recognized the value of management, they must take a leading role in the promotion of knowledge management building the necessary mechanisms that favor this process; empowering employees to proactively participate in knowledge creation and transfer through the decentralization of the decision-making process (autonomy); promoting corporate socialization with the aim of creating a work context in which closer relationships between employees are possible; and combining internal and external ways of creating and/or acquiring knowledge.

We have structured the chapter in five sections. After the introduction, there is a literature review which highlights the strategic nature of knowledge, along with the role of knowledge management in the creation of sustainable competitive advantages. A detailed description of the qualitative research work follows, the findings being reported in the next section. Finally, the closing section summarizes the main conclusions drawn from the study, along with its limitations, and suggests future research lines.

LITERATURE REVIEW

Nobody can deny the transformation experienced by present-day society, where business success no longer derives essentially from production factors, but from knowledge, which arises as the basic production and wealth creation factor

(Drucker, 1993; Sveiby, 1997). Due to such aspects as globalization, market deregulation and access to information, firms' competitive advantages are no longer sustainable, knowledge appearing as a fundamental concept in order to understand the evolution of the economy in general and of economic change in particular. Although according to most of the literature, knowledge management processes have largely had at its basis a technological or information-systems approach (Wilson, 2002; Alvesson & Kärreman, 2002), this study's focus is on the emergent *knowledge-based view of the firm*, whereby knowledge has become one of the most important resources from a strategic point of view (Grant, 1996; Spender, 1996, Tyre & von Piel, 1997; Teece, Pisano & Shuen, 1997; Zack, 1999). Scholars refer to knowledge in several ways, the most commonly-used terms being competencies, capabilities, routines or innovation. Knowledge originates from creativity, individual experiences and organizational learning, and we can often find the sources of knowledge not only in the written documents but also in the routines, tasks, processes, practices, rules and values that shape an organization (Bhagat, Kedia, Harveston & Triandis, 2002). Knowledge is therefore a dynamic concept resulting from the interactions between individuals and organizations and is also specific to a context defined by some particular time and place circumstances (Hayek, 1945; Nonaka, Toyama & Konno, 2000).

Nelson and Winter (1982) point out that this resource is the fruit of experiences developed by company members over time, and Hoskisson, Hitt, Wan and Yiu (1999, p. 442) state that "due to its tacit and socially complex character, a company's knowledge stock is a crucial determining factor in its competitive advantage". Figure 1 expresses it graphically.

Knowledge management has consequently turned into a fundamental task —and simultaneously into one of the most outstanding challenges of our time— its global aim being both to maximize the company's effectiveness and income levels arising from its knowledge assets and to succeed in constantly renewing them (Wiig, 1997; Shariq, 1997). Knowledge management, along with the initial set of resources and capabilities owned by the firm, emerges as a source of heterogeneity inside the organization and, therefore, as the main cause of its competitive advantages (Hill & Deeds, 1996).

Based on the contributions made by various authors, among whom stand out Quintas, Lefrere and Jones (1997), Wiig (1997), Davenport, De Long and Beers (1998), and Guns and Välikangas (1998), knowledge management could be defined as *the set of business policies and actions undertaken to aid the creation of knowledge, its transfer to all members of the company, and its subsequent implementation, with the aim of achieving distinctive competencies that provide the company with a*

Figure 1. The knowledge-based competitive advantage causality chain

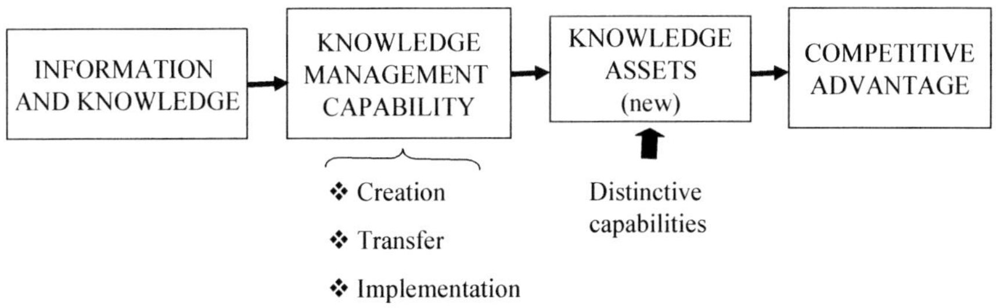

Source: Adapted from Grant (1991), Helleloid & Simonin (1994), and Nonaka & Takeuchi (1995).

long-term competitive advantage. Such corporate policies deal, among other things, with human resources management, corporate culture, organizational design, and technological platforms, all of them crucial aspects shaping the necessary infrastructure and the appropriate environment to support knowledge management processes.

We have already shown in the introduction that, due to their unique characteristics, MNCs provide the adequate field to carry out knowledge creation, transfer and implementation processes. In this context, Almeida, Song and Grant (2002) highlight the superiority of MNCs in the creation and transfer of international knowledge, both over the market and over alliances. These authors argue that this superiority has to do with the fact that MNCs can achieve knowledge combinations which markets would find it impossible to achieve. This last idea has its origin in the arguments of Kogut and Zander (1993, 1995), according to whom firms are social communities acting as efficient mechanisms for the creation and transfer of knowledge without the need for market failures to occur.

Along these lines, we are now going to develop a qualitative research work that will make it possible to develop theory from the results obtained.

METHOD AND DATA

Introduction

The reason for using a qualitative research lies in the fact that, although there are numerous theoretical works in the field of knowledge management, only few of them empirically specify the set of practices applied by firms when undertaking this process or the mechanisms through which they can create and transfer new knowledge.

We decided to use the case study as our research method throughout the development of the empirical work because the characteristics of case studies make it possible to come closer to the study object. Hamel, Dufour and Fortin (1993, p. 34) emphasize the descriptive nature of this approach and consider it an "in-depth study of a specific case". Yin (1994, p. 13) defines it as an "empirical study that examines a contemporary phenomenon within its real context, especially when the limits between the phenomenon and its scope are not clearly defined and multiple sources of evidence are used". Finally, Eisenhardt (1989) considers that a case study is a research strategy focused on understanding the dynamics produced in specific contexts. This author sees the case study as a fundamental mechanism, not for testing theories but for theory-building.

In order to answer the three questions posed at the introduction section, we chose to use the multiple case study as opposed to the single-case one, always seeking to find behavior patterns that allow a generalization of the results ("replication logic", Yin, 1994, 1998) based on the evidence obtained in various economic, organizational and sectorial contexts. A single case would have a low degree of representativeness, confining the scope of the conclusions to a specific type of organization and industry.

In the absence of an initial hypothesis, the inductive method became especially relevant, as it enabled us to create a basis for a future theory. It was an exploratory case study meant to find practical evidence of knowledge management processes undertaken by large prestigious MNCs located in Spain, characterized by their high competitiveness and the level of success reached in knowledge management practices. The study actually reveals how these organizations set up their best practices in the field of knowledge.

The qualitative research work went through a number of stages. The first one consisted in the examination of the most relevant concepts and theories linking the areas of knowledge management and MNCs in the literature. The second included the preparation of a standardized interview customized for each firm depending on its industry. During the third stage, we held interviews with managers, visited premises (facilities), and compiled secondary data. In the fourth stage, we sent the elaborated case to the interviewees so that they could okay it or correct certain aspects, if necessary. The fifth stage focused on comparative studies. Finally, after the results observed, we "built theory" developing a conceptual framework which makes it possible to state a number of propositions that will be subject to verification in a future quantitative stage.

Population

The basis for the selection of the cases was a non-random sample. We chose those cases which offered good opportunities for learning, and followed the recommendation that their number should be neither less than four nor more than ten (Eisenhardt, 1989). The process led to the selection of six Spanish enterprises from different industries which had as their two main features: (a) that they showed a pro-active attitude in the field of knowledge; and (b) that they made a great effort to inform their stakeholders about their experiences in this field. Their proactivity becomes clear in the fact that these are companies where knowledge management has become a part of their daily life in a planned or deliberate way; they characteristically perform actions to create, transfer and apply knowledge insofar as is possible. Additionally, these firms often attend conferences, gatherings and seminars that link knowledge to the business context, and actively collaborate with universities in the development of joint projects, which allows them to shed light on this emergent area of firm

Table 1. Technical specifications card for qualitative research

Target enterprises	ELECTROTÉCNICA ARTECHE HERMANOS S.A. (EAHSA) (Manufacture of electric motors, transformers and generators)
	UNIÓN FENOSA (UF) (Production and distribution of electricity, gas, and professional services (SOLUZIONA))
	PricewaterhouseCoopers (PWC) (Management and business assessment. Auditing)
	SIEMENS ESPAÑA S.A. (Electrical installations. Manufacture of electric motors, transformers and generators)
	TELEFÓNICA GROUP (Fixed and mobile telephone services, Internet, content production and dissemination and directories.)
	SANTANDER GROUP (Banking activities in general and activities related to the management of investment and pension funds in particular)
Unit of analysis	(Parent or subsidiary) enterprise
Geographical area	Munguía (Biscay, Basque Country) – ARTECHE
	Madrid- UNIÓN FENOSA
	Madrid- PRICEWATERHOUSECOOPERS
	Tres Cantos (Madrid)- SIEMENS S.A.
	Madrid-Telefónica Group
	Madrid-Santander Group
Time period during which fieldwork took place	March – September 2004
Type of interview	Semi-structured or in-depth interview

strategic management. The reason for choosing Spanish firms was our interest in identifying the link between knowledge and MNCs in Spain, as no empirical works had linked these two topics until now. Table 1 shows the technical specifications card for this research.

Information Collection

In order to avoid a potential bias introduced by researchers themselves and/or by informants, we collected the data using the "triangulation technique", which combines three methodologies:

- *In-depth interview*, with the Chief Knowledge Officer (CKO) or the person responsible for matters related to knowledge management at the firm. We used a standard questionnaire with open-ended questions, adapted and customized for each one of the enterprises. We recorded the interviews —which lasted four hours on average— and later transcribed them, always with the interviewees' consent. We kept in touch with interviewees via telephone or e-mail to clarify any aspects that might arise right up until they completed and approved the final report on each case.
- *Observation*, which implies visits to the premises and contacts with the workforce. Although this is a secondary source to obtain data, it not only enables the researcher to discover the truth about the study object but also to achieve a better understanding of the case.
- *Consulting documents* extracted from the Internet and publications –both internal (Intranet, formal and informal reports) and external (websites, books, published articles, annual reports and corporate management reports).

Due to the qualitative character of most data, triangulation permits to increase construct validity. As for internal validity, the researcher can ensure it being in permanent contact with the interviewees during the process of analysis, because they can provide more data to fill any new possible information gaps that might arise. In turn, external validity comes as a result of multiple case studies and comparative result analyses. As for the reliability problem, we have made an effort to alleviate it, first preparing a detailed case study protocol that is common to all enterprises, and then taking very much into account the information obtained from the documents and the later transcript of the interviews. Finally, we sent the case study to the interviewees so that they could supervise and okay it or make any comments, if necessary, in the hope that this would make our results more reliable.

QUALITATIVE RESEARCH: RESULTS

The multiple case study about six renowned, internationally prestigious, and proactive Spanish firms has highlighted that these organizations regard knowledge as a very valuable strategic resource that they permanently need to create, transfer, store and enlarge in order to survive to the dynamism and turbulence that characterize the present-day competitive environment. The replication logic appeared during the research work, showing in most cases similar behavior patterns in the performance of the enterprises analyzed, even though they belonged to different industries.

Knowledge Management in MNCs

Activities focused on creating and sharing knowledge at EAHSA started already in 1995 with the aim of developing a set of values which had proved necessary for the survival of the enterprise. EAHSA undertook actions to create and transfer knowledge, all of them backed up by an infrastructure that enabled their introduction; its organizational structure became increasingly horizontal —practically no hierarchies existed— with a stable structure and another more flexible *ad hoc* one; and its culture emphasized tolerance with mistakes, encouraged trust and dialogue, and gave an impulse to learning. As for its human resources policy, EAHSA had as its priorities to attract and retain talent —always selecting and recruiting its staff with a knowledge creation and transfer viewpoint in mind, and recognizing training as a well-established cultural value— and to develop a technological platform that enabled knowledge-sharing through contributions made both on an individual scale and at a work team level.

In the case of UF, when the organization had to face the integration of two different companies after the merger[a] in 1982, it reflected on the importance of looking after its personnel as a strategic factor. This led the company's senior management to set up activities meant to generate and share knowledge. Thus, UF stands out as having the necessary degree of socialization for the transfer of tacit knowledge, as well as the capability required to elaborate its own intellectual capital model to face the challenges of identifying, ordering, and measuring strategic intangibles. This is, therefore, an enterprise that likes to change and has initiative, and in which, although hierarchies still exist, the relationship and communication between chiefs and collaborators has been constantly improving. It places a strong emphasis on training, has established a competence-based management, and uses audio-conferences, an Intranet and a knowledge portal to transfer and acquire knowledge.

PWC decided that the knowledge management project was very important to help with the merger[b] in 1998; from then on, the firm has assigned resources and created positions associated with knowledge management. As a consequence, there is a vision of knowledge and its objectives on an international scale, and the firm has even developed its own knowledge management model. International practice communities reveal the strengths and weaknesses of subsidiaries' knowledge, thus leading to the transfer and exploitation of best practices. The efforts made in the field of knowledge are remarkable; however, PWC still does not seem to have the most appropriate infrastructure to support them. It is an enterprise where a lot of hierarchy still remains —with a lot of supervision and control— and it is only over the last few years that its corporate culture and human resources policy have started to become more receptive to new ideas, more flexible, and more willing to value emotional competencies. From a technological point of view, PWC uses technology as much as possible, basically to store and retrieve specific knowledge that other people might need to use later.

The subject of knowledge management has a long tradition at Siemens, and the global, knowledge-intensive nature of its sector justifies the considerable attention given to this resource. This became apparent when the firm created a Knowledge Management Team (including a Human Resources Manager, an Information Technology Manager and a Processes Area Manager) and undertook several initiatives meant to emphasize the relevance of practice communities. The enterprise made it clear that knowledge had become a priority, the proposed objectives being: (a) to start to develop a culture which valued the importance of knowledge; (b) to stimulate the provision of ideas along with knowledge transfer; and (c) to get to know the strengths of the enterprise regarding knowledge. Siemens has a technological platform which distinguishes between its storage section and the section for chats and forums, the latter being crucial for tacit knowledge transfer. It equally appears as an enterprise that its employees find very attractive, as shown by its low employee turnover rate. Its organizational structure shows no hierarchies, and teamwork as well as the dialogue-based organizational culture emerge as outstanding features of a company that incorporates a strong innovation and experimentation component too.

As a result of the deregulation of Spain's telecommunications sector in 2000, along with the ever-increasing globalization, Telefónica lost its monopoly over Spanish telecommunications and suddenly found itself before a large number of competitors. Faced with this new situation, Telefónica undertook a deep organizational transformation, betting on change and realizing that the knowledge of their employees was the most valuable resource owned by the company and that it could help the organization to obtain a competitive advantage. This knowledge, derived from the experience in the telecommunications sector, served as a guide for good practices that the company implemented in the organization as a whole, thus capitalizing on the existing knowledge. The creation of new knowledge and the transfer of best practices required a relatively hierarchy-free organizational structure and a business culture open to change. Consequently, Telefónica reduced the number of hierarchical levels, thus favoring the formation of multidisciplinary work teams and the development of inter-area transversal projects. At the same time, its once very conservative culture became more participative and collaborative. Employees' professional development became an essential value, which led the company to increase the number of training hours, to improve the feedback level, and to make a strong bet on coaching and e-learning, all of which seeking to develop competencies at all levels.

The same as UF and PWC, Santander Group arose from the merger of two large organizations —two important Spanish banks— in 1999[c]. The new company realized that the traditional management systems did not suffice to provide an efficient response to an increasingly complex and dynamic environment and, considering that knowledge and intangibles formed the basis of its competitive success, it structured its vision and mission around the need to manage these resources efficiently. Santander Group considers that employees are its most important asset because they allow the company to generate middle-term and long-term value. This is why the organization strives to attract and retain its talented professionals, ensuring their adequate professional development. The company's organizational structure is now more horizontal, betting on a higher degree of flexibility and communication, all of which has materialized in an increased number of multifunctional work teams. Its culture focuses on corporate social responsibility and identifies as its essential values dynamism, strength, innovation and leadership. Santander Group usually employs as its main technological tools the Internet, an Intranet and videoconferencing. The knowledge forums, the knowledge portal and the practice communities form part of the first two.

Knowledge Creation in MNCs

Creating knowledge implies both an individual and a shared reflection on the new working processes, on the products and services that a firm delivers, on the understanding of business strategy and, last but not least, on the analysis of the environment.

Knowledge creation strategies seek to create new knowledge or to acquire existing one. Exploration and exploitation are not mutually exclusive, as the same organization may need to develop an area of knowledge and simultaneously exploit others; the ideal is to maintain a balance between the two. On an internal level, knowledge creation takes place through R&D activities, learning by doing, or team work, but the difficulties encountered by companies when they try to generate internally all the knowledge required to face market circumstances lead them to create new knowledge or to acquire existing knowledge from external sources.

Knowledge creation becomes especially relevant among the enterprises studied, as they all operate in global knowledge-intensive sectors and constantly need to generate new knowledge inputs through which they can remain competitive and face any potential new dynamics.

The knowledge creation capability largely depends on the characteristics of the MNC (be it a parent or a subsidiary corporation) and on both the actions undertaken in its internal environment and those carried out through its external network.

Characteristics of the Enterprise

As explained above, the six enterprises under analysis are characteristically proactive in the implementation of activities meant to leverage knowledge. All of them show a strong initiative thanks to which they can constantly create knowledge and assume increasingly higher responsibilities. EAHSA started to deal with knowledge issues in 1995 seeking to develop a set of values considered important for the survival of the company; UF as well as PWC decided to develop a knowledge management scheme in order to help with their respective mergers. Siemens has always paid a lot of attention to knowledge as a strategic resource which allows continuous innovation. Telefónica's initiative to implement knowledge management processes stemmed from the need to become an *e-company*, that is, a *learning organization* which could not only exploit to the full the existing knowledge but also make the most of new knowledge creation. The initiatives undertaken by Santander Group in relation to intellectual capital and knowledge management are historic. Already before the merger, one of the two banks involved, Banco Central Hispano, started to develop a number of activities which sought to identify the best practices among its most excellent staff, to transfer them to the rest of employees, and to follow up the results. Such activities implied entering an area which would eventually become an essential part of all the firms belonging to Santander Group, always under the coordination and supervision of the Group's intellectual capital manager.

In addition to initiative, it is necessary to highlight leadership and autonomy in the enterprises analyzed. Leadership materializes in top management's support, which in turn leads to an encouragement of employee initiative (Birkinshaw, Hood & Jonsson, 1998; Birkinshaw, 1996). All the enterprises examined claim to have: internationally respected leaders; a top management with a high level of credibility; and senior managers who closely collaborate with the executives to accomplish the company's objectives. Anyway, this forms part of the organizational culture and structure that characterize each enterprise.

Regarding autonomy, Foss and Pedersen (2002) point out that the problem of organizational design lies, among other things, in choosing the organizational tools related to such aspects as control, motivation, and context, so that subsidiaries can have access to knowledge and produce it. From the perspective of knowledge management, Nonaka, Toyama and Konno (2000) state that autonomy improves the chances to find valuable information and encourages organization members to produce new knowledge. With the exception of PWC, which still keeps a certain degree of hierarchy because of its actual partnership structure, all the firms have a considerable degree of freedom to adopt decisions about their products and/or processes. All this is possible thanks to their organizational design, which mainly revolves around teamwork, collaboration and empowerment.

It is therefore easy to identify the characteristics of the enterprises analyzed (initiative, leadership and autonomy) that have made the creation of knowledge and the assumption of additional responsibilities become basic dynamic capabilities of these organizations. We can consequently state the following propositions:

P_1: The firm's initiative positively influences its knowledge creation capability

P_2: The firm's leadership positively influences its knowledge creation capability

P_3: The firm's autonomy positively influences its knowledge creation capability

Internal Environment and External Network

The MNC's internal environment, formed by the investments[d] made in the different functional areas, is an essential aspect in the knowledge creation process (Foss & Pedersen, 2002; Lane & Lubatkin, 1998; Cohen & Levinthal, 1990; Dyer & Singh, 1998). That knowledge is not only useful to overcome the existing shortages but also for the potential exploitation in other multinational units located elsewhere. Nevertheless, the difficulty to generate all the knowledge required makes firms resort to external sources, e.g. the knowledge coming from the local clusters or that resulting from the relationships between the enterprise and the agents in its supply chain (Porter, 1990; Sanna-Randaccio & Veugelers, 2007). In fact, absorption capacity and social capital appear as determining factors for the exchange of knowledge within and between organizations (Frost & Zhou, 2005).

EAHSA has learned to successfully combine the exploitation of its knowledge in geographical areas outside Spain with the creation of new knowledge. The latter is possible through: R&D, to which the company dedicates permanent efforts; the acquisition of plants in Mexico, Argentina and Brazil; the establishment of joint ventures; the external relationships with R&D centers, electrical and business management organizations, quality institutions, universities and other academic institutions; the interaction with customers, who provide specific details about the products they require; and the use of transnational teams and centers of excellence.

UF uses knowledge exploitation especially in the energy business. The parent company (located in Spain) is the one where the distinctive competencies and accumulated knowledge in the generation, commercialization and distribution of electric power remain, thus providing the starting point for the development of similar businesses in Latin America. UF leaves its place of origin to acquire competencies that it does not have, undertaking joint ventures in Egypt and Oman and purchasing companies in various countries. The company complements the exploitation of knowledge with its generation, where new knowledge forms the basis for new businesses. Creation also takes place through R&D, connections with other organizations and universities, relationships with suppliers and customers, a suggestions box (the "Innowatio Award" for the best idea), expertise centers (at SOLUZIONA-professional services), and international work teams.

PWC is an organization which excels for its knowledge exploitation rather than for exploration, as its work practices are global and there is a tendency to maximize returns from the already existing ones. Nevertheless, exploration allows it to take over new market segments. That is why innovation, work teams (both national and international), relationships with universities and business schools, as well as the attendance to seminars and conferences, all prove useful to create knowledge whenever possible. On a lesser scale, centers of excellence, transnational teams, and company acquisitions also help PWC to create or achieve new knowledge.

The need to constantly create, share and apply knowledge becomes vital for Siemens. Creation is mainly possible through R&D. Innovation is one of the main pillars for this firm's level of competitiveness. That is why it constantly works on the development of new products and innovative solutions that will make it possible to expand the current business lines, giving rise to a high number of registered patents. Suggestions boxes equally represent a significant source of knowledge, as they boost the generation of ideas. For the purpose of achieving external knowledge, Siemens resorts to collaboration with customers and suppliers, company acquisitions, setting up of joint ventures (mainly in African and Middle-East countries), centers of excellence, and relationships with external R&D centers.

Telefónica creates knowledge by means, meanly, of R&D. Investment in technological innovation is very high and enables the company to launch into the market a considerable number of new products and services seeking to satisfy customer demand in the areas of Internet, broadband, voice market and mobile services. However, Telefónica has also put in practice various projects meant to reward good ideas among its employees, including Idealab!, Patenta, Penthalón (in Argentina), Champions Race (in Brazil), Líder.es and Comex (in Latin America). R&D is so important for Telefónica that it even has its own subsidiary: *Telefónica R&D*. From the external point of view, Telefónica attends meetings, forums, conferences, international organisms, associations, etc., all of which allows the company to obtain knowledge about best practices in other firms. Customers equally represent an important source of knowledge for Telefónica, since their needs and demands always lead this company to constant innovation and to a permanent search for new solutions.

Two of the most important tools used by Santander Group to create knowledge are teamwork and the suggestions box system. The former serves to share the ideas of different groups in order to achieve global solutions with a high added value. The suggestions box system in turn makes it possible to take into consideration people's perceptions and ideas, which can become an important motivating element. Externally, the Group acquires new knowledge thanks to its relationships with business schools, universities, forums, conferences, customers as well as benchmarking.

Various mechanisms, either internal or external to the company, seem to contribute to knowledge creation in MNCs, and we can expect creation to have even more support in companies where the entire necessary infrastructure to start up knowledge management already exists.

The reasoning above leads to make the following two propositions:

P_4: The firm's internal environment positively influences its knowledge creation capability

P_5: The firm's external network positively influences its knowledge creation capability

Knowledge Transfer in MNCs

In MNCs, with resources scattered geographically, the transfer of knowledge becomes one of the key activities facilitating the creation of knowledge-based value. Relationships between MNCs' units become important insofar as they are the channels enabling the flow of useful knowledge and information (Hansen 1999). This section focuses on identifying the factors which make possible the transfer within the MNC's internal structure, that is, between the parent company and its subsidiaries and between the latter. Gupta and Govindarajan (1991, p. 773) call this transfer an "intracorporate knowledge flow", and define it as "the transfer of either expertise (e.g., skills and capabilities in product and process design or marketing know-how) or external market data (information on customers, competitors or suppliers) with a high strategic value". This has to do with the boundary-spanning practices involved in working across multiple intra-organizational boundaries (Balogun, Gleadle, Hailey & Willmott, 2005). Our interest lies in getting to know the variables which facilitate the transfer of the most tacit knowledge and in verifying that, although information and communication technologies are the mechanisms most commonly used at transfer processes, they have limitations to share this type of knowledge, due to its peculiar characteristics. For that reason, the enterprises examined use mechanisms that enable individuals to develop closer relationships.

We can thus say that the knowledge transfer capability has a strong dependence on the firm's autonomy, on its corporate socialization, and on the use of expatriates.

Autonomy

The same as in knowledge creation, the study shows that autonomy has a positive effect on the transfer of knowledge across the MNC's units. Thus, Hedlund (1986), as well as Ghoshal and Bartlett (1990) and Tsai (1997), state that centralization is a constraint upon the initiatives undertaken by subsidiaries and upon communication with the other units.

EAHSA does not usually find great barriers to transfer knowledge. The way in which the company organizes its structure, its homogeneous operating style at all its plants and its capability to ensure dialogue and understanding among all its members removes the main obstacles to transfer. Its subsidiaries enjoy a high level of autonomy. There are some patterns common to the different locations and, on the basis of that shared operating style, each firm assumes its own management. EAHSA considers that the option of increasing autonomy as opposed to exerting more control is positive and largely helps encourage knowledge creation and transfer.

UF is a firm that pursues a common culture and operating style, although its subsidiaries have a certain degree of autonomy when they do business. For UF, it is very important to have a business model, a middle-term business plan, and an annual strategic plan, but once the company has defined this and has set a number of objectives, it gives itself some leeway to achieve them, to act, to innovate, and to improve.

On some occasions, knowledge flows in PWC may face limitations due to issues of control over subsidiaries, but a high level of autonomy usually exists in the area of knowledge management. Within this context, the Spanish subsidiary is fully autonomous, as the knowledge management project depends on the top management and there is a department, and some resources, associated with that project, which greatly encourages activities linked to knowledge sharing. In the rest of areas, a number of common policies and patterns with some global services seem to exist, though each subsidiary follows its own management approach.

Knowledge transfer within Siemens does not often have to face great complications. Neither best practice encouragement nor capability-sharing between sender and receiver or the knowledge coding level appear to constitute significant barriers to transfer. There is a high level of autonomy in the different units, though we should distinguish two realities: that of the Spanish subsidiary, which may differ a little from what the parent company dictates in Germany; and the vertical areas, that is, the various business divisions which must follow more closely the guidelines established by the parent company for a specific business.

The changes occurred in Telefónica modified its internal structure in such a way that, although a certain degree of hierarchy continues to exist due to its peculiar culture and traditional civil-service-inspired nature, the creation of working groups along with the closer relationships between firm members has led to a more horizontal, and more flexible, organization. This increasingly flat structure facilitates the active participation of the whole company, an essential aspect being the use of the top-bottom management methodology, combined with the down-top approach, in which the middle management becomes a key element within the communication process.

As for Santander Group, because the parent company is in Spain, the transfer from this country to the rest of units tends to be much higher. Nevertheless, all subsidiaries transfer knowledge to a greater or lesser extent, as shown by the fact that some of them have achieved great recognition for their best practices in certain activities and, consequently, share these activities openly. On the whole, there are some common patterns and values which are compatible with the autonomy given by the parent company for the development of activities in the different areas and countries.

After analyzing these six companies, it becomes clear that the autonomy awarded to the different units largely encourages knowledge transfer inside the MNC, which leads us to state the following proposition:

P_6: The firm's autonomy positively influences its knowledge transfer capability

Corporate Socialization

Regardless of the formal organizational structure, informal lateral relationships emphasize a more voluntary, personal and intensive cooperation mode. Thus, teams, networks, and all other forms of interaction between different units, promote the trust required for inter-unit knowledge transfer. We can define "corporate socialization" as "the set of mechanisms developing interpersonal ties within the multinational" (Van Maanen & Schein 1979) and its purpose partly coincides with that of corporate culture. It aims to establish a set of values, aims and beliefs common to all the units forming the MNC (Nohria and Ghoshal 1994; Schein 1999).

Strong links exist between the different units in EAHSA, as shown by the continuous visits that the staff pays to the various plants of the Group, the frequent telephone calls, and the use of the corporate Intranet and the e-mail, as well as by the permanent coordination that is at place for the implementation of joint projects.

In UF, the socialization and spread of a common culture are essential for the transfer of knowledge and its later absorption. The training programs imparted at UF's Corporate University (Spanish initials, *UCUF*) which last several months, permit physical proximity between the individuals as well as the transfer of experiences that are impossible to find in textbooks or manuals. In addition to that, the strong links developed between the units through the visits to plants, the frequent telephone calls and the audio-lectures make it easier to assimilate the competencies and know-how transferred.

The links between the units in PWC tend to be very strong, especially for those participating in international practice communities, which represent an important meeting point to share experiences and many other aspects. In this case, constant visits between subsidiaries take place, as well as permanent contacts via telephone, the information and communication technologies, the e-mail and to seek advice about certain issues.

Siemens copes with the difficulty of coding knowledge bringing individuals closer to one another and paying constant visits to its various units. The company is aware of the need for a high degree of *face to face* contact if it wants to bring together the experience and capabilities still scattered at the moment. For that reason, the development of links takes place not only through trips but also with meetings, practice communities, and the use of information and communication technologies.

Telefónica is now fully aware of the potentialities that socialization offers to share the most tacit knowledge and, consequently, never misses any chances to bring its employees closer to one another, regardless of the country they come from. The annual conventions organized by the Group often serve to transfer its best practices and values. These conventions bring together various groups and offer people the opportunity to meet and get to know each other, to establish links of friendship, and to encourage dialogue, all of which largely helps knowledge transfer.

The same as Telefónica, Santander Group perfectly knows the extent to which conventions can help bring individuals closer to one another.

That is why conventions take place throughout the year in which managers meet to analyze the achievements of their units and to design action plans for the future. The most important one is Santander Group Managers' Convention, which gathers 1,000 managers from all over the world, though the Commercial Banking Convention and the America Division Managers' Convention are also worth mentioning. These meetings serve to transfer a lot of information; they provide a chance to know what is happening in other countries and additionally improve the levels of trust among group members, thus favoring later contacts between them.

It follows from the reasoning above that transfer knowledge in MNCs takes place within a shared social context, which leads us to the formulation of another proposition:

P_7: The firm's corporate socialization positively influences its knowledge transfer capability

Expatriates

The topic of expatriates has received a lot of attention in the literature on MNCs (Edström & Galbraith, 1977; Boyacigiller, 1990; O'Donnell, 2000). Human resources are a basic component of knowledge management, since individuals are the ones who possess the knowledge required, and it is the period spent at the corporation that enables them to create an organizational memory. Therefore, a leading factor in the internationalization of corporations, especially in MNCs, is that concerning the choice between local or expatriate staff for activities abroad. The latter transfers the knowledge obtained at the point of origin to another destination and gains experience from working with a multicultural workforce and dealing with different languages, attitudes and behaviors. This not only contributes to their personal development but also boosts the international activities of the organization as a whole (Bender & Fish 2000).

Although EAHSA uses expatriates, this group of employees represents a very small proportion of its total staff. We are, therefore, referring both to parent company employees who go to foreign subsidiaries and to subsidiary employees who move into the parent company in Spain. The expatriation period normally lasts three or four years. Those traveling abroad have as their main task to manage the external plants in order to transfer the group's operating style and cohesion rules. In turn, those coming to Spain learn about a number of aspects that they later transfer back to their place of origin.

Expatriates, though used in the past, are currently less and less common in UF, since the company has replaced them with local staff already trained by the *UCUF*. Expatriates were needed at first, but in recent years only those employees who are strictly necessary stay to transfer the knowledge required to manage and control the different units.

Though not very often, PWC uses expatriates too. The company employed them especially to set in motion the knowledge management project in Europe, sending expatriates from Spain to Brussels and Holland with the task of developing certain stages of the project.

Siemens equally uses expatriates as a means of transferring successful competencies. Expatriates at Siemens Spain have as their main task to implement in other countries the same that they do in Spain, as well as to provide the knowledge that they own within their area of activity. These are individuals with a high level of competencies, whose importance continues to be recognized when they return to their place of origin. The company always strives to ensure that expatriates and their families can quickly adapt to their new situation.

As for Telefónica, it also uses expatriates to take to target countries values, knowledge and management practices from its country of origin.

Thus, when Telefónica acquires a firm in a foreign country, several Spanish employees travel to that country and, during a period of time, shape a management scheme, as well as the work team required to make it operate as any other firm within the Group.

Unlike what happens in other MNCs, most of the people belonging to Santander Group work in their country of origin, since the group believes that the best way to attend to the local interests is doing it from a local perspective. Thus, expatriates are rather unusual, though over a hundred Spaniards work in banks of the Group located outside Spain, holding various levels of responsibility. These people are in charge of transferring the knowledge and cultural values from Spain to their respective destinations.

It follows from the above that, though not to a large extent, the companies examined use expatriates as a way of transferring their most strategic knowledge. Hence our last proposition:

P_8: The use of expatriates by the firm positively influences its knowledge transfer capability

CONCLUSION

The exploratory study carried out in the preceding pages starts to provide the answers to the research questions posed, simultaneously offering a global vision of firms totally integrated into the New Economy and proactive in knowledge matters. The six firms examined have been able to recognize the role played by knowledge in recent years and are well aware of the fact that they have to compete for knowledge at present. Innovation, along with the development of new competencies and capabilities and the generation of added value for the customer, has become the main aim to achieve, for which it becomes essential to implement activities focused on knowledge management.

The motivation for this research work had to do with a growing interest in getting to know how MNCs treat knowledge inside their organizations. The objective was to answer the following questions: (a) what actions do MNCs undertake to set knowledge management processes in motion? (b) what main variables impact on their knowledge creation capability? and (c) what main variables impact on their knowledge transfer capability? For that purpose, and taking as a reference both the knowledge theory and the MNC theory, we decided to use a qualitative research method based on a multiple case study.

We have carried out an in-depth examination of six MNCs characterized by being knowledge-intensive and proactive in the field of knowledge management. After a comparative study of the cases, the results showed that all the firms analyzed own a vision which recognizes the importance of knowledge; their human resources management policies seek to attract, retain and develop talent; their organizational structures have become increasingly horizontal and encourage the formation of multifunctional work teams; and the organizational culture is open to new, enterprising and learning-oriented ideas. It also became visible that knowledge creation largely depends on certain characteristics of the MNC, its internal environment, and its external network. The study showed that knowledge transfer also has to do with such aspects as autonomy, corporate socialization and the use of expatriates. All this materialized in the formulation of eight propositions.

As we pointed out in the introduction, this study contributes to the literature in two ways: from the empirical point of view, it increases the empirical evidence within the knowledge-MNC link through a focus on the actions undertaken for the purpose of managing knowledge and on the mechanisms which make possible the generation and transfer of this resource; and from a practical perspective, it provides the basis for an exploratory study which shows that management is facing new patterns. Managers need to build the necessary mechanisms that favor knowledge management, empowering employees to proactively participate in knowledge creation and transfer through the decentralization of the decision-making process (autonomy), promoting corporate socialization for the purpose of creating a work context where closer relationships between employees are possible, and combining internal and external ways of creating and/or acquiring knowledge.

Despite all the above, this study has faced a limitation due mainly to the research methodology used. Although we applied the case study method as opposed to the single case approach with the aim of preventing a potential lack of representativeness, the study does not permit to generalize the findings. Likewise, other types of variables which can differ from one company to another may affect knowledge creation and transfer. Therefore, as future research lines, we suggest an in-depth examination of other firms for the purpose of checking whether or not their variables coincide with those already studied here, as well as the implementation of some quantitative research work that can make it possible to generalize the results to a larger population.

REFERENCES

Abell, A., & Oxbrow, N. (1999). Skills for the knowledge economy: the reality of the market place. *Business Information Review, 16*(3), 115-121.

Almeida, P., Song, J., & Grant, R. (2002). Are firms superior to alliances and markets? An empirical test of cross-border knowledge building. *Organization Science, 13*(2), 147-161.

Alvesson, M., & Kärreman, D. (2005). Odd couple: making sense of the curious concept of knowledge management. *Journal of Management Studies, 38*(7), 995-1018.

Bhagat, R., Kedia, B., Harveston, P., & Triandis, H. (2002). Cultural variations in the cross-border transfer of organizational knowledge: an integrative framework. *Academy of Management Review, 27*(2), 204-221.

Balogun, J., Gleadle, P., Hailey, V., & Willmott, H. (2005). Managing change across boundaries: boundary-shaking practices. *British Journal of Management, 16*(4), 261-278.

Bender, S., & Fish, A. (2000). The transfer of knowledge and the retention of expertise: the continuing need for global assignments. *Journal of Knowledge Management, 4*(2), 125-137.

Birkinshaw, J. (1996). How multinational subsidiary mandates are gained and lost. *Journal of International Business Studies, 27*(3), 467-495.

Birkinshaw, J., Hood, N., & Jonsson, S. (1998). Building firm-specific advantages in multinational corporations: the role of subsidiary initiative. *Strategic Management Journal, 19*(3), 221-241.

Boyacigiller, N. (1990). The role of expatriates in the management of interdependence, complexity and risk in multinational corporations. *Journal of International Business Studies, 21*(3), 357-381.

Cohen, W., & Levinthal, D. (1990). Absorptive capacity: a new perspective on learning and innovation. *Administrative Science Quarterly, 35*(1), 128-152.

Davenport, T., De Long, D., & Beers, M. (1998). Successful knowledge management projects. *Sloan Management Review, 39*(2), 43-57.

Drucker, P. (1993). *Post-capitalist so*ciety. New York: HarperCollins.

Dyer, J., & Singh, H. (1998). The relational view: cooperative strategy and sources of interorganizational competitive advantage. *Academy of Management Review, 23*(4), 660-679.

Edström, A., & Galbraith, J. R. (1977). Transfer of managers as a coordination and control strategy in multinational organizations. *Administrative Science Quarterly, 22*(2), 248-268.

Eisenhardt, K. (1989). Building theories from case study research. *Academy of Management Review, 14*(4), 532-550.

Foss, N., & Pedersen, T. (2002). Transferring knowledge in MNCs: the role of sources of subsidiary knowledge and organizational context. *Journal of International Management, 8*(1), 49-67.

Frost, T., & Zhou, C. (2005). R&D co-practice and 'reverse' knowledge integration in multinational firms. *Journal of International Business Studies, 36*(6), 676-687.

Ghoshal, S., & Bartlett, C. A. (1990). The multinational corporation as an interorganizational network. *Academy Management Review, 15*(4), 603-625.

Grant, R. (1991). The resource-based theory of competitive advantage: implications for strategy formulation. *California Management Review, 33*(3), 114-135.

Grant, R. (1996). Toward a knowledge-based theory of the firm. *Strategic Management Journal, 17*(winter special issue), 109-122.

Gupta, A., & Govindarajan, V. (1991). Knowledge flows and the structure of control within multinational corporations. *Academy of Management Review, 16*(4), 768-792.

Guns, W., & Välikangas, L. (1998). Rethinking knowledge work: creating value through idiosyncratic knowledge. *Journal of Knowledge Management, 1*(4), 287-293.

Hamel, J., Dufour, S., & Fortin, D. (1993). *Case study methods.* Newbury Park: SAGE Publications.

Hansen, M. (1999). The search-transfer problem: the role of weak ties in sharing knowledge across organization subunits. *Administrative Science Quarterly, 44*(1), 82-11.

Hayek, F. A. (1945). The use of knowledge in society. *The American Economic Review*, 35(September), 519-530.

Hedlund, G. (1986). The hypermodern MNC- A heterarchy? *Human Resource Management, 25*(1), 9-35.

Helleloid, D., & Simonin, B. (1994). Organizational learning and a firm's core competence. In G. Hamel & A. Heene (Eds.), *Competence-based competition*, (pp. 213-239). Wiley, Chichester.

Hill, C., & Deeds, D. (1996). The importance of industry structure for the determination of firm profitability: a neo-Austrian perspective. *Journal of Management, 33*(4), 429-451.

Hoskisson, R., Hitt, M., Wan, W., & Yiu. D. (1999). Theory and research in strategic management: swings of a pendulum. *Journal of Management, 25*(3), 417-456.

Kogut, B., & Zander, U. (1993). Knowledge of the firm and the evolutionary theory of the multinational corporation. *Journal of International Business Studies, 24*(4), 625-645.

Kogut, B., & Zander, U. (1995). Knowledge, market failure and the multinational enterprise: a reply. *Journal of International Business Studies, 26*(2), 417-426.

Lane, P., & Lubatkin, M. (1998). Relative absorptive capacity and interorganizational learning. *Strategic Management Journal, 19*(5), 461-477.

Nelson, R., & Winter, S. (1982). *An evolutionary theory of economic change.* Cambridge, MA: Harvard University Press.

Nohria, N., & Ghoshal, S. (1994). Differentiated fit and shared values: alternatives for managing headquarters-subsidiary relations. *Strategic Management Journal, 15*(6), 491-503.

Nonaka, I., & Takeuchi, H. (1995). *The knowledge-creating company.* New York: Oxford University Press.

Nonaka, I., Toyama, R., & Konno, N. (2000). SECI, Ba and leadership: a unified model of dynamic knowledge creation. *Long Range Planning, 33*(1), 5-34.

O'donnell, S. W. (2000). Managing foreign subsidiaries: agents of headquarters, or an interdependent network? *Strategic Management Journal, 21*(5), 525-548.

Porter, M. (1990). The competitive advantage of nations. *Harvard Business Review*, 68(2), 73-94.

Quintas, P., Lefrere, P., & Jones, G. (1997). Knowledge management: a strategic agenda. *Long Range Planning, 30*(3), 385-391.

Sanna-Randaccio, F., & Veugelers, R. (2007). Multinational knowledge spillovers with decentralised R&D: a game-theoretic approach. *Journal of International Business Studies, 38*(1), 47-63.

Schein, J. (1999). What is corporate culture anyway? In *The corporate culture survival Guide*, chapter 2, , CA: Jossey-Bass, San Francisco.

Shariq, S. (1997). Knowledge management: an emerging discipline. *Journal of Knowledge Management, 1*(1), 75-82.

Spender, J. C. (1996). Making knowledge the basis of a dynamic theory of the firm. *Strategic Management Journal, 17*(winter special issue), 45-62.

Sveiby, K. (1997). *The new organizational wealth. Managing and measuring knowledge-based assets.* San Francisco, CA: Berret-Koehler Publishers, Inc.

Teece, D., Pisano, G., & Shuen, A. (1997). Dynamic capabilities and strategic management. *Strategic Management Journal, 18*(7), 509-533.

Tsai, W. (1997). Leveraging global knowledge: an empirical study of inter-unit knowledge sharing in a multinational corporation. *Strategic Management Society Conference*, October, Barcelona, Spain.

Tyre, M. J., & Von Hippel, E. (1997. The situated nature of adaptive learning in organizations. *Organization Science, 8*(1), 71-83.

Van Maanen, J., & Schein, E. H. (1979). Toward a theory of organizational socialization. In B. M. Staw (Ed.), *Research in organizational behaviour*. Greenwich, CT.

Wiig, K. (1997). Knowledge management: an introduction and perspective. *Journal of Knowledge Management, 1*(1), 6-14.

Wilson, T. D. (2002). The nonsense of 'knowledge management. *Information Research, 8*(1), paper 144.

Yin, R. (1994). *Case study research: design and methods.* 2nd edition. Newbury Park: Sage Publications.

Yin, R. (1998). The abridged version of case study research. In L. Bickman, & D. Rog (Eds.), *Handbook of applied social research methods* (pp. 229-259). Thousand Oaks, CA: Sage Publications.

Zack, M. (1999). Developing a knowledge strategy. *California Management Review, 41*(3), 125-145.

KEY TERMS

Case Study: According to Yin (1994) it is an empirical study that examines a contemporary phenomenon within its real context, especially when the limits between the phenomenon and its scope are not clearly defined and multiple sources of evidence are used.

Corporate Socialization: Set of mechanisms developing interpersonal ties within the multinational (Van Maanen & Schein 1979) and its purpose partly coincides with that of corporate culture.

Knowledge Creation: It implies both an individual and a shared reflection on the new working processes, on the products and services that a firm delivers, on the understanding of business strategy and, last but not least, on the analysis of the environment. It takes place through R&D activities, learning by doing, team work, strategic alliances, and benchmarking.

Knowledge Management: Set of business policies and actions undertaken to aid the creation of knowledge, its transfer to all members of the company, and its subsequent implementation, with the aim of achieving distinctive competencies that provide the company with a long-term competitive advantage.

Knowledge Transfer: In the case of this chapter, the concept of knowledge transfer is similar to the concept of "intracorporate knowledge flow" given by Gupta and Govindarajan (1991). It is defined as the transfer of either expertise (e.g., skills and capabilities in product and process design or marketing know-how) or external market data (information on customers, competitors or suppliers) with a high strategic value.

Knowledge: Knowledge originates from creativity, individual experiences and organizational learning, and it can be found not only in the written documents but also in the routines, tasks, processes, practices, rules and values that shape an organization (Bhagat, Kedia, Harveston & Triandis, 2002). Knowledge is therefore a dynamic concept resulting from the interactions between individuals and organizations and is also specific to a context defined by some particular time and place circumstances (Hayek, 1945; Nonaka, Toyama & Konno, 2000).

Triangulation Technique: It is the combination of three methodologies during the research in order to avoid a potential bias introduced by researchers themselves and/or by informants. In this study, triangulation technique is carried out using: in-depth interviews, observation and consulting documents.

ENDNOTES

[a] UF is the result of the merger between Unión Eléctrica Madrileña, S.A. and FENOSA.

[b] PWC is the result of the merger between Price Waterhouse and Coopers & Lybrand.

[c] Santander Group is the result of the merger between Banco Santander and Banco Central Hispano Americano.

[d] The investments undertaken refer to expenses on: R&D, production, marketing and training.

Chapter XX
Culture as a Dynamic Capability:
The Case of 3M in the United Kingdom

Cliff Bowman
Cranfield School of Management, UK

Pauline Gleadle
The Open University, UK

ABSTRACT

The chapter addresses a central dilemma from the viewpoint of dynamic capabilities and the resource based view of the firm: how to manage creativity within New Product Development without sacrificing financial control. The empirical evidence examined concerns 3M's NPD activity in the United Kingdom from a holistically viewed management control perspective at the organizational level, and a study of the development and launch of a highly successful and radically new product, Genesis. It is concluded that NPD processes within 3M in the United Kingdom display a large measure of coherence juxtaposed with flexibility through the manner in which controls, holistically viewed, are embedded within organizational routines. Using case evidence clear distinctions can be made between dynamic capabilities, resources and product outcomes, and the elements of 3M's capability can be discerned. The authors conclude that a dynamic capability can consist of both replicable elements, and elements embedded in the culture and routines of the firm that are difficult to imitate.

INTRODUCTION

This paper addresses a dilemma facing many firms: how to manage creativity within new product development processes without sacrificing financial control. It draws on arguments from the new product development (NPD) and managerial control literatures, and relates these to the recent work on dynamic capabilities. Insights from these research areas are drawn on to help us interpret NPD processes at 3M.

The empirical evidence examined concerns the development and launch of the Genesis product line, a radically new version of the industrial respirator or face-mask, substantially differentiated from the competition. While Genesis cannot be described as an 'emotional product' in design terms compared to a car for example, it was ground-breaking in concept.

This focus on a particular product launch is in line with Floyd and Wooldridge's (2000) call for strategy process studies in which the 'strategic initiative' is the primary unit of analysis. The discussion then builds on the case evidence of 3M, focussing on how the corporation handles uncertainty whilst enabling flexibility in its NPD processes, with a view to establishing whether 3M practice can be said to constitute a dynamic capability in terms of its organizational coherence. Implications of the findings for the management of 3M in the UK and the corporation are explored including in terms of whether the outcomes discussed are either replicable or path dependent (Dierickx & Cool, 1989).

"CONTROLLING" NEW PRODUCT DEVELOPMENT

On the one hand, many have argued the basic incompatibility between creativity and financial control from an essentially cultural viewpoint (Armstrong and Tomes, 1996), whilst others focus on the key role of uncertainty in new product development (Cooper, 2001).

The cultural barriers discussed by Armstrong and Tomes (1996) are set out in Table 1. They argue that design within new product development follows quite different imperatives from those of management control, with the designer being akin to 'hero artist.' Once it is attempted to render design accountable to managerial control, Armstrong and Tomes argue that outstanding financial returns are unlikely because such bastardized design is likely to be so watered down that the resulting new product is predictable, and so little different to that offered by the competition. It is the very unpredictability of outcomes

Table 1. The incompatibility of design and managerial control (Armstrong & Tomes, 1996)

Design	Managerial control
Language of design as 'quite incommensurate with written and verbal language' (Armstrong & Tomes, p. 115)	Languages of audit are those of word and number (Armstrong & Tomes, p. 122)
Communication achieved by design does not work on the rational level (A&T, p. 117).	Accountable design unlikely to achieve outstanding financial returns as likely to be the result of 'corporate-level group-think' and so 'to relate to the product field in predictable ways.'(A&T, p.123)
The designer as hero artist (A&T, p. 117)	'Self-defeating nature of accountable design stems from the impossibility of planning for an outcome which depends, in its nature, on unpredictability.'(A&T, p.123)

of the design activity that make it both difficult to manage, but also as offering the possibility of super normal profits.

Armstrong and Tomes' views as to the potentially huge divide existing between those responsible for the creative aspects of new product development and accountants seeking to control the activity are echoed in Lothian (1984), who comments:

'*[Accountants] must beat the drum about cost control and the role of profit. They must re-educate the naïve university science graduate who supposes that research resources materialise from some non-corporate source.*'(Lothian, 1984:105)

Lothian continues:

'*Accountants will get immediate co-operation from their industrial colleagues if they spell out the consequences of having* ***tight R&D targets and strong controls*** *(emphasis in bold by current authors), and of using existing resources of people and equipment efficiently.*'(1984:106)

Both Armstrong and Tomes and Lothian, speaking from different sides of the fence, therefore recognize the potential cultural divide existing between those acting within the new product development activity, and those seeking to manage it. Accordingly, Lothian argues the necessity of 'strong' controls while recognizing that this is a difficult case to make to R&D staff.

New product development (NPD) is therefore fraught with difficulty, particularly as commented upon by Drury (1996) when he notes that businesses in such situations face uncertainty, rather than risk:

'*Risk is applied to a situation where there are several possible outcomes and there is relevant past experience to enable statistical evidence to be produced for predicting possible outcomes. Uncertainty exists where there are several possible outcomes, but there is little previous statistical evidence to enable the possible outcomes to be predicted. Most business decisions can be classified in the uncertainty category.*"

DYNAMIC CAPABILITIES

Teece, Pisano and Shuen (1997) identify the "dynamic capabilities" firms require to enable them to continually refresh their resource stocks. A vital capability in this regard would be the processes that generate valuable innovations. Moreover, both Teece, Pisano and Shuen and Amit and Schoemaker (1993) identify uncertainty itself as a potential source for the creation of economic rents for firms who are capable of approaching the future more flexibly and imaginatively than their competitors (Amit and Schoemaker 1993), and 'from managerial efforts to strategically deploy these assets (of differentiated capabilities) in coordinated ways' (Teece, Pisano and Shuen 1997). Key to the creation of economic rents in this analysis therefore is both flexibility and imagination, coupled with a stress on coordination. Teece, Pisano and Shuen locate such coherence within organizational processes or routines (Nelson and Winter, 1982), which offer opportunities for superior financial performance. A successful synthesis of these seemingly conflicting requirements of flexibility and imagination coupled with coordination or control should therefore lead to such firms being able to innovate in valuable ways over long periods of time, which could be a dynamic capability in Teece et al's terms.

The key argument of this paper is that such coherence juxtaposed with flexibility and imagination is achieved in the case of 3M in the UK through the manner in which controls, holistically viewed are embedded within organizational routines, encouraging a climate of creativity. In this connection, Barney (1986) argues that core values fostering innovativeness and flexibility in firms, when linked with management control, are likely to lead to sustained superior financial performance. Whilst use is made of aspects of 'advanced' management accounting techniques in 3M, feedback from senior management in both the UK and the US indicates that 3M tends to emphasise achieving a high level of coherence among the various congruences and complementarities to be exploited in the tricky and highly uncertain process of new product development, rather than trying to attain technical accounting excellence for its own sake.

The overall aim of the paper is to fill something of a gap in the literature, following Teece, Pisano & Shuen (Page 530), who in their conclusion call for empirical research in

'...helping us understand how firms get to be good, how they sometimes stay that way, why and how they improve, and why they sometimes decline. Researchers in the field of strategy need to join forces with researchers in the fields of innovation, manufacturing, and organizational behavior and business history if they are to unlock the riddles that lie behind corporate ... competitive advantage.'

DYNAMIC CAPABILITIES: FINANCIAL CONTROL OF NPD

Against the background of widely increased perceived risk in the business environment at large (e.g. see Tidd, Bessant and Pavitt, 1997), some commentators such as Ghemawat et al (2001) stress the importance of dynamic analysis in seeking explanations for how value is built up and how organizations deal with change, especially of a fundamental nature. Accordingly, they argue that a fully dynamic view of strategy should seek to link what a company did yesterday to what it can do well today, and importantly, also to what it can accomplish well tomorrow. It is this last link that Ghemawat et al see as lacking in traditional RBV theory. Ways of dynamizing RBV and dynamic capabilities arguments are seen by these authors as including reviewing the process of making commitments and developing capabilities in the context of environmental changes and of the irreversibility of choices made by the firm:

'Choices concerning activities, resources, commitments and capabilities must be examined in depth, with an eye towards (the) tests of economic value.' (Ghemawat et al 2001:132)

They, like Teece, Pisano and Shuen, raise the issue of uncertainty and its role in the development of these superior capabilities, a crucial aspect of the dynamic capabilities argument. Moreover, Teece, Pisano and Shuen stress *coherence* within organizational processes or routines as a major means of dealing with uncertainty.

A dynamic capabilities perspective locates coherence within organizational processes or routines, which may offer opportunities for superior financial performance. This is because replication of such coherence by other firms can be tricky, requiring as it does systemic changes throughout the organization as a whole and changes to linkages with outsiders. But there is a debate within the dynamic capabilities literature as to the extent to which the capability to create and reconfigure resources can be repeated internally, or copied (replicated) externally. For something to be judged to be an organizational capability we would expect there to be evidence of repeated performance. So a 'one-off' reconfiguration of the firm's resource base would probably not be considered to be a dynamic capability. Where there is evidence of repeated performance, and possibly the accumulation of expertise and know-how through these experiences, we would consider the firm to have built a dynamic capability. The second question relates to whether this capability could be replicated by rival firms. Eisenhardt and Martin (2000) suggest that most dynamic capabilities are not unique in the RBV sense, as they can be found across a number of competing firms. Competing firms may indeed have 'generic' dynamic capabilities, e.g., they all engage in R and D, but the broad generic categorization of an activity masks important differences in the execution and performance impact of a specific set of activities within a particular firm viz. all pharmaceutical firms engage in R and D but some are clearly more successful at benefiting from R and D activity than others.

The particular enactment of a dynamic capability is sensitive to firm context. The impact of the capability will be determined in part on the presence or absence of complementary capabilities and circumstances, which would include aspects of the firm's history and its culture. Thus to progress our understanding of dynamic capabilities we need to investigate specific firm contexts in ways that enable us to account for complementarities and coherence within the organization.

The view of the necessity of coherence within organizational processes or routines is arguably compatible with more recent developments in management control theory, which stress the importance of understanding management control in terms of management control *packages* (Otley, 1999), incorporating an accumulation of both informal and formal control mechanisms. Weber's (1947) concept of collegiality as a strong informal mechanism of control is well recognized within universities, for example, and more recently Simons (1991 & 1995) has identified further mechanisms of informal control. He argues that in innovative firms in particular, senior managers may use quite standard profit-planning information *interactively*, rather that diagnostically as is traditionally the case, in dealing with more junior staff. The objective of such interactive control, rather than being that of diagnosing problems, becomes that of interrogating the environment, via the perceptions of staff closer to the customer, in order to remain alert to emerging threats and opportunities in a rapidly changing environment.

However, arguably such use of interactive control mechanisms will only be possible where Finance acts as something of an 'integrating vernacular' (Nixon & Innes, 1998), linking different levels of staff across functional areas through a common language. In such circumstances therefore, it is not the sophistication of controls from a purely technical accounting viewpoint that is important. Rather what counts is their embeddedness within organizational routines at large in an environment that prioritizes, in equal measure, creativity and financial control. If such a level of embeddedness is achieved, then this is argued to go far beyond the purely systemic approach advocated by some management writers (e.g. Keating, Oliva, Repenning, Rockart & Sterman, 1999) and instead, firms approach the level of the coherence required to achieve superior financial performance in RBV terms.

Finally, in the context of risk reduction in NPD, a further mechanism involves the use of cross-functional teams (Doucherty, 1992), which are argued to effect risk minimization through harnessing the phenomenon of team members having to understand the 'thought worlds' of others. Doucherty suggests that these thought worlds are usually coherent in themselves for team members from different functional areas. However, they will tend to be necessarily partial, 'partitioning the product into separate sources of uncertainty' (Doucherty, Page 187), a phenomenon that may prevent the development of a more comprehensive understanding of the market. Accordingly, through the effective use of cross-functional teams in new product development, companies can reduce risk by building a more complete picture of both the risks and opportunities inherent in the process.

The next section reviews briefly evidence from three corporations researched by Tushman and O'Reilly (1996) which are judged to have track records of successful NPD: Hewlett Packard (HP), AB&B and Johnson & Johnson. This is followed by a summary of prior research into 3M.

EVIDENCE OF SUCCESSFUL NPD CAPABILITIES

Tushman and O'Reilly (1996) discuss the necessity for an increasing alignment between strategy, structure and processes in organizations whilst they simultaneously prepare for revolutionary change necessitated by discontinuities in the environment, an alignment that could be interpretable in dynamic capabilities terms as coherence. They describe this as the ability of the firm to be 'ambidextrous.' Like Barney (1986), they argue that culture can provide competitive advantage, although it can also create obstacles to innovation. However, an important commonalty that they identify in HP, AB&B and Johnson & Johnson, which they regard as being examples of ambidextrous organizations, concerns the creation of small autonomous units within the context of a much larger organization. Moreover, they also highlight the co-existence of strong continually reinforced social or 'soft' controls alongside 'harder' clear mechanisms for 'killing' projects.

With regard to 3M in particular, the company has been extensively written about in the management literature (e.g. see Peters and Waterman, 1982; Kanter, 1984; Shaw, Brown and Bromiley, 1998; Brown and Eisenhardt, 1998; Von Hippel et al, 1999) and tends to be viewed primarily as an innovator, strategic thinker or as a company otherwise adept at the use of 'soft' cultural mechanisms in promoting innovation. These include its almost explicit encouragement of a culture of 'bucking the system' by individuals determined to have their own projects implemented despite official obstacles. Indeed, 3M senior management is famous for such remarks as:

'We want to institutionalize a bit of rebellion in our labs.'

and

'It has been said that the competition never knows what we are going to come up with next. The fact is, neither do we.'

(Both remarks attributable to John Mueller, Chairman and former CEO of 3M Company's UK operations, cited in Gleadle (1999)).

One of the few exceptions to this emphasis on 3M's 'softer' aspects and so arguably, a more complete picture of the company is to be found in Brown and Eisenhardt (1998).

Importantly, while Brown and Eisenhardt (Page 15) describe 3M as

'...a bit bipolar...poised at the edge of chaos'

they indicate that this popular conception of the company does not represent the full story. They refer to the importance of cost management at 3M, and to the company's essentially risk-averse culture, despite appearances to the contrary in the management literature:-

'Managers rarely make huge moves and rarely place risky bets; instead, they relentlessly change the company year after year.'(Brown and Eisenhardt, 1998:15).

Tellingly, Brown and Eisenhardt refer to 3M's 'sophisticated financial controls and information systems' despite their view of 3M strategy as a

'...loosely coherent direction ....' (Brown and Eisenhardt, 1998:17)

according to which 3M follows 'internally generated rhythm' (Brown and Eisenhardt, 1998:180), arising partly from the fixed percentage of sales targeted every year to be derived from new products.

While Brown and Eisenhardt's picture of 3M is the most consistent with the views of the authors found to date within the management literature, the current chapter attempts to develop understanding of 3M's processes for dealing with uncertainty, a key issue in NPD. Specifically, in contrast to Brown and Eisenhardt's vision of 3M as employing 'sophisticated financial controls', this paper argues instead that the financial controls in themselves are *not* that sophisticated in a purely technical sense. Instead, what is argued to represent a dynamic capability for 3M is the holistic manner in which these controls are embedded within the company's organizational routines.

RESEARCH METHOD

The current longitudinal historical case study is the result of a long-standing involvement with 3M in the UK, stretching over a period of seven years. Over the course of this period, different aspects of management and management accounting practice have been studied, primarily through use of semi-structured interviews with individuals at different levels in the organizational hierarchy, across three 3M locations in the UK and covering the Finance, Sales & Marketing, Manufacturing and various UK R&D-related functions. Additionally, there has been some limited feedback on the issue of the NPD: Finance interface from a senior 3M source in the US, which has provided useful corroboration of the findings within 3M in the UK.

For the current researcha pilot study was conducted with the aim of compiling an 'explanatory' case study (Yin, 1984) at the organizational level as to how 3M in the UK sought to encourage innovation whilst exercising sufficient financial control. Managers from a variety of R&D-related functions were interviewed at the UK R&D site in Swansea and these findings were written up in Gleadle (1999). Subsequently, a historical case study was conducted at the project level in order to understand the more detailed mechanisms involved from concept to product launch and beyond in terms of how 3M managed the Finance: NPD interface. For this more detailed study, members of the Core Team were interviewed and re-interviewed, both individually and as a team,, related documentation was reviewed and the processes involved discussed with 3M senior management in the UK, thereby triangulating findings against each other. Moreover, whenever any academic presentations or conference papers have been written by the authors on the subject of 3M's NPD activity, these have always been cleared by the company, both in terms of checking the accuracy of the detail as well as for reasons of company confidentiality.

CASE EVIDENCE: 3M'S NEW PRODUCT DEVELOPMENT ACTIVITY IN THE UK

While it is evident that 3M staff tend to be quite proud about the wealth of stories within the company concerning successful products that had to 'buck the system' in order to be implemented, there are nonetheless well-established NPD processes within 3M. At an organizational level, the overriding performance measure of Economic Profit is cascaded throughout the Group as a whole. However, in contrast with some other strategic financial control mechanisms such as Economic Value Added® (EVA® Stern Stewart, 1995), Economic Profit is quite deliberately loosely implemented in the view both of one senior corporate manager and also of local 3M management in the UK. This loose implementation is designed so as not to stifle innovation. Moreover, an additional support mechanism of Pacing Plus (P+) strategic recognition (Tidd et al 1997) by the Centre is in place for facilitating the progress of promising projects, which is explored in detail later in the context of the Genesis project. (Note that subsequently the Pacing Plus was replaced by a similar programme, 3M Acceleration).

As discussed in Gleadle (1999), perhaps surprisingly at first sight, the UK R&D function is characterized by a lack of formal financial control mechanisms. However, what emerges on closer examination is a wealth of self-reinforcing processes of collegial control (Weber, 1947), such as the existence of quarterly Technical Forum conferences for R&D staff. Moreover, UK R&D staff in 3M appear considerably more financially literate as a group than their comparators in other knowledge-intensive firms researched by the authors, as well as being more closely linked into the Sales and Marketing function. This linkage into Sales and Marketing manifests itself for example in the common career path of industrial chemists moving from UK R&D into Sales and Marketing, a move generally viewed positively in career development terms, and also in the role of the UK Technical Director. His remit is to liaise with customers so as to inform them of new applications of 3M's range of over 55,000 products, as well as remaining alert to the changing requirements of lead users in particular, who are the most demanding customers and therefore also the best source of new ideas for future NPD. This is important in the case of complex products where potential users may not be able to articulate their needs. Therefore successful innovators need to be able to lead existing customers and identify potential new customers. These potential users may need to be 'educated' which creates a situation where conventional market research techniques are of little use. This is a process referred to by Hamel & Prahalad (1994) as 'expeditionary marketing.'

Should a project pass successfully through the hurdles examined in the next sub-section of the case evidence, then a *cross-functional* Business Team may be established to develop the product. These teams traditionally enjoy a high level of operating autonomy in having the freedom to behave in an almost entrepreneurial fashion, but within corporate constraints. While this might appear at first sight unrelated to issues of risk management, Doucherty has argued that such cross-functional teams act as an important risk reduction mechanism in harnessing the quite different perspectives of team members so as to build a more cross-functionally complete profile of risks inherent in a project. Moreover, in terms of flexibility, Gleadle (1999) has commented that this practice of establishing a small business team early on in a project's life, enables 3M to benefit from the very real advantages afforded by much smaller firms in terms of speed of response. However, crucially such 3M Business Teams continue to benefit from the advantages of belonging to a major multinational.

Within the Business Team, a key member is the Financial Analyst whose job it is to act as educator for the team in transmitting the organizational vernacular of Finance (Nixon and Innes, 1998). As with the common 3M-career move from R&D into Sales and Marketing, the role of the Financial Analyst tends to be prized by accountants within the group who regard it as being a good move because of the Financial Analyst's proximity to Sales and Marketing within the business teams. Crucially however, as with 3M's deliberately loose implementation of Economic Profit, the emphasis by the Finance function tends to be upon adopting what are perceived to be the useful comprehensible aspects of 'advanced' accounting techniques such as Activity Based Costing, rather than seeking theoretical perfection in implementation. This emphasis on widespread comprehensibility of financial information is crucial in 3M's use of interactive control (Simons, 1991 & 1995) by senior managers who in their ongoing product viability reviews, use quite standard profit-planning information. Through regular reviews with more junior staff closer to the customer, profit-planning information is used interactively in order to probe for emerging threats and opportunities in the environment.

At the project level, further mechanisms exist for managing uncertainty whilst enabling the necessary flexibility for the majority of standard non-Pacing Plus designated projects.

THE PROGRESS OF A SUCCESSFUL PROJECT THROUGH 'THE SYSTEM' IN 3M (UK)

At the concept stage, project ideas are filtered through the cross-functionally managed New Product Introduction (NPI) system, and those passing this test will be subject to continued scrutiny as to whether they fulfil financial criteria in terms of meeting Economic Profit targets. The main form of this financial scrutiny is the ongoing product viability reviews by senior management already described. Should an individual project pass these tests, both of an NPI and financial nature, and also show signs of particular promise, then a cross-functional business team may be established. However, despite a project being managed by a business team, unless it has been designated Pacing Plus (P+), it will continue to be subject to scrutiny under the system of product viability reviews.

Additionally however, an important support mechanism exists as while products belong to the divisions within 3M, technology is owned by the Corporation. This means that technical managers work for the centre and are allocated as necessary to projects needing technical help, so that these managers may spend their careers working across a range of divisions. Accordingly, this has important implications even for non-P+ projects with respect to the technical support they are afforded in enabling them to react flexibly and speedily to technical problems and perceived changes in the environment.

For Pacing Plus projects however, progress through the system in 3M in the UK is substantially different in many respects.

THE SELECTION AND MANAGEMENT OF PACING PLUS PROJECTS

A project is designated Pacing Plus (P+) only if two conditions are satisfied. First, financial forecasts should indicate super-normal profitability according to corporate criteria. Secondly, the project should be of a sufficiently ground-breaking nature so as to 'change the basis of competition.' The second condition refers to the requirement that development of a project should be so substantially different from what is currently on the market that it will take the competition some years to catch up, thereby guaranteeing 3M an element of sustained competitive advantage. Arguably in terms of the resource based view, 3M's mechanism of strategic recognition of projects as being P+ is important in understanding the process of economic rent creation. Specifically, the operation of this second condition is an attempt to identify projects that satisfy the RBV "VRIN" criteria (the resource is simultaneously valuable, rare, inimitable and non-substitutable).

Once a project is recognized as being P+, this has at least four major implications. Firstly, the project is ring-fenced from the product viability review process so that its future existence is not jeopardized. Secondly, a Business Team will be formed, often with substantial Sales and Marketing input. In the case of Genesis, an S&M manager was allocated to the project for 50% of his time early on in the project's life, and he was subsequently given full-time responsibility for the project. Given that it has been argued that the successful handling of uncertainty is an aspect of resource creating capabilities, this high level of S&M input had important implications for Genesis. As a major issue in NPD concerns uncertainty regarding sales income forecasts, this heavy level of S&M involvement throughout the project helped ensure that actual financial outcomes were very close to forecasts This is particularly remarkable given the ground-breaking nature of the Genesis respirator, and therefore the lack of comparable market information available.

The two further important implications of P+ designation for a project concern the level of extra resources forthcoming from the centre should these be needed. These resources may be of a financial nature, as when the Accelerating Program was introduced in order to bring Genesis to market more quickly than originally planned. Finally, these extra resources from the centre may also be of a technical nature. In the case of Genesis, problems were encountered in the course of its development with a particular component part, which were resolved relatively speedily with special technical assistance from the US.

Importantly, therefore because Genesis had been designated P+, it was offered protection from potential cutbacks throughout its development. Moreover, being designated P+ also afforded the project real benefits in terms of the extra resources it was allocated both of a technical and a financial nature. It has been argued that an important element of these extra resources concerns the dedicated S&M expertise afforded early on in the project, which was crucial in addressing the key issue of uncertainty in financial forecasts in such a radically new product. This accuracy in financial projections had major knock-on effects in terms of planning for other aspects of the project's implementation e.g. from a manufacturing and logistics standpoint to name just two of the areas affected.

Table 2 sets out a time line for the Genesis project. The idea for Genesis originated during one of the 3M technical conferences, argued to be indicative of collegial control within the R&D areas of the company. Importantly, there was substantial Sales and Marketing input very early on in Genesis' life, with a dedicated Marketing Manager being assigned to the project for 50% of his time, as befits Genesis' P+ status. Other

Table 2. The sequence of events for the Genesis Project

START	**Conference in US on manufacturing technologies. Decision to look for new technologies for identical processes (i.e. rather than improve current processes). UK technical team chosen to implement this for new type of respirator. (Concurrently, Team drawing on US expertise through 3M's system of global conferences). UK Marketing Manager assigned to team for 50% of his time. EBOC (European Business Operating Committee) asked Core Team to accelerate introduction to market because of increased competition. Second request for capital funding to the US. New full-time Marketing Manager assigned to team. Product Launch Team formed. Technical problems with component part of respirator. US involvement in identifying necessity of entirely new approach to problem's resolution and in coming up with solution. Product Launch Team delivered integrated launching scenario for approval by MD of the European Business Centre (EBC). Product launched at German business fair.**

crucial factors include the Core Team's successful request for extra funds to accelerate introduction to market because of increased competitive pressures plus US/Corporate involvement in resolving technical problems with a component part of the respirator.

DISCUSSION

From the evidence presented, it has been argued that 3M deals with the apparently irresolvable dilemma (Armstrong and Tomes, 1996) of how to manage creativity within New Product Development without sacrificing financial control by means of the manner in which controls, holistically viewed, are embedded within organizational routines in a culture fostering innovation. This is evident at the organizational level within 3M, lending support to Barney's contention that core values fostering innovativeness and flexibility in firms, when linked with management control, are likely to lead to sustained superior financial performance. The case of the Genesis project and how it was both accommodated and nurtured within 3M, with its highly satisfactory financial outcomes, is argued to provide a useful mini case study illustrating Barney's contention. This is all the more remarkable because of the ground-breaking nature of the Genesis design so that this appears to overcome Armstrong and Tomes' contention as to the 'self-defeating nature of accountable design' (Armstrong and Tomes, 1996:123). Moreover, it is argued that the current study adds to the existing literature on what 'makes 3M good' to paraphrase Teece, Pisano and Shuen (1997), in that it explores further Brown and Eisenhardt's (1998) picture of the company as one managing to combine an almost restless search for further innovation, with management control. However, in contrast to Brown and Eisenhardt's view of 3M as exercising sophisticated financial controls and information systems, it has been argued that the techniques and controls themselves are not 'advanced' in a purely technical sense. Instead, the strength of the NPD process in 3M in the UK lies in the apparently holistic view of management control underlying the combination of controls, both formal and informal, that goes beyond the merely systemic approach advocated in much of the management literature. This speaks of a degree of coherence as the various congruences and complementarities within the NPD process are exploited, whilst concurrently apparently allowing both R&D Technical staff in the UK and the Genesis Core Team the necessary room for manoeuvre so as to work effectively without undue senior management interference.

At the organizational level in 3M, the dual threats and opportunities inherent in an uncertain business environment are managed mainly through informal control mechanisms, aspects of a culture which continues to encourage an element of 'bucking the system'. Accordingly, while UK technical staff are subject to collegial control (Weber 1947), they are also financially literate to a degree unusual in other companies researched by the authors. Moreover, further congruence is evident in the linkages that exist and are nurtured between the UK R&D functions and Sales and Marketing for example, in terms of the common career path of R&D scientists moving across to the Sales and Marketing function and in the UK Technical Director's role in facilitating 'expeditionary marketing'(Hamel & Prahalad, 1994).

Within the more commercial areas of the company, this degree of financial literacy manifests itself in senior managers' use of quite standard profit-planning information. Following Simons (1991; 1995), this financial information, which is widely understood at more junior levels within the company, is used as a mechanism of interactive control so as to enable senior managers to interrogate the environment via the perceptions of lower-level staff closer to the customer, both as to emerging threats and opportunities. Finance therefore appears to fulfil some of its promise noted by Nixon and Innes (1998) in acting as an effective 'integrating vernacular,' linking creativity with management control.

This high degree of financial literacy is encouraged through other mechanisms embedded in day-to-day organizational routines, rather than through a great stress on formal financial training. Accordingly, the Financial Analyst present on every Business Team plays a key role in disseminating knowledge about such matters as the calculation of Economic Profit, Group capital approval methodologies and Unit Cost policies, which in any case tend to stress comprehensibility and usefulness rather than theoretical rigour relentlessly pursued for its own sake.

At the project level, the focus of this study has been upon the process of making commitments or of ratification processes. Here, it has been argued that a primary mechanism of addressing uncertainty is to be found again in the strength of intra-company linkages so that the cross-functional nature of both the New Product Introduction system at the earliest stages and of the business team later, use Doucherty's (1992) notion of risk minimization through capitalizing on the different 'thought worlds' of employees from quite distinct functional areas. Moreover, these processes function under the overall umbrella of Economic Profit, loosely implemented though it may be, which acts as a filter to screen out projects not forecast to meet Group financial objectives.

However, as well as these measures for risk minimization, it has been argued also that a further support mechanism is in place encouraging potentially radical innovation in the form of Pacing Plus designation. As described and illustrated in the case of Genesis, being designated Pacing Plus had major implications for the success of the project in terms of the extra sales and marketing support afforded from very early on its life as well the extra financial and technical resources it was able to command from the Centre at critical points in its development. However, in understanding coherence within the management control processes involved in NPD in 3M at the local UK level, it is perhaps the early injection of dedicated sales and marketing expertise from staff who had the necessary technical background that stands out as a key factor in deciding the eventual accuracy of the sales income forecasts, usually one of the major sources of uncertainty in the financial planning of New Product Development.

The overall picture of 3M from a management control perspective emerges as being remarkably similar in some important respects to the three companies studied by Tushman and O'Reilly (1996). Specifically, like Tushman and O'Reilly's three companies studied, 3M favours the creation of small autonomous units, the use of strong and continually reinforced social controls as well as 'harder' clear mechanisms for 'killing' projects. However, what this study has attempted to contribute is an illumination of the juxtaposition of these 'softer' and 'harder' controls embedded within day-to-day practices in the overall operation of the 3M management control system from an NPD perspective.

In terms of dynamic capabilities, this combination of a climate of creativity allied with financial control would appear to offer a significant source of sustainable competitive advantage in that it is not easily replicable (Dierickx & Cool, 1989) by other firms. Moreover, path dependency is evident in the manner in which this culture of creativity allied with financial control is so embedded within organizational practice at all levels with 3M. As explained by Zollo and Winter "a dynamic capability is a *learned and stable pattern of collective activity* through which the organization systematically generates and modifies its operating routines in pursuit of improved effectiveness" (Zollo and Winter 2002, 340, emphasis added). This culture of creativity has clearly been 'built' rather than bought (Makadok, 2001) and is embedded in the firm (Eisenhardt and Martin, 2000).

Given the evidence presented, could other firms could copy what 3M have done and how they would do this? The R&D linkages to Sales and Marketing and the common use of the financial vernacular in the R&D function would take some time to be built up by another company, so that this capability exhibits some elements of path dependency, and so of a potential lack of immediate imitability. Moreover, it is also doubtful whether the effects of this capability in terms of producing valuable innovation, could be easily substituted by other means e.g. simply through acquiring other companies who have successfully developed particular products, rather than nurturing and integrating the NPD activity in-house. With regard to other aspects of 3M practice discussed, the Technical Director's 'expeditionary marketing' activity and the technical nature of most sales and marketing staff hardly count as dynamic capabilities in themselves. On the other hand, 3M's tradition of setting up autonomous teams, empowering staff to behave in an entrepreneurial fashion, might count to some extent as a dynamic capability, as might the widespread cultural acceptance of bucking the system to get your own project accepted. By way of contrast, explicit systems such as P+ and the product viability reviews are highly imitable individually in themselves, but what is argued to constitute a dynamic capability, is the *combination* of these processes, some of which have been argued to be path dependent.

Moreover, to date we have little theoretical or empirical evidence to base any suggestions as to how dynamic capabilities can be deliberately built. Eisenhardt and Martin (2000) take the view that dynamic capabilities might be commonly found within an industry, and that they may not be differentiated across a collection of firms. They conclude that dynamic capabilities are equifinal, substitutable and fungible: many firms will have similar dynamic capabilities. Smart, Bessant and Gupta (2007) found some evidence of network level dynamic capabilities in the biotech industry and Lampel and Shamsie (2003) provide some evidence of industry dynamic capabilities in the Hollywood movie industry.

This would imply that dynamic capabilities might be relatively easy to build. However, and invoking an RBV perspective on uniqueness, we would argue that dynamic capabilities are only likely to be similar across firms if we describe them in broad aggregated terms. Feldman and Pentland (2003) distinguish between ostensive and performative aspects of routines. The ostensive aspect of the routine is the structure or abstract understanding of the routine, and the performative aspect is the actual performance of the routine (Feldman and Pentland 2003). If dynamic capabilities are indeed repeated performances they are akin to high level organisational routines (Collis 1994; Zott 2003). The ostensive routine i.e. the abstract description of the dynamic capability might be very similar across competing firms e.g. 'we all do R&D'. However, we would expect that the performative aspect of the routine, the dynamic capability *in practice*, would display subtle but important differences between firms. In addition, even where the performative capability was identical across firms, the supporting and complementary processes and assets are most likely to be differentiated, thus the effect of the common capability would be variable.

This study therefore enables us to elaborate and extend the concept of dynamic capability. First, it is important to distinguish between a dynamic capability and a resource. Although a dynamic capability may display some of the characteristics of a resource, for example, it might be difficult to imitate, it is a fundamentally different construct. In order for a resource to generate rents it must be directly connected to the production of a product or service that produces a revenue stream for the firm. In contrast, a dynamic capability is a process that *creates* resources. In this respect the dynamic capability is one step removed from the direct production of products and services. It operates outside or alongside the rent generating resources. In the case of 3M, the dynamic capability explored in this paper created resources which produced an innovative, rent generating product.

Secondly, the study suggests that a dynamic capability is most likely to be complex, thus restricting the ability of competitors to replicate the process. But although the capability may be complex, elements of it may well be easily replicable. This would indicate that there may be several forms of dynamic capability:

a. A capability may comprise some elements that are replicable with other elements that are very difficult to imitate.
b. A capability may be constructed around a set of replicable elements, but it is the particular configuration of elements that is difficult to replicate.
c. A capability may consist both of elements and configurations that are difficult to replicate.

It would seem that in 3M we have an example of a category c) capability. Some elements of the NPD process are easily understandable and hence replicable in other firms, for example the use of cross-functional business teams or the use of a mechanism similar to Pacing Plus designation, but they are embedded in a culture that is peculiar to 3M. This culture establishes the context wherein these elements can configure to deliver a stream of profitable product innovations. So the use of hurdle rates, routine financial information, and cross-functional teams are all individually replicable in other firms. These are unremarkable elements of most screening processes, likely to be common to many corporations. But the culture in which these knowable elements are embedded is idiosyncratic. Similarly, practices that create the culture may themselves be understandable and replicable, like the movement of staff between functions. But the pursuit of these and other practices consistently over long periods results in the establishment of a cultural context that enhances the value of more standardised and replicable practices. The fact that R and D staff can see that others have made successful moves into the sales area gives them confidence and reassurance to make the move themselves. But a history of successful transitions takes time to be established. Thus the cultural context is a path dependent aspect of the capability.

Thirdly, the study helps us to understand in more detail important distinctions between dynamic capabilities, resources and products/services. Specifically, from the case we can identify the elements of a dynamic capability which produces resources. But the produced face mask itself is *not* a resource. A stream of rents can only flow from the repeated production and sale of these products. The capabilities to produce valued products over time are the firm resources in this case. So the resources involved in generating a rent stream from the Genesis project would be: a patented product *concept*; the manufacturing know-how to produce this product in large volumes to a tight quality specification; the sales and marketing capability to achieve the required sales volumes and prices. The last two resources combine to produce sales volumes and margins.

Fourthly, this study provides an example of where existing resources are extended or leveraged through the dynamic capability processes. It is arguable in the case of 3M that manufacturing and marketing resources existed in some form prior to the Genesis project. Indeed, in any established firm any new product is likely to be leveraging some extant resources to some degree. The *specific* resources created via Genesis would be the *particular* know-how required to mass produce the face mask, and the particular expertise required to market it. Clearly we can add to this list of resource increments the patented product concept itself. But to be entirely clear we would have to recognize that the firm's extant resources are already engaged in the production of a saleable product, which generates the rent stream. If this resource can be leveraged or extended in some way, the process whereby this takes place is a dynamic capability. With the development of Genesis, the development process benefited from

Figure 1. The elements of 3M's dynamic capability

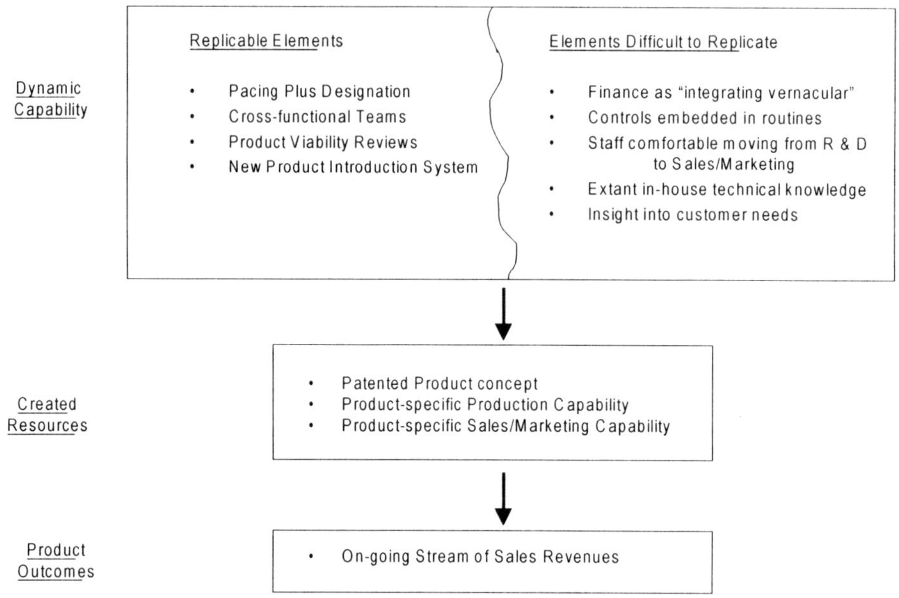

extant technical expertise that has been built up in the firm through prior product development processes. In addition, the past experience of the UK technical director provided beneficial insights into customer needs.

So dynamic capabilities create resources that may be incremental extensions of existing resource capabilities, or be entirely new to the firm. Where the firm embarks on a truly unrelated product development process it is likely that whole new set of resources would be developed, which of course is likely to be extremely difficult to achieve and hence would be very risky.

In figure 1 we have summarised our analysis of the Genesis product innovation process. The dynamic capability consisted of replicable systems operating within an idiosyncratic cultural context. The resources produced by this process were the patented product *concept*, the technical capability to produce this product in the required volumes, and the marketing and sales expertise to sell it at the required prices and volumes. So these newly created resources generate an on-going stream of revenues, a proportion of these revenues being *rents*.

CONCLUSION

We have aimed to fill something of a gap in the literature identified by Teece, Pisano & Shuen (1997) in their call for empirical research in helping us understand 'how firms get to be good.' The handling of uncertainty in terms of enabling flexibility and imagination, but under the umbrella of a coherent view of management control and organizational coordination has formed the focus of this paper. Moreover, ratification processes have been examined in some detail, particularly with reference to Genesis, a highly successful strategic new product.

It has been argued that New Product Development processes within 3M in the UK display a large measure of coherence juxtaposed with flexibility through the manner in which controls, holistically viewed, are embedded within organizational routines. This supports Barney's (1986) view that core values fostering innovativeness and flexibility in firms, when linked with management control, are likely to lead to sustained superior financial performance.

Thus a dynamic capability is not a single organizational process. In the case of 3M it is a product of a complex interaction or interchange between explicit, managed systems, and embedded routines, values and behaviours that are mutually reinforcing. It is valuable, in that it *creates* resources, which produce a stream of revenues from the sale of patented products. These products are financially successful and cannot be readily reproduced in another substitute way.

ACKNOWLEDGMENT

This paper is based on two studies, the first funded by the Chartered Institute of Management Accountants (CIMA) in the UK and the second, jointly by CIMA and the Design Council, also in the UK. We would like to thank Naomi Gornick of Naomi Gornick Associates in the UK for her help with this project.

REFERENCES

Amit, R., & Schoemaker, P. J. H. (1993). Strategic assets and organizational rent. *Strategic Management Journal, 14*, 33-46.

Armstrong, P., & Tomes, A. (1996). Art and accountability: the languages of design and management control. *Accounting, Auditing & Accountability Journal, 9*(5), 114-125.

Barney, J. B. (1989). Asset stocks and sustained competitive advantage: a comment. *Management Science, 35*(12), 1511-1513.

Barney, J. B. (1991). Firm resources and sustained competitive advantage. *Journal of Management, 17*, 99-120.

Barney, J. B. (1986). Organizational culture: can at be a source of sustained competitive advantage? *Academy of Management Review, 11*(3), 656-666.

Barney, J. B. (2001). Is the resource-based "view" a useful perspective for strategic management research? Yes. *The Academy of Management Review, 26*(1), 41-56.

Brown, S. L., & Eisenhardt, K. M. (1998). *Competing on the edge: strategy as structured chaos.* Harvard Business School Press.

Collis, D. J. (1994). Research note: how valuable are organizational capabilities? *Strategic Management Journal, 15*(S1), 143-152.

Cooper, R. (2001). *Winning at new products: accelerating the process from idea to Launch* (3rd Edition). Perseus Publishing.

Dierickx, I., & Cool, K. (1989). Asset stock accumulation and sustainability of competitive advantage. *Management Science, 35*(12), 1504-1511.

Doucherty, D. (1992). Interpretive barriers to successful product development in large firms. *Organization Science, 3*(2), 179-202.

Drury, C. (1996). *Management and Cost Accounting* (4th Edition). Thomson Business Press.

Eisenhardt, K. M., & Martin, J. A. (2000). Dynamic Capabilities: What are They? *Strategic Management Journal, 21*, 1105-1121.

Feldman, M. S., & Pentland, B. T. (2003). Reconceptualizing organizational routines as a source of flexibility and change. *Administration Science Quarterly, 48*(1), 94-118.

Floyd, S. W., & Wooldridge, B. (2000). *Building strategy from the middle: reconceptualizing the strategy process.* Sage.

Ghemawat, P., Collis, D. J., Pisano, G. P., & Rivkin, J. W. (2001). *Strategy and the business landscape: core concepts*. Prentice Hall.

Gleadle, P. (1999). The interface between Finance and New Product Development: encouraging a climate of innovation. *Management Accounting* July/August, (pp. 24-25).

Hamel, G., & Prahalad (1994). *Competing for the future*. Harvard Business School Press.

Kanter, R. M. (1984). *The change masters: corporate entrepreneurs at work.* George Allen & Unwin, UK.

Keating, E., Oliva, R., Repenning, N., Rockart, S., & Sterman, J. (1999). Overcoming the Improvement Paradox. *European Management Journal, 17*(2), 120-134.

King, A. W., & Zeithaml, C. P. (2001). Competencies and firm performance: examining the causal ambiguity paradox. *Strategic Management Journal, 22*, 75-99.

Lampel J. and Shamsie, J. (2003). Capabilities in motion: new organizational forms and the reshaping of the Hollywood movie industry. *Journal of Management Studies*, *40*(8), 2189-2210.

Lothian, N. (1984). *How companies manage R&D: a survey of major UK companies.* The Institute of Cost and Management Accountants.

Macintosh, N. B. (1994). *Management accounting and control systems: an organizational and behavioral approach.* Wiley.

Makadok, R. (2001). Towards a synthesis of the resource-based and dynamic capability views of rent creation. *Strategic Management Journal, 22*, 387-401.

Nelson, R., & Winter, S. (1982). *An evolutionary theory of economic change.* Belknap Press: Harvard University Press.

Nixon, W., & Innes, J. (1998). Management accountants and design. *Management Accounting*, June 1998.

Ouchi, W. G. (1980). Markets, bureaucracies and clans. *Administrative Science Quarterly, 25*, 129-141.

Peters, T. J., & Waterman, R. H. (1982). In search of excellence: lessons from America's best-run companies. Harper Collins.

Priem, R. L., & Butler, J. E. (2001). Is the resource-based "view" a useful perspective for strategic management research? *Academy of Management Review, 26*(1), 22-40.

Rumelt, R. P. (1991). How much does industry matter? *Strategic Management Journal, 12*, 167-185.

Shaw, G., Brown, R., & Bromiley, P. (1998). Strategic stories: how 3M is rewriting business planning. *Harvard Business Review,* May-June 1998, (pp. 41-50).

Simons, R. (1991). Strategic orientation and top management attention to control systems. *Strategic Management Journal,* (pp. 49-62).

Simons, R. (1995). Control in an age of empowerment. *Harvard Business Review*, March-April.

Simons, R. (2000). *Performance measurement and control systems for implementing strategy: text and cases.* Prentice Hall.

Smart P., Bessant, J., & Gupta, A. (2007). Towards technological designing innovation a dynamic capabilities. *International Journal of Operations and Production Management*, 27(10), 1069-1092

Stern, S. (1995). What's your company's EVA®? What you don't know may be hurting you. *Advertisement in the Harvard Business Review*, July-August, (p. 143).

Teece, D. J., Pisano, G., & Shuen, A. (1997). Dynamic capabilities and strategic management. *Strategic Management Journal, 18*(7), 509-533.

Tidd, J., Bessant, J., & Pavitt, K. (1997). *Managing innovation: integrating technological, market and organizational change*. John Wiley.

Tushman, M. L., & O'Reilly, C. A. (1996). Ambidextrous organizations: managing evolutionary and revolutionary change. *California Management Review, 38*(4), 8-30.

Von Hippel, E., Thomke, S., & Sonnack, M. (1999). Creating breakthroughs at 3M. *Harvard Business Review,* September-October, (pp. 47-57).

Weber, M. (1947). T. Parsons (Ed.), *The Theory of Social and Economic Organization.* Oxford University Press.

Yin, R. K. (1984). *Case study research: design and methods*. Sage.

Zollo, M., & Winter, S. (2002). Deliberate learning and the evolution of dynamic capabilities. *Organization Science*, *13*(3), 339-351.

Zott, C. (2003). Dynamic Capabilities and the emergence of intra-industry differential firm performance: Insights from a simulation study. *Strategic Management Journal*, *24*, 97-125.

KEY TERMS

Collegial Control: A form of management control where peer review constitutes an important part e.g. as in universities or in Research & Development departments.

Dynamic Capability: (Following Zollo & Winter, 2002, 340, emphasis added) '*a learned and stable pattern of collective activity* through which the organization systematically generates and modifies its operating routines in pursuit of improved effectiveness.'

Economic Profit: This is a general term which can be defined broadly as Net profit after tax less risk-adjusted cost of capital.

Ostensive Versus Performative Aspects of Routines Ostensive: This is the structure or abstract understanding of the routine.

Performative: The actual performance of the routine(Feldman & Pentland, 2003).

Chapter XXI
Cultural Issues, Organizations and Information Fulfillment:
An Exploration towards Improved Knowledge Management Relationships

Maria E. Burke
University of Salford, UK

ABSTRACT

The purpose of this chapter is to consider an original way of improving Knowledge Management relationships. This is done within the context of an aspect of Information behaviour, known as Information Fulfillment. The chapter presents the cultural results of a three-year study into the concept of information fulfillment, and considers the impact of culture on levels of information fulfillment. Ethnographic studies were undertaken within higher education institutions in four countries and the social and symbolic meanings that underpinned the culture of information in the chosen institutions are presented followed by a section of "raw data" from the ethnographic field. Culture impacted significantly in all the studies, and each study had its own unique character and provided rich insights into the culture and contexts of the fields. The relationships between the cultures and the levels of information fulfillment are reported with suggestions re helping build KM systems that deliver higher levels of information fulfillment.

INTRODUCTION

Knowledge management (KM) systems may fail or be abandoned if they do not result in the information fulfillment that they promise. However, levels of information fulfillment are affected by cultural factors, which differ between institutions, and to understand this relationship it is necessary to bring together aspects of information seeking and to establish what kinds of relationships can be found between types of organization structure and levels of information fulfillment, while taking into account cultural differences. This chapter focuses upon the impact of culture on levels of information fulfillment, through presentation and analysis of the cultural results of a three-year study into the concept of information fulfillment, using case studies of higher education institutions in four countries.

Between 2002 and 2005, a funded research project explored issues surrounding organization structures, and examined levels of information fulfillment in microsubstantive settings, within institutions in Poland, Hungary, Russia and the UK. Interpretive ethnographic studies were undertaken by examining each organization's structure (e.g. bureaucratic, matrix etc.) and comparing this with the level of information fulfillment achieved. It is the social and symbolic meanings that underpinned the culture of information in the chosen institutions that form the basis of this chapter. By understanding how cultural factors can affect information fulfillment it becomes possible to see what determines whether a KM system is hailed a success or branded a failure by those who use it, and how to build KM systems associated with high levels of information fulfillment.

The impact of culture on levels of information fulfillment is considered throughout six stages. First, a discussion is presented of the relationship between information fulfillment and knowledge management. Second, a review is given of the place of information fulfillment in established information models. This is followed by the third section, which contains a discussion of the cultural frameworks used to underpin each of the institutions. The fourth part of the chapter allows for analysis of the way in which the term was interpreted and used in each of the cultural environments. The fifth part of the chapter presents an assessment of the impact of the cultures on the levels of information fulfillment. Finally, the chapter closes with a discussion regarding the building of knowledge management systems that can be designed to encourage and achieve high levels of information fulfillment.

Defining Culture, Information Fulfillment and Knowledge Management

Whilst defining culture is a difficult task, it is important to do so in order to put the research into context. Allaire (1984) provided a typology of school of thought in cultural anthropology and found that a useful metaphor for viewing culture is about "decay, (of one culture), adaption (to a new culture), resulting in radical cultural shifts and change".

Whilst metaphors of culture are useful Adler (1983) created a typology of management studies involving culture and defined culture as all embracing, atmospheric and about the fundamentals of values and beliefs. This definition is more useful for our studies in this paper and so we will use this as the main definition.

The second concept, information fulfillment can be defined by taking a step back and considering first a wider view – that of information systems. Systems utilize the available technology in order to undertake particular parts of the information management process - including careful planning of the way in which the information flows within the organization structure - resulting in overall improved control of the way in which the information is managed. Due to the continuous nature of change in the external environment of an organization, it is critical that managers of the organization are able to respond quickly to these changes by making prompt good quality decisions. To enhance this process, an area of research within information management known as "information seeking", or more properly as "information seeking behavior", examines the ways in which people find the information they require. Information seeking can itself be defined as a study of how and where people look for solutions to information problems.

One of the major purposes of information in organizations is to allow members of that organization to fulfil the duties of their role. This is done by having the correct information, in the correct format, at an appropriate time. Each person within the organization needs complete information fulfillment, i.e. to consider that "all their information needs are truly satisfied, which will allow them to complete any task associated with their role". [Burke, 2005] The challenge is not only to provide sufficient information but also to avoid a situation in which bureaucratic complexity leads to information overload, in which users "satisfice". [Simon, 1957]

Knowledge management, on the other hand, can be defined in a number of ways. Building on earlier approaches of data management and information management, it adds a higher level of complexity with the inclusion of meaning, networking, collaboration and business process improvement. KM employs techniques to manage the common base of organizational knowledge and encourage its sharing and re-use. According to Civi (2000) it is a business process through which firms create and use their institutional or collective knowledge. This can take many forms, but will often include the identification and mapping of intellectual assets within an organization, the generation of new knowledge for competitive advantage, making large amounts of corporate information accessible, sharing of best practices, and related technology, such as intranets and groupware. [Barclay and Murray, 97] Therefore, it may be loosely defined as a way of storing information in a manner that is easily retrievable.

How then can the two areas of information fulfillment and knowledge management be linked? Even technology-based KM systems must take into account the psychological and social needs of the users. [Dougherty, 1999] Without KM there can be no true information fulfillment and without information fulfillment the purpose of a KM system is pointless and without a "raison d'être". The information system must therefore be designed to ensure that the end user is able to function effectively within the organization and can access all the information necessary to complete a task.

Review of Information Fulfillment in Established Information Models

There has been a variety of information models proposed, most notably those by Wilson and Ellis (Wilson & Spink, 1981; Wilson 1987; 1999, Ellis, 1989; 1993, Ellis, Cox and Hall, 1993) whose ideas are concerned with modelling the sequence of events from the initial information seeking to information finding, and what was then regarded as the final phase of seeking, known as "information satisfaction". However, there had been little research published that linked the ultimate part of the information seeking process, i.e. the level of fulfillment experienced by those members of an organization who actually use the information at the end of the entire information seeking process. Papers have been published on specific aspects of information seeking such as "Uncertainty" (Ingression, 1996; Kuhlthau, 1993) "Serendipity" (Rice et. al., 1991; Foster, 2003) and "Browsing" (Levine, 1969). Models such as that proposed by Kuhlthau (1991) have considered the emotional aspects of information seeking and proposed six stages: initiation, selection, exploration, formulation, collection, and presentation. Kuhlthau also presented a final stage of "relief, satisfaction and a sense of direction", but again no mention of fulfillment of information needs.

Jarvelin and Wilson (2003) provide a synthesis of the literature containing analysis of information seeking in a place of employment. [Auster and Choo, 1994; Fabritius, 1998; Herner and Herner, 1967; Siatri, 1998; Timko and Loynes, 1989; Wilson and Strearfield, 1980] These studies included a wide range of contexts, from prairie farmers to news reading, and a comparative study of electronic seeking in Greek and British universities. Other studies of information seeking within workplaces have included Bawden (1997) on midwifery, Cobbledick (1996) on artists, Futas & Vidor (1986) on business managers using libraries, Gorman (1995) and Lundeen et.al.(1994) on doctors and others in the medical profession and Nichols and Martin (1997) on the information seeking behavior of journalists.

The aim of the entire Information Fulfillment project has been to bring together aspects of information seeking and to establish what kinds of relationships can be found between levels of information fulfillment and types of organization structures, taking into account the cultural differences in each of the case studies. As established earlier, the aim of this chapter is specifically to consider one aspect of the project - the impact of culture on levels of information fulfillment. The influence of cultural values and norms is critical for several reasons: for a system to be actively used, for a system to encourage information storing and information seeking, and for a system that will ultimately give true information fulfillment to the user.

The chapter has now set into context the relationship between Information Fulfillment and Knowledge Management and considered the literature, and thus the place of Information Fulfillment in established information models. Having established this important background, the next part of the chapter will concentrate on the cultural issues of the project.

CULTURAL FRAMEWORKS

The studies took place in radically different cultures, which affected the chosen research approach (ethnography) and thus the outcome of each of the studies. It was important to find cultural frameworks that could be used to assist with the analysis of each of the studies. As it was difficult to identify a single cultural framework that would encapsulate the myriad of issues arising within each of the ethnographies, the following five frameworks were chosen, as they represent different perspectives of culture. The frameworks chosen were from the mid 1980's before the "fall" of communism, which have a very appropriate fit to the reality of organizational cultures found in the universities observed.

The first cultural framework is that put forward by Kets de Vries and Miller (1984) whose work linked neurotic styles with organizational functioning. They identified what they saw as five common neurotic styles taken from the psychiatric discipline and then discussed the parallels within organizational behaviors, strategy, culture, structure and behavior. The five cultural styles are:

Paranoia. An emphasis on an organization's intelligence, worry and mistrust that nothing is quite as it seems, that others have power. An atmosphere of secrecy is likely to operate within this culture.

Avoidant. characterized by a lack of control and power. Avoidance of conflict, just doing the job, agreeing to changes with little or no consultation.

Charismatic. An emphasis on strong leadership skills, success, a penchant for drama and a need to be followed by a cohort of supporters.

Bureaucratic. A culture which is rule bound, rigid and detailed.

Schizoid. A culture which suffers from a leadership vacuum – a culture in which members are withdrawn and detached – no excitement or enthusiasm.

This cultural framework emphasizes the negative aspects of a culture, yet it is a realistic view of organizations held by many. It is an inflexible, cynical view, but nevertheless useful in identifying problems – and hopefully solutions.

The second of the five frameworks is that devised by Mitroff and Kilmann (1975) who base their cultural analysis on that of the four main personality types identified by that of C.G. Jung. Jung identified two types of decision making "sensing" and "thinking" found in managers. He postulated that "thinking" types use logic as reason whilst "sensing" types use personal considerations as reasons for decisions. The two types were further subdivided into four categories, as follows:

Sensation thinking, where work roles are impersonal and authoritarian; *Intuitive thinking,* where work roles are flexible and goal driven; *Intuitive feeling,* when the role is seen as that of caring and decentralized and *Sensation feeling,* where the culture is "homelike" and relationship driven. While there is a danger in this model of overgeneralizing Jung's work, this is a useful analytical framework where a culture is much politicized and there are contradictory personalities working within an unstable environment.

The third framework was posited by Sethia and Von Gilnow in 1985. They identified two important criteria that help to define an organization's culture – its concern for its people and its concern for performance of its members. Within these levels they identified the four cultures of *Caring, Apathetic, Integrative,* and *Exacting.* The apathetic culture shows little concern for people, whereas the integrative culture is the ideal culture, which gives equal weight to both people and performance. Finally the exacting culture is centered on performance and has little regard for people.

This cultural framework allows for analysis in an environment where there may be motivational issues. It is a useful model but does not allow for any issues related to leadership which would are likely to be present in the kind of environment Sethia and Von Gilnow describe.

The fourth framework deals with more traditional views of culture and is based on ideas put forward by Deal and Kennedy (1982). They identified five elements of culture: an *organizational environment* which, for example, can lead to a strong ingrained culture or to a lacklustre ambiguous culture; the *core beliefs* of the culture; the *heroes of the culture* e.g. the key champions who can act as role models; the *folklore, myths, rites and rituals* of culture; and finally the importance of the *cultural network,* the informal communication which takes place within the organization.

This culture can be seen as dangerous as it does not allow for change. Although people will change as they leave and join the organization, the stories and the myths are likely to remain and grow, resulting in either organizational stagnation, or, if the stories and beliefs are positive rather than negative then the organization may flourish. However this is a high risk culture as the organization needs to adapt to the environment rather than rely for values on rites and rituals

The fifth framework is that proposed by Jaeger (1978) who classify cultures into three distinct types: types A, J and Z. Type As exist in a culture which is strongly controlled, but allows some element of decision making. Type J was identified in cultures which had "tribal control" with general decision making as a group and Type Z was about "tribal decision making" and decision making in a patient and consenting way.

This model assumes that the culture is based on two issues – personality types and decision making. Whilst this is useful in categorizing the "appropriate" people to make "good" decisions it does not allow for the values and beliefs systems which for example, Deal and Kennedy identify in their model. This fifth culture is useful but has limitations in that it does not (nor does it aspire to) cover all the intangible aspects of culture.

Although each of the frameworks has limitations they provided a useful way of extending the analysis of each of the organizations used in the ethnographies. It was not an easy decision to "categorize" each organization, but by using these models it was possible to at least propose an idea of the type of organizational culture in which the "actors" were immersed.

THE CULTURAL ENVIRONMENTS

This section will now present the cultural findings from three of the case studies. Within each of the studies there is a brief discussion of the way in which information fulfillment was translated, as inevitably the translation and the understanding varied in each country and it was vital to establish a common understanding and definition. This is followed by a reproduction of the original field notes and a discussion of which cultural framework seemed to best fit the organization.

A Brief Introduction to Ethnographic Field Notes

It is worth considering here the view posited by Atkinson (1992) on ethnographic field notes i.e. that they "should first be constructed through the ethnographers gaze - as what the researcher sees is how the field is defined; second, that the field is then reconstituted through his or her ability to construct a text and finally that the ethnography is reconstituted and recontextualized through the readers work of interpretation and contextualisation." This problem of interpretation and contextualization is on the part of the both the researcher and the reader inevitably mean that two "world views" are likely to be part of the ethnography. However, given that this was a known issue a certain degree of objectivity was able to be maintained. The originality of the ethnography is therefore of critical importance - and a sample of the raw (condensed) field notes are reproduced below in order to give a flavour of the location and atmosphere of the study. This was vital, vibrant part of the ethnography and the text has been deliberately preserved as originally written in note format. The headings used are based on suggestions by Spradley (1980) and Milofsky & Schneider (2003): fieldwork period, local commitments, description of the setting, the community and the atmosphere, the people, and the overall analysis of the culture.

RUSSIAN CULTURAL ENVIRONMENT

The Russian University had strong traditional and historical associations, and in order to put into context the cultural elements it is useful to say a few words about what was understood by the term Information fulfillment within the Russian field. The term "information fulfillment" was translated by members of the Russian organization as "Pol'naia nuzhnaia Informatsiia" (Complete needed information). Most organizational members responded in a very serious, indignant manner that the term meant "having everything that they need to be a 'proper' student or staff member". When questioned further on the term "proper student" they defined this as being correct, punctual, and having the complete set of necessary documents to complete their tasks. Others were more nonchalant and guessed that the term meant "knowing everything" – just getting what they needed to do their jobs/studies. Discussion took place and an agreement was then reached on a definition of the term.

Having established a common definition of Information Fulfillment, time was spent in the field collecting relevant data. Out of the chosen five cultural frameworks, the two which seemed to best fit the Russian study were those of Mitroff and Kilmann (1975) "Sensation – Thinking Roles" – whereby work roles are seen as impersonal and authoritarian (which leads to a powerless and rigid organization culture) and Kets de Vries' (1984) cultural "Paranoia" typology where there is an emphasis on organizational intelligence, combined with an atmosphere of fear and mistrust that "nothing is at it seems." Although the culture had been stagnant for a long time there were signs that things were changing and there was evidence of hope/wishes for more flexibility in the future.

These frameworks became apparent during the time of the study and can be evidenced by the following description and analysis of the culture within the University during the time of the study.

Cultural Ethnographic research field notes: Russian Study

(Condensed Raw Data)

Methodology: Participant Observation

Field Work Period: March 2003

Local City Commitments: Much of the City was preparing for a major event in May 2003 so many buildings covered in plastic sheeting – air of excitement, yet at times felt flat and very quiet, almost a City lost and forgotten.

A description of the setting, the physical space, furniture, décor, repair, smells, lighting etc.

There was snow on the ground. Roads were flooded as the sewers could not cope with the amount of melted snow on top of the normal sewerage. The University grounds were dirty, wet and muddy with many temporary planks of wood nailed together to make a temporary "raft" and thrown in a cavalier fashion around the University buildings in order to enhance access from one building to the next. The University was cold and had a lost, isolated, gloomy feeling. Students were wrapped up in heavy coats, scarves and hats which made it difficult to see faces adding to the atmosphere of secrecy and depression.

Inside the buildings ceilings were vaulted which made for strange acoustics. The many corridors were dimly lit and surprisingly quiet for the middle of a busy spring term. The staff offices had brown faded padded inner and outer doors – presumably for sound proofing (?) The padding was pinned to the door with silver clips placed at strategic points on the door.

The academic offices varied in size and light depending on seniority of the inhabitant. Most contained quite standard 1950'soffice furniture, table, chairs, computer, green bakelite telephones and a heavy duty coat stand which was in constant use.

The community and the atmosphere.

Atmosphere was dark and foreboding. Feeling of impending doom. The academic community seemed small – yet quite close with a hidden impression of care.

Description of the people in the setting – initial notes – list of people and their roles, short descriptive portraits and their relations with each other – 1st names can be used.

(Confidential)

Comments on culture, background, pertinent observations of relevance to study

State owned, large University, little money. Staff seemed to have pride however in their work. The term "scientist" was the word most favoured for those qualified in the area of information science. The organization chart of the University was often to be seen framed and hung on the corridor walls complete with heraldic crest.

Students and staff displayed a keen interest and enthusiasm in learning and improving their prospects. No real alternatives available to them. A very controlled environment. Everyone knew very precisely what their job was - and aimed to do it well.

Information for staff was available but only on a need to know basis – if there was not seen as any need – there was no flexibility on this. They had been taught (socialized) to work like this and so were unaware of alternative methods of working. Information cascaded down the organization in a pure hierarchical (downwards) direction. There was also still a sense of fear that pervaded the western "working the system attitude" – nothing could be exaggerated or implied – all reports had to be factual and evidence linked.

During the time spent with the students staff members were present for some of the time. Students reacted to this and became very subdued. Tendency to "show off" and ask what they considered to be "illicit questions when "alone" i.e. without staff present.

Ethnographic Research Field Notes - Study 1: Russia

From the evidence in the cultural sample and the time spent undertaking the participant observation both the cultural framework offered by Mitroff and Kilmann (1975) and the one offered by Kets deVries (1984) seemed to present a good fit. The sense of a rigid bureaucratic organization structure coupled with the sense of awe of powerful figures (supervisors, heads, deans etc) created a culture that was tense and typified by Kets de Vries' cultural paranoia. However, the constant discussions regarding the name change of the University and the desire to increase cooperation with western Universities were two tangible signs of the push towards change which may help to move the University towards a more flexible culture in the future.

POLISH CULTURAL ENVIRONMENT

The Polish translation of the term information fulfillment was stated as "dostarczanie informacji", meaning the literal delivery of information. About 60% responded that the term meant for them, "being able to attend work/ classes", "knowing where to go at what time", "knowing what work to complete", and "knowing what they had to do in order to undertake tasks". It was interesting to note that the term "knowing" was used extensively in the Polish study. Although there were no direct references to knowledge management, it was clear that a knowledge management framework of some kind was used, albeit on a collegiate basis. Others commented that to them the term "information fulfillment" meant "being organized" and "fulfilling the duties set by the University". Again, after discussion, a common ground was established as to the definition of information fulfillment.

Having established the definition the next stage was to consider the cultural issues. The importance of the "atmosphere" of the University, the emotional issues, the attitudes of the staff and students, were important parts of the Polish ethnography and a sample of the collected raw data evidencing this is given below. Ritual and ceremony held important roles in this University. Oil paintings of past and present Rectors were hung on walls and previous Rectors were also displayed in the form of magnificent bronze busts. Treasures of the University such as gold wine goblets, antique astronomical models, tapestries, rare books, solid gold sceptres were prevalent and were displayed in the University Museum. The wealth of the University was significant in this setting.

The framework that best fits this culture (from the chosen five) is that of Deal and Kennedy's (1982) five elements of culture. Their proposition of the five elements of culture, i.e. environment, core beliefs of the culture, the heroes of the cultures, the champions who can act as models, and the importance of folklore and myth, are an appropriate analysis for the culture of the University. The organizational environment is that of a historical, traditional organization that aims to move forward and cater for modern times. The core beliefs of the culture are about "distinctiveness" - in Polish terms about "being special". Education is seen as "special", as a privilege, and the University is "special" due to its long history of survival, which is reflected in the strong sense of Polish pride. The champions who act as models for others can be identified as a variety of key staff, and younger staff, in particular, "are put on pedestals" and seen as important as role models for the students. Finally, the importance of folklore is demonstrated by the telling of stories about the University, (in particular the survival of the University over so many hundreds of years and the restoration after WW2), the prestige of being associated with the University and the sense of belonging to an elite group.

This framework has its roots in the following evidence noted during the ethnographic field study.

Ethnographic Research Field Notes: Study 2: Poland

(Condensed Raw Data)
Methodology: Participant Observation
Field work period: Autumn 2003

Local City Commitments: Several large marquees erected in the main square ("Marketplace") dedicated to presenting Information Fairs concerning the Accession of Poland to the European Union. General feeling of excitement. Carnival atmosphere. Entrance was free, displays inside the marquee neat, well laid out, free glasses of champagne offered.

Autumn fairs of toffee apples, baked potatoes and fragrances of freshly baked Polish bread emanated from the Market square.

Awareness of new students around. Tourist season beginning to close, still quite busy.

A description of the setting, the physical space, furniture, décor, repair, smells, lighting etc.

The Medieval University setting

The old University is full of examples of its historical setting such as red wax historic seals, gothic arches and shady courtyards. Magnificent mahogany staircases, carved figures of important historical figures. Beautiful sections of inlaid wooden flooring with intricate designs, gothic silver candelabras, silver candle chandeliers. Ornate door mouldings, valuable paintings, a piano reputed to have been played by Chopin, antique furniture, original medieval painted ceilings. Examples of University dress worn in medieval times.

The New University

The new building was clean, shiny, all walls painted brilliant white, both inside and outside. A remarkable transformation from the previous dark cramped location of the Department. All staff offices fitted with new furniture, new computers, and smelled of furniture polish and new carpets. All staff doors also fitted with key code locks. Feeling of security. No feelings of threat. Very warm, welcoming atmosphere. High quality finish of building.

Although building work was still ongoing on the site, there was little noise or disruption. Notable attention to detail in all classroom facilities e.g. blinds fitted to windows which cast shadows on to projector screens.

Still tendency for students to sit in rows. Not aware of classrooms where furniture had been moved to circle or small group positions.

All the spaces in the new building bright and airy with very high ceiling in the public areas of 20ft or so.

Staff had however juxtaposed the new with the old, for example, a large marble statue of a famous Pole and two large Roman pictures of mosaics had been brought over from the old building and stood in the reception area presumably as a timely reminder of the heritage of the University.

The community and the atmosphere.

The atmosphere was one of joy and happiness that the new home for the Department was so lovely. However, behind the scenes among more senior members of staff there were worries about the future, as the move to this building is in fact, only temporary until the permanent home for the Department is found elsewhere in the new buildings. So, some staff were aware that this was only a temporary stay and were politically active in resolving the more permanent home.

The community is one of care about the students – the personal tutor system is well in evidence and staff were aware of particular students with difficulties. Students in general work hard and consider it a privilege to be attending the University.

Comments on culture, background, pertinent observations of relevance to study

University state owned and fiercely proud of the achievements of the University. University quite controlled. Example - student attendance keenly monitored. All students own a small book (called an Index) with the times of lectures preprinted. At the end of a lecture each individual book must be signed by the lecturer to show that they have in fact attended – books not signed carry severe penalties – and could in exceptional cases lead to the withholding of the degree.

The culture of the lecture times is radically different from the UK. Lectures start at 6am until lunch time, break a couple of hours for lunch and then can continue until 8pm in the evening. Students are on the premises for considerable time.

Notice boards quite important. All notices are current – no out-of-date material is left on boards.

Use of email quite high.

However the telecoms communication infrastructure was surprisingly weak, For example, trying to make a phone call or a fax to a company in the city centre was difficult as many phones are set up for internal calls only, Finding a phone that would dial outside numbers was a difficult problem that involved 3 members of staff and took one and a half hours to resolve. In the end the system did not work as could not get through. Availability of outside lines therefore stills a problem. How this is resolved with internet access was not particularly made known to me, although the students did not report this as a problem.

Food is seen as a way of welcoming visitors. Food and drink were consumed consistently with many courses (usually about five). Placing of cups and saucers was done with great care. Very proud of possessions. Care about books. Treat them very carefully as treasured objects.

Ethnographic Research Field Notes - Study 2: Poland

The major issues and observations from the Polish fieldwork were the emotional aspects of pride in the University and care about fellow academics; the issues concerning the contradiction between the central control of the University and freedom to initiate new ideas; the value placed on the opinions of colleagues and the need for students to be accepted by their peers. Deal and Kennedy's cultural analysis which is about folklore and heroes fits the setting although there are issues (as analysed above) behind the elements they identify. The sense of pride was strong in Poland and the sense of a huge effort to modernize the country and the particular city where the fieldwork took place. Similar field studies have shown that people in organizations where society is beginning to alter aim to have enthusiasm and take pride in their work (Applebaum, 1981) and this was certainly demonstrated in the Polish study.

BRITISH CULTURAL ENVIRONMENT

The UK respondents were familiar with the concept concerning "information fulfillment". Nevertheless, it was important that the same discussion took place concerning meaning in order to ensure consistency throughout the entire study.

The cultural framework which most closely matches the British University is that of Ouchi and Jaeger (1978) who analysed culture as primarily being concerned with belonging or not belonging to an identifiable group of people and with types of decision making found in each group. They further classified culture into the three distinct types of control and decision making. Type A organizations had a culture which was controlling, but allowed some decision making, Type J organizations tended to arise in a culture which had overall "tribal control" and group decision making and Type Z organizations "combined a basic cultural commitment to individualistic values with a highly collective, non –individual pattern of interaction". Type Z organizations were categorised by decisions made "as an entire tribe", for the good of all.

A mix of all these types of decision making characteristics was found in the UK study. The holistic decisions made by Senior Management levels could be identified as Type A, whilst Faculty decisions tended to fit into Type J and Departmental decision into Type Z.

However this is a neat, "boxed" analysis and on further study of the field it was found that Type Z decisions, although purported to be "for the good of all" were often made to fulfil Faculty requirements that in turn were keen to fulfil senior University requirements. The culture of belonging, the sense of community was strong in the Department and Ouchi and Jaeger's analysis provides a way of initially identifying a complex culture.

The chosen cultural framework can be analysed from the following evidence noted during the ethnographic field study.

Ethnographic Research Field Notes: Study 3: Britain

(Condensed Raw Data)
Methodology: Participant Observation
Field work period: Summer 2004

Local City Commitments: Touring Art Exhibition of Colorful Artificial Cows. The cows were displayed in various colours and at busy venues e.g. Town Hall, Music Halls, Shopping Centres.

A description of the setting, the physical space, furniture, décor, repair, smells, lighting etc.

Cramped, untidy, old, not particularly clean, no sense of any attention paid to design. People attempt to improve the environment with lush foliage plants and comfortable chairs. Old computers on floors in classrooms, odd chairs in lecture theatres, old signs and posters which are not always removed after events.

All four buildings were of a different design, no sense of unity.

New areas in the library which housed a teaching and learning centre. Good quality finish.

The community and the atmosphere.

Community was strong, if divided, very much technical versus soft approach. However within the communities commitment and loyalty seemed to be very high.

Recent events of loss of staff still keenly felt, yet made for situation of "us and them" and a strong will to be the best.

Community quite cooperative. Most people willing to help out and take on extra work (several examples noted during 10 day period.)

Visiting professor present on some days. Much attention and organization focused around his visit to endure the Department was seen in the best light.

Comments on culture, background, pertinent observations of relevance to study

Currently undergoing financial crisis, difficult decisions to be made re voluntary redundancy resulting in loss of staff. Some staff worries about coping with workload.

Most staff highly respected seen to be "at top of profession" and very well known in relevant disciplines.

Considerable autonomy given to staff. General lack of control noted, but this seemed to result in excellent output and high creativity. All staff seemed to be self motivated.

Decision making process appeared democratic but within constraints of the Faculty and University.

Some expressed regret that there was no staff room.

Culture was that of joint decisions within a bureaucratic organization. A sense of tribal "belonging" seems to exist within the Department both within the University and within the groups of colleagues nationally and internationally who work within the discipline.

High use made of email, low use of noticeboards.

Communication sporadic, difficult to judge.

Ethnographic Research Field Notes. Study 3: Britain

Relationship between Culture and Information Fulfillment

Significant further studies were completed in each of the countries and many charts and matrices drawn up which have been reported elsewhere (Burke, 2005). As it is not the intention of the chapter to convey the statistical analysis, the results are presented in the paragraphs below in narrative form with an emphasis on the cultural aspects of the results.

RUSSIA

These results were gained from a study where immersion in the field was classified as "New: New" which allowed for good, relatively easy levels of objectivity. The major issues and observations arising out of the Russian ethnography were the formality and bureaucracy of the context, the significantly low levels of information fulfillment regarding informal academic information together with the suspicion and curiosity that surrounded the study. In addition the two opposite attitudes of optimism and pessimism divided the community. These attitudes were at different ends of the spectrum with little evidence of any "middle" attitudes. Finally all the participants had issues surrounding trust which affected the levels of information fulfillment. This fits with Kets de Vries "Paranoia" typology of the cultural environment.

POLAND

Immersion in the Polish field was Familiar: New – where the researcher was familiar with the University but new to the city and surroundings. These results were interesting, and quite different from those found in the first study. Results showed that both informal and formal academic information score highly in information fulfillment within this structure, but that the social information does not always give full satisfaction, with informal social actually scoring the lowest of all. This is reflective of a culture which is controlled and which views higher education as a "special privilege". The organization structure was more difficult to identify as there are many layers and different sections of the University, although all sections report to the central powerful figure of the Rector.

BRITAIN

Immersion in this field was categorised as Native: Familiar which was the most difficult field in which to operate. The limitations placed on the researcher were considered and the interpretative stance of the research was helpful in placing the study within an objective context. The major issues and observations arising out of the British ethnography were the strong sense of community spirit, the success of the informal sources of information, the importance placed on tribal belonging and the contradictions between a sense of pessimism and optimism for the future of the

Department. The cultural framework devised by Ouchi and Jaeger (1978) which examined decision making in different levels of the organization provided an interesting analysis between the kind of tribal decisions making which was purported to be "for the good of all" (and which fit within the informal, democratic nature of the organization) and decisions made to fulfil Faculty and University obligations.

CONCLUSION

Culture impacted significantly in all the studies, and notably each study had its own unique character and provided rich insights into the culture and contexts of the fields. In each case, the relationships between the culture and the levels of information fulfillment have been reported. The culture in the organization has an impact on the processes and on the likelihood of either high or low levels of information fulfillment. By understanding the culture within an organization, information fulfillment can be enhanced by appropriate KM management. KM systems can only transform the workplace, so that workers feel that all their information needs are truly satisfied, allowing them to complete any task associated with their role, if the culture of an organization is fully considered.

Information fulfillment is vital in today's world of information overload. There needs to be a planned strategy which takes into account all the variables which affect information processing, including the design of the organizational structure, consideration of the environment of the industry, and of the different types of information needed by members of the organization. Moreover, the strategist also needs to be involved in the decision making processes surrounding these issues. A robust Knowledge Management system which takes this into account is sorely needed by today's society, and one which is designed to take care of individual cultures would be helpful and very much welcomed in different societies, and at different stages of development in those societies.

Inevitably, this research is a report of a small section of a much larger project, and has attempted to "separate" the cultural aspects from other aspects of the project. The work, however, continues – recent work has been completed in Hungary and work is planned in Holland and Denmark. It is therefore an evolving project and one which is filled with different patterns, of culture, of information use, and of fulfillment. The patterns within this work have been interesting, fascinating, contradictory and ultimately illuminating, and it is hoped that through the appropriate use of KM tools, all these aspects will be linked to ensure the ultimate achievement of information fulfillment for all that work within organizations.

REFERENCES

Adler, N. J. (1983). A typology of management studies involving culture. *Journal of International Business, 14*(2), 29-47.

Allaire, Y., & Firsirotu, M. (1984). Theories of organizational culture. *Organization Studies, 5*(3), 193-226.

Applebaum, H. (1981). *Royal blue: the culture of construction workers*. New York: Holt.

Atkinson, P. (1992). Understanding ethnographic texts. *Qualitative research methods, 25*. Sage Publications.

Auster, E., & Choo, C. (1994). How senior managers acquire and use information in environmental scanning. *Information Processing and Management, 30*(5), p607-618.

Bawden, D., & Kay, R. (1997). Information Behaviour in Nursing Specialties: A Case Study of Midwifery. *Journal of Information Science, 23*(6), 407-421.

Blumer, H. (1969). *Symbolic Interactionism: Perspective and Method.* Englewood Cliffs, NJ: Prentice-Hall.

Burke, M. (2005). Reflections on structures and solutions regarding information fulfillment in organisations. *Proceedings of Information Management Resources Association 2005.* San Diego (CD)

Civi, E. (2000). Knowledge management as a competitive asset: a review. *Marketing Intelligence & Planning, 18/4,* 166-174.

Cobbledick, S. (1996).The Information-Seeking Behavior of Artists: Exploratory Interviews. *Library Quarterly,* 66(4), 343-372.

Deal, T. E., & Kennedy, A. A. (1982). *Corporate cultures: the rites and rituals of corporate life.* Reading MA: Addison Wesley.

Dougherty, V. (1999). Knowledge is about people, not databases. *Industrial and Commercial Training, 31*(7), 262-266.

Ellis, D. (1993). Modelling the information seeking patterns of academic researchers: a grounded theory approach. *The Library Quarterly, 63*(4), 469-486.

Ellis, D., Cox, D., & Hall, K. (1993). A comparison of the information seeking patterns of researchers in the physical and social sciences. *Journal of Documentation, 49*(4), 356-369

Ellis, D. (1989). A behavioural approach to information retrieval design. *Journal of Documentation, 46,* 318-338.

Fabritius, H. (1998). Information seeking in the newsroom: application of the cognitive framework for analysis of the of the work context. *Information Research, 4*(2) Retrieved 12 Oct 2004 from http://informationr.net/ir/

Foster, A., & Ford, N. (2003). Serendipity and information seeking: An empirical study *Journal of Documentation, 59*(3), 321-340.

Futas, E., & Vidor, D. (1986). How Business Professionals Use Libraries. *Library Journal, 1*(11), 112-121.

Gorman, P. (1995). Information Needs of Physicians. *Journal of the American Society for Information Science, 46*(10), 729-736.

Herner, ., & Herner, M. (1967). Information needs and uses in science and technology. *Annual Review of Science and technology, 2,* 1-34.

Ingwersen, P. (1996). Cognitive perspectives of information retrieval interaction: elements of a cognitive IR theory. *Journal of Documentation, 51,* 2-50.

Jarvelin, K., & Wilson, T. D. (2003). On conceptual models for information seeking and retrieval research. *Information Research, 9*(1). Retrieved on 10 Oct 2004 from http://informationr.net

Kets de Vries, M. F. R., & Miller, D. (1984). *The Neurotic organization.* San Francisco, CA: Jossey Bass.

Kuhlthau, C. (1993). A principle of uncertainty for information seeking. Journal of Information seeking. *Journal of Documentation, 49*(4), 39-55.

Kutlhau, C. (1991). Inside the search process: information seeking from the user's perspective. *Journal of the American Society for Information Science, 42,* 361-371.

Levine, M. M. (1969). An essay on browsing . *Research Quarterly,* 9(1), 35-6.

Lundeen, G., Tenopir, C., & Wermager, A. (1994). Information Needs of Rural Health Care in Hawaii. *Bulletin of the Medical Library Association 82*(2), *197-205.*

Milofsky, C., & Schneider, J. (2002). *The field notes manual. Doing ethnography in sociology and anthropology.* Lewisburg, PA: Bucknell Univ Press.

Mitroff, I., & Kilmann, R. (1975). Stories managers tell: a new tool for organisational story telling. *Management Review* (pp. 18-28).

Nicholas, D., & Martin, H. (1997). Assessing Information Needs: A Case Study of Journalists. *Aslib Proceedings, 49*(2), 43-52.

Ouchi, W. G., & Jaeger, A. M. (1978). Type Z organisations: stability in the midst of mobility. *Academy of Management Review, 3*, 18-28.

Rice, R., & Aydin, C. (1991). Attitudes toward new organisational technology: network proximity as a mechanism for social information processing. *Administrative Science Quarterly,* 36(2), 219-226.

Sethia, N. K., & Von Glinow, M. A. (1985). Arriving at four cultures by managing the reward system. In R. H. Kilmannet al.(Eds.), *Gaining control of the corporate culture* (pp. 400-20). San Francisco, CA: Jossey Bass.

Siatri, R. (1998). Information seeking in an electronic environment: a comparative investigation among computer scientists in British and Greek Universities. *Information Research, 4*(2). Retrieved 12 October 2004 from htpt://information.net/ir

Simon, H. (1957). *Models of Man – Social and Rational.* New York: John Wiley & Sons.

Spradley, J. P. (1980). *Participant Observation.* New York: Holt Rhinehart and Winston.

Timko, M., & Loynes, R. M. A. (1989). Market information needs for prarie farmers. *Canadian Journal of Agricultural Economics,* 37, 609-627.

Wilson, T. D., & Spink, A. (1981). *Uncertainty in information seeking.* Library and Information Commission Research Report 59 ISSN 1466 2949

Wilson, T. D. (1981). On user studies and information needs. *Journal of Documentation, 37*(1), 3-15

Wilson, T. D. (1987). Information behaviour: an interdisciplinary perspective. *Information Processing and Management, 33*(4), 551-572.

Wilson, T. D. (1999). Models in information behaviour research. *Journal of Documentation, 55*(3), 249-270.

Wilson, T. D., & Streatfield, D. R. (1980). A *study of information use in local authority social services departments.* conducted by Project INNIS Sheffield, University of Sheffield, School of LIS, occasional paper no 12. Retrieved 12 October 2004 at http://informationr.net/tdw

KEY TERMS

Culture: The values and beliefs within an organisation.

Ethnography: A study of people in their natural habitat

Information Fulfillment: A concept of emotion with regard to fulfilling need for information

Chapter XXII
Engineering Design at a Toyota Company:
Knowledge Management and the Innovative Process

Darius Mehri
University of California, Berkeley, USA

ABSTRACT

The author worked in the research and design department at a large Toyota company in the late 1990s and experienced an innovative process where engineers worked in tightly knit groups where monitoring, the informal hierarchy and dependence resulted from an emphasis on collective work. In the approach to innovation during the design process, the Toyota engineers were found to engage in an inductive process that placed an emphasis on the concrete and an orientation toward the field as a result of an approach that relied on experience based knowledge. The use of tacit and explicit knowledge is discussed within the context of the design process and the author finds that explicit knowledge dominates the improvement of productivity and organizational learning. The latest research in the sociology of culture and cultural psychology is used to highlight the cognitive approach to problem solving during the innovative process.

INTRODUCTION

With the rise of Toyota's renowned position as a producer of high quality automobiles, the past two decades has seen a dramatic increase in the study of the company's use of knowledge and organizational learning (Cusumano and Nobeoka 1998; Keeney and Florida 1993; Monden 1993; Womack, Jones and Roos 1991). The literature primarily focuses on the principles of the Toyota Production System and it's unique blend of human resource and management techniques. Scholars claim that Toyota's success stems from employing principles of continuous improvement and problem solving in what is known as "lean production". Although the studies initially focused on manufacturing techniques, such as just-in-time manufacturing and continuous improvement (kaizen) to reduce waste and increase quality, scholars claim that management's use of knowledge in the research and design stage in the Toyota organization is an important aspect of implementing the best practices of lean production. (Liker 2004) suggests that one of the keys to Toyota's success lies in its ability to create an organizational culture focused on problem solving, continuous improvement and organizational learning implemented at all levels of product development.

Another stream of literature focuses on the cognitive processes behind the use of knowledge in organizations. The use of tacit verses explicit knowledge initially discussed by Michael Polanyi has become the basis for studies in knowledge management in Japanese organizations. Tacit knowledge is defined as knowledge known only to an individual by experience. Explicit knowledge, on the other hand, is knowledge that is available in written form and can therefore easily transferred to others. (Nonaka and Takeuchi 1995) claim that Japanese firms do not employ the Western, hierarchical top-down management structure where selected knowledge flows from below to top management who use the information to devise corporate strategy, nor do they employ a bottom up strategy where employees are independent, and the hierarchy and the division of labor are eliminated. Japanese firms instead employ a middle-up down process of knowledge creation where middle managers are at the center of knowledge management and are best able to exploit the use of both tacit and explicit knowledge to improve organizational learning and productivity.

Many of these studies developed in part as a consequence of Japanese manufacturing industries posing a threat to American companies and the turn to investigating intellectual resources and organizational learning during the 1990s (Styhre and Sundgren 2005). Although studies of management and the Toyota Production System have contributed to the understanding of knowledge management in Japan, they are pointed toward learning specific management techniques and rarely focus on the micro-social processes behind the dynamics of innovation. In this paper I will discuss the use of knowledge and innovation through an ethnographic analysis of my experience working at a Toyota company in Japan. I will draw on the Toyota scholarship while discussing the cognitive turn in sociology and the latest findings in cultural psychology.

Current research in the sociology of culture and cultural psychology suggest that culture influences the way actors interpret and use knowledge. Sociologists believe that actors' thoughts, motives and intentions are constituted by the cultures and social institutions of their society and that cultures and institutions are reproduced by the structurally shaped and constrained actions of those actors (Sewell 2005). Structures consist of available rules and schemas (procedures or principles of action), capable of being put into practice in a range of different circumstances. (Swidler 1986) suggests that strategies of action are cultural products which are derived from practices of a group or society that create ways of organizing experience and evaluating reality. Culture shapes a "tool kit" of habits and skills in which individuals construct a strategy of action.

Research in cultural psychology suggest that a "person is a social and collective construction made possible through an individual's participation in the practices and meanings of a given cultural context." Many of the studies in cultural psychology are aimed at investigating the cognitive process in a comparative context. For instance, studies by Peng and Nisbett evaluate the cognitive and cultural differences between East Asians and Westerners. They suggest that there are two culturally bound ways of approaching problem solving – an East Asian way of dialectical reasoning, a compromise approach that retains elements of two opposing perspectives and the

European-American way that polarizes contradictory perspectives to determine which perspective is correct (Peng and Nisbett 1999). In a follow-up investigation on how cognitive processes influence formal versus intuitive reasoning among East Asians and European Americans showed that European Americans favored rule-based, formal and deductive reasoning whereas East Asians tended to favor intuition and contextualization in problem solving (Norenzayan et al. 2002).

Studies by Markus and Kitayama show that individuality is an essential element of the self-constructs of Americans whereas it is much less relevant for members of a more collectivist society such as Japan (Markus and Kitayama 1991). For example, in response to a question "What is a person" Japanese responded that an individual is a connected and committed being that is bound to others whereas Americans tended to respond that a person is a being that is independent and enters social relations with others by mutual consent. With respect to problem solving within the context of an organization, we would expect Japanese to be inclined toward a compromise approach, to favor intuition and contextualization and to lean toward collectivism in work activities. Individual action in the organization will be based on rules and schemas, or a cultural tool kit of habits and skills.

METHODOLOGY

After graduating with a masters degree in mechanical engineering at the University of Wisconsin-Madison I obtained a job in the research and design laboratories at a Toyota company in Japan (from now referred to as Nizumi) and I worked there from April of 1996 to July of 1999. It was a second tier company that employed over 8000 people and had over 5 billion dollars in sales. I was assigned to the computational fluid dynamics (CFD) group I was responsible for using computer tools to improve the design process and to come up with innovative ideas that could be incorporated into new products.

This study is based on my years as a participant-observer. In addition to the direct observation I recorded in my field notes, I also conducted over thirty interviews related to the engineering work and its environment and collected hundreds of pages of information freely distributed to employees. The interviews ranged in duration from ten minutes to two hours. About three quarters of those interviewed were Nizumi workers. I interviewed engineers, temporary laborers, contract employees, and mid to high level managers. Some 20% of the workers I interviewed were foreign, temporary workers, while the rest were permanent Japanese workers. I conducted approximately two-thirds of the interviews on company grounds. These were informal talks. The remaining third were held outside the company and were more formally structured. I have not included anything in this book that I did not personally observe or that did not come from at least two sources. My own observations and experiences have almost always been confirmed by those of my interviewees.

ETHNOGRAPHIC ANALYSIS

The Group and Monitoring

When I initially entered the Nizumi offices I was amazed at its size—it was absolutely enormous and completely open. There were no interior walls. The sections were organized into separate entities by desks jammed close together, carving out a space on the floor and a narrow path through which employees could pass. Although the office was open, there seemed to be complete order, with employees communicating politely and efficiently. With managers and their subordinates working shoulder to shoulder in a space without walls, it seemed that the office had been designed to embody egalitarianism but I would soon learn that it served other functions.

I was soon immersed in the company design process, but for me the most striking aspect of being at Nizumi was not my actual job but the work environment. For one thing, the close proximity of lower ranked engineers and higher ranked managers all facilitated discussion with other engineers or with my boss with whom I felt at ease to approach. For instance, while working on improving the design of a flagship product I immediately approached him and other engineers in the section for technical advice. This arrangement also allowed for the easy distribution of announcements and technical information that was passed from desk to desk. It was common for engineers and managers to distribute data or reports that was of interest to others in this manner. On the other hand, there was a total lack of privacy. Since every section was entirely open, there was not one place in the whole office that could not be seen by all members of the section. All desks were arranged in blocks of four and they all faced inward. The managers' desks were located on the outer edge of each section making a large rectangle that surrounded the inner blocks. Each manager's desk faced the lower-ranked workers. The resulting formation meant that everyone could see what each other was doing, and in many cases, what they were reading as well.

There was one minor exception for my section only. Each desk was separated from the next by a partition nine inches high from the desktop of the desk, partially blocking what the others could see. I surmised that since we were the research division some of our information was proprietary. Nevertheless, I always felt I was being watched. As I sat at my desk, the top of the wall was at eye level, so when I looked up, I always saw the eyes of my facing colleagues over the top edge of the wall.

As an American socially conditioned to value privacy, I was uncomfortable with the lack of walls, but what made me even more anxious was the way I was constantly being monitored by my colleagues. It was common practice for employees to look over the shoulders of their colleagues and to poke their noses into their computers or personal documents. Members of the section commonly opened each others' desk drawers and read each other's notes, letters, and papers. Nothing was private. My mild-mannered boss, Higuchi, would routinely approach me from behind and stick his face directly into my work to see what I was doing. This was standard management practice.

This monitoring unnerved me. At first, I would frequently go to the toilet to be in the one place where I could have privacy, if only for a few minutes. I however eventually became used to the monitoring and soon discovered that it was an integral part of group dynamics at the company. The engineering group, in which all engineers belonged, was to function in solidarity since if one member fell behind on a project, the engineers in his group were required to help him catch up by staying late at work to collectively gather and analyze data. Service overtime, a rule requiring engineers to stay after hours at the company without pay, was enforced particularly when the company had an important project with a strict deadline. I later discovered that if employees did not follow these rules, the entire group could be punished. Michael Hechter describes monitoring as a form of control to ensure compliance within a group. "A group must be able to detect whether individuals comply with their obligations or not." For those who chose to free ride, exclusion was the primary form of punishment. Deviants were moved to the corner of the office and were referred to as "members of the window watching" group (mado giwa zoku).

The office arrangement had a dual purpose for the management of knowledge – it functioned as a way for engineers and managers to share information and as a tool for monitoring employees. The open interaction of both management and engineers in a single space facilitated continuous improvement and organizational learning since engineers readily received the latest technical information and frequently used it to improve product designs. Both knowledge acquisition and monitoring was however a group activity and those who did not participate were openly punished indicating that my colleagues saw themselves collectively bound to others in the group.

Hierarchy, Training and Knowledge Acquisition

After I had been at Nizumi a few weeks, my boss whose name was Higuchi called me to his desk. The upper level managers had decided on using CFD and CAD to improve one of the company's flagship products, the XT37 -- part of the drive-train. Higuchi explained my role in the project and what he expected of me – to use the latest in computer simulation technology to create a more innovative product. He was confident that I had acquired the skills to begin working on my first assignment. I was pleased to be getting my career off the ground and excited that I would be learning how to design in Japan, where they made the best products in the world.

Nizumi implemented all of the five environmental components important for creativity and innovation (Amabile 1988; Styhre and Sundgren 2005). These include the encouragement of creativity where the company creates an environment where new ideas can be passed freely to all levels of the organization. Autonomy so that employees feel individually free to express their ideas. Resources in the form of technology to carry out the work. Pressures in the form of positive challenges such as the requirement to produce patents for the company and the avoidance of organizational obstacles to creativity such as influences of a conservative perspective to new ideas.

Getting my career moving in Japan, however, required me to adjust to the Japanese way of doing things. I learned early on that Higuchi was my only source of information regarding the technology I was using. Since Japanese engineers are not required to be at all knowledgeable before entering a company, on-the-job training by one's immediate superior was the norm for all engineers at the company. Since Higuchi was responsible for educating me, that meant we needed to develop a traditional Japanese relationship where the superior functioned as the mentor, or senpai, and the subordinate was the kohai. As a kohai and a new recruit, I was very dependent on Higuchi. Since much of the information was proprietary, only Higuchi, with his in-house experience at Nizumi, could provide the education I needed to design the part.

As I worked on designing the part for the new drive-train, I became frustrated by the lack of information that Higuchi provided. I always received information on a piece- meal basis. At times it was as if he was giving me secret "hints" about the technology, and when he finished, there was often an awkward silence as I waited for more information that never came. When we discussed design options, I did express my disagreement sometimes, but this was invariably frustrating and time-consuming. Higuchi was usually surprised that I would question his wisdom at all. Although much of his knowledge transferred to me was tacit knowledge in the form of experience with designing products, all employees at the company, including Higuchi, were required to document their engineering knowledge and skills in written form for management to evaluate, or as educational reports for lower ranked engineers.

Even the engineers in my section were not as forthcoming as I expected. One day Erberto came to my desk and told me that Kurata was holding a contest to come up with the best new drive-train designs. At the meeting to discuss the details, I was surprised when Kurata, who was highly-placed Director of the Design Division, bluntly stated that the company's foreign competitors had moved ahead of Nizumi. When I returned from the meeting, I approached members of my section and asked them what they thought about the new designs. To my surprise, they reacted defensively and avoided discussion, as if I was trying to steal their secrets.

Because of my frustrations with Higuchi, I was interested in learning how my colleagues interacted with their bosses, so I observed them closely. A superior would yell out the name of an engineer, who would drop what he was doing and rush to his desk. They would talk about the issue – usually loudly enough for everyone in the section to hear. Although the engineers would sometimes raise issues and make objections, in the end, they deferred to what their bosses said. Finally, the superior would give the subordinate a direct order and the engineer would respond with a "hai wakarimashita" and walk away. Both sides avoided a direct clash of ideas. Now I saw why Higuchi was surprised at some of my objections. Although I was only trying to create the best design, I was breaking the rules of social conduct.

The steel name-board reified the hierarchy. The names of all the employees in the section were printed on thin magnets. Upon entering or leaving the company, you moved your magnet to a column showing whether you were in the office, at home, or away on business. The names were arranged vertically by rank. The Section Manager was placed at the top of the board, with his direct subordinates placed under him, etc. The name board reflected some of the subtleties in the system. Since I was the newest member of the section, I was placed toward the bottom – but higher than a technician who had been there for several years, but who was part of a lower-ranked subsidiary company. The office lady was at the lowest position on the name board.

The acquisition of knowledge was highly embedded within the formal and informal hierarchy of the organization. The formal hierarchy consisted of the rankings of employees while the informal hierarchy involved the relationship between the engineer and the manager. Management would guide engineers on how to go about designing products but the knowledge transfer was highly dependent on developing a close relationship with one's superior. The senpai/kohai relationship was particularly important for career advancement since white collar, full-time employees were expected to stay at the company for the duration of their career and the lack of an external labor market prevented the movement to another company. On-the-job training was the norm at the company and although it was highly context oriented and developed tacitly (i.e. specific computer simulation tools were used to design certain products) knowledge acquisition and knowledge transfer from one employee to another was mostly carried out explicitly. Since middle managers interacted with both higher level management and engineers who did most of the research and design work, and were thus at the center of the knowledge management, explicit knowledge in the form of simulation tools, reports and explicit guidelines were used to improve productivity and organizational learning.

Concrete vs. the Abstract

Although my relationship with Higuchi was congenial, the way I discussed the technology with was very different than the way I learned in America. I would frequently ask him questions about design considerations. He would respond with very specific answers, never discussing the concepts abstractly. All discussions about technology were concrete. While I would always begin my talks with Higuchi with a discussion of basic ideas, he would immediately focus on the details. Once when I brought him 3D pictures of a design I was considering, Higuchi bent forward and put his head right up to a small part of the model. He said, "What about this?"

"What?"

"This," he said, pointing to a tiny speck on the model. I thought he was pulling my leg -- but he was serious. I was beside myself that he would consider such a small detail while ignoring the beauty of my overall design. But remembering I was a kohai, I just said I would look at it and went back to work.

I did express my disagreement sometimes, but this was invariably frustrating and time-consuming. Higuchi was usually surprised that I would question his wisdom at all, and we would discuss the issue at length, arguing back and forth, with me focusing on the abstract and him on the details. In the end, he wouldn't budge, so we would end up right where we had started.

In retrospect, most of the time he was correct. After all, he was the more experienced engineer. But what I found irritating was the assumption that there was only one way to approach the design project – his way: focus on the concrete. He always remained affable and patient while hearing me out, but I soon saw that our discussions were mostly a way for me to get things off my chest. Unless I had concrete results to show him, he wouldn't even consider what I had to say. However, if I could prove my ideas with results, he would affably and easily change his mind. Higuchi was open to new ideas -- as long as I could prove them.

I observed a similar emphasis on detail during the Friday technical meetings. Everyone in our section was required to present his research and a discussion would follow but a debate about the basic physics of the engineering phenomena rarely occurred. Only concrete information that could be validated through experiments or through previous designs was considered acceptable for discussion. A manifestation of the emphasis on the concrete was the language used during discussion such as katachi, meaning the form of an object in Japanese, and the gutaikeki, what is concrete or the tangible characteristics of an object.

Western engineers from foreign companies who entered Nizumi faced similar problems. When a German engineer named Rolf from a consulting company came to discuss a project he experienced substantial frustration related to cross-cultural communication. A number of engineers including myself were assigned to an advanced design project for a product that was planned to be released in five years. The company did not have some of the key technology so they hired a consultant to transfer the technology. When the Japanese engineers presented their designs, laying out CAD drawings of the assembly showing every bolt, curve, and surface. The level of detail was impressive, but Rolf asked how the parts could work together without major malfunctions. His idea of the product was different from theirs. He presented a fundamental reason why they should design it his way, but they did not agree. Rolf gave another reason, and they argued back and forth. During the discussion, the Japanese engineers would always drag Rolf into talking about the details. Rolf, however, would discuss the basics of the design, backing his reasoning with fundamentals. His voice got louder and he began acting agitated.

I empathized with him, because for months I had experienced the same frustration. The Japanese engineers argued with Rolf, back and forth, for every component in the product.

Then Rolf pointed to a part of the design that would dramatically reduce its efficiency, offering logical reasons why it would not work well. Saiki asked "How do you know it will be inefficient if you don't have any data?"

"I don't need data!" Rolf was getting angry. He explained yet again what was wrong.

The conversation continued for a number of minutes but the lesson from this encounter and others that I experienced or observed was that neither approach was the "correct" way of going about the design process.

This vignette suggests an emphasis on concrete knowledge in the way that engineers at Nizumi approached the design of their products. Abstract knowledge, unless it could be proven with empirical data, was not acceptable. Engineers at Nizumi always contextualize the object during the analysis and would rarely focus the analysis on the object to debate the fundamentals.

Induction vs. Deduction

While I worked on the flagship product my boss wanted me to create many models of various designs. Then we would choose the best among the many options available. The aim was to design a part with the highest efficiency while keeping manufacturing costs down. During the design process, we were required to sit down with engineers in production who explained the manufacturing process and costs.

For most projects I my task was to improve the technology or the product (a process famously referred to as kaizen), but once I was assigned to design a completely new product. The project involved designing a device to reduce the aerodynamic drag of the vehicle. The aerodynamic drag is the amount of force pushing on a vehicle in the opposite direction to which the car is moving. Reducing the drag results in better gas mileage. Although drag reducers existed in the industry, Nizumi had never designed one, so we would have to start from scratch (or so I thought).

For inspiration, I consulted my fluid mechanics textbook. I thought about the basic physics of the design problem and worked out some equations. I again focused on the object as the point of analysis and refused to look at other designs to maximize the ability to be creative. After a few days, I approached Higuchi with my ideas. Higuchi looked at me askance and demanded, "How do you know this? We've never designed a drag-reducer before."

Now I was confused. Hadn't he expected me to use my engineering education and experience to develop a creative design? No, he had not. The next day I discovered the approach he preferred. An engineer who was working on the project named Suzuki walked into the office with a large cardboard poster showing pictures of all of the drag-reducing products currently used in the industry. He'd gotten these pictures from industry magazines. Higuchi got very excited and studied each one, while Suzuki looked on proudly. It was an excellent display; the color photographs revealed every detail of the products. We discussed the merits of some specific designs, then Higuchi told us to create CAD models and analyze them using CFD software on all of the them so we could compare and see which was best.

During the weekly technical meetings I continued to learn how my Japanese colleagues approached problem-solving. To arrive at the best design, the engineers would gather huge amounts of information, comparing new designs with previous designs. If the technology unearthed by their research could benefit the product in any way, they would include it in the many alternatives they were considering.

Ward, Sobek, Cristiano and Liker's research describe Toyota's approach to product development as set-based design where "designers think and reason about sets of design alternatives. Over time, these sets are gradually narrowed as the designers eliminate inferior alternatives until they find a final solution." They claim this method differs from the practice called "point-based" design common in many American and Western manufacturing companies that involves choosing a single design early on and iterating until a solution is obtained. I would soon learn that set-based design was used extensively at Nizumi. Comparing one design to another was considered the best way to evaluate the advantages of each. A high level manager named Abe in charge of designing the wind deflector once distributed a memo called "The Vision Method." This was a step-by- step directive about engaging engineers in the set-based process. One of the steps was "Deciding the Subject": "To achieve the goal, you must think about as many ideas as you can and write them down. Then you must choose the best idea from all of the ideas."

Abe planned a brainstorming meeting for the new drag reducer Nizumi would produce. I spent many days thinking of the basic physics of the product and engaging in analysis. When the day came, Abe called on each of us to present our new product designs. I was surprised when all the other engineers brought in designs of products that had already been developed or manufactured by other companies. Suzuki and another engineer showed a design that came from a company's brochure. When my turn came, I presented some novel ideas based on my analysis alone. My proposals were not as clever as some of the others, but they were certainly more original.

It was important for a base of knowledge to be obtained from competitor products in the field before a new product was to be developed. Explicit knowledge was used to create a new product while improving the design by investigating the advantages and disadvantages of products that existed in the field. I believe the cognitive approach to product design used by my Toyota colleagues indicated a far different conception of innovation. They used an inductive process, while as an American-educated engineer and a recent university graduate, I had a far different cultural-tool kit in that I had been trained to use deduction.

Organizational Learning and the Benchmarking Process

The process of comparing designs of products from various companies in the field is commonly referred to as benchmarking. Benchmarking was the topic a number of department meetings and one day I had a birds eye view to the amount of effort that went into the process. The section manager announced we would benchmark a European competitor's product, which was rumored to incorporate the most advanced technology in the industry.

When I entered the chop shop later that day, my mouth dropped. Enormous effort had been expended in displaying how the European design compared with the Nizumi's and other competitor's similar products. Large, excruciatingly detailed charts filled the walls, comparing efficiency, gas mileage, etc. All the relevant parts had been cut up and placed on a table for us to examine. Each part was compared with the corresponding parts of the competition's products. The benchmark was so thorough that there was even a comparison of the number of bolts used to put the products together. All parts on display were documented and filed on the intranet so that any engineer in the company could have access to the information at any time. I was amazed.

At Nizumi, benchmarking was a crucial part of the design process. During design meetings, each engineer was required to show the main design parameters for the optimal design of the product. For example, if product efficiency was the main criterion, the chart would be a spreadsheet consisting of the design parameters in the columns and the manufacturer's design of that parameter in the rows, with each cell containing the numerical efficiency. Each design parameter was graded according to efficiency, cost and ease of manufacture. From this information, a preliminary prototype was produced, and after further investigation, the final prototype was made. Then the engineers would improve the design in the technical lab or on the computer by tweaking various design parameters and adding new technology when needed. After further testing, the part was then manufactured.

Benchmarking was used at all levels of product development: in research and development, in product design, and in market analysis. It was not necessarily used to copy other products but was thought to speed up the design process while generating new ideas. Analysis of and experiment on an existing product was the basic approach to designing a new one. There were several technicians at the company whose only job was to take apart the competitor's products, test them, and write up the results for engineers.

After benchmarking and design iterations the final design decisions occurred in the "big room". A lower level manager who worked for Abe named Watanabe called a group of us together to discuss the drag reducer. He brought in the analysis information that I had worked on. A Design Manager contributed extremely detailed drawings showing exactly how the product should be designed. An engineer from the industrial design group brought in his own set of drawings.

It was Watanabe's project, so he directed the meeting and spoke first, presenting the analysis information. Then the Design Manager took the floor and we discussed his drawings. A technician remarked that a design would be difficult to include because of noise problems. Other engineers wanted a feature that would benefit the customer, while the design guys wanted to make the vehicle more efficient. The meeting went on and on, as we discussed in minute detail every aspect of the product -- while continually making comparisons to competitor products.

Watanabe took out a chart showing the number of vehicles that would include the drag reducer and the number that would not. He held up another detailed chart, comparing the drag reducer with all the other products Nizumi made. Both charts were incredibly beautiful, with neatly drawn, detailed illustrations of the drag reducer. Finally, Watanabe pointed to pictures on the chart and said, "O.K., let's try this one, that one and this one."

DISCUSSION

The use of knowledge management in Toyota has garnered much interest in the past two decades but I believe this paper has raised important issues as to how knowledge is used in a Toyota organization. The open office space facilitated the sharing of knowledge for continuous improvement and organizational learning but monitoring was an important element in controlling knowledge and ensuring that employees who did not participate were openly ostracized (see Figure 1 below for schematic of knowledge management). Company hierarchy also played a large role in the management of knowledge. Important to engineers was the informal hierarchy. Management would guide engineers on how to design products but the knowledge transfer was highly dependent on developing a tight relationship with one's superior in a traditional senpai/kohai relationship. Although an informal hierarchy of knowledge transfer from superior to inferior is not unique to Toyota organizations, what made it exceptional was that employees were expected to stay at the company for their career and dependence on a superior for the acquisition of knowledge was particularly important.

On-the-job training was the norm at the company and although it was highly context oriented and existed in both tacit and explicit form, the most important knowledge existed explicitly in the form of training material, presentations to employees and computational tools used for the research and design process. Although middle level managers worked in the world between high level managers and engineers who conduced the research and design, they primarily relied on explicit knowledge to improve productivity and organizational learning.

Cognition significantly shaped the way knowledge was used at Nizumi to design products. Abstract knowledge was considered suspicious unless engineers could prove their claims with empirical data and contextualizing an object during the analysis was the primary way engineers would approach the design process. A base of knowledge was obtained from competitor products in the field before a new product was developed. The most important aspect of the design process was the use of explicit knowledge to improve the design of products while continuously taking into consideration the advantages and disadvantages of design characteristics of products that existed in the field. I believe the cognitive approach to product design by my Toyota colleagues – the use of induction and benchmarking - indicated a conception of innovation that differed significantly from the approach implemented by foreign educated engineers. To be sure, a single case study cannot be used to make generalizations about design at Japanese companies or to establish a

Figure 1. Step by step knowledge management during the design process

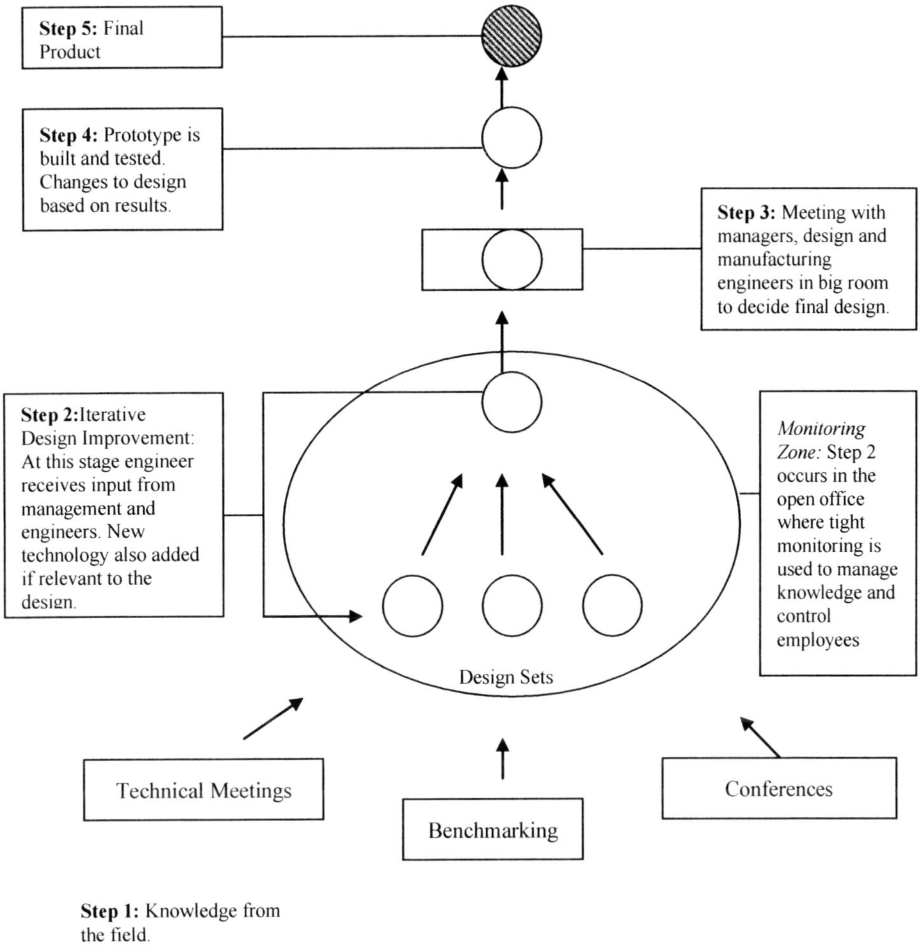

direct causal link between cognition and innovation at Nizumi. The data however is consistent with the latest research in the sociology of culture and cultural psychology.

REFERENCES

Amabile, T. (1988). A model of creativity and innovation in organizations. *Research in Organizational Behavior, 10*, 123-67.

Cusumano, M., & Kentaro, N. (1998). *Thinking Beyond Lean.* New York, London, Toronto, Sydney, Singapore: The Free Press.

Hechter, M. (1987). *Principles of Group Solidarity.* Berkeley, Los Angeles and London: University of California Press.

Keeney, M., & Richard, F. (1993). *Beyond Mass Production*: Oxford University Press.

Liker, J. K. (2004). *The Toyota Way: 14 Management Principles from the World's Greatest Manufacturer.* McGraw-Hill.

Liker, J. K., Ettlie, J. E., &Campbell, J. C. (Eds.) (1995). *Engineered in Japan: Japanese Technology Management Practices.* New York and Oxford: Oxford University Press.

Markus, H. R., & Shinobu, K. (1991). Culture and the Self: Implications for Cognition, Emotion and Motivation. *Psychological Review, 98*, 224-253.

Markus, H. R., & Shinobu, K. (1998). The Cultural Psychology of Personality. *Journal of Cross-Cultural Psychology,* 29, 63-87.

Monden, Y. (1993). *Toyota Management System: Linking the Seven Key Functional Areas*. Portland, Oregon: Productivity Press.

Nonaka, I., & Hirotaka, T. (1995). *The Knowledge-Creating Company: How Japanese Companies Create the Dynamics of Innovation.* Oxford University Press.

Norenzayan, A, Smith, E. E., Beom, J. K., &Nisbett, R. E. (2002). Cultural Preferences for Formal Versus Intuitive Reasoning. *Cognitive Science, 26*, 653-684.

Peng, K., &Nisbett, R. E. (1999). Culture, Dialectics, and Reasoning About Contradiction. *American Psychologist, 54*, 741-754.

Sewell, W. H. (2005). *Logics of History: Social Theory and Social Transformation.* University of Chicago Press.

Styhre, A., & Sundgren, M. (2005). *Managing Creativity in Organizations: Critique and Practices.* Palgrave Macmillan.

Swidler, A. (1986). Culture in Action: Symbols and Strategies. *American Sociological Review,* 51, 273-286.

Womack, J., Jones, D., &Roos, D. (1991). *The Machine That Changed the World: The Story of Lean Production.* Harper Perennial.

KEY TERMS

Cognitive Processes: Refers to the faculty for the processing of information and applying knowledge.

Culture: Culture consists of such symbolic vehicles of meaning, including beliefs, ritual practices, as well as informal cultural practices such as language, gossip, and rituals of daily life. These symbolic forms are the means through which shared modes of behavior and outlook in a community take place.

Explicit Knowledge: Knowledge that can be articulated, codified, and stored in certain media and that can be readily transmitted to others in an organization.

Kaizen: Continuous improvement.

Lean Production: Practice of production that considers the expenditure of resources, on such things as equipment or the transfer of knowledge, for any means other than the creation of value for the customer to be wasteful, and therefore, should be the target of elimination.

Monitoring: To watch and keep track of.

Tacit Knowledge: Knowledge only known by an individual through experience and that is difficult to communicate to the rest of an organization.

ENDNOTES

1 Markus, Hazel R., and Shinobu Kitayama. 1998. "The Cultural Psychology of Personality." *Journal of Cross-Cultural Psychology* 29:63-87. p.63.

2 Hechter, Michael 1987. *Principles of Group Solidarity.* Berkeley, Los Angeles and London: University of California Press. p. 51

3 Liker, Jeffrey K., John E. Ettlie, and John C. Campbell (Eds.). 1995. *Engineered in Japan: Japanese Technology Management Practices.* New York and Oxford: Oxford University Press. p. 192.

Chapter XXIII
Critical Analysis of International Guidelines for the Management of Knowledge Resources

Federica Ricceri
University of Padova, Italy

James Guthrie
The University of Sydney, Australia

ABSTRACT

The shift towards a knowledge based economy is at the core of the debate of contemporary management and accounting literature and organisations are challenged by the need to manage their knowledge resources. Several national and international institutions have produced authoritative "guidelines" to facilitate the management and reporting of KR. Many of these guidelines are the result of co-operation between researchers, companies, industry organisations and consultants and have, therefore, been informed by practice. However, to date, there has been no serious critique of these guidelines. The main objective of this chapter is to provide an in-depth analysis of six contemporary guidelines. By reviewing these guidelines, this chapter explores how each of these addresses the MKR and therefore facilitates the management and reporting of KR. Therefore, this chapter will establish some of the key issues involved in understanding MKR. It will also provide an overview of how these issues are addressed or otherwise in the six guidelines. Two key messages of this chapter are the followings: first, MKR and its elements are embedded in various ways into the international guidelines examined; second, that a key policy issue is international harmonisation.

INTRODUCTION

Over the past few decades, the world has rapidly moved from its industrial economic base, in which economic growth was considered to be mostly determined by the use of tangible resources. Instead, many organisations have shifted towards a knowledge base, in which wealth creation is associated with the challenge of developing and managing knowledge resources (KR). These are commonly visualised using the tripartite classification of intellectual capital (IC)[a] (see, among others, MERITUM, 2002; SKE, 2005; EC, 2006; Guthrie et al., 2007; Unermann *et al.* 2007).

Some knowledge-intensive organisations have responded to this challenge by adopting matrix structures in order to foster knowledge flows and innovation and enhance 'value creation' (Mouritsen *et al.*, 2005: 4). Others have sought to manage KR by applying information technology. In these and other cases, organisations are responding to major changes in their external environment by using knowledge management tools (e.g. intranet, open plan offices) to attempt to manage KR, but in a non-systematic way. The management of KR (MKR) is central to the way in which an organisation is made up and, therefore, it cannot be separated out and acted upon in the same way as a single business process or management system (Ricceri, 2008).

Several national and international institutions have produced authoritative 'guidelines' for MKR. These guidelines aim to facilitate the management and reporting of KR by framing IC with sets of metrics and narratives. Many of these guidelines are the result of co-operation between researchers, companies, industry organisations and consultants and have, therefore, been informed by practice.

However, to date, there has been no serious critique of these guidelines and the main objective of this chapter is to provide an in-depth analysis of six contemporary guidelines. By reviewing several of these guidelines, this chapter aims to explore how each of these addresses the MKR and therefore facilitates the management and reporting of KR. Therefore this chapter will establish some of the key issues involved in understanding MKR. It will aso provide an overview of how these issues are addressed or otherwise in the six guidelines, and identify gaps in these contemporary guidelines.

The chapter is structured as follows. Section two discusses the context in which the guidelines have been developed. Section three outlines the six contemporary guidelines from different geographic areas and the management issues that will be used for their analysis. Section four analyses how these management issues are incorporated into the contemporary guidelines. Finally, section five discusses the lessons learned from the analysis and provides a conclusion to the chapter.

INTERNATIONAL KNOWLEDGE RESOURCES FRAMEWORKS

The challenge of understanding MKR has been addressed by many KR frameworks. One common characteristic of these frameworks is that they use measurement as a way to make IC visible. Sveiby[b] identifies many frameworks and more have been added to make a comprehensive list of 36.

These frameworks can be collapsed into two different approaches: the '*stock approach*' and the '*flow approach*' (see, Guthrie and Ricceri, 2002). Under the '*stock approach*', KR are thought to be static and able to be assigned a monetary value. Table 1 highlights eighteen '*stock approach*' KR frameworks that could provide a traditional 'financial view' of KR. The underlying assumption of the '*stock approach*' is that KR are recognised mainly on the basis of their market value or for their contribution to the generation of revenue, earnings or cash flows. Therefore, KR are contextualised within a traditional financial accounting frame.

Table 1. 'Stock approach' KR frameworks

Year	Framework	Proponent
2001	Inclusive Valuation Methodology (IVM)	M'Pherson and Pike
2000	The Value Explorer™	Andriessen and Tiessen
2000	Intellectual Asset Valuation	Sullivan
2000	Total Value Creation, TVC™	Anderson and McLean
2000	Value Added Intellectual Coefficient (VAIC™)	Pulic
1999	Knowledge Capital Earnings	Lev
1998	Accounting for the Future (AFTF)	Nash
1998	Investor Assigned Market Value (IAMV™)	Standfield
1997	Market-to-Book Value	Stewart (1997); Luthy (1998)
1997	Economic Value Added (EVA™)	Stewart
1997	Calculated Intangible Value	Stewart (1997); Luthy (1998)
1997	IC-Index™	Roos, Roos, Dragonetti, and Edvinsson
1996	Technology Broker	Brooking
1996	Citation- Weighted Patents	Bontis, Dragonetti, Jacobson and Roos
1996	Human Resource Costing & Accounting (HRCA)	Gröjer and Johanson
1990	The Invisible Balance Sheet	Sveiby
1985	Human Resource Accounting	Flamholtz
1950s	Tobin's Q	Tobin

Under the *'flow approach'*, KR are contextualised within the organisation for understanding their links to organisational performance, via KR metrics and narratives, rather than assigning a specific monetary value. As will be observed later in this chapter, the *'flow approach'* supports the idea that metrics by themselves are not informative, as they can capture only the measurable part of KR. For instance, assume that a research organisation is developing a new drug for treating patients with a particular disease and that, for this project to succeed, new competencies are needed. In order to acquire the necessary competencies, the research organisation has to employ five PhD students. Does the metric '5 new PhD students' represent this situation? A more useful approach would be to integrate the metric with narratives that link to the organisational context (e.g., strategy to focus on this project, the strategic choice of employing the PhD students with specific competencies). Therefore, narratives provide a context for understanding the meaning of the metrics for the specific organisation.

The KR frameworks which adopted a *'flow approach'* are illustrated in Table 2. Pioneers of this approach were: the Balanced Scorecard (1992); the Intangible Asset Monitor (1997); and the Skandia Navigator (1997). The underlying assumption of the *'flow approach'* is that KR have to be understood and managed in order to create

Table 2. 'Flow approach' KR frameworks

Year	Framework	Proponent
2002-2006	Austrian Universities Act	Federal Ministry of Education, Science and Culture (FMESC)
2005	Japanese Guidelines	Ministry of Economy, Trade and Industry (METI)
2005	Australian Guiding Principles	Society for Knowledge Economics (SKE)
2005	Intellectual Capital Management Process	Roos, Pike and Fernstrom
2004	German Guideline	Federal Ministry of Economics and Labour (FMEL)
2004	Performance Prism	Neely, Adams and Kennerly
2004	Value+ä Model	Bygdås, Røyvrik and Gjerde
2004	Strategy Maps	Kaplan and Norton
2004	Topplinjen/ Business IQ	Sandvik
2003	IC-dVAL	Bonfour
2003	Danish Guideline	Mouritsen et al.
2002	European Meritum Guidelines	MERITUM
2002	IC Rating™	Edvinsson
2001	Value Chain Scoreboard™	Lev
2001	Knowledge Audit Cycle	Schiuma and Marr
1999	Intellectual Capital Navigator (ICN)	Roos and Jacobsen
1997	Skandia Navigator™	Edvinsson
1997	Intangible Asset Monitor	Sveiby
1992	Balanced Scorecard	Kaplan and Norton

value for the organisation and its stakeholders. Given the difficulties associated with determining monetary values for KR, most of the metrics considered by these frameworks do not attempt to put a monetary figure on KR. The *'flow approach'* attempts to untangle the KR puzzle and provides insight into how KR can be managed, measured and reported.

The next section will describe the six contemporary guidelines that were selected within the *'flow approach'* frameworks and then present the management issues used to analyse them.

RESEARCH METHODS

As indicated above, six contemporary *'flow approach'* frameworks have been selected for examination. These frameworks have been developed by national or international bodies to guide organisations in the management and reporting of KR. The six selected guidelines are listed in Table 3.

Each of the guidelines was subjected to detailed analysis by using four management issues. These were established in Ricceri (2008) as important

Table 3. The six guidelines

Year	Guideline	Proponent
2003	Danish Guideline: "Intellectual Capital Statement – The New Guideline",	The Danish Ministry of Science, Technology and Innovation (DMSTI)
2004	German guideline: "Intellectual capital statement – Made in Germany"	Federal Ministry of Economics and Labour (FMEL)
2002-2006	"Austrian Universities Act"	Federal Ministry of Education, Science, and Culture (FMESC)
2002	European Meritum Guidelines: "MERITUM (Measuring Intangibles to Understand and Improve Innovation Management) Guidelines"	European Union - MERITUM Project
2005	Australian Guiding Principles: "Australian Guiding Principles on Extended Performance Management" (SKE, 2005)	The Australian Society for Knowledge Economics (SKE)
2005	Japanese Guidelines: "Guidelines for Disclosure of Intellectual Assets Based Management"	Ministry of Economy, Trade and Industry (METI)

elements for the MKR. The four management issues are: organisational strategy; resources interactions; measurement; and reporting.

Organisational strategy aims to investigate if and how KR are considered in strategy formulation. The basic assumption here is that considering KR when formulating organisational strategy is fundamental for sustainable organisational performance. Although strategy has been recognised as the most important context for guiding MKR, the link between MKR and organisational strategy has been widely ignored in practice (Zack, 1999: 125-126). Managers do not have well developed strategies that help to link knowledge oriented processes to strategy and are unsure of how to translate the goal of making their organisation more "intelligent" into a strategic course of action (Zack, 1999: 126).

Theoretically, the relevance of considering KR and their management within organisational strategy is grounded in the resource-based literature, which assumes that organisational performance can be explained by an organisation's resources portfolio (Dierickx and Cool, 1989) and its deployment. In particular, it is recognised that knowledge is a main strategic asset of the organisation (Itami and Roehl, 1987; Grant, 1991; Hall, 1993).

The resource-based literature also states that bundles of resources impact upon performance (Lippman and Rumelt, 1982) and it is difficult to identify the contribution of individual elements without taking into account the transformations between various resources (Dierickx and Cool, 1989; King and Zeithaml, 2001). Therefore an understanding of resources flows is of critical importance for strategy formulation and for making an effective use of KR.

The second MKR issue, **resources interactions**, highlights the relevance of understanding flows within resources and these are also known as resources transformations.

Within the IC literature, the existence of resources interactions has been highlighted by several contributions (e.g., Nonaka and Takeuchi, 1995; Roos and Roos, 1997; Roos *et al.*, 2005). In particular, Roos *et al.* (2005: 109) indicate that value is created through the transformation of one resource into the other. However, Sveiby

(2001: 348) states that despite the relevance of transformations between KR, they tend not to be co-ordinated and systematically managed because senior managers lack an understanding of the 'full perspective'. Therefore, resources interactions should be identified, mapped and assessed for an understanding of their contribution to organisational performance (Ricceri, 2008).

Transformations (see, also Roos and Jacobsen, 1999; Gupta and Roos, 2001; Marr *et al.*, 2004; Roos *et al.*, 2005) are defined as resources flows that affect different organisational resources types, being tangible assets or KR (see, Roos *et al.*, 2005: 109-110; Ricceri, 2008). Whilst transformations within tangible resources (physical or financial) are, in most cases, observable and measurable, transformations which involve KR are difficult to identify. For example, consider the brand Nike. There is a transformation between Nike's brand (structural capital) and Nike's revenues (financial resources – cash flows or credit instruments), but this transformation is not easily measurable, nor specifically tracked by financial transactions and the resultant financial documents.

The third MKR issue, **measurement**, refers to the use of KR metrics and narratives to support MKR and, in particular, to assess performance. Many organisations are integrating traditional accounting-based performance measures with strategic performance measures (or key performance indicators). As Ittner and Larker (2003: 88) highlighted, in the past decades, an increasing number of organisations has been using strategic performance measures to monitor multiple performance perspectives (e.g., customers and innovation) and related drivers (e.g., customer loyalty and employee satisfaction) that do not follow traditional financial management accounting practices. Bontis (2001: 57) reports that top executives in large US and Canadian businesses agree that IC measures are required to manage knowledge assets. He analyses the strengths and weaknesses of six IC frameworks and highlights critical issues in their operationalisation. Also, he establishes that part of the complexity of IC measurement is related to the fact that it should attempt to capture not only forms of individual IC resources but also changes in these stocks of capital, i.e. the flows or transformations of intellectual capital (Bontis, 2001: 58).

The integration of strategic performance measurement (SPM) into organisations' measurement systems is aimed at capturing the factors leading to the "creation of value in the business" (Ittner and Larcker, 1998: 217) and responding to shortcomings in traditional financial performance measures.

The fourth MKR issue, **reporting**, relates to the construction of the reporting devices which can be used for external and internal communication. A common device used to provide internal and external stakeholders with an extended view of organisational performance by focusing on the efforts to manage and develop KR is the Intellectual Capital Statement (ICS) (Mouritsen, 2004: 259).

An ICS provides information about how KR are created, developed and applied in the organisation (Edvinsson and Malone, 1997; Sveiby, 1997; Bontis *et al.* 1999; Mouritsen, 2004; Mouritsen and Larsen, 2005). Also, it summarises the firm's efforts to develop and use KR and puts evaluative managerial questions that help managers to change KR and/or direct them towards new strategies (Mouritsen, 2004: 259). Therefore, the ICS has two main functions: a descriptive function and an enabling one. First, the descriptive function relates to the description of KR and their management. This function is mainly related to the ability of the ICS to provide a picture of KR and their management to internal and external stakeholders. Therefore, ICS can be considered as a descriptive device for understanding KR and their management. Second, the enabling function relates to the knowledge that derives from the ICS and, in particular, to if and how this knowledge enables managerial intervention.

Ideally, KR information should be reported and used internally and a selected set should also be reported externally. Reporting should be done in a consistent manner, using a model that links metrics and narratives.

The remaining part of this section is devoted to a brief presentation of the six international guidelines that were selected within the *'flow approach'* frameworks and listed in table 3.

Danish Guideline

The Danish Ministry of Science, Technology and Innovation (DMSTI) has published the "Intellectual Capital Statement – The New Guideline", which was the output of a project over several years, based on the experiences of over 100 organisations. This guideline, issued in 2003, was for public and private organisations, large and small. Its aim was to foster the companies' ability to manage KR that create value for society. The Danish Guideline stimulates organisations "to work more systematically and comprehensively with the main initiatives within knowledge management" (Mouritsen *et al.* 2003: 3). It also aimed to provide a reporting tool for communicating knowledge management to existing and potential internal and external stakeholders via Intellectual Capital Statements (ICS), as part of organisations' knowledge management strategy.

The Danish Guideline provided a way of managing and reporting IC. This process is based on four interrelated elements "which together express the company's knowledge management" (Mouritsen *et al.*, 2003: 2). They are the knowledge narrative; management challenges; initiatives; and indicators.

The process for preparing the ICS helps to systematise knowledge management by finding consistency within the four elements and making them work together. Therefore, the preparation of the ICS requires going from one element to the other.

German Guideline

The German guideline (i.e. "Intellectual capital statement – Made in Germany") was issued in 2004 by the Federal Ministry of Economics and Labour to foster "the implementation of the intellectual capital statement and of knowledge management in both small and medium-sized enterprises, and in the trades sector" (FMEL, 2004: 3). The Guideline targets small and medium-sized enterprises (SMEs). The German Guideline was based on the Danish Guideline and a pilot project was established to adjust it for German SMEs, 13 of which were using the ICS for internal management and 10 for external reporting purposes (FMEL, 2004: 10).

Austrian Universities Act

The Austrian Universities Act (FMESC, 2002) and its related Regulation (FMESC, 2006) are the first mandatory requirements to produce an Intellectual Capital Report (ICR). The Act came into force in 2004 and was aimed at restructuring the educational and legal framework of universities (Altenburger and Schaffhauser-Linzatti, 2006). According to this directive, universities were granted autonomy from the Federal Ministry of Education, Science, and Culture (FMESC) and universities' budgets were placed on a performance-oriented basis.

The Regulation states that a university's ICR is aimed at "presenting, evaluating and communicating intangible assets, performance processes and their consequences and serves as a qualitative and quantitative basis for generating and entering a performance agreement" (FMESC, 2006: 1).

One consequence of this was the introduction of new forms of reporting. External reports were required to be standardised. The four new external reports introduced were: the performance report; intellectual capital reports (ICR); the evaluation report; and the financial statement.

European MERITUM Guidelines

The MERITUM (Measuring Intangibles to Understand and Improve Innovation Management) Guidelines for managing and reporting on IC were established in 2002. These Guidelines are the result of a 30-month (1998-2001) project funded by the European Union within the Targeted Socio-Economic Research (TSER) program. These Guidelines aim to assist organisations to develop their IC by its identification, measurement and control. Also, they aim to assist organisations in the external disclosure of the intangible determinants of their value creation capability (MERITUM, 2002: 56).

The MERITUM Guidelines are divided into three sections: the conceptual framework; the management of intellectual capital; and the intellectual capital report.

Australian Guiding Principles

The Australian Society for Knowledge Economics (SKE) produced the "Australian Guiding Principles on Extended Performance Management" (SKE, 2005), with the objective of inspiring Australian organisations to measure, organise and report their knowledge-intensive resources. The principal aims were to: provide a broad and balanced perspective on organisational health and wealth; better define the capacity an organisation has to create value in the future; and make visible knowledge-intensive organisational resources, identifying new opportunities for management intervention and financial valuation (SKE, 2005: 4). The Principles use the term "Extended Performance Management" (EPM) to describe the framework developed. Also, they highlight three main management phases that are used to operationalise EPM: (1) Business Orientation; (2) Business Analysis; and (3) Performance Assessment.

The Principles can be used from two main perspectives (SKE, 2005: 9). First, they take an internal management perspective, which provides managers with a practical tool for gaining a better understanding of knowledge-intensive resources and business performance. Therefore, internally, EPM represents a useful device for improving strategy formulation and resource allocation processes as well as for motivating employees. Second, an external reporting perspective, which organisations can use to disclose information to stakeholders through extended performance accounts. These communicate the organisation's knowledge-intensive resources which are not included in traditional financial accounts.

Japanese Guidelines

The Japanese Industrial Structure Council issued an Interim Report on Intellectual Assets (IA) which examined measures to promote Japan "to become a society where higher added value is realised" (SMIA, 2005: 5).

The Council promoted the management and reporting of IA, which represents the beginning of a "virtuous cycle" of benefits for the organisation, capital markets and Japanese national wealth (SMIA, 2005: 27).

However, the main point of the Interim Report was not disclosure, but rather the management of IA (SMIA, 2005: 47-48). The Council stated that in a knowledge-based society, Intellectual Assets Based Management (IABM), in which corporations accurately recognise and utilise their potential, was becoming increasingly important (SMIA, 2005: 63).

In response to the Council's Interim Report, the Ministry of Economy, Trade and Industry (METI) released the "Guidelines for Disclosure of Intellectual Assets Based Management" (METI, 2005). The focus of these Japanese Guidelines was on IA management of companies, rather than just IA reporting (METI, 2005: 1).

The four MKR issues identified above, will now be used to analyse the selected KR international guidelines.

A CRITICAL AND COMPARATIVE ANALYSIS OF THE GUIDELINES

The following analysis was driven by a desire to understand how MKR was incorporated into the various guidelines. For the purpose of understanding MKR in the various KR guidelines, the four MKR issues discussed in detail above are now used to provide a critical and comparative analysis. Table 4 summarises the findings of the analysis of the six individual guidelines and provides an overview of each MKR issue in the examined set.

The specific observations in relation to the four MKR issues are now discussed in detail to highlight key points from the analysis. These points are then used to highlight several important observations at the conclusion of this section.

a. Organisational strategy

Concerning strategy, all the guidelines (except the Austrian and the Japanese) address the relevance of considering KR in the organisation's strategy. The Austrian and Japanese guidelines are focused on performance assessment and reporting and do not address the need to include KR into strategy formulation and implementation.

In the Danish Guideline, the formulation and implementation of the strategy for MKR plays a central role and is derived from the construction of a knowledge narrative. The knowledge narrative is centred on the KR required to create 'use value' and considers users as the main stakeholders. The knowledge narrative is specified, in terms of KR requirements, by the management challenges which are then operationalised by a set of initiatives. Initiatives consist of the activities that compose, develop and procure KR.

The German Guideline identifies a strategy cycle, in which the knowledge strategy is derived from the business strategy and describes the organisation's position with regards to subareas of IC. The business strategy is derived from the analysis of environmental factors and the organisation's vision. This is informed by the ICS which, in this Guideline, measures and evaluates the success of the knowledge strategy. The analysis of the organisation's environment considers the social and the political context and therefore, also information about stakeholders (e.g., customer, suppliers, competitors). Also, the issue of undertaking actions in order to achieve the knowledge strategy is not addressed in detail. It states that the "management of IC" focuses on the identification, mapping and assessment of resources transformations.

Table 4. Guidelines and management issues

Guidelines/ management issues	Organisational strategy	Resources interactions	Measurement	Reporting
1. Danish Guideline	✓	X	✓	✓
2. German Guideline	✓	✓	✓	✓
3. Austrian Universities Act	X	X	✓	✓
4. European MERITUM Guidelines	✓	X	✓	✓
5. Australian Guiding Principles	✓	X	✓	✓
6. Japanese Guidelines	X	X	✓	✓

In the MERITUM Guidelines, the vision of the firm is about how the customers and other (market) stakeholders benefit from the firm's knowledge production activities. This is the starting point for the identification of strategic objectives and intangible resources. Customers and suppliers are considered by this framework, but other stakeholder groups are not taken into account in the strategy formulation. Also, all the illustrations provided about "other stakeholders" relate to market stakeholders. The implementation of the strategy is then undertaken via intangibles activities that aim to acquire and develop critical intangibles in order to achieve strategic objectives. Also, the Guidelines identify processes that can facilitate the integration of IC management within the firm's managerial processes.

In the Australian Principles, the identification of gaps to be addressed by MKR is informed not only by market analysis, but by the analysis of the perspectives and needs of a range of internal and external stakeholder groups. The organisation's strategy is expressed in terms of "use value" to be delivered to stakeholders. Therefore, the Australian framework is the only one that provides guidance on how to consider the interests of various stakeholder groups in strategy formulation. In relation to strategy implementation, these Principles identify five activities for managing KR: acquisition, development, utilisation, maintenance, and disposal of KR.

In summary, the majority of KR guidelines highlight the need for considering KR within organisational strategy in different ways. Also, the Australian framework provided some guidance for considering a wide range of stakeholder interests along with KR in strategy formulation.

b. Resources interactions

Only one framework details the tools for identification, assessment and mapping of KR transformations. The German Guideline addresses, in a systematic way, the issue of resources transformations. According to these guidelines, without understanding resources interactions, KR cannot be "sensibly" managed (FMEL, 2004: 33). Therefore, the analysis and assessment of interdependencies is considered in this guideline as an important prerequisite for managerial action. The identification of "influencing factors" (e.g., building up employees' experience) is the starting point. Then, the Guideline proposes two tools for mapping and assessing interdependencies between influencing factors: the matrix; and the interdependencies network.

Nearly all the guidelines consider flows between resources as important. It is acknowledged that all organisations have a unique set of tangible and KR that are interconnected in various ways and value is created through the transformations of these resources. Therefore, an understanding of the 'value creation' process can be achieved via the mapping of resources interactions.

In summary, the relevance of Resources interactions for 'value creation' is acknowledged by nearly all the frameworks. However, only the German Guideline provides tools for managers to map and assess resources transformations and therefore consider in a systematic way the contribution of KR to 'value creation'.

c. Measurement

All the frameworks use KR metrics and accompanying narratives for identifying, measuring and assessing IC and provide examples of financial and non-financial KR metrics. Not all of them provide examples about accompanying narratives (e.g., Austrian and MERITUM). Also, the majority of the guidelines recognise that KR metrics are organisationally specific. The Austrian framework provides a generally applicable set of IC indicators for the university sector. Moreover, some of the frameworks identify specific characteristics that the metrics should have (e.g., Danish, MERITUM and Australian).

The Danish Guideline uses narratives and indicators for a qualitative assessment and a quantitative assessment of performance. The first, qualitative assessment uses narratives to assess the effectiveness and the level of ambition of existing initiatives for knowledge management. The second, quantitative assessment uses a set of indicators to specify the management challenges, initiatives and results. Also, for this guideline, indicators should be calculated on a systematic basis to allow for comparability over time and can be defined *ex ante* in terms of target scores.

The German Guideline defines indicators as an absolute or relative benchmark that serves to describe a circumstance. Indicators refer to the main IC category to which they belong (i.e., human capital, relational capital and structural capital) and are defined in relation to an influencing factor. Also, for the indicators the Guideline outlines the need for the following: (a) integrating indicators with a qualitative assessment of the degree of achievement of stated objectives; (b) presenting indicators over different reporting periods; and (c) defining the desired trend of the indicators for the future. Also, indicators should be supplemented by narratives; these describe the context, interpret the results and show the consequences from the point of view of the organisation and highlight future trends.

In the regulated Austrian framework, universities must provide a mandatory list of KR metrics. The metrics refer to three main areas: intellectual property, core processes and output and impacts. Therefore, metrics relate to resources (e.g., number of students), activities (e.g., number of doctoral programs) and results (e.g., number of awarded degrees). Also, narrative information should be provided for an understanding of universities' strategies and performance.

The MERITUM Guidelines propose the use of narratives for describing an organisation's vision and strategic objectives, whilst indicators relate to intangible resources and intangible activities. Also, these guidelines highlight the relevance of using indicators for assessing performance over time.

The Australian Principles identify three main categories of indicators (i.e., measurement areas): stocks of KR, investments in KR, and effects on KR. Moreover, they briefly state several critical issues related to the choice of the indicators. These are issues associated with validity, objectivity and accuracy, incomparability in time and space, and availability of information. Also, the Principles support the integration of indicators and narratives to measure and assess performance and highlight the need to define targets.

The Japanese Guidelines support the need to integrate metrics and narratives to 'tell a story' about value creation. In this story, indicators support the narratives and it is through their inter-relationships that their meaning can be understood. Moreover, these guidelines specify that, in order to enhance the credibility of the indicators, these should be subject to internal control and historical changes should be reported. Also, targets for indicators should be defined.

In summary, all the guidelines recognise the relevance of the provision of KR metrics and narratives for understanding and managing IC.

d. Reporting

All of the guidelines analysed focus on reporting and provide models for this purpose. These models include KR and their management via financial and non-financial metrics and narratives. The Danish Guideline promotes the ICS for internal and external use. The ICS is designed so that IC components (which can be modified by each organisation) are reported against knowledge narratives, management challenges, initiatives and results. These are interrelated elements which together express the company's knowledge management. Also, for external reporting, this framework compares IC and other "supplementary accounts" and addresses the issue of the choice of reporting media.

The German Guideline promotes the use of the ICS for internal and external reporting purposes. The ICS shows the links between organisational goals, IC and performance, using indicators and narratives. This framework states that it is not possible to define a generally valid structure for the ICS. However, in the illustration provided for a sample ICS, seven parts are used: (1) Foreword – Why an ICS in our organisation?; (2) Company description; (3) Business success and challenges; (4) Business and knowledge strategy; (5) Our intellectual capital; (6) Future perspectives and measures; (7) Collection of indicators. The Guideline highlights the need to identify internal and external target groups and criteria for communications and provides a help table for this. Issues about reporting media and differences between internal and external ICS are not discussed in detail.

The Austrian Act focuses on external reporting. The ICR it proposes identifies five sections: (a) Scope of application objectives and strategy; (b) Intellectual property (divided into human, structural and relational capital); (c) Core processes (divided into education and continuing education, and research and development); (d) Output and impact of core processes; and (e) Summary and prospects. This framework is strongly measurement-oriented and most of the ICR sections contain metrics. Only the first section, "Scope of application objectives and strategy", and the last one, "Summary and prospects", state that narratives should be used, but no illustration of these is supplied. Probably, the use of the ICR for government funding and performance agreements requires a standardisation of the information reported for the university sector.

The MERITUM Guidelines promote the use of the ICS for internal and external reporting purposes. Three main reporting areas are identified: vision of the firm (including strategic objectives and critical intangibles); summary of intangible resources and activities; systems of indicators for intangible resources and activities. The guidelines also tackle the issue of the reporting media and recommend the use of a stand-alone ICS.

The Australian Principles propose the use of Extended Performance Accounts for internal and external reporting. The reporting structure consists of three KR components which are reported against: strategic objectives; managerial efforts (i.e., current and planned actions); and indicators (i.e., internal and external). Also, the principles contain a brief review of other forms of reporting that highlight the increasing number of international guiding principles on how to manage, measure and report knowledge intensive organisational resources.

The Japanese Guidelines focus on the IABM Report for external reporting. The main body of the report is divided into: (a) general; (b) from past to present; (c) from present to future. The report contains narratives and indicators in the main body and, in the attachment, a list of other indicators and calculation formula. Also, the Guidelines consider other forms of reporting and, in particular, compare IA and corporate social responsibility reporting.

All the frameworks provide detailed guidance for reporting. As indicated above, the various guidelines promote the use of a stand-alone ICS as the media for internal and external reporting. It was clear from the analysis that the various guidelines envisage an ICS as including MKR objectives, processes, results and IC components. A variety of narratives and metrics were used.

The findings from this analysis highlight several important general observations. First, that the main focus of most of these guidelines is on external reporting. However, they also provide guidance internally of how the management of KR can be undertaken. Second, all of these guidelines, except the Australian Principles, assume 'value creation' as one of the main objectives for which KR should be managed. Third, the guidelines are similar in that they deal with the issues of strategy and actions, performance assessment and reporting, and consider these as parts of a process for

MKR. Fourth, the majority did not address the important issue of Resources interactions. In particular, only the German guidelines addressed the issue of resources transformations and provided guidance on how to identify and visualise them. Fifth, only one guideline refers to organisational sustainability (the Australian Principles), which was expressed in terms of an extended view of organisational performance and considered the analysis of various stakeholder interests for the identification of the organisation's objectives. In general, from these observations a main conclusion is that only one of these frameworks, the German Guideline, covers all the MKR issues.

The relevance of KR and their management in a knowledge-based economy has been recognised by various international guidelines. Nearly 40 KR frameworks, all of which aim to make IC some how visible, were classified for consideration in this chapter on the basis of their measurement approach: the stock approach versus the flow approach. The above analysis focuses on the six contemporary guidelines of the flow approach using four critical MKR issues.

CONCLUSION

Two key messages of this chapter are that: first, MKR and its elements are embedded in various ways into the international guidelines examined; second, that a key policy issue is international harmonisation.

This chapter discussed how MKR was incorporated into the six international guidelines. Four key lessons from the analysis are now highlighted. First, many of the guidelines have a view of strategy as an incremental process that starts with management formulation and flows to KR actions. Also, many of the guidelines accept that strategy formulation leads to deliberate actions and this is coupled with an acceptance that an application of knowledge and leverage of resources enhances organisational performance. It was found that these frameworks view strategy and the MKR based on the notion of intended strategies. Therefore, it was assumed that all these frameworks had a common view of MKR, which was to achieve intended strategies.

Second, most of the guidelines recognise the importance of KR transformations for organisational performance, however, only the German Guideline includes an analysis of resources transformations. What is missing in most of the guidelines is the analysis of resources transformations. Third, the majority of the guidelines use KR metrics and narratives for describing and measuring IC and/or assessing performance. Also, the frameworks recognise that KR information is organisationally specific. However, KR information in many of these guidelines is limited to describing and assessing MKR for senior management use and there is no mention of the importance of the use of KR information by the workforce. In light of this, the role of visuals should be considered. What is missing in the guidelines is the availability of KR information, so that it can be used by a variety of stakeholders.

Fourth, the various guidelines promote the use of an ICS for internal and external reporting purposes. These guidelines generally envisage an ICS as including KR components, MKR objectives, initiatives and results. They did not include stakeholders, economic, social and environmental concerns. What is missing in the guidelines is the inclusion of a wider perspective of organisational concerns and performance.

Therefore, the above analysis has highlighted what is included or not included internationally in a selection of KR guidelines.

We now turn to harmonisation. The above analysis of the six guidelines suggests that there is significant and varied international practice when the guidelines are examined in-depth. When practice leads policy there are numerous issues that need to be agreed upon.

First, experimentation with MKR is increasing in Europe, Japan and Australia. However, there is still little comparative work that looks at the diversity in practice and the motivation for organisations to report this material.

Second, experimentation within MKR under a specific guideline should be studied over time to see the developments of practice, both in terms of the adoption of MKR and the use of the information both internally and externally.

Third, should policy and the guidelines be prescriptive or normative? If guidelines are developed, will they specify certain types of elements and the formatting of reporting?

Fourth, an important issue is the need for greater education as to the precise nature of KR and how to manage them. This will lead to an increase in practical uptake and a broader understanding of the issues associated with the MKR.

Fifth, presumably, given the differences in organisational types and activities considerable fluidity and flexibility will have to be built into any policy arrangement. For instance, the only regulated guideline (Austrian) specifically sets individual metrics for Universities to report against. This may be because these guidelines are specifically industry-based (e.g. university), whereas the other guidelines only illustrate some metrics, possibly because they are trying to cover a universal set of organisational types and business activities.

The diversity in guidelines and practice signals an urgent need for debate about harmonisation. Harmonisation may depend upon the creation of international communities of practice, which bring together practitioners, policy makers and thought leaders from around the world. For instance, Boedker et al. (2008: 21) indicate that the World Intellectual Capital Initiative by OECD and others provides an example of an appropriate vehicle for facilitating debates, mediating knowledge and practice, and improving international collaborations and harmonisation. Further, harmonisation suggests that one framework would fit all circumstances. As indicated above, the current frameworks are different and further research should be undertaken into the theoretical and empirical underpinnings of these to gauge if it is possible to have one meta-framework.

REFERENCES

Altenburger, O. A., & Schaffhauser-Linzatti, M. (2006). *The Order on the Intellectual Capital Statements of Austrian Universities – A Critical Analysis.* Paper presented at the 2nd Workshop on the Process of Reform of University Systems, CINI Foundation, Venice, Italy, May 4th – May 6th.

Boedker, C., Mouritsen, J., & Guthrie, J. (2008). Enhanced business reporting: international trends and possible policy directions. *Journal of Human Resource Costing & Accounting*, 12(1), 14-25.

Bontis, N., Dragonetti, N. C., Jacobsen, K., & Roos, G. (1999). The knowledge toolbox: a review of the tools available to manage and measure intangible resources. *European Management Journal*, 17(4), 391-402.

Dierickx, I., & Cool, K. (1989). Asset stock accumulation and sustainability of competitive advantage. *Management Science*, 35(12), 1504-1511.

Edvinsson L., & Malone M. (1997). *Intellectual Capital: Realising Your Company's True Value by Finding its Hidden Brainpower.* New York, NY: Harper Collins.

European Commission (EC) (2006). *RICARDIS: Reporting Intellectual Capital to Augment Research, Development and Innovation in SME's*, Brussels, June.

Federal Ministry of Economic and Labour (FMEL) (2004). *Intellectual Capital Statement – Made in Germany*, Berlin.

Federal Ministry of Education, Science and Culture (FMESC), (2002). *Federal Act on the Organisation of the Universities and their Studies (Universities Act 2002)*, available at http://www.bmbwk.gv.at (last accessed in February 2007).

Federal Ministry of Education, Science and Culture (FMESC), (2006). *63rd Regulation: Regulation on Intellectual Capital Reports*, available at http://www.bmbwk.gv.at (last accessed in February 2007).

Grant, R. M. (1991). The resource-based theory of competitive advantage: implications for strategy formulation. *California Management Review, 33*(3), 114-135.

Gupta, O., & Roos, G. (2001). Mergers and acquisitions through an intellectual capital perspective. *Journal of Intellectual Capital*, 2(3), 297-309.

Guthrie, J., & Ricceri, F. (2002). *Quantify Intellectual Capital: Measuring and Reporting to Demonstrate Value of KM to Stakeholders.* Paper presented at KM Australia: Building and improving on knowledge management initiative for commercial proficiency conference, Merchant Court Hotel, Sydney, 4 December.

Guthrie, J., Petty, R., & Ricceri, F. (2007). *Intellectual Capital Reporting: Lessons from Hong Kong and Australia.* Research Monograph, The Institute of Chartered Accountants of Scotland, Edinburgh.

Hall, R. (1993). A framework linking intangible resources and capabilities to sustainable competitive advantage. *Strategic Management Journal*, 14(8), 607-618.

Itami, H., & Roehl, T. W. (1987). *Mobilizing Invisible Assets.* Cambridge, MA: Harvard University Press.

Ittner, C. D., & Larker, D. F. (1998). Innovation in performance measurement: trends and research implications. *Journal of Management Accounting Research*, 10, 205-238.

King, A. W., & Zeithaml, C. P. (2001). Competencies and firm performance: Examining the causal ambiguity paradox. *Strategic Management Journal*, 22(1), 75-99.

Lippman, S. A., & Rumelt, R. P. (1982). Uncertain imitability: An analysis of interfirm differences in efficiency under competition. *Bell Journal of Economics*, 13(2), 418-438.

Marr, B., Schiuma, G., & Neely, A. (2004). The dynamics of value creation: mapping your intellectual performance drivers. *Journal of Intellectual Capital* , 5(2), 312-325

MERITUM, (2002), *Guidelines for Managing and Reporting of Intangibles*, Fundacion Airtel Movil, Madrid.

Ministry of Economy, Trade and Industry (METI), (2005). *Guidelines for Disclosure of Intellectual Assets Based Management*, October.

Mouritsen, J. (2004). Measuring and intervening: how do we theorise intellectual capital management, *Journal of Intellectual* Capital, 5(2), 257-267.

Mouritsen, J., & Larsen, H. T. (2005). The second wave of knowledge management: The management control of knowledge resources through intellectual capital information. *Management Accounting Research*, 16, 371–394.

Mouritsen, J., Bukh, P., and Kaasgaard B. H. (2005), *Understanding Intellectual Capital in an Innovative Medium-sized Firm: The Case of Maxon*, The Aarhus School of Business, Copenhagen.

Mouritsen, J., Bukh, P. N., Flagstad, K., Thorbjørnsen, S., Rosenkrands Johansen, M., Kotnis, S., Thorsgaard Larsen, H., Nielsen, C., Kjærgaard Jensen, I., Krag, L., Jeppesen, G., Haisler J., & Stakemann, B. (2003). *Intellectual Capital Statements - the New Guideline.* Published by the Danish Ministry of Science, Technology and Innovation (DMSTI), http://www.videnskabsministeriet.dk/cgi-bin/theme-list.cgi?theme_id=100650&_lang=uk , retrieved in April, 2004

Nonaka, I., & Takeuchi, H. (1995). *The Knowledge Creating Company*. Oxford: Oxford University Press.

Ricceri, F. (2008). *Intellectual Capital and Knowledge Management: Strategic Management of Knowledge Resources*. London and New York: Routledge.

Roos, G., & Jacobsen, K. (1999). Management in a complex stakeholder organization: a case study of the application of the IC-process to a branch of the Commonwealth Public Service. *Monash Mt. Eliza Business Review, 2*(1), 82-93.

Roos, G., & Roos, J. (1997). Measuring your company's intellectual performance. *Long Range Planning*, 30(3), 413-426.

Roos, G., Pike, S., & Fernström, L. (2005). *Managing Intellectual Capital in Practice*. Oxford: Elsevier.

Society for Knowledge Economics (SKE),(2005). *Australian Guiding Principles on Extended Performance Management*. Sydney: SKE.

Subcommittee on Management & Intellectual Assets (SMIA) (2005). *Interim Report by Subcommittee on Management & Intellectual Assets*, August, Japan.

Sveiby K. E. (1997). *The New Organizational Wealth: Managing and Measuring Knowledge Based Assets*. San Francisco: Berret Koehler.

Sveiby, K. E. (2001). A knowledge-based theory of the firm to guide in strategy formulation. *Journal of Intellectual Capital*, 2(4), 344-358.

Unerman, J., Guthrie, J., & Striukova, L. (2007). *UK Reporting of Intellectual Capital*, Institute of Chartered Accountants in England and Wales Centre for Business Performance.

Zack, M. H. (1999). Developing a knowledge strategy, *California Management Review*, 41(3), Spring, 125-145.

KEY TERMS

Intellectual Capital (IC): A framing device for understanding Knowledge Resources and related elements. See also Knowledge Resources.

Intellectual Capital Statement (ICS): Provides information via metrics and narratives about how KR are created, developed and applied in the oganisation. Also, it summarises the firm's efforts to develop and use KR and puts evaluative managerial questions that help managers to change KR and/or direct them towards new strategies.

Knowledge Resources (KR): Non tangible organisational resources that can be classified into three main components: human resources; structural resources; and relational resources:

> Human resources refer to internal stakeholders, such as senior managers and employees, and to their attributes, that is knowledge, abilities, skills, experiences and innovativeness. These are becoming critical resources for oganisations, particularly because they contribute to the ability to respond and adapt to a changing environment.
>
> Structural resources consist of all those things that remain in the oganisation when the employees have left the building and are in some way owned or controlled by the oganisation. Structural resources include 'intellectual property' and 'infrastructural resources'. Intellectual property is owned by the company and protected by law and includes elements such as patents, trademarks and copyrights. Infrastructural resources consist of oganisational characteristics such as methods and procedures and the oganisational context provided to individuals to achieve strategic objectives. Therefore, structural resources include, but are not limited to, culture, processes, routines, and information and networking systems.

Relational resources include the organisation's brand and image in the marketplace, as well as its relationships with external stakeholders (such as government, customers, partners and retailers, suppliers, residents, etc.). Some of these resources are not owned by the oganisation, but are relationships that are significant and require management.

This tripartite classification of knowledge resources is known as intellectual capital and is a framing device for understanding KR and related elements. As a result, the concepts of knowledge resources and intellectual capital embrace all kinds of non tangible oganisational resources, either formally owned or used, or informally deployed and mobilized.

Guidelines: Best examples of flow approach frameworks developed by national and international institutions as guidelines for oganisations to manage, measure and report IC. Many of these frameworks use intellectual capital statements as a way of embarking on the management of knowledge resources and for understanding the relationship between measurement and management on the one side and operational activities, strategies and context on the other.

Management of Knowledge Resources (MKR): Refers to the dynamic capability of managing KR in a changing environment for achieving oganisational sustainability. The management of knowledge resources involves addressing four basic issues: (1) considering the relevance of KR and their management when formulating and implementing oganisational strategy; (2) understanding resources interactions via their identification, mapping and assessment; (3) measuring KR to monitor multiple performance perspectives and related drivers; and (4) reporting to internal and external stakeholder an extended view of oganisational performance by focusing on the efforts to manage and develop KR.

Measurement: Refers to the use of KR metrics and narratives to support MKR and, in particular, to assess performance. For KR measurement, the aim is not to assign a financial value to KR but to create a set of metrics (or indicators) based around the individual KR elements within each KR component (e.g. customers' satisfaction within the relational KR). Many metrics are context-specific and therefore there are no widely accepted standards available to help readers understand the meaning of the reported metrics. Therefore, metrics must be accompanied by narratives which explain the metrics' meaning and their relationships with oganisational context and performance.

Oganisational Strategy: The factor that combines the dynamic context in which the oganisation operates and its resources and capabilities. In this chapter oganisational strategy refers both to the formulation of strategic objectives and to the implementation of plans and actions for acquiring, deploying and maintaining KR in order to achieve oganisational sustainability.

Reporting: Relates to the construction of the reporting devices which can be used for external and internal communication. A common device used to provide internal and external stakeholders with an extended view of oganisational performance by focusing on the efforts to manage and develop KR is the intellectual capital statement (ICS).

Resources Interactions: Relates to flows within resources and these are also known as resources transformations. Transformations are defined as resources flows that affect different oganisational resources types, being tangible assets or KR. Whilst transformations within tangible resources (physical or financial) are, in most cases, observable and measurable, transformations which involve KR are difficult to identify map, and assess.

ENDNOTES

[a] IC is a tripartite classification for KR and is a framing device for understanding KR. IC is made up of three main components: human resources, structural resources, and relational resources (Ricceri, 2008).

[b] See, Karl-Erik Sveiby http://www.sveiby.com/Portals/0/articles/IntangibleMethods.htm last accessed in March 2008.

Section VI
The Knowledge Worker

Chapter XXIV
Strategic Alliance Capability: Bringing the Individual Back into Inter-Organizational Collaboration

Christiane Prange
EM Lyon Business School, France

ABSTRACT

Internationalization has accelerated the speed of knowledge generation and innovation. Thus, companies increasingly need to pool and create new resources by engaging in alliances with various partners. However, high failure rates of strategic alliances imply that the degree of a company's collaboration success is related to the level of its alliance capability. While "alliance capability" has largely been conceptualized from within the resource based and the dynamic capability view, one of the major drawbacks is the lack of micro-foundations, i.e. an explanation of individual knowledge and actions, which drive the development of alliance capability. A modified approach to the capability life-cycle is introduced, which aims at filling this gap. Finally, some implications for managerial practice and for future research are addressed.

INTRODUCTION

In the global marketplace, competitive advantages have become increasingly difficult to realize and many firms strive for new sources of knowledge and corporate growth. For many companies, strategic alliances have become a cornerstone in their expansion efforts because they facilitate access to new resources and wealth creation. Indeed, strategic alliances[a] can be considered a critical issue in the network economy, which is evidenced by both their rise in number and the variety of emerging forms, such as 'value networks', 'alliance networks' or 'alliance constellations' (Gomes-Casseres, 2003; de Man, 2005).

Motives for those 'loosely-coupled arrangements' (Weick, 1976) include easier access to foreign markets, economies of scale, accelerated development of technological capabilities, risk reduction and the acquisition and transfer of knowledge embedded in respective partners (e.g., Hamel, Doz and Prahalad, 1989; Larsson, Bengtsson et al. 1998). Yet, there is also widespread recognition that firms fail with roughly half of the alliances they form and there is considerable heterogeneity in terms of reported performance results (Bleeke and Ernst, 1993). Indeed, the inherent instability of strategic alliances has led both practitioners and researchers to focus on the intriguing question of what firms can do to enhance alliance results (Chang, Chen and Lai, 2008).

Previous research on the success factors of alliances has largely focused on structural and cultural aspects, presuming that these are the major drivers of effectiveness (Cartwright and Cooper, 1993). Only recently has attention been drawn to the fact that some firms are considerably more successful in managing alliances than others and the degree of a company's collaboration success has been linked to specific capabilities involved in managing these relationships (Wuyts, Dutta and Stremersch, 2004). With the recent hype of both the resource-based view (RBV) and the dynamic capability view (DCV) in strategy research, firm-specific factors, such as routines and capabilities, have been highlighted as antecedents of rent differentials (Nelson and Winter, 1982; Barney, 1991).

In this stream of research, the unit of analysis is no longer the relationship between firms, but a distinct organizational-level capability that is subject to dynamic processes of development, change, and improvement. Consequently, subsequent work has emphasized that alliance capability positively contributes to firm-level competitive advantage (Anand and Khanna, 2000).

However, it has also been suggested that the construct of alliance capability should be conceptualized on multiple levels, spanning individuals, groups, and organizations (Blomqvist and Levy, 2006). Unfortunately, studies which refer to *individual* alliance capability, or even comprise multiple level issues, are sparse and firms are left in the dark about adequate action perspectives for the individual manager (Johnson, Melin and Whittington, 2003). Part of the problem is due to the fact that traditional capability research adopts a collectivist focus, while neglecting micro-level foundations (Felin and Foss, 2004; Teece, 2007).

By building on these omissions, a deliberately individual focus is adopted to investigate the micro-foundations of alliance capability. This article provides the following contributions: *First*, a synopsis of previous research on alliance capability is presented and contributions and shortcomings are discussed. *Second*, by highlighting theoretical contributions from the RBV and the DCV, it will be shown that both offer valuable contributions to the conceptualization of alliance capability but do not sufficiently explain how capabilities develop. *Third*, by building on these omissions, a framework is proposed that considers individual contributions to the development of organizational alliance capabilities more thoroughly. *Finally*, some avenues for future research and some practical managerial implications will be suggested.

Strategic Alliance Capability: A Synthesis of the Literature

In this article, the terms of 'alliance capability' and 'strategic alliance capability' are used synonymously to signify those capabilities required to successfully manage a strategic alliance. 'Managing' is used as a generic term to incorporate all activities of an alliance life-cycle (see subsequent paragraphs). This section consists of a literature synopsis of the discourse domain (main terms, constructs, and developments). It further locates an important research gap in the lack of clear interrelations between individual-level origins and organizational-level alliance capability.

Definitions of Strategic Alliance Capability: The Formation of a Research Field

The recent literature on strategic alliances has paid considerable attention to either the very beginning of a collaborative activity and/or the ultimate end of the venture, while managerial issues in-between have been left understudied (Doz, 1996; Kandemir, Ghauri, and Cavusgil, 2002). For instance, Kogut (1988) adopts a life-cycle approach and describes the development sequences of joint ventures as those of creation, institutionalization and termination. Van de Ven and Walker (1984) introduce a stage model that explains the frequent decline of collaborative endeavours. They argue that the reason for the eventual dissolution is implicit in the formation stage, where structures are formalized and control mechanisms agreed. A number of authors have also gone beyond traditional linear stage models by suggesting cyclic relationships. For instance, Zajac and Olsen (1993) relate to the stages of initializing, processing and reconfiguration. During the initializing stage initial conditions are set. In the processing stage, learning takes place and first behaviour patterns evolve. Finally, in the reconfiguration stage, the collaboration is evaluated and this may lead to a revision of the original conditions. While all these research efforts have offered valuable insights into a large task-set associated with collaborative ventures, they fail to provide detailed knowledge of managerial responsibilities.

With the advent of 'alliance or collaborative capability', initial efforts were undertaken to fill this void. Focusing on specific capabilities to mange relationships became popular in academic discussion in the mid-1990s (Bucklin and Sengupta, 1993; Simonin, 1997; Lorenzoni and Lipparini, 1999). In the marketing and sales literature, interest concentrates on improving relationships between firms and their customers (Day, 1994; Storbacka, Strandvik and Grönroos, 1994; Crosby, Evans and Cowles, 1990; Sivadas and Dwyer, 2000). With regard to a firm's business-to-business relations, Håkansson (1987: 124) defines 'networking ability' as "a firm's ability to improve its position in a network (with regard to resources and activities) and its ability to handle individual relationships." However, the concept remains rather vague and lacks operationalization.

In the management and strategy literature, Simonin (1997: 1151) was among the first to empirically investigate 'collaborative know-how', which he measures as the extent to which firms have skills in identifying, negotiating, managing, monitoring, and terminating collaborations. Subsequently, a large array of heterogeneous terms emerged, which amply illustrates the pre-paradigmatic stage of research. Some authors refer to 'relational capability' and argue that the ability to interact and share knowledge with other companies is a distinctive organizational competence for firms transactionally intensive in nature (Lorenzoni and Liparini, 1999; Dyer and Singh, 1998). Others use terms, such as 'network management capability' (Birkinshaw, 2000), or 'network capability' (Ritter, 1998; Walter, Auer and Ritter, 2006), 'network ability' (Håkansson, 1987; Hamel, 1991; Hamel, Doz and Prahalad, 1989) or 'alliance capability' (Draulans, de Man and Volberda, 2003; Kale, Dyer and Singh, 2002; Kale and Singh, 1999; Khanna, 1998). While the normal convention seems to be that alliances refer to bilateral and networks to multilateral relations, the use of terms has remained rather ambiguous.

Further research referred to 'learning to manage alliances' (Anand and Khanna, 2000) as an ability to anticipate and respond to contingencies that cannot be pre-specified in a formal contract. While the learning focus connects to dynamic cycles of alliance development, it has also been related to experience necessary to build alliance capability (Simonin, 1997; Kale, Dyer and Singh, 2002; Heimeriks and Duysters, 2007). Simonin concludes that a firm should first internalize collaborative experience before the lessons learned become useful for a firm's future alliances. Others also focus on experience and learning effects and their presumed translation into future alliance success (Gulati, 1999; Kale, Singh and Perlmutter, 1999), but do not explain the associated aggregation problem. For instance, Gulati (1995) investigates the importance of prior ties and their influence on future modes of cooperation but does not explain *how* firms can successfully internalize experience. Anand and Khanna (2000) argue that experience plays an important role in the stability of inter-firm collaborations. As firms accumulate experience, their increasing abilities to anticipate and respond to critical contingencies are likely to enhance the chances of success in subsequent alliances.

In short, the majority of studies finds a positive and linear relationship between experiences and alliance performance (Anand and Khanna, 2000; Heimeriks and Duysters, 2007). However, it has also been argued that greater experience may be a necessary but an insufficient condition for firms to build alliance capability. This has been explained by the fact that firms differ in their abilities to appropriate knowledge from alliances (Kumar and Nti, 1998). As Chang, Chen and Lai (2008: 299) argue, "prior experience ...may at best be a crude proxy for the precise mechanisms that build alliance capability [and] further alliance capability enhancement may rest upon how effectively a firm is able to capture, share, and disseminate the learnt know-how associated with prior experience". In a related vein, relations between alliance experience and alliance performance have been found to follow a curvilinear pattern (Deeds and Hill, 1996; Hoang and Rothaermel, 2005) based on increasing conflict-resolution skills (Mohr and Spekman, 1994) and accumulated process know-how (Simonin, 1997).

Taken collectively, previous research has widely contributed to the formation of a new research field but developments have been hampered by scant attention given to precise definitions of alliance capability and its constituting elements. However, minimum consensus exists on the issue of alliance capability as being related to the stages of the alliance life-cycle. As succinctly summarized by Lambe, Spekman and Hunt (2002: 142) alliance capability is the "organizational ability to find, develop and manage relationships". While this definition is useful because it includes dynamic aspects of change - which preview an investigation from a dynamic capability perspective (see subsequent chapters) -, it does not provide much insight into what *exactly* constitutes the construct of alliance capability.

Elements of Strategic Alliance Capability

What makes up alliance capability has so far remained rather elusive (Gulati, 1998). However, there have been a few selected attempts to more precisely identify its elements. For instance, Ritter and Gemünden (2003) distinguish between the tasks that need to be performed in order to manage a company's technological network and the qualifications, skills, and knowledge that are required in order to perform these tasks. More precisely, tasks refer to relation-specific (e.g. initiation of first partner-contacts, exchange of products and information, coordination of exchange) and cross-relational tasks (e.g. analysis and planning, organizing and staffing). Network management qualifications involve a complex process, which requires specialist knowledge of the technical side of the relationship and social qualifications. Both types of elements are seen as being highly interdependent. While the authors conclude that their study highlights a firm's ability to initiate, handle, and use a portfolio of inter-organizational relationships, they seem to confuse the individual and organizational units of analysis. Related research proposes that cooperative competency consists of the ability of the partners to trust, communicate, and coordinate

(Sivadas and Dwyer, 2000) with social skills being explicitly emphasized as a complement to structure-related elements of alliance capability (Lawler and Thye, 1999; Prange, Bojkowszky and Wieshofer, 2004).

One of the most comprehensive investigations of alliance capabilities and their elements has been provided by Schreiner and Corsten (2004) and Schreiner (2004), who empirically investigated the components of what they call 'collaborative capability'. They suggest that capabilities in a collaborative context consist of structural, cognitive, and affective elements.

Structural capabilities, according to their view, include the build-up and maintenance of human resources, partner-specific tangible and intangible assets, as well as time-management and investment strategy (so-called resourcing elements). Further, coordinative elements are subsumed under this category, e.g. partnership and task management, interaction routines, process standardization and personnel continuance. *Cognitive capabilities* refer to the existence of absorptive capacity as the ability to assimilate and exploit new information to foster learning (Cohen and Levinthal, 1990) and the potential to effectively communicate. Finally, *affective capabilities* consist of care-giving and empathic abilities. Again, this study provides important input for a better understanding of alliance capability but suffers from two major drawbacks: It does not clearly link alliance capabilities to the associated alliance life-cycle, and, more importantly, it neglects the linkage between individual skills and organizational routines.

Levels of Strategic Alliance Capability

The previous omissions are also prevalent in subsequent work, where either life-cycle and *organizational* capabilities or *individual* skills are emphasized. The former most often suggests improving specific tasks, such as the codification and transfer of information within 'dedicated alliance functions' (Anand and Khanna, 2000; Dyer, Kale and Singh, 2001) or implementing 'organizing principles' for the internalization of alliance management know-how (Kale, Dyer and Singh, 2002). These capabilities are seen as being embedded in organizational routines, which are repetitive activities a firm applies in order to deploy its resources available in and through alliances (Nelson and Winter, 1982). In addition, alliance training, alliance metrics and evaluation systems, best practice programmes as well as external support by consultants, lawyers, and financial specialists have been suggested to support those routines (Heimeriks and Duysters, 2007). Taken collectively, the locus of this stream of research remains an abstract phenomenon of alliance capability, which almost completely neglects the concrete contribution of the individual in inter-organizational research.[b]

On the other hand, there is a variety of studies, which places major emphasis on *individual* skills and their impact on collaboration. Scholars have argued that strong interpersonal ties provide channels through which partners learn about other firm's competencies and reliability (Gulati, 1999). From this perspective, relational capital which rests upon close interpersonal ties at the dyadic level can also play an important role in creating and building larger alliance networks (Kale, Singh and Perlmutter, 2000: 218). Draulans, deMan and Volberda (2003) examine whether it may be useful to concentrate alliance knowledge and experience in certain individuals. While middle management is regarded as potentially suitable for such activities, they focus less on the respective capabilities for managing relations. McGee, Dowling and Megginson (1995) concentrate on experience-based collaborative capabilities and analyze the question as to whether inexperienced managers should cooperate to gain new knowledge or rather avoid it unless they are experienced enough to know what they don't know.

In short, various research has emphasized elements and levels of alliance capability albeit in a rather disconnected manner. However, preliminary suggestions have been made to consider alliance capability as a *multi-dimensional* and *multi-level construct,* in which elements and levels are closely interlinked and mutually reinforcing (Schreiner, 2004; Blomqvist and Levy, 2006; Dansereau,Yammarino and Kohles, 1999). While studies tend to emphasize single levels of analysis or refrain from clear level specifications, a notable exception is the research by Buckley, Glaister and Husan (2002), who investigate managers' 'partnering skills' in cross-cultural joint ventures and distinguish between national and macro elements, industry or sector level factors, organizational and firm levels, and the perceptions of individual managers.

Figure 1 builds on this approach and provides a generic overview of the previous debate with a particular emphasis on the levels of the individual and the organization. Categorical labels for elements are borrowed from Schreiner (2004) but clearly relate to the individual. Further, the notion of structural elements is replaced by 'technical' because the former has too close an association with organizational structures. Arrows in the figure indicate that linkages between individual elements and organizational alliance capability are largely missing in the literature.

Part of the confusion on levels and definitions can be traced back to the theoretical origin of resource and capability definitions within strategic management research. Indeed, as research within the RBV and the DCV itself can still be considered in its infancy (Helfat, 2000), it is not surprising that theoretical contributions lack precise insights into the black box of alliance capability (Priem and Butler, 2001).

Figure 1. Elements of strategic alliance capability

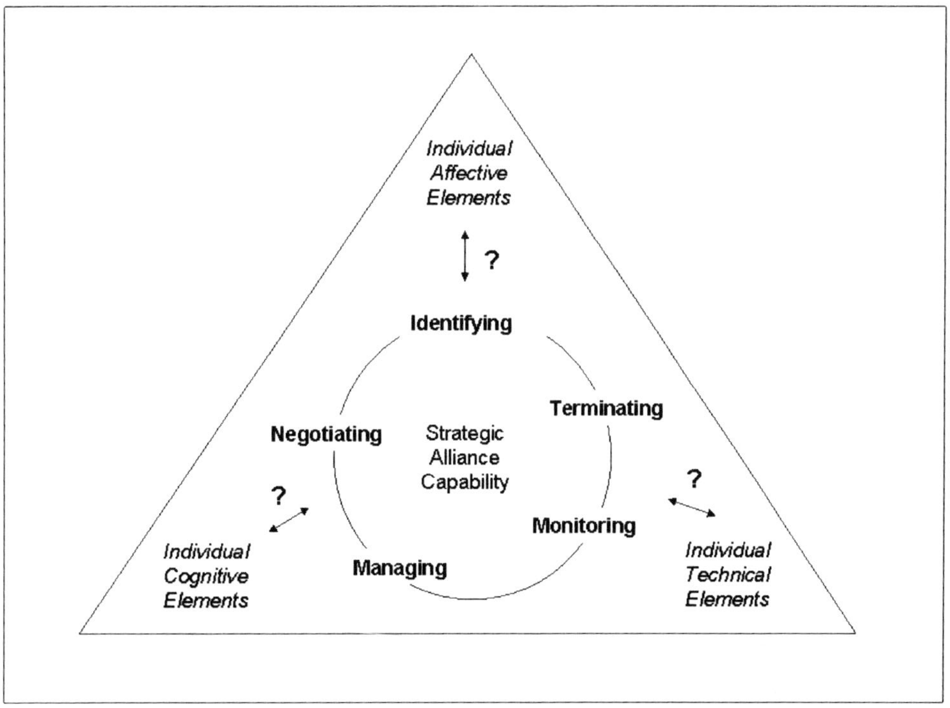

THEORETICAL FOUNDATIONS OF STRATEGIC ALLIANCE CAPABILITY

As a theoretical foundation of explaining alliance capability, both the resource-based view and the dynamic capability view of strategy have been suggested (Kale and Singh, 2007). The dynamic capability view extends the argument by departing from the static notion of resources. As capabilities for new market entry relate to multiple environments, it is important for a firm to constantly reconfigure its alliance capability. Hence, a dynamic capability view offers a suitable theoretical foundation as it suggests some leeway for learning, integrating, building and reconfiguring internal and external competencies (Teece, Pisano and Shuen, 1997).

Resource-Based View

The RBV considers firms as bundles of resources, which form a prerequisite for achieving and sustaining competitive advantage (Rumelt, 1984; Wernerfeld, 1984; Barney, 1991; Prahalad and Hamel, 1990; Amid and Schoemaker, 1993). The major argument of the RBV is that firms are able to accumulate resources and capabilities that are rare, valuable, imperfectly inimitable and imperfectly substitutable (Barney, 1991; Wernerfeld, 1984). Consequently, a firm's performance is fundamentally due to the heterogeneity of its resources and their persistence over time rather than to industry structure as argued in the market-based view of the firm (Porter, 1980). In exploring this approach, I concur with recent contributors to the literature, who distinguish capabilities from resources (Grant, 1991; Mahoney and Pandian, 1992; Teece, Pisano and Shuen, 1997). *Resources* refer to "all assets, capabilities, organizational processes, information, knowledge, etc. controlled by a firm that enable the firm to conceive and implement strategies" (Barney 1991: 101), i.e. assets pose an input to production. In contrast to resources, organizational *capabilities* refer to an organization's ability to perform a coordinated set of tasks, utilizing and leveraging organizational resources, for the purpose of achieving a particular end result (Amit and Schoemaker, 1993; Helfat and Peteraf, 2003).

The distinction is not completely selective but it has been recognized that capabilities are required to leverage resources and it is therefore capabilities, which provide the essential basis of competitive advantage. As related to alliances, it has been argued that the factual collaborative relationship should be considered a resource, while alliancing as a managerial process has tentatively been mentioned as a capability (Eisenhardt and Martin, 2000:1106). Further, it has been suggested to consider alliance capability as a *meta-capability* (Blomqvist and Levy 2006), directed at improving the lower-order capability of alliancing (Winter, 2000; Kale and Singh, 2007).

According to Simonin (1997), 'collaborative know-how' or 'alliance capability' also fits each of the criteria for turning resources into competitive advantage.[c] Managing alliances is obviously valuable as collaboration enhances a company's flexibility required for building future options. According to conventional logic, it is also a very rare capability given the extensive failure rates of cooperative undertakings. The third criterion, imperfect inimitability, relates to the fact that alliance capability is often complex knowledge rooted in the social fabric of an organization. Finally, alliance capability is difficult to substitute because it is acquired during a period of experiential learning, which is most likely company-specific.

Whether alliance capability is completely experience-based or can be acquired via training (Draulans, de Man and Volberda, 2003) and whether this knowledge can be transferred across companies is an issue which requires further research. This also refers to the nature of alliance capability as related to its transfer among different units within or between companies. The literature is full of classification schemes and examples of both resources and capabilities, which provide helpful guidance. Amit and Schoemaker (1993), for example, refer to capabilities as tangible or intangible assets, which are firm-specific and created over time. Hall (1992, 1993) further distinguishes between intangible/tangible and person-/non-person-based resources and capabilities. Tangible resources include technology, production machinery, facilities, etc. whereas intangible resources range from property rights, trade secrets, public knowledge to know how, organizational culture, etc. (Hall 1992: 135). Intangible resources, in contrast, rely more on a personal momentum whether this be perception, implicit knowledge or person-based learning (Itami and Roehl, 1987). Generally, it has been accepted that the value of a company derives to an increasing degree from its availability of those 'intangible assets' as proven in the difference between market and book value. The related distinction between person and non person-based resources and capabilities resembles the recent discussion in organizational learning and knowledge management. In this stream of research, scholars accept that organizational level constructs rely on individual processes, which have become institutionalized over time (e.g. Kim, 1993; Prange, 1999; Maier, Prange, von Rosenstil, 2001).

Dynamic Capability View

The DVC defines 'dynamic capabilities' as "the firm's ability to integrate, build, and reconfigure internal and external competences to address rapidly changing environments" (Teece, Pisano and Shuen, 1997: 516). It is explicitly mentioned that dynamic capabilities consist of specific strategic and organizational processes that create value for firms within dynamic markets by manipulating resources into new value-creating strategies (Eisenhardt and Martin 2002: 1106). Despite slight variations in definitions, consensus has emerged that capabilities are made up of organizational routines, which make use of and deploy combinations of various assets. Eisenhardt and Martin (2002) further argue that dynamic capabilities as such cannot be a source of competitive advantage, instead they need to be applied and the ability to change them quickly is a major asset. Collis (1994) is particularly explicit in making the point that dynamic capabilities govern the rate of change in ordinary capabilities given path dependencies and market positions.

Draulans, de Man and Volberda (2003) present an exceptional case, when they consider alliance capability from a DCV-perspective, emphasizing the development of capabilities by the absorption of inside and outside knowledge. This process supposedly consists of identifiable and specific routines which, at best, are deeply anchored within the organization. At a more strategic level, dynamic capabilities involve those routines that are required to reconnect single relationships into a web of collaborations between alliance partners to generate ever changing resources among businesses. In stable markets, alliance capability resembles the traditional concept of routines, i.e. repetitive action based on sophisticated organizing processes that rely on existing knowledge (Nelson and Winter, 1982; Eisenhardt and Martin, 2000). The situation is different, when firms operate in dynamic markets where capabilities require adaptation. As dynamic markets are not always predictable, these 'routines' are often simple, exhibit experiential components and are situation-specific applied (Eisenhardt and Galunic, 2000). This is why Eisenhard and Sull (2001) introduce the concept of 'simple rules' where competitive advantages come from successfully seizing fleeting opportunities. Guided by a few strategic processes, these simple rules should place a company where new challenges are swiftest and deepest.

This also previews particular developmental processes, which require multiple testing and imply several pathways to successfully creating relevant knowledge.

Figure 2 summarizes the previous discussion and presents some examples, where a distinction is drawn between both an alliance relationship (a resource) and the skills of managing it (a capability). Resource and capability are inextricably intertwined and exhibit both tangible and intangible components.

For instance, alliance mindset incorporates an understanding of alliances as 'first best strategy', which has been regarded as an important precondition for successful collaboration. Similarly, commitment and trust are further implicit components of alliance capability. These are complemented by hard factors, such as handbooks, guidelines, benchmarking procedures as to how alliances can best be implemented. These manifestations of alliance capability only contribute to performance outputs if related to the resources of the alliance, which consist of the factual alliance, i.e. its strategies, human resources, structures and governance issues, etc.

The resulting challenge for managerial practice remains how heterogeneous (alliance) capabilities like routines, guidelines or simple rules are supposed to be created by homogeneous individuals in firms - an implicit, but questionable, assumption of resource-based theorizing (Henderson and Cockburn, 1994) - , and how individual action can be transferred into successful organizational behaviour within inter-organizational settings. An answer to these questions is likely to arise from insights into how the collective construct of alliance capability emerges.

DEVELOPING ALLIANCE CAPABILITY: THE CONTRIBUTIONS OF THE INDIVIDUAL

Little is known so far how capabilities arise in the first place. Research from within the resource-based tradition has provided a few hints that, taken together with traditional approaches of knowledge management, present some input into the evolutionary process of alliance capability. Building on these inputs, I suggest a model of alliance capability development, which adds individual knowledge and action as antecedents. I further suggest a more detailed analysis of micro-foundations in order to understand alliance capability differentials between firms.

The Process of Capability Development

The process of capability development can start from different vantage points and often takes unique paths, i.e. it exhibits high degrees of equifinality (Eisenhardt and Martin, 2000). While the literature does not offer straightforward answers

Figure 2. Alliances as resources and alliance capabilities

	Alliances as a Resource	**Alliance Management as a Capability**
Intangible	Culture, alliance strategy, human resources dedicated to the alliance, etc	Alliance mindset (commitment/ trust); implicit and explicit learning about alliances, etc.
Tangible	Structure (nature of contract, governance structure, facilities, IT infrastructure), location, etc.	Codified alliance knowledge (alliance functions, databases, handbooks, guidelines), etc.

to the question of how capabilities are generated, authors seem to agree on repeated practice and experience. Thus, new routines or capabilities build on previous ones, i.e. "firms tend to do what they have done before" (Kogut and Zander, 1995: 425). In a similar vein, Zollo and Winter (2004) argue that 'experience accumulation' constitutes organizational routines by skill building based on the repeated execution of similar tasks, an insight shared with the literature on learning curves (Argote, 1999). They further emphasize that experiential learning is largely based on tacit knowledge, which is often applied in a semi-automatic way. Apart from experiential learning, the authors introduce two further learning processes, borrowed from Nonaka's (1994) conception of knowledge management. First, 'articulation' is seen as a deliberate process by which individuals share their knowledge on what works and what does not. This may be facilitated through collective discussions, debriefing sessions, and performance evaluation processes which help to make implicit knowledge more transparent. Second, 'codification' occurs when individuals transfer their understanding into written tools, such as manuals, blueprints, or decision support systems. Through the co-evolution of these processes capability development is presumed to occur.

One of the few studies, which explicitly refers to alliance capability and its *developmental process* via institutionalizing was undertaken by Dyer, Kale and Singh (2001). The authors empirically investigated 78 companies and indicated that the investment in an alliance function serves as a vehicle for transferring individual into company-based collaborative know-how. Draulans, de Man and Volberda (2003: 152) argue that "like any other competence, the management of alliances is a skill that can be built up and can become a significant source of competitive advantage." Ritter and Gemünden (2003) relate to 'organizational' antecedents of network competence and identify access to resources, network orientation of human resource management and the integration of formal and informal structures as well as an openness of organizational culture as being important.

While there have been several attempts at explaining capability development, there is only anecdotal evidence of the important role of the individual. This is not surprising given the fact that collectivist notions of capability research typically sidestep critical individual-level considerations, including individual action and heterogeneity (Felin and Foss, 2004, 2005). But as the authors remark:

"individuals matter…[and] to fully explicate organizational anything – whether identity, learning, knowledge or capabilities – one must fundamentally begin with and understand the individuals that compose the whole, specifically their underlying nature, choices, abilities, propensities, heterogeneity, purposes, expectations and motivations" Felin and Foss (2005: 441).

The Capability-Life-Cycle Revisited: Towards Micro-Foundations of Alliance Capability

In order to more fully capture the role of individuals in the development of capabilities, the life-cycle approach, as suggested by Helfat and Peteraf (2003), is used as a basic model. Each stage of the original model will be complemented by individual antecedents that help to explain heterogeneity in alliance capability.

The concept of the capability life-cycle "depicts a general pattern and set of possible paths that characterize the evolution of an organizational capability" (Helfat and Peteraf, 2003: 1000), which can be related to the development-cycle of an alliance (see introductory sections) even though the two need not necessarily coincide. Organizations with no heritage in collaboration ('new to the world of alliances') start in the *founding phase* with no previous alliance experience that might influence alliance capability development.

However, this stage cannot be seen as a clean slate as individuals may have previous experience with alliances obtained elsewhere.

Individual Level Contributions in the Founding Phase

Before joining an organization, several of the key elements of alliance capability may be influenced by individuals' earlier skills and knowledge related to specific alliance partners and individuals in partner firms. Adner and Helfat (2003) refer to this as 'managerial human capital', i.e. learned skills based on some investment in education, training, or learning. As identified earlier, there may be different types of individual skills, which influence the development of alliance capability. For instance, in a more general way, Castanias and Helfat (1991) distinguish between generic, industry-specific, and firm-specific skills. As shown elsewhere (Prange, Bojkowszky, & Wieshofer, 2004), there are some industries – like biotechnology – where industry-specific skills dominate all other elements of alliance capability. Thus, industry experience may be a selection criterion for prospective alliance managers.

Further, specific alliance roles may exist, e.g. as negotiator or implementer of an alliance, which require some leadership experience or the existence of specific personal traits. Indeed, Rosenbloom (2000: 1102) suggests that leadership by individuals may be a 'central element' in the more general dynamic capability development. There may also be self-selection processes in that only those individuals who have the presumed skills to manage an alliance enter the firm. This initial endowment with skills provides a source of heterogeneity to alliance capability development.

Iindividuals check available knowledge (e.g. via observation) and start a learning process on which they build their action ('learn-act-sequence'). This is the typical incremental and largely cognitive learning approach, which gradually develops knowledge through training and information search. From this initial starting point, two trajectories are possible. First, after reflection and continuous successful action, knowledge is transferred into organizational capabilities by processes of articulation and codification (Zollo and Winter, 2004). Installing these processes adds to the strategic development of knowledge in and about the alliance. As a result, emerging capabilities are made up of routines derived from thorough reflection and stable behaviour patterns. With repeated experience, accumulated knowledge eventually transfers into sedimented knowledge from which quasi-automatic behaviour is generated. In turn, these organizational routines influence individual action.

Secondly, when transferring experience in rather volatile environments, individual experimentation ('act-learn') may also lead to the establishment of simple rules as an expression of alliance capabilities. These are the bases of competitive advantage, where companies simply 'jump' into the market, experiment, test opportunities and shift frequently among partners and businesses as circumstances dictate. Still, there are some principle rules underlying this seemingly chaotic process, which could be the conscious play with market uncertainty, the seizing of several selected opportunities, strategic creativity induced on a permanent basis or the introduction of 'serious play' (Schrage, 2000) as a means of strategy formulation. All these simple rules open up scenarios without limiting a company's future choices by deadlocked routines.

Both reflective action and experimentation lead to different manifestations of alliance capabilities. In the same way as individual learning modes are dominated by one process or build on the logic of both 'thinking and experiencing', these different types of capabilities may interact over time, when flexible rules become more stabilized and stable routines need to be broken up to allow for more flexibility. For instance, when a firm opts to increase the heterogeneity of its alliance partners, past routines may prove detrimental as they do not capture what is new. When firm-level routines turn negative, differing personal endowments can prevent such a lock-in.

Individual Level Contributions in the Development Phase

Pursuing experimental learning processes in order to build 'simple rule-based capabilities' is closely linked to an individual's risk propensity as performance outcomes are highly uncertain. As outputs cannot be anticipated, a tolerance for mistakes is important. Most often, simple rules are tacit and it takes conscious effort to make them explicit and extend them as business unfolds. At the same time, these capabilities consist of a few rules that make them amenable for easy adoption. For instance, CEO Meg Whitman made Ebay's values explicit in simple rules that helped managers to predict what opportunities would work for the company and how they could be adapted (Eisenhardt and Sull, 2001). Given the fact that individuals need to actively engage in the articulation of tacit knowledge, motivational incentives become important (Osterloh and Frey, 2000) as well as cognitive skills, i.e. mental models and beliefs, which determine information search and opportunity seizing in the process of updating existing knowledge components (Hambrick and Mason, 1984).

In contrast, the emergence of stable routines may rather start from initial imitation of already existing capabilities in other organizations (benchmarking of best-practice alliance capabilities), where less individual creativity is required. In order to arrive at sufficient diversity in individual knowledge input, alliance human resource management is challenged to control adequate knowledge inflows. These are presumably tied to different types of motivational incentives.

Reaching maturity with a selected partnership, the development of capabilities may either come to a standstill as there may be satisfaction with what can be achieved, or is deliberately ceased in the process of alliance capability development. While current capabilities may be perceived as influential for performance outputs, this relationship could be blurred by perception gaps or aspiration level definitions. Therefore, complacency with existing capabilities could easily incur lock-in effects, which negatively impact alliance results.

Individual Level Contributions in the Maturity Phase

Individuals may exhibit different levels of skilfulness prior to reaching the full technical limits of capability development (Helfat and Peteraf, 2003: 1002). This may be due to differences in previous education and learning behaviour. Personal satisfaction levels may also differ due to cognitive processes like perception, sensing, opportunity seizing (Teece, 2007). When capabilities consist of simple rules, the problem of causal ambiguity emerges, i.e. comprehensive experiencing activities obscure the fundamental commonalities that drive the effectiveness of the capability. Thus, managers may not know themselves whether and why capabilities are successful and more cognitive effort is required to critically challenge established rules. Also, hierarchical positions in the organization may influence how far capability development is continued. For instance, the strength of influence from the top may have relevant consequences on capability development (Adner and Helfat, 2003: 24). Managers' ability to interpret their company's previous alliance experience also varies profoundly across hierarchical levels, with higher-level actors having more difficulty interpreting feedback from action than lower-level actors (Gavetti, 2005). Thus, variability in decision-making style, speed and implementation act as a driver of heterogeneity in alliance capabilities. Further, aspects of power and incentive systems are supposed to play a crucial role which warrants further attention (Shenkar and Ellis, 1995).

Figure 3 provides a summary of individual actions and some of their micro-foundations that influence the development of alliance capabilities.

In short, the learn-act sequence pays attention to the fact that there are 'intendedly rational' individuals, who cognitively engage in knowledge generation as a basis for alliance capabilities. With a lower cognitive involvement, experimentation and tacit learning through trial and error contribute to a more flexible type of alliance capability, which is less subject to routine but could be equally effective in turbulent markets. This act-learn sequence can be characterized by an ongoing process of experimentation accompanied by retrospective sense-making and the repetition of successful behaviour sequences. In fact, different learning mechanisms contribute to different manifestations of capabilities (simple rules and routines) mutually related over time to avoid the pitfalls of over- or under-specification. While the role of the individual is emphasized in this figure and attention is directed to several micro-foundations, the opposite process from organizational capabilities driving individual behaviour, as one of the traditional assumptions of resource-based theorizing, still holds true but is neglected in the figure.

DISCUSSION AND CONCLUSION

This article has provided a discussion of the recently fashionable construct of 'strategic alliance capability', its conceptualization and theoretical origin. Resource-based and dynamic capability approaches were used to incorporate 'alliance capability' into the overall framework of resource and capability-based theories. Thereby, an analysis

Figure 3. Individual foundations and processes of alliance capability development

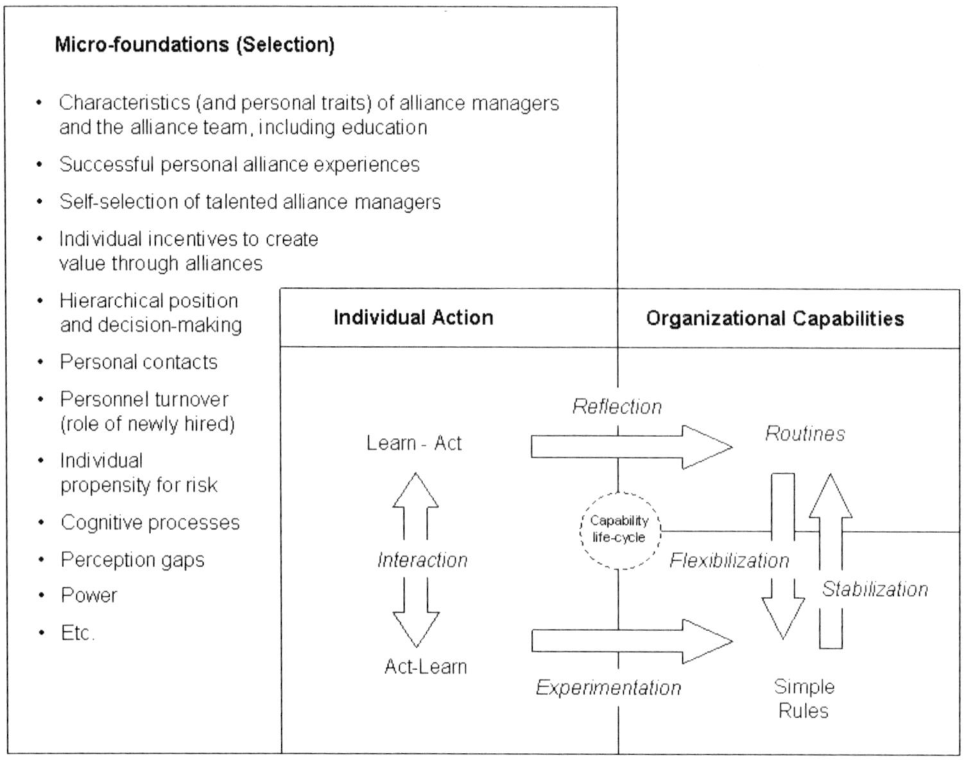

of alliance capability both benefits and suffers from the theoretical promises and pitfalls of resource-based theorizing.

As one of the major difficulties, it has been mentioned that the RBV defines resources and capabilities in a conceptually vague and non-operational way (e.g. Priem and Butler, 2001). Yet, strategic alliance capability exists in several exactly identifiable elements along the cooperative life cycle, which have selectively given rise to empirical studies. Further, the RBV has been criticized as being relevant only for stable markets. This criticism has been encountered by the DCV, which modifies the quest for sustainable advantage into a temporary one as resources and capabilities undergo constant changes. One of the major omissions in both the RBV and the DCV relates to the lack in dealing with individual-level antecedents of alliance capability. In order to fill this void, individual contributions on each stage of the alliance capability life cycle have been introduced.

Several questions can be derived from this model, constituting a future promising research agenda. First, differential learning processes pose several challenges, e.g. how do managers react to environmental turbulences and update their individual knowledge portfolio? Is there an optimal speed for experimental learning and are there given boundaries to the codification of individual knowledge into organizational routines? How do cognitive constraints influence processes like rapid learning, real-time information, multiple options and their impact on existing routines within an organization? When referring to reflective cognitive learning, it would be interesting to know how far previous education or industrial affiliation influences reflection processes? Further, are there previous personal contacts, which facilitate (or impede) the building of social skills as an important element of alliance capability?

As the concept of simple rules illustrates, there are different manifestations of capabilities and further research should more closely match these types of capabilities to specific contingencies. Closely related is the question whether it is generally valid to institutionalize knowledge in rapidly changing environments? Whereas previous studies suggest the implementation of a dedicated alliance function, which coordinates all alliance-related activity within the organization and initiates the transfer of both tacit and explicit alliance knowledge, the flexibility aspect has not been considered. The inherent danger might be inflexibility and overly bureaucratic procedures, which retard or prevent corporate flexibility. Thus, an important research direction is the exact interplay of more stable (routines) and flexible (simple rules) types of capabilities.

Finally, the exact sequence and the particular form of knowledge created and transferred in each step of the cooperative life-cycle both require further empirical analysis. This includes a specific emphasis on the contribution of individual knowledge components and learning processes as well as hierarchical positions and power relations which may have an impact. In more detail, several of the aforementioned micro-foundations pose a research agenda in their own right depending on the research question. For instance, hierarchical roles may serve as an important element of heterogeneity, which may be tailored to specific environmental setting and subsequent performance results. Also, the issue of personal traits offers intriguing challenges for future research, e.g. whether someone is particularly suited for combining different learning processes or whether these should be split between different people in order to guarantee a variety of alliance capabilities at the organizational level.

Also, several managerial implications spring to mind. Once precise micro-foundations of alliance capabilities are identified, human resource practices (selection, incentive systems, motivation) within alliances could be tailored to promote the development of required organizational level routines. As a result, the capability-performance link might be more effectively managed as the relation is highly dependent on environmental conditions and specific types of alliance capabilities. Finally, potential negative effects of (alliance) routines could be avoided by paying attention to those individual antecedents which stir up the system of stable but unproductive capabilities. Thus, management can add more flexibility to the process of capability generation and its dynamic adaptation to changing contingencies.

REFERENCES

Adner, R., & Helfat, C. (2003). Corporate effects and dynamic managerial capabilities. *Strategic Management Journal, 24*, 1011-1025.

Amit, R., & Schoemaker, P. J. (1993). Strategic assets and organizational rent. *Strategic Management Journal, 17*, 33-46.

Anand, B. N., & Khanna, T. (2000). Do firms learn to create value: The case of alliances. *Strategic Management Journal, 21*, 295-315.

Argote, L. (1999). Organizational Learning: Creating, Retaining and Transferring Knowledge. Kluwer: Newell, MA.

Barney, J. B. (1991). Firm resources and sustained competitive advantage. *Journal of Management, 17*, 99-120.

Birkinshaw, J. (2000). Network Relationships Inside and Outside the Firm, and the Development of Capabilities. In J. Birkinshaw, & P. Hagström (Eds.), *The Flexible Firm: Capability Management in Network Organizations, 4-17.* Oxford: Oxford University Press.

Bleeke, J., & Ernst, D. (1993). *Collaborating to Compete: Using Strategic Alliances and Acquisitions in the Global Market Place.* New York: Wiley.

Blomqvist, K., & Levy, J. (2006). Collaborative capability – a focal concept in knowledge creation and collaborative innovation in networks. *International Journal of Management Concepts and Philosophy, 2*, 31- 48.

Bucklin, L. P., & Sengupta, S. (1993). Organizing successful co-marketing alliances. *Journal of Marketing, 57*, 32-42.

Buckley, P. J., Glaister, K.W., & Husan, R. (2002). International joint ventures: partnering skills and cross-cultural issues. *Long Range Planning, 35*,113-134.

Cartwright, S., & Cooper, G. (1993). If cultures don't fit, mergers may fail. *New York Times, 15*,August, 51.

Cohen, W. M., & Levinthal, D. A. (1990). Absorptive capacity: A new perspective on learning and innovation. *Administrative Science Quarterly, 35*, 128-152.

Chang, S-C., Chen, S-S., & Lai, J.-H. (2008). The effect of alliance experience and intellectual capital on the value creation of international strategic alliances. *Omega, 36*, 298-316.

Collis, D. J. (1994). How valuable are organizational capabilities? *Strategic Management Journal, 15*/special issue, 143-152.

Contractor, F., & Lorange, P. (1988). *Cooperative Strategies in International Business: Joint Ventues and Technology Partnerships between Firms.* Lexington, MA: Lexington Books.

Crosby, L. A., Evans, K. R., & Cowles, D. (1990). Relationship quality in services selling. An interpersonal influence perspective. *Journal of Marketing, 54*(3), 68-81.

Danserau, F., Yammarino, F. J., & Kohles, J. C. (1999). Multiple levels of analysis form a longitudinal perspective: Some implications for theory building. *Academy of Management Review, 24*, 346-357.

Day, G. S. (1994). The capabilities of market-driven organizations. *Journal of Marketing, 58*, 37-53.

Deeds, D. L., & Hill, C. W. L. (1996). Strategic alliances and the rate of new product development: an empirical study of entrepreneurial biotechnology firms. *Journal of Business Venturing, 11*, 41-55.

De Man, A. P. (2002). How to analyze alliance networks. *Competitive Intelligence Magazine. July/August 2002, 5*, 14-29.

Dyer, J. H., & Singh, H. (1998). The relational view: Cooperative strategy and sources of inter-organizational competitive advantage. *Academy of Management Review, 23*, 660.

Dyer, J. H., Kale, P., & Singh, H. (2001). How to make strategic alliances work. *Sloan Management Review, 42*, 37-43.

Draulans, J., deMan, A.-P., & Volberda, H. W. (2003). Building alliance capability: Management techniques for superior alliance performance. *Long Range Planning, 36*, 151.

Eisenhardt, K., & Galunic, D. C. (2000). Co-evolving. At last, a way to make synergies work. *Harvard Business Review, January-February, 2000*, 91-101.

Eisenhardt, K. M., & Martin, J. A. (2000). Dynamic capabilities: what are they? *Strategic Management Journal, 21,* 1105-1121.

Eisenhardt, K., & Sull, D. N. (2001). Strategy as simple rules. *Harvard Business Review, January 2001*, 107-116.

Felin, T., & Foss, N. J. (2005). Strategic organization: A field in search of micro-foundations. *Strategic Organization, 3*, 441-455.

Felin, T., & Foss, N. J. (2004). *Methodological individualism and the organizational capability approach.* Working Paper Copenhagen Business School, No.5/2004.

Gavetti, G. (2005). Cognition and hierarchy: Rethinking the micro-foundations of capability development. *Organization Science, 16*, 599-617.

Gomes-Casseres, B. (2003). Competitive advantage in alliance constellations. *Strategic Organization, 1*, 327-335.

Grant, R. M. (1991). The resource-based theory of competitive advantage: implications for strategy formation. *California Management Review, 33*, 114-135.

Gulati, R. (1995). Does familiarity breed trust? The implications of repeated ties for contractual choice in alliances. *Academy of Management Journal, 38*, 85-112.

Gulati, R. (1998). Alliances and networks. *Strategic Management Journal, Special Issue, 19*, 293-318.

Gulati, R. (1999). Network location and learning: The influence of network resources and firm capabilities on alliance formation. *Strategic Management Journal, 20*, 397-421.

Håkansson, H. (1987). *Industrial Technological Development: A Network Approach.* London: Croom Helm.

Hall, R. (1992). The strategic analysis of intangible resources. *Strategic Management Journal, 13*, 135-144.

Hall, R. (1993). A framework linking intangible resources and capabilities to sustainable competitive advantage. *Strategic Management Journal, 14*, 607-618.

Hamel, G. (1991). Competition for competence and inter-partner learning with international strategic alliances. *Strategic Management Journal,* (pp. 83-103).

Hambrick, D. C., & Mason, P. A. (1984). Upper echelons. The organization as a reflection of its top managers. *Academy of Management Review, 9*, 193-206,

Heimeriks, K. H.., & Duysters, G. (2003). Experience and capabilities to explain alliance performance: Substitutes or complements? *Eindhoven Centre for Innovation Studies (ECIS)*, The Netherlands.

Heimeriks, K. H., & Duysters, G. (2007). Alliance capability as a mediator between experience and alliance performance: An empirical investigation into the alliance capability process. *Journal of Management Studies, 44*, 25-49.

Helfat, C. E. (2000). Guest editor's introduction to the special issue: The evolution of firms capabilities. *Strategic Management Journal, 21*, 955-960.

Helfat, C. E., & Peteraf, M. A. (2003). The dynamic resource-based view: Capability lifecycles. *Strategic Management Journal, 24*, 997-1010.

Henderson, R., & Cockburn, I. M. (1994). Measuring competence? Exploring firm effects in pharmaceutical research. *Strategic Management Journal, 15*, 63-84.

Hoang, H. T., & Rothaermel, F. T. (2005). The effect of general and partner-specific alliance experience on joint R&D project performance. *Academy of Management Journal, 48*, 332-45.

Ireland, R. D., Hitt, M. A., & Vaidyanath, D. (2002). Alliance managers as a source of competitive advantage. *Journal of Management, 28*, 413-447.

Itami, H., & Roehl, T. W. (1987). *Mobilizing Invisible Assets.* Cambridge, Mass: Harvard University Press.

Johnson, G., Melin, I., & Whittington, R. (2003). Guest Editors introduction: Micro strategy and strategizing: Towards an activity-based view. *Journal of Management Studies, 40*, 3-22.

Kale, P., & Singh, H. (2007). Building firm capabilities through learning: The role of the alliance learning process in alliance capability and firm-level alliance success. *Strategic Management Journal, 28*, 981-1000.

Kale, P., & Singh, H. (1999). *Alliance capability and success: A knowledge-based approach.* Paper presented at the Academy of Management Annual Meeting, Chicago, IL.

Kale, P., Dyer, J. H., & Singh, H. (2002). Alliance capability, stock market response, and long-term alliance success: The role of the alliance function. *Strategic Management Journal, 23*, 747-767.

Kale, P., Singh, H., & Perlmutter, H. (2000). Learning and protection of proprietary assets in strategic alliances: Building relational capital. *Strategic Management Journal, 21*, 217-237.

Kandemir,D., Ghauri, P., Cavusgil, T. (2002). The strategic role of organizational learning in relationship quality in strategic alliances. In: Contractor, F., & P.Lorange (Eds.), Cooperative strategies, Amsterdam, Elsevier, (pp. 799-828).

Khanna, T. (1998). The scope of alliances. *Organization Science, 9*, 340-355.

Kim, D. H. (1993). The link between individual and organizational learning. *Sloan Management Review, Fall*, (pp. 37-50).

Kogut, B., & Zander, U. (1995). Knowledge, market failure and the multinational enterprise: A reply. *Journal of International Business Studies, 26*, 417-426.

Kumar, R., & Nti, K. O. (1998). Differential learning and interaction in alliance dynamics: A process and outcome discrepancy model. *Organization Science, 9*, 356-66.

Lambe, C. J., Spekman, R. E., & Hunt, S. D. (2002). Alliance competence, resources, and alliance success: conceptualization, measurement, and initial test. *Academy of Marketing Science, 30*, 141-158.

Larson, A. (1992). Network dyads in entrepreneurial settings: A study of the governance of exchange relations. *Administrative Science Quarterly, 37*, 76-104.

Larsson, R., Bengtsson, L., Henriksson, K., & Sparks, J. (1998). The inter-organizational learning dilemma: Collective knowledge development in strategic alliances. *Organization Science, 9*, 285- 305.

Lawler, E. J., & Thye, S. R. (1999). Bringing emotions into social exchange theory. *Annual Review of Sociology, 25*, 217-244.

Lorange, P., & Roos, J. (1992). *Strategic Alliances: Formation, Implementation, and Evolution*. Cambridge, Mass: Blackwell.

Lorenzoni, G., & Lipparini, A. (1999). The leveraging of inter-firm relationships as a distinctive organizational capability: A longitudinal study. *Strategic Management Journal, 20*, 317-338.

Macpherson, A., Jones, O., & Zhang, M. (2004). Evolution or revolution? Dynamic capabilities in a knowledge dependent firm. *R&D Management, 34*, 161.

Mahoney, J. T., & Pandian, J. R. (1992). The resource-based view within the conversation of strategic management. *Strategic Management Journal, 13*(363), 380.

Maier, G. W., Prange, C., & von Rosenstil, L. (2001). Psychological perspectives of organizational learning. In M. Dierkes, ABerthoin Antal, J. Child, & I. Nonaka (Eds.), *Psychological perspectives of organizational learning and knowledge*, (pp. 14-34).

McGee, J. E., Dowling, M. J., & Megginson, W. L. (1995). Cooperative strategy and new venture performance: The role of business strategy and management experience. *Strategic Management Journal, 16*, 565-580.

Möller, K. K., & Halinen, A. (1999). Business relationships and networks: Managerial challenge of the network era. *Industrial Marketing Management, 28*, 413-427.

Mohr, J., & Spekman, R. (1994). Characteristics of partnership success: partnership attributes, communication behaviour and conflict resolution. *Strategic Management Journal, 15*, 135-52.

Nelson, R., & Winter, S. (1982). *An Evolutionary Theory of Economic Change*. Cambridge, MA: Belknap Press.

Nonaka, I. (1994). A dynamic theory of knowledge creation. *Organization Science, 5*, 14-37.

Osborn, R.N., & J. Hagedorn (1997). The institutionalization and evolutionary dynamics of inter-organizational alliances and networks. *Academy of Management Journal, 40*, 261-278.

Osterloh, M., & Frey, B. (2000). Motivation, knowledge transfer and organizational form. *Organization Science, 11*, 538-550.

Porter, M.E. (1980). *Competitive strategy*. Free Press, New York.

Prahalad, C.K., & Hamel, G. (1990). The core competence of the corporation. *Harvard Business Review*, May/June 1990, 68, 79-91.

Prange, C. (1999). Organizational learning – desperately seeking theory. In: Easterby-Smith, M., Araujo, L., & Burgoyne, J. (Eds.), *Organizational learning and the learning organization*. Thousand Oaks, Sage Publications, 23-42.

Prange, C., Bojkowsky, B., & Wieshofer, B. (2004). *Networking capability as a prerequisite for cooperative innovation success - An individual manager's perspective*. IASTED-Conference, Cambridge, MIT.

Priem, R.L., & Butler, J.E., (2001). Is the resource-based "view" a useful perspective for strategic management research? *Academy of Management Review, 26*, 22-40.

Reilly, N.H., Brad, J.M., & Stroh, L.K. (1993). The impact of corporate turbulence on managers' attitudes. *Strategic Management Journal, 14*, 167-179.

Ritter, T. (1998). *Innovationserfolg durch Netzwerkkompetenz – Effektives Management von Unternehmensnetzwerken*. Gabler, Wiesbaden.

Ritter, T., & Gemünden, H.G. (2003). Network competence: Its impact on innovation success and its antecedents. *Journal of Business Research, 56*, 745-755.

Rosenbloom, R.S. (2000). Leadership, capabilities, and technological changes: the transformation of NCR in the electronic era. *Strategic Management Journal, Special Issue, 21*, 1083-1104.

Rumelt, R.P. (1984). Towards a strategic theory of the firm. In Lamb, R.B. (Eds), *Competitive strategic management*. Prentice-Hall: Englewood Cliffs, NJ, 556-570.

Schrage, M. (2000). *Serious play: How the world's best companies simulate to innovate*. Harvard Business School, Cambridge, MA.

Schreiner, M. (2004). *Collaborative capability in vendor-service provider relationships: Construct development and empirical analysis in the software service industry*. Doctoral Thesis, Universität St. Gallen.

Schreiner, M., & Corsten, D. (2004). Integrating perspectives: A multidimensional construct of collaborative capability. In: Beyerlein, M. Johnson, D., & Beyerlein, S. (Eds), *Complex collaboration: Building the capabilities to work across boundaries*. JAI Press, 125-159.

Shenkar, O., & Ellis, S. (1995). Death of the "organization" man: Temporal relations in strategic alliances. *The International Executive, 37*, 537-553.

Simonin, B. (1997). The importance of collaborative know-how. *Academy of Management Journal, 40*, 1150-1174.

Sivadas, E., & Dwyer, F.R. (2000). An examination of organizational factors influencing new product success in internal and alliance-based processes. *Journal of Marketing, 64*, 31-49.

Spekman, R.E., Forbes, T.M.III, Isabelly, L.A., & MacAvoy, T.C. (1998). Alliance management: A view from the past and a look to the future. *Journal of Management Studies, 35*, 747-772.

Storbacka, K., Strandvik, T., & Grönroos, C. (1994). Managing customer relationships for profit: The dynamics of relationship quality. *International Journal of Service Industry Management, 5*, 21-38.

Teece, D.J. (2007). Explicating dynamic capabilities: The nature and micro-foundations of (sustainable) enterprise performance. *Strategic Management Journal, 28*, 1319-1350.

Teece, D.J., Pisano, G., & Shuen, A. (1997). Dynamic capabilities and strategic management. *Strategic Management Journal, 18*, 509-533.

Van de Ven, A.H., & Walker, G. (1984). The dynamics of inter-organizational coordination. *Administrative Science Quarterly, 29*, 598-621.

Walter, A., Auer, M., & Ritter,M. (2006). The impact of network capabilities and entrepreneurial orientation on university spin-off performance. *Journal of Business Venturing, 21*, 541-567.

Weick, K. (1976). Educational organizations as loosely coupled systems. *Administrative Science Quarterly, 21*, 1-19.

Wernerfeld, B. (1984). A resource-based view of the firm. *Strategic Management Journal, 3*, 147-158.

Winter, S. G. (2000). The satisfying principle in capability learning, *Strategic Management Journal, 21*(10/11), Oct-Nov Special Issue, 981-996.

Williamson, O.E. (1991). Comparative economic organization: The analysis of discrete structural alternatives. *Administrative Science Quarterly, 36*, 269-296.

Wuyts, S., Dutta, S., & Stremersch, S. (2004). Portfolios of inter-firm agreements in Technology-intensive markets: Consequences for innovation and profitability. *Journal of Marketing, 68*, 88- 102.

Yoshino, M.Y., & Rangan, U.S. (1995). *Strategic alliances: An entrepreneurial approach to globalization*. Boston, MA: Harvard University Press.

Zajac, E.J., & Olsen, C.P. (1993). From transaction cost to transactional value analysis: Implications for the study of inter-organizational strategies. *Journal of Management Studies, 30*, 131-145.

Zollo, M., & Winter, S.G. (2002). Deliberate learning and the evolution of dynamic capabilities. *Organization Science, 13*, 339-351.

ENDNOTES

[a] In this research, 'strategic alliance' is used as a generic term to signify voluntary and planned inter-organizational collaboration between, at least, two partners (e.g. Contractor and Lorange, 1988; Yoshino and Rangan, 1995) and does not consider differences within individual forms, such as joint ventures (JVs), licensing arrangements, partnerships, and others. However, the researcher wants to attract attention to the fact that this is a worth-while effort, which should be undertaken in other studies.

[b] This is a typical approach in inter-organizational research. As Osborn and Hagedorn (1997: 271) in citing Larson (1992) say: "Almost lost in the empirical study of alliances is the importance of the experience and predisposition of the individual using them…The potentially important role of individuals in operating alliances remains virtually unexplored".

[c] Even though he does not further distinguish between resources and capabilities, in principle, I share his argument as applied to alliance management as a capability.

Chapter XXV
Automation vs. Human Intervention:
Is There any Room Left for the Analyst in the Data Mining Process?

Meryem Sevinc
Georgia Southern University, USA

Lawrence Locker
Georgia Southern University, USA

John D. Murray
Georgia Southern University, USA

ABSTRACT

In the contemporary context of knowledge discovery, the amount of information and the process itself has increased in complexity. Relevant to the present chapter is the increased reliance on automaticity in knowledge discovery. Although, there are positive benefits of automation, there is reason to believe that a process that emphasizes greater human participation may produce more meaningful results. Through a description of the human information processing system and its attributes, this chapter discusses why an analyst-centered approach to a knowledge discovery system is a desirable goal. We argue that a perspective based on cognitive psychology can serve as a useful guide in achieving a desirable synergy between automated knowledge discovery tools and the human analyst.

INTRODUCTION

In the present technological age, there is an increasing need in complex organizations for the rapid acquisition, interpretation, and practical application of data. Fifty years ago, it was considered a great success for organizations to be able to answer a question such as what their revenue had been over the previous four years. Today however, the questions are much more sophisticated, such as "What are the estimated unit sales over the next ten months?" and "What are the reasons behind these projections?" Technological advances such as efficient computer systems and the World Wide Web (WWW), now allow organization analysts to access easily enormous data sets which can, in turn, be analyzed in any number of ways that can be helpful to an organization. For example, a retail company could use available data to gain a better understanding of customer preferences, leading to more effective use of advertising dollars and overall improvement of marketing strategies. Alternatively, companies could use data for information about internal functioning that could lead to a better understanding of employee communication or effective use of technology. Indeed, in an age of competitive global markets, effective acquisition and use of data is not only a benefit, but may actually be necessary for an organization to stay competitive. Such a climate has led to the label "inquiring organizations" which refers to organizations that are involved in the creation of knowledge (e.g., data) that serves their mission to stay current and competitive (e.g., Churchman, 1971; Murray, Case, & Gardiner, 2005). Technological processes that are critical to inquiring organizations are Knowledge Discovery in Databases (KDD) and Data Mining (DM).

KDD refers to the general process of discovering useful information and patterns in datasets. DM is a specific form of KDD involving the use of computational algorithms to extract from large data sets information and statistical patterns that directly point to actionable findings. In this chapter we focus on the role of the data mining analyst, the individual who applies the computational algorithms to a data set and then interprets the output in light of the organizational goals for strategic change or improvement. Currently, there is a trend in DM towards a greater reliance on automation. That is, once the analyst selects the appropriate algorithms, their execution is largely automated (e.g., Murray et al., 2005). Consequently, the search for meaningful patterns is computer-based, whereas the role of the analyst is centered primarily on interpretation of outcomes. The heavy reliance on automation and relatively low analyst involvement in DM has benefits and liabilities. The benefits of a heavy reliance on automation include speed and efficiency with which data analytic processes can be executed. In contrast, a liability of an automated algorithm-execution stage is that the analyst is unable to flexibly employ and interject into the process valuable background experiences and domain knowledge. For example, in the "data extraction process" low analyst involvement may be associated with missed data or patterns. Stated differently, if pattern detection is left solely to a computer-based algorithm, then it is probable that many patterns will be discarded. Furthermore, some of these (discarded) patterns might, to a human analyst, be judged to be important based on the background knowledge of the analyst (e.g., an insight that might indicate a new approach to the data and consequently new model parameters that might lead to the identification of statistical patterns that might otherwise never be considered). We would argue that although automaticity has an invaluable pragmatic value in its ability to reduce large bodies of data to manageable proportions, it is also important to determine how the typically automated components of DM can be augmented by potentially valuable human (i.e., analyst) involvement given the rich knowledge and inferential abilities that humans bring to any task[1]. In this chapter, we will attempt to articulate why a heavily automated approach to

KDD and DM is not an ideal goal and that such an approach diminishes the contributions from the (human) analyst.

To make our case, let us first turn to a discussion of KDD and the current state of DM. We will then turn to a description of the human information processing system in order to illustrate its strengths and flexibility. Finally we will discuss the importance of integrating the analyst into the DM process and how this might be accomplished.

STEPS IN DATA MINING

As outlined in Murray et al. (2005), there are five steps or stages in KDD. The first is *Task and Data Discovery*, involving the identification of task requirements and the nature of the relevant data sets. This stage of the process, as one would expect, is analyst-centered as the analyst attempts to understand and evaluate the available data sets. Also involving the analyst is the second step of *Data Cleaning*, which involves preparation of the data for analyses (e.g., identification of outliers). The third is *Model Development* in which hypotheses or models are developed. However, this is phase is largely driven by the data rather than by a prior assumptions (Murray et al., 2005). That is, rather than necessarily approaching the analysis with prior hypotheses, the interpretation is guided by the outcome of the analysis. The final stages are *Data Analysis* and *Output Generation* in which some algorithm is used to analyze the data; results are derived from the analysis and ultimately utilized for some relevant purpose such as strategic planning (Murray et al., 2005).

If one considers these steps, the process begins and ends in an analyst-centered fashion. That is, an analyst evaluates data sets, performs data cleaning, and ultimately makes interpretations of the outcome with follow-ups appropriate to the particular organization (e.g., development of reports or marketing plans). On the surface, then, this would seem to be a highly analyst-centered process and in many ways it is. However, underlying these steps is the actual process of mining the data (i.e., the extraction of patterns from the data set). As a consequence, between initial evaluation of the data set and the final interpretation, the role of the analyst is actually considered less important in regard to this DM process. This is because once a relevant data set is identified; *automated* analysis techniques are applied to the data set (e.g., an algorithm that identifies correlational patterns within the data). Once the analysis is complete, an output is provided that can be interpreted. At first glance, this might seem reasonable as analysts often do not approach data sets with prior hypotheses (Murray et al., 2005). Therefore, the complex process of data analysis can be left to a computer system (i.e., that implements some algorithm) and the analyst need simply make decisions concerning the validity, relevance, and importance of the outcome. Thus, the current approach places the *identification* of patterns largely on an automated system, whereas drawing conclusions concerning the patterns is left to the analyst.

Obviously, the complex statistical analyses involved in DM are best left to a computer software program. However, by emphasizing automation at this stage (i.e., identification of important data patterns), the analyst is left to make decisions or draw conclusions concerning data patterns that they have had a *minimal role* in identifying. Hypothetically, the application of purely automated algorithms leaves the analysis software as the *sole* determinant of which aspects of the data are deemed important. Given a highly complex data set, computer identification of relevant patterns in the data is a necessity. However, at some point, there is a benefit in the analyst taking a role in determining which patterns or variables are relevant[2]. A question at this point is, given the computational power and sophistication of DM software, why would increased automation be considered a negative aspect? That is, what further benefit can an analyst bring to a computational process? To begin to answer this question we will now turn to a discussion of the human information processing system to illustrate its strengths.

THE HUMAN INFORMATION PROCESSING SYSTEM

Generally speaking, like the KDD process the human information processing system is one that extracts data from the external environment, detects patterns, retains or rejects information relative to the current context, processes this information at a "high-level" (e.g., extracting meaning from input such as words, sentences, etc), and draws conclusions or engages in behavior. However, the human information processing system is a dynamic one that is not passive, but an active processor of environmental data. This system draws upon a rich base of knowledge and complex systems of rapid inferential processes. This system is not infallible; errors can arise at a number of points in the system (e.g., misperceiving a word on a grocery list). Despite possible errors, the human information processing system is impressive in its capabilities.

Although there are a number of models that have been put forth to describe the human information processing system, models of memory proposed by Atkinson and Shiffrin (1971) and Baddeley (e.g.,1992) are among the most comprehensive without being either overly complex or overly simple. Atkinson and Shiffrin describe three architectural components of the human memory system: The first is sensory memory, a brief memory store in which sensory information is initially held for further processing by the brain. The second component is short-term memory, which is the active (i.e., conscious) component of the memory system. It is in short-term memory where an individual might, for example, rehearse a phone number obtained from an operator and keep it active until the number is dialed. As the name implies, short-term memory is limited in both capacity and duration of information processing. The third component of the model is long-term memory, which is the permanent memory store. New information can be transferred from short-term memory to long-term memory (e.g., if one were to remember the phone number in the example described above) and information is continually retrieved from long-term memory (e.g., knowledge of what a "telephone" is). In terms of the flow of information through the system, environmental input (e.g., a visual image or auditory pattern) enters the appropriate sensory memory buffer for that sense and is held long enough to be transferred to short-term memory. In short-term memory, the information can be interpreted using knowledge and experience contained in long-term memory. Depending on a number of factors involved in processing the experience, the information might be stored permanently in long-term memory and consequently be available for later retrieval.

A compelling re-conceptualization of short-term memory (working memory) was put forth by Alan Baddeley (e.g., Baddeley, 1992). This re-conceptualization expanded the original notion of short-term memory to better reflect the high-level control processes that appear to occur within this level of processing. Baddeley's model of working memory (so named to reflect the conscious activity individuals engage in) is more complex than Atkinson and Shiffrin's unitary conceptualization of short-term memory. The primary component of working memory is the central executive, a control component responsible for controlling attentional resources and executing complex skills (e.g., reasoning or problem solving). The central executive also coordinates the activities of two so-called "slave systems", the articulatory loop and the visuospatial sketchpad. The articulatory loop is responsible for the rehearsal of verbal information (e.g., repeating a phone number long enough to dial it) and the visuospatial sketchpad manipulates visual information (e.g., mentally retracing one's steps trying to find a lost item). The central executive performs high-level processing, engaging the slave systems as needed. Thus, structurally, the human information processing system can be viewed as a flow of information through a short, temporary sensory store as well as a short-term, but highly active conscious stage that can manipulate information, execute complex skills, and draw upon a large permanent memory store (e.g., Atkinson & Shiffrin, 1971; Baddeley, 1992).

There are two additional properties of this system that merit elaboration. The first is that the components of this system are highly interactive and operate in a parallel fashion (e.g., Locker, Simpson, & Yates, 2003; Pexman & Lupker, 1999). That is, this system does not operate as a simple one-way flow of information from input to conscious perception, but as a dynamic system in which there is overlap in processing between stages such, that "higher" level stages (e.g., prior conceptions or knowledge) can influence "lower" level stages (e.g., incoming data from the environment). To illustrate, consider the two following examples. At the simplest level, this interactive effect is evident even when reading a single word. In word recognition studies, a common finding is that the *meaning* of the word can influence the individual's ability to recognize it (i.e., in terms of speed and accuracy). Generally, the finding is that words that are somehow more "meaningful" by some metric are recognized more efficiently (e.g., see Balota, Ferraro, & Connor, 1991 for a review). How can word meaning have an influence on the *process* of recognizing a word? One answer is based in the assumption that the human information processing system is a highly efficient, interactive system in which knowledge at all levels becomes available immediately in processing. Thus, as the system begins to process the visual input of the word, it immediately begins activation of the meaning, which in turn can influence the process of recognition of the visual input (e.g., Locker et al., 2003). This interactive, parallel processing aspect of the human information processing system illustrates that even at the simplest level, humans make use of a myriad of information not only from the environment, but also internally such that perception of events is rendered as efficient as possible. Consider another example in an environmental context. When entering a *new* restaurant, we automatically have certain expectations and in a sense seem to "know what to do" although we have never been in that particular establishment. Unless, these expectations are violated, we most likely give them little explicit thought, simply expecting certain events to occur (e.g., that a menu will be available at some point). Why would this occur? Again, it has to do with the rich body of background knowledge we immediately bring to any processing situation. Upon entering the restaurant, we immediately draw upon prior experiential knowledge of restaurants that guides our expectations (this experiential knowledge is sometimes referred to as "scripts", e.g., see Schank & Abelson, 1977). If one considers going to a new airport, restaurant, school, job, etc., we can, based on our long-term knowledge, quickly know what to do or what to expect, not having to treat each of these experiences as *new*. Again, our use of long-term memory knowledge renders our perceptual experiences more efficient and, indeed, it is difficult to imagine how one would navigate the experiences of life without this ability.

Another overall property of the human information processing system that merits elaboration is that it has highly developed inferential abilities that quickly allow individuals to comprehend information that was *not* explicitly experienced or stored as facts. Mark Ashcraft, a well known textbook author, uses an excellent example of an individual asked the question "How many hands did Aristotle have?" (p. 4, 2006). The obvious answer is two, but it is unlikely that anyone was ever explicitly exposed to this information (i.e., one was told explicitly that Aristotle had two hands). Although this inference is relatively complex in terms of a verbal explanation, the efficiency of our information processing system is such that the actual inference occurs virtually without awareness, or largely *automatically*. That is, such inferences generally occur rapidly and without conscious awareness, thus minimizing the mental resources they might require (Posner & Snyder, 1975). Thus, although processes implicated in human information processing are quite complex, a great deal of these processes occur at an automatic level, allowing conscious processes to be devoted to higher level reasoning, skills, etc. This division between automatic and conscious abilities accounts for a great deal of the efficiency by which the human information processing system operates.

Thus, not only do humans have available an impressive bank of experiential knowledge, but can utilize this knowledge quickly and with relatively little burden on processing resources. Of course, conscious processes play a role as well. In the above example concerning Aristotle, we might consciously consider information such as the speaker's intent or consciously consult other knowledge within our system that might support or question the conclusion (Ashcraft, 2006). However, automaticity allows us to devote our mental resources to these more complex tasks or thought processes while at the same time performing impressive processing tasks with little or no awareness.

In sum, the human information processing system is a highly advanced and complex system that benefits from the rapid interaction of input from the environment and stored knowledge. Not only is this system impressive in its capabilities, but also its *flexibility*. This flexibility is a function of the interactive nature of the system in that a perception is not entirely data-driven (i.e., environmental input), but is dynamically manipulated and interpreted. That is, our internal knowledge and interpretation of the contextual situation will modulate our perception to a greater or lesser degree (e.g., Palmer, 1975). Given that our perception is influenced by a myriad of information beyond the simple sensory input, one's interpretation of an event might even be radically altered.

To illustrate, consider observing a painting and forming a perception about its design. The perception will be based, of course, on the visual input of the painting. However, the observer will simultaneously draw upon their stored knowledge about painting in general, etc. All of these inputs might lead the painting to be judged as nonsensical or badly designed. However, if the observer obtained additional knowledge (e.g., an explanation about the painting from a museum) this perception might be altered substantially. In this case, the input (i.e., the painting) while static, was interpreted and reinterpreted based on knowledge beyond that input, whether from the environmental or an internal source. Clearly, perception is a dynamic process as individuals are capable of combining multiple sources of information into a flexible experience and interpretation.

It seems then, that the KDD process could benefit from being as analyst-centered as possible. This is because any automated algorithm, while highly efficient, is ultimately constrained by its parameters, whereas the analyst can be highly fluid in their processing of the same information. We will now turn to a discussion of how a balance between automation and analyst-centered approaches might be achieved.

AN ANALYST-CENTERED APPROACH TO DATA MINING

Unlike the human information processing system described above, computer data mining involves the application of algorithms that are not dynamic in nature. That is, algorithm parameters are established and remain fixed throughout the data analysis process. The challenge then, is to make the DM process as dynamic as possible. Given that an algorithm is based on pre-established parameters, the solution is to interface the process to as great an extent as possible with the human analyst, who does process information in a dynamic fashion.

However, an analyst-centered focus at all stages of data mining is not a simple approach. As noted above, human working memory is limited in both duration and capacity. Consequently, as the size and complexity of a data base increases, the role of the analyst diminishes and increased automation becomes more necessary (Fayyad, n.d.). Research, therefore, must be aimed at a means by which the increased reliance on automation in handling massive data sets can still be, to some degree, analyst centered. In his editorial, Fayyad includes a discussion of *data visualization* as a means of facilitating user interface with large data sets. From a cognitive perspective, a focus on some form of interactivity based on visualization between a data mining program and the analyst would seem to be a viable approach, as humans have a highly developed visual system, and indeed the majority of information processed by human beings is via the visual modality (Eisenhauer, Hoffman, & Kretschmer, 2002).

Shneiderman (2001) discuss some excellent arguments in favor of an analyst-centered approach to DM including visualization. First, the use of visualization tools in data mining facilitates an analyst's understanding of the data set. The greater involvement of the analyst consequently allows the user to more easily identify new data analysis possibilities and discard those that are not fruitful. Finally, Schneiderman makes the point that if the tools utilized by the analyst are not well understood, confidence in the results is diminished, whereas greater analyst involvement decreases the possibility of error. As the current paper illustrates, these recommendations are sound not only from an analytical perspective, but also a cognitive one.

Although in practice DM is quite complex, a very simple example from statistics might illustrate the effectiveness of visualization. Consider a program in which an algorithm computes Pearson correlations among sets of variables. Assume that for a set of calculations, the computer produced three hypothetical correlations (e.g., .88, .75, & .95) that are tagged as statistically significant. As part of the analysis, it would be important to examine the relationship among the variables visually (scatterplots or tables) in order to assess such issues as linearity or outliers as well as examine the substantive relationships among the variables (e.g., Wilson, 2005). For example, consider the above correlation of .88. Assume that this correlation is based on the following pairs of hypothetical numbers (2,4; 3,6; 2,4; 10,12; 5,4; 4,4). A correlational analysis would yield a conclusion that the variables are significantly related. However, a visual examination of the scatterplot *immediately* indicates that the linear relationship is driven by a pair of outliers (10, 12; see Figure 1). Although this example is extremely simple, it illustrates that a visual representation is an important and necessary component of an analysis in regard to understanding the outcome and identifying potentially problematic issues. In this example, based on the visual representation, the analyst could immediately discount this particular correlation as spurious, or based on the background knowledge of the situation, choose to explore the outliers. This simple example can be generalized to more complex situations in which visualization is an integral component of data assessment and interpretation.

Shneiderman (2001) notes, however, that researchers investigating data mining techniques and information visualization are often working in independent domains and indeed may disagree as to the importance of human intervention. DM researchers may place less emphasis on human intervention and a greater reliance on machine algorithms, whereas the information visualization approach places a greater value on the human component. Since these two communities are influenced by differing ideals, a clearer understanding of the role of human cognition in the KDD process might help clarify the role of the analyst and lead the data mining process to a whole new dimension.

We believe that cognitive psychology can serve as a useful research domain in regard to the investigation of how DM methods can capitalize on the benefits of automation while at the same time developing means by which the analyst can actively guide the process, rather than be a passive recipient of the results. In the current paper, we have discussed one possible avenue; an emphasis on the incorporation of visualization into the process. In regard to research concerning an interactive visualization approach, there are a number of issues to be considered that could benefit from cognitive psychology. For example, any visualization approach must take into consideration the limitations of human working memory in regard to capacity, duration, and attentional resources. That is, the aim of interactive visualization should be to allow for the most ideal perception possible without overwhelming the human information processing system. Long-term memory is also of importance. How can visual displays be constructed that facilitate the transfer of information into long-term storage, allowing the analyst to more easily construct mental models of the data set as the analysis proceeds? What mental models might analysts construct as they perform DM and how do these models relate to their long-term knowledge? As these few examples illustrate, an interactive visual approach to DM is a rich avenue of research that has both theoretical and practical benefits (see also Murray et al., 2005 for a discussion of cognitive issues in relation to KDD and DM).

There are also important implications regarding a research endeavor that links business organizations and the domain of cognitive psychology. Firstly, this approach facilitates a strong *interdisciplinary* avenue to research between cognitive psychology, statistics, and business. Cognitive psychologists can further approach traditional questions regarding memory, language, etc. from the perspective of applications in business organizations and approaches to data analysis. This would facilitate collaboration between cognitive scientists and members of the business community, enriching the knowledge of both domains. Secondly, this approach leads to new avenues of research and questions that could be addressed specifically within the context of business organizations. One could envision numerous studies that could be pursued within the business environment. Additionally, this approach would facilitate better understanding of the approaches of the science of psychology for members of business organizations, facilitating collaborative efforts, improving data analysis approaches, and perhaps suggesting new approaches that could be considered within organizations. Thus, an interdisciplinary, research-based approach could prove invaluable both to cognitive psychologists that aim to apply their research to real-world issues, as well as members of organizations that can use this knowledge to increase productivity and profits through a better understanding of and accessibility to patterns in the available data.

In summary, in the traditional KDD process, the search for patterns within a large data set is mostly accomplished by computer methods, whereas the involvement of the analyst is generally limited to reviewing the output and forming new sets of questions to refine the search or elaborate on some aspects of the findings. However, with the interactive visual data mining approach, the analyst can contribute to the process *from the beginning*. The advantage is the synergy between the processing power of a computer and the flexible use of domain knowledge by the analyst. Although increased automation in the KDD process may seem to be a reasonable goal in regard to efficiency or reduced cost, we would argue that ultimately the opposite is true. As automated algorithms lack the ability to mimic the dynamic aspect of human thought processes, a great deal could be lost in an automated approach. Automation minimizes at least two important components that the analyst can bring to the DM process: a

Figure 1. Scatterplot based on hypothetical correlational data (generated by the authors)

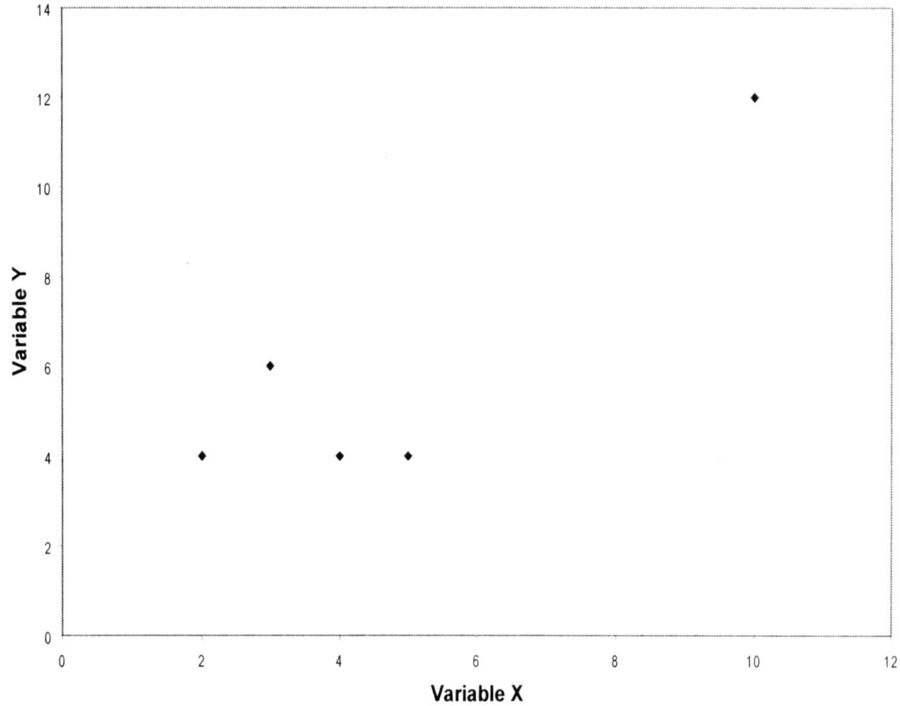

vast experiential knowledge base and flexible use of that knowledge. As has been argued (e.g., Schneiderman, 2001), greater analyst involvement may lead to greater confidence in results and more rapid identification of data patterns that could benefit an organization. Thus, it is likely that the *quality* of the KDD process can be enhanced to a great degree through an analyst-centered approach. Businesses hire employees on the basis of experience and talent. Underlying these overt abilities is the human information processing system, which exceeds any computer program in terms of the ability to apply knowledge and perceive events in a flexible way.

From an organizational point of view, the cost/benefits must be weighed with these arguments in mind. Of course, there are limitations that should also be considered given such an approach. As noted above, the goal of automation is to facilitate analysis in terms of efficiency and rapidity. Greater integration of the analyst may, in the short-term at least, not appear to be as cost effective. Furthermore, funding would be needed for basic research relating to the issues discussed above. Undoubtedly, this creates front-end costs that may not immediately translate to increased profits. It is the belief of these authors, however, that long-term benefits would compensate for these short comings. First, development of an interdisciplinary approach between cognitive researchers in academia, for example, and individuals in applied areas of business could create an infrastructure of cooperation that could conceivably be quite beneficial from both intellectual and economic standpoints (e.g., effective application of research monies by R & D divisions). Secondly, successful implementation of optimal DM approaches (in our view, analyst-driven) by an organization could enhance profits over the long-term due to efficient analysis and interpretation of data in an ever increasingly complex and competitive global market.

Our argument, from a cognitive perspective, is that it is more likely that interesting trends in data would be identified by the analyst as opposed to an automated program. If one also considers such ill-defined concepts as insight or creativity, it becomes evident that the potential of the analyst should not be underestimated. Rather the analyst should be the user of a powerful, but ultimately subordinate tool (the analysis program). In future research endeavors it is likely that the human information processing system can serve as a point of reference when considering the role of the analyst in DM and what benefit this role may bring to the process.

REFERENCES

Ashcraft, M. (2006). Cognitive Psychology: An introduction. *Cognition* (4th ed., pp. 1-33). Upper Saddle River, NJ: Prentice Hall.

Atkinson, R. C., & Shiffrin, R. M. (1971). The control of short-term memory. *Scientific American, 225,* 82-90.

Baddeley, A. (1992). Working Memory. *Science, 255,* 556-559.

Balota, D. A., Ferraro, F. R., & Connor, L. T. (1991). On the early influence of meaning in word recognition: A review of the literature. In P. J. Schwanenflugel (Ed.), *The Psychology of word meanings* (pp. 187-222). Hillsdale, NJ: Earlbaum.

Churchman, C. W. (1971). *The design of inquiring systems: Basic concepts of systems and organizations.* New York: Basic Books.

Eisenhauer, M., Hoffman, B., & Kretschmer, D. (2002). *State of Art Human Computer Interaction.* Retrieved February 18, 2007, from Telematica Institute, Giga Mobile Web Site: https://doc.telin.nl/dscgi/ds.py/GetRepr/File-25715/html

Field, A. P. (2005). Regression. *Discovering Statistics Using SPSS.* (2nd ed.). (pp. 143-218). London: Sage.

Fayyad, U. (n.d.). Data Mining and Knowledge Discovery. *DMKD Journal, 1(1).* Retrieved February 22, 2007, from http://research.microsoft.com/research/datamine/vol1-1/editorial3.htm

Locker, L., Simpson, G. B., & Yates, M. (2003). Semantic neighborhood effects on the recognition of ambiguous words. *Memory and Cognition, 31,* 505-515.

Murray, J. D., Case, T. L., & Gardiner, A. B. (2005). Knowledge creation in inquiring organizations using KDD: Re-focusing research on the analyst. In J. Courtney, J.Haynes, & D. Paradice (Eds.), *Inquiring Organizations: Moving from knowledge management to wisdom* (pp. 133-153). Hershey, PA: Idea Publishing Group.

Posner, M. I., & Snyder, C. R. R. (1975). Facilitation and inhibition in the processing of signals. In P. M. A. Rabbitt & S. Dornic (Eds.), *Attention and Performance V* (pp. 669-682). New York: Academic Press.

Palmer, S. E. (1975). The effects of contextual scenes on the identification of objects. *Memory and Cognition, 3,* 519-526.

Pexman, P. M., & Lupker, S. J. (1999). Ambiguity and visual word recognition: Can feedback explain both homophone and polysemy effects? *Canadian Journal of Experimental Psychology,* 53, 323-334.

Schank, R. C., & Abelson, R. P. (1977). *Scripts, plans, goals, and understanding.* Hillsdale, NJ: Erlbaum.

Shneiderman, B. (2001). *Inventing Discovery Tools: Combining Information Visualization with Data Mining.* Retrieved March 6, 2007, from University of Maryland, Department of Computer Science Web site: http://hcil.cs.umd.edu/trs/2001-16/2001-16.pdf

Wilson, J. H. (2005). Correlational Data. *Essential Statistics.* (pp. 201-223). Upper Saddle River, NJ: Prentice Hall.

ENDNOTES

1 It should be noted as discussed in Murray et al. (2005) that human involvement could also at times lead to error in analysis. For example, data that are deemed by the analyst to be unimportant that are in fact of potential interest. Thus, as noted above, it is important to strike a proper balance between automaticity in the DM process and analyst centered activities as either have potential benefits as well as liabilities.

2 An analogy to statistics might be of use at this point. In building a regression model, computer based analysis can be used to identify important predictor variables based purely on statistical considerations (i.e., the strength of correlations). However, it may be ideal beyond an exploratory stage for the analyst to utilize theory as a guide in building the regression model (e.g., see Field, 2005 for discussion). In the theory-driven case, the analyst plays an active role in building the regression model as well as final interpretation of the results.

Chapter XXVI
Temporality and Knowledge Work

Johanna Shih
Hofstra University, USA

ABSTRACT

The hi-tech firms that predominate in Silicon Valley contain a large proportion of knowledge workers—employees with high levels of education and expertise. The region is subsequently a useful prism by which to explore the shift in the pace of work and ideologies of labor control. Engineers in Silicon Valley are a prototypical example of "knowledge workers;" they are valued for their ability to contribute to firms' competitive advantage via their expertise and innovation. This chapter reports on fifty four semi-structured interviews of high-skilled, white and Asian men and women engineers who worked in the hi-tech industry of Silicon Valley, focusing on the issue of work temporality. Temporality has long been understood as central to the labor process, and as inextricably linked to the mode of production. Here, I highlight the problematic aspects of the shift from the routinized schedule of "clock time", characterized by rigid temporal boundaries between work and home, and "project time," characterized by an erratic and increasing pace of work that appears to be largely unfettered by boundaries between private and work time.

INTRODUCTION

This chapter explores the temporal experiences of engineers in the hi-tech industry of Silicon Valley. Engineers in this region are a prototypical example of "knowledge workers", because they are valued for their ability to contribute to firms' competitive advantage via their expertise and innovation. While Silicon Valley has been the subject of intensive scrutiny, both popular press and academic research have primarily focused their analyses on how the particular economic structure of the region has contributed to the region's rapid growth. In contrast, relatively less attention has been paid to the experiences of the workers who, after all, undergird the region's economy. While important studies have documented the conditions faced by low skill, contingent and itinerant workers (Barley and Kunda, 2004; Carnoy, Castells and Benner 1997, Hossfeld 1988) the experiences of hi-skill workers have generally been assumed to be uniformly positive.

Here, I subject the work lives of hi-tech engineers to greater scrutiny, focusing in particular on their temporal experiences. Three related questions are explored. First, how is the pace of work organized, and what factors shape it? Second, why do hi-skilled workers comply with an increasingly hectic work schedule? Third, how do the demands of work impact upon other temporal worlds of engineers?

TEMPORALITY AND MANAGERIAL IDEOLOGIES OF CONTROL DURING INDUSTRIALIZATION

Temporality has long been understood as central to the labor process, and as inextricably linked to the mode of production. For example, in an agricultural based economy, the pace of work can be characterized as seasonal. In contrast, the emergence of large factories during industrialization brought about a linear and rigid sense of time embodied by the clock, where workers' time was "bought" and thus controlled by and subject to manipulation by owners (Mumford 1934, Thompson 1993). The inculcation of clock time was critical for capitalists, because it allowed them to synchronize workers to the coordination requirements of technologies in mass production, and also allowed them to obtain greater control over workers by creating increasingly rigid steps and specifications for the labor process that must be met within fixed units of time. By exercising minute control over the labor process, productivity gains, and thus, capital accumulation were achieved (Thrift 1990). Clock time was thus part of the larger project of industrialization that transferred the control of production from craftsmen to managers (Braverman 1974).

Divested of their autonomy, workers may still, of course, resist, by slowing down the pace of production (Burawoy 1979; Roy 1952). Thus labor theorists have detailed the transformation of managerial ideologies from a direct and open form of "simple" authority (Edwards, 1979) to ideologies that emphasized cooperation, posing workers' and managers' interests as either the same, or at least mutually beneficial. Starting with Frederick Taylor's strategy of "scientific management" that depicted workers and managers as partners in increasing productivity efficiency, to the human relations model of Elton Mayo and Chester Barnard, who believed that organizations could satisfy individuals' need to be part of a larger collective and that managers should shoulder the responsibility of "taking care" of their workers, there was a shift towards understanding how compliance is obtained internally. Similarly, Edwards (1979) argued that the development of "structural or bureaucratic control" was important towards securing compliance, because authority is vested in the "rules of the company", rather than any one individual.

Bureaucratic control thus equates workers' interests with the interests of the company, building incentives via an internal labor market that rewards employees for demonstrating "desirable" work traits and creating organizational cultures that socialize workers into identifying with their companies. Whyte's (1956) "organization men" are thus created—workers who replace their individual identities with collective, organizational identities. Furthermore, the concept of a "career" became central to employees' experiences, creating a stake in the reproduction of the industrial order, since their own rewards are dependent on the stability of this structure (Zussman, 1985). Ironically, we come full cycle, because what potentially saves individuals from being completely consumed is the organization of work around the clock, which distinguished personal time from work time (Zerubavel 1981, 1979). This split has the potential to protect "the modern individual from being entirely 'swallowed' by what Coser has called 'greedy institutions'" (Zerubavel 1981, p. 166). Recent studies, however, have documented that white collar workers are not protected by "clock time", but rather are increasingly working longer hours with less vacation or leisure time (Schor, 1991), and are subjected to "normative" control via strong organizational cultures (Kunda, 1992).

THE POST-INDUSTRIAL ERA: TEMPORALITY, IDEOLOGIES OF CONTROL AND KNOWLEDGE WORKERS

The post-industrial era is characterized by a shift towards specialization, innovation and customization. Piore and Sabel (1984) argued that the shift was a response to a change in consumption patterns that arose with the improvement in the technologies of communication (and the advent of "real time"). Given the more ephemeral tastes of consumers, mass production using expensive, rigid machinery became less profitable, especially within the context of rising international competition. Silicon Valley's hi-tech industry exemplifies this emerging type of knowledge-driven economy, where organizations are reliant on knowledge or expertise to achieve high "value added" in products and services. Thus the hi-tech firms that predominate in Silicon Valley contain a large proportion of knowledge workers—employees with high levels of education and expertise. The region is subsequently a useful prism by which to explore the shift in the pace of work and ideologies of labor control.

There are two important changes to highlight. First, as an archetype of flexible specialization (Saxenian, 1990), one of the ways in which Silicon Valley is able to adapt quickly to the global marketplace is by creating a "flexible" workforce characterized by a high proportion of contingent workers (Kunda, Barley and Evans 2002; Barley and Kunda, 2004) and fluid organizational boundaries. This weakens the "contract" between employees and employers, such that employers no longer believe it is their responsibility to "take care" of their workers, and individuals are expected to be responsible for maintaining their own careers. The result is a growing proportion of part time and temporary workers, and more generally a labor force that "job hops" frequently.

Second, in contrast to mass production, profit is highly dependent upon innovation. Knowledge workers thus hold a crucial position in the firms, as their knowledge work—the intellectual skills and creativity they bring towards developing a service or product, is one of the means of production (Drucker 1993) of the firm. Take, for example the development of the personal computer: high profit in computer hardware companies is dependent upon the ability of their engineers to design faster and cheaper chips. Another example is the proliferation of MP3 devices—each version adding yet another function that whet consumers' appetites. It is also worth noting that knowledge work is generally autonomous in nature. Unlike mass production, where the steps for production are elaborated and dictated to workers, the process of production for design work, however, is achieved primarily without specific instructions from managers. In other words, engineers work autonomously in using their intellectual skills towards achieving a goal.

So how do these two shifts—the flexible workforce that de-links workers with organizations, and the autonomous nature of knowledge work mean for the experiences of hi-skill workers? I turn now to the case of Silicon Valley to explore these questions.

BACKGROUND: SILICON VALLEY'S HI-TECH INDUSTRY

The region known as Silicon Valley is located in Northern California and encompasses more than 1,300 square miles and 15 cities. Bounded by Palo Alto in the North, Milpitas in the East, and Gilroy in the South, it is home to cities well known for hi-tech development such as Cupertino, Sunnyvale, and Santa Clara. While Santa Clara County is at the heart of Silicon Valley, development has also spread into the neighboring counties of Alameda and San Mateo. Once an agricultural center, in fact, the "prune capital" of America, the origins of hi-tech development in this region are rooted in the development of the microelectronics and then the semi-conductor industries. Silicon Valley became the spotlight of international attention in the 1980's when its hi-tech economy achieved a turnaround in the nation-wide industrial recession, striking a path that was markedly different from other hi-tech regions such as Boston's Route 88 (Saxenian, 1994). In doing so, it became the community to imitate because it appeared to represent a model that could succeed in the face of growing international competition. Within a number of years, the area's hi-tech economy became one of the fastest growing in the nation, was host to one fifth of the nation's top hi-tech firms, and had wage rates that were 60% above the national average (Markoff, 1999). The region also drew considerable investment capital. In the first quarter of 1999, investors poured well over one billion dollars into the valley (Markoff, 1999). It became a public phenomenon as well, as "valley watchers" told stories of the seemingly boundless riches that the industry could bestow on any individual with talent, ingenuity and dedication.

Researchers widely viewed Silicon Valley's economic structure-- characterized by flexible and decentralized organizational structures, specialized firms, and dense and overlapping networks--as critical to its success as a leader in hi-tech innovation (Rogers and Larsen, 1984; Packard, 1996; Saxenian, 1994). Flexible specialization was viewed as the antithesis of production in the "Fordist" state, with its accompanying bureaucratic and hierarchically structured organizations (Harvey, 1989:147). Flexible specialization, in contrast to mass production, is a "strategy of permanent innovation: an accommodation to ceaseless change, rather than an effort to control it." (Piore and Sabel, 1984:17)

Between March 1999 and January 2001, I conducted fifty four semi-structured interviews of high-skilled, white and Asian men and women engineers who worked in the hi-tech industry of Silicon Valley. With the exception of four interviews, the data were collected before the "internet bust" of late 2000. Interviewees were chosen using a snowball method. Initial respondents were located from a number of sources, including contacts I garnered from attendance at specialised engineering society functions, solicitation of professors at major universities in Taiwan and India for referrals to graduates they sent abroad, an ad in an alumni magazine, and referrals from acquaintances. Interviews typically ranged from one to two hours, and occurred primarily at interviewees' workplaces. They were audio taped, and fully transcribed.

All respondents had college degrees, and half had advanced graduate degrees. Thirty-two of the respondents were women. Nineteen of the respondents were Chinese/Taiwanese, nineteen were white, thirteen were Indian, two were Filipino, and one was Vietnamese. Twenty-four of the respondents were U.S. born (including all of the whites); the remainder were foreign born. The average age of the respondents was 36.3, which approximates the average age of high-skilled workers in Silicon Valley (Alarcon 1999). The respondents worked (or were entrepreneurs) at 39 different firms, representing both larger, well established organizations and smaller firms or start-ups. However, the majority of the respondents had worked in the past for both established and newer firms, and almost all the respondents had worked for more than one company. The average number of years in the work force for respondents was over eleven years.

The interview schedule was divided into three sections designed to elicit information on three domains: the respondents' career trajectory, their perceptions of gender and ethnic inequality in job hiring and mobility in the hi-skilled sector of Silicon Valley, and their experiences with work-life balance with respect to the pace of work in the region. These were semi-structured interviews—with the exception of demographic questions, all questions were open ended. As the interviews proceeded, I identified main coding and conceptual themes, wrote memos that facilitated the analysis of the data, and adapted some of the initial questions on the interview schedule to reflect the findings from the data. This follows the procedures of Glaser and Strauss' influential constant comparison method of qualitative data analysis, where data, findings, and theory occur in a continuous feedback loop. Indeed, the findings that form the basis of this chapter were unexpected and emerged from the respondents' answers, and I have documented that analytical and methodological "trail" (along with two other examples from this project) in another paper (Shih, 2007).

THE ORGANIZATION OF WORK FOR ENGINEERS IN SILICON VALLEY

In contrast to this linear and fixed conception of time described by industrial sociologists, engineers in Silicon Valley typically describe their work-time as organized not by the clock, but by the project they are on. This was exemplified to me when respondents could not answer what I viewed as a standard question about the average hours worked per week. They explained that their hours varied widely, from 30 hours a week to one hundred, because work was guided by the cycle or stage of the project they were working on. The length of a project (for example, designing a more efficient version of a microprocessor, creating a piece of voice technology, producing a more effective cooling system for a personal computer, and developing new educational software) can vary anywhere from three months to a year, and the project deadline coupled with coordination of work within project groups organizes work time. In this manner, work-time is organized in a cyclical fashion, where the beginnings of a project are typically characterized by relatively fewer hours and a relaxed pace of work, which then escalates rapidly towards the end of the project, which is described as hectic and breathless.

A typical explanation of the variation of work hours that can occur throughout one project cycle was given by this software architect. She says, "Usually, the cycle, there are ups and downs, and at the end it always gets crunchy... longest crunch time I had was 4 months and I was so burned...one week I had a 100 hour week, it was really bad, pulled a couple of all nighters. Then you have to slow down for a while because you just can't keep it up. Sometimes its really low though, at 30 hours."

The uneven pace of work reflects the fact that engineers are typically given assignments, but are expected to accomplish their tasks with little guidance from their managers. This type of managerial organization is exemplified by William Hewlett's description of Hewlett-Packard's "management by objective." Hewlett writes that it is "a system in which overall objectives are clearly stated and agreed upon, and which gives people the flexibility to work toward those goals in ways they determine best for their own areas of responsibility." (1996:153) Hewlett-Packard pioneered this type of management in Silicon Valley, and it characterizes most companies in the region today. One can note that this shift in the organization of work is not merely philosophical: the actual work and the tools used for work (computer or computer-based) in hi-tech are inherently autonomous, since they are knowledge intensive and conceptual in nature (Piore and Sabel, 1984). Even if one were to attempt to set guidelines and procedures, the rapid change in products and services in hi-tech would make this a fairly impossible task.

Respondents' description of their daily work activities depict a relatively informal work process, and confirm that engineers of all levels have a large degree of autonomy both in terms of how they do their work, and also how a project is completed. Respondents indicate that "there is a lot of flexibility in terms of what we can do," and that the organization is structured into work groups including people of varying levels, which are "very informal" and where "everyone gives input." Most believe that more "bureaucracy will ultimately slow a company down" and agree that there is "not much hierarchy" at work.

Respondents also say that there is little formal training or guidance. For instance, Alix, an immigrant Chinese engineer says that the norm is "training by doing, hands on, so I'm assigned to a project and start doing it, if I don't know something and there's someone in the group or company that has experience then I ask that person. If it's a new technology, then (I go to) outside sources." As this comment suggests, in-house help is often insufficient, so employees use their own network resources to figure out a technological problem, calling up a past professor or mentor, or acquaintances and friends who might have expertise in the area in question. In this sense, employees appear to be more "on their own", independently seeking solutions to achieve their project goals.

The organization of work via projects were generally satisfying to the engineers I spoke with because it allowed them to have significant autonomy to apply their knowledge and skills set to a problem. This process, and the feeling of ownership over the product, was typically described as fulfilling and interesting. However, the clear downside to the use of "project-time" versus clock time is that it unleashed the number of hours a high-skill worker might have to devote to completing a project. Take, for example, the description of this respondent of her first month at a start up. She says about when she first started:

"They really needed a demo to go on the sales calls to venture capitalists....so my first job was basically to get a demo together, build a demo which basically displays the technology. So we have to build it, one of the sexiest pitches is airplane delays for example—if your flight was delayed a certain amount of time, wouldn't you want a phone call? So anyway, showing that this is technically possible. Someone can do the voice technology here, so I work with him on how to integrate the web. My other charter was to work with a more junior person and get him up to speed. So we built something which was pretty successful at showing what we could do. We started in april and we had something to show in under a month, a few weeks, and I was working pretty late hours because I hadn't worked on the latest version of this and was trying to teach the other woman and had all these interruptions and I was pretty much working all the time (laughs)! I would get in at 9 or 10, maybe a little earlier, and I would leave at, ugh, sometimes it was 5 AM, sometimes it was 2AM, 3AM five days a week plus I would come in on weekends too but wouldn't stay until 5 AM. So it was pretty intense."

As this description indicates, a "charter" or a "goal" is rather loosely defined, in this case, building a demonstration to present to venture capitalists, and it was up to her and her project group to coordinate and accomplish the tasks. This included the work of informally training others in the group, and resulted in what was rather typical among respondents' descriptions—a hectic end of a project cycle. Thus the organization of work by the project, rather than by a 9-5 routine of clock time, enables managers to garner more hours of work from their employees. The porous division between work and home is also clearly enabled by advances in communication technology: respondents typically described checking emails every night and weekend, and working from home via telecommuting.

The lack of rigid temporal boundaries that protect private time is further exacerbated by the fact that knowledge work can happen "anywhere". For example, an engineer working on chip design says, "you know we are in the hi-tech business, so sometimes if you have a problem, it may take a couple days to figure it out, so even when I'm driving I'm still thinking about it!" Similarly, a hardware engineer notes, "nobody dictates a specific schedule, but you are trying to get the work done...you are pretty much tied to the email. If an emergency comes up, for instance, when we had a big review for an executive board meeting there are a lot of finalizing, so if the presentation is on Monday and if it's not done on Friday, you'll be on conference all weekend. It happens more than I like."

Furthermore, managers can easily manipulate the time engineers spent on work by simply shortening project deadlines. Matt, a senior network engineer, who works for a large networking organization, explains,

The nature of engineering is that it's imprecise, and so deadlines and schedules are all just best guesses about when it will be accomplished. So managers, they like to play head games with people. They say, okay, we need something done by this date, and then people feel constrained to really deliver by then, and then family just gets trashed... You can't deny that it works. You tell someone that it needs to be done in two months, and it takes six months or a year... So for a person who is really driven, they compromise everything.

As Matt notes, the fact that engineering is "imprecise" is key to the ability to manipulate deadlines. Since the work taken to achieve the goal is not specifically determined by managers and because the application of "knowledge" or "skills" to a particular problem is amorphously defined, managers can increase their time demands on workers by shortening project deadlines.

This "imprecise" nature of work is exacerbated in start-ups, where responsibilities are not well defined given the typically small number of initial employees. One entrepreneur explains "The biggest thing at a start up is that there is always more work to do than you can...The other thing is that it is very informal, not many processes, informal networks are very very very strong in startups....there are no established procedures or rules, if there is a problem you just get people together in a room and let it happen."

Chen, an Chinese immigrant engineer who had recently become vice president of a new start-up company when he spoke with me exemplifies how start-ups in particular can co-opt the time of employees. When I met him on a Sunday afternoon at his sparsely furnished company, he and many of his employees were busy working, and it is evident that this is a regular routine. He was a gregarious and friendly man, but when I asked him what hours he asks of his employees, he skirts the question by exclaiming "Whatever it takes!" When I asked him to clarify, he is initially evasive and then answers,

I am looking for a person who is committed to the company, who is committed to the project, who believes that the idea can really take off in the marketplace. In terms of absolute time commitment, I don't have any numbers. You can work like... in this day and age, it's very hard to tell when people are working and when people are not working.

This description effectively describes the substitution of an objective work schedule bound by clock time with the subjective demand for commitment when work is typically organized around projects or goals. Chen further explained,

Over here, [it's] like teaching my daughter to swim, just dump [her] into the water! You must be independent and motivated. I always tell my engineers, you are your own managers. There is a pile of work on the table and I don't want to give you the deadline to finish the work because the work is almost infinite at this point in time so why don't you just dive in, and find your own work and deadlines and it's up to you to figure out how to swim.

Chen's expectation that workers must be their own managers is significant, reflecting the burden placed on employees in the absence of rigid temporal boundaries and clearly elaborated responsibilities. He has effectively created a situation where the time dedicated to work is limitless. And because workers are managing their own time, the time put in becomes interpreted as a show of commitment.

PROJECT CYCLES IN THE AGE OF THE HI-TECH GOLD RUSH

Of course the shortening of project deadlines by managers and the breathless pace at start-ups is not simply motivated by some Machiavellian desire to extract more labor from employees. Rather, the hi-tech sector is embedded within a global hi-tech market that is rapidly developing. In this situation where time to market is key and where "things get obsolete very fast", managers and entrepreneurs are externally pressured to develop new products and services at a quickening pace. Perlow's study (1999) of a software engineering group has documented how a shortened development cycle leads to extraordinary time pressures. As a senior manager I spoke with notes, "the issue of current engineering is how to speedily get the product from concept to market," while a successful entrepreneur notes that "the high tech stuff is moving fast enough, you can't just take it as 8-5, and I'm not going to think about work after 5 o clock." Since the growth of hi-tech is not limited by material goods, but instead includes the development of services and the "space" of the internet, these are "boundless markets" to conquer (Harvey, 1989).

That the hi-tech economy relies on and capitalizes on being able to respond and define market needs is reflected in a conversation I had with an entrepreneur of a start up, which began with his explaining to me in detail the service niche they will fulfill is to build a platform that can facilitate the collaboration needed to customize a product. He then says,

"So it may be easy now for me to describe to you, but just a couple minutes ago I was in a meeting trying to decide what kind of niche we should fill. To start a company you have to constantly move around things to figure out what exactly the market needs and what kinds of tools, applications you will develop to help. So that its not that nothing is on the paper, but its not concrete, we have to figure out how to do it. So that's why our company is exciting, we are much closer to the real market... it's like you and your friends and your whole group are going into war. You have to cover your area, if you cannot cover it... we'll get killed. So today's environment, the pressure is high."

His emphasis on being attuned to the market, and being able to respond quickly to the market underlines what is viewed as a strength of flexible specialization. But it also, as is evident, underlines the increasing pressure on workers.

Respondents were aware of the impact that the accelerating pace of hi-tech had on their work lives. Raj, an Indian software engineer who works at a mid sized company talked about upper managements' expectations:

These are unrealistic timelines... They are not set by product specifications, but what competitors are coming out with for the market, so it's really demanding. I mean, if a product should take ten

months to finish, there's often a six-month deadline, and you just have to finish it to meet the market…It's a gold rush scenario, which makes it different, I think, because there's also extra pressure on the company. It [comes from] much higher, from the investors…and that trickles down to the employees.

As Raj's comments suggest, the speed-up of the high-tech market sets deadlines for project cycles that are difficult for engineers to meet. Clearly, the "gold rush scenario," that is, the competition for market share, affects the rhythms of work, and this pressure from competition is refracted at several levels, from investors to management to employees.

In a similar account, Shelley, a senior design engineer at a microprocessor manufacturer, spoke about the impact of increasing competition in the high-tech industry and the subsequent escalating pace of development. She related its effect on project cycles, especially in "money maker" groups such as the one in which she worked.

In this business, the design cycle is getting shorter, shorter, shorter, shorter. You have to do more things in that time because, I mean, time to market, getting it out, quicker and quicker, better, faster, smaller. In the last eight years, the first projects, the cycle was this long [holds hands wide apart]. Now it's this long [holds hands much closer] but you have to do more, so it's like, really, cranking it out.

As Shelley noted, the design cycle is shaped by the demands of "time to market," a phrase meant to denote the amount of time one needs to design and develop a product for the market. In her particular field, microprocessors are quickly becoming "better, faster, smaller," and she and her colleagues are pressured by the heavy competition and increasing pace of innovation in the microprocessor market. As the pace of development in high-tech quickens, project deadlines shorten, increasing the pace of work in Silicon Valley.

In this situation, all time is potentially defined as work time, to the detriment of families and personal lives. This was mentioned by almost all the respondents. In one particularly stressful example, a white female engineer, who is married to a systems engineer explained that when she went into labor with her daughter, her husband was still at work at 2:30 in the morning. She called him at the lab to pick him up, and although he took only three days of paternity leave, he was told that he "wasn't reliable" when he returned, and was removed from the project. His boss explained to him that "you can spend time with your children when you're rich".

EVERYONE IS AN ENTREPRENEUR IN AN ENTERPRISE CULTURE

When I ask respondents why they agree to work the hours they do, they typically mentioned that financial incentives, specifically, stock options, tied them to the success of their companies. They said, for example, that "I have stock options in the company so I want it to do well obviously", that "all of us….are emotionally and financially tied to the futures of the company" or that "realistically I'm in a good position to capitalize…you can make a lot of money." In other words, the ubiquity of stock options, which directly links the company's success to workers' economic fortunes clearly drives workers. Of course, as the post-boom downturn has shown, this position is overly optimistic. Yet almost everyone I spoke with had the hope that perhaps he or she would be one of those who "made it," in part because most people knew of someone who was worth millions, at least on paper. This mood is exemplified by one respondent, who wryly noted about living in the region:

A lot is different, it changes you…being surrounded by people who make millions, if you're not doing that, well then something's wrong with you, you're doing something wrong. It's unspoken, but its definitely there. I mean, you think, my friend, today he's worth ten thousand, and then tomorrow he's worth ten million!"

However, while financial incentives were generally first acknowledged, respondents typically proceeded into more elaborate explanations of why they were willing to work at such a hectic pace that reflected their concerns about managing their career development, their identity as an engineer, or feeling a sense of accomplishment.

First, respondents repeatedly voiced the need to continually develop their skills and marketability, in part by taking "risks". This is in contrast, of course, to the Fordist organizational model where companies trained their employees, and dedication to the company was rewarded by moving up an internal labor market. Reflecting this shift, in response to a question about what determines career mobility, one senior manager of a major hardware company explains

I think to move up in this environment is different from my previous environment (at a construction engineering firm in the East Coast). In this one its more a function of contributions, being willing to take risks and perform....part of contribution is taking some risk, the assignments you take, whether they are secure or really on the edge, being in pilot manufacturing as opposed to volume manufacturing).

This perspective is confirmed in my conversation with a recruiter for one of the most successful companies in the region. When I ask him what characteristics he looks for in candidates, he says that they are looking for people who "demonstrate control of their career, rather than an applicant who has been in a job for 15 years as opposed to an applicant who has been at 3 different positions in 5 years who has grown. Its more ideal, (it's not) stability or loyalty."

Respondents' identity seems to revolve around the conception of themselves as continuously growing. Several engineers explained switching jobs because they felt they needed to "broader horizons". For example, a female engineer who specializes in artificial intelligence explained that she left her previous job because she was not learning anything new. At her current job, she "basically insisted that I get through the training, because I though it was important and thought I wasn't growing, wasn't learning more stuff. [At my previous job] I basically got stuck training them, rather than being trained to build up my technical skills. [My current job involves] an internet project which was a good move for me, because it was good for me to rebuild my technical skills."

Similarly, a mid level manufacturing engineer also says she left her previous job because she "had nothing to do." As she switched to a new job, she says "I was very specific about what I will be doing, what projects are there, who will I be responsible for, what are my day to day responsibilities. I made sure this was going to be something I liked". This type of consideration was reflected at all seniority levels. A junior engineer similarly explained that she carefully chose the company she is currently at because "they are very good in technology, they have very good engineers here so I think this will be a good place for me to learn....I feel I want to learn more before I go out and do it, and people are really smart here. In other words, respondents are aware that as knowledge workers, they had to maintain their marketability by continuously expanding their knowledge and skills base, and to have "an inventive mind".

Indeed, workers who do not "initiate" learning new skills can find themselves in a difficult position. A senior vice president at a major hardware firm talked matter-of-factly about letting go of forty percent of their staff when the company was experiencing financial difficulties, because their skills were in older, obsolescent technologies. He explained that while, in the past, people may have been able to spend their careers working on one type of technology, the current environment is quite different:

For many years technology did not change very fast so the person who was interested in technology could probably have their entire technical life working in that technology...Today in many fields, hardware and software, in the computer and biotech industry, things are advancing so well that the technological underpinnings change every couple [of] years. So if you are just in one technical discipline you may find yourself high and dry.

This executive's perspective reflects companies' relinquishing of responsibility for their workers and the expectation that employees should be self-reliant. He continued:

[The] thing in the valley is that it is not the company's responsibility, it's the individual's responsibility. The quid pro quo here is that in return for opportunity, the individual has to make choices, unless you want to go back to a slower, more idyllic time where the company takes care of you...So the individual has to take responsibility.

What these engineers describe reflect an increased emphasis on individual performance and contribution, which is also reflected in the increasing norm of merit-based pay (Kanter 1995), instead of pay that is based on rank or seniority. In the context of Silicon Valley, employees are encouraged to be "entrepreneurial" in their work by "adding value" through new ideas. Harvey writes, for instance, that flexible specialization shifts what is valuable in workers, it "...has put a premium on 'smart' and innovative entrepreneurialism, aided and abetted by all of the accoutrements of swift, decisive, and well informed decision making (Harvey, 1989:157)." Given the emphasis on innovation in the rapidly developing hi-tech industry, high-skill workers are thus expected to make individual contributions.

The fact that it is the employees' task to "prove their worth" to the company and to remain marketable, without any long-term expectations in return, reflects the de-linking of individuals and organizations, at the very least on a psychological level. This is a marked departure from a human relations model (Bendix 1956; Perrow 1972; Barley and Kunda 2000) of managerial ideology, which views membership in an organization as inherently beneficial to humans and managers' responsibilities as creating collectivity within organizations. In Silicon Valley, neither appears to owe the other side any promises, and each is understood as motivated by maximizing their own outcomes.

THE OUTCOME: DISRUPTED AND DESYNCHRONIZED TEMPORAL WORLDS

The stories of these respondents illustrate how the absence of clock time, the autonomy of knowledge work, and hi-tech's intimate link to global marketplace, the de-linking of organizations and workers, and an entrepreneurial culture collectively blurred the boundaries between work time and private time. Here, I consider the outcome of this blurring by exploring how the encroachment of work time disrupts other temporal worlds that the respondents inhabited. Perlow's (1998) study of a software engineering group has documented how time pressures at work could impact upon spouses and on family time. Here, I broaden "private time" to reflect a multiplicity of temporal worlds that include bodily rhythms, family time, and the rhythms of social relationships.

In Silicon Valley, the cyclical aspect of projects, and in particular, the "burn out" reported by respondents suggests that the routine of care for physical bodies is being displaced. Take, for instance, the comments of Shelley, the engineer I quoted earlier, who observed that project cycles were shortening. As she talked to me about these project cycles, her vivacious manner diminished as she lost her composure and became quite upset.

I've been in this industry for eight years. I've worked the long hours. I've worked the grind, I've given a period of my life to this company as I'm sure you have heard others say...Basically, I remember being young [laughs] and getting here at 7, say, outta here 9, 10, 11, 12, 1, okay, and doing this for prolonged periods of times for extensive deadlines, for big projects and stuff. So you can imagine that doing this for a number of projects, it can take its toll.

Shelley is an engineer in her early thirties, yet the fact that she no longer saw herself as "young" and that she experienced work as giving a "period of my life" to the company reflects the physical toll taken by the demands of project cycles and the tremendous growth of the high-tech industry.

In another example, Caren, a senior research and development engineer, spoke about her experiences in a large hardware manufacturing company that she had just left, and about the prioritization of work over any physical needs. A talkative, bright woman, she spoke about the consuming nature of her work: "When I worked at [this company], I woke up thinking about work, and I went to bed thinking about work. It was totally consuming and there were very few moments when I wasn't thinking about work." Caren continued to describe its demands:

[My company is] very demanding in that this is a highly competitive environment. So if you leave at 5 or 5:30, you feel you are sneaking out! You feel "this is going to reflect on me" in this way, so I would work until 8:30...I just could never say, "You know what, I can't do that because I need to rest." It just didn't seem like the right thing to say there. You were admitting to physical problems...[My company] is a place that depends on people being there when they are supposed to be. It's a manufacturing environment—if something goes wrong, you are there; you are there until the problem is fixed. You know they will pay you for it, they will praise you for it, but if you are not there, you can bet you will be...Because your job is to be there, and a lot of times at [company] your job should come before your life.

The fact Caren felt that it was not "okay" to admit to physical problems suggests that a stratification of temporal worlds—where the time demands of work, where leaving at 5 is "sneaking off"—takes priority over the demands of the body. Caren eventually left her company because she could no longer face the physical toll and opted to become a technical writer at another company where she could have a well-defined work schedule.

The erratic nature of project cycles also disrupted social relationships, including relationships with family members. After answering my question of why people agree to work such long hours, an engineer in her thirties, for example, spoke of how the region breeds people who are young and single:

That's what people talk about. We don't have a life. We don't have free time, you just go home and sleep, and on weekends you just recuperate, or you have to work. And a lot of people travel...and that takes a lot out of you. It's nomadic, people traveling all the time, so there is no home base. It's very hard to maintain a relationship that way.

Alex, an engineer who has worked for both an established company and now a start-up and whose wife stayed at home to care for their children, commented somewhat regretfully about the loss of his regular interaction time with his family.

I've seen a significant difference since joining a start-up in terms of balance. I used to spend a lot of time with my kids before I started my own start-up, and what I noticed, just a month ago I think, is that, when I come home and try to pick up things with my kids from where we left off, that the thing would be gone in their minds already. Because you know, in the past I would have daily contact with them. Now my contact has gone down to once a week or even sometimes not even that much. And the kids just got used to me not being around. And in a way it's good because they've become independent and at this age it's good for them. But four to five years from now, they'll be gone, and I'll probably remember that I had this opportunity to spend this time with them and I didn't take it.

His example reflected the suspension of interaction time with family due to the erratic and exhaustive temporal rhythms of work.

One can note here, that it is likely that the pace of work might have precluded my interviewing those who have primary child care responsibilities, since the work of rearing children typically requires a more regular schedule. Indeed, several female engineers noted that their female colleagues in their 30s seemed very likely to leave the labor market, either to care for children in the home, or to segue into another occupation that has more well defined work schedules.

CONCLUSION

In this chapter, I considered how the organization of work via projects impacts on the experiences and lives of hi-tech engineers. Engineers represent the burgeoning numbers of "knowledge workers" whose intellectual skills contribute to their firms' competitive advantage. Here, I highlighted the problematic aspects of the shift from the routinized schedule of "clock time", which is characterized by rigid temporal boundaries between work and home, and "project time", which is characterized by an erratic and increasing pace of work that appears to be largely unfettered by boundaries between private and work time.

The organization of work around projects reflects the autonomous nature of knowledge work, as well as a marked emphasis on individual performance (rather than "time put in"). The nature of this type of work enabled managers to demand increasing amounts of work from engineers, both because technologies of communication infiltrate the home and because much of the intellectual component of the project could happen "anywhere". Furthermore, managers could easily pressure workers to put in more hours by shortening the project cycles, a common practice in the hi-tech industry. Thus, in the same way the flexibly organized economies are well suited to adapt to the vicissitudes of consumer tastes, engineers' pace of work was thus linked to the escalating rhythms of the global capitalist economy. These findings complement research on itinerant hi-skilled workers in Silicon Valley (Barley and Kunda, 2004; Evans et al (2004). Barley and Kunda (2004) have found that in contrast to the optimistic view that hi-skilled contractors could use the market to achieve greater flexibility over their time, these workers instead work longer hours than employees, and try to minimize the "down time" between jobs.

Workers comply with this escalating pace both because stock options link their fortunes directly with those of their companies (particularly in start-up firms), but also because the region espouses an individualist ideology that sees workers as entrepreneurs of their own careers. This ideology functions as an effective mode of control because it posits this labor as being in the worker's own interest, as an entrepreneurial activity rather than one embedded within relations of control. Thus unlike organization men, who could count on the paternalistic care taking of their companies, engineers in Silicon Valley were driven by their desire to remain marketable and their identity as engineers, continuously looking for ways to develop their knowledge base and skills.

There is clearly a downside to this story. In Silicon Valley, linking workers to the rhythms of the global capitalist market does not simply limit personal time. Rather, their erratic and escalating nature disrupted or precluded other temporal worlds that respondents inhabit. As Larry Ellison, CEO of Oracle, has suggested, it seems to have become a "Darwinian capitalism" out there, a survival of the fittest, or perhaps the survival of those who can subsist with the least amount of sleep.

REFERENCES

Alarcon, R. (1999). Recruitment Processes Among Foreign Born Engineers and Scientists in Silicon Valley. American Behavioral Scientist 42(9), 1381-1397.

Barley, S., & Kunda, G. (2000). Design and devotion: Surges of rational and normative ideologies of control in managerial discourse. In K. Grint (Ed.), *Work and society* (pp. 303-342). Malden, MA: Blackwell Publishers.

Barley, S., & Kunda G. (2004). *Gurus, warm bodies and hired guns: Itinerant experts in the knowledge economy.* Princeton: Princeton University Press.

Bendix, R. (1956). *Work and authority in industry.* Berkeley: University of California Press.

Braverman, H. (1974). *Labor and monopoly capital.* New York: Monthly Review Press.

Burawoy, M. (1979). *Manufacturing consent.* Chicago: University of Chicago Press.

Carnoy, M., Castells, M., & Benner, C. (1997). Labor markets and employment practices in the age of flexibility: A case study of Silicon Valley. *International Labor Review, 136*, 27-48.

Drucker, P. (1993). *Post-Capitalist Society.* New York: Harper Business.

Edwards, R. (1979). *Contested terrain.* New York: Basic Books.

Evans, J. A., Kunda, G., & Barley, S. (2004). Beach time, bridge time, and billable time: The temporal structure of technical contracting. *Administrative Science Quarterly, 49*, 1-38.

Harvey, D. (1989). *The conditions of post modernity.* Oxford: Basil Blackwell.

Hossfeld, K. (1988). *Divisions of labor, divisions of lives: Immigrant women workers in Silicon Valley.* Dissertation, University of California at Santa Cruz.

Kanter, R. M. (1995). *When giants learn to dance.* New York: Simon and Schuster.

Kunda, G. (1992). *Engineering Culture: Control and Commitment in a High-Tech Corporation.* Philadelphia: Temple University Press.

Kunda, G., Barley, S., & Evans, J. (2002). Why Do Contractors Contract? The Experience of Highly Skilled Technical Professionals in a Contingent Labor Market. *Industrial and Labor Relations Review, 55*(2), 234-261.

Markoff, J. (1999). Boom Mind-Set Deeply Etched in Chip Capital. *New York Times*, June 16.

Mumford, L. (1934). *Technics and civilization.* New York: Harcourt, Brace and Company.

Packard, D. (1995). *The HP Way: How Bill Hewlett and I Built Our Company.* New York: Harper Business.

Perlow, L. (1998)."Boundary Control: The Social Ordering of Work and Family Time in a High-tech Corporation. *Administrative Science Quarterly, 43*(2, 328-357.

Perlow, L. (1999). The time famine: toward a sociology of time. *Administrative Science Quarterly, 44*, 57-81.

Perrow, C. (1972). *Complex organizations: A critical essay.* Glenview, IL: Scott, Foresman and Company.

Piore, M., & Sabel, C. (1984). *The second industrial divide: Possibilities for prosperity.* New York: Basic Books.

Rogers, E., & Larsen, J. (1984). *Silicon Valley fever.* New York: Basic Books.

Roy, D. (1952). Quota restriction and goldbricking in a machine shop. *American Journal of Sociology, 57,* 427-442.

Saxenian, A. (1994). *Regional advantage.* Cambridge: Harvard University Press.

Schor, J. (1991). *The Overworked American.* New York: Basic Books.

Thompson, E. P. (1993). Time, work-discipline and industrial capitalism. In E. P. Thompson, *Customs in common* (pp. 352-403). New York: The New Press.

Thrift, N. (1990). Owners' time and own time: The making of a capitalist time consciousness, 1300-1800. In J. Hassard (Ed.), *The sociology of time.* New York: St. Martin's Press.

Whyte, W. (1956). *The organization man.* New York: Simon and Schuster.

Zerubavel, E. (1979). *Patterns of time in hospital life: A sociological perspective.* Chicago: University of Chicago Press.

Zerubavel, E. (1981). *Hidden rhythms.* Chicago: University of Chicago Press.

Zussman, R. (1985). *Mechanics of the middle class.* Berkeley: University of California Press.

KEY TERMS

Flexible Specialization: (Also known as flexible production, or flexibly organized economies). It is a form of economic organization characterized by decentralized and fluid organizational structures, designed to adapt rapidly to variations in consumer demands. Flexible specialization is viewed as a shift away from the mass production and relatively rigid organizational hierarchies of the Fordist era.

Project Time: refers to the organization of time at work via project cycles, which are cyclical in nature.

Silicon Valley: The popular term for the hi-tech region in Northern California that is primarily centered in Santa Clara County.

Temporal Worlds: this term is intended to highlight the different (and non-linear) conceptions of time in individuals' lives. For example, temporality at work, that is, the experience of time at work, is organized differently from the experience of time at home, or in one's life course. It also highlights the question of whether these various temporal worlds can be synchronized.

Chapter XXVII
Knowledge Intensive Work in a Network of Counter-Terrorism Communities

Alice MacGillivray
www.4km.net, Canada

ABSTRACT

Knowledge management is often associated with the need for change and related shifts in ontologies, ways of knowing and ways of working. Combine the centuries-old debates about what defines knowledge with proposed paradigm shifts to become knowledge-oriented, focused on inter-relationships, and cognisant of the complex and voluntary nature of knowledge work, and there is bound to be controversy and ambiguity. However, knowledge management research and practice becomes more focused and less ambiguous when set in the context of an urgent need. This chapter describes a study of a Canadian public sector science initiative. The terrorist attacks of 9/11 catalyzed ripples of reflection and innovation over great distances. In Canada, the federal government initiated the Chemical, Biological, Radiological and Nuclear (CBRN) Research and Technology Initiative (CRTI) to enable learning and progress, using what is essentially a communities of practice model. CRTI established a knowledge management office, to help this network of communities generate, share and use tacit and explicit knowledge. Some aspects of the initiative were working better than others and I was asked to conduct research to explore how CRTI members understand their work in a complex, knowledge-rich environment. I collected data through interviews and observation, and used phenomenography: a qualitative methodology from Scandinavia, which reveals qualitatively different ways of understanding phenomena. Phenomenography is usually driven by the desire to improve something, rather than simply to deepen understanding. As part of the analysis, I used a model for understanding communities of practice that was developed by [then] Major Pete Kilner in his work with the internationally respected CompanyCommand community.

Participants who understood their work as complex and unpredictable tended to emphasize connections and relationships, focused on learning more than doing, spontaneously referenced all aspects of Kilner's model, saw knowledge as more of a flow than a thing, and were more satisfied with their individual and community effectiveness. This research had added value in that CRTI is considered successful and is being considered as a potential model for other science and technology work in the Canadian public service. The research has implications for knowledge-intensive work in complex environments and suggests that there is fertile ground for more qualitative research that integrates thinking from knowledge management and complexity thinking.

INTRODUCTION

Senior managers often initiate knowledge management work because issues or crises push them to think in new ways and to encourage their staffs to innovate and adapt. The terrorist attacks of 9/11 were one such crisis, which led to ripples of reflection and innovation far from the physical impacts of the planes. Canadian officials recognized the need to improve counter-terrorism capacity and capability and launched the Chemical, Biological, Radiological and Nuclear (CBRN) Research and Technology Initiative (CRTI) to enable learning and capacity-building. CRTI is now situated in a unit called the Centre for Security Science. They employ what is essentially a *communities of practice* model in which a threat type (such as radiological/nuclear) forms the domain of each community. Community members who work in different parts and levels of government interact in these communities to learn from each other, and they undertake projects that make sense to the members. The named leaders of these communities work without positional authority. When I conducted research in CRTI, there were four such communities. The original three were threat-based: chemical, biological and radiological/nuclear. The newer forensics community focused on front line response and procedures for gathering evidence so that it would stand up in a court of law. Since then, an explosives community—which was approved in principle at the time of the interviews—has been formalized, expanding the acronym to CBRNE. Members of these groups often refer to them as clusters, so I retain this term where it was used in direct quotes.

CRTI's knowledge management office helps this network of communities generate, share and use tacit and explicit knowledge. They have taken on initiatives as diverse as the development of a portal, support of scientific and social science research, and the organization of an annual symposium, the goal of which is "to provide a forum to share and exchange the knowledge created by CRTI partners and to learn about related allied work in CBRN" (*Proceedings of the 2006 CRTI Summer Symposium*).

CRTI knowledge management leader Susan McIntyre contacted me in 2005 when I was directing knowledge management graduate programs at Royal Roads University. She wanted to better understand why some aspects of CRTI were working better than others. She also relayed her interest in spanning disciplines and her desire to ground her work in theory.

Susan said the comments and case studies in my response whetted her appetite. I had written that the highly contextual nature of the work is what makes knowledge management so interesting. "Part of it is a function of the newness of the field; part of it is the complex and messy nature of human beings, organizational cultures and emergent needs." In 2006, our conversations gelled in the form of a research project to explore how CRTI members understood their work in a "complex, knowledge-rich environment."

SCOPE OF STUDY AND CHAPTER

In the full study, I focused on overlaps between and amongst the fields of knowledge management, leadership and complexity. They are intertwined in many ways. For example, knowledge—particularly tacit knowledge—is shaped by an individual's experience and context. Knowledge sharing is a voluntary activity inspired by context and enabled by trust. In knowledge-intensive work, the shift from a "things" mindset to a mindset of intangibles and human relationships typically involves leadership at many levels of an organization. The variables involved in individual experience, relationships, leadership, trust and context make knowledge-intensive work complex. I am using the term "complex" as used in complexity theory and thinking. These involve the study of environments in which there are many interacting entities, which exhibit emergence and where results are difficult to predict with any degree of accuracy. In this chapter, I am focusing primarily on the knowledge management sphere with some reference to overlaps with leadership and the complex, knowledge-intensive nature of CRTI work.

Knowledge Management Research

Knowledge management is often associated with the need for change and related shifts in ontologies, ways of knowing and ways of working. Combine the centuries-old debates about what defines knowledge with proposed paradigm shifts to become knowledge-oriented, focused on interrelationships, and cognisant of the complex and voluntary nature of knowledge work, and there is bound to be controversy. Verna Allee writes about the shifting foci of organizations in the industrial era from "plan, organize and control" to "vision, values and empowerment," and the further shift in the knowledge era to "emergence, integrity and relationships" (2003, p. 30). Simon Lelic outlines experts' perspectives on new generations of knowledge management, including Snowden's observation that context was gaining ground over

Figure 1. Scope of study

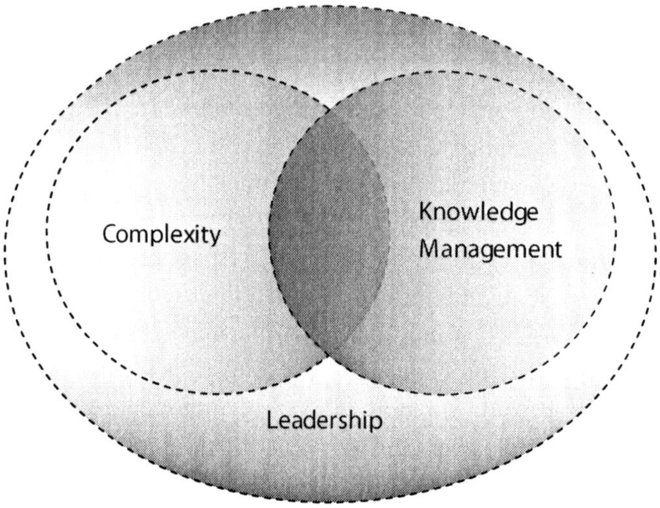

information distribution for decision support and McElroy's view that there is a shift from supply- to demand-oriented knowledge processing (2002). Snyder and Wenger write:

No formal structure can fully address problems that are too complex to predict or standardize. Moreover, these problems invariably require a configuration of disciplines and resources that are rarely contained in any one agency, level, or sector. This calls for the explicit cultivation of knowledge-based, boundary-crossing structures such as communities of practice to complement formal agency and program structures. (2003, p. title page)

These scholar-practitioners paint pictures of increasingly multi-faceted, dynamic knowledge landscapes. In a culture where uncertainty is to be eliminated, knowledge management looks bad, or at least immature.

Some authors have dealt with uncertainties and ambiguities by drawing firm boundaries around descriptors of knowledge or knowledge management and by developing associated models or processes (e.g., Firestone & McElroy, 2003; Koenig, 1996). Others have created conceptual landscapes that accommodate various definitions and descriptors (e.g., Davenport & Prusak, 1998; Rumizen, 2002; Wiig, 2002).

Knowledge management research is still in its infancy. A scan of papers in one peer-reviewed journal provides insights into the nature of the current literature. Figure 2 shows the types of papers, as defined by the authors and journal in the abstracts, in recent issues of the Emerald Journal of Knowledge Management. Papers in the "Other" category were—in order of frequency—literature reviews, general reviews, technical papers and one viewpoint paper.

Within the research paper category, there is a mixture of quantitative studies working towards prediction, qualitative studies working towards understanding and other papers in which the approach is not as clear cut. These papers frequently include reviews of literature or other documents, exploration of concepts and sometimes preliminary development work towards a model or framework. The breakdown of research paper types (the 58% pie wedge in Figure 2) is shown in Figure 3. For the quantitative and qualitative categories, the authors often stated this explicitly. If they did not, I used information they provided about method (a small number of in-depth interviews as evidence of qualitative work, for example) or next steps (the need for further statistical validation as evidence of quantitative work, for example.)

Few of the qualitative papers explicitly state a methodology or culture of inquiry; when they do, it is typically grounded theory or ethnography. So, based on this sample—*even when mixed method and action research projects are included*—fewer than 20% of all the papers in these issues are qualitative studies that might deepen our understanding of any aspect of knowledge management.

Furthermore, nine of the 129 papers reference complexity theory or science, and about half of those references were simply titles of papers in the reference list or brief mentions of complexity in the body of the paper. Similarly, of 570 knowledge management theses and dissertations in the ProQuest database, nine include "complexity

Figure 2. Types of papers in Journal of Knowledge Management, n=129

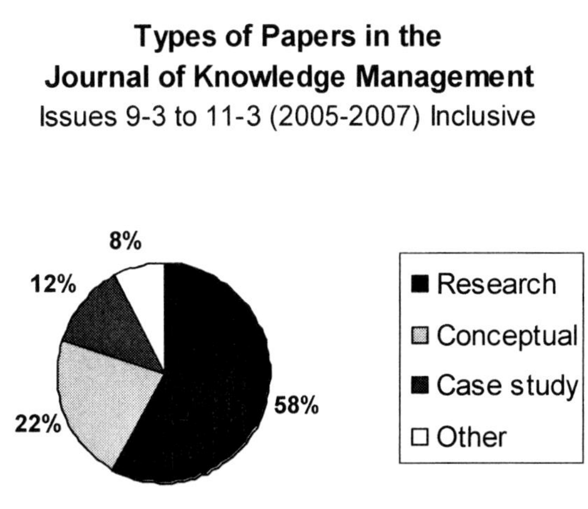

Figure 3. Types of research papers in Journal of Knowledge Management n=76

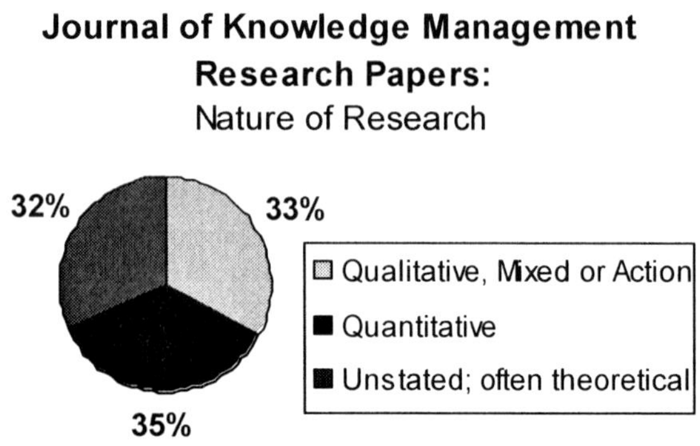

theory," "complexity science" or "complex adaptive system*" in the citation or abstract.

In other words, if these theses, dissertations and recent papers in the Journal of Knowledge Management are typical, we are still in the early stages of exploring how knowledge management and complexity inform each other and in using qualitative cultures of inquiry to deepen our understanding of work in complex, knowledge intensive environments. Because many papers are conceptual or theoretical and attempting to make sense of trans-disciplinary literature, scholarly work in knowledge management can appear ambiguous. Some practitioners prefer to rely on literature from fields that seem simpler and more predictable, and some academics adopt positivist views, hoping to find theories that can be applied in many varied contexts.

In my practitioner role, many knowledge management ambiguities fade in specific contexts. Such contexts are often shaped by challenges or crises, which catalyze pioneering efforts in the generation, sharing and use of knowledge. In the case of CRTI, scientists needed to learn about and from each other to increase counter-terrorism capability and capacity. Their outputs might include increased common knowledge, new knowledge, newly defined roles and responsibilities, intellectual capital, expanded networks and social capital, new vehicles for collaboration, and innovations such as new technologies and practices. In some cases, outputs would need to flow out well beyond the boundaries of CRTI into their home organizations, other groups, universities, first responders, the public, and so on. So there were uncertainties, but there was no need to debate—for example—whether the field of knowledge management includes the acquisition or creation of new knowledge. New knowledge was either needed or not, and tools and techniques for knowledge acquisition and generation would be used as and when needed.

PURPOSE OF RESEARCH

This research was driven by the Centre for Security Science Knowledge Management office and their need to better understand what was working well in the CRTI communities, what was working less well, and why, so that they could provide better support. From that practical perspective, I was exploring how individuals understood their work in the CRTI communities, and potential relationships between perceived effectiveness and literatures from complexity, knowledge management and leadership. As mentioned previously, this chapter focuses primarily on knowledge management.

METHODOLOGY

This research project uses phenomenography, which explores qualitatively different ways of understanding a phenomenon such as knowledge generation and sharing ("Phenomenography"). Like ethnography, it is considered qualitative, empirical and interpretive. Phenomenography is relatively young and there are debates about details of how to use it, so I will provide context for the decisions I made.

Marton and Pang (1999) explain that phenomenography does not have an *either/or* view of the world and respects the different ways in which our backgrounds and perceptions shape our understandings. It emerged in Sweden as a pragmatic methodology in the early 1970s through the work of Marton, Säljö, Dahlgren and Svensson (Bowden & Walsh, 2000; "Phenomenography"). Early applications grew from observations that some students learned better than others. It explored students' different ways of understanding a concept, with the goal of helping them learn more effectively. It has since been used in several continents to explore many topics and issues (Bowden & Walsh, 2000) including health care (Larsson, Holmström, & Rosenqvist, 2003) and organizational change (Wagner, 2006). It is an intriguing approach for work in complex systems, because of its systemic, non-dualist orientation and its recognition of diversity, which is important in complex systems (McKelvey, 2002; Michaels, 2002). Because CRTI wanted to support positive change, the action-oriented history of phenomenography was a good fit.

Phenomenographers usually collect data through interviews. Questions are very open-ended so that participants have the freedom to decide on the scope and focus of their responses (Bowden, 1996 citing Marton). Data are analyzed for patterns in ways of understanding. A way of understanding is the normal unit of analysis; individuals could span more than one. The coding approach resembles that of grounded theory in that researchers code, re-code and refine their framework over time. Inter-rater reliability is uncommon, because most experts agree that good researchers could work with participants to come to different, defensible conclusions about how to categorize ways of understanding (true to phenomenographic assumptions). Researchers should be transparent about how they create categories and illustrate them with quotes.

Work with about 15–20 participants (Sandberg, 2000; Wagner, 2006) usually achieves saturation. Sandberg's findings of workers' conceptions of competence at Volvo became repetitive after 15 participants. In this study, I interviewed each of 14 participants for about an hour, with the longest interview being an hour and a half. Because I adjusted some questions after the first interview, the first participant's responses are only included where the questions matched. Interview data were supplemented by observations during a week-long symposium.

Because phenomenography is a qualitative methodology—intended to deepen understanding more than to predict—it does not employ representative samples. Sampling in exploratory research is strategic (Palys, 1997); a diverse sample illuminates the variation that phenomenography seeks to reveal. If some ways of understanding are more effective than others, the categories become catalysts for dialogue about knowledge sharing and mobilization.

To select participants, I used a combination of purposeful sampling (more specifically intensity sampling (Palys, 1997)) by working with the CRTI Secretariat and snowball sampling to broaden out from the core of the network. My CRTI contact, Susan McIntyre, sent community participants a note about the research and provided me with a list of potential participants whom I contacted by electronic mail. She announced the study at the 2006 CRTI symposium in Ottawa-Gatineau, Canada, encouraging individuals to volunteer. If those approaches did not yield enough variation, CRTI members suggested other individuals. Some of them agreed to participate and others did not. Three interviews took place in offices, nine at the symposium and two by telephone.

Participants were stationed in at least three provinces, two jurisdictions and at least seven organizations. I say at least, because some organizations were huge and individuals identified with a subsection of the larger entity. Almost all participants considered themselves scientists, though the type of science varied from relatively pure laboratory-centred work to applied field work. Men and women, and Francophones and Anglophones, participated in the study. Experience in the field ranged from decades to a few years. Some individuals had worked in one community of practice (with biological threats, for example) in relative isolation; others were familiar with the workings of other communities. Typically, participants were in key places in their organizations—for example, working as senior managers or senior scientists, sometimes leading their area of specialization for the country, and frequently working in international circles.

The interview questions were open-ended and of two types. An example of the first type follows:

Your goal is to provide science solutions to CBRN terrorist threats, through linkages among non-traditional partners and across organizational boundaries. That seems like a field with many variables and uncertainties. How to you deal with that uncertainty in your work?

These questions got people talking about their experiences. In response to the question above, some spoke at length about the complexity and unpredictability of their work, with stories to illustrate their points. Others spoke about how there really was no uncertainty, and described the sequential processes they employed.

In the second type of question, participants had sheets of paper on which lines were drawn, with contrasting statements at the ends of the lines. They were asked to make a mark on the line to illustrate where they thought they were in their community at present, and to explain why. Later they were asked where they would like to be in an ideal world, to be as effective as possible. A sample of these somewhat contradictory statements is shown in Table 1. These questions elicited interesting insights, especially when the questions surprised participants. They also provided data for descriptive statistics and content analysis, which some phenomenographers consider appropriate, particularly if the participants' contexts are kept in mind during the analysis.

Both question types were informed by literatures from knowledge management, complexity and leadership. Where a transcript in isolation would be stripped of some obvious context, I probed in order to make non-verbal reactions and emotions behind words more explicit.

Transcripts and related pseudonyms were stored in a password-protected folder, with qualitative data analysis supported by Atlas.ti™ software. In the first coding pass, I highlighted phrases that seemed significant as a reference point rather than as a formal part of the analysis. I then coded the text with straightforward items, such as the name of the community, whether the person was a formal leader, and how each portion of the narrative linked to specific interview questions.

Table 1. A sample of somewhat oppositional statements from interview questions

We interact when we formally meet face to face		We interact regularly in different ways
Our ideas spread easily to the people who need them		Our ideas stay within our group
In our meetings, we stick to a pre-determined agenda		In our meetings, the agenda evolves as we interact
We try things out (as long as they are safe) and see what happens		Before trying things out we carefully plan and analyze
Because we are such a diverse group, we confine our conversations to common ground, where it's easy to understand each other and work is efficient		Because we are such a diverse group, we spend a lot of time trying to understand each other and establish new common context
We focus on doing		We focus on learning

I then moved into conceptual coding. Some was unplanned; for example, participants often made emotional statements about their experiences, so I coded for different types of emotions. Other coding was linked to the literature. Because this work was qualitative, exploratory and inductive, I began with a broad review of the literature, but did not set out to fill a targeted theoretical gap. Rather, I iteratively referenced various theories, descriptors, studies, frameworks and issues, bringing them to the foreground when it made sense to elicit new information or make sense of what I heard. For example, I drew on a community of practice model—referred to as the C4P model—developed in the U.S. military. The model, described below, had not yet been published in peer-reviewed journals. I selected it because of links to 1) a successful community of practice and 2) a promising model deserving of testing and 3) another North American community with military elements. Leaders of this community were offered full professorships at the United States Military Academy (USMA) and have pursued doctoral studies as part of that move (pers. comm. Pete Kilner 2004).

The CompanyCommand (CC) community began in 2000 as a labour of love, when a few individuals in the U.S. Army recognized the importance of new ways of learning for the knowledge-intensive work of company commanders. I watched their online portal with interest until it was closed to participants who did not have a U.S. military e-mail address, and later narrowed to persons with specific responsibilities in the army. Core members say the community is still thriving, with thousands of members in over one hundred countries, though it has shifted from off-the-sides-of-desks to a U.S. Military Academy-supported community. Vice-Dean for Education George Forsythe recently wrote, "I can only imagine what the Army profession will be like when Soldiers who have grown up with these professional forums are leading the profession in the years to come. I'm inspired and encouraged by the possibilities" (Dixon, Allen, Burgess, Kilner, & Schweitzer, 2005, p. viii).

The name C4P comes from the interactions of Content, Connections, Conversation and Context around the community's Purpose. The importance of a central purpose, as emphasized by many authors, cannot be understated. Through experience, Major Pete Kilner had found that these four other elements and their interrelationships are also important.

In this model, *content* refers to explicit knowledge that can be codified and stored, in databases: standard operating procedures, for example. This information is pushed out in one direction, in contrast to *conversation*, which involves dialogue. *Connections* describe contacts that involve relationships between community members. *Context* "is the who, what, where, when, why, and how that enables community members to assess whether and how information is relevant to them" (Hoadley & Kilner, 2005, p. 34).

Kilner describes what happens if elements are missing:

If content is absent, conversation is likely to have difficulty getting started and staying focused on the community's purpose. If conversation is missing, knowledge may transfer but is unlikely to be generated. If connections are absent, there will be fewer contributions of content and conversation, and the contributions will have less context. If information context is absent, the community is prone to misinterpret content or apply knowledge inappropriately to new situations. Finally, without purpose, knowledge building will founder. A clear communal purpose gives meaning to content, provides direction to conversation, fosters connections, and is the unifying context for all activities in the community (2005, p. 33).

In my coding, I looked for narrative that described content, conversation, connections and context as defined by Kilner and Hoadley.

Figure 4. C4P model of community leadership

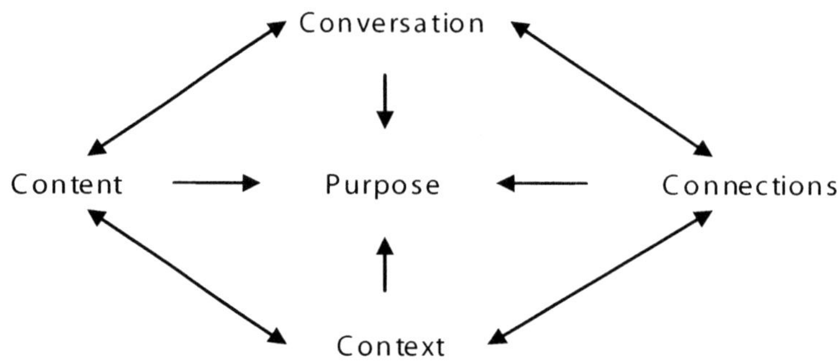

FINDINGS

Phenomenography seeks to find qualitatively different ways of understanding, and these ways of understanding are normally labelled using participants' terms. CRTI community members understood their work with knowledge in three ways, labelled *free-flowing, increasing* and *stuck.* Although I did not set out to explore the concept of boundaries, it emerged—explicitly or implicitly—during interviews. Ways of understanding boundaries are labelled *integrated, overlapping* and *constrained.* These are shown in table 2 and described below. The ways of understanding are grouped to reflect the conceptual coherence between free-flowing and integrated, and between constrained and stuck. Most individuals' comments fit consistently into a single way of understanding for each concept. There were also patterns within each community or cluster.

Ways of Understanding Knowledge Management

Use of the C4P model helped to highlight the variations in the breadth and variations of perspectives about knowledge work.

In the *free-flowing* category of knowledge management, participants

- made statements relating to all four Cs: context, content, connection and conversation;
- said they interacted in many different ways;
- contextualized their responses to whether they focus on *learning or doing* with specific examples of where each was appropriate; and
- contextualized their responses to the question about the nature of conversation ("Because we are such a diverse group...") with specific examples of where each was appropriate.

Sample quote from *free-flowing* category of knowledge management:

Lloyd talked about the importance of knowledge flow within clusters on several levels:

Lloyd: so we're looking for ways to draw out those new ideas. And so my personal belief from my involvement in science has been that one of the fastest ways to get new ideas to the forefront is to have lots of interaction with people. And to generate lots of ideas—and to do that people have to be knowledgeable about what other people are doing—so the goal is really by bringing these people together and you have to balance off enough structure, so that you're accountable but sufficiently loose structure that you don't prevent the free flow of ideas and the innovation that needs to come forward.

Statements from the free-flowing category showed fluidity, resilience and thoughtful flex-

Table 2. CRTI members' ways of understanding boundaries and knowledge management

	Ways of Understanding Research Elements		
Research Element	**Category I**	**Category II**	**Category III**
Knowledge Management • from flowing to static	Free-flowing	Increasing	Stuck
Perceived Nature of Boundaries • from permeable to impermeable	Integrated	Overlapping	Constrained

ibility when dealing with different contexts and types of knowledge.

In the *increasing* category of knowledge management, participants

- made statements relating to three of the four Cs;
- with one exception, said they interacted in many different ways; and
- with one exception, emphasized learning in the learning-doing spectrum, often tied to specific contextualized examples of where each was appropriate.

Sample quote from *increasing* category of knowledge management:

Some spoke about improved flow in professional networks. Martin talked about how it can take a long time for organizations and jurisdictions to really connect, but he gives an example of doors opening in a conversation with a Defence Innovation member, as soon as that person knew Martin was in a CRTI cluster.

Martin: It simplifies the few contacts there.
Alice: Okay.
Martin: If nobody has heard about you—well at least you're in the [community name]—"Ah you're in the [community name]!" This is not because you are John Smith or you're Rita Boubeau; it's ... as if you went through a kind of filter system.

Statements in the *increasing* category showed some of the diversity and resilience of the *free-flowing* category, but their stories were also interwoven with struggles to overcome barriers, perhaps because several people in this category tended to think about a very broad range of responsibilities from prevention to prosecution. Despite the challenges, participants spoke as change leaders who were experiencing benefits and who were confident they would enable progress in the future. Sometimes they expressed concern that if they could no longer participate, there were few people with the perspectives and tenacity to carry on with the work.

In the *stuck* category of knowledge management, participants

- made statements relating to two of the four Cs;
- on the *learning vs. doing* focus spectrum, responded on the *doing* half of the spectrum;
- on the methods of interaction spectrum, responded on the *few* half of the spectrum;
- on the nature of conversation question, responded on the *confined to common ground* half of the spectrum; and
- on the *ideas spread easily to those who need them* spectrum, responded on the *stay within the group* half of the spectrum and they had much larger gaps than other categories between current and desired states.

Sample quotes from *stuck* category of knowledge management:

David spoke about a range of challenges in the production and application of knowledge. An example follows:

David: We've had to tackle a lot of issues and some are still far from being resolved. For example, there are a lot of requests from some of the provincial labs—what tests should they use? There are different commercial tests. As a cluster, how can we recommend tests? Well, then we have legal issues, and my God ... it's a really ugly one. It's almost a no-win situation.
Alice: Hmmm.
David: If you recommend one test in particular, you can have the other competitors on your back, and if it's being used and somehow it's not performing, then you could be blamed legally. You could be liable, because you recommended that test ... So it's a kind of a no-win situation. We have a lot of issues like this.

Statements from this *stuck* perspective showed participants' struggles. These individuals cared very much about their work, realized there were gaps between the current and ideal state—of knowledge sharing, for example—but had not been able to find their ways out of patterns and perspectives that were not serving them well.

WAYS OF UNDERSTANDING BOUNDARIES

The topic of boundaries is more prominent in complexity literature than in traditional management and leadership literature. Richardson (2001) states that "the boundaries delimiting subsystems in a complex system are emergent and temporary." In the *integrated* category of boundaries

- over 70% of their boundary-related statements were about permeable boundaries;
- permeability was generally seen as positive; and
- the focus of permeable boundaries varied considerably and included boundaries between different identities, roles and perspectives; the cluster and participating organizations; between clusters; between countries and cultures; and between the cluster and other communities or networks, including universities and international organizations.

Sample quotes from *integrated* category of boundaries:

Brad is among many participants who describe how the CRTI initiative has facilitated the creating of more permeable boundaries:

Brad: I think CRTI is well placed to link agencies together... we're not hampered by formality and structure.... It's comfortably loose and people are very open in their comments.

Barrett describes some of the linkages at an interpersonal level:

Barrett: People assume that the [discipline/cluster name] program in Canada was well-connected, but in point of fact, I think I met [name] once before CRTI started. And people like [name] at [organization] and [name] at [organization], I never worked with these people before. So they're brand new and they're very good relationships.

Barrett also described new and productive connections nationally and internationally.

Statements from the *integrated* category of boundaries held a kind of energy, similar to the free-flowing statements about knowledge and learning. Many seemed oblivious to boundaries. Their stories suggested they had used well-developed skills to engender recognition and trust; perhaps others saw no need to block their work or communication. I heard a few stories about problems and conflicts, and it was interesting to note that statements in this category had nothing to do with retrenching or competing. The default strategy was to collaborate with the group that initiated the difficulty so that their collective efforts would be stronger.

In the *overlapping* category of boundaries:

- 50%–70% of their boundary-related statements were about permeable boundaries;
- permeability was generally seen as positive; and
- the focus of permeable boundaries varied somewhat and included boundaries between the cluster and participating organizations, between clusters, and between the cluster and other communities or networks.

Sample quotes from *overlapping* category of boundaries:

Although Ken described cluster work as "onerous" and "absolute overhead," he also saw it overlapping in some ways with his regular work:

Alice: So I'm curious, how in the [community name] you see that division or boundary between cluster work, and line organization work?
Ken: In many ways there's significant overlap. I mean, what I do for example ... We've just extended to a field capability that we didn't have before.
Alice: In your organization?
Ken: For my particular group. For other groups, they basically beefed up capacity, so they just can do more.

The *overlapping* category sits between the permeable character of the *integrated* category and the closed, *constrained* category. However, it felt distinctive enough to have its own category.

In the *constrained* category of boundaries,

- under 40% of their boundary-related statements were about permeable boundaries;
- binary thinking was common in their world of primarily impermeable boundaries—whether they be desirable or undesirable, imposed or created, real or assumed. A task was either the responsibility of x or y; one can either do work for one's organization or work for CRTI, etc.;
- permeability was frequently seen as a negative thing or as a symptom of something negative in relation to other categories; and
- the focus of permeable boundaries was usually localized (specifically, the boundaries between the cluster the secretariat or participating organizations).

Sample quotes from *constrained* category of boundaries:

David speaks to perspectives of boundaries constraining progress on a practical level:

David: Okay, just the movement of money from department to department... financial mechanisms... just the plain day-to-day bureaucracy of doing something like this is so difficult. There are days... why should I bother?
Alice: Yes.
David: It's a lot easier to do my own work in [names setting and organization]. But when you're trying to do something at this level... [name of central agency] is really hard to work with, so the... getting security clearance because were trying to get outside people in there...

It's just one piece of bureaucracy after another. It's a killer. To the point where we're delayed, and people know; it doesn't look good.

Some of the *constrained* statements were based on standard principles of government structures: divisions and lines of authority are created intentionally, and one is not supposed to duplicate or usurp responsibilities of other units. Such statements were along the lines of "We can't do that...that is Organization X's role." Others, such as David's above, showed emotional, financial or workload costs associated with firm boundaries in boundary-spanning environments.

WAYS OF UNDERSTANDING SATISFACTION AND EFFECTIVENESS

Because the CRTI Secretariat was interested in building on successes, I explored participants' perceptions of satisfaction and effectiveness and links between these perceptions and the ways in which they understood their knowledge work. I therefore asked questions and prompted conversations in ways that revealed how they felt and where they would like to see improvements. For example, one question read, "What three words or phrases best describe your experience in this group?" and one of the spectrum questions in this category used the phrases "I think I am a worthwhile contributor" and "I think my expertise is not well used." Analysis of these and all other parts of the narrative yielded three ways of conceptualizing their satisfaction and sense of effectiveness. The satisfaction and effectiveness categories are labelled *mutual benefit*, *shared opportunity* and *difficult*. Sample quotes from each category follow.

Ken described the early momentum of counter-terrorism work in the *mutual benefit* category of satisfaction and effectiveness:

Ken: I have to give it to the Canadian government. They reacted extremely quickly. When I was in [location outside Canada] giving talks about the work we were doing with the money we received from CRTI, the [nationality], at least in the early days, came up to me and said, "how the devil did you get to do this so quickly?"
Alice: Wow.
Ken: We were a year, if not 18 months ahead of [the country] in getting this thing rolling.

Stan was one of many participants to discuss scope-related challenges. His portrayal of challenges, coupled with plans to overcome them, was typical of the *shared opportunity* category of satisfaction and effectiveness:

Stan: A lot of that work has been done and there's still a lot more that has to be done, but moving more now towards prevention, disruption, interdiction the intelligence side of things and moving it further in advance of the event is I think probably the priority that we're looking at now.
Alice: Do you find it's different working with the [names of other] clusters?... On the prevention side vs. the reaction side?
Stan: (Deep breath). We really haven't gone far enough down that road with any of the...clusters.

The energy in *shared opportunity* comments was similar to the increasing category of knowledge management. As exemplified by Stan's statements above, these individuals seemed to be climbing a steep hill, struggling with challenges, but with no sense of feeling defeated. They didn't speak about distant goals or vision; it was more of a step-by-step process, scanning the environment, watching for opportunities, and recruiting allies through successes en route.

Jordan was one of the individuals who spoke about how difficult it can be to get good conversation going in the *difficult* category of satisfaction and effectiveness.

Jordan: Or the tendency too is if you don't understand the common ground... you maybe get too quiet instead of saying, 'well, I don't understand where you're going.'

As a researcher, it was difficult to hear some of the stories and statements in the *difficult* category. I was there to help deepen understanding; this was not an action research project, and my results were compiled in a way that would maintain participant and community anonymity. The most striking characteristic of this category was the emotion with which people spoke and the palpable tension between their hopes and their experience.

This research did not include external measures of satisfaction or effectiveness. However, individuals sometimes introduced them to the conversation. Barrett—in the *mutual benefit* category—stated:

Barrett: We are the strongest cluster. We always have been, for five years now.
Alice: Hmmm.
Barrett: And I'm not just saying that... [Name of senior person] said that and other people.
Alice: What kinds of criteria are you thinking about?
Barrett: Exercises; publicity; CRTI awards; we're well above what our quota would be.

Satisfaction and effectiveness categories are included in Table 3.

As mentioned earlier, individual participants tended to have a consistent way of understanding for each research element such as knowledge management. When ways of understanding were mapped for the four communities, interesting patterns emerged. The profiles of communities three—in Table 4—and one—in Table 5--were the least similar:

If we contrast these two communities—which had developed distinctive cultures—we see that participants who perceived their work (individually and in the community) to be satisfying and effective were in Community 3. Most individuals in this community conveyed ideas about the importance of three elements in the context, conversation, connections and content model, said they interacted in their community in many ways, and emphasized learning over doing. They also tended to ignore boundaries or worked to span or integrate in ways that would facilitate learning and effectiveness.

Community 1 participants perceived their work as relatively unsatisfying and ineffective, though they did considered it important. With the exception of the named leader, their perceptions of knowledge work were in the "stuck" category. Members of this community focused on doing rather than learning, interacted in relatively few ways, said they focused primarily on common ground in conversations and in comparison with the other three communities saw the most room for progress in having their ideas flow out to those who need them. They felt constrained by boundaries, such as limits imposed by organizational mandates and procedures, and yet spoke about reinforcing boundaries more than opening them, as in Jordan's response to a member's suggestion: "But isn't that [named organization's] responsibility or mandate?"

Another aspect of this study—not included here—explored the ways in which participants understood leadership, and how that wove into patterns within communities.

It is interesting to note that regardless of which community participants were in, they rarely spoke about data or information management or the im-

Table 3. CRTI members' ways of understanding facets of their work

	Ways of Understanding Research Elements		
Research Element	**Category I**	**Category II**	**Category III**
Perceived Satisfaction and Effectiveness • from most to least	Mutual benefit	Shared opportunity	Difficult
Knowledge Management • from flowing to static	Free-flowing	Increasing	Stuck
Perceived Nature of Boundaries • from permeable to impermeable	Integrating	Overlapping	Constrained

Table 4. Community 3 profile with high level of satisfaction

	Ways of Understanding Research Elements		
Research Element	**Category I**	**Category II**	**Category III**
Perceived Satisfaction and Effectiveness • from most to least • mutual benefit, shared opportunity & difficult			
Knowledge Management • from flowing to static • free-flowing, increasing and stuck			
Perceived Nature of Boundaries • from permeable to impermeable • integrating, overlapping and constrained			

Table 5. Community 1 profile with low level of satisfaction

	Ways of Understanding Research Elements		
Research Element	**Category I**	**Category II**	**Category III**
Perceived Satisfaction and Effectiveness • from most to least • mutual benefit, shared opportunity & difficult			
Knowledge Management • from flowing to static • free-flowing, increasing and stuck			
Perceived Nature of Boundaries • from permeable to impermeable • integrating, overlapping and constrained			

Table 6.

Formal community leader's way of understanding

Community participants' way of understanding

Single community participant's way of understanding

Formal leader and community participants' way of understanding portance of codifying knowledge. In one respect, this surprised me, given the scientific nature of their domains and the tendencies for governments to store information. They did store and access some important documents. But in our conversations, they chose to focus on the importance of tacit knowledge and expertise, especially when innovation was required. This fits with many studies such as Tom Allen's book *Managing the Flow of Technology (1984),* in which he wrote that scientists approached individuals for important information much more often than using codified sources such as files or databases. Later, when knowledge repositories had become much more sophisticated, Cross, Parker, Prusak and Borgatti researched the practices of 40 Fortune 500 managers and found that "these managers overwhelmingly indicated (and supported with vivid stories) that they received this information from other people far more frequently than impersonal sources such as their personal computer archives, the Internet or the organization's knowledge management database" (2001). This reflects a trend in knowledge management research to focus more on human and social capital, networks, communities of practice and the complex systems in which knowledge is generated and shared, even if this research is not embraced by consultants and organizations craving quick fixes and technology solutions.

CONCLUSIONS AND REFLECTIONS

Rigorous qualitative research deepens understanding through exploration with relatively few participants. CRTI managers found that this research enriched their understanding and was of immediate value. Qualitative research does not seek universal laws or definitive cause and effect relationships, so the findings from one context may not transplant to another without adaptation. However, it can be worthwhile to hold up the results of such studies against theories, frameworks and models from related disciplines.

This study helped us gain insights into an interdisciplinary knowledge-intensive network of counter-terrorism communities, and has implications for any complex, knowledge-intensive work, such as work with public sector challenges relevant to different governments, ministries and stakeholder groups. Participants dealt with uncertainties ranging from the challenges of trans-organizational collaboration to the difficulty predicting if, when, where or how terrorists might attack. Watching their work from the periphery, I consider it to be classically complex: having many interacting entities and systems in which emergence and unexpected results are commonplace. However, I must point out that participants' views about the degree of complexity varied, depending—in part—on how they drew boundaries around the scope of their work.

Using Dave Snowden's Cognitive Edge (formerly Cynefin) model (2002), one would expect formal or informal leaders to work in fluid ways: probing, watching for patterns and supporting the growth of positive results. In Community 3, where members felt most effective, this is similar to the way in which the formal leader described their work, with narrative such as the following:

...so the goal is really by bringing these people together and you have to balance off enough structure, so that you're accountable but sufficiently loose structure that you don't prevent the free flow of ideas and the innovation that needs to come forward.

One Community 3 participant spoke about stimulating knowledge generation and sharing by "increasing the complexity" in the work as they progress, by introducing risks and human factors in exercises. This comfort with complexity is also reflected in Community 3 members' unsolicited thinking about the application of connection, conversation, context and/or content to their purpose, and their desire to expand conversations and understanding beyond comfortable common ground.

Knowledge management authors (Davenport & Prusak, 1998; Kock, McQueen, & Baker, 1996) have written about knowledge being different, and more human, than information. Some have written about knowledge as a flow rather than a thing (Currie & Kerrin, 2004; Halal, 2005; Snowden, 2002) and the pitfalls of emphasizing "knowledge stock to the detriment of knowledge flow" (Fahey & Prusak, 1998, p. 266). These perspectives overlap with those depicting knowledge and learning as being embedded in practice (Lave & Wenger, 1991; Wenger, 1998). Portrayals of knowledge as highly contextualized and flowing imply that boundaries can be permeable or temporary and emphasize relationships amongst entities. In his reflections on complex organizational work, Kurt Richardson writes, "A clear lesson, which follows directly from complex versions of management theory, is that project boundaries (if one chooses to organize around the notion of a project) must not be reified, they must not be taken too seriously; they need to be allowed to flow" (2005, p. viii).

My research in the counter-terrorism communities shows that in the CRTI context, the individuals who felt most satisfied with their contributions and the effectiveness of their community (perceptions supported anecdotally by their examples of evidence) understood their environments as complex. They learn through largely unplanned stimulations of the flow of knowledge, in practice-oriented contexts such as exercises and through collaborative innovations. This contributes to the strength of several authors' conceptual publications, and suggests there is fertile ground for more exploration of decision-making and innovation in complex, knowledge-rich environments.

ACKNOWLEDGMENT

I would like to acknowledge the DRDC Centre for Security Science (CRTI unit) and Fielding Graduate University for supporting aspects of this research.

REFERENCES

Allee, V. (2003). *The Future of Knowledge: Increasing prosperity through value networks*. Amsterdam: Butterworth-Heinemann.

Allen, T. J. (1984). *Managing the Flow of Technology: Technology Transfer and the Dissemination of Technological Information Within the R&D Organization* (2nd ed.). Cambridge MA: The MIT Press.

Bowden, J. A. (1996). Phenomenographic research: Some methodological issues. In G. Dall'Alba & B. Hasselgran (Eds.), *Reflections on phenomenography: Toward a methodology?* Goteborg: Kompendiet.

Bowden, J. A., & Walsh, E. (Eds.). (2000). *Phenomenography*. Melbourne: RMIT University Press.

Cross, R., Parker, A., Prusak, L., & Borgatti, S. P. (2001). Knowing what we know: Supporting knowledge creation and sharing in social networks. *Organizational Dynamics, 30*(2), 100-120.

Currie, G., & Kerrin, M. (2004). The limits of a technological fix to knowledge management: Epistemological, political and cultural issues in the case of intranet implementation. *Management Learning, 35*(1), 9-29.

Davenport, T. H., & Prusak, L. (1998). *Working knowledge: How organizations manage what they know*. Boston: Harvard Business School Press.

Dixon, N. M., Allen, N., Burgess, T., Kilner, P. G., & Schweitzer, S. (2005). *CompanyCommand: Unleashing the power of the army profession*. West Point: The Center for the Advancement of Leader Development and Organizational Learning.

Fahey, L., & Prusak, L. (1998). The eleven deadliest sins of knowledge management. *California Management Review, 40*(3), 265-276.

Firestone, J. M., & McElroy, M. W. (2003). *Key Issues in the New Knowledge Management*. Burlington, MA: Butterworth-Heinemann.

Halal, W. E. (2005). Knowledge management: how to foster creation and flow. *Handbook of Business Strategy, 6*(1), 297-301.

Hoadley, C. M., & Kilner, P. G. (2005). Using technology to transform communities of practice into knowledge-building communities. *ACMSIGGROUP Bulletin, 25*(1), 31-40.

Kock, N. F., McQueen, R. J., & Baker, M. (1996). Learning and process improvement in knowledge organizations: a critical analysis of four contemporary myths. *The Learning Organization, 3*(1), 31-42.

Koenig, M. E. D. (1996). Intellectual capital and knowledge management. *IFLA Journal, 22*(4), 299-301.

Larsson, J., Holmström, I., & Rosenqvist, U. (2003). Professional artist, good Samaritan, servant and co-ordinator: Four ways of understanding the anaesthetist's work. *Acta Anaesthesiologica Scandinavica, 47*, 1-7.

Lave, J., & Wenger, E. (1991). *Situated learning: Legitimate peripheral participation*. Cambridge: Cambridge University Press.

Lelic, S. (2002). Inside knowledge editorial. *Knowledge Management,* 4.

Marton, F., & Pang, M. F. (1999). *Two Faces of Variation*. Paper presented at the Conference Name|. Retrieved Access Date|. from URL|.

McKelvey, B. (2002). Chapter 9 Complexity and Leadership In M. Lissack & J. Rivkin (Eds.), *The interaction of complexity and management* (pp. 85-90). Westport: Quorum Books.

Michaels, M. (2002). A Practitioner's Perspective. In M. Lissack & J. Rivkin (Eds.), *The interaction of complexity and management* (pp. 173-181). Westport: Quorum.

Palys, T. (1997). *Research Decisions: Quantitative and Qualitative Perspectives* (Second ed.). Toronto: Harcourt Brace.

Phenomenography. from http://www.ped.gu.se/biorn/phgraph/home.html

Phenomenography. Retrieved December 5 2005, from http://www.ped.gu.se/biorn/phgraph/civil/main/1res.appr.html

Proceedings of the 2006 CRTI Summer Symposium. (2006). Paper presented at the CRTI Summer Symposium, Aylmer, Quebec.

Richardson, K. A. (2001). *On the status of natural boundaries: A complex systems perspective*. Paper presented at the Systems in management: 7th annual ANZSYS Conference.

Richardson, K. A. (2005). Volume Introduction. In K. A. Richardson (Ed.), *Managing the Complex: Philosophy, Theory and Application* (Vol. One, pp. iii-viii). Greenwich Connecticut: IAP Information Age Publishing.

Rumizen, M. C. (2002). *The complete idiot's guide to knowledge management*. Madison: Alpha Books.

Sandberg, J. (2000). Understanding human competence at work: An interpretative approach. *Academy of Management Journal, 43*(1), 9-25.

Snowden, D. (2002). Complex acts of knowing: Paradox and descriptive self-awareness. *Journal of Knowledge Management, 6*(2), 100-111(112)

Snyder, W. M., & Wenger, E. (2003). Communities of practice in government: the case for sponsorship (pp. 86).

Wagner, R. S. (2006). *The human element of organizational transformation: A phenomenographic study of how internal stakeholders in federal defense organizations experience and make sense of planned organizational change*. Fielding Graduate University, Santa Barbara.

Wenger, E. (1998). *Communities of practice: Learning, meaning, & identity.* Cambridge: Cambridge University Press.

Wiig, K. (2002). Knowledge management has many facets. Retrieved January 2003, from http://www.krii.com/downloads/Four_KM_Facets.pdf

KEY TERMS

Boundaries: Are [often socially constructed] areas of discontinuity containing or dividing entities.

Communities of Practice: Groups of people who engage in ongoing, voluntarily interaction to learn from each other and improve their work in a given field or domain.

Complex System: A complex system has many elements involved in non-linear interactions, making precise predictions impossible.

Counter-Terrorism Work: Work that improves capability and capacity for prevention of, preparedness for, and response to terrorism-related threats to public safety and security.

Effectiveness: Improvement that is broader than efficiency. Improvements can include increased relevance, perceived value, acceptance by stakeholders, protection of assets, achievement of results, secondary benefits, and so on.

Knowledge Management: In this paper I draw on work of Snowden and McElroy to describe knowledge management as work that helps to establish common context in order to enable organizational learning. Resulting activities could include knowledge generation, acquisition, sharing, re-use, and mobilization for decision-support and innovation.

Phenomenography: A qualitative research methodology originating in Scandinavia, which seeks to reveal qualitatively different ways of understanding concepts.

Chapter XXVIII
Tensions between Knowledge Creation and Knowledge Sharing:
Individual Preferences of Employees in Knowledge-Intensive Organizations

Tatiana Andreeva
Graduate School of Management, St. Petersburg State University, Russia

ABSTRACT

Contemporary literature usually views knowledge creation and knowledge sharing as either independent or positively related processes. However, based on the review of the literature on the organizational conditions aimed to support these processes, the author challenges this view at the individual level of analysis and suggests that an individual employee can hardly simultaneously combine features that support both knowledge creation and knowledge sharing and thus can hardly be efficient in both processes at the same time. The data from the survey of 120 employees from 5 knowledge-intensive companies supported this idea, and the author discusses its implications for further research and for management practice in knowledge-intensive organizations.

INTRODUCTION

Managing knowledge-related processes in organizations is one of the hotly discussed themes of the last decade. Both management practitioners and academics claim that these processes are crucial for creating and maintaining a competitive advantage in the post-industrial era (see, e.g., Nonaka, 1994; Davenport & Prusak, 2000). Another topical issue for organizations is managing their human resources, as people are now recognized as being the most valuable asset of the modern organization (see, e.g., Becker & Gerhart, 1996; Lepak & Snell, 1999). Interestingly, the tasks and problems of these two approaches to sustaining a company's competitiveness, knowledge management and human resource management, are deeply interrelated, as the efficiency of knowledge employment is highly dependent upon the good will of the employees (Husted & Michailova, 2002; Minbaeva et al., 2003; Storey, 2005). Yet, despite the obvious significance of individual-level factors for knowledge management, they are poorly discussed in contemporary literature and there is a lack of empirical evidence on the effects of these factors (Foss & Felin, 2006).

Though considered relevant for most contemporary organizations, these issues are especially critical (and even more intertwined) for so-called "knowledge-intensive organizations" — firms whose main activity is based on the employment of knowledge (Starbuck, 1992; Alvesson, 1995; Nurmi, 1998). In fact, employees with their knowledge and skills form the key capital of such a company and determine its unique competitive advantages, with its other assets playing only an auxiliary role. Thus, an understanding of individual knowledge-related behaviour and the grounded design of human resource management practices are strategically important for the competitiveness of knowledge-intensive firms (KIFs) (Boxall & Steeneveld, 1999; Robertson & Hammersley, 2000; Swart & Kinnie, 2003).

This paper presents some findings from research on Russian knowledge-intensive companies, and is aimed at shedding more light on peculiarities of individual behaviors related to two key knowledge-related processes: knowledge creation and knowledge sharing. I start with a presentation of the theoretical grounds of this research, which include a critical analysis of the relationship between knowledge creation and knowledge sharing, a discussion of the role of an individual in these processes; and a formulation of research questions. Further on, I present the research strategy, including data collection methods and sample characteristics. Then I turn to research findings, and conclude the paper with a discussion of them and of implications for further research and for management practice in knowledge-intensive organizations.

THEORETICAL GROUNDS

Contemporary management theory views knowledge as one of the key sources for the creation and maintenance of a sustainable competitive advantage in a post-industrial economy (Kogut & Zander, 1992; Grant, 1996; Teece, 2004). Consequently, the tasks of managing various knowledge-related processes in an organization are brought to the forefront. Two knowledge-related processes — knowledge creation (Nonaka, 1991) and knowledge sharing (Husted & Michailova, 2002) — dominate the literature on the issue.

Why are these processes in particular so widely discussed by both academics and practitioners? New knowledge allows a company to leave its competitors behind by undertaking innovative actions, and thus to appropriate so-called Schumpeterian rents (Schumpeter, 1934). A number of economists believe that innovation-based competition can serve as a basis for successful development in the post-industrial knowledge economy (Romer & Kurtzman, 2004). Sharing existing knowledge within an organization helps the company use available resources in the most efficient way by transferring the best practices — those that have proven to bring the best results, lower costs, or very satisfied customers — from one department to another, from one project or client to another, etc. Thus both of these processes are viewed as very significant for the competitiveness of an organization in the modern knowledge economy.

Knowledge creation and knowledge sharing: clarifying the terms. For the sake of further discussion, some clarification of terms is needed at this point. The processes of "moving" *existing* knowledge around organizations have been labelled in the literature in a variety of ways; for example, as knowledge *sharing* (e.g. Hansen et al., 2005), knowledge *exchange* (e.g. Christensen, 2005), knowledge *transfer* (e.g. Argote & Ingram, 2000) and knowledge *replication* (e.g. Szulanski, 1996). Despite having closely-related meanings, these concepts are not identical, and the fact that they are often used interchangeably in the literature may lead to some confusion. I suggest that, at least linguistically, *sharing* implies dissemination of knowledge by a knowledge "sender" without any specification of a knowledge "receiver's" reaction to this act. It means that when we call some effort "knowledge sharing", we actually specify neither if "sent" knowledge was applied, nor if it was perceived, or even if it reached anybody. Knowledge *exchange* indicates some reciprocity of actions, implying that knowledge (or something else in exchange for knowledge) has been moved each way within the same pair of organizational actors; but this does not say anything about further action upon this knowledge. Knowledge *transfer* suggests that a receiver at least absorbed "sent" knowledge and probably even acted somehow upon it, or, as Argote and Ingram put it, that he/she was "affected by the experience" of a sender (Argote & Ingram, 2000, p.151). *Replication* points to a specific type of knowledge transfer, in which a receiver acts upon "sent" knowledge by trying to "copy" a sender's experience. Thus we may conclude that the terms "sharing" and "exchange" refer primarily to the "knowledge-moving" process itself, while the terms "transfer" and "replication" also specify results of this process. Such a distinction also shows that sharing appears to be the most generic (as it is the least specific) among the discussed terms — and this fact probably explains why it is used in the literature much more often than the others.

Discourse on the development of new knowledge in organizations tends to use fewer terms to describe the phenomenon it analyses, with *knowledge creation* (e.g., Nonaka, 1991) and *innovation* (e.g., Van de Ven, 1986) being the two most frequently used ones. Though they are often used interchangeably, one can identify the difference between these two terms in a manner similar to the distinction between sharing/exchange and transfer/replication: while knowledge creation refers primarily to the process of development of new ideas, innovation is used in the literature to describe this process, its results (e.g., new products), or both.

In this paper I use "knowledge sharing" to identify the process of moving *existing* knowledge, and "knowledge creation" to identify the process of development of *new* knowledge. I will refer to the results of these two processes as knowledge transfer (or replication) and innovation. However, there are still ambiguities with these terms, as the degree of knowledge "novelty" can be very difficult to identify. For example, should we treat as innovation or replication a divisional organizational structure, which is not an innovation itself but was never used before in this particular company? This problem raises the question of how to draw the line between replication and innovation, which deserves a separate discussion. That is why, for the sake of brevity, I will not approach in this paper the borderline cases where replication approaches innovation and vice-versa, but will treat them as the two opposite poles, replication being the usage of something that *existed* before in a particular company, and innovation being the creation of something *new* for a particular company.

The relationship between knowledge creation and knowledge sharing processes in organizations. If these two processes are so essential for contemporary organizations, it is important to understand how they are related to each other. The literature usually treats them as independent from each other and as equally important for an organizational knowledge management strategy. However, let us take a closer look, for example, at Nonaka's model of organizational knowledge creation (Nonaka, 1991). Developing the distinction between tacit and explicit knowledge, Nonaka suggested that the creation of new knowledge in organizations can be described with a four-stage spiral model. It starts with a socialization phase, in which tacit knowledge of individuals is exchanged. This is followed by an articulation phase, in which new tacit knowledge is translated into explicit knowledge. This explicit knowledge is pooled with existing explicit knowledge in the next, combination, phase; and the turn of the spiral concludes with an internalization phase, in which this new explicit knowledge is absorbed by individuals and enriches their tacit knowledge base. Then the tacit knowledge is exchanged again, and the knowledge creation process continues along the spiral. Nonaka does not use the term "knowledge sharing" in his model; however one can see that two of the stages, in fact, are based on intensive knowledge sharing processes. The first phase, socialization, includes intensive sharing of tacit knowledge among employees, mainly among close colleagues. The third phase, combination, concerns sharing of explicit knowledge that may involve a broader set of employees through the whole organization. Taking into account that Nonaka postulates each stage of his model as essential for successful knowledge creation, we can conclude that in his view efficient knowledge sharing processes are one of the prerequisites for efficient knowledge creation in an organization. In so far as "efficient" implies that the process brings some results, this also means that knowledge-transfer (as a result of knowledge sharing) is one of the prerequisites for innovation (a result of knowledge creation). Hence, according to Nonaka knowledge creation and knowledge sharing processes are closely interrelated, and this interplay is positive.

As both knowledge creation and knowledge sharing are considered very significant for contemporary companies, a practical question arises: what should managers do in order to ensure the best possible flow of these processes in their companies? Prerequisites for, and barriers to, knowledge creation or knowledge sharing are discussed intensively in the literature (e.g., Nonaka & Konno, 1998; Brown & Duguid, 2002). A large part of this discussion is focused on various organizational conditions, or factors, that may influence these processes, including organizational culture (DeLong & Fahey, 2000; Alavi et al., 2006), organizational structure (Hedlund, 1994; Miles et al., 1997; Tsai, 2002), and work space design (Davenport et al., 2002), among others.

Most of this literature supposes that managers should make efforts to increase the efficiency of knowledge sharing and knowledge creation *simultaneously*, and this is true irrespectively of whether the authors understand these processes as independent or positively related (where knowledge sharing represents a part of knowledge creation). However, a more detailed comparative analyses of organizational conditions and recommendations for managers, developed by "knowledge creation" and "knowledge sharing" authors, reveals some contradictions.

Let us take organizational culture as an example. Nonaka and Konno stress that in order to support innovations in an organization, managers should nurture a special culture that treats innovation as a key value and intensively encourages knowledge-creating processes (Nonaka & Konno, 1998). At the same time, Szulanski and Winter note that a strong innovation-oriented culture tends to make employees and whole departments more focused not on replication, i.e., not on intensive knowledge sharing and application of others' experience in their work, but rather on development of competencies and solutions of their own (Szulanski & Winter, 2002).

Thus we can see potential contradiction between managers' efforts aimed at supporting innovative processes on the one hand and their efforts aimed at supporting replicative processes on the other. Organizational conditions that promote creation of new knowledge may become barriers to knowledge sharing. And vice-versa: factors aimed at facilitating knowledge sharing may suppress or, at least not support, innovation. Despite the fact that the conflict between knowledge creation and knowledge sharing processes is not evident on the conceptual level, turning to another level of analysis, that of applied conditions for the intensification and efficiency of these processes, we can suppose that the relationship between them is more complex than it is usually understood to be, and that in some cases they may contradict each other, as I have demonstrated above. Hence, we can hypothesize that the same factors may influence knowledge creation processes positively and knowledge sharing negatively, and vice-versa.

Though this statement sounds novel in relation to the knowledge-management literature, in fact a similar problem has been widely discussed within other fields of management discourse, as the exploration versus exploitation dilemma (March, 1991; Gupta et al., 2006). Exploration refers to an organizational strategy focused on creating value through searching for new knowledge and opportunities, while exploitation means a strategy concentrated on utilization of existing ones. Thus we can logically link a focus on knowledge-creating processes with exploration, and focus on knowledge sharing processes with exploitation. What is interesting in relation to the possibility of potential contradictions between practices that support knowledge sharing and knowledge creation processes is that many earlier studies of the exploration/exploitation dilemma often regarded controversies between these two strategies as insurmountable. However, more recent research has suggested that organizations can overcome these difficulties, and the term "ambidextrous" was coined to describe companies that know how to successfully combine both orientations (Tushman & O'Reilly, 1996; Gibson & Birkinshaw, 2004; Van Looy et al., 2005). I suggest that these findings from exploration/exploitation research both support the notion of contradictions between knowledge sharing and knowledge creation and provide some hope that they can be balanced. Still, it is necessary to mention that the "ambidexterity" discussion is based on an organizational level of analysis. Now let us turn to the individual level.

The role of the individual in knowledge creation and knowledge sharing. One can distinguish two different levels of analysis within discussions of factors that support or hinder knowledge creation and knowledge sharing processes: the organizational and the individual levels. While the former concerns the organizational conditions mentioned above, the latter focuses on issues having to do with the knowledge-related behaviour of an individual — his/her intentions, motives, fears, etc. (e.g, Husted & Michailova, 2002; Bock et al., 2005; Cabrera et al., 2006).

The above-mentioned organizational factors for knowledge creation and knowledge sharing can be viewed as organizational conditions that can be purposefully created by company managers. Though they differ in the effort and time needed to change them (for example, it is usually easier to change organizational structure than organizational culture), still they depend mainly on a manager's will and are defined by his/her vision.

But taking into account only these factors oversimplifies the essence of managing knowledge, as not only managers but every employee can significantly influence knowledge-related processes in an organization. Knowledge and experience in an organization initially belong not to the organization itself, but to the individuals it employs. Though organizational knowledge is not a simple sum of the knowledge of its employees, and transformation of individual knowledge into organizational knowledge is an important task for companies (see, e.g., Tsoukas & Vladimirou, 2001; Nonaka, 1991), many authors admit that the extent to which knowledge can be detached from an individual is very limited (Grant, 1996; Flood et al., 2001). That is why the efficiency of knowledge employment depends highly on the good will of individuals, both to share knowledge and to apply it in the best way. Thus knowledge creation and knowledge sharing processes depend to a great extent not only on management decisions but on the personal features and preferences of company employees.

Despite the obvious significance of these individual factors, they are poorly discussed in contemporary literature (Foss & Felin, 2006). Foss and Felin emphasize the importance of developing theory and practice in this area and call for more research on the micro-foundations of knowledge-related processes. Taking into account this standpoint, I shall focus attention on the frameworks of research on individual preferences for participation in knowledge creation and knowledge sharing processes.

In order to see if the above-stated hypothesis about a potential contradiction between conditions for knowledge creation and knowledge sharing can be justified at an individual level of analysis, let us turn to an overview of the literature. Theory and research on creativity consider, among other issues, features of an individual that support knowledge creation (see, e.g., Barron & Harrington, 1981; Ford, 1996; Oldham& Cummings, 1996; Ruscio et al., 1998; Amabile et al., 2002). For example, Sternberg distinguishes, based on his research, the following components (features) of creativity in an individual: lack of conventionality, unorthodox thinking, readiness to question common norms, ability to put old information together in a new way and make connections between seemingly different things, aesthetic taste and imagination, flexibility (including ability to change directions), and drive for accomplishment and recognition (Sternberg, 1986). Other authors mention similar features, along with originality of thinking, risk taking, internal locus of control, metaphoric thinking, ability to find order in chaos, emotional instability, and others (Barron & Harrington, 1981; Amabile, 1988; Woodman, 1993; Oldham & Cummings, 1996; Amabile et al., 2005).

Now let us consider features of an individual who is disposed to knowledge sharing and is capable of participating in it successfully. An inclination to put forward and develop one's own ideas and an orientation to self-interests are considered to be significant individual barriers to knowledge sharing (Husted & Michailova, 2002). In contrast, an orientation to group interests and group recognition, an inclination toward cooperation, valuing group relationships, emotional stability, and extraversion facilitate participation

Table 1. Characteristics of an individual inclined to one of the knowledge-related processes

Characteristics	*Inclined to knowledge creation, oriented to innovation*	*Inclined to knowledge sharing, oriented to replication*
Thinking	Original	Standardized
Group behaviour	Independent, non-conformist	Group affiliation, conformist
Authority	Self-oriented	Oriented on external authorities
Motivation	Self-actualization, recognition	Safety, group affiliation
Value system	Values achievement	Values relations
Attitude to goals	Hard-hitting goals motivate	Hard-hitting goals de-motivate

in knowledge sharing (Husted & Michailova, 2002; Bock et al., 2005; Cabrera et al., 2006). Table 1 presents a brief summary of a comparative analysis, in which some of the above-mentioned features are grouped in pairs.

Comparing the two columns of the table, one can conclude that an individual can hardly simultaneously combine features that support knowledge creation and knowledge sharing, as this would imply an inclination towards contradictory values and behaviours. Thus, the table provides vivid illustration of the idea that individual level factors promoting knowledge creation and knowledge sharing may contradict each other. In terms of the discussion of ambidexterity above, I suggest that while organizations can try to combine both orientations, for an individual this task is extremely arduous if indeed it is ever possible. So, based on the above analysis, I formulated the following hypothesis to be examined:

There are two clusters of individuals: those more inclined towards knowledge creation, and those more inclined towards knowledge sharing. These two clusters are non-overlapping, meaning that a person cannot be oriented to both innovation and replication at the same time.

I supposed that an individual can switch his/her orientation from one process to another during his/her life, but that at every specific moment he/she is inclined towards behaviour that mainly supports only one of the knowledge-related processes in question. I was also interested to discover whether this orientation to one of the processes depends on the socio-demographic characteristics of an individual. The results of the research are given in the following sections.

RESEARCH STRATEGY

I explored this hypothesis within the research project that I conducted during 2006-2007, which covered a wide range of questions on knowledge management in Russian knowledge-intensive companies. In this section I will introduce research methodology issues that are relevant to the above hypothesis.

I chose to focus this research on knowledge-intensive companies for two reasons. First, by the very nature of their business, these companies represent a fertile field for research on knowledge-related processes and, in particular, on individual participation in these processes, as they constitute core business activities in these companies. Second, as mentioned in the Introduction, the understanding of individual knowledge-related behaviour is of strategic importance for the competitiveness of knowledge-intensive firms.

Focusing on knowledge-intensive companies, I needed to identify particular companies as the object of the research, and this required defining the concept of a "knowledge-intensive company." This question does not have a self-evident solution, as this concept "does not lend itself to precise definition or delimitation," as Alvesson (2000, p. 1103) notes. The term is usually applied to those firms in which most work is of an intellectual nature and in which knowledge is more important than other resources (Starbuck, 1992; Alvesson, 1995). Yet on the level of empirical research, the common approach is to define "knowledge-intensive companies" as those having well-educated, highly qualified employees as the major part of the workforce (Alvesson, 2000). For instance, Starbuck (1992) in his study defined a "knowledge-intensive firm" as a company in which not less than one-third of the workforce consists of specialists with an education at the doctoral level. I believe that this approach is not unproblematic (see, e.g., Swan & Kinnie, 2003). One of the counterarguments is that a doctoral-level education differs in ease of access in different countries, with the result that similar companies from different countries may differ significantly according to this criterion. In Russia, university and doctoral-level education has been widely accessible (Andreeva, 2007). That is why in my research I followed the approach proposed by Swan and Kinnie, who defined "knowledge-intensive firms" "as the organisations . . . that employ highly skilled individuals and therefore create market value through the application of knowledge to novel, complex client demands." They urged the application of these criteria to each individual organization (Swan & Kinnie, 2003, p. 15).

Research procedures. I developed a questionnaire for gathering data on the hypothesis. To meet the research goals, based on a literature analysis (Barron & Harrington, 1981; Sternberg, 1986; Amabile, 1988; Oldham & Cummings, 1996; Ford, 1996; Ruscio et al., 1998; Amabile et al., 2002; Husted & Michailova, 2002; Amabile et al., 2005; Bock et al., 2005; Cabrera et al,. 2006), I formulated a number of questions (21 in total) covering different aspects of individuals' preferences regarding participation in knowledge creation and knowledge sharing processes. The questions were primarily of the closed multiple-choice type. In designing the questionnaire I shuffled randomly characteristics representing knowledge creation and knowledge sharing profiles in order to avoid respondent biases.

I was also interested in discovering by which characteristics the two different groups of individuals differ from each other, assuming they exist as hypothesised. For this reason, I added to the questionnaire two more sections: one on the socio-demographic characteristics of respondents (age, education level, years of experience in profession, etc.), and another on work-related motives. Measuring motivation for work is not unproblematic, and knowledge work is not an exception (Kubo & Saka, 2002; Amar, 2004; Hendriks & Sousa, 2006). Among the various theories of human motivation developed by psychologists, A. Maslow's pyramid of human needs (or, to be precise, the need to revise the order of needs he suggested) has been often cited in relation to knowledge work (e.g. Miller, 2002; Brelade & Harman, 2003; Dunkin, 2003). For this reason, I decided to base the motivational section on Maslow's five-factor motivation model (though not replicating it precisely), and the questions on motives referred to these five motives: stability, material well-being, group affiliation, social recognition, and self-actualization. The motivational section of our questionnaire cannot be treated as a comprehensive tool for studying work-related motivation, as it may provide only partial insight, but I believe that it fits the purposes of this research, which is primarily concerned with the knowledge management issues in Russian knowledge-intensive firms.

The questionnaire was pilot-tested with a number of experts as well as with a number of employees from knowledge-intensive companies. The follow-up interviews with these respondents suggested some minor improvements in the wording and format of questions to ensure that they would be properly understood. The questionnaire was run with the help of the Web interface in order to ensure the anonymity of answers.

Research sample. As the research involved individuals from various knowledge-intensive firms, there are two samples within the data: one of the individual employees, and one of the companies.

Sample of companies. Taking into account the above-described considerations on the identification of knowledge-intensive organizations, I used a selective approach to choose the companies for the research, with the first stage involving the analysis of secondary information about target companies, as well as primary information obtained in direct contact with representatives of the companies to make sure that the company fits the criteria. I ended up with five participating firms, small and medium-sized Russian companies (with from 20 to 200 employees), having knowledge-based activities as the core of their business, employing highly-skilled individuals, and regularly dealing with novel and unique client demands. Industry-wise, two of them provide management consulting, the other two offer engineering services, and the fifth is engaged in software development.

Sample of individuals. One hundred and twenty respondents filled in the questionnaire. 42.5% of respondents were women and 57.5% men. 69% of the respondents were in the 20–34 age range. The majority of the respondents had at least one higher education degree (84%). 34% of the respondents had been working in their profession for 4 to 10 years, and 29% for 1 to 3 years.

Table 2. Results of factor analysis

No	Question	Component		
		1	2	3
1	I like working with what I already have and do not spend time on fantasies. (-) / I like working with imaginary situations. (+)			-,559
2	I try to control any situation; it makes my actions more efficient. (-) / I do not spend effort on controlling all situations; uncertainty always means some new chances. (+)		,306	-,536
3*	I like working in a constantly changing environment, when I cannot predict how the situation will change and which task will become topical.			,552
4*	I enjoy revising customary work methods constantly.			,654
5*	I enjoy solving totally new, atypical tasks.			,470
6	Most valuable ideas for my work were inspired by different fields unrelated to my profession. (-) / Most valuable ideas for my work I borrowed from colleagues and experts in my field or from special literature in my field. (+)			,381
7*	I work more effectively alone, even if I am surrounded by specialists with whom I have good relationships.	,526		
8	***How do you typically solve the tasks that are new for you?***			
8.1.	I perform task analysis and find a solution on my own.	-,410		-,422
8.2.	I start with task analysis on my own, then check my ideas with colleagues and experts, and then formulate a solution.		-,597	
8.3.	I search for experts who have already faced similar tasks and adopt their experience.		-,411	
8.4.	Such tasks are solved in group work and solutions are developed by the group.	,524	-,382	
9	***If you feel a need for development of your professional knowledge, what do you usually do?***			
9.1	I search our company information base.	,560		
9.2	I search for books, manuals, and information on the Internet and study them on my own.			-,379
9.3	I turn to colleagues from my department for their advice and experience.	,743		
9.4	I turn to experts in the field I am interested in for their advice and experience, irrespectively of which department of my company they belong to.		-,499	
9.5	I turn to experts from other organizations (to my professional community) for their advice and experience.		-,702	
9.6	I turn to my direct boss for his advice and experience.	,640		
10*	***If I develop or master a new way of solving my professional tasks, I willingly share it with…***			
10.1*	colleagues from my department.	-,454	,430	
10.2*	specialists from other departments of our company.		,593	
10.3*	specialists from other companies.		,604	

** Questions marked with an "*" have an inverted scale. This means that the maximum value corresponds to a fully negative answer to this question.*

As the financial motives of the respondents are a significant factor, to be discussed below, the level of material well-being of the respondents in the sample is relevant. With regard to average monthly income per family member, no specific income grouping dominated the sample: 25% of the respondents reported 300–450 euros and 23% 600–900 euros per month per family member.

RESEARCH FINDINGS AND DISCUSSION

Individual orientation towards different knowledge-related processes. In order to examine the hypothesis, I performed consequent factor and cluster analysis of the data. Factor analysis of the data (using principal factor analysis) showed that the questionnaire I had developed measured characteristics of an individual's behaviour along three independent, non-overlapping axes (factors) (Table 2).

Analyzing the content of the questions within each factor, I identified them as follows: factor 1: individual orientation to group interactions in knowledge-related processes; factor 2: individual orientation to independent (self-dependent) work in knowledge-related processes (with a negative sign); factor 3: individual orientation to creative, innovative activities versus replication (with a negative sign). Negative signs are technical consequences of the questionnaire design, as some of the questions had an inverted measurement scale in order to ensure maximum objectivity of the responses.

Further, I performed cluster analysis, taking these three factors as variables. I used the hierarchical clustering method and measured the distance by the square of the Euclidian distance. The results of this analysis are provided in Table 3.

As one can see from Table 3, the cluster analysis resulted in five clusters, two of which (#1 and #4) are large enough for further statistical analysis. The other three clusters are too small, so they were disregarded in the next stage of the analysis. Further, I compared these two groups of respondents in terms of three factors identified earlier, as represented in Table 4.

Table 4 demonstrates that these two clusters differ significantly in only one factor, factor 3.

Table 5 shows that cluster #4 is statistically significantly different from cluster #1, but only in terms of one factor, factor 3. Taking into account the meaning of the factors, this means that cluster #4 includes individuals who are more inclined towards innovation, while cluster #1 includes individuals who are more inclined towards knowledge sharing and replication. Thus the hypothesis about

Table 3. Identified clusters of individuals

Cluster #	Number of respondents	Sample %	Valid sample %
1	***43***	***35.8***	***58.1***
2	1	.8	1.4
3	4	3.3	5.4
4	***25***	***20.8***	***33.8***
5	1	.8	1.4
Total*	74	61.7	100.0

** The total number of cases (individuals) who were included in the cluster analysis is smaller than the total sample size (74 versus 120), as the rest of the cases were excluded because of missing data for some of the factors.*

Table 4. The significance of differences between clusters #1 and #4

Factor: individual orientation to specific behaviour in knowledge-related processes:	t-criterion of equality of means		
	t	Degrees of freedom	Significance (2-sided)
Factor 1: orientation to group interactions	.107	66	.915
Factor 2: orientation to independent work	1.244	66	.218
Factor 3: orientation to innovative/ replicative activities	12.255	66	*.000*

Table 5. Descriptive statistics for factor 3

Factors	Clusters	Cluster size	Mean	Standard deviation	Standard mean error
Factor 3: orientation to innovative/ replicative activities	#1	43	.6733220	.57427753	.08757650
	#4	25	-1.0850069	.56371864	.11274373

two non-overlapping groups of individuals, those more inclined towards knowledge creation and those more inclined towards knowledge sharing, is confirmed within the sample.

Differences between identified clusters. As I have addressed this hypothesis within the framework of a large research project on the specifics of knowledge management in Russian knowledge-intensive companies, the project questionnaire included also a number of questions on the work-related motives of individuals. A detailed discussion of the results of this aspect of my research is beyond the focus of this paper. Here I concentrate on the findings that are related to the clusters of individuals that have been identified.

I was interested to check whether my suppositions concerning the significance of the different motives of individuals with different preferences towards knowledge-related processes were validated by this sample. Based on the literature analysis, I proposed (see Table 1) that employees more inclined towards knowledge creation tend to value self-actualization more than the other motives, while employees more inclined towards knowledge sharing tend to value group affiliation more than the other motives. The questionnaire included three items to measure each of the five motives that I had identified. For this reason, the first step in examining these ideas was to carry out a factor analysis to minimize the number of variables. Factorization by the principal-factor analysis method demonstrated that the questionnaire items grouped together exactly as they were designed to do; thus, five factors measuring five motives emerged out of this. The next step was to compare clusters #1 and #4 according to these factors. The results of the data analysis are presented in Tables 6 and 7.

One can see from the above tables that the clusters that were identified statistically differ in the significance of two motives, the motive of group affiliation and the motive of self-actualization. Individuals from cluster #4 (those more inclined towards knowledge creation) placed a

Table 6. The significance of differences in motives between clusters of respondents

		t-criterion of equality of means		
#	Factors (Motives)	t	Degrees of freedom	Significance (2-sided)
1	*Group affiliation*	*2.345*	*65*	*.022*
2	Stability	1.591	65	.116
3	*Self-actualization*	*-2.133*	*65*	*.037*
4	Social recognition	.406	65	.686
5	Material well-being	.490	65	.626

Table 7. Descriptive statistics for motives 1 and 3

Factors (Motives)	Clusters	Cluster size	Mean	Standard deviation	Standard mean error
Group affiliation	#1	43	.3347992	.93898099	.14319326
	#4	24	-.2029679	.82463946	.16832883
Self-actualization	#1	43	-.1312698	1.17351283	.17895903
	#4	24	.4203101	.62980875	.12855917

comparatively higher value on the motive of self-actualization, while individuals from cluster #1 (those more inclined towards knowledge sharing and replication) placed a comparatively higher value on the motive of group affiliation. These results confirmed my suppositions about the features of individuals belonging to the clusters I identified.

I was also interested in checking whether an individual's affiliation with one of the identified clusters was related to his/her socio-demographic characteristics. A data analysis revealed no relationships between individual inclination towards one of the knowledge-related processes and such characteristics as sex, age, level of education, or work experience. Statistically significant differences between two clusters of respondents were found with regard to the "average monthly income per family member" variable: this income was found to be relatively higher for cluster #4 (those more inclined towards knowledge creation) than for cluster #1 (those more inclined towards knowledge sharing) ($p = 0.012$ by the Mann-Whitney criterion). This finding looks very interesting in the light of the common view that the creative orientation of an individual does not depend on his/her material well-being (the so-called "hungry artist paradox"). The explanation of this result may be found in the opposite direction: it is not better material well-being that stimulates creativity, but inclination toward knowledge creation that finally brings better salaries, as people with such an inclination may purposefully seek specific jobs that are usually better paid by knowledge-intensive organizations.

The clusters showed differences with regard to one other variable: the "number of companies the respondent has worked for during his/her professional life," though these differences were only at the level of a statistical trend ($p = 0.060$). Most individuals from cluster # 1 (inclined towards knowledge sharing) had worked in fewer then three companies, while most of those in cluster #4 (inclined towards knowledge creation) had worked in three to five companies. One of the potential explanations for this is that individuals oriented towards knowledge creation are inclined to change their jobs more often in search of new tasks and new experience. Still, this cluster did not correlate with the largest number of companies an individual has worked for on the scale that was used. Probably this is because a higher rate of changing jobs (over five companies, taking into account that 69% of respondents were under 35 years old) would tend to indicate not an aspiration for new things but an inability to settle down or adapt in any organization.

Discussion and research limitations. One of the important questions that arise from these findings concerns the other three clusters, which were too small for further analysis (two clusters with one individual and one cluster with four individuals). Do these clusters appear just as a consequence of accidental deviations in the data, or do they represent some other behavioural intentions, though very rare, that could have been revealed if the sample was significantly bigger? Splitting all individuals into two broad categories obviously represents some simplification of a complex reality, and I can suggest there are at least two potential groups of individuals that may stand behind these clusters. First, these may be individuals who experienced a change in their behavioural inclination exactly during the time of the research and thus were caught "in the middle" between the two orientations we discuss. Secondly, these may be individuals who succeeded in efficiently combining and maintaining simultaneously both orientations, though in my opinion such an "ambidextrous" behavioural orientation would be too difficult for an individual to maintain. These questions call for further research with the bigger sample.

The fact that the questionnaire's items were grouped into three factors, while I found differences between clusters of individuals only with regard to one factor, bears important implications for future research design. It means that for the purposes of verifying the hypothesis a much shorter questionnaire, covering only the items that were included in factor 3, might be enough.

The presented findings should of course be considered only within the scope of the limitations of the research design. One limitation lies in the number of firms within the sample of companies, which was quite small. This fact may have affected the findings by limiting them to demonstrating situations in particular companies instead of more general trends. However, as the sample of five companies represents three industries and organizations of different size, life cycle, and overall strategy, I suggest that the findings may indicate some general tendencies. Another limitation lies in the size of the sample of individuals, which, though being much larger than that of the companies, is not very large. It is possible that the size of the sample of individuals was the reason I was able to identify only two significant clusters. However, I suggest that this sample is suitable for the exploratory stage of this research.

One other limitation can be seen in the quantitative research method. Closed questions in an anonymous written survey certainly have a limited capacity for measuring individual intentions and motives. Thus I suggest that further research in this area needs to combine both quantitative and qualitative methods, such as interviews with employees.

IMPLICATIONS AND CONCLUSION

In this section, I first propose some implications of the findings for knowledge management theory. Next, I formulate some implications for the management of knowledge-intensive organizations.

Implications for knowledge management theory. The findings suggest that individuals can be inclined primarily towards either creating new knowledge or sharing and applying existing knowledge, and that a person can hardly be inclined to (and thus, be efficient in) both processes at the same time. This means that at least on the micro-level of analysis, there is a certain tension between knowledge creation and knowledge sharing processes. This idea challenges the common view in the contemporary knowledge management literature, which holds that knowledge creation and knowledge sharing processes are positively interrelated. Evidently the research and its results have certain limitations in terms of sample size and data collection tools. Yet, I believe it can serve to initiate further discussion and research on this topical issue that will lead to a more comprehensive understanding of the interrelationship between these two key knowledge-related processes.

I also suggest that these results should be of interest for another conceptual discussion: namely, the definition of "knowledge worker." Although this term has been circulating in the literature for a few decades already (starting with Drucker, 1959), up to now there has been no single and precise understanding of it (Kelloway & Barling, 2000; Joseph, 2005). Various authors used different characteristics to identify this group; for example, the share of mental work out of all work performed (Flood et al., 2001), level of education (more precisely, an advanced degree) (Flood et al., 2001; Starbuck, 1992; Drucker, 2002), and profession (e.g. Davenport et al., 1996). The "capability to create new knowledge" is one of the characteristics which is very often ascribed to knowledge workers. For example, Miller suggests that knowledge workers are those "workers who are not normally following a defined procedure, but exploiting all their creativity, knowledge and skills to move the business forward" (Miller, 2002, p.17). The respondents within our sample can be qualified as knowledge workers according to certain criteria, but above all due to the fact that they are engaged in knowledge-intensive companies and thus are deeply involved in knowledge work (Kelloway & Barling, 2000). Yet our findings suggest that individuals who work with knowledge may differ in their inclination towards knowledge creation, and thus such criterion should be used in defining this group of employees with great care.

Implications for the management of knowledge-intensive organizations. On the practical level, the existence of two non-overlapping groups of employees with different orientations towards knowledge creation and knowledge sharing processes has a number of implications for managerial practices in knowledge-intensive firms, especially in the human resource management area.

First of all, I suggest that a KIF needs to analyse its particular industry/business as well as its strategy from this point of view in order to understand which of the two knowledge-related processes — knowledge creation or knowledge sharing and replication — is more critical for the achievement of its current strategic goals. Although KIFs are commonly thought of as focused on knowledge creation, the answer to this question is not as evident as it may seem. For example, a company's priorities in relation to these two processes may change over time as the company passes through different stages of its lifecycle. Using Greiner's model as a framework (Greiner, 1972), I speculate that in the stage of growth through creativity (the first stage in Greiner's model) knowledge creation is the key, while in the stage of growth through co-ordination (the fourth stage) knowledge sharing and replication come to the foreground. Another example of the shift in priorities between these two processes involves the change in the competitive environment when, with the maturing of a company's industry and/or the intensification of the price competition in the industry, focus on knowledge creation may become too costly and weaken a company's bottom line. Yet even KIFs operating at the same time within the same industry may have different priorities regarding knowledge creation and knowledge sharing, depending on their strategy. For instance, in the management consulting industry, some companies focus on providing standardized services, while others position themselves as providers of unique client solutions.

A company's human resource management priorities need to be aligned with its strategic focus on one of these knowledge-related processes. I believe that any knowledge-intensive organization needs both types of the employees I have identified, but their optimal proportions within the total workforce may vary among different organizations depending on their current strategic focus, as described above. Moreover, the intensity of demand for employees more inclined either towards knowledge creation or towards knowledge-replication may vary among different departments within the same organization. Thus, staffing decisions need to fit into an organization's strategic priorities regarding knowledge creation versus knowledge sharing, and at the same time ensure that both types of employees are represented in a company. Though this recommendation may sound self-evident, both my current research and my consulting experience demonstrate that knowledge-intensive organizations tend to over-focus in their staffing policies (especially in their selection procedures) on those individuals who are more inclined towards knowledge creation, irrespectively of the realistic needs of their business, which in turn results in frequent (and sometimes costly!) cases of "reinventing the wheel."

Another implication of my findings for human resource management practices in knowledge-intensive organizations is that managers should not expect or require from their employees an equally high level of performance for both processes. This understanding has to be incorporated into employee assessment criteria and procedures, as well as into remuneration schemes. For instance, I encountered during my research a knowledge-intensive company that desperately needed to focus on replication in order to cut product costs and maintain its competitive position, but its bonuses system included only bonuses for various types of knowledge creation, such as proposals for new product solutions.

Extrapolating these findings from the individual to the organizational level of analysis concerning the interrelations between knowledge creation and knowledge sharing and replication, I suggest that managers' efforts to develop organizational structure, culture, communication systems, etc. aimed at supporting these knowledge-related processes cannot focus on both of these processes simultaneously and be efficient. However, this proposition needs further empirical research.

ACKNOWLEDGMENT

I would like to thank Andrei D.Nasledov, PhD, Associate Professor, St. Petersburg State University, for his help in statistical data analysis; Vasily E. Raskov, for fruitful discussions of ideas for Table 1; and anonymous reviewers for their valuable comments.

REFERENCES

Alavi, M., Kayworth T. R., & Leidner, D. E. (2006). An Empirical Examination of the Influence of Organizational Culture on Knowledge Management Practices. *Journal of Management Information Systems, 22*(3), 191-224.

Alvesson, M. (1995). *Management of Knowledge Intensive Companies*. Berlin and New York : De Gruyter.

Alvesson, M. (2000). Social Identity and the Problem of Loyalty in Knowledge-Intensive Companies. *Journal of Management Studies, 37*(8), 1101-1123.

Amabile, T.M. (1988). A Model of Creativity and Innovation in Organizations. In B. M. Staw & Cummings, L. L. (Eds.), *Research in Organizational Behavior, 10*. Greenwich, CT: JAI Press, 123-167.

Amabile, T. M., Barsade, S. G., Mueller, J. S., & Staw, B.M. (2005). Affect and Creativity at Work. *Administrative Science Quarterly, 50*(3), 367-403.

Amabile, T. M., Hadley, C. N., & Kramer, S. J. (2002). Creativity Under the Gun. *Harvard Business Review, 80*(8), 52-61.

Amar, A.D. (2004). Motivating Knowledge Workers to Innovate: A Model Integrating Motivation Dynamics and Antecedents. *European Journal of Innovation Management, 7*(2), 89-101.

Andreeva, T. (2007). Rabotnik intellectualnogo truda: podhod k opredeleniju. ("Knowledge Worker: An Attempt to Define the Phenomena"). *Vestnik St. Peterburgskogo Gosudarstvennogo Universiteta, Serija Management, 4*, 32-49.

Argote, L., & Ingram, P. (2000). Knowledge Transfer: A Basis for Competitive Advantage in Firms. *Organizational Behavior and Human Decision Processes, 82*(1), 150-169.

Barron, F. B., & Harrington, D. M. (1981). Creativity, Intelligence, and Personality. *Annual Review of Psychology, 32*, 439-476.

Becker, B., & Gerhart, B. (1996). The Impact of Human Resource Management on Organizational Performance: Progress and Prospects. *Academy of Management Journal, 39*(4), 779-801.

Bock, G.-W., Zmud, R. W., Kim Y.-G., Lee, J.-N. (2005). Behavioral Intention Formation in Knowledge Sharing: Examining the Roles of Extrinsic Motivators, Social-psychological Forces, and Organizational Climate. MIS Quarterly, 29(1), 87-111.

Boxall, P. & Steeneveld, M. (1999). Human Resource Strategy and Competitive Advantage: A Longitudinal Study of Engineering Consultancies. *Journal of Management Studies, 36*(4), 443-63.

Brelade, S., & Harman, C. (2003). Knowledge Workers Want to Reap Rewards. *Strategic HR Review. 2*(2), 18-21.

Brown, J. S., & Duguid, P. (2002). Balancing Act: How to Capture Knowledge without Killing It. *Harvard Business Review. 78*(3), 73-80.

Cabrera A., Collins, W. C., & Salgado, J. F. (2006). Determinants of Individual Engagement in Knowledge Sharing. *International Journal of Human Resource Management, 17*(2), 245-264.

Christensen, P. H. (2005). Facilitating knowledge sharing — conceptual framework. (Copenhagen Business School Working paper SMG WP 4/2005).

Davenport, T., & Prusak, L. (2000). *Working Knowledge: How Corporations Manage What They Know*. Boston: Harvard Business School Press.

Davenport, T. H., Thomas, R. J., & Cantrell S. (2002). The Mysterious Art and Science of Knowledge-Worker Performance. *MIT Sloan Management Review, 44*(1), 23-30.

DeLong, D., & Fahey L. (2000). Diagnosing Cultural Barriers to Knowledge Management. *Academy of Management Executives, 14*(4), 118-127.

Dunkin, R. (2003). Motivating Knowledge Workers: Lessons to and from the Corporate Sector. Higher Education Management and Policy, 15(3), 41-49.

Flood, P. C., Turner, T., Ramamoorthy, N., & Pearson, J. (2001). Causes and Consequences of Psychological Contracts among Knowledge Workers in the High Technology and Financial Services Industries. *International Journal of Human Resource Management, 12*(7), 1152-1165.

Ford, C. M. (1996). A Theory of Individual Creative Action in Multiple Social Domains. *Academy of Management Review, 21*(4), 1112-1142.

Foss N., & Felin, T. (2006). Individuals and Organizations: Thoughts on a Micro-Foundations Project for Strategic Management. *Research Methodology in Strategy and Management, 3*, 253-288.

Gibson, C. B., & Birkinshaw, J. (2004). The antecedents, Consequences and Mediating Role of Organizational Ambidexterity. *Academy of Management Journal, 47*, 209-226.

Grant, R. M. (1996). Toward a Knowledge-based Theory of the Firm. *Strategic Management Journal, 17*, 109-122.

Greiner, L. (1972). Evolution and Revolution as Organizations Grow. *Harvard Business Review* (July–August), 37-46.

Gupta, A., Smith, K. G., & Shalley, C. E. (2006). The Interplay between Exploration and Exploitation. *Academy of Management Journal, 49*(4), 693-706.

Hansen, M. T., Mors, M. L., Løvås, B. (2005). Knowledge Sharing in Organizations: Multiple Networks, Multiple Phases. *Academy of Management Journal, 48*(5), 776-793.

Hedlund, G. (1994). A Model of Knowledge Management and the N-form Corporation. *Strategic Management Journal, 15*(5), 73-90.

Hendriks, P., & Sousa, C. (2006). Motivation for Knowledge Work." In David G. Schwartz (Ed.) *Encyclopedia of Knowledge Management*. Hershey, PA: Idea Group Publishing, (pp. 656-664).

Husted, K., & Michailova, S. (2002). Diagnosing and Fighting Knowledge-sharing Hostility. *Organizational Dynamics 31*(1), 60-73.

Kelloway, E., & Barling, J. (2000). Knowledge Work as Organizational Behavior. *International Journal of Management Reviews, 2*(3), 287-304.

Kogut, B., & Zander, U. (1992). Knowledge of the Firm, Combinative Capabilities, and the Replication of Technology. *Organization Science, 3*(3), 383-397.

Kubo, I., & Saka, A. (2002). An Inquiry into the Motivations of Knowledge Workers in the Japanese Financial Industry. *Journal of Knowledge Management*, *6*(3), 262-271.

Lepak, D. P., & Snell, S. (1999). The Human Resource Architecture: Toward a Theory of Human Capital Allocation and Development. *Academy of Management Review, 24* (1), 31-48.

March, J. G. (1991). Exploration and Exploitation in Organizational Learning. *Organization Science, 2*(1), 71-87.

Maslow, A. (1954). *Motivation and Personality.* New York: Harper & Row.

Miles, R. E., Snow, C. S., Mathews, J. A., Miles, G., & Coleman Jr., H. J. (1997). Organizing in the Knowledge Age: Anticipating the Cellular Form. *Academy of Management Executives, 11*(4), 7-20.

Minbaeva, D., Pedersen, T., Björkman, I., Fey, C. F, & Park, H. J. (2003). MNC Knowledge Transfer, Subsidiary Absorptive Capacity, and HRM. *Journal of International Business Studies, 34*(6), 586-599.

Nonaka, I. (1991). The Knowledge-Creating Company. *Harvard Business Review 69*(6), 96–104.

Nonaka, I., & Konno, N. (1998) The Concept of 'Ba': Building a Foundation for Knowledge Creation. *California Management Review, 40*(3), 40-54.

Nurmi, R. (1998). Knowledge-intensive Firms. *Business Horizons 41*(3), 26-32.

Oldham, G. R., & Cummings, A. (1996). Employee Creativity: Personal and Contextual Factors at Work. *Academy of Management Journal, 39*(3), 607-634.

Robertson, M., & Hammersley, G. O. (2000). Knowledge Management Practices within a Knowledge-Intensive Firm: The Significance of the People Management Dimension. *Journal of European Industrial Training, 24*(2-4), 241-254.

Robertson, M., & Swan, J. (2003). Control—What Control? Culture and Ambiguity within a Knowledge Intensive Firm. *Journal of Management Studies, 40*(4), 831-858.

Romer, P.M., & Kurtzman, J. (2004). In *Handbook on Knowledge Management,* Chapter 1: Knowledge Matters, (pp. 73-87).

Ruscio, J., Whitney, D. M., & Amabile, T .M. (1998). Looking inside the Fishbowl of Creativity: Verbal and Behavioral Predictors of Creative Performance. *Creativity Research Journal, 11*(3), 243-263.

Schumpeter, J. A. (1934). *The Theory of Economic Development*. Cambridge, MA: Harvard University Press.

Starbuck, W. H. (1992), Learning by Knowledge-intensive Firms. *Journal of Management Studies 3*(4), 262-275.

Sternberg, R. J. (1986). Intelligence, Wisdom, and Creativity: Three is Better than One. *Educational Psychologist 21*(3), 175-190.

Storey, J. (2005). Human Resource Policies for Knowledge Work. In T. Ray, P. Quintas & S. Little (Eds.), *Managing Knowledge: An Essential Reader*. London: Sage, (pp. 199-219).

Swart, J., & Kinnie, N. (2003). HR Policies and Processes in Knowledge Intensive Organisations. *Human Resource Management Journal, 13* (2), 13-28.

Szulanski, G. (1996). Exploring Internal Stickiness: Impediments to the Transfer of Best Practice within the Firm. *Strategic Management Journal, 17*, 27-43.

Szulanski, G., & Winter, S. (2002). Getting it Right the Second Time. *Harvard Business Review, 80* (1), 63-69.

Teece, D. J. (2004). Knowledge and Competence as Strategic Assets. In *Handbook on Knowledge Management,* Chapter 1: Knowledge Matters, (pp. 129-152).

Tsai, W. (2002). "ocial Structure of 'Competition' within a Multiunit Organization: Coordination, Competition, and Intraorganizational Knowledge Sharing. *Organization Science 13* (2), 179-190.

Tsoukas, H., & Vladimirou, E. (2001). What is Organizational Knowledge? *Journal of Management Studies 38*(7), 973-993.

Tushman, M. L., & O'Reilly, C. A. (1996). Ambidextrous Organizations: Managing Evolutionary and Revolutionary Change. *California Management Review 38*, 8-30.

Van de Ven, A. (1986). Central Problems in the Management of Innovation. *Management Science, 32*(5), 590-607.

Van Looy, B., Martens, T., & Debackere, K. (2005). Organizing for Continuous Innovation: On the Sustainability of Ambidextrous Organizations. *Creativity and Innovation Management, 14*(3), 208-221.

Woodman, R. W., Savyer, J. E., & Griffin, R. W. (1993). Toward a Theory of Organizational Creativity. *Academy of Management Journal 18*(2), 293-321.

KEY TERMS

Ambidexterity: Organizational characteristic, that defines that companies that know how to successfully combine both exploration and exploitation (related term - ambidextrous organization).

Exploitation: An organizational strategy concentrated on utilization of existing knowledge and opportunities.

Exploration: An organizational strategy focused on creating value through searching for new knowledge and opportunities.

Knowledge-Intensive Organization: A firm whose main activity is based on the employment of knowledge.

Knowledge Creation: The process of development of new knowledge.

Knowledge Exchange: Type of knowledge sharing, characterized by some reciprocity of actions, implying that knowledge (or something else in exchange for knowledge) has been moved each way within the same pair of actors.

Knowledge Replication: Type of knowledge transfer, in which a receiver acts upon "sent" knowledge by trying to "copy" a sender's experience. It refers to the usage of something that existed before in a particular company.

Knowledge Sharing: The process of moving existing knowledge between different agents (either within organization or beyond its borders). It implies dissemination of knowledge by a knowledge "sender" without any specification of a knowledge "receiver's" reaction to this act.

Knowledge Transfer: Type of knowledge sharing, in which a receiver at least absorbed "sent" knowledge and probably even acted somehow upon it.

Innovation: Refers either or both -to the process of development of new knowledge or results of this process.

Section VII
Discussing Knowledge

Chapter XXIX
The 'Value' of Knowledge:
Reappraising Labour in the Post-Industrial Economy

Steffen Böhm
University of Essex, UK

Chris Land
University of Essex, UK

ABSTRACT

Knowledge is implicitly assumed to form an increasingly important, or even the dominant source of values for today's knowledge based organizations. It is rare, however, to encounter writings questioning what is 'value', enquiring into its provenance, or examining its distribution amongst organization's stakeholders. This chapter asks these very questions, focusing on Marx's (1976) formulation of value theory. Divided into four parts, it begins by giving a basic overview of the labour theory of value, as developed by Marx in mid 19th century, industrialised England. The second part examines Roy Jacques' (2000) critique of Marx, his rejection of the adequacy of 'labour' as a concept for analysing contemporary value production, and his call for a 'knowledge theory of value'. The third section focuses on labour process theorist Paul Thompson (2005) and his challenge to the idea that labour and knowledge are fundamentally different. The fourth part extends this concern with 'other' forms of contemporary labour to a more global level by examining De Angelis' (2006) and Retort's (2005) suggestion that the global economy today is driven by acts of enclosure and 'primitive accumulation.'

INTRODUCTION

For writings on knowledge management, knowledge based organizations, the knowledge economy and knowledge intensive firms, it is an implicit assumption that knowledge is an increasingly important, perhaps even the dominant, source of value for organizations today (Drucker, 1968; Leadbeater, 1999; Tapscott, 1996; Wenger et al, 2002). Knowledge, it is assumed, can create value in a number of ways: increasing access to cheaper resources or to new markets; fostering technical and organizational innovation; enhancing awareness of, and responsiveness to, the demands of customers; reducing the inefficiencies of repeatedly reinventing the wheel, especially in large, multi-national, distributed organizations. The list goes on. What is rare, however, is for such writings to ask exactly what 'value' is, to enquire into its provenance, or to question its distribution amongst the various stakeholders that constitute 'the organization' in its broader sense. This is despite value-creation being one of the key objectives of management, at least within capitalist enterprises (Jacques, 2000).

In this chapter we want to open up this discussion of value and knowledge by connecting with a set of well established debates over the locus of value in the economy. As we are concerned here with the substance of value – what value is and how it is created – we start not with neo-classical economics and marginalism but rather with the labour theory of value, as developed by Adam Smith, David Ricardo and Karl Marx. In this paper we focus on Marx's (1976) formulation of value theory for three reasons. First, as he was writing after Smith and Ricardo and built upon their ideas, his formulation of the labour theory of value is arguably the most developed. Second, Marx's critical perspective on political economy offers a critical leverage that allows us, even today, to address questions of social *values* alongside technical considerations of economic *value*. Third, and finally, Marx's legacy has been 150 years of intense theoretical exegesis, commentary, critique and development so that lines of analysis can be followed to examine the relevance of his ideas today.

The structure of the chapter is in four parts. The first gives a basic overview of the labour theory of value, as developed by Marx (1976) in mid 19th century, industrialised England. This provides the theoretical basis for the following discussions as well as indicating some points of continued relevance in Marx's theory today. The second part of the chapter examines Roy Jacques' (2000) critique of Marx, his rejection of the adequacy of 'labour' as a concept for analysing contemporary value production, and his call for a 'knowledge theory of value'. This is the section that is closest to conventional concerns with knowledge work and management. Jacques' critique of Marx resonates with other writings on the knowledge economy by suggesting a recent rupture, associated with the development of Information and Communication Technologies (ICT), between industrial capitalist and post-industrial forms of organization and value production. His critique of Marx thus provides us with a basis for evaluating Marx's theory of value, and its applicability to the world today. It also provides us with a counterpoint from which to evaluate the more contemporary Marxist perspectives examined in the third and fourth parts of the chapter. The third section examines labour process theorist Paul Thompson (2005) and his colleagues' (e.g., Warhurst and Thompson, 1998; Thompson et al., 2001) challenge to the idea that labour and knowledge are fundamentally different. This section draws attention to the empirical realities of work for the majority of people today, including those in so-called 'advanced' capitalist economies. Focusing on the UK, evidence is presented that suggests knowledge work has too readily been conflated with service work in general, despite much work in this sector being highly routinised, poorly paid, and sharing little with the dominant representations of knowledge work found in mainstream managerial writings.

The fourth section extends this concern with 'other' forms of contemporary labour to a more global level by examining De Angelis' (2006) and Retort's (2005) suggestion that the global economy today is driven by acts of enclosure and 'primitive accumulation' (Marx, 1976) whereby labour, resources and markets are expropriated for private profit through the exercise of naked power, predominantly through privatisation and military activity.

Throughout the development of these perspectives on value production we hope to perform the kind of inversion of traditional Marxist value theory that Diane Elson (1979) and David Harvey (1999) have referred to as a 'value theory of labour'. In part this is done through our critique of the suggestion that 'knowledge' is the dominant source of value today. By drawing attention to the economic significance of more traditional, industrial, or even pre-industrial, forms of value production and accumulation we hope to revalue those activities not as backwards and anachronistic but as an integral part, perhaps even the dominant reality, of today's so-called 'knowledge economy'. In addition to this empirical critique we also want to draw a cautionary note for our own labour as academics. By focusing so much of our attention on knowledge work, our research and teaching often functions to valorise knowledge work and thereby denigrate and marginalise the work of those who are not knowledge workers. In this sense our choices in deciding what to study, what to write about, and how to anatomise contemporary political-economic formations[a], help reproduce the very conditions that value the work of some and not others. Our 'knowledge work' legitimates and reproduces the hierarchies of evaluation that privilege the immaterial labour of 'knowledge workers' in the city of London over that of Coltan miners in the Congo, landless peasants in Brazil, or steel workers in China. This paper is intended, in part, as a corrective to this myopia in academic writings on knowledge work, and to function as a revaluation of these 'other' forms of work.

THE CLASSICAL MARXIST PERSPECTIVE: LABOUR IS THE SOLE SOURCE OF VALUE

When discussing the question of value production within capitalist economies it is impossible to exorcise the spectre of Marx that still haunts the dreams of political economists (and perhaps the nightmares of 'straight' economists) (Derrida, 1994). In the first volume of *Capital*, Marx (1976, see also 1985) offers us an extended meditation on the capitalist production of value. Starting with an analysis of the commodity form, Marx spirals out through a series of perspectival shifts to discover the source of value in 'living labour' (Marx, 1973: 361; Marx, 1976: 342). Marx starts his analysis by interrogating the commodity form and its circulation, working on the assumption that goods exchange upon some kind of rational basis of equivalence. If there was no basis for equivalence, then commodities could not be exchanged in a market relationship, or even in primitive barter, as there would be no ground upon which to claim that good x is equivalent to good y or two of good z. But such exchange does occur and Marx deduces that this is because they share a common 'value' that renders the commodities to be exchanged commensurable. But what is this value?

Today mainstream economists and management theorists have shifted this question of value to the sphere of exchange and consumption, resolving it in terms of the perceived utility of a commodity for the person buying or selling it[b]. This might well work in the context of primitive barter or in the context of a child's playground swap, but does it hold under conditions of monetised exchange? Where money, traditionally gold, has become a universal equivalent, the 'value' of a specific commodity has an external and objective measure in the money form. Under the conditions of perfect markets, artificial scarcity and monopoly should also no longer apply, so that a commodity will exchange, in the balance of supply and demand, at its value equivalent to other commodities. If this is the case, and commodities do indeed exchange, on average, at their value, then profit is inexplicable. Mercantile profit depends upon bringing commodities into a market where they are scarce, from one where they are abundant. Monopoly profits work by distorting exchange so that goods are artificially scarce and can be traded above their value. In both cases wealth can be redistributed but not created. Someone pays over the odds so another can profit. Hence, exploitation and profit are the result of distorted market functioning.

Marx finds the resolution to this problem by discovering one commodity with a unique property. The commodity is 'labour power' and its property is 'superadequacy' (Spivak, 1985). Arguably Marx's most significant theoretical insight was into the dual and indeterminate nature of labour as a commodity (Braverman, 1974). When exchanged upon a labour market, what the labourer sells and the capitalist purchases is the capacity to work, or 'labour power', but the utility of labour power is inherently indeterminate and open to negotiation and contestation. If the employee is worked harder and longer, then their labour power will offer the capitalist greater utility as a greater quantity of labour will be performed in exchange for their wage. This use value of labour power – 'labour' itself – is distinct from its exchange value, which determines a wage. For Marx, the exchange value of labour power is determined by the value of goods required for its maintenance and reproduction; in other words, the amount of money a worker requires to house, clothe and feed themselves at such a level that they are able to return to work day after day. Of course, this level is the basic 'value' of labour power. In reality the level of wages is socially determined through political struggle over wages, working conditions and living standards.

For Marx, then, it is labour time that is the ultimate measure of value. Like labour power itself, the value of a commodity is determined by the amount of labour time put into producing it, plus the value of any materials and tools used up in the course of its production. The latter can only have their value transferred to the new commodity but the labour time put into producing the new commodity creates new value. This is the heart of Marx's 'labour theory of value': labour is the only source of new value and, by dint of its ability to produce more value than it costs, labour power is at the heart of capitalist production. Of course, Marx spends over 1000 pages working through the implications of this idea in *Capital*, and the reality is rather more complex than this deceptively simple outline suggests. The main complication is that value is not determined by concrete labour time but by abstract, or 'socially necessary', labour time. This avoids the absurdity of suggesting that a less efficient worker, who takes longer to produce a given commodity, would thereby produce a commodity of greater value. Instead, the capitalist, by setting the speed of work and controlling it through direct supervision and the employment of machinery, sets the average rate of productivity and thereby determines the value of commodities through controlling the productivity of labour. In this respect Marx's labour theory of value also explains the capitalist imperative to innovate and accelerate the rate of commodity production. If an individual capitalist (or their managerial representative) can increase the productivity of the labour power they employ above the social average then, for a while at least, they will be able to enjoy super-profits. Capitalist and self-employed producers who are less able to invest in organizational and technological innovations will find themselves producing below the socially average rate and thus will suffer from a lower rate of profit and be less able to innovate and compete in the future.

So, how might Marx's labour theory of value inform our understanding of the role of knowledge in the economy today? A conventional Marxist interpretation would suggest that labour remains the source of all value as we are still living in a capitalist economy. Developments in techno-science and organizational innovations such as knowledge management might increase the productivity of labour power but they do not ultimately present a new source of value, just an improved means of exploiting labour. Nevertheless, such innovations are imperative from the point of view of capital. Unless an organization remains at the cutting-edge of technological development, its profitability will suffer. This is fairly obviously the case for new product development but it also applies to process innovation where the main goal is to improve the process of production and delivery, either by reducing waste or by increasing productivity. Waste reduction ensures that the maximum value of raw materials used is transferred to saleable commodities. Productivity increases reduce the labour time required to produce each commodity below the social average and thereby secure super-profits or a larger market share. In either case the additional value realised through knowledge and innovation is to make labour more productive.

In summary then, for Marx, 'knowledge' remains an adjunct to the productive power of labour[c]. Whilst techno-scientific and organizational knowledges are a part of labour-power insofar as they determine its socially average rate of productivity, it remains labour itself, and only labour, that produces value. This traditional Marxist interpretation has been found wanting by several commentators, particularly as it applies to the age of high-tech, informational capitalism. It is to one such critique that we now turn.

THE POST-INDUSTRIAL PERSPECTIVE: KNOWLEDGE HAS REPLACED LABOUR AS THE DOMINANT SOURCE OF VALUE

In Marx's conception, commodities exchange under capitalist conditions as a result of an underlying equivalence. That equivalence is the result of their being the expression of a common substance: labour. Crucially, labour power itself is one such commodity and, once brought to the labour market for exchange, loses its distinctive character as concrete labour process and becomes labour in general, at least for the purposes of value production (Marx, 1976: 142). It is this homogenization of all labour that many commentators find unsuitable in the current economic context.

There are several forms of argument in the literature on knowledge management that seek to distinguish the industrial 'labour in general' that Marx was concerned with in the mid 19th century from contemporary knowledge work. Perhaps the most facile of these is the suggestion that knowledge is the inalienable property of the knowledge worker. The argument here is that whilst an industrial worker was dependent upon the capitalist to provide the machinery necessary for them to work (at least, to work at the socially average rate and thereby produce a competitive level of value), the knowledge worker needs nothing but their brain. This 'knowledge capital' gives them a more equal bargaining position with employers so knowledge workers are not exploited in the same way as industrial workers and may even be in a position to rent capital and machinery from owners (e.g., Drucker, 1992: 147). Unfortunately, such utopian thinking bears little empirical scrutiny. Knowledge workers are, on the whole, dependent upon an organizational infrastructure to provide them with competitive marketing and access to clients and projects, as well as to provide the funding to keep their skills set up to date, for example by paying for costly training, professional development, membership of professional associations, libraries, and mentoring and development.

A rather more sophisticated line of reasoning is presented by Roy Jacques (2000). Jacques argues, like Drucker, that Marx's labour theory of value is no longer relevant, but he does so through direct engagement with the substance of Marx's arguments in volume 1 of *Capital*. Jacques rejects both utility theory and labour theory as effective explanations of value production today. Utility theory is dismissed because of its tautological structure whereby value is "defined as a function of utility (which is defined as what is valued)" (Jacques, 2000: 200). Labour theory is rejected for five distinct reasons: Marx's relativistic definitions of 'necessary' and 'surplus' labour; the elision of distinctions between 'labour power' and 'labour knowledge'; Marx's inability to account for knowledge exercised except in the direct production of commodities; concerns over the productive value of machinery; and an exclusive focus on machine based production. Given that Jacques' claim for the necessity of a new, 'knowledge theory of value' is premised upon the validity of his rejection of labour theory, it is worth examining these criticisms in detail. For the purposes of this paper, however, we will focus on the third and fourth criticisms as these are the most relevant for our understanding of knowledge based organizations. The first criticism is not central to Jacques' argument that knowledge is the source of all value, only his concerns with the equitable distribution of surplus value. The second is a circular criticism that begs the question, essentially criticising Marx for not having a concept of knowledge that is separate from labour power. No clear grounds are given as to why this is desirable, so the main problem seems to be that Marx doesn't deliver what Jacques wants (i.e. a knowledge theory of value). The final criticism relates to the fact that Marx's analysis is dominated by machine production, on the basis of which Jacques, conveniently ignoring the last 150 years of commentary, exegesis and development of labour theory (Jacques, 2000: 210), determines that the 'metaphor' of labour "is of extremely limited usefulness" (Jacques, 2000: 213). Of course, for Marx 'labour' was not a metaphor so much as an analytical and political category and at least some engagement with the structure and function of 'labour' as such would be necessary before it could be dismissed as no longer relevant. The third and fourth criticisms, however, are of more significance. It is to these that we now turn, in reverse order.

For Jacques, the productive value of the machine, "is the foremost limitation of labour theory" (2000: 212) and one that is especially significant in the context of seeking to understand the production of value in the age of information technology. According to Jacques:

For Marx, the tool or the machine is nothing but dead labour. If a thousand hours were required to produce it, then it is assumed to transfer the value of one thousand hours' labour into the products it is used to produce over its lifetime. (2000: 212)

Thus far his reading is accurate. Unfortunately, he quite misunderstands the implications of this. Jacques believes, on the basis of this inability of machinery to produce new value, that Marx was claiming that technology cannot increase the productivity of labour. He gives the example of a front-end loader, asking "who says that, for instance, a front-end loader built with a thousand hours of labour cannot replace ten thousand hours of hand shovelling?" The simple answer would be no one, least of all Marx. Unfortunately, Jacques gives us no references in his account to indicate where he believes Marx to have made such a claim, so it is not possible to address the details of his interpretation. It is possible, however, to contrast it with Marx's own words:

It is evident that whenever it costs as much labour to produce a machine as is saved by the employment of that machine, all that has taken place is a displacement of labour. Consequently, the total labour required to produce a commodity has not been lessened, in other words, the productiveness of labour has not been increased. However, the difference between the labour a machine costs and the labour it saves, in other words the degree of productivity the machine possesses, does not depend on the difference between its own value and the value of the tool it replaces. As long as the labour spent on a machine is such that the portion of its value added to the product remains smaller than the value added by the worker to the product with his tool, there is always a difference of labour saved in favour of the machine. The productivity of the machine is therefore measured by the human labour-power it replaces. (1976: 513)

For Marx, the explicit purpose of machinery is to make labour more productive, specifically more productive of surplus value. It can do this in a number of ways. It can deskill labour and enable the employment of unskilled, and therefore cheaper, labour power. It can lighten the physical burden of work and enable the employment of women and children, thereby removing the necessity for a family wage. It can increase the intensity of labour and seal up the porosity of the working day. And, of course, it can augment the productive powers of labour by enabling it to produce greater quantity of commodities in a given period of time. It is this last point that has eluded Jacques in Marx's writing but it is central to his whole understanding of machine based production. Machines can, and do, increase the productivity of labour but in so doing they simply spread the value that labour produces over a greater number of commodities, cheapening them. This cheapening of commodities through industrialisation is a regular feature of capitalist economies, enabling the mass production and consumption of goods like automobiles, washing machines, electrical fridges, microwaves, televisions, DVD players and personal computers. This has the additional advantage for capital of reducing the value of labour power by reducing the value of the commodities required for its reproduction. This in turn reduces the part of the working day given over to necessary labour and increases the part given 'freely' to the capitalist as surplus labour.

Jacques' second example of Marx's 'failure' to understand the productive power of machinery is specific to the use of knowledge in production, what Jacques refers to as 'machine intelligence':

What about the increasing ability of machines to exert knowledge power? What is the value to a fishing trawler of a radar system that senses fish that unaided humans would not know was there? (2000: 212)

Here Jacques makes the basic error of assuming that the qualitative aspects of labour and machinery make any kind of difference to production and value. The value of fish on the market is unaffected by the means by which it was caught. If the radar increases the productivity of fishers' labour power, then the value of the fish caught will be reduced and they will become cheaper as the socially average labour time required to catch a fish is reduced. Fish will become cheaper, people will eat more, and stocks will be depleted, eventually leading to the need for more effective radar systems to maintain productivity levels. If productivity cannot be maintained, the value and price of fish will increase as a greater amount of labour time will be given to each fish/commodity. Again, the technology may increase productivity, but from the point of view of market values a fish is a fish is a commodity, regardless of the 'machine intelligence' required to catch it. As the above discussion suggests, Marx's labour theory is far from unable to address the question of the value of machinery to capitalist production. If there is something distinct that has changed in the production of value through information and communication technologies, this is not made clear in critiques like Jacques'.

In the last of Jacques' refutations of Marx he shifts his attention away from technology and on to the form of labour, claiming that "Marx accords no portion of the value of a product to functions such as management, marketing, product development and accounting" (2000: 211). Although Jacques recognises that much of this labour may be devoted to the maximisation and expropriation of *surplus* value, as opposed to value per se, Jacques is insistent upon the idea that indirect labour contributes to the value of commodities. There has been a significant debate over this point in Marxist theory in recent years, most often couched in terms of productive versus unproductive labour (Harvie, 2006), and much contemporary Marxist thought would recognise that value is produced by more than just the waged labour directly employed in manufacturing commodities. Feminist writers have emphasised the, usually unwaged, reproductive labour that women provide for capital in doing housework (Dalla Costa and James, 1975). Consumption and unwaged 'cultural' and knowledge work can contribute to the production of value, whilst falling outside traditional Marxist categories of 'labour' (Terranova, 2004; Ross, 2000; Lazzarato, 1996). In the wake of Baudrillard (1981) and postmodernism, Marxism has had to address the social production of symbolic systems of meaning that give brands and other forms of consumption their sign-value. This includes, of course, the work of marketers but also the labour of consumption and the (re)production of cultural values, work that requires a significant expenditure of time and effort and is often collectively and cooperatively performed without direct financial recompense (Arvidsson, 2006). In all of these areas, contemporary Marxist thought has made significant inroads into the set of problems that Jacques addresses and even gone further than he suggests by moving beyond the narrowly circumscribed limits of 'the organization' as the unit of production of value, to recognise the wider, social circuits of value-production (Dyer-Witheford, 1999). Indeed, if we wanted only to recognise the indirect labour expended on production in an organization characterised by a complex division of labour then we do not need to move beyond *Capital*, where Marx (1996: 354) develops the concept of the 'collective labourer'. With this concept, Marx recognises that the production of value under capitalism increasingly becomes a collective effort and produces a hierarchy of labour powers, from the highly skilled, knowledgeable worker down to the 'unskilled' labourer. Rather than assuming that we can apportion an element of the productivity that results from this division of labour as 'necessary' and a separate portion of it as productive only of 'surplus', however, Marx recognises that the subsumption of the labour process under capital transforms the form and content of this process. Without appreciating how capital has reconfigured the entire labour process in its image it is impossible to understand the full implications of Marx's analysis. The question is not which portion of labour is productive of necessary, and which of surplus value, and therefore determining its equitable distribution, but of how capital has redesigned the entire labour process toward the production of surplus value, and how labour can resist and challenge this form of social organization.

This observation leads in two different possible directions. On the one hand we can pursue the autonomist Marxist analysis of how activities like marketing are now part of the 'real subsumption' of labour under capital and actively serve to extend subsumption to the whole of social reproduction, including the production of consumption (Dyer-Witheford, 1999; Arvidsson, 2006). On the other hand we can pick up on Marx's observation that capitalism itself produced the 'unskilled' labourer, a category that did not exist, at least in manufacturing, prior to the establishment of the capitalist division of labour (Marx, 1996: 355). Here the concept of 'knowledge' is opened up to a political analysis of what counts as knowledge and what is rewarded as 'knowledgeable' work, as well as to the recognition that deskilling is still, perhaps, the dominant logics of capitalist organization, even in the most 'advanced' economies. It is to this second idea that we now turn.

THE LABOUR PROCESS PERSPECTIVE: 'KNOWLEDGE' AIN'T ALL THAT

Whilst the gurus of the virtual, networked, knowledge based organization proclaim that we have moved into a post-industrial age, or even left the logics of capitalism behind us (Drucker, 1992), the prevalence and universality of this tendency have been questioned on a number of grounds (Warhurst and Thompson, 1998; Thompson, 2005). Empirical evidence suggests that changes in the form and content of contemporary labour processes vary by firm, sector and country, so claims of a universal 'paradigm shift' to knowledge work are overstated (Warhurst and Thompson, 1998: 19). In this part of the chapter we examine two main concerns with the knowledge economy thesis reviewed in the last section: that 'knowledge work' has been conflated with 'services' in a way that overplays the evidence for a significant rise in 'knowledge work' and hides a reality of routinised service work in the fastest growing areas of employment today; and that where tacit, endogenous knowledge is required from employees it is often in the form of culturally specific and aesthetic knowledge, rather than technical, scientific or academic knowledge.

In the UK at least, the economy has changed enormously over the last century. In a comparison of labour market statistics between 1900 and 2000 in the UK, Craig Lindsay (2003) found that employment and relative contribution to the economy had fallen dramatically in both the primary and secondary sectors. In agriculture, forestry and fishing the contribution to the national economy fell from 11% in 1900 to a mere 2% in 2000 and employment from 12% to 2%. A similar, though less dramatic decline, occurred in manufacturing, which saw its share of economic output fall from 28% to 22% and its share of employment fall from 24% to 14%. Services, on the other hand, grew from 50% of the economy in 1900 to 66% in 2000, by which time it accounted for around 75% of employment compared to only 34% in 1901 (Lindsay, 2003: 134; 137). According to Lindsay, this shift is at least partly accounted for by changes in the technological composition of production and the international division of labour. On the one hand, new technology increased productivity in the primary and secondary sectors, freeing up labour to work in the services. On the other hand, routinised work, particularly in manufacturing, relocated to countries where labour was cheaper. This "pattern was to be repeated across a number of industries, and the economy moved to focus on those areas where it had more of a competitive advantage, such as services or those manufacturing industries that required higher skills" (Lindsay, 2003: 138).

This is precisely the pattern of industrial re-composition that Daniel Bell (1974) referred to in terms of the coming of a 'post-industrial society' in the 1970s and later in terms of an 'information society' (Bell, 1981). By increasing productivity in the primary and secondary sectors, Bell predicted a progressive decline in employment in these sectors as employees moved into the service sector and leveraged technical and scientific knowledge to innovate and plan production more effectively. In Bell's framework, services equated with knowledge work. The assumption was that this burgeoning sector required higher skill levels and expertise as society was rationally planned, policies implemented, and innovation pursued to increase productivity.

A quick look at the composition of services in labour market statistics belies this benign image of a coming 'information society'. Between 1978, shortly after Bell's first formulation of the post-industrial society thesis, and 2007, the fastest growing category in the UK government's labour market statistics was 'Finance and Business Services' (ONS, 2008), which increased by 135% during this period (ONS, 2008). Included in this category are activities like 'industrial cleaning', 'investigation and security services', 'data processing' and the full range of financial and banking services, including insurance and pensions (ONS, 2006). Whilst some of the growth in this sector of the economy is undoubtedly high-end knowledge work, the aggregation of figures means that it also includes the growth of security services, for example night-club bouncers and private security workers on minimum wage, patrolling car-parks and shopping malls in the hope of apprehending juvenile delinquents. It also includes the huge growth in call centre operatives, who now provide the majority of both back and front office service provision for banking and financial services. The second largest growth area in the UK service sector labour market between 1978 and 2007 was 'distribution, hotels and restaurants' which grew by some 33% (ONS, 2008). This category includes the retail sector, hotels, bars, 'take-away food shops' and 'canteens'. In the time during which the knowledge economy was booming, then, the UK saw a 1/3 increase in employment in jobs like burger flipping at McDonalds, working on the check-out at Tesco, cleaning hotel rooms and serving beer.

Together these two areas account for the bulk of growth in service sector employment in the UK over the last twenty years but they are by no means dominated by knowledge work. Rather, much of the work in these sectors is highly routinised, deskilled and controlled through a factory-like, Taylorist management of the labour process (Thompson, 2005; Leidner, 1993; Taylor and Bain, 1999; Warhurst and Thompson, 1998; Garson, 1989). The figures suggest that at most 7-10% of the working population in 'advanced' capitalist economies like the UK and USA are 'knowledge workers' whose main job involves the manipulation and analysis of information, symbols and knowledge (Thompson, 2005: 84; Thomson et al, 2001). This small number of 'iMac jobs' are dwarfed by the huge growth in 'McJobs' and even in areas like software programming the labour process has been subjected to Taylorised control, deskilling and automation reminiscent of traditional industrial forms of control in manufacturing (Beirne et al, 1998). Such evidence suggests that rather than 'knowledge' or 'learning' becoming ever more central to contemporary value production, low skill, routinised work with little scope for autonomy, creativity or innovation still dominates the labour market even in advanced, post-industrial economies. Even areas that were traditionally thought of as knowledge work, like computer programming, are subject to the logic of deskilling and control identified by Braverman (1974) as the defining features of the capitalist labour process. What is usually thought of as 'knowledge intensive' work is, then, at best a minority concern or perhaps even a temporary anomaly in an emerging sector to which the logic of deskilling and control has not yet been applied. At the very least, valorising 'knowledge work' as the main source of economic value today draws attention away from the realities of work facing the majority of the population and, by holding out the ideal of knowledge work as the norm in advanced capitalist economies, devalues the significant economic role played by such work.

To temper this suggestion slightly and to acknowledge that, as Warhurst and Thompson (1998: 6) put it, "there are only a few diehards clinging to the view that nothing really has changed and that it is still just the same old capitalist labour process", it is worth considering one distinct shift within contemporary service work. In interactive service work in retailing, hotels and catering, some employees *are* recruited for their tacit knowledge. This is not the technical or scientific knowledge, expertise or learning, however, but a specific set of social, cultural and aesthetic accomplishments. In their studies of Scottish hotels, for example, Thompson and his colleagues (2001) found that front-line service workers were recruited for their cultural capital and aesthetic sensibilities. An ability to dress and comport oneself well, coupled with an attractive (at least to North American tourists) Edinburgh brogue assured an employee of a place on the reception desk or in another customer facing role. A more working class appearance, coupled with a thick Glaswegian accent would relegate an employee to the lower status areas of service work, like the kitchen, where work does not involve interaction with customers. In high-end retail outlets, for example in designer fashion stores, young, middle-class students are often recruited as they have the correct appearance, carriage and attitude to sell clothes to affluent consumers (Warhurst and Nickson, 2007). Such employees comprise a 'new labour aristocracy' as they not only get the best jobs in the service sector, but do so on the basis of their skills and knowledge. This is not a technical or formal knowledge, however, but the cultural and aesthetic knowledge that comes from class background and upbringing, rather than from formal training or schooling. In this sense, as Thompson and his colleagues argue, knowledge is indeed central to the production of value in the 'new' economy as aesthetic and cultural values drive high-end, value-added service interactions, but this is not the kind of knowledge conventionally associated with knowledge intensive firms (Thompson et al, 2001; Thompson, 2005).

THE GLOBAL PERSPECTIVE: MILITARISTIC NEO-LIBERALISM AND THE RETURN OF PRIMITIVE ACCUMULATION

The last hypothesis on the value of knowledge that we discuss in this chapter takes the labour process critique of knowledge work further by focussing on the global dimensions of the production of capitalist value. The Retort Collective (2005), as well as other writers (see, for example, De Angelis, 2001, 2006), have recently suggested that rather than a clear line of development from primary, through secondary, to the tertiary sector (whether as knowledge or service work), the current global political economy is dominated by a return to coercive international relations, often under conditions of outright warfare, to secure a new round of what Marx (1976) referred to as 'primitive accumulation'. This line of argument highlights the aggressive, militarised and violent nature of the way global capitalism and its double, the liberal democratic state, are spread across the globe. Contemporary neo-liberal capitalism is therefore directly linked to a politics of imperialism on the world stage.

Of course this is not a new argument. Marx (1996: 747) was acutely aware of the fact that the value produced in Manchester's factories was only half the story of the industrial revolution. Manchester's other half was Liverpool's port, which was at the centre of the slave trade triangle between England, Africa and the Americas. The slave trade was one of the earliest forms of global free trade and based on the brutal force of primitive accumulation, which separated people from their homeland and their means of production in order to turn them and their land into commodities (Rediker, 2007). In Latin America, for example, millions of hectares of land were colonised by European farmers who killed or enslaved indigenous people, the original 'owners' of that land, in order to enclose the land and turn it into capitalist property from which rent could be earned and on which commodities, such as sugar cane, could be grown and exported to Europe. The violent process of primitive accumulation is therefore targeted at those people who have direct access to means of production, and the aim for the colonisers is to separate them from these means in order to turn them into means of capitalist production themselves (De Angelis, 2006). When today we hear about the much advertised advantages that global free trade, democratisation and deregulated markets are supposed to deliver, we need to remember the violence that is at the origin of this very process of globalisation.

Many liberal commentators would argue that, putting the regrettable violence that has occurred in the past aside, globalisation is at heart a force of human, social, cultural and economic development that eventually will produce benefits for everyone. As De Angelis (2006) points out, even classic Marxist understandings of development would argue that the enclosures of land and primitive accumulation are the starting points for a process that eventually leads to a 'transition' from feudalism to capitalism and then onto higher stages of capitalist development. This is sometimes referred to as 'stage theory', implying the gradual development from primary, through secondary, to the tertiary sector. With the latter, characterised by the dominance of knowledge and service industries, we have supposedly reached the so far most 'advanced' stage of capitalist development. The underlying ideology of stage theory is that development is a linear, gradual process, and if 'developing' countries manage their economies and political systems well enough, they too can reach the pinnacle of the tertiary development stage and become knowledge economies.

The realities of the so-called 'developing' world paint a different picture. Reflecting on their continent's chronic underdevelopment, Latin American writers, such as Furtado (1967) and Cardoso and Faletto (1979), started to critique the stage theory of development in the 1950s and 1960s. In what they termed 'dependency theory' they outlined the continuing dependency of Latin American countries on Europe and North America, which in turn were only able to develop themselves because of the violent exploitation of Latin America's riches. Dependency here is equal to underdevelopment, which, for these writers, stands in a dialectical relationship with development. In other words, rather than being 'developing' countries, Latin American and other Southern countries need to be seen as chronically underdeveloped, as they are embedded in a world system of value accumulation based on international divisions of labour dictated by the powerful elites in the 'developed' North and West (Wallerstein, 1974; Amin, 1974).

De Angelis (2006) equally points out that there are no distinct and linear stages or transitional paths that countries can take towards the desired goal of full capitalist development. In his view, primitive accumulation sits side by side with more advanced knowledge production, meaning that underdevelopment and development are dependent on each other. He calls this the 'continuous character of primitive accumulation' (2006: 136). In such an account the knowledge work of consultants and call-centre operatives alike is impossible without the military enforced expropriation of land in the Niger Delta for oil production, the civil war around Coltan (a necessary raw material for the production of mobile phones) and Uranium mining in the Congo, or GM soya production in Brazil.

The knowledge economy in the rich world is hence dialectically related to, and dependent upon, violent processes of primitive accumulation in the poor world. Put differently, the tertiary sector (where knowledge and information work supposedly rule) would not be possible without a primary sector dependent upon the primitive accumulation of raw materials. This is even acknowledged by the stock markets around the world, which, after the 'dot.com bubble' burst in 2001, have mainly been thriving on the back of growth in the primary sector (energy, mining, agro-business, raw commodities, etc). Fuelled by the growth in China, India and other emerging markets, which produce the technology gadgets that Western/Northern labourers need for their knowledge work and affluent patterns of consumption, stock prices of mining and oil companies and other primary sector industries have rocketed. As stock market traders in the City of London try to make a profit by trading in commodities and companies' shares, the computers, mobile phone and other ICT gadgets that enable them to do their knowledge work will have to be produced 'somewhere'. This 'somewhere' has always included far away countries in the South that provide raw materials, cheap labour, and other commodities shipped to the North so that the 'centre' can be 'developed' further.

We need to be careful not to draw this line between North and South, centre and periphery, too firmly. As De Angelis (2006) argues, the process of primitive accumulation is continuous, and it also continues in the North. That is, enclosures of what used to be public goods continue to take place even in the most 'advanced' economies. We could name here the privatisation of what used to be public services; for example, transport, health and education. We could also mention the newly created carbon trading mechanisms, which aim to establish new markets to exploit a completely new commodity: pollution. Carbon is a new commodity, a form of primitive accumulation that sits alongside the knowledge economy. Particularly relevant, given the focus of this book, is the enclosure of the 'knowledge commons' (De Angelis, 2006: 149) whereby the autonomous reproduction of cultural and technical knowledge is increasingly subordinated to the capitalist imperative of privatisation and accumulation, through copyright legislation, corporate control over cultural reproduction, corporate sponsorship of research and education, and through newly established forms of intellectual property rights.

Like the last section, what all of the examples discussed in this section of the paper, and the overall framework of 'primitive accumulation', demonstrate is that the accumulation of 'value' in contemporary capitalism is not a simple matter of the application of knowledge contained in individual knowledge workers' brains. Knowledge, both in its technical and cultural variants, is increasingly subject to processes of enclosure and control. Perhaps more significantly, for the purposes of this chapter, this knowledge represents only one aspect of value production today. Corporate sponsored knowledge work runs alongside widespread processes of industrial deskilling and violent, often militarised, expropriation of the raw materials of production. And as land is expropriated for mining, building pipelines, and growing bio-fuels, soya, or carbon-capture plantations, so those previously dependent upon that land for their subsistence are 'set free' to work in capitalist labour markets in the very moment that they are liberated from any other options but wage labour.

CONCLUSION

In this review of four perspectives on value production, and the role of knowledge in that process, we have sought to highlight aspects of the contemporary global economy that escape the lens of 'knowledge work'. But perhaps this does not go quite far enough. In focussing on 'knowledge' as the key driver of economic development and wealth, processes of primitive accumulation, routinised service work and deskilling are relegated to history. It has been the argument of this paper that these processes are very much alive and kicking and that the 'knowledge discourses' actively contribute to their neglect by legitimating a developmental logic, a linear narrative of history in which the future is a rosy world of empowered immaterial labourers, self-actualising through their work.

Whilst management gurus fill the shelves of airport bookshops with their prognostications on knowledge and the latest organizational forms, as academics it is incumbent upon us to both interrogate the evidence for their claims and to situate their examples and ideas in a wider, historically and geographically located political, economic and social context. Paying attention to the international division of labour and the current rounds of militarised expropriation occurring in the global peripheries reminds us of the violence with which capitalist social relations have always established themselves, and still do in extending their coverage today. By examining the realities of work in the 'new economy', and seeing it dominated by deskilled, routine service work, rather than autonomous knowledge work, we can peel back the facade of democratic upskilling that legitimates the knowledge economy and attend to the forms of knowledge and distinction that characterise work for the majority of employees in 'advanced' economies today. By returning to Marx's labour theory of value, we can ask whether the commodity form of labour/knowledge has really changed in the contemporary economy, or whether the basic dynamics of industrial capitalism are still with us today. By exploring the changes that the political concept of labour has undergone in relation to both new technology and to the extension of capitalist subsumption into ever new aspects of social life, we can develop concepts of work and organization adequate to contemporary political-economic realities.

REFERENCES

Amin, S. (1974) *Accumulation on a World Scale*. New York, NY: Monthly Review Press.

Arvidsson, A. (2006) *Brands: Meaning and Value in Media Culture*. Abingdon: Routledge.

Baudrillard, J. (1981) *For a Critique of the Political Economy of the Sign*. St. Louis: Telos.

Beirne et al (1998). Developments in Computing Work: Control and Contradiction in the Software Labour Process. In P. Thompson & C. Warhurst (Eds.), *Workplaces of the Future*. Basingstoke: MacMillan.

Bell, D. (1974) *The Coming of Post-Industrial Society*. New York: Harper Colophon Books.

Bell, D. (1981). The Social Framework of the Information Society. In T. Forester (Ed.), *The Microelectronics Revolution*. Cambridge, MA: MIT Press.

Böhm, S. (2002). The Consulting Arcade: Walking Through Fetish-Land. *Tamara: Journal of Critical Postmodern Organization Science*, *2*(2), 20-35.

Braverman, H. (1974) *Labor and Monopoly Capital: The Degradation of Work in the Twentieth Century*. London: Monthly Review Press.

Cardoso, H., & Faletto, E. (1979). *Dependency and Development in Latin America*. Berkeley, CA: University of California Press.

Dalla Costa, M., & James, S. (1975). *The Power of Women and the Subversion of Community*. Berlin: Falling Wall Press.

De Angelis, M. (2001). Marx and primitive accumulation: The continuous character of capital's enclosures. *The Commoner*, www.thecommoner.org.

De Angelis, M. (2006). *The Beginning of History: Value Struggles and Global Capital*. London: Pluto.

Derrida, J. (1994). *The Specters of Marx*. trans. Peggy Kamuf. London: Routledge.

Drucker, P. (1968). *The Age of Discontinuity: Guidelines to our Changing Society*. New York: Basic Books.

Drucker, P. (1992). The New Society of Organizations. *Harvard Business Review*, Sept-Oct, 95.

Dyer-Witheford, N. (1999) *Cyber-Marx*. Urbana: University of Illinois Press.

Elson, D. (1979). The value theory of labour. In D. Elson (Ed.), *Value: The Representation of Labour in Capitalism*. London: CSE Books.

Furtado, C. (1967). *Development and Underdevelopment*. Berkeley, CA: University of California Press.

Garson, B. (1989). *The Electronic Sweatshop: How Computers are Transforming the Office of the Future into the Factory of the Past*. New York : Simon & Schuster.

Harvie, D. (2006). Value production and struggle in the classroom: Teachers within, against and beyond capital. *Capital & Class*, *88*, 1-32.

Harvey, D. (1999). *The Limits to Capital*. London: Verso.

Jacques, R. (2000). Theorizing knowledge as work: The need for a 'knowledge theory of value. In C. Pritchard, R. Hull, M. Chumer & H. Willmott (Eds.), *Managing Knowledge: Critical Investigations of Work and Learning.* Basingstoke: Macmillan.

Lazzarato, M. (1996). Immaterial Labour. In P. Virno & M. Hardt (Eds.), *Radical Thought in Italy.* Minneapolis: University of Minnesota Press.

Leadbeater, C. (1999). *Living on Thin Air: The New Economy.* London: Viking.

Leidner, R. (1993). *Fast Food, Fast Talk: Service Work and the Routinisation of Everyday Life.* Berkeley: University of California Press.

Lindsay, C. (2003). A century of labour market change: 1900 to 2000. *Labour Market Trends*, March 2003.

Marx, K. (1973). *Grundrisse: Foundations of the Critique of Political Economy*, trans. Martin Nicolaus. London: Penguin.

Marx, K. (1976). *Capital: A Critique of Political Economy*, Vol. 1, trans. Ben Fowkes. London: Penguin.

Marx, K. (1985). Value, price and profit. In K. Marx and F. Engels *Collected Works*, Volume 20: Marx and Engels 1864-1868. London: Lawrence and Wishart.

Marx, K. (1996) *Capital, vol. 1* in *Marx and Engels Collected Works Volume 35.* London: Lawrence and Wishart.

Noble, D. (2001). *Digital Diploma Mills: The Automation of Higher Education.* New York: Monthly Review Press.

Office of National Statistics (2006). *Labour Force Survey User Guide – Volume 5: LFS Classifications.* London: National Statistics. Web version at http://www.statistics.gov.uk/statbase/Product.asp?vlnk=1537. Accessed 1/3/08.

Office of National Statistics (2008). Labour Market Statistics. London: National Statistics. Online at: http://www.statistics.gov.uk/statbase/TSDdownload2.asp. Accessed 1/3/08.

Poulter, D. and Land, C. (2008). Preparing to work: dramaturgy, cynicism and normative 'remote' control in the socialization of graduate recruits in management consulting. *Culture and Organization, 14*(1), 65-78.

Rediker, M. (2007). *The Slave Ship: A Human History.* London: John Murray.

Retort Collective (2005). *Afflicted Powers: Capital and Spectacle in a New Age of War.* London: Verso.

Ross, A. (2000). The Mental Labor Problem. *Social Text, 18*(2), 1-31.

Spivak, G. C. (1985). Scattered Speculations on the Question of Value. *Diacritics, 15*(4), 73-93.

Tapscott, D. (1996). *The Digital Economy.* New York: McGraw Hill.

Taylor, P., & Bain, P. (1999). An assembly line in the head': work and employee relations in the call centre. *Industrial Relations Journal, 30*(2), 101-117.

Terranova, T. (2004). *Network Culture: Politics for the Information Age.* London: Pluto.

Thompson, P. (2005). Foundation and Empire: A critique of Hardt and Negri. *Capital & Class, 86*, 73-100.

Thompson, P., Warhurst, C., & Callaghan, G. (2001). Ignorant theory and knowledgeable workers: Interrogating the connections between knowledge, skills and services. *Journal of Management Studies, 38*(7), 923-942.

Wallerstein, I. (1974). *The Modern World-System.* New York, NY: Academic Press.

Warhurst, C., & Nickson, D. (2007). A new labour aristocracy? Aesthetic labour and routine interactive service. *Work, Employment and Society, 21*(4), 785-798.

Warhurst, C., & Thompson, P. (1998). Hands, hearts and minds: changing work and workers at the end of the century. In P. Thompson & C. Warhurst (Eds.), *Workplaces of the Future*. Basingstoke: Macmillan.

Wenger, E., McDermott, R., & Snyder, W. (2002). *Cultivating Communities of Practice: A Guide to Managing Knowledge*. Boston, MA: Harvard Business School Press.

KEY TERMS

Jacques: A management and organisation theorist who has put forward a 'knowledge theory of value'.

Knowledge: A person's expertise and skills knowledge economy: A term used in the last two decades to point to developments in primiarly Western economies that are said to be more dependent on the economic exploitation of people's knowledge and continuous learning.

Labour: also, wage labour: Work done by humans as workers who have to sell their labour to employers to make a living.

Marx: One of the most important political economists who analysed the workings of the commodity form in capitalism.

Primitive Accumulation: A classical politico-economic term used by Marx and others to define the enclosure of 'the commons' and hence the starting point of private property and capitalist profit making.

Value: An ethical as well as economic term to express a degree of worthiness or importance.

Work: A general term to define all types of paid activity by humans.

ENDNOTES

[a] For example, by splitting the economy into primary, secondary and tertiary sectors, or dividing the globe into 'more' and 'less' developed nations, both of which presuppose hierarchical forms of evaluation and privilege such formulations over more process orientated, commodity chain (or supply chain) analyses.

[b] One of the great advantages of Marxist value theory over marginalist conceptions, at least for students of management and organization, is that it focuses on the production of value: how value is created rather than just realised in the marketplace. By taking us into 'the hidden abode of production', Marx (1976: 195) provides an answer to the question of how managers can organize their employees so as to create value, a question to which marginalist supply and demand curves offer little leverage.

[c] The obvious exception here would be where 'knowledge' itself is the commodity being produced, as is the case for academics and consultants for example. In such cases there is little reason to believe that the same basic logic of productivity does not apply so long as such services are provided in the context of a capitalist enterprise (see, for example, Harvie (2006) and Noble (2001) on the academic labour process and Böhm (2002) and Poulter and Land (2008) on management consulting).

Chapter XXX
New Media and Knowledge Work

Alexander Styhre
Chalmers University of Technology, Sweden

ABSTRACT

This chapter discusses the use of media in knowledge-intensive organizations. Media is defined here as the integration of technologies, practices, and institutions serving to record, inscribe and circulate speech, writing, and images. The presence of media in organized activities remains relatively unexplored, even though various media "enframe" the life-world of the organization. New media do not only constitute assemblages of integrated technologies and tools (e.g. the telephone, the computer, pens and pencils) which are used en route in day-to-day work, they also gradually break down the line of demarcation between inside and outside, between embodied and technological matter.

INTRODUCTION

The concept of knowledge has from the outset been of central interest within philosophy and social theory. Plato addressed the nature of knowledge in some of his dialogues (e.g. *Theaetetus, Protagoras,* and *Meno*) but failed to establish a clear and unambiguous line of demarcation between knowledge and non-knowledge. In contemporary times, the sociologist Karl Mannheim (1936) instituted what the called "sociology of knowledge" in the field of academic sociology, a tradition that Robert Merton (1957) then continued. In the 1960s, Fritz Machlup published a seminal work in which he conceived of knowledge as a major production factor in American industry and society. In organization theory, knowledge has always been an "absent present", that which is always present yet rarely articulated, in the analysis of organizational practice. In the mid-1990s, arguably with the publication of a special issue of the *Strategic Management Journal* edited by Robert Grant and

J.-C. Spender (1995), the idea of a specific and privileged theoretical perspective on organizations known as "knowledge management" (or "the knowledge-based view of the firm" (Foss, 1996), drawing on the debate on the "resource-based view of the firm" in strategic management quarters, e.g., Barney, 1991) was proposed. However, a few significant contributions to the field were published prior to 1995, perhaps the most notable of which being Nonaka's (1994) discussion about the conversion of forms of knowledge. Since 1995, the knowledge management perspective has become established as a legitimate component of mainstream organization theory and management studies. Journals, conferences, and professional associations are dedicated to the topic and no less that two handbooks have been published, aimed at providing state-of-the-art overviews of the field (Dierkes, Berthon, Child and Nonaka, 2001; Easterby-Smith and Lyles, 2003). Today, knowledge management is a progressive and heterogeneous field of research hosting a great variety of theoretical, methodological, and practical orientations (for an overview, see Tsoukas and Vladimirou, 2001; Newell, Robertson, Scarborough and Swan, 2002; Styhre, 2003).

In this paper, knowledge management and knowledge work will be examined as something fundamentally shaped and influence by media; technologies that are capable of producing, manipulating, distributing, and storing information in various forms (i.e. as text, images, sounds, symbols). To date, the knowledge management literature has only addressed to a limited extent the central importance of media in the constitution of knowledge, knowledge work and, most importantly, the subject-position of the knowledge worker. In this paper, media are defined as "enframing" and structuring knowledge work; they constitute the infrastructure of most knowledge work and thus media need to be carefully examined. While there is a substantial literature exploring the co-alignment of new technology and organization (Barley, 1986, 1990; Prasad, 1993; Woicehyn, 2000; Orlikowski, 2000; Edmonson, Bohmer, and Pisano, 2001; Lanzara and Patriotta, 2001; McGail, 2002), the interest in media in the humanities and social sciences (e.g. McLuhan, 1962, 1964; Kittler, 1990, 1997, 1999; Bolter, 1991; Bolter and Grusin, 1999; Hayles, 2002, 2005) has only been restrictedly mirrored in organization theory. One exception to this is the interest in actor-network theory in organization studies, a theoretical perspective that points to the mutual constitution of knowledge, inscription procedures, media, and organization. Scientific knowledge is embedded in procedures of inscription (Latour, 1987, Latour, 1991), that is, the rendering of what is contested and not-yet-fixed immutable or possible to circulate in the form of mathematical formulae or visual representations (or in a more mundane case, in the inscriptions on a bottle of water; Joerges and Czarniawska, 1998); such inscriptions are the outcome of the effective alignment of organization and technology. Technoscience, in actor-network theory, is an assemblage composed of humans, technologies (e.g. media), and inscription procedures (Law, 1986; Lenoir, 1998). Seen in this way, actor-network theory bridges knowledge management and media theory in terms of emphasizing the use of media and technology when "inscribing the world".

Media and their accompanying instances of speech, writing, and code are inextricably entangled with the process of organizing. The presence of new media (a term reserved for media based on digital technologies) such as electronic mail (e-mail) and computer-based information technologies in organizations implies new *modi operandi* in organizations (Brown and Lightfoot, 2002; Kallinikos, 1996a). For instance, the use of e-mail, representing a form of the inscription of everyday conversations into computer systems (Lee, 1996), implies a new set of problems and challenges for organizations; e-mail systems demand certain procedures, agreed upon routines for handling incoming and outgoing mail, and an ethos guiding the thoughtful use of the system. An e-mail system, like any other new medium, does not operate all by itself or "by necessity", but is instead anchored in pre-existing institutions. This paper aims to discuss the recent media studies represented by scholars like Marshall McLuhan, Katherine Hayles, Friedrich Kittler, and David Jay Bolter and to examine implications for organization theory. This recent body of work is transdisciplinary and addresses a range of the social, cultural, and philosophical implications emanating from the new media. Above all, media are conceived of as that which is recursively constituted by predominant regimes of representation and inscription, but they also constitute such practices.

MEDIA THEORY

A recent corpus of literature examines the influence of new media on society. This literature is perhaps best described as transdisciplinary and includes technology analyses, literature theory, sociological writing, anthropological research, and historical studies (Hansen, 2006). In the literature, the three dominant forms of what Luhmann (1995: 161) calls "media of dissemination" are writing, printing, and electronic broadcasting. Hayles (2002) refers to "speech, writing, and code" as "the three worldviews" of media. Mark Poster (2001), discussing the constitution of the subject as a mediated process, shares this view in which three forms of media are clearly separated:

Every age employs forms of symbolic exchange which contains internal and external structures, means and relations of significations. Stages in the mode of information may be tentatively designated as follows: face-to-face; orally mediated exchange; written exchanges mediated by print; and electronically mediated exchanges. If the first stage is characterized by symbolic correspondences, and the second stage is characterized by representation of signs, the third is characterized by informational simulations. In the first, oral stage the self is constituted as a position of enunciation through its embeddedness in a totality of face-to-face relations. In the second, print state the self is constructed as an agent centered in rational/imaginary autonomy. In the third, electronic state the self is decentered, dispersed, and multiplied in continuous instability. (Poster, 2001: 6-7)

Rather than representing a gradual progression towards more technologically-advanced forms of media, media studies suggest that the three forms are of necessity always interrelated and mutually constitutive (Gitelman, 1999; Aaseth, 2003). Speech is at times regarded as something which precedes writing, or, as in the Derridean critique of logocentrism (Derrida, 1976, 1981), conversely deemed to be something which is more authentic and original than writing. The code of the computer language is what represents a machine-like language devoid of meaning deeper than its functions in the sequence of programming instructions (Piñeiro, 2007: 106). Rather than being three separated and disjointed categories, speech, writing, and code coexist in simultaneity. In what follows, we adhere to Krämer's (2006: 93) definition of media: "'Media' are first and foremost cultural techniques that allow one to select, store, and produce data and signals".

The first and most generic innovation in terms of media is the invention of writing. Anthropologists and historians account for the radical implications of practices of writing in terms of being a media for "collective memory", a form of storage enabling know-how and experience to be disseminated within broader communities. Bolter (1991: 33) writes: "Writing is a technology for collective memory, for preserving and passing on human experience . . . Eventually writing also becomes the preserver and extender of other technologies as an advanced culture develops a technical literature". Anthropologists like Lévi-Strauss (1979) even distinguish between societies capable of writing and those incapable of writing using this as a significant line of demarcation. Flusser (2000) discusses the relationship between writing and images. For Flusser (2000), human thinking began with images, serving as "mediations between humans and the world". However, since images are not "denotative" (unambiguous) but "connotative", and open to interpretation, the invention of "linear writing" is a new medium for interpreting images. As a consequence, Flusser (2000) sees an irreconcilable conflict between image and text:

The struggle of writing against the image—historical consciousness against magic—runs throughout history. With writing, a new ability was born called conceptual thinking, which consisted of abstracting lines from surfaces, i.e., producing and decoding them . . . Thus with the invention of writing, human beings took one step further back from the world. Texts do not signify the world; they signify the images they tear up. Hence, to decode texts means to discover the images signified by them. The interpretation of texts is to explain images, while that of concepts is to make ideas comprehensible. In this way, texts are a metacode of images. (Flusser, 2000: 11)

In Flusser's (2000, 2002) media philosophy, texts and images based respectively on "surface codes" and "linear codes", are complementary or even incommensurable media used by humans.

The second radical shift in the history of media is the innovation of printing (Eisenstein, 1983; Burns, 1989; Febvre and Martin, 1997). McLuhan (1962: 155) suggests that Johann Gutenberg's printing technology represented a "move into the age of the machine": "The principle of segmentation of actions and functions and roles became systematically applicable wherever desired . . . The Gutenberg technology extended this principle to writing and language and the codification and transmission of every kind of learning." While speech and handwriting were essentially marked by individual skills and capacities, printing technology "technologized the word" (in Ong's, 1982, apt phrase) and separated it from its spokesman in time and space. Even though the very act of writing per se represents a technological form, it is printing technology that makes media a self-perpetuating force in society. The German media analyst Friedrich Kittler (1990, 1997, 1999) examines the expansion of media into other domains than the written word, e.g. the aural and visual fields. In the nineteenth century, media like the phonograph, the gramophone, the photograph, the mechanical typewriter, and the cinematograph were invented (Crary, 1990: 107-109; Gitelman and Pingree, 2003). For Kittler, such media constituted a new "discourse network", that is, a "network of technologies and institutions that allow a given culture to select, store, and process relevant data" (Kittler, 1990: 116). For Kittler, each media and its technologies were coupled with specific institutions (the printed book and the university; the cinematograph and the entertainment industry, etc.) and thus constituted social practices and new industries stretching outside of the narrower range of the focal technology. Among other things, the new media enabled the reproduction of individual works (Benjamin, 1973). Media became a major social force in the nineteenth century. For contemporary critics, new media are not regarded as mere blessings, instead being greeted with skepticism (see, for instance, Williams, 1990; Bourdieu, 1996; Merrin, 1999; Whelan, 2002, on television). For instance, Heidegger, long after the introduction of the mechanical typewriter—a technological innovation that Nietzsche, perhaps, was the first major thinker to use—argued that "mechanical writing deprives the hand of its rank in the realm of the written word and degrades the word to a means of communication" (Heidegger, cited in Kittler, 1999: 199). Over the course of time, new media are examined in terms of *inauthenticity*, and merely serve as means of disseminating copies. However, we learn from history that new media sooner or later become more widely acclaimed as helpful tools, enabling faster and more reliable communication or providing opportunities for entertainment and new experiences.

The third shift, from printed to electronic texts, is discussed by Katherine Hayles (2002a, b). Hayles speaks more generally about *inscription technologies* as devices capable of initiating "material changes that can be read as marks" (Hayles, 2002: 24. original emphasis omitted). Some examples of such inscription technologies are telegraphy, film, video, and medical devices such as X-rays and CAT scans (as well as other forms of what Gaston Bachelard, 1984, calls *phénomenotechniques* in scientific practice). Hayles argues that literary studies have largely been ignorant of the inscription technologies per se. She also argues that "when a literary work interrogates the inscription technology that produces it, it mobilizes reflexive loops between its imaginative world and the material apparatus embodying that creation as a physical presence" (Hayles, 2002: 25). Then, media are not solely a means of communication but are, in fact, inherent in the literary work per se. Hayles (2002: 25. Emphasis in the original) contends: "[M]y claim is that *the physical form of literary artifact always affects what the word (and other semiotic components) mean*". Hayles (2002: 26) reserves the concept of "writing machines" not just for the nineteenth century mechanical typewriter but also for any inscription technology capable of producing literary texts, including "printing presses, computers, and other devices". What is of interest to Hayles (2002), then, is the very *materiality* of the text, the technological aspects of the literary work:

Materiality thus emerges from interaction between physical properties and a work's artistic strategies. For this reason, materiality cannot be specified in advance, as if it preexisted the specificity of the work. As emergent property, materiality depends on how the work mobilizes its resources as a physical artifact as well as on the user's interactions with the work and the interpretative strategies she develops—strategies that include physical manipulations as well as physical frameworks. In its broadest sense, materiality emerges from the dynamic interplay between the richness of a physically robust world and human intelligence as it crafts this physicality to create meaning. (Hayles, 2002: 33)

A specific type of materiality is the use of programming code, a form of inscription technology carrying little meaning outside of its function. The software engineer Ellen Ullman (cited in Hayles, 2002: 48) says: "We can use English to invent poetry, to try to express things that are hard to express. In programming you really can't. Finally, a computer program has only one meaning: what it does. It isn't a text for an academic to read. Its entire meaning is its function". Dodge and Kitchin (2005), examining a variety of coded objects and processes, define code accordingly:

Code consists of instructions and rules that, when combined, produce programs capable of complex digital functions that operate on computer hardware. We therefore use the term code in a restricted sense to refer to the rules and instructions of software rather than broader notions of codes as sociocultural structures and technical/legalistic protocols of ordering and control, such as national laws, international treaties, etiquette, standards, systems of measurements, institutional customs, and professional codes of conduct. (Dodge and Kitchin, 2005: 163)

Code is not, in Dodge and Kitchin's (2005) analysis, something which is detached from everyday human life but is instead something which constitutes and structures social spaces: "Code is bound up in, and contributes to, complex discursive and material practices, relating to both living and non-living humans and technology, which work across scales and time", contend Dodge and Kitchin (2005: 164). Ellen Ullman may be right in emphasizing that the "meaning of the code is its function", but it also produces meaning as something that constitutes the infrastructure of everyday life. Or, as Dodge and Kitchin (2005: 178) put it: "Code and human life are produced through or folded into each other, taking the form of coded practices". Texts embedded in code are electronic texts or *hypertexts*, that is, "[t]ext composed of blocks of texts . . . and the electronic links that join them" (Landow, 2006: 3), While the printed text was, as Bolter (1991: 9) says, "a great homogenizer of writing", the hypertext is "fragmentary" and composed of "self-contained units" rather than being an "organic, developing whole". Hypertexts are thus "infinitely variable" (Landow, 2006: 36); when manipulating the code, the text is changed. Landow writes:

Hypertext . . . provides an infinitely recenterable system whose provisional point of focus depends on the reader, who becomes the truly active reader in yet another sense. One of the fundamental characteristics of hypertext is that it is composed of bodies of linked texts that have no primary axis of organization. (Landow, 2006: 56)

Thus, in the hypertext medium, the text is no longer unified or integrated, but can evolve along unlimited lines of reading; it is "always open, unbordered, unfinished and unfinishable, capable of infinite extension" (Landow, 2006: 196). For Landow (2006), hypertext undermines the conventional distinction between authors and readers; to read hypertexts is to serve as an author, that is, to actively influence the text and choose paths to follow. In Bolter's (1991: 9) term, to author/read a hypertext is to engage in a "writing space", that is, "in a perpetual state of reorganization".

Manovich (2001) provides a comprehensive formalistic overview of the functioning of new, coded media, identifying five principles for all media. First, all media are based on "numerical representations", that is, they can be "described formally" in a mathematical language and be "subject to algorithmic manipulation". Second, media are based on "modularity":

The principle can be called the 'fractal structure of new media'. Just as a fractal has the same structure on different scales, a new media object has the same modular structure throughout. Media elements, be they images, sounds, shapes, or behaviours, are represented as collectives of discrete samples (pixels, polygons, voxels, characters, scripts). These elements are assembled into larger-scale objects but continue to maintain their separate identities. (Manovich, 2001: 30)

As a consequence of the two first characteristics, media are (3) possible to manipulate through automatic operations, and (4) possible to modify infinitely: "A new media object is not something fixed once and for all but something that can exist in different, potentially infinite versions", argues Manovich (2001: 36). Finally, new media are subject to what Manovich (2001) calls *transcoding*, i.e. forging a close relationship between the cultural and technological layers of the media. On the basis of these principles, a great variety of technological applications are developed and integrated.

Media studies enable us to see not just the disruptive changes supposedly introduced by new technologies but also the substantial continuity between the elementary forms of writing and the use of binary codes structured into different computer languages in contemporary software engineering (Gitelman, 1999). In addition, media studies address what may be called an *epistemology of inscription*; the claims of authenticity of any established and preexisting media vis-à-vis new forms, as well as the anxieties expressed when language and inscription devices are blended, are representative of a credo of purity of thought and language that influences any reception of a new media. Moreover, media studies make the media per se an object of investigation, instead of it being some residual factor. For instance, for

Hayles (2002), the materiality of the text is just as central to a literary work as its content; form and content are again examined in comparative terms.

Knowledge Work and Media: New Drug Development and Sound Engineering

In this section, the close entanglement of new media and knowledge work will be examined. in order to indicate the scope of media, two rather different domains of knowledge work are examined: new drug development work and sound engineering and recording. While these two cases differ substantially, they are indicative of the increased reliance on media in knowledge-intensive work.

The Work of Developing New Drugs

New media are used in a broad variety of settings and industries. In scientific work, it is virtually impossible to separate media from scientific work, and thus the notion of *technoscience*, conflating the two terms, is widely used today. Many students of scientific work in laboratory milieus thus emphasize mediated inscription work as central to "fact-making". For instance, Lenoir (1998: 8) says: "[L]aboratory studies observe the striking congruence between literary inscriptions and 'facts': discussions about facts are inseparable from their inscriptions; the acceptance of a scientific fact is tied to the strength of its links to layers of texts; the ostensibly factual nature of a statement can be undermined by drawing attention to the process of its inscriptions". Scientific work and medical practice are heavily mediated. For instance, in surgery, VR (virtual reality technology) has been used to simulate operations since it was introduced in 1991 (Gallagher and Cates, 2004). It is estimated that medical errors cause 44,000-94,000 deaths annually in the US, and, argue Gallagher and Cates (2004: 1538), "many medical errors are caused by human factors associated with invasive image-guided techniques" such as arthroscopy, laparoscopy, and flexible endoscopy. Research shows that training in a VR environment yielded "significantly fewer" inoperative errors than the conventionally-trained reference group. In another study, the VR-trained group made six times fewer inoperative errors and worked 30% faster than did the reference group (Gallagher and Cates, 2004: 1538). Another domain where VR techniques and other new computer-mediated technologies are used in new drug development, and more specifically in what is called "virtual screening", when detecting molecules that can be further explored during what is called "lead optimisation" in new drug development (Eckert and Bajorath, 2007; Walters, Stahl and Murcko, 1998). Since synthesis chemists engaged in identifying promising molecules operate in what Walters, Stahl, and Murcko (1998) call a "virtual chemistry space" that includes 10^{100} potential molecules, there is a great need to reduce the number of interesting molecules. Bensaude-Vincent and Stengers ([1993] 1996: 255) emphasize the need to reduce the number of investigated molecules:

Since the beginning of synthetic chemistry, some ten million different molecules have been 'invented', and this number grows by more than a thousand a day. The production of a new molecule is no more than the background noise for other stories—and these stories do not relate first to chemistry as a science but to the interests and need of industry. For one substance used by the pharmaceutical industry, nearly ten thousand have been tested and declared without intrinsic or commercial value.

Drug discovery, in Nightingale's (1998: 704) formulation, thus "[i]nvolves reducing the 'molecular space' that profitable drugs will be found in, to a small enough volume that empirical testing can take place". Even though synthesis chemists use what Nightingale (1998) calls "chemical intuition" to detect promising molecules, the virtual chemistry space/molecular space needs to be reduced. Virtual screening means that technologies are used to automatically examine a library of molecules in a 2-D setting to identify potentially interesting molecules. Selected molecules are then further examined using 3-D visualization technologies. Even though virtual screening is capable of reducing the number of investigated molecules, there are significant methodological concerns regarding this gradual reduction and the method is being debated in the pharmaceutical industry (see, for instance, Oprea. 2002; Hindmarch, Heath, and Fraser, 2006). Draws (2000) points to the limited effect on the actual output:

The advent of genomic sciences, rapid DNA sequencing, combinatorial chemistry, cell-based assays, and automated high-throughput screening (HTS) had led to a new concept of drug discovery. In this new concept, the critical discourse between chemists and biologists and the quality of scientific reasoning are sometimes replaced by the magic of large numbers... So far, this several hundredfold increase in the number of raw data has not yet resulted in a commensurate increase in research productivity, As measured by the number of new compounds entering the market place, the top 50 companies in the pharmaceutical industry collectively have not improved their productivity during the 1990s. (Drews, 2000: 1962)

Despite failing to live up to the promises of its spokesmen, the virtual screening technologies are expected to play a central role in the pharmaceutical industry of the future. *The Science 2020* report issued by Microsoft Research, Cambridge, UK, and the *Bioscience 2015* report issued by the British Bioscience and Innovation Growth Team, commissioned by the British government, both strongly emphasize a mediated pharmaceutical industry, mentioning "bioinformatics" and "e-science" as important tools when developing new and safe drugs (see also The Economist, June 14th, 2007, on "Biology's Big Bang").

In summary, the entire process of detecting new chemical entities is increasingly being shaped by the use of various media, including high-throughput screening and visualization technologies. Media are defined here in terms of offering opportunities for reducing the number of molecules under investigation through automatic processes of molecule selection. The knowledge involved in synthesis chemistry work is therefore increasingly becoming entangled with the understanding, use, and maintenance of advanced media.

Sound Engineering and Recording

In sound engineering and recording, a "mediatization" similar to that in other fields has taken place. Among other things, the recent "digitalisation" (Greffe, 2004) of sound engineering and recording has brought new opportunities, but it also demands new skills. In her analysis of the historical development of sound engineering and recording, Horning (2004) emphasizes the move from "acoustic recording" to "digital recording" as a major technological leap. In acoustic recording, the engineer was trained to position instruments and voices in the studio so as to achieve the best mix of instruments. In addition, being capable of "reading the grooves" off the record was important since recordings were directly scripted onto the wax (Horning, 2004: 706). With electric recording, studio engineering changed from being a "craft" to a "profession" on the basis of being "[g]rounded increasingly in scientific, mathematical, and systems engineering methods and knowledge" (Horning, 2004: 708). Under the electronic recording regime, studio engineers were trained to select equipment (e.g. microphones) that suited a particular sound or voice. In general, the entire profession was based on the ability to combine musical instruments, voices, equipment, and technology into a functional unit that produced the "sound" aimed at. In the more recent digitalisation of recording work, where continuous sounds are transformed into digital and discrete units, the ability to manipulate and modify recorded sounds increases almost infinitely. However, this growth in the opportunities for producing and manipulating sounds makes new demands of the recording engineers. Porcello (2004), himself a former studio engineer, emphasizes the need to develop a seamless web consisting of vocabularies, aural capacities, and technologies in recording work. For instance, in musical training (e.g. in master's programs in studio engineering) in "aural perception classes", students are trained not only to hear sounds but also to identify how to modify them in order to achieve the desired sound:

In an aural perception class, students do not only learn how to hear sound; in studying the electrical and acoustic principles underlying limiters, compressors, equalizers, and so forth, not only do they learn how sound waves are modified and their effects on achieving a balanced musical mix; when studying circuits, they do not simply memorize information and electrical current flow. In each case, they simultaneously learn a complex technical discourse—a way of talking about and hence conceptualizing the relevant phenomena—then translating them into significant communicative resources to be deployed in situated sessions studio work. (Porcello, 2004: 738)

Porcello (2004: 746-747) especially emphasizes the communicative skills of the sound engineers. Since they are constantly collaborating and interacting with musicians not necessarily trained or skilled in expressing how they want the final record to sound, sound engineers draw on a variety of resources. First, they use "singing/vocables", that is "phonetic and phonological work" to mimic musical sounds. For instance, in Porcello's case, a sound engineer discusses the sound of the bass drum with a drummer and here uses sounds like "hm", "pz", "dz" to convey meanings and "images of sounds". Second, they use what Porcello (2004) calls "lexical onomatopesis", "words that bear at least a partial acoustic resemblance to the sound to describe, but which are simultaneously metaphors that more abstractly describe the sound". Third, sound engineers use "'pure' metaphors", that is, "words such as 'pitch-bend', 'tight' or 'deep' are used to describe timbral characteristic, but do *not* bear any acoustic similarity to the sound in question (which distinguishes them from lexically onomatopoetic words). Finally, associations that involve citing other musicians (e.g. Jimi Hendrix or Miles Davis), "classic albums" (e.g., the Beach Boys' *Pet Sounds*), sounds (e.g. a "roots reggae drum and bass sound"), or time periods ("60s pop music", "70s funk", "80s hip-hop"); The use of associations helps to define "[a] common frame of reference from which to describe the timbres in question, and, implicitly, where this band will fit into the larger world of musical styles and commodities". These associations thus function "indexically", involving other "styles, musicians, or production technologies" (Porcello, 2004: 747). When speaking with colleagues and peers, sound engineers use a more esoteric (in the true sense of the term) vocabulary which includes product names (e.g. a "Shure microphone sound" or a "telecaster sound") as shorthand descriptors of specific sounds. Since virtually the entire recording process is reliant on digital media, the sound engineer needs to have an intimate knowledge of how to produce the desired sound using the technological apparatus at hand in the studio. The manipulation of frequencies and beats is embedded in the use of advanced media, providing endless possibilities for manipulation of the incoming signal (i.e. the recorded sound).

In both Horning's (2004) and Porcello's (2004) accounts, audio engineering work includes the skill of bridging the aural, lexical, and technological—what is non-linguistic (sounds) using linguistic and technological resources. In addition, the aural is always mediated, that is, produced, manipulated, stored, and distributed through the use of media. Although work on new drug development and audio engineering represents two wholly different domains of expertise, relying on idiosyncratic demands for education and training, skills, communication patterns, and creativity, they are still two professions—or professional domains—where molecules and sounds are increasingly mediated; perception and cognition are in both cases embedded in the thoughtful and informed use of advanced media. Just as the synthesis chemist is capable of operating virtual screening technologies, identifying promising molecules for further investigation, the sound engineer is trained in manipulating analogue or digital signals through the use of media. In both cases, media and knowledge are closely bound together and mutually constitutive. Knowledge is not "external" to media but is instead constituted as the very ability to operate the media and to communicate the meaning of the images and sounds produced by media. When synthesis engineers inspect a molecule, they make use of their "chemistry intuition" to sort out what they deem to be interesting molecules. This "chemistry intuition" includes the ability to communicate the ideas and beliefs, often in a tacit form, to peers and decision-makers in the industry. Similarly, sound engineers develop a certain tacit skill in shaping sounds to accomplish the desired outcomes. Their communication with musicians and various experts includes a wide variety of lexical resources ranging from onomatopoetic sounds via references to product names. Seen in this way, knowledge management is the ability to bring together media, communication, and propositional and tacit knowledge in one functional unit; functional in terms of being able to produce new approved drugs for the market and advanced recordings meeting the expectations of artists and audiences.

Comparing the Two Cases

The knowledge work done by a synthesis chemist in the pharmaceutical industry and that done by a sound engineer is representative of two rather different domains of the "knowledge economy" or "knowledge society". While the synthesis chemist is a practicing scientist who operates in a technoscientific field that is determined by a range of technologies and procedures, the sound engineer engages in what may be termed "aesthetic work", i.e. work that is more complicated to evaluate on the basis of fixed or widely agreed upon standards (Taylor and Hansen, 2005). However, the two professional groups share the predicament, or the opportunity, associated with operating in a life-world highly determined by the use of new media, media that are capable of storing, retrieving, manipulating, and circulating data and information in "universalized packages". For instance, in the new visualization technologies used by synthesis chemists, a specific molecule may be rotated and examined from various angles; it may be de-composed and modified; it can easily be circulated between co-workers and peers. Similarly, sound engineers work with digital sound files that may be endlessly manipulated. Signals may be amplified, cut up into sequences, inverted, and so forth, all enabling new sounds to be produced. In both cases, the focal knowledge worker is provided with media that extend the scope of what is possible to do and thus knowledge work is increasingly becoming a matter of choice and selection. Media offer so many choices and therefore the mark of the true knowledge worker is the ability to take proper action in a multiplicity of competing alternatives. In addition, such choices cannot be conducted by media but are always a matter of what Daston and Galison (2007) call "trained judgment", i.e. the ability to make a choice on the basis of incomplete or, on the contrary, excessive information. For the synthesis chemist, identifying the most promising molecule is not achieved by the media but by something which is part of one's professional training and work experience. For the seasoned sound engineer, choosing a microphone and what frequencies to eliminate in order to accomplish the desired "sound" are based on past experience of operating the media available. Therefore, knowledge work is embedded in media but is never wholly determined by media; instead, knowledge work is the ability to bridge and align skills, experiences, technology, media, and preferences and trained judgment in order to accomplish the desired objectives.

DISCUSSION AND CONCLUSION

This paper has examined the transdisciplinary (rather than multidisciplinary) literature dealing with media and has pointed to the need to inform organization theory using such alternative and complementary views of media and their roles. The concept of media used here does not simply refer to the technology, nor to the social production of information and entertainment (Luhmann, 2000; Kellner, 1995) provided by television, radio, newspapers, or the film industry, rather it denotes what Hayles (2002) calls *inscription technologies*, integrating information, technology, and social institutions into one single process. Media, then, are assemblages which are part technological, part informational, and part social, with the boundaries between these different components being complicated to separate, both practically and analytically. In addition, media draw on the three worldviews of speech, writing, and code. It is a mistake to confuse technology and media; media is a broader construct, extending outside of the mere technological artifact, no matter how delicate and advanced such an artifact may be (Kallinikos, 1995). For instance, Kittler's (1999) analysis of the gramophone, the cinema, and the typewriter draws on the Lacanian registers of the imaginary, the symbolic and the Real, and conceives of these inscription technologies as capable of representing images, sounds, and noises previously unheard and unseen. In this view, media are not uncomplicated technological devices representing an extension or mechanization of the human body—e.g. the typewriter replacing the hand and the pen (McLuhan, 1964; Flusser, 2000: 23)—but are to be examined in terms of having significant social, cultural, and psychological implications. Media produce social effects that are not always possible to predict or control, and thus it is important to critically examine them from a variety of perspectives. In organization theory and management studies, media tend to be taken for granted and are thus naturalized as a part of the organizational lifeworld. Contrary to such a view, media need to be de-familiarized anew so that their full scope can be examined in a new light. If it is true, as McLuhan (1964) suggested, that "media is the message", then media deserve a proper analysis and a proper theoretization.

In the knowledge management literature, media tend to be naturalized and taken for granted. Rather than assuming that knowledge work exists detached from the use of media and that media are resources "added on top" of preexisting knowledge work, media are regarded here as integral components of knowledge work. Expressed differently, knowledge is mediated and constituted through media; knowledge and knowledge work are the result of the very use of media. For instance, in the case of virtual screening in the pharmaceutical industry, synthesis chemists are trained to identify opportunities for synthesizing new promising molecules on the basis of interaction with the screening technologies. Rather than complement the conventional laboratory procedures, the virtual screening techniques "enframe" and structure all synthesis chemistry work. Seen in this way, a key skill in the synthesis chemist's portfolio of expertise and experience is the ability to interpret and evaluate the output from the virtual screening procedure. The virtual screening of molecule libraries is an inscription technology, a media capable of inscribing potentiality into an epistemic object such as a molecule. In the case of recording engineers, a category of workers who can be grouped under knowledge work, the recent digitalization of sound recording has brought with it an immense set of possibilities for the manipulation of analog or digital signals. If we assume that the recording studio is, to use the vocabulary of Flusser (2000) in his analysis of the camera, an "apparatus" endowed with a "program", a fixed set of possibilities, recording engineers must learn to master at least a selection of the actions provided by the program. First, they learn to manipulate sound signals in order to accomplish the desired effects and soundscapes. Second, they need to enact a linguistic system that denotes the various operations and manipulations. More specifically, they need to develop both an esoteric and an exoteric vocabulary. The esoteric vocabulary operates with the minimum of articulations; the exoteric vocabulary brings the amateur into the conversation and must thus make use of all the available resources. In this particular type of mediated knowledge work, two abstract domains, i.e. aural perception and a linguistic system, are constantly intersecting. Media theory and studies constitute a domain of research and thinking that is of great interest to knowledge management researchers. Rather than rendering media as black boxes whose internal logic and functioning are essentially unproblematic, knowledge management researchers should pay more attention to the mediation of knowledge work; media are not additional or a complement to knowledge work, but precisely its very infrastructure (Star and Bowker, 2002), that which enframes and structures knowledge work without always being noticed in day-to-day practices. As media theorists such as Mosco (2004) have pointed out, the real power of media and technology emerges when they become familiarized and taken for granted:

The real power of new technologies does not appear during their mythic period, when they are hailed for their ability to bring world peace, renew communities, or end scarcity, history, geography, or politics; rather, their social impact is greatest when technologies become banal—when they literally (as in the case of electricity) or figuratively withdraw into the woodwork. (Mosco, 2004: 19)

Taking media for granted makes us susceptible to various myths and ideologies relating to media (Coyne, 1999; Stivers, 1999; Ullman, 1997), e.g. what Aaseth calls the "teleological myth of media convergence" in which "[a]ll old media come together in the dawn of the high-tech era and are subsumed by the new digital supermedium" (Aaseth, 2003: 416). Not all digitial media share basic characteristics, argues Aaseth (2003: 416), but various hypertext media have as little in common as printed documents like "telegrams, lecture notes, and restaurant menus". Aaseth argues: "The functional difference between old and new media, paper and digitality, could not be drawn clearly . . . some paper media had more in common with some digital media than certain digital media had with each other . . . the analog/digital distinction in media is overrated and uninformative and breaks down under scrutiny" (Aaseth, 2003: 418). In knowledge management theory and research, the role of media deserves to be recognized and the black boxes need to be opened. Knowledge is mediated and technologically constituted and must therefore be examined on the basis of these premises.

REFERENCES

Aaseth, E. (2001). We all want to change the world: The ideology of innovation in digital media. In G. Liestøl, A. Morrison, & T. Rasmussen (Eds.), (2003), *Digital media revisited.* (pp. 415-439). Cambridge & London: MIT Press.

Bachelard, G. (1934/1984). *The New Scientific Spirit.* Boston: Beacon Press.

Barley, S. R. (1986). Technology as an occasion of structuring: Evidence from observations of CT scanners and the social order of radiology departments. *Administrative Science Quarterly, 31,* 78-108.

Barley, S. R. (1990). The alignment of technology and structure through roles and networks. *Administrative Science Quarterly, 35*, 61-103.

Barney, J. (1991). Firm resources and sustained competitive advantage. *Journal of Management, 17*, 99-120.

Benjamin, W. (1973). The work of art in the age of mechanical reproduction. In W. Benjamin (Ed.) (1973), *Illuminations*. London: Fontana Press.

Biocca, F. (1992). Virtual reality technology: A tutorial. *Journal of Communication, 42*(4), 23-74.

Bioscience 2015, (2003). *Bioscience and Innovation Growth Team, UK.* (Available at http://www.bioindustry.org/bigtreport/index2.html Accessed March 9, 2007)

Bolter, J. D. (1991). *Writing space: the computer, hypertext, and the history of writing.* Hillsdale, Hove and London: Lawrence Erlbaum.

Bolter, J. D., & Grusin, R. (1999). *Remediation. Understanding new media.* Cambridge: The MIT Press.

Bourdieu, P. (1996).*On television.* New York: The New Press.

Brown, S. D., & Lightfoot, G. (2002). Presence, absence, and accountability: E-mail and the mediation of organizational memory. In S. Woolgar (Ed.), (2002), *Virtual society? Technology, cyberbole, reality.* Oxford & New York: Oxford University Press.

Bud, R. (1983). *The uses of life: A history of biotechnology.* Cambridge: Cambridge University Press.

Burns, A. (1989). *The power of the written word: the role of literacy in the history of Western civilization.* New York: Peter Lang.

Clarke, A. E., Mamo, L., Fishman, J. R., Shim, J. K., & Fosket, J. R.(2003). Biomedicalization. Technoscientific transformations of health, illness, and U.S. biomedicine. *American Sociological Review, 68*, 161-194.

Coyne, R. (1999). *Technoromanticism: Digital narrative, holism, and the romance of the real.* Cambridge & London: The MIT Press.

Crary, J. (1990). *Techniques of the observer: On vision and modernity in the nineteenth century.* Cambridge & London: The MIT Press.

Daston, L., & Galison, P. (2007). *Objectivity.* New York: Zone Books.

Derrida, J. (1976). *Of Grammatology.* Baltimore: John Hopkins University Press.

Derrida, J. (1981). *Dissemination.* Chicago: The University of Chicago Press.

Dierkes, M., Berthon, A., Child, J., & Nonaka, I. (Eds.), (2001). *Handbook of organizational learning & knowledge.* Oxford: Oxford University Press.

Dodge, M., & Kitchin, R. (2005). Code and the transduction of space. *Annals of the American Geographers, 95*(1), 162-180.

Drews, J. (2000). Drug discovery: a historical perspective. *Science, 287*, 1960-1964.

Easterby-Smith, M., & Lyles, M. A. (2003). *Handbook of organization learning and knowledge management.* Oxford & Malden: Blackwell.

Eckert, H., & Bajorath, J. (2007). Molecular similarity analysis in virtual screening: foundations, limitations and novel approaches. *Drug Discovery Today, 12*(5-6), 225-233.

Edmonson, A. C., Bohmer, R. M., & Pisano, G. P. (2001). Disrupted routines: Team learning and new technology implementation in hospitals. *Administrative Science Quarterly, 46*, 685-716.

Eisenstein, E. (1983). The *printing revolution in early modern Europe.* Cambridge: Cambridge University Press.

Febvre, L., & Martin, He-J. ([1958]1997). *The coming of the book: The impact of printing 1450-1800*, trans. by David Gerard, London & New York: Verso.

Flusser, V. (1983/2000). *Towards a philosophy of photography*. London. Reaktion Books.

Flusser, V. (2002). *Writings*, Edited by Andreas Ströhl, trans. by Erik Eisel, Minneapolis & London: The University of Minnesota Press.

Foss, N. J. (1996). Knowledge-based approaches to the theory of the firm: Some critical remarks. *Organization Science*, *7*(5), 470-476.

Gallagher, A., & Cates, C. (2004). Virtual reality training for the operating room and cardiac catheterisation laboratory. *The Lancet*, *364*, 1538-1540.

Gane, N. (2005). Radical post-humanism. Friedrich Kittler and the primacy of technology. *Theory, Culture & Society*, *22*(3), 25-41.

Gergen, K. J., & Thatchenkery, T. J. (1996). Organizational science as social construction. In the *Journal of Applied Behavioural Science*, *32*(4), 356-277.

Gitelman, L. (1999). *Scripts, grooves, and writing machines. Representing technology in the Edison era.*Stanford: Stanford University Press.

Gitelman, L., & Pingree, G. B. (Eds.), (2003). *New media, 1940-1915*. Cambridge & London: The MIT Press.

Greffe, X. (2004). Artistic work in the digital age. *Journal of Arts Management, Law, and Society*, *34*(1), 79-94.

Hansen, Mark B. N. (2006). Media theory. *Theory, Culture & Society*, *23*(2-3), 297-306.

Haraway, D. J. (1991). *Semians, Cyborgs, and Women: The Reinvention of Nature*. London: Free Association Books.

Hayles, N. K. (2005). *My mother was a computer: Digital subjects and literary texts*. Chicago & London: The University of Chicago Press.

Hayles, N. K. (1999). *How we became posthuman: Virtual bodies in cybernetics, literature, and informatics*. Chicago & London: The University of Chicago Press.

Hayles, N. K. (2002). *Writing machines*. Cambridge & London: The MIT Press.

Hedgecoe, A., & Martin, P. (2003). The drugs don'twork: Expectations and the shaping of pharmacogenetics. *Social Studies of Science*, *33*(3), 327-364.

Heidegger, M. (1977). *The Question Concerning Technology and Other Essays*. New York: Harper and Row.

Horning, S. S. (2004). Engineering the performance: Recording engineers, tacit knowledge and the art of controlling sound. *Social Studies of Science*, *34*(5), 703-731.

Joerges, B., & Czarniawska, B. (1998). The question of technology, or how organizations inscribe the world. *Organization Studies*, 19(3), 363-385.

Jones, R. A. (2004). *Soft machines: Nanotechnology and life*. Oxford & New York: Oxford University Press.

Kay, L. E. (2000). *Who wrote the book of life? A history of the genetic code*. Stanford & London: Stanford University Press.

Kallinikos, J. (1995). The archi-tecture of the invisible: Technology is representation. *Organizations*, *2*(1), 117-140.

Kallinikos, J. (1996a). *Organizations in an age of information*. Lund: Academia Adacta.

Kallinikos, J. (1998). Organized complexity: Posthumanist remarks on the technologizing of intelligence. *Organization*, *5*(3), 371-396.

Kellner, D. (1995). *Media culture: Cultural studies, identity and politics between the modern and the postmodern*. London & New York: Routledge.

Kittler, F. (1990). *Discourse networks 1800/1900*, trans. by Michael Metteer & Chris Cullens, Stanford: Stanford University Press.

Kittler, F. A. (1997). *Essays. Literature, media, information systems*. Ed. by John Johnston, Amsterdam: G+B Arts International.

Kittler, F. (1999). *Gramophone, film, typewriter*, trans. by Geoffrey Winthrop-Young and Michael Wutz, Stanford: Stanford University Press.

Krämer, S. (2006). The cultural techniques of time axis manipulation: On Friedrich Kittler's conception of media. *Theory, Culture and Society, 23*(7-8), 93-109.

Landow, G. P. (2006). *Hypertext 3.0: Critical theory and new media in an era of globalization*. Baltimore: the Johns Hopkins University Press.

Lanzara, G. F., & Patriotta, G. (2001). Technology and the courtroom: An inquiry into knowledge making in organizations. *Journal of Management Studies, 38*(7), 943-971.

Lash, S. (2006). Life (Vitalism). *Theory, Culture & Society, 23*(2-3), 323-329.

Latour, B. (1987). *Science in Action*. Cambridge: Harvard University Press.

Latour, B. (1991). Technology is society made durable. In J. Law (Ed.), *A sociology of monsters: Essays on power, technology and domination*. London & New York: Routledge.

Law, J. (Ed.) (1986). *Power, Action, and Belief: A New Sociology of Knowledge*. London: Routledge and Kegan Paul.

Lenoir, T. (1998). Inscription practices and materialities of communication. In T. Lenoir (Ed.), (1999), *Inscribing science: Scientific texts and the materiality of communication* (pp. 1-19). Stanford: Stanford University Press.

Lee, J. Y. (1996). Charting the codes of cyberspace: A rhetoric of electronic mail. In L. Strate,, R. Jacobson, & S. B. Gibson Eds.), *Communication and cyberspace: Social interaction in an electronic environment* (pp. 275-296). Cresskill, NJ: Hampton Press.

Lévi-Strauss, C. (1979). *Myth and Meaning: Cracking the Code of Meaning*. New York: Shocken Books.

Luhmann, N. (1995). *Social Systems*. Stanford: Stanford University Press.

Luhmann, N. (2000). *The reality of the mass media*. Cambridge: Polity Press.

Lykke, N., & Braidotti, R. (1996). *Between Monsters, Goddesses and Cyborgs: Feminist Confrontations with Science, Medicine, and Cyberspace*. London: Zed Books.

Machlup, F. (1962). *The production and distribution of knowledge in the United States*. Princeton: Princeton University Press.

Mannheim, K. (1936). *Ideology and utopia*. London: Kegan Paul.

Manovich, L. (2001). *The language of new media*. Cambridge & London: The MIT Press.

McGail, B. A. (2002). Confronting electronic surveillance: Desiring and resisting new technologies. In S. Woolgar (Ed.), (2002). *Virtual society? Technology, cyberbole, reality*. Oxford & New York: Oxford University Press.

McLuhan, M. (1962). *The Gutenberg galaxy: The making of typographic man*. London: Routledge & Kegan Paul.

McLuhan, M. (1964). *Understanding Media*. New York: Signet Books.

Merrin, W. (1999). Television is Killing the Art of Symbolic Exchange: Baudrillard's Theory of Communication. *Theory, Culture & Society, 16*(3), 119-140.

Merton, R. K. (1957). Karl Mannheim and the sociology of knowledge. In *Social Theory and Social Structure*. Glencoe: Free Press.

Michaels, M. (2000). *Reconnecting culture, technology and nature: From society to heterogeneity*. London & New York: Routledge.

Milburn, C. (2004). Nanotechnology in the age of posthuman engineering: Science fiction as science. In K. N. Hayles (Ed.), (2005), *Nanoculture: Implications of the new technoscience*. (pp. 109-129). Bristol: Intellect Books.

Mosco, V. (2004). *The digital sublime: Myth, power and cyberspace*. Cambridge & London: The MIT Press.

Newell, S., Robertson, M.,Scarborough, H., & Swan, J. (2002). *Managing knowledge work*. Basingstoke: Palgrave.

Ong, W. J. (1982). *Orality and Literacy: The Technologizing of the Word*. London: Routledge.

Oprea, T. I. (2002). Virtual screening in lead discovery: A viewpoint. *Molecules,* 7, 51-62.

Orlikowski, W. J. (2000). Using technology and constituting structures: A practice lens for studying technology in organizations. *Organization Science, 11*(4), 404-428.

Piñeiro, E. (2007). Aesthetics at the heart of logic: On the role of beauty in computing innovation. P. Guillet de Monthoux, C. Gustafsson, & S-E. Sjöstrand (Eds.), (2007), *Aesthetic leadership: Managing fields of flow in art and business* (pp. 105-127). Basingstoke: Palgrave Macmillan.

Plato (1921). *Theaetetus*. Indianapolis and Cambridge: Hackett Publishing.

Plato (1956). *Protagoras & Meno*. London: Penguin.

Porcello, T. (2004). Speaking of sound: Language and the professionalization of sound-recording engineers. *Social Studies of Science, 34*(5), 733-758.

Poster, M. (2001). *The information subject: Essays*. Amsterdam: G+B Arts.

Prasad, P. (1993). Symbolic process in the implementation of technological change: A symbolic interactionist study of work computerization. *Academy of Management Journal, 36*(6), 1400-1429.

Schrödinger, E. (1946). *What is life? Physical aspects of the living cell*. Cambridge: Cambridge at the University Press.

Science 2020 (2006). Microsoft Research, Cambridge, UK. (Available at http://research.microsoft.com/towards2020science/ Accessed March 9, 2007)

Spender, J.-C., & Grant, R. M. (1996). Knowledge and the firm: Overview. *Strategic Management Journal, 17*(Winter Special Issue), 5-9.

Star, S. L., & Bowker, G. C. (2002). How to infrastructure. In L. A. Lievrouw & S. Livingstone (Eds.), (2002), *Handbook of new media: Social shaping and consequences of ICT.* (pp. 151-162). London, Thousand Oaks & New Delhi: Sage.

Stengers, I. (1997). *Power and invention: Situating science*. Minneapolis & London: Minnesota University Press.

Steuer, J. (1992). Defining Virtual Reality: Dimensions Determining Telepresence. *Journal of Communication, 42*(4), 73–93.

Stivers, R. (1999). *Technology as magic: The triumph of the irrational*. New York: Continuum.

Styhre, A. (2003). *Understanding knowledge management: Critical and postmodern perspectives.* Malmö: Liber; Oslo: Abstrakt; Copenhagen: Copenhagen Business School Press.

Taylor, S. S., & Hansen, H. (2005). Finding form: Looking at the field of organizational aesthetics. *Journal of Management Studies, 42*(6), 1211-1231.

Thomas, T. C., & Acuña-Narvaez, R. (2006). The convergence of biotechnology and nanotechnology: Why here, why now? *Journal of Commercial Biotechnology, 12*(2), 105-110.

Tsoukas, H., & Vladimirou, E. (2001). What is organizational knowledge? *Journal of Management Studies, 38*(7), 973-993.

Ullman, E. (1997). *Close to the machine: Technophilia and its discontents*. San Francisco: City Lights Book.

Walters, W. P., Stahl, M. T., & Murcko, M. A. (1998). Virtual screening - An overview. *Drug Discovery Today, 3*, 160-178.

Wiener, N. (1950). *The human use of human beings*. London: Eyre and Spottiswoode.

Whelan, G. (2002). Appropriat(e)ing Wavelengths: On Bourdieu's *On Television*. *Ephemera, 2*(2), 131-148.

Williams, R. (1974/1990). *Television Technology and Cultural Form*. 2nd Edition, London & New York: Routledge.

Wise, J. M. (1997). *Exploring technology and social space*. Thousand Oaks, London & New Delhi: Sage.

Woicehyn, J. (2000). Technology adoption: Organizational learning in oil firms. *Organization Studies, 21*(6), 1095-1118.

Vattimo, G. (1992). *The Transparent Society*. Cambridge: Polity Press.

Chapter XXXI
Knowledge Management: The Construction of Knowledge in Organizations

Ben Tran
Alliant International University, USA

ABSTRACT

This chapter examines knowledge and innovation as invaluable factors affecting the longevity of large organizations. It presents the history and evolution of the concepts of knowledge and learning within organizations to provide grounds for establishing crucial factors affecting the development and maintenance of competitive advantage for large contemporary organizations. Thus the purpose of this chapter is to address the evolution of knowledge management, the meaning and purpose of knowledge management, and the organizational structure that supports such knowledge.

INTRODUCTION

Knowledge and innovation are widely known as invaluable factors in the longevity of large organizations. Managers in large organizations have been attempting to utilize and capitalize on these factors so that they can best leverage the knowledge base of their organizations to build competitive advantages for their firms. In so doing, organizations are struggling to understand, and address some of their knowledge and innovation concerns. These concerns are: 1) What is organizational knowledge?; 2) Where does it reside?; and 3) How does organizational learning take place and how does it generate knowledge?

In order to address and understand knowledge and innovation as invaluable factors that affect the longevity of large organizations, to utilize and capitalize on these factors so that they can leverage the knowledge base of their organizations to build competitive advantages for their firms, one must understand what they are and their evolution. Thus the purpose of this paper is to address the evolution of knowledge management, the meaning and purpose of knowledge management, and the organizational structure that supports such knowledge. In turn, organizations striving for competitiveness and longevity will be able to have their concerns addressed.

THE HISTORY OF KNOWLEDGE MANAGEMENT

Some may argue that consultants developed knowledge management (KM) to replace declining revenues from the waning re-engineering movement. Others may feel that knowledge management is just a "re-bagging" of earlier information and data management methods (Prusak, 2001). According to Larry Prusak (2001), knowledge management, like any system of thought that has value, is both old and new, and its combination of new ideas with ideas that "everyone has known all along" should reassure practitioners rather than unnerve them. While the idea of consultants looking for a profitable new subject to replace an expiring one has some credibility, the fact is that knowledge management is not just a consultants' invention but a practitioner-based, substantive response to real social and economic trends.

Thus, knowledge management describes both a business practice and an emerging theoretical field of study (Anonymous, 2000; McInerney, 2002; Southon, Todd, & Seneque, 2002). The desire to share knowledge is something so natural that it seems strange that knowledge management has emerged as something newly invented by corporations. Clearly, the thinking about knowledge management has resided in commerce and industry, and that is where most of the writing on the topic has been published, but recently literature on knowledge management has began to cross boundaries, and scholars in many disciplines have shown an intense interest in the creation of knowledge and its value and power when it can be shared across the organization. Since knowledge management theory is still developing, it is especially appropriate for those in the information and technology professions to examine knowledge management and offer analytical frameworks that can guide thoughtful and humane knowledge practices (McInerney, 2002). As such, knowledge management is an interdisciplinary field that draws on a variety of business activities and academic specializations. As its name suggests, knowledge management is concerned with systematic, effective management, and the utilization of an organization's knowledge resources. It encompasses the creation, storage, arrangement, retrieval, and distribution of an organization's knowledge (Anonymous, 2000).

The growing awareness and value of specialized knowledge in its various forms has been recognized in an emerging discourse known as knowledge management (Amidon, 1997; Hansen, Nohria, & Tierney, 1999; Nonaka & Takeuchi, 1995; Quinn, 1992; Sieloff, 1999; Wiig, 1993). Knowledge management is also known as organizational knowledge, for knowledge management is to theorists, as organizational knowledge is to practitioners (Anonymous, 2000; Duffy, 2000; Prusak, 2001; Yakel, 2000). This discourse, primarily conceptualizing knowledge as embedded in the experience, skills, wisdom, and capabilities of people, as well as in the processes, routines, and the tangible artifacts produced in an organization, is diffuse and complex, providing not only multiple perspectives of what constitutes knowledge management, but also different underpinning assumptions about its nature, contextualization, role, and indeed, the meanings of its constituent terms "knowledge" and "management" (Southon, Todd, & Seneque, 2002).

THE BIRTH OF KNOWLEDGE

Information and library science, information systems, computer science, engineering, communication, cognitive science, and organizational science have all laid claim to some aspect of knowledge management (Borghoff & Pareschi, 1998; Dienes & Perner, 1999; DiMattia & Oder, 1997; Dutta, 1997; Koenig, 1996; Parikh, 2001; Streng, 1999; Zack, 1999). Despite their differences, the practitioners of these disciplines have a common interest in knowledge and knowledge sharing. Consequently, it is reasonable that the study of knowledge management should begin with the study of knowledge itself. Knowledge is the awareness of what one knows through study, reasoning, experience or association, or through various other types of learning. It is "acquaintance with or understanding of a science, art, or technique" (Merriam Webster's Collegiate Dictionary, 2003).

The Oxford English Dictionary (1989) presents the word "knowledge" as meaning "acknowledging...recognizing...inquiring...being aware...understanding...information acquired through study, and learning." The verb forms used in defining knowledge show how knowledge is a result of a varied set of processes, processes that also demonstrate the active nature of knowledge. Another dictionary, according to Anonymous (2000), equates knowledge with the accumulation and understanding of facts, ideas, principles, or skills. So defined, knowledge may be acquired through study, observation, and/or experience. On the other hand, Richard Daft (2001: 258) defines knowledge as a conclusion drawn from information that has been linked to other information and compared to what is already known.

Although dictionary definitions of knowledge recognize slight variations in usage, the state of knowing is distinguished from a body of knowledge. For example, all definitions imply insight, comprehension, and mastery of recorded information as key characteristics and essential attributes of knowledge. Such insight, comprehension, and mastery clearly distinguish knowledge from information. Thus, unlike static information that can be held in database and on paper, knowledge is based in sentient beings, or emanates from them, and thus, it is always changing with the human experience. Within organizations where work depends on personal interactions with others, knowledge has both an active and a social dimension (Brown & Duiguid, 2000).

KNOWLEDGE: SUBJECTIVE VS. OBJECTIVE

Congruent to Polyani's paradigm, according to Tsoukas (2005: 143), granted that there is a common structure underlying all kinds of knowledge, knowledge is anything but "objective, self-contained, detaches, and independent of human action." This is due to the fact that "all knowing involves skillful action," as well as the fact that the all living organisms are subjectively opinionated. Subjective opinionated organisms are what attribute to the fact that "all knowing is personal knowing" (Polyanyi & Prosch, 1975: 44) and "personal knowing" is "subjective knowing," and "subjective knowing" is subjective knowledge." Thus, knowledge is not objective, but subjective.

TYPES OF KNOWLEDGE

Knowledge is acquired actively and dynamically through sensory stimulation, listening to and observing others, reading and retaining, being aware of feelings, life experience, and all the processes related to learning. It is this dynamic nature of knowledge that leads to the question of how something in flux, in movement and action, can be managed. In a knowledge management program it is the knowledge artifact, or the thing, that is managed, not knowledge itself, and the knowledge representation must reflect the action of knowledge acquisition. For example, if records of the lessons that people learn in the course of a project are collected, subtleties of efforts with clients or colleagues must be captured and reported along with a write up of conclusion.

Artifacts as explicit expressions of knowledge are still dependent on the human attributes embodied in the personal knowledge of a knower. Michael Polanyi (1958) has created an exhaustive catalog of knowledge categories in his signature project *Personal Knowledge*, a work that consumed him for nearly nine years (p. ix). Other authors often invoke his work, but practically speaking, all of Polyani's intricate categories are seldom differentiated in organizational knowledge management. Polyani's greatest contribution to understanding knowledge is his explication of tacit (internal) and explicit (external) knowledge. In his essays published in 1969 as *Knowledge and Being*, Polanyi emphasizes the importance of tacit knowledge, and he says, "The ideal of a strictly explicit knowledge is indeed self-contradictory. Deprived of their tacit co-efficients, all spoken words, all formulae, all maps and graphs are strictly meaningless" (p. 195). Admittedly, Polanyi's view is a somewhat sanitized version of knowledge (Prichard, 2000), but because he was an early theorist of tacit/explicit knowledge, his framework has proven useful to others.

Tacit Knowledge: According to Haridimos Tsoukas (2005: 143), Polanyi was the inventor of the term tacit knowledge, but the term was made famous by Ikujiro Nonaka and Hirotaka Takeuchi's (1995) influential book titled *The Knowledge-Creating Company* (p. 142). Ever since Nonaka and Takeuchi helped popularize the concept of tacit knowledge in management studies, their interpretation has been adopted by several management authors (e.g. Ambrosini & Bowman, 2001; Banmard, 1999; Boisot, 1995; Davenport & Prusak, 1998; Devlin, 1999; Dixon, 2000; Krogh, von Ichijo, & Nonaka; 2000; Leonard & Sensiper, 1998). Polanyi's bifurcation of tacit knowledge and explicit knowledge is a division seen throughout the seminal knowledge management literature (Broadbent, 1998; Davenport & Prusak, 1998; Dienes & Perner, 1999; Nonaka & Takeuchi, 1995; Whitley, 2000, etc.). Tacit knowledge, sometimes known as implicit knowledge, is unspoken and hidden. It is the expertise and assumptions that individuals develop over the years that may never have been recorded or documented. In other words, according to Richard Daft (2001: 258), tacit knowledge is often very difficult to put into words. Tacit knowledge is based on personal experience, rule of thumb, intuition, and judgment. It includes professional know-how and expertise, individual insight and experience, and creative solution that are often difficult to communicate and pass on to others.

In other words, tacit knowledge, according to Tsoukas (2005: 146), is like a triangle, at the three concerns of which are the *subsidiary particulars*, the *focal target*, and the *knower* who links the two (Figure 1).

The structure of tacit knowing has three aspects: the functional, the phenomenal, and the semantic. The functional aspect consists in the *from-to* relation of particulars (or subsidiaries) to the focal target. Tacit knowing is a from-to knowing: we know the particulars by relying on our awareness of them for attending to something else. Human awareness has a "vectorial" character (Polanyi, 1969: 182): it moves from subsidiary particulars to the focal target (Gill, 2000: 38-39). Or, to repeat the words of Polanyi and Prosch (1975: 37-38): "Subsidiaries exists as such by bearing on the focus *to* which we are attending *from* them" (emphasis in the original). The phenomenal aspect involves the transformation of subsidiary experience into a new sensory experience. The latter appears through—it is created out of—the tacit integration of subsidiary sense perceptions. Finally, the semantic aspect is the meaning of subsidiaries, which is the focal target on which they bear (147-148).

Figure 1. Personal knowledge

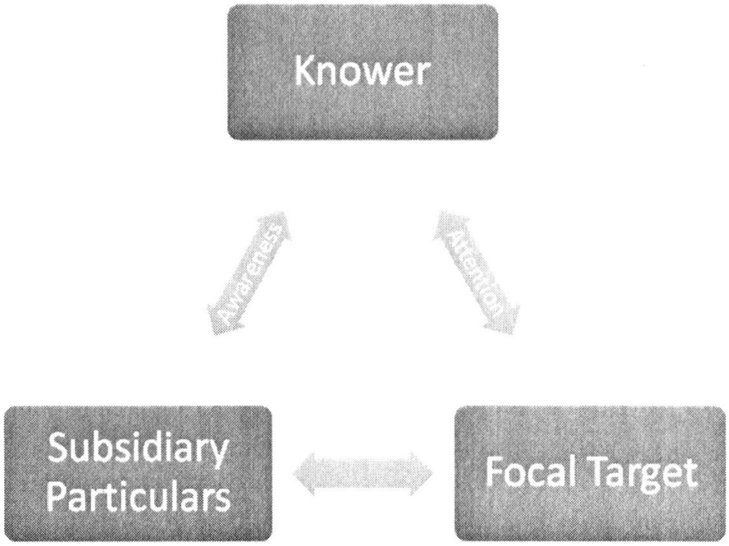

On the other hand, Nonaka and Takeuchi assume that tacit knowledge is knowledge-not-yet-articulated: a set of rules incorporated in the activity an actor is involved in, which it is just a matter of time for him/her to first learn and then formulate. Nonaka and Takeuchi seem to think that what Ikuro Tanaka learned through her apprenticeship with the master can be ultimately crystallized in a set of propositional "if, then" statements (Tsoukas, 1998: 44-48), or what Michael Oakeshott (1991: 12-15) called "technical knowledge" and Gilbert Ryle (1963: 28-32) "knowing that." In that sense the tacit knowledge involved in mapping that Tanaka picked up through one's apprenticeship—in Oakeshott's terms, (1991: 12-15), the "practical knowledge" of mapping, and in Ryle's terms (1963: 28-32), "knowing how" to map—the sort of knowledge that exists only *in use* and cannot be formulated in rules, is equivalent to the set of statements that articulate it, namely to technical knowledge.

Tacit knowledge is thought to have the structure of a syllogism, and as such can be reversed and, therefore, even mechanized (Polanyi & Prosch, 1975: 40). According to Tsoukas (2005), what Tanaka was missing, the authors imply, were the premises of the syllogism, which one acquired through one's sustained apprenticeship. Once they have been learned, it was a matter of time before one could put them together and arrive at the conclusion that "twisting stretch" and "the (right movements required for the kneading propeller" (Nonaka & Takeuchi, 1995: 103-106).

Explicit Knowledge: Explicit knowledge, as the first word in the term implies, is knowledge that has been articulated and, more often than not, captured in the form of text, tables, diagrams, product specifications and so on. In a well-known and frequently cited 1991 Harvard Business Review article titled The Knowledge Creating Company, Ikujiro Nonaka refers to explicit knowledge as "formal systematic " and offers product specifications, scientific formulas and computer programs as examples (Nickols, 2003). In other words, explicit knowledge is knowledge that has been explained, recorded, or documented (Figure 2). Figure 2 is adopted from Fred Nickols's (2003) *The Knowledge in Knowledge Management.*

When tacit knowledge has not been represented and made explicit in an organization, there

Figure 2. Explicit, implicit, and tacit knowledge

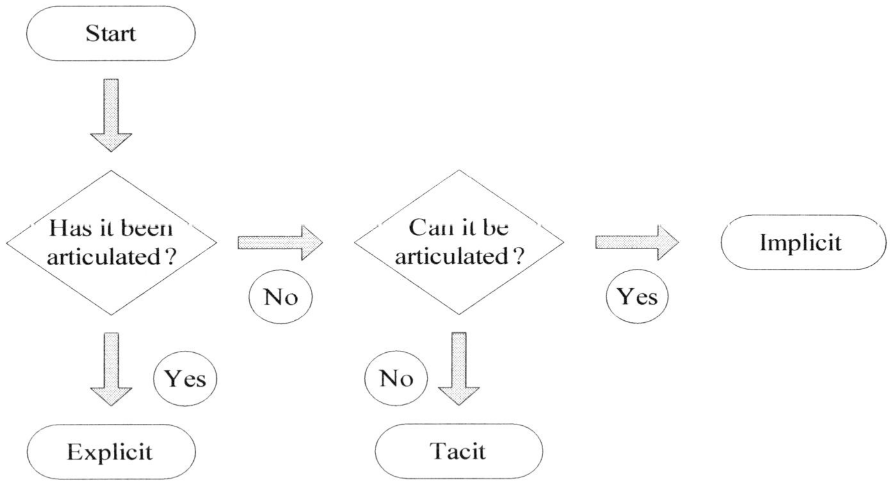

could be lost opportunities in performance, opportunities that other organizations may exploit for their own purposes. Michael Zack (1999) explains that:

Potentially explicable knowledge that has been articulated represents a lost opportunity to efficiently share and leverage that knowledge. If competitors have articulated and routinized the integration and application of similar knowledge, then they may obtain a competitive advantage (p. 47).

This advantageous use of knowledge in the marketplace is usually referred to as using the organization's "intellectual capital" (Koenig, 1996; Stewart, 1998, 2001). Some businesses have captured knowledge previously thought to be intuitive or simply "business know-how," and have made financial gains this way. As such, Daft (2001: 258) defines explicit knowledge as a formal, systematic knowledge that can be codified, written down, and passed on to others in documents or general instructions. With that said, there are three other types of knowledge in knowledge management that are less well known, and often not mentioned mention but are worth mentioning here. Cognitive psychologists acknowledge these three types of knowledge as declarative, procedural, and strategic knowledge.

Declarative Knowledge. Declarative knowledge has much in common with explicit knowledge in that declarative knowledge consists of descriptions of facts and things or of methods and procedures. The person most closely associated with the distinction between declarative and procedural knowledge is John Anderson of Carnegie-Mellon University. He has been writing about these two notions for almost 25 years (Anderson, 1976; 1993; 1995). Being able to state the cut-off date for accepting applications is an example of declarative knowledge. It is also an instance of explicit knowledge. For most practical purposes, declarative knowledge and explicit knowledge may be treated as synonyms. This is because all declarative knowledge is explicit knowledge, that is, it is knowledge that can be and has been articulated (Figure 3). Figure 3 is adopted from Fred Nickols's (2003) *The Knowledge in Knowledge Management.*

Procedural Knowledge. One view of procedural knowledge, according to Nickols (2003), is that it is knowledge that manifests itself in the

Figure 3. Declarative and procedural knowledge

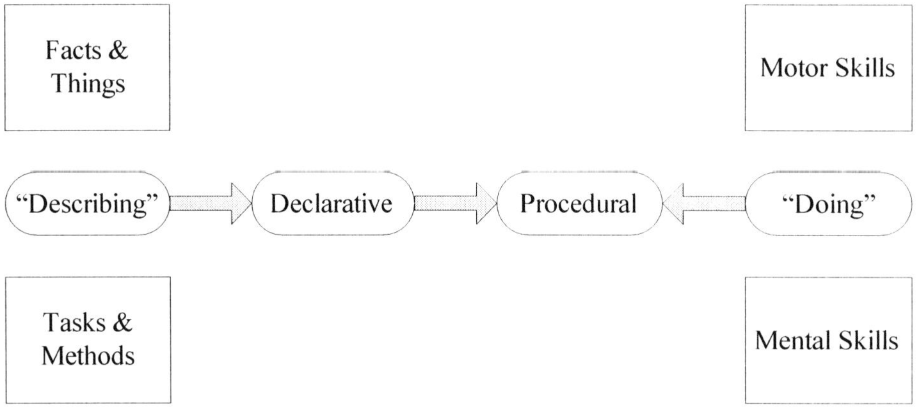

doing of something. As such it is reflected in motor or manual skills and in cognitive or mental skills. For an example, we think, we reason, we decide, we dance, we play the piano, we ride bicycles, we read customers' faces and moods (and our bosses' as well), yet we cannot reduce to mere words that which we obviously know or know how to do. Attempts to do so are often recognized as little more than after-the-fact rationalizations. This knowing-is-in-the-doing view of procedural knowledge is basically the view of John Anderson, the Carnegie-Mellon professor mentioned earlier. Another view of procedural knowledge is that it is knowledge about how to do something. This view of procedural knowledge accepts a description of the steps of a task or procedure as procedural knowledge. The obvious shortcoming of this view is that it is no different from declarative knowledge except that tasks or methods are being described instead of facts or things.

Strategic Knowledge. Strategic knowledge is a term used by some to refer to what might be termed know-when and know-why. Although it seems reasonable to conceive of these as aspects of doing, it is difficult to envision them as being separate from that doing. In other words, we can separate out strategic knowledge only in the describing, not the doing. Consequently, strategic knowledge is probably best thought of as a subset of declarative knowledge instead of its own category (Figure 4). Figure 4 is adopted from Fred Nickols's (2003) *The Knowledge in Knowledge Management*.

THE RELATIONSHIP BETWEEN TACIT KNOWLEDGE AND EXPLICIT KNOWLEDGE

According to Tsoukas (2005), the cornerstone of Nonaka and Takeuchi's theory of organizational knowledge is the notion of "knowledge conversion"—how tacit knowledge is "converted" to explicit knowledge, and vice verse. This interaction is known as "knowledge conversion" (Tsoukas, 2005: 151). With that said, Noaka and Takeuchi distinguish four modes of knowledge conversion: from tacit knowledge to tacit knowledge (socialization); from tacit knowledge to explicit knowledge (externalization); from explicit knowledge to explicit knowledge (combination); and from explicit knowledge to tacit knowledge (internalization).

Tacit knowledge is converted to tacit knowledge through observation, imitation, and practice, in those cases where an apprentice learns from a

Figure 4. Integration

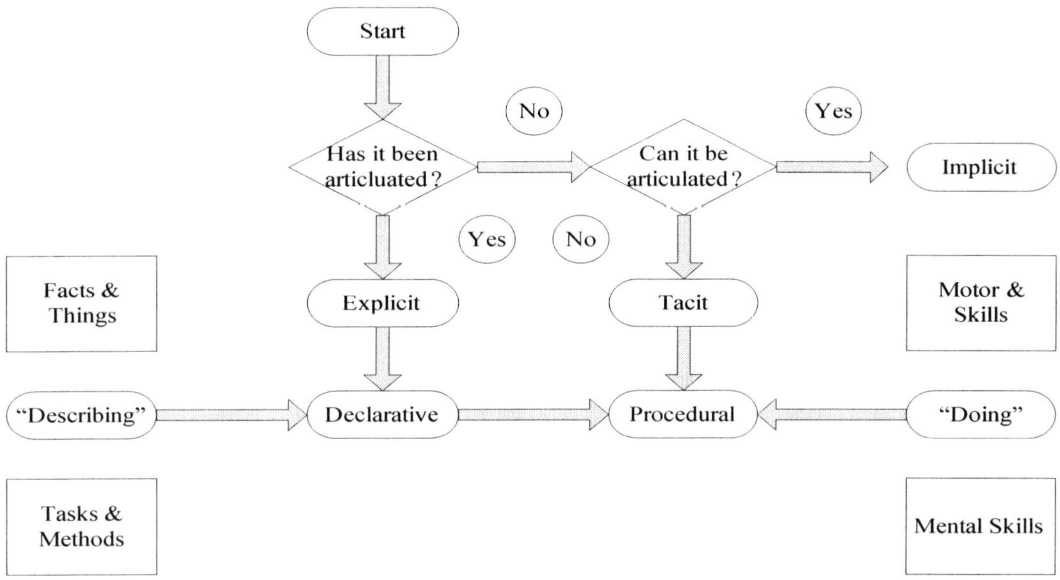

master. Tacit knowledge is converted to explicit knowledge when it is articulated and it takes the form of concepts, models, hypotheses, metaphors, and analogies. Explicit knowledge is converted to explicit knowledge when different bodies of explicit knowledge are combined. Explicit knowledge is converted to tacit knowledge when it is first verbalized and then absorbed, internalized by the individuals involved (Nickols, 2003: 6; Tsoukas, 2005: 151-152).

Take the organizational knowledge-creation process for an example, the process proceeds in cycles (in a spiral-like fashion), with each cycle consisting of five phases: the sharing of tacit knowledge among the members of a team; the creation of concepts whereby a team articulates its commonly shared mental model; the justification of concepts in terms of the overall organizational purposes and objectives; the building of an archetype which is a tangible manifestation of the justified concept; and the "cross-leveling" of knowledge, whereby a new cycle of knowledge creation may be created elsewhere in (or even outside) the organization (Tsoukas, 2005: 152). As such, congruent to Tsoukas (2005), Nonaka and Takeuchi's interpretation of tacit knowledge as knowledge-not-yet-articulated—namely, knowledge awaiting its "translation" or "conversion" into explicit knowledge—an interpretation that has been widely adopted in management studies, is erroneous: it ignores the essential ineffability of tacit knowledge, thus reducing it to what can be articulated. Tacit and explicit knowledge are not two ends of a continuum but two sides of the same coin: even the most explicit kind of knowledge is underlain by tacit knowledge. As a result, the misunderstanding of the concept of the knowledge apprentice, are touched upon.

KNOWLEDGE ORIGINATES AND RESIDES IN THE HUMAN MIND

Although Davenport and Prusak (1998) and others write about knowledge processes operating in the mind, in such phrases as "knowledge originates...in the minds of knowers," this concept is problematic because it restricts knowledge to being exclusively an intellectual activity. Knowledge goes beyond mind activity. Knowledge is based on sensory experience and physical activity, as well as mindful cognition. As D. H. Lawrence (1928, 1980) said, "Real knowledge comes out of the whole corpus of consciousness...the mind can only analyze and rationalize." Knowing involves the whole person, as mind and body where emotion, cognition, and physicality together create what is known.

In one of the central essays of Managing Knowledge, a critical look at knowledge management, Craig Prichard (2000) argues that the body needs to be put back into knowledge management. He alludes to knowledge management literature that recommends that conversation is the key to sharing knowledge (Davenport & Prusak, 1998), and he cites other writings from business that indicate that people to people communication and face-to-face meetings are necessary to stimulate innovation through knowledge. In many of these cases Prichard maintains, the emphasis on physicality is obvious, but it is not acknowledged. He goes on to say that the importance of tacit knowledge, as Polyani and others have shown, proves that the body cannot be separated from the mind in knowledge management frameworks if we want meaningful knowledge sharing.

Feminist authors also see the difficult in separating mind and body when conceptualizing knowledge. Allison Jaggar (1989) exposes the myth of dispassionate investigation" in necessary not only for knowledge acquisition, but for human survival itself. In western culture, Jaggar points out, people have been encouraged to "control" or "suppress" their emotions, and therefore, they may not be consciously aware of their emotions or their importance in knowing. Jaggar says:

But lack of awareness of emotions certainly does not mean that emotions are not present subconsciously or unconsciously or that subterranean emotions do not exert a continuing influence on people's articulated values and observations, thoughts, and actions (p. 155).

KNOWLEDGE MANAGEMENT

Knowledge management (KM), also known as knowledge sharing (KS) (McInerney, 2002) and personal knowledge management (PKM) (Miller, 2005), was relatively unknown just a few years ago, but it is fast becoming one of the most widely publicized business initiatives. Knowledge management concepts and methods are enjoying the same enthusiastic reception that was given to business process reengineering in the 1990s, to office automation in the early 1980s, and to distributed computing in the early 1970s (Anonymous, 2000). Anonymous (2000) defines knowledge management as a concern with systematic, effective arrangement, retrieval, and distribution of an organization's knowledge. Jan Duffy (2000) defines it as a process of locating, organizing, transferring, and using information.

On the other hand, Daft (2001: 257) defines knowledge management as the efforts to systematically find, organize, and make available a company's intellectual capital and to foster a culture of continuous learning and knowledge sharing so that organizational activities build on existing knowledge. Gareth R. Jones (2004: 381), however, defines it as the sharing and integrating of expertise within and between functions and divisions through real-time interconnected information technology (IT). Last but not least, Ron Miller (2005) defines it as individual workers who try to keep track of the information they encounter in their daily work lives, and more importantly, make intelligent use of that information.

THE RESIDENTS OF KNOWLEDGE MANAGEMENT

The power of knowledge management resides in three forms. The first two are knowledge spillovers and inherited knowledge (Agarwal, Echambadi, Franco, & Sarkar, 2004) and the third is what I refer to as knowledge apprenticeship. Knowledge spillovers have focused on the treat of voluntary exists from firms of experts who possess critical know-how, a threat causing technology-rich firms to be known as "precarious monopolies" (Stinchcombe & Heimer, 1988; Zucker, Darby, & Brewer, 1998). A firm's tacit knowledge is not only team-based and socially embedded in routines (Nelson & Winter, 1982), but also resident in individual human capital (Bermna, Down, & Hill, 2002; Hitt, Bierman, Shimizu, & Kochhar, 2001; Lepak & Snell, 1999; Szulanski, 1996). As employees internalize an organization's culture (Inzerille & Rosen, 1983; Meek, 1988), they imbibe procedural and declarative knowledge related to functional capabilities such as R&D and marketing. Human capital is mobile since employees are under limited organizational control and free to resign at will (Aldrich & Pfeffer, 1976; Boeker, 1997; Coff, 1997).

Inherited knowledge focused on knowledge transfer from a recipient organization's perspective and investigated knowledge diffusion and the interorganizational social structure created by executive migration (Aldrich & Pfeffer, 1976; Boeker, 1997). Various difficulties involved in the transfer of "sticky" tacit knowledge have been acknowledged (von Hippel, 1994), but research has emphasized that organizational blueprints can transfer across firm boundaries, in a manner analogous to the reproduction and transmission of biological genes (Winter, 1991). These transfer may include unique insights and decision rules used to transform resources into action (Prahalad & Bettis, 1986), cognitive dimensions of competency (Fiol, 1991), and specific knowledge and information (Boeker, 1997). Since "what an organization knows at its birth will determine what it searches for, what it experiences, and how it interprets what it encounters" (Huber, 1991: 91), one implication is that a spin-out's capability accumulation may be linked to its inherited knowledge and that the agent of transfer may have an impact in efficacy of transfer.

The apprenticeship knowledge is the knowledge spillovers and the inherited knowledge "to-be." The knowledge apprentice is the trainee and the future of the knowledge spillovers and the inherited knowledge. Through training and experience gained in one's profession, the knowledge apprentice will then become an expert who possesses critical know-how, and thus a knowledge spillover or an inherited knowledge. However, past research automatically assumed that the succession of the apprenticeship knowledge is emanated upon the apprenticeship with a master. This assumption is fallacious.

One must understand and acknowledge that no two knowledge apprentices will achieve equivalent succession upon completion of the apprenticeship under the same master. For instance, the map example mentioned by Tsoukas (2005), no two apprentices will view, process, and interpret the map, in relations to the physical world the same way. As such, the prerequisite of the journey of a knowledge apprentice rests on two critical factors: the ability and willingness of the knowledge apprentice to achieve successions and an organization's support and the organization's willingness to learn. This factor is known as organizational learning.

ORGANIZATIONAL LEARNING

The connection between knowledge and organizational learning is inevitable because knowledge is what has been learned (Kofman & Senge, 1993). Organizational learning is about people and organizational goals. The work of Peter Senge, Chris Agyris, and others has explored how organization s learn (Agyris, 1991, 1993; Senge, 1990a, b; Senge, Kleiner, Roberts, Roth, Ross, & Smith, 1999) and the importance of organizational learning in being able to adapt to change and being resilient enough to weather uncertain economic climates. Due to the fact that knowledge and organizational learning are closely tied (McInerney & LeFevre, 2000), it is doubtful that any organization can succeed in sharing knowledge and managing knowledge artifacts well without a commitment to learning.

Learning and knowledge management are processes that involve change and movement to new levels of cognition and understanding among individuals in an organization. One working definition that we might use for knowledge management incorporates what we know about the theory and practice of knowledge management and its connections to learning. In simple language, according to McInerney (2002):

Knowledge management is an effort to increase useful knowledge within the organization. Ways to do this include encouraging communication, offering opportunities to learn, and promoting the sharing of appropriate knowledge artifacts (p. 1014).

Organizational learning, sometimes described as intellectual capital (Anonymous, 2000), has been defined in more ways than one. According to Jones (2004), organizational learning is the process through which managers seek to improve organizational members' desire and ability to understand and manage the organization and its environment so that they make decisions that continuously raise organizational effectiveness (p. 376). Duke Okes (2005) defines it as the focuses on learning that occurs through interactions among members of an organization, such as cross functional teams and communities of practice. On the other hand, intellectual capital, according to Okes (2005), is the focusing on techniques. This view of knowledge management tries to quantify the value of the organization's intellectual assets, such as its patents and unique understanding of customer needs.

TYPES OF ORGANIZATIONAL LEARNING

James March proposed that two principal types of organizational learning strategies can be approached: exploration and exploitation (Jones, 2004). *Exploration* involves organizational members searching for and experimenting with new kinds or forms of organizational activities and procedures to increase effectiveness. Learning that involves exploration might involve finding new ways of managing the environment—such as experimenting with the use of strategic alliances and network organizations—or inventing new kinds of organizational structures for managing organizational resources—such as product team structures and cross-functional teams (Jones, 2004).

Exploitation involves organizational members learning ways to refine and improve existing organizational activity procedures in order to increase effectiveness. Learning that involves exploitation might involve implementing a total quality management program to promote the continuous refinement of existing operating procedures, or developing an improved set of rules to perform specific kinds of functional activities more effectively. *Exploration* is therefore a more radical learning process than *exploitation*, although both are important in increasing organizational effectiveness (Jones, 2004).

It is based on these two principal types of organizational learning strategies that enable organization to purposefully design and construct its structure, culture, and strategy so as to enhance and maximize the potential for organizational learning to take place. In so doing, the organization increases the ability of its employees, at every level in the organization, to question and analyze the way an organization currently performs its activities and to experiment with new ways to change it to increase effectiveness. In creating this learning organization, managers are to encourage learning at four levels: individual, group, organizational, and interorganizational. Some principles for creating a learning organization at each level have been developed by Senge (Jones, 2004).

FOUR LEVELS OF ORGANIZATIONAL LEARNING

Individual: According to Jones (2004), at the individual level, managers need to do all they can to facilitate the learning of new skills, norms, and values so that individuals can increase their own personal skills and abilities and thereby help build the organization's core competences. Senge has argued that for organizational learning to occur, each person in an organization needs to develop a sense of personal mastery, by which he means that organizations should empower individuals and allow them to experiment and create and explore what they want. The goal is to give employees the opportunity to develop an intensive appreciation for their work that translates into a distinctive competence for the organization. As part of attaining personal mastery, and to give employees a deeper understanding of what is involved in a particular activity, organizations need to encourage employees to develop and use complex mental models that challenge them to find new or better ways of performing a task.

Group: At the group level, according to Jones (2004), managers need to encourage learning by promoting the use of various kinds of groups—such as self-managed groups or cross-functional teams—so that individuals can share or pool their skills and abilities to solve problems. Groups allow for the creation of synergism—the idea that the whole is much more than the sum of its parts—which can enhance performance. "Group routines" and "shared pools of collective meaning" that enhance group effectiveness may develop from such group interactions. Senge refers to this kind of learning as team learning and he argues that team learning is more important than individual-level learning to promoting organizational learning because most important decision are made in subunits such as groups, functions, and divisions.

Organization: At the organization level, managers can promote organizational learning through the way they create an organization's structure and culture. An organization's structure can be designed to inhibit or facilitate intergroup communication and problem solving, and this effects team members' approach to learning. Mechanistic and organic structures, for example, encourage different approaches to learning. The design of a mechanistic structure seems likely to facilitate explorative learning, while the design of an organic structure seems more likely to facilitate explorative learning. Indeed, organizations need to strike a balance between a mechanistic and an organic structure in order to take advantage of both types of learning (Jones, 2004).

According to Jones (2004), culture, too, is likely to be an important influence on learning at the organizational level. Another of Senge's principals for designing a learning organization emphasizes the importance of building shared vision, by which he means building the ongoing frame of reference or mental model that all organizational members use to frame problems or opportunities and that binds them to an organization. At the heart of this vision is likely to be the set of terminal and instrumental values and norms that guide behavior in a particular setting and that affect the way people interact with individuals and groups outside an organization, that is, organizational culture. Thus yet another important aspect of organizational culture is its ability to promote or inhibit organizational learning and change.

Interorganizational: Organizational structure and culture not only establish the shared vision or framework of common assumptions that guide learning inside an organization, but also determine how learning takes place at the interorganizational level. In general, interorganizational learning is important because organizations can improve their effectiveness by copying and imitating each other's distinctive competences (Jones, 2004).

THE FEEDING OF KNOWLEDGE

The strategic value of knowledge and knowledge management have almost become a given. In this environment, organizations that master the challenge of developing a successful knowledge management have a competitive advantage and also produce a superior products to sell to their consumers. There is another key driver that should be considered. Today's high-speed, volatile work environment demands that everyone be willing and able to rethink situations almost as each decision is made. The orderly decision-making process if our business predecessors are no longer the norm. Circumstances change almost on a minute-by-minute basis existing knowledge needs to be viewed through a new lens in each new set of circumstances (Duffy, 2000).

Organizations must provide employees with all the help they can. Access to what is already known and the tools and environment to take advantage of this store of knowledge are critical. It is important to recognize that different people use the same lessons in different ways. They develop new context and this, in turn, becomes new knowledge. The benefit is that this knowledge and experience continues to add to the knowledge within the organization.

Further complicating the situation is the need for employees (particularly those who are front-line customer contacts) to be increasingly responsive. It is no longer enough to provide a simple answer to a simple question. Everyone needs to feel comfortable with helping resolve problems or issues on the spot. This suggests that employees need access to a wide variety of information, knowledge, and tools to help them. This need can be satisfied to some extent by a well-designed knowledge management environment.

However, success also requires that the employees have the ability to quickly assess a situation and then suggest the most appropriate solution. Often there is no time to ask whether the picture is complete because there is little time to think. Different perspectives produce a different result. The need to interpret, analyze, and synthesize is challenging the abilities of many organization's knowledge workers. Thus, the feeding of organizational knowledge, and the organizational structure that encourages and supports organizational knowledge, is a "flat" organizational structure.

CONCLUSION

Knowledge management (KM), also known as knowledge sharing (KS) (McInerney, 2002) and personal knowledge management (PKM) (Miller, 2005) to theorists as organizational knowledge is to practitioners (Anonymous, 2000; Duffy, 2000; Prusak, 2001; Yakel, 2000). Knowledge has been widely defined, but although dictionary definitions of knowledge recognize slight variations in usage, the state of knowing is distinguished from a body of knowledge. Nevertheless, knowledge is acquired actively and dynamically through sensory stimulation, listening to and observing others, reading, being aware of feelings, life experience, and all the processes related to learning. It is this dynamic nature of knowledge that leads to the question of how something in flux, in movement and action, can be managed. Knowledge as such, resides in three forms, knowledge spillovers and inherited knowledge (Agarwal, Echambadi, Franco, & Sarkar, 2004) and the third is what I refer to as knowledge apprentice. An organizational learning environment that embraces, encourages, and supports such building, sharing, and creating of knowledge is a "flat" organizational structure.

REFERENCES

Agarwal, R., Echambadi, R., Franco, A. M., & Sarkar, M. B. (2004). Knowledge transfer

through inheritance: Spin-out generation, development, and survival. *The Academy of Management Journal, 47, 4,* 501-522.

Agyris, C. (1993). On organizational learning. Cambridge, MA: Blackwell Publishers.

Agyris, C. (1991). Teaching smart people how to learn. *Harvard Business Review, 69, 3,*99-109.

Aldrich, H. E., & Pfeffer, J. (1976). Environments of organizations. In A. Inkeles (Ed.), *Annual Review of Sociology, 2,* 79-105.

Ambrosini, V., & Bowman, C. (2001). Tacit knowledge: Some suggestions for operationalization. *Journal of Management Studies, 38*, 811-829.

Amidon, D. A. (1997). *Innovation strategy for the knowledge economy: The ken awakening.* Boston: Butterworth-Heinemann.

Anonymous. (2000). Knowledge management: An overview. *Information Management Journal, 34,* 4-7.

Banmard, P. (1999). *Tacit knowledge in organizations* (Translated by S. Wanchope). London: Sage.

Berman, S. L., Down, J., & Hill, C. W. L. (2002). Tacit knowledge as a source of competitive

advantage in the national basketball association. *Human Resource Management Journal, 45,* 13-31.

Boeker, W. (1997). Executive migration and strategic change: The effect of top manager movement on product-market entry. *Administrative Science Quarterly, 42,* 213-236.

Boisot, M. H. (1995). *Information space: A framework for learning in organizations, institutions and culture.* London: Routledge.

Borghoff, U. M., & Pareschi, R. (1998). Information technology for knowledge management (Eds.). Berlin: Springer-Verlag.

Broadbent, M. (1998). The phenomenon of knowledge management: What does it mean to the information profession? *Information Outlook, 2*(5), 23-35.

Brown, J. S., & Duguid, P. (2000). The social life of information. Boston: Harvard Business School Press.

Coff, R. W. (1997). Human assets and management dilemmas: Coping with hazards on the road to resource-based theory. *Academy of Management Review, 22,* 374-402.

Daft, R. L. (2001). Organization theory and design (7th Eds.). South-Western College Publishing.

Davenport, T. H., & Prusak, L. (1998). Working knowledge: How organizations manage what they know. Boston, MA: Harvard Business School Press.

Devlin, K. (1999). *Infosense*. New York, NY: Freeman.

Dienes, Z., & Perner, J. (1999). A theory of implicit and explicit knowledge. *Behavioral and Brain Sciences, 22*(5), 735-808.

DiMattia, S., & Oder, N. (1997). Knowledge management: Hope, hype, or harbinger? *Library Journal, 122*(5), 33-36.

Dixon, N. M. (2000). *Common knowledge*. Boston, MA: Harvard Business School Press.

Duffy, J. (2000). Knowledge management: What every information professional should know. *Information Management Journal, 34*(3), 10-14.

Dutta, S. (1997). Strategies for implementing knowledge-based systems. *IEEE Transactions on Engineering Management, 44*(1), 79-90.

Fiol, C. M. (1991). Managing culture as a competitive resource: An identity-based view of sustainable competitive advantage. *Journal of Management, 17,* 191-211.

Gill, J. H. (2000). *The tacit mode.* Albany, NY: State University of New York Press.

Hansen, M. T., Nohria, N., & Tierney, T. (1999). What's your strategy for managing knowledge? *Harvard Business Review, 77*(2), 106-116.

Hitt, M. A., Bierman, L., Shimizu, K., & Kochhar, R. (2001). Direct and moderating effects of human capital on strategy and performance in professional service firms: A resource-based perspective. *The Academy of Management Journal, 44,* 13-28.

Huber, G. P. (1991). Organizational learning: The contributing processes and the literatures. *Organization Science, 2,* 88-115.

Inzerille, G., & Rosen, M. (1983). Culture and organizational control. *Business Research, 17,* 281-292.

Jaggar, A. M. (1989). Love and knowledge: Emotion in feminist epistemology. In A. M. Jaggar & S. R. Bordo (Eds.), *Gender/body/knowledge: Feminist reconstructions of being and knowing.* New Brunswick, NJ: Rutgers University Press.

Jones, G. R. (2004). *Organizational theory, design, and change: Text and cases* (4th Eds.). Pearson Education, Inc.

Koenig, M. E. D. (1996). Intellectual capital and knowledge management. *IFLA Journal, 22*(4), 299-301.

Kofman, F., & Senge, P. M. (1993). Communities of commitment: The heart of learning organizations. *Organization Dynamics, 22*(2), 5-23.

Krogh, G., von Ichijo, K., & Nonaka, I. (2000). *Enabling knowledge cognition.* New York, NY.: Oxford University Press.

Lawrence, D. H. (1929, 1980). Lady chatterly's lover. New York: Bantam Books.

Leonard, D., & Sensiper, S. (1998). The role of tacit knowledge in group innovation. *California Management Review, 40*(3), 112-132.

Lepak, D. P., Snell, S. A. (1999). The human resource architecture: Toward a theory of human capital allocation and development. *Academy of Management Review, 24,* 31-48.

McInerney, C. (2002). Knowledge management and the dynamic nature of knowledge. *Journal of the American society for information science and technology, 53*(12), 1009-1018.

McInerney, C., & LeFevre, D. (2000). Knowledge managers: History and challenges. In C. Prichard, R. Hull, M. Chumer, & H. Willmott (Eds.), *Managing knowledge: Critical investigations of work and learning.* London: Macmillan Business.

Meek, V. (1988). Organizational culture: Origins and weaknesses. *Organization Studies, 9,* 453-473.

Merrian-Webster (2003). Merrian-Webster's Collegiate Dictionary (11th Ed.).

Miller, R. (2005). The evolution of knowledge management: This time it's personal. *EContent, 28*(11), 38-41.

Nelson, R. R., & Winter, S. G. (1982). An evolutionary theory of economic change. Cambridge, MA: Harvard University Press.

Nickols, F. (2003). *The knowledge in knowledge management.* Retrieved June 4, 2008, from http://home.att.net/~OPSINC/knowledge_in_KM.pdf

Nonaka, I., & Takeuchi, H. (1995). The knowledge-creating company: How Japanese companies create the dynamics of innovation. Oxford: Oxford University Press.

Oakeshott, M. (1991). *Rationalism in politics and other essays, new and expanded edition.* Indianapolis, IN: Liberity.

Okes, D. (2005). Corral your organization's knowledge. *Quality Progress, 38, 10,* 25-30.

Parikh, M. (2001). Knowledge management framework for high-tech research and development. *Engineering Management Journal, 13*(3), 27-33.

Polanyi, M. (1969). Knowing and being: Essays by michael polyani. London: Routledge.

Polanyi, M. (1958). Personal knowledge: Towards a post-critical philosophy. Chicago: The University of Chicago Press.

Polanyi, M. & Prosch, H. (1975). *Meaning*. Chicago, IL: University of Chicago Press.

Prahalad, C. K., & Bettis, R. A. (1986). The dominant logic: A new linkage between diversity and performance. *Strategic Management Journal, 7*, 485-502.

Prichard, C. (2000). Know, learn and share! The knowledge phenomenon and the construction of a consumptive-communicative body. In C. Prichard, R. Hull, M. Chumer, & H. Willmott (Eds.), *Managing knowledge: Critical investigations of work and learning*. London: Macmillian Business.

Prusak, L. (2001). Where did knowledge management come from? *IBM Systems Journal, 40*(4), 1002-1017.

Quinn, J. B. (1992). Intelligent enterprise: A knowledge and service based paradigm for industry. New York: The Free Press.

Ryle, G. (1963). *The concept of mind*. London: Penguin.

Senge, P. M. (1990a). The fifth disciple: The art and practice of the learning organization. New York: Doubleday.

Senge, P. M. (1990b). The leader's new work: Building learning organizations. *Sloan Management Review, 32*(1), 7-22.

Senge, P. M., Kleiner, A., Roberts, C., Roth, G., Ross, R., Smith, B. (1999). The dance of change: The challenges to sustaining momentum in learning organizations. New York: Currency/ Doubleday.

Sieloff, C. G. (1999). If only hp knew what hp knows: The roots of knowledge management at Hewlett-packard. *Journal of Knowledge Management, 3*(1), 47-53.

Simpson, J. A., & Weiner, E. (1989). The oxford english dictionary (2nd Ed.). Oxford University Press.

Southon, F. C. G., Todd, R. J., & Seneque, M. (2002). Knowledge management in three organizations: An exploratory study. *Journal of the American Society for Information Science and Technology, 53*(12), 1047-1059.

Spender, J. C. (1996). Making knowledge the basis of a dynamic theory of the firm. *Strategic Management Journal, 17*, 45-62.

Stewart, T. A. (2001). The wealth of knowledge: Intellectual capital and the twenty-first century organization. New York: Currency.

Stewart, T. A. (1998). Intellectual capital: The new wealth of organizations. New York: Bantam.

Stinchcombe, A. L., & Heimer, C. A. (1988). Interorganizational relations and careers in computer software firms. In I. H. Simpson & R. L. Simpson (Eds.), *Research in the sociology of work, 5,* 179-204.

Streng, D. J. (1999). Knowledge management: An essential framework for corporate library leadership. *Advances in Library Administration and Organization, 16,* 1-30.

Szulanski, G. (1996). Exploring internal stickness: Impediments to the transfer of best practice within the firm. *Strategic Management Journal, 17 (special issue),* 27-43.

Tsoukas, H. (2005). Do we really understand tacit knowledge. In Haridimos T. *Complex knowledge:*

Studies in organizational epistemology. New York, NY.: Oxford University Press.

Tsoukas, H. (1998). Forms of knowledge and forms of life in organized contexts. In R. C. H. Chia, *In the realm of organization* (43-66). London: Routledge.

Von Hippel, E. (1994). "sticky information" and the locus of problem solving: Implications for innovation. *Management Science, 40,* 429-439.

Whitley, E. A. (2000). Tacit and explicit knowledge: Conceptual confusion around the commodification of knowledge. Presented at the Knowledge Management: Concepts and Controversies Conference. http://is.lse.ac.uk/staff/whitley/. Accessed January 5, 2006.

Wiig, K. (1993). Knowledge management foundations. Arlington, TX: Schema Press.

Winter, S. G. (1991). On coase, competence, and the corporation. In O. E. Williwamson & S. G. Winter (Eds.), *The nature of the firm: Origins, evolution and development (179-195).* Oxford, England: Oxford University Press.

Yakel, E. (2000). Knowledge management: The archivist's and records manager's perspective. *Information Management Journal, 34*(3), 24-29.

Zack, M. (1999). Managing codified knowledge. *Sloan Management Review, 40*(4), 45-58.

Zucker, L. G., Darby, M. B., & Brewer, M. B. (1998). Intellectual human and the birth of US biotechnology enterprises. *American Economic Review, 88,* 290-306.

KEY TERMS

Explicit Knowledge: Knowledge that has been articulated and, more often than not, captured in the form of text, tables, diagrams, product specifications and so on

Knowledge: Acknowledging… recognizing… inquiring… being aware… understanding… information acquired through study, and learning

Knowledge Management: Concerned with systematic, effective management, and the utilization of an organization's knowledge resources. It encompasses the creation, storage, arrangement, retrieval, and distribution of an organization's knowledge

Organizational Learning: The process through which managers seek to improve organizational members' desire and ability to understand and manage the organization and its environment so that they make decisions that continuously raise organizational effectiveness

Procedural Knowledge: Knowledge that manifests itself in the doing of something

Strategic Knowledge: What might be termed know-when and know-why

Tacit Knowledge: Based on personal experience, rule of thumb, intuition, and judgment. It includes professional know-how and expertise, individual insight and experience, and creative solution that are often difficult to communicate and pass on to others

Chapter XXXII
Redefining Professional:
The Case of India's Call Centre Agents

Premilla D'Cruz
Indian Institute of Management, Ahmedabad, India

Ernesto Noronha
Indian Institute of Management, Ahmedabad, India

ABSTRACT

Scholars researching the area of the sociology of professions had earlier predicted that as occupations seek to improve their public image, professionalism would embrace all their incumbents. It is therefore no revelation that call centre agents in India identify themselves as professionals. Using van Manen's hermeneutic phenomenological approach, we explored this dimension with 59 call centre agents located in Mumbai and Bangalore, India. The findings demonstrate that neither the trait nor the power approaches drawn from the traditional literature on the sociology of professions explain call centre agents' identification with professional work. Instead, agents' experiences validate the contemporary explanation that emphasises the appeal of professionalism used by employer organisations as a means to convince, cajole, and persuade their employees to perform and behave in ways which the employer organisation deems appropriate, effective and efficient. It is in this context that agents accept stringent work systems and job design elements, techno-bureaucratic controls and the primacy of the customer in return for the privileges bestowed upon them by way of being professionals. While professional identity thus serves as a means of socio-ideological control facilitating the realisation of the organisation agenda, it is not all-encompassing as agents simultaneously show signs of resistance.

INTRODUCTION

Several years ago, Wilensky (1964) predicted that professionalism would eventually embrace everyone with some claim to specialised knowledge or practice. The basis for this observation was the rapid spread of the forms of professional organisation among occupational groups, which were not professions (Marshall, 1962). Even the most unlikely occupations were becoming candidates for professionalisation as a high degree of technical competence, sophistication, and complexity became increasingly characteristic of the vast majority of work activities (Pavalko, 1971). Others argued, that it was not technical competencies alone that was claimed but occupations also claimed professional status by announcing that they were trustworthy, had a code of ethics, a professional association, and performed important services which only they were qualified to do, and were therefore deserving of autonomy and prestige (Klegon, 1978; Crompton, 1990). Thus, virtually every occupation seeking to improve its public image claimed to be a "profession" (Friedson, 1970). The spread of this phenomenon had Larson (1977) ask why and how a set of work practices and relations that characterised medicine and law came to become a rallying call for a whole set of knowledge-based occupations in very different employment conditions. More recently, Evetts (2003) argues that the word "professional" is increasingly being used in all work contexts. Not surprisingly then, in India, it is commonplace to refer to call centre agents as professionals (See D'Cruz & Noronha, 2006; Ramesh, 2004). So entrenched is this perception in the Indian call centre industry that even trade unionists trying to organise call centre agents have named their organisation as UNITES Professionals (Union for Information Technology Enabled Services Professionals) or Young Professionals Collective. It would therefore be important at this stage to refer to the sociology of professions literature.

PROFESSIONS AND PROFESSIONALISM: UNDERSTANDING THE PHENOMENA

Traditionally, there have been two approaches in the sociology of professions: the trait or attribute approach and the power approach. Until the early 1970's, the trait approach dominated the academic literature. Numerous efforts along functionalist lines (See, for example, Barber, 1963; Carr-Saunders & Wilson, 1933; Goode, 1969; Greenwood, 1962; Harris-Jenkins, 1970; Kornhauser, 1962; Marshall, 1962; Moore, 1970; Parsons, 1951; Wilensky, 1964) were devoted to isolating and listing attributes that served to distinguish professions from nonprofessional occupations. This school of thought believed that the sociological task was to list the characteristics of an ideal-typical profession against which actual examples of occupational groups could then be assessed as more or less professional (MacDonald, 1995). The trait model of professions included two core characteristics – a body of theoretical and technical knowledge and a service orientation. On the basis of these characteristics, the profession claimed and acquired other properties. This included professional autonomy which was the right accorded by society to members of a profession to determine the nature of problems with which they were concerned, the appropriate procedures by which these would be solved, and the evaluation of professional performance. In addition, the professions were characterised by control over recruitment and licensing of new members, a long period of training and socialisation, monopoly over the performance of certain tasks, authority recognised by clients and the public, a belief in the importance of their function, a sense of community, formal associations and a code of ethics (Latham, 2002; Leicht & Fennell, 2001; Toren, 1975;).

However, by the early 1970's, this functional orthodoxy was increasingly criticised and rejected

(MacDonald, 1995). The revisionists abandoned the idea that professions could be distinguished from other expert occupations on any empirically essential or analytically invariant grounds (Sciulli, 2005). According to Dietrich and Roberts (1999), trait approaches provide mere descriptions of professions, rather than bases for analysis. The trait approach was not considered to be sufficiently dynamic or process-oriented. That is, it took no account of the unequal distribution of power between professionals and customers of professional services, but saw the relation between the professions and society as an exchange, in the process obscuring the historical conditions under which occupational groups become professions. Thus, instead of concentrating on abstract traits of an occupation, it was necessary to recognise that resources contributing to successful professionalisation stem from linkages to the wider social structure (Klegon, 1978).

Accordingly, the power approach gained ground. The analytical focus shifted from professions as central functional structures in society to the study of professionalism, professionalisation and professional projects (Henriksson, 2006). As Dietrich and Roberts (1999) point out, the power approach to understanding the professions states that the distinguishing feature of the professions is purely their ability to gain societal recognition as professions. It was now increasingly proposed that professions are simply expert occupations that happen, by one strategic means or another, to establish and maintain particularly well-patrolled, yet structurally unnecessary, monopolies in the labour market for expert services (Sciulli, 2005). These post-functionalist studies of the professions tended to see the professions as centres of power claiming exclusive ownership of particular areas of expertise and to raise the status and prestige of their practice while subjecting the public and other occupations to their dominating rules (See, for example, Abbott, 1988; Freidson, 1970; Johnson, 1972; Larson, 1977; Macdonald, 1995). The relevant question was therefore not to determine what a profession is in an absolute sense but to consider how society determines who and what is professional.

Moving away from the two traditional approaches, recent literature in the sociology of professions focuses on the contemporary appeal of the discourse of professionalism in all occupations (Evetts, 2006). For instance, Evetts (2003) argues that despite the different interpretations of the word professional, the appeal of the idea of profession and professionalism is increasingly used in all work contexts. The word professional is gradually used as a marketing device to appeal to customers, in mission statements and organisational aims and objectives to motivate employees, and as a disciplinary mechanism for governing at a distance. It is an attractive prospect for an occupation to be considered a profession and for occupational workers to be identified as professionals. The reconstitution of employees as professionals involves more than just a process of relabeling, it also involves the delineation of "appropriate work identities." Thus, service and knowledge workers are having to and, indeed, choosing to reconstitute themselves as self-managing and self-motivated employees (Fournier, 1999). In effect, professionalism is being used to convince, cajole, and persuade employees to perform and behave in ways which the organisation deems to be appropriate, effective and efficient (Evetts, 2003). In addition, the customer is granted a sovereign position in the organisation's discourse, made explicit in the core values of the organisation. One such value relates to the emotionalisation of work deemed central for satisfying customers. Employees are urged to "own customers' problems," "see through the eyes of the customers," and "do whatever it takes to satisfy customers' needs." Thus, the appeal to professionalism serves to efface direct organisational control through the articulation of the needs of and in the name of customers (Fournier, 1999).

METHODOLOGY

The present article is part of a larger inquiry whose focus was to understand subjective meanings and interpretations of work experiences of employees in the Information Technology Enabled Services–Business Process Outsourcing (ITES-BPO) sector in Mumbai and Bangalore, India. The mandate of the study deemed the adoption of phenomenology as its research strategy, and van Manen's (1998) hermeneutic phenomenology which explores participants' lived experiences was used. Following van Manen's (1998) approach, conversational interviews were used to explore and gather experiential narrative material that would serve as a resource for developing a richer and deeper understanding of the experience being studied. Though unstructured, the process was disciplined by focusing on the fundamental question that prompted the research. Yet the clarity of the research question did not preclude exploring issues, such as being professional, that emerged during the interview because the researchers were aware that they could generate important insights into the phenomenon under study.

As is the case in the phenomenological tradition, participants in the study should be people who have experienced the phenomenon. Potential participants were identified through snowball sampling. All interviews were conducted in English, recorded and transcribed. Of the 59 call centre agents whose experiences are presented in this article, 34 were from Mumbai and 25 were based in Bangalore. Thirty nine worked in inbound processes, 12 in outbound processes and 8 in both inbound and outbound processes. While there were 29 women and 30 men whose ages ranged from 20 to 55 years, the largest number of participants were in the 22 to 25 years age group. Forty participants were unmarried and forty were graduates. The average monthly salary of participants was approximately Indian Rupees (INR) 12,900, based on a range of INR 8,000 to INR 25,000. All the participants were employed by either MNC (multinational corporation) captive, MNC third party or Indian third party call centre organisations and served overseas clients and customers. None of the participants were members of any unions.

The treatment and analysis of participant narratives followed Van Manen's (1998) thematic analyses. Sententious and selective approaches were used to identify the core theme and other themes that captured the essential meaning of participants' experiences. Being professional emerged as the core theme that described agents' lived experience. Following the identification of the core theme, agents' experiences were analysed in the light of the academic literature on the sociology of professions.

FINDINGS

In the findings presented below, the comparison between agents' description of being professional and the sociological literature emphasising the trait and power approaches is first elaborated upon. This is followed by an elucidation of how agents' lived experience demonstrates contemporary employer organisations' growing reliance on the appeal of professionalism (Evetts, 2003 & 2006; Fournier, 1999) as a means of identity regulation and socio-ideological control in order to achieve the organisational agenda.

Indian Call Centre Agents as Professionals: A View from the Trait and Power Approaches

As mentioned earlier, the trait approach stressed that there was some general consensus that a profession is based upon a body of knowledge of an intellectual nature (Snider, 1963). The expertise possessed by professionals is said to consist of a set of esoteric and abstract principles that have been mastered and organised by the profession into a theory under its exclusive control (Baer, 1986;

Khurana et al, 2005). Theory serves as a base in terms of which professionals rationalise their operations in concrete situations. Preparation for a profession, therefore, involved a considerable preoccupation with systematic theory, a feature virtually absent in the training of nonprofessionals (Greenwood, 1962). Further, a system of licensure is available to the professions in order to establish certain standards of proficiency and ensure that at least a minimum degree of competence exists. Usually, examinations conducted by professional associations or by the state must be successfully completed before being allowed to practice a profession (Snider, 1963). Interestingly, while our participants considered themselves to be professionals, none of these features were present in their case.

To elaborate, though call centre agents considered themselves to be possessing superior cognitive abilities, advanced qualifications and performing highly skilled jobs, in reality, mass customised call centres such as those included in this study, were characterised by low autonomy, low complexity and low variety, and hence the skills required for task performance included computer literacy, familiarity with typing, communication abilities and fluency in English (Cowie, 2007; Ramesh, 2004; Taylor & Bain, 2005). Job positions could thus easily be filled with people having high school diplomas, and advanced training beyond that was not needed. It was the peculiarities of the Indian context that resulted in so many university graduates taking up employment in the call centre industry. Nonetheless, as Russell (2006) notes, though call centre work entails greater skill than the blue-collar operator positions of the factory era, it cannot be considered as knowledge work.

Mostly, calls used to be the same type. While we started, it was interesting, but after sometime, the same old story... the longer the agents worked, their boredom increased.

Given the circumstances, call centre jobs did not fulfill the requisite belief that professional expertise was based on the performance of a vital function in society which required specialised knowledge and skill, through prolonged education and experience (Kornhauser, 1962). There was no legal or political position of privilege that protected call centre jobs from being encroached upon by other occupations. The functions of licensure, which provides a profession with a legal monopoly over the performance of some strategic aspect of its work and effectively prevents free competition from other occupations (Freidson, 1970), were not available to call centre agents. NASSCOM's[1] (National Association of Software and Services Companies) Assessment of Competence (NAC) initiative, launched in 2006, focused on the issue of addressing attrition and not licensure. It endeavoured to operate as an industry standard assessment and certification programme to ensure the transformation of a "trainable" workforce into an "employable" workforce with a view to helping call centre employers reduce their hiring costs, improve efficiencies, enlarge the candidate pool and perhaps more importantly to control the escalation of entry level wages (NASSCOM, 2007). Moreover, in the wider job market, work experience in a mass customised call centre was not considered to be of much value even in related industries like information technology (IT). Therefore, it was a job that neither enhanced the status of employees nor promoted their careers in occupations where sound and specialised theoretical knowledge was required.

If you are into computer field or in any other profession, you everyday learn something new... but after working for a year in the call centre, I have learnt more about ____ (employer organisation), nothing else. Today if I quit the call centre, and I want to work as a computer operator, nobody would employ me. I might have good English accent or may be I understand the nuances of being a professional but I have no technical skills…that's what I think about my experience in call centres.

Moreover, professions are closely tied to the issue of autonomy which stems from the belief that qualified practitioners are best able to determine how a function ought to be performed and hence must be free to exercise their own judgment in specific cases (Kornhauser, 1962). The low levels of control associated with call centre jobs raises questions about autonomy. In fact, techno-bureaucratic control was institutionalized through technology and strengthened and deepened by the use of bureaucratic procedures in shaping the social and organisational structure of the workplace (Callaghan & Thompson, 2001). Thus, as an occupational group, call centre agents were not able to be self-directing as they could not control the production process, particularly the application of knowledge and skill in the work they perform. Moreover, the substance of their knowledge and skill was known to others - in this case, their superiors including the quality personnel, their clients and their customers - who could legitimately criticise and evaluate the way work was carried out.

Further, as Korczynski (2001) states, contemporaneously, the increasing importance accorded to customers entails a significant shift in the fabric of the employer organisation from the uncontested dominance of the bureaucratic paradigm to the prevalence of a hybridisation of bureaucracy and service orientation. Bureaucracy, representing a rational, efficient and routine authority, is combined with a customer focus, representing a more variable and unpredictable authority, resulting in the need for employee self-control while simultaneously fulfilling bureaucratic requirements. In the ensuing performance of emotional labour via remote mode in the context of techno-bureaucratic controls, call centre employees met the norm of professionalisation as expressed by the degree to which work groups adhere to both the service ideal and professional conduct (Wilensky, 1964). However, the situation of call centre employees was far from Hughes's (1963) requirement that professionals seek to replace the usual stricture of caveat emptor (let the buyer beware) with the norm of credit emptor (let the buyer trust).

Instead of the customer acceding to the professional judgment of the call centre employee, the former appraised their own needs and judged the potential of the service provided to them. In other words, call centre agents could not profess to know better than their customers. On the contrary, the customer was able to evaluate the performance of the professional and was considered a true judge of the value of the service received. In fact, Indian call centre agents feared overseas customers suing the client which, in turn, would impact the business prospects of the Indian ITES-BPO sector and, subsequently, their own employment. Deference to the customers, to the extent of altering cultural and linguistic orientation including adoption of accents and pseudonyms and engaging in locational masking (See D'Cruz & Noronha, 2006), predominated agents' jobs.

Going further, agents did not enjoy the authority vested in professionals, with customers expressing doubts over their competence and distrust over divulging personal and sensitive information. Cross-cultural factors complicated the situation. Under these circumstances, customers' insubordination to agents' professional authority divested them of the monopoly of judgment associated with a profession. This was contrary to Freidson's (1970) formulation that influence is not exerted by adducing persuasive evidence that professional advice is valid and, therefore, worth obeying. A professional's advice should be obeyed because it is a professional who gives it. Not surprisingly, Nanda (2005) put call centre agents outside the realm of those delineated as professionals. In his work, call centre agents relying on algorithm-based inference to provide services that are useful but not highly valued by customers, are not professionals.

The real challenge on the job is that people in the UK (United Kingdom) think that we Indians are not competent to help them. As soon as we speak to them, they realise that we are not based in the UK, making them insecure and hesitant to divulge information like bank details.

When I was working for American Express, some customers abused me when they figured out that I was an Indian. However much you try to put on their accent, they neither want to talk to you, nor trust you.

Further, customers' claims of Indian agents' incompetence and deceit have been buttressed by the fact that, every few months, there have been allegations appearing in the media that personal data of customers handled by Indian call centres were at risk. On all such occasions, NASSCOM has not only insisted that the perpetrators of these alleged frauds be brought to book, but has also set up the National Skill Registry (NSR) - a centralised database of employees of the IT and ITES-BPO companies - to ensure that there is a verified database (with independent background checks) of the human resources present within the industry. The registration for the NSR touched the 125,000 mark as of July 2007, and NASSCOM's target was to take this number 5 times over to touch 500,000 by December 2007. This initiative, according to NASSCOM, would reduce the risk of appointing employees on the basis of fake/forged documents, lessen the cost and time involved in conducting background checks independently, facilitate faster completion of human resource (HR) processes that depend on background checks, ensure customer information is in safe and secure hands, allow the Indian IT and ITES-BPO industry to confidently claim higher standards of recruitment practices and allow international customers to view employee information directly (NASSCOM, not dated a/n.d. a).

Besides, NASSCOM has been working very closely with Indian law enforcement organisations and has set up cyber training labs in Mumbai, Thane, Pune and Bangalore to train police officers in cyber crime investigation. Further, the Data Security Council of India - a self-regulatory body for the Indian IT and ITES-BPO industry - was set up in April 2007 to popularise, monitor and enforce privacy and data protection standards for India's IT and ITES-BPO industry (NASSCOM, not dated b & c/n.d. b & c). Thus, while there are no ethical codes governing the work ethos among call centre agents from within their own occupation as is the case with other professions, control is being imposed from outside. To elaborate, call centre agents have no governing body, composed of respected members of the profession, that oversees adherence to a code of conduct by establishing monitoring mechanisms, reviewing complaints, and administering sanctions normally associated with professionals as a formal method of declaring to all that the occupation can be trusted and thereby of persuading society to grant the special status of autonomy.

In matters relating to the lifestyle of professionals, one aspect of Indian call centre agents' lives attest to the academic conceptualisation. Self-immersion in one's work, reflecting personal involvement such that strain is absorbed and work-life imbalance is accepted was visible, in keeping with the notion of professionalism that for a professional person, his/her work becomes his/her life (Greenwood, 1962).

Beyond this, however, the lifestyle associated with call centres does little to promote a professional image. The general opinion of call centres among the Indian public is that the young men and women working the phones at night constantly party and enjoy themselves, engaging in sex and drug-taking (Khaleej Times Online, 2006). Media reports suggest that call centre employees have come to acquire a reputation of having "licentious lifestyles" (The Sydney Morning Herald, 2006) with stories of used condoms blocking call centre restroom drains and drug taking during night shifts (Farrell, 2006). Some reports appearing in the press suggest that call centre staff have been caught by hidden cameras having sex in cubicles. Not only is such uninhibited conduct bewildering for middle-class India (The Sydney Morning Herald, 2006), but also the Catholic Church in India has announced its intentions to address the problem of call centre promiscuity (Haines, 2006).

While many call centre agents included in this article maintained that these images, though not incorrect, were exaggerated, older agents were unforgiving in their comments. According to them, the young workforce joining the industry was uncouth, uncultured, casual, irresponsible, carefree and extravagant. Call centre agents saw too much of money and freedom at a young age, both of which they were unable to handle. The money they earned was considered to be pocket money which they spent on excessive drinking, partying, dating, smoking and living lavishly. Overspending, rather than saving, was the norm. Older agents rued the overemphasis on unfavourable Western practices creeping into Indian society, wishing that Indian youth would emulate positive Western values. Older agents pointed out that from the moment young people took up jobs in the call centres, parents lost control. Young agents often lied to their parents about working on night shifts, when they actually partying with friends. Moreover, older agents were aghast with the overemphasised collegial organisational culture and the lack of respect shown to the superiors which, in their view, stemmed from the independence agents had achieved vis-a-vis their parents.

People have this negative view about call centres. Lot of my friends say that I am in a bad industry. Call centres have this reputation about themselves – there are only parties and the ITES-BPO industry has somewhat created a scandal.

Undoubtedly, this public image of call centre employees, coupled with lack of expertise, authority and autonomy, stringent monitoring, customer control and absence of a code of conduct, does not compare with the image building activity that occupations require to pursue in order that the public recognises the occupation to be a profession. The image building activity requires professionals to display service as essential, exclusive, and complex to the public, with successful public recognition resulting in the award of autonomy (Forsyth & Danisiewicz, 1985). The ambivalence with which call centre agents are regarded perhaps further complicates matters. To quote Cowie (2007), "the way that these new workers are described in the English language broadsheets such as *Times of India* or *Asian Age* is ambivalent. On the one hand, they are the cool new generation, symbolic of India's economic growth, who have 'work hard play hard' lifestyles and are financially independent. On the other hand, they are 'cyber coolies' who are 'not in a real job'."

Agents' Lived Experience and the Appeal of Professionalism

Nonetheless, following van Manen's (1998) hermeneutic phenomenological approach, the essential structure of agents' experiences was found to be embodied in the core theme of being professional. The notion of professionalism embraced agents' identity, altering their self-concept and enhancing their self-esteem. According to agents, professionals possess superior cognitive abilities, advanced qualifications and a sense of responsibility and commitment to work. They prioritise work over personal needs and pleasure, behaving in a dignified and restrained manner and performing optimally and rationally while on the job. Professionals comply with job and organisational requirements, absorbing emergent strain. Under such circumstances, not only do agents perceive gains accruing from their job as consistent with the notion of professionalism but also transactional psychological contracts of employment as means of discipline are similarly justified. Though resistance is displayed by some agents a few times, this is described as a temporary outlet to ease job-related strain, co-existing with professional identity – it is not an indicator of anti-work or anti-employer sentiment.

Through agents' narratives, the context surrounding their professional identity came out vividly. Organisations cultivated the notion of professionalism in employees through induction training, on-going socialisation, performance evaluation mechanisms and other elements of organisational design, with a view to gain their compliance and commitment to the realisation of the organisation's agenda. That professional identity is greatly valued as a symbol of social status and upward mobility in the Indian context facilitated the process. Indeed, professional identity allowed agents to accept task and organisational demands in spite of the strain they engendered. Material artifacts and organisational processes were cited as proof of organisation's espousal of professionalism.

Undoubtedly, agents' lived experience demonstrates contemporary employer organisations' growing reliance on the appeal of professionalism (Evetts, 2003 & 2006; Fournier, 1999) as a means of identity regulation and socio-ideological control in order to achieve the organisational agenda.

Justifying Organisational Requirements, Task-Related Demands and Techno-Bureaucratic Controls

Agents' professional identity coloured their perceptions of and responses to organisational and job demands. Being employed by international facing call centres, agents served overseas clients and customers. That is, whether the firm they were employed with was MNC captive, MNC third party or Indian third party, the clients were based either in the USA (United States of America), Canada, UK or Australia and had a formalised relationship (also known as a service level agreement/SLA), either temporal or project based, with participants' employer organisations (the offshored Indian/India-based service providers) to deliver stipulated services to their customers who were also located overseas. The service level agreement (SLA) between the client and the employer organisation laid down the process and outcome requirements of the particular service, the fulfillment of which was critical to the continuity and/or renewal of the contractual relationship between the two parties. With competitive advantage being the key focus, employer organisations diligently implemented client expectations and this set the work context for participants.

Adherence to job and organisational demands as well as discipline at and priority towards work were constantly emphasised, linked to the notion of professionalism. That is, employer organisations cultivated the notion of professionalism in their agents in order to gain the latter's compliance and commitment to the realisation of organisational goals. It was thus not surprising that agents, while acknowledging the nature and requirements of their jobs, saw nothing amiss in their work situation, maintaining that the acceptance and fulfillment of such job-related demands formed an integral part of a professional's life. Clearly, agents' professional sense of self worked in a pervasive manner, disciplining them on the job and ensuring that they behaved objectively and rationally and performed optimally.

We have to stick to what we have to do. Don't go out of it, unless we are asked. Do your best, that's it. You will be recognised. Be in good terms with your seniors. Don't be harsh in the team. That is professional.

Job design elements and techno-bureaucratic controls together contributed to a high stress work environment for agents. In other words, though on the one hand, participants' tasks lacked variety, complexity and autonomy resulting in a routinised monotony, on the other hand, stringent quality and quantity parameters enforced via technology-based monitoring and surveillance ensured that agents met organisational and client expectations. Notwithstanding the intense pressure, rationality, objectivity and optimal performance always took precedence, being described as indicators of professionalism. Emotions, subjectivity and relationships were accorded secondary status.

My TL (team leader) is very close to me. We are like friends. He is younger to me. He is 21 and I am 23. He was my trainer. When he was a trainer, I was in his batch. When I came to the call floor, he was promoted as a TL, and luckily, he became my TL. We became very close friends. But he was very professional. I have never seen a person who is professional like him. Before we enter the call floor, we have to leave our mobile phones in the locker - if we fail to do so, a fine has to be paid. On one particular day, I carried the phone to the floor. My friend (the TL) caught me and asked me to hand over the phone to him. I told him not to tell anybody about it but he insisted that I hand over the phone to him. When I handed over the phone, he told me to pay the fine. He told me, "Friendship outside, be professional inside". I was lucky because I was in his team and I learned many things.

Participants' initial reactions to the intensive and constant monitoring and surveillance were mixed. On the one hand, it unnerved them. Reports of self-consciousness and nervousness were common. On the other hand, they believed that not only were such measures part of client requirements specified in the SLAs and hence an unavoidable part of the work context but also that the feedback they received from such measures facilitated their performance and ensured their career progress. As professionals, they had to put organisational interests and work demands above their personal discomfort. At the same time, task performance could be scaled up to higher levels of professionalism via the feedback received. Professionalism involved a concern for standards, not only in the final delivery of a service but in the process leading to that delivery (Swailes, 2003).

As participants elaborated, feedback emanating from monitoring helped agents to understand their shortcomings, overcome deficiencies and enhance their capacity to handle calls and iron out errors. In other words, feedback had no negative connotation attached to it but was seen as being supportive of the agents' effort, serving as an opportunity to learn from those who had a sound knowledge about the process, to improve oneself and to take advantage of further training and coaching and performance improvement plans, if required.

There is a quality management team who records and hears your calls and gives feedback. Sometimes, while on the call, they will cut it and talk to you over the phone itself, saying, "This is the mistake you made. Otherwise, you would have got the sale."

Feedback was also seen as helpful to distinguish between good performers and average ones, encouraging those with drive and dedication to move up the organisation while preventing shirking. In the same vein, poor performers who did not meet expectations in spite of being put on performance improvement plans, received no sympathy. Dismissing them was considered to be an appropriate step. Indeed, these values espoused by call centre agents were in keeping with merit based practices of professionals (Raelin, 1989).

It is relevant to mention that in addition to demands and requirements directly related to task performance, employer organisations laid down general etiquette rules which were strictly maintained. Agents were expected to behave politely, displaying respect towards everyone at the workplace in spite of the informal atmosphere.

Professionalism means punctuality, doing your job to the best of your ability, the way you dress, the way you move with people... Bringing in personal grudges, favouritism – that is not professionalism.

Further, dressing "provocatively" was seen as both causing a distraction from work and creating an unprofessional atmosphere, and could invite punishment.

One of the clients has settled down in Bangalore, so they might walk in any time. They say that they want us to be professional, they want to see British influence here. So if you are wearing jeans, they might think that you are a casual kind of guy. But if you are in formals, they will feel that you are a decent guy.

Apart from being well-groomed and appropriately dressed, agents were expected to conduct themselves in a dignified manner. Participants provided an illustration of the latter by citing the case of workplace romances. They highlighted that public displays of affection, flirtatious behaviour and acts of intimacy between couples were not tolerated during office hours and were treated with warnings and even dismissals. Romantic relationships were part of personal life and did not concern the organisaton – hence they should not impinge on task performance but should be reserved for non-office hours. Professionalism required that they manage conflicts and tensions in their personal and working lives (Swailes, 2003).

The company tells us to be professional. They say, "You may have your girlfriend working with you. But in the workplace, she is only your colleague." I deserve to be thrown out if I kiss her on the floor.

The Primacy of the Customer

Emotional labour remains central to task performance in call centres. Located at the customer-service provider organisation/client interface, call centre agents represent the service provider organisation/client to customers and hence how they behave during these encounters becomes critical (Ashforth & Humphrey, 1993; Morris & Feldman, 1996). Not surprisingly, then, service provider organisations/clients are increasingly willing to direct and control how employees present themselves to customers (Hochschild, 1983). Agents included in this article described organisational endeavours and related employee training undertaken towards this end. Incorporation of emotional labour requirements into performance measures, especially qualitative parameters, reinforced the position. With customer satisfaction being as important as production levels, employer organisations monitor agent interactions with customers, rewarding those who perform emotional labour as expected and punishing those who do not. This notion of the customer now being fundamental to current management paradigms as a means of analysing and defining work performance and work relations is dominant in call centres (Du Gay & Salaman, 2002). Participants, viewing the primacy accorded to the customer through the lens of their professional identity, accepted both the gains and demands of emotional labour. According to them, complying with the requirements associated with emotional labour was part of being professional.

Communicating effectively with customers was emphasised. This encompassed clarity and accuracy of communication, adherence to scripts such that providing wrong information and misleading customers was avoided, politeness, cordiality, sensitivity and patience (particularly with irate customers). All this had to be accomplished in a virtual context, concomitant with other process requirements, in real time. In keeping with

Belt, Richardson and Webster (1999), agents had to smile down the phone. Agents were trained to believe that since customers could decipher their moods, the espousal and display of a positive frame of mind was important to induce a similar demeanour in customers, to enhance the perceived quality of the service interaction and to leave behind a favourable impression about the client. To this end, agents were encouraged to empathise with and absorb customer reactions, apologising to them for any perceived or attributed problem or inconvenience even if it was not their fault. At the same time, maintaining objectivity was emphasised. That is, agents were not allowed to develop personal relationships with customers or display any partiality towards them. Interactions had to be limited to the business at hand. Agents thus had to relate to customers enough to perform effective emotional labour, ensure customer satisfaction and promote client interests while simultaneously meeting other qualitative and quantitative performance criteria. Clearly, as earlier stated by Houlihan (2000), conflicting role requirements were imposed on agents in terms of the challenge of trying to get closer to the customer while reducing costs, prescribing standards and meeting targets.

In a call centre, you are forced to finish the call and even if the customer wants to be personal, you cannot be so. You need to tell him, "Hey! my time limit is going up." You also have the quality in your mind, AHT (average handling time of the call) and all that stuff. In a call centre, time is the most important factor because, based on the AHT, they analyse you and mark your ratings.

Moreover, agents were trained to set aside their own emotions prior to the shift, in a bid to focus their energies on the task. Professionalism involved an ability to suppress emotions that might otherwise get in the way of delivering quality services (Swailes, 2003). Being preoccupied with personal affective issues during the shift was described by superiors as interfering with optimal performance and as unprofessional. The ability to remain calm under pressure and to maintain a friendly and tactful attitude while at the same time being psychologically disengaged from the customer, as noted by Rose and Wright (2005), was emphasised. Agents who were seen as being unable to comply with the foregoing requirements were invited to share and work out their problems with TLs and other superiors so that they could eliminate impediments to the performance of emotional labour.

When you come to call centres, you become professional. You forget about your emotions and everything. We don't think even what we did in the last call.

For Indian agents working in international facing call centres, training in emotional labour skills went beyond the scope of customer interaction and satisfaction, as described above, to embrace cultural, linguistic and geographical dimensions linked to the lives of their overseas customers (See D'Cruz & Noronha, 2006). Clients had laid down these latter set of requirements to ensure that customers remained comfortable with and willing to divulge personal information during service interactions, apart from continuing to harbour perceptions of satisfaction over service quality, in spite of migration of services via offshoring and outsourcing (Taylor & Bain, 2005). Through the training, agents not only acquired the requisite skills and abilities but also learnt to accept them as part of the job, being linked to SLAs, process continuity/renewal, organisational success and their own positions. Accordingly, appropriate measurement parameters and related rewards and punishments formed part of agents' evaluation. Not surprisingly, agents viewed these requirements as part of their professional sense of self.

Further, cultural and linguistic requirements, adoption of pseudonyms and engaging in locational masking, being seen as a part of the job, were accepted within the realm of professionalism. According to agents, it was easier for client and organisational objectives, and, in turn, their own evaluation criteria, to be met, with the assumed identity. Indeed, acceding to these demands did not adversely affect agents' sense of self. Instead, it resembled donning a persona that, in reflecting various characteristics of the customer, allowed service interactions to proceed smoothly, simultaneously putting customers at ease and serving organisational and client objectives. Some agents claimed that job-related cultural and linguistic requirements, pseudonyms and locational masking augmented their professional identity. They derived pride from their association with overseas clients and customers. Becoming Westernised was equated with sophistication and success in the Indian context (Cohen & El-Sawad, 2007). For agents, then, identity posing clearly made their task easier (Poster, 2007), though a few doubted whether such strategies were completely effective, reflecting Taylor and Bain's (2005) view that cultural and linguistic differences are not readily overcome.

Agents' responses to abusive customers (whom agents usually referred to as irate customers) covered various dimensions. Instruction during the training phase prepared agents for such an eventuality. It was made clear to agents that abusive customers had to be handled with empathy, tact, patience and detachment – even hints of reciprocating customers' negative backlash (whether through abuse in English/an Indian language, non-verbal cues or cutting off the call) would invite termination of employment. Agents were further told that generally customer tirades stemmed from reasons not linked to them such as long call waiting queues, poor service/product quality which prompted the call, personal stressors, repeated disturbances via phone calls and so on) but were being displaced on to them, and hence they should not take the experience personally. On the contrary, they should allow the customer to calm down and then proceed with the business at hand.

The way you talk is very important. No profanity. No matter what the customer tells, he may curse you, get very personal with you. You have to keep your cool and it is a part of your job. That guy may be frustrated, he had a bad day, whatever... If you retaliate, you use profanity to them, the company could be sued, and you could be thrown out.

Agents accepted organisational directives about customer abuse, recognising the role of client requirements, organisational survival and process retention in this. Consequently, they concurred with the position that agents abusing customers should be dismissed. Over time, they learnt to distinguish between customers whose rudeness arose due to a genuine problem and customers whose personality predisposed them to anger and irritability. Additionally, in instances where agents' coping broke down, they were advised to take a break and regain their equilibrium so that subsequent task performance was not hampered. With experience, agents coped effectively with customer abuse. In fact, Poster (2007) points out that it was quite a sobering experience for her as an American to listen to the steadfast composure and professionalism of Indian employees. Being able to handle the situation effectively as outlined above was seen as a measure of professionalism and resulted in high performance ratings. Moreover, it was here that the adoption of pseudonyms proved worthwhile – agents were reminded that customers were not shouting at them but at their assumed selves.

PRIVILEGES OF PROFESSIONALISM

Artifacts of the organisation, typically associated with high status, supported the notion of professionalism, strengthening agents' identification and compliance. The infrastructure was a case in point. Employer organisations were located in ultra-modern buildings, offering state-of-the-art infrastructure and facilities, as also reported by Ramesh (2004) and Mirchandani (2004). Concrete and glass were aesthetically combined in constructing the outer structure of the buildings while elevators, air-conditioning and artistic interiors characterised by wooden/marble/granite bases, bright lighting, elegant but comfortable furniture, decorative artifacts and electronic gadgets installed for security purposes completed the internal environment. The overall impression conveyed was that of efficiency, progress, class and neatness. Facilities within the office premises included individual lockers, cafeterias with wide-ranging menus at reasonable prices, recreation and de-stress rooms with bean bags, computers with internet access, music systems, televisions, indoor games such as carrom boards, table tennis, chess, pool, etc., video games and reading spaces. Gymnasiums, badminton courts and sleep facilities were also provided by a few organisations. Most employer organisations sought to provide physical work environments of international standards resembling those in the West, with some clients insisting that the call floor be an exact replica of the identical process being executed overseas.

When the company is in a posh locality or office, with good exteriors and interiors, proper furniture, etc., then the moment a person enters the company, he would feel that he is a professional. That environment makes you feel that. Plus you are in a good post so that also makes you feel that you are responsible. He feels that he is worth something, the company has valued him. He definitely feels that he is a true asset to the company.

Apart from adding to their sense of professionalism, the physical work environment triggered favourable self-comparisons with people in the West and with Indian IT professionals. Moreover, agents considered themselves to be superior to employees in the government/public sector and the traditional industrial and service sectors. According to them, these groups were not only less educated and less motivated than them but also their work involved less skill and low returns. In addition, the physical work environment here was described negatively, highlighting its regressive and decrepit nature.

A government office is a place where papers are piled up and people sit there aaram se (leisurely). You need to pass some kind of bill in order to get your work done - people are so relaxed, and there is nothing like a professional environment. In contrast, view the people in a modern, good-looking office that looks so professional, so dignified, so clean, so prominent - automatically even your work sense changes. These buildings actually exude a professional attitude and cause you to feel like a professional - that's what I believe. And these well-designed buildings give you a feeling that you are working in a very dignified organisation wherein everything is spic and span, everything is disciplined, and that's why you are a professional. All of us have the feeling to live the way we are in our jobs because this gives us a professional attitude. Even if you look at our pantry cleaners and cafeteria boys, they are so well dressed, they are so professional.

Gains from the job further nurtured agents' professional identity. Designations attached to call centre agents' tasks such as customer care officer, call centre executive, customer care executive, contact centre representative and customer support executive invoked images of white-collared, professional work and upward mobility, enhancing agents' self-esteem. As observed by Poster (2007), our participants too experienced status enhancement because of association with overseas clients and customers and employment with MNC organisations, where applicable, as well as opportunities to visit client locations in foreign countries for training purposes, where applicable. Moreover, participant narratives underscored the extent to which the ITES-BPO sector, especially global offshoring, had altered India's job market. Employees in this sector, particularly those working for MNC captives, MNC third party and Indian third party organisations, received attractive pay packages. In addition to their salary, agents received performance incentives in financial and material forms such as gift vouchers, clothes and accessories, movie and entertainment tickets, landline phone sets, cordless phone sets, mobile handsets, i-pods, DVD (digital versatile disc) players, etc. Various allowances such as food allowance, night shift allowance (for those working in the night shift), transport facilities and medical/health services (including a doctor, a counselor and a nutritionist on call) formed part of the package.

The money is good. As a fresher in any company, you won't get this much of money initially. And there are good incentives, pick-up and drop facilities, medical benefits, food. We save a lot of money on traveling. Plus you are paid well and other benefits. So I think it is pretty good way to start off. And there are growth opportunities in the company - you can always grow because they are looking for people who can perform well.

Given the limited employment opportunities for those with a liberal arts/science degree as well as the poor returns at the entry level in many technical/professional fields, it is not surprising that the ITES-BPO sector is widely regarded as the most viable means currently available to achieving a decent quality of life. Agents elaborated on the contemporary lifestyle which, in its inclusion of pubs, discos, parties, weekend outings and credit cards, displayed Western leanings. Those who had prior work experience in other sectors, which paid meagerly, compared the returns received from both the sectors, highlighting in the process the reasons why the ITES-BPO sector was so much sought after in spite of the challenges it presented. Participants emphasised the sense of independence and self-reliance that their income allowed them, demonstrating changes in their self-concept.

This boom happening in call centres and BPOs... for a normal graduate, you can't get a job like this. What is this ITES-BPO doing? It's actually getting them jobs very easily. So repeating 10 lines a day, I will get paid INR 10000-12000 - amazing, believe me, it is amazing. Because even a guy who works from morning to evening, say in a garment or textile shop, he wouldn't have been paid even more than INR 3000 and he can't even live properly. Here you get a good income, plus allowances, transport, good office... So somewhere down the line, independence and self-sufficiency, a good life...

That agents abhorred nomenclatures such as "cyber coolies" and "slaves on Roman ships" (See Ramesh, 2004), often used to describe them, testifies to the pride they derived from their professional identity.

The notion of professionalism was seen as being pervasive throughout the organisation. Organisational processes were seen as exemplifying the organisation's espousal of professionalism. Besides, various initiatives, cited as illustrations of the employer organisation's commitment to employees' well-being, were viewed through this perspective. Apart from the type of designations used and the nature of returns provided, the organisation's concerns for agents' professional development and career growth were mentioned. Many organisations had tie-ups with educational institutions for business administration and management courses, and agents availing of this opportunity were usually fully or partially funded by their employers. Similarly, agents reported that organisations created avenues for vertical movement. Through internal job postings (IJPs) circulated every quarter, communication about promotion opportunities was shared. Organisations emphasised that career growth was determined by performance and not by sociodemographic factors, seniority or intra-organisational social networks. Organisational claims that merit and objectivity (a value common among professionals, as noted by Raelin [1989]) influenced promotion decisions were interpreted by agents as testimony of its professional orientation. In addition, the possible pace of movement added to this perception, with agents being told that, for top performers, the transition from an entry level post to a junior level supervisory post occurred within a year of joining the organisation. The view that anyone whose performance was superior could quickly move up the organisational hierarchy inspired positive images of the employer in agents' minds, strengthening their loyalty towards the organisation and increasing their willingness to accept job-related demands and strain.

Creating an atmosphere of congeniality and camaraderie testified to organisation's professional orientation. Fun initiatives at the workplace not only served as evidence of the organisation's recognition of work-life balance but also provided opportunities for employees to behave as responsible professionals who knew how and where to draw the line between work and pleasure. By and large, call centre organisations were portrayed by their management as extensions of college where work and enjoyment were combined. While task-related requirements remained unrelenting, concerted efforts were put in to create and maintain a vibrant environment to energise as well as de-stress employees. Various competitions, entertainment programmes, hobby classes, birthday celebrations, festival celebrations and so on were conducted during work hours, apart from activities such as team outings, team parties and office gatherings (including picnics, treks, family days, etc.) held during weekly and public holidays. Indeed, organisations employed fun officers, fun squads and event managers to manage these roles. The underlying message here, in addition to those of employer concern for employees, professionalism and work-life balance, was that employers were willing to spend on and invest in employees' well-being. Ramesh (2004) asserts that the portrayal of "work as fun" and "workplace as yet another campus" was the central logic through which potential employees were attracted to the ITES-BPO sector.

The informal nature of workplace relationships, particularly between superiors and subordinates, helped to highlight the contours of professionalism. That is, it is common practice to address everyone, including one's superiors, by first name in a call centre organisation, thereby downplaying hierarchy and promoting integration. Indeed, agents reported instances where employees were reprimanded for using prefixes such as "sir" or "madam" when interacting with their superiors. Yet, behaving disrespectfully and overstepping boundaries is not tolerated.

We are very friendly with our superiors but they that does not mean leniency in performance or disrespect. There are certain limits and one cannot forget that. One has to maintain the professional touch.

The professional approach adopted by call centre organisations extended to employee redressal opportunities. Indeed, call centre organisations prided themselves on the number and nature of grievance avenues they provided their agents with. According to them, in keeping with a professional style of management, openness of communication in terms of content, form, style and route were valued. Therefore, in addition to periodic employee satisfaction surveys, skip-level meetings and open fora with superiors, employees with grievances could approach anyone in the organisation whether the CEO (chief executive officer), the TL or someone in between via email, letters, telephone conversations or face-to-face meetings. That the professional atmosphere in the organisation precluded the complainant's victimisation was strongly emphasised. Under such circumstances, not only did agents feel valued and empowered, considering employers in a positive light and displaying greater commitment to them, but also any third party intervention including legal protection and collectivist groups were seen as redundant. In other words, with their employers taking such great care of their interests, alternative mechanisms were not required.

We have an open door policy. If one is not happy with the immediate supervisor, we can go and discuss with the senior management, who will not only give a patient listening, but try to solve the problems.

Resisting the Appeal of Professionalism

However, the appeal to professionalism was not all-encompassing: the techno-bureaucratic control mechanisms used in call centres simultaneously helped to challenge the notion of professionalism. That a few agents rely on various outlets to cope with work-related strain was pointed out by some of our participants. Extending the call wrap-up time during which relevant information from the phone conversation is keyed into the system, altering their position in the call distribution queue by pressing the release button on their phone, entering wrong customer email addresses into the system if the call did not proceed satisfactorily (so that feedback could not be obtained from the particular customer), extending restroom breaks, unnecessarily transferring customers' calls and delaying the disconnection of calls were some of the ways in which a few agents got some breathing space.

Team members are all good friends. We will be talking about a good topic. In the midst of the topic, some call comes. By the time I finish the call, the topic will be over and I miss the conversation. So we play some tricks. If we disconnect the call, what happens is that if the call gets monitored, it becomes a serious issue. Better than that, do a double click, you are now the last person in the queue... One can at least get some breathing time that way.

Further, customer abuse was dealt with either by placing the phone in mute mode and cursing the customer aloud in the presence of team members or by pressing the mute button and enabling the loudspeaker so that the team could collectively listen to, make fun of and enjoy the customer's tirade.

Sometimes one gets tired of so much work and then, on top of it, a customer starts abusing. So what some people do – they put the customer on mute and curse him back. There he is thinking that we are listening to the scolding but actually we are giving it back to him.

Agents were able to decipher when their calls were being monitored either because of an echoing or beeping sound that accompanied such activity or from the call monitoring data sheet, and they would take special care to ensure their optimal performance during that time. In their own words, "they played the game once they got a hang of it".

Monitoring times are fixed for each shift and for each team – one can come to know from the monitoring sheet. So whenever I go into a new shift, I keep a watch for this by studying the monitoring sheet. In the monitoring sheet, it will be there. This call is monitored, by this person, on this day, everything will be there. For different teams, different days, calls get monitored. First week, I will make a note. Second week, I will see again and I will find it to be the same pattern. Last shift, we used to get monitored every Monday. So I knew that. So that day, I will be perfect. Otherwise, I would not bother that much.

Sometimes, agents also helped ease their team members' strain. That is, when agents filled in for TLs who, for some reason, could not monitor calls, they manipulated the entire system by telling their team members to give a list of calls on which they had performed well.

For about three months, I used to complete my shift and used to barge the agents. I have to sit on the TL spot, which the TL has entrusted to me. You won't believe me but I used to barge all the 20 agents on a single process and complete this within two hours. I will come and tell each and every team member before log in, I need four rated calls in which you gave perfect information to the customer. And I would send that in for the performance purposes.

CONCLUSION

"Professionalisation" is the process by which an occupation becomes a profession or stakes a claim to professionalism. Although the act of professionalising an occupation is most compatible with the power approach (as in politically agitating to establish an occupation in the public's eye as critical and exclusive), it may also adhere to the trait/attribute approach (Raelin, 1989). Going by this, Indian call centre agents, though referred to as professionals, meet neither of the two approaches appropriately. Not only was the power approach not even considered by call centre agents but also there was no attempt by them to use strategies and tactics to gain control over the market for their services or enlist state support for self-regulation. Turning to the trait approach, call centre agents' expertise was not esoteric, nor did they possess the requisite autonomy, code of ethics, professional association or system of certifying professionals. On the contrary, they were trapped within techno-bureaucratic control mechanisms and had to be subservient not only to their employer organisations but also to customers.

Thus, as Evetts (2003) states, what is relevant here is to consider the appeal of the concepts of "profession", and particularly of "professionalism". In the context of Indian call centre agents, a professional is defined as a person who has the desire to satisfy customers, puts aside personal problems and concentrates on service, accepts stringent monitoring and shift timings, is able to withstand strains and pressures of work, and is receptive to the idea of taking on another identity in the interest of the organisation and the customer. The appeal to professionalism is one such new software of socio-ideological control that invited employees to re-imagine themselves (Fournier, 1999). Thus, control was sought to be accomplished through the self-positioning of employees within managerially inspired discourses about work and organisation (Alvesson & Wilmott, 2002). However, Schwartz's (1987) argument that control in contemporary organisations is totalising does not hold true in the case of call centre agents. The several signs of resistance displayed by agents highlight gaps in the organisational control process.

ACKNOWLEDGMENT

This research was funded by the Indo-Dutch Programme on Alternative Development Project 5.5.26.)

REFERENCES

Abbott, A. (1988). *The system of the professions: An essay on the division of expert labour.* Chicago: University of Chicago Press.

Alvesson, M., & Karreman, D. (2004). Interfaces of control: Technocratic and socio-ideological control in a global management consultancy firm. *Accounting, Organisations and Society,* 29(3-4): 423-444.

Alvesson, M., & Willmott, H. (2002). Identity regulation as organisational control: Producing the appropriate individual. *Journal of Management Studies*, 39(5): 619-644.

Ashforth, B.E., & Humphrey, R.H. (1993). Emotional labour in service roles: The influence of identity. *Academy of Management Review*, 18(1): 88-115.

Baer, W. (1986). Expertise and professional standards. *Work and Occupations*, 13(4): 532-552.

Barber, B. (1963). Some problems in the sociology of professions. *Daedal us*, 92 (Fall): 669-688.

Belt, V., Richardson, R., & Webster, J. (1999). Smiling down the phone: Women's work in telephone call centres. Workshop on Call Centres, March 1999. London: London School of Economics.

Callaghan, G., & Thompson, P. (2001). Edwards revisited: Technical control and call centres. *Economic and Industrial Democracy*, 22(1): 13-37.

Carr-Saunders, A.M., & Wilson, P.A. (1933). *The professions*. Oxford: Clarendon.

Cohen, L., & El-Sawad, A. (2007). Accounting for 'us' and 'them': Indian and UK customer service workers' reflections on offshoring. *Economic and Political Weekly*, 42(21): 1951-1957.

Cowie, C. (2007). The accents of outsourcing: The meanings of neutral in the Indian call centre industry. *World Englishes*, 26(3): 316-330.

Crompton, R. (1990). Professions in the current context. *Work, Employment and Society*, 4(5): 147-166.

D'Cruz, P., & Noronha, E. (2006). Being professional: Organisational control in Indian call centres. *Social Science and Computer Review*, 24(3): 342-361.

Dietrich, M., & Roberts, J. (1999). Beyond the economics of professionalism. In J. Broadbent, M. Dietrich & J. Roberts (Eds.), *The end of the professions? The restructuring of professional work*. Oxon, UK: Routledge.

Du Gay, P., & Salaman, G. (1992). The cult(ure) of the customer. *Journal of Management Studies*, 29(5): 615-633.

Evetts, J. (2003). The sociological analysis of professionalism: Occupational change in the modern world. *International Sociology*, 18(2): 395-415.

Evetts, J. (2006). The sociology of professional groups: New directions. *Current Sociology*, 54(1): 133-143.

Farrell, N. (2006). Indian call centres are both Sodom and Gomorrah: Take Archbishop of Bangalore notions with a pillar of salt. Retrieved 28 August 2008 from http://www.theinquirer.net/default.aspx?article=35715

Forsyth, P., & Danisiewicz, T. (1985). Toward a theory of professionalisation. *Work and Occupations*, 12(1): 59-76.

Fournier, V. (1999). The appeal to "professionalism" as a disciplinary mechanism. *The Sociological Review*, 47(2): 280-307.

Freidson, E. (1970). *Professional dominance: The social structure of medical care*. New York: Atherton Press.

Goode, W. (1969). The theoretical limits of professionalisation. In A. Etzioni (Ed)., *The semi-professions and their organisation*. New York: Free Press.

Greenwood, E. (1962). Attributes of a profession. In S. Nosow & W. H. Form (Eds.), *Man, work and society*. New York: Basic Books.

Haines, L. (2006). Catholic church bemoans call centre Bacchanalia: Indian "dens of iniquity". Retrieved 28 August 2008 from http://www.theregister.co.uk/2006/10/09/dens_of_iniquity/

Harris-Jenkins, G. (1970). Professionals in organisations. In J.A Jackson (Ed.), *Professions and professionalisation*. Cambridge: Cambridge University Press.

Henriksson, L. (2006). Understanding professional projects in welfare service work: Revival of old professionalism? *Gender, Work and Organisation,* 13(2): 174-192.

Hochschild, A.R. (1983). *The managed heart.* Berkeley: University of California Press.

Houlihan, M. (2000). Eyes wide shut? Querying the depth of call centre learning. *Journal of European Industrial Training,* 24(2/3/4): 228-40.

Hughes, E. (1963). Professions. *Daedalus*, 92 (Fall): 655-668.

Johnson, T. (1972). *Professions and power.* London: Macmillan.

Khaleej Times Online (2006). Sex life of call centre workers fascinates India. Retrieved 28 August 2008 from http://www.khaleejtimes.com/DisplayArticle.asp?xfile=data/todaysfeatures/2006/November/todaysfeatures_November28.xml&section=todaysfeatures

Khurana, R., et al (2005). Is business management a profession? *Harvard Business School Working Knowledge.* Retrieved 20 August 2007 from http://hbswk.hbs.edu/item/4650.html

Klegon, D. (1978). The sociology of professions: An emerging perspective. *Sociology of Work and Occupations,* 5(3): 259-283.

Korczynski, M. (2001). The contradictions of service work: Call centre as customer oriented bureaucracy. In A. Sturdy, I. Grugulis & H. Willmott (Eds.), *Customer service: Empowerment and entrapment.* London: Palgrave.

Kornhauser, W. (1962). *Scientists in industry: Conflict and accommodation.* Berkeley: University of California Press.

Larson, M. (1977). *The rise of professionalism: A sociological analysis.* London: University of California Press.

Latham, S. R. (2002). Medical professionalism: A Parsonian view. *The Mount Sinai Journal of Medicine*, 69(6), 363-369.

Leicht, K.T., & Fennell, M.L. (2001). *Professional work: A sociological approach.* Oxford: Blackwell.

Macdonald, K. (1995). *The sociology of professions.* London: Sage.

Marshall, T.H. (1962). Professionalism and social policy. In S. Nosow & W. Form (Eds.), *Man, work and society.* New York: Basic Books.

McPhail, B. (2002). What is on the line in call centre studies? Retrieved 10 August 2005 from http://www.fis.utoronto.ca/research/iprp/publications/mcphail-cc.pdf

Middlehurst, R., & Kennie, T. (1999). Leading professionals. In J. Broadbent, M. Dietrich & J. Roberts (Eds.), *The end of the professions? The restructuring of professional work.* Oxon, UK: Routledge.

Mirchandani, K. (2004). Practices of global capital: Gaps, cracks and ironies in transnational call centres in India. *Global Networks,* 4 (4): 355–373.

Moore, W. (1970). *The professions: Roles and rules.* New York: Russell Sage.

Morris, J.A., & Feldman, D.C. (1996). The dimensions, antecedents and consequences of emotional labour. *Academy of Management Review,* 21(4): 986-1010.

Nanda, A. (2005). Who is a professional? *Harvard Business School Publishing, Product Number 9-904-047.* Boston: Harvard Business School.

NASSCOM (2006). *Strategic review 2006.* New Delhi: NASSCOM.

NASSCOM (2007). *Strategic review 2007.* New Delhi: NASSCOM.

NASSCOM (Not dated/n.d. a). *National skills registry: Fact sheet* Retreived 28 August 2008 from http://www.nasscom.in/upload/5216/Factsheet-NSR%20Aug%2023%202007.doc

NASSCOM (Not dated/n.d.b). *Indian security environment: Fact sheet.* Retreived 28 August 2008 from http://www.nasscom.in/upload/5216/Indian%20Security%20Environment%202005-06%20July%2006.pdf

NASSCOM (Not dated/n.d. c). *Data security council of India: A self-regulatory initiative in data security and privacy protection.* Retreived 28 August 2008 from http://www.nasscom.in/upload/5216/Datasecurity.pdf

Parsons, T. (1951). *The social system.* New York: Free Press.

Pavalko, R.M. (1971). *Sociology of occupations and professions.* Itasca: FE Peacock.

Poster, W. (2007). Who's on the line? Indian call centre agents pose as Americans for US outsourced firms.*Industrial Relations,* 46 (2): 271-304.

Raelin, J.A. (1989). Unionisation and deprofessionalisation: Which comes first? *Journal of Organisational Behaviour,* 10(2): 101-115.

Ramesh, B. (2004). Cybercoolies in BPOs. *Economic and Political Weekly,* 39(5): 492-497.

Rose, E., & Wright, G. (2005). Satisfaction and dimensions of control among call centre customer service representatives. *International Journal of Human Resource Management,* 16(1): 136-160.

Russell, B. (2006). Skill and info-service work in Australian call centres. In J. Burgess & J. Connell (Eds.), *Developments in the call centre industry: Analysis, changes and challenges.* London: Routledge.

Schwartz, H.S. (1987). On the psychodynamics of organisational totalitarianism. *Journal of Management,* 13(1): 41–54.

Sciulli, D. (2005) Continental sociology of professions today: Conceptual contributions. *Current Sociology,* 53(6): 915-942.

Snider, H. W. (1963). Problems of professionalism. *Journal of Insurance,* 30(4): 563-572.

Swailes S. (2003). Professionalism: Evolution and measurement. *The Service Industries Journal,* 23 (2): 130-149.

Taylor, P., & Bain, P. (1999). "An assembly line in the head": Work and employment relationships in the call centre. *Industrial Relations Journal,* 30(2): 101-117.

Taylor, P., & Bain, P. (2005). India calling to the faraway towns: The call centre labour process and globalisation. *Work, Employment and Society,* 19(2): 261-282.

The Sydney Morning Herald (2006). Call centre girls have more fun, but it's blamed for rise of New Delhi belly. Retrieved 28 August 2008 from http://www.smh.com.au/news/world/call-centre-girls-have-more-fun/2006/10/10/1160246130071.html

Toren, N. (1975). Deprofessionalisation and its sources *Sociology of Work and Occupations,* 2(4): 323-337.

Van Manen, M. (1998). *Researching lived experience.* Canada: Althouse.

Wilensky, H. (1964). The professionalisation of everyone? *American Journal of Sociology,* 70(2): 137-158.

KEY TERMS

Call Centre: A call centre is a specialised office where employees (also known as call centre agents) remotely provide information, deliver services, and/or conduct sales, using some combination of integrated telephone and information technologies, typically with an aim to enhancing customer service while reducing organisational costs (McPhail, 2002).

Organisational Control: Organisation control has been defined in numerous ways but most definitions seem to agree that organisational control includes the exercise of power (influence) in order to secure sufficient resources, and mobilise and orchestrate individual and collective action towards (more or less) given ends. Organisational control typically includes an apparatus for specifying, monitoring and evaluating individual and collective action. It focuses on worker behaviour, output and/or the minds of the employees. Sometimes it attempts to focus on all three. Managerial activity that attempts to control behaviour typically includes designing and supervising work processes. This is usually carried out in a way that attempts to make work processes as simple and transparent as possible, thereby lowering knowledge thresholds (and the price of labour) (adapted from Alvesson & Karreman, 2004). Socio-ideological and techno-bureaucratic controls (defined below) are two forms of organisational control.

Socio-Ideological Control: Socio-ideological control can be defined as efforts to persuade employees to adapt to certain values, norms and ideas about what is good, important, praiseworthy, etc., in terms of work and organisational life (Alvesson & Karreman, 2004).

Techno-Bureaucratic Control: Technical control is embedded in the technology of work, moving the direction and pace of work from the control of the supervisor to the production line. Bureaucratic control is carried out through rules, policies, formal incentives and other impersonal devices. Thus, techno-bureaucratic control is institutionalised through technology and this is strengthened and deepened by bureaucratic control in shaping the social and organisational structure of the workplace (Callaghan & Thompson, 2001).

Professions: Occupations that perform tasks of great social value because those enacting them possess knowledge and skill that in some way set them apart from other kinds of workers and that entail a self-regulating form of social control are known as professions (Freidson, 1984).

Professionals: Those who perform the tasks associated with the professions are called professionals. They also display the characteristics expected of the members of specific professions (Middlehurst & Kennie, 1999).

Professionalism: Professionalism not only embraces the belief that certain work is so specialised as to be inaccessible to those lacking the required training and experience and the belief that such work cannot be standardised, rationalised and commodified, but also represents the occupational control of work where workers enjoy the autonomy to organise and control their own work as against customer or managerial control where customers or employers choose who is to perform what tasks and how much will be paid, on what terms, for performing them (Freidson, 2001).

Professionalisation: Professionalisation captures the process whereby work groups attempt to actually change their position on one or more dimensions of the occupation-profession continuum, moving towards the professional pole (Pavalko, 1971).

ENDNOTE

[1] NASSCOM is India's National Association of Software and Service Companies, the premier trade body and the chamber of commerce of the IT/information technology software and services industry in India. As of 31st December 2005, NASSCOM had over 950 members, of which over 150 are global companies from the USA (United States of America), UK (United Kingdom), EU (European Union), Japan and China. NASSCOM's member companies are in the business of software development, software services, software products and ITES-BPO services. A not-for-profit organisation, NASSCOM's primary objective is to act as a catalyst for the growth of the software-driven IT industry in India. Other goals include facilitation of trade and business in software and services, encouragement and advancement of research, propagation of education and employment, enabling the growth of the Indian economy and provide compelling business benefits to global economies by global sourcing (NASSCOM, 2006).

Chapter XXXIII
Knowledge Management: Fad or Enduring Organizational Concept?

Dariusz Jemielniak
Kozminski University, Poland

Jerzy Kociatkiewicz
University of Essex, UK

ABSTRACT

Knowledge management and knowledge-intensive work are two of today's hot buzzwords, though both already have a history of managerial usage. While some authors claim that knowledge is the most important organizational asset in contemporary society, others retort that much of knowledge management literature and practical solutions are just perfunctory and propagandist and many, if not most, managerial polices rely on manipulation of emotions and identity creation. This chapter aims to capitalize on this fascinating and timely research area. We want to present the current business fad of knowledge-management in terms of excess and forgetful repetition of ideas. We look at knowledge management as an idea of highly suspect utility, and search for explanations for and possible counterbalances to its ubiquity.

INTRODUCTION

The concepts of knowledge management and knowledge-intensive work have been developing for quite a while. Some authors claim that knowledge is the most important organizational asset in contemporary society, and that as a result, knowledge workers are crucial for a company's success (e.g. Stewart, 1997). Others claim that much of the knowledge management literature and practical solutions are just perfunctory and propagandist (Styhre & Sundgren, 2005). Many managerial policies rely on the manipulation of emotions and identity creation (Kärreman & Alvesson, 2004).

Another interesting issue is that knowledge-workers are perceived and presented as the most valued members of an organization, leading and defining it; at the same time they are manipulated, "engineered," overworked until they burn out, and deprived of family life (Perlow, 1997). The conflict between the worker and manager is often more obvious than in other settings (Roscigno & Hodson, 2004). These and other paradoxes mark knowledge work and knowledge-intensive companies as a particularly worthwhile object of study.

This short chapter, which concludes this book, capitalizes on this fascinating and timely research area. We want to present the current business fad of knowledge-management in terms of excess and forgetful repetition of ideas, dating back not only to Mallet (1975), but also perhaps to Plato. We believe that the praise for excessive consumption has also been taken to the world of ideas, and that knowledge management is a conspicuous example of the overproduction of notions, old crumbs of wisdom infinitely regurgitated into a pop-culture pulp – all done in the name of promoting knowledge-intensive organizations.

KNOWLEDGE MANAGEMENT AS PULP FICTION

One of the most disingenuous characteristics of knowledge management literature is the fact that its content can be often reduced to a truism: knowledge is good, so make people share it.

Alexander Styhre and Mats Sundgren (2005) describe this phenomenon, characteristic of the pop-management literature on creativity and knowledge in organizations, by merciless exposure of arbitrary references, wishful thinking, methodological ridicule, and obtrusive didacticism of William C. Miller's *Flash of Brilliance* (1999). Indeed, all too many knowledge management books resemble children's storybooks: they are full of colorful images and diagrams, they are written in a simplified language (do the authors of books on knowledge management really think that their readers are so stupid?), and include simplistic advice that is little different from what is found in the bestselling Chicken Soup series (Canfield & Hansen, 1993).

This has been confirmed by our short, and mostly anecdotal, research experiment at the 2008 Standing Conference for Management and Organization Inquiry (SCMOI) meeting in Philadelphia. We looked up "knowledge" and "knowledge management" in books.google.com. From the eight top books in both categories we chose one sentence with the word "knowledge" (not "knowledge management"). We distributed the sentences among SCMOI participants and asked them to try to determine whether or not the quotation had been taken from the knowledge management literature. The examples included such obvious sentences as:

- "knowledge evolves as our purposes change in creative response to our environment" (Alle, 1997, p. 19)
- "'maps' to knowledge experts are useless if these experts cannot be reached at the moment when knowledge is needed" (Malhotra, 2000, p. 124)
- "the knowledge transfer process involves the transmission of knowledge from the initial location to where it is needed and is applied" (Easterby-Smith & Lyles, 2003, p. 110).

We contrasted these with statements like:

- "the boundaries of distinct disciplines became a more entrenched feature of the production of knowledge, embodied in the constitution of university" (Goliński, 1998, p. 67),
- "the behavioral account of knowledge has considerable plausibility with respect to third-person epistemic judgments" (Kornblith, 2002, p. 91)

- "perceptual knowledge cannot be reconstructed in terms of inductive reasons" (Pollock & Cruz, 1999, p. 43).

It was not surprising that about 75% of the conference participants were correct in their guesses. While the results of this quick poll do not prove anything, they may indicate that the knowledge management literature uses the word "knowledge" in contexts that are very different, and perhaps significantly simpler, than does the literature of other fields.

Some authors interpret this guilelessness as yet another managerial fad (Fotache, 2005; Klincewicz, 2004). Indeed, management is a field that has a constant demand for new ideas and notions, cycling as often as every 5-10 years (Abrahamson, 1991). The proposed concepts cannot be overly sophisticated, as they have to resonate well with the mass audience. In fact, they need to be repetitive and rephrase the general truths. In this sense, knowledge management can be perceived as totally separate from organizational reality, being more like a well propagated mem than anything more serious (Ponzi & Michael, 2002).

There is nothing new in the need to handle information and encourage employees' collaboration. The Egyptians invented papyrus, and the Chinese invented paper for the purpose of storing data. They did not have Peter Drucker to call them knowledge workers (after elegantly borrowing the idea from Fritz Machlup), but they did employ methods that were contemporaneously associated with knowledge management (Cortada, 1998).

Another argument in favor of treating knowledge management as just a literary fashion is the fact that the notion of "knowledge management" is used arbitrarily. It functions in many contexts and has a plethora of meanings (Wilson, 2002). This may suggest that, while knowledge management is a bestselling brand, there is no grounded meaning behind the slogan: it can be used conveniently to mean almost anything.

Finally, the knowledge element in knowledge management is often dubious. In this part of KM literature, which tries to approach the subject more scientifically, the inconsistencies and lack of common methodological ground accumulate (Alvesson, Kärreman, & Swan, 2002; Styhre, 2003). So do the discrepancies with information theory, from which KM eagerly draws. Thus, knowledge management is a rhetorically attractive term, one that is neither related to knowledge nor to management per se.

That said, we believe that knowledge management is more than just a fad. We will try to explain the potential usefulness of this concept over and above its status as a platitude.

While it is possible to scour historical records for evidence of precedents of contemporary social arrangements, such an activity is both entertaining and pointless. Robert Merton's (1965) magisterial *On The Shoulders of Giants*, an erudite search of the origin of the titular phrase, is perhaps the most accomplished illustration of both qualities. Few, if any, social institutions appear out of nowhere, but their significance and prevalence varies by context. Through a combination of factors such as the growing complexity and dominance of technoscience (Haraway, 2008), the development of widespread global communication and large-scale network forms of organization (Castells, 1996), and, at least in the West, a shift away from manufacturing, (certifiable and certified) knowledge has become the prime characteristic and requirement of valued, and well paid, work. While the present period has also seen massive growth in unskilled service desk and call center McJobs, these carry low prestige and remuneration and, as such, much more rarely capture public, not to mention managerial imagination. It is the professional, knowledge-based work that defines the current epoch. Knowledge management is therefore of both practical and academic interest, both as a practice and as a discourse.

KNOWLEDGE AS A FUZZY BLOB

At the heart of any discussion of knowledge management lie assumptions about knowledge and its place in organizations. As we have already noted, there is a number of distinct, partial conceptualizations of the idea, usually vaguely rooted in information theory. A common typology follows Michael Polanyi (1967) in distinguishing explicit from tacit knowledge, with the former characterized as easily codified and transferable, and the latter portrayed as vague, context-bound, and often tied to physical activities. Elaborate schemes have been devised to explain and facilitate learning, creating, and transformation of one type of knowledge into another--Nonaka and Takeuchi's (1995) Socialization, Externalization, Combination, Internalization (SECI) model is among the most popular. But, as Brown and Duguid (2000) ironically comment, there is little inherent difference between the two types, and knowledge is defined as "sticky" (tacit) or tied to its context, whenever the managerial intent is to facilitate its dissemination and "leaky" (explicit), or decontextualized, when the aim is to stem the spread of valuable knowledge. They argue that the confusion has, at its root, the failure to identify patterns of social interaction among professionals who tend to communicate each other through the frequently trans-organizational, informal Communities of Practice rather than through formal organizational channels. Furthermore, defining knowledge as tacit or explicit might have more to do with power relations and workplace asymmetry, than with its inherent features. After all, the right to recognize knowledge as such is an important managerial privilege, a useful weapon against the new experts (Brint, 1994), who admittedly are carriers of knowledge, but need to be supervised and controlled to allow knowledge transformations.

FIRE AND FORGET

That said, most of the attention in the knowledge management literature focuses on the acquisition and (internal) sharing of knowledge, where management of the latter appears largely equivalent to hoarding: organizations are expected to gather, create, and combine knowledge, building systems that are conducive to quick and easy access to this treasure trove of competitive advantage. Several scholars, however, argue that an equally, if not more, crucial aspect of organizational life is organizational forgetting, the loss of institutional knowledge. While the traditional approach (Pollitt & Bouckaert, 2000) laments organizational amnesia (referred to interchangeably as a "phenomenon" and as a "problem") for squandering a precious resource, de Hollan and Philips (2004) note that purging of knowledge is a vital activity, enabling organizations to forget, to adapt to changing circumstances by shedding assumptions, procedures, and rituals that have ceased to be useful for current performance. Without forgetting, no change is possible (Lewin, 1951). Losing knowledge seems to be as important as acquiring it, although knowledge management mainstream literature does not seem to have recognized this yet. Although knowledge creation is clearly serendipitous and contingent (Barber & Fox, 1958), in management it still is depicted as a rational, systematic and planned process, which can be easily controlled if certain rules are followed.

Geoffrey Bowker (1997) distinguishes processes of clearance (creation of time barriers to retention of knowledge) from erasure (eradication of current knowledge). The former, allowing for the creation of a blank slate and for preempting attacks on the present based on the logic of the past, is a hallmark of radical change. The latter, used to edit out narratively inconvenient details, perpetuates the current order. Both, although time- and resource-intensive, are common in the organizational world. In 1969, Karl Weick raised this issue:

Has an organization ever failed to survive because it forgot something important? More likely is the possibility that organizations fail because they remember too much too long and persist too often doing too many things the way they've always done them. (1969, p. 224)

Taking the logical next step in knowledge management repertoire, John Landry (1999) looks for ways to design forgetting into technological systems for data storage and retrieval. Since the sites of knowledge are important for knowledge management, they are rarely barred from reappropriation into the domain of management.

TOTAL CONTROL

Knowledge and the attempts to control it have been found in many corners of contemporary organization by its numerous scholars (cf. Kostera, 2003 on the interplay between management and control) have targeted diverse aspects of organizational life. We have already proposed technological solutions as one nexus of organizational knowledge and control. Yet, as much of the research in Science and Technology Studies (Law, 1991) shows, technology is always open to reinterpretation by its local context, and especially by its users. Similarly, solutions rooted in organizational structure and procedures (Van Maanen, 1991), innovative spatial arrangements (Brown & Duguid, 2000), quality-assuring audits (Power, 1997) have all been found to be prone to subversion, misuse, and outright destruction at the hands of the human beings (and their non-human: economic discursive, and technological allies: cf. Latour, 1993) subjected to the regimes of knowledge management. On the one hand, the rise of flexible, geographically distributed forms of organizing (Castells, 1996, 2004) and general dissolution of the seemingly immovable social structures (Bauman, 2007) have undermined the confidence in solutions bypassing the human element. On the other hand, management control over workers presents its own set of vicissitudes. Foucault (1976/2000) meticulously chronicled attempts to control and discipline human bodies lying at the heart of the modern project, and the shift towards the disciplined internalizing control mechanisms. The process is all the more pertinent as regards knowledge workers (people who work more with their brains and less with their hands). In case of knowledge management, external control makes little sense, as it is impossible to tell a hard-working employee from one who is slacking. The process of labor is a black box for any bystanders and thus the management needs to rely much more on the eagerness of the subordinates to work efficiently by themselves.

KNOWLEDGE WORKERS

The link between knowledge and knowledge workers is particularly interesting and bears further exploration. The latter are usually presented as the bearers, if not necessarily the creators, of organizational knowledge, while at the same time they can be depicted as untrustworthy and liable to divulge organizational secrets to strangers while withholding vital information from coworkers. Consider the following passage, emblematic in its attitude towards knowledge workers:

While there is no doubt that knowledge is the most important asset for modern firms, it cannot be denied that managing knowledge is the most formidable task they face.... While it is well recognized that social interactions are vital for real knowledge exchange, unfortunately most firms leave social interactions to their employees' informal, chance discussion with peers in their social networks (Mitra & Kumar, 2007: 156).

Workers' autonomy has always troubled the managerialist project, though different forms of work engendered different foci of managerial oversight. Whether Frederick Taylor's behavioral supervision or Arlie Russell Hochschild's mandated emotional labor (1983) control over all assets of production has long been seen as the ultimate goal of management. Knowledge work is commonly framed as involving extensive formal and informal networking (e.g. Quinn, 1992; Sveiby, 2007) through which knowledge is acquired, developed, and shared. It is not surprising, then, to see managerialist prescriptions of exerting control over the totality of employees' social exchanges (the quoted passage comes from an article entitled "Managed Socialization"). At the same time, such attempts are often couched in the discourse of providing the workers with respite from unduly intrusive regulations. Indeed, as Boltanski and Chiapello (1996) argue, these new forms of control may well spring from the critique of earlier manifestations of managerial power. Yet, the results are seldom beneficial:

Flexibility was oriented strongly to firms and to the needs of production because, via the 'accommodation' of workers, the boundaries between work and home time and space are collapsed. While this loosening of boundaries between home and work is cast as a perk of for workers, it also means that personal time and space are eclipsed (MacEachen et al., 2008: 1030)

Thus, what the assembly line did to blue collar workers, knowledge management attempts to do to the rest (Braverman, 1974); knowledge management is the new version of scientific management, but for knowledge workers.

CONCLUSION

As Stephen Barley and Gideon Kunda observed, management science has been experiencing surges of rational and normative control (Barley & Kunda, 1992). Over at least the last half century we can observe a battle of conflicting paradigms: the so-called X and Y theory, as described by Douglas McGregor, one of the founding fathers of human relations approach (McGregor, 1960).

Theory X, epitomized in Frederick Taylor's work, relies on strict external control and standardization of behavior. Its contemporary representations include total quality management (TQM), reengineering, or just-in-time production, all requiring firm supervision of the worker.

Theory Y, often associated with the stream of human relations, relies on norms internalized by the worker. Instead of close observation (and punishment when instructions are not followed) it is based on the ability of workers to discipline themselves. It is loosely associated with organizational learning, as the authors interested in participative management and empowerment were also the ones who started the discussion on knowledge in organizations (Greenwood & Levin, 1998; Lewin, 1951). Contemporary literature on organizational learning draws heavily on the foundations of action research (Argyris, 1982; Schön, 1983).

The difference between the two is, however, entirely superficial. Both, as well as Theory Z proposed by Ouchi (1981), presuppose the managerial ability to define organizational reality. The goal of (and the right to) organizational despotism, benevolent or otherwise, is seen as part and parcel of managerial responsibilities.

Modern organizations follow the neo-Platonic rational principle, but, as Nils Brunsson convincingly shows, the practice of forcing rationalizations and repetitive reforms deepens, rather than diminishes the divide between the theory and practice of organizing (Brunsson, 2006). Failures in building rationalizing models lead, paradoxically, to the conclusion that the reality and practice are wrong (not corresponding with the model), not to the refutation of the theory itself. This leads to the non-learning cycle: organizations unlearn from their mistakes, and plunge into absurdity. Knowledge management, as a prevailing organizational theory, fits this image well.

Naturally, the difference between official organizational rhetoric and common practice is certainly not new (Höpfl, 1995; Knights & Willmott, 1999), but in knowledge-intensive companies, in particular high-tech environments, the difference is extremely conspicuous.

This is because contemporary knowledge management is an attempt to combine the best of both worlds: it uses the language of industrial democracy and sells itself under the label of empowering the workers, but at the same time it focuses on providing functional tools to exert more control over the workers. All capitalists need to make the employees exceed their productivity (Marx, 1867/1992). This paradox was pointed out as early as the 1950s by Reinhard Bendix, who wrote that (1956/2001, p. 327)

... in the words used to describe "two-way" communication, subordinates are expected to listen so they may learn, while managers merely receive information which they can use. (...) The fact is that Mayo's synthesis has been capable of making widely divergent managerial approaches sound alike, and this capacity is one of the tests of a successful ideology. His contribution may well be to have brought about a change of outlook among American managers as a whole, a possibility which is obscured by the appearance of hypocrisy which a mere use of his language implies. For it may not be inconsequential that even those who remain hostile to the human-relations approach adopt some of its language. In the long run, the use of a terminology may exert a cumulative pressure toward the acceptance of new practices which differ from those previously regarded as inviolate, even if they also differ from the words used to describe them.

Half a century later, it is quite clear that the ideological change remained mostly rhetorical. The pseudo-democratic discourse, visible in knowledge management and in the mainstream literature on knowledge-intensive organizations, has a very important role: by taking a stance that seemingly resembles the real industrial democracy and cooperatives theory (Greenwood, González Santos, & Cantón, 1991; Whyte & Whyte, 1991), it squeezes it out of the market. As silly as the knowledge management literature may sound, it still reinforces the managerial importance in organizations and the asymmetry of power. Apparently, knowledge management is sometimes much more than a rhetorical fad: it is a cover-up theory, used to prevent knowledge-intensive organizations from relying on the knowledge workers, and not on the managers.

REFERENCES

Abrahamson, E. (1991). Managerial Fads and Fashion: The Diffusion and Rejection of Innovations. *Academy of Management Review, 16*(3), 586-612.

Alle, V. (1997). *The Knowledge Evolution: Expanding Organizational Intelligence*. Boston: Butterworth-Heinemann.

Alvesson, M., Kärreman, D., & Swan, J. (2002). Departures from Knowledge and/or Management in Knowledge Management. *Management Communication Quarterly, 16*(282-291).

Argyris, C. (1982). *Reasoning, learning, and action: individual and organizational* (1st ed.). San Francisco: Jossey-Bass.

Barber, B., & Fox, R. C. (1958). The Case of the Floppy-Eared Rabbits: An Instance of Serendipity Gained and Serendipity Lost. *The American Journal of Sociology, 64*(2), 128-136.

Barley, S. R., & Kunda, G. (1992). Design and Devotion: Surges of Rational and Normative Control in Managerial Discourse. *Administrative Science Quarterly, 37*, 363-399.

Bauman, Z. (2007). *Liquid times: living in an age of uncertainty*. Cambridge: Polity Press.

Bendix, R. (1956/2001). *Work and authority in industry; ideologies of management in the course of industrialization*. New Brunswick, N.J.: Transaction Publishers.

Bowker, G. C. (1997). *Social science, technical systems, and cooperative work: beyond the great divide*. Mahwah, N.J.: Lawrence Erlbaum Associates.

Braverman, H. (1974). *Labor and monopoly capital. The degradation of work in the twentieth century*. New York: Monthly Review Press.

Brint, S. G. (1994). *In an age of experts: the changing role of professionals in politics and public life*. Princeton, N.J.: Princeton University Press.

Brown, J. S., & Duguid, P. (2000). *The social life of information*. Boston.: Harvard Business School Press.

Brunsson, N. (2006). *Mechanisms of hope: maintaining the dream of the rational organization*. Copenhagen: Copenhagen Business School Press.

Canfield, J., & Hansen, M. V. (1993). *Chicken soup for the soul: 101 stories to open the heart & rekindle the spirit*. Deerfield Beach, FL: Health Communications.

Castells, M. (1996). *The rise of the network society*. Cambridge, Mass.: Blackwell Publishers.

Castells, M. (Ed.). (2004). *The network society: a cross-cultural perspective*. Cheltenham, UK - Northampton, MA: Edward Elgar Pub.

Cortada, J. W. (1998). Introducing the Knowledge Worker. In J. W. Cortada (Ed.), *Rise of the knowledge worker* (pp. xix, 240). Boston: Butterworth-Heinemann.

Easterby-Smith, M., & Lyles, M. A. (2003). *The Blackwell Handbook of Organizational Learning and Knowledge Management*. Malden: Blackwell.

Fotache, M. (2005). Knowledge Management Between Fad and Relevance. *Information, 8*(2), 255-268.

Foucault, M. (1976/2000). *Historia seksualności (Histoire de la sexualité)*. Warszawa: Czytelnik.

Goliński, J. (1998). *Making Natural Knowledge: Constructivism and the History of Science*. Cambridge, UK: Cambridge University Press.

Greenwood, D. J., González Santos, J. L., & Cantón, J. (1991). *Industrial democracy as process: participatory action research in the Fagor Cooperative Group of Mondragón*. Assen/Maastricht-Stockholm: Van Gorcum Arbetslivscentrum.

Greenwood, D. J., & Levin, M. (1998). *Introduction to action research: social research for social change*. Thousand Oaks, Calif.: Sage Publications.

Haraway, D. J. (2008). *When species meet*. Minneapolis: University of Minnesota Press.

Hochschild, A. R. (1983). *The managed heart: commercialization of human feeling*. Berkeley: University of California Press.

Höpfl, H. (1995). Rhetoric and the threat of ambivalence. *Studies in Cultures, Organizations and Societies, 1*(2), 175-187.

Kärreman, D., & Alvesson, M. (2004). Cages in Tandem: Management Control, Social Identity, and Identification in a Knowledge-Intensive Firm. *Organization, 11*(1), 149-176.

Klincewicz, K. (2004). *Management Fashions: Turning Best-selling Ideas into Objects And Institutions*. New Brunswick, N.J.: Transaction Publishers.

Knights, D., & Willmott, H. (1999). *Management lives: power and identity in work organizations*. London - Thousand Oaks, Calif.: Sage.

Kornblith, H. (2002). *Knowledge and Its Place in Nature*. Oxford: Oxford University Press.

Kostera, M. (2003). Managing Professional Identities: Knowledge, Performativity and the New Professional, edited by M. Dent and S. Whitehead. Routledge, 2002. 262 pp. *Gender, Work and Organization, 10*(1), 120-125.

Landry, J. R. (1999). Forgetful or bad memory? *System Sciences, 1999. HICSS-32. Proceedings of the 32nd Annual Hawaii International Conference on.*

Latour, B. (1993). *We have never been modern*. Cambridge, Mass.: Harvard University Press.

Law, J. (1991). *A Sociology of monsters: essays on power, technology, and domination*. London; New York: Routledge.

Lewin, K. (1951). *Field theory in social science; selected theoretical papers*. New York: Harper & Row.

Malhotra, Y. (2000). *Knowledge Management and Virtual Organizations*. Hershey: Idea Group Publishing.

Mallet, S. (1975). *Essays on the new working class*. St. Louis: Telos Press.

Marx, K. (1867/1992). *Capital: Volume I: A Critique of Political Economy (Das Kapital. Kritik der politischen Oekonomie)*. Harmondsworth: Penguin.

McGregor, D. (1960). *The Human Side of the Enterprise*. New York: McGraw Hill.

Merton, R. K. (1965). *On the shoulders of giants: a Shandean postscript*. New York: Harcourt Brace & World.

Nonaka, I. o., & Takeuchi, H. (1995). *The knowledge-creating company: how Japanese companies create the dynamics of innovation*. New York: Oxford University Press.

Ouchi, W. G. (1981). *Theory Z: how American business can meet the Japanese challenge*. Reading, Mass.: Addison-Wesley.

Perlow, L. A. (1997). *Finding time: how corporations, individuals, and families can benefit from new work practices*. Ithaca, NY: ILR Press.

Polanyi, M. (1967). *The tacit dimension*. Garden City, N.Y.,: Anchor Books.

Pollitt, C., & Bouckaert, G. (2000). *Public management reform: a comparative analysis*. Oxford; New York: Oxford University Press.

Pollock, J. L., & Cruz, J. (1999). *Contemporary Theories of Knowledge*. Lanham: Rowman&Littlefield.

Ponzi, L. J., & Michael, K. (2002). Knowledge management: another management fad? *Information Research, 8*(1), retrieved from http://informationr.net/ir/8-1/paper145.html.

Quinn, J. B. (1992). *Intelligent enterprise: a knowledge and service based paradigm for industry*. New York: Free Press.

Roscigno, V. J., & Hodson, R. (2004). The Organizational and Social Foundations of Worker Resistance. *American Sociological Review, 69*(1), 14-39.

Schön, D. (1983). *The Reflexive Practitioner. How Professionals Think in Action*. New York: Basic Books.

Stewart, T. A. (1997). *Intellectual capital: the new wealth of organizations*. New York: Doubleday/Currency.

Styhre, A. (2003). *Understanding Knowledge Management: Critical and Postmodern Perspectives*. Copenhagen: Copenhagen Business School Press.

Styhre, A., & Sundgren, M. (2005). *Managing creativity in organizations: critique and practices*. Basingstoke - New York: Palgrave Macmillan.

Sveiby, K. E. (2007). Disabling the context for knowledge work: the role of managers' behaviours. *Management Decision, 45*(10), 1636-1655.

Van Maanen, J. 1991 The smile factory: Work at Disneyland. In P.J. Frost, L.F. Moore, M.R. Louis, C.C.Lundberg & J.Martin (eds.), *Refraining organizational culture* (pp. 58-76). Newbury Park: Sage.

Weick, K. E. (1969). *The social psychology of organizing*. Reading, Mass.: Addison-Wesley Pub. Co.

Whyte, W. F., & Whyte, K. K. (1991). *Making Mondragon: the growth and dynamics of the worker cooperative complex* (2nd, rev. ed.). Ithaca, NY: ILR Press.

Wilson, T. D. (2002). The nonsense of 'knowledge management'. *Information Research, 8*(1), retrieved from http://www.informationr.net/ir/8-1/paper144.html.

KEY TERMS

Knowledge Management: The notion of a special managerial toolset applicable only in contemporary organizations, particularly those of the high-tech sector

Knowledge Worker: Employees whose most important organizational asset is their knowledge and their ability to manipulate it.

Management Fad: Management concept rising quickly to mainstream prominence, expected to equally quickly disappear into obscurity

Compilation of References

Aaseth, E. (2001). We all want to change the world: The ideology of innovation in digital media. In G. Liestøl, A. Morrison, & T. Rasmussen (Eds.), (2003), *Digital media revisited.* (pp. 415-439). Cambridge & London: MIT Press.

Abbott, A. (1988). *The system of professions. An essay on the division of expert labor.* The University of Chicago Press.

Abell, A., & Oxbrow, N. (1999). Skills for the knowledge economy: the reality of the market place. *Business Information Review*, *16*(3), 115-121.

Abrahamson, E. (1991). Managerial Fads and Fashion: The Diffusion and Rejection of Innovations. *Academy of Management Review*, *16*(3), 586-612.

Abrahamson, E., & Fairchild, G. (1999). Management Fashions: Lifecycles, Triggers, and Collective Learning Processes. *Administrative Sciences Quarterly, 44*, 708-740

Abram, D. (1996). *The Spell of the Sensuous.* New York: Pantheon Press.

Acar, B. S. (1966). A new model for the design process. *Proceedings of the Institute of Mechanical Engineers, Series E*(210), 135-138.

Adler, N. J. (1983). A typology of management studies involving culture. *Journal of International Business*, *14*(2), 29-47.

Adner, R., & Helfat, C. (2003). Corporate effects and dynamic managerial capabilities. *Strategic Management Journal, 24*, 1011-1025.

advantage in the national basketball association. *Human Resource Management Journal, 45,* 13-31.

Agarwal, R., Echambadi, R., Franco, A. M., & Sarkar, M. B. (2004). Knowledge transfer

Agyris, C. (1991). Teaching smart people how to learn. *Harvard Business Review, 69, 3,*99-109.

Agyris, C. (1993). On organizational learning. Cambridge, MA: Blackwell Publishers.

Ahmed, P. X. (1998). Culture and climate for innovation. *European Journal of Innovation Management, 1*(1), 30-43.

Ahonen, H., Engeström, Y., & Virkkunen, J. (2000). Knowledge management – The Second Generation: Creating Competencies Within and Between Work Communities in the Competence Laboratory. In Y. Malhotra (Ed.), *Knowledge Management and Virtual Organizations.* London, UK: Idea Group Publishing (IGP).

Akella, D. (2003). *Unlearning the Fifth discipline: Power, Politics and Control in Organizations.* New Delhi: Response Books.

Akella, D. (2007). Learning organizations: managerial control systems? *Global Business Review, 8*,13-28.

Akgun, A. E., Lynn, G. S., & Byrne, J. C. (2004). Taking the guesswork out of new product development: how successful high-tech companies get that way. *The Journal of Business Strategy, 25*(4), 41-48.

Alarcon, R. (1999). Recruitment Processes Among Foreign Born Engineers and Scientists in Silicon Valley. American Behavioral Scientist 42(9), 1381-1397.

Alavi, M., & Leidner, D. (2001). Knowledge Management and Knowledge Management Systems: Conceptual Foundations and Research Issues. *MIS Quarterly*, *25*(1), 107-136.

Alavi, M., & Tiwana, A. (2003). Knowledge Management: The Information Technology Dimension. In M. Easterby-Smith & M. A. Lyles (Eds.), *Organizational Learning and Knowledge Management* (pp. 104-121). London: Blackwell Publishing.

Alavi, M., Kayworth T. R., & Leidner, D. E. (2006). An Empirical Examination of the Influence of Organizational Culture on Knowledge Management Practices. *Journal of Management Information Systems, 22*(3), 191-224.

Aldrich, H. E., & Pfeffer, J. (1976). Environments of organizations. In A. Inkeles (Ed.), *Annual Review of Sociology, 2,* 79-105.

Alexander, M., & Young, D. (1996). Outsourcing: Where's the Value? *Long Range Planning, 29*(5), 728-730.

Allaire, Y., & Firsirotu, M. (1984). Theories of organizational culture. *Organization Studies, 5*(3), 193-226.

Alle, V. (1997). *The Knowledge Evolution: Expanding Organizational Intelligence.* Boston: Butterworth-Heinemann.

Allee, V. (2000). The value evolution: addressing the larger implications of an intellectual capital and intangibles perspective. *Journal of Intellectual Capital 1*(1), 17-32.

Allee, V. (2003). *The Future of Knowledge: Increasing prosperity through value networks.* Amsterdam: Butterworth-Heinemann.

Allen, T. J. (1977). *Managing the flow of technology.* Cambridge, MA, USA: MIT Press.

Allen, T. J. (1984). *Managing the Flow of Technology: Technology Transfer and the Dissemination of Technological Information Within the R&D Organization* (2nd ed.). Cambridge MA: The MIT Press.

Almeida, P., Phene, A., & Grant, R. (2003). Innovation and Knowledge Management: Scanning, Sourcing and Integration. In M. Easterby-Smith & M. A. Lyles (Eds.), *Organizational Learning and Knowledge Management*, (pp. 356-371). London: Blackwell Publishing.

Almeida, P., Song, J., & Grant, R. (2002). Are firms superior to alliances and markets? An empirical test of cross-border knowledge building. *Organization Science, 13*(2), 147-161.

Altenburger, O. A., & Schaffhauser-Linzatti, M. (2006). *The Order on the Intellectual Capital Statements of Austrian Universities – A Critical Analysis.* Paper presented at the 2nd Workshop on the Process of Reform of University Systems, CINI Foundation, Venice, Italy, May 4th – May 6th.

Alvesson M. (2000). Social Identity and the Problem of Loyalty in Knowledge-Intensive Companies). (8), December. *Journal of Management Studies, 37*

Alvesson M.(1995). *Management of Knowledge-Intensive Companies.* Berlin: Walter de Gruyter..

Alvesson M., 2004, 'Interfaces of control. Technocratic and socio-ideological control in a global management consultancy firm', *Accounting, Organizations and Society*, 29:3-4, April/May.

Alvesson, M. (2000). Social Identity and the Problem of Loyalty in Knowledge-Intensive Companies. *Journal of Management Studies, 37*(8), 1101-1123.

Alvesson, M. (2004). *Knowledge Work and Knowledge-Intensive Firms.* Oxford, Oxford University Press.

Alvesson, M., & Kärreman, D. (2000). Varieties of discourse: On the study of organizations through discourse analysis. *Human Relations*, *53*(9), 1125-1149.

Alvesson, M., & Kärreman, D. (2001). Odd couple: making sense of the curious concept of knowledge management. *Journal of Management Studies, 38,* 995-1018.

Alvesson, M., & Willmott, H. (1996). *Making Sense of Management.* London: Sage.

Alvesson, M., & Willmott, H. (2002). 'Identity regulation as organizational control: Producing the appropriate Individual', *Journal of Management Studies*, 39 (5): 619-644.

Alvesson, M., Kärreman, D., & Swan, J. (2002). Departures from Knowledge and/or Management in Knowledge Management. *Management Communication Quarterly, 16*(282-291).

Amabile, T. (1988). A model of creativity and innovation in organizations. *Research in Organizational Behavior, 10*, 123-67.

Amabile, T. M., Barsade, S. G., Mueller, J. S., & Staw, B.M. (2005). Affect and Creativity at Work. *Administrative Science Quarterly, 50*(3), 367-403.

Amabile, T. M., Hadley, C. N., & Kramer, S. J. (2002). Creativity Under the Gun. *Harvard Business Review, 80*(8), 52-61.

Amabile, T.M. (1988). A Model of Creativity and Innovation in Organizations. In B. M. Staw & Cummings, L. L. (Eds.), *Research in Organizational Behavior, 10*. Greenwich, CT: JAI Press, 123-167.

Amar, A.D. (2004). Motivating Knowledge Workers to Innovate: A Model Integrating Motivation Dynamics and Antecedents. *European Journal of Innovation Management, 7*(2), 89-101.

Ambrosini, V., & Bowman, C. (2001). Tacit knowledge: Some suggestions for operationalization. *Journal of Management Studies, 38*, 811-829.

Amidon, D. A. (1997). *Innovation strategy for the knowledge economy: The ken awakening.* Boston: Butterworth-Heinemann.

Amigoni F. (1979). *I sistemi di controllo direzionale.* Giuffré,Varese.

Amin A., & Cohendet P. (2000). How to Govern Simultaneously Transactions and Competencies: Should Organisational Learning Rely on Isolated Properties or Embedded Practices. *Journal of Management and Governance.*

Amin, S. (1974) *Accumulation on a World Scale.* New York, NY: Monthly Review Press.

Amit, R., & Schoemaker, P. J. (1993). Strategic assets and organizational rent. *Strategic Management Journal, 17*, 33-46.

Anand, B. N.., & Khanna, T. (2000). Do firms learn to create value: The case of alliances. *Strategic Management Journal, 21*, 295-315.

Ancori, B., Bureth, A., & Cohendet, P. (2000). The Economics of Knowledge: The Debate about Codification and Tacit Knowledge. *Industrial and Corporate Change, 9*(2).

Anderson, C., & Bieniaszewska, R. (2005). The Role of Corporate Social Responsibility in an Oil Company's Expansion into New Territories. *Corporate Social Responsibility and Environmental Management, 12*, 1-9.

Andreeva, T. (2007). Rabotnik intellectualnogo truda: podhod k opredeleniju. ("Knowledge Worker: An Attempt to Define the Phenomena"). *Vestnik St. Peterburgskogo Gosudarstvennogo Universiteta, Serija Management, 4*, 32-49.

Andreu, R., & Ciborra, C. (1996). Organizational Learning and Core Capabilities Development: The Role of Information Technology. *Journal of Strategic Information Systems*, June, (pp. 117-127).

Andrews, K. (1971). *The Concept of the Corporate Strategy.* Homewood: IL, Irwin.

Andriessen, D. (2004). IC Valuation and Measurement: Classifying the State of the Art. Journal of Intellectual capital, *5*(2), 230-242.

Anonymous. (2000). Knowledge management: An overview. *Information Management Journal, 34*, 4-7.

Ansoff, H. I. (1965). *Corporate Strategy.* New York: McGraw-Hill.

Ansoff, H. I. (1965). The firm of the future. *Harvard Business Review, 43*(5), (Sept-Oct), 162-178.

Anthes, G. H. (1997). The Gartner Gods. *Computerworld*, March 3, 87-89

Antonacopoulou, E. P., & Gabriel, Y. (2001). Emotion, Learning and Organizational Change: Towards an integration of Psychoanalytic and Other Perspectives. *Journal of Organizational Change Management, 14*(5). 435-451.

Applebaum, H. (1981). *Royal blue: the culture of construction workers*. New York: Holt.

Argote, L. (1999). Organizational Learning: Creating, Retaining and Transferring Knowledge. Kluwer: Newell, MA.

Argote, L., & Ingram, P. (2000). Knowledge Transfer: A Basis for Competitive Advantage in Firms. *Organizational Behavior and Human Decision Processes, 82*(1), 150-169.

Argote, L., & McGrath, J. E. (1993). Group processes in organizations: continuity and change. *International Review of Industrial and Organizational Psychology, 8*, 333-89.

Argyris, C. (1982). *Reasoning, learning, and action: individual and organizational* (1st ed.). San Francisco: Jossey-Bass.

Argyris, C., & Schön, D. (1996). *Organizational Learning II*. Reading, MA: Addison-Wesley.

Argyris, C., & Schön, D. A. (1978). Organizational Learning: A Theory of Action Perspective. London: Addison-Wesley.

Armstrong, P., & Tomes, A. (1996). Art and accountability: the languages of design and management control. *Accounting, Auditing & Accountability Journal, 9*(5), 114-125.

Arrow, K. J. (1974). *The Limits of Organization*. New York: Norton.

Arundel, A. (2001). The relative effectiveness of patents and secrecy for appropriation. *Research Policy, 30*(4), 611-624.

Arvidsson, A. (2006) *Brands: Meaning and Value in Media Culture*. Abingdon: Routledge.

Ashcraft, M. (2006). Cognitive Psychology: An introduction. *Cognition* (pp. 1-33). Upper Saddle River, NJ: Prentice Hall.

Ashforth, B.E., & Humphrey, R.H. (1993). 'Emotional labour in service roles: The influence of identity', *Academy of Management Review,* 18 (1): 88-115.

Atkinson, P. (1992). Understanding ethnographic texts. *Qualitative research methods, 25*. Sage Publications.

Atkinson, R. C., & Shiffrin, R. M. (1971). The control of short-term memory. *Scientific American, 225*, 82-90.

Auster, E., & Choo, C. (1994). How senior managers acquire and use information in environmental scanning. *Information Processing and Management, 30*(5), p607-618.

Austin, J. L. (1975). How to do things with words. In J. O. Urmson & M. Sbisà, (Eds.), *The William James Lectures delivered at Harvard University in 1955*. Oxford University Press,.

Autio, E., Sapienza, H. J., & Almeida, J. G. (2000). Effects of Age at Entry, Knowledge Intensity, and Imitability on International Growth. *Academy of Management Journal, 43*(5), 909-924.

Bachelard, G. (1934/1984). *The New Scientific Spirit*. Boston: Beacon Press.

Backen, T., & Hernes, T. (2003). *Autopoietic Organization Theory*. Copenhagen: Abstract, Liber, Copenhagen Business School.

Baddeley, A. (1992). Working Memory. *Science, 255*, 556-559.

Baer, W. (1986). 'Expertise and Professional Standards', *Work and Occupations,* 13(4): 532-552.

Baeten, E. M. (1996). The Magic Mirror: Myth's Abiding Power. *Suny series in the Philosophy of the Social Sciences*. New York Press.

Baker, C. M., Pesut, D. J., McDaniel, A. M. & Fisher, M. L. (2007). Evaluating the impact of problem-based learning on learning styles of master's students in nursing Administration. *Journal of Professional Nursing, 23*(4), 214-219.

Balogun, J., Gleadle, P., Hailey, V., & Willmott, H. (2005). Managing change across boundaries: boundary-shaking practices. *British Journal of Management, 16*(4), 261-278.

Balota, D. A., Ferraro, F. R., & Connor, L. T. (1991). On the early influence of meaning in word recognition: A review of the literature. In P. J. Schwanenflugel (Ed.), *The Psychology of word meanings* (pp. 187-222). Hillsdale, NJ: Earlbaum.

Banks, A., & Banks, S. P. (1998). *Fiction and research By Ice or Fire*. Walnut Creek: Sage publications.

Banmard, P. (1999). *Tacit knowledge in organizations* (Translated by S. Wanchope). London: Sage.

Bannon, L. (2000). Understanding Common Information Spaces in CSCW. Paper presented at the Workshop on Cooperative Organisation of Common Information Spaces. Technical University of Denmark. Available at http://dmm.cti.dtu.dk/position/bannon.pdf.

Bannon, L., & Bødker, S. (1997). Constructing common information spaces. In Proceedings of the 5th European Conference on CSCW (ECSCW'97) Dordrecht/Kluver, (pp. 81-96).

Barber, B. (1963). 'Some Problems in the Sociology of Professions', *Daeda us*, 92 (Fall): 669-688.

Barber, B., & Fox, R. C. (1958). The Case of the Floppy-Eared Rabbits: An Instance of Serendipity Gained and Serendipity Lost. *The American Journal of Sociology, 64*(2), 128-136.

Barber, F., & Strack, R. (2005).The surprising economics of a "People Business". *Harvard Business Review*, June.

Barinaga, E. (2002). *Levelling Vagueness – A study of cultural diversity in an international project group*. Stockholm: EFI.

Barley, S. R. (1986). Technology as an occasion of structuring: Evidence from observations of CT scanners and the social order of radiology departments. *Administrative Science Quarterly, 31*, 78-108.

Barley, S. R. (1990). The alignment of technology and structure through roles and networks. *Administrative Science Quarterly, 35*, 61-103.

Barley, S. R. (1997). In L. A. Perlow (Foreowrd), *Finding Time. How Corporations, Individuals, and Families Can Benefit from New Work Practices*. Ithaca-London: ILR Press.

Barley, S. R., & Kunda, G. (1992). Design and Devotion: Surges of Rational and Normative Control in Managerial Discourse. *Administrative Science Quarterly, 37*, 363-399.

Barley, S. R., & Kunda, G. (2004). *Gurus, Hired Guns, and Warm Bodies. Itinerant Experts in a Knowledge Economy*. Princeton: Princeton University Press.

Barley, S., & Kunda G. (2004). *Gurus, warm bodies and hired guns: Itinerant experts in the knowledge economy*. Princeton: Princeton University Press.

Barley, S., & Kunda, G. (2000). Design and devotion: Surges of rational and normative ideologies of control in managerial discourse. In K. Grint (Ed.), *Work and society* (pp. 303-342). Malden, MA: Blackwell Publishers.

Barney, J. (1991). Firm resources and sustained competitive advantage. *Journal of Management, 17*, 99-120.

Barney, J. B. (1986). Organizational culture: can at be a source of sustained competitive advantage? *Academy of Management Review, 11*(3), 656-666.

Barney, J. B. (1989). Asset stocks and sustained competitive advantage: a comment. *Management Science, 35*(12), 1511-1513.

Barney, J. B. (1991). Firm resources and sustained competitive advantage. *Journal of Management, 17*(1), 99–120.

Barney, J. B. (2001). Is the resource-based "view" a useful perspective for strategic management research? Yes. *The Academy of Management Review, 26*(1), 41-56.

Barras, R. (1986). Towards a theory of innovation in services. *Research Policy, 15*(4), 161-173.

Barras, R. (1990). Interactive innovation in financial and business services: The vanguard of the service revolution. *Research Policy, 19*(3), 215-237.

Barron, F. B., & Harrington, D. M. (1981). Creativity, Intelligence, and Personality. *Annual Review of Psychology, 32*, 439-476.

Barthelemy, J. (2001). The hidden costs of IT outsourcing. *Sloan Management Review, 42*(3), 60-69.

Barthelemy, J., & Geyer, D. (2000). It outsourcing: findings from an empirical survey in France and Germany. *European Management Journal, 19*(2), 195-202.

Baszanger, I., & Dodier, N. (1997). Ethnography. Relating the Part to the Whole. In D. Silverman (Ed.), *Qualitative Research. Theory, Method and Practice* (pp. 8-23). London: SAGE.

Baudrillard, J. (1981) *For a Critique of the Political Economy of the Sign*. St. Louis: Telos.

Bauman, Z. (2007). *Liquid times: living in an age of uncertainty*. Cambridge: Polity Press.

Baumann, Z. (2000). *Liquid Modernity*. Cambridge: Policy Press.

Bawden, D., & Kay, R. (1997). Information Behaviour in Nursing Specialties: A Case Study of Midwifery. *Journal of Information Science, 23*(6), 407-421.

Beard, C., & Easingwood, C. (1996). New Product Launch: Marketing Action and launch tactics for high technology products. *Journal of Industrial marketing Management, 25*, 87-103.

Becker, B., & Gerhart, B. (1996). The Impact of Human Resource Management on Organizational Performance: Progress and Prospects. *Academy of Management Journal, 39*(4), 779-801.

Beckett, D., & Hager, P. (2002). *Life, Work and Learning*. London: Routledge

Beirne et al (1998). Developments in Computing Work: Control and Contradiction in the Software Labour Process. In P. Thompson & C. Warhurst (Eds.), *Workplaces of the Future*. Basingstoke: MacMillan.

Bell, D. (1973). *The Coming of Post-Industrial Society: A Venture in Social Forecasting*. New York: Basic Books.

Bell, D. (1974) *The Coming of Post-Industrial Society*. New York: Harper Colophon Books.

Bell, D. (1981). The Social Framework of the Information Society. In T. Forester (Ed.), *The Microelectronics Revolution*. Cambridge, MA: MIT Press.

Belt, V., Richardson, R., & Webster, J. (1999). Smiling down the phone: Women's work in telephone call centres. Workshop on Call Centres, March 1999. London: London School of Economics.

Bender, S., & Fish, A. (2000). The transfer of knowledge and the retention of expertise: the continuing need for global assignments. *Journal of Knowledge Management, 4*(2), 125-137.

Bender, T. (1988). Introduction. In T. Bender (Ed.), *The university and the city, from medical origins to the present* (pp. 3-10). New York: Oxford University Press.

Bendix, R. (1956). *Work and authority in industry*. Berkeley: University of California Press.

Bendix, R. (1956/2001). *Work and authority in industry; ideologies of management in the course of industrialization*. New Brunswick, N.J.: Transaction Publishers.

Benjamin, W. (1973). The work of art in the age of mechanical reproduction. In W. Benjamin (Ed.) (1973), *Illuminations*. London: Fontana Press.

Berger, A. A. (1998). *Media Analysis Techniques*. Thousand Oaks-London-New Delhi: Sage Publications.

Berger, P., & Luckmann, T. (1966). *The Social Construction of Reality*. New York: Anchor Books.

Bergson, H. (2001). *Time and Free Will: An essay on the immediate Data of Consciousness*. Dover Publications (ISBN: 0480417670).

Berman, S. L., Down, J., & Hill, C. W. L. (2002). Tacit knowledge as a source of competitive

Bertelsen, O., & Bødker, S. (2001). Cooperation in Massively Distributed Information Spaces. In Proceedings of the European Conference on Computer Supported Cooperative Work (ECSCW'01), Dordrecht/Kluver, (pp. 1-17).

Beveridge, W. I. B. (1957). *The art of scientific investigation* (3rd ed.). New York: Vintage.

Bhagat, R., Kedia, B., Harveston, P., & Triandis, H. (2002). Cultural variations in the cross-border transfer of organizational knowledge: an integrative framework. *Academy of Management Review, 27*(2), 204-221.

Bierly, P., & Chakrabarti, A. (1996). Generic Knowledge Strategies in the US Pharmaceutical Industry. *Strategic Management Journal, 17*(1), 123-135.

Bijker, W. E. (1993). Do not despair: there is life after constructivism. Science, Technology, & Human values, 18(1), 113-138.

Bijlsma-Frankema, K., Rosendaal, B., & Taminiau, Y. (2006). Acting on Frictions: Learning Blocks and Flows in Knowledge Intensive Organizations. *Journal of European Industrial Training, 30*(4), 291-309.

Biocca, F. (1992). Virtual reality technology: A tutorial. *Journal of Communication, 42*(4), 23-74.

Bioscience 2015, (2003). *Bioscience and Innovation Growth Team, UK.* (Available at http://www.bioindustry.org/bigtreport/index2.html Accessed March 9, 2007)

Birkinshaw, J. (1996). How multinational subsidiary mandates are gained and lost. *Journal of International Business Studies, 27*(3), 467-495.

Birkinshaw, J. (2000). Network Relationships Inside and Outside the Firm, and the Development of Capabilities. In J. Birkinshaw, & P. Hagström (Eds.), *The Flexible Firm: Capability Management in Network Organizations, 4-17.* Oxford: Oxford University Press.

Birkinshaw, J., Hood, N., & Jonsson, S. (1998). Building firm-specific advantages in multinational corporations: the role of subsidiary initiative. *Strategic Management Journal, 19*(3), 221-241.

Blacker, F., Crump, N., & McDonald, S. (1999). Managing experts and competing through innovation: an activity theoretical analysis. *Organization, 6*(1), 5-31.

Blackler, F. (1995). Knowledge, knowledge work and organizations: an overview and interpretation. *Organization Studies, 16*, 1021-46.

Blackler, F. (1995). Knowledge, Knowledge Work and Organizations: An Overview and Interpretation. Organization Studies, *16*(6),1021-1046.

Bleeke, J., & Ernst, D. (1993). *Collaborating to Compete: Using Strategic Alliances and Acquisitions in the Global Market Place*. New York: Wiley.

Blind, K., & Thumm, N. (2004). Interrelation between patenting and standardisation strategies: Empirical evidence and policy implications. *Research Policy, 33*(10), 1583-1598.

Blomqvist, K.., & Levy, J. (2006). Collaborative capability – a focal concept in knowledge creation and collaborative innovation in networks. *International Journal of Management Concepts and Philosophy, 2*, 31- 48.

Blomqvist, K.-M., & Pöyhönen, A. (2006). *Knowledge-Based View of the Firm – Theoretical Notions and Implications for Management.* Working paper, Lappeenranta University of Technology.

Blumer, H. (1969). *Symbolic Interactionism: Perspective and Method.* Englewood Cliffs, NJ: Prentice-Hall.

Bock, G.-W., Zmud, R. W., Kim Y.-G., Lee, J.-N. (2005). Behavioral Intention Formation in Knowledge Sharing: Examining the Roles of Extrinsic Motivators, Social-psychological Forces, and Organizational Climate. *MIS Quarterly, 29(1), 87-111.*

Boedker, C., Mouritsen, J., & Guthrie, J. (2008). Enhanced business reporting:international trends and possible policy directions. *Journal of Human Resource Costing & Accounting*, 12(1), 14-25.

Boeker, W. (1997). Executive migration and strategic change: The effect of top manager movement on product-market entry. *Administrative Science Quarterly, 42,* 213-236.

Böhm, S. (2002). The Consulting Arcade: Walking Through Fetish-Land. *Tamara: Journal of Critical Postmodern Organization Science*, *2*(2), 20-35.

Boisot M. H. (1998). *Knowledge assets – Securing Competitive Advantage in the Information Economy.* Oxford: Oxford University Press.

Boisot, M. H. (1995). *Information space: A framework for learning in organizations, institutions and culture*. London: Routledge.

Boje, D. M. (1991). The storytelling organization: A study of story performance in an office-supply firm. *Administrative Science Quarterly, 36*, 106-126.

Boje, D. M. (2001). *Narrative Methods for Organizational & Communication Research*. London-Thousand Oaks-New Delhi: Sage Publications.

Boje, D. M. (2006). Breaking out of narrative's prison: Improper story in Storytelling Organization. *Storytelling, Self, Society: An Interdisciplinary Journal of Storytelling Studies, 2*(2), 28-49.

Boje, D. M. (2006). Pitfalls in Storytelling Advice and Praxis. *Academy of Management Review, 31*(1), 218-224.

Boje, D. M. (2006). The Dark Side of Knowledge Reengineering Meets Narrative/Story. *Organization: The Critical Journal of Organization, Theory and Society* (forthcoming, accepted 2006). http://business.nmsu.edu/~dboje/690/papers/Knowledge_Reengineering_Review_Boje.pdf

Boland Jr., R. J., & Tenkasi, R. V. (1995). Perspective Making and Perspective Taking in Communities of Knowing. *Organization Science*, *6*(4), July-August, 350-372.

Bollinger, A. S., & Smith, R. D. (2001). Managing Organizational Knowledge as a Strategic Asset. *Journal of Knowledge Management, 5*(1), 8-18.

Bolter, J. D. (1991). *Writing space: the computer, hypertext, and the history of writing*. Hillsdale, Hove and London: Lawrence Erlbaum.

Bolter, J. D., & Grusin, R. (1999). *Remediation. Understanding new media*. Cambridge: The MIT Press.

Bonora, E. A., & Revang, O. (1993). A framework for analysing the storage and protection of knowledge in organizations: strategic implications and structural arrangements. In P. Lorange, B. Chakravarthy, J. Roos, & A. Van de Ven, (Eds.), *Implementing Strategic Processes: Change, Learning and Co-operation* (pp. 190-213). Blackwell, Oxford.

Bontis, N. (1999). Managing Organizational Knowledge by Diagnosing Intellectual capital: Framing and Advancing the State of the Field. *International Journal of Technology Management, 18*(5-8), 433-462.

Bontis, N., Dragonetti, N. C., Jacobsen, K., & Roos, G. (1999). The knowledge toolbox: a review of the tools available to manage and measure intangible resources. *European Management Journal*, 17(4), 391-402.

Booz, A., & Hamilton (1991). *New Product Management*. New York, USA: Booz, Allen and Hamilton Inc.

Borghoff, U. M., & Pareschi, R. (1998). Information technology for knowledge management (Eds.). Berlin: Springer-Verlag.

Bossen, C. (2002). The Parameters of Common Information Spaces: The Heterogeneity of Cooperative Work at a Hospital Ward. In Proceedings of Computer Supported Cooperative Work (CSCW'02), (pp. 176-185). New York: ACM Press.

Bourdieu, P. (1996).*On television*. New York: The New Press.

Bowden, J. A. (1996). Phenomenographic research: Some methodological issues. In G. Dall'Alba & B. Hasselgran (Eds.), *Reflections on phenomenography: Toward a methodology?* Goteborg: Kompendiet.

Bowden, J. A., & Walsh, E. (Eds.). (2000). *Phenomenography*. Melbourne: RMIT University Press.

Bower, D. J., & Keogh, W. (1997). Conflict and cooperation in technology-based alliances. *International Journal of Innovation Management, 11*(4), 387-409.

Bowker, G. C. (1997). *Social science, technical systems, and cooperative work: beyond the great divide*. Mahwah, N.J.: Lawrence Erlbaum Associates.

Boxall, P. & Steeneveld, M. (1999). Human Resource Strategy and Competitive Advantage: A Longitudinal Study of Engineering Consultancies. *Journal of Management Studies, 36*(4), 443-63.

Boyacigiller, N. (1990). The role of expatriates in the management of interdependence, complexity and risk in multinational corporations. *Journal of International Business Studies, 21*(3), 357-381.

Boyatzis, R. E. (1982). *The Competent Manager.* New York: John Wiley & Sons.

Bradshaw, M. T. (2004). How Do Analysts Use Their Earnings Forecasts in Generating Stock Recommendations. *The Accounting Review, 79*(1), 25-50.

Brandes, H., Lilliecreutz, J., & Brege, S. (1997). Outsourcing- success or failure? Findings from five case studies. *European Journal of Purchasing & Supply Management, 3*(2),63-75.

Braverman, H. (1974) *Labor and Monopoly Capital: The Degradation of Work in the Twentieth Century.* London: Monthly Review Press.

Brelade, S., & Harman, C. (2003). Knowledge Workers Want to Reap Rewards. *Strategic HR Review. 2*(2), 18-21.

Brint, S. G. (1994). *In an age of experts: the changing role of professionals in politics and public life.* Princeton, N.J.: Princeton University Press.

Broadbent, M. (1998). The phenomenon of knowledge management: What does it mean to the information profession? *Information Outlook, 2*(5), 23-35.

Brookes, F. P. (1995). *The Mythical Man-Month.* Reading, Massachusetts: Addison- Wesley.

Brown, J. S., & Duguid, P. (1991). Organizational Learning and Communities-of-Practice: Toward a Unified View of Working, Learning, and Innovation. *Organization Science, 2*(1), 40-57.

Brown, J. S., & Duguid, P. (2000). *The social life of information.* Boston.: Harvard Business School Press.

Brown, J. S., & Duguid, P. (2002). Balancing Act: How to Capture Knowledge without Killing It. *Harvard Business Review. 78*(3), 73-80.

Brown, S. D., & Lightfoot, G. (2002). Presence, absence, and accountability: E-mail and the mediation of organizational memory. In S. Woolgar (Ed.), (2002), *Virtual society? Technology, cyberbole, reality.* Oxford & New York: Oxford University Press.

Brown, S. L., & Eisenhardt, K. M. (1997). The Art of Continuous Change: Linking Complexity Theory and Time-paced Evolution in Relentlessly Shifting Organizations. *Administrative Science Quarterly, 42,* 1-34.

Brown, S. L., & Eisenhardt, K. M. (1998). *Competing on the edge: strategy as structured chaos.* Harvard Business School Press.

Bruner, J. (1986). *Actual Minds, Possible Worlds Cambridge.* Massachusetts: Harvard University Press.

Bruner, J. (1990). *Acts of Meaning.* Cambridge, Mass: Harvard University Press.

Brunsson, N. (2006). *Mechanisms of hope: maintaining the dream of the rational organization.* Copenhagen: Copenhagen Business School Press.

Bruun, H., & Hukkinen, J. (2003). Crossing boundaries: An integrative framework for studying technological change. *Social Studies of Science, 33*(1), 95-116.

Bruun, H., & Langlais, R.(2003). On the Embodied Nature of Action. *Acta Sociologica, 46*(1), 31-49.

Buckley, P. J., Glaister, K.W.,., & Husan, R. (2002). International joint ventures: partnering skills and cross-cultural issues. *Long Range Planning, 35,*113-134.

Bucklin, L. P.., & Sengupta, S. (1993). Organizing successful co-marketing alliances. *Journal of Marketing, 57,* 32-42.

Bud, R. (1983). *The uses of life: A history of biotechnology.* Cambridge: Cambridge University Press.

Budden, R. (January 6, 2003). Life for 3 G without Killer Application. *Financial Times.*

Burawoy, M. (1979). *Manufacturing consent.* Chicago: University of Chicago Press.

Burch, S. (2005). The Information Society/ the Knowledge Society. In *A. Ambrosi, V. Peugeot, & D. Pimienta (Eds.), Word Matters: Multicultural perspectives on information societies. Paris:* C & F Éditions.

Burgoyne, J. (1999). Design of the times. *People Management, 5*(11), 38-44.

Burgoyne, J., Pedlar, M., & Boydell, T. (1994). *Towards the Learning Company*. McGraw Hill.

Burke, J., & Ornstein, R. (1995/1997). *The Axemaker's Gift: Technology's Capture and Control of Our Minds and Culture*. New York: Penguin Putnam.

Burke, M. (2005). Reflections on structures and solutions regarding information fulfillment in organisations. *Proceedings of Information Management Resources Association 2005*. San Diego (CD)

Burns, A. (1989). *The power of the written word: the role of literacy in the history of Western civilization*. New York: Peter Lang.

Burns, T. R., & Stalker, G. M. (1961). *The Management of Innovation*. London: Tavistock.

Burrell, G. (1998). Linearity, control and Death. In D. Grant, T. Keenoy, & C. Oswick (Eds), *Discourse and Organization*. In London: Sage.

Burt, R. (2002). *The social capital of structural holes, new directions in economic sociology*. New York: Russel Sage.

Butler, R. (1991). *Designing Organizations: A Decision Making Perspective*. London: Routledge.

Cabrera A., Collins, W. C., & Salgado, J. F. (2006). Determinants of Individual Engagement in Knowledge Sharing. *International Journal of Human Resource Management, 17*(2), 245-264.

Caldwell, F. (2002). *Knowledge Management Scenario: What's Next*? Gartner Symposium ITxpo (Orlando, Florida), 26F-SYM12, October 6-11, 2002.

Caldwell, F. (2003). *From Enterprise Content Management to the SES and Beyond*. Gartner Symposium ITxpo (Florence, Italy), 26F-SPR4, March 10-12, 2003.

Caldwell, F., & Andrews, W. (2002). Update on Search Technology. *Gartner Letter From the Editor, LE-16-9553*, June 7, 2002.

Caldwell, F., & Harris, K. (2002). Hype Cycle for Knowledge Management 2002. *Gartner Research Note, SPA-15-0651*, January 3, 2002.

Caldwell, F., & Logan, D. (2002). Powerhouse Vendors Move to Knowledge Management. *Gartner Letter From the Editor, LE-18-6080*, November 12, 2002.

Caldwell, F., & Shegda, K. (2002). BEA Participates in High-Growth Area of Knowledge Management. *Gartner FirstTake, FT-15-3652*, January 25, 2002.

Caldwell, F., Gilbert, M., & Hayward, S. (2002). CM, Portals and Collaboration Fading: Enter 'Smart' Suite. *Gartner Letter From the Editor, LE-16-6229*, May 10, 2002.

Caldwell, F., Gilbert, M., Hayward, S., Logan, D., & Lundy, J. (2002). *New Focus on Knowledge and Collaboration Begins in 2002*. January 7, 2002.

Caldwell, F., Linden, A., Miklovic, D., Morello, D., Knox, R., Logan, D., Grey, M., Gilbert, M., Harris, K., Andrews, W., Lundy, J., Hayward, S., Bell, M., Latham, L., & Shegda, K. (2003). Hype Cycle for Knowledge Management 2003. *Gartner Strategic Analysis Report, R-20-0010*, June 6, 2003.

Callaghan, G. & Thompson, P. (2001). 'Edwards revisited: technical control and call centres', *Economic and Industrial Democracy*, 22 (1), 13-37.

Callon, M. (1986). Some Elements of a Sociology of Translation: Domestication of the Scallops and the Fisherman of St Brieuc Bay. In J. Law (Ed.), *Power, Action and Belief: A New Sociology of Knowledge* (pp. 196-233). London: Routledge & Kegan Paul.

Callon, M. (1986). The sociology of an Actor-network: The case of the electric vehicle. In M. Callon, J. Law, & A. Rip (Eds.), *Mapping the Dynamics of Science and Technology: Sociology of Science in the Real World* (pp. 19-34). London: Macmillan.

Callon, M. (1987). Society in the Making. In W. E. Bijker, T. P. Hughes, & T. J. Pinch (Eds.), *The Social Construction of Technological Systems* (pp. 83-103). Cambridge: MIT Press.

Cambridge NY: Cambridge University Press.

Campion, M. A., Papper, E. M., & Medsker, G. J. (1996). Relations Between Work Team Characteristics and Effectiveness: A Replication and Extension. Personnel Psychology, *49*(2), 429-440.

Canfield, J., & Hansen, M. V. (1993). *Chicken soup for the soul: 101 stories to open the heart & rekindle the spirit.* Deerfield Beach, FL: Health Communications.

Cantillon, P., & Jones, R. (1999). Does continuing medical education in general practice make a difference? *British Medical Journal, 318*, 1276-1277.

Cardoso, H., & Faletto, E. (1979). *Dependency and Development in Latin America.* Berkeley, CA: University of California Press.

Carnoy, M., Castells, M., & Benner, C. (1997). Labor markets and employment practices in the age of flexibility: A case study of Silicon Valley. *International Labor Review, 136*, 27-48.

Carreau, D., & Logan, D. (2001). With SharePoint, Microsoft Blurs Portals and Knowledge Management. *Gartner FirstTake, FT-12-9070*, January 25, 2001.

Carr-Saunders, A.M & Wilson, P.A. (1933). *The Professions.* Oxford: Clarendon.

Carter, C. F., & Williams, B. R. (1959). The characteristics of technically progressive firms. *Journal of Industrial Economics*, March, (pp. 87–104).

Cartwright, S.., & Cooper, G. (1993). If cultures don't fit, mergers may fail. *New York Times, 15*,August, 51.

Cassel, C., & Gillian, S.(Eds.) (1994). *Qualitative Methods in Organisational Research: A Practical Guide.* London: Sage.

Castells, M. (1996). *The Information Age. Economy, Society and Culture, 1: The rise of the network society.* Oxford: Blackwell Publishers

Castells, M. (1996). *The Rise of Network Society.* MA: Blackwell, Cambridge.

Castells, M. (1999). *The Information Age: Economy, Society and Culture*. Oxford: Blackwell Publishers.

Castells, M. (Ed.). (2004). *The network society: a cross-cultural perspective*. Cheltenham, UK - Northampton, MA: Edward Elgar Pub.

Castells, M., & Himanen, P. (2002). *The Information Society and the Welfare State: The Finnish Model.* Oxford: Oxford University Press.

Chandler, A. D. (1962). *Strategy and Structur.* Caembridge, MA: The MIT Press..

Chang, S-C., Chen, S-S.,. & Lai, J.-H. (2008). The effect of alliance experience and intellectual capital on the value creation of international strategic alliances. *Omega, 36*, 298-316.

Cheetham, G., & Chivers, G. (2001). How professionals learn in practice. *Journal of European Industrial Training, 24*(7), 247-292.

Chesborough, H. (2003). *Open Innovation: The new imperative for creating and profiting from technology.* Boston, MA: Harvard Business School Press.

Chia, R. (1992). Foundations of Management Knowledge: Assumptions and Limitations. Paper number 01/ 04, University of Exeter paper series.

Chia, R. (2000). Discourse analysis as organizational analysis. *Organization, 7*(3), 513-518.

Chia, R. (2003). From knowledge creation to the perfection of action: Tao, Basho and pure experience as the ultimate ground of knowing. *Human Relations, 56*(8): 953-981

Chia, R. (2003). Organization Theory as a Postmodern Science. In H. Tsoukas & C. Knudsen, (Eds.), *The Oxford Handbook of Organization Theory: Meta-theoretical Pespectives* (pp. 113-143). Oxford: Oxford University Press (2005 paperback edition).

Chiva, R., & Alegre, J. (2006). Organizational Learning and Organizational Knowledge. Towards the Integration of Two Approaches. *Management Learning 36*(1), 49-68.

Choi, B., & Lee, H. (2003). An Empirical Investigation of Knowledge Management Styles and Their Effect on Corporate Performance. *Information & Management, 40*, 403-417.

Christensen, P. H. (2005). Facilitating knowledge sharing — conceptual framework. (Copenhagen Business School Working paper SMG WP 4/2005).

Churchman, C. W. (1971). *The design of inquiring systems: Basic concepts of systems and organizations.* New York: Basic Books.

Ciborra, C. U. (Ed) (2000). From Control to Drift: The Dynamics of Corporate Information Infrastructures. Oxford/Oxford University Press.

Civi, E. (2000). Knowledge management as a competitive asset: a review. *Market Intelligence & Planning, 18,* 166-74.

Clark, B. (1983). *The Higher Education System: Academic Organization in Cross-National Perspective.* Berkeley: University of California Press.

Clarke, A. E., Mamo, L., Fishman, J. R., Shim, J. K., & Fosket, J. R.(2003). Biomedicalization. Technoscientific transformations of health, illness, and U.S. biomedicine. *American Sociological Review, 68*, 161-194.

Clarke, J., & Turner, P. (2004). Global Competition and the Australian Biotechnology Industry: Developing a Model of SMEs Knowledge Management Strategies. *Knowledge and Management Process, 11*(1), 38-46.

Clegg, R. S., Kornberger, M., & Rhodes, C. (2005). (referred to as Clegg, 2005). Learning/Becoming/Organizing. Organization, *12*(2), 147-167.

Clegg, S. (2000). Globalising the intelligent organisation. In J. Garrick & C. Rhodes, (Eds.), *Research and Knowledge at Work: Perspectives, Case-studies and Innovative strategies*(pp. 77-99). London and New York: Routledge.

Clegg, S. R. (2005). Learning/Becoming/Organizing. *Organization, 12*(2), 147-167.

Cobbledick, S. (1996).The Information-Seeking Behavior of Artists: Exploratory Interviews. *Library Quarterly,* 66(4), 343-372.

Coff, R. W. (1997). Human assets and management dilemmas: Coping with hazards on the road to resource-based theory. *Academy of Management Review, 22,* 374-402.

Coghlan, D., & Brannick, T. (2005). *Doing Action Research in your own Organization.* London: Sage publishers

Cohen, L., & El-Sawad, A. (2007). 'Accounting for 'us' and 'them': Indian and UK customer service workers' reflections on offshoring', *Economic and Political Weekly, 42*(21): 1951-1957.

Cohen, W. M., & Levinthal, D. A. (1990). Absorptive capacity: A new perspective on learning and innovation. *Administrative Science Quarterly, 35*, 128-152.

Cohen, W., & Levinthal, D. (1989). Innovation and Learning: the two faces of R&D. *The Economic Journal, 99*, 569-596.

Cohen, W., & Levinthal, D. (1990). Absorptive capacity: a new perspective on learning and innovation. *Administrative Science Quarterly, 35*(1), 128-152.

Cohendet, P., & Steinmuller, E. (2000). The Codification of Knowledge: A Conceptual and Empirical Exploration. *Industrial and Corporate Change, 9*(1), March.

Coleman, J. S. (1990). *Foundations of Social Theory.* Cambridge, MA: Harvard University Press.

Collins, H. (2007). Bicycling on the Moon: Collective Tacit Knowledge and Somatic-limit Tacit Knowledge. *Organization Studies, 28*(2), 257-262.

Collis, D. J. (1994). How valuable are organizational capabilities? *Strategic Management Journal, 15*/special issue, 143-152.

Collis, D. J. (1994). Research note: how valuable are organizational capabilities? *Strategic Management Journal, 15*(S1), 143-152.

Common, R. (2004). Organizational Learning in a Political environment. *Policy Studies, 25*(1), 35-49

Connel, C. (2001). *Why Software Is (Almost) Always Late*. Presentation of CHC-3 Consulting at http://www.chc-3.com/talk/why_software_late.ppt. (accessed 01.10.2008).

Conner, K. (1991). A historical comparison of resource-based theory and five schools of thought within industrial organization economics: do we have a new theory of the firm? *Journal of Management, 17*(1), 121–154.

Conner, K. R., & Prahalad, C. K. (1996). A Resource-based Theory of the Firm: Knowledge Versus Opportunism. *Organization Science, 7*(5), September-October, 477-501.

Contractor, F.,., & Lorange, P. (1988). *Cooperative Strategies in International Business: Joint Ventues and Technology Partnerships between Firms*. Lexington, MA: Lexington Books.

Contu, A., & Willmott, H. (2003). Re-embedding situatedness: The importance of power relations in learning theory. *Organization Science*, **14**, 283-296.

Cook, S. D. N., & Brown, J. S. (1999). Bridging epistemologies: The generative dance between organizational knowledge and organizational knowing. *Organization Science 10*, 381-400.

Cook, S. D. N., & Yanow, D. (1993). Culture and organizational learning. *Journal of Management Inquiry, 2*, 373-90.

Cooper, D., Greenwood, R., Hinings, C. R., & Brown, J. (1996). Sedimentation and transformation in organizational change: the case of Canadian law firms. *OrganizationStudies, 17*(4), 623-647

Cooper, M. (2000). Being the "Go-To Guy": Fatherhood, Masculinity, and the Organization of Work in Silicon Valley. *Qualitative Sociology*, 23/4: 379-405.

Cooper, R. (1989). The visibility of the Social Sciences. In M. C. Jackson, P. Keys, & S. A. Cropper (Eds.), *Operational Research and the Social Sciences* (pp. 51-57). New York and London: Plenum Press.

Cooper, R. (1992). Formal Organization as Representation: Remote Control, Displacement and Abbreviation. In J. Hassard & D. Pym (1990, reprinted 1992), (Eds.), *Theory and Philosophy of Organizations*. London: Routledge.

Cooper, R. (1999). The invisible success factors in product innovation. *Journal of Product Innovation Management, 16*(2).

Cooper, R. (2001). *Winning at new products: accelerating the process from idea to Launch* (3rd Edition). Perseus Publishing.

Cooper, R. G. (1994). Perspective: Third generation new product processes. *Journal of Product Innovation Management, 11*(1), 3-14.

Cooper, R. G. (1999). From Experience: the invisible success factors in product innovation. *Journal of Product innovation Management, 16*(4), 333-351.

Cooper, R. G. (2001). *Winning at New Products: Accelerating the process from idea to launch*, 3rd Edition. Perseus Books.

Cooper, R. G., & Edgett, S. J. (2003). Overcoming the crunch in resources for new product development. *Research Technology Management, 46*(3), 48-59.

Cooper, R. G., & Kleinschmidt, E. J. (1996). Winning businesses in product development: The critical success factors. *Research Technology Management, Jul/Aug, 39*(4), 18-30.

Cooper, R. G., & Kleinschmidt, E. J. (2000). New product performance: What distinguishes the star products? *Australian Journal of Management, 25*(1), 17-46.

Cooper, R. G., Edgett, S. J., & Kleinschmidt, E. J. (1997). Portfolio management in new product development: Lessons from the leaders – Part I. *Research Technology Management, Sep/Oct, 40*(5), 16- 30.

Cooper, R. G., Edgett, S. J., & Kleinschmidt, E. J. (2002). Optimising the stage-gate process: What best practice companies do – II. *Research Technology Management*, Nov/Dec, *45*(6), 43-51.

Cooper, R., Wooton, B., & Bruce, M. (1998). Requirements Capture: Theory and Practice. *Technovation, 18*(8/9), 497-511.

Cooperrider, D. L, Sorenson, P. F. Jr., Whitney, D., & Yaeger, T. F. (Eds.) (2000). *Appreciative Inquiry: Rethinking Human Organization Toward a Positive Theory of Change.* Champaign, IL: Stipes Publishing L.L.C.

Cooperrider, D. L., & Avital, M. (Eds.) (2004). *Advances in Appreciative Inquiry Volume 1: Constructive Discourse and Human Organization.* Oxford: Elsevier Ltd.

Cooperrider, D. L., Whitney, D., & Stavros, J. M. (2003). *Appreciative Inquiry Handbook: The First in a Series of AI Workbooks for Leaders of Change.* Ohio: Lakeshore Publishers Inc.

Coopey, J. (1998). Learning to trust and trusting to learn: a role for radical theatre. *Management Learning, 29,* 365-82.

Cooren, F. (2000). The organizing property of language. Philadelphia: John Benjamins.

Cooren, F. (2001). Acting and Organizing: How speech acts structure organizational interactions. *Concepts and Transformations, 6*(3), 275-293.

Cooren, F. (2004). Textual agency: How texts do things in organizational settings. *Organization, 11*(3), 373-393.

Cortada, J. W. (1998). Introducing the Knowledge Worker. In J. W. Cortada (Ed.), *Rise of the knowledge worker* (pp. xix, 240). Boston: Butterworth-Heinemann.

Coser, L. (1974). *Greedy Institutions.* New York: Free Press.

Cowan, R., David, P. A., & Foray, D. (2000). The Explicit Economics of Knowledge Codification and Tacitness. *Industrial and Corporate Change*, 9(2).

Cowie, C. (2007). 'The accents of outsourcing: The meanings of neutral in the Indian call centre industry', *World Englishes,* 26(3): 316-330.

Coyne, R. (1999). *Technoromanticism: Digital narrative, holism, and the romance of the real.* Cambridge & London: The MIT Press.

Crary, J. (1990). *Techniques of the observer: On vision and modernity in the nineteenth century.* Cambridge & London: The MIT Press.

Crompton, R. (1990). 'Professions in the Current Context', *Work Employment and Society,* (Special Issue): 147-166.

Crosby, L. A., Evans, K. R.., & Cowles, D. (1990). Relationship quality in services selling. An interpersonal influence perspective. *Journal of Marketing, 54*(3), 68-81.

Cross, R., Parker, A., Prusak, L., & Borgatti, S. P. (2001). Knowing what we know: Supporting knowledge creation and sharing in social networks. *Organizational Dynamics, 30*(2), 100-120.

Crossan, M., Lane, H., & White, R. (1999). *An Organizational Learning Framework: from Intuition to Institution.* Academy of Management Review, *24*(3), 522-537.

Currie, G., & Kerrin, M. (2004). The limits of a technological fix to knowledge management: Epistemological, political and cultural issues in the case of intranet implementation. *Management Learning, 35*(1), 9-29.

Currie, W. L., & Willcocks, L. P. (1998). Analysing four types of IT sourcing decisions in the context of scale, client/supplier interdependency and risk mitigation. *Information Systems Journa*l, *8*(2), 119-1434.

Customer Oriented Bureaucracy', in A. Sturdy, I. Grugulis and H. Willmott (eds.) *Customer Service: Empowerment and Entrapment,* pp. 79–101. London: Palgrave.

Cusumano, M., & Kentaro, N. (1998). *Thinking Beyond Lean.* New York, London, Toronto, Sydney, Singapore: The Free Press.

Cyert, R. M., & March, J. G. (1963). *A Behavioral Theory of the Firm.* Englewood, NJ: Prentice-Hall.

Czarniawska, B. (1997). *Narrating the Organization: Dramas of Institutional Identity.*

Czarniawska, B. (1998). A Narrative Approach to Organization Studies. Thousand Oaks, CA: Sage.

Czarniawska, B. (1999). *Writing Management.* Oxford: Oxford University Press.

Czarniawska, B. (2000). *The uses of Narrative in Organization Research.* Gothenburg: GRI.

Czarniawska, B., & Joerges, B. (1996). Travels of Ideas. In B.Czarniawska & G. Sevón, (Eds.), *Translating Organizational Change* (pp. 13-48). Berlin-New York: de Guyter.

Czarniawska-Joerges, B. (1988). *Ideological control in non-ideological organizations*. New York: Praeger.

Czarniawska-Joerges, B. (1992). *Exploring complex organizations: a cultural perspective*. Newbury Park, CA: Sage Publications.

D' Cruz, P. & Noronha, E. (2006). 'Being professional: Organisational control in Indian call centres', *Social Science and Computer Review*, 24(3): 342-361.

Daft, R. L. (2001). Organization theory and design (7th Eds.). South-Western College Publishing.

Dalla Costa, M., & James, S. (1975). *The Power of Women and the Subversion of Community*. Berlin: Falling Wall Press.

Daniels, H. (2004). Cultural historical activity theory and professional learning. *International Journal of Disability, Development and Education, 51*(2), 185-200.

Danserau, F., Yammarino, F. J.., & Kohles, J. C. (1999). Multiple levels of analysis form a longitudinal perspective: Some implications for theory building. *Academy of Management Review, 24*, 346-357.

Das, T. K., & Teng, B.-S. (1998). Between trust and control: developing confidence in partner cooperation in alliances. In *Academy of management review, 23*(3), 491-512 (Special topic forum on trust in and between organisations).

Das, T. K., & Teng, B.-S. (2001). Trust control and risk in strategic alliances: an integrated framework. *Organizational Studies, 22*(2), 251-283.

Daston, L., & Galison, P. (2007). *Objectivity*. New York: Zone Books.

Davenport, T. (2001). Knowledge Workers and the Future of Management. In W. Bennis, G. Spreitzer, & T. Cummings (Eds.), *The Future of Leadership – Today's Top Leadership Thinkers Speak to Tomorrow's Leaders* (pp. 41-58).

Davenport, T. H. (2001). *From Data to Knowledge*. San Jose, CA: Oracle Inc.

Davenport, T. H. (2005). Thinking for a living: how to get better performances and results from knowledge workers. Cambridge: Harvard Business School Press.

Davenport, T. H., & Prusak, L. (1998). *Working Knowledge: How Organizations Manage What They Know*. Boston: Harvard Business School Press.

Davenport, T. H., Thomas, R. J., & Cantrell S. (2002). The Mysterious Art and Science of Knowledge-Worker Performance. *MIT Sloan Management Review, 44*(1), 23-30.

Davenport, T., & Prusak, L. (1998). *Working Knowledge*. Cambridge, MA: Harvard Business School Press.

Davenport, T., & Prusak, L. (2000). *Working Knowledge: How Corporations Manage What They Know*. Boston: Harvard Business School Press.

Davenport, T., DeLong, D., & Beers, M. (1998). Successful Knowledge Management Projects. *Sloan Management Review, 39*(2), 43-57.

David, P. A., & Foray, D. (1995). Accessing and expanding the science and technology knowledge base. *STI-Review, 16*, 13-68.

Davis, E. (1998). *TechGnosis: Myth, Magic and Mysticism in the age of Information*. New York: Harmony Books, Crown Publishers.

Dawson, R. (2000). *Developing Knowledge-Based Client Relationships*. Butterworth-Heinemann, Woburn.

Day, G. S. (1994). The capabilities of market-driven organizations. *Journal of Marketing, 58*, 37-53.

Day, J. D., & Wendler, J. C. (1998). Best practices and Beyond: Knowledge Strategies. *The McKinsey Quarterly, 1*, 19-25.

De Angelis, M. (2001). Marx and primitive accumulation: The continuous character of capital's enclosures. *The Commoner*, www.thecommoner.org.

De Angelis, M. (2006). *The Beginning of History: Value Struggles and Global Capital.* London: Pluto.

De Man, A. P. (2002). How to analyze alliance networks. *Competitive Intelligence Magazine. July/August 2002, 5*, 14-29.

de Woot, P. (1990). *High Technology Europe: Strategic issues for global competition.* Oxford: Basil Blackwell.

Deakin, S., Lane, C., & Wilkinson, F. (1994). 'Trust' or Law? Towards an integrated theory of contractual relations between firms. *Journal of Law and Society, 21*(1), 329-349.

Deal, T. E., & Kennedy, A. A. (1982). *Corporate cultures: the rites and rituals of corporate life.* Reading MA: Addison Wesley.

DeCarolis, D. M., & Deeds, D. (1999). The Impact of Stocks and Flows of Organizational Knowledge on Firm Performance: An Empirical Investigation of the Biotechnology Industry. *Strategic Management Journal, 20*, 953-968.

Deeds, D. L.., & Hill, C. W. L. (1996). Strategic alliances and the rate of new product development: an empirical study of entrepreneurial biotechnology firms. *Journal of Business Venturing, 11*, 41-55.

Deetz, S. (1992). *Democracy in an age of corporate colonization: Developments in communication and the politics of everyday life.* Albany, NY: State University of New York Press.

Deetz, S. (2003). Reclaiming the legacy of the linguistic turn. *Organization, 10*(3), 421-429.

Dekker, H. C. (2001). *Control of inter-organizational relationships.* Theoretical frameworks and an empirical investigation. ARCA Research Memoranda, Vrije Universiteit Amsterdam, ARCA-RM 01-12.

DeLong, D., & Fahey L. (2000). Diagnosing Cultural Barriers to Knowledge Management. *Academy of Management Executives, 14*(4), 118-127.

Denning, S. (2001). *The Springboard: How Storytelling Ignites Action in Knowledge-Era Organizations.* Boston: Butterworth-Heinemann.

Denning, S. (2005). *The Leaders's Guide to Storytelling: Mastering the Art and Discipline of Business Narrative.* San Francisco: Jossey-Bass.

Denning, S. (2007). *The Secret Language of Leadership: How Leaders Inspire Action through Narrative.* San Francisco: Jossey-Bass.

Derrida, J. (1976). *Of Grammatology.* Baltimore: John Hopkins University Press.

Derrida, J. (1981). *Dissemination.* Chicago: The University of Chicago Press.

Derrida, J. (1994). *The Specters of Marx.* trans. Peggy Kamuf. London: Routledge.

Devlin, K. (1999). *Infosense.* New York, NY: Freeman.

Di Bernardo, B., & Rullani, E. (1990). *Il management e le macchine. Teoria evolutiva dell'impresa*, Il Mulino, Bologna.

Dienes, Z., & Perner, J. (1999). A theory of implicit and explicit knowledge. *Behavioral and Brain Sciences, 22*(5), 735-808.

Dierickx, I., & Cool, K. (1989). Asset stock accumulation and sustainability of competitive advantage. *Management Science, 35*(12), 1504-1511.

Dierkes, M., Berthon, A., Child, J., & Nonaka, I. (Eds.), (2001). *Handbook of organizational learning & knowledge.* Oxford: Oxford University Press.

Dietrich, M. & Roberts, J. (1999). Beyond the economics of professionalism. In Broadbent, J., Dietrich, M. & Roberts, J. (Eds.) *The End of the Professions?: The restructuring of professional work.* Oxon, UK: Routledge.

Dillon, T. A., Lee, R. K., & Matheson, D. (2005). Value Innovation: Passport to wealth creation. *Research Technology Management, 48*(2), 22-36.

DiMattia, S., & Oder, N. (1997). Knowledge management: Hope, hype, or harbinger? *Library Journal, 122*(5), 33-36.

Ditillo A. (2005). Management control in knowledge-based organizations. In C. Clubb (Ed), *Accounting – The*

Blackwell Encyclopaedia of Management. Second Edition, Blackwell Publishing.

Ditillo, A. (2004). Dealing with uncertainty in knowledge-intensive firms: the role of management control systems as knowledge integration mechanism. *Accounting, Organizations and Society*, *29*(3-4), April/May.

Dixon, N. M. (2000). *Common knowledge*. Boston, MA: Harvard Business School Press.

Dixon, N. M., Allen, N., Burgess, T., Kilner, P. G., & Schweitzer, S. (2005). *CompanyCommand: Unleashing the power of the army profession*. West Point: The Center for the Advancement of Leader Development and Organizational Learning.

Dodge, M., & Kitchin, R. (2005). Code and the transduction of space. *Annals of the American Geographers*, *95*(1), 162-180.

Doig, S. J., Ritter, R. C., Speckhals, K., & Woolson, D. (2001). Has outsourcing gone to far? *McKinsey Quarterly, 4,* 24-37.

Donate, M., & Guadamillas, F. (2007). The Relationship between Innovation and Knowledge Strategies: its Impacts on Business Performance. *International Journal of Knowledge Management Studies*, *1*(3/4), 388-422.

Doucherty, D. (1992). Interpretive barriers to successful product development in large firms. *Organization Science, 3*(2), 179-202.

Dougherty, D. (1992). A Practice-Centered Model of Organizational Renewal through Product Innovation. *Strategic Management Journal, 13*, 77-92.

Dougherty, V. (1999). Knowledge is about people, not databases. *Industrial and Commercial Training, 31*(7), 262-266.

Douglas, M. (1966). *Purity and Danger: An Analysis of the Concepts of Pollution and Taboo*. London: Routledge & Kegan Paul.

Douma, S., & Schreuder, H. (2004). *Economic Approaches to Organizations*. Third Edition, New York: Prentice Hall.

Draulans, J., deMan, A.-P., & Volberda, H. W. (2003). Building alliance capability: Management techniques for superior alliance performance. *Long Range Planning, 36*, 151.

Drews, J. (2000). Drug discovery: a historical perspective. *Science, 287*, 1960-1964.

Droege, S. B., & Hoobler, J. M. (2003). Employee turnover and tacit knowledge diffusion: a network perspective. *Journal of Managerial Issues, 15*(1), 50-64.

Drucker, J. (1999). *The Alphabetic Labyrinth: the letters in History and Imagination*. London: Thames and Hudson.

Drucker, P. (1959). *Landmarks of Tomorrow: A Report on the New "Post-Modern" World*. New York: Harper Colophon Books.

Drucker, P. (1968). *The Age of Discontinuity: Guidelines to our Changing Society*. New York: Basic Books.

Drucker, P. (1992). The New Society of Organizations. *Harvard Business Review*, Sept-Oct, 95.

Drucker, P. (1993). *Post-Capitalist Society*. London: Butterworth Heinemann..

Drucker, P. (1993/1999). *Społeczeństwo pokapitalistyczne*. Warszawa: PWN.

Drucker, P. F. (1959). *Landmarks of Tomorrow: A Report on the New "Post-Modern" World*. New York: Harper & Row.

Drucker, P. F. (1968). *The Age of Discontinuity*. New York: Harper and Row

Drucker, P. F. (1988). The Coming of the New Organization. *Harvard Business Review, 66*(1), 45-54.

Drucker, P. F. (1993). The Rise of the Knowledge Society. *Wilson Quarterly, 17*(2), 52-70.

Drucker, P. F. (1998). The coming of the new organization. *Harvard Business Review, 66*(1), 1-19.

Drucker, P. F. (1999). Knowledge-Worker Productivity: The Biggest Challenge. *California Management Review, 41*(2),: 79-95.

Drury, C. (1996). *Management and Cost Accounting* (4th Edition). Thomson Business Press.

Du Gay, P. & Salaman, G. (1992). 'The cult(ure) of the customer', *Journal of Management Studies*, 29 (5): 615-633.

Duffy, J. (2000). Knowledge management: What every information professional should know. *Information Management Journal, 34*(3), 10-14.

Dunkin, R. (2003). Motivating Knowledge Workers: Lessons to and from the Corporate Sector. Higher Education Management and Policy, 15(3), 41-49.

Dutta, S. (1997). Strategies for implementing knowledge-based systems. *IEEE Transactions on Engineering Management, 44*(1), 79-90.

Dyer, J. H., & Hatch, N. W. (2006). Relation-specific capabilities and barriers to knowledge transfers: Creating advantage through network relationships. *Strategic Management Journal, 27*(8), 701-19.

Dyer, J. H., & Singh, H. (1998). The relational View: Cooperative Strategy and Sources of Competitive Advantage. *Academy of Management Review, 23*, 660-679.

Dyer, J. H., & Singh, H. (1998). The relational view: Cooperative strategy and sources of inter-organizational competitive advantage. *Academy of Management Review, 23*, 660.

Dyer, J. H., Kale, P.., & Singh, H. (2001). How to make strategic alliances work. *Sloan Management Review, 42*, 37-43.

Dyer, J., & Singh, H. (1998). The relational view: cooperative strategy and sources of interorganizational competitive advantage. *Academy of Management Review, 23*(4), 660-679.

Dyer-Witheford, N. (1999) *Cyber-Marx*. Urbana: University of Illinois Press.

Earl, M. (1996). The risks of outsourcing IT. *Sloan Management Review*, Spring 1996, (pp. 26-32).

Earl, M. (2001). Knowledge Management Strategies: Toward a Taxonomy. *Journal of Management Information Systems, 18*(1), 215-233.

Easterby-Smith, M., & Lyles, M. A. (2003). *Handbook of organization learning and knowledge management.* Oxford & Malden: Blackwell.

Easterby-Smith, M., & Lyles, M. A. (2003). *The Blackwell Handbook of Organizational Learning and Knowledge Management.* Malden: Blackwell.

Easterby-Smith, M., Crossan, M., & Nicolini, D. (2000). Organizational learning: debates past, present and future. *Journal of Management Studies, 37*, 783-96.

Easterby-Smith, M., Crossan, M., Nicolini, D. (2000). Organizational learning: Debates past, present and future. *Journal of Management Studies, 37*(6), 783-796.

Eccles, R. G. (1991). The Performance Measurement Manifesto. *Harvard Business Review, 69*, January-February, 131-137.

Eckert, H., & Bajorath, J. (2007). Molecular similarity analysis in virtual screening: foundations, limitations and novel approaches. *Drug Discovery Today, 12*(5-6), 225-233.

Edgerton Jr., S. Y. (1975). *The Renaissance Rediscovery of Linear Perspective.* New York: Icon Editions, Harper and Row.

Edmondson, A. C. (2003). Speaking up in the operating room: How team leaders promote learning in interdisciplinary action teams. *Journal of Management Studies, 40*(6), 1419-52.

Edmonson, A. C., Bohmer, R. M., & Pisano, G. P. (2001). Disrupted routines: Team learning and new technology implementation in hospitals. *Administrative Science Quarterly, 46*, 685-716.

Edström, A., & Galbraith, J. R. (1977). Transfer of managers as a coordination and control strategy in multinational organizations. *Administrative Science Quarterly, 22*(2), 248-268.

Edvinsson L., & Malone M. (1997). *Intellectual Capital: Realising Your Company's True Value by Finding its Hidden Brainpower.* New York, NY: Harper Collins.

Edvinsson, L., & Malone, M. (1997). *Intellectual capital: Realising Your Company's True Value by Finding its Hidden Brainpower.* New York: Harper Collins.

Edwards, R. (1979). *Contested terrain.* New York: Basic Books.

Eijnatten, F. M. van (1993). *The Paradigm That Changed the Work Place.* Assen, Van Gorcum.

Eikeland, O. (2006). Phrónêsis, Artistotle, and Action Research. *International Journal of Action Research, 2*, 15-53.

Eisenhardt, K. (1989). Building theories from case study research. *Academy of Management Review, 14*(4), 532-550.

Eisenhardt, K. M.., & Martin, J. A. (2000). Dynamic capabilities: what are they? *Strategic Management Journal, 21,* 1105-1121.

Eisenhardt, K., & Galunic, D. C. (2000). Coevolving. At last, a way to make synergies work. *Harvard Business Review, January-February, 2000*, 91-101.

Eisenhardt, K., & Martin, J. (2000). Dynamic Capabilities: What Are They? *Strategic Management Journal, 21*, 1105-1121.

Eisenhardt, K.., & Sull, D. N. (2001). Strategy as simple rules. *Harvard Business Review, January 2001*, 107-116.

Eisenhauer, M., Hoffman, B., & Kretschmer, D. (2002). *State of Art Human Computer Interaction.* Retrieved February 18, 2007, from Telematica Institute, Giga Mobile Web Site: https://doc.telin.nl/dscgi/ds.py/GetRepr/File-25715/html

Eisenstein, E. (1983). The *printing revolution in early modern Europe*. Cambridge: Cambridge University Press.

Elisa (2006). *Annual Report.* [http://www.elisa.com/english/docimages/attachment/Elisa_vk2006_uk.pdf].

Elisa (2007). *Presentation.* [http://www.elisa.com/english/docimages/attachment/Q2%202007%20English.pdf]

Elisa (2008). [http://www.elisa.com/english/]

Elkjaer, B. (2004). Organizational Learning. The 'Third Way'. *Management Learning, 35*(4), 419-434.

Elliott, P. (1972). *The Sociology Of The Professions.* Basingstoke: Macmillan.

Ellis, D. (1989). A behavioural approach to information retrieval design. *Journal of Documentation, 46*, 318-338.

Ellis, D. (1993). Modelling the information seeking patterns of academic researchers: a grounded theory approach. *The Library Quarterly, 63*(4), 469-486.

Ellis, D., Cox, D., & Hall, K. (1993). A comparison of the information seeking patterns of researchers in the physical and social sciences. *Journal of Documentation, 49*(4), 356-369

Ellis, N., & Watterson, C. (2001). Client perceptions of regional law firms and their implications for marketing management. *Service Industries Journal, 21*(4), 100-118

Elmholdt, C. (2003). Metaphors for Learning: cognitive acquisition versus social participation. *Scandinavian Journal of Educational Research, 47*(2), 115-131.

Elson, D. (1979). The value theory of labour. In D. Elson (Ed.), *Value: The Representation of Labour in Capitalism.* London: CSE Books.

Engeström, Y. (1995). Objects, contradictions and collaboration in medical cognition: an activity-theoretical perspective. *Artificial Intelligence in Medicine, 7*, 395-412.

Engeström, Y. (2001). Expansive learning at work: toward an activity theoretical reconceptualisation. *Journal of Education and Work, 14*(1), 133-156.

Engeström, Y. (2004). New forms of learning in co-configuration work. Paper presented to the Department of Information Systems. *ICTs in the contemporary world.* seminar, LSE, January 2004

Engeström, Y., Virkkunen, J., Helle M., Pihlaja J., & Poikela, R. (1996). The change laboratory as a tool for transforming work. *Lifelong Learning in Europe, 2*, 10-16.

Entman, R. M. (1993). Framing: Toward Clarification of a Fractured Paradigm. *Journal of Communication, 43*(4), 51-58

Eraut, M. (2000). Non-formal learning and tacit knowledge in professional work. *British Journal of Educational Psychology, 70*, 113-136.

Eraut, M. (2000). Non-formal learning, implicit learning and tacit knowledge in professional work. In F. Coffield (Ed.), *The Necessity of Informal Learning.* Bristol: Policy Press.

Erickson, T., &. Kellog, W. A. (2003). Social Translucence: Using Minimalist Visualisations of Social Activity to Support Collective Interaction. In K. Höök, D. Benyon, & A. J. Munro (Eds.), Designing Information Spaces: The Social Navigation Approach (pp. 17-42). Berlin: Springer,.

Eskola, A. (1982). *Vuorovaikutus, muutos, merkitys* [Interaction, Change, Significance]. Helsinki: Tammi.

European Commission (EC) (2006). *RICARDIS: Reporting Intellectual Capital to Augment Research, Development and Innovation in SME's*, Brussels, June.

Evans, J. A., Kunda, G., & Barley, S. (2004). Beach time, bridge time, and billable time: The temporal structure of technical contracting. *Administrative Science Quarterly, 49*, 1-38.

Evetts, J. (2003). 'The sociological analysis of professionalism: Occupational change in the modern world', *International Sociology*, 18 (2): 395-415.

Evetts, J. (2006). 'Short Note: The Sociology of Professional Groups: New Directions', *Current Sociology*, 54(1): 133 – 143.

Fabritius, H. (1998). Information seeking in the newsroom: application of the cognitive framework for analysis of the of the work context. *Information Research, 4*(2) Retrieved 12 Oct 2004 from http://informationr.net/ir/

Fahey, L., & Prusak, L. (1998). The eleven deadliest sins of knowledge management. *California Management Review, 40*(3), 265-276.

Fairclough, N. (1995). *Critical discourse analysis: The Critical Study of Language*. London: Longman.

Farrell, N. (2006). Indian call centres are both Sodom and Gomorrah Take Archbishop of Bangalore notions with a pillar of salt. Tuesday 14 November 2006, Retrieved on 28 August, 2008 from http://www.theinquirer.net/default.aspx?article=35715

Fayol, H. (1987). *General and industrial management: Henri Fayol's classic revised by Irwin Gray.* Belmont, CA: David S. Lake Publishers.

Fayyad, U. (n.d.). Data Mining and Knowledge Discovery. *DMKD Journal, 1(1).* Retrieved February 22, 2007, from http://research.microsoft.com/research/datamine/vol1-1/editorial3.htm

Febvre, L., & Martin, He-J. ([1958]1997). *The coming of the book: The impact of printing 1450-1800*, trans. by David Gerard, London & New York: Verso.

Federal Ministry of Economic and Labour (FMEL) (2004). *Intellectual Capital Statement – Made in Germany*, Berlin.

Federal Ministry of Education, Science and Culture (FMESC), (2002). *Federal Act on the Organisation of the Universities and their Studies (Universities Act 2002)*, available at http://www.bmbwk.gv.at (last accessed in February 2007).

Federal Ministry of Education, Science and Culture (FMESC), (2006). *63rd Regulation: Regulation on Intellectual Capital Reports*, available at http://www.bmbwk.gv.at (last accessed in February 2007).

Feldman, M. S., & Pentland, B. T. (2003). Reconceptualizing organizational routines as a source of flexibility and change. *Administration Science Quarterly, 48*(1), 94-118.

Felin, T.., & Foss, N. J. (2004). Methodological individualism and the organizational capability approach. Working Paper Copenhagen Business School, No.5/2004.

Felin, T.., & Foss, N. J. (2005). Strategic organization: A field in search of micro-foundations. *Strategic Organization, 3*, 441-455.

Fenwick, J., & McMillan, J. (2005). Organizational Learning and Public Sector Management: An alternative view. *Public Policy Administration, 20*(3), 42-55.

Fenwick, T. (1998). Questioning the concept of the learning organization. In S. M. Scott, B. Spencer, & A. M. Thomas (Eds.), *Learning for Life: Canadian Readings in Adult Education*, (pp. 140-52). Toronto: Thompson..

Fermine, M. (2001). *Snow*. Surrey, UK: Acorn Book Company.

Field, A. P. (2005). Regression. *Discovering Statistics Using SPSS*. (2nd ed.). (pp. 143-218). London: Sage.

Filion, N., & Rudolph, H. (1999). *Power, control and organisational learning. Discussion paper no. FS I 99 - 104*. Institut de sciences sociales Raymond-Ledrut.

Financial Times (2004, November). *Lex Column: Equity Research*.

Fiol, C. M. (1991). Managing culture as a competitive resource: An identity-based view of sustainable competitive advantage. *Journal of Management, 17*, 191-211.

Firestone, J. M., & McElroy, M. W. (2003). *Key Issues in the New Knowledge Management*. Burlington, MA: Butterworth-Heinemann.

Firth, D. R., & Swanson, E. B. (2002). *IT Research and Analysis Services: Surveying their Use and Usefulness*. Working Paper, May 2002, Los Angeles: The Anderson School at UCLA

Firth, D. R., & Swanson, E. B. (2005). How useful are IT research and analysis services? *Business Horizons, 48*, 151-159

Fisher, C. D., & Ashkanasy, N. M. (2000). The emerging role of emotions in working life: An introduction. *Journal of Organizational Behavior, 21*, 123-129.

Fisher, S. R., & White, M. A. (2000). Downsizing in a learning organization: are there hidden costs? *Academy of Management Review, 25*(1), 244-51.

Flood, P. C., Turner, T., Ramamoorthy, N., & Pearson, J. (2001). Causes and Consequences of Psychological Contracts among Knowledge Workers in the High Technology and Financial Services Industries. *International Journal of Human Resource Management, 12*(7), 1152-1165.

Floyd, S. W., & Wooldridge, B. (2000). *Building strategy from the middle: reconceptualizing the strategy process*. Sage.

Flusser, V. (1983/2000). *Towards a philosophy of photography*. London. Reaktion Books.

Flusser, V. (2002). *Writings*, Edited by Andreas Ströhl, trans. by Erik Eisel, Minneapolis & London: The University of Minnesota Press.

Flyvbjerg, B. (2001). Making Social Science Matter: Why Social Inquiry Fails and How It Can Succeed Again (Translated by Steven Sampson) Cambridge: Cambridge University Press.

Foerster, H. von (1991). Through the Eyes of the Other. In F. Steier (Ed.), *Research and Reflexivity* (pp. 21-28). London: Sage.

Fong, P. S. W. (2003). Knowledge- creation in multidisciplinary project teams: An empirical study of the processes and their dynamic interrelationships. *International Journal of Project Management, 21*(7), 479-86.

Fontana, A., & Frey, J. (1994). Interviewing. The art of science. In Denzin, N. & Lincoln, Y. (eds.) *Handbook of Qualitative Research* (pp. 361-376).Thousand Oaks, London, New Delhi: Sage.

Foray, D. (2004). *The Economics of Knowledge*. Cambridge: MIT Press.

Ford, C. M. (1996). A Theory of Individual Creative Action in Multiple Social Domains. *Academy of Management Review, 21*(4), 1112-1142.

Forsyth, P. & Danisiewicz, T. (1985). 'Toward a theory of professionalization', *Work and Occupation*, 12(1): 59-76.

Foss N., & Felin, T. (2006). Individuals and Organizations: Thoughts on a Micro-Foundations Project for Strategic

Management. *Research Methodology in Strategy and Management, 3*, 253-288.

Foss, N. (1996). Knowledge-Based Approaches to the Theory of the Firm: Some Critical Comments. *Organization Science, 7*(5), 470-476.

Foss, N. (2005). *Strategy, Economic Organization and the Knowledge Economy.* The Coordination of Firms and Resources. Oxford: Oxford University Press.

Foss, N. J. (1996). Critical Comments on Knowledge-based Theories of the Firm.*Organization Science*, 7(5), September-October, 519-523.

Foss, N. J., & Mahnke, V. (2003). Knowledge Management: What Can Organizational Economics Contribute? In M. Easterby-Smith & M. A. Lyles (Eds.), *Organizational Learning and Knowledge Management.* (pp. 78-103). London: Blackwell Publishing.

Foss, N., & Pedersen, T. (2002). Transferring knowledge in MNCs: the role of sources of subsidiary knowledge and organizational context. *Journal of International Management*, *8*(1), 49-67.

Foster, A., & Ford, N. (2003). Serendipity and information seeking: An empirical study *Journal of Documentation*, *59*(3), 321-340.

Fotache, M. (2005). Knowledge Management Between Fad and Relevance. *Information, 8*(2), 255-268.

Foucault, M. (1969/2002). *Archeologia wiedzy.* Warszawa: De Agostini.

Foucault, M. (1976/2000). *Historia seksualności (Histoire de la sexualité).* Warszawa: Czytelnik.

Fournier, V. (1999). 'The appeal to "professionalism" as a disciplinary mechanism', *The Sociological Review*, 47 (2): 280-307.

Franson, P. (1997). The Market Research Shell Game. Upside, March 1997, (pp. 78-82 & 106-116).

Freeman, C. (1982). *The Economics of Industrial Innovation.* 2nd edn, Frances Pinter, London.

Freidson, E. (1970). *Professional Dominance: the Social Structure of Medical Care.* New York: Atherton Press.

Freidson, E. (1994). *Professionalism reborn. Theory, prophecy and policy.* The University of Chicago Press.

Freidson, E. (2001). *Professionalism.* Cambridge: Polity Press

Freyens, B., & Martin, M. (2007). Multidisciplinary knowledge transfer in training multimedia projects. *Journal of European Industrial Training, 31*(9), 680-705.

Frost, T., & Zhou, C. (2005). R&D co-practice and 'reverse' knowledge integration in multinational firms. *Journal of International Business Studies, 36*(6), 676-687.

Furtado, C. (1967). *Development and Underdevelopment.* Berkeley, CA: University of California Press.

Futas, E., & Vidor, D. (1986). How Business Professionals Use Libraries. *Library Journal, 1*(11), 112-121.

Gabe, J. et al (2004). *Key Concepts in Medical Sociology.* London: Sage Publications.

Gabriel, Y. (2000). *Storytelling in Organizations: Facts, Fictions, and Fantasies.* Oxford University Press.

Galbraith, J. R. (1974). Organization design: An information processing view. *Interfaces, 3*, 28-36.

Gallagher, A., & Cates, C. (2004). Virtual reality training for the operating room and cardiac catheterisation laboratory. *The Lancet, 364*, 1538-1540.

Gane, N. (2005). Radical post-humanism. Friedrich Kittler and the primacy of technology. *Theory, Culture & Society, 22*(3), 25-41.

Garavelli, C., Gorgoglione, M., & Scozzi, B. (2004). Knowledge Management Strategy and Organization: a Perspective of Analysis. *Knowledge and Process Management, 11*(4), 273-282.

Garratt, B. (1990). *Creating a Learning Organisation: A Guide to Leadership, Learning and Development.* Cambridge, UK: Director Books.

Garson, B. (1989). *The Electronic Sweatshop: How Computers are Transforming the Office of the Future into the Factory of the Past.* New York : Simon & Schuster.

Gartner (1999). 1999 Worldwide Collaborative Workplace Software Program Market Definitions. *Gartner Dataquest Guide,* January 11, 1999.

Gartner Research note. (2001, June).

Gartner Research report. (2001, December).

Gartner Strategic Analysis report. (2001, May).

Garvin, D. A. (1993). Building a learning organization. *Harvard Business Review, 71*(4), 78-91.

Gasser, L. (1986). The Integration of Computing and Routine Work. ACM Transactions on Office Information Systems 4(3), 205-225.

Gavetti, G. (2005). Cognition and hierarchy: Rethinking the micro-foundations of capability development. *Organization Science, 16*, 599-617.

Gehani, R. R. (1996). Concurrent product development for fast track corporations. In S. J. Hart (Ed.), *New product development* (pp. 184-197). Dryden Press.

Gergen, K. J., & Thatchenkery, T. J. (1996). Organizational science as social construction. In the *Journal of Applied Behavioural Science*, *32*(4), 356-277.

Geroski, P. (1993). Technology and Markets. In P. Stoneman (Ed.), *Handbook of the Economics of Innovation and technical change*. London, Basil Blackwell.

Gerwin, D., & Barrowman, N. J. (2002). An evaluation of research on integrated product development. *Management Science, 47*(7), 938-953.

Gerwin, D., & Ferris, S. J. (2004). Organising New Product Development Projects in Strategic Alliances. *Organisation Science, 15*(1), 22-38.

Ghalayini, A., & Noble, J. (1996). The Changing Basis of Performance Measurement. *International Journal of Operations & Production Management, 16*(8): 63-80.

Ghemawat, P., Collis, D. J., Pisano, G. P., & Rivkin, J. W. (2001). *Strategy and the business landscape: core concepts.* Prentice Hall.

Gherardi, S. (1999). Learning as problem-driven or learning in the face of mystery. *Organization Studies, 20*(1), 101-124.

Gherardi, S., & Nocolini, D. (2001). The Sociological Foundations of Organizational Learning. In M. Dierkes, A. Berthoin Antal, J. Child, & I. Nonaka (Eds.), *Handbook of Organizational Learning and Knowledge.* Oxford: Oxford University Press.

Gherardi, S., Nicolini, D., & Odella, F. (1998). Toward a social understanding of how people learn in organizations: the notion of situated curriculum. *Management Learning, 29*, 273-97.

Ghoshal, S., & Bartlett, C. A. (1990). The multinational corporation as an interorganizational network. *Academy Management Review, 15*(4), 603-625.

Ghoshal, S., & Moran, P. (1996). Bad for Practice: A Critique of the Transaction Cost Theory. *Academy of Management Review, 21*(1), 13-47.

Gibbons, M., Nowotny, H., & Limoges, C. (1994). *The New Production of Knowledge the New Production of Knowledge: The Dynamics of Science and Research in Contemporary Societies.* London: Sage.

Gibson, C. B., & Birkinshaw, J. (2004). The antecedents, Consequences and Mediating Role of Organizational Ambidexterity. *Academy of Management Journal, 47*, 209-226.

Giddens, A. (1984). *The Constitution of Society. Outline of the Theory of Structuration.* Cambridge: Polity Press.

Gilbert, M., Caldwell, F., & Hayward, S. (2002). The Smart Enterprise Suite Is Coming: Do We Need It? *Gartner Article Top View, AV-16-2189*, May 10, 2002.

Gilbert, M., Phifer, G., Hayward, S., Latham, L., & Lheureux, B. (2002). Vignette to Buy Epicentric, Move Toward Smart Enterprise Suite. *Gartner FirstTake, FT-18-7281*, November 4, 2002.

Gill, J. H. (2000). *The tacit mode.* Albany, NY: State University of New York Press.

Gitelman, L. (1999). *Scripts, grooves, and writing machines. Representing technology in the Edison era.* Stanford: Stanford University Press.

Gitelman, L., & Pingree, G. B. (Eds.), (2003). *New media, 1940-1915.* Cambridge & London: The MIT Press.

Glaser, B. G., & Strauss, A. L. (1967). *The discovery of grounded theory: strategies for qualitative research.* Hawthorne, NY: Aldine de Gruyter.

Glasner, H. (1979) Professional Power and State Intervention in Medical Practice, *Journal of Sociology,* 15: 20-29

Gleadle, P. (1999). The interface between Finance and New Product Development: encouraging a climate of innovation. *Management Accounting* July/August, (pp. 24-25).

Gloor, P., Laubacher, R., Dynes, S., & Zhao, Y. (2003). Visualization of Communication Patterns in Collaborative Innovation Networks: Analysis of some W3C working groups. *Proc. ACM CIKM 2003*, New Orleans, November 5-6.

Gold, J., Thorpe, R., Woodall, J. & Sadler-Smith, E. (2007). Continuing professional development in the legal profession: a practice-based-learning perspective. *Management Learning, 38*(2), 235-250.

Goliński, J. (1998). *Making Natural Knowledge: Constructivism and the History of Science*. Cambridge, UK: Cambridge University Press.

Gombrich, E. H. (1960). *Art and Illusion.* New York: Pantheon Books, Bollinger Series xxxc. 5.

Gomes-Casseres, B. (2003). Competitive advantage in alliance constellations. *Strategic Organization, 1,* 327-335.

Goode, W. (1969). 'The theoretical limits of professionalization'. in A. Etzioni (ed). *The Semi-Professions and Their Organization.* New York: Free Press. 266-313.

Goodman, R. S., & Kruger, E. J. (1988). Data Dredging or Legitimate Research Method? Historiography and Its Potential for Management Research. *The Academy of Management Review, 13*(2), 315-325.

Goold M., & Luchs, K. (1993). Why diversify? Four decades of management thinking. *Academy of Management Executive,* 7(3), 7–25.

Gopalakrishnan, S., & Bierly, P. (2001). Analysing Innovation Adoption Using a Knowledge-based Approach. *Journal of Engineering and Technology Management, 18*, 107-130.

Gorman, P. (1995). Information Needs of Physicians. *Journal of the American Society for Information Science, 46*(10), 729-736.

Grandori, A. (1997). An Organizational Assessment of Inter-Firm Coordination Modes.*Organization Studies* (pp. 897-925).

Granovetter, M. (1985). Economic action and social structure: a theory of embeddedness. *American Journal of Sociology, 91*, 481-510.

Grant, J., Chambers, E., & Jackson, G. (Eds) (1999). *The Good CPD Guide: A Practical Guide to Managed CPD.* Surrey: Reed Business Information.

Grant, R. (1991). The resource-based theory of competitive advantage: implications for strategy formulation. *California Management Review, 33*(3), 114-135.

Grant, R. (1996). Prospering in Dynamically-Competitive Environments: Organizational Capability as Knowledge Integration. *Organization Science,* 7(4), 375-387.

Grant, R. (1996). Toward a knowledge-based theory of the firm. *Strategic Management Journal, 17*(winter special issue), 109-122.

Grant, R. M. (1991). The resource-based theory of competitive advantage: implications for strategy formulation. *California Management Review, 33*(3), 114-35.

Grant, R. M. (1996). Prospering in Dynamically-competitive Environments: Organizational Capability as Knowledge Integration. *Organization Science*, 7(4), July-August, 375-387.

Grant, R. M. (1996). Toward a knowledge based theory of the firm. *Strategic Management Journal, 17*,109-122

Grant, R. M. (1997). The Knowledge-based View of the Firm: Implications for Management Practice. *Long Range Planning, 30*(3), 450-454.

Grant, R. M. (2002). *Contemporary Strategy Analysis. Concepts, Techniques and Applications (Fourth Edition).* Boston: MA, Blackwell Publishers.

Grant, R. M., & Baden-Fuller, C. (2004). A Knowledge Accessing Theory of Strategic Alliances. *Journal of Management Studies, 41*(1), 61-79.

Gray, J. H., & Densten, I. L. (2006). Towards an integrative model of organizational culture and knowledge management. *International Journal of Organizational Behavior, 9*(2), 594-603.

Greenwood, D. (1985). *The Taming of Evolution: The Persistence of Nonevolutionary Views in the Study of Humans.* Ithaca, Cornell University Press.

Greenwood, D. (n.d.). *Why Universities are Not Learning Organizations and What Can Be Done About It: An International Action Research Approach to Higher Education Reform.* unpublished manuscript.

Greenwood, D. J., & Levin, M. (1998). *Introduction to action research: social research for social change.* Thousand Oaks, Calif.: Sage Publications.

Greenwood, D. J., González Santos, J. L., & Cantón, J. (1991). *Industrial democracy as process: participatory action research in the Fagor Cooperative Group of Mondragón.* Assen/Maastricht-Stockholm: Van Gorcum Arbetslivscentrum.

Greenwood, D., & Levin, M. (2006). Introduction to Action Research. London: Sage.

Greenwood, D., & Levin, M. (2007). *Introduction to Action Research: Social Research for Social Change*, 2nd edition. Thousand Oaks, CA: Sage Publications.

Greenwood, D., *et al.* (1992), *Industrial Democracy as Process: Participatory Action Research in the Fagor Cooperative Group of Mondragón.* Assen-Maastricht: Van Gorcum.

Greenwood, E. (1962). Attributes of a profession. In S. Nosow and W. H. Form (Eds.), *Man, Work, and Society,* New York: Basic Books, 206-218.

Greenwood, R., Hinings, C. R., & Brown, J. (1990). P2 Form' strategic management: Corporate practices in professional partnerships. *Academy of Management Journal, 33*(4), 725-755.

Greffe, X. (2004). Artistic work in the digital age. *Journal of Arts Management, Law, and Society, 34*(1), 79-94.

Greimas, A. J., & Courtés, J. (1982). *Semiotics and Language. An Analytical Dictionary.* Bloomington, IN: Indiana University Press.

Greiner, L. (1972). Evolution and Revolution as Organizations Grow. *Harvard Business Review* (July–August), 37-46.

Griffin, A. (1997). PDMA research on new product development practices. *Journal of Product Innovation Management, 14*(6), 429-458.

Grisham, G. (2006). Metaphor, poetry, story telling and cross-cultural leadership. *Management Decision, 44*(4), 486-503.

Grisoni, L. (2006). *Poetic bridges between Knowledge and Practice.* Art of Management Conference Krakow, Poland 5-8 September 2006.

Grisoni, L. (2008). Poetry. In M. Broussine (Ed.), *Creative methods in Organizational Research* (pp. 108-127). London: Sage publications.

Grisoni, L., & Kirk P. (2006). Voice, Verse and Va va voom: Iluminating Management processes through Poetry. *Management Decision, 44*(4), 512 -525.

Guadamillas, F., & Donate, M. (2006). Conocimiento organizativo, innovación y crecimiento empresarial: el caso del Grupo Tecnobit. *Universia Business Review, 12*, 50-65.

Gulati, R. (1995). Does familiarity breed trust? The implications of repeated ties for contractual choice in alliances. *Academy of Management Journal, 38*, 85-112.

Gulati, R. (1998). Alliances and networks. *Strategic Management Journal, Special Issue, 19*, 293-318.

Gulati, R. (1999). Network location and learning: The influence of network resources and firm capabilities on alliance formation. *Strategic Management Journal, 20*, 397-421.

Guns, W., & Välikangas, L. (1998). Rethinking knowledge work: creating value through idiosyncratic knowledge. *Journal of Knowledge Management, 1*(4), 287-293.

Gupta, A., & Govindarajan, V. (1991). Knowledge flows and the structure of control within multinational corporations. *Academy of Management Review, 16*(4), 768-792.

Gupta, A., Smith, K. G., & Shalley, C. E. (2006). The Interplay between Exploration and Exploitation. *Academy of Management Journal, 49*(4), 693-706.

Gupta, O., & Roos, G. (2001). Mergers and acquisitions through an intellectual capital perspective. *Journal of Intellectual Capital*, 2(3), 297-309.

Gurteen, D. (1998). Knowledge, Creativity, and Innovation. *Journal of Knowledge Management, 2*(1), 5-13.

Guthrie, J., & Ricceri, F. (2002). *Quantify Intellectual Capital: Measuring and Reporting to Demonstrate Value of KM to Stakeholders.* Paper presented at KM Australia: Building and improving on knowledge management initiative for commercial proficiency conference, Merchant Court Hotel, Sydney, 4 December.

Guthrie, J., Petty, R., & Ricceri, F. (2007). *Intellectual Capital Reporting: Lessons from Hong Kong and Australia.* Research Monograph, The Institute of Chartered Accountants of Scotland, Edinburgh.

Haas, M. R., & Hansen, M. T. (2005). When Using Knowledge Can Hurt Performance: The Value of Organizational Capabilities in a Management Consulting Company. *Strategic Management Journal, 26*, 1-24.

Haendly, M. (2002). *SAP Exchange Infrastructure. Enabling Process-Centric Collaboration.* Presentation at SAPPHIRE, Lisbon, September 4-6, 2002, http://www.sap.com/community/events/2002_lisbon/pdf/d2_t12_17.pdf, access date 3.10.2003.

Haines, L. (2006). Catholic Church bemoans call centre Bahanalia Indian 'dens of iniquity'. Monday 9th October 2006. Retrieved on 28 August, 2008 from http://www.theregister.co.uk/2006/10/09/dens_of_iniquity/

Håkansson, H. (1987). *Industrial Technological Development: A Network Approach.* London: Croom Helm.

Håkansson, H., & Lundgren, A. (1995). Industrial Networks and Technological Innovation. In K. Möller & D. Wilson (Eds.), *Business Marketing: An Interaction and Network Perspective.* London: Kluwer Academic Publishers.

Halal, W. E. (2005). Knowledge management: how to foster creation and flow. *Handbook of Business Strategy, 6*(1), 297-301.

Hall, R. (1992). The strategic analysis of intangible resources. *Strategic Management Journal, 13*, 135-144.

Hall, R. (1993). A framework linking intangible resources and capabilities to sustainable competitive advantage. *Strategic Management Journal*, 14(8), 607-618.

Hambrick, D. C.., & Mason, P. A. (1984). Upper echelons. The organization as a reflection of its top managers. *Academy of Management Review, 9*, 193-206,

Hamel, G. (1991). Competition for competence and interpartner learning with international strategic alliances. *Strategic Management Journal,* (pp. 83-103).

Hamel, G., & Prahalad (1994). *Competing for the future.* Harvard Business School Press.

Hamel, G., & Prahalad, C. K. (1989). Strategic Intent. *Harvard Business Review, 67*, May-June, 63-78.

Hamel, J., Dufour, S., & Fortin, D. (1993). *Case study methods.* Newbury Park: SAGE Publications.

Hammer, M., & Champy, T. (1993). Reengineering the Corporation: a manifesto for business revolutions. New York: Nicolas Brealey.

Hammersley, M., & Atkinson, P. (1995). Ethnography: principles in practice (2nd ed.). London, New York: Routledge.

Hanlon, G. (1998). Professionalism as enterprise: service class politics and the redefinition of professionalism. *Sociology, 32*(1), 43-63.

Hansen, M. (1999). The search-transfer problem: the role of weak ties in sharing knowledge across organization subunits. *Administrative Science Quarterly, 44*(1), 82-11.

Hansen, M. T., Mors, M. L., Løvås, B. (2005). Knowledge Sharing in Organizations: Multiple Networks, Multiple Phases. *Academy of Management Journal, 48*(5), 776-793.

Hansen, M. T., Nohria, N., & Tierney, T. (1999). What's Your Strategy for Managing Knowledge. *Harvard Business Review*, March-April, (pp. 106-116).

Hansen, Mark B. N. (2006). Media theory. *Theory, Culture & Society, 23*(2-3), 297-306.

Haraway, D. J. (1991). *Semians, Cyborgs, and Women: The Reinvention of Nature*. London: Free Association Books.

Haraway, D. J. (2008). *When species meet*. Minneapolis: University of Minnesota Press.

Harborne, P., & Johne, A. (2003). Creating a project climate for successful product innovation. *European Journal of Innovation Management, 6*(2), 118-133.

Harris, K. (2003). Success or Failure in KM, CM, Collaboration and E-Learning. *Gartner Article Top View, AV-19-2417*, February 11, 2003.

Harris, K., & Jacobs, J. (2000). Knowledge Management vs. Information Management. *Gartner Commentary, COM-11-9460*, November 3, 2000.

Harris, K., Kolsky, E., & Lundy, J. (2003). The Case for Knowledge Management in CRM. *Gartner Article Top View, AV-19-5592*, April 21, 2003

Harris-Jenkins, G. (1970). 'Professionals in Organizations', in J.A Jackson (ed). *Professions and Professionalization*. Cambridge: Cambridge University Press. 53-107

Harrison, S., & Dourish, P. (1996). Re-Placing Space: The Roles of Place and Space in Collaboration Systems. In Proceedings of the CSCW 96, New York: ACM Press.

Hart, S. J. (1995). Where we've been and where we're going in new product development research. In M. Bruce & W. G. Biemens (Eds.), *Product development – Meeting the challenge of the design-marketing interface* (pp. 13-43). Chichester, UK: John Wiley and Sons.

Hart, S. J. (1996). *New Product Development: A Reader*. The Dryden Press, Harcourt Brace and Company Limited.

Hart, S. J., & Baker, M. J. (1996). The multiple convergent processing model of new product development. In S. J. Hart (Ed.), *New Product Development* (pp 151-166). London: TheDryden Press.

Hart, S. J., Hutlink, E., Tzokas, N., & Commandeur, H. (2003). Industrial Companies' Evaluation Criteria in new Product Development gates. *Journal of Product Innovation Management, 20*(1), 22-36.

Hart, S., & Hogg, G. (1998). Relationship marketing in corporate legal services. *The Service Industries Journal, 18*(1), 55-69.

Hartley, J. F. (1994). Case studies in organisational research. In C. Cassel & G. Symon, (Eds.), *Qualitative Methods in Organisational Research: A Practical Guide*. London: Sage.

Harvey, D. (1989). *The conditions of post modernity*. Oxford: Basil Blackwell.

Harvey, D. (1999). *The Limits to Capital*. London: Verso.

Harvie, D. (2006). Value production and struggle in the classroom: Teachers within, against and beyond capital. *Capital & Class, 88*, 1-32.

Hatch, M. J. (1997/2002). *Teoria organizacji*. Warszawa: PWN.

Hatch, M. J., Kostera, M., & Kozminski, A. (2005). *The Three Faces of Leadership: Manager, Artist, Priest.* Oxford: Blackwell Publishing

Hatch, N. W., & Dyer, J. H. (2004). Human Capital and Learning as a Source of Sustainable Competitive Advantage. *Strategic Management Journal, 25*, 1155–1178.

Havelok, E. A. (n.d.). *The Muse Learns to Write; Reflections on Orality and Literacy from Antiquity to the Present.* New Haven, USA: Yale University Press.

Hayek, F. A. (1945). The use of knowledge in society. *The American Economic Review*, 35(September), 519-530.

Hayles, N. K. (1999). *How we became posthuman: Virtual bodies in cybernetics, literature, and informatics.* Chicago & London: The University of Chicago Press.

Hayles, N. K. (2002). *Writing machines.* Cambridge & London: The MIT Press.

Hayles, N. K. (2005). *My mother was a computer: Digital subjects and literary texts.* Chicago & London: The University of Chicago Press.

Hayward, S., & Austin, T. (2001). IBM to Integrate Lotus More Closely. *Gartner FirstTake, FT-12-8860*, January 12, 2001

Hayward, S., Gilbert, M., Phifer, G., & Caldwell, F. (2003). The Smart Enterprise Suite Magic Quadrant for 2003. *Gartner Research Note M-19-3949*, March 4, 2003

Hayward, S., Graff, J., & Grey, M. (2002). Oracle Has a Chance to Challenge in the Collaboration Market. *Gartner FirstTake, FT-17-4164*, July 12, 2002

Hayward, S., Shegda, K., Logan, D., & Gilbert, M. (2002). Documentum Aims for Smart Enterprise Suite with eRoom Deal. *Gartner FirstTake, FT-18-4537*, October 8, 2002

Hechter, M. (1987). *Principles of Group Solidarity.* Berkeley, Los Angeles and London: University of California Press.

Hedberg, B. (1981). How organizations learn and unlearn. In P. C. Nystrom & W. H. Starbuck (Eds.), *Handbook of Organizational Design* (pp. 3-27). Oxford: Oxford University Press.

Hedgecoe, A., & Martin, P. (2003). The drugs don't work: Expectations and the shaping of pharmacogenetics. *Social Studies of Science, 33*(3), 327-364.

Hedlund, G. (1986). The hypermodern MNC-A heterarchy? *Human Resource Management, 25*(1), 9-35.

Hedlund, G. (1994). A Model of Knowledge Management and the N-form Corporation. *Strategic Management Journal, 15*(5), 73-90.

Heer, J., & Boyd, D. (2005). *Vizster: Visualizing Online Social Networks. In InfoVis 2005, IEEE Symposium on Information Visualization.*

Heide, J. B., & John, G. (1995). Measurement issues in research on interfirm relations. In K. Möller & D. Wilson (Eds.), *Business Marketing: An interaction and network perspective* (pp. 531-554). Boston: Kluwer Academic Publishing.

Heidegger, M. (1977). *The Question Concerning Technology and Other Essays.* W. Lovitt (transl.). New York: Harper & Low.

Heimeriks, K. H.., & Duysters, G. (2003). Experience and capabilities to explain alliance performance: Substitutes or complements? *Eindhoven Centre for Innovation Studies (ECIS)*, The Netherlands.

Heimeriks, K. H.., & Duysters, G. (2007). Alliance capability as a mediator between experience and alliance performance: An empirical investigation into the alliance capability process. *Journal of Management Studies, 44*, 25-49.

Helfat, C. E. (2000). Guest editor's introduction to the special issue: The evolution of firms capabilities. *Strategic Management Journal, 21*, 955-960.

Helfat, C. E.., & Peteraf, M. A. (2003). The dynamic resource-based view: Capability lifecycles. *Strategic Management Journal, 24*, 997-1010.

Helleloid, D., & Simonin, B. (1994). Organizational learning and a firm's core competence. In G. Hamel &

A. Heene (Eds.), *Competence-based competition*, (pp. 213-239). Wiley, Chichester.

Henderson, R. M., & Cockburn, I. (1994). Measuring competence? Exploring firm effects in pharmaceutical research. *Strategic Management Journal, 15*(Winter Special Issue), 63-84.

Hendriks, P., & Sousa, C. (2006). Motivation for Knowledge Work." In David G. Schwartz (Ed.) *Encyclopedia of Knowledge Management*. Hershey, PA: Idea Group Publishing, (pp. 656-664).

Henriksson, L. (2006). 'Understanding Professional Projects in Welfare Service Work: Revival of Old Professionalism?', *Gender, Work and Organization,* 13 (2): 174-192.

Hepsø, V. (2006). When are we going to address organizational robustness and collaboration as something else than a residual factor? Society of Petroleum Engineers-paper SPE-100712.

Hepsø, V., & Botnevik, R. (n.d.). *Improved Crane Operations and Competence Development in a Community of Practice through CSCW and CSCL.* unpublished manuscript.

Hermans, J. A. (1999). Catch the knowledge management wave. *Library Journal, 124*(14), 161-63.

Herner, ., & Herner, M. (1967). Information needs and uses in science and technology. *Annual Review of Science and technology, 2*, 1-34.

Hibbard, J. (1997). Search for Differentiation. *InformationWeek*, October 6, 68 and 72.

Hill, C., & Deeds, D. (1996). The importance of industry structure for the determination of firm profitability: a neo-Austrian perspective. *Journal of Management, 33*(4), 429-451.

Himmelfarb, P. A. (1992). *Survival of the fittest – New product development during the 90's.* Englewood Cliffs, NJ, USA: Prentice-Hall International.

Hinings, C. R., Greenwood, R., & Cooper, D. (1999). The Dynamics of Change in Large Accounting Firms. In D. M. Brock, M. J. Powell & C. R. Hinings (Eds.), *Restructuring the Professional Organization.* London: Routledge.

Hirschhorn, L. (1997). *Reworking Authority: Leading and Following in the Post-Modern Organization.* Cambridge: MIT Press.

Hitt, M. A., Bierman, L., Shimizu, K., & Kochhar, R. (2001). Direct and moderating effects of human capital on strategy and performance in professional service firms: A resource-based perspective. *The Academy of Management Journal, 44,* 13-28.

Hitt, M. A., Ireland, R. D., & Santoro, M. D. (2004). Developing and Managing Strategic Alliances, Building Social Capital and Creating Value. In A. Ghobadian *et al.* (Eds.), *Strategy and Performance: Achieving Competitive Advantage in the Global Marketplace.* New York: Palgrave, (pp. 1-14).

Hjorth, D. (2005). Organizational entrepreneurship with de Certeau on creating heterotopias (or spaces for play). *Journal of Management Inquiry, 14*(4), 386-398.

Hoadley, C. M., & Kilner, P. G. (2005). Using technology to transform communities of practice into knowledge-building communities. *ACM SIGGROUP Bulletin, 25*(1), 31-40.

Hoang, H. T.., & Rothaermel, F. T. (2005). The effect of general and partner-specific alliance experience on joint R&D project performance. *Academy of Management Journal, 48*, 332-45.

Hochschild, A. R. (1983). *The managed heart. Commercialization of human feeling.* Berkley, Los Angeles, London: University of California Press.

Hochshild, A. R. (1997). *The Time Bind: When Work Becomes Home and Home Becomes Work.* New York: Metropolitan.

Hoecht, A. (2004). Control in collaborative research and technology development. A case study in the chemical industry. *Journal of Managerial Psychology, 19*(3), 218-234.

Hoecht, A., & Trott, P. (1999). Trust, risk and control in the management of collaborative technology development. *International Journal of Innovation Management, 3*(1), 257-270.

Hollins, W., & Pugh, S. (1990). *Successful product design*. London, UK: Butterworth.

Holman, D. (2003). 'Call centres', in Holman D., Wall, C., Sparrow, C., and Howard, A. (eds). *The new work place: A guide to the human impact of modern working practices*. Chichester, UK: Wiley.

Holt, K., Geschka, H., & Peterlongo, G. (1984). *Need assessment – A key to user orientated product innovation*. John Wiley and Sons Ltd.

Hölttä, P. (2000). *Piimäki 2000: Laajakaistaisen alueverkon uudet palvelut. tuotekehityshakemuksen liite 2*. Tutkimus- ja kehitysprojektisuunnitelma TEKESin 'Tietoliikenteellä maailmalle' teknologiaohjelmaan. HPY Tutkimuskeskus. (Unpublished reference).

Hong, J., & Ståhle, P. (2005). The Coevolution of Knowledge and Competence Management. *Int. J. Management Concepts and Philosophy, 1*(2).

Höpfl, H. (1995). Organizational rhetoric and the threat of ambivalence. *Studies in Cultures, Organizations and Societies, 1*(2), 175-187.

Höpfl, H. (1995). Rhetoric and the threat of ambivalence. *Studies in Cultures, Organizations and Societies, 1*(2), 175-187.

Hopwood, A. G. (1976). *Accounting and Human Behavior*. Englewood Cliffs: NJ: Prentice Hall..

Horning, S. S. (2004). Engineering the performance: Recording engineers, tacit knowledge and the art of controlling sound. *Social Studies of Science, 34*(5), 703-731.

Hoskisson, R., Hitt, M., Wan, W., & Yiu. D. (1999). Theory and research in strategic management: swings of a pendulum. *Journal of Management, 25*(3), 417-456.

Hossfeld, K. (1988). *Divisions of labor, divisions of lives: Immigrant women workers in Silicon Valley*. Dissertation, University of California at Santa Cruz.

Houlihan, M. (2000). 'Eyes Wide Shut? Querying the Depth of Call Centre Learning', *Journal of European Industrial Training*, 24(2/3/4): 228-40.

http://www.khaleejtimes.com/DisplayArticle.asp?xfile=data/todaysfeatures/2006/November/todaysfeatures_November28.xml&section=todaysfeatures

Huber, G. P. (1991). Organizational learning: The contributing processes and the literatures. *Organization Science, 2*, 88-115.

Hughes, E. (1963). 'Professions', *Daedalus*, 92(Fall): 655-668.

Hultink, E. J., & Hart, S. (1998). The world's path to the better mousetrap: myth or reality? An empirical investigation into the launch strategies of high and low advantage new products. *European Journal of Innovation Management, 1*(3), 106-121.

Humphrey, J., & Schmitz, H. (1996). *Trust in economic development*. Brighton, University of Sussex: IDS paper 355.

Hunt, B. (May 15, 2002). Multimedia Messaging: Operators hope for Many Happy Returns. *Financial Times*.

Huplic, V., Pouloudi, A., & Rzevski, G. (2002). Towards an Integrated Approach to Knowledge Management: 'Hard', 'Soft' and 'Abstract' Issues. *Knowledge and Process Management, 9*(2), 90-102.

Husted, K., & Michailova, S. (2002). Diagnosing and Fighting Knowledge-sharing Hostility. *Organizational Dynamics 31*(1), 60-73.

Iansiti, M., & Clark, K. B. (1994). Integration and Dynamic Capability: Evidence from Product Development in Automobiles and Mainframe Computers. *Industrial and Corporate Change, 3*(3).

Ingwersen, P. (1996). Cognitive perspectives of information retrieval interaction: elements of a cognitive IR theory. *Journal of Documentation, 51*, 2-50.

Inzerille, G., & Rosen, M. (1983). Culture and organizational control. *Business Research, 17*, 281-292.

Ireland, R. D., Hitt, M. A.., & Vaidyanath, D. (2002). Alliance managers as a source of competitive advantage. *Journal of Management, 28*, 413-447.

Irvine, P. J. (2004). Analysts' Forecasts and Brokerage-Firm Trading. *The Accounting Review, 79*(1), 125-149.

Iscnson, R. (1968). *Technology in retrospect and critical events in science (Project Traces).* Chicago: Illinois Institute of Technology/National Science Foundation.

Itami, H., & Roehl, T. W. (1987). *Mobilizing Invisible Assets*. Cambridge, MA: Harvard University Press.

Ittner, C. D., & Larker, D. F. (1998). Innovation in performance measurement: trends and research implications. *Journal of Management Accounting Research*, 10, 205-238.

Ives, W., Torrey, B., & Gordon, C. (1998). Knowledge management: an emerging discipline with a long history. *Journal of Knowledge Management, 1*, 269-74.

Jackall, R. (1988). *Moral Mazes: The World of Corporate Managers.* New York: Oxford University Press

Jacobs, J. A., & Gerson, K. (2001). Overworked Individuals or Overworked Families? *Work and Occupations, 28*(1), 40-63.

Jacques, R. (2000). Theorizing knowledge as work: The need for a 'knowledge theory of value. In C. Pritchard, R. Hull, M. Chumer & H. Willmott (Eds.), *Managing Knowledge: Critical Investigations of Work and Learning*. Basingstoke: Macmillan.

Jaggar, A. M. (1989). Love and knowledge: Emotion in feminist epistemology. In A. M. Jaggar & S. R. Bordo (Eds.), *Gender/body/knowledge: Feminist reconstructions of being and knowing.* New Brunswick, NJ: Rutgers University Press.

James, J., & Weir, D. (2006). Special issue on poetry, organization, emotions, management and enterprise – POEME. *Management Decision, 44*(4).

Janz, B. D., Colquitt, J. A., & Noe, R. A. (1997). Knowledge Worker Team Effectiveness: The Role of Autonomy, Interdependence, team Development, and Contextual Support Variables. *Personnel Psychology, 50*(4).

Jarvelin, K., & Wilson, T. D. (2003). On conceptual models for information seeking and retrieval research. *Information Research, 9*(1). Retrieved on 10 Oct 2004 from http://informationr.net

Jaworski, J., & Scharmer, C. O. (2000). *Leadership in the Digital Economy: Sensing and Seizing Emerging Futures.* http://www.ottoscharmer.com/LeadingDigitalEconomy.pdf.

Jaynes, J. (1976, reprinted 1991). *The Origin of Consciousness in the breakdown of the Bicameral Mind.* London: Penguin.

Jemielniak, D., & Kociatkiewicz, J. (Eds.) (2008). *Management Practices in High-Tech Environments.* Hershey: Information Science Reference.

Jenkins, S., Forbes, S., Durrani, T. S., & Banerjee, S. K. (1997). Managing the product development process [Part I: An assessment]. *International Journal of Technology Management, 13*(4), 359-378.

Jennings, D. (1997). Strategic guidelines for outsourcing decisions. *Journal of Strategic Change, 6*, 85-96.

Jobber, D. (1998). *Principles and Practice of Marketing,* Second Edition. McGraw-Hill Publishing Company, International Editions.

Joerges, B., & Czarniawska, B. (1998). The question of technology, or how organizations inscribe the world. *Organization Studies*, 19(3), 363-385.

Johannessen, J., Olaisen, J., & Olsen, B. (2001). Management of tacit knowledge: the importance of tacit knowledge, the danger of information technology, and what to do about it. *International Journal of Information Management, 21*(1), 3-20.

Johnson, G., Melin, I.., & Whittington, R. (2003). Guest Editors introduction: Micro strategy and strategizing: Towards an activity-based view. *Journal of Management Studies, 40*, 3-22.

Johnson, T. (1972). *Professions and Power.* London: Macmillan

Jones, A. M., & Hendry, C. (1992). *The learning organization: a review of literature and practice*. Unpublished report, The HRD Partnership, London.

Jones, A. M., & Hendry, C. (1994). The learning organization: adult learning and organizational transformation. *British Journal of Management, 5,* 153-62.

Jones, G. R. (2004). *Organizational theory, design, and change: Text and cases* (4th Eds.). Pearson Education, Inc.

Jones, M. O., Moore, M. D., & Snyder, R. C. (1988). *Inside Organizations Understanding the Human dimension.* New York: Sage publications.

Jones, R. A. (2004). *Soft machines: Nanotechnology and life*. Oxford & New York: Oxford University Press.

Juntunen, A. (2005). *The emergence of a new business through collaborative networks: a longitudinal study in the ICT sector.* Acta Universitatis Oeconomicae Helsingiensis. Printed in HSEPrint. A-series, no 256, ISSN 1237-556X. ISBN: 951-791-957-3/1.

Juntunen, A. (2008). Data Warehouse in the Finnish Police - A Case Study, In John Wang (Ed.) *Encyclopedia of Data Warehousing and Mining: 2nd Edition.* Idea Group Publishing. Forthcoming.

Kakabadse, A., & Kakabadse, N. (2002). Trends in outsourcing. *European Management journal, 20*(2), 189-198.

Kale, P., Dyer, J. H.., & Singh, H. (2002). Alliance capability, stock market response, and long-term alliance success: The role of the alliance function. *Strategic Management Journal, 23*, 747-767.

Kale, P., Singh, H.., & Perlmutter, H. (2000). Learning and protection of proprietary assets in strategic alliances: Building relational capital. *Strategic Management Journal, 21*, 217-237.

Kale, P.., & Singh, H. (1999). *Alliance capability and success: A knowledge-based approach.* Paper presented at the Academy of Management Annual Meeting, Chicago, IL.

Kale, P.., & Singh, H. (2007). Building firm capabilities through learning: The role of the alliance learning process in alliance capability and firm-level alliance success. *Strategic Management Journal, 28*, 981-1000.

Kallinikos, J. (1995). The archi-tecture of the invisible: Technology is representation. *Organizations, 2*(1), 117-140.

Kallinikos, J. (1996). *Organizations in an age of information.* Lund: Academia Adacta.

Kallinikos, J. (1998). Organized complexity: Posthumanist remarks on the technologizing of intelligence. *Organization, 5*(3), 371-396.

Kalyanaram, G., & Krishnan, V. (1997). Deliberate product definition: Customising the product definition process. *Journal of Marketing Research, 34*(2), 276-286.

Kandemir,D., Ghauri, P.., Cavusgil, T. (2002). The strategic role of organizational learning in relationship quality in strategic alliances. In: Contractor, F., & P.Lorange (Eds.), Cooperative strategies, Amsterdam, Elsevier, (pp. 799-828).

Kanter, R. (1983). *The Changemasters.* New York: Simon and Schuster.

Kanter, R. M. (1984). *The change masters: Corporate Entrepreneurs at Work.* London, Routledge.

Kanter, R. M. (1995). *When giants learn to dance.* New York: Simon and Schuster.

Kanter, R. M. (1998). When a thousand flowers bloom: structural, collective, and social conditions for innovation in organisation. *Research in Organisational Behaviour, 10*, 169-211.

Kaplan, R. (1986). Accounting Lag: The Obsolescence of Cost Accounting Systems. *California Management Review, 28*(2):174-199.

Kaplan, R. S., & Norton, D. P. (1993). Putting the Balanced Scorecard to Work', *Harvard Business Review.*

Kaplan, R. S., & Norton, D. P. (1993). The Balanced Scorecard – Measures That Drive Performance. *Harvard Business Review.*

Kaplan, R., & Norton, D. (1992). The Balanced Scorecard: Measures that Drive Performance. *Harvard Business Review* Jan-Feb, (pp. 71-79).

Karreman, D., & Alvesson, M. (2004). *Cages in Tandem: Management Control, Social Identity, and Identification in a Knowledge-Intensive Firm Organization. 11*(1), 149 - 175.

Kasvi, J. J. J., Vartiainen, M., & Halikari, M. (2003). Managing knowledge and knowledge competences in projects and project organisations. *International Journal of Project Management, 21*(3), 571-82.

Katz, R. (1997). *The human side of managing technological innovation*. New York: Oxford University Press.

Kay, L. E. (2000). *Who wrote the book of life? A history of the genetic code*. Stanford & London: Stanford University Press.

Keating, E., Oliva, R., Repenning, N., Rockart, S., & Sterman, J. (1999). Overcoming the Improvement Paradox. *European Management Journal, 17*(2), 120-134.

Keeney, M., & Richard, F. (1993). *Beyond Mass Production*: Oxford University Press.

Kellner, D. (1995). *Media culture: Cultural studies, identity and politics between the modern and the post-modern*. London & New York: Routledge.

Kelloway, E., & Barling, J. (2000). Knowledge Work as Organizational Behavior. *International Journal of Management Reviews, 2*(3), 287-304.

Kelly, P., & Kranzberg, M. (Eds.) (1978). *Technological Innovation: A Critical Review of Current Knowledge.* San Francisco: San Francisco Press.

Kennerley, M., & Neely, A. (2003). Measuring Performance in a Changing Business Environment. *International Journal of Operations & Production Management, 23*(3): 213-229.

Kessler, E. H., Bierly, P. E., & Gopalakrishnan S. (2000). Internal vs. External Learning in New Product Development: Effects on Speed, Cost and Competitive Advantage. *R& D Management, 30*(3), 213-223.

Kesteloot, L. (2003). *Why Software is Late?* http://www.teamten.com/lawrence/writings/late_software.html. (accessed 01.10.2008).

Kets de Vries, M. F. R., & Miller, D. (1984). *The Neurotic organization.* San Francisco, CA: Jossey Bass.

Kettunen, J. (2005). Implementation of strategies in continuing education. *The International Journal of Educational Management, 19*(3), 207-217.

Kettunen, J. (2006). Strategies for the cooperation of educational institutions and companies in mechanical engineering. *The International Journal of Educational Management, 20*(1), 19-28.

Kettunen, J. (2007). Strategies of Regional Development. In A. Ghosh & G. Banerjee (Eds.), *Strategic Management for Firms in Developing Countries* (pp. 520-530). New Delhi: Allied Publishers.

Kettunen, J. (2007). The Strategic Evaluation of Academic Libraries. *Library Hi Tech, 25*(3), 409-421.

Khaleej Times Online (2006). Sex life of call-centre workers fascinates India. 13 November 2006. Retrieved on 28 August, 2008 from

Khanna, T. (1998). The scope of alliances. *Organization Science, 9*, 340-355.

Khurana, R. et al (2005). 'Is Business Management a Profession?' HBS Working Knowledge, http://hbswk.hbs.edu/item/4650.html

Kianto, A. (2007). What do we really mean by dynamic intellectual capital? *International Journal of Learning and Intellectual Capital, 4*(4), 342-356.

Kianto, A. (2008). Development and validation of a survey instrument for measuring organizational renewal capability. *International Journal of Technology Management, 42*(1/2): 69-88.

Kickert, W. J. M. (1993). Autopoiesis and the Science of (Public) Administration; Essence, Sense and Nonsense. In *Organisation Studies*, 14(2), 261-278.

Kiechel III, W. (1990). The organization that learns. *Fortune, 121*(6), 75-7.

Kieser, A. (1996). Moden & Mythen des Organisierens. *Die Betriebswirtschaft, 56*(1), 21-39.

Kim, C. W., & Mauborgne, R. (1999). Strategy, Value Innovation, and the Knowledge Economy. *Sloan Management Review, 40*(3), 41-54.

Kim, D. H. (1993). The link between individual and organizational learning. *Sloan Management Review, 35,* 37-50.

King, A. W., & Zeithaml, C. P. (2001). Competencies and firm performance: examining the causal ambiguity paradox. *Strategic Management Journal, 22,* 75-99.

Kirp, D. (2003). *Shakespeare, Einstein, and the Bottom Line: The Marketing of Higher Education.* Cambridge: Harvard University Press.

Kirton, M. (1980). Adaptors and innovators in organisations. *Human Relations, 3*(4), 213-224.

Kittler, F. (1990). *Discourse networks 1800/1900,* trans. by Michael Metteer & Chris Cullens, Stanford: Stanford University Press.

Kittler, F. (1999). *Gramophone, film, typewriter,* trans. by Geoffrey Winthrop-Young and Michael Wutz, Stanford: Stanford University Press.

Kittler, F. A. (1997). *Essays. Literature, media, information systems.* Ed. by John Johnston, Amsterdam: G+B Arts International.

Klegon, D. (1978). 'The Sociology of Professions- An Emerging Perspective', *Sociology of Work and Occupation,* 5(3): 259-283.

Klemp, G. O. Jr. (Ed.) (1980). *The Assessment of Occupational Competence.* Washington, DC: National Institute of Education.

Klincewicz, K. (2004). *Management Fashions: Turning Best-selling Ideas into Objects And Institutions.* New Brunswick, N.J.: Transaction Publishers.

Knights, D., & Willmott, H. (1999). *Management Lives: Power and Identity in Work Organisations.* London, Sage

Knowledge Management (1997). 1997 Knowledge Management Insight Report – Summary, PC Week, August 18, http://ntsrv2000.educ.ualberta.ca/nethowto/urlsubmit/knowledge/hype/delphi%20survey.htm, access date 20.08.2003

Kock, N. F., McQueen, R. J., & Baker, M. (1996). Learning and process improvement in knowledge organizations: a critical analysis of four contemporary myths. *The Learning Organization, 3*(1), 31-42.

Koenig, M. E. D. (1996). Intellectual capital and knowledge management. *IFLA Journal, 22*(4), 299-301.

Kofman, F., & Senge, P. M. (1993). Communities of commitment: The heart of learning organizations. *Organization Dynamics, 22*(2), 5-23.

Kogut, B., & Kulatilaka, N. (2001). Capabilities as Real Options. *Organization Science, 12*(6), 744-759.

Kogut, B., & Zander, U. (1993). Knowledge of the firm and the evolutionary theory of the multinational corporation. *Journal of International Business Studies, 24*(4), 625-645.

Kogut, B., & Zander, U. (1995). Knowledge, market failure and the multinational enterprise: a reply. *Journal of International Business Studies, 26*(2), 417-426.

Kogut, B., & Zander, U. (1996) What Firms Do? Coordination, Identity, and Learning. *Organization Science, 7*(5), September-October, 502-518.

Kogut, B., & Zander, U. (1996). What Firms Do? Coordination, Identity, and Learning. *Organization Science, 7*(5), 502-518.

Kogut, B., Zander, U. (1992). Knowledge of the Firm, Combinative Capabilities and Replication of Technology. *Organization Science, 3*(3), 383-397.

Kogut, B.., & Zander, U. (1995). Knowledge, market failure and the multinational enterprise: A reply. *Journal of International Business Studies, 26,* 417-426.

Kolb, D. (1984). *Experiential Learning.* Englewood Cliffs: Prentice Hall.

Komumunyakaa, Y. (2001). *Pleasure Dome: New and Collected Poems*. In G. Grisham (2006) *Metaphor, poetry, storytelling and cross-cultural leadership', Management Decision, 44*(4), 486-503. Wesleyan University Press, Middletown CT cited.

Konecki, K. (2000). *Studia z metodologii badań jakościowych. Teoria ugruntowana.* Warszawa: PWN.

Konicki, S. (2003). The Reality of Research. *InformationWeek*, September 10, 2001, www.informationweek.com, access date: 14:08.2003

Kor, Y. Y., & Mahoney, J. T. (2005). How Dynamics, Management, and Governance of Resource Deployments Influence Firm-Level Performance. *Strategic Management Journal, 26*, 489-496.

Korczynski, M. (2001). 'The Contradictions of Service Work: Call Centre as

Kornblith, H. (2002). *Knowledge and Its Place in Nature*. Oxford: Oxford University Press.

Kornhauser, W. (1962). *Scientists in Industry: Conflict and Accommodation.* Berkley: University of California Press.

Koskinen, K. U., Pihlanto, P., & Vanharanta, H. (2003). Tacit knowledge acquisitions and sharing in a project work context. *International Journal of Project Management, 21*(4), 281-90.

Kostera, M. (1997). Personal Performatives: Collecting Poetical Definitions of Management. *Organization, 4*(3), 345-353.

Kostera, M. (2003). Managing Professional Identities: Knowledge, Performativity and the New Professional, edited by M. Dent and S. Whitehead. Routledge, 2002. 262 pp. *Gender, Work and Organization, 10*(1), 120-125.

Krämer, S. (2006). The cultural techniques of time axis manipulation: On Friedrich Kittler's conception of media. *Theory, Culture and Society, 23*(7-8), 93-109.

Krogh, G., von Ichijo, K., & Nonaka, I. (2000). *Enabling knowledge cognition*. New York, NY.: Oxford University Press.

Kubo, I., & Saka, A. (2002). An Inquiry into the Motivations of Knowledge Workers in the Japanese Financial Industry. *Journal of Knowledge Management*, *6*(3), 262-271.

Kuhlthau, C. (1993). A principle of uncertainty for information seeking. Journal of Information seeking. *Journal of Documentation, 49*(4), 39-55.

Kuhn, T. S. (1962/1996). *The Structure of Scientific Revolutions*. Chicago, ILL.: University of Chicago Press.

Kumar, R.., & Nti, K. O. (1998). Differential learning and interaction in alliance dynamics: A process and outcome discrepancy model. *Organization Science, 9*, 356-66.

Kunda, G. (1992). *Engineering Culture: Control and Commitment in a High-Tech Corporation.* Philadelphia: Temple University Press.

Kunda, G., Barley, S., & Evans, J. (2002). Why Do Contractors Contract? The Experience of Highly Skilled Technical Professionals in a Contingent Labor Market. *Industrial and Labor Relations Review, 55*(2), 234-261.

Kurtz, C. F., & Snowden, D. J. (2003). The new dynamics of strategy: Sense-making in a complex and complicated world. *IBM Systems Journal,* 42(3).

Kusunoki, K., Nonaka, I., & Nagata, A. (1998). Organizational capabilities in product development of Japanese firms: a conceptual framework and empirical analysis. *Organization Science*, *9*(6), 699-718.

Kutlhau, C. (1991). Inside the search process: information seeking from the user's perspective. *Journal of the American Society for Information Science*, *42*, 361-371.

Labouvie-Vief, G. (1994). *Psyche and Eros: Mind and Gender in the Life Course*. New York: Cambridge University Press.

Lacity, M., & Hirschheim, R. (1993). Information Systems Outsourcing: Myths, Metaphors and Realities. Chichester: John Wiley Publishers.

Lacity, M., & Willcocks, L. (1998). An empirical investigation of information technology sourcing practices: lessons from experience. *MIS Quarterly*, *22*(3), 363-408.

Laet, M., & Mol, A. (2000). The Zimbabwe Bush Pump: Mechanics of a fluid technology. Social Studies of Science, 30(2), 225-263.

Lam, A. (2000). Tacit knowledge, organizational learning and societal institutions: an integrated framework. *Organization Studies, 21*, 487-513

Lambe, C. J., Spekman, R. E.., & Hunt, S. D. (2002). Alliance competence, resources, and alliance success: conceptualization, measurement, and initial test. *Academy of Marketing Science, 30*, 141-158.

Lampel J. and Shamsie, J. (2003). Capabilities in motion: new organizational forms and the reshaping of the Hollywood movie industry. *Journal of Management Studies*, *40*(8), 2189-2210.

Landers, G. (2002). *Extracting Value: Document Management and Imaging.* Gartner Symposium ITxpo (Orlando, Florida), 02E-SYM12, October 6-11, 2002

Landow, G. P. (2006). *Hypertext 3.0: Critical theory and new media in an era of globalization.* Baltimore: the Johns Hopkins University Press.

Landry, J. R. (1999). Forgetful or bad memory? *System Sciences, 1999. HICSS-32. Proceedings of the 32nd Annual Hawaii International Conference on.*

Lane, C., & Bachmann, R. (Eds) (1998). Trust within and between Organizations. *Conceptual Issues and empirical applications.* Oxford: Oxford University Press.

Lane, P., & Lubatkin, M. (1998). Relative absorptive capacity and interorganizational learning. *Strategic Management Journal, 19*(5), 461-477.

Langfield-Smith, K., & Smith, D. (2003). Management Control Systems and Trust in Outsourcing Relationships. *Management Accounting Research, 14*(3), *281-307.*

Langrish, J., Gibbons, M., Evans, W. G., & Jevons, F. R. (1972). *Wealth from Knowledge.* London: Macmillan.

Lanzara, G. F., & Patriotta, G. (2001). Technology and the courtroom: An inquiry into knowledge making in organizations. *Journal of Management Studies, 38*(7), 943-971.

Larson, A. (1992). Network dyads in entrepreneurial settings: A study of the governance of exchange relations. *Administrative Science Quarterly, 37*, 76-104.

Larson, M. (1977). *The rise of Professionalism: A Sociological Analysis.* London: University of California Press.

Larsson, J., Holmström, I., & Rosenqvist, U. (2003). Professional artist, good Samaritan, servant and co-ordinator: Four ways of understanding the anaesthetist's work. *Acta Anaesthesiologica Scandinavica, 47*, 1-7.

Larsson, R., Bengtsson, L., Henriksson, K.., & Sparks, J. (1998). The inter-organizational learning dilemma: Collective knowledge development in strategic alliances. *Organization Science, 9*, 285- 305.

Lash, S. (2006). Life (Vitalism). *Theory, Culture & Society, 23*(2-3), 323-329.

Latham, S. R. (2002). Medical professionalism: A Parsonian view. *The Mount Sinai Journal of Medicine*, 69, 363-369.

Latour, B. (1986). The Powers of Association. In J. Law (Ed.), *Power, Action and Belief.* London: Routledge.

Latour, B. (1987). *Science in action. How to follow scientists and engineers through society.* Cambridge, Mass: Harvard University Press.

Latour, B. (1991). Technology is society made durable. In J. Law (Ed.), *A sociology of monsters: Essays on power, technology and domination.* London & New York: Routledge.

Latour, B. (1993). *We have never been modern.* Cambridge, Mass.: Harvard University Press.

Latour, B. (1995). Mixing Humans and Nonhumans Together: The sociology of a Door-Closer. In S. L. Star (Ed.), *Ecologies of Knowledge, Work and Politics in Science and Technology.* New York: State University of New York Press.

Latour, B. (1999). *Pandora's Hope. Essays on the Reality of Science Studies.* Harvard University Press.

Latour, B., & Woolgar, S. (1979). *Laboratory life: the social construction of scientific facts.* Beverly Hills: Sage.

Lave, J., & Wenger, E. (1991). *Situated Learning: Legitimate Peripheral Participation.* Cambridge: Cambridge University Press.

Law, J. (1991). *A Sociology of monsters: essays on power, technology, and domination.* London ; New York: Routledge.

Law, J. (2003). Ladbroke grove, or how to thing about failing systems. http://www.comp.lancs.ac.uk/sociology/papers/lawladbroke-grove-failing-systems.pdf Revised December 2003, (last accessed December 2004).

Law, J. (Ed.) (1986). *Power, Action, and Belief: A New Sociology of Knowledge.* London: Routledge and Kegan Paul.

Law, J., & Singleton, W. (2005). Objects lessons. Organization, 12(3), 331-355.

Lawler, E. J.., & Thye, S. R. (1999). Bringing emotions into social exchange theory. *Annual Review of Sociology, 25*, 217-244.

Lawrence, D. H. (1929, 1980). Lady chatterly's lover. New York: Bantam Books.

Lazaroff, M., & Snowden, D. (2006). Anticipatory modes for Counter Terrorism. In R. Popp, & J. Yen (Eds.), *Emergent Information Technologies and Enabling Policies for Counter-Terrorism.* Wiley-IEEE Press http://www.research.ibm.com/journal/sj/423/kurtz.html

Lazzarato, M. (1996). Immaterial Labour. In P. Virno & M. Hardt (Eds.), *Radical Thought in Italy.* Minneapolis: University of Minnesota Press.

Leadbeater, C. (1999). *Living on Thin Air: The New Economy.* London: Viking.

Lee, J. Y. (1996). Charting the codes of cyberspace: A rhetoric of electronic mail. In L. Strate,, R. Jacobson, & S. B. Gibson Eds.), *Communication and cyberspace: Social interaction in an electronic environment* (pp. 275-296). Cresskill, NJ: Hampton Press.

Lee, N., & Hassard, J. (1999). *Organization Unbound: Actor-Network Theory, Research Strategy and Institutional Flexibility, 6*(3), 391-404.

Leicht, K.T., & Fennell, M.L. (2001). *Professional work: A sociological approach.* Oxford: Blackwell.

Leidner, D., Alavi, M., & Kayworth, T. (2006). The Role of Culture in Knowledge Management: A Case Study of Two Global Firms. *International Journal of e-Collaboration, 2*(nº 1) 17-40.

Leidner, R. (1993). *Fast Food, Fast Talk: Service Work and the Routinisation of Everyday Life.* Berkeley: University of California Press.

Leifer, R., Colarelli O'Connor, G. Peters, L. S., Rice, M., Veryzer, R. W., McDermott, C. M., (2000). *Radical Innovation.* Boston, Mass.: Harvard Business School Press.

Lelic, S. (2002). Inside knowledge editorial. *Knowledge Management,* 4.

Lengrand, L., & Chartrie, I. (1999). *Business Networks and the Knowledge-Driven Economy.* Brussels: European Commission.

Lenoir, T. (1998). Inscription practices and materialities of communication. In T. Lenoir (Ed.), (1999), *Inscribing science: Scientific texts and the materiality of communication* (pp. 1-19). Stanford: Stanford University Press.

Leonard, D. A. (1998). *Wellsprings of Knowledge: Building and Sustaining the Sources of Innovation.* Boston: Harvard Business School Press.

Leonard, D., & Sensiper, S. (1998). The role of tacit knowledge in group innovation. *California Management Review, 40*(3), 112-132.

Leontyev, A. N. (1978). *Activity, Consciousness and Personality.* Englewood Cliffs: Prentice-Hall.

Lepak, D. P., Snell, S. A. (1999). The human resource architecture: Toward a theory of human capital allocation and development. *Academy of Management Review, 24,* 31-48.

Levin, M. (2002) *Researching Enterprise Development - Action Research on the Cooperation Between Management and Labor in Norway.* Amsterdam: John Benjamins.

Levine, M. M. (1969). An essay on browsing . *Research Quarterly,* 9(1), 35-6.

Lévi-Strauss, C. (1979). *Myth and Meaning: Cracking the Code of Meaning.* New York: Shocken Books.

Levitt, B., & March J. G. (1988). Organizational learning. *Annual Review of Sociology, 14,*319-40.

Lewin, K. (1951). *Field theory in social science; selected theoretical papers.* New York: Harper & Row.

Li, T. (1999). The impact of the marketing-R&D interface on new product export performance: A contingency analysis. *Journal of International Marketing,* 7(1), 10-34.

Liebeskind, J., & Oliver, A. (1998). From handshake to contract: intellectual property, trust and the social structure of academic research. In C. Lane & R. Bachman (Eds.), *Trust within and between organizations. Conceptual issues and empirical applications* (pp. 118-145). Oxford, Oxford University Press.

Liker, J. K. (2004). *The Toyota Way: 14 Management Principles from the World's Greatest Manufacturer.* McGraw-Hill.

Liker, J. K., Ettlie, J. E., &Campbell, J. C. (Eds.) (1995). *Engineered in Japan: Japanese Technology Management Practices.* New York and Oxford: Oxford University Press.

Linde, C. (1993). *Life Stories: The Creation of Coherence.* New York: Oxford University Press.

Lindlof, T. R. (1995). Qualitative Communication Research Methods. Thousand Oaks-London-New Delhi: Sage Publications.

Lindsay, C. (2003). A century of labour market change: 1900 to 2000. *Labour Market Trends*, March 2003.

Linstead, S., & Mullarkey, J. (2003). Time, creativity and culture: introducing Bergson. *Culture and Organization,* 9(1), 3-13.

Lippman, S. A., & Rumelt, R. P. (1982). Uncertain imitability: An analysis of interfirm differences in efficiency under competition. *Bell Journal of Economics,* 13(2), 418-438.

Locker, L., Simpson, G. B., & Yates, M. (2003). Semantic neighborhood effects on the recognition of ambiguous words. *Memory and Cognition, 31,* 505-515.

Logan, D., & Caldwell, F. (2002). Knowledge Management Attracts Powerhouse Vendors. *Gartner Article Top View, AV-17-7196,* November 12, 2002,

Logan, D., Caldwell, F., & Young, C. (2001). New Rules for Measuring and Managing Intellectual Capital. *Gartner Research Note, SPA-12-7644,* March 13, 2001,

Lohmann, S. (n.d.). How Information Flows From Those Who Have It to Those Who Need It: The Information Ecology of the Large Public State University. *Conference on Herding Cats, Moving Cemeteries, and Hauling Academic Trunks: Managing Change in Higher Education,* UCLA.

Lönnqvist, A. (2004). *Measurement of Intangible Success Factors: Case Studies on the Design, Implementation and Use of Measures.* Tampere University of Technology, Publication 475. Tampere: Tampere University of Technology.

Lorange, P.., & Roos, J. (1992). *Strategic Alliances: Formation, Implementation, and Evolution.* Cambridge, Mass: Blackwell.

Lorenzoni, G.., & Lipparini, A. (1999). The leveraging of inter-firm relationships as a distinctive organizational capability: A longitudinal study. *Strategic Management Journal, 20,* 317-338.

Lothian, N. (1984). *How companies manage R&D: a survey of major UK companies.* The Institute of Cost and Management Accountants.

Lovejoy, A. (1936). *The Great Chain of Being: A Study of the History of an Idea.* Cambridge: Harvard University Press.

Luhmann, N. (1979). *Trust and Power.* Chichester: John Wiley.

Luhmann, N. (1995). *Social Systems*. Stanford, CA: Stanford University Press.

Luhmann, N. (2000). *The reality of the mass media*. Cambridge: Polity Press.

Luhmann, N. (ed.) (2002). *Theories of Distinction. Redescribing the Descriptions of Modernity*. Stanford, CA: Stanford University Press.

Lundeen, G., Tenopir, C., & Wermager, A. (1994). Information Needs of Rural Health Care in Hawaii. *Bulletin of the Medical Library Association 82*(2), *197-205.*

Lundvall, B. A. (1988). Innovation as an interactive process: From user producer interaction to the national system of innovation. In Dosi et al., (Eds.), *Technical Change and economic Theory*. London and New York: Pinter Publishers.

Lundvall, B. A. (1992). Introduction to national systems of innovation. In B. A. Lundvall (Ed.), *National systems of innovation* (pp. 1-22). London: Pinter.

Lundy, J., & Herschel, G. (2003). Making Knowledge Part of CRM. *Gartner Letter From the Editor, LE-19-8729*, April 21, 2003

Lykke, N., & Braidotti, R. (1996). *Between Monsters, Goddesses and Cyborgs: Feminist Confrontations with Science, Medicine, and Cyberspace*. London: Zed Books.

Lynn, G. S., & Akgun, A. E. (1999). Launch your new products/services better, faster. Research Technology Management, 46(3), 21-26.

Lyon, D. (2004). How Can You Help Organisations Change to Meet the Corporate Responsibility Agenda? *Corporate Social Responsibility and Environmental Management, 11*, 133-139.

Lyotard, J. F. (1979/1984). *The Postmodern Condition.* Translated by Geoff Bennington and Brian Massumi. Minneapolis, Minnesota: University of Minnesota Press. 1979 in French edition and 1984 English edition.

MacDonald, K. M. (1995). *The sociology of the professions*. London, Thousand Oaks, New Delhi: Sage Publications.

Machlup, F. (1962). *The production and distribution of knowledge in the United States*. Princeton: Princeton University Press.

Macintosh, N. B. (1994). *Management accounting and control systems: an organizational and behavioral approach*. Wiley.

Macpherson, A., Jones, O.., & Zhang, M. (2004). Evolution or revolution? Dynamic capabilities in a knowledge dependent firm. *R&D Management, 34*, 161.

Madique, M. A. (1988). Entrepreneurs, champions and Technological development. In M. L. Tushman & W. L. Moore (Eds.), *Readings in the management of innovation* (2nd ed) (pp. 565-584). New York: Harper Business.

Mahoney, J. T.., & Pandian, J. R. (1992). The resource-based view within the conversation of strategic management. *Strategic Management Journal, 13*(363), 380.

Maier, G. W., Prange, C.., & von Rosenstil, L. (2001). Psychological perspectives of organizational learning. In M. Dierkes, A Berthoin Antal, J. Child,., & I. Nonaka (Eds.), *Psychological perspectives of organizational learning and knowledge*, (pp. 14-34).

Maier, J. L., Rajner Jr., R. K., & Snyder, C. A. (1997). Environmental scanning for information technology: An empirical investigation. *Journal of Management Information Systems, 14*(2), 177-200.

Maier, R., & Remus, U. (2002). Defining Process-Oriented Knowledge Management Strategies". *Knowledge and Process Management, 9*(2), 103-118.

Major, E., & Cordey-Hayes, M. (2003). Encouraging innovation in small firms through externally generated knowledge. In L. Shavinina (Ed.), *International Handbook on Innovation*. Oxford: Elsevier.

Makadok, R. (2001). Towards a synthesis of the resource-based and dynamic capability views of rent creation. *Strategic Management Journal, 22*, 387-401.

Malerba, F., & Orsenigo, L. (2000). Knowledge, Innovative Activities and Industrial Evolution. *Industrial and Corporate Change, 9*(2).

Malhotra, Y. (1998). Knowledge Management for the New World of Business. *Asian Leadership Institute Review (Business Studies Special Issue), 20*, 489-514.

Malhotra, Y. (2000). Knowledge Management and New Organization Forms: A Framework for Business Model Innovation. *Information Resources Management Journal, 13*(1), 5-14.

Malhotra, Y. (2000). *Knowledge Management and Virtual Organizations*. Hershey: Idea Group Publishing.

Mallet, S. (1975). *Essays on the new working class*. St. Louis: Telos Press.

Mann, J. (2003). Knowledge Management Is Not a „Market". *META Group Analyst Insights* (METAbits), 21 February, www.metagroup.com, access date: 8.08.2003

Mannheim, K. (1936). *Ideology and utopia*. London: Kegan Paul.

Manovich, L. (2001). *The language of new media*. Cambridge & London: The MIT Press.

March, J. G. (1991). Exploration and exploitation in organizational learning. *Organization Science, 2*, 71-87.

Marchant, F. (2005). Night Visions. *New England Journal of Public Policy, 19*(2), 285-295. In G. Grisham (2006). *Metaphor, poetry, story telling and cross-cultural leadership. Management Decision, 44*(4), 486-503.

Margolis, J., & Walsh, J. P. (2003). Misery Loves Companies: Rethinking Social Initiatives by Business. *Administrative Science Quarterly, 48*, 268-305.

Mark, A., & Snowden, D. (2004). *Researching practice or practising research - innovating methods in healthcare the contribution of Cynefin.* Presented paper at the Organisational Behaviour in Health Care Conference on the theme of Innovation held by the Centre for Health and Policy Studies (CHAPS) University of Calgary at the Banff Centre Alberta Canada

Markoff, J. (1999). Boom Mind-Set Deeply Etched in Chip Capital. *New York Times*, June 16.

Markus, H. R., & Shinobu, K. (1991). Culture and the Self: Implications for Cognition, Emotion and Motivation. *Psychological Review, 98*, 224-253.

Markus, H. R., & Shinobu, K. (1998). The Cultural Psychology of Personality. *Journal of Cross-Cultural Psychology,* 29, 63-87.

Marquardt, M., & Reynolds, A. (1994). *Global Learning Organization: Gaining Advantage through Continuous Learning.* New York: Irwin.

Marr, B. (2005) (Ed) *Perspectives on Intellectual capital.* Oxford: Elsevier.

Marr, B., Schiuma, G., & Neely, A. (2004). The dynamics of value creation: mapping your intellectual performance drivers. *Journal of Intellectual Capital* , 5(2), 312-325

Marshak, R. J. (2006). *Covert Processes at Work: Managing the Five Hidden Dimensions of Organizational Change.* San Francisco: Berret-Kohler.

Marshall, J., & Reason, P. (1993). Adult Learning in Collaborative Action Research:

Marshall, T.H. (1962) 'Professionalism and Social Policy'. In: S. Nosow and W. Form (eds.), *Man, Work and Society* (New York: Basic Books)

Marton, F., & Pang, M. F. (1999). *Two Faces of Variation.* Paper presented at the Conference Name|. Retrieved Access Date|. from URL|.

Marx, K. (1867/1992). *Capital: Volume I: A Critique of Political Economy (Das Kapital. Kritik der politischen Oekonomie).* Harmondsworth: Penguin.

Marx, K. (1973). *Grundrisse: Foundations of the Critique of Political Economy*, trans. Martin Nicolaus. London: Penguin.

Marx, K. (1976). *Capital: A Critique of Political Economy*, Vol. 1, trans. Ben Fowkes. London: Penguin.

Marx, K. (1985). Value, price and profit. In K. Marx and F. Engels *Collected Works*, Volume 20: Marx and Engels 1864-1868. London: Lawrence and Wishart.

Marx, K. (1996) *Capital, vol. 1* in *Marx and Engels Collected Works Volume 35.* London: Lawrence and Wishart.

Maskell, B. H. (1991). *Performance Measurement for World Class Manufacturing*, Cambbridge, MA: Productivity Press, Inc.

Maslow, A. (1954). *Motivation and Personality.* New York: Harper & Row.

Matsumoto, I. T., Stapleton, J., Glass, J., & Thorpe, T. (2005). A knowledge-capture report for multidisciplinary design environments. *Journal of Knowledge Management, 8*(3), 83-92.

Matthew-Maich, N., Mines, C., Brown, B., Lunyk-Child, O., Carpio, B. Drummond-Young, M., Noesgaard, C., & Linton, J. (2007). Evolving as nurse educators in problem-based learning through a community of faculty development. *Journal of Professional Nursing, 23*(2), 75-82.

Maturana, H. R. & Varela, F. J. (1987/1992). *The Tree of Knowledge: The Biological Roots of Human Understanding*, Transl. Paolucci, R. Boston. Shambhala, Boston & London: New Science Library.

Maturana, H. R. (1981). Autopoiesis. In M. Zeleny (Ed.), *Autopoiesis: A theory of Living Organisation.* New York, North Holland.

Maula, M. (1999). *Multinational Companies as Learning and Evolving Systems.* Helsinki: Helsinki School of Economics and Business Administration.

Maula, M. (2000). The senses and memory of a firm - implications of autopoiesis theory for knowledge management. *Journal of Knowledge Management, 4*(2), 157-161.

Maykut, R., & Morehouse, R. (1994). *Beginning Qualitative Research: A Philosophical and Practical Guide.* London: The Falmer Press.

McClelland, D. C. (1973). Testing for competence rather than for "intelligence'. *American Psychologist, 1*,1-14.

McCloskey, d. N. (1986). *The Rhetoric of Economics.* Brighton: Wreatsheaf Books Ltd.

McCombs, M. E. (1997). Building Consensus: The News Media's Agenda-Setting Roles. *Political Communication, 14,* 433-443

McCombs, M. E., & Shaw, D. L. (1972). The Agenda-setting Function of Mass Media. *Public Opinion Quarterly, 36*(2), 176-187.

McDonough, B. (2002). Knowledge Management. *eINFORM, 3*(8). http://www.kmcenter.info/Documents/IDC_april_2002.pdf, access date: 12.05.2003

McEvily, S. K., & Chakravarthy, B. (2002). The Persistence of Knowledge-based Advantage: An Empirical Test for Product performance and Technological Knowledge. *Strategic Management Journal*, *23*(4), 285-305.

McGail, B. A. (2002). Confronting electronic surveillance: Desiring and resisting new technologies. In S. Woolgar (Ed.), (2002). *Virtual society? Technology, cyberbole, reality.* Oxford & New York: Oxford University Press.

McGee, J. E., Dowling, M. J.., & Megginson, W. L. (1995). Cooperative strategy and new venture performance: The role of business strategy and management experience. *Strategic Management Journal, 16*, 565-580.

McGill, M. E., & Slocum Jr., J. W. (1993). Unlearning the organization. *Organizational Dynamics, 22*(2), 52-66.

McGrath, M. E., Anthony, M. T., & Shipiro, A. R. (1992). Product development: Success through cycle time excellence. PRTM Butterworth-Heinemann Publishing.

McGrath, R., MacMillan, G., & Venkataraman, S. (1995). Defining and developing competence: A strategic process paradigm. *Strategic Management Journal, 16*, 251-275.

McGregor, D. (1960). *The Human Side of the Enterprise.* New York: McGraw Hill.

McInerney, C. (2002). Knowledge management and the dynamic nature of knowledge. *Journal of the American society for information science and technology, 53*(12), 1009-1018.

McInerney, C., & LeFevre, D. (2000). Knowledge managers: History and challenges. In C. Prichard, R. Hull, M. Chumer, & H. Willmott (Eds.), *Managing knowledge: Critical investigations of work and learning.* London: Macmillan Business.

McIvor, R. (2000). Strategic Outsourcing: Lessons from a systems integrator. *Business Strategy Review, 11*(3), 41-50.

McKelvey, B. (2002). Chapter 9 Complexity and Leadership In M. Lissack & J. Rivkin (Eds.), *The interaction of complexity and management* (pp. 85-90). Westport: Quorum Books.

McKnight, C., Dillon, A., & Richardson, J. (1991). *Hypertext in Context.* Cambridge: Cambridge University Press.

McLuhan, M. (1962 reprinted 1967). *The Gutenberg Galaxy: The making of Typographic Man.* London: Routledge and Kegan Paul.

McLuhan, M. (1962). *The Gutenberg galaxy: The making of typographic man.* London: Routledge & Kegan Paul.

McLuhan, M. (1964). *Understanding Media: The extensions of Man.* McGraw-Hill, Toronto.

McLuhan, M. (1969). *Counter Blast.* Toronto: McClelland and Stewart.

Meek, V. (1988). Organizational culture: Origins and weaknesses. *Organization Studies, 9,* 453-473.

Merchant, K. A. (1985). Control in business organizations. Boston: Pitman.

MERITUM, (2002), *Guidelines for Managing and Reporting of Intangibles*, Fundacion Airtel Movil, Madrid.

Merrian-Webster (2003). Merrian-Webster's Collegiate Dictionary (11th Ed.).

Merrin, W. (1999). Television is Killing the Art of Symbolic Exchange: Baudrillard's Theory of Communication. *Theory, Culture & Society, 16*(3), 119-140.

Merton, R. K. (1957). Karl Mannheim and the sociology of knowledge. In *Social Theory and Social Structure.* Glencoe: Free Press.

Merton, R. K. (1965). *On the shoulders of giants: a Shandean postscript.* New York: Harcourt Brace & World.

Meyer, M. H., Anzani, M., & Walsh, G. (2005). Innovation and Enterprise Growth: It took courage, focus and commitment at all levels for IBM to develop its next-generation product lines. *Research Technology Management, 48*(4), 34-44.

Michaels, M. (2000). *Reconnecting culture, technology and nature:From society to heterogeneity.* London & New York: Routledge.

Michaels, M. (2002). A Practitioner's Perspective. In M. Lissack & J. Rivkin (Eds.), *The interaction of complexity and management* (pp. 173-181). Westport: Quorum.

Milburn, C. (2004). Nanotechnology in the age of post-human engineering: Science fiction as science. In K. N. Hayles (Ed.), (2005), *Nanoculture: Implications of the new technoscience.* (pp. 109-129). Bristol: Intellect Books.

Miles, I. (2003). Services and the knowledge based economy. In J. Tidd & F. Hull (Eds.), *Service Innovation: Organizational Responses to Technological Opportunities and Market Imperatives* (pp. 1-34). London: Imperial College Press.

Miles, M. B., & Huberman, A. M. (1994). *Qualitative data analysis: an expanded sourcebook.* 2nd edition. CA: Sage Publications.

Miles, R. E., Snow C. C., & Miles, G. (2000). TheFuture.org. *Long range Planning, 33*, 300-321.

Miles, R. E., Snow, C. S., Mathews, J. A., Miles, G., & Coleman Jr., H. J. (1997). Organizing in the Knowledge Age: Anticipating the Cellular Form. *Academy of Management Executives, 11*(4), 7-20.

Miller, R. (2005). The evolution of knowledge management: This time it's personal. *EContent, 28*(11), 38-41.

Milofsky, C., & Schneider, J. (2002). *The field notes manual. Doing ethnography in sociology and anthropology.* Lewisburg, PA: Bucknell Univ Press.

Minbaeva, D., Pedersen, T., Björkman, I., Fey, C. F, & Park, H. J. (2003). MNC Knowledge Transfer, Subsidiary Absorptive Capacity, and HRM. *Journal of International Business Studies, 34*(6), 586-599.

Mingers, J. (1995). *Self-Producing Systems. Implications and Applications of Autopoiesis*. New York and London: Plenum Press.

Ministry of Economy, Trade and Industry (METI), (2005). *Guidelines for Disclosure of Intellectual Assets Based Management*, October.

Mintzberg, H. (1983). *Structure in Fives: Designing Effective Organisations*. Englewood Cliff, NJ: Prentice-Hall.

Mintzberg, H. (1989). *Mintzberg on management*. New York: the Free Press.

Mintzberg, H., Ahlstrand, B., & Lampe, J. (1998). *Strategy Safari. The complete guide through the wilds of strategic management*. London: Prentice Hall Financial Times.

Mirchandani, K. (2004). 'Practices of global capital: gaps, cracks and ironies in transnational call centres in India,' *Global Networks* 4(4): 355–373.

Mitroff, I., & Kilmann, R. (1975). Stories managers tell: a new tool for organisational story telling. *Management Review* (pp. 18-28).

Moellering, G. (2006). Trust: Reason, Routine, Reflexivity. Oxford: Elsevier.

Mohr, J.., & Spekman, R. (1994). Characteristics of partnership success: partnership attributes, communication behaviour and conflict resolution. *Strategic Management Journal, 15*, 135-52.

Mol, A. M. (2003). The Body Multiple: Ontology in Medical Practice. New York: Duke University Press.

Möller, K. K.., & Halinen, A. (1999). Business relationships and networks: Managerial challenge of the network era. *Industrial Marketing Management, 28*, 413-427.

Möller, K., & Svahn, S. (2006). Role of Knowledge in Value Creation in Business Nets. *Journal of Management Studies, 43*(5), 985-1007.

Monden, Y. (1993). *Toyota Management System: Linking the Seven Key Functional Areas*. Portland, Oregon: Productivity Press.

Moore, W. (1970). *The Professions: Roles and Rules*. New York: Russell Sage.

Morgan, G. (1986). *Images of Organization*. Beverly Hills, CA: Sage.

Morgan, G. (1988). *Riding the waves of change: Developing managerial competences for a turbulent world*. San Francisco: Jossey-Bass.

Morgan, G. (1997). *Images of Organization*. London: Sage.

Morgan, G. (1997). *Images of Organization. New Mindsets for Seeing, Organizing and Managing*. San Fransisco, Thousand Oaks, CA: Berrett-Koehler and Sage Publishers.

Morgan, G. (1997/2001). *Wyobraźnia organizacyjna. Nowe sposoby postrzegania, organizowania i zarządzania*. Warszawa: PWN.

Morris, J.A., & Feldman, D.C. (1996). 'The dimensions, antecedents and consequences of emotional labour', *Academy of Management Review*, 21(4): 986-1010.

Morris, M. H., Allen, J., Schindeutte, M., & Avila, R. (2006). Balanced Management Control Systems as a Mechanism for Achieving Corporae Entrepreneurship. *Journal of Managerial Issues, XVIII*(4), 468-493.

Mosco, V. (2004). *The digital sublime: Myth, power and cyberspace*. Cambridge & London: The MIT Press.

Mouritsen J. and Thorsgaard Larsen H., 2005, 'The 2nd wave of knowledge management: The management control of knowledge resources through intellectual capital information', Management Accounting Research, 16, 371-394.

Mouritsen, J., Bukh, P. N., Flagstad, K., Thorbjørnsen, S., Rosenkrands, Johansen, M., Kotnis, S., Thorsgaard Larsen, H., Nielsen, C., Kjærgaard Jensen, I., Krag, L., Jeppesen, G., Haisler J., & Stakemann, B. (2003). *Intellectual Capital Statements - the New Guideline*. Published by the Danish Ministry of Science, Technology and Innovation (DMSTI), http://www.videnskabsministeriet.dk/cgi-bin/theme-list.cgi?theme_id=100650&_lang=uk , retrieved in April, 2004

Mouritsen, J. (2004). Measuring and intervening: how do we theorise intellectual capital management, *Journal of Intellectual* Capital, 5(2), 257-267.

Mouritsen, J., & Larsen, H. T. (2005). The second wave of knowledge management: The management control of knowledge resources through intellectual capital information. *Management Accounting Research*, 16, 371–394.

Mouritsen, J., Bukh, P., and Kaasgaard B. H. (2005), *Understanding Intellectual Capital in an Innovative Medium-sized Firm: The Case of Maxon*, The Aarhus School of Business, Copenhagen.

Mumford, L. (1934). *Technics and civilization.* New York: Harcourt, Brace and Company.

Murray, J. D., Case, T. L., & Gardiner, A. B. (2005). Knowledge creation in inquiring organizations using KDD: Re-focusing research on the analyst. In J. Courtney, J.Haynes, & D. Paradice (Eds.), *Inquiring Organizations: Moving from knowledge management to wisdom* (pp. 133-153). Hershey, PA: Idea Publishing Group.

Nanda, A. (2005). 'Who is a professional?', *Harvard Business School Publishing, Product Number 9-904-047.* Boston: Harvard Business School.

NASSCOM (2007). *Strategic Review 2007.* New Delhi: NASSCOM

NASSCOM (Not dated/n.d. a). National Skills Registry - Fact sheet Retreived on 28 August 2008 http://www.nasscom.in/upload/5216/Factsheet-NSR%20Aug%2023%202007.doc

NASSCOM (Not dated/n.d. c). Data Security Council of India (DSCI): A Self Regulatory initiative in Data Security and Privacy Protection. Retreived on 28 August 2008 www.nasscom.in/upload/5216/Datasecurity.pdf

NASSCOM (Not dated/n.d.b). Indian Security Environment – Fact Sheet. Retreived on 28 August 2008 www.nasscom.in/upload/5216/Indian%20Security%20Environment%202005-06%20July%2006.pdf

Neef, D. (1997). *The Knowledge Economy.* Oxford: Butterworth-Heinemann.

Neely, A. (1999). The Performance Measurement Revolution: Why Now and What Next? *International Journal of Operations & Production Management, 19*(2), 205-228.

Neely, A. (2005). The Evolution of Performance Measurement Research. Developments in the Last Decade and a Research Agenda for the Next. *International Journal of Operations & Production Management, 25*(12), 1264-1277.

Nelson R. R. and Winter S. G., 1982, *An Evolutionary Theory of Economic Change* Belknap Press, Cambridge.

Nelson, R. R. (Ed.) (1993). *National Systems of Innovation: A Comparative Study.* Oxford: Oxford University Press.

Nerkar, A., & Roberts, P. W. (2004). Technological and Product-Market Experience and the Success of New Product Introductions in the Pharmaceutical Industry. *Strategic Management Journal, 25*, 779-799.

Nerney, C. (1997). Search Engines. Searching for true knowledge. *Network World, 42.*

Nerney, C. (1998). They're not start-ups anymore. BackWeb pulls back on push. *Network World, 26.*

Newell, S., Robertson, M.,Scarborough, H., & Swan, J. (2002). *Managing knowledge work.* Basingstoke: Palgrave.

Newfield, C. (2004). *Ivy and Industry: Business and the Making of the American University, 1880-1980.* Durham: Duke University Press.

Nicholas, D., & Martin, H. (1997). Assessing Information Needs: A Case Study of Journalists. *Aslib Proceedings, 49*(2), 43-52.

Nickols, F. (2003). *The knowledge in knowledge management.* Retrieved June 4, 2008, from http://home.att.net/~OPSINC/knowledge_in_KM.pdf

Nixon, W., & Innes, J. (1998). Management accountants and design. *Management Accounting*, June 1998.

Noble, D. (1977). *America By Design: Science, Technology, and the Rise of Corporate Capitalism.* New York: Alfred Knopf.

Noble, D. (1984). *Forces of Production: A Social History of Industrial Automation.* New York: Alfred Knopf.

Noble, D. (2001). *Digital Diploma Mills: The Automation of Higher Education.* New York: Monthly Review Press.

Nohria, N., & Ghoshal, S. (1994). Differentiated fit and shared values: alternatives for managing headquarters-subsidiary relations. *Strategic Management Journal, 15*(6), 491-503.

Noke, H., & Radnor, Z. J. (2004). Navigating innovation: a diagnostic tool supporting the process. *Journal of Manufacturing Technology Management, 15*(2), 172-185.

Nonaka I., 1994, 'A Dynamic Theory of Organizational Knowledge Creation', *Organization Science,* Vol. 5, No. 1, February: pp. 15-37.

Nonaka I., Toyama R. and Nagata A., 2000, 'A Firm as a Knowledge-creating Entity: A New Perspective on the Theory of the Firm, *Industrial and Corporate Change,* Vol. 9, No. 1, March.

Nonaka, I. (1991). *The knowledge creating company.* Harvard Business Review, *69*, Nov-Dec, 96-104.

Nonaka, I. (1994). A dynamic theory of organizational knowledge creation. *Organization Science*, *5*, 67-77.

Nonaka, I. o., & Takeuchi, H. (1995). *The knowledge-creating company: how Japanese companies create the dynamics of innovation.* New York: Oxford University Press.

Nonaka, I., & Konno, N. (1998) The Concept of 'Ba': Building a Foundation for Knowledge Creation. *California Management Review, 40*(3), 40-54.

Nonaka, I., & Takeuchi, H. (1995). *The Knowledge Creating Company: How Japanese Companies Create the Dynamics of Innovation.* Oxford: Oxford University Press.

Nonaka, I., Reinmöller, P., & Toyama, R. (2001). Integrated Information Technology Systems for Knowledge Creation. In M. Dierkes, B. A. Antal, J. Child, & I. Nonaka (Eds.), *Handbook of organizational learning & knowledge*. New York: Oxford University Press, (pp. 827-848).

Nonaka, I., Sasaki, K., & Ahmed, M. (2003). Continuous innovation: The power of tacit knowledge. In L. Shavinina (Ed.), *International Handbook on Innovation.* Oxford: Elsevier Science.

Nonaka, I., Toyama, R., & Konno, N. (2000). SECI, Ba and leadership: a unified model of dynamic knowledge creation. *Long Range Planning, 33*(1), 5-34.

Nonaka, I., Toyama, R., & Konno, N. (2001). SECI, ba and leadership: a unified model of dynamic knowledge creation. In I. Nonaka & D. Teece, (Eds.), *Managing Industrial Knowledge: Creation, Transfer and Utilization* (pp. 13-43). London: Sage.

Nordhaug, O. (1998). Competence specificities in organizations. *International Studies of Management and Organization, 28*(1), 8-29.

Norenzayan, A, Smith, E. E., Beom, J. K., & Nisbett, R. E. (2002). Cultural Preferences for Formal Versus Intuitive Reasoning. *Cognitive Science, 26*, 653-684.

Norman, P. A., & Peterson, T. (1999). Quality improvement through innovation. In S. K. Ho (Ed.), *TQM and Innovation Proceedings of the fourth international conference on ISO 9000 and TQM* (pp 64-70). HKBU press.

Nowotny, H., Scott, P., & Gibbons, M. (2001). *Re-thinking Science: Knowledge and the Public in an Age of Uncertainty.* London: Polity Press.

Nurmi, R. (1998). Knowledge-intensive Firms. *Business Horizons 41*(3), 26-32.

O'Dell, C., & Grayson, C. J. (1998). If Only We Knew What We Know: Identification and Transfer of Internal Best Practices. *California Management Review, 40*(3), 154-174.

O'donnell, S. W. (2000). Managing foreign subsidiaries: agents of headquarters, or an interdependent network? *Strategic Management Journal, 21*(5), 525-548.

Oakeshott, M. (1991). *Rationalism in politics and other essays, new and expanded edition.* Indianapolis, IN: Liberity.

Oakley, M. (1990). Design and design management. In M. Oakley (Ed.), *Design management: A handbook of issues and methods* (pp 3-15). Oxford, UK: Basil Blackwell Ltd.

OECD (2000). *Chairman's conclusions. International symposium Measuring and Reporting Intellectual capital: Experiences, Issues, and Prospects.* 9-11 June, Amsterdam, Netherlands. Available at: http://www.oecd.org//dsti/sti/industry/indcomp/act/ams-conf/conclusions.htm.

OECD (2005). OECD Science, Technology and Industry Scoreboard 2005. Executive Summary. Available at: http://www.oecd.org/dataoecd/59/52/35465901.pdf.

OECD (2007). *Higher education and regions, globally competitive, locally engaged.* Organisation for Economic Co-operation and Development, Paris.

OECD. (1996). *The Knowledge-based Economy.* Paris: STI Outlook.

Office of National Statistics (2006). *Labour Force Survey User Guide – Volume 5: LFS Classifications.* London: National Statistics. Web version at http://www.statistics.gov.uk/statbase/Product.asp?vlnk=1537. Accessed 1/3/08.

Office of National Statistics (2008). Labour Market Statistics. London: National Statistics. Online at: http://www.statistics.gov.uk/statbase/TSDdownload2.asp. Accessed 1/3/08.

Okes, D. (2005). Corral your organization's knowledge. *Quality Progress, 38, 10,* 25-30.

Oldham, G. R., & Cummings, A. (1996). Employee Creativity: Personal and Contextual Factors at Work. *Academy of Management Journal, 39*(3), 607-634.

OLF (2005). Integrated Work Processes: Future work processes on the Norwegian continental shelf. On-line: http://www.olf.no/?28867.pdf.

Oliveira, M. (1999). Core Competencies and the Knowledge of the Firm. in Hitt, M.A. *et al.* (Eds.): *Dynamic Strategic Resources: Development, Diffusion and Integration.* (pp. 17-41). New York: John Wiley & Sons.

Oliver, N., & Blakeborough, M. (1998). Innovation Networks: The view from inside. In J. Greive Smith & J. Michie (Eds.), *Innovation, co-operation and growth.* Oxford: Oxford University Press.

Ong, W. (1956). System, Space, and Intellect in Renaissance Symbolism. Bibliotheque d' Humanisme et Renaissance, no. 18, (pp. 222-239).

Ong, W. J. (1982). *Orality and Literacy: The Technologizing of the Word.* London: Routledge.

Oprea, T. I. (2002). Virtual screening in lead discovery: A viewpoint. *Molecules,* 7, 51-62.

Orlikowski, W. J. (2000). Using technology and constituting structures: A practice lens for studying technology in organizations. *Organization Science, 11*(4), 404-428.

Orlikowski, W. J. (2002). Knowing in practice: enacting a collective capability in distributed organizing. *Organization Science, 13,* 249-73.

Osborn, R.N., & J. Hagedorn (1997): The institutionalization and evolutionary dynamics of inter-organizational alliances and networks. Academy of Management Journal, 40, 261-278.

Osterloh, M., & Frey, B. (2000): Motivation, knowledge transfer and organizational form. Organization Science, 11, 538-550.

Osterlund, J. (1997). Competence management by informatics in R&D: The corporate level. *IEEE transactions on Engineering Management, 44*(2), 135-145.

Ouchi W. G., 1979, 'A conceptual framework for the design of organizational control mechanisms', *Management Science*, 25:9, 833-848.

Ouchi, W. G. (1980). Markets, bureaucracies and clans. *Administrative Science Quarterly, 25*, 129-141.

Ouchi, W. G. (1981). *Theory Z: how American business can meet the Japanese challenge*. Reading, Mass.: Addison-Wesley.

Ouchi, W. G., & Jaeger, A. M. (1978). Type Z organisations: stability in the midst of mobility. *Academy of Management Review, 3*, 18-28.

Owens, J. D. (2004). An evaluation of Organisational groundwork and learning objectives for New Product Development. *Journal of Enterprising Culture, 12*, 303-325.

Owens, J. D. (2004b). World Class Supply: Is it just a question of effective partnership? *Management Services Journal, 48, 8-15.*

Owens, J. D., & Davies, J. (2000). The Importance of a New Product Development (NPD) Process: Getting Started. *First European Conference on Knowledge Management*, Bled School of Management, Bled, Slovenia, 26-27 October.

Ozer, M. (1999). A Survey of New Product Evaluation Models. *Journal of Product Innovation Management, 16*, 77-94.

Ozer, M. (2004). Managing the selection process for new product ideas. *Research Technology Management, 47*(4), 10-15.

Packard, D. (1995). *The HP Way: How Bill Hewlett and I Built Our Company.* New York: Harper Business.

Palmer, S. E. (1975). The effects of contextual scenes on the identification of objects. *Memory and Cognition, 3,* 519-526.

Palys, T. (1997). *Research Decisions: Quantitative and Qualitative Perspectives* (Second ed.). Toronto: Harcourt Brace.

Parikh, M. (2001). Knowledge management framework for high-tech research and development. *Engineering Management Journal, 13*(3), 27-33.

Parolini, C. (1999). *The Value Net: A Tool for Competitive Strategy.* Chichester: Wiley.

Parsons, T. (1951). *Social System.* New York: Free Press.

Patel, P., & Pavitt, K. (1994). The continuing widespread (and neglected) importance of improvements in mechanical technologies. *Research Policy, 23*, 533-545.

Paul, L. G. (2001). *How IT Managers Can Get The Most Out of Analyst Services Firms*. CIO, July 15, http://www.cio.com/article/30383/How_IT_Managers_Can_Get_The_Most_Out_of_Analyst_Services_Firms, access date: 21.11.2007

Pavalko, R.M. (1971). *Sociology Of Occupations and Professions.* Itasca: : FE Peacock.

Pavitt, K. (1984). Patterns of technological change: towards a taxonomy and a theory. *Research Policy, 13*(6), 343-373.

Pearce, C. L. (2004). The Future of Leadership: Combining Vertical and Shared Leadership to Transform Knowledge Work. *Academy of Management Executive, 18*(1), 47-57.

Peng, K., & Nisbett, R. E. (1999). Culture, Dialectics, and Reasoning About Contradiction. *American Psychologist, 54*, 741-754.

Penrose, E. (1959). *The Theory of the Growth of the Firm.* Oxford: Oxford University Press.

Perlow, L. (1998)."Boundary Control: The Social Ordering of Work and Family Time in a High-tech Corporation. *Administrative Science Quarterly, 43*(2, 328-357.

Perlow, L. (1999). The time famine: toward a sociology of time. *Administrative Science Quarterly, 44*, 57-81.

Perlow, L. A. (1997). *Finding time: how corporations, individuals, and families can benefit from new work practices*. Ithaca, NY: ILR Press.

Perlow, L. A. (2004). *When You Say Yes But Mean No.* New York: Crowns Business

Perrow, C. (1972). *Complex organizations: A critical essay*. Glenview, IL: Scott, Foresman and Company.

Peteraf M. A., 1993, 'The Cornerstones of Competitive Advantage: a Resource-based View', *Strategic Management Journal*, Vol. 14: pp. 179-191.

Peters, T. J., & Waterman, R. H. (1982). In search of excellence: lessons from America's best-run companies. Harper Collins.

Pettigrew, A. M. (1997). What is a processual Analysis? *Scandinavian Journal of Management, 13*, 337-348.

Pexman, P. M., & Lupker, S. J. (1999). Ambiguity and visual word recognition: Can feedback explain both homophone and polysemy effects? *Canadian Journal of Experimental Psychology, 53*, 323-334.

Phenomenography. Retrieved December 5 2005, from http://www.ped.gu.se/biorn/phgraph/civil/main/1res.appr.html

Phenomenography. from http://www.ped.gu.se/biorn/phgraph/home.html

Pinch, T. J., & Bijker, W. E. (1987). The Social Construction of Facts and Artifacts: Or How the Sociology of Science and the Sociology of Technology Might Benefit Each Other. In W. E. Bijker, T. P. Hughes, & T. J. Pinch (Eds.), *The Social Construction of Technological Systems* (pp 17-50). Cambridge: MIT Press.

Piñeiro, E. (2007). Aesthetics at the heart of logic: On the role of beauty in computing innovation. P. Guillet de Monthoux, C. Gustafsson, & S-E. Sjöstrand (Eds.), (2007), *Aesthetic leadership: Managing fields of flow in art and business* (pp. 105-127). Basingstoke: Palgrave Macmillan.

Pinnington, A., & Morris, T. (2003). Archetype change in professional organizations. *British Journal of Management, 14*(1), 85-99.

Pio, E. (2005). What's Stopping you? Find out through Haiku. *Workplace Spirituality*. www.workplacespirituality.info/haiku.html. (Accessed 02.02.05)

Piore, M., & Sabel, C. (1984). *The second industrial divide: Possibilities for prosperity*. New York: Basic Books.

Pirenne, M. H. (1964). The Scientific Basis for Leonardo Da Vinci's Theory of Perspective. *The British Journal for the Philosophy of Science, 3* (1952-1953), 169-185.

Plato (1921). *Theaetetus*. Indianapolis and Cambridge: Hackett Publishing.

Plato (1956). *Protagoras & Meno*. London: Penguin.

Polanyi, M. & Prosch, H. (1975). *Meaning*. Chicago, IL: University of Chicago Press.

Polanyi, M. (1958). Personal knowledge: Towards a post-critical philosophy. Chicago: The University of Chicago Press.

Polanyi, M. (1964). *Personal Knowledge*. New York: Harper and Row.

Polanyi, M. (1966). *The Tacit Dimension*. Gloucester, MA: P. Smith.

Polanyi, M. (1967). *The tacit dimension*. Garden City, N.Y.,: Anchor Books.

Polanyi, M. (1969). Knowing and being: Essays by michael polyani. London: Routledge.

Polanyi, M., & Prosch, H. (1975). *Meaning*. Chicago: University of Chicago Press.

Pollitt, C., & Bouckaert, G. (2000). *Public management reform: a comparative analysis*. Oxford ; New York: Oxford University Press.

Pollock, J. L., & Cruz, J. (1999). *Contemporary Theories of Knowledge*. Lanham: Rowman&Littlefield.

Polyani, M. (1966). *The Tacit Dimension*. London: Routledge & Kegan.

Ponzi, L. J., & Michael, K. (2002). Knowledge management: another management fad? *Information Research, 8*(1), retrieved from http://informationr.net/ir/8-1/paper145.html.

Porcello, T. (2004). Speaking of sound: Language and the professionalization of sound-recording engineers. *Social Studies of Science, 34*(5), 733-758.

Porter, M. (1980). *Competitive strategy: techniques for analysing industries and competitors.* New York: The Free Press.

Porter, M. (1985). *Competitive advantage.* New York: The Free Press.

Porter, M. (1990). *Competitive Advantage of Nations.* New York: Macmillan.

Porter, M. (1998). *On competition.* Boston: Harvard Business School Press.

Porter, M.E. (1980): Competitive strategy. Free Press, New York.

Posner, M. I., & Snyder, C. R. R. (1975). Facilitation and inhibition in the processing of signals. In P. M. A. Rabbitt & S. Dornic (Eds.), *Attention and Performance V* (pp. 669-682). New York: Academic Press.

Poster, M. (2001). *The information subject: Essays.* Amsterdam: G+B Arts.

Poster, W. (2007). 'Who's on the line? Indian call centre agents pose as Americans for US outsourced firms', *Industrial Relations,* 46(2): 271-304.

Potter, J. (1997). Discourse analysis as a way of analysing naturally occurring talk. In D. Silverman (Ed.), *Qualitative research* (pp. 144-160). London: Sage.

Potter, J., & Wetherell, M. (1987). *Discourse and social psychology. Beyond attitudes and behaviour.* London: Sage.

Poulter, D. and Land, C. (2008). Preparing to work: dramaturgy, cynicism and normative 'remote' control in the socialization of graduate recruits in management consulting. *Culture and Organization, 14*(1), 65-78.

Powell W. W. (1990). Neither market nor hierarchy: network forms of organisations. In *Research in organisational behaviour, 12*, 95-336.

Powell, W., Koput, K., & Smith-Doerr, L. (1996). Interorganizational collaboration and the locus of innovation: networks of learning in biotechnology. In *Administrative Science Quarterly, 41*(1), 116-146.

Pöyhönen, A. (2004). *Modeling and Measuring Organizational Renewal Capability.* Doctoral Dissertation. Acta Universitatis Lappeenrantaensis 200. Lappeenranta: Lappeenranta University of Technology.

Pöyhönen, A. (forthcoming). *Development and Validation of a Method for Measuring Organizational Renewal Capability.*

Prahalad, C. K., & Bettis, R. A. (1986). The dominant logic: A new linkage between diversity and performance. *Strategic Management Journal, 7,* 485-502.

Prahalad, C., & Hamel, G. (1990). 'The Core Competence of the Corporation. *Harvard Business Review* May-June: (pp. 79-91).

Prange, C. (1999): Organizational learning – desperately seeking theory. In: Easterby-Smith, M., Araujo, L., & Burgoyne, J. (eds.): Organizational learning and the learning organization. Thousand Oaks, Sage Publications, 23-42.

Prange, C./Bojkowsky, B./Wieshofer, B.(2004): Networking capability as a prerequisite for cooperative innovation success - An individual manager's perspective. IASTED-Conference, Cambridge, MIT

Prasad, P. (1993). Symbolic process in the implementation of technological change: A symbolic interactionist study of work computerization. *Academy of Management Journal, 36*(6), 1400- 1429.

Price, J. (1997). Handbook of Organizational Measurement. *International Journal of Manpower, 18*(4/5/6), 305-558.

Prichard, C. (2000). Know, learn and share! The knowledge phenomenon and the construction of a consumptive-communicative body. In C. Prichard, R. Hull, M. Chumer, & H. Willmott (Eds.), *Managing knowledge: Critical investigations of work and learning.* London: Macmillian Business.

Prichard, C., Hull, R., Chumer, M., & Willmott, H. (Eds.) (2000). *Managing knowledge: Critical investigations of work and learning.* London: MacMillan.

Priem, R. L., & Butler, J. E. (2001). Is the resource-based "view" a useful perspective for strategic management research? *Academy of Management Review, 26*(1), 22-40.

Proceedings of the 2006 CRTI Summer Symposium. (2006). Paper presented at the CRTI Summer Symposium, Aylmer, Quebec.

Prusak, L. (2001). Where did knowledge management come from? *IBM Systems Journal, 40*(4), 1002-1017.

Pugh, S. (1991). *Total design – Integrated methods for successful product engineering.* UK: Addison-Wesley Publishing.

Pugh, S., & Moreley, I. E. (1988). *Total Design: Towards a theory of total design and Total Design: Some questions and some answers.* Design division, University of Strathclyde, UK.

Quelin, B., & Duhamel, F. (2003). Bringing together strategic outsourcing and corporate strategy: outsourcing motives and risks. *European Management Journal, 21*(5), 647-661.

Quinn, J. B. (1991). Managing innovation: controlled chaos. In H. Mintzberg & J. B. Quinn (Eds.), *The strategy process: concepts, contexts & cases* (2nd ed) (pp. 746-758). Englewood Cliffs, NJ: Prentice Hall.

Quinn, J. B. (1992). *Intelligent enterprise: a knowledge and service based paradigm for industry.* New York: Free Press.

Quinn, J. B. (1999). Strategic outsourcing: leveraging knowledge capabilities. *Sloan Management Review,* summer 1999, (pp. 9-21).

Quinn, J. B., Anderson, P., & Finkelstein, S. (1996). Leveraging Intellect. *Academy of Management Executive, 10*(3), 7-27.

Quinn, J., & Hilmer, F. (1994). Strategic outsourcing. *Sloan Management Review,* summer 1994, 43-55.

Quintas, P., Lefrere, P., & Jones, G. (1997). Knowledge management: a strategic agenda. *Long Range Planning, 30*(3), 385-391.

Raelin J. A., 1985, 'The Basis for the Professional's Resistance to Managerial Control', *Human Resource Management*, Summer, Vol. 24, Number 2: pp. 147-175.

Raelin, J.A. (1989). 'Unionization and Deprofessionalization: Which Comes First?',

Ramesh, B. (2004). 'Cybercoolies in BPOs', *Economic and Political Weekly*, 39 (5): 492-497.

Ramsey, C. (2005). Narrative: From Learning in Reflection to Learning in Performance. *Management Learning, 36*, 219 - 235.

Reason, P. (2001). Learning and Change through action research. In J. Henry (Ed.), *Creative Management.* London: Sage Publications.

Rediker, M. (2007). *The Slave Ship: A Human History.* London: John Murray.

Reich, R. (1992). *The Work of Nations.* New York: Random House.

Reid, S. E., & Brentani, U. de (2004). The fuzzy front end of the new product development for discontinuous innovations: a theoretical model. *Journal of Product Innovation Management, 21*(3), 170-198.

Reilly, N.H., Brad, J.M., & Stroh, L.K. (1993): The impact of corporate turbulence on managers' attitudes. Strategic Management Journal, 14, 167-179.

Retort Collective (2005). *Afflicted Powers: Capital and Spectacle in a New Age of War.* London: Verso.

Reve, T. (1990). The firm as a nexus of internal and external contracts. In M. Aoki (Ed.), *The firm as a nexus of treaties.* London: Sage.

Ricceri, F. (2008). *Intellectual Capital and Knowledge Management: Strategic Management of Knowledge Resources.* London and New York: Routledge.

Rice, R., & Aydin, C. (1991). Attitudes toward new organisational technology: network proximity as a mechanism for social information processing. *Administrative Science Quarterly,* 36(2), 219-226.

Richardson, K. A. (2001). *On the status of natural boundaries: A complex systems perspective.* Paper presented at the Systems in management: 7th annual ANZSYS Conference.

Richardson, K. A. (2005). Volume Introduction. In K. A. Richardson (Ed.), *Managing the Complex: Philosophy, Theory and Application* (Vol. One, pp. iii-viii). Greenwich Connecticut: IAP Information Age Publishing.

Richter, I. (1998). Individual and organizational learning at the executive level: towards a research agenda. *Management Learning, 29*, 299-316.

Ricoeur, P. (1984/2003). *Time and Narrative, 3.* Chicago: Univ. of Chicago Press.

Ricoeur, P. (1995). Manifestation and Proclamation. In D. M. Pellauer (trans.) & I Wallace (Ed.), *Figuring the Sacred.* U.S.A.: Fortress Press.

Riiter, T. et al (2002). Measuring network competence: some international evidence. *Journal of Business & Industrial Marketing, 17*(2/3), 119-138.

Ritter, T. (1998): Innovationserfolg durch Netzwerkkompetenz – Effektives Management von Unternehmensnetzwerken. Gabler, Wiesbaden.

Ritter, T., & Gemünden, H.G. (2003) Network competence: Its impact on innovation success and its antecedents. Journal of Business Research, 56, 745-755.

Robertson, M., & Hammersley, G. O. (2000). Knowledge Management Practices within a Knowledge-Intensive Firm: The Significance of the People Management Dimension. *Journal of European Industrial Training, 24*(2-4), 241-254.

Robertson, M., & Swan, J. (2003). Control — What Control? Culture and Ambiguity within a Knowledge Intensive Firm. *Journal of Management Studies, 40*(4), 831-858.

Robinson, W. T., & Chiang, J. (2002). Product development strategies for established market pioneers, early followers, and late entrants. *Strategic Management Journal, 23*(9), 855-864.

Rogers, E. M., Dearing, J. W., & Bregman, D. (1993). The Anatomy of Agenda-Setting Research. *Journal of Communication, 43*(2), 68-84.

Rogers, E., & Larsen, J. (1984). *Silicon Valley fever.* New York: Basic Books.

Rolland, K., Hepsø, V., & Monteiro, E. (2006). (Re)conceptualizing Common Information Spaces Across Heterogeneous Contexts: im/mutable mobiles and imperfection. Proceedings of the CSCW 2006 New York: ACM Press.

Romberg, D. (1998). *Knowledge management market to hit $5 billion.* Computing Canada, September 11, http://ntsrv2000.educ.ualberta.ca/nethowto/urlsubmit/knowledge/hype/5%20billion.htm, access date: 5.05.2003

Romer, P.M., & Kurtzman, J. (2004). In *Handbook on Knowledge Management,* Chapter 1: Knowledge Matters, (pp. 73-87).

Roos, G., & Jacobsen, K. (1999). Management in a complex stakeholder organization: a case study of the application of the IC-process to a branch of the Commonwealth Public Service. *Monash Mt. Eliza Business Review, 2*(1), 82-93.

Roos, G., & Roos, J. (1997). Measuring your company's intellectual performance. *Long Range Planning,* 30(3), 413-426.

Roos, G., Pike, S., & Fernström, L. (2005). *Managing Intellectual Capital in Practice.* Oxford: Elsevier.

Roos, J., Roos, G., Dragonetti, N. C., & Edvinsson, L. (1998). *Intellectual capital: Navigating in the New Business Landscape.* New York: New York University Press.

Roscigno, V. J., & Hodson, R. (2004). The Organizational and Social Foundations of Worker Resistance. *American Sociological Review, 69*(1), 14-39

Rose, E., & Wright, G. (2005). 'Satisfaction and dimensions of control among call centre customer service representatives', *International Journal of Human Resource Management,* 16 (1): 136-160.

Rosenbloom, R. S. (2000). Leadership, Capabilities, and Technological Change: The Transformation of NCR in the Electronic Era. *Strategic Management Journal, 21*, 1083-1103.

Ross, A. (2000). The Mental Labor Problem. *Social Text, 18*(2), 1-31.

Rothman, R. A. (1984). 'Deprofessionalization: the case of law in America', *Work and Occupations,* 11(2): 183-206.

Rothwell, R. (1992). Successful industrial innovation: critical success factors for the 1990s. *R&D Management, 22*(2), 221-239.

Rothwell, R., Freeman, C., Horlsey, A., Jervis, V. T. P., Robertson, A. B., & Townsend, J. (1974). SAPPHO updated: Project SAPPHO phase II. *Research Policy, 3*, 258–91.

Rousseau, D.M. (1990). 'New hire perceptions of their own and their employer's obligations: a study of psychological contracts', *Journal of Organisational Behaviour* 11(5):389–400.

Roy, D. (1952). Quota restriction and goldbricking in a machine shop. *American Journal of Sociology, 57,* 427-442.

Rumelt, D. P. (1984). Towards a Strategic Theory of the Firm. Alternative theories of the firm, (2), 286-300, *Elgar Reference Collection. International Library of Critical Writings in Economics, 154*. Cheltenham, U.K. and Northampton, Mass.: Elgar; distributed by American International Distribution Corporation, Williston.

Rumelt, R. P. (1991). How much does industry matter? *Strategic Management Journal, 12,* 167-185.

Rumelt, R.P. (1984): Towards a strategic theory of the firm. In: Lamb, R.B. (eds): Competitive strategic management. Prentice-Hall: Englewood Cliffs, NJ, 556-570.

Rumizen, M. C. (2002). *The complete idiot's guide to knowledge management.* Madison: Alpha Books.

Ruscio, J., Whitney, D. M., & Amabile, T .M. (1998). Looking inside the Fishbowl of Creativity: Verbal and Behavioral Predictors of Creative Performance. *Creativity Research Journal, 11*(3), 243-263.

Ruuska, I. E., & Vartiainen, M. (2005). Characteristics of knowledge-sharing communities in project organizations. *International Journal of Project Management, 23*(5), 374-9.

Ryle, G. (1949). *The Concept of Mind.* London: Hutchinson.

Sadler-Smith, E., & Badger, B. (1998). HR practitioners' attitudes to continuing professional development. *Human Resource Management Journal, 8*, 66-75.

Sadler-Smith, E., Allinson, C. W., & Hayes J. (2000). Cognitive style and learning preferences: some implications for CPD. *Management Learning, 31*, 239-256.

Saint-Onge, H., & Wallace, D. (2003). *Leveraging Communities of Practice for Strategic Advantage*. Amsterdam: Butterworth-Heinemann.

Sako, M. (1992). Prices, Quality and Trust: inter-firm relations in Britain and Japan.

Salzer-Mörling, M. (1998). Murderous Ink: A Case of Rhetorical Killing. *Studies in Cultures, Organizations and Societies, 4*, 125-145.

Sandberg, J. (2000). Understanding human competence at work: An interpretative approach. *Academy of Management Journal, 43*(1), 9-25.

Sanna-Randaccio, F., & Veugelers, R. (2007). Multinational knowledge spillovers with decentralised R&D: a game-theoretic approach. *Journal of International Business Studies, 38*(1), 47-63.

Saren, M. A. (1984). A classification and review of models of the intra-firm innovation process. *R&D Magazine, 14*(1), 11-24.

Saxenian, A. (1994). *Regional advantage.* Cambridge: Harvard University Press.

Scarbrough, H. (1995). Blackboxes, hostages and prisoners. *Organization Studies, 16*(6), 991-1019.

Scarbrough, H. (1998). Path(ological) dependence? Core competencies from an organizational perspective. *British Journal of Management, 9,* 219-32.

Schank, R. C., & Abelson, R. P. (1977). *Scripts, plans, goals, and understanding.* Hillsdale, NJ: Erlbaum.

Scharmer, O. (2001). Self-Transcending Knowledge: Sensing and Organizing around Emerging Opportunities. *Journal of Knowledge Management, 5*(2), 137-151.

Schein, E. H. (1985). *Organizational culture and leadership.* San Francisco: Jossey-Bass.

Schein, J. (1999). What is corporate culture anyway? In *The corporate culture survival Guide*, chapter 2, , CA: Jossey-Bass, San Francisco.

Schienstock, G. (2004). *Embracing the Knowledge Economy.* Cheltenham: Edward Elgar.

Schmidt, K., & Bannon, L. (1992). Taking CSCW seriously - Supporting articulation work. Computer Supported Cooperative Work (CSCW), 1(1), 7-40.

Schön, D. (1983). *The Reflective Practitioner: How Professionals Think in Action.* New York: Basic Books.

Schon, D. (1985). *The Design Studio.* London: RIBA Publications.

Schön, D. (1987). *Educating the Reflective Practitioner.* San Francisco: Jossey-Bass.

Schön, D. (Ed.) (1991). *The Reflective Turn.* New York: Teachers College Press.

Schor, J. (1991). *The Overworked American.* New York: Basic Books.

Schor, J. (1991). *The Overworked American: The Unexpected Decline of Leisure.* New York: Basic Books.

Schrage, M. (2000): Serious play: How the world's best companies simulate to innovate. Harvard Business School, Cambridge, MA.

Schreiner, M. (2004): Collaborative capability in vendor-service provider relationships: Construct development and empirical analysis in the software service industry. Doctoral Thesis, Universität St. Gallen.

Schreiner, M., & Corsten, D. (2004): Integrating perspectives: A multidimensional construct of collaborative capability. In: Beyerlein, M. Johnson, D., & Beyerlein, S. (eds): Complex collaboration: Building the capabilities to work across boundaries. JAI Press, 125-159.

Schreyögg, G., & Koch, J. (2005). *Knowledge Management and Narratives: Organizational Effectiveness Through Storytelling.* Edited by (Berlin: Erich Schmidt Verlag GmbH & Co).

Schrödinger, E. (1946). *What is life? Physical aspects of the living cell.* Cambridge: Cambridge at the University Press.

Schroeder, A., & Pauleen, D. (2007). KM Governance: Investigating the Case of Knowledge Intensive Research Organization. *Journal of Enterprise Information, 20*(4), 414-431.

Schultze, U., & Stabell, C. (2004). Knowing what you don't know? Discourses and contradictions in knowledge management research. *Journal of Management Studies, 41*, 549-73.

Schulz, M., & Jobe, L. A. (2001). Codification and Tacitness as Knowledge Management Strategies: An Empirical Exploration. *Journal of High Technology Management Research, 12*, 139-165.

Schumpeter, J. A. (1934). *The Theory of Economic Development.* Cambridge, MA: Harvard University Press.

Schwartz, H.S. (1987). 'On the psychodynamics of organizational totalitarianism', *Journal. of Management*, 13(1): 41–54.

Science 2020 (2006). Microsoft Research, Cambridge, UK. (Available at http://research.microsoft.com/towards2020science/ Accessed March 9, 2007)

Sciulli, D. (2005) 'Continental Sociology of Professions Today: Conceptual Contributions', *Current Sociology,* 53(6): 915-942.

Searle, J. R. (1969). *Speech Acts: An Essay in the Philosophy of Language.* London: Cambridge University Press.

Searle, J. R. (1995). *The construction of social reality.* New York: Free Press.

Seely-Brown, J., & Duguid, P. (2000). *The Social Life of Information.* Boston: Harvard Business School Press.

Senge, P. (1990). *The Fifth Discipline-The Art and Practice of the Learning Organization.* New York: Doubleday/Currency, cop.

Senge, P. (1990/2006). *Piąta dyscyplina. Teoria i praktyka organizacji uczących się.* Kraków: Wolters Kluwer.

Senge, P. M., Kleiner, A., Roberts, C., Roth, G., Ross, R., Smith, B. (1999). The dance of change: The challenges to sustaining momentum in learning organizations. New York: Currency/Doubleday.

Sethi, R. (2000). New product Quality and Product Development Teams. *Journal of Marketing, 64*(2), 1-14.

Sethia, N. K., & Von Glinow, M. A. (1985). Arriving at four cultures by managing the reward system. In R. H. Kilmannet al.(Eds.), *Gaining control of the corporate culture* (pp. 400-20). San Francisco, CA: Jossey Bass.

Sewell, W. H. (2005). *Logics of History: Social Theory and Social Transformation.* University of Chicago Press.

Shapiro, S. (1987). The social control of impersonal trust. *American Journal of Sociology, 93*(3), 623-58.

Shariq, S. (1997). Knowledge management: an emerging discipline. *Journal of Knowledge Management, 1*(1), 75-82.

Shaw, G., Brown, R., & Bromiley, P. (1998). Strategic stories: how 3M is rewriting business planning. *Harvard Business Review,* May-June 1998, (pp. 41-50).

Shaw, P. (2002). *Changing Conversations in Organizations: A complexity Approach to Change.* London: Routledge.

Shenhar, A. J. (2001). One size does not fit all projects: Exploring classical contingency domains. *Management Science, 47*(3), 394-414.

Shenkar, O., & Ellis, S. (1995): Death of the "organization" man: Temporal relations in strategic alliances. The International Executive, 37, 537-553.

Sheth, J. (1996). Organizational buying behaviour: past performance and future expectations. *Journal of Business and Industrial Marketing, 11*(1), 7-24.

Shields, R. (n.d.). The Ethic of the Index and its space-time effects. (details of paper not known at this point).

Shlain, L, (1998). *The Alphabet versus the Goddess: Male Words and Female Images.* London: Allen Lane, The Penguin Press.

Shneiderman, B. (2001). *Inventing Discovery Tools: Combining Information Visualization with Data Mining.* Retrieved March 6, 2007, from University of Maryland, Department of Computer Science Web site: http://hcil.cs.umd.edu/trs/2001-16/2001-16.pdf

Siatri, R. (1998). Information seeking in an electronic environment: a comparative investigation among computer scientists in British and Greek Universities. *Information Research, 4*(2). Retrieved 12 October 2004 from htpt://information.net/ir

Sieloff, C. G. (1999). If only hp knew what hp knows: The roots of knowledge management at Hewlett-packard. *Journal of Knowledge Management, 3*(1), 47-53.

Silverman, D. (1993). *Interpreting qualitative data: Methods for analysing talk, text and interaction.* London: Sage.

Simon H. A. (1979), 'The architecture of complexity the sciences of artificial', Cambridge: MIT Press.

Simon, H. (1955. A Behavioral Model of Rational Choice. *Quarterly Journal of Economics, 69,* 99-118.

Simon, H. (1957). *Models of Man – Social and Rational.* New York: John Wiley & Sons.

Simonin, B. (1997): The importance of collaborative know-how. Academy of Management Journal, 40, 1150-1174.

Simons, R. (1991). Strategic orientation and top management attention to control systems. *Strategic Management Journal,* (pp. 49-62).

Simons, R. (1995). Control in an age of empowerment. *Harvard Business Review,* March-April.

Simons, R. (2000). *Performance measurement and control systems for implementing strategy: text and cases*. Prentice Hall.

Simpson, J. A., & Weiner, E. (1989). The oxford english dictionary (2nd Ed.). Oxford University Press.

Sitkin, S., & Roth, N. (1993). Explaining the limited effectiveness of legalistic "remedies" for trust/distrust. *Organization Science*, *4*, 367-392.

Sitkin, S., & Stickel, D. (1996). The road to hell: the dynamics of distrust in an era of quality. In R. Kramer & T. Tyler (Eds.), *Trust in Organizations. Frontiers of theory and Research*. Thousand Oaks: CA: Sage.

Sivadas, E., & Dwyer, F.R. (2000): An examination of organizational factors influencing new product success in internal and alliance-based processes. Journal of Marketing, 64, 31-49.

Smart P., Bessant, J., & Gupta, A. (2007). Towards technological designing innovation a dynamic capabilities. *International Journal of Operations and Production Management*, 27(10), 1069-1092

Smith, K. G., Collins, C. J., & Clark, K. D. (2005). Existing Knowledge, Knowledge Creation Capability, and the Rate of New Product Introduction in High-Technology Firms. *Academy of Management Journal*, *48*(2), 346-357.

Snell, R., & Chak A. M. (1998). The learning organization: learning and empowerment for whom? *Management Learning*, *29*, 337-64.

Snider, H. W. (1963). 'Problems of professionalism' *Journal Of Insurance*, 30 (4): 563-572.

Snow, C. C., & Hrebiniak, L. G. (1980). Strategy, distinctive competence, and organizational performance. *Administrative Science Quarterly*, *25*, 317-336.

Snowden, D. (2000). Cynefin: a sense of time and space, the social ecology of knowledge management In C. Despres & D. Chauvel (Eds.), *Knowledge Horizons: The Present and the Promise of Knowledge Management*. Butterworth-Heinemann: Oxford.

Snowden, D. (2002). Complex Acts of Knowing: Paradox and Descriptive Self-Awareness. *Journal of Knowledge Management*, *6*(2), 100-111.

Snowden, D., & Boone, M. (2007). A Leader's Framework for Decision Making. *Harvard Business Review*. November 2007.

Snyder, W. M., & Wenger, E. (2003). Communities of practice in government: the case for sponsorship (pp. 86).

Society for Knowledge Economics (SKE),(2005). *Australian Guiding Principles on Extended Performance Management*. Sydney: SKE.

Souder, W. E. (1987). *Managing new product innovations*. Lexington, MA: Lexington Books.

Southon, F. C. G., Todd, R. J., & Seneque, M. (2002). Knowledge management in three organizations: An exploratory study. *Journal of the American Society for Information Science and Technology*, *53*(12), 1047-1059.

Spekman, R.E., Forbes, T.M.III, Isabelly, L.A., & MacAvoy, T.C. (1998): Alliance management: A view from the past and a look to the future. Journal of Management Studies, 35, 747-772.

Spencer, L. M., & Spencer, S. M. (1993). *Competence at Work: Models for Superior Performance*. New York: John Wiley & Sons.

Spender, J. C. (1996). Competitive Advantage form Tacit Knowledge? Unpacking the Concept and Its Strategic Implications. In B. Moingeon & A, Edmondson (Eds.), *Organizational Learning Competitive Advantage*, (pp. 56-73). London: Sage Publications.

Spender, J. C. (1996). Making knowledge the basis of a dynamic theory of the firm. *Strategic Management Journal*, *17*(winter special issue), 45-62.

Spender, J.-C. (1996). Making Knowledge the Basis of a Dynamic Theory of the Firm. *Strategic Management Journal*, *17*, 45-62.

Spender, J.-C. (1996). Organizational Knowledge, Learning and Memory: Three Concepts in Search of a Theory. *Journal of Organizational Change*, *9*(1), 63-78.

Spender, J.-C., & Grant, R. (1996). Knowledge and the Firm: An Overview. *Strategic Management Journal, 17*, 5-9.

Spender, J-C. (1996). Making Knowledge the Basis of a Dynamic Theory of the Firm. *Strategic Management Journal, 17*, 45-62.

Spender. J.-C., & Marr, B. (2006). How a Knowledge-Based Approach Might Illuminate the Notion of Human Capital and its Measurement. *Expert Systems with Applications, 30(*2), 265-271.

Spivak, G. C. (1985). Scattered Speculations on the Question of Value. *Diacritics, 15*(4), 73-93.

Spradley, J. P. (1980). *Participant Observation.* New York: Holt Rhinehart and Winston.

Stacey, R. D. (2003). Learning as an Activity of Interdependent People. *The Learning Organization, 10*(6), 325-331.

Stacey, R. D. (2005). *Experiencing Emergence in Organizations: Local Interactions and the Emergence of Global Pattern.* Abingdon: Routledge.

Stacey, R. D. (2006). The Science of Complexity: An Alternative Perspective for Strategic Change Processes. In R. MacIntosh *et al* (Eds.), *Complexity and Organizations: Readings and Conversations.* Abingdon: Routledge.

Ståhle, P., & Grönroos, M. (2000). *Dynamic Intellectual capital.* Knowledge Management in Theory and Practice. Porvoo: WSOY.

Ståhle, P., Ståhle, S., & Pöyhönen, A. (2003). *Analyzing Dynamic Intellectual capital: System-Based Theory and Application.* Acta Universitatis Lappeenrantaensis, 152. Lappeenranta: Lappeenranta University of Technology.

Star, S. L., & Bowker, G. C. (2002). How to infrastructure. In L. A. Lievrouw & S. Livingstone (Eds.), (2002), *Handbook of new media: Social shaping and consequences of ICT.* (pp. 151-162). London, Thousand Oaks & New Delhi: Sage.

Star, S. L., & Griesemer, J. R. (1989). Institutional Ecology, Translations, and Boundary Objects: Amateurs and Professionals in Berkeley's Museum of Vertebrate Zoology, 1907-1939. Social Studies of Science, 19(3), 387-420.

Starbuck, W. H. (1992), Learning by Knowledge-intensive Firms. *Journal of Management Studies 3*(4), 262-275.

Steiner, L. (2003). Roots of Identity in Real Estate Industry. *Corporate Reputation Review, 6*(2) (March), 178-196.

Steinmueller W. E, 2000, 'Will New Information and Communication Technologies Improve 'Codification' of Knowledge?', *Industrial and Corporate Change,* Vol. 9, No. 2, March.

Stengers, I. (1997). *Power and invention: Situating science.* Minneapolis & London: Minnesota University Press.

Stern, S. (1995). What's your company's EVA? What you don't know may be hurting you. *Advertisement in the Harvard Business Review*, July-August, (p. 143).

Sternberg, R. J. (1986). Intelligence, Wisdom, and Creativity: Three is Better than One. *Educational Psychologist 21*(3), 175-190.

Sternberg, R. J., Forsythe, G. B., Hedlund, J., Horvath, J. A., Wagner, R. K., Williams, W. M., Snook, S., & Grigorenko, E. L. (2000). *Practical Intelligence in everyday life*. Cambridge: Cambridge University Press.

Steuer, J. (1992). Defining Virtual Reality: Dimensions Determining Telepresence. *Journal of Communication, 42*(4), 73–93.

Stewart, T. A. (1997). *Intellectual capital: The New Wealth of Organizations.* New York: Doubleday

Stewart, T. A. (1998). Intellectual capital: The new wealth of organizations. New York: Bantam.

Stewart, T. A. (2001). The wealth of knowledge: Intellectual capital and the twenty-first century organization. New York: Currency.

Stinchcombe, A. L. (1965). Social Structure and Organizations. In J. G. March (Ed.), *Handbook of Organizations* (pp. 142-193). Chicago: Rand McNally.

Stinchcombe, A. L., & Heimer, C. A. (1988). Interorganizational relations and careers in computer software firms. In I. H. Simpson & R. L. Simpson (Eds.), *Research in the sociology of work, 5,* 179-204.

Stivers, R. (1999). *Technology as magic: The triumph of the irrational.* New York: Continuum.

Stoneman, P. (1983). *The Economic Analysis of Technological Change.* Cambridge: Cambridge University Press.

Storbacka, K., Strandvik, T., & Grönroos, C. (1994): Managing customer relationships for profit: The dynamics of relationship quality. International Journal of Service Industry Management, 5, 5, 21-38.

Storey, J. (2005). Human Resource Policies for Knowledge Work. In T. Ray, P. Quintas & S. Little (Eds.), *Managing Knowledge: An Essential Reader.* London: Sage, (pp. 199-219).

Stovel, M., & Bontis, N. (2002). Voluntary turnover: knowledge management – friend or foe? *Journal of Intellectual Capital, 3*(3), 303-322.

Strannegård, L., & Friberg, M. (2001). *Already elsewhere. Play, identity and speed in the business world.* Sweden: Raster Forlag.

Strati, A. (1999). *Organization and Aesthetics.* London, Sage publishing.

Streatfield, P. J. (2001). *The Paradox of Control in Organizations.* London: Routledge.

Streng, D. J. (1999). Knowledge management: An essential framework for corporate library leadership. *Advances in Library Administration and Organization, 16,* 1-30.

Striukova, L. (2007). Patents and corporate value creation: theoretical approach. *Journal of Intellectual Capital, 8*(3), 431-443.

Styhre, A. (2003). *Understanding Knowledge Management: Critical and Postmodern Perspectives.* Copenhagen: Copenhagen Business School Press.

Styhre, A. (2003). *Understanding knowledge management: Critical and postmodern perspectives.* Malmö: Liber; Oslo: Abstrakt; Copenhagen: Copenhagen Business School Press.

Styhre, A., & Sundgren, M. (2005). *Managing Creativity in Organizations. Critique and Practices.* New York: Palgrave Macmillan

Subcommittee on Management & Intellectual Assets (SMIA) (2005). *Interim Report by Subcommittee on Management & Intellectual Assets,* August, Japan.

Subramanian, M., & Youndt, M. A. (2005). The Influence of Intellectual Capital on the Types of Innovative Capabilities. *Academy of Management Journal, 48*(3), 450-463.

Sullivan, P. H. (1998). *Profiting from Intellectual capital - Extracting Value from Innovation.* New York: Wiley.

Suomala, P., & Jokionen, I. (2003). The pattern of success in product development: a case study. *European Journal of Innovation Management, 6*(4), 213-227.

Sveiby K. E. (1997). *The New Organizational Wealth: Managing and Measuring Knowledge Based Assets.* San Francisco: Berret Koehler.

Sveiby, K. E. (2001). *A knowledge-based theory of the firm to guide strategy formulation.* Journal of Intellectual Capital, *2*(4), 344-358.

Sveiby, K. E. (2007). Disabling the context for knowledge work: the role of managers' behaviours. *Management Decision 45*(10), 1636-1655.

Sveiby, K-E. (2008). www.sveiby.com, © March 1996. Updated 1 March 1998, 3 June 1998 20, March 1999, April 2000, and April 2001.

Swailes S. (2003). 'Professionalism: Evolution and Measurement', t*he Service Industries Journal,* 23 (2): 130-149.

Swan, J., Newell, S., Scarbrough, H., & Hislop, D. (1999). Knowledge management and innovation: networks and networking. *Journal of Knowledge Management, 3,* 262-75.

Swan, J., Robertson, M., & Bresnen, M. (2001). Knowledge Management and the colonization of knowledge.

CMS Conference: The Dissemination of Management Knowledge Stream, July 2001

Swanson, E. B. (2000). *Information Systems as Buzz*. Information Systems Working Paper 1-00. Los Angeles: The Anderson School at UCLA.

Swanson, E. B., & Ramiller, N. C. (1997). The Organizing Vision in Information Systems Innovation. *Organization Science, 8*(5), 458-474.

Swart, J., & Kinnie, N. (2003). HR Policies and Processes in Knowledge Intensive Organisations. *Human Resource Management Journal, 13* (2), 13-28.

Swidler, A. (1986). Culture in Action: Symbols and Strategies. *American Sociological Review,* 51, 273-286.

Swieringa, J., & Wierdsma, A. (1992). Becoming a Learning Organization: Beyond the Learning Curve. Wokingham, UK: Addison-Wesley.

Szulanski, G. (1996). Exploring internal stickness: Impediments to the transfer of best practice within the firm. *Strategic Management Journal, 17 (special issue),* 27-43.

Szulanski, G., & Winter, S. (2002). Getting it Right the Second Time. *Harvard Business Review, 80* (1), 63-69.

Szulanski, G., Cappetta R., Jensen R. J. (2004). 'When and how trustworthiness matters: knowledge transfer and the moderating effect of causal ambiguity', *Organization Science*, Volume 15, Numeber 5, pp. 600-613.

Takeuchi, H., & Nonaka, I. (2004). *Hitotsubashi on Knowledge Management*. Singapore: John Wiley & Sons.

Tannenbaum S. I. (1997). Enhancing Continuous Learning: Diagnosis Finding from Multiple Companies. *Human Resource Management, 36*(4), 437-452.

Tapscott, D. (1996). *The Digital Economy*. New York: McGraw Hill.

Taylor, N. (1996). Professionalism and Monitoring CPD: Kafka Revisited. *Planning Practice and Research, 11*(4), 379-389.

Taylor, P. and Bain, P. (2005). 'India calling to the faraway towns": The call centre labour process and globalisation', *Work, Employment and Society,* 19(2):261-282.

Taylor, P., & Bain, P. (1999). An assembly line in the head': work and employee relations in the call centre. *Industrial Relations Journal, 30*(2), 101-117.

Taylor, S. S., & Hansen, H. (2005). Finding form: Looking at the field of organizational aesthetics. *Journal of Management Studies, 42*(6), 1211-1231.

Tecnobit (2007). *Tecnobit Report.*

Teece D. J. and Pisano G., 1994, 'The Dynamic Capabilities of Firms: an Introduction', *Industrial and Corporate Change*, Volume 3, Number 3.

Teece, D. J. (1998). Research Directions for Knowledge Management. *California Management Review, 40*(3), 289-292.

Teece, D. J. (2000). *Managing Intellectual Capital.* Great Britain: Biddles Ltd., Guildford & King's Lynn.

Teece, D. J. (2003). Explicating Dynamic Capabilities: Asset Selection, Coordination, and Entrepreneurship. *Strategic Management Theory* (August 2003).

Teece, D. J. (2004). Knowledge and Competence as Strategic Assets. In *Handbook on Knowledge Management,* Chapter 1: Knowledge Matters, (pp. 129-152).

Teece, D. J., Pisano, G., & Shuen, A. (1997). Dynamic Capabilities and Strategic Management. *Strategic Management Journal, 18*(7), 509-533.

Teece, D.J. (2007): Explicating dynamic capabilities: The nature and micro-foundations of (sustainable) enterprise performance. Strategic Management Journal, 28, 1319-1350.

Teece, D.J., Pisano, G., & Shuen, A. (1997): Dynamic capabilities and strategic management. Strategic Management Journal, 18, 509-533.

Templeton, G., & Snyder, C. (1999). A model of organizational learning based on control. *International Journal of Technology Management, 18,* 705-19.

Terranova, T. (2004). *Network Culture: Politics for the Information Age*. London: Pluto.

The Sydney Morning Herald (2006) Call centre girls have more fun, but it's blamed for rise of New Delhi belly. 11 October 2006. Retrieved 28 August 2008 from http://www.smh.com.au/news/world/call-centre-girls-have-more-fun/2006/10/10/1160246130071.html

Thomas, R. (1992/1995). *Literacy and Orality in Ancient Greece*. Cambridge, England: Cambridge University Press.

Thomas, T. C., & Acuña-Narvaez, R. (2006). The convergence of biotechnology and nanotechnology: Why here, why now? *Journal of Commercial Biotechnology, 12*(2), 105-110.

Thomke, S., & Kuemmerle, W. (2002). Asset Accumulation, Interdependence and Technological Change: Evidence from Pharmaceutical Drug Discovery. *Strategic Management Journal, 23*, 619-635.

Thompson, E. P. (1993). Time, work-discipline and industrial capitalism. In E. P. Thompson, *Customs in common* (pp. 352-403). New York: The New Press.

Thompson, P. (2005). Foundation and Empire: A critique of Hardt and Negri. *Capital & Class, 86*, 73-100.

Thompson, P., Warhurst, C., & Callaghan, G. (2001). Ignorant theory and knowledgeable workers: Interrogating the connections between knowledge, skills and services. *Journal of Management Studies, 38*(7), 923-942.

Thorpe, R., & Cornelissen, J. (2003). Visual media and the construction of meaning. In D. Holman & R. Thorpe (Eds.), *Management and Language*. London: Sage.

Thrift, N. (1990). Owners' time and own time: The making of a capitalist time consciousness, 1300-1800. In J. Hassard (Ed.), *The sociology of time*. New York: St. Martin's Press.

through inheritance: Spin-out generation, development, and survival. *The Academy of Management Journal, 47, 4,* 501-522.

Tidd, J. (2000). *From knowledge management to strategic competence: Measuring technological, market and organisational innovation*. London: Imperial College Press.

Tidd, J., Bessant, J., & Pavitt, K. (1997). *Managing innovation: integrating technological, market and organizational change*. John Wiley.

Tienari, J., Holgersson, C., Meriläinen, S., & Höök P. (n.d.). *Gender relations and market discourse: the case of gender quotas in the Swedish and Finnish media.*

Timko, M., & Loynes, R. M. A. (1989). Market information needs for prarie farmers. *Canadian Journal of Agricultural Economics*, 37, 609-627.

Toffler, A. (1990). *Powershift: knowledge wealth and violence at the edge of the 21st century.* New York: Bantam Books.

Toren, N. (1975). 'Deprofessionalization and its sources', *Sociology of Work and Occupations*, 2(4): 323-337.

Törmänen, A. (2003). *Tietovarastoinnin kehitys poliisiorganisaatiossa 1992-2002.* Sisäasiainministeriö, poliisiosaston julkaisusarja 11/2003. ISBN 951-734-513-5.

Totterdell, P., Leach, D., Birdi, K., Clegg, C., & Wall, T. (2002). An investigation of the contents and consequences of major organizational innovations. *International Journal of Innovation Management, 6*(4), 1-26.

Toulmin, S. (1990). *Cosmopolis: The Hidden Agenda of Modernity.* Chicago: University of Chicago Press.

Toulmin, S., & Gustavsen, B. (1996). *Beyond Theory: Changing Organizations Through Participation, Dialogues on Work and Innovation 2.* Amsterdam: John Benjamins.

Tracey, M. (2004). A holistic approach to New Product Development: New Insights. *Journal of Supply Chain Management, 40*(4), 37-56.

Tripp, R. (1996). *Action Inquiry* www.parnetorg/PARchive/docs/tripp_96/ (Accessed 05.05.2007).

Trott, P. (2008). *Managing Innovation and New Product Development* 4th ed. London: Prentice Hall.

Trott, P., & Hoecht, A. (2004). *A Preliminary study of Enterprise Resource Planning (ERP) and its impact on the innovative capability of firms.* Paper presented at Irish Academy of Management Conference, Trinity College, Dublin, Sept 2-4.

Tsai, W. (1997). Leveraging global knowledge: an empirical study of inter-unit knowledge sharing in a multinational corporation. *Strategic Management Society Conference*, October, Barcelona, Spain.

Tsai, W. (2002). "ocial Structure of 'Competition' within a Multiunit Organization: Coordination, Competition, and Intraorganizational Knowledge Sharing. *Organization Science 13* (2), 179-190.

Tsoukas, H. (1996). Firm as a Distributed Knowledge System: A Constructionist Approach. *Strategic Management Journal, 17*, 11-25.

Tsoukas, H. (1998). Forms of knowledge and forms of life in organized contexts. In R. C. H. Chia, *In the realm of organization* (43-66). London: Routledge.

Tsoukas, H. (2003). *Handbook of Organizational Knowledge*. London: Blackwell.

Tsoukas, H. (2005). *Complex knowledge: studies of organizational epistemology.* Oxford, UK: Oxford University Press.

Tsoukas, H. (2005). Do we really understand tacit knowledge. In Haridimos T. *Complex knowledge: Studies in organizational epistemology.* New York, NY.: Oxford University Press.

Tsoukas, H., & Chia, R. (2002). On Organizational Becoming: Rethinking Organizational Change. *Organization Science, 13*(5), 567-582.

Tsoukas, H., & Vladimirou, E. (2001). What is organizational knowledge? *Journal of Management Studies, 38*(7), 973-993.

Tulin, M. F. (1997). Talking organization: Possibilities for conversation analysis in organizational behavior research. *Journal of Management Inquiry, 6*, 101-119.

Tuomi, I. (1999). *Corporate Knowledge: Theory and Practice of Intelligent Organizations.* Helsinki: Metaxis.

Tuomi, I. (2002). The future of knowledge management. *Lifelong Learning in Europe, 2*, 69-79.

Tushman, M. L., & O'Reilly, C. A. (1996). Ambidextrous organizations: managing evolutionary and revolutionary change. *California Management Review, 38*(4), 8-30.

Tushman, M., & Nadler, D. (1986). Organizing for innovation. *California Management Review, 28*(3) 74-88.

Twiss, B. (1992). *Managing Technological Innovation* 4th edn. London: Pitman.

Tyler, J. A. (2006). Only the shadow knows: Increasing organizational polyphony with liminal storytelling. *Tamara Journal, 5*(3)

Tyler, J. A. (2007). Incorporating Storytelling into Practice: How HRD Practitioners Foster Strategic Storytelling. *Human Resource Development Journal, 18*(4).

Tyler, J. A. (2007). Storyaliveness and powerful listening. *Electronic Journal of Radical Organizational Theory: Fifth International Conference on Critical Management Studies Proceedings.* Available online at http://www.mngt.waikato.ac.nz/ejrot/cmsconference/2007/proceedings.asp

Tynjälä, P. (2003). Developing Vocational Expertise in the Knowledge Society. In J. Kirjonen (Ed.), *Knowledge Work and Occupational Competence*, (pp. 85-108).

Tyre, M. J., & Von Hippel, E. (1997. The situated nature of adaptive learning in organizations. *Organization Science, 8*(1), 71-83.

Ullman, E. (1997). *Close to the machine: Technophilia and its discontents.* San Francisco: City Lights Book.

Un, C. A., & Cuervo-Cazurra, A. (2004). Strategies for Knowledge Creation in Firms. *British Journal of Management, 15*, 27-41.

Unerman, J., Guthrie, J., & Striukova, L. (2007). *UK Reporting of Intellectual Capital*, Institute of Chartered

Accountants in England and Wales Centre for Business Performance.

Utterback, J. (1994). *Mastering the dynamics of innovation.* Boston, Mass: Harvard Business School Press.

Van de Ven, A. (1986). Central Problems in the Management of Innovation. *Management Science, 32*(5), 590-607.

Van de Ven, A. H., & Poole, M. S. (1990). Methods for Studying Innovation Development in the Minnnesota Innovation Research Program. *Organization Science, 1*(3), 313-335.

Van de Ven, A., Polley, D., Garud, R., & Venkataraman, S. (1999). *Innovation Journey.* New York: Oxford University Press.

Van de Ven, A.H., & Walker, G. (1984): The dynamics of inter-organizational coordination. Administrative Science Quarterly, 29, 598-621.

van der Meer-Kooistra, J., & Vosselman, E. G. (2000). Management control of interfirm transactional relationships: the case of industrial renovation and maintenance. *Accounting, Organizations and Society, 25,* 51-77.

Van der Panne, G., Van Beers, C., & Kleinknecht, A. (2003). Success and failure of innovation: A literature review. *International Journal of Innovation Management, 7*(3), 309-338.

Van Dijk, T. (1993). Principles of critical discourse analysis. *Discourse & Society, 4*, 249-283.

Van Looy, B., Martens, T., & Debackere, K. (2005). Organizing for Continuous Innovation: On the Sustainability of Ambidextrous Organizations. *Creativity and Innovation Management, 14*(3), 208-221.

Van Maanen, J. & Barley, S. R. (1984). Occupational communities: Culture and control in organizations. In L. L. Cummings & B. M. I. Staw (Eds.), *Research in organizational behavior, 6*, 287-365. Greenwich, CT: JAI Press.

Van Maanen, J. (1979). Reclaiming qualitative methods for organizational research: a preface. *Administrative Science Quarterly, 24*, 520-526.

Van Maanen, J. 1991 The smile factory: Work at Disneyland. In P.J. Frost, L.F. Moore, M.R. Louis, C.C.Lundberg & J.Martin (eds.), *Refraining organizational culture* (pp. 58-76). Newbury Park: Sage.

Van Maanen, J., & Kunda, G. (1989). Real feelings: Emotional expression and organizational culture. In L.L. Cummings & B.M. I. Staw (Eds.), *Research in organizational behavior, 11*, 43-103. Greenwich, CT: JAI Press.

Van Maanen, J., & Schein, E. H. (1979). Toward a theory of organizational socialization. In B. M. Staw (Ed.), *Research in organizational behaviour.* Greenwich, CT.

Van Manen, M. (1998). *Researching lived experience.* Canada: Althouse.

Vattimo, G. (1992). *The Transparent Society.* Cambridge: Polity Press.

Vicari S., 1992, 'Risorse aziendali e valore', *Sinergie*, n. 29 Settembre-Dicembre: pp. 81-94.

Victor, B., & Boynton, A. (1998). *Invented Here: Maximizing Your Organization's Internal Growth and Profitability.* Boston: Harvard Business School Press.

Virkkunen, J., & Ahonen, H. (2000). *Knowledge Management as Creative Dialogue about the Future.* Paper presented in Knowledge Management conference in Sao Paulo, Brazil, 7/2000.

Virkkunen, J., & Ahonen, H. (2004). Transforming learning and knowledge creation on the shop floor. *International Journal of Human Resources Development and Management 2004, 4(1)*, 57–72.

von Hippel E., 1993, 'Trading in Trade Secrets', *Harvard Business Review*, February/March.

Von Hippel, E. (1994). "sticky information" and the locus of problem solving: Implications for innovation. *Management Science, 40,* 429-439.

Von Hippel, E., Thomke, S., & Sonnack, M. (1999). Creating breakthroughs at 3M. *Harvard Business Review,* September-October, (pp. 47-57).

von Krogh, G. (1999). *Developing a knowledge-based theory of the firm.* Available at: http://www.dialogon-leadership.org/vonKrogh-1999cp.html.

Von Krogh, G., Ichijo, J., Nonaka, I., & Ichijo, K. (2000). Enabling Knowledge Creation: How to Unlock the Mystery of Tacit Knowledge and Release the Power of Innovation. Oxford, UK:Oxford University Press.

Von Krogh, G., Ichijo, K., & Nonaka, I. (2001). *Facilitar la Creación de Conocimiento.* México: Oxford University Press.

Wagner, R. S. (2006). *The human element of organizational transformation: A phenomenographic study of how internal stakeholders in federal defense organizations experience and make sense of planned organizational change.* Fielding Graduate University, Santa Barbara.

Wallerstein, I. (1974). *The Modern World-System.* New York, NY: Academic Press.

Walter, A., Auer, M., & Ritter,M. (2006): The impact of network capabilities and entrepreneurial orientation on university spin-off performance. Journal of Business Venturing, 21, 541-567

Walters, W. P., Stahl, M. T., & Murcko, M. A. (1998). Virtual screening - An overview. *Drug Discovery Today, 3*, 160-178.

Warhurst, C., & Nickson, D. (2007). A new labour aristocracy? Aesthetic labour and routine interactive service. *Work, Employment and Society, 21*(4), 785-798.

Warhurst, C., & Thompson, P. (1998). Hands, hearts and minds: changing work and workers at the end of the century. In P. Thompson & C. Warhurst (Eds.), *Workplaces of the Future.* Basingstoke: Macmillan.

Warmington, P., Daniels, H., Edwards, Leadbetter, A., Martin, J., Brown, D., & Middleton, D. (2004). Learning in and for interagency working: conceptual tensions in 'joined up' practice. Paper presented to the *TLRP Annual Conference.* Cardiff, November

Washburn, J. (2005). *University, Inc.: The Corporate Corruption of American Higher Education.* New York: Basic Books.

Watkins, K. E., & Marsick, V. J. (1993). Sculpting the Learning Organization: Lessons in the Art and Science of Systemic Change. San Francisco: Jossey-Bass.

Weber, M. (1922/2002). *Gospodarka i społeczeństwo.* Warszawa: PWN.

Weber, M. (1947). T. Parsons (Ed.), *The Theory of Social and Economic Organization.* Oxford University Press.

Weick, K. (1976). Educational organizations as loosely coupled systems. *Administrative Science Quarterly, 21*, 1-9.

Weick, K. E. (1969). *The social psychology of organizing.* Reading, Mass.: Addison-Wesley Pub. Co.

Weick, K. E. (1991). The Nontraditional Quality of Organizational Learning. *Organization Scienc, 2*(1), 116-123.

Weick, K. E. (2006). Organizing and Failures of Imagination. *Public Management Review, 8*(3), 425-439.

Weick, K. E., & Quinn, R. E. (1999). Organizational Change and Development' *Annual Review of Psychology, 50*(1), 361-386.

Weinert, F. E. (2001). Concept of competence: a conceptual clarification. In D.S. Rychen & L. H. Salganik (Eds.), Defining and Selecting Key Competence, (pp. 45-65). Seattle: Hogrefe & Huber Publishers.

Weintraub, A., Shegda, K., & Landers, G. (2000). Universal IDM Vendors Define Their Survival Strategies. *Gartner Research Note, M-10-4123*, November 1, 2000.

Wenger E., 1998, 'Communities of Practice; Learning as a Social System', *Systems Thinker,* June.

Wenger, E. (1991). *Communities of practice: where learning happens* (pp. 6-8). Benchmark, Fall.

Wenger, E., McDermott, R., & Snyder, W. (2002). *Cultivating Communities of Practice: A Guide to Managing Knowledge.* Boston, MA: Harvard Business School Press.

Wernerfelt, B. (1984). A resource-based view of the firm. *Strategic Management Journal, 5*(2), 171–180.

Wertheim, M. (1999). *The Pearly Gates of Cyberspace: A history of space from Dante to the Internet.* England: Little Brown and Company, Virago Press.

Wheelwright, S., & Clark, K. (1992). *Revolutionising Product Development.* New York: Free Press.

Whelan, G. (2002). Appropriat(e)ing Wavelengths: On Bourdieu's *On Television. Ephemera, 2*(2), 131-148.

White, H. C. (1992). *Identity and Control: A Structural Theory of Social Action.* Princeton, NJ: Princeton University.

Whitley, E. A. (2000). Tacit and explicit knowledge: Conceptual confusion around the commodification of knowledge. Presented at the Knowledge Management: Concepts and Controversies Conference. http://is.lse.ac.uk/staff/whitley/. Accessed January 5, 2006.

Whitney, D., & Trosten-Bloom, A. (2003). *The Power of Appreciative Inquiry: A Practical Guide to Positive Change.* San Francisco: Berret-Kohler.

Whyte, D. (1994). *The Heart Aroused: Poetry and the Preservation of the Soul in Corporate America.* New York: Doubleday.

Whyte, W. (1956). *The organization man.* New York: Simon and Schuster.

Whyte, W. F., & Whyte, K. K. (1984). *Learning from the field: a guide from experience.* Beverly Hills: Sage Publications.

Whyte, W. F., & Whyte, K. K. (1991). *Making Mondragon: the growth and dynamics of the worker cooperative complex* (2nd , rev. ed.). Ithaca, N.Y.: ILR Press.

Wiener, N. (1950). *The human use of human beings.* London: Eyre and Spottiswoode.

Wiig, K. (1993). Knowledge management foundations. Arlington, TX: Schema Press.

Wiig, K. (1997). Knowledge management: an introduction and perspective. *Journal of Knowledge Management, 1*(1), 6-14.

Wiig, K. (2002). Knowledge management has many facets. Retrieved January 2003, from http://www.krii.com/downloads/Four_KM_Facets.pdf

Wilensky, H. (1964). 'The professionalization of everyone?', *American Journal of Sociology*, 70(2): 137-158.

Willcocks, L., & Lacity M. (1999). IT outsourcing in insurance services: risk, creative contracting and business advantage. *Information Systems Journal, 9*, 163-180.

Williams, R. (1974/1990). *Television Technology and Cultural Form.* 2nd Edition, London & New York: Routledge.

Williamson, O. E. (1979). The economics of organization: the transaction cost approach. *American Journal of Sociology, 87*, 548-577

Williamson, O. E. (1993). Opportunism and its critics. *Managerial and Decision Economics, 14*, 97-107.

Williamson, O.E. (1991): Comparative economic organization: The analysis of discrete structural alternatives. Administrative Science Quarterly, 36, 269-296.

Wilson, J. H. (2005). Correlational Data. *Essential Statistics.* (pp. 201-223). Upper Saddle River, NJ: Prentice Hall.

Wilson, T. D. (1981). On user studies and information needs. *Journal of Documentation, 37*(1), 3-15

Wilson, T. D. (1987). Information behaviour: an interdisciplinary perspective. *Information Processing and Management, 33*(4), 551-572.

Wilson, T. D. (1999). Models in information behaviour research. *Journal of Documentation, 55*(3), 249-270.

Wilson, T. D. (2002). The nonsense of 'knowledge management. *Information Research, 8*(1), 144. Available at http://InformationR.net/ir/8-1/paper144.html

Wilson, T. D., & Spink, A. (1981). *Uncertainty in information seeking.* Library and Information Commission Research Report 59 ISSN 1466 2949

Wilson, T. D., & Streatfield, D. R. (1980). A *study of information use in local authority social services departments.* conducted by Project INNIS Sheffield, University of Sheffield, School of LIS, occasional paper no 12. Retrieved 12 October 2004 at http://informationr.net/tdw

Winter, S. G. (1987). Knowledge and Competence as Strategic Assets. In D. J. Teece (Ed.), *The Competitive Challenge: Strategies for Industrial Innovation and Renewal.* (pp. 159-184). Cambridge, MA: Ballinger Publishing Company.

Winter, S. G. (1991). On coase, competence, and the corporation. In O. E. Williwamson & S. G. Winter (Eds.), *The nature of the firm: Origins, evolution and development (179-195).* Oxford, England: Oxford University Press.

Winter, S. G. (2000). The satisfying principle in capability learning, Strategic Management Journal 21(10/11), Oct-Nov Special Issue, 981-996.

Wise, J. M. (1997). *Exploring technology and social space.* Thousand Oaks, London & New Delhi: Sage.

Wittgenstein, L. (1953). *Philosophical Investigations.* G. E. M. Anscombe (transl.). Oxford: Blackwell.

Wittgenstein, L. (1958). *The Blue and Brown Books.* HarperCollins Publishers.

Woicehyn, J. (2000). Technology adoption: Organizational learning in oil firms. *Organization Studies, 21*(6), 1095-1118.

Wolfe, R. A. (1994). Organisational innovation: review and critique and suggested research directions. *Journal of Management Studies, 31*(3) 405–31.

Womack, J., Jones, D., &Roos, D. (1991). *The Machine That Changed the World: The Story of Lean Production.* Harper Perennial.

Wong, K. Y., & Aspinwall, E. (2004). Knowledge Management Implementation Frameworks: A Review. *Knowledge and Process Management, 11*(2), 93-104.

Wong, V. (2002). Antecedents of international new product rollout timeliness. *International Marketing Review, 19*(2/3), 12-132.

Woodilla, J. (1998). Workplace conversations: The text of organizing. In D. Grant, D., Keenoy, T., & Oswick, C. (Eds.), *Discourse and Organization* (pp. 31-50). London: Sage.

Woodman, R. W., Savyer, J. E., & Griffin, R. W. (1993). Toward a Theory of Organizational Creativity. *Academy of Management Journal 18*(2), 293-321.

Woolgar, S., Vaux J., Gomes, P., Ezingeard, J.-N., & Grieve, R. (1998). Knowledge and the speed of transfer and imitation of organisational capabilities: An empirical test. *Organisation Science, 6*(1), 76-92.

Wright, I. C. (1998). *Design Methods in engineering and product design.* UK: McGraw Hill.

Wright, I. C., & Swain, E. (1995). New product engineering: The quality paradox. *Journal of Engineering Design, 6*(1), 49-56.

Wuyts, S., Dutta, S., & Stremersch, S. (2004). Portfolios of inter-firm agreements in Technology-intensive markets: Consequences for innovation and profitability. Journal of Marketing, 68, 88- 102.

Yakel, E. (2000). Knowledge management: The archivist's and records manager's perspective. *Information Management Journal, 34*(3), 24-29.

Yakhlef, A., & Salzer-Mörling, M. (2000). Intellectual capital: Managing by numbers. In C. Prichard, R. Hull, M. Chumer & H. Willmott (Eds.), *Managing knowledge: Critical investigations of work and learning* (pp. 20-36). London: MacMillan.

Yin, R. (1994). *Case study research: design and methods.* 2nd edition. Newbury Park: Sage Publications.

Yin, R. (1998). The abridged version of case study research. In L. Bickman, & D. Rog (Eds.), *Handbook of applied social research methods* (pp. 229-259). Thousand Oaks, CA: Sage Publications.

Yin, R. K. (1984). *Case study research: design and methods.* Sage.

Yli-Renko, H., Autio, E., & Tontti, V. (2002). Social Capital, Knowledge, and the International Growth of

Technology-Based Firms. *International Business Review*, *11*, 279-304.

Yoshino, M.Y., & Rangan, U.S. (1995): Strategic alliances: An entrepreneurial approach to globalization. Boston, MA: Harvard University Press.

Zack, M. (1999). Developing a knowledge strategy. *California Management Review*, *41*(3), 125-145.

Zack, M. (1999). Managing codified knowledge. *Sloan Management Review*, *40*(4), 45-58.

Zajac, E.J., & Olsen, C.P. (1993): From transaction cost to transactional value analysis: Implications for the study of inter-organizational strategies. Journal of Management Studies, 30, 131-145.

Zander U. and Kogut B., 1995, 'Knowledge and the Speed of the Transfer and Imitation of Organizational Capabilities: An Empirical Test', *Organization Science*/Vol. 6, No. 1, January-February: pp. 76-92.

Zenger T. R. and Hesterly W. S., 'The Disaggregation of Corporations: Selective Intervention, High-powered Incentives, and Molecular Units', *Organization Science*/ Vol. 8, No. 3, May-June 1997.

Zerubavel, E. (1979). *Patterns of time in hospital life: A sociological perspective*. Chicago: University of Chicago Press.

Zerubavel, E. (1981). *Hidden rhythms*. Chicago: University of Chicago Press.

Zhao, Z., Yap, C. M., & Ang, B. W. (1999). A framework for facilitating quality tools' applications in new product development. In S. K. Ho (Ed.), *TQM and Innovation proceedings of the fourth international conference on ISO 9000 and TQM* (pp. 455-461). HKBU press.

Zollo, M., & Winter, S. (2002). Deliberate learning and the evolution of dynamic capabilities. *Organization Science*, *13*(3), 339-351.

Zollo, M., Reuer, J. J., & Singh, H. (2002). Interorganisational routines and performance in strategic alliances. *Organisational Science*, *13*(6), 701-713.

Zott, C. (2003). Dynamic Capabilities and the emergence of intra-industry differential firm performance: Insights form a simulation study. *Strategic Management Journal*, *24*, 97-125.

Zuboff, S. (1984). *In the Age of the Smart Machine: The Future of Work and Power*. New York: Basic Books.

Zucker, L. (1986). *Production of trust; institutional sources of economic structure, 1840-1920. Research in Organizational Behaviour*, *8*, 53-111.

Zucker, L. G., Darby, M. B., & Brewer, M. B. (1998). Intellectual human and the birth of US biotechnology enterprises. *American Economic Review*, *88*, 290-306.

Zucker, L., Darby, M., & Yusheng, P. (1996). Collaboration structures and information dilemmas in biotechnology: organizational boundaries of trust production. In R. Kramer & T. Tyler (Eds.), *Trust in Organizations: Frontiers of theory and Research* (pp. 90-113). London: Sage.

Zussman, R. (1985). *Mechanics of the middle class*. Berkeley: University of California Press.

About the Contributors

Dariusz Jemielniak is an assistant professor of Management and the Academic Director of international programs at Kozminski University (Poland). 2004-2005 he spent as a Fulbright visiting scholar at Cornell University. He was also a visiting researcher at Harvard University (2007) and at University of California, Berkeley (2008). His main research focuses on workplace relations and occupational culture, especially in knowledge-intensive environment, which he studies by ethnographic and action research methods. He authored over 30 publications in English and in Polish, including a recent volume co-edited with Jerzy Kociatkiewicz on *Management Practices in High-Tech Environments* (Information Science Reference, 2008).

Jerzy Kociatkiewicz is a lecturer in Management at the University of Essex. He holds a PhD in sociology from the Polish Academy of Science. His main research interests include the social construction of high-tech workplaces, organizational space, narrativity, and science fiction He has published his work in journals such as *Qualitative Sociology, Human Resource Development International, Knowledge Transfer,* and *Ephemera.* With Dariusz Jemielniak, he recently edited "Management Practices in High-Tech Environments." He can be reached at kociak@kociak.org

* * *

Tatiana Andreeva is a senior lecturer at the Organizational behaviour and Human Resources Management Department, Graduate School of Management, St. Petersburg State University, Russia. She received her Master in International Business and PhD in Economics at the same school. Dr. Andreeva is currently involved in teaching, research and management consulting. Her key research interests are knowledge management, change management, and cross-cultural issues in management.

Ester Barinaga BA, MBA, PhD is currently a Wallander Fellow at the Economic Research Institute at the Stockholm School of Economics. From January 2007 until May 2008 she was a visiting scholar at Stanford University. Previously she was a researcher at the Department of Industrial Economics and Management at the Royal Institute of Technology in Stockholm. She obtained her PhD from the Stockholm School of Economics. She has published in Human Relations and in the autumn of 2008 has published a book on *Powerful dichotomies – Inclusion and exclusion in the information society.* Her research interests include cultural diversity, the information society, and the intersection between technology and culture. She can be reached at ester.barinaga@hhs.se

David M. Boje is endowed Bank of America professor in the Management Department at New Mexico State University, and past holder of the Anderson professorship. His main research is the interplay of storytelling methods and ethics. His current books (for Sage) *The Storytelling Organization* and *Critical Theory Ethics for Business and Public Administration* (Information Age Press), and just released *Handbook of Managerial Psychology* (with co-editors). Boje books include *Managing in the Postmodern World* (with Dennehy), *Narrative Methods in Organization and Communication Research.* He has published over 120 journal articles, including ones for *Administrative Science Quarterly, Management Science, Management Communication Quarterly, Organization Studies, Leadership Quarterly*, and other fine journals. He is President of Standing Conference for Management & Organization Inquiry (http://scmoi.org), editor of Tamara Journal (http://tamarajournal.com) and associated editor for *Qualitative Research in Organization & Management* (QROM) and *Journal of Organization Change Management.* He serves on 14 other editorial boards.

Cliff Bowman BA, MBA, PhD is professor of Strategic Management at Cranfield School of Management, UK. His research interests include competitive strategy, dynamic capabilities, strategy processes and the development and leveraging of strategic assets. He has undertaken consulting assignments for a wide range of organizations and is the author of eight books and over sixty articles.

Steffen Böhm is senior lecturer in Management at the University of Essex. He holds a PhD from the University of Warwick. His research focuses on critiques of the political economy of organization and management. He is co-founder and member of the editorial collective of the open-access journal *ephemera: theory & politics in organization* (www.ephemeraweb.org), and co-founder and co-editor of the new open publishing press mayflybooks (www.mayflybooks.org). He has recently published two books: *Repositioning Organization Theory* (Palgrave) and *Against Automobility* (Blackwell).

Maria E. Burke is an experienced senior lecturer at Salford Business School. Her research area is Information Management and she is the known for work on Information Models. Within this remit her work also examines the relationships between strategy and Knowledge Management. She has published books, papers given several keynote speeches and has presented her work at many international conferences. She has worked in China and is a Visiting Fellow at the Polish Jagiellonian University in Krakow. She holds numerous grants, is a member of two of the leading UK Research Councils and often a Panel member at various Seminars. She has won several awards for her work including Russian Diploma awards, the prestigious John Campbell prize awarded by the Institute of Information Scientists; the Emerald Highly Commended Journal Paper; and Best Chair awards at various conferences.

Enrique Claver PhD (University of Valencia, Spain) is a professor and Head of the Department of Management at the University of Alicante, Spain. His primary research interests are strategic management, knowledge management, and international management. He has published research papers in international journals including *Information & Management, Total Quality Management & Business Excellence, International Business Review, Asia Pacific Journal of Management, Emerging Markets Finance and Trade, Journal of General Management, Journal of Asia Business Studies, Revue Française de Gestion, Cross Cultural Management: An International Journal, International Journal of Contemporary Hospitality Management, Journal of Small Business and Enterprise Development,* and *International Journal of Knowledge Management Studies.*

Angelo Ditillo is an assistant professor of Management Accounting and Control at Università Bocconi and Professor of SDA Bocconi School of Management. He has published several contributions in academic journals, including *Accounting, Organizations and Society*. His current research interests relate to inter-organizational management accounting, and management control in knowledge-intensive firms and innovative settings.

Mario J. Donate-Manzanares is a lecturer at the University of Castilla-La Mancha. He teaches courses on Strategic Management, Ethics and Entrepreneurship at the Faculty of Law and Social Sciences in Ciudad Real, Spain. His research mainly focuses on knowledge management, technological innovation and social responsibility issues. He recently obtained his PhD from the University of Castilla-La Mancha. His works have been published in specialised journals and books.

Pauline Gleadle is lecturer in Management at the Open University in the UK. Her research interests include financialization, debates around enterprise, and the role of knowledge workers. She has been lead guest editor for a special issue of the *Journal of Organizational Change Management* on change, identity, and employment and is currently (lead) guest editing a special issue for "*Organization*" on enterprising selves. She has published in the British Journal of Management and in Critical Perspectives on Accounting.

Jeff Gold is principal lecturer in Organisation Learning at Leeds Business School, Leeds Metropolitan University and Leadership Fellow at Leeds University where he co-ordinates the Northern Leadership Academy. He has led a range of seminars and workshops on leadership with a particular emphasis on participation and distribution. He is the author of *Management Development, Strategies for Action* (with Alan Mumford), published by the Chartered Institute of Personnel and Development in 2004 and the fourth edition of his textbook on *Human Resource Management* (with John Bratton) was published in 2007 with Palgrave Macmillan. He is also co-author with Richard Thorpe and Alan Mumford of the *Gower Handbook of Leadership and Management Development* to be published in 2009.

Davydd J. Greenwood is the Goldwin Smith professor of Anthropology at Cornell University where he has served as a faculty member since 1970. He has been elected a Corresponding Member of the Spanish Royal Academy of Moral and Political Sciences. He served as the John S. Knight professor and director of the Mario Einaudi Center for 10 years and as director of the Cornell Institute for European Studies for 8 years. His work centers on action research, political economy, ethnic conflict, community and regional development, and neo-liberal reforms of higher education. He has worked in the Spanish Basque Country, Spain's La Mancha region, and the Finger Lakes region of Upstate New York. The author of 8 books and over 40 articles on agricultural industrialization, the use of biological ideologies to support political economic regimes, industrial cooperatives, and action research, he is currently working on the role of action research in developing creative responses to neo-liberal reforms in higher education.

Louise Grisoni has been head of the School of Organization Studies, Bristol Business School for seven years and Director of Learning and Teaching and assessment in 2006-2007. Her teaching interests include inquiry based methodologies, organisational analysis and behaviour, organisational learning and leadership. Her research interests include group and intergroup dynamics, leadership and gender, experiential learning and creative research methods. She has presented regularly at conferences nationally and internationally, including co-stream organiser with Per Darmer (CBS) for the 'Poetry' stream at three Art of Management conferences. Working with poetry as a creative research method has become a principal focus for her work, using poetic forms such as Haiku to access organisational knowledge and for making sense of personal organisational experience.

Fátima Guadamillas-Gómez is a professor of Strategic Management at the Faculty of Law and Social Sciences in Toledo, Spain. She has a degree in Economics and obtained her PhD from the University of Castilla-La Mancha. She coordinates the MBA on Human Resources Management of this University. She teaches courses at the degree level on strategic and general management and on knowledge management, innovation and strategic management at the MBA and PhD levels. Her research focuses on innovation, knowledge management strategies and ethics and social responsibility in businesses. Her works have been published in specialised journals and books.

James Guthrie is a professor of Accounting at the University of Sydney and chair of the Discipline of Accounting. His research and teaching interests include public sector accounting, auditing, accountability and management, social and environmental reporting and auditing, management of knowledge and intellectual capital and the measurement of intangibles. He also consults on public and private sector management, management of knowledge, intellectual capital, budget performance, and annual reporting strategies. James is also coeditor of seven public sector management and accounting books. He is the co-editor of Accounting, Auditing and Accountability Journal. James previously held posts at the University of New South Wales and Deakin University, prior to taking up his professorship at the Macquarie Graduate School of Management in 1995. Before commencing his academic career, James worked in a chartered accounting firm and has been made a Fellow of the Australian Society of CPAs and a Fellow of the Institute of Chartered Accountants in Australia.

Vidar Hepsø has worked as researcher and project manager in StatoilHydro, the state oil company of Norway, since 1991. Main research issues are virtual organizations, computer supported cooperative work, communities of practice and organizational culture. Through his career has been highly involved in planning and implementation of virtual or physical collaborative spaces. This includes the development, deployment and evaluation of groupware based systems. Hepsø has a PhD in anthropology from NTNU (Norwegian University of Science and Technology) on the subject "new collaborative practices enabled by new information and communication technology". In addition to his job in StatoilHydro, Dr Hepsø is adjunct professor at the Norwegian School of Management (BI) in Oslo within the field of leadership and organisational management

Andreas Hoecht PhD is a principal lecturer at the Business School, University of Portsmouth. He is an economist and political scientist with a particular research interest in the role of trust in (inter-) business relations. He also has a research interest in innovation management and has published in a range of innovation managementjournals.

Jianzhong Hong is a senior lecturer of knowledge management in the School of Business at Lappeenranta University of Technology. His articles have appeared in several international journals, including those in the areas of Psychology, Education and Management. His prime teaching is related to organizational learning and competence development, and his current research focuses on the impact of culture on cross-border knowledge interaction and collaborative innovation.

Arla Juntunen's main research interests are management of technology and knowledge, business networks, values and capabilities. She graduated from the Department of Marketing and Management at the Helsinki School of Economics. She is also a post-graduate student at the Political Science Department at the University of Helsinki in 2005. Currently, she works as a senior adviser at the Ministry of the Interior at the Supreme Command of the Police. She is a well-known speaker both on academic and business arenas. Her recent articles and other publications have been published by Finland's Ministry of the Interior in their own publication series and also by IGI in Information Science Reference-series and other publications.

Aino Kianto is a professor of Knowledge Management in the School of Business at Lappeenranta University of Technology, Finland. Her teaching and research focus on knowledge management, intellectual capital, creativity, innovation and organizational renewal. Her current interests include the knowledge-based view of the firm and measurement of knowledge-related phenomena in organizations. She has authored and co-authored several academic articles, papers, books and book chapters related to knowledge management, intellectual capital and innovation. In addition to the academia, she also has worked with the Future committee of the Finnish parliament and regularly lectures for companies.

Krzysztof Klincewicz is an associate professor at the Faculty of Management, University of Warsaw. He specializes in management of technology and innovation. Dr Klincewicz has many years of experience in IT industry in Poland, Finland and in the UK, confirmed by the professional title of chartered marketer, awarded by the British Chartered Institute of Marketing. Author of numerous articles and conference papers, as well as three management science books: "Knowledge management. Development, diffusion and rejection" (WZUW 2004), "Strategic alliances in the high-tech industry" (Logos Verlag 2005) and "Management fashions. Turning bestselling ideas into objects and institutions" (Transaction Publishers 2006).

Juha Kettunen is the Rector of Turku University of Applied Sciences, Finland and the Adjunct Professor at the University of Jyväskylä, Finland. He was previously the director of the Vantaa Institute for Continuing Education, University of Helsinki and director of the Advanced Management Education Centre, University of Jyväskylä. He holds a PhD from the University of Bristol, UK, and a DSc from the University of Jyväskylä, Finland.

Chris Land is a lecturer in Management at the University of Essex. His research is concerned primarily with the question of 'value' and organization. Here value should be understood in the broadest sense, including both economic value and the more philosophical or ethical values that motivate organizing and behaviour. Much of his recent research has therefore been concerned with explicitly values-driven forms of organization, such as communes, communities and social movement organizations.

Lawrence Locker Jr. earned a bachelor's degree in psychology from Fort Hays State University and a doctoral degree in cognitive psychology from the University of Kansas. He is currently on faculty at

Georgia Southern University. His research and teaching interests include language processing, memory, and the application of statistical techniques in psychology.

Alice MacGillivray is a consultant and associate faculty member and former director of Knowledge Management graduate programs at Royal Roads University. Alice is a doctoral candidate in Human and Organizational Systems at Fielding Graduate University, with a concentration in knowledge organizations. Her research interests cluster around the intersections of knowledge management, complexity thinking and leadership. She is currently researching perceptions and uses of boundaries. For more information, see www.4KM.net.

Darius Mehri is the author of "Notes from Toyota-land: An American engineer in Japan" (Cornell 2005). He is currently a PhD student in sociology at the University of California-Berkeley where his current interests include organizations, culture and economy and society.

John Murray PhD currently serves and professor and chair of the Department of Psychology at Georgia Southern University, in Statesboro GA, USA. A cognitive psychology by training, he has done research in the area of psycholinguistics and discourse processing since the early 1990s. More recently, he has ventured into the area of Knowledge, Discovery, and Databases (KDD) and is pursing issues connecting cognitive psychology to KDD applications.

Jonathan D. Owens is a senior lecture in Operations and Logistics Management at the Lincoln Business School, University of Lincoln, UK. His research interests are in New Product Development issues and the appreciation of having a structured technology roadmap incorporated into the process and the learning issues to be understood in the design process. He is chartered engineer and currently a visiting professor for the Tecnologico de Monterrey University, Mexico. He is a member of the editorial panel for numerous journals and a member of the Chartered Institute of Purchasing and Supply (CIPS) logistics forum.

Anders Örtenblad is a researcher and teacher at Halmstad University, Sweden. His main research interests are management ideas connected to knowledge and learning, and the spread and popularity of these and other management ideas. He has published articles on these subjects in e.g. *Human Relations, Human Resource Development Quarterly, International Journal of Management Reviews, International Journal of Management Concepts and Philosophy, Management Learning, Philosophy of Management and The Learning Organization.* Anders Örtenblad is a member of the International Editorial Board of Management Learning, Sage Publications, of the Editorial Advisory Board of The Learning Organization, Emerald, and of the Editorial Board of the *International Journal of Quality and Innovation* (Inderscience). In 2004 he was awarded the journal of Management Learning's Reviewer Annual Prize for "your sound intellectual work in helping pursue our joint field by way of your reviews". He has been teaching in organizational behaviour, organizational theory and leadership since 1990."

Agnieszka Postula received her master's degree from the School of Management, Warsaw University, Poland in 2000. In 2007, she received PhD ("IT professionals' role in organizations") at the same faculty. From 2000, she works as an assistant professor at Management Systems Department. Her main research interests lie in the area of organizational anthropology, communication and socio-professional roles in Polish organizations. Other interests and experience of Agnieszka Postula include team building trainings, group work, interpersonal communication, and negotiations which she uses in coaching. She teaches negotiation, international negotiation, organization and management theory, organizational anthropology and cross-cultural management at several faculties.

Christiane Prange is an associate professor of International Marketing and Strategy at the EM Lyon Business School. She obtained her PhD from Geneva University in Switzerland and previously worked at Vienna University of Economics and Business Administration in Austria. Over the past, she has gained considerable experience in management consultancy and with SAP AG. She is also the director of an international consultancy firm which specialises in international strategy projects in high-velocity environments, strategic market planning, and innovation management. Her current research revolves around international innovation strategies, strategic alliances, and industry disruption. Christiane has published five books as well as numerous papers both in academic and practitioner journals.

Diego Quer PhD (University of Alicante, Spain) is an associate professor in the Department of Management at the University of Alicante, Spain. His primary research interests include several topics of international management, such as entry modes, emerging markets, and the internationalization process. He has published research papers in international journals including *International Business Review, Asia Pacific Journal of Management, Emerging Markets Finance and Trade, Journal of General Management, Journal of Asia Business Studies, Revue Française de Gestion, Cross Cultural Management: An International Journal, International Journal of Contemporary Hospitality Management, Journal of Small Business and Enterprise Development,* and *International Journal of Knowledge Management Studies.*

Federica Ricceri is an associate professor of Accounting at the University of Padova. Her research and teaching interests include strategic performance measurement, management and financial accounting, extended performance reporting, intellectual capital, the strategic management of knowledge resources, and finance and valuation. She has published several articles in both international and national refereed and professional journals focusing on intellectual capital and the strategic management of knowledge resources. She has also published several chapters in international and national books focusing on strategic performance measurement and financial accounting. She has presented her ideas and research findings to national and international gatherings. She is a member of the editorial board of the *Journal of Human Resource Costing and Accounting.*

Meryem Sebnem Sevinc has interests in both business and psychology. She completed her MBA at Georgia Southern University where she was also active in the psychology department, particularly in psychological research. She is currently working in the state of Virginia in the United States.

Stephen Sheard is currently employed as an associate lecturer in HRM by Bradford Business School. He gained a PhD in Management from Canterbury Business School, Kent University in 1999. He has published in a number of academic journals, including the *Journal of Philosophy of Management, E: CO (Emergence)*, and the *Journal of Management History.* He has varied research interests in areas of organizational theory which include the application of ideas of philosophy to organization and scrutiny of these ideas (especially phenomenology/poststructuralism). His studies have included the areas of complexity theory/socio-technical and symbolic aspects of e-commerce/business, and evaluations of areas like critical realism/postmodernism; in which areas he is currently working. He likes to cultivate an individual critical/creative style relative to contemporary ideas in organization.

Johanna Shih is an assistant professor of Sociology at Hofstra University, NY. Her areas of research specialization include the sociology of work, racial and ethnic inequality, racial attitudes, and issues pertaining to the post-1965 immigration.

Lars Steiner, Ekon.Dr is a lecturer in Business and Real Estate Management at the University of Gävle in Sweden. Previously he worked at the Universities of Umeå and Sundsvall, Economic Research Institute (EFI) at Stockholm School of Economics (HHS), Royal Institute of Technology (KTH) and at the Chancellor for the Swedish Universities. Basically being an organization theorist, his research covers the fields of knowledge management and organization growth, learning and identity transformation in small and medium seized businesses and Real Estate.

Alexander Styhre PhD (Lund University, 1999) is professor and chair of Operations Management the Department of Technology Management and Economics at Chalmers University of Technology, Gothenburg, Sweden. Alexander is interested in knowledge-intensive organizations and innovation work. He has published a number of papers and book in the field of organization theory including his most recent books *Science-based innovation* (Palgrave, 2008) and *Perception and Organization: Art, Music, Media* (Palgrave, 2008).

Richard Thorpe is professor of Management Development and a deputy director of the Keyworth Institute. He began his career as a management trainee in the footwear industry before using his industrial engineering skills firstly in the water industry and then in the Highlands of Scotland where he managed a small clothing company manufacturing outdoor protective clothing. It was there that he completed an MSc at Strathclyde University Business School, the research focus being payment systems. From Strathclyde he moved to Glasgow University and began to research Small Firm Growth and Development. Moving south he worked at the North West Regional Management Centre on a collaborative MSc in Management delivered by action learning and for eighteen years worked at Manchester Metropolitan University where his interest in management and organisational learning.

Paul Trott is a reader in Innovation Management at the Business School, University of Portsmouth and Professor of Innovation & Entrepreneurship at Delft University of Technology, The Netherlands. He received his PhD from Cranfield University. He has published over thirty articles on innovation management. He has published in *R&D Management, Technology Analysis & Strategic Management, Journal of Marketing Theory, International Journal of Innovation Management.*

Ben Tran received his Doctor of Psychology (PsyD) in organizational consulting from the Marshall Goldsmith School of Management at Alliant International University in San Francisco, California, United States of America. Dr. Tran has presented articles on topics of, but not limited to, business and management ethics, (expatriate) recruitment, selection and retention, knowledge management, and gender and minorities in multinational corporations at the Academy of Management (AOM), Society for Advancement of Management (SAM), International Standing Conference on Organizational Symbolism, and International Association for Chinese Management Research just to name a few. Dr. Tran has also published articles with the Social Responsibility Journal (published by Emerald). Dr. Tran can be reached at tranconsulting@gmail.com

Jo Tyler is assistant professor at Pennsylvania State University where she teaches in the MEd program in Training and Development. A corporate practitioner for 25 years, most recently as a vice president of organization and management development at Armstrong World Industries, she now consults with organizations interested in the influence and interplay of their stories, storytelling and organizational narratives. She has published articles and book chapters on storytelling in organizational settings and other topics related to organizational development. She can be reached at jat235@psu.edu.

Patrocinio Zaragoza PhD (University of Alicante, Spain) is an associate professor in the Department of Management at the University of Alicante, Spain. Her primary research interests include several topics of knowledge management and international management, such as knowledge creation and transfer in multinationals and the knowledge management process. She has published research papers in international journals including *Journal of Knowledge Management, Journal of Intellectual Capital* and *International Journal of Knowledge Management Studies.*

Index

Symbols

3M in the United Kingdom 330–347

A

actor network theory (ANT) 67
alliance capability 395, 398, 400
alliance capability development 402, 403, 404, 405, 406
alliance life-cycle 395, 397, 398
analyst 153, 154, 167, 168, 205, 337, 341, 414, 415, 419
analyst-centered 416
animism 148
appeal of professionalism 529, 532, 536, 537
automation 16, 414, 415, 421, 493
automation vs. human intervention 414–424
autopoiesis 67, 69, 74, 75, 77, 78

B

bicamerality 148
boundary objects 281, 282, 288, 289, 292, 294
British cultural environment 357

C

call centre 529, 532, 550
capability development 195, 402, 403, 404, 405, 406, 409
case study 70, 79, 127, 190, 191, 203, 328, 360, 362
Chemical, Biological, Radiological and Nuclear (CBRN) initiative 440
Chemical Research and Technology Initiative (CRTI) 440
cognition 246, 250, 268, 372, 374, 409, 418, 423
coherence 36, 84, 85, 87, 90, 91, 187, 330, 331, 332, 333, 334, 335, 340, 341, 344, 448
collaborative experience 397
combination 10, 13, 21, 22, 29, 91, 135, 185, 187, 209, 244, 251, 252, 253, 295, 300, 307, 329, 340, 341, 342, 445, 462, 513, 518, 550, 554
combination phase 29
common information spaces (CIS) 279, 280, 281, 282, 283, 284, 291, 293
communities of knowing 246, 252, 280, 281, 282, 283, 285, 286, 287, 288, 289, 291, 292, 294
communities of practice 7, 177, 181, 194, 195, 237, 238, 239, 245, 269, 281, 388, 440, 441, 443, 455, 457, 522
comparisons of competing vendors 154
competence development 259, 260, 263, 266, 269, 270, 271, 272, 273, 277, 284
competence measurement and development 264, 265, 277
complex system 458
contemporary management theory 460
contextual knowledge 234, 236, 238
continuing professional development 30, 46
control over knowledge 229, 230
cooperative life cycle 407
cooperrider's appreciative inquiry 89
corporate knowledge management platform 193–207
corporate socialization 323, 328

counter-terrorism communities 455, 456
creativity and/vs. control 297
cultural environments 349, 353
cultural historical activity theory 30, 36, 46
culture 28, 29, 32, 74, 93, 99, 100, 107, 133, 134, 135, 137, 138, 139, 140, 141, 145, 169, 170, 174, 175, 179, 180, 181, 185, 186, 187, 191, 233, 235, 267, 299, 303, 305, 307, 308, 314, 317, 318, 319, 322, 323, 325, 328, 329, 330, 334, 335, 340, 341, 343, 345, 348, 349, 351, 352, 353, 354, 355, 357, 358, 359, 360, 362, 363, 364, 373, 390, 401, 403, 435, 443, 462, 463, 473, 497, 498, 509, 510, 520, 521, 522, 523, 525, 526, 536, 553, 561
culture as a dynamic capability 330–347
customer primacy 539

D

data mining 178, 415
dedicated alliance functions 398
Denning's springboard stories 88
dualism 143, 144
dynamic capabilities 328, 331, 347, 401, 409, 411, 412

E

E and M Commerce 134
enterprise resource planning systems 48
equifinality 402
ethnography 130, 308, 362
european electronic commerce 134
experiential learning 275, 403
explicit knowledge 29, 374, 516, 518, 528
externalization 21, 22, 29, 177, 185, 518
externalization phase 29

F

feeding of knowledge 524
flow approach 376, 377, 378, 381, 387, 391

G

gaming industry 48

H

higher education institutions 9, 197, 348, 349
human memory 417
human resources 169, 170, 174, 175, 180, 183, 186, 187, 191, 314, 317, 325, 390, 392, 398, 402, 460, 535

I

ICT-sector 193, 194
identity 77, 78, 95, 96, 190, 254, 256, 275, 283, 473, 547, 559
immutable mobiles 294
individual alliance capability 395
information communication technologies 48, 65
information fulfillment 348, 349, 348, 350, 351, 353, 359, 362, 348, 350, 351, 353, 359, 362
information society 4, 261, 487
information technology 6, 9, 14, 50, 62, 67, 68, 71, 72, 167, 171, 193, 194, 376, 484, 520, 533, 551
innovation co-operation 67, 69, 70, 72, 73, 76
innovation intensive firms, KM implementation 169–192
inscription technology 499, 505
integrating knowledge, through communication and cognition 246
intellectual capital (IC) 112, 160, 256, 259, 260, 261, 263, 264, 266, 269, 270, 271, 272, 273, 275, 278, 317, 319, 376, 380, 381, 382, 386, 389, 391, 408, 444, 517, 520, 522
inter-relationship 134
internalization 21, 22, 398, 462, 518
internalization phase 29
international knowledge resources frameworks 376
IT professional communities, creativity and control 295–310
IT Research & Analysis 152, 153, 156, 158, 162, 164, 168
IT specialists 295, 296, 297, 298, 299, 300, 302, 303, 304, 305, 306, 307

J

Jacques 479, 480, 483, 484, 485, 486, 493, 494
jnowledge intensive work 116–132

K

KM platform, benefits and usage 199
KM platform, development and implementation 196
KMS implementation, case studies 179
KMS implementation, elements 175
knowledge 31
knowledge, narrative and story theory 86
knowledge, subjective vs. objective 514
knowledge-based view 169, 194, 260, 266, 267, 268, 269, 270, 273, 278, 313, 496

knowledge-intensive companies 254, 460, 473
knowledge-intensive firms, stability and innovation 243–258
knowledge-intensive organisations have responded to this challenge by adopting m 376
knowledge-intensive organizations 1, 2, 3, 4, 5, 6, 7, 8, 13, 14, 15, 18, 20, 24, 26, 27, 67, 280, 459, 460, 466, 470, 471, 472, 473, 495, 553, 558
knowledge birth 514
knowledge construction in organizations 512–528
knowledge control 242
knowledge conversion 21, 253, 258, 518
knowledge creation 96, 99, 107, 113, 114, 131, 167, 190, 191, 256, 318, 329, 459, 475, 476
knowledge creation 8, 15, 19, 20, 21, 22, 26, 29, 40, 53, 63, 99, 101, 102, 109, 110, 111, 112, 114, 115, 129, 171, 173, 177, 178, 179, 180, 185, 194, 203, 204, 241, 246, 250, 251, 261, 279, 282, 311, 312, 314, 317, 318, 319, 320, 321, 322, 325, 326, 328, 364, 408, 411, 456, 459, 460, 461, 462, 463, 464, 465, 466, 469, 470, 471, 472, 473, 519, 555
knowledge creation and sharing, tensions 459–478
knowledge intensive work 116, 117, 126
knowledge management 9, 19, 20, 21, 26, 28, 64, 67, 68, 69, 70, 71, 72, 74, 75, 76, 78, 79, 81, 82, 83, 86, 87, 88, 93, 94, 96, 133, 134, 142, 143, 146, 149, 152, 153, 156, 157, 158, 159, 160, 161, 162, 163, 164, 165, 168, 169, 170, 173, 178, 179, 182, 183, 184, 185, 186, 191, 192, 193, 194, 195, 196, 201, 229, 230, 231, 233, 234, 235, 236, 238, 239, 241, 242, 256, 266, 277, 279, 281, 282, 291, 311, 312, 313, 314, 315, 316, 317, 319, 321, 322, 324, 325, 326, 328, 349, 350, 355, 364, 368, 372, 373, 376, 381, 385, 389, 401, 402, 403, 423, 440, 441, 442, 443, 444, 446, 448, 449, 452, 453, 455, 456, 457, 458, 460, 462, 465, 466, 469, 471, 472, 480, 483, 496, 504, 505, 506, 507, 510, 512, 513, 514, 515, 517, 520, 522, 524, 525, 526, 527, 552, 553, 554, 555, 556, 557, 558, 561
knowledge management, history 513
knowledge management, qualitative study 311–329
knowledge management, story and narrative 87
knowledge management as pulp fiction 553
knowledge management perspective 69
knowledge management platform 194
knowledge management research 442
knowledge management strategies 171
knowledge management strategy 170
knowledge outside the individual, storing 232
knowledge redundancy 234, 235, 236, 238
knowledge replaces labour 483
knowledge resources, international guidelines 375–393
knowledge sharing (KS) 7, 19, 20, 21, 22, 26, 30, 40, 46, 53, 82, 89, 93, 104, 177, 185, 186, 195, 196, 200, 229, 231, 235, 238, 322, 328, 445, 450, 459, 460, 461, 462, 463, 464, 465, 466, 468, 469, 470, 471, 472, 473, 474, 477, 514, 520, 524
knowledge society 1, 4, 98, 230
knowledge types 514
knowledge workers 5, 81, 82, 92, 246, 261, 262, 269, 275, 278, 293, 393, 425, 427, 434, 437, 472, 474, 481, 483, 488, 491, 524, 531, 552, 554, 556, 557, 558, 559, 561

L

Labour 107, 126, 378, 379, 381, 388, 479, 481, 483, 484, 487, 492, 493, 494
labour, source of value 481
labour process perspective 487
language as alien or entitative 143
lean production 364
learning organizations 2, 3, 5, 7, 8, 18, 526, 527
legal profession 31, 33, 34, 35, 45
levels of alliance capability 399
limited liability partnership (LLP) 37

M

management fad 561
management fashion arena 153
managing knowledge-related processes 460
market sizing 154, 160
Marx 267, 479, 480, 481, 482, 483, 484, 485, 486, 489, 492, 493, 494, 558, 560
Marxist perspective, classical 481
McLuhan 138
measurement 202, 255, 256, 259, 260, 261, 263, 264, 265, 266, 268, 272, 273, 274, 275, 276, 277, 278, 383, 384, 391
media theory 496, 497
micro-foundations of alliance capabilities 407
micro-level foundations 395
militaristic neo-liberalism 489
mind control 234, 238
MNCs, knowledge creation 318
MNCs, knowledge transfer 321

mobile telephony, role in sensibility 136
multi-dimensional 195, 399
multi-level construct 399
multinational corporations (MNCs) 311
multiple convergent model 214

N

negotiating knowledge 123
new media and knowledge work 495
new organizational learning 242
new product? 209
new product development (NPD) 208, 331
new product development, "controlling" 331
new product development process 208–228, 209
NPD capabilities, evidence of success 335

O

oil and gas industry 51, 279, 283, 284
old organizational learning 242
Organisational Control 550
Organizational Independence 242
organizational independence 231, 242
organizational learning 5, 7, 63, 98, 99, 100, 108, 109, 110, 111, 167, 195, 197, 198, 229, 230, 231, 232, 233, 234, 237, 238, 239, 240, 241, 242, 313, 329, 363, 364, 366, 368, 372, 401, 410, 411, 458, 507, 512, 521, 522, 523, 524, 525, 557
organizational learning, types 522
organizational life 4, 70, 98, 100, 101, 110, 303, 304, 305, 307, 309, 555, 556
organizational measurement, knowledge-based approach 259–278
organizational memory 242
organizational routines 7, 251, 253, 330, 332, 334, 336, 340, 341, 345, 398, 401, 403, 404, 407
organizing process 117, 120, 130, 161
outsourcing 47, 49, 47, 49, 51, 55, 57, 60, 62, 63, 66, 122, 532

P

performative view of language 116, 117, 129, 130
perspective making and taking 282
phenomenography 440, 444, 445, 448, 456, 457, 458
poetic expression 100
poetry 98, 99, 100, 101, 102, 103, 104, 107, 109, 110, 111, 112, 113, 114, 115, 499
Polanyi's theory of tacit knowing 82
Polish cultural environment 355
popular knowledge management approaches, implications 93
Post-Industrial Era 427
post-Industrial perspective 483
power approach 530, 531, 532, 546
primitive accumulation 489, 494
product and cycle-time excellence model 216
professional, redefining 529–551
professional community 297
professionalisation 546, 550
professionalism 44, 45, 308, 536, 538, 539, 540, 545, 548, 549, 550
professionalism 33, 34, 35, 45, 529, 530, 531, 532, 535, 536, 537, 538, 539, 541, 542, 543, 544, 545, 546, 547, 548, 549
professionalism, resisting the appeal 545
professionalism appeal 536
professionalism privileges 541
professionals 17, 282, 294, 295, 297, 301, 361, 438, 530, 532, 536, 548, 550, 560
professions 31, 34, 35, 44, 298, 300, 308, 504, 513, 529, 530, 531, 532, 533, 534, 535, 546, 547, 548, 549, 550
proto-alphabetical culture by cyberspace 141

Q

qualitative study of knowledge management 311–329

R

research and technology initiative (CRTI) 440, 441
residents of knowledge management 520
Russian cultural environment 353

S

Shared Situational Awareness 294
Silicon Valley's hi-tech industry 428
simple rules 75, 401, 402, 404, 405, 406, 407, 409
socialization 21, 177, 185, 192, 245, 250, 253, 312, 317, 322, 323, 324, 325, 326, 328, 462, 493, 518
socialization phase 29
social theory of autopoiesis 67, 69
socio-ideological control 550
stage gate model 212
strategic alliances 189, 225, 275, 394, 408, 411
strategic client learning 41, 43, 46
subjective knowledge 229, 230, 231, 232, 233, 234, 236, 237, 238, 239, 242, 514
symbolic form 149

T

tacit knowing, Polanyi's theory 82
tacit knowledge 3, 4, 20, 21, 22, 23, 24, 29, 33, 37, 43, 45, 62, 63, 81, 82, 87, 89, 92, 94, 98, 99, 102, 107, 108, 109, 111, 114, 129, 160, 177, 181, 185, 233, 240, 250, 251, 270, 271, 317, 321, 323, 367, 403, 405, 442, 455, 462, 488, 504, 508, 515, 516, 517, 518, 519, 520, 521, 526, 527, 555
tacit knowledge and explicit knowledge 518
techno-bureaucratic control 529, 534, 537, 545, 546, 550
TECNOBIT case 182
temporality 122, 425, 426, 439
third generation new product processes 221
total design 211, 217, 218, 219, 220, 226
Toyota, engineering design 363–374
Toyota production system 363
trait approach 530, 531, 532, 546
trend forecasting 154
triangulation technique 329
tyranny of the eye 134, 147

V

vagueness 116–132
value of knowledge 479–494
visualism and cyberspace 145
visualization 138, 288, 420, 421, 502, 504

W

Wenger's communities of practice 91